THE OXFORD HANDBOOK ON THE

WORLD TRADE ORGANIZATION

THE OXFORD HANDBOOK ON THE

WORLD TRADE ORGANIZATION

Edited by

AMRITA NARLIKAR
MARTIN DAUNTON
and
ROBERT M. STERN

OXFORD
UNIVERSITY PRESS

OXFORD
UNIVERSITY PRESS

Great Clarendon Street, Oxford ox2 6DP

Oxford University Press is a department of the University of Oxford.
It furthers the University's objective of excellence in research, scholarship,
and education by publishing worldwide in

Oxford New York

Auckland Cape Town Dar es Salaam Hong Kong Karachi
Kuala Lumpur Madrid Melbourne Mexico City Nairobi
New Delhi Shanghai Taipei Toronto

With offices in

Argentina Austria Brazil Chile Czech Republic France Greece
Guatemala Hungary Italy Japan Poland Portugal Singapore
South Korea Switzerland Thailand Turkey Ukraine Vietnam

Oxford is a registered trade mark of Oxford University Press
in the UK and in certain other countries

Published in the United States by Oxford University Press Inc., New York

British Library Cataloging in Publication Data
Data available

Library of Congress Cataloging in Publication Data
Data available

Typeset by SPI Publisher Services, Pondicherry, India

ISBN 978-0-19-958610-3

ACKNOWLEDGMENTS

....

This project would not have been possible without the splendid cooperation of our contributors. We were greatly saddened by the passing of our contributor, Professor Robert Baldwin. This volume carries the last piece that he wrote, and it displays the same intellectual verve and clarity for which he won the respect of economists and non-economists alike. While his passing will be an irreplaceable loss to the field, his work will continue to influence and inspire future generations of students and scholars.

We are also very grateful for the comments of three anonymous referees whose constructive and thoughtful comments contributed to several improvements in the project design and content. We thank the efficient and helpful team at Oxford University Press, and particularly Dominic Byatt for his enthusiastic support and efficiency, which were vital in all stages of the making of this volume.

This Oxford Handbook brings together the cooperation of a political scientist, a historian, and an economist. All three of us have had a penchant for interdisciplinarity, and this volume provided us with a unique and special opportunity to join the forces of the three disciplinary approaches and apply them to a shared puzzle. Working on this project together has been an intellectual treat for us. We hope that the readers will enjoy the end product as much as we enjoyed the process.

Contents

PART I THEORY OF MULTILATERAL TRADE LIBERALIZATION

PART II INSTITUTIONAL EVOLUTION: BUILDING UP THE WTO

PART III PROCESS BEHIND THE WORKINGS OF THE WTO

PART IV AGENCY IN THE WTO

PART V SUBSTANCE OF THE AGREEMENTS

PART VI IMPLEMENTATION AND ENFORCEMENT

PART VII CHALLENGES
TO THE SYSTEM

PART VIII NORMATIVE ISSUES

PART IX REFORM OF THE WTO

LIST OF FIGURES

LIST OF TABLES

LIST OF ABBREVIATIONS

AAA	US Agricultural Adjustment Act
ACP	African, Caribbean, and Pacific countries
ACWL	Advisory Centre on WTO Law
AD	anti-dumping
AFL–CIO	American Federation of Labor—Congress of Industrial Organizations
AfT	Aid for Trade
AGOA	African Growth and Opportunity Act
AMS	Aggregate Measure of Support
ANZCER	Australia–New Zealand Closer Economic Relations Agreement
AoA	WTO Agreement on Agriculture
APEC	Asia-Pacific Economic Cooperation
ASCM	Agreement on Subsidies and Countervailing Measures
ASEAN	Association of Southeast Asian Nations
ASP	American Selling Price
ATC	Agreement on Textiles and Clothing
AWG–LCA	Ad Hoc Working Group on Long-Term Cooperative Action
BATNA	best alternative to negotiated agreement
BFC	Better Factories Cambodia
BICs	Brazil, India, and China
BIT	bilateral investment treaties
BRIC	Brazil, Russia, India, and China
CACM	Central American Common Market
CAP	Common Agricultural Policy
CARICOM	Caribbean Community and Common Market
CBD	UN Convention on Biological Diversity
CDP	Committee for Development Policy
CDR	carbon dioxide removal
CEFTA	Central European Free Trade Agreement
CEMAC	Communauté Économique et Monétaire de l'Afrique Centrale
CHF	Swiss francs
CIEL	Center for International Environmental Law
CIS	Commonwealth of Independent States (made up of former Soviet republics)
CITAC	Consuming Industries Trade Action Coalition

CITES	Convention on International Trade in Endangered Species of Wild Fauna and Flora
Codex	Codex Alimentarius Commission
COMESA	Common Market for Eastern and Southern Africa
CPA	corporate political activity
CSR	corporate social responsibility
CTE	Committee on Trade and Environment
CTESS	Committee on Trade and Environment Special Session
CU	customs union
CVD	countervailing duties
DA	Development Agenda
DDA	Doha Development Agenda
DDG	Deputy Director-General
DFQF	duty-free and quota-free
DG	Director-General
DM	Deutsche Mark
DR–CAFTA	Dominican Republic–Central America Free Trade Agreement
DSB	Dispute Settlement Body
DSM	dispute settlement mechanism
DSU	Dispute Settlement Understanding
DTIS	Diagnostic Trade Integration Study
EAC	East African Community
EC	European Community/Communities
ECJ	European Court of Justice
ECOSOC	United Nations Economic and Social Council
ECOWAS	Economic Community of West African States
EEC	European Economic Community
EFTA	European Free Trade Association
EHS	environment, health and safety
EIF	Enhanced Integrated Framework
EPA	Environmental Protection Agency
ERT	European Round Table of Industrialists
EU	European Union
EVI	economic vulnerability index
FAO	Food and Agriculture Organization of the United Nations
FIPs	Five Interested Parties
FDI	foreign direct investment
FLEGT	Forest Law Enforcement, Governance, and Trade (EU)
FOGS	Negotiating Group on the Functioning of the GATT System
FTA	free trade agreement
GATS	General Agreement on Trade in Services
GATT	General Agreement on Tariffs and Trade

GCC	Gulf Cooperation Council
GDP	gross domestic product
GHG	greenhouse gases
GM	genetically modified
GNI	Gross National Income
GI	geographical indication
GMO	genetically modified
GNI	Gross National Income
GPA	Government Procurement Agreement
GSP	Generalized System of Preferences
HAI	human asset index
HOPE	II Haitian Hemispheric Opportunity through Partnership Encouragement
HR	human resource
HS	World Custom Organization's Harmonized Commodity Coding and Classification System
HTS	harmonized tariff system
IBSA	India, Brazil, and South Africa
ICA	international commodity agreement
ICANN	Internet Corporation for Assigned Names and Numbers
ICJ	International Court of Justice
IEA	International Energy Agency
IF	Integrated Framework
IFC	International Finance Corporation
IGO	international governmental organization
IISD	International Institute for Sustainable Development
ILO	International Labour Organization
IMF	International Monetary Fund
IP	intellectual property
IPPC	Secretariat of the International Plant Protection Convention
IPR	intellectual property rights
IR	international relations
ISEAL	International Social and Environmental Accreditation and Labelling
ISO	International Organization for Standardization
ITC	International Trade Centre
ITO	International Trade Organization
ITU	International Telecommunication Union
JECFA	Joint FAO/WHO Expert Committee on Food Additives
LDC	least-developed country
LTFR	less than full reciprocity principle
MAI	Multilateral Agreement on Investment
MEA	multilateral environmental agreement

Mercosur	Southern Common Market
MFA	Multifibre Arrangement
MFN	most-favoured nation
MNE	multinational enterprise
MRA	mutual recognition agreement
MTN	multilateral trade negotiations
MTS	multilateral trading system
NAFTA	North American Free Trade Agreement
NAMA	non-agricultural market access
NFIC	net food-importing countries
NGMA	Negotiation Group on Market Access
NGO	non-governmental organization
NIEO	New International Economic Order
NIS	newly independent states
npr-PPMs	non-product-related production and processing methods
NSMD	non-state market driven
NTB	non-tariff barrier
ODA	Official Development Assistance
OECD	Organization for Economic Cooperation and Development
OIE	World Organization for Animal Health
PBM	political bargaining model
PI	parallel imports
PPM	process and production method/production processes and method[s]
PRSPs	Poverty Reduction Strategy Papers
PTA	preferential trade agreement
OIE	World Organization for Animal Health
QIZ	Qualified Industrial Zone
QR	quantitative import restriction
R&D	research and development
RAM	recently-acceded member to the WTO
RTA	regional trade agreement
RTAA	Reciprocal Trade Agreements Act
S&D	special and differential
SACU	South African Customs Union
SADC	Southern African Development Community
SAPTA/SAFTA	South Asian Preferential (Free) Trade Arrangement
SCM	Subsidies and Countervailing Measures
SDT	special and differential treatment
SPS	Sanitary and Phytosanitary Measures
SRM	solar radiation management
SSM	Special Safeguard Mechanism

STDF	Standards and Trade Development Facility
STOs	specific trade obligations
STR	special representative for trade negotiations (US)
SVE	small and vulnerable economies
TAFTA	Transatlantic Free Trade Agreement
TBT	Technical Barriers to Trade
TFEU	Treaty on the Functioning of the European Union
TNC	Trade Negotiations Committee
TPR	trade policy review
TPRB	Trade Policy Review Body
TPRD	Trade Policies Review Division
TPRM	Trade Policy Review Mechanism
TPSC	Trade Policy Staff Committee
TRAPCA	Trade Policy Training Centre in Africa
TRIPS	Trade-Related Aspects of Intellectual Property Rights
TRIMs	Trade-Related Investment Measures
TRQ	tariff rate quota
TRTA	Transparency Mechanism for Regional Trade Agreements, Trade-Related Technical Assistance
TTMRA	Trans-Tasman Mutual Recognition Arrangement
UAW	United Auto Workers
UDRP	Uniform Domain-Name Dispute-Resolution Policy
UEMOA	Union Économique et Monétaire Ouest Africaine
UN	United Nations
UNCTAD	United Nations Conference on Trade and Development
UNDP	United Nations Development Programme
UNECA	United Nations Economic Commission for Africa
UNEP	United Nations Environment Programme
UNFCCC	United Nations Framework Convention on Climate Change
UNIDO	United Nations Industrial Development Organization
UPOV	International Union for the Protection of New Varieties of Plants
USAID	United States Agency for International Development
USDA	United States Department of Agriculture
USITC	US International Trade Commission
USTR	United States Trade Representative
VCLT	Vienna Convention on the Law of Treaties
VER	voluntary export restraint
VPA	voluntary partnership agreement
WAEMU	West African Economic and Monetary Union
WIPO	World Intellectual Property Organization
WSSN	World Standards Services Network
WTO	World Trade Organization

About the Contributors

Amrita Narlikar is Reader in International Political Economy at the Department of Politics and International Studies, University of Cambridge, and the Director of the Centre for Rising Powers. She is also an Official Fellow of Darwin College, Cambridge.

Martin Daunton is Professor of Economic History and Master of Trinity Hall in the University of Cambridge. He has written extensively on British economic history since 1700, concentrating on the formation of economic and social policy. He is currently writing a book on the economic government of the world since 1933.

Robert M. Stern is Professor Emeritus of Economics and Public Policy, University of Michigan, and currently Visiting Professor, Goldman School of Public Policy, University of California, Berkeley.

Rudolf Adlung is Counsellor (Senior Economist) in the Trade in Services Division of the WTO Secretariat.

Todd Allee is Assistant Professor of Government and Politics at the University of Maryland. His research focuses on the World Trade Organization, international trade, US trade policy, foreign direct investment, and dispute settlement.

Richard Baldwin is Professor of International Economics at the Graduate Institute in Geneva, Policy Director of the Centre for Economic Policy Research, and founder and Editor-in-Chief of the policy portal, VoxEU.org.

The late Robert Baldwin was Professor of Economics, Emeritus, at the University of Wisconsin–Madison. He received his PhD in Economics from Harvard in 1950, and served in President Kennedy's Special Trade Representative Office as Chief Economist.

Thomas Bernauer is Professor of Political Science at ETH Zurich.

Steven Bernstein is Associate Professor in the Department of Political Science, and Director, Master of Global Affairs, at the University of Toronto.

Richard Blackhurst is an Adjunct Professor at The Fletcher School, Tufts University. He was Director of Economic Research and Analysis at the GATT/WTO Secretariat (1985–97) and the founding editor of the World Trade Review.

Andrew G. Brown is a former Director in the Department of Economic and Social Affairs at the United Nations, New York.

Drusilla Brown is an Associate Professor of Economics at Tufts University and is the Director of the International Relations Program.

Helen Coskeran is a PhD student at the Department of Politics and International Studies, University of Cambridge.

Thomas Cottier is Professor of European and International Economic Law, and Managing Director of the World Trade Institute, University of Bern, Switzerland.

Cédric Dupont is Professor of Political Science at the Graduate Institute of International and Development Studies in Geneva.

Manfred Elsig is Assistant Professor in International Relations at the World Trade Institute, University of Bern.

Meera Fickling is a graduate student studying energy and environmental policy at Duke University. She was a Research Analyst at the Peterson Institute for International Economics from 2008 to 2011.

Joseph Michael Finger organized the first Trade Policy Research Group at the World Bank and served as Lead Economist and Chief of that group. Since retiring from the World Bank in 2001 he has done work for the Asian Development Bank, the United Nations Food and Agricultural Organization, the UN Millennium Project Task Force on Trade, the UK Department for International Development, and for several developing country governments.

Judith Goldstein is the Janet Peck Professor of International Communication and Professor of Political Science at Stanford University, California. She is also a Senior Fellow at the Stanford Center for Economic Policy Research and, by courtesy, the Freeman Spogli Institute for International Studies.

Erin Hannah is Assistant Professor in the Department of Political Science, King's University College, at the University of Western Ontario.

Bernard Hoekman is Director of the International Trade Department at the World Bank. He is also a Research Fellow at the Centre for Economic Policy Research, London, and a Senior Associate in the Economic Research Forum for the Middle East, Iran, and Turkey.

Robert Howse is Lloyd C. Nelson Professor of International Law and Faculty Co-Director of the Institute for International Law and Justice, New York University Law School.

Gary Hufbauer is the Reginald Jones Senior Fellow at the Peterson Institute for International Economics. He has written extensively on international trade, international taxation, economic sanctions, and climate change.

Marion Jansen is the Head of the Trade and Employment Programme in the International Labour Office. She is currently on leave from her position as a Counsellor in the Economic Research and Statistics Division of the World Trade Organization.

Tim Josling is Senior Fellow, Freeman Spogli Institute for International Studies, Stanford University, and Professor Emeritus, Food Research Institute, Stanford University.

Dan Kim is Research Associate at the Centre for Rising Powers, and is in the final year of his doctorate as a Jack Kent Cooke Foundation Graduate Scholar at the Department of Politics and International Studies, University of Cambridge.

Sam Laird is Special Professor of International Economics, University of Nottingham, Visiting Professor, Trade Policy Training Centre in Africa (TRAPCA), Arusha, and a former staff member of the Trade Policies Review Division.

Steven McGuire is Professor of Management and Director, Centre for International Business and Public Policy at the School of Management and Business, Aberystwyth University. He is also Visiting Professor at the Audencia Nantes School of Management. He has published extensively on firms and the international trade system, and on technology policy in Europe and the United States.

Keith Maskus is Professor of Economics and Associate Dean for Social Sciences at the University of Colorado at Boulder. He is also an Adjunct Professor at the University of Adelaide and a frequent consultant for the World Bank and World Intellectual Property Organization.

Mitsuo Matsushita is Professor Emeritus of Tokyo University and a former member of the WTO Appellate Body.

Patrick Messerlin is Professor of Economics at Sciences Po Paris, and the Director of Groupe d'Économie Mondiale at Sciences Po. He is also a member of the Trade Council of the World Economic Forum.

Joost Pauwelyn is Professor of International Law at the Graduate Institute of International and Development Studies in Geneva.

Ernest Preeg is Senior Adviser for International Trade and Finance, Manufacturers Alliance, Arlington, Virginia, and author of *Traders in a Brave New World: The Uruguay Round and the Future of the International Trading System*.

Shishir Priyadarshi is the Director of the Development Division of the World Trade Organization in Geneva. He has written extensively on a wide range of WTO topics, including international trade and development, and regularly lectures in WTO training programmes all over the world.

Taufiqur Rahman is a Counsellor in the Development Division of the World Trade Organization in Geneva. He is responsible for the work of the WTO's Committee on least-developed countries (LDCs)—a dedicated forum to address issues of interest to LDCs in the multilateral trading system. He regularly contributes to studies on LDC issues undertaken by the WTO Secretariat.

Gregory Shaffer is Melvin C. Steen Professor of Law at the University of Minnesota Law School. He has written extensively on international trade law, transatlantic relations, transnational law and legal process, hard and soft law in global governance, empirical work in international law, and legal realism.

Jens Steffek is Professor of Transnational Governance at the Institute for Political Science, Technische Universität Darmstadt, Germany. He is also a Principal Investigator in the Cluster of Excellence, 'The Formation of Normative Orders', hosted by the Goethe Universität, Frankfurt am Main.

Alan Sykes is James and Patricia Kowal Professor of Law, Stanford Law School, and directs the Masters Program in International Economic Law, Business and Policy. He is a leading expert on the application of economics to legal problems, and his writing and teaching have encompassed international trade, torts, contracts, insurance, antitrust, and economic analysis of law.

Richard Toye is Professor of Modern History at the University of Exeter. His books include *The Labour Party and the Planned Economy, 1931-1951* and (with John Toye) *The UN and Global Political Economy*.

Joel Trachtman is Professor of International Law at The Fletcher School of Law and Diplomacy, Tufts University.

Raymundo Valdés is a staff member of the Trade Policies Review Division at the WTO.

Brendan Vickers is Head of Research and Policy in the International Trade and Economic Development division of the Department of Trade and Industry in South Africa, and a Research Associate of the Department of Political Sciences, University of Pretoria, South Africa. He writes in his personal capacity.

Thomas Zeiler is Professor of History and International Affairs at the University of Colorado at Boulder, and the Director of the Global Studies Residential Academic Program.

INTRODUCTION

AMRITA NARLIKAR, MARTIN DAUNTON,
ROBERT STERN

THE World Trade Organization (WTO) came into existence in 1995, but behind its apparent youth lie over five decades of institutional history, learning, and evolution that have made the multilateral trading system what it is today. This volume grapples with this critical, complex, and controversial organization.

Of all the international organizations and regimes that were negotiated at the end of the Second World War, at least in fulfilling their immediate mandate, few have had as successful a record as the multilateral trade regime. Governed first by the General Agreement on Tariffs and Trade (GATT), and succeeded by the WTO, the regime has facilitated an impressive reduction in tariff and non-tariff barriers to international trade. The regime ensures that its members enjoy the benefits of freer trade and more open markets, access to which is negotiated on a multilateral basis. Further, they do so in a consistent and reliable manner due to the enforceable rules that underpin the multilateral trading system. This resilience of the system came to the fore most visibly in the aftermath of the global financial crisis: despite predictions of the return to the protectionism of the 1930s and all its devastating consequences, markets have remained open and trade has continued to provide a vital route of recovery.[1] The demand for the regime is evident in the large and growing number of countries clamouring to become its members: the original contracting parties to the GATT numbered 23; today the WTO has 153 members, and 31 countries with observer status.[2] And yet, not all is well with the organization.

The trading system, even in the days of the GATT, was subject to ill-informed attacks and accusations from the outside. The replacement of the GATT with a full-blown organization and a strengthened dispute settlement mechanism (DSM) brought the WTO even more into the public eye. But the difficulties that afflict the WTO today

---

[1] Eichengreen and O'Rourke 2010.

[2] Acquiring 'observer status' is not an empty commitment: with the exception of the Holy See, all governments are required to start negotiating their accession within five years of acquiring their observer status.

derive not just from crackpot and opinionated outsiders, but also well-meaning critics; the malaise that grips the organization now is thus more serious. Its manifestation in the early 2000s took the shape of the demand for improved processes of participation by its own members from the developing world. Despite the responsiveness of the organization to these demands, dissatisfaction and disengagement persist (and now pervade through not just its developing country members, but also the industrialized countries). Their most visible symptom can be found in the deadlocks that have marred the negotiations of its Doha Development Agenda (the first round of trade negotiations to be launched since the creation of the WTO in 2001 was due for completion in 2005; almost a decade after its launch, agreement is proving elusive).[3] Repeatedly missed deadlines not only delay the significant gains to be had from agreement, but also undermine the credibility of the organization. Disengaged politicians turn to less efficient but easier bilateral and regional alternatives, which reinforces the disengagement with the WTO.

The purpose of this handbook is to provide a holistic understanding of what the WTO does, how it goes about fulfilling its tasks, why it has reached the point of crisis today despite having a long history of achievements behind it, and how might it contend with current and new challenges. To effectively address the key academic and policy debates that surround the WTO, an interdisciplinary perspective is indispensable. The editorial team thus comprises a political scientist, a historian, and an economist; our distinguished and international team of authors includes political scientists, historians, economists, lawyers, and practitioners working in the area of multilateral trade.

Our interdisciplinary approach is complemented by our explicit attempt to bring together a diversity of perspectives on the WTO. Some of us are more committed to the cause of free trade than others; for some, issues of distributive justice are central, while others are more engaged with questions of efficiency and feasibility; we are all cautiously sanguine, but in different degrees, about the possibility of institutional reform. We believe that this pluralism is one of the strengths of the book: it allows us a more comprehensive understanding of the politics of the WTO where an even bigger diversity of approaches is bubbling away, and it ensures that the volume brings together the cutting-edge and leading research in the field irrespective of the personal ideological leanings of authors.

The result of our collective endeavours is this volume, which we believe provides an authoritative reference point for all those interested in working in and around the specific organization, as well as others interested more generally in multilateral economic institutions. All the chapters present original and state-of-the-art research material. They critically engage with existing academic and policy debates, and also contribute to the evolution of the field by setting the agenda for current and future WTO studies. All

---

[3] An example of the ferocity of debate in the trade policy circles on the possibility and implications of Doha crashing can be found on <http://groups.google.com/group/cuts-tradeforum> accessed on 15 April 2011.

the chapters also include extensive bibliographies that will be indispensable for the reader wishing to follow up on any of the key issues addressed.

We have divided the subject matter of this handbook into an introduction followed by 34 chapters, which are categorized under nine parts. The driving logic of the nine parts stems from five fundamental puzzles: the theory behind the institution (Part I), negotiation of the agreements (Parts II, III, and IV), the substance of the agreements (Part V), implementation and enforcement (Part VI), and reform of the system (Parts VII, VIII, and IX). What follows below is a brief outline of this logic and the puzzles that underlie it. Section 2 of this introduction offers a brief overview of the chapters. Section 3 concludes with a summary of the major themes that emerge from the collection.

1 THE DRIVING PUZZLE

The case in favour of free trade is theoretically clear and empirically rich.[4] We know that, bar a few exceptions, trade liberalization is a welfare-maximizing pursuit. But the benefits from free trade do not lie in the material sphere or 'universal opulence' alone. For over three centuries, classical–liberal economists have been pointing to the pacifying effects of trade. The cataclysmic costs of ignoring this wisdom were illustrated most visibly in the interwar years, when the beggar-thy-neighbour policies across nations worsened the Great Depression and set the stage for the Second World War. The hard lessons of rampant protectionism struck deep, and leading negotiators of the post-war economic system displayed an explicit recognition of the wide-ranging costs that illiberal trade policies could yield. Henry Morgenthau (the US Secretary for the Treasury), for instance, at the opening of the Bretton Woods conference, declaimed the following conviction:

> All of us have seen the great economic tragedy of our time. We saw the worldwide depression of the 1930s. We saw currency disorders develop and spread from land to land, destroying the basis for international trade and international investment and even international faith. In their wake, we saw unemployment and wretchedness— idle tools, wasted wealth. We saw their victims fall prey, in places, to demagogues and dictators. We saw bewilderment and bitterness become the breeders of fascism, and, finally, of war.[5]

The imperatives that guided politicians and policymakers seeking to resurrect the war-torn economic system in 1944 of course differed significantly from the imperatives that guided their successors in 1994. But particularly striking in the Agreement Establishing the WTO, too, is (a) the continued commitment to trade liberalization, and (b) the recognition that free trade is not an end in itself but a means towards achieving a

---

[4] For a particularly readable and lucid account of both the classical case for free trade, and its relevance today, see Bhagwati 2003.

[5] Morgenthau 1944.

multiplicity of goals. These goals include and go beyond the economic realm, ranging from 'raising standards of living, ensuring full employment and a large and steadily growing volume of real income and effective demand, and expanding the production of, and trade in, goods and services', to 'sustainable development' and ensuring that 'developing countries...secure a share in the growth in international trade commensurate with the needs of their economic development'. Importantly, the WTO does not attempt to secure all these aspirations directly; its action is firmly focused in the domain of trade governance. It thus expresses the commitment of members to achieve these several noble objectives via 'the substantial reduction of tariffs and other barriers to trade' and resolves 'to develop an integrated, more viable and durable multilateral trading system'.[6] Given the historical experience and also the epistemic consensus, neither the trade-specific objectives of the WTO, nor the more general aspirations that they aim to secure via freer trade, should be controversial. That they provoke extreme passions nonetheless can be explained by five sets of issues that can serve as roadblocks on the pathway of good intentions: (1) caveats regarding the theory; (2) controversies over process; (3) contestation over substance; (4) issues of implementation and enforcement; and (5) contested directions of reform (that overlap somewhat with the first four sets of problems, but also include additional issues).

1.1 Rider to the theory

The intuition behind the argument in favour of free trade is beautiful and simple. Specialization on the basis of comparative (rather than absolute) advantage allows for the gains from trade. In fact, as classical liberal economists have pointed out convincingly and repeatedly, bar a few exceptions, the gains from trade accrue to any country that lowers trade barriers, irrespective of what other countries do. Paul Krugman was not far off the mark when he claimed, 'If economists ruled the world, there would be no need for a World Trade Organization.'[7] But the world is not ruled by economists, and convincing theory is difficult to translate into practice for at least two reasons.

First, while trade liberalization almost always improves aggregate national welfare, it also produces winners and losers within societies. And not all the winners and losers are equally well organized or equally able to articulate their interests into policy. Producer interests that stand to lose from market opening, for example, tend to be more concentrated, better organized, and more vocal than the consumer interests that stand to win from the process. States that have more articulate exporter interests and consumer interests are likely to face an easier task selling liberalization at home, as are also states that have effective compensation mechanisms that can secure buy-in from potential losers. But effectively, much depends on the domestic configurations of interests: the promise

---

[6] WTO 1994.   [7] Krugman 1997.

of significant collective gains from free trade may remain unfulfilled if better organized, small-group, protectionist interests carry more influence in policy. Herein lies the first important deterrent to the exploitation of the gains from free trade: the economist proposes, the politician disposes.

Related to the above are the several domestic bottlenecks that can prevent the translation of the gains from trade among large groups (thereby creating a backlash against trade liberalization). Examples of such bottlenecks include high levels of corruption that render compensation schemes ineffective, and low levels of education and poor infrastructural facilities that disallow labour mobility. International trade agreements (such as those governed by the WTO) become the easy scapegoats for failures of public policy.

Second, while the aggregate benefits of free trade for states per se are clear, trade policy does not operate in a vacuum. Governments, even if cognizant of the benefits of lowering their barriers to trade, may attach greater and more immediate priority to alternative or competing goals such as self-sufficiency in a dangerous political context abroad (or deeply embedded historical concerns such as national food security), or full employment in hard times at home. Further, to be effective, free trade policies need to be balanced by complementary policies in related areas: the trade-creating effects of low tariffs can, for example, be countered by currency manipulation. Depending on the policy trade-offs that governments are willing to make, free trade might win—but it also might not.

1.2 The process of freeing up trade

There are several routes to achieving the goal of international cooperation on multilateral trade, and some are more effective than others. We are directly concerned in this handbook with three aspects of the negotiation process: historical process, decision-making and negotiation process, and process as agency.

Attention to the historical process whereby multilateral trade negotiations have been conducted takes us into the heart of institutional evolution. Through an examination of the failed negotiations of the International Trade Organization (ITO), the eight successful trade rounds of the GATT, and the establishment of the WTO, we can find some important continuities and changes that explain the anachronisms and inconsistencies that the organization faces today.

The history of the GATT also holds the key to understanding peculiarities of decision-making and negotiation processes in the WTO. The WTO stands out in the universe of the international organizations as being a 'member-driven' organization, where the members themselves are responsible for all decision-making (rather than an executive board or a secretariat to which such powers might be delegated). Even today, despite the wide reach and enforceability of its mandate, its Secretariat remains quite small when compared to other international organizations. The reason for this lies in the roots of the WTO in the GATT. As the GATT was not a proper organization, it was unable to create its own secretariat; the solution that was resolved through the continued existence of the Interim Commission for the International Trade Organization (even after the ITO negotiations had failed) which provided the basis for the GATT Secretariat.[8]

Another particularly interesting example is consensus-based decision-making. The text of GATT 1947 accorded each contracting party one vote, and Article XXV:4 stated that, except when specified otherwise, all decisions would be arrived at through a majority vote. In practice, however, the norm of decision-making in the GATT was consensus, which acquired formal recognition in the Agreement Establishing the WTO (Article IX:1).[9] The practice of consensus diplomacy worked well in the days of the GATT, when most decisions were arrived at through consultations among the 'Quad' (the EU, US, Canada and Japan), and when the rest of the contracting parties were willing to stand on the margins in return for a free ride on concessions exchanged among the major players. It has, however, proven to be a considerably less effective method of decision-making in the WTO, where even the core group of countries is much more diverse than the old Quad, and even smaller players recognize the importance of exercising their voice over rules that have the potential to be strictly enforced.

This brings us to the third aspect of process, which is agency. Quad-dominated diplomacy was one of the reasons why developing countries would refer to the GATT as the 'Rich Man's Club'. Changes—both in terms of balance of power, and ideas of development and fairness—have resulted in a dramatic change in the main actors in the WTO. The old Quad has been replaced in the Doha negotiations by permutations of a new core group that has consistently included Brazil, India, and China, besides the EU and the US. Nor are the voices of the emerging markets the only new voices in key WTO processes. Particularly after the collapse of the Seattle Ministerial, and amidst a changing normative context internationally (that attaches increasing importance to development concerns, such as the Millennium Development Goals), the WTO has addressed many of the criticisms that it had encountered over marginalization of smaller developing countries. As a result of these institutional changes, as well as their own initiatives, many of the smaller players—including the least-developed countries (LDCs)—have come to exercise an unprecedented agency in the organization. And developing countries—ranging from the rising powers of Brazil, India, and China (BICs),[10] to the LDCs—have had their agency in the WTO further reinforced through the coalitions that they operate in. These are very important and positive developments, especially for those traditionally concerned with the democratic deficit of international organizations. But they come at a cost.

Increasing multipolarity at the core of the organization (which comes hand in hand with not just a larger number of powerful players, but players at differing levels of development and visions of development) improves fairness of process. But its coexistence

---

[8] Hudec 1998.

[9] Consensus is reached if no member 'formally objects to the proposed decision'.

[10] Note that the 'R' is missing from the acronym; the reason why we refer to the BICs rather than the BRICs is because Russia became a member of the WTO only in December 2011. It is too early to analyse or predict its behaviour in the organization as a full member.

with GATT-derived decision-making and negotiation approaches (e.g. consensus, single undertaking) also means that the organization is much less efficient in arriving at decisions, and is more prone to the recurrence of deadlock.[11] A study of the different aspects of the WTO's process—historical and current—is essential to explaining the institutional evolution of the organization thus far, and also exploring directions for reform.

1.3 The substance of the agreements

If the process underpinning the workings of the WTO has proven conflict prone, the substance of its agreements has been no less controversial. Dating back to the ITO negotiations, states have fought hard over what is covered by the rules, and how the rules themselves are framed. The distributive consequences of these rules can be profound in their own right, and are even more so in a system driven primarily by a mercantilist logic (where acquiring market access is seen as a win, but opening up one's own market is seen as a 'concession'). While the content and implications of the main agreements are explored in specific chapters in the handbook, we highlight below a broad set of problems in the area of substance and their impact on institutional evolution.

The success of the early rounds of the GATT lay in the fact that its coverage was limited to the area of tariffs and trade in goods (in contrast to the ITO, which had sought to cover a much bigger terrain that included employment, development, restrictive business practices, and commodities). But the GATT, in later years, and the WTO today, are in some ways victims of these past successes. As tariffs fell, both the GATT and the WTO had to go into more difficult areas of negotiation. The GATT began its foray into addressing non-tariff barriers (or behind-the-border measures) in the Kennedy Round; the Uruguay Round saw its agenda expand beyond the traditional domain of goods to include the 'new issues' of trade in services, Trade-Related Aspects of Intellectual Property Rights (TRIPS), and Agreement on Trade-Related Investment Measures (TRIMs). The conflict over what was included in the GATT, and what was excluded, was fought along North–South lines. Developing countries repeatedly pointed to the exclusion of areas in which their comparative advantage lay (such as textiles and agriculture), and the inclusion of areas that were of advantage to the North (such as TRIPS). They also resented the increasing intrusiveness of some GATT rules, which usually involved requirements for developing countries to bring their own standards (e.g. on customs valuation, or Sanitary and Phytosanitary standards) in line with those of the developed countries. The dissatisfaction of the developing countries with the substance of the Uruguay Round agreements heightened their expectations and also increased their distrust.[12]

The WTO is in even more difficult terrain than the GATT was in the Uruguay Round. When the Doha Development Agenda (DDA) was launched, it promised to be the most ambitious of all trade rounds negotiated in the multilateral trade regime. Even the more streamlined DDA is proving to be a challenge though. Having already bound their tariffs

---

[11] Narlikar 2010.   [12] Narlikar 2005.

on industrial goods, members must now agree to reduce the 'water in the tariffs', with developed countries anxious to secure real tariff cuts and market access in the emerging economies. Agriculture—the bête noire of the GATT—can no longer be brushed under the carpet with exceptions, with developing countries particularly enraged by the agricultural protectionism of the EU and the US. Progress in services negotiations (an area where potential gains are still high) has been slow, partly due to the request–offer negotiation method. The focus on development, while essential to bringing the developing world on board, has muddied the waters further in at least two serious ways. First, and unlike a precise and quantifiable commitment to lowering tariff barriers, the commitment to development is vague and subject to many different interpretations. This strategy of deliberate vagueness in framing can work well in securing buy-in in the agenda-setting stage, but as trade negotiators are learning the hard way, it can allow expectations to snowball in many different and even incompatible directions, and thereby make it harder to reach an agreement. Second, the focus on development may have contributed to the misperception in the developed economies—and particularly business groups within them—that the round is based on charity (not reciprocity) and offers them little gains. The vital domestic support for trade liberalization in the developed world, which was vital in the launch of the Uruguay Round, is missing in the case of the DDA.

The above examples are instances of the difficulties associated with negotiating the substance of WTO agreements, even if members are agreed upon the broad issue. And in many instances, even agreeing on the broader agenda can be difficult—recall, for instance, the furore over the inclusion of services, TRIPS, and TRIMs in the Uruguay Round, and the Singapore Issues in the DDA. Trade liberalization may be a welfare-maximizing pursuit, but there is nothing automatic or obvious in the prioritization of issue areas or the rules whereby market opening is facilitated.

1.4 Implementation and enforcement

As a member-driven organization, the WTO places the onus of implementing and enforcing its agreements on the members themselves. But it does provide strengthened mechanisms that members can use in this process in the form of a strengthened Trade Policy Review Mechanism and a much more powerful Dispute Settlement Mechanism (DSM). The far-reaching automaticity and enforceability of the WTO's DSM is one reason why advocates of non-trade concerns (ranging from labour standards and human rights, to environment, sustainable development and climate change) are so keen to have these issues included within the mandate of the WTO. Members of the WTO are certainly much more inclined to use the DSM than they were in the GATT: since the founding of the WTO to April 2011, 427 dispute cases have been brought to the DSM, in contrast to just 101 panel reports that were adopted by the DSB in the entire life of the GATT. Several important concerns remain, however. The major ones are highlighted below.

First, even though the number of developing countries (particularly the BICs) using the DSM has increased, litigation remains an expensive and technical business that many weaker developing countries are ill-equipped to take on. This is reflected in the figures: the most frequent users of the DSM are the US and the EU, which appear as complainants in 97 and 83 cases respectively; Brazil and India have the highest usage amongst developing country members, with 25 and 19 cases brought to the DSM as complainants; LDCs appear sparsely, and mainly as third party litigants (with the exception of Bangladesh, which brought a case in 2004 as complainant). Second, if a ruling goes in a country's favour, and the respondent fails to comply, the complainant is granted the right to retaliate. But this method of enforcement sometimes acts as a deterrent to smaller countries, which can seldom hope to impact the economies of a much larger respondent. Third, the logic of the enforcement mechanism—retaliation—is inherently trade-distorting. This is in keeping with the aforementioned mercantilism underpinning the system, but makes little sense from a trade-liberalizing perspective as retaliation thus undertaken is welfare-reducing for the complainant too. Fourth, the WTO faces an imbalance in that its relatively efficient DSM is not matched by equal efficiency in the organization's negotiation function. The temptation for countries to litigate the way out of deadlock is high, when they are unable to reach the solutions they desire via the negotiation process.[13] This raises some fundamental questions that go to the heart of what the functions of the WTO are, and how it can and should go about fulfilling them. It also raises implications for power distributions within the WTO: especially from the perspective of developing countries, whose effective use of the negotiation process is quite recent, potential forum-shifting from the General Council to the Dispute Settlement Body would be quite detrimental.

1.5 Contested directions for reform

The impressive record of the WTO in fostering multilateral trade liberalization (in good times and bad) notwithstanding, the organization faces several new challenges. The fifth and final set of problems driving this handbook relates to the practical and normative challenges that the WTO faces, and takes us into an examination of the directions of institutional reform.

The problem of institutional reform derives from several sources. In part, as mentioned earlier, the WTO is a victim of its own success: its impressive record in addressing issues such as the binding of tariffs necessarily brings it into the more contested and controversial areas (such as agriculture). On process too, it is one of the few international organizations to adapt so readily to the changing balance of power and also evolving norms of greater inclusiveness and transparency. But here too, this adaptability has generated costs that include declining efficiency, and also declining support from almost all its constituencies. The main challenge lies in finding appropriate reform measures that

---

[13] Gehring 2010.

can harness and strengthen the very significant progress that the institution has made, while countering some of the unintended costs that this progress has generated. It is not our task in this handbook to recommend a particular set of policies. But we do see it very much within our collective mandate to analyse the leading research in this area, and comment on comparative strengths, weaknesses, and overall workability of various proposals. We believe that such an analysis is a timely and urgent step not only in WTO studies, but one that bears relevance for other institutions of global economic governance.

2 OUTLINE OF THE BOOK

The book is divided into nine parts, which fit within the five puzzles identified in the previous section (see Table 1, which highlights the structure of the book). A brief outline of each of the nine parts follows.

Table 1 Book outline

Puzzles	Parts	Chapter topics
Puzzle 1 Riders to the Theory	Part I Theory of Multilateral Trade Liberalization	1 The Case for a Multilateral Trade Organization (Baldwin)
		2 The Inconsistent Quartet (Daunton)
		3 Trade Liberalization and Domestic Politics (Goldstein)
Puzzle 2 Process: Challenges and Opportunities	Part II Institutional Evolution: Building up the WTO	4 The International Trade Organization (Toye)
		5 The Expanding Mandate of the GATT (Zeiler)
		6 The Uruguay Round Negotiations and the Creation of the WTO (Preeg)
	Part III Process Behind the Workings of the WTO	7 The Role of the Director-General and the Secretariat (Blackhurst)
		8 Defining the Borders of the WTO Agenda (Jansen)
		9 Bargaining Coalitions in the WTO (Narlikar)
	Part IV Agency in the WTO	10 The Influence of the EU (Messerlin)
		11 The Role of the US (Allee)
		12 The Role of the BRICS in the WTO (Vickers)
		13 Least-Developed Countries in the WTO (Priyadarshi and Rahman)
		14 NGOs and Social Movements at the WTO (Steffek)
		15 Corporations and Organized Labour in the WTO (McGuire)

Puzzles	Parts	Chapter topics
Puzzle 3 Substance of the Agreements	Part V Substance of the Agreements	16 Trade in Manufactures and Agricultural Products (Coskeran, Kim, and Narlikar)
		17 Trade in Services (Adlung)
		18 Trade-Related Intellectual Property Rights (Maskus)
		19 Flexibilities, Rules, and Trade Remedies (Finger)
		20 Regulatory Measures (Howse)
Puzzle 4 Enforcement	Part VI Implementation and Enforcement	21 The Trade Policy Review Mechanism (Laird and Valdés)
		22 Dispute Settlement Mechanism (Bernauer, Elsig, and Pauwelyn)
		23 The Appellate Body (Matsushita)
		24 Interpretation and Institutional Choice (Shaffer and Trachtman)
		25 Ensuring Compliance? (Sykes)
Puzzle 5 Institutional Reform	Part VII Challenges to the System	26 Persistent Deadlock (Elsig and Dupont)
		27 The Role of Domestic Courts in the Implementation of WTO Law (Cottier)
		28 Preferential Trading Arrangements (Baldwin)
		29 Food, Agriculture, and Natural Resources (Josling)
	Part VIII Normative Issues	30 Fairness in the WTO Trading System (Brown and Stern)
		31 Labour Standards and Human Rights (Brown)
		32 Trade and the Environment (Hufbauer and Fickling)
	Part IX Reform of the WTO	33 Proposals for WTO Reform (Hoekman)
		34 The WTO and Institutional (In)Coherence (Bernstein and Hannah)

Part I: Theory of multilateral trade liberalization

Part I corresponds with Puzzle 1, and comprises three chapters. Chapter 1, by Robert Baldwin, presents us with an eloquent case for the GATT and the WTO by highlighting their successful empirical record in achieving trade liberalization. He also engages with theories of political economy to explain why countries need to form trade agreements at all (and why they do not commit readily to unilateral trade liberalization, despite the promise of its benefits). Having a multilateral basis to trade liberalization helps countries overcome the risks associated with unilateral market opening. But the path to free trade never does run smooth, and as Martin Daunton argues persuasively in Chapter 2, trade is only one of several competing goals that governments pursue. He expands the discussion of the 'trilemma' to focus on the 'Inconsistent Quartet' to highlight the trade-offs that have to be made between trade, exchange rates, capital controls, and domestic monetary policy. He further gives us historical examples and engages with current problems to shed new light on the conditions in which free trade triumphed over some of these other goals, and lost out in others. Chapter 3, by Judith Goldstein, analyses the domestic constraints on trade liberalization. Using the lens of economic interests, political institutions, and ideas, Goldstein demonstrates the constraining effects of domestic politics, particularly in democratic societies. She also explains how these constraints were overcome, and liberalization made more politically stable, with the help of the rules and norms of the GATT, and identifies new dangers to further liberalization that are rooted in the legalization of the multilateral trading regime of the WTO.

Part II: Institutional evolution: building up the WTO

While three parts of the handbook (II, III, and IV) deal with Puzzle 2—i.e. the evolution and impact of process—Part II focuses on the historical processes of the failed ITO and the more successful GATT, which hold the key to understanding many institutional peculiarities of the WTO.

In Chapter 4, Richard Toye presents an analysis of the unsuccessful attempt to create the ITO, and carefully traces the negotiation processes that contributed to this failure. Interestingly, in the conclusion, he engages in counterfactual analysis to argue, 'the ITO might have produced a more inclusive, productive, orderly and just world economy than that which in fact emerged'. This argument, in fact, also points towards one of the sources of the successes of the GATT—its lower ambition and comparatively weaker enforceability allowed for a successful negotiation in the first instance, while its de facto functioning as a 'Rich Man's Club'—for all its problems—did contribute to its sustained efficiency.

Chapter 5, by Thomas Zeiler, focuses on the first seven rounds of GATT, and presents a fascinating account of the reasons and (often fraught) processes whereby the mandate of the GATT expanded, and also why it took the particular directions that it did. Inherent in this expansion were also several problems, all of which contributed to the search for a solution that would eventually take the shape of the WTO. Several of the issues that Zeiler raises are picked up by the following chapter.

Chapter 6, by Ernest Preeg, studies the Uruguay Round—a round with a deeper and wider reach than all previous rounds, and the round that also led to the creation of the WTO. Preeg presents a lively analysis of the controversies that dogged the Uruguay Round each step of the way. He also examines the processes that led to the creation of the WTO. Preeg's analysis of the distinctive characteristics of the WTO and his brief overview of the expanse of its agreements (along with the previous two chapters, which highlight the difficulties that former trade negotiators had faced in their pursuit of a fully fledged organization) provide an indication of just how momentous an achievement the creation of the WTO was. His final note is sombre, however, where he analyses the problems associated with the altered balance of power in the WTO, the rise of regionalism, and the persistence of what he calls the 'irrational dichotomy between developed and developing economies'. Variants of these themes recur in several chapters of the book.

Part III: Process behind the workings of the WTO

This group of chapters focuses on the processes that underlie the everyday functioning of the WTO. It comprises three chapters, which focus on the role of the Director-General and Secretariat, the process of agenda-setting, and the role of coalitions respectively.

The role of the Director-General and the Secretariat forms the focus of Chapter 7 by Richard Blackhurst. Blackhurst provides a valuable overview of the WTO's relatively small bureaucracy, and its roots in the GATT. Interestingly, altered circumstances in the WTO—expanded membership, expanded agenda, a strengthened DSM, behind-the-border reach of its rules (and into domestic regulations and values), and the rise of developing countries—have been accompanied by a diminished role for the Secretariat. Blackhurst identifies this trend as almost inevitable, and examines proposals for reform. His conclusion, however, is that the Secretariat has consistently and successfully acted as the 'guardian' of the system for at least three decades, and that the direction for reform should lie elsewhere.

Chapter 8, by Marion Jansen, addresses the process of agenda-setting in the WTO. Defining the borders of the regime was, and remains, a deeply contested issue, and particularly controversial is the link between trade liberalization and behind-the-border measures. As Jansen rightly points out, the 2008–9 financial crisis demonstrated that strong liberalization in a weak regulatory environment can lead to global economic instability. But encroaching into the domestic regulatory environment of states can be sensitive: not only are domestic regulations often embedded in a particular cultural heritage, but changes to the regulatory status quo also generate costs. After providing us with the rationale for linking domestic regulations to trade negotiations, she traces the process whereby the trade agenda has expanded in the GATT and the WTO. Note that this chapter offers particularly useful background for Part V on the substance of the agreements.

The focus of Chapter 9 is the role of coalitions in the institutional processes of the WTO. Amrita Narlikar argues here that while bargaining coalitions, especially of developing countries, are first and foremost agents of the power that stems from collective agency (and hence the link between this chapter and the actor-focused chapters in Part IV), they have come to acquire a vital role in the WTO's decision-making and negotiation processes. Narlikar traces the changing rationale and structure of coalitions, from the Uruguay Round to the DDA, and also investigates the bargaining strategies that the DDA coalitions have used, both to preserve unity among their own members, and also in dealing with the outside parties. These strategies have contributed to the emergence of 'strong' coalitions, which have become an integral part of the negotiation and decision-making process, and which are, as a result, more inclusive than ever before. But as Narlikar argues, according such a role to coalitions is not without problems: the most serious is their contribution to the making of an organization that is more deadlock-prone and conflict-ridden. The final section of the chapter offers possible solutions.

It is worth mentioning that the fourth factor that underpins the everyday workings of the WTO is the decision-making process. We chose not to have a separate chapter on this aspect of process in Part III of the volume because other chapters (within Part II, as well as Chapter 9) discuss this issue in the context of the institutional evolution of the organization. Chapter 33, by Bernard Hoekman, (in Part IX on Institutional Reform) further provides a succinct analysis of decision-making in the WTO before discussing proposals for reforming this, and could be read just as easily in tandem with Part III as a part of Part IX.

Part IV: Agency in the WTO

The member-driven nature of the WTO means that we must pay considerable attention to key players in the process, and the changing imperatives driving them. This part of the volume focuses on both state and non-state agency in the organization. Our country-specific chapters cover the EU and the US (both members of the former Quad and all permutations of the new Quad), the BICs (as the rising powers in the world trading system), and the LDCs (as among the weakest players in the trading system, but still providing us with instances of growing voice and influence). Part IV also includes two chapters on the non-state actors that have attempted, with varying degrees of success, to influence the workings of the organization: business and organized labour groups on the one hand, and non-governmental organization (NGOs) and social movements on the other. While this part of the volume studies the central players in the WTO from a process perspective, these actors and their interests reappear in several other chapters of this volume.

Chapter 10, by Patrick Messerlin, studies the influence of the European Union as an actor in the WTO. Messerlin starts off with an important observation: the EU's influence in the GATT and the WTO has been quite different from that of other powers (such as the US). The uniqueness of its influence derives from the particular tools that it evolved—and continues to evolve—to facilitate its integration process. Further, this influence varies according to issue areas. For instance, Messerlin points out that the EU's influence is particularly visible in some of the more difficult areas, such as Technical Barriers to Trade, and the relatively newer areas, such as services, which the EU has already tackled successfully for its internal market. Of course, not all such strategies translate effectively at the multilateral level; Messerlin highlights examples where the EU's experience has been useful for trade liberalization in the WTO, and others where it has been less relevant.

Todd Allee, in Chapter 11, systematically analyses the changing role of the United States in the WTO system. The ambivalence of the US towards the system was reflected even at the time of the ITO negotiations: the US can in good measure be blamed for scuppering the Havana Charter through its failure to ratify it, and yet it played a vital role in the creation and maintenance of the GATT. Indeed, as Allee rightly points out, the US provided leadership and support for the GATT system for the first 30 years, but its role in the last 30 years of the regime has become 'more complicated and at times more contentious'. Allee's multi-causal analysis for decline in US support towards the regime includes three factors: (a) the decline in US hegemony; (b) the role of ideas, and particularly the change in the 'free trade mentality' to one that focuses more on the 'unfair practices' of other nations; and (c) the role of domestic interest groups, and particularly the increasing effectiveness of import-competing interests.

The focus of Chapter 12, by Brendan Vickers, is on the rising powers of Brazil, India, and China. All three, while still presenting themselves as members of the developing world, have come to acquire an unprecedented influence in the WTO. Their rise offers several new opportunities for the trading system, but also poses serious and unanticipated challenges. Vickers offers us two compelling reasons for studying the WTO diplomacy of the BICs: economically, the three have captured large shares of global trade, and politically, their growing voice in the WTO is reshaping at least some of the rules of the game. After a brief overview of the trade policies of the BICs, the chapter investigates the impact of the rising powers on the WTO along three fronts: rule-making, rule-enforcement, and coalitions. Vickers is careful to distinguish between the behaviours of Brazil, India, and China on all three fronts, while also highlighting some important similarities. And while all three show greater activism in the organization, activism does not equate with leadership.

Chapter 13, by Shishir Priyadarshi and Taufiqur Rahman, focuses on the least developed countries in the WTO. In some ways, this group forms the opposite end of the spectrum of the developing world from the BICs: neither do the LDCs enjoy remotely comparable market shares to the BICs, nor do they occupy a comparable position of importance in the key processes of the WTO. Priyadarshi and Rahman provide a brief overview of the trade profiles of the LDCs, and the constraints that they face in the trading system. But as the rest of the chapter demonstrates, the LDC story in the WTO is one that offers us cause for at least cautious optimism for two reasons. First, the WTO system has several flexibilities and other provisions that apply to the LDCs, and the attempts of the Doha negotiations to go even further to integrate them more effectively into the system through provisions like duty-free and quota-free market access and Aid for Trade. Second, the LDCs themselves have shown considerable initiative and agency through collective bargaining and building alliances with other developing countries. Even though the LDCs have not managed to acquire the clout that some of their counterparts from the developing world have, Priyadarshi and Rahman give a convincing account of their increasing empowerment in the WTO.

In Chapter 14, Jens Steffek analyses the role of NGOs and social movements in the WTO. After providing a theoretical overview that outlines the rationale for NGO involvement in intergovernmental organizations, Steffek traces the role of the NGOs in the multilateral trading system from a historical perspective. The GATT offered little scope for NGO involvement, but the WTO accorded some recognition to NGOs through a vague reference to the possibility for consultation by the General Council in the Marrakesh Agreement. This relationship was clarified through the 1996 guidelines on arrangements for relations with NGOs. Though the WTO offered more engagement with NGOs than the GATT, they still had no place in the 'inner sanctum' of its decision-making. Following criticism regarding its lack of transparency (criticism that was especially vociferous at the time of the Seattle Ministerial in 1999), the WTO has taken several other measures to improve participation through representation and information access. Steffek acknowledges these 'incremental' (rather than 'revolutionary') steps towards opening the organization to non-state actors, examines which NGOs have secured access to the WTO, and also traces their achievements. In his conclusion, he cautions against overplaying the direct impact that NGOs have had on policy decisions, even though they have had some successes in placing issues on the agenda and triggering public debate.

Chapter 15, by Steven McGuire, addresses the fundamental problem of the declining voice of business interests and organized labour in the WTO. Domestic interests, which form the subject of McGuire's study, are traditionally seen as a deterrent to trade liberalization (as argued by Goldstein in Chapter 3, and further illustrated by Allee in Chapter 11). Interestingly, however, the lack of engagement by domestic interests is now often cited as a cause for deadlock in the Doha negotiations. McGuire explains the causes of this disengagement in terms of the oft-ignored heterogeneity of corporate actors. He argues that for corporate actors, the broad sweep of the negotiations and the numerous non-state actors from civil society make it difficult to keep the negotiations focused on the technical aspects of business regulation. Regional trade agreements and the DSM offer more opportunity than the Doha negotiation process. Further, organized labour groups—with their agenda for labour standards—find their position weakened by the rise of the emerging markets (which see this set of demands as a form of protectionism). And the contribution of trade to poverty alleviation has blunted the case of labour activists in developing countries.

Part V: Substance of the agreements

All the chapters in Part V relate to Puzzle 3 about the content of the agreements, how this was negotiated, and what kinds of distributive implications these agreements generate.

Chapter 16, by Helen Coskeran, Dan Kim, and Amrita Narlikar, examines the negotiations on non-agricultural market access and agriculture, in the past and the DDA. Both areas, as the authors point out, belong to the conventional area of goods, i.e. familiar terrain even for the GATT. And yet, these are also the two issues over which the DDA negotiations have repeatedly broken down. Coskeran, Kim, and Narlikar address two puzzles in the chapter: (a) why, after a very successful record of bringing down trade barriers in the previous rounds, have the NAMA negotiators faced repeated deadlock in the DDA? And (b) how far are the difficulties in the agricultural negotiations a continuation of the

problems that previous rounds encountered, or are they a product of interests and processes specific to the DDA? The chapter presents a historical account of the negotiations
in each area before examining the problems of the DDA. The authors illustrate how traditional methods that negotiators use to break deadlock—such as issue linkage, Chair's
texts, variations in formulae to facilitate an acceptable distribution of costs—have all
failed to deliver a compromise in the DDA. They attribute these difficulties to two fundamental causes. First, the difficulties encountered in NAMA and agriculture are a
reflection of the more general problems of the WTO that derive from the altered balance
of power (see also Chapter 6 by Preeg, Chapter 9 by Narlikar, and Chapter 12 by Vickers).
Second, the ambition of the DDA negotiations in these areas is deeper than any of the
previous rounds, and automatically takes negotiators into much more difficult terrain.

Rudolf Adlung, in Chapter 17, explores trade in services. In contrast to NAMA and
agriculture, for example, services is a relatively new area for the multilateral trading system, and Adlung notes that the General Agreement on Trade in Services (GATS) is a
young and incomplete agreement. Moreover, market access offers in the Doha Round
compare poorly against the autonomous moves towards liberalization taken on by
members. Adlung explores the reasons for this, and further analyses why, notwithstanding the poor substance of offers under GATS, a lot has happened in terms of liberalization at the ground level. In doing so, the chapter also takes into account the
implications of services liberalization as part of Bilateral Investment Treaties and preferential trade agreements (PTAs). While services PTAs might be less trade distorting than
their counterparts in merchandise trade, Adlung identifies several important costs that
they generate in the form of their 'GATS-minus' commitments, as well as the deflection
of resources away from the multilateral process. The chapter also raises broader questions of policy coherence within countries and at the multilateral levels, and as such res-
onates with Chapter 28 on regionalism and Chapter 34 on the coherence of trade within
the broad area of global economic governance.

Chapter 18 by Keith Maskus examines the Agreement on Trade-Related Aspects of
Intellectual Property Rights (TRIPS). Maskus starts off by identifying TRIPS as the most
important agreement on intellectual property for three reasons: its comprehensive
nature, its near-universal reach, and its enforceability via the DSM. After providing an
overview of the principles and major requirements of TRIPS, the chapter also analyses
the flexibilities allowed by the agreement and its application under the DSM through a
discussion of landmark cases. The chapter is particularly effective in bringing out the
different political interests and processes that underpin the agreement, and how they
contribute to current controversies and negotiations in the DDA.

In Chapter 19, Michael Finger provides us with an analysis of the flexibilities, rules,
and trade remedies that form a part of the WTO agreements. Provisions such as safeguards and anti-dumping are important in that they provide governments the necessary
flexibilities to deal with internal pressures and still maintain a generally liberal trade
policy. While acknowledging their benefits, however, Finger argues that they are 'an
embarrassment to both legal and economic theory': the discipline that the system applies
is more about fewer restrictions than good restrictions versus bad. Rather than simply a

description of such provisions, the chapter analyses their evolving usage. The chapter calls for 'analytic reform' rather than just 'policy reform' of the trade remedy system, which includes a closer attention to the national institutions that manage trade remedies.

Chapter 20, by Robert Howse, focuses on the issue of regulatory measures in the WTO (and thereby also addresses some of the issues that are raised in Chapter 8). Howse gets to the heart of one of the key problems: it is extremely difficult to distinguish between measures that are a legitimate exercise of domestic regulatory autonomy from others that may be seen as a form of protectionism. Even in the early years of the regime, when the reach of the GATT behind the borders was minimal, Howse points to the difficulties associated with determining impermissible versus permissible discrimination, without reference to some standards. The chapter then goes on to address agreements that deal with these concerns, including the Agreements on Sanitary and Phytosanitary Measures, Technical Barriers to Trade, and GATS. Finally, the chapter investigates the implications that the WTO's regulatory measures generate for the organization's democratic deficit (thereby linking up with several of the issues raised in Part IX of the handbook).

Part VI: Implementation and enforcement

While the previous chapters deal broadly with issues of rule-making, all the chapters in Part VI examine the implementation and enforcement of the rules and norms of the WTO. The focus here is particularly on the Trade Policy Review Mechanism (TPRM) and the Dispute Settlement Mechanism (DSM).

While the WTO's DSM has attracted much attention, this is not the only mechanism available in the organization's toolbox to implement and enforce its rules. Chapter 21, by Sam Laird and Raymundo Valdés, highlights the purpose, main features, functioning, and limitations of the TPRM. This 'transparency mechanism' is not a part of the enforcement process of the WTO, but the information that it provides can be used to assess compliance; as such, its role is particularly important in a member-driven organization, besides the fact that efforts to enhance transparency go back to the creation of the regime. The chapter traces the evolution of the TPRM, from the ad hoc surveillance schemes of the GATT in its early years, to its establishment on a provisional basis in 1989, and institutionalization on a permanent footing with the creation of the WTO. Laird and Valdés carefully trace the workings of the TPRM, and also highlight the results of various appraisal procedures. The achievements of the TPRM are significant, which include the creation of an extensive resource base on trade policies. But as the chapter explains, it also faces challenges, including demands on it to fulfil a technical assistance role. At least some of the challenges relate to the capacity and limited resources of the Secretariat (also see Chapter 7 by Blackhurst).

The focus of Chapter 22, by Thomas Bernauer, Manfred Elsig, and Joost Pauwelyn, is on the DSM. After a brief overview of the workings of the DSM, the greater part of the chapter offers an analytic and interdisciplinary literature review. The authors address major conceptual and theoretical issues associated with the DSM, including the fundamental question of why international trade agreements need dispute settlement provisions, and what shape might they take. They further provide an overview of scholarship on major questions on the WTO's DSM, such as legalization, dispute initiation, and third party litigation. Finally, they address gaps in the literature, thereby setting an agenda for future work in the field.

Chapter 23, by Mitsuo Matsushita, studies the role of the Appellate Body in the WTO. If members are not satisfied with the rulings of the dispute settlement panel, they can appeal to the Appellate Body, which reviews the panel reports, and can uphold, modify, and reverse them. Matsushita provides an overview of the major principles of WTO jurisprudence that have been established by the Appellate Body. This jurisprudential role of the Appellate Body has proven to be controversial (see also, Chapter 22). The chapter addresses two sets of critiques: for some the Appellate Body has been too literal in its interpretations, whereas for others the Appellate Body has overstepped its mandate by going beyond interpretation and into rule-making. Matsushita explains that though these two criticisms seem to contradict each other, in fact they address different functions of the Appellate Body. Finally, the chapter addresses possible directions for reform.

In Chapter 24, Gregory Shaffer and Joel Trachtman provide an analytic framework for describing and assessing the consequences of choices in treaty interpretation. They do so by referring to examples from WTO case law. The chapter assesses interpretive decisions by examining how they allocate authority between different social decision-making processes. Focusing on the welfare and participatory implications of these choices, the authors offer two important conclusions. First, these choices impact upon social decision-making in terms of transparency, accountability, and legitimacy. Second, the choice of institutional alternatives—such as incorporation of international standards, judicial balancing, delegation to markets, national deference, and process-based review—can determine which social decision-making process decides a particular policy issue, thereby affecting the institutional mediation of individual preferences.

Alan Sykes, in Chapter 25, investigates the extent to which the purpose of the DSM is to 'ensure compliance'. The answer is less straightforward than it would appear to be at first glance. While all scholars agree that one purpose of the DSM is to encourage compliance with WTO obligations at least some of the time, Sykes points to differing views on whether the system is meant to facilitate efficient breach (and hence the limits of retaliation) or if it is meant to rebalance concessions following breach of obligations. The chapter, after providing a brief historical overview, takes us to the heart of the legal debate on the purpose of the DSM, and explains how it allows members the option to violate WTO obligations for a measured 'price' that is tied to the harm done by the violation to the complainants. Sykes argues that the logic of the system can be best understood 'as a way to facilitate efficient adjustment of the bargain over time'.

Part VII: Challenges to the system

The final set of puzzles addressed in the volume has to do with the challenges to the system, and possible directions of institutional reform that incorporate both practical and normative concerns. Part VII deals specifically with the practical challenges to the system, which include the problem of recurrent deadlock, the call by certain interests to expand the reach of the WTO into new and non-trade issues (and thus related to Part V) and also the role of domestic courts in implementing WTO commitments.

Chapter 26, by Manfred Elsig and Cédric Dupont, traces and explains the recurrent deadlock in the Doha negotiations. They identify four structural/contextual factors—ideas, institutions, interests, and information—as necessary for understanding and anticipating potential deadlocks. They further incorporate the intervening variable of behavioural choices by actors to explain deadlocks, using a simple game theoretic model to outline the logic of their argument. The chapter concludes by outlining two general scenarios for the DDA, and discusses their implications for the WTO.

In Chapter 27, Thomas Cottier addresses the complex problem of the domestic–international interface in implementing the obligations of the WTO. Specifically, he examines the role of domestic courts in assessing claims brought to them on the basis of WTO law. In doing so, he addresses the vital question of how far a domestic court can enforce international law, and further produce compliance from its legislative and executive branches. Other relevant questions include the comparative effectiveness of WTO law in different jurisdictions. Cottier demonstrates that traditional doctrines of dualism and monism in international law no longer provide an adequate framework in dealing with WTO law. Based upon the premise of the unity of all law, he argues in favour of the development of a doctrine in the process of dialogue and interaction of courts which may eventually also find its way into explicit principles and rules within the WTO.

Chapter 28, by Richard Baldwin, addresses the issue of regionalism. Several other chapters in the volume also touch upon the dangers that the turn to preferential trading arrangements poses for the multilateral trading regime. Baldwin systematically unpacks the political economy of regionalism. He distinguishes between the twentieth century regionalism—which dealt primarily with tariff preferences—and the twenty-first century regionalism that deals with the new disciplines that underpin the deeper and more complex patterns of commerce today. His analysis points to a serious risk: 'regionalism is creating new rules governing international commerce, including international trade. These are being decided outside of the WTO in a setting of massive power asymmetries and without basic principles of non-discrimination and reciprocity in concessions.' The resulting challenge for the WTO is either to multilateralize some of the deeper disciplines, or somehow retain its vibrancy within the narrower mandate that was set for it with the signing of the Uruguay Round agreements in 1994.

Chapter 29, by Tim Josling, addresses one of the emerging challenges for the WTO, and focuses on the nexus between food, agriculture, and natural resources. In food trade, he identifies a vital need for rules that reflect the globalization of food systems, including the emergence of private food standards, and the possible updating of the Sanitary and Phytosanitary Measures (SPS) Agreement. Agriculture raises questions about the appropriateness of current trade rules as a backdrop for investments in agriculture, food production, and marketing in developing countries. In the area of natural resources, the development of rules on government ownership, or investment in land and other resources in other countries, could become an issue. And extending to several areas of primary products' trade is the need to strengthen the rules that constrain the use of export restrictions and taxes when commodity prices are high. The chapter further explores some of the specific considerations in each that would have to be negotiated, often related to environmental and social factors. As Josling argues, together these issues offer an opportunity to complete the integration of developing countries into the WTO agenda, though much will depend on the shape that these rules end up taking.

Part VIII: Normative issues

The issue of fairness in trade has attracted many interpretations and controversies. In Chapter 30, Andrew Brown and Robert Stern unpack the concept of fairness. They provide a brief critique of the utilitarian principle as a guide to fairness in the world trading system. They then offer an alternative conception of fairness in terms of economic equity. In doing so, they focus on two of its components: equality of opportunity and distributive justice, and further specify the conditions of autonomy and reciprocity that have to be met to achieve greater fairness in multilateral trade negotiations. The authors also comment on aspects of procedural justice that are necessary for the functioning of a fair trading system. They substantiate this normative analysis through an assessment of fairness considerations achieved in the Uruguay Round and the implications that they generate for the conclusion of the DDA.

Chapter 31, by Drusilla Brown, addresses the deeply divisive issue of the links between international trade, and human rights and labour standards. As she points out, the integration of global markets in goods and service, facilitated first by the GATT and then the WTO, has been correlated with a decline in poverty, and a general improvement in the status of women and children. But as cases of poor labour standards and human rights violations also abound, activists have argued for the establishment of international labour standards linked to market access within the WTO to remedy some of the gross violations of human rights that can accompany international trade. After providing a brief historical overview of the scant provisions on this subject in the multilateral trade regime, and the theoretical case for such standards, Brown systematically analyses seven labour standard categories, the link between globalization and human rights violations, and the market inefficiency or inequity that a standard would remedy. Finally, the chapter investigates and assesses the implementation of labour standards in practice, focusing particularly on the Generalized System of Preferences and the Better Factories Cambodia initiative.

Chapter 32 is the final chapter in Part VIII, where Gary Hufbauer and Meera Fickling examine the relationship between international trade and environmental concerns in the context of the WTO. This is another controversial area for the WTO, and one that has often been afflicted by serious North–South divisions. The authors highlight some of the key provisions of the WTO that relate to environmental concerns, and further discuss proposals that have been made whereby the WTO could deal with this issue more effectively. Particularly interesting are the chapter's proposals on eliminating tariffs on environmental goods, and also addressing the issue of environmentally harmful subsidies. The chapter also addresses the issue of climate change, and investigates how far it can and should be dealt with in the WTO. The authors offer a 'Code of Good Practice' among the major emitting countries to guide their trade-related climate change measures, and also touch upon the trade implications of geoengineering.

Part IX: Reform of the WTO

The final part of this volume deals with the question of how the WTO might be reformed. Chapter 33, by Bernard Hoekman, is a perfect complement to the issues addressed in Part III, and should ideally be read in parallel with the other chapters on process. In this chapter, Hoekman provides an overview of the modus operandi of the WTO (e.g. decision-making procedures, negotiating modalities, and dispute settlement), and also summarizes the major arguments and proposals to reform them. Hoekman rightly points out that much has already been done to improve the internal and external transparency of World Trade Organization processes. He offers a constructive critique of key proposals: for instance, he argues that some proposals for structural reform ignore incentive constraints and the fact that the World Trade Organization is an incomplete contract that must be self-enforcing. Others—such as calls for a 'critical mass' approach to negotiations—can be pursued (and have been). The agenda for international cooperation increasingly revolves around 'behind-the-border' regulatory externalities that do not necessarily lend themselves to binding commitments in a trade agreement. He makes the case for a focus on strengthening notification/surveillance and developing more effective mechanisms for dialogue on regulatory policies that sometimes create negative spillovers.

In Chapter 34, Steven Bernstein and Erin Hannah explore institutional cooperation in global economic governance to address two fundamental questions: (a) where do the rules of the WTO overlap or compete with those of other institutions and (b) what explains institutional coherence/incoherence between the WTO and other international organizations? Bernstein and Hannah explore the relationship of the WTO with different institutions and over different issue areas, ranging from finance and aid, to intellectual property rights, and environmental and social regulations. In doing so, they touch upon and further develop some of the mandate-related concerns that were raised in Chapters 2, 8, and also chapters 16–20. They argue that in certain areas, which parties have directly targeted to facilitate trade liberalization (e.g. intellectual property rights, finance, and aid), the WTO has a regulatory role to play in cooperation with other relevant institutions. But in areas such as social and environmental regulation, where 'the goal of regulation is to "embed" economic governance in broader societal goals', they argue that coherence would be best achieved if states ensured that WTO rules continued to leave space for a global division of labour and allowed alternative institutions to do the regulating.

3 Conclusion

As the previous section illustrates, the 34 chapters in this volume cover a wide range of topics. All the authors, despite some differences in their disciplinary backgrounds and normative starting points, acknowledge the achievements of the WTO. The regime has played a key instrumental role in facilitating trade liberalization, and thereby provided the global economy with the foundations for economic growth, prosperity, and overall stability since the end of the Second World War. It has ensured the evolution of a rules-based system to govern multilateral trade, which has proven resilient to the onslaught of global economic crises. It is true that even the WTO's most ardent supporters would find it difficult to claim that it has managed to achieve the ideal levels of participation or the optimal outcomes for the world's poorest countries and people. But no fair assessment of the WTO could ignore the quantum leap that it has made (from the days of the GATT, and indeed in comparison to most other international organizations) in ensuring greater inclusiveness and prioritizing development. All the chapters in this volume, in one way or another, recognize these achievements.

That said, the volume also highlights many of the problems that the WTO faces today. Obvious symptoms of the problems are the recurrence of deadlock in the Doha negotiations, and the proliferation of regional and bilateral alternatives. Many of the chapters keep an eye on these issues as they address some of the bigger debates. At least four major themes emerge from the collective analysis, which offer an agenda for future research and also implications for the policy world.

First, freer trade is a necessary—but not sufficient—condition for equitable growth. Especially when growth is unevenly distributed *within* countries, trade is seldom the culprit, but it does make an easy scapegoat. To avoid misallocation of blame, and indeed ensure the necessary support for the system, it is extremely important that trade governance takes place in cooperation with other economic (and indeed social) goals, with a clear and identifiable allocation of responsibilities. Intellectually, this requires more empirical studies at the domestic level that identify the policy trade-offs that governments make, and how they justify them to their publics. This needs to be accompanied by analyses at the international level on the available and prospective tools for greater coherence in global economic governance.

Second, many of the controversies of the GATT—and indeed current ones at the WTO—have to do with the mandate of the organization. Here opinion is divided among scholars on how the reach of the organization should be defined, not only over behind-the-border measures, but in several new areas such as climate change. While the WTO will need to move with the changing imperatives of trade, any proposed expansion in its agenda needs to be justified theoretically and conceptually. A close eye also needs to be kept on feasibility: the WTO is arguably already overstretched through its expansion into trade-related aspects of development, while its Secretariat and resources have not expanded comparably. Several of the chapters in this volume suggest ways in which the WTO's agenda can be defined and limited, such that it remains in step with the organization's structures and capabilities but also works hand in hand with other institutions and regimes of global governance.

Third, the handbook illustrates both the efficiencies and flaws of the processes of the WTO, and in doing so, also provides an indication of the normative balancing act that previous, current, and indeed any future reform measures, must entail. As several of the chapters demonstrate, the WTO today is a considerably more inclusive and transparent organization, at least as far as its members are concerned. But the unintended cost of ensuring fairness of process has been a decline in the efficiency of its functioning, and hence also the multiple problems of deadlock, regionalism, and rule-making through litigation that ensue.

Finally, all the chapters are cognizant of the *political bargains* that underpin the WTO. These are reflected in the domestic political economy of trade liberalization, the historical failures and successes that eventually led to the formation of the WTO, the negotiation and decision-making processes at the organization, and indeed in the substance of the agreements. They even appear in the most legalized arm of the organization—the DSM—which for all practical purposes *encourages* rather than *enforces* compliance. This allows us some editorial satisfaction at least in our initial intuition on the relevance of interdisciplinarity for this project. It also suggests that both theorists and policymakers would be well served to learn from cognate disciplines as they seek to analyse and reform the WTO.

REFERENCES

Bhagwati, Jagdish. 2003. *Free Trade Today*. Princeton: Princeton University Press.

Eichengreen, Barry, and Kevin O'Rourke. 2010. A Tale of Two Depressions: What do the New Data Tell Us? February update. VoxEU (10 March). Available from <http://voxeu.org/index.php?q=node/3421>. Accessed on 15 May 2011.

Gehring, Markus W. 2010. Litigating the Way Out of Deadlock: The WTO, the EU and the UN. In *Deadlocks in Multilateral Negotiations: Causes and Solutions*, edited by Amrita Narlikar, 96–120. Cambridge: Cambridge University Press.

Hudec, Robert. 1998. The Role of the GATT Secretariat in the Evolution of the WTO Dispute Settlement Procedure. In *The Uruguay Round and Beyond: Essays in Honour of Arthur Dunkel*, edited by Jagdish Bhagwati and Mathias Hirsch, 101–20. Heidelberg: Springer-Verlag.

Krugman, Paul. 1997. What Should Trade Negotiators Negotiate About? *Journal of Economic Literature* 35 (1):113–20.

Morgenthau, Henry Jr. 1944. Inaugural Address. United Nations Monetary and Financial Conference, July, Bretton Woods. Available from <http://www.ena.lu/inaugural_address_henry_morgenthau_jr_july_1944-020005008.html> Accessed on 12 April 2010.

Narlikar, Amrita. 2005. *The World Trade Organization: A Very Short Introduction*. Oxford: Oxford University Press.

Narlikar, Amrita, ed. 2010. *Deadlocks in Multilateral Negotiations: Causes and Solutions*. Cambridge: Cambridge University Press.

WTO. 1994. The Agreement Establishing the World Trade Organization. Available from <http://www.wto.org>. Accessed on 11 April 2011.

PART I

THEORY OF MULTILATERAL TRADE LIBERALIZATION

CHAPTER 1

....

THE CASE FOR A MULTILATERAL TRADE ORGANIZATION

....

ROBERT E. BALDWIN

1.1 INTRODUCTION

....

THE General Agreement on Tariffs and Trade (GATT) and its successor, the World Trade Organization (WTO), are generally regarded as the most successful international economic organizations established in the post-First World War period.[1] Most agree that the two other most prominent international institutions established in the period, namely the International Monetary Fund and the World Bank, have both fallen short of fulfilling the roles for which they were created. The most important accomplishment of the GATT/WTO has been a significant reduction in the levels of tariffs and non-tariff trade barriers that had emerged during the great depression of the 1930s. Average tariff levels on manufactured goods in most industrial countries have fallen from 40–50 per cent in 1948 to about 3–5 per cent today through a series of eight multilateral negotiating rounds.

A second major accomplishment of the GATT/WTO has been the establishment of a reasonably successful self-enforcing system of settling disputes among members in which panels of trade experts and, more recently, an appellate body, render judgments concerning the consistency of particular trade measures with GATT/WTO principles. Adherence by members to the two basic principles of GATT/WTO, namely that in the absence of a free-trade agreement or customs union the most favourable tariff treatment extended to one country must be extended to all countries (the most-favoured nation principle), and that foreigners must receive the same treatment as domestic citizens (the

---

[1] The GATT took effect in 1948 with 23 countries signing the Agreement. The WTO was established in 1995 with 113 countries signing the Uruguay Round Agreement.

national treatment clause), has also proved to be very successful in reducing tensions among trading countries.

Thus, one approach to making the case for a multilateral trade organization is to provide a historical description of the various trade negotiating efforts of GATT/WTO members that have led to the significant liberalization achieved. Another approach is theoretical, namely to investigate the trade policy actions that welfare-maximizing governments, who preside over large countries, will take, as well as their effects on world welfare. The following two sections present the theoretical cases for trade agreements, while Sections 1.4–1.6 review the main trade-liberalizing and dispute resolution accomplishments achieved under the GATT/WTO framework. Section 1.7 briefly summarizes the main points of the chapter.

1.2 TERMS OF TRADE EXTERNALITIES

As Bagwell and Staiger[2] have pointed out, a problem that arises when large countries set tariff rates so as to maximize national welfare is that they become involved in pursuing 'beggar-my-neighbour' trade policies. This occurs because the imposition of a tariff by a large country gives rise to an externality that reduces the national welfare of other countries and increases economic welfare in the tariff-setting country. This is because the prices received by foreign exporters fall as a consequence of tariffs being imposed on their exports, i.e. the terms of trade of foreign exporters decline, and the terms of trade of the tariff-imposing country improve.

Consequently, in unilaterally setting its tariffs, a large country engages in beggar-my-neighbour activities by imposing import duties on imports whose supply prices can be influenced in this manner. However, other large countries will also engage in beggar-my-neighbour policies in the process of maximizing their national welfare, and will impose tariffs on their imports of products from the initial tariff-raising country. By lowering the supply prices of these imports, this retaliation process offsets the terms of trade improvement for the initial beggar-my-neighbour country so that on balance no one tends to gain. It is usually assumed that a Nash equilibrium position is eventually reached when further increases in tariffs no longer reduce the economic welfare of other countries. However, the distortions brought about by the retaliatory tariff-raising process result in the economic welfare of all the participants being reduced below their free trade levels.

The essential point can be seen from a simple supply and demand diagram.[3] In Figure 1 let the curve D_M be the net import demand curve of a large country (country 1) for a

---

[2] Bagwell and Staiger 2000, 2009.
[3] Harry Johnson presented the first formal explanation of the terms-of-trade argument in general equilibrium terms (Johnson 1953–4).

particular product (shoes, for example) and S_x be the net export supply curve of other countries for this product. In the absence of any tariff, the equilibrium price paid by the importing country (and received by the exporting countries) for the product will be Op, and the volume of trade will be Oa.[4] Now assume that importing country (country 1) imposes a specific duty equal to p'p" on its imports of the product. The import supply curve will shift upward by this amount to S_{x+T}, with the price paid by the importing country rising to Op' and the volume of trade declining to Oh. The price paid by the importing country does not increase by the full amount of the duty but only by pp', since the cost of producing the export good falls from Op to Op" as demand is reduced from Oa to Oh. The tariff revenue collected by the importing country equals the area p'cep". Thus, part of the burden of the tariff falls on the exporters of the good, namely the area pdep". The other part of the tariff, an amount equal to the area pp'cd, is borne by consumers in the importing country who pay a higher price for the traded good. The government of the importing country gains revenue equal to the area p'cep", which exceeds this amount by pdep". This sum, which is assumed to be distributed to the consumers of the taxed product through a costless lump-sum redistribution process, represents a gain in national welfare for the tariff-imposing country.[5]

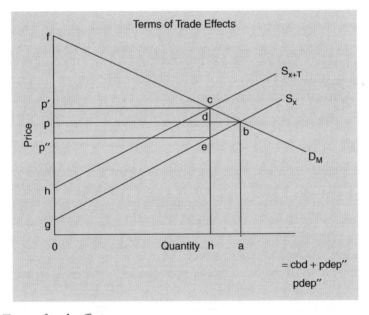

FIGURE 1 Terms of trade effects

⁴ The consumer surplus initially received by the importing country is equal to the area fbp.
⁵ The change in national welfare for the tariff-imposing country equals the sum of the change in its consumer surplus, namely minus the area p'cbp, and the increase in its tariff revenue, namely p'cep" or an amount equal to pdep" minus cbd. The decrease in national welfare for the exporting countries equals the change in their producer surplus, namely minus pbep".

The sequence of events will not end here, however. Other large countries will take retaliatory action in an effort to increase their national welfare. Since the imports of these countries include the exports of the initial tariff-imposing country, this latter country faces decreases in the prices of its exports, which offset the improvement in its terms of trade when it alone imposes import duties. The end result of this beggar-my-neighbour process will be welfare levels for all the participating countries that are lower than their initial free trade levels.

A trade agreement provides the means by which welfare levels can be restored to their free trade levels. If countries engage in negotiations with each other to reduce their tariffs on a reciprocal basis, both further adverse terms of trade effects will be avoided for any particular country, and trade and welfare levels will move back toward their free trade levels.

1.3 THE POLITICAL ECONOMY AND COMMITMENT APPROACHES TO TRADE AGREEMENTS

Although there is no dispute over the logic of the terms of trade argument, there is disagreement over its practical relevance for trade agreements. In tariff-setting discussions among policymakers, one does not typically observe any reference to the terms of trade. Instead, in providing protection to particular sectors, policy makers cite such justifications as equity considerations, e.g. protecting employment and income levels of unskilled labour, offsetting unfair practices on the part of foreign countries, such as dumping, and responding to the pressures of politically powerful industries such as the textile sector. In other words, governments pursue political objectives in their tariff-setting actions.

Bagwell and Staiger recognize the importance of political economy considerations in the real world tariff-setting process. The only structure they place on government preferences is the weak condition that, with domestic prices held constant, welfare increases with an improvement in the terms of trade. They then proceed to show that with such preferences a political economy approach to trade agreements does not offer any separate political purpose for a trade agreement.

Another argument for trade agreements stresses the difficulty that governments have in making policy commitments to the private sector, and suggests that trade agreements may provide a way to enhance policy credibility. Suppose that a government sets its trade policy after producers make their production decisions. As Bagwell and Staiger explain:

> In this case, the governments may have an incentive to surprise producers with a level of protection that it would not choose ex ante, when producers selections are still unsettled. The government's preferred ex ante and ex post tariff decisions differ, since, once producer decisions are determined, the government recognizes that its choices only affect consumption decisions. Of course, if producers understand the

government's incentives, they will alter their production decisions in anticipation of the government's actions, and production decisions are therefore distorted. This production distortion is the real cost of trade-policy flexibility, and the identification of this cost suggests that a trade agreement would increase (*ex ante*) government welfare if it enables the government to commit to its (*ex post*) preferred tariff.[6]

1.4 OFFSETTING MARKET IMPERFECTIONS AND LONG-TERM PROTECTIONISM

Unlike the theoretical world we often postulate, the real world in which economic agents operate is characterized by such conditions as the lack of perfect knowledge and the lack of perfect mobility among productive factors. As a result of these conditions, underlying market opportunities among countries go unexploited that could increase collective economic welfare across countries. However, the formation among countries of international institutions such as the GATT and the WTO can serve to offset the consequences of these market imperfections. For example, with the establishment of government offices to collect and process relevant data needed to conduct trade-liberalizing negotiations, mutually beneficial trading opportunities can be revealed and exploited. These include not only income-increasing opportunities arising from current market imperfections, but welfare-increasing opportunities associated with protectionist measures taken in previous periods. Thus, as the preamble to the General Agreement of Tariffs and Trade states, 'relations within the field of trade and development should be conducted with a view to raising standards of living, ensuring full employment and a large and steadily growing volume of real income and effective demand, developing the full use of the resources of the world and expanding the productions and exchange of goods'.

1.5 NEGOTIATING TECHNIQUES AND RESULTS

In the early days of the GATT, members first exchanged lists indicating the goods on which they were willing to offer tariff reductions and the goods on which they were seeking reductions from other countries. They then negotiated bilaterally with the principal suppliers of the goods on which they sought tariff reductions. The goal was to achieve a balance of concessions made and received.

While this procedure worked reasonably well in the early rounds of GATT negotiations, it was hampered by the fact that the volume of imports for which one country was

---

[6] Bagwell and Staiger 2000, 21.

the principal supplier to another country could differ widely from the volume of imports for which the second country was the principal supplier to the first. This limited the depth of the average tariff cut at which it was possible to achieve a balance of concessions received and granted to others. For example, while the average cut in all duties achieved in the first GATT round of negotiations in 1947 was 32 per cent, subsequent trade-liberalizing rounds utilizing the same principal-supplier approach reduced average duties by only 1.9 per cent in a second round in 1949, by 3.0 per cent in a third round in 1950–51, by 3.5 per cent in a fourth round in 1955–56, and 2.4 per cent in a fifth round held in 1961–62.

Thus, in the following round of negotiations, the so-called Kennedy Round (1964–67), the United States proposed that, as a means of achieving a meaningful average tariff reduction, the major trading countries reduce their industrial tariffs by 50 per cent across the board, with a minimum number of exceptions. This proposal was essentially accepted by other GATT members and, as a result, average duties were reduced in the trade negotiations by 36 per cent.

While this result left average tariffs on industria goods roughly the same among the major participants in the negotiations—the United States, the European Community and Japan—the dispersion of the rates around the means differed widely. This was because the Common External Tariff of the EC was formed by averaging member country rates, a procedure that resulted in a concentration of rates in the 10 to 15 per cent range. The United States had over 900 tariff line items over 30 per cent, whereas there were only a handful of such rates in the EC's tariff schedule. Community members argued that this was unfair because an equal cut in high US and middle level EC rates would increase US exports to the Community much more than EC exports to the United States. It was simultaneously argued that cuts in the larger number of low-duty US rates were not worth much in terms of increased exports for the EC, because these low duties were already only a minor obstacle to trade. Furthermore, an equal cut would increase imports into the EC from third countries more than such imports into the United States. In other words, exports from third countries would be diverted (in relative terms) from the United States to the EC.

While the US did not buy these arguments, it agreed in the following round of negotiations, the Tokyo Round (1973–9), to a tariff-reducing formula that cut high duties by a greater percentage than low duties after it found from test runs on a representative sample of US and EC imports that the EC proposal actually resulted in a smaller balance-of-payments deficit.

The tariff-cutting formula for industrial products accepted by all participants in the Tokyo Round negotiations was proposed by the Swiss, namely:

$$Z = AX/(A + X)$$

where Z is the new tariff rate, A is a constant and X is the current tariff rate. The constant was set at 14 for the US and 16 for the EU. Thus, a US duty of 20 per cent was reduced to 14x20/(14 + 20) = 8.23 per cent. The United States was somewhat constrained by this formula, in that it could not cut duties more than 60 per cent, but it was able to raise its average rate of reduction to the levels achieved by other industrial countries by utilizing its statutory power to reduce duties of 5 per cent and below by up to 100 per cent. Taking into account the various exceptions to applying the Swiss formula, the average reduction in tariffs on industrial products in the Tokyo Round was about 35 per cent for both the US and EC.[7]

Besides achieving a significant average duty reduction in the Tokyo Round, GATT members also negotiated a series of detailed codes covering non-tariff measures that set forth permissible and non-permissible GATT-consistent behaviour. The main subjects covered were subsidies and countervailing duties, anti-dumping practices, government procurement policies, valuation and licensing practices, and technical barriers to trade (standards). Signing the codes was made voluntary on the part of the participants in the negotiations.

The most successful post-World War II multilateral trade negotiation, as measured by the depth and scope of liberalization, was the Uruguay Round (1986–93). Three new subjects not covered in previous negotiating rounds were introduced: trade in services, trade-related intellectual property rights, and trade-related aspects of investment measures. In addition, a special effort was made that brought agriculture and textiles/apparel under GATT discipline. The negotiations also covered such traditional topics as tariff liberalization, subsidies, dumping, government procurement policy, technical barriers to trade, dispute settlement, and institutional reform.

An important feature of the framework agreement negotiated for services is that it covers not only cross-border trade in services, but services supplied by foreign firms within a country to consumers in that country and services supplied by domestic firms to nationals of other countries who are visiting the country. The General Agreement on Trade in Services (GATS) commits WTO signatories to a set of general principles which includes most-favoured nation treatment, transparency with regard to domestic laws affecting trade in services, and the progressive liberalization of traded services.

In fashioning policies covering intellectual property, namely creations of the mind such as inventions, literary and artistic works, and symbols, names, images, and designs used in commerce, society must balance two output-creating forces. One is the output gains that comes about from distributing an existing body of knowledge as widely as possible. The other is the output gains that arises because inventors and other creators of intellectual property are granted temporary monopolies that prevent others from copying their intellectual creations before they have had a chance to reap the monetary gains that make their creative efforts worthwhile. The Uruguay Round Agreement on the Trade-Related Aspects of Intellectual Property attempted to overcome some of the drawbacks of the existing system. For example, all countries are now

---

[7] Winham 1986, 267. The EC consisted of nine countries by the end of the Tokyo Round, with Denmark, Ireland, and the United Kingdom becoming members in 1972.

required to provide copyright, trademark, and patent protection on goods and services for a specified number of years. However, developing countries and the least developed countries were given extra time to implement this requirement. In addition, countries are required to establish civil judicial procedures whereby individuals and firms can seek to enforce their intellectual property rights. Criminal procedures must also be put in place to deal with wilful trademark counterfeiting or copyright piracy on a commercial scale. In a notable ruling in 2009, a WTO dispute-settlement panel ruled that China violated WTO rules by barring copyright protection for movies, music, and books that have not been approved for publication or distribution in China.

1.6 Dispute settlement procedures

Equally important to achieving a significant degree of trade liberalization by establishing a multilateral trade organization is the goal of successfully resolving disputes that arise among GATT/WTO members as they apply the basic rules of these institutions. Most of these rules were agreed to by 1947 and set forth in the Articles of the General Agreement on Tariffs and Trade. New rules were added when the World Trade Organization replaced the GATT in 1994 and a new agreement covering trade in services was approved. GATT/WTO rules were also routinely modified in the various rounds of trade negotiations.

The basic rule governing trade is set forth in the first Article of the GATT and the WTO as the most-favoured nation principle. It states that the most favourable treatment with respect to any charges imposed on imports or exports by a country shall be the treatment granted to all other countries. However, there is an exception to this rule if a country enters into a free trade agreement or customs union with another country. Thus, trade is free among members of the European Union or members of the North American Free Trade Agreement, namely the United States, Canada, and Mexico. Since the early 1990s, free trade agreements have become a very prominent feature of the multilateral trading system. As of July 2010, 574 regional trade agreements have been notified to the GATT/WTO. It is not as yet clear just what the long-run effect of this trend will be on the degree of liberalization achieved under the GATT/WTO system.

Among the other rules of the GATT/WTO are:

- when governments can levy anti-dumping and countervailing duties on foreign exports to offset dumping by foreign firms and subsidization by foreign governments;
- when governments can withdraw tariff concession because an industry is seriously injured;
- the conditions under which governments can grant subsidies to their domestic industries;

- the permissible procedures for valuing imports for the purpose of levying import duties;
- when governments can impose quantitative restrictions on imports; and
- the extent to which purchases from domestic firms are provided with a price preference compared with purchases from foreign firms when it comes to purchases by government agencies.

If a GATT/WTO member believes that benefits to which it is entitled from the GATT/WTO agreements are being nullified by an action on the part of another member (perhaps because this other member believes the country is not following the rules of the organization), the country may request a formal consultation from the country taking the action. If the dispute is not resolved through consultation, the two disputants may then request that a panel of experts be appointed to investigate the case and render a decision. The members of the panel must be agreed upon by both disputants. If, after their investigation, the panel rules in favour of the party initiating the case, the GATT/WTO can then authorize the winner of the dispute to impose sanctions on the losing party.

Unfortunately, prior to the Uruguay Round Agreement in 1994 this procedure was deeply flawed because decisions by GATT members required unanimity. Thus, the losing party in a panel report could block adoption of the report and even block the winning party's request to retaliate if the losing party did not comply with a panel report that was adopted. The Understanding on Rules and Procedures Governing the Settlement of Disputes reached in the Uruguay Round significantly changed the previous dispute settlement process. Most importantly, the principle of 'automaticity' was introduced into the new Agreement. Now, formation of panels, adoption of their reports, and, if a panel ruling is not complied with, retaliations are all automatic. These changes in themselves greatly strengthen the dispute settlement process.

There are several other ways in which the process has been strengthened. A unified system to settle disputes arising under the various agreements replaces the various different procedures for settling disputes under the Tokyo Round agreements. This system even applies to disputes arising over issues on which there are no legal obligations under the GATT. Time limits have also been established for carrying out the various steps in the settlement process. For example, panels appointed by the Dispute Settlement Body to render a decision on the merits of a complaint must normally report their findings within six months and in no longer than nine months. Another important change is the creation of an Appellate Body to review panel decisions that are appealed. This body has seven members who are appointed for a four-year term. The decision of this body must be made within 60 and 90 days.

It should be noted that panel rulings are *not* self-executing. If a country chooses not to change its laws or regulations to conform to a panel ruling, the penalty it will incur will be the possibility of retaliatory actions by its trading partners. However, such a country is likely to find it more difficult to persuade other countries of the merits of the cases it brings before the Dispute Settlement Body.

1.7 Summary

The strongest case for a multilateral trade organization can be made simply by chronicling the history of the GATT and WTO in achieving trade liberalization actions since 1948. The increased communications among countries that resulted from establishing the GATT and WTO has revealed a steady stream of mutually beneficial trading opportunities that have been exploited through a series of eight multilateral trade negotiations. This liberalization has covered both tariffs and non-tariff trade barriers and involved a variety of trade-liberalizing techniques. Significant progress has also been made over the period in developing dispute resolution methods that have served to strengthen the multilateral trade system.

There are also theoretical reasons why countries form trade agreements. Consider a situation in which goods are produced under increasing cost conditions and countries are large in the sense that their purchases of goods from other countries affect the international prices of these goods. Under these conditions, welfare-maximizing governments are likely to become involved in beggar-my-neighbour trade policies. This occurs because by imposing tariffs on foreign imports and reducing output in these industries each large country can improve its terms of trade, that is, reduce the prices at which it purchases imports relative to the prices at which it sells its exports. The net result of each country taking actions to improve its terms of trade will be a situation in which world welfare declines below its free trade level. At this stage governments realize that forming a trade agreement and reducing import duties on a reciprocal basis can increase the volume of trade without worsening their terms of trade.

A separate approach to the theory of trade policy can be made if it is posited that the purpose of a trade agreement is to tie the hands of member governments against private agents in the economy, and thereby offer an external commitment device.[8] There exists the possibility that an anticipated trade-policy-lobbying relationship between the government of a small country and producers in one of its sectors could distort the equilibrium in allocation of resources in the economy toward the sector with the active lobby. The government will be compensated by the lobby for the *ex post* distortions its trade policy choices impose on the economy. But the lobby will not compensate the government for the *ex ante* distortions in the sectoral allocation of resources created by the anticipation of the government's relationship with the lobby, and this provides an opening for the government to wish to tie its hands *ex ante* against the possibility of being influenced by *ex-post* lobbying. A possible commitment role for a trade agreement is thereby identified.

---

[8] The wording of this paragraph closely follows Bagwell and Staiger 2009, 12–13.

References

Bagwell, Kyle, and Robert W. Staiger. 2000. GATT-Think. NBER Working Paper 8005. Cambridge MA: National Bureau of Economic Research.

Bagwell, Kyle, and Robert W. Staiger. 2009. The WTO Theory and Practice. NBER Working Paper 15445. Cambridge MA: National Bureau of Economic Research.

Johnson, Harry G. 1953–4. Optimum Tariffs and Retaliation. *Review of Economic Studies* 21 (2):142–53.

Winham, Gilbert R. 1986. *International Trade and the Tokyo Round Negotiation*. Princeton: Princeton University Press.

CHAPTER 2

....

THE INCONSISTENT QUARTET: FREE TRADE VERSUS COMPETING GOALS

....

MARTIN DAUNTON

2.1 INTRODUCTION

....

THE World Trade Organization (WTO) is obviously concerned with trade policy, and this volume focuses on the ways it has operated in dealing with the highly contentious issues of multilateral trade liberalization, the shaping of rules and the balancing of interests, the creation of coalitions, and the nature of dispute resolution. These issues are complex and difficult, and are made even more so by the expansion of the remit of the WTO to cover services and intellectual property, and the extension of the agenda to include development. Yet we should consider not only trade policy, for a full understanding of the operation of the WTO—as of earlier episodes in the history of trade policy—should place trade in a wider context of policy choices.

Politicians and officials, interest groups, and advocates must always think about other elements of economic policy which affect both the domestic and international economies. At the most basic level, should priority be given to the pursuit of domestic considerations which might tip over into destructive economic nationalism as in the 1930s, or to cosmopolitan or international concerns which might be seen as sacrificing important domestic interests?[1] And when this fundamental policy choice has been made, how does the pursuit of free or multilateral trade connect with two other aspects of international economics: exchange rates and capital flows? The implications of free or multilateral

---

[1] For two studies of the ways in which globalization faced the challenge of nationalism, see James 2001; O'Rourke and Williamson 1999.

trade for both the domestic and international economy differed depending on its relationship with other policy choices concerning exchange rates, capital controls, and domestic monetary policy. By focusing only on trade, there is a serious danger of misunderstanding the processes that shape policy outcomes.

2.2 THE 'TRILEMMA', INCONSISTENT QUARTET, AND BALANCE OF PAYMENTS

The trade-off between fixed (or flexible) exchange rates, free (or controlled) movement of capital, and an active (or passive) domestic monetary policy forms the so-called 'trilemma' or 'unholy trinity' as set out in the Mundell–Fleming model.[2] In a dilemma, a choice has to be made between two possible courses of action; in a 'trilemma', one desideratum out of three must be abandoned.[3] Suppose that an economy faces a recession and rising unemployment. One obvious response is to stimulate activity by reducing interest rates. Such a policy might work if capital movements are limited, but in the absence of controls the result might be an outflow of capital in search of higher returns elsewhere. The pursuit of an active domestic monetary policy therefore required the imposition of capital controls. Furthermore, if exchange rates are fixed, low interest rates might push the currency down, which would soon require an increase in interest rates to bolster the exchanges. Hence, an active domestic monetary policy would not be possible unless fixed exchanges were abandoned. The converse also applies: if the economy was overheating, higher interest rates, designed to deflate the economy, would lead, in the absence of controls, to an influx of capital and an appreciation of the exchange rate above the fixed parity. Hence, one of the three elements of the 'trilemma' had to be sacrificed: an active domestic monetary policy was not compatible with both fixed exchanges and free movement of capital.

The 'inconsistent quartet' adds a fourth variable, trade policy, which is of particular significance for this volume. Regardless of the choice made in the 'trilemma', a country could opt for either protection or free trade. In Britain before 1914, the choice of fixed exchange rates and capital mobility was linked with free trade, which had, by the end of the nineteenth century, hardened into a dogmatic adherence to unilateralism as other countries moved to protectionism.[4] But in the case of the USA, adherence to the gold standard from 1873 was associated with a much more protectionist trade policy: in the UK import duties were 5.6 per cent of total imports in 1913, whereas in the USA they were 21.4 per cent.[5] The same point applied to Germany. Trade policy may vary independently of the trade-offs within the 'trilemma', with differing relationships. In the 1930s, many countries adopted protectionism with floating exchanges (often designed to undervalue currencies and so encourage exports and discourage imports); at present,

---

[2] Mundell 1963; Fleming 1962.   [3] Obstfeld and Taylor 2004.   [4] Trentmann 2008.
[5] Estevadeordal 1997.

floating exchanges are complemented by trade liberalization (unless attempts to hold down the value of currencies to secure export markets spill over into trade war). These relationships are historically contingent, depending on the interplay between domestic and international politics.

These trade-offs had considerable influence on the way in which balance of payments were brought into equilibrium, and hence on trade policy, which affects the work of the WTO. Under the fixed exchange rate system of the gold standard, the adjustments were—at least in principle—implemented through the specie-flow mechanism. A country with a balance of payments deficit would send gold to the country with a surplus; prices would fall in the former economy so that its exports became more competitive, and rise in the latter so that its goods became less competitive on international markets. This adjustment mechanism could lead to considerable social and economic disruption in the domestic economy, as happened in the 1920s in Britain, so contributing to nationalistic pressure against the global economy.[6] The same process would apply where currencies were pegged to each other: the deficit country would lose foreign exchange reserves and the amount of money in circulation would decline, with deflationary consequences. It could also borrow from abroad to cover the deficit, or reduce its foreign lending to compensate for the weakening in the current account, so that international capital movements would play a role in creating balance on current account. (The exception was that under the fixed exchange rate regime of Bretton Woods, the USA, as the provider of the major international currency, could simply print more dollars, for it was not so rigidly tied to holdings of gold as under the classic gold standard. Hence, the American government could avoid deflation at home and export inflation to the rest of the world.) Meanwhile, a country with a surplus could lend to the deficit countries or purchase assets, so that the balance on current account was covered through the capital account; failing this, the country with a deficit would run down its foreign reserves to pay for the goods. The difference from the gold standard was that a country was permitted to devalue its currency to prevent domestic deflation from threatening political stability or economic welfare.

Adjustment under a flexible exchange rate regime operates in a different manner. Although countries might borrow or lend capital, buy or sell assets, there is no need to maintain the exchange rate. A firm purchasing goods turns to the foreign exchange market to secure currency of the surplus country, whose price will rise relative to that of the deficit country, so making the price of goods in the surplus country rise compared with those in the deficit country. The exchange rate is set by the demand and supply of currencies, leading to appreciation of the currency in the surplus and depreciation in the deficit country, which should then adjust the relative price of goods and bring the system back into equilibrium. Of course, some surplus countries might try to manipulate their currency to prevent this happening, intervening to hold the currency stable so that goods remain competitive. In other words, within a floating system it is still possible to peg currencies for reasons of national economic policy.

[6] Keynes 1925.

These considerations affect the way in which trade policy operates. In a regime of fixed rates on the gold standard, tariffs could be used to prevent a deficit from mounting and to limit the importation of goods of more competitive economies, but it was not possible to use the exchange rate as an alternative or supplementary policy option. In the system of fixed but variable rates from the Second World War to the early 1970s, the use of tariffs was more difficult as a result of the drive for open markets for goods and the creation of General Agreement on Tariffs and Trade (GATT). Neither was currency manipulation a policy option, beyond occasional devaluations when a country's goods became uncompetitive or, more significantly, through the disinclination of surplus countries to revalue. In the case of flexible rate regimes, tariffs could in theory be used as they were in the 1930s—but, given the trade liberalization policies associated with GATT and the WTO, in the current period of flexible rates it might be easier to manipulate exchange rates as a substitute for trade policy. The formation of the WTO came in a world of flexible exchange rates, with the possibility that national governments could intervene in currency markets. Consequently, the creation of a level playing field in trade policy could be contradicted by biases in the exchange rates which are outside the remit of the WTO. It is not clear that a country is permitted to react to a deliberate undervaluation of a competitor's currency by imposing countervailing duties. The exchange rate regime therefore creates the context for trade policy. The following sections of this chapter outline, in a necessarily selective manner, the historical evolution of these trade-offs and interrelationships. The chronology of these trade-offs is set out in Table 2.

2.3 THE INCONSISTENT QUARTET AND THE GOLD STANDARD BEFORE 1914

In the first peak of globalization prior to the First World War, Britain was the centre of the world economy. Britain adhered to the gold standard and fixed exchange rates from 1821 to the First World War; at the same time, it permitted complete freedom in capital movements. The outflow of capital was counter-cyclical, with domestic investment falling from 62 per cent of gross domestic fixed capital formation in the late 1880s to 37 per cent in the 1890s, before rising to as much as 76 per cent of gross domestic fixed capital formation between 1905 and 1914; by the outbreak of war, overseas investment amounted to about a third of all British capital.[7] Critics argued that the outflow of capital led to a low level of investment in social overhead capital at home, and to income disparities between wealthy investors and workers who did not benefit from the creation of domestic employment. Supporters argued that the outflow of capital led to the production of cheap food for domestic consumers, the creation of markets for British goods, and an inflow of interest payments, which created a balance

---

[7] Stone 1999; Simon 1967.

Table 2 Policy trade-offs between domestic economic policies, capital mobility, and fixed exchanges (c.1870–1990)

	Fixed exchanges	Capital mobility	Active economic policies
Gold standard			
to 1913	yes	yes	no
1925–31	yes	less	tentatively
Off gold, 1931–39	no	no	yes
Bretton Woods to 1973	yes	no	yes
Float from 1974	no	yes	yes

Source: Adapted from Obstfeld and Taylor 2004, 40.

of payments surplus.[8] What the outflow of capital did mean for the international economy was that Britain returned its massive surplus to create liquidity in the world economy, and by keeping its own markets open, the borrowing countries were able to sell their goods to service the debt. The counter-cyclical nature of investment also meant that a recession in Britain, with potentially harmful effects on the demand for foreign and colonial goods, was offset by an outflow of capital to stimulate demand in those areas of the world that benefited from British investment.

The adoption of these two policies of fixed exchange rates and capital movements meant that it was impossible for the British government—or more accurately the Bank of England—to pursue an active domestic monetary policy. Let us suppose that Britain faced a recession and rising unemployment, which might be mitigated by reducing interest rates to stimulate demand, employment, and investment. Given the free movement of capital around the world under the gold standard, the result would be an outflow of capital to secure higher rates of return elsewhere so that the benefit of domestic investment would be reduced, and the London money market would be less attractive to short-term deposits. Consequently, the exchange rate faced downward pressure, which could not be permitted with the fixed exchange rates of the gold standard. Interest rates would therefore have to rise. Similarly, the use of higher interest rates to prevent the economy from overheating would lead to an increase in short-term deposits on the London money market, and might keep funds at home, so leading to upward pressure on the pound which was not permitted under the gold standard. Furthermore, the very high level of overseas investment in the decade before the First World War could have a crowding-out effect on spending on social overhead capital at home. Although the Chancellor of the Exchequer, David Lloyd George, and his economic adviser, George Paish, believed that overseas investment would create demand for British exports (and

---

[8] The argument was made at the time by Giffen 1905, Chiozza Money 1905, and Hobson 1902, and has continued ever since, such as in Pollard 1985.

so increase employment), and produce more cheap food (and so lead to a recovery in real wages), there was a very real possibility that it increased the cost of borrowing for spending on public health, schools and housing to which the Liberal government was committed.[9] Hence, the option of fixed exchange rates and free movement of capital came at the cost of an active domestic monetary policy and constraints on social spending.

This choice within the 'trilemma' must be explained by the nature of domestic politics—and the interpretation is a matter of controversy. The explanation, in the opinion of some historians, is simple: policy was dominated by 'gentlemanly capitalists', comprising the financiers of the City of London and the landed aristocracy, who shared a common educational background and intermarried in response to the agricultural depression of the last quarter of the nineteenth century, dominating the Court of the Bank of England and Parliament, excluding the concerns of domestic industry and the working class in favour of the pursuit of a cosmopolitan economic policy.[10]

Eichengreen puts the argument in a slightly different, though closely related, way. He suggests that those who stood to lose from fixed exchanges (to which we might add capital mobility), and to gain from an active domestic monetary policy (and investment at home) lacked voice. They could not press their case that a different trade-off would benefit employment and domestic economic stability because the franchise was limited, and in any case industrialists and workers lacked a theoretical understanding of the links between international monetary policy, high interest rates and domestic stability to create a powerful counterargument. Furthermore, he argues that the maintenance of fixed exchange rates before the war rested on a particular institutional system: central banks in the major economies were able to cooperate to maintain the system without the intrusion of national politics. On this view, the trade-off changed after the First World War with the adoption of universal manhood suffrage, a growing understanding by economists of the impact of high interest rates, and the collapse of cooperation between central bankers with the erosion of their autonomy through the intrusion of national politics.[11]

These arguments are not entirely convincing, and a more plausible approach would run as follows: workers and industrialists did have considerable voice, and politicians were concerned about the great industrial towns of Lancashire where national elections were won and lost. Further, workers and industrialists expressed their voice in support of the gold standard, which was far from being merely an ideology of 'gentlemanly capitalists'. The gold standard was a cultural symbol as much as an economic policy that favoured particular interest groups: it was an automatic device immune to manipulation by financiers and speculators; it offered access to the world's largest trade bloc of prosperous countries; it was an expression of peace and civilization; and it offered workers higher real wages as prices fell. The gold standard and the free movement of capital with which it was associated seemed to make sense, and the reduction of unemployment was

---

[9] Offer 1983.   [10] Cain and Hopkins 1993; Cassis 1985; Green 1988.   [11] Eichengreen 1992.

expected to come about through other policies designed to remove inflexibilities in the labour market.[12] Of course, American populists in the later nineteenth century gave gold a very different cultural meaning so that we need to be alert to the distinctive interpretations of gold within national politics.[13]

In the case of Britain prior to the First World War, this particular choice within the trilemma was firmly associated with free trade, which was introduced in stages from the early nineteenth century. Free trade was symbolized by the repeal of the corn laws in 1846, which seemed to guarantee peace and prosperity, to purge politics of special interests, to benefit the consumer, and to permit free association of citizens.[14] Although free trade came under threat from the advocates of imperial preference in the decade before the First World War, it survived whilst at the same time undergoing internal change. Progressive 'new' Liberals and Labour continued to support free trade, but within a different ideological framework from Richard Cobden's minimalist state based on retrenchment. Increasingly, the progressives argued that free trade should be linked with a just distribution of income and wealth within Britain so that exports did not rest on domestic poverty, and imports did not reflect the luxury consumption of the rich. Free trade should therefore be linked with redistribution at home—and, similarly, it should not rest on the exploitation of countries overseas, and might require the planning of the international economy. The alliance in support of free trade held up to 1914, but these internal tensions contributed to its dissolution after the war when new challenges appeared.[15]

As noted above, in some countries the same trade-off within the trilemma was linked with protectionism, which at first sight seems contradictory. According to one calculation, countries on the gold standard traded almost 30 per cent more amongst themselves than with non-gold countries, and global trade would have been 20 per cent lower between 1880 and 1910 without the widespread adoption of the gold standard.[16] Hence, membership of the fixed exchange rate regime of the gold standard was a trade-creating policy, giving access to the largest and most prosperous trade area in the world. Nevertheless, in some cases—such as Germany and the United States—the adoption of gold was associated with a move towards protectionism.

On closer inspection, the ability of trade policy to vary independently of the other policy choices is less surprising. The countries adopting gold in the 1870s seem to have made the decision without considering trade policy, and subsequently compensated those who lost from the adoption of gold by introducing tariffs. The outcome reflected different alignments of interests, so that the supporters of a cosmopolitan international economy might win on exchange rates and lose on trade policy. Thus the adoption of gold could mean downward pressure on wages to maintain competitiveness under the fixed exchange rate, which was then compensated by protection against cheaper imports. Again, a link between fixed exchanges under the gold standard and protection could be

---

[12] Daunton 2006.   [13] Goodwyn 1976.   [14] Trentmann 2008.   [15] Trentmann 2008.
[16] Lopez-Cordova and Meissner 2003; Meissner 2005.

part of a policy of economic development. In the case of Japan, for instance, adoption of the gold standard meant that the government could raise funds more cheaply on the London market, for the gold standard was a credible commitment to creditors to make loans.[17] These funds were invested in militarism and in the infrastructure, and the goods produced by 'infant' industries needed protection from cheaper imports from more advanced industrial countries. Trade policy, then, should be understood in terms of the other policy choices within the 'inconsistent quartet'.

2.4 THE INCONSISTENT QUARTET BETWEEN THE WORLD WARS

After the First World War, these trade-offs changed in significant ways. Tensions were already appearing before the First World War, for the policy choices had differential impacts on countries and economic interests. European farmers and landowners threatened by the importation of cheap grain from the new world pressed for protection, as did industrial workers facing increased competition. Labour mobility was a further important factor, for the large-scale movement of workers from Europe pushed up wages there and held them down in the new world. European farmers and landowners faced lower profits and higher wages, and so demanded protection; new world farmers and landowners experienced higher profits and land values, whereas workers feared an erosion of their standard of living, and so demanded restriction on immigration. The gap between the income levels of the two sides of the Atlantic narrowed—but in the old world, income differentials fell whilst in the new world they rose.[18] As Harold James argues, nation states acted as defence mechanisms against the threat of globalization through tariffs, controls on migration, or welfare policies. At the same time, nation states provoked nationalism which led to an uneasy relationship with globalization.[19] Up to the First World War, the forces of nationalism were held in check; after the war, the balance shifted.

The war led to serious problems, for many countries abandoned the gold standard and even Britain, the main proponent of free trade, introduced protectionist policies. This modest wartime shift in policy was followed by political battles over protectionism in the 1920s, and resulted in the adoption of imperial preference in the early 1930s. Progressive support for free trade was supplanted by a growing emphasis on redistribution and planning by the state as a better route towards fairness, and the post-war collapse of export industries weakened the rationale for open markets.[20] At the same time, commitment to the gold standard became more problematic. Eichengreen argues that the extension of the franchise destabilized the pre-war policy choices. As we noted, he

[17] Bordo and Rockoff 1996; Sussman and Yafeh 2000.
[18] O'Rourke and Williamson 1999; Aghion and Williamson 1999.
[19] James 2001.   [20] Trentmann 2008.

claims that workers suffered from the lack of an active domestic monetary policy before the war, and restoration of the gold standard after the war meant that they paid the price through unemployment and the need for wage flexibility to maintain competitiveness. In his view, workers gained voice and political power after the war through the expansion of the franchise and increased unionization and militancy. Furthermore, he argues that economists before 1914 had only a limited understanding of the link between international monetary policy, high interest rates and domestic economic stability. Now there was a better theoretical understanding of the implications of the policy which gave workers the ability to express their concerns. Furthermore, he argues that the cooperation of central bankers was no longer possible as it had been before the war. Before the First World War, the gold standard was a 'contingent rule' which might be abandoned in times of war or emergency, with a strong presumption that it would be restored. It was not underwritten by international institutions. After the war, the rule was weakened for central banks were constrained, particularly as a result of high levels of inflation in the early 1920s, which led to the imposition of stricter controls on their discretion. At the same time, international institutions were not created with sufficient force to deal with nationalistic pressures. Consequently, the pre-1914 trade-off was under considerable pressure.[21]

This interpretation should be revised to take account of the comments made earlier about the explanation of the trade-offs before 1914. Rather than pre-existing hostility to the gold standard now being expressed because workers secured voice, the benefits and losses of the gold standard had changed. The nation state now succumbed to domestic political pressures in the absence of constraints from commitment mechanisms and international institutions. The attempt to return to the gold standard in the 1920s imposed strains in the 'trilemma', for the war and post-war boom led to changes in pre-war parities and the attempt to return to the gold standard at pre-existing rates created serious problems. In Britain, where costs and wages had risen faster than in the USA, it was necessary to deflate the economy and to support sterling by high interest rates, which exacerbated social tensions. High interest rates made the costs of debt service—a serious problem after the war for all the combatants—more onerous, both for industrialists and the government, which squeezed investment and welfare spending. The use of interest rates to defend the pound was now constrained. In Britain, the high level of debt owed by export industries to banks meant that higher interest rates threatened default and a financial crisis, so that the Bank of England had to be much more concerned about the needs of domestic industry than it had before the war. The persistence of unemployment was also a serious social and political issue. Hence, even when Britain returned to the gold standard in 1925, greater attention was paid to the domestic impact of monetary policy.[22]

Similarly, the free movement of capital was more problematical. Since it was not possible to sustain the pound by raising interest rates as far as was necessary, because of the

---

[21] Eichengreen 1992; James 2001.   [22] Solomou 1996; Moggridge 1972; Tolliday 1987.

threat to industry and the domestic economy, attention turned to an alternative approach: restricting capital mobility. According to a United Nations report of 1949, the net capital exports of the United Kingdom between 1911 and 1913 were $1,042 m. During the First World War, the UK disposed of $4,000 m of its accumulated overseas investment to pay for the war effort. After the war, capital exports resumed and reached $881 m in 1921, but then fell to only $407m between 1922 and 1928, before turning negative in the 1930s. Controls were imposed during the First World War, and were not entirely removed in the interwar period. There were several motivations. After the war, overseas loans were limited in order to permit local authority borrowing for the construction of social housing to resolve the serious housing shortage, and to allow the conversion of short-term government debt into longer-term funded debt. Although the embargo on foreign loans was removed in 1924, it was reinstated by the end of the year in preparation for the return to the gold standard, and it was soon extended to loans to the dominions and colonies. Capital mobility was sacrificed to maintain the gold standard—a deeply controversial policy, for a reduction in foreign loans might harm industrial exports, and the limitation of colonial and dominion capital exports might weaken the empire by driving borrowers to the United States. Although the embargo was removed again in November 1925, freedom was not restored as before 1914: instead, there was concern for the benefits to the economy as a whole and an assessment of the political consequences at home and abroad.[23]

The abandonment of the gold standard by Britain in 1931 marked a further shift. Instead of defending the exchange rate, the pound was devalued and held down in order to simulate exports and limit imports—a strategy linked with the introduction of higher import duties and imperial preference. Low interest rates were attractive as a means of holding down the value of the pound, permitting a conversion of the national debt to lower interest, and encouraging investment in housing and consumer goods. Hence there was a shift towards an active domestic monetary policy. Capital mobility remained a concern, for the government wished to retain funds at home to assist in the conversion of the national debt, and when controls slackened priority was given to loans that would assist domestic employment.[24]

The trade-off therefore changed in the interwar period, in ways that were later interpreted as harmful. The outcome was seen as being just as bad as the earlier trade-off when priority was given to international considerations. In the opinion of many participants in the debates over the reform of the international economy, the shortcoming of the interwar period was that the pursuit of active domestic monetary policies gave priority to economic nationalism over international concerns, and led to 'beggar-my-neighbour' policies. The abandonment of fixed exchange rates meant that competitive devaluation could be used to secure export markets and exclude competition from foreign suppliers—a strategy linked with a shift to protectionism such as the Smoot-Hawley tariff in the USA, imperial preference in Britain, and Schachtianism in Germany.

[23] Atkin 1970; Clarke 1990.   [24] Solomou 1996.

The attempt of each country to find salvation at home meant that everyone suffered as world trade shrank.

At least, such was the assumption of later commentators. Eichengreen and Sachs argue that reality might be different. Whereas protectionism leaves everyone worse off, devaluation does lead to the benefits of lower interest rates, high domestic investment, and increased demand in the depreciating country. Hence countries that departed from gold early (such as Britain and Scandinavia) made a swifter recovery of industrial output and exports than those which delayed (such as France). In the countries that remained on gold, industrial production fell by 13.9 per cent between 1929 and 1936, whereas in the sterling block, which devalued in 1931, the growth rate was 27.8 per cent. The extent to which depreciation 'beggared' other countries depends on whether it was a corrective to price disparities (beneficial) or an aggressive act to secure market share (harmful). In the 1930s, the absence of coordination meant that there was always a danger that it could tip over into being harmful,[25] which explains the attempt after 1944 to control depreciation, confining it to correcting imbalances and preventing manipulation to secure market share.

2.5 THE INCONSISTENT QUARTET AND BRETTON WOODS, 1944–1971

The solution adopted during the Second World War rested on a new trade-off within the 'trilemma' and the inconsistent quartet. The main desideratum was to return to multilateral trade and reject protectionism through tariffs, preferences, and controls. The leading ideologue of the return to open markets was Cordell Hull, the US Secretary of State from 1933 to 1944, who wished to reduce US protectionism from the heights of the Smoot-Hawley tariff and to destroy British imperial preference. In Hull's opinion, 'unhampered trade dovetailed with peace; high tariffs, trade barriers and unfair economic competition with war'.[26] Hull was Richard Cobden reincarnated—but as we have seen, the interpretation of free trade in Britain had shifted away from Cobdenism towards a concern for redistribution and coordination. A commitment to multilateral trade could mean different things to different people.

It was not enough simply to reduce trade barriers without a fundamental change in other elements of the inconsistent quartet: multilateral trade could not be achieved without restoring liquidity and preventing disruptive movements in exchange rates. It was necessary to contain the economic nationalism that had destroyed the global economy between the wars: the contingent commitment of the gold standard could no longer be relied upon, and the absence of formal institutional commitments between the wars meant that economic nationalism was not constrained. Hence it was considered

---

[25] Eichengreen and Sachs 1985; Solomou 1996.   [26] Hull 1948.

imperative to stop competitive devaluations by returning to a fixed exchange rate, but now with a degree of flexibility in the event of disequilibria which would otherwise require severe deflation and recession, with the danger of a recurrence of economic nationalism. The dollar was pegged to gold and other currencies were pegged against the dollar, with the ability to alter the rate when it would create serious domestic problems. The aim was to create a balance between exchange rate stability, which was seen as vital for the restoration of international trade, and domestic welfare, which was seen as equally necessary to prevent a nationalistic backlash against globalization.

Henry Morgenthau, Secretary of the Treasury, believed that the depression of the 1930s started with currency disorders and then spread to trade; it was therefore necessary to fix exchange rates first to allow multilateral trade to recover. As he said at the Bretton Woods conference in 1944:

> All of us have seen the great economic tragedy of our time. We saw the worldwide depression of the 1930s. We saw currency disorders develop and spread from land to land, destroying the basis for international trade and international investment and even international faith. In their wake, we saw unemployment and wretchedness— idle tools, wasted wealth. We saw their victims fall prey, in places, to demagogues and dictators. We saw bewilderment and bitterness become the breeders of fascism, and, finally, of war.[27]

Of course, fixed exchange rates had proved dangerous in the 1920s by requiring deflation and attacks on wage rates in order to remain competitive, so leading to a nationalistic backlash against globalization. The same problem would recur after the Second World War if serious balance of payments disequilibrium were to lead to attacks on costs and wages in order to gain markets. What was needed, in the words of Ragnar Nurkse in his analysis of interwar currency, 'was to find a system of international currency relations compatible with the requirements of domestic stability'.[28] Hence the first Article of the International Monetary Fund (IMF) was a commitment to 'the promotion and maintenance of employment and real income, and to the development of the productive resources of all members as primary objectives of economic policy'.[29]

How was this to be done? The commitment to develop productive resources proved to be highly controversial. To the British, multilateral trade should rest on a commitment to full employment within domestic economies, an approach that many Americans feared as socialist. It also brought the needs of developed and underdeveloped countries into conflict in the discussions to create the International Trade Organization (discussed in Chapter 4),[30] and continued through the proposals of the United Nations Conference on Trade and Development and into the Doha Development Agenda. More practically and immediately, the rules of the IMF allowed currencies to be devalued in the event of disequilibrium, and permitted controls over capital exports, which allowed the pursuit of active domestic economic policies in combination with a commitment to

---

[27] United States Department of State 1948.   [28] League of Nations 1944.
[29] Horsefield 1969.   [30] Daunton 2010.

open international markets for goods fostered by stable exchange rates. Nationalism and internationalism were brought into balance.

Arguably, capital exports from Britain before 1914 were a source of stability in the international economy. As we noted, the export of this capital was counter-cyclical: when Britain was experiencing prosperity, its open market meant that the goods of the world had an outlet and previous loans could be serviced; when Britain was less prosperous, it invested overseas and so helped to stabilize the international economy. Furthermore, overseas investment was largely in social overhead capital—and above all in railways—in temperate zones of recent settlement which produced food and raw materials for the developed economies, with general benefit to the recipients.[31] However, in the interwar period capital movements were seen as the cause of difficulties, taking the form of 'hot' money fleeing from uncertainty in one part of the world or the other. Capital movements meant disruptive speculative flows rather than the preservation of stability and prosperity. In the trade-off of the 'trilemma', domestic prosperity could only be combined with fixed (though now flexible) exchange rates by sacrificing capital mobility in order to use interest rates to maintain domestic stability without provoking an export of capital and downward pressure on the exchange rates. Keynes realized that 'the whole management of the domestic economy depends upon being free to have the appropriate rate of interest without reference to the rates prevailing elsewhere in the world. Capital control is a corollary to this.'[32] Similarly, Bertil Ohlin remarked that the movement of goods 'is a prerequisite of prosperity and economic growth' whereas the movement of capital was not.[33] Article VI section 3 of the IMF Agreement specified that 'members may exercise such controls as are necessary to regulate international capital movements.'[34] Hence, the post-war restoration of multilateral trade and the emergence of the General Agreement on Tariffs and Trade were linked with fixed (though variable) exchange rates, capital controls, and active domestic policies. The form taken by GATT presupposed the existence of these other elements.

The post-war trade-off of fixed exchange rates, capital controls and an active domestic monetary policy with trade liberalization was linked with domestic institutional arrangements between the state, labour, and capital. Recovery after the war rested on convincing workers to accept lower current wages for higher living standards in the future created by reinvesting profits. But could labour trust management to deliver on the promise in the future? The state underwrote the bargain by encouraging ploughback of profits through tax policies and creating stable markets, and offered welfare schemes to workers. The result was an 'institutional exit barrier'.[35] Whether it could hold indefinitely as political and economic conditions changed was to be put to the test by the late 1960s.

The trade-off continued into the 1960s, as is apparent during the Kennedy Round of GATT trade talks which came to a conclusion in 1967, marking the single most

---

[31] Nurkse 1954; Singer 1950.   [32] Moggridge 1980.   [33] Helleiner 1994.
[34] Horsefield 1969.   [35] Eichengreen and Braga de Macedo 2001.

substantial reduction in tariffs since the war.[36] At the same time, Presidents Kennedy and Johnson were extending controls on American capital exports. They wished to make the American economy more competitive and efficient by stimulating domestic investment, utilizing capacity to the full, and increasing public spending to remove the problems of poverty at home. They embarked on a policy of tax breaks on depreciation to stimulate investment, improved welfare benefits and minimum wages to boost workers' efficiency, and raised investment in human resources. This policy was associated with capital controls. In his advice to Kennedy, J. K. Galbraith argued that restriction on capital flows was the least damaging option in preserving the American balance of payments, and that the alternatives were not politically feasible. A reduction in overseas military spending would be opposed by the State Department and was scarcely possible at the height of the Cold War. Deflation of the domestic economy was not electorally desirable at a time of political unrest, and it would conflict with the administration's policies of reducing poverty. In Galbraith's view, the Treasury's preference for free capital movements was a case of 'banker syndrome', and he argued that it made more sense to invest at home to improve the efficiency of the American economy and so make its goods more competitive in export markets.[37] Such arguments led to the Interest Equalization Tax of 1963, which raised the cost of borrowing to foreigners above the domestic rate. In 1965, Johnson went still further and introduced direct controls on capital exports.

Although Richard Nixon promised to end capital controls during his election campaign, the task proved difficult. In 1969, Henry Kissinger warned that free movement of capital would weaken America's strategic position, for it would lead to a deterioration of the balance of payments and allow European governments to criticize the Americans for irresponsibility. Kissinger argued that capital controls were preferable to cutting military spending or forcing allies to pay more of the costs, which would risk alienating them or giving them more power over American policy.[38] Of course, Nixon was also trying to build a new electoral coalition at home, based on the South and blue-collar workers, which made him extremely reluctant to respond to the weakening of the balance of payments by deflating the domestic economy.[39] Although capital controls were retained for some time, the trade-off proved to be unstable, and not only because of the ideological commitment to the free movement of capital espoused by many economists and politicians. Capital controls were more difficult to enforce with the widespread adoption of convertibility from 1958. Capital could move via the current account, and controls could be evaded by holding dollars offshore through the emerging Euro–dollar market. The greater mobility of capital put pressure on the maintenance of fixed exchange rates—and when these collapsed in the early 1970s, the rationale for capital controls largely disappeared.[40]

On 15 August 1971, Nixon suspended the convertibility of dollars into gold, so triggering a period of uncertainty in international monetary policy. The problem with the

---

[36] Zeiler 1992.   [37] FRUS 1961–3, Volume IX.   [38] FRUS 1969–76, Volume III.
[39] Matusow 1998.   [40] Helleiner 1994; Obstfeld and Taylor 2004.

Bretton Woods system of fixed exchange rates was that it allowed countries with weak currencies to devalue, with the exception of the United States which provided the peg against which other countries were fixed; it did not require countries with strong currencies—such as West Germany and Japan—to revalue. As a result, major changes in relative economic performance created serious disequilibria in exchange rates which were not easily resolved through the existing institutional machinery of the IMF, and led to concern by the Americans that undervaluation of the Deutsche Mark (DM) and yen amounted to a return of beggar-my-neighbour policies designed to engross international trade. Equally, other countries accused America of irresponsibility in failing to act on its overvalued currency, and for indulging in 'greenback imperialism' by printing dollars to finance military adventures, purchase European firms, and export inflation.[41] More realistically, Robert Triffin pointed to the dilemma that the world needed liquidity provided by dollars if it were to continue to grow—but the provision of liquidity by means of an American deficit undermined confidence in the dollar.[42] The failure of the IMF or G8 to produce a realistic reform of the international currency system led to a policy of 'benign neglect'. A crisis was allowed to develop without taking action to avert it, in the hope of creating an opportunity to realign currencies and reform the international monetary system.[43] It meant the demise of the trade-off in the 'trilemma' that was created at Bretton Woods.

2.6 THE INCONSISTENT QUARTET AND THE DEVELOPMENT OF FLOATING EXCHANGES

The closing of the gold window was followed by the Smithsonian Agreement of December 1971 which attempted to reinstate the Bretton Woods system of fixed but variable exchange rates. It revalued the yen by 16.9 per cent and the DM by 13.57 per cent, and devalued the dollar against other G10 currencies by 10 per cent.[44] The attempt to preserve Bretton Woods at new parities did not succeed and a new trade-off within the 'trilemma' emerged, after a period of considerable tensions and confusion.

The collapse of the regime of fixed exchange rates was not the result of intellectual conversion, despite the advocacy of some leading economists—and above all Milton Friedman—for floating. As Gottfried Haberler pointed out, it was not a system but a 'non-system', which arose by default.[45] The explanation was, in large part, the failure of the Nixon administration to take domestic action as the balance of payments continued to deteriorate and an expansive monetary policy was pursued to prevent a domestic recession, with inflation held in check by controls over prices and wages. How long these controls would succeed was doubtful: Friedman warned that 'all previous attempts to

---

[41] Rueff 1972.   [42] Triffin 1960.   [43] Matusow 1998; James 1996.   [44] James 1996.
[45] Quoted in James 1996.

freeze prices and wages have ended, from the time of the Roman Emperor Diocletian to the present, in utter failure and the emergence into the open of suppressed inflation'.[46] George Shultz, the Secretary of the Treasury, agreed: 'a freeze will stop when labor blows it up with a strike. Don't worry about getting rid of it—labor will do that for you.'[47] Much the same could be said of Britain in the early 1970s, where the Conservative administration of Edward Heath was 'blown up' by the unions, and the succeeding Labour administration attempted to contain inflation and wage demands by a 'social contract' with unions.

The comments of Shultz and the experience of Britain called into question the institutional arrangements between the state, labour, and capital that had lain at the basis of the Bretton Woods regime. By the late 1960s, strains were appearing in this institutional system. Until this point, higher capital inputs provided increasing marginal returns which allowed a combination of outcomes: the payment of higher wages; stable prices for consumer goods; and sufficient profits to allow continued investment. The inflationary potential of full employment was therefore mitigated, and high demand from consumers and for capital goods meant that full employment was maintained in a virtuous circuit of growth. By the late 1960s, the marginal productivity of capital was declining so that it was no longer possible to pay higher wages without inflation or a squeeze on profits. This outcome was particularly marked in Britain and the USA compared with West Germany and Japan, where there was greater potential for structural transformation from agriculture into industry. In the case of the UK, the rate of profit on the net assets of industrial and commercial companies fell, after tax, from 7.1 per cent to 4.1 per cent.[48]

The question that faced governments in Britain and other countries was how to handle the trade-off between exchange rates and domestic policy. Should exchange rates be fixed, which would impose an external restraint on inflation and wage demands because of the priority to protect the value of the pound? Or were the consequences for domestic stability so serious that exchange rates should be allowed to depreciate in order to make British goods more competitive and allow an active domestic policy designed to stimulate growth? If such a policy were pursued, would floating exchanges lead to economic growth or to inflation fuelled by monetary expansion, and to continued wage increases and continued depreciation of the currency to maintain competitiveness?

The initial policy choice in Britain was to join the European currency 'snake' on 1 May 1972, which pegged currencies in a narrower band within the wider 'tunnel' of the Smithsonian Agreement. On 23 June 1972, Britain left the snake and allowed the pound to float. These policy choices were deeply contentious. The attempt to keep the pound within a narrow band relative to other European currencies constrained policies designed to reduce unemployment and to set interest rates for domestic reasons. The Chancellor of the Exchequer made his doubts about the trade-off clear in March 1972 when he commented that 'it is neither necessary nor desirable to distort domestic economies to an unaccountable extent in order to retain unrealistic exchange rates'. The case

---

[46] Friedman 1975.   [47] Matusow 1998.   [48] Glyn and Sutcliffe 1972.

for joining (or rejoining) the snake was that a completely free float led to the danger that the money supply could be expanded without constraint, and that there was therefore less reason to restrain wages and prices since the exchanges could take the strain. The snake would impose discipline on the domestic economy, obliging the government to contain costs and wages in order to remain within the currency band. But could it work?

The Treasury was sceptical: an attempt to refix the rate was doomed for it could only be held through tough counter-inflationary measures (which would be deeply unpopular) and without strikes, which would be provoked by the attempts to control inflation. Furthermore, fixed rates would mean cutting public expenditure, which would prevent improvements to the infrastructure and harm growth, and would require higher interest rates to support the pound and so hit investment and employment. A decision to return to the snake meant greater priority given to external exchanges than to employment and growth; floating meant a higher priority given to employment and growth than to maintaining a fixed parity within the European system. But was it obvious that floating would indeed be beneficial? The ability of the pound to float meant that there was less incentive to control wages, with the result that profits, investment, and competitiveness would be under threat. The outcome was that Britain remained outside the snake and opted to float.

The balance of payments situation remained parlous, leading to intervention by the IMF in 1976 and to a divisive debate within the government which had major implications for the 'inconsistent quartet'. Rather than budgetary restraint and tighter monetary policy with serious domestic consequences, why not adopt a 'siege economy' and reject the whole project of open markets pursued since the Second World War? Protective barriers would cure the trade deficit, increase profits and investment, and allow planning of the economy. This so-called 'alternative economic strategy' was defeated, but the debate does highlight the trade-offs within the 'inconsistent quartet' which were contested in the 1970s as the Bretton Woods regime ended.[49]

The USA followed a similar path to Britain, for similar reasons, when it allowed the dollar to float in 1973. By contrast, the government of West Germany maintained monetary control, contained inflation and costs, so remaining competitive in export markets and absorbing the impact of the OPEC oil shock. The explanation was, in part, the adoption of the 'social market' which gave unions a role on the advisory boards of companies with a commitment to raising productivity. West Germany retained a trade surplus and strong currency which placed strain on the 'snake', for other members, such as France and Italy, were less successful in absorbing the oil shock, and opted for looser monetary policies and inflation. Their currencies therefore moved outside the bounds of the snake. Priority was given to domestic concerns and politics rather than to the maintenance of fixed exchange rates. Nevertheless, the commitment mechanisms of GATT meant that protectionism was held in check, and the tensions in the monetary system ran alongside the Tokyo round.

[49] Daunton 2009.

In both Britain and the United States, the results were problematical: there was no constraint on monetary expansion or on wages, with the result that inflation reached high levels. The solution was to reimpose external constraint through tighter monetary policy in the 'shock' administered by Paul Volcker of the Federal Reserve on 16 October 1979, when high interest rates and tight money squeezed inflation out of the economy at the cost of recession and unemployment. The same approach was followed by the government of Margaret Thatcher after the election of a Conservative government in Britain in 1979. Higher levels of unemployment weakened the power of trade unions, and legislation was amended to reduce the threat of strike action and to create a more 'flexible' labour market. At the same time, taxation was reduced on higher incomes and shifted towards indirect taxes in an attempt to restore incentives to the economy. The process continued with the liberalization of financial markets in both Britain and the United States, with 'big bang' in the City of London in 1986 and the repeal of the Glass-Steagall Act in 1999. By the 1990s, international capital movements reached levels not seen since the period before the First World War.[50] A new trade-off had emerged: capital was highly mobile; exchange rates were free to vary in most countries; and monetary policy could be used for domestic reasons. The Federal Reserve was expected to maintain employment and control inflation; the Bank of England had a narrower remit from 1997 to keep inflation below a threshold figure. In neither case were the central banks required to maintain the external exchange rate—nor, for that matter, did they play a very active role in regulating the activities of the financial sector.

A new trade-off had emerged since the demise of the Bretton Woods regime established after 1944—a system that is sometimes called 'Bretton Woods II'. The events of 2008 posed the question of whether the trade-off of Bretton Woods II could survive. Globalization led to major shifts in patterns of employment as the opening of international markets and the freer movement of capital allowed production of many industrial commodities to move to low-cost countries. The rules of GATT meant that workers and businesses affected by these changes could not introduce protective duties as in previous periods. But will the rules hold, and are there other ways of responding to domestic political pressures? A new trade-off might emerge within the 'trilemma' and inconsistent quartet.

2.7 THE INCONSISTENT QUARTET AND THE GREAT RECESSION

Trade wars and a rise in protectionism were avoided in the 'great recession' after 2008, unlike in the great depression of the 1930s. A WTO report of November 2010 estimated that new trade restrictions since October 2008 amounted to 1.8 per cent of G20 imports

[50] Obstfeld and Taylor 2004.

and 1.4 per cent of total world imports, and as a result trade remains more open than it has ever been. Although the report commended the restraint shown by countries, it still warned of the dangers of protectionism from exchange rate manipulation, trade imbalances and high levels of unemployment.[51] Politicians were extremely conscious that trade barriers led to the great depression, and on the whole were careful not to give in to domestic pressure groups. They were less concerned at the impact of their domestic policies on international trade. Ben Bernanke of the Federal Reserve was technically correct when he claimed that quantitative easing was designed to deal with domestic inflation and unemployment, and that the external value of the dollar was outside his remit. Nevertheless, depreciation of the dollar was a natural consequence of his actions, as the Chinese and Germans were quick to point out. Protectionism can be achieved by other strategies than trade barriers.

In the absence of the Bretton Woods regime of fixed though variable exchange rates, there was scope for 'currency manipulation' as a way of increasing the competitiveness of exports and the unattractiveness of imports. In September 2010, the finance minister of Brazil warned that 'international currency wars' had broken out. In January 2011 he went further and argued that currency war was turning into trade war. The claim was melodramatic, but was widely repeated. The complaint was that China suppressed the value of the renminbi against the dollar so that their goods were cheaper in the United States and more competitive than those from Japan, South Korea, Taiwan, or Brazil, where exchange rates were left to the market so that their currencies appreciated. As the Brazilian finance minister pointed out, the real was not pegged to the dollar and had appreciated by 25 per cent since the beginning of 2009, whereas the renminbi hardly moved. Such complaints led the House Ways and Means Committee to name China a currency manipulator and to request a 20 per cent appreciation of the renminbi.[52]

Although the People's Bank of China was more sympathetic to currency appreciation, the Chinese government was naturally cautious and feared serious unrest or at least hardship if exports declined—a threat it used against the American administration. Wen Jiabao, the Chinese premier, warned that exporting firms would close and workers return to the country: 'If China saw social and economic turbulence, it would be a disaster for the world.'[53] The appreciation of the Japanese yen after the Plaza accord of 1985 offered a warning of economic stagnation and the dangers of succumbing to external pressure. Instead, the Chinese government criticized the US government for failing to deal with its own internal fiscal deficit and for its role in causing the financial crisis. The Chinese argued—with some justice—that the high level of American unemployment did not arise from their manipulation of the renminbi but rather from the low interest rate policy of the Federal Reserve under Allan Greenspan, with consequent speculation, overconsumption and a mounting trade deficit. On this view, there was nothing 'manipulative' about maintaining a peg between the renminbi and dollar as had been the policy

---

[51] WTO 2010.
[52] *Financial Times*, 27 and 28 September 2010, 10 January 2011.
[53] *Financial Times*, 7 October 2010.

under the Bretton Woods system; the solution was for the United States to become more competitive and reduce its costs. Of course, domestic deflation is never an appealing option, and in any case poses major political problems, with the Democrats reluctant to cut welfare spending and the Republicans reluctant to increase taxation to balance the budget.

Protection by means of tariff barriers was contained after 2008 as a result of the warning provided by the great depression of the 1930s and the existence of commitment mechanisms through GATT and the WTO, but international rivalries were displaced to other elements of the 'inconsistent quartet'. A focus on trade policy alone is misleading. The use of currency manipulation in order to secure trade falls outside the rules of the WTO, and the attempts of countries to manage their exchange rates, are very difficult to coordinate in global economic institutions—as they were in 1971. What is needed is a means of joining the concern of IMF for currencies with the WTO's concern with trade, but the proposal of Brazil to change WTO rules to cover undervaluation of exchange rates as a form of export subsidy and protection is likely to be vetoed by China.[54]

Not everyone is alarmed. As we have seen, Eichengreen argued that competitive devaluation in the 1930s was not necessarily a destructive policy of 'beggar-my-neighbour' and could help recovery by realigning currencies. He follows the same line for the present, arguing that recent competitive devaluations have a similar effect in creating more currency, which acts as a form of monetary easing. Nevertheless, the strategy is dangerous. Uncoordinated intervention by individual countries in the foreign exchange markets leads to conflict rather than cooperation. Ted Taylor of the Peterson Institute rightly points to the danger of confusing intervention in exchange rates with monetary policy. In his view, monetary easing is better achieved by central banks in each country adopting policies within their own domestic markets rather than through international currency markets. The Europeans and Americans are less willing to intervene to hold down their own currencies than are their counterparts in Asia (and Brazil), with the possibility of international instability and conflict.[55]

The concerns about currency manipulation also connect with another element of the inconsistent quartet: capital controls. The adoption of easy monetary policy and low interest rates in the United States means that money flows to emerging economies with higher returns, with the potential consequence of currency appreciation and a loss of competitiveness. A country such as Brazil might therefore find that its goods are even more expensive in export markets, leading it to adopt capital controls in the form of an increased tax on purchases of bonds by foreigners. Other countries have adopted similar policies to control the inflow of capital and appreciation of their currencies: South Korea imposed a withholding tax on foreign holders of government bonds, and Indonesia and Thailand took similar action. Although long-term investment is desirable, the flow of funds in search of higher interest rates is potentially destabilizing and risks a repeat of the Asian financial crisis of 1997/8. When Asian countries turned to capital controls in response to that crisis, the IMF was hostile; now, it is more measured in its views. Ken

[54] *Financial Times* 10 January 2011.   [55] *Financial Times* 28 September 2010.

Rogoff, formerly the chief economist of the IMF, suggests that the benefit of capital account liberalization to emerging markets is, at best, unproven. Although the IMF does not consider that capital controls are universally or even normally successful, strong support for financial liberalization and open capital accounts has given way to at least an acceptance that controls might be sensible to shield emerging economies from surges in short-term capital inflows which may lead to asset bubbles and currency appreciation. In 2010, the IMF admitted that capital controls could be a useful part of the policy mix when carefully assessed against their distortions and implementation costs, and in particular in containing the disruptive effects of temporary, large increases in inflows; more permanent increases in inflows caused by fundamental factors are a different matter. It was precisely the short-term flows of funds in the 1930s that were criticized by Keynes and others, and allowed the imposition of capital controls in the agreement at Bretton Woods. In 2011, the IMF might be going further in the direction of capital controls, with senior economists such as Bhagwati complaining that free trade has been wrongly equated with capital account liberalization. Of course, complaints about capital flows could be used to justify protection of domestic financial services, so that care is needed about the precise reasons for controls; it remains to be seen whether they can work in financial markets that are more developed and sophisticated than after the Second World War.[56]

2.8 Conclusion

This chapter has explained how policies on trade should be placed in a wider context of exchange rates, capital controls, and domestic policies. The trade-off in the policy choices shifted over time and varied between countries. The policy mix reflected the balance between domestic and international concerns at any time and place, reflecting the impact on particular interest groups in society and their ability to express their concerns in the political arena. The outcome also reflected the existence of international agreements, for credible rules on trade after the formation of GATT limited the ability to impose protective duties, and the regime of fixed though variable exchanges from the end of the Second World War to the early 1970s limited the ability to manipulate currencies. The recession after 2008 has placed new strains on the trade-off: protectionism has been contained, but currency manipulation and capital controls have been used to address some of the difficulties. The operations of the WTO should be placed within this wider context of divided responsibilities with the IMF for the operation of the world economy. There is no doubt that two fundamental issues facing the world in the future are: how can the international ramifications of domestic policies be controlled; and how can the interplay between trade and monetary or financial issues be understood?

---

[56] International Monetary Fund 2010a and 2010b; *Financial Times* 10 January 2011.

References

Aghion, Phillipe, and Jeffrey G. Williamson. 1999. *Growth, Inequality and Globalization: Theory, History and Policy*. Cambridge: Cambridge University Press.

Atkin, J. 1970. Official Regulation of British Overseas Investment, 1914–31. *Economic History Review* 23 (2):324–35.

Bordo, Michael, and Hugh Rockoff. 1996. The Gold Standard as a 'Good Housekeeping Seal of Approval'. *Journal of Economic History* 56 (2):389–428.

Cain, Peter J., and Anthony G. Hopkins. 1993. *British Imperialism: Innovation and Expansion, 1688–1914*. Harlow: Longmans.

Cassis, Youssef. 1985. Bankers in English Society in the Late Nineteenth Century. *Economic History Review* 38 (2):210–29.

Chiozza Money, Leo. 1905. *Riches and Poverty*. London: Macmillan.

Clarke, Peter F. 1990. The Treasury's Analytical Model of the British Economy between the Wars. In *The State and Economic Knowledge: The American and British Experience*, edited by Mary O. Furner and Barry Supple, 171–207. Cambridge: Cambridge University Press.

Daunton, Martin. 2006. Britain and Globalisation since 1850: I Creating a Global Order, 1850–1914. *Transactions of the Royal Historical Society (Sixth series)* 16: 1–38.

Daunton, Martin. 2009. Britain and Globalisation since 1850: IV The Creation of the Washington Consensus. *Transactions of the Royal Historical Society (Sixth series)* 19: 1–35.

Daunton, Martin. 2010. From Bretton Woods to Havana: Multilateral Deadlocks in Historical Perspective. In *Deadlocks in Multilateral Negotiations: Causes and Solutions*, edited by Amrita Narlikar, 47–78. Cambridge: Cambridge University Press.

Eichengreen, Barry. 1992. *Golden Fetters: The Gold Standard and the Great Depression, 1919–1939*. New York and Oxford: Oxford University Press.

Eichengreen, Barry, and J. Braga de Macedo. 2001. *The European Payment Union: History and Implications for the Evolution of the International Financial Architecture*. Paris: OECD Development Centre.

Eichengreen, Barry, and J. D. Sachs. 1985. Exchange Rates and Economic Recovery in the 1930s. *Journal of Economic History* 45 (4):925–46.

Estevadeordal, A. 1997. Measuring Protection in the Early Twentieth Century. *European Review of Economic History* 1 (1):89–125.

Fleming, J. Marcus. 1962. Domestic Financial Policies under Fixed and Floating Exchange Rates. *IMF Staff Papers* 9: 369–79.

Friedman, Milton. 1975. *There's No Such Thing as a Free Lunch*. La Salle, IL: Open Court.

FRUS. 1961–3. *Foreign Relations of the United States 1961–63, Volume IX: Foreign Economic Policy*. Document 30. Letter from John Kenneth Galbraith to President Kennedy, 28 August 1963.

FRUS. 1969–76. *Foreign Relations of the United States 1969–76, Volume III. Foreign Economic Policy: International Monetary Policy 1969–72*. Document 12. Memoranda from the President's Assistant for National Security Affairs (Kissinger) to President Nixon, 17 March 1969.

Giffen, Robert. 1905. Notes on Imports versus Home Production and Home Versus Foreign Investment. *Economic Journal* 15 (60):483–93.

Glyn, Andrew, and Robert Sutcliffe. 1972. *British Capitalism, Workers and the Profits Squeeze*. Harmondsworth: Penguin.

Goodwyn, Lawrence. 1976. *Democratic Promise: The Populist Moment in America*. New York: Oxford University Press.

Green, Ewen H. H. 1988. Rentiers versus Producers? The Political Economy of the Bimetallic Controversy. *English Historical Review* 103 (408):588–612.

Helleiner, Eric. 1994. *States and the Re-emergence of Global Finance from Bretton Woods to the 1990s.* Ithaca: Cornell University Press.

Hobson, John A. 1902. *Imperialism: A Study.* London: James Nisbet and Co.

Horsefield, J. Keith. 1969. *The International Monetary Fund, 1945–65, III: Documents.* Washington, DC: IMF.

Hull, Cordell. 1948. *The Memoirs of Cordell Hull, I.* London: Hodder and Stoughton.

International Monetary Fund. 2010a. *Global Financial Stability Report: Meeting New Challenges to Stability and Building a Safer System.* Washington, DC: IMF.

International Monetary Fund. 2010b. *Capital Inflows: The Role of Controls.* IMF Staff Position Note. SPN/10/04. Washington, DC: IMF Research Department.

James, Harold. 1996. *International Monetary Cooperation Since Bretton Woods.* Oxford: Oxford University Press.

James, Harold. 2001. *The End of Globalization: Lessons from the Great Depression.* Cambridge, MA: Harvard University Press.

Keynes, John Maynard. 1925. *The Economic Consequences of Mr Churchill.* London: Hogarth Press.

League of Nations. 1944. *International Currency Experience: Lessons of the InterWar Period.* Geneva: League of Nations.

Lopez-Cordova, J. E., and Christopher M. Meissner. 2003. Exchange Rate Regimes and International Trade: Evidence from the Classical Gold Standard Era. *American Economic Review* 93 (1):1259–75.

Matusow, Allan J. 1998. *Nixon's Economy: Booms, Busts, Dollars and Votes.* Lawrence: Kansas University Press.

Meissner, Christopher M. 2005. A New World Order: Explaining the International Diffusion of the Gold Standard, 1870–1913. *Journal of International Economics* 66 (2):285–406.

Moggridge, Donald E. 1972. *British Monetary Policy 1924–1931: The Norman Conquest of $4.86.* Cambridge: Cambridge University Press.

Moggridge, Donald E., ed. 1980. *The Collected Writings of John Maynard Keynes, Vol. 26: Activities 1943–46. Shaping the Postwar World. Bretton Woods and Reparations.* London: Macmillan.

Mundell, Robert A. 1963. Capital Mobility and Stabilization Policy under Fixed and Flexible Exchange Rates. *Canadian Journal of Economic and Political Science* 29 (4):475–85.

Nurkse, Ragnar. 1954. International Investment Today in the Light of Nineteenth-Century Experience. *Economic Journal* 64 (256):744–58.

Obstfeld, Maurice, and Alan M. Taylor. 2004. *Global Capital Markets: Integration, Crisis and Growth.* Cambridge: Cambridge University Press.

Offer, Avner. 1983. Empire and Social Reform: British Overseas Investment and Domestic Politics, 1908–14. *Historical Journal* 26 (1):119–38.

O'Rourke, Kevin H., and Jeffrey G. Williamson. 1999. *Globalization and History: The Evolution of a Nineteenth-Century Atlantic Economy.* Cambridge, MA: MIT Press.

Pollard, Sidney. 1985. Capital Exports 1870–1914: Harmful or Beneficial? *Economic History Review* 38 (4):489–514.

Rueff, Jacques. 1972. *The Monetary Sin of the West.* New York: Macmillan.

Simon, Matthew. 1967. The Pattern of New British Portfolio Foreign Investment, 1865–1914. In *Capital Movements and Economic Development*, edited by J. H. Adler. London: Macmillan.

Singer, Hans W. 1950. The Distribution of Gains Between Investing and Borrowing Countries. *American Economic Review* 40: 473–85.

Solomou, Solomos. 1996. *Themes in Macroeconomic History: The UK Economy, 1919–1939*. Cambridge: Cambridge University Press.

Stone, I. 1999. *The Global Export of Capital from Great Britain, 1865–1914: A Statistical Survey*. Basingstoke: Macmillan.

Sussman, N., and Y. Yafeh. 2000. Institutions, Reforms and Country Risk: Lessons from Japanese Government Debt in the Meiji Era. *Journal of Economic History* 60 (2):442–67.

Tolliday, Steven. 1987. *Business, Banking and Politics: The Case of British Steel, 1918–39*. Cambridge, MA: Harvard University Press.

Trentmann, Frank. 2008. *Free Trade Nation: Commerce, Consumption, and Civil Society in Modern Britain*. Oxford: Oxford University Press.

Triffin, Robert. 1960. *Gold and the Dollar Crisis: The Future of Convertibility*. New Haven: Princeton University Press.

United States Department of State. 1948. *United Nations Monetary and Financial Conferences, Proceedings and Documents, I.* International Organizations and Conferences Series. Washington DC: US Department of State.

WTO. 2010. *Report on G20 Trade Measures (May 2010 to October 2010)*. Geneva: WTO.

Zeiler, Thomas W. 1992. *American Trade and Power in the 1960s*. New York: Columbia University Press.

....

CHAPTER 3

TRADE LIBERALIZATION AND DOMESTIC POLITICS

....

JUDITH GOLDSTEIN

3.1 INTRODUCTION

....

ECONOMIC theory makes the unambiguous claim that nations maximize their welfare by pursuing a policy of open trade. In fact, support for free trade may be one of the few policy prescriptions to which all economists subscribe. Policymakers, however, rarely heed this injunction. Even though the economics community argues that governments that abstain from using border measures to influence trade flows will be rewarded with rising national incomes, policymakers regularly enact a variety of trade barriers. Trade policy is an arena in which theory and politics diverge widely.

Why does state policy so often diverge from well-supported economic advice? The explanation is straightforward. In the aggregate, nations gain from open borders. The gain, however, is never equally distributed among social groups. This asymmetry leads to an organizational bias in favour of those who are hurt by trade. Protectionist interests are concentrated and highly motivated while free trade interests are diffuse and subject to 'free rider' problems. The result of this particular political economy is an overrepresentation of protectionist interests and pressure on governments to close markets.

This bias towards pro-protection policy is especially evident in democratic regimes. In the absence of some institutional mechanism to either diffuse pro-protectionist groups or to overcome the barriers to collective action facing those who would gain from free trade, political factors will make it difficult for politicians to consistently support open borders to trade. Simply, political factors trump economic rationality.

The logic of this underlying political constraint makes recent history remarkable: since the end of the Second World War, nations have increasingly opened their borders to trade in goods and services. While market liberalization in Britain in the 1840s occurred in the absence of a full franchise, the current wave of liberalization is even more remarkable because it occurred among democracies as well as autocracies, accelerating at the end of the twentieth century.[1] This change in policy reflects the adopting of rules and norms now identified with the General Agreement on Tariffs and Trade (GATT)/World Trade Organization (WTO) system, enabling politicians to support trade openness.

This chapter explains the origin of these rules and norms, via a study of the politics of trade in the United States (US) at the time of the regime's creation. While centring on initial post-Second World War trade liberalization in the US, the chapter argues that explanations of subsequent trade flows must consider three key variables: the distribution of economic interests, collective action costs of organizing, and the institutional rules and norms that channel social forces into policy. Together, economic interests, political institutions, and ideas about how markets function all played a part in the creation of the trading regime and continue to influence the regime today. This chapter takes up each in turn to demonstrate how key decisions in the past continue to influence contemporary trade policymaking. Today, the extant rules and norms that constitute the trade regime encourage open trade by facilitating policies that would be unstable in the absence of institutional support; as well, however, the legalization of the regime has undermined flexibility and the ability of the regime to accommodate members' varied political constraints.

3.2 WHY IS FREE TRADE POLICY UNSTABLE IN DEMOCRACIES?

The history of trade policy in the US illustrates the more general theoretical issue of why free trade policymaking is problematic in democracies.[2] The American Constitution granted the right to set the tariff schedule to Congress. Given that tariffs were considered a 'tax', initial authority was granted to the House of Representatives. Although a co-equal with the Senate in legislative authority, House members answer to smaller constituencies and face significantly shorter electoral cycles. In general, as district size increases in a representational system, leaders are more willing to think about the welfare of society as a whole—a reflection of the ability to make trade-offs between competing groups with cross-cutting interests.[3] Thus, the president, who serves the largest constituency in the US, has historically been more willing to support free trade than has Congress. Among congressional representatives, the Senate is more free trade oriented than is the House.

On the other hand, with very small districts, House members have a greater difficulty ignoring organized groups within their constituency. Even though a majority may exist

---

[1] On the classic study of the domestic roots of British liberalization, see Polanyi 1944; on the current wave, see Milner and Kubota 2005.

[2] Barton et al. 2006.

[3] The relationship between district size and trade politics has been noted broadly. See McGillivray 2004; Milner 1997; Bailey, Goldstein, and Weingast 1997; Verdier 1994 as examples.

in their district that would benefit from trade liberalization, it is more likely that the voice of import-competing groups will determine the votes of those representatives. Compounding this protectionist bias, when aggregated together, House votes often form a log roll in which all interests are accommodated. When asked to set border measures for the country as a whole, this means that representatives help each other appease constituents by supporting each other's needs for a restrictive trade measure.

The most often cited example demonstrating the effect of short electoral cycles, small districts and log rolling in the US is the passage of the Smoot-Hawley Tariff in 1929–30.[4] This was the last tariff act in which congress set rates product by product, and the end result was the highest tariff level of the century. Passage of this Tariff Act has often been cited as a signal of a lack of American commitment to keeping its market open. America's abandonment of liberal trade policies turned out to have devastating consequences, as closure of the US market and rising tariffs elsewhere contributed factors to the onset of the Great Depression and the Second World War.[5]

When historians look for an exemplar of the politics of tariff-setting, they most often turn to the circumstances around the passage of this last US tariff act. In part, this reflects the intractability of the dilemma faced by elected officials, even those that do not support the height of the tariff wall. In the US the Smoot-Hawley tariff became akin to a morality play, warning later leaders against the temptation of log rolled tariffs.

The Smoot-Hawley legislative history began as an inconspicuous response to a long-term decline in agricultural prices, which was, in part, a result of slow economic growth in European markets after the First World War. To counteract the drop in demand, the House entertained a limited revision of the tariff for agricultural products. Once debate began on the measure, however, organized and vocal protectionist groups throughout the country lobbied in support of an increase in the tariff for their own particular commodity. In the House Ways and Means Committee, more than 1,100 people attempted to give testimony. Even with a time limitation of two minutes per witness, almost 11,000 pages of testimony were heard, almost all of which argued for more protection. The bill was finally voted up and sent to the Senate, where the same political forces were present. The already high tariff bill was amended over 1,500 times, further raising rates. Each representative had some group to appease and, in the end, each supported the need of their fellows to placate a constituent. Arthur Vandenberg, then a freshman Republican senator, would later lament that, 'it lacked any element of economic science or validity'.[6]

Given the historical evidence of political dynamics at play in 1930, it is surprising that four years later, in 1934, the US embarked upon a programme that led to radical tariff

---

[4] Schattsneider wrote the now classic analysis of congressional politics and the passage of the Act (Schattsneider 1935); Bauer, Pool, and Dexter looked at congressional politics and the passage of the subsequent Trade Act (Bauer, Pool, and Dexter 1972).

[5] As Kindleberger noted, one nation was willing but unable. Britain, and the other, the US, was able but unwilling, to provide the collective goods necessary to maintain international markets (Kindleberger 1986).

[6] Goldstein 1993, 125.

cuts over the next decade. Even before the creation of the GATT, US tariffs declined from an *ad valorem* average of over 50 per cent to about a 19 per cent *ad valorem* level. This ability to reduce trade barriers was prefaced by a shift in agenda control over tariff-setting from Congress to the President, and a change from item-by-item tariff-setting to the bundling of tariff rates in a series of international bilateral swaps. This transformation in US policy has engendered much research and is perhaps a model example of both the constraints and possibilities nations face in setting trade policy.

3.3 WHOSE INTERESTS?

The political analysis of trade policymaking is based upon an assumption of voter preferences that reflects, to a great extent, whether or not they will benefit or lose from a change in the tariff level. Taxes at the border have differential effects on different groups. Consumers are always net beneficiaries of low rates—the absence of a tariff will mean more and varied products on the market for a lower price. The interests of producers are more complex. If a producer is import-competing, then the border measure may raise the price on the home market for his good and allow him to continue to produce and/or increase his profits. However, if he is producing a final product that relies on imports as inputs, then trade restrictions will increase his costs of production. Similarly, exporters are less interested in border measures at home unless they are importing material used in production, or other nations retaliate against the home tariff by raising rates in the foreign export market. Elected and other government officials may align their interests with one or the other of these groups depending upon campaign donations and/or economic factors in districts in which production occurs.[7]

If we imagine that countries vary on three input factors of production—land, labour, and capital—then, groups who produce goods or services based on these endowments will be affected differently by the opening up of their home market to foreign products. Producers with relatively abundant factors of production are well served by competition from abroad; those employing scarce factors lose from competition with global forces.

In general, an individual's position on whether open borders offer opportunities for growth, or the opposite, will depend upon which factors they employ and the relative endowments held by the nation in which they reside.[8]

Two sets of predictions follow from the integration of factor endowments and the consideration of an individual's dependence on that factor for economic gain. In one, the prediction is of political activity to be organized within a factor. Here, the interests of labourers in a labour-scarce nation, for example, are the same, no matter their sector of

---

[7] Alt and Gilligan provide one of the best reviews of the alternative explanations for the economic basis of trade politics (Alt and Gilligan 1994).

[8] For a more comprehensive overview, see Alt and Gilligan 1994.

employment. In the other, the prediction is that coalitions will form within sectors. Even in labour-scarce nations, it is not surprising to find that labour's interests align with the producers who employ them. For example, labour could be in a coalition with owners in a capital-intensive industry because of a shared interest in import protection. The difference between the two approaches turns on the degree of labour mobility incorporated in the model. Ron Rogowski derives a set of predictions on what groups should be found in what coalitions based on the Stolper-Samuelson theorem, which relates factor endowments to relative wages and returns to capital, and assumes mobility.[9] Jeff Frieden, relying on a Ricardo-Viner model in which labour is less mobile, predicts that alliances should and will form within sectors.[10] Both suggest that we look first at which groups are hurt or benefited, and then at potential coalition patterns, in order to understand the roots of political activity and thus the constraints a government would face when attempting to open markets to foreign goods and services. They vary in that Rogowski assumes much more mobility within factors than does Frieden.

These economic pressures on trade politics are evident throughout recent history. For example, the German author Gerschenkron noted, in his history of the integration of the German nation, the importance of the 'marriage of iron and rye'.[11] The tariff position of iron producers, or the Junker class, follows from competition with Britain and their relatively higher wages. Consistent with Stolper-Samuelson logic, any producer that used land intensively in Germany would also have been harmed by free trade, because its scarcity made agricultural products less competitive on world markets. The result was a coalition between two otherwise unlikely groups who shared an interest in having a closed German market. In that era, the same logic explains a different position for England. The British government was able to support free trade because business and labour were both served by open markets, again reflecting the nation's endowments. The opposition in both periods, labour in Germany and farmers in Britain, were unable to have the government support their preferred position—in the former, free trade, and the latter, protectionism.

At other times, coalition patterns have deviated from what a factor approach would predict. The most common deviation is that groups do often align by sector, as Frieden has suggested. One recent example is the coalition on trade that formed on the question of trade protection for the US auto industry. While a factor approach would have labour and capital on opposite sides of this policy question, unions and owners jointly and repeatedly petitioned Washington for protection in the face of increasing pressure from Japanese exports. Even though the US is scarce in labour and rich in capital, the immobility of jobs, at least in the short term, led industry and labour to identify a joint interest in closing the US market.

The observation shared by all analysts is that trade policy has different effects on groups in society. The existence of these differences explains why individual interests diverge so markedly within nations on trade policy.

---

[9] Rogowski 1989.   [10] Frieden and Rogowski 1996.   [11] Gerschenkron 1943.

3.4 WHEN DO GROUPS ORGANIZE?

The existence of an interest in protectionism, whether due to your nation's endowment or increasing import pressure on your sector, is still only a partial explanation for a nation's trade policy. To be effective, groups must recognize their shared interest, organize and articulate their preferred policy. In general, groups face differing costs to organizing, and these collective action costs deter some groups from political participation.[12]

The varying nature of organization costs makes the pattern of mobilization hard to predict—the large and diffuse nature of some of these economic interests, the lack of information about what is at stake, and/or uncertainty about the probable success of lobbying activities may lead some groups and not others to calculate that it is not worthwhile to organize because the potential gains are small. Thus, although having a shared interest may be a necessary component of political action, it is the articulation of that interest that is the more important part of the political process, at least from the perspective of the policymaker.

The greatest impediment to organizing is the incentive to free ride. When groups reach some size, it is difficult, if not impossible, to organize the group, even with a shared interest. Organizing is a costly task. As interests become more diffuse, these costs rise. If the policy 'good' to be obtained is not excludable, that is, members of the group get the benefit even if they do not participate in the political process, each individual will find it rational to free ride on others. The result is that certain groups do not form, and particular interests are under-represented. To the extent that free trade is such a 'good', it is not surprising that members of groups that could benefit from open borders are under-represented.

Policymakers that want to maintain open markets then face a difficult task. They understand that both, free trade, and pro-protection groups, face collective action costs, and that there are these collective action issues that intervene to influence the probability that a group will pressure them for a particular policy. Because of the particularistic gains from protectionism, minorities who are hurt by trade policy or the potential of a change in policy have a greater incentive to organize to gain increased protection and/or to become a veto player in attempts to liberalize policy. Those who benefit from low tariffs, either as consumers of final or intermediate import products or as exporters, may be large in number but accrue a relatively smaller benefit from the low tariff and thus, have less of an incentive to organize in their own interests.

This variation means that even if a majority of people in a nation would benefit from free trade, the intensity of the potential loss by one group could lead their voice to be the only one heard. The group that always benefits from lower prices, consumers, has huge collective action problems. Consumers are widely dispersed and gain perhaps but a

---

[12] Olson 1965. Olson argued that the cost of organizing also led to 'free-riding', even under the situation of perfect information.

small increment from a reduced tariff on any particular product. In fact, given the costs of organizing, the probability of a benefit and the small increment of value, it may well be irrational for any particular consumer to expend energy to lobby for the lower tariff. Such is not the case for those employed in a job that will disappear if a tariff is lowered (or is not increased). An individual employed in an industry that suffers job losses because of foreign competition will have an intensity to his or her preference that will make it rational to expend costs to organize and voice their preferences politically.

In addition, informational characteristics of the policymaking environment will affect a group's ability to overcome the collective action problem. For example, if groups know for certain that they will be hurt by some action on the part of their leaders they are more likely to expend the collective costs. The psychology of this is well documented. Those who are facing a certain loss will be far more sensitive to that loss than would be those who were benefiting from an equal gain.[13] Thus the extent to which the distributional implications of policy are either revealed or hidden will influence incentives to mobilize.

The characteristics of a particular group (e.g. size) are not the only determinants of a group's ability to organize politically. Policymakers—nominally the targets of collective action—can also influence the messages they receive. Policymakers are not blank slates: rather, they provide information to others about their own intentions and their own preferences. Such information, by biasing expectations about the probability of success at pressuring for a policy, will influence groups' calculations about whether or not to organize in the first place. If there is a low chance of success, they may choose not to expend resources to change policy.

Generally in the United States today, the pro-protection lobby is more fully mobilized than is the lobby for those that favour openness. Elected officials repeatedly face pressures from a range of groups who prefer a policy biased towards domestic production, or who demand action on the part of the WTO in response to a perception of unfairness on the part of a nation or foreign producer. The process of obtaining protection today may be more difficult than in the past for import-competing groups, but pro-protection pressures continue and regularly erupt, as in 1999 at the ministerial meeting of the WTO in Seattle, or more recent attempts by the US Congress to force the President to use the WTO dispute system to force a change in the exchange rate of the Chinese renminbi.

The effects of the political environment on the incentive to organize can be seen in changes in US tariff history. Before 1934, groups were likely to organize and articulate their pro-protection position to their representatives for two reasons. First, they knew for certain that the legislation would influence their particular tariff level, and second, they knew that the log rolling process meant that they would have a high probability of influencing their tariff level, provided they could first win over their congressman. Given

---

[13] Kahneman and Tversky 1979. Kahneman and Tversky first showed that individuals react differently to risk in the realm of gains and losses. This individual response is consistent with the group logic offered by Olson (Olson 1965). Both predict an asymmetry in who will be interested in, and willing to, lobby for trade policy.

this environment, no one should be surprised that any group that felt international competition (or the threat of that competition) would organize and ask for a tariff hike. The Smoot-Hawley experience may have been extreme, but it is consistent with politics in America. If groups feel that organizing is efficacious, they will expend the time and effort to garner their preferred policy.

The importance of the institutional setting is evidenced by what occurred four years after Smoot-Hawley, when in 1934 Congress again considered a tariff act. Unlike in the previous debate, only 14 witnesses (six of whom were from the administration) testified in the House, and the Senate committee considered the bill and sent it to the floor within a week of its arrival. The mayhem of social activism so present in the earlier legislation was gone. What changed between 1930 and 1934?

Whether knowingly or not (and there is some debate about this), Congress had fundamentally changed the information environment, and thus the probability that import-competing groups would expend resources on lobbying efforts.[14] The 1934 legislation mandated a reduction in tariffs of up to 50 per cent, but with no designation of who would suffer the reduction. In effect, tariff setting became less transparent to any one particular producer. Given that there was more uncertainty that a particular product would be part of a tariff reduction, it was less likely that groups would expend the costs and organize in defence of their tariff. The 1934 law also changed the locus of authority, moving it from Congress to the President—the elected official with the largest of all constituencies. Overall, delegation increased the costs of organizing for import protection.

For export groups, however, the incentives went in the opposite direction. The method mandated for tariff setting in the 1934 Act provided them with a direct interest in domestic tariff levels. The legislation delegated authority to the President, but not without constraints—he needed to set rates through a process of bilateral treaty negotiations in which the US gave access to its home market on the condition that reciprocal access be granted by a trading partner. This had two effects. First, exporters gained a direct, material stake in trade liberalization, since openness at home was tied to market access abroad; second, by mandating only reciprocal agreements, the 1934 Act changed the information environment in which exporters made decisions about whether or not to be part of a low-tariff coalition.[15] By changing the information environment in which exporters made decisions about whether or not to be part of a low tariff coalition, politicians heard not only from import-competing groups but also from exporters whose interests were tied to increasing access to the US market.

Between 1934, when Congress first mandated such agreements, and 1947, when the GATT was negotiated, the United States concluded 32 treaties with 28 countries. In each, both signatories reduced their tariff schedule on a particular set of products in return for access for a set of other products. At the start of a negotiation, governments relied on their export sector to guide them in making demands for access into the foreign market,

---

[14] On the 1934 Act see: Haggard 1988; Bailey, Goldstein, and Weingast 1997; and Hiscox 1999.
[15] Gilligan 1997.

thereby activating producer groups and creating an interest in the treaty. By congressional mandate, the treaties needed to be reciprocal, that is, each needed to be a bundle of measures that allowed access to new markets in return for reciprocal access to their own market. As in the past, import-sensitive groups complained, but now elected leaders found support in the newly mobilized exporters, who had a reason to want the treaty signed and enforced. By design, these treaties were balanced in terms of group mobilization, that is, their distributional implications were not biased towards either import sensitive or export groups.

Thus, for the first time and as a result of mandating only reciprocal agreements, the potential gains from organizing and articulating their pro-trade interests were transparent to exporters. Where exporters had no reason to organize in the preceding century, they now had a stake in the tariff-setting process, and a reason to organize in defence of trade liberalization at home. The lesson from the US case is that, to the extent that information activates protectionists, other things being equal, nations will find it harder to build a consensus around a new liberalizing agreement.[16] But if export groups or others who benefit from open borders organize and balance the pro-protection interests, then open trade becomes possible even in a political system that allows social voice to influence economic policy.

In sum, the literature on domestic politics and trade liberalization assumes that groups differ on how they will be affected by trade. Thus they hold varying and often divergent intrinsic interests regarding a particular trade policy. Whether or not a group will organize in order to convince decision makers to enact a policy of their choosing, however, depends upon a number of factors that relate to the probability of success and the costs of organizing members of the group. Taken together, the expectation is that pro-protection groups are more likely to organize and effect policy unless incentives exist for other groups, such as exporters, to organize and counterbalance these interests. The information environment is key—if groups know with certainty that they will be hurt or helped by an act of government, they will be more likely to expend the collective action costs. To the extent that government can change the amount of such information available to groups, they will influence what voices they will activate, and thus need to respond to.

3.5 INSTITUTIONAL SETTING: RULES AND NORMS MATTER

Given the importance of government incentives in explaining when economic interests will motivate collective action, a large literature has developed on the effects of various institutional settings on trade policymaking. One of the more general models was

---

[16] This logic is derived from and is expanded in Goldstein and Martin 2000.

offered by Grossman and Helpman.[17] In their model, interest groups make political contributions to government officials in return for influence in trade policymaking. Interest groups 'bid' for protection and decision makers, who care about their own re-election, will respond to whoever makes the biggest contribution. The idea of contributions could be thought of broadly. Politicians are welfare maximizers whose utility functions take into account a variety of things that may influence their re-election or their general level of governing authority. As McGillivray details in her examination of protectionism in the United Kingdom, officials consider a range of factors in deciding whether or not to increase protection on a good.[18] These factors include industry size, whether or not producers are losing market share, the degree of concentration of the industry, firm heterogeneity, and geographic location. Each factor has a different effect across electoral units depending upon the specifics of the region, suggesting that knowing the interests of a producer and the costs of organization is still insufficient to explain government policy. As well, we need to consider the specific incentives of government officials and when local social 'voices' lead them to adhere to the interests of a group.

The US case is suggestive of the importance of both particular rules and norms in the determination of the country's trade policy.[19] As previously noted, the US constitution created a system of governance that made it difficult for the country to support open trade. Given the penetration of Congress by organized interests, it is not surprising that, except for a brief period in the early nineteenth century, the US existed behind a high tariff wall. But after 1934 Congress rewrote the institutional script that dictated tariff setting, and in effect made it more difficult for themselves to adhere to vocal groups' demands for tariff relief. While adhering to constitutional constraints, Congress was able to grant new powers to the Office of the President. This delegation of authority facilitated trade liberalization by granting the President agenda-setting powers on trade matters. This allowed executive officials to mould 'the agenda and policy process to their own ideological, bureaucratic and above all, international interests'.[20]

If pro-protection groups controlled Congress, why did they support delegation to the President? Delegation was possible for two reasons. First, one party controlled all parts of government and a powerful President was able to elicit his preferred policy from both houses of Congress.[21] But, more importantly, as suggested earlier on, the delegation was done under a 'veil of ignorance' of exactly which industries would or would not be touched by tariff changes. No particular product suffered a reduced rate in the 1934 Act and so no groups had an incentive to organize and pressure their representative. The absence of pressure allowed the President to ask and receive authorization to negotiate

[17] Grossman and Helpman 1994.

[18] McGillivray 2004; Barton et al. 2006; Goldstein 2000.

[19] A large literature exists on institutional foundations for foreign economic policy. See, for example, Verdier 1994; O'Halloran and Lohmann 1994; Haggard 1988.

[20] Haggard 1988, 91. For more detail see Goldstein 1998; Bailey, Goldstein, and Weingast 1997; Hiscox 1999.

[21] Hiscox 1999. Hiscox argues that delegation was possible only because one party controlled both the legislature and the presidency.

these treaties. These tariff agreements then became law without returning to Congress or obtaining a super majority (as with other treaties).

Once granted authority, the President was able to craft bills that were immune from being picked apart by pro-protection groups. Presidential agenda control undercut the organizational bias held by pro-protection groups in two distinct ways. First, these trade treaties were able to elicit majority support because they changed the nature of coalitional politics. The process of tariff setting created a disincentive for import-competing groups to organize, while increasing access for export groups. The balance of social 'power' thus shifted. Second, the President crafted agreements that were bundles of tariff changes that were impossible to 'unpack'. Congress could not cherry pick—their choice was to take the agreement as negotiated or reject the entire treaty. As long as the President crafted an agreement in which at least 51 per cent of the districts (or 51 per cent of those in each district) benefited from tariff reductions, the treaty was acceptable to Congress.

This process was for the most part adopted in the creation of the GATT. The GATT itself should be viewed as a response to domestic politics, mostly in the US. The 1934 Act had stipulated that the President needed to seek advice from the Tariff Commission, the Departments of State, Agriculture and Commerce, and from all other appropriate sources before lowering a tariff. To accommodate this mandate, a series of committees— the Trade Agreements Committee, country-specific committees and the Committee for Reciprocity Information—were assembled to give interested parties the opportunity to present their views. They took briefs and held public hearings. Until 1937, a formal announcement of intent to negotiate was accompanied by a list of the principal producers who could potentially get a tariff cut; after this date, the list was replaced by a general or 'public' list which signalled all items that were under consideration in any negotiation. The result of committees, notices, and hearings, both before the negotiations and after a list of products was tentatively accepted, was a glut of information for producer groups. Interest groups operated not solely in Congress but moved to pressuring the bureaucracy throughout the negotiating process. Even with exporters' participation in the debate, the process was again creating incentives that made liberalization difficult.

This is the context in which the US supported international delegation. In 1945, the President asked Congress for negotiating authority to lower rates an additional 50 per cent from those then in effect. Congress granted the request but set a three-year renewal. This time constraint was not new. Congress had repeatedly kept the President on a 'short leash' and renewals were a regular part of the trade agreements programme. As in the past, the President needed to 'use up' his authority. Thus, in order to show progress before the 1948 renewal, the US pre-empted the International Trade Organization (ITO) process and called for multilateral talks in 1947 in Geneva.[22]

In substance, the GATT was modelled on the Reciprocal Trade Agreements Act (RTAA) agreements. The bilateral treaties had consisted of two parts—a series of general

---

[22] The International Trade Organization was to be the trade equivalent of the IMF. Although debated in a number of international meetings, it was not until 1948 in Cuba that those attending initialled the final document.

provisions, and the particular negotiated schedules. The general provision section was oriented towards making the tariff reduction meaningful—rules were set that defined what were, and were not, allowable exceptions and safeguards, prohibitions against other forms of discrimination, and the conditions under which the agreements could be breached and/or terminated. The GATT included, in a somewhat more expanded form, this structure of rules that had successfully finessed domestic political pressures in the US.[23]

There are a number of reasons why moving the context of trade negotiations into a multilateral format made liberalization politically more stable. First, the GATT made it difficult for the US to renegotiate a particular treaty. As opposed to the bilateral treaties, which each had a sunset provision, joining the GATT meant adhering to all treaties negotiated among and between members. The new rules increased the 'shadow of the future' that encouraged cooperation and ultimately investment in export trade. Of course, countries could always leave the GATT with six months' notice. However, by making the options to either adhere to all agreements or exit and lose all the benefits, the political power shifted towards compliance. Delegation to a multilateral organization also made it more difficult for US interest groups to veto trade agreements. Although the Tariff Commission, at least in the early days, was assigned the task of setting 'peril point' limits for certain products, the process of tariff negotiation was far more closed than was its bilateral predecessor, and much of the access that groups had in the RTAA years became unavailable.

Second, since the GATT was multilateral, both principal suppliers and any country that accounted for 15 per cent of imports needed to give a concession. This expanded the number of markets open to US producers and balanced the losses from increased import penetration at home. The effect was not only to speed up the process of liberalization, something noted by Irwin,[24] but also to expand the interconnectedness of the treaties GATT members signed, making it difficult to renege on an agreement.

---

[23] Part I of the GATT included the most-favoured nation (MFN) provision and gave legal effect to the lower tariff schedules (Articles 1, 2). Unlike the bilateral agreements, but indicative of the times, there was a strict prohibition against an increase in preferences on all Articles; earlier treaties only covered specified products. The GATT also prohibited export taxes, not covered in any earlier agreement. Similar to the earlier agreements, the GATT spells out the prohibition on monetary manipulation as a means of protecting producers (Article 2), the specific rules for nullification (Article 23), the escape clause procedures (Article 19), and the exception for economic development (Article 18). The language and intent was familiar to all countries that had a treaty with the US. Similarly, Part II of the GATT repeated language from the bilateral treaties. This section dealt with barriers to trade and forbade the use of barriers that would undermine a tariff reduction. Articles 3–23 were also found in very similar form in previous agreements. New was the extension of national treatment to imported articles (Article 3) and more narrow rules on anti-dumping and countervailing duties (inserting the need for the product to not only be dumped or subsidized but to hurt a domestic industry as a result of the action) and the details on custom rules (Article 7). The GATT also stipulated a balance-of-payments exception, reflecting the policy of the new IMF.

[24] Irwin 2002.

Third, through multilateral bargaining, the US was able to finesse some of the problems created by the bilateral agreements; enlarging the number of participants at the table, the US changed the information environment in which import-competing groups operated and increased the number of exporters with a stake in the process. The structure of multilateral trade negotiations made it more difficult to predict the depth of cuts from any particular product, and over time the notification process became increasingly less predictive for producers, undercutting their ability to make an accurate forecast of their interest in political action. As a result, officials heard less often from those hurt by open trade and more often from exporters, now willing to voice support for liberalization.

The GATT, then, was a necessary part of the creation of a domestic coalition in support of free trade. Although the US had been a world economic power for a generation, it was only in the midst of the Great Depression that a coalition emerged in favour of trade liberalization. For the first 150 years of its history, US trade policy was partisan and erratic; trade agreements were repeatedly enmeshed in larger disputes of party, region, and power haggling among the branches of government. A year before Roosevelt's election, the US showed no sign of internationalism and, instead, had abandoned the London Conference. The policy shift that occurred in 1934 and then again in 1947, given this history, is remarkable and reflects the importance of institutional structures, both domestic and international, in creating political coalitions in favour of trade.

3.6 INTERESTS ALONE?

The specific changes in coalition politics in the US and elsewhere were important in the worldwide liberalization of trade that occurred after the Second World War. The GATT, and later the WTO, encouraged nations to participate in agreements that opened up their markets to trade in goods and services. This new attitude reflected the changing interests of groups in trade openness. As well, coalition politics was influenced by changing ideas about the efficacy of liberal trade and the association between trade politics and more general foreign policy.[25] Today, there is general agreement that market-driven trade policy is far more efficient than are the pro-protection policies of the last century. In fact, certain market interventions by governments are considered illegitimate, both by WTO rules and by conventional notions of the appropriate role of governments which may be pressured to respond to groups who demand aid in the face of international import pressures but that are far more constrained in comparison to earlier eras by the fear that protectionism would undercut growth.

In the last quarter of the twentieth century, politicians came increasingly to accept economists' predictions about the relationship between trade and growth. In part, this

---

[25] Goldstein 1989.

reflected the shared educational background of leaders around the globe, increasingly trained by neoclassical economists; as well, the failure of the Soviet model gave increased credence to market-driven policy. Whatever the cause, this change in orientation led to a fundamental shift in economic policy in the developing world in the 1990s, with many previously closed economies shifting policy to a programme sometimes referred to as the Washington Consensus. The set of policies, pithily summarized by Dani Rodrik as 'stabilize, privatize and liberalize', is attributed to John Williamson, who, in 1989, pre-scribed ten specific economic polices to reform developing nations.[26] These policies, reinforced by technocrats within the developing world and bureaucrats in the WTO, highlighted the virtues of market-driven border policies.

This was not always the case. In the US, for example, free trade ideas were scarcely taught at the turn of the nineteenth century, and by the twentieth century were still con-tested. Only in the wake of the Great Depression did policymakers adhere to policies then being supported by the economics profession. In fact, over 1,000 economists famously signed a petition against Smoot-Hawley, predicting dire results upon its pas-sage.[27] Tariff policy, however, had deep roots in the US—protectionist ideas were like glue, holding a coalition of groups together. Protectionism, like the Washington Consensus a century later, acted, in Max Weber's terms, as 'switchmen', determining the 'tracks along which action [was] pushed by the dynamic of interest'.[28]

Once the US and her trading partners accepted the tenets of free trade, the policy was self-enforcing. In the US, legislation that hinted at closing markets elicited quick response from export groups who would label it as a step towards Smoot-Hawley, with the potential of sending the world down a slippery slope to beggar-thy-neighbour poli-cies and economic depression. Free trade became equated with the 'free world' and poli-ticians were quick to decry any pro-tariff legislation as undermining pro-Western foreign policy goals. Foreign economic trade policy and foreign policy in general became enmeshed in the Soviet era; when the Soviet Union broke apart, democratization and free trade were argued as companion programmes. Free trade ideals were being prac-tised in the expanded EU and were being taught in Geneva by the WTO Secretariat.

Free trade ideals, however, did not extend to policies considered orthogonal to open markets. Nations that did not adhere to their WTO obligation on subsidies could be punished through a host of measures, which effectively differed little from a traditional tariff. For example, nations who trumpeted the virtues of free trade also maintained sup-port for anti-dumping activities under the heading of either 'levelling the playing field' or in defence of free and 'fair' trade. Congress could feel it improper to increase tariffs on goods from China because of competition but they would not hesitate from raising bar-riers if convinced that the Chinese were unfairly subsidizing their producers and/or their currency. Free trade ideals remain a potent constraint on policymakers but in a

---

[26] See Williamson 1990, chapter 2, for original version, and Rodrik 2006 for interpretation of its effects.

[27] Goldstein 1993.

[28] Weber 1958, 280.

somewhat new form. Governments see themselves as having the right, and perhaps obligation, to retaliate against governments who, for whatever reason, are not living up to those ideals.

3.7 THE GATT/WTO AND DOMESTIC POLITICS OF TRADE TODAY

Today, the GATT/WTO has evolved from its origins as a decentralized and relatively powerless institution into a powerful legal entity. The number of country members has increased and the amount of trade covered has expanded greatly from the original 1947 GATT. The regime's elaborate set of rules on commerce has implications for domestic politics in member nations. What is unclear is whether or not this increased legalization and judicialization of trade has increased support for free trade or the opposite—that is, created incentives for domestic groups to mobilize and pressure their government to adopt policies that favour them once again. Three effects are noteworthy.

First, and most directly, nations that accede to the WTO need to conform their institutional structures to accommodate WTO rules and adjudication procedures. Legalization of the trade regime has changed the entry barriers for membership. In the early GATT days, joining the organization was a relatively easy process—nations negotiated on their tariff schedule and signed on to loosely defined procedures of monitoring. For a class of nations, ex-colonies and other small developing nations, accession was even easier, with the GATT waiving substantive changes in tariff level. Today, however, acceding to the trade regime can entail a fundamental and intrusive restructuring of domestic trade institutions.

Since the 1980s, the process of accession has become more regularized and demanding. As the nature of the regime has changed, focusing increasingly on production methods, nations have been asked to reform fundamental parts of their governing structures. For example, the Trade-Related Aspects of Intellectual Property Rights (TRIPS) Agreement requires that members enact substantive laws guaranteeing protections for patents, copyrights, trademarks, and other such intellectual properties. To accomplish this, a patent office must be created and there must be some means to enforce new rules. Likewise, the WTO mandates oversight of health and safety standards, areas in which many nations have either few laws or weak enforcement. The WTO is not alone in its influence on domestic politics in member states. Regional and preferential trade agreements have made similar demands on members.[29]

Second, the WTO influences domestic politics because increased rule precision has led to more and better information about the distributional implications of commercial

---

[29] See Steinberg 2010 for examples of how WTO participation directly influences the creation of domestic institutions in member nations.

agreements.[30] Since information on who will gain and lose from some international action affects the incentives of groups to mobilize for and against trade agreements, WTO membership affects social mobilization. In general, legalization appears to have empowered protectionists relative to free traders on issues relating to the conclusion of new agreements, and free traders relative to protectionists on issues of compliance to existing agreements.

The information available to members about the effects of policies potentially enacted by the multilateral regime has risen dramatically over time. In the initial GATT rounds, tariff information was not systematically collected. Nations relied on data supplied by their negotiating partners, and thus the computation of offers and counter-offers relied on often incomplete statistics. Over time, the secretariat began to compile data on tariff and non-tariff barriers in a more systematic fashion. In 1989, the Trade Policy Review Mechanism was authorized, and this began a process of regular country studies, providing sector and product information on practices of GATT members. All countries were regularly reviewed—the four largest, every two years; the next sixteen by trade volume, every four years; and all other members, every six years. The result has been a richer and more symmetric information environment for trade policymaking in member nations.

There have been two effects of this increasingly rich information environment. First, access to information on potential new agreements may have made it more difficult for members to sign on to new agreements. Domestic groups, now more certain than ever before of how they will be affected by a new agreement, have often become 'veto' players, making it uncomfortable for their leaders to sign on to a new agreement. Where early rounds were often quiet deals among a few like-minded nations, contemporary politics demands informed consent on the part of affected groups. This transparency has meant more, and more open, meetings and constant press coverage. In that delegates have always worried about domestic constituents, early liberalization in Geneva may have benefited from the ability of delegates to obfuscate on exactly who would benefit and lose from a deal until the 'bundle' was initialled by attendees. Today, it is impossible to enact such deals. Group resistance at home translates into national paralysis in Geneva.

Second, while the availability of information on the distributional effects of a round may undermine new deals, information on behaviour may lead to more adherence to existing WTO obligations. Although only nations have standing in the WTO, most monitoring occurs in a decentralized manner within member states and is often undertaken by private parties. These parties turn to their own governments for redress against some behaviour on the part of an importing nation. Home governments then petition the trading partner for a change in the policy that is viewed as transgressing a WTO obligation. Monitoring costs are significant. In the past, they were borne by private domestic actors, but today these costs are partially borne by the regime, making it easier for a range of parties—unions, producers, NGOs and the like—to force their governments to use WTO dispute procedures in order to get protection from what is perceived as an illegal behaviour. In this sense, the formalization of the regime has changed the

---

[30] This section is derived from Goldstein and Martin 2000.

nature of pro-protection politics. Some behaviours are now more difficult—there are time limits on the use of remedies such as the escape clause. This constrains domestic politicians. However, it also empowers groups to make claims on other nations that they are not abiding by an agreement.

Third, tightly bound trade rules in the more formalized WTO has another unintended effect, which also may make nations unwilling to expand on the liberalization agenda. In the new regime, dispute settlement is far more binding than in the past. Leaders have a far harder time ignoring mandates from Geneva to change an illegal trade act. The downside of this increased legalization lies in the inevitable uncertainties of economic interactions between states and the need for domestic political actors to be able to have flexibility to deal with economic shocks. Legalization, at its core, refers to *pacta sunt servanda*, or the presumption that once signed, nations will adhere to treaty obligations. Lawyers using a discourse focusing on rules—their exceptions and applicability—and not on interests typically remedy interpretations of this responsibility. This has created a new constraint on governments, who may fear having their hands tied in case of some economic problem facing their nation; this fear may well explain the limited interest in further expansion of the regime's reach.[31]

Whether or not binding rules are good for future liberalization is still an open question. If the rules can be accommodated without rising domestic tension, then governments will continue to push liberalization forward. On the other hand, if they are so tightly construed that politicians have no flexibility, this may lead nations not only to refuse more liberalization but also to abandon the regime itself. The problem is that if agreements are impossible to breach, either because of their level of obligation or because the transparency of rules increases the likelihood of enforcement, elected officials may find that the costs of signing such agreements and/or adhering to existing agreements outweigh the benefits.

3.8 Conclusion

Trade policy has always been, and will always remain, a hostage to domestic politics. Leaders want their nations to benefit from trade with other nations but they must also have a 'toolkit' of remedies for groups that suffer because of foreign competition. Finding the balance between the need to placate powerful groups and the economic incentives to trade broadly is often difficult for politicians. Support for liberalization will vary depending upon how leaders choose to balance these two factors.

To some extent, delegation to the GATT/WTO regime has empowered leaders in their quest to keep markets open. The regime has provided access to markets by bringing exporters into the free trade coalition to balance the voice of the pro-protection

---

[31] See Downs and Rocke 1997 on issues related to the political issues surrounding overly inflexible rules.

lobby. However, economic shocks cannot be ignored and politicians who want to retain support must be able to shelter their economy, when necessary, for legitimate domestic reasons. Leaders remain wedded to the regime because it helps them solve a domestic problem—that is, how to overcome the bias of organization that leads to the over-representation of pro-protection groups. But when the regime creates problems by forcing compliance in a mechanistic manner, it may no longer be viewed as useful in support of open markets.

References

Alt, James, and Michael Gilligan. 1994. The Political Economy of Trading States: Factor Specificity, Collective Action Problems, and Domestic Political Institutions. *Journal of Political Philosophy* 2 (2):165–92.

Bailey, Michael, Judith Goldstein, and Barry Weingast. 1997. The Institutional Roots of American Trade Policy: Politics, Coalitions, and International Trade. *World Politics* 49 (3):309–38.

Barton, John, Judith Goldstein, Timothy Josling, and Richard Steinberg. 2006. *The Evolution of the Trade Regime: Politics, Law and Economics of the GATT and the WTO*. Princeton: Princeton University Press.

Bauer, Raymond, Ithiel de Sola Pool, and Lewis Dexter. 1972. *American Business and Public Policy: The Politics of Foreign Trade*. Chicago: Aldine Atherton.

Downs, George, and David Rocke. 1997. *Optimal Imperfection? Domestic Uncertainty and Institutions in International Relations*. Princeton: Princeton University Press.

Frieden, Jeffry, and Ron Rogowski. 1996. The Impact of the International Economy on National Policies: An Analytical Overview. In *Internationalization and Domestic Politics*, edited by Keohane and Milner, 25–47. New York: Cambridge University Press.

Gerschenkron, Alexander. 1943. *Bread and Democracy in Germany*. Ithaca: Cornell University Press.

Gilligan, Michael. 1997. *Empowering Exporters: Delegation, Reciprocity and Collective Action in Twentieth Century American Trade Policy*. Ann Arbor: University of Michigan Press.

Goldstein, Judith. 1989. The Impact of Ideas on the Origin of Trade Policy. *International Organization* 43 (1):31–72.

Goldstein, Judith. 1998. International Institutions and Domestic Politics. In *The WTO as an International Organization*, edited by Anne Krueger, 133–60. Chicago: University of Chicago Press.

Goldstein, Judith. 1993. *Ideas, Interests, and American Trade Policy*. Ithaca: Cornell University Press.

Goldstein, Judith. 2000. The United States and World Trade: Hegemony by Proxy? In *Strange Power: Shaping the Parameters of International Relations and International Political Economy*, edited by Thomas Lawton, 249–74. Aldershot: Ashgate Publishing Ltd.

Goldstein, Judith, and Lisa Martin. 2000. Legalization, Trade Liberalization and Domestic Politics: A Cautionary Note. *International Organization* 54 (3):603–32.

Grossman, Gene, and Helpman, Elhanan. 1994. Protection for Sale. *American Economic Review* 84 (4):833–50.

Haggard, Stephan. 1988. The Institutional Foundations of Hegemony: Explaining the Reciprocal Trade Agreements Act of 1934. *International Organization* 42 (1):91–119.

Hiscox, Michael J. 1999. The Magic Bullet? The RTAA, Institutional Reform, and Trade Liberalization. *International Organization* 53 (4):669–98.

Irwin, Douglas A. 2002. *Free Trade Under Fire*. Princeton: Princeton University Press.

Kahneman, Daniel, and Amos Tversky. 1979. Prospect Theory: An Analysis of Decision under Risk? *Econometrica* 47 (2):263–92.

Kindleberger, Charles. 1986. *The World in Depression, 1929–1939*. Berkeley: University of California Press.

McGillivray, Fiona. 2004. *Privileging Industry: The Comparative Politics of Trade and Industrial Policy*. Princeton: Princeton University Press.

Milner, Helen. 1997. Democratic Politics and International Trade Negotiations: Elections and Divided Government as Constraints on Trade Liberalization. *Journal of Conflict Resolution* 41 (1):117–46.

Milner, Helen, and Keiko Kubota. 2005. Why the Move to Free Trade? Democracy and Trade Policy in the Developing Countries. *International Organization* 59 (4):107–43.

O'Halloran, Sharon, and Susanne Lohmann. 1994. Divided Government and U.S. Trade Policy: Theory and Evidence. *International Organization* 48 (4):595–632.

Olson, Mancur. 1965. *The Logic of Collective Action: Public Goods and the Theory of Groups*. Cambridge: Harvard University Press.

Polanyi, Karl. 1944. *The Great Transformation: The Political and Economic Origins of Our Time*. 2nd edition, 2001. Boston: Beacon Press.

Rodrik, Dani. 2006. Goodbye Washington Consensus, Hello Washington Confusion. *Journal of Economic Literature* 44 (4):973–87.

Rogowski, Ronald. 1989. *Commerce and Coalitions: How Trade Affects Domestic Political Alignments*. Princeton: Princeton University Press.

Schattsneider, E. E. 1935. *Politics, Pressure and the Tariff*. New York: Prentice Hall.

Steinberg, Richard, 2010. Power, International Trade Law, and State Transformation. Unpublished manuscript, University of California, Los Angeles.

Verdier, Daniel. 1994. *Democracy and International Trade: Britain, France and the United States, 1860–1990*. Princeton: Princeton University Press.

Weber, Max. 1958. The Social Psychology of the World's Religions. In *From Max Weber: Essays in Sociology*, edited by H. H. Gerth and C. Wrights Mills. New York: Oxford University Press.

Williamson, John. 1990. *Latin American Adjustment: How Much Has Happened?* Washington, DC: Institute for International Economics.

PART II

INSTITUTIONAL
EVOLUTION:
BUILDING UP
THE WTO

CHAPTER 4

···

THE INTERNATIONAL
TRADE ORGANIZATION

···

RICHARD TOYE

4.1 Introduction

THE International Trade Organization (ITO)—an intellectual precursor of the WTO—
never existed. During and after the Second World War, extensive efforts were made to
bring it into being, culminating in the multilateral negotiation of a charter for the organization at Havana in 1947–8. However, the Havana Charter was never ratified, chiefly
because domestic opposition within the United States led the Truman administration to
drop its efforts to win congressional backing for the ITO by the end of 1950.

Although the attempt to create the ITO failed, it was nonetheless significant for two
reasons. The first of these was its relationship with the General Agreement on Tariffs and
Trade (GATT), which was designed as an interim measure to regulate international
trade in the period before the ITO came into effect (see Chapter 5). In other words, the
effort to establish the ITO brought the GATT into being, and this in turn had consequences for the eventual creation of the WTO. The second reason is that the idea of the
ITO marks an important staging post in the shift between two contrasting types of trade
liberalism. Late nineteenth century free trade arguments were strongly influenced by
moral internationalism, the assumption that global economic well-being was best
secured by governments reducing trade barriers unilaterally out of enlightened self-
interest. After 1945, by contrast, arguments for freer trade were almost always based on
institutional internationalism, which assumed, more pessimistically, that successful liberalization required an international regulatory framework in order to avoid free riding
and enforce good behaviour.[1] Although the ITO itself proved a dead letter, the underlying idea persisted, and today has hegemonic status.

---

[1] For the distinction between the two types of internationalism, see Sylvest 2009, 10.

William Diebold's *The End of the ITO*[2] provided a classic contemporary analysis for the failure to ratify the charter, which in his view was determined by American domestic politics. The plan was derailed by an unholy alliance between supporters of protectionism and free trade purists who objected to exceptions to laissez-faire within the proposed ITO rules. This assessment, although capable of refinement, still holds good today. However, the considerable literature on the ITO tends to be very US-centred in terms of its focus and ideological outlook. For example, the role of poorer countries, which successfully pressed for exemptions in the charter for the purposes of economic development, is often treated dismissively. This chapter offers a more rounded treatment. It examines:

(1) the origins of the ITO
(2) the negotiation of the charter
(3) the failure to ratify the charter.

The conclusion considers the ITO's legacy. It places the relevant diplomatic negotiations within the context of trade culture and politics in the US, the UK and elsewhere, and explains them in relation to contemporary understandings of the concept of economic underdevelopment and attitudes to international organizations in general. It has recently been argued that there is a mistaken tendency to romanticize the supposedly 'wise and prudent internationalists' of the 1940s at the expense of the politicians of more recent times.[3] The ITO episode reminds us that, if its proponents were in some respects unusually far-sighted, they were also at the mercy of events and subject to pragmatic political considerations not dissimilar to those experienced today.

4.2 THE ORIGINS OF THE ITO

The idea of an international organization to regulate trade received a major boost from the perceived economic failures of the interwar years, but it had earlier antecedents. In 1847, the year after the British anti-protectionist lobby secured the goal of abolishing the Corn Laws, an international free trade congress met at Brussels; further congresses met at irregular intervals in the years before the First World War and again thereafter. This, however, was not an intergovernmental body, but was rather a means for individual free traders to meet to promote their cause in what was arguably a rather self-congratulatory atmosphere. The idea that free trade helped promote international peace was of course a familiar trope from the rhetoric of Richard Cobden. By the 1850s, free trade was being discussed in the same breath as proposals to settle diplomatic disputes by arbitration, although no one yet suggested that international trade disputes could be resolved in this

---

[2] Diebold 1952.   [3] Mazower 2009, 6.

way.[4] In fact, in the late nineteenth and early twentieth centuries, the very concept of international trade agreements was seen as suspect by many British free traders. The 1902 Brussels Sugar Convention was an agreement by ten countries, including Britain, to work together to tackle export bounties that destabilized the international market. The effort was a success, but it was opposed by Liberals who, prizing cheap sugar for British consumers above all else, portrayed involvement in an international commission as an attack on British sovereignty. In 1912 the Liberal government denounced the convention.[5] During the Great War, however, British progressives were amongst the proponents of international government and the concept of a League of Nations, although the consequences of this in the sphere of trade were not yet clear.

The first concrete proposal for a recognizably ITO-type body came from within the United States. In 1916, Democratic Congressman, Cordell Hull, argued for the establishment of 'a permanent international trade congress'. (Later, in 1925, he used the term 'International Trade Organization'.) As a native of Tennessee, Hull shared the common sense of grievance that high US tariffs favoured Northern manufacturers to the detriment of Southern agriculture; but he also developed Cobdenite opinions about the link between trade barriers and war. The purpose of his proposed organization was to reach agreements 'designed to eliminate and avoid the injurious results and dangerous possibilities of economic warfare', and to promote fair and friendly international trade relations.[6] Hull's ideas may have influenced the third of President Woodrow Wilson's famous Fourteen Points—the third point called for the removal of economic barriers and 'the establishment of an equality of trade conditions' between all the nations consenting to the eventual peace treaty.[7] Hull's contribution thus marked a shift in the American trade debate. The focus until this point had largely been on whether or not a particular tariff level was beneficial for the United States; with America's global power increasing, there was now some consideration of the impact of trade barriers on the good of the world as a whole.[8] It should be noted, though, that Hull had no clear concept of the mechanisms by which the planned organization would actually operate. Furthermore, with the US shift to isolationism in the 1920s, and with the Democratic party showing increased sympathy for protectionism as the decade went on, Hull remained an isolated if respected voice until appointed as Franklin D. Roosevelt's Secretary of State in 1933.

Meanwhile, the economic machinery of the League of Nations provided a potential arena for international cooperation on trade, American failure to join the League notwithstanding.[9] John Maynard Keynes' *The Economic Consequences of the Peace* (1919) included a proposal for the creation of a 'free trade union' under the auspices of the League of Nations. Members would 'impose no protectionist tariffs whatever against the

[4] *The Times*, 23 September 1856, 5.
[5] Trentmann 2008, 154–61.
[6] Hull 1948 volume I, 81–2; Toye and Toye 2004, 19. See also Miller 2003, chapter 2.
[7] Toye and Toye 2004, 20.
[8] Hull 1948 volume I, 83.
[9] *Florence Times-News*, 2 June 1931, 1.

produce of other members of the union'.[10] Subsequent League efforts to establish a 'tariff truce' failed, partly because of the lack of any means of enforcement, but principally because of the growing protectionist sentiment in the world at large in the aftermath of the Great Crash of 1929.[11]

In 1930, the United States adopted the Smoot-Hawley tariff, which is frequently alleged to have deepened the depression and is often mistakenly stated to have been unprecedentedly high. In fact, Smoot-Hawley was less significant for its direct economic consequences than for the mythical status it achieved as an emblematic policy failure, which was used by later policymakers to justify support for international trade cooperation.[12] In the wake of a serious political and financial crisis in 1931 (and not in obvious retaliation for Smoot-Hawley), Britain extended significantly its existing system of imperial tariff preferences. Traditional opposition to British imperialism helped fuel US resentment of imperial preference, which became Hull's special bugbear.[13] The elimination of such forms of 'discrimination' was to become at least as important an object of US policy as the reduction of average tariff levels. Ironically, though, the 1932 Ottawa accords—a series of bilateral deals between Britain and its self-governing dominions—formed a model of sorts for the GATT/ITO experience. The Ottawa conference was, in a sense, a precursor of later forms of multilateral negotiation, even though it represented an attack on free trade rather than an attempt to extend it. The failure of the 1933 World Economic Conference, however, demonstrated that at this time there was no capacity or political will for economic cooperation on a global scale.

Although humiliated by the circumstances of the conference's collapse, Hull, as Secretary of State, was able to pursue his vision of freer trade on a more piecemeal basis through the Reciprocal Trade Agreements Act (RTAA) of 1934. The act virtually handed the power to alter the tariff from Congress to the administration. It empowered the President (in practice the State Department) to enter into trade agreements with foreign countries for the reciprocal reduction of tariffs and other trade restrictions. The powers it granted were initially for three years only, but the act was successively renewed for further fixed terms. In the decades to come, the deadlines set by the expiry of presidential tariff-cutting powers affected negotiating positions and substantive outcomes. Moreover, the diminution of congressional influence was significant. As Stephen Haggard notes, 'With the transfer of tariff-making authority to the executive, the United States could make credible commitments and thus exploit its market power to liberalize international trade.'[14] The act permitted the reduction of US tariffs on an item-by-item basis (in contrast to the more sweeping powers granted under later legislation), although no one duty could be reduced by more than 50 per cent. Any such reductions of duty would be extended to all other countries, although these benefits could be withheld from countries that discriminated against American commerce.

[10]   Keynes 1919, 248.
[11]   Mathias and Pollard 1989, 92.
[12]   Eckes 1995, chapter 4.
[13]   Rooth 1993, 285–6.
[14]   Haggard 1988, 91.

By 1938, Hull had succeeded in bringing 60 per cent of the foreign trade of the USA within the scope of the trade agreements. However, the average level of US tariffs remained high, and Hull made little if any progress in reversing the trend towards discrimination and bilateralism in world trade in general.[15] Although the RTAA was to become central to later efforts to create the ITO, it was not originally imagined that it could form any kind of basis for the establishment of an international organization. After the outbreak of the Second World War, therefore, State Department planning for the post-war world was initially based on the assumption that future progress towards freer trade would be founded on a straightforward extension of the RTAA programme.

The planning process was further stimulated when, in August 1941, the British and American governments issued the Atlantic Charter, in which the two countries stated their 'desire to bring about the fullest collaboration between all nations in the economic field, with the object of securing for all improved labour standards, economic advancement and social security'.[16] The Japanese attack on Pearl Harbor on 7 December that year gave further stimulation to US internationalism, in economic relations as well as in foreign policy.[17] And in 1942, Britain committed herself to Article VII of the Mutual Aid Agreement, whereby as 'consideration' for American lend-lease aid, the UK would work with the USA towards 'the elimination of all forms of discriminatory treatment in international commerce, and to the reduction of tariffs and other trade barriers'.[18] There followed a drawn-out process of Anglo-American negotiation as to the form this consideration should take.

Up until this point, as we have seen, the Roosevelt administration had pursued its substantial objective—an increase in global multilateral trade—via a bilateral procedure, under the RTAA. The 1942–3 period saw a shift towards support for procedural multilateralism as the means to achieve substantive multilateralism. By the end of the war, in other words, it was envisaged that many countries would negotiate bilateral trade agreements amongst themselves, simultaneously, before generalizing the results of each deal to the other participant nations, and that a new international organization would be required to make this process work. To a considerable extent, this important departure was the result of thinking by British officials, who approached their negotiations with the US with two tactical objectives in mind. First, they wanted future trade deals to be carried out on a multilateral basis, as they hoped that this would help Britain form a united front with the Commonwealth countries, combating possible US attempts to play them off against one another. The Americans were prepared to accede to this, as they were aware of the importance of appearing to treat each of their allies alike. Second, the British were keen to take the initiative in the wartime discussions. Deeply conscious of

---

[15] Arndt 1944, 81–8.

[16] 'Joint declaration by the President of the United States of America and Mr Winston Churchill, representing His Majesty's government in the United Kingdom known as the Atlantic Charter', Cmd. 6321, 1941.

[17] Toye and Toye 2004, chapter 1.

[18] 'Agreement between the Governments of the United Kingdom and the United States of America on the principles applying to mutual aid', Cmd. 6341, 1942, 3.

their own country's likely post-war economic weakness, they chose to make bold proposals to the Americans while writing their own safeguards and 'escape' clauses.[19]

One key British proposal was the plan designed by James Meade, a Keynesian economist and wartime civil servant, for an international commercial union. This was intended as the complement of John Maynard Keynes' contemporaneous plan for an international clearing union. The purpose of the commercial union was to create a multilateral trading system, from which, Meade believed, Britain was likely to benefit. However—and here were the safeguards—both state trading and 'the continuation of a moderate degree of Imperial Preference' would be permitted.[20] Meade's ideas were recognizably similar to Hull's original idea of a permanent trade congress but they were much more detailed and concrete. His proposals formed the framework of the Anglo-US Article VII discussions that took place in the autumn of 1943; the British found that they were knocking at an open door.[21] The multilateral economic regime that emerged after the war is often portrayed as a product of American hegemonic imposition. In the case of trade, however, Britain—a substantially weaker power—played an important (if self-interested) role in promoting the multilateral agenda.

There was also a limited amount of input into the discussions from countries other than the USA and the UK. By the end of 1945, the Americans and the British had agreed on a set of 'proposals for consideration by an international conference on trade and employment'. The emphasis on employment reflected pressure from, in particular, the Australian government, for the international coordination of Keynesian-style full employment. Although this demand was sidelined in subsequent negotiations, it did reflect a significant strand of contemporary thought (not least among British Keynesian economists and politicians) and illustrates the divergent and potentially conflictual approaches to international economic reform that were in circulation at the end of the war.[22] More generally, the 'Proposals' outlined the need for 'an International Trade Organization of the United Nations, the members of which would undertake to conduct their international commercial policies and relations in accordance with agreed principles [...] in order to make possible an effective expansion of world production, employment, exchange and consumption'.[23] The ITO was thus intended, like the Bretton Woods institutions, to be a UN specialized agency, that is to say, part of the UN system but independent in terms of operational control. Like them, too, it was seen as an essential part of a broad-ranging multilateral, international economic regime that would encompass both trade and payments.

---

[19] This paragraph draws substantially on Miller 2003, chapter 4. For an example of British official thinking at this time, see 'Draft Minutes, First Meeting of the Inter-Departmental Committee on Post-War Commercial Policy', 24 November 1942, UK National Archives, Kew London (henceforward TNA), BT 61/79/6.

[20] Howson 1988, 27–35.

[21] Miller 2003, 199.

[22] Hudson and Way 1989, 90–1.

[23] 'Proposals for consideration by an international conference on trade and employment', Cmd. 6709, December 1945, 3–4.

4.3 THE NEGOTIATION OF THE CHARTER

Although the 'Proposals' seemed to show outward harmony between Britain and America, there were tensions between the two countries that would come to pollute the subsequent ITO discussions. There was indeed agreement over the general desirability of the ITO, but progress on the issue was inseparable from arguments over specific trade practices (notably imperial preference) and tariff levels, and from the new Labour government's need for American help to prop up the British economy. Indeed, acceptance of the 'Proposals' was one of the conditions of the $3.75 billion loan by America to Britain agreed in December 1945. Over time, Anglo-American trade diplomacy became soured by the Truman administration's growing irritation at Britain's demands (made in consciousness of her own economic weakness) that the ITO rules include various departures from free trade principles. In the end, the US successfully mobilized a coalition of nations against Britain's demands, but at the cost of including other exemptions in the charter that made it unacceptable to American domestic opinion.

The 'Proposals' were subsequently elaborated in a draft ITO charter, which was then discussed at the first session of the preparatory committee to the UN conference on trade and employment. This met in London in October–November 1946, attended by 18 countries. Widening participation in the discussions had the effect of altering their tone. Although concerns about the stability of international demand raised their head, being reflected in the 'full employment' issue, the most pregnant topic raised was that of special treatment of underdeveloped countries. The concept of 'economic underdevelopment' was a relatively new one and did not have any substantial body of theory behind it. However, the inclusion of a significant number of poorer countries in the UN gave it a considerable political salience in the era of decolonization. Changes in terminology were related to political sensitivities; as more and more nations became independent the interests of tact dictated that countries previously described as economically 'backward' should now be referred to as 'undeveloped' or 'underdeveloped', and later as 'developing' or 'less developed'. Increasingly, countries became willing to identify themselves as belonging to some of these latter categories, and the corollary of this was usually the claim that the richer states bore some measure of responsibility for the condition of the poorer and should be prepared to do something about it. State-led, import-substituting industrialization was often the development model of choice for these poorer countries. Accordingly, at the London conference, India, China, Lebanon, Brazil, and Chile argued that the charter should allow countries to promote industrialization by using import quotas. Australia, which at this time was perceived (at least by its own negotiators) as an underdeveloped country, also supported the use of quotas. In order to meet this demand, the US delegation drafted a new chapter on economic development, recognizing 'that special governmental assistance may be required in order to promote the establishment or reconstruction of particular industries and that such assistance may take the form of protective measures'. The ITO itself would be responsible for judging countries' applications to be allowed to take such measures.[24] Therefore, although the Americans had made some concessions to the underdeveloped countries' point of view, they could expect, given their likely dominant role in the ITO's governance, to have considerable influence on the way that these provisions were actually used.

The second session of the preparatory committee met in 1947 in Geneva. Twenty-three countries, 11 of which could be classed as underdeveloped, were now represented.[25] Talks to refine the draft charter took place simultaneously with the first round of negotiations aimed at achieving mutual tariff concessions. The Geneva conference needs to be understood in the context of both the emerging Cold War and the severe economic plight of European countries—not least Britain. These factors triggered the American Marshall Aid programme, announced during the conference, and this came with an ancillary US agenda for European economic integration. Although the tariff talks would almost certainly have failed in the absence of the Marshall Plan, this support for a form of regional integration to some extent undercut the global ambition of the ITO project. The dynamics of multilateral negotiation also had a significant impact on the shape of the charter, leading to the inclusion of some provisions which the developed countries' representatives believed to be inconsistent with the basic principles of multilateral trade.

At Geneva, the developing countries continued their efforts to secure for themselves greater freedom to use devices such as quantitative import restrictions (QRs), differential internal taxation, mixing regulations, and preferences between neighbouring states for the purposes of development. The Americans were forced to yield on these matters, more or less reluctantly, although the concessions on regional preferences were in harmony with their own ideas on European integration.[26] Thus far, the British had favoured the freedom to discriminate and to employ QRs in the interests of solving balance-of-payments problems, but had worked with the Americans in attempting to resist pressure from the less-developed nations. However, the sterling convertibility crisis of July–August 1947, which severely drained Britain's dollar reserves, weakened the UK's commitment to the ITO. Just as the draft charter was completed, and in the immediate aftermath of the crisis, the British warned publicly that for the time being, in order to safeguard their balance of payments, they would have to use methods which 'may appear to be opposed to the principles and methods of the draft charter'.[27]

Britain's growing doubts about her economy's ability to sustain the full obligations of ITO membership in the near future were matched by her increasing scepticism—fuelled by the experience of the tariff talks—of America's willingness to reduce her own trade barriers substantially. Unless this were done, British policymakers believed, the conditions for the ITO's success would not exist. Therefore, they followed a dual strategy. On the one hand, whilst accepting ITO principles, they asked for application of the most burdensome obligations to be postponed; on the other, they resisted American demands for the substantial elimination of the imperial preference system, insisting that the

---

[24] United Nations 1946, 27–8.
[25] Srinivasan 1999, 1054.
[26] Gardner 1980, 361–7; United Nations 1947.
[27] Speech by Harold Wilson at the second session of the preparatory committee of the UN conference on trade and employment, 6th meeting, 23 August 1947, WTO archive, Geneva.

proposed reductions in US tariffs, offered as a *quid pro quo*, were insufficient to justify this. In the short term, this strategy worked well. The British secured US agreement that there should be a breathing space before the nondiscrimination provisions of the GATT—the terms of which were also agreed at the Geneva talks—came into effect. They also called the Americans' bluff when faced with the threat that Marshall Aid would be withheld from Britain unless a substantial move was made towards the abolition of imperial preference.[28] At the Havana conference, however, these previous successes led the British to push their luck. Their demands for further concessions infuriated the Americans. The resulting collapse in mutual trust had significant repercussions for the final form, and thus the eventual fate, of the ITO charter.

The Havana conference opened in November 1947.[29] The chairman of the US delegation was the 'tall, strikingly handsome, beautifully attired, articulate, affable, assured' Will Clayton, formerly Under Secretary of State for Economic Affairs.[30] Clayton and his team of officials have often been characterized as free trade ideological visionaries. Yet they themselves stressed that complete free trade was not practical; they were pursuing only *freer* trade.[31] And when domestic political interests (notably agricultural ones) were at stake, the representatives of the US proved just as willing as those of other countries to modify free trade principles to suit themselves. Therefore, the real issue at Havana was not whether free trade principles would be modified, but in what ways, and to what extent, this should be done. And because the majority of the 56 countries present were, or at least classed themselves as, economically underdeveloped, the question of development became central to discussion. The informal leadership of the underdeveloped group was now taken by the Latin Americans.

At the time, US officials portrayed the views these countries expressed at the conference as 'extreme', and historians have tended to accept this picture.[32] Yet, although there was indeed an unreasonable and erratic element amongst the leadership of the poorer countries, this does not mean that all of their arguments were unsound. Many such countries had experienced severe economic dislocation during the war and post-war period, and this conditioned their attitude to the ITO. They argued that the charter in its existing form was devised for the benefit of the developed countries (which would benefit from let-outs when in economic difficulties), but that the underdeveloped did not have the necessary exemptions to enable them to develop their own economies. As the delegate of El Salvador put it, 'The industrialized countries' concept of equilibrium was very formal, while the underdeveloped countries felt that there should be a basic criterion—unequal treatment for unequally developed countries.'[33]

The conference quickly became bogged down, the major stumbling block to progress being the issue of QRs. These were governed by Article 13 of the draft charter, which

[28] Toye 2003a.

[29] For a comprehensive account, see Toye 2003b.

[30] Galbraith 1983, 181.

[31] See, for example, Clayton's remarks quoted in telegram from UK delegation in Geneva to Foreign Office, 17 April 1947, TNA FO 371/62291.

[32] Wilcox 1949, 32, 48.

[33] Records of Havana Conference (E/Conf.2/23: Heads of delegations: summary record of meeting), 24 December 1947, p. 6, WTO archive.

provided an escape from the general embargo on QRs for the purposes of protection, but required that its use be approved by the ITO in advance. (This Article had been added to the charter in Geneva.) The underdeveloped bloc rejected this rule of 'prior approval', as they wanted more or less unrestricted freedom to use QRs for the purposes of economic development. For their part, the British feared that allowing such freedom on QRs would severely damage UK exports. The question also intersected with the UK's objectives on non-discrimination. Its delegation attempted to secure continuation until March 1952 of the suspension, agreed at Geneva, of non-discrimination obligations. This demand was likely to try the Americans' patience, not least because it would encourage the underdeveloped countries to demand a *quid pro quo*, making it more difficult for the developed countries to hold the line on the QRs. As one Foreign Office official noted at the end of the month, 'While the Americans are beginning to recognize that we have a good case' for a complete waiver until 1952, 'the arguments for it unfortunately provide the "developers" with a first-class weapon in their attack on us'.[34] British insistence on pushing for this contributed much to their own isolation at the Havana talks.

In spite of the seeming deadlock, the Americans in Havana pressed on in their bid to secure an acceptable charter, even though their superiors in Washington, distracted by the Marshall Aid programme, were no longer taking much interest in the ITO. The eventual completion of the charter, however, was dependent on a change in US strategy. Rather than force a showdown over QRs, it was decided to offer a package of concessions to the underdeveloped countries on a take-it-or-leave-it basis. Cold War concerns played some part in the decision to take this approach, which successfully exploited the divisions between these countries. It was feared that an overt confrontation with the Latin American nations would have damaging consequences in the Western Hemisphere and that the collapse of the conference would hand a propaganda victory to the Soviets. However, the Cold War cannot be used as a monocausal explanation for the US delegation's decision to adopt a less directly confrontational position towards the developing countries. Britain was an important Cold War ally but the Americans had no hesitation in squeezing them at Havana. It was impossible to satisfy in full the competing demands of the developed and the underdeveloped countries, and in choosing to look for some degree of compromise with the latter, the interests of the former had to some degree to be sacrificed. Although the underdeveloped countries were by no means an entirely cohesive bloc, the outcome of the ITO talks did reflect their growing political power, independent of purely Cold War issues.

The Americans were now prepared to concede ground on QRs. Article 13, as finally embodied in the charter, meant that the ITO would be expected to give automatic approval to quantitative restrictions on commodities not covered by existing trade agreements if any of a number of conditions were filled. Among these conditions was that the industry was started between 1939 and 1948, this being intended to cover the case of uneconomic industries started during the war or immediate post-war periods.[35] The British

---

[34] C.T. Crowe, 'ITO', 29 December 1947, TNA FO 371/68873.
[35] Gardner 1980, 368.

delegation, at least at first, fought determinedly against the US attempt to reach this compromise with the Latin American and other underdeveloped countries. But they found themselves 'almost alone in seeking to restrain the Americans from progressive weakening of the text of Article 13', receiving only moderate support from the Canadians and the French. 'In our view the United States have been astonishingly feeble in their approach to this whole problem, and we have been led to the conclusion that their attitude was dictated primarily by a wish to gain credit with the Latin American countries.'[36]

The British believed that they were being asked to agree to concessions to underdeveloped countries on QRs (under Article 13), whilst receiving, in her own view, insufficient rights to discriminate (under Article 23). They also objected to another US concession, under Article 15, that the ITO would be expected to give automatic approval to new regional preference agreements, created for the purposes of economic development, if they conformed to certain agreed standards.[37] The British felt that the American position on this involved a double standard. The USA was now sympathetic to the idea of preference, in the form of a customs union for Western Europe, in the interests of boosting the region's prosperity as an antidote to the Cold War communist threat. However, US policymakers remained implacably hostile to Britain's imperial preference system, even though, in terms of economic theory, it was arguably no more objectionable than a customs union. But British protests were to no avail. As Clair Wilcox, Clayton's deputy, observed with glee: 'The UK is trying to pressure us at the last minute but they cannot get away with it since the US has fifty countries lined up to support the Charter, including the rest of the British Commonwealth and Europe. The UK is absolutely isolated and their position is as impossible as that of a small boy standing in front of a steam roller.'[38] The British did receive some minor concessions on non-discrimination and regional preferences, but were obliged to accept the provisions on QRs. When the conference finally reached agreement on the charter in March 1948, therefore, the British were downbeat. Clayton, by contrast, was jubilant: 'This may well prove to be the greatest step in history toward order and justice in economic relations among the members of the world community and toward a great expansion in the production, distribution and consumption of goods in the world.'[39]

4.4 FAILURE TO RATIFY THE CHARTER

From the point of view of the Americans, however, the outcome was mixed. They had been defeated or outmanoeuvred on some issues, such as how the exports of the occupied areas (Germany and Japan) were to be treated. They were forced to abandon what

---

[36] UK Delegation in Havana to Foreign Office, 20 February 1948, TNA FO 371/68883.

[37] Gardner 1980, 366–7.

[38] Minutes of US Delegation Meeting, 19 February 1948, United States National Archives, College Park, Maryland (henceforward NA) RG 43 International Trade Files (henceforward ITF) Box 148.

[39] 'Statement by the Honourable William L. Clayton at final plenary session, on 23 March 1948', NA RG 43 ITF Box 145.

proved to be a short-lived conversion to the principle of weighted voting—as opposed to one vote for each country—in the ITO. (This was potentially problematic for the USA, which risked being outvoted, although how things would have worked out in practice had the ITO come into being is hard to say. Under the GATT, decision-making generally proceeded by consensus rather than by formal voting, but the ITO could have created a different dynamic, as transpired later with the WTO.) Having been persuaded by US business interests to include in the charter provisions on the security of foreign investment, the provisions that were actually negotiable proved, from the point of view of those interests, unacceptably weak.[40] The charter's insistence that foreign investments could not be expropriated or nationalized except under 'just', 'reasonable', or 'appropriate' conditions could be interpreted as weakening the protection that US investments abroad had previously enjoyed.[41] The charter had other aspects which the US found unpalatable, but to which its negotiators had long since reconciled themselves. For example, from the American point of view, agreements for the stabilization of commodity prices were fundamentally inconsistent with the other provisions of the charter; but, believing that primary producing countries would inevitably enter into them, they accepted that it was desirable to lay down 'rules of the road' and thus eliminate some of the worst characteristics of such agreements as had been seen in the past. These and other provisions became the subject of intense criticism within the United States.

Fifty-three countries, including Britain, signed the final act of the conference. However, the ITO charter would not come into effect until it was ratified, and other countries generally held back from doing so until it was clear how the United States would act. Even though the Democrats regained control of Congress in 1948, the Truman administration hesitated to put the issue to the test. US public opinion was not well informed on trade issues. Opinion polls in 1947–8 showed that only about one-third of respondents had heard of the GATT or of the reciprocal trade agreements programme; and whereas 59 per cent agreed that it was important to establish an organization to increase global trade, it would not necessarily be easy to translate this general backing into support for a specific plan.[42] Nevertheless, historical criticisms of weaknesses in the administration's public relations efforts on behalf of the ITO are somewhat misplaced. These were doubtless imperfect but they were substantial, and it is doubtful that an improved effort would have made a difference to the final outcome. More significant was the fact that the ITO lacked powerful advocates in Washington, its main State Department champions (including Clayton) having left the administration after the Havana conference. Dean Acheson, who became Secretary of State in 1949, was prepared to send the charter for congressional consideration, and to speak in favour of it, but lacked Clayton's drive and conviction on the subject.[43]

[40] Zeiler 1999, 140–2; Aaronson 1996, 90–1; Diebold 1952, 18–19.
[41] Odell and Eichengreen 1998, 186.
[42] Aaronson 1996, 100.
[43] Leddy 1973, 74.

Clayton did, however, testify during relevant Senate hearings. The exchanges between him and the Republican Senator Eugene D. Millikin were illustrative of the differences between the administration and one of its key protectionist critics. Clayton had argued that other countries' exchange controls, import quotas, and other restrictions were a consequence of the war, and that they would disappear under the ITO as the world recovered its economic health. 'I suggest to you that the tendency will be entirely the other way', Millikin responded. 'We are off on a great international movement toward state socialism and toward stateism.'[44] Protectionists, of course, felt that (some forms of) state intervention in foreign trade matters was acceptable, but saw any kind of international trade organization as an incipient 'superstate' that would infringe American national sovereignty.[45] What they had in common with free trade enemies of the ITO was support for domestic free enterprise, to which—both groups of opponents claimed—the Havana Charter posed a threat.

Groups such as the National Association of Manufacturers, which supported free trade but which came out against the charter, have been cast in the literature as 'purists'. Arguably, this requires qualification. They were not pure believers in moral internationalism—as British Edwardian opponents of the Sugar Convention were—but saw a role for international institutions in the governance of trade. They thought that *some* kind of ITO was desirable, but felt that the plans that had actually been drawn up would do more harm than good. With some sections of organized labour opposing the ITO too, the charter was up against a formidable coalition.[46]

Diebold's 'unholy alliance' explanation for the failure is then not in need of serious amendment, but it may be added to. In May 1948 Clair Wilcox, the US negotiator who had done much to secure the final deal at Havana, gave a presentation on the charter to non-governmental advisers who had also been at the conference. After acknowledging that it was hard for America to criticize the underdeveloped countries' strong sentiment in favour of protectionism for purposes of development 'in view of our own history of policy during our period of industrialization', he offered a 'sweeping generalization' which was 'not for publication'.

> This Charter is very one-sided. It will impose restraints and limitations on one side and leave almost absolute freedom on the other side. And the way it is one-sided is this: It imposes on most of the other countries in the world limitations on their freedom to do a lot of things they have been doing, are doing, want to do, otherwise will do, without this Charter. Now these limitations are also imposed on us, but they are things we haven't done, aren't doing, and don't intend to do. And the Charter, as far as I can see, is not going to prevent us from doing anything that we are doing or intend to do or want to do.[47]

---

[44] US Senate 1949, 174–5.
[45] *Milwaukee Journal*, 9 November 1948, 41.
[46] *Bend Bulletin*, 18 January 1950, 6.
[47] 'Meeting with Non-Governmental Advisors on ITO', 5 May 1948, ITF Box 1, NA.

Wilcox was obviously attempting to put the best possible gloss on the outcome, so his analysis may well have been too optimistic. It is very difficult to say how the charter would have operated in practice had it come into effect, given that the countries that negotiated it interpreted many of its provisions very differently. The crucial point, however, is that Wilcox's arguments were ones that could not, as he pointed out, be made in public, at least not explicitly. Although potentially persuasive to a US home audience, they would alienate the other countries which also had to ratify the charter and which would only do so if they continued to believe that they had secured a good deal. Thus, the administration's domestic efforts to secure ratification were hampered by the game it needed to play at the international level.

The outbreak of the Korean War in June 1950, which meant that congressional time had to be devoted to emergency business, sealed the ITO's fate: in December, the administration announced it would not proceed with ratification. To the extent that the ITO was deprioritized by the Truman administration because of more pressing concerns, it can be seen as a victim of the Cold War. This dimension, however, should not be overstated. The Soviet Union had not taken part in the charter talks, although it left open the chance it would do so until just a few weeks before the Havana conference. As Diebold reflected in 1994, this actually made things simpler: 'Had the USSR joined, the cold war would have fuelled Congressional, and other, resistance to full American support for the ITO and perhaps blocked other trade measures as well. As it was, the obstacles to the adoption of the ITO that proved impossible to overcome were rooted in American relations with the rest of the world, not the Communist countries.'[48]

4.5 CONCLUSION

The standard view of the post-Second World War global economic settlement is that 'America...invented multilateralism';[49] but, as G. John Ikenberry has noted, 'the system was shaped by the United Kingdom as well as by the United States and in ways that would be unanticipated by simple considerations of power'.[50] As we have seen, the case of the GATT/ITO demonstrates this point. It also shows that countries beyond the Anglo-American axis could have an impact on negotiations via the new multilateral procedures. At Havana, the United States was still learning to play the multilateral game—successfully in terms of securing international agreement, but at the price of alienating its own domestic opinion.

In spite of its failure, the ITO had a number of legacies for the politics of international trade. In 1955—in what appears to have been an opportunistic bid to secure the

---

[48] Diebold 1994, 342.
[49] 'Hightable talk: Lunch with the *FT*: Chris Patten', *Financial Times* magazine, 9 August 2003, issue 16.
[50] Ikenberry 1993, 61.

support of underdeveloped countries—the Soviet Union declared that the Havana Charter should be ratified and that it was itself willing to join the ITO.[51] More significantly, chapter 6 of the charter continued to serve as a general guide to commodity problems during intergovernmental consultations on the issue, and thus influenced the various international price stabilization agreements that were reached in the years following Havana. The most obvious significance of the ITO, however, is that the attempt to create it gave birth to the GATT, which continued as the basis on which world trade was regulated until it was superseded by the WTO in 1995. As the 1947 GATT rules (as subsequently amended) were nested inside the Marrakesh Agreement of 1994, it could be argued that the spirit of the ITO—as well as that of the GATT— lives on in the WTO.

It is worth asking whether or not the ITO's failure should be seen as a missed opportunity. The ITO might well have had a wider membership than the GATT, which came to be perceived as a 'rich men's club'.[52] It was not that poor countries were excluded from GATT membership, but that the organization's activities gave them little motive for joining: during the 1950s, it concentrated its efforts on reducing tariffs on industrial goods, an issue of limited importance to the many underdeveloped countries which had yet to industrialize. An ITO might have been a more attractive organization for underdeveloped countries to join, and that might have promoted less autarchic/anarchic trade policies in such countries, with additional growth benefits. This might have given a further boost to the impressive post-Second World War growth in world trade that took place under the auspices of GATT. At the same time, the Havana Charter's exceptions to free trade rules, especially those made in the interests of economic development of poorer countries, might have helped reduce global inequalities. Conceivably, then, the ITO might have produced a more inclusive, productive, orderly, and just world economy than that which in fact emerged.

This, however, remains speculative, given the difficulties noted above of saying with confidence how the Havana Charter would have operated in practice. It is equally possible that, even on the optimistic assumptions about the way it would have worked, the ITO would not have proved to be a substantially more economically productive regime than the GATT. This is not to say that the charter should not be commended as a forward-looking document. The debates surrounding it provided some of the inspiration for the radical thinking on economic development that spurred the creation of the UN Conference on Trade and Development (UNCTAD) in 1964. It is, however, worth noting some of its limitations. For example, questions of intellectual property and the environment did not find any more place in the charter than they did in the original GATT.[53] At the time, of course, no one suggested that they should be included in either document.

A crucial difference between the charter and the GATT, though, was that the former allowed disputes to be referred to the International Court of Justice, the recommendations

---

[51] Bronz 1956, 443.   [52] Eckes 2000, 20.   [53] Diebold 1994, 344.

of which would be binding (Chapter VIII, Article 96). By contrast, the GATT's dispute settlement mechanism could easily be ignored because of its voluntary nature.[54] That a compulsory mechanism was written into the charter, even though it did not come into effect, signifies how much progress the institutional version of trade liberalism had made since the pre-1914 era. Today, the assumptions of institutional trade liberalism are so hegemonic that the common equation made between the WTO and 'free trade' seems an entirely natural one. Some defenders of classical free trade, such as the Ludwig Von Mises Institute, denounce the WTO as a Trojan horse for mercantilism and economic planning. Such views, precursors of which were part of the mainstream in Edwardian Britain and even 1940s America, are nowadays marginal. Perhaps they are absurd. They do, however, help remind us that free trade and international organization, however desirable it may be, did not always go hand in hand. The link between them had to be invented—and it was for this accomplishment that the designers of the ITO were to a great extent responsible.

REFERENCES

Aaronson, Susan Ariel. 1996. *Trade and the American Dream: A Social History of Postwar Trade Policy*. Lexington, KY: University Press of Kentucky.

Arndt, H.W. 1944. *The Economic Lessons of the Nineteen-Thirties*. London: Oxford University Press.

Bronz, George. 1956. An International Trade Organization: The Second Attempt. *Harvard Law Review* 69 (3):440–82.

Diebold, William. 1952. *The End of the ITO*. Princeton: Princeton University.

Diebold, William. 1994. Reflections on the International Trade Organization. *Northern Illinois University Law Review* 14 (2):335–46.

Drache, Daniel. No date. The Short But Amazingly Significant Life of the International Trade Organization (ITO): Free Trade and Full Employment: Friends or Foes Forever? Toronto: Robarts Centre for Canadian Studies, York University. Available from <http://www.yorku.ca/robarts/projects/wto/pdf/apd_ito.pdf>. Accessed 27 July 2010.

Eckes, Alfred E. 1995. *Opening America's Market: US Foreign Trade Policy Since 1776*. Chapel Hill and London: University of North Carolina Press.

Eckes, Alfred E., ed. 2000. *Revisiting U.S. Trade Policy: Decisions in Perspective*. Athens, Ohio: Ohio University Press.

Galbraith, John Kenneth. 1983. *A Life In Our Times: Memoirs*. London: Corgi.

Gardner, Richard N. 1980. *Sterling–Dollar Diplomacy in Current Perspective: The Origins and the Prospects of our International Economic Order*. 3rd edition. New York: Columbia University Press.

Haggard, Stephan. 1988. The Institutional Foundations of Hegemony: Explaining the Reciprocal Trade Agreements Act of 1934. *International Organization* 42 (1):91–119.

Howson, Susan, ed. 1988. *The Collected Papers of James Meade, iii: International Economics*. London: Unwin Hyman.

Hudson, W. J., and Wendy Way, eds. 1989. *Documents on Australian Foreign Policy 1937–49, viii: 1945*. Canberra: Australian Government Publishing Service.

---

[54] Drache (no date), 22.

Hull, Cordell. 1948. *The Memoirs of Cordell Hull* (two volumes). London: Hodder and Stoughton.

Ikenberry, G. John. 1993. Creating Yesterday's New World Order: Keynesian 'New Thinking' and the Anglo-American Postwar Settlement. In *Ideas and Foreign Policy: Beliefs, Institutions, and Political Change*, edited by Judith Goldstein and Robert O. Keohane, 57–86. Ithaca and London: Cornell University Press.

Keynes, John Maynard. 1919. *The Economic Consequences of the Peace*. London: Macmillan.

Leddy, John M. 1973. Oral history interview by Richard D. McKinzie. Harry S. Truman Library, Independence, MO.

Mathias, Peter, and Sidney Pollard. 1989. *The Cambridge Economic History of Europe, viii: The Industrial Economies: The Development of Economic and Social Policies*. Cambridge: Cambridge University Press.

Mazower, Mark. 2009. *No Enchanted Palace: The End of Empire and the Ideological Origins of the United Nations*. Princeton: Princeton University Press.

Miller, James N. 2003. The Anglo-American Origins of Multilateralism. Unpublished Ph.D. dissertation, University of Cambridge.

Odell, John, and Barry Eichengreen. 1998. The United States, the ITO and the WTO: Exit Options, Agent Slack, and Presidential Leadership. In *The WTO as an International Organization*, edited by Anne O. Krueger, 181–209. Chicago: University of Chicago Press.

Rooth, Tim. 1993. *British Protectionism and the International Economy: Overseas Commercial Policy in the 1930s*. Cambridge: Cambridge University Press.

Srinivasan, T. N. 1999. Developing Countries in the World Trading System: From GATT, 1947, to the Third Ministerial Meeting of WTO. *The World Economy* 22 (8):1047–144.

Sylvest, Casper. 2009. *British Liberal Internationalism, 1880–1930: Making Progress?* Manchester: Manchester University Press.

Toye, Richard. 2003a. The Attlee Government, the Imperial Preference System and the Creation of the GATT. *English Historical Review* 118 (478):912–39.

Toye, Richard. 2003b. Developing Multilateralism: The Havana Charter and the Fight for the International Trade Organization, 1947–1948. *International History Review* 25 (2):282–305.

Toye, John, and Richard Toye. 2004. *The UN and Global Political Economy: Trade, Finance and Development*. Bloomington, IN: Indiana University Press.

Trentmann, Frank. 2008. *Free Trade Nation: Commerce, Consumption, and Civil Society in Modern Britain*. Oxford: Oxford University Press.

United Nations. 1946. *Report of the First Session of the Preparatory Committee of the United Nations Conference on Trade and Employment*. Document number E/PC/T/33. London: United Nations.

United Nations. 1947. *Report of the Second Session of the Preparatory Committee of the United Nations Conference on Trade and Employment*. Document number E/PC/T/186. No place: United Nations.

US Senate. 1949. Hearings on ITO. 81st Congress, 1st sess., 17 February.

Wilcox, Clair. 1949. *A Charter for World Trade*. New York: Macmillan.

Zeiler, Thomas W. 1999. *Free Trade, Free World: The Advent of GATT*. Chapel Hill, NC: University of North Carolina Press.

....

CHAPTER 5

THE EXPANDING MANDATE OF THE GATT: THE FIRST SEVEN ROUNDS

....

THOMAS W. ZEILER

5.1 INTRODUCTION

....

BORN in an era of international economic and political turmoil caused by the destruction of the Second World War and the advent of the Cold War, the General Agreement on Tariffs and Trade (GATT) improbably lasted for nearly half a century as the chief multilateral forum for negotiating the reduction of trade barriers of its member states. The GATT was originally conceived as the tariff-bargaining forum for a more comprehensive trade body, yet that big institution did not exist until the World Trade Organization came into being in 1995. In the meantime, the GATT operated as a trade treaty, a forum—it was an agreement rather than a formal organization—approximating the Bretton Woods monetary institutions of the IMF and World Bank. But, unlike these financial mechanisms (which did not last past the 1970s), the GATT endured because it became more than an effective tool for reducing tariffs and promoting global growth in trade. It was also a means of discussing a wide range of international economic problems and a weapon in the security arsenal of the Free World against communism.

The GATT's long span of success derived mainly from its focused effort to reduce trade barriers, and mainly tariff levels, and the steady institutional, structural, and programmatic growth that derived from the expansion in world trade. This happened in two stages—over the first seven rounds of negotiations during which the GATT evolved—that will serve as the chronological framework of this chapter. From the first negotiations in 1947 at Geneva through talks concluded in 1961, the GATT placed trade and tariffs in the context of post-Second World War *recovery* in Europe and Asia. This reconstruction era was the formative stage of the forum, as the GATT added new members and fixed tariff levels in Western Europe as its primary aims. When recovery was evidenced by the vigour of the European Economic Community as well as the reinstitution of currency convertibility, the GATT entered its second phase of *competition*. In this period, it adapted the trading system to growing trade pressures on the hegemonic United States from Europe and Asia, as well as to demands for equity from the burgeoning Third World. The competition phase began with the Kennedy Round in the mid-1960s and lasted through the late 1970s. By the time of the Uruguay Round, the eighth set of negotiations (see Chapter 6), the GATT was poised for a new phase of expansion.

The GATT added members and changed according to demands and the economic needs and requirements of various nations, but it remained single-minded in its pursuit of addressing a myriad of trade barrier issues in a multilateral fashion. Over the years, GATT negotiating 'rounds', as the eight multilateral meetings that occurred from 1947 to 1994 were called, considered a host of topics. But the forum's mission of trade liberalization was so entrenched that many of the top concerns of nations—such as Third World development—became the responsibility of other organizations. In the end, nations easily inserted the GATT into the larger World Trade Organization (WTO). Before it ended its reign after the Uruguay Round as a stand-alone forum, the GATT incorporated trade rules, customs, and barrier reductions—along with institutions to maintain and enhance such liberalization—into the capitalist world economy. This was all the more remarkable if one considers that, when it began, GATT lacked an institutional framework, a secretariat to administer it, and legal ties to an organization (because its parent body, the International Trade Organization, never materialized). It was simply an agreement, but it did more than survive. The GATT became a 'major force' in the international economy.[1]

5.2 THE GATT PHILOSOPHY

The GATT developed from fears of a return to the 'beggar-thy-neighbour' protectionism of the Great Depression and the need to bring recovery, stability, and growth to the world economy in the wake of the Second World War. The United States and the United Kingdom orchestrated its creation. American Secretary of State, Cordell Hull, was a staunch believer in the link between liberal trade and national security. He did not pursue the impossible dream of outright free trade, for politics in all nations inhibited a dramatic lifting of tariff and other protection for domestic producers. However, Hull did tie a philosophy of fair treatment (non-discrimination), equal opportunities, and orderly exchanges in national markets to the promotion of peace. In his view, an open-door commercial system, based on multilateral negotiations of trade barriers and a market

---

[1] Jackson 2000, 18.

ethic, would prevent a headlong descent into regimentation that led 'to the suppression of human rights, and all too frequently to preparations for war and a provocative attitude toward other nations'.[2] He also frowned on restrictions on the flow of gold, but detested even more the economic nationalism implied in the British system of imperial trade preferences. As the chief trade negotiating arm of the government, the Department of State followed his lead in working to pry open closed doors to trade around the world. Hull set the standard for the pursuit of market capitalism as a pillar of US trade policy, and as a foundation for the process of later globalization under the WTO.

The British held to the same general philosophy of seeking lower trade barriers and the promotion of global prosperity through multilateral commercial agreements, but they stomached discriminatory policies because of their prostration from the Second World War. During the war, British leaders such as James Meade and John Maynard Keynes had produced the first templates for a trade negotiation forum and a larger commercial union during the war. They also determined to protect Britain's vulnerable economy by guarding its imperial trade networks through discriminatory practices. While not necessarily preferring state trading, Britain nonetheless accepted regulations on imports, special arrangements for agricultural trade, and even government-run trade regimes as permanent fixtures in the trade system. In its feeble economic state, the country simply could not yet join the type of multilateral commercial system, based on large-scale and largely unfettered trade barrier reductions, that the Americans desired. Anglo-American debates over the purpose, course, and nature of the trade system resulted in an approach of 'modified multilateralism'. British protectionism would temper the American push for free trade, although the United States was not an advocate of an outright embrace of unfettered markets either. Freer trade and protectionism were juxtaposed; politics sometimes trumped economics under the modified multilateral regime. The GATT—the tariff negotiation protocol designed to bind or reduce rates— would push forth as vigorously as possible with bilateral cuts, multilateralized to other partners, amidst the political pressures surrounding the trade regime.[3]

The modified multilateral order that evolved in the post-war period under the GATT was less an assault on national sovereignty—for recovery and reconstruction demands required countries to protect their economies—than a general thrust towards opening markets. Essentially, all nations did not pretend to seek unregulated commercial relations. Each had domestic constituencies vulnerable to import competition, each struggled to normalize their economies during peacetime, and each had interests that superseded the theory behind market ideology. In short, there was never a chance for pure economics to dominate the politics and diplomacy of trade; the GATT occupied a place where globalization emerged between trade and diplomatic visionaries and pragmatic politicians. The advent of the GATT in 1947 involved a multilateralist drive for installing free enterprise practices, which themselves were buffeted by protectionism. In doing so, the GATT 'set out principles for the conduct of commercial policy' to ensure

---

[2] Kimball 1991, 44–5.   [3] Irwin, Mavroidis, and Sykes 2008, 12–73; Zeiler 1999, 41–58.

that the cardinal post-war objectives of trade liberalization, and the avoidance of another Great Depression, came to pass.[4]

5.3 THE RECOVERY PHASE

5.3.1 Geneva Round, 1947

As the drama played out over the ill-fated International Trade Organization (ITO), the GATT pressed on with trade liberalization, although not at a universal level. That is, the advent of the Cold War narrowed the GATT's mission to the recovery of the Western nations allied with the United States against Soviet-led communism, along with other major regional initiatives in trade and finance (such as the European Payments Union) promulgated by the European Recovery Act, or Marshall Plan. Thus, the American-led GATT pressed for European regionalism as a means of recovery, and ultimately the political stability, of the Free World. Such an approach also allowed for discrimination against US goods within Europe, as the means of boosting reconstruction of industries and agriculture, and aimed to ensure that governments remained liberal and leaned towards a pro-capitalist ideology. From its very inception, the GATT allowed for the exception of discriminatory customs unions and free trade areas (under Article 24) because contracting parties believed that such trade arrangements would contribute to world growth and lead to further liberalization at the multilateral level. Both reasons supported the security argument.[5] In the first rounds, the goal was to 'bind'—or fix— national tariff levels in place so they could not rise. This entailed negotiations through the 1950s that froze European tariffs at existing levels, binding them as the European countries gradually removed quantitative barriers and foreign exchange controls.[6] In this way, the United States linked diplomatic concerns over the Cold War to the GATT trade system by maintaining the drive toward liberalism while encouraging European integration to solidify the Western alliance against communism.

The landmark Geneva Round of 1947 set the initial rules for the GATT and principles under 24 Articles, with the stress first on liberalizing trade but not to the exclusion of protective measures. The first, and most fundamental, Article called for general most-favoured-nation treatment. All the GATT signatories (called 'contracting parties') would not discriminate against others, so that all received the same treatment. The GATT devised an innovative way to facilitate the non-discrimination principle in trade negotiations by having pairs of countries deal bilaterally with products in which each was the other's principal supplier. Then, under the most-favoured-nation process, con-cessions granted in these bilateral deals would extend to all participants. Another Article

---

[4] Irwin 2009, 223.   [5] WTO 2007, 133.
[6] Coppolaro 2010, 5. See also Asbeek Brusse 1997.

provided for equal, non-discriminatory 'national treatment' when it came to the regulatory standards for imports competing with domestic goods. Other Articles allowed for deviations from the most-favoured-nation clause, such as allowing for measures to safeguard payments balances, use of subsidies, and resort to state-trading practices. And Articles 14, 20, and 21 explicitly permitted exceptions to the principle of non-discrimination on specific grounds of security or simply on a general basis. Customs unions—inherently discriminatory—were also allowed, while there would be a gradual, and not immediate, elimination of quantitative barriers.[7]

Multilateralism was modified even in the very process of bargaining. For example, contracting parties adhered to reciprocal (not unilateral) negotiations, then spread concessions reached through the bilateral talks on a multilateral basis. This proved to be a cumbersome method of reducing or binding duties. It reflected protectionist pressures, especially in the United States, where trade law prohibited sweeping tariff cuts. Nonetheless, strict reciprocity and the bilateral–multilateral approach allowed the American State Department to take the lead and push for GATT-wide concessions. Seven months of discussions in 1947 in Geneva resulted in 45,000 tariff concessions that affected $10 billion in trade. This was a notable achievement considering the enfeebled post-war state of European economies and a US Congress that hesitatingly accepted freer trade and sapped the political will to lower trade barriers.

The actual results for trade at this first Geneva Round were not as important as the acceptance of the GATT itself as the global trade institution. Indeed, the GATT did not enter definitively into force because the 23 nations that participated at Geneva would not subject all of their trade to the Agreement. Article XXVI of the GATT protocol required the GATT to remain provisional until negotiations covered at least 85 per cent of world trade. There were also major gaps in the GATT's coverage—economic development, cartels, trade in services, state-trading—that were controversial and the responsibility of the stillborn ITO. The GATT stuck to tariffs and trade for the near future, although its lengthy and non-binding dispute settlement mechanism proved a weakness, because it allowed nations to prevent decisions arising from negotiations from going into force.[8] Provisional and purposefully weak—but flexible and adaptable—the GATT conceived at Geneva compromised between classical economics and politics to facilitate movement towards freer trade.

5.3.2 Annecy and Torquay Rounds

In 1948, the GATT was officially born when the Geneva concessions came into effect, and the timing of international events, mainly the intensifying Cold War and the rejection of the ITO, influenced the two following rounds. Both granted some additional tariff concessions (5,000 and 8,700 concessions respectively), but their main

---

[7] Irwin 2009, 223–4; Riesman 1996, 84; Barton et al. 2006, 35–42.
[8] Jackson 1989, 33, 303.

accomplishments lay in the additional countries added to the list of contracting parties. Eleven nations acceded to the GATT at Annecy in 1949, where the United States proved to be the only nation willing to cut tariffs significantly. Britain still faced economic collapse at this point and therefore insisted that America grant more concessions to close the dollar gap that put its currency at risk. Compared to the Geneva Round, Annecy's results were modest. All nations hoped that the passage of the ITO would further the cause of comprehensive multilateral trade liberalization, but that was not to be. The United States withdrew support from the ITO in 1950.

The same year, the Torquay Round, where six more nations acceded to the GATT, reduced tariff levels of 1948 by one quarter, but it, too, was an unimpressive show for the new forum. The British Commonwealth permitted no more than nominal tariff concessions on its discriminatory imperial preference system. The Americans again stepped forward with a healthy list of concessions, most of them tariff cuts and not bindings, but the Europeans believed the United States should do much more. When the British would not budge on their offers, Washington aborted talks with London, and the Torquay Round of 1950 came to a sputtering end that raised questions about the very relevance of the GATT.[9] The forum awaited a more peaceful climate and, above all, more favourable news of European recovery. Nonetheless, as one trade historian has noted, the GATT was a 'political miracle' considering the political and economic problems facing the transatlantic partners in the post-war world.[10]

5.3.3 Geneva II and Dillon Rounds

By the mid-1950s, as the reconstruction of Western Europe emerged and the region forged its customs union, Geneva hosted another GATT round. Twenty-six nations cut $2.5 billion worth of tariffs, but US reciprocal trade legislation limited American offers, to the chagrin of the Eisenhower administration. The White House sought vigorous trade liberalization, but congressional protectionists—many in the President's own Republican Party—were wary of the GATT and other internationalist organizations. Much of the momentum forward for concessions arose from the accession of West Germany and Japan to the forum. Their membership indicated the reconstruction of the post-war world, though not without controversy. The British Commonwealth especially resisted Japanese membership because of wartime memories of Japan's barbarity and predatory economic practices. Admitting Japan to the GATT after the American occupation was over in 1951, however, was critical to an Eisenhower administration that sought to link free trade to security in Asia. Japan became a contracting party in 1955, in readiness for the Geneva II Round, but only after a series of bilateral tariff negotiations with the United States pointed Tokyo towards liberalization.[11] By this time, there were

---

[9] Zeiler 1999, 170–9, 180–3.   [10] Gardner 1996, 182.
[11] Forsberg 1998, 186–7; Shimizu 2001, 29–48.

added problems related to Japanese competition, such as growing concern in the United States towards the inflow of cheap textiles from the country.

Textiles, the rising European Economic Community (EEC), and an emerging imbalance in American international payments prompted by European reconstruction were the subjects of the 11-month long Dillon Round (named after the US Secretary of State) in 1960–1 that concluded the first, or 'recovery', phase of the GATT. The prime focus was on the New Europe of the Six and American concerns about the transformation in the balance of economic power among the capitalist nations. Despite some $4.9 billion of tariff concessions, it was clear by the end of the Dillon negotiations that a reform, if not an overhaul, of the GATT system was in order. By this time, the United States suffered an increasingly severe balance-of-payments deficit, and consequent drain of gold from its coffers, as Western Europeans cashed in their glut of dollars for bullion. That this deficit might lead to lessening America's security commitments overseas was a frightening prospect for Washington as well as its allies. An answer lay with the rising EEC, or Common Market. This customs union discriminated against outsiders by favouring treatment of internal trade and establishing both a common external tariff for manufactures and a highly protectionist common levy and quota system on agriculture imports. The Americans welcomed the EEC as a powerful trading partner but realized the time had arrived when Europe (and Japan) had recovered from the war. Thus the GATT regime moved into a new era. The old GATT-security nexus held: as President Dwight Eisenhower announced in 1959 on the eve of the Round, the objective was 'the establishment of a less restricted international trade which will foster greater strength and solidarity among the nations of the free world'.[12] But now there would be more competition.

In 1961, as the Kennedy administration readied bold liberal trade legislation to address the altered economic order wrought by the Common Market, negotiators at the Dillon Round realized they were playing with an old deck of cards. Tariffs were still significant barriers to trade, but the EEC's agricultural policy and continuing American protection of its farm sector was one area in which non-tariff obstacles had become obstinate problems in the GATT. The contracting parties had never dealt with a customs union of such magnitude as the EEC. The Dillon Round centered on bilateral talks between the United States and the Common Market that revealed that modified multilateralism was as strong as ever. America, however, woefully lacked negotiating authority equal to the task of meeting the EEC's dynamic challenge. The GATT, moreover, had to expand its mandate to range into a host of global trade issues. The Dillon Round marked the end of the era of recovery, and the beginning of the age of competition in the GATT system.

This was no more clear than in the US–EEC bilaterals. GATT rules stipulated that the Common Market had to compensate other nations faced with higher duties because the Six were poised, on 1 January 1962, to adjust tariffs upward. The low-tariff Germany and the Benelux nations had to raise their individual tariff rates towards the higher French and Italian duty levels to establish the common external tariff. To do so, the Six broke

---

[12] Catudal 1960, 1.

prior tariff-binding commitments amounting to $2 billion worth of imports, and were thus required to offer compensatory concessions to other nations on other EEC products to offset the losses. The Common Market resisted, however, arguing that lowering Franco-Italian duties in the common external tariff was compensation enough for outsiders. The Americans finally wrangled $1.6 billion in concessions, but much less than they had originally sought. The Six refused to bargain further.

The Dillon Round extended four months past its original deadline because of this compensation issue, as well as obstacles to liberal trade in the farm sector and a stymied bargaining process itself. The round ended in autumn 1961 after a severely circumscribed deal on agriculture that gained the United States duty-free bindings on a handful of goods, including soya beans and cotton. Although commodities were of the utmost importance to the Americans because the EEC bought nearly one-third of US farm goods, the Common Market offered no more because its common agricultural policy (CAP) levies were still in the design and discussion stage. For its part, the EEC chafed at the timidity of the US tariff-negotiating authority that prohibited the broad, sweeping cuts by sectors and categories used by the Six. Because American law permitted only item-by-item reductions, the EEC withdrew some of its concessions. The Dillon Round, like its predecessor, ground to a halt. All sides realized reform, prompted by new competitive pressures, was in order in the GATT system.[13]

The need for an overhaul was all the more pressing because of the emergence of Third World nations by this time. Many of them were fresh from colonialism. They joined others to raise demands in the United Nations and elsewhere for aid through special trade arrangements because they participated in the GATT regime. The emerging nations spoke directly to the modified multilateral ethic, for many sought preferential trade ties that smacked squarely up against the GATT's non-discrimination clauses. Yet they also asked for other help in light of their needs and lack of options after their failed attempt at import substitution during the 1950s. The Bandung conference of 1955 had set out their neutralist agenda in the Cold War, and in trade they hoped to diverge from the GATT regime by demanding that the advanced nations set aside their insistence on reciprocity to boost infant industries. They targeted the American-led GATT, but soon realized that this forum of traditional trade liberalization would offer little assistance short of minor concessions.

The way forward for the Third World was to create an organization separate from the GATT—the United Nations Committee on Trade and Development (UNCTAD)—in the following decade and gain preferential treatment that way. The United Nations, which had declared the 1960s to be the Decade of Development, would be the tool for prosperity and reform of the GATT system. The push by the Third World for special development provisions would continue in the succeeding decades, and most recently as a special agenda at the Doha Round in 2001 (see later in this volume). The Dillon Round revealed that the GATT—and the United States—faced challenges from all quarters at the end of the recovery era.

[13] Zeiler 1992, 59–63.

5.4 THE COMPETITION PHASE

5.4.1 Kennedy Round, 1963–7

Agreement between the United States and the Common Market was the focal point of the Kennedy Round, the sixth set of GATT talks. Armed with President John Kennedy's bold Trade Expansion Act, American negotiators aimed to slash tariffs on manufactures by half (and minimize protectionist exceptions), liberalize the Common Market's agricultural policy, take GATT's initial major stab at reducing and preventing non-tariff barriers, and meet some of the demands of the Third World. As in earlier rounds, the bilateral results would be multilateralized to the eventual 62 participants at the Kennedy Round, including seven members of the other European trade bloc, the European Free Trade Association.

The Kennedy Round lasted 37 months, 11 months longer than the previous record set at the Dillon Round. It yielded tariff concessions amounting to $40 billion of world trade—four times the previous mark set at Geneva in 1947. The deal encompassed 80 per cent of world trade. Because it occurred during a major transformation in global economic power, due to the rise of the EEC and accompanying challenges to the hegemonic position of the United States in the Western alliance, it was a pioneering round of the GATT. Also, as America's lead negotiator later reflected, it occurred when 'economic issues were not understood to be that critical politically'. Thus, policymakers made decisions regarding the GATT that had a bearing on future international relations at a time (unlike the following decade) when the world economy took centre stage.[14] Still, the Kennedy Round also reflected hard-fought progress, won against a backdrop of rising global protectionism. Modified multilateralism not only seemed the order of the day in the GATT, but the doctrine veered the trade forum towards more discrimination despite the Kennedy Round's healthy dose of liberalization.

This first round of the GATT's era of competition began with strategies designed to adjust nations to a transformed economic world. The Americans linked trade firmly to security, arguing that faster growing Western Europe was fully capable of bearing a greater share of the alliance burden by absorbing more US exports, particularly in the agricultural sector. Washington launched its first trade challenge against a post-war Europe in which it had tolerated discrimination because this approach encouraged regional integration and enhanced competitive capabilities. The Europeans would now have to acknowledge that trade went hand in hand with security, and therefore help to rectify the US payments deficit. In the EEC and Free Trade Association, the goal at the Kennedy Round was to raise exports to the lucrative American market. The Common Market, in particular, realized it had leverage because it was negotiating for six nations as one unit. After much (and continuing) internal strife over the extent of the common

[14] Eckes 2000, 79.

agricultural policy, the EEC would be armed with a protectionist bargaining chip with which it could confront the United States.[15] The GATT negotiations witnessed the clash of two competitors playing on the most equal ground since the war.

In industrial sectors, the Kennedy Round reaped some major rewards for traders. Although the Common Market claimed that its rates on manufactures were generally lower than America's, the disparity did not preclude a robust agreement that slashed duties on industrial products by an average of over one-third of their previous levels— and on a value of goods eight times the amount of the Dillon Round. Disparities among nations disappeared. America's highest tariff rates fell, and, in general, US duties plunged by nearly two-thirds of their previous levels. European tariffs fell by half. In Tokyo, Japanese officials applauded as their bilateral deals, especially with the United States, yielded largely one-sided benefits for their country. Regarding non-tariff barriers, officials reached a compromise on chemicals. The Europeans lowered their tariffs in exchange for America converting its pernicious American Selling Price (ASP) to a normal customs valuation method. (The ASP was a protectionist measure that originated in 1922 to protect American chemical producers from German competition.) The provision jacked up tariffs by 60 per cent, basing duties on the current US price of chemicals rather than the value of the imports, and thereby severely limited imports. Congress refused to eliminate the ASP, thus undercutting the deal, but in the process spurred the White House to adopt the fast-track process before the Tokyo Round in 1974 to avoid protectionist interference. Most noteworthy was an Anti-Dumping Code that was later revised at the Tokyo Round and indicated the GATT's new interest in addressing non-tariff barriers. In reality, the significant lowering of traditional tariffs in the GATT had prompted the rise of non-tariff barriers; the trade forum was a victim of its own success.

Yet the EEC's common agricultural policy proved to be the biggest disappointment for the United States. The CAP proved that GATT's modified multilateral approach did not always result in progress towards liberalization. The average tariff cuts in the sector were a measly 20 per cent of prior levels. The maintenance of CAP levies on grains and poultry, among other major items, meant that the United States received no access guarantees to assure future sales. As a result, American farm trade to the region began to stagnate, putting greater pressure on the payments deficit (and on presidential initiatives at home to pursue liberal trade policies). Agriculture promised to be the major issue facing the advanced nations in the GATT in the next decade, but the tone had been set: no country was willing to subjugate its farmers to the winds of free trade competition.[16] As serious, the failure in the sector gave rise to the notion among American congressional critics that the GATT regime's leader, the United States, had given 'away the store for the sake of gaining political foreign policy advantages'.[17] Protectionists and free-traders alike accused the Kennedy and Johnson administrations of allowing gains for trade partners at the expense of the home market to ease relations within NATO and

---

[15] Coppolaro 2010, 9–10.
[16] Preeg 1970, 159–236. See also Josling, Tangermann, and Warley 1996, 69–71.
[17] Eckes 2000, 90.

further security commitments. Not undercutting the CAP was the prime example of a supposedly soft-pedalling negotiation strategy on the part of the United States. The failure against the CAP raised the ire of producers and Congress, and fuelled protectionist attempts to gut trade liberalism and the GATT itself.

The Kennedy Round fell short of the high ambitions set for it by American and European leaders, so much so that some analysts began questioning whether the GATT itself had outlived its usefulness. Slashing tariffs overall by over a third still fell short of the halving sought under the Trade Expansion Act. Certainly, the GATT had an 'unquestioned achievement', wrote expert William Diebold, of producing major reductions in trade barriers while solving disagreements and avoiding others.[18] But trade in farm goods turned into a bête noire within GATT, as a myriad of creative protectionist devices guarded home producers. Traders from the poor and developing world welcomed an aid commitment of ten million tons of grain (one quarter sent by the EEC and two-fifths by the United States), but they made little headway in using the GATT as a platform to push for preferential trade arrangements. And the Americans sought the donation to keep surplus European grains off commercial markets, while the ten million tons fell short of the initial goal targeted for development aid. The contracting parties settled on an International Grain Agreement but the price levels were too high and thus distorted trade in favour of less efficient producers in Europe and elsewhere. In addition, the EEC refused to open its market to outsiders enough to give them a greater quota on grains. Fighting back protectionist thrusts at home (where tariff hike and quota bills numbered over 700 in Congress), President Lyndon Johnson warned of the stress in the GATT as well as the greater free world alliance. 'We can emerge stronger and more mature', he said, 'or we can dissolve into rival islands.'[19]

The security–trade nexus was as present as before. In fact, general foreign policy objectives had driven Kennedy to propose his ambitious programme of trade liberalization in the GATT in the first place. In 1962, the Trade Expansion Act had transformed US law by allowing for sweeping, across-the-board tariff cuts of up to 50 per cent; previous legislation going back to the advent of the Reciprocal Trade Agreements Act of 1934 had granted the President authority to bargain down duties only on a cautious, item-by-item basis. But Congress required a trade-off by tempering such a push for free trade with a significant reorganization of the liberalization programme. A special United States trade representative (USTR), operating out of the White House, would handle negotiations. Rather than the foreign policy (and liberal) State Department, the USTR, from this point forward, would have an eye on the politics of trade and on the interests of domestic producers and labour, rather than the State Department's traditional perspective on the impact of trade policy on other nations. By the later 1960s, trade expansion did not seem to be an answer to protectionist trends. Domestic producer and labour outcries, slowing growth, and competition altered the international economic landscape, and certainly the American political scene when it came to trade. Congress

---

[18] Diebold 1996, 158.   [19] Zeiler 1992, 240.

refused to renew trade negotiating authority until 1974, and when it did, it insisted on the USTR as representative for the United States. If indeed there was warfare, it was between Congress and the President, and between GATT partners themselves, rather than against the communist enemy.

The Common Market had not fallen apart (an earlier concern of policymakers) but instead had changed the course of history within the GATT. That transformation pointed to larger concerns. Were the founding principles of GATT, non-discrimination (including non-preferential trade under the most-favoured-nation practice and cautious allowances for customs unions) and outlawing of quantitative restrictions, obsolete? Were GATT rules against the necessary exceptions due to payments difficulties, poverty, or limitations on regional trade blocs outmoded? Was the equanimity of shared ambitions, values, and goals of 1947 a figment of the past? In the words of one analyst, was this the 'Twilight of the GATT'?[20]

Reform of the entire GATT system was in order. Officials turned to the seventh round to effect such change. The Kennedy Round had been the first GATT negotiations to go beyond tariffs to deal with non-tariff barriers, and the first to address the concerns of the developing world. It was the first to be bogged down by agricultural trade conflict and the first round in which Europeans had crafted policies challenging the hegemony of the United States.[21] The Kennedy Round, therefore, indicated that the GATT must, once again, adapt to new circumstances and pressures.

5.4.2 Tokyo Round, 1973–9

In the face of heightened calls for protectionism at home, Washington restarted the momentum for trade liberalization through modified multilateralism in the GATT by calling for a new trade round. Congress passed the Trade Act of 1974, which armed the United States with tools to combat protectionism at home and abroad. To answer domestic outcries, the legislation required deeper and quicker investigations into protests by industry about imports and also authorized the president to find ways to eliminate unfair practices abroad against US exports and investment. Free traders got satisfaction, too. For the first time, the power of Congress to amend or filibuster against a trade agreement was reduced; the president could 'fast-track' GATT accords through the legislative process, on an up or down vote, without fear of a long debate inspired by protectionists. It was likely that Congress would pass through most agreements. That Congress granted fast-track authority to the Executive branch at the very time President Richard Nixon was being removed from office stunned the contracting parties. (Although preoccupied with the impeachment process, Congress managed to carry on with normal business through legislation that a majority agreed needed reform. Trade fell into the category of economic policy deemed to be above the partisan fray.) They welcomed the development

---

[20] Evans 1971, 318.   [21] WTO 2007, 184.

of sweeping powers granted to American officials, nonetheless. The Nixon, Ford, and Carter administrations used the Trade Act to negotiate in Tokyo.

The results of the Tokyo Round in terms of trade concessions were sizable, and remarkable given the economic climate. Over the 74 months of talks (nearly double the Kennedy Round duration), the Tokyo Round of multilateral trade negotiations was bookended by two oil crises, followed the collapse of the dollar and the Bretton Woods system, and finished during a deep recession. Nonetheless, the GATT regime adjusted, in this era of duress, to produce over $300 billion in tariff reductions. The 102 nations that participated in the round had even larger ambitions than in the previous GATT talks. The negotiators took their usual stance to reduce tariffs and quotas and to implement and enforce GATT rules and principles, but they then sailed into the uncharted waters of non-tariff barriers on a broader and more numerous scale than ever before. For their part, the Ford and Carter administrations decided to make the Tokyo Round so expansive in terms of adding more issues to the table that, in the words of the chief of the delegation, USTR Robert Strauss, it would 'be so big that no one can stand the failure'. As a consequence, the Americans 'kept loading the table' with suggestions for codes on non-tariff barriers before the Europeans and Japanese realized that such provisions played to US strengths by reducing pernicious obstacles to trade.[22] These included voluntary export restraints and a host of barriers on agricultural products. The contracting parties also finally addressed, in a meaningful way, the interests of developing nations.

In addition to large tariff cuts, negotiators established several codes that transformed the GATT from a tariff reduction body to a trade management forum, and thus anticipated the WTO. These codes related to government procurement, subsidies and dumping, product standards, customs valuation, and import licensing. That is, the GATT had long dealt with tariffs; now non-tariff barriers were fair game. The code on subsidies and countervailing duties addressed national industrial policies by acknowledging that subsidies on manufactures were trade barriers, and not just domestic policies. Countries could impose unilateral countervailing duties if a foreign subsidy created material injury to a home producer. With the agreement of others, such duties could be slapped on a third party. There was an important exception, as agricultural export subsidies were exempt from the code, but there was a pay-off for domestic producers. That is, it was clear that the code meant not a change in flows of trade (due to lessened subsidies) but a promise that implementing legislation could aggressively turn to using countervailing duty laws. Because subsidies were too embedded in politics and domestic business and industrial constituencies to alter significantly, they would emerge as major problems for the GATT in the decades ahead. Indeed, the code highlighted the fact that, considering the myriad of government practices, the very definition of a subsidy was confusing.[23]

Other codes also addressed the politics of trade, and the modified multilateral balancing act between liberalism and protection. Anti-dumping rules were tightened under

---

[22] Eckes 2000, 119, also 125.   [23] Jackson, Louis, and Matsushita 1984, 13.

one code, though not easily. Because the concept of 'injury' was transferred from the subsidies code, private and government practices were jumbled together in ways that made enforcement difficult. State purchasing policies were also recognized as a non-tariff barrier under a code on government procurement. Rules followed to give national and foreign firms equal treatment when bidding on contracts. The number of government agencies so covered was small, but this code paved the way for later expansion by adhering to standards of conditional most-favoured-nation treatment. That meant that non-signatories might not necessarily have access to the government procurement markets of this code's signatories, although the initial list of 12 members covered some two-thirds of world traders who could buy abroad. The customs valuation code took another stab at the American Selling Price that has so bothered competitors to the US chemical industry and that the Kennedy Round had failed to phase out. The result was the conversion of some of these egregious protective devices to tariffs on an *ad valorem* basis, which were then easier to reduce. Surveillance and dispute mechanism rules were set under other non-tariff barrier codes, each of which established a committee of members who could oversee and consult about their implementation but could not, in general, rule on disputes. Thus, improving dispute mechanisms and settlement procedures made limited headway, although the modest steps set a precedent for future action.

The expansion of the GATT's purview, through the non-tariff barrier codes, opened the door to an ITO-type organization, of which the WTO was the result 15 years later. By no means did the codes solve all the problems caused by non-tariff barriers. In large part, their value lay in heading the contracting parties in the direction of solutions that required even more expanded powers and rules by the GATT. The forum also deviated from its hallmark principle of non-discrimination because only signatories of the codes, and not the entire GATT membership, were governed by the new regulations. Thus, most of the Third World nations saw the codes as too restrictive and refused to sign them, even though they were susceptible to discrimination by code signatories under GATT rules. More detailed work on these measures was also needed because some left vague the forms of government intervention that were considered violations of non-tariff barrier rules. The Tokyo Round also did not adequately apply the non-discrimination/most-favoured-nation rule to safeguards, such as the rising number of voluntary export restraints, because of selective, rather than universal, treatment.[24]

In the difficult trials over agriculture, there were few successes because contracting parties could not agree on whether liberalization of trade (the American position) or stable prices and supply (the European Community's goal under the CAP, with Japan's backing) should prevail. This was a fundamental disagreement that spoke to the GATT's ethic of modified multilateralism, but disputes in the farm sector had become seemingly insurmountable obstacles to any progress in trade negotiations. The US Department of Agriculture saw no purpose in the GATT round other than to destroy the CAP, and thus enthusiasm for the Tokyo talks dwindled in this important constituency. It was all the

---

[24] Winham 1986, 212–55. See also Jackson, Louis, and Matsushita 1984, 14–15.

more serious because the developing nations depended on access to the agricultural consumer markets of the advanced countries. Only an agreement to consult on certain commodities was attained in Tokyo because the European Community wanted stabilization of commodity trade. Such a conservative approach was not acceptable to major exporters, including Australia which sought special exceptions to export subsidies. Modest gains in tariff cuts and trade in grains were the order of the day, yet the Tokyo Round also proved to be the last time that agriculture was exempted from multilateral trade negotiations. It was the last gasp of domestic protectionists to expand subsidies and the like. The succeeding Uruguay Round would heed the call to attack such farm-sector protectionism.[25]

At the Tokyo Round, the Third World received a pledge for differential treatment that would exempt them from GATT rules on reciprocity and non-discrimination, and that would make the generalized system of preferences negotiated under UN auspices legal in the GATT regime. Under this plan, as development proceeded, such treatment would gradually be withdrawn and these nations would assume the obligations of regular GATT members. The terms of withdrawal were left vague, however, and many of the Third World nations remained mired in poverty or struggled with other models of growth (export drives or debt) to facilitate development. However, they gained greater access to GATT rule-making itself. For example, the forum had created two deputy director positions, one of which was responsible solely for the developing nations. Yet adhering to principles was another matter entirely. The emerging countries were unable to adjust to the notion that, for the first time, the contracting parties were asking all nations to submit to codes that impinged on sovereignty. Most of the Third World countries were simply not ready to permit such a course because their internal political structures, which were highly protective, prohibited such action. A handful—India, Brazil, Korea, and Argentina—at the last minute embraced the customs valuation code under a special protocol that permitted them to take five years to implement the obligation (rather than do so immediately). That was one of the very few instances of agreement between the advanced and developing world at the Tokyo Round.

In the eyes of the Third World nations, the GATT still failed many of them, and the advanced countries took note. The Americans, for one, noted that with respect to the non-tariff barrier codes, 'there was very little developing-country participation'. The GATT forged agreements among the rich countries in North America, Europe,

---

[25] At the Uruguay Round, negotiators made an extra effort to end trade-distorting arrangements that had plagued the agricultural sector. The later WTO created an Agriculture Committee to oversee commitments to less protectionism and more market access for all nations, although poor countries were given more time to adjust. Nonetheless, at WTO talks in the first decade of the new millennium the farm sector continued to defy reforms. The EU managed to liberalize somewhat its domestic subsidies but the United States and Japan only slowly, if at all, lowered such supports that had long plagued the GATT trade regime. The Third World nations, most of which could not afford to subsidize commodity producers, were forced to buy cheaper goods from abroad and thus had trouble competing on the international market or even staying in business at home. Agricultural issues remained largely unchanged from the 1950s onward, as the farm sector remained resistant to reform.

and Asia (Japan), and the developing world was not brought into the process until the end. Thus, the United States and other nations believed the Third World got a 'free ride at the Tokyo Round', or received benefits without obligations. Meanwhile, most of the developing countries believed that tariff concessions awarded to them were so modest as not to 'justify their participation in some of these non-tariff measure agreements.'[26] The next round of the GATT, at Uruguay (see Chapter 6), Tokyo negotiators pledged, would include a wider array of nations on these important issues, but the Tokyo Round also highlighted the difficulty for the Third World nations of achieving their ends. Coalitions were hard to build, particularly among countries at varying stages of development and with divergent interests according to export and import needs (as Amrita Narlikar and Ernest Preeg explain in Chapter 9 and Chapter 6). In addition, until the Uruguay Round, the GATT had not been an effective tool for the reforms sought by the developing nations: bargaining in the GATT had long focused on industrial goods (in which the Third World was less involved than the advanced countries) and the list of countries participating in negotiations was largely limited to the rich powerhouses. Thus, the GATT continued to be both an engine of growth but an unsatisfactory avenue to prosperity for the poorer and developing countries.

In the end, the Tokyo Round changed the course of the GATT by opening up the forum to more countries, more issues, and more means of solving problems. Concrete accomplishments (such as an agreement to liberalize the civilian aircraft industry) and the various codes were abundant. Indeed, the codes themselves transformed GATT rules, in the words of one expert, 'from statement of broad principle to more detailed regulations relating to domestic and international procedures.'[27] Contracting parties recognized that the GATT needed to change with the times of new demands, constraints, and shifting fortunes of nations, including the leaders in world trade. The GATT had exhausted its usefulness as merely a tariff-reduction forum. Now it would attack the newer, more pernicious non-tariff trade barriers. The American fast-track authority was one example of the needed change. It endured into the next rounds and proved even dramatically helpful by granting authority that provided for a congressional–executive branch partnership to preserve trade agreements.

In fact, the Tokyo Round actually legitimized the GATT itself. For instance, US trade law in 1979, at the conclusion of the negotiations, mentioned it throughout its provisions for the first time in history. Keeping with the rising interest of Congress in trade policy, the 1979 law also gave the President (under section 301) the authority to enforce US rights on a unilateral basis; now, the US could retaliate against what it deemed as unreasonable and discriminatory practices, at the same time that the push for fast-track trade liberalization continued. By the time of the Uruguay Round, in the midst of the Reagan administration, the dual position of liberalization tempered by retaliatory threats and cushioning domestic producers had strengthened. The President also signed bilateral trade pacts (Israel, 1985, and Canada, 1988) that protected certain industries and

---

[26] Eckes 2000, 156, also 122, 145, 150, 155, 158, 160–1, 172; WTO 2007, 188.
[27] Winham 1986, 17.

included items not covered by the GATT, such as trade in services and intellectual property rights, while he pushed for lower trade barriers in general. The Tokyo Round was also a transitional launching pad to the Uruguay Round that established the World Trade Organization. That round dealt with such issues as opening Japanese financial markets and setting accords in the telecommunications sector that would not have been possible without the big step of the Tokyo Round codes.

Transitional, not transformational, best describes the Tokyo Round. There was not enough notice of Japan's new-found economic might, or for Asian power in general. Agricultural problems also went largely unresolved, as did issues affecting the developing world. The dispute settlement code proved to be a mark of progress, but it was not strong enough. Although solutions were imperfect, they were groundbreaking in advancing the forum towards more concrete, workable solutions in future rounds. Multilateralism prevailed. In addition, the commitments made in the Tokyo Round continued into the Uruguay Round, and were accepted under the WTO. Actually, four agreements—in civil aircraft, government procurement, dairy products, and bovine meat—bucked the trend towards multilateralism and remained 'plurilateral', or limited to a narrow group of signatories. The former two gained more adherents as time went on, and the dairy and meat plurilaterals were absorbed into other agreements.[28] In general, most experts agreed that the Tokyo Round served 'as a halfway point to the Uruguay' talks in terms of settling outstanding issues and beginning negotiations on new, more enduring and relevant ones that continued the GATT's progress forward as a vehicle of modified trade liberalization.[29]

5.5 CONCLUSION

By the end of the Tokyo Round, the General Agreement on Tariffs and Trade had been in existence for over 30 years. During that time, its mandate for multilateral trade liberalism had expanded as the forum adjusted to new pressures and circumstances in global commerce and balanced between the market ethic and protectionism. During the four decades of its existence, the GATT had succeeded in addressing key points of discord in the trading system, such as quantitative barriers, which were thorns in the 1940s but had largely disappeared as problems by the 1960s. By that time as well, the forum had largely neutralized the chronic problem of tariffs that had so terrorized the world since the Great Depression. Thus, GATT's signature achievement was engaging in an 'unprecedented amount of tariff disarmament' by the end of the 1960s.[30]

That the globalization of the 1980s onward rendered the GATT less important, because such key aspects of the world economy as trade in services were not addressed

---

[28] WTO, *Plurilaterals*. See also Winham 1986, 21, 57.
[29] John Greenwald, USTR, in Eckes 2000, 165–71.
[30] Gardner 1996, 197.

by the forum, showed that its mandate had not grown sufficiently. Failure to stop agricultural protectionism and the emergence of trade agreements outside of the GATT—such as the Multiber Arrangement on textiles—threatened its relevance. Third World nations largely worked outside of its purview, believing that the GATT did not serve their interests because they were not principal suppliers and lacked leverage and the institutional capacity to effect change within the forum.[31] Criticism from classical economists also buffeted the GATT. By granting exceptions and waivers to the non-discrimination rule, the GATT, they argued, had abandoned 'price-oriented' policy and 'bent' to protectionism to preserve 'harmony' among nations. Doing so had slowed trade liberalization and world growth. Their views unrealistically neglected the forum's role in facilitating *political* agreement, as well as economic cooperation, however.[32] Modified multilateralism promoted growth, but also security, alliances, and domestic peace. The GATT had long been placed in service to NATO, foreign policy agendas, and, at least in part, to the whims of national legislatures.

By the 1980s, the forum's historic role simply pointed to the need for extending the GATT system into even more economic arenas than before, and stimulated calls for another round of negotiations to address new and more issues. A legal overhaul was in order: GATT required the formalization of rules and enforcement mechanisms. In short, it needed to move from a forum to a more formal body.[33] The GATT had long served as a flexible instrument to help with the recovery of the world economy after the Second World War. It then helped to adjust the economic system to transformations in power among nations that led to new competitive pressures and patterns. It had carried out these roles successfully. By the time of the Uruguay Round in 1986, the world trade forum itself had transformed into a larger, more complex organization that contracting parties would reform further. Along the way, the GATT emerged as the midwife of a comprehensive global economic organization—the WTO—that had long been the goal of its founders half a century before.

REFERENCES

Asbeek Brusse, W. 1997. *Tariffs, Trade, and European Integration: From Study Group to Common Market*. New York: St. Martin's Press.

Baldwin, Robert E. 2000. Pragmatism Versus Principle in GATT Decision-Making: A Brief Historical Perspective. In *From GATT to the WTO: The Multilateral Trading System in the New Millennium*, edited by the WTO Secretariat, 35–44. The Hague: Kluwer Law International.

Barton, John, Judith Goldstein, Timothy Josling, and Richard Steinberg. 2006. *The Evolution of the Trade Regime: Politics, Law and Economics of the GATT and the WTO*. Princeton: Princeton University Press.

---

[31] Oyejide 2000, 116.
[32] Baldwin 2000, 37.
[33] WTO, *The GATT Years*; Barton et al. 2006, 23.

Catudal, Honoré M. 1960. *The 1960–61 GATT Tariff Conference*. Department of State Bulletin 6958. Washington, DC: Office of Public Services.

Coppolaro, Lucia. 2010. Trade, Security, and GATT: The United States, Western Europe, and the Political Economy of Trade Liberalisation (1947–1972). Paper presented at Unpeaceable Exchange: Trade and Conflict in the Global Economy workshop, July, Lisbon, Portugal.

Diebold, William, Jr. 1996. From the ITO to GATT—and Back? In *The Bretton Woods–GATT System: Retrospect and Prospect after Fifty Years*, edited by Orin Kirshner, 152–73. Armonk, NY: M. E. Sharpe.

Eckes, Alfred E., Jr. 2000. *Revisiting U.S. Trade Policy: Decisions in Perspective*. Athens, Ohio: Ohio University Press.

Evans, John W. 1971. *The Kennedy Round in American Trade Policy: The Twilight of the GATT?* Cambridge, MA: Harvard University Press.

Forsberg, Aaron. 1998. The Politics of GATT Expansion: Japanese Accession and the Domestic Political Context in Japan and the United States, 1948–1955. *Business and Economic History Review* 27 (1):185–95.

Gardner, Richard. 1996. The Bretton Woods–GATT System after Fifty Years: A Balance Sheet of Success and Failure. In *The Bretton Woods–GATT System: Retrospect and Prospect after Fifty Years*, edited by Orin Kirshner, 181–212. Armonk, NY: M. E. Sharpe.

Irwin, Douglas A. 2009. *Free Trade Under Fire*. 3rd edition. Princeton: Princeton University Press.

Irwin, Douglas A., Petros C. Mavroidis, and Alan O. Sykes. 2008. *The Genesis of the GATT*. Cambridge: Cambridge University Press.

Jackson, John. 1989. *The World Trading System: Law and Policy of International Economic Relations*. Cambridge, MA: MIT Press.

Jackson, John H. 2000. *The Jurisprudence of GATT and the WTO: Insights on Treaty Law and Economic Relations*. Cambridge: Cambridge University Press.

Jackson, John H., Jean-Victor Louis, and Mitsuo Matsushita. 1984. *Implementing the Tokyo Round: National Constitutions and International Economic Rules*. Ann Arbor: University of Michigan Press.

Josling, Timothy E., Stefan Tangermann, and T. K. Warley. 1996. *Agriculture in the GATT*. Houndsmill: Macmillan.

Kimball, Warren F. 1991. *The Juggler: Franklin Roosevelt as Wartime Statesman*. Princeton: Princeton University Press.

Oyejide, T. Ademola. 2000. Low-Income Developing Countries in the GATT/WTO Framework: The First Fifty Years and Beyond. In *From GATT to the WTO: The Multilateral Trading System in the New Millennium*, edited by the WTO Secretariat, 113–22. The Hague: Kluwer Law International.

Preeg, Ernest H. 1970. *Traders and Diplomats: An Analysis of the Kennedy Round of Negotiations under the General Agreement on Tariffs and Trade*. Washington, DC: The Brookings Institution.

Riesman, Simon. 1996. The Birth of a World Trading System: ITO and GATT. In *The Bretton Woods–GATT System: Retrospect and Prospect after Fifty Years*, edited by Orin Kirshner, 82–8. Armonk, NY: M. E. Sharpe.

Shimizu, Sayuri. 2001. *Creating People of Plenty: The United States and Japan's Economic Alternatives, 1950–1960*. Kent, Ohio: Kent State University Press.

Winham, Gilbert R. 1986. *International Trade and the Tokyo Round Negotiation*. Princeton: Princeton University Press.

WTO. *The GATT Years: From Havana to Marrakesh.* Available from <http://www.wto.org/ english/thewto_e/whatis_e/tif_e/fact4_e.htm>. Accessed 6 November 2011.

WTO. *Plurilaterals: Of Minority Interest.* Available from <http://www.wto.org/english/ thewto_e/whatis_e/tif_e/agrm10_e.htm>. Accessed 6 November 2011.

WTO. 2007. *World Trade Report 2007: Six Decades of Multilateral Trade Cooperation: What Have We Learnt?* Geneva: WTO Publications.

Zeiler, Thomas W. 1992. *American Trade and Power in the 1960s.* New York: Columbia University Press.

Zeiler, Thomas W. 1999. *Free Trade, Free World: The Advent of GATT.* Chapel Hill, NC: University of North Carolina Press.

CHAPTER 6

THE URUGUAY ROUND NEGOTIATIONS AND THE CREATION OF THE WTO

ERNEST H. PREEG

6.1 INTRODUCTION

THE Uruguay Round, launched at Punta del Este, Uruguay, in September 1986, and concluded at Marrakesh, Morocco, in March 1994, was the most important and successful of the eight General Agreement on Tariffs and Trade (GATT) rounds of multilateral negotiations. Tariffs on non-agricultural trade were reduced substantially and a trade liberalization framework for agriculture was adopted. Trade in services and intellectual property rights were incorporated within the trading system. Dispute procedures were strengthened greatly and bilateral import quotas for textiles were phased out. Other noteworthy agreements were reached for trade-related investment measures, export subsidies, anti-dumping, government procurement, safeguards, sanitary and phytosanitary measures, and technical barriers to trade. And, although not part of the original negotiating mandate, the World Trade Organization (WTO) was created during the final phase of the negotiations, which incorporated all elements of the Uruguay Round Agreement and the long-standing provisions of the GATT.[1]

The presentation here is mostly chronological, with specific issues addressed as they reached a decisive point, for two reasons. First was the progressive course of the negotiations, with significant achievements during each stage, which stands in contrast with the prolonged Doha Round impasse over initial modalities for later specific negotiation. And second, the evolution of participation by developing countries, and differing posi-

---

[1] This chapter is based principally on Preeg 1995. Some footnotes refer to fuller presentations in the book, which include documentation and references. See also Preeg 2008.

tions within the grouping, provide relevant historical context for what subsequently happened in the WTO through a more rigid political dichotomy between developed and developing countries.

6.2 LAUNCHING THE URUGUAY ROUND (1979–86)

The Uruguay Round agenda began to take shape when the previous Tokyo Round was concluded in 1979.[2] Developing countries were greatly disappointed by the failure to agree on a more disciplined multilateral safeguards system, which permitted developed countries to impose temporary import restrictions to avoid injury to domestic industry, including a broad network of bilateral import quotas for textiles and apparel. The developing countries boycotted the ceremony to initial the final agreement, and negotiations were to continue on safeguards. Another unresolved issue was a strengthening of the GATT dispute settlement mechanism.

The initiative for a new round, as in the past, came from the United States, and in 1981 the new Reagan administration prepared a bold trade agenda, leading to a new GATT round that would concentrate on new issues—trade in services, trade-distorting investment measures, trade in high-technology industries, counterfeit goods, and transition of the more advanced developing countries to fuller compliance with GATT obligations—as well as on long-standing problems of agricultural subsidies and safeguards.

The new assault on agricultural subsidies was not welcomed by the Europeans, while developing countries wanted action on safeguards before opening a new round, which led to the failure of the US attempt to launch a new round at the November 1982 GATT ministerial meeting in Geneva. Despite the diplomatic disarray, however, ministers did agree on a comprehensive 1983–4 GATT work programme, including safeguards, textiles, dispute settlement, trade in services, and counterfeit goods, which was to set the stage for launching a new round.

A decisive point was the US call in April 1985 for a new round, in large part to counter growing protectionism in the United States. The US trade deficit was growing, and the 'bicycle theory' advised that the best way to counter protectionist forces was to roll forward with trade liberalization rather than to stand still. Continued US pressure led to agreement in October to begin formal preparation of the agenda for a new round, for adoption at a ministerial meeting at Punta del Este in September 1986. Negotiations over the new round agenda among the industrialized nations were contentious, especially over agriculture and a European Community (EC)[3] proposal for a 'balance of benefits' provision directed at Japanese non-tariff barriers, but progress was made during 1986. The participation of

---

[2] For an account of this initial period, see Preeg 1995, 24–59.

[3] The name change to European Union (EU) occurred in November 1993, towards the end of the Uruguay Round, and this name sequence is followed here.

developing countries in a new round was more complex, and a split in the grouping emerged. A group of 47 (G47) industrialized and developing countries submitted an ambitious draft ministerial declaration in July, while a hardline group of ten (G10) developing countries, headed by Brazil and India, provided an alternative draft with a far more limited scope of negotiation. Latin American nations were evenly split, with Chile, Colombia, and Mexico in the G47 and Argentina, Brazil, and Peru in the G10. Among the Asians, India alone was in the G10, while ten East and South Asians were among the strongest supporters of the G47 draft. China, of course, was not yet a member of the GATT.

The showdown meeting at Punta del Este was basically a victory for the comprehensive G47 agenda, whose membership had grown to 60, while the G10 became more and more isolated, and Brazil became more amenable to compromise.[4] For developing countries, the final provisions included liberalized textile and apparel import quotas, a reduction in barriers for tropical products, and a 'standstill' on new and a 'roll-back' of existing safeguard restrictions, although this immediate commitment was largely ignored in practice. The new issues of trade in services, investment measures, and more recent proposals for protection of intellectual property, were adopted. For agriculture, the United States and the Cairns group of developed and developing country agricultural exporters successfully pressed the EC to accept a three-pronged approach to liberalization, dealing with internal price supports, access for imports, and export subsidies. Other provisions of the declaration included reductions in non-agricultural tariffs, export subsidies and countervailing duties, strengthening of dispute settlement procedures, and improvements in various existing GATT codes and procedures. There was no mention, however, of possibly creating a new WTO.

The Punta del Este meeting was a watershed for the world trading system, for reducing barriers to trade and for broadening and strengthening the rules-based trading system. The prospect for success, however, was greeted with considerable scepticism, as by the *Financial Times*: 'Setting an agenda is one thing: repairing that worn fabric of the GATT by rewriting the rules and negotiating mutual concessions that would liberalize trade is another.'[5]

6.3 Specifying objectives and early harvest (1987–8)

Negotiations got off to a quick start. Fifteen negotiating groups were established by January 1987 to address the specific issues in the Punta declaration, and a mid-term ministerial meeting in Montreal in December 1988 was agreed. The United States pressed for an 'early harvest' of results to open export markets as a counter to growing protectionist

---

[4] For a detailed, primary source account of the Punta del Este meeting, see Preeg 1995, xi–xiv.
[5] *Financial Times*, 22 September 1986.

pressures from the record $150 billion US trade deficit in 1986. These pressures were to surface in the 1988 Omnibus Trade and Competitiveness Act, which gave President Reagan 'fast-track' authority for a prompt, up or down Congressional vote, without amendments, on the final agreement,[6] but also greatly expanded Section 301 authority for more aggressive unilateral actions to open foreign markets for US exports and investment, including protection of intellectual property. Section 301 became a factor in the Uruguay Round negotiations, whereby multilateral concessions in the round were viewed by some others as preferable to threatened unilateral US actions.

A broader cloud rising over the multilateral GATT negotiations, adding urgency to the Uruguay Round, was the prospect of competing bilateral and regional free trade agreements (FTAs). The emerging EC arrangement for market unification was viewed, especially among Asian exporters, as a growing 'Fortress Europe' against imports. President Reagan spoke of expanding free trade in the Western Hemisphere from Tierra del Fuego to the Arctic Circle, while the American Ambassador in Tokyo called for a US–Japan FTA. The Japanese Ministry of International Trade and Industry developed a New Asian Industrial Development Plan, which reminded some of the East Asia Co-Prosperity Sphere of the 1930s. Canadian Trade Minister, John Crosbie, opened the Montreal meeting proclaiming the recently concluded US–Canada FTA a catalyst and building block for multilateral trade liberalization, but many delegates were not convinced of the desirability of this two-track approach.

Another challenge for the negotiators was the status of the more advanced, and increasingly export-competitive, developing countries. GATT Part IV on trade and development elaborates special and differential (S&D) treatment for developing countries, including not to expect 'reciprocity for commitments during GATT negotiations', but the Punta declaration restated the 'Enabling Clause' of the previous Tokyo Round, that 'with the progressive development of their economies and improvements in their trade situation, developing countries would be expected to participate more fully in the framework of rights and obligations'. Greater reciprocity was pressed by the United States and the EC, especially with South Korea, other East Asians, and Brazil. Acting US Secretary of the Treasury, Peter McPherson, who had previously served for six years as the Administrator of the US Agency for International Development, condemned import substitution policies of some developing countries as 'built on false assumptions', and concluded that GATT S&D provisions 'are used as cover for protectionism that has nothing to do with development'.[7] Progressively greater reciprocity by the more

---

[6] In earlier rounds, the American president had limited negotiating authority, and the Kennedy Round final agreement included two provisions that required post-agreement Congressional approval. The Congress, however, did not approve them, simply by not bringing them to a vote. Therefore, to restore the president's negotiating credibility, the 'fast track' was created in the 1974 Trade Act for the Tokyo Round and repeated in the 1988 Trade Act.

[7] This 14 September 1988 speech was the final product of a post-Punta US interagency task force on Uruguay Round strategy and objectives for developing country participation in the round, chaired by the author, who was then serving as Chief Economist of the United States Agency for International Development (USAID).

advanced developing countries became a leitmotiv throughout the round, which stands in contrast to the 2001 Doha Development Agenda, which established a categorical dichotomy between developed and developing nations with respect to reciprocity.

The Montreal meeting produced mixed results. In terms of early harvest, import barriers were lowered for tropical products, of benefit to developing countries, although the trade impact was small, and strengthened GATT dispute procedures were implemented, for further development later in the negotiations. A comprehensive framework for trade in services was agreed, although commitments by sector, for actual market access, were left for later. Little reported at the time, bilateral textile and apparel import quotas were to be phased out, but with the schedule still to be agreed. Less progress was made on tariff reductions, beyond a 33 per cent average overall target, and no significant progress was made on anti-dumping and safeguards more broadly. Negotiation of an agreement on intellectual property rights also remained at the preliminary stage, with a number of developing countries, and India in particular, voicing strong reservations or opposition.

The central impasse at Montreal, however, was agriculture, which pitted the United States against the EC, with other agricultural exporters highly critical of both parties. The United States proposed total elimination of protection by 2000, which was clearly unacceptable to the EC, while the EC, in turn, proposed a freeze on current protection and some modest short-term reductions. Australian Trade Minister, Michael Duffy, referred to the United States and the EC as 'a pair of rippers', and concluded: 'I think we're staring down the barrel of an all-out farm trade war.'[8]

Principally as a result of the agricultural impasse, on 9 December 1988 GATT Director-General, Arthur Dunkel, suspended the Montreal mid-term review until April, and most press reports concluded that the meeting had been a failure. Lester Thurow, Dean of the Sloan School of Management at MIT, came close to impinging on Nieztschean intellectual property in pronouncing: 'GATT is dead.'[9] This obituary, however, was premature. One reason for suspending the talks was that both the US and the EU representatives were lame ducks. After winning re-election in November, President Reagan's new trade representative would not take over until early in the new year, as would a new EC Commission. Another positive result was that Dunkel was given the task of consulting in capitals to bring the positions closer together, which he did with consummate skill. And thus, by mid-April a mid-term package of agreements was reached. For agriculture, a freeze in support prices for 1989–90 was coupled with commitments for substantial progressive reductions of up to 100 per cent, including for export subsidies, while work was to begin on a multilateral framework for sanitary and phytosanitary regulations. As for intellectual property, India and other earlier resistors to any agreement accepted 'the importance of the successful conclusion of the multilateral negotiations' for trade-related aspects of intellectual property rights.

---

[8] *Journal of Commerce*, 12 December 1988.
[9] The Thurow statement was circulated in copier form. For reactions, see *Journal of Commerce*, 30 January 1989.

6.4 SHAPING THE FINAL PACKAGE (1989–90)

The second half period of negotiating group meetings, from April 1989 to summer 1990, was definitive in shaping the final Uruguay Agreement, scheduled for conclusion at a ministerial meeting in Brussels in December.[10] Among the issues that moved towards majority if not consensus support:

- a draft comprehensive agreement on safeguards, including time limits for temporary import restrictions
- a six- to ten-year phase-out of textile quotas
- an export subsidy agreement based on three categories of subsidies, one of which was 'actionable', meaning subject to countervailing duties
- general provisions for the framework agreement for trade in services
- alternative draft texts for a comprehensive intellectual property agreement.

Agriculture, however, remained at an impasse, and differences remained as to whether the one-third reductions in non-agricultural tariffs should be made on a formula basis or through itemized offer lists. In April 1990, Canada proposed the creation of a new World Trade Organization, although it was received coolly, as explained in Section 6.5 below. In any event, Director-General Dunkel instructed all negotiating groups to submit clearly defined issue 'profiles' as a basis for decision-making at senior levels, with only the most difficult issues left for the ministerial meeting in Brussels.

The Uruguay Round prospect leading up to the Brussels meeting was influenced by dramatic developments elsewhere, to both positive and negative effect. Most dramatic was the collapse of the Berlin Wall and communist regimes throughout Eastern Europe, replaced by democratically elected governments committed to market-oriented economic reforms, including free trade. Similar movements to elected governments and economic reform took place in South Korea, Taiwan, and throughout Latin America. GATT membership was growing, including Chinese accession negotiations and observer status for the Soviet Union. The principles of liberal trade and market-oriented prices, embedded in the GATT, became mainstream thinking for economic reform almost everywhere.

The precise role of the GATT multilateral trading system within a vaguely defined 'new world order', however, was less clear. Momentum continued to build for bilateral and regional free trade. The EC became deeply engaged in adjusting to a unified German economy and developing initiatives for broadening and deepening regional economic integration. The US–Canada FTA moved towards a North American agreement, including Mexico, and in June 1990 President Bush proposed an Enterprise for the Americas, with 'a comprehensive free trade zone for the Americas our long term goal'.[11] In

---

[10] For a detailed account of the Brussels meeting, see Preeg 1995, 100–21.
[11] White House press release, 27 June 1990.

November 1989, the Asia-Pacific Economic Cooperation (APEC) grouping had been established, which began discussion of more open, if not free, trade across the Pacific, and in December 1990 Malaysian Prime Minister, Mahathir Mohamad, proposed an East Asian economic grouping excluding the United States.

These far-reaching developments, while broadly supportive of more open trade, also competed with the multilateral approach pursued in the Uruguay Round, and distracted leaders from giving priority to the GATT negotiations. European leaders clearly gave top priority to developments within Europe. US leadership in the Uruguay Round faltered in the face of having to make difficult decisions, such as for the phase-out of textile quotas and reductions in farm subsidies. Projections of an increase in the US trade deficit as a result of the final agreement reduced political support further. The informal 'Quad' framework—the United States, the EC, Japan, and Canada—that had provided active joint leadership during the earlier phases, was relatively quiescent in 1989–90. Nevertheless, despite inner doubts, official optimism was widely expressed as the Brussels meeting approached, and, at its opening, the ubiquitous official poster blazoned the conference motto: 'World Trade: The Courage To Go Further.'

The objective of the Brussels meeting was for ministers to resolve the most difficult outstanding issues, leaving the final negotiations and conclusion of the agreement for early 1991, before US fast-track negotiating authority expired on 31 May. It was not an unreasonable goal, given sufficient political will, or 'courage'. The GATT Secretariat had prepared a heavily bracketed 391-page draft comprehensive agreement, and by the second day of the meeting reports indicated progress in most of the seven consolidated negotiating groups. Agriculture, however, remained at an impasse, with the EC more and more isolated, causing the other groups to begin to hold back. On the final day, the EC negotiators indicated that they could be more flexible on agriculture if other areas of the negotiation moved forward as well, and guarded relief permeated the conference centre as the late night final negotiating session approached.

The next morning, 7 December, the headline, 'Concessions break trade talks deadlock' led a *Financial Times* story that opened: 'The deadlock was broken in the Uruguay Round of talks to reform the world trade system last night after the European Community offered concessions on farm support and the United States shifted its position on services such as banking, telecommunications, and insurance.' The *Financial Times* prided itself on its full coverage of GATT issues, and all week free copies had been distributed at breakfast in hotels housing conference guests. Unhappy hubris. The story, signed by three reporters, got it wrong.

The press misreading stemmed from faulty EC decision-making. The Commission negotiators believed they had greater flexibility on agriculture and communicated this to others, but member state approval was still lacking, despite a prominently reported meeting between French President Mitterand and German Chancellor Kohl, and France still objected to any further concessions. During the night meeting, the EC simply restated its existing position, the US delegation became exasperated, and the Argentine and Brazilian delegates refused further negotiations. The following morning, amid gloom and confusion, the conference chairman suspended the negotiations and, once again, Director-General Dunkel was requested to pursue intensive consultations to resolve outstanding differences. Recriminations abounded and press reports were overwhelmingly negative. Much criticism focused on the EC and agriculture, while the United States stepped back as champion of last resort for the GATT multilateral system. US Secretary of Commerce, Robert Mosbacher, when asked about multilateral versus regional agreements, replied: 'We could be okay either way... In all truth, we're doing that now.'[12]

Ministers at Brussels failed to exhibit courage, and it would take another two years to resolve the agricultural impasse. And yet the Brussels negotiators did narrow the gaps on many issues and shaped the framework for the final agreement.

6.5 CONCLUDING THE AGREEMENT (1991–4)

Basic agreement could have been reached in December 1990 at Brussels if the agricultural impasse had been resolved, but the result would have been considerably narrower in scope than the final agreement ultimately signed in Marrakesh in April 1994. The extra three years of negotiation enabled substantial broadening and deepening of commitments on a number of fronts. Most importantly, the creation of the WTO to replace the GATT would not have happened if basic agreement had been reached at Brussels.[13]

Director-General Dunkel consulted in capitals and intensified negotiating group meetings during the spring and summer of 1991. Significant progress was made in most areas. One noteworthy breakthrough, with relevance to the long-standing Doha Round impasse, was for reduction of non-agricultural tariffs. The target of a one-third average reduction had bogged down over various formula proposals and the US preference for specific offer lists. Industrialized country private sector organizations then proposed a sectoral approach of 'zero-for-zero' free trade for some sectors, including farm machinery and toys, and harmonized low rates for other sectors, such as pharmaceuticals. This proved to be a more practical approach to demonstrate reciprocity and was pursued with success.

Agriculture, however, as well as a few other difficult issues, remained at an impasse. To force participants to move towards a package deal consensus, in December 1991 the Director-General circulated his 436-page 'Dunkel draft', which the EC found 'not acceptable' and the United States only supported with reservations. The text did focus the minds, however, and by late 1992 almost all issues had moved towards consensus, with the intent of reaching agreement by December so that the US Congress could approve it under the two-year extension of fast track authority, which expired in April 1993. But agriculture remained under intense negotiation as the French became more obdurate,

---

[12] *New York Times*, 4 December 1990.
[13] See Preeg 1995, 127–80, on this final phase of the negotiations.

and, on 5 November, EC Agricultural Commissioner, Ray MacSharry, resigned, accusing the French of sabotaging the negotiations.

At this point the agricultural impasse was broken through an extraordinary US diplomatic manoeuvre which demonstrated that history is often made, not through the dialectical forces in play, but by individual initiative. George Bush lost the presidential election on 3 November, and the expectation was for a hiatus in the Uruguay Round until the new Clinton administration was in place in early 1993. But Bush, and his Trade Representative, Carla Hills, continued on with a strong and credible ultimatum to the EC. The Uruguay Round agricultural package had always been linked to a bilateral problem over a $1 billion US loss of oilseed exports through the workings of the EC agricultural policy, on which GATT dispute panels had twice found in favour of the United States. On 6 November, Hills announced a 200 per cent oilseed retaliatory tariff on $300 million of white wine and other agricultural imports from the EC, effective from 5 December, with another $700 million of retaliation to follow. This was a make or break showdown for the Uruguay Round, since there was no way the lame duck American president would reverse this decision, and President Clinton, once in office, would be greatly reluctant to do so before consultations with the new, more protectionist Congress. Meanwhile, French wine and other EC farm exports would be paying 200 per cent extra duties. As a result, the French blinked, Mac Sharry was reinstated with a new mandate, and the 'Blair House Accord' of 20 November resolved the long-standing agricultural impasse, including deeper cuts in EC export subsidies and a compromise on US oilseed exports to the EC.

The Blair House agricultural accord opened the way to the final stage of Uruguay Round negotiations. President Clinton obtained yet another one-year extension of negotiating authority from the Congress, and his Trade Representative, Mickey Kantor, the 'fixer', worked closely with the new EC Trade Commissioner, Leon Brittan, the liberal trade 'ideologue'. A new GATT Director-General, former Irish Prime Minister, Peter Sutherland, added political forcefulness to the negotiating process. Progress was made on all fronts. Compromises were necessary on a number of issues, including some weakening of the Blair House agricultural accord.

In any event, time was short and final agreement had to be reached by 15 December 1993, in order to meet notification requirements of the US trade legislation. The two final substantive issues were not resolved until the night of 14 December. The ten-year phaseout of textile quotas was agreed when the Indian delegate accepted a commitment to 'achieve improved access' for imports by textile exporters, although this reciprocal commitment was never implemented. And for the Anti-Dumping Agreement, the United States obtained agreement for no changes in two key provisions, standards of review and anti-circumvention actions, which weakened enforcement. As for organizational reform, the creation of a new WTO was only approved by the United States on 15 December, when Director-General Sutherland was then able to announce, live on CNN, that a very far-reaching and historic trade accord had been achieved.

There were still many loose ends to resolve before the signing of the final agreement at Marrakesh, but no major problems were encountered. The sectoral lists for inclusion in the Services Agreement were broadened substantially, although they remained limited in scope by developing countries. An agreement on the relationship between trade and environmental policies was adopted—another example of a late-starting initiative that would not have been included at the time of the Brussels meeting. Implementation of this agreement, however, was left for a new WTO Committee, and its operations in practice have been lacklustre.

At the signing ceremony on 14 April, Moroccan King Hassan II welcomed this 'gigantic step forward towards broader and more intensive international cooperation'. The new challenges for cooperative leadership in world trade, however, under circumstances far different from those that prevailed during the Uruguay Round, would prove to be daunting and not long in coming.

6.6 THE CREATION OF THE WORLD TRADE ORGANIZATION

The creation of the WTO during the course of the Uruguay Round, with its far-reaching implications for the world trading system, deserves a more detailed presentation to conclude this historical account.[14]

The failure of governments to ratify the International Trade Organization (ITO) in 1948, while adopting the provisional GATT framework, with limited membership, led to four decades of discussion and proposals for a permanent trade organization. Some called for UN-style global membership. Others, especially after the failed 1982 GATT ministerial meeting, proposed a more restricted membership of like-minded free traders. As late as 1989, a study by American economist, Gary Hufbauer, in collaboration with a task force of 12 distinguished US trade experts, recommended the creation of an OECD Free Trade and Investment Area.

The 1986 Uruguay Round mandate did not include the creation of a new trade organization, but there were several objectives for institutional reform, including a more effective dispute settlement mechanism, country trade policy reviews by the GATT Secretariat, and ministerial meetings at regular intervals. Discussion of a new, permanent trade organization began in the Quad framework, in October 1989, at Canadian initiative, with support from the EC. The United States, however, was decidedly cool, if not negative, concerned about Congressional opposition over loss of sovereignty and the possibility that negotiations would shift towards institutional reform and away from the substantive objectives for trade liberalization.

In April 1990, Canada formally proposed the creation of the WTO, based largely on a January book by the American legal scholar, John Jackson, who served as a consultant to

---

[14] See Preeg 1995, 122–6 and 207–10, in particular.

the Canadian delegation.[15] Little headway was made through the December Brussels meeting, but more serious negotiations got underway during 1991–3, first in the Quad, and then in an expanded Geneva-based negotiating group.

Three issues became central to the outcome:

- *Decision-making.* The United States pressed for continuation of the GATT consensus approach, with qualified majority voting when necessary, on key issues. Others supported UN-style one-nation-one-vote majority voting, although in 1994 50 per cent of GATT members accounted for only 1 per cent of GATT exports. The final result was for decisions to be made by consensus or, failing this, on a one-nation-one-vote basis, with key decisions requiring a two-thirds or three-quarters vote, and with amendments to certain articles of agreement subject to unanimity.
- *Single undertaking membership.* There had been uncertainty as to how new agreements for trade in services and protection of intellectual property would relate to existing obligations for trade in goods. The WTO resolved this issue by bringing all provisions of the final Uruguay Round Agreement, as well as existing GATT commitments, within a single WTO undertaking, subject to the overall WTO management structures. Moreover, membership of the new organization required agreement on almost all provisions of the single undertaking. This was very different from earlier GATT rounds, where some developing countries did not sign the final agreement, and from earlier proposals, including the original Canadian proposal to have WTO global membership, with or without agreement to the final Uruguay Round obligations.
- *Strengthened and integrated dispute settlement procedures.* This had been the most important organizational objective throughout the Round, and dispute procedures were strengthened greatly in the final Agreement. The new WTO dispute mechanism tightened procedural disciplines, dropped earlier GATT veto power over the establishment of a dispute panel, even by the accused party, and established an appellate review procedure. The Agreement also permitted 'cross-retaliation' among components of the single undertaking, whereby, for example, retaliatory sanctions on traded goods could be applied for violation of intellectual property rights.

The final results from these three issues constituted a political trade-off between the developing countries, who wanted a stronger multilateral organization with enhanced influence within it, and the industrialized countries, who insisted on agreement to the full range of Uruguay Round commitments by developing countries as the price for WTO membership.

The United States continued to resist agreement on the WTO during the final phase of the negotiations, in part over continuing concern about Congressional support, and in part as a tactical ploy to gain concessions on other issues, but, as stated earlier, it finally

---

[15] See Jackson 1990. This book was the product of a public/private sector study group sponsored by Chatham House.

agreed to WTO creation on the final day of the negotiations. President Clinton did have difficulties with Congress, and had to make some concessions, including the establishment of a panel of retired US judges to monitor WTO dispute panel findings, followed by a Congressional vote on withdrawal from the WTO if the judges disagreed with the WTO panels three times in five years, but this never happened. Congress approved the Uruguay Round Agreement with large majorities, 288–146 in the House and 76–24 in the Senate.

Many questions remained as to how the WTO would operate in practice, and the first important decision, on selection of the first WTO Director-General, resulted in discord. Competing Italian, Mexican, and South Korean candidates eluded consensus, and the EU insisted on a one-nation-one-vote majority vote. The EU had 17 member state votes, ten pending new member votes, and numerous associated African state votes, and this carried the day for the Italian, Renato Ruggiero. It was a disturbing harbinger for WTO decision-making, on a different track from the long-standing GATT consensus approach.

6.7 THE FINAL AGREEMENT: A FORWARD-LOOKING ASSESSMENT

A full assessment of the final Agreement is beyond the scope of this chapter, and is, in fact, the substance of a number of other chapters in this work. The presentation here is limited to a brief listing of the principal elements of the final Agreement, to show the broad scope of accomplishment, and commentary on three overarching issues that have influenced the course of the WTO during its initial 15 years.

The principal elements of the final Agreement were:[16]

- *Market access for non-agricultural products.* The industrialized countries reduced tariffs on industrial products by 40 per cent, from 6.3 per cent to 3.8 per cent, and developing countries reduced their tariffs by 20 per cent, from 15.3 per cent to 12.3 per cent.
- *Agriculture.* Non-tariff import barriers were converted to tariffs, and all tariffs were reduced by 36 per cent for industrialized countries and 24 per cent for developing countries. Industrialized countries reduced export subsidies by 36 per cent in value and 21 per cent in quantity, and internal support prices by about 20 per cent.
- *Textiles and apparel.* Industrialized country import quotas were phased out over ten years.
- *Services.* The General Agreement on Trade in Services (GATS) provided a framework of rules and principles for trade in services, including most-favoured-nation

---

[16] See Preeg 1995, 190–201, for expanded summaries of these principal elements.

treatment, national treatment, safeguards, transparency, dispute settlement, and the free flow of payments and transfers. The framework agreement was complemented by country sectoral schedules of applicability, with coverage relatively complete for industrialized countries, but far less so for developing countries. The sectoral agreements for financial and telecommunications services were negotiated post-Uruguay Round.

- *Intellectual property rights.* The Agreement on Trade-Related Aspects of Intellectual Property Rights (TRIPS) established strengthened standards and the enforcement of these standards, including for patents, copyrights, trademarks, and geographic indicators.

- *Trade-related investment measures.* The Agreement on Trade-Related Investment Measures (TRIMs) reinforced GATT provisions, specifically including local content, trade-balancing, and foreign exchange-balancing requirements.

- *Anti-dumping.* The revised Anti-Dumping Agreement provided greater transparency and specification for anti-dumping procedures, but did little to strengthen the disciplines to restrict dumping and anti-dumping duties.

- *Export subsidies and countervailing duties.* The Agreement established clearer rules and stronger disciplines for subsidies related to trade, while exempting certain subsidies from countervailing duties.

- *Government procurement.* The Agreement strengthened the disciplines applicable to government procurement and expanded coverage to new areas of procurement. It was the only major part of the overall Uruguay Round Agreement that allowed voluntary rather than full participation by WTO members, with participation limited predominantly to industrialized nations.

- *Safeguards.* The safeguard provisions of GATT Article XIX were elaborated to ensure that such temporary import restrictions are transparent, temporary, degressive, and subject to review and termination.

- *Sanitary and phytosanitary measures.* This Agreement established rules and disciplines for measures taken to protect human, animal, and plant life and health in the areas of food safety and agriculture.

Other noteworthy sections of the Agreement dealt with import licensing procedures, customs valuation, pre-shipment inspections, rules of origin, technical barriers to trade, and revisions of various Articles of the GATT.

Three overarching and interacting issues, as they developed during the course of the Uruguay Round, have had follow-on importance for the course of the WTO trading system:

The WTO as an international institution. The WTO has risen towards becoming a global trade organization as membership has grown to include almost all substantial trading nations. The strengthened dispute settlement procedures have played a central and largely successful role in enforcing trade liberalization obligations and the rules-based system, both greatly extended in the Uruguay Round Agreement. Management and decision-making, however, have moved towards UN-style political groupings, principally on a developed versus developing country basis, which has slowed down and weakened further progress towards multilateral trade liberalization. Decision-making has tended towards a one-nation-one-vote basis rather than the dominant consensus process under the GATT, where major trading nations would not be voted down on significant issues. The informal yet decisive Quad leadership role during the Uruguay Round is no longer viable and needs to be replaced, most sensibly by a sextet leadership grouping consisting of Brazil, China, the EU, India, Japan, and the United States.

Multilateral trade liberalization versus bilateral and regional free trade agreements. This two-track trade policy path was largely competitive during the course of the Uruguay Round, and the competition has intensified post-Uruguay Round, with momentum clearly on the FTA track as the Doha Round bogged down in a ten-year impasse.[17] Most recently, FTA proliferation has centred on Asia. South Korea has concluded comprehensive free trade and investment agreements with the United States, the EU, and India, and is pursuing others, including with Japan and possibly China. India, in addition to South Korea, has concluded such an agreement with Singapore, is well advanced in negotiations with the EU, Japan, and Malaysia, and is pursuing others with South-east Asian trading partners and Canada. The obvious resolution to this competitive movement towards free trade would be to consolidate all existing FTAs within a multilateral, or plurilateral, FTA for non-agricultural trade, including at least the mature and newly industrialized nations that account for 90 per cent of global trade. This idea received noteworthy post-Uruguay Round attention. Fred Bergsten, director of the Washington-based Peterson Institute for International Economics, proposed such a free trade 'Grand Bargain' in 1996.[18] The opening US position in the Uruguay Round for non-agricultural trade was multilateral free trade, which was supported by some other nations, but rejected by the EU, China, and India. A book-length assessment, *From Here to Free Trade in Manufactures: How and Why*, was presented by the author at the WTO Cancún Ministerial in 2004.[19] Since 2004, however, there has been little official interest in consolidating the ever-growing number of FTAs.

The increasingly irrational dichotomy between developed and developing economies. This has become the most detrimental issue for an effectively functioning WTO, including its impact on the two previous issues. Greater obligations by the more advanced and export-competitive developing countries towards 'graduation' was a major issue throughout the Uruguay Round, as recounted here, and the more advanced developing countries did take on relatively greater obligations. The North–South dichotomy issue, moreover, in stark and ironic contrast, has largely disappeared on the FTA track, wherein both developed and developing country participants see a mutual interest in going to

[17] For the initial post-Uruguay Round interaction between the WTO and FTAs, see Preeg 1998, especially essays 3, 4, and 5, which deal with Transatlantic, Western Hemisphere, and Transpacific regional trade relations respectively.

[18] Bergsten 1996.

[19] Preeg 2004. The book elicited some lively discussion among observers and media representatives at Cancún, but official delegates quickly became sidetracked and secluded in futile debate over agriculture.

free trade, usually resulting in the developing country undertaking relatively greater reductions in import and investment barriers because its barriers were much higher to begin with. In the Doha Round, however, the Tokyo and Uruguay Round Enabling Clause provision for more trade-competitive developing countries 'to participate more fully in the framework of rights and obligations' was jettisoned and replaced by a categorical dichotomy, most graphically illustrated by the differential formulas proposed for trade liberalization, with much weaker obligations for all developing countries.

The increasing irrationality of this categorical dichotomy is highlighted by China's dramatic rise during the first decade of the twenty-first century, which coincided with the troubled course of the Doha Round, to displace the United States as the number one exporter of manufactures, the dominant sector of trade. In 2000, US global exports of manufactures were three times larger than Chinese exports, while by 2010 Chinese exports were half as large again as US exports, and on track to double them in two to three years. In parallel, China has maintained an unprecedented trade surplus in manufactures, and the United States an unprecedented deficit.[20]

'What's to be done?', to borrow from Lenin. In simplest terms, the three issues presented here need to be addressed as the integrated challenge they pose.[21] Restoration of the WTO as the dominant centre of a multilateral trading system will require bold and concerted leadership, especially among the big six. The principal objective should be the consolidation of the ever-growing number of FTAs within a multilateral free trade agreement for non-agricultural trade, that includes at least the mature and newly industrialized country groupings. Such an agreement would also facilitate substantial trade liberalization for agriculture and services. And these two steps, by definition, would greatly reduce the divisive North–South dichotomy issue, except for warranted special treatment for the poorest, least developed countries.

The outlook for this actually happening is bleak. The big Six, in particular, would need to display far more courage and foresight than they have yet done. But a starting point, at least, would be serious discussion of the lessons of history, and why, in particular, the Uruguay Round was a sweeping success, while the Doha Round appears to be headed towards a modest, face-saving conclusion, or worse.

REFERENCES

Bergsten, C. Fred. 1996. Globalizing Free Trade: The Ascent of Regionalism. *Foreign Affairs* 75 (3):105–20.

Jackson, John. 1990. *Restructuring the GATT System*. London: Royal Institute of International Affairs.

Preeg, Ernest H. 1995. *Traders in a Brave New World: The Uruguay Round and the Future of the International Trading System*. Chicago: University of Chicago Press.

---

[20] For a full analysis of this dramatic changing of places, including the large and growing majority of Chinese exports in high-tech industries, see Preeg 2005, 2011.

[21] For a more detailed and broader assessment of the content of this paragraph, see Preeg 2010.

Preeg, Ernest H. 1998. *From Here to Free Trade: Essays in Post-Uruguay Round Trade Strategy.* Chicago: University of Chicago Press, and Washington, DC: The Center for Strategic and International Studies.

Preeg, Ernest H. 2004. *From Here to Free Trade in Manufactures: How and Why.* Washington, DC: Manufacturers Alliance/MAPI.

Preeg, Ernest H. 2005. *The Emerging Chinese Advanced Technology Superstate.* Washington, DC: Manufacturers Alliance/MAPI and the Hudson Institute.

Preeg, Ernest H. 2008. *India and China: An Advanced Technology Race and How the United States Should Respond.* Washington, DC: Manufacturers Alliance/MAPI and the Center for Strategic and International Studies.

Preeg, Ernest H. 2010. *Restoring Bretton Woods: An International Economic System Overtaken by Success.* Washington, DC: Manufacturers Alliance/MAPI.

Preeg, Ernest H. 2011. *The United States and China Trade Places: Trade in Manufactures During the First Decade of the Twenty-First Century and How the United States Should Respond.* Washington, DC: Manufacturers Alliance/MAPI.

PART III

PROCESS BEHIND THE WORKINGS OF THE WTO

CHAPTER 7

....

THE ROLE OF THE DIRECTOR-GENERAL AND THE SECRETARIAT

....

RICHARD BLACKHURST[*]

7.1 INTRODUCTION

....

THE World Trade Organization (WTO) serves two principal functions: it provides (1) a set of multilaterally agreed rules governing policies affecting both trade in goods and services, and the protection of intellectual property; and (2) a forum for administering the rules, settling trade disputes, and pursuing negotiations to reduce trade barriers and strengthen and extend the multilateral rules.

Two groups of specialists are, in turn, involved in carrying out the second of these two functions—the member countries, or more specifically their representatives in Geneva plus support staff in capitals, and the WTO Secretariat headed by the Director-General (DG).[1] From the perspective of the member countries, the DG and the Secretariat exist primarily to service the day-to-day needs of the member countries, as defined by those countries. To flag a theme that will reoccur in this chapter, there is less agreement on whether the DG and the Secretariat also have a responsibility to act as independent guardians of the WTO system.

---

[*] I am indebted to the GATT/WTO experts (mostly former Secretariat colleagues) who very kindly agreed to comment on an earlier version of this chapter. They will remain anonymous because the chapter may contain one or more conclusions that some of them either disagree with or would not like to be publicly associated with, even if the conclusions in question draw on their comments. I am, of course, fully responsible for any errors or shortcomings.

[1] 'Member countries' is not a technically correct term since the WTO includes some non-countries, such as Hong Kong, but it's less stuffy than the formal 'members'.

The chapter begins with a review of the DG's responsibilities and activities, first during the Uruguay Round years, and then during the years since the creation of the WTO in 1995. This is followed by a similar examination of the role of the Secretariat. Noting that the GATT is widely considered to have been one of the most successful of the post-war international organizations, the chapter considers the factors behind this success. The next section takes up the question of the present day role of the DG and the Secretariat, first by asking if the GATT model is working for the WTO, and then—faced with evidence that the influence of both on the work of the WTO has been declining in recent years—by evaluating proposals for strengthening the role of the DG and the Secretariat. The principal findings are summarized in the concluding section.

7.2 RESPONSIBILITIES AND ACTIVITIES

7.2.1 Director-General

Counting the current DG, Pascal Lamy (France), there have been five WTO DGs in 16 years: Peter Sutherland (Ireland), who was also the last DG of the General Agreement on Tariffs and Trade (GATT, the WTO's predecessor), Renato Ruggiero (Italy), Mike Moore (New Zealand), and Supachai Panitchpakdi (Thailand).[2]

The ad hoc procedures for selecting the DG that evolved under the GATT worked much less well in the selection of Sutherland's three successors,[3] with the result that in December 2002 the member countries adopted a set of formal rules and procedures for appointing DGs.[4] They specify a term of four years, with the possibility of reappointment for a second term not exceeding four years (Lamy was reappointed for four years in 2009).

A starting point for a discussion of the role of the DG is to note that the member countries have never provided the DGs with a specific job description. This lacuna was supposed to have been corrected in the WTO, with the Marrakesh Agreement establishing the WTO stating 'The Ministerial Conference shall...adopt regulations setting out the powers, duties, conditions of service and term of office of the Director-General.'[5]

---

[2] Including Sutherland, the GATT had four DGs in 46 years: Eric Wyndham White (United Kingdom), Olivier Long (Switzerland), and Arthur Dunkel (Switzerland). All references to the GATT in this chapter are to GATT 1947—that is, to the original GATT as amended (GATT 1994 is part of the WTO and is the umbrella treaty covering trade in goods). See World Trade Organization 1995, 485–558, for the full text of GATT 1947 as amended.

[3] For example, a deadlock over who would replace Ruggiero was resolved by having Moore and Supachai each serve a 'non-renewable' three-year term rather than either of them getting a four-year term with a strong likelihood of renewal for another four years (thus they were lame ducks from day one). It's not an accident that one was from a developed country and one from a developing country. It's also not an accident that all the DGs prior to Moore were Europeans.

[4] WTO 2003.

[5] WTO 1995, Article VI.2.

While the easy parts of this task have been, necessarily, fulfilled, the important part—setting out in writing the powers and duties of the DG—has not.[6]

With little or nothing in the way of a written job description, a discussion of the role of the DG necessarily turns to actual experience. What, exactly, have DGs spent their time doing?

7.2.1.1 *The Uruguay Round years*

It's useful to begin by looking at the Uruguay Round years, including the preparatory period prior to the formal launch of the negotiations in 1986. Along with providing a better perspective, including the activities of the DG in the last years of the GATT allows us to take advantage of a detailed, virtual diary-like record of the Uruguay Round years (there is nothing comparable for the WTO years).[7]

In the early 1980s, when the system was in very serious trouble, Dunkel visited capitals to discuss the state of the trading system, the underlying purpose being to develop working relationships and trust with trade ministers—when problems arise in Geneva, the DG needs to be able to deal directly with ministers. The visits very often included public speeches on the state of trade relations and, later, on progress in the negotiations.

As an ad hoc initiative in 1983, on his own authority and financed independently, Dunkel appointed seven eminent persons to 'study and report on problems facing the international trading system'. The Leutwiler Group's report put forth 15 recommendations that are generally credited with helping to shape the negotiations leading to the launch of the Uruguay Round.[8] Two years later he openly supported the need for a new round of negotiations. This action, which angered many developing countries—they accused him of taking sides on a very divisive issue—illustrates perfectly the potential for tension between the DG's role as an 'honest broker' and proposals that he (and the Secretariat) should also act as independent guardians of the WTO system.

Another, closely related, example of such a tension occurred in 1986 in connection with his role in putting forward a draft of the ministerial declaration to be issued at the end of the ministerial meeting that would launch the new round (the declaration outlined the structure, topics, and goals of the new round). As Croome notes, this earned

---

[6] The resulting impact on the DG's activities is one of the issues addressed in a 2004 report by a Consultative Board appointed by DG Supachai (WTO 2004). While the Board's report criticized the failure to provide a job description for the DG, a common view among several of the WTO experts who commented on a draft of this chapter was that a formal written job description would tie the DG's hands more than those of the member countries. One of them added, 'A job description will not help a DG who doesn't understand how to plan and lead a negotiation and one who does will not need a job description.' In a similar vein—and anticipating a discussion in the latter part of this chapter—more than one commentator expressed the view that a DG's independence and authority are mainly a function of his abilities, rather than something that is formally 'granted'.

[7] Croome 1995. Croome's account focuses on activities related to the new round, rather than on routine day-to-day responsibilities.

[8] GATT 1985.

him 'a series of rebukes in formal letters from the representatives of Brazil, India and other members of the hardliners as having, in their view, departed from total even-handedness'.[9]

Both before and after the launch of the new round, Dunkel chaired many informal meetings of senior officials on a variety of issues, including especially the many 'Green Room' meetings in the DG's small private conference room. These informal, off-the-record meetings, involving 20 to 30 heads of the main delegations interested in the particular issue being discussed, played an essential role in the negotiations. Once the new round was launched, he formally chaired important committees—in particular, the Trade Negotiations Committee at non-ministerial level meetings, and the Group on Negotiations on Goods.

On numerous occasions, Dunkel served as a 'mediator', including, importantly:

- in efforts to relaunch the Uruguay Round after the suspension in Brussels in December 1990
- in coordinating the preparation of the Draft Final Act Embodying the Results of the Uruguay Round of Multilateral Trade Negotiations (December 1991)
- as chair of the agriculture negotiating group—always the most contentious topic in the GATT—acting as an arbitrator and conciliator in the preparation of the draft agricultural agreement (he was the only DG to ever chair an agricultural negotiating group)
- in suggesting ways out of apparent impasses, particularly in the cases of the proposed Trade Policy Review Mechanism and the Agreement on Textiles and Clothing.

Occasionally a Director-General will set deadlines to pressure member countries to reach agreement, as Sutherland did in a general way after taking office in July 1993 and in a very specific way in November 1993, which led to the successful conclusion of the round in December. This effort was helped by Sutherland's personal stature as a former senior politician—at the time unprecedented for a GATT DG—which gave him access to the top levels of government.[10]

7.2.1.2 *The WTO years*

The DGs' principal activities from the birth of the WTO at the beginning of 1995 until the launching of a new round of negotiations in 2001—the Doha Development Agenda (DDA)—included implementing the Uruguay Round agreements, assisting with the negotiations on the Financial Services Agreement (which had not been completed in the Uruguay Round) and the Information Technology Agreement, as well as negotiations leading to the Singapore Ministerial Declaration (1996) and subsequent work programme, to the Protocol on Basic Telecommunications (1998), to the Seattle Ministerial meeting (1999), and to the launch of the DDA.

---

[9] Croome 1995, 30.

[10] He had been Ireland's Attorney General, and a Commissioner of the European Communities, where he was responsible for competition policy (his other Commission dossiers were Social Affairs, Education and Relations with the European Parliament).

With the launch of the Doha Round, the DGs once again chaired the Trade Negotiations Committee (TNC) at non-ministerial level meetings, and used 'Green Room' meetings and public speeches to try to move the negotiations forward. As has already been noted, in 2003 Supachai put together a Consultative Board, chaired by former DG Sutherland, to examine the WTO and 'clarify the institutional challenges that the system faced and to consider how the WTO could be reinforced and equipped to meet them'.[11]

The Doha Round negotiations have not gone well, and much of the current DG's time has been devoted to keeping the round alive, particularly in his capacity as Chairman of the TNC. Other activities include acting as the principal coordinator of the Aid for Trade programme and, in response to the financial and economic crises that began in 2008, developing a programme for monitoring trade policy developments more frequently. He also represents the WTO at meetings of the G20, the International Monetary Fund (IMF)-World Bank and OECD ministers.

An important dimension of the DG's day-to-day activities involves his relations with the heads of the Geneva delegations, typically ambassadors. Prior to Sutherland's taking over in July 1993, GATT DGs had been relatively senior civil servants who dealt with the Geneva ambassadors from a position of more or less 'equal rank'.

The relationship with the Geneva ambassadors became more complicated when senior political figures took over the DG's job, beginning with Sutherland, followed by Ruggiero (former Director-General for regional policy at the European Commission, Italy's Ambassador to the EC, and Italy's Minister for Foreign Trade), Moore (former Minister of Foreign Affairs and Prime Minister of New Zealand), Supachai (former Deputy Prime Minister of Thailand and Minister of Commerce), and Lamy (Trade Commissioner at the European Commission). Relative to the previous DGs, they were in a much better position to cultivate personal working relationships with trade ministers in capitals—relationships that can be, as was noted above, very valuable when negotiations in Geneva are not going well. At the same time, those relationships complicate the DG's working relations with the Geneva ambassadors, who understandably resent anything that suggests the DG is going 'over their heads' or 'behind their backs'. A closely related factor in their willingness to work with him is the extent of the DG's willingness to work with them as 'equals'. It's a delicate balancing act that some DGs have been better at than others.

7.2.2 The Secretariat

For an international organization regularly mentioned in the popular as well as financial press, the WTO has a surprisingly small secretariat.[12] From Table 3 we see that the

---

[11] WTO 2004, 2.

[12] Exactly who is counted as part of the WTO Secretariat varies among different writers. Some include the DG while others do not. The same holds for the Deputy Directors-General and for members of the Appellate Body Secretariat. In this chapter I include everyone except the DG and the seven Appellate Body jurists.

Table 3 Staff of selected international economic organizations

Organization	Staff in 2008/09
World Food Programme	10,197
World Bank	10,000
International Organization for Migration	7,127
United Nations Office for Project Services	6,000
Food and Agriculture Organization of the United Nations	3,418[a]
United Nations Development Programme	3,289[b]
Organization for Economic Cooperation and Development	2,500
Asian Development Bank	2,500
International Monetary Fund	2,478
International Labour Organization	1,900
European Bank for Reconstruction and Development	1,407
World Intellectual Property Organization	1,318
United Nations Environment Programme	1,089
United Nations Population Fund	1,031[c]
International Telecommunications Union	702
United Nations Industrial Development Organization	690
World Trade Organization	**621**
Bank for International Settlements	550
International Civil Aviation Organization	503
United Nations Conference on Trade and Development	400

a Figure for 2003
b Figure for 2007
c Figure for 2007

Secretariat's 621 full-time employees rank it 17th out of 20 major international economic organizations.[13] There are some organizations in the table ranked well ahead of the WTO that are virtually unknown outside their area of expertise. The staffs of its two 'sister' organizations, the World Bank and the IMF, are, respectively, 16 times larger and four times larger.

Secretariat staff members can be divided loosely into four broad groups by function. The activities of the first two—*senior management* (the four Deputy Directors-General and their office staffs) and *Secretariat-wide services* (administration,

---

[13] The figures in Table 3 were obtained primarily from the respective organizations' websites. They are not fully comparable for at least three reasons: some are only estimates (two are rounded to the nearest thousand, and four to the nearest hundred), it was not possible to put the figures for each institution onto a fully comparable basis (in terms of how consultants, temporary employees, and so forth are counted), and three figures are not current. In short, the figures indicate only approximate orders of magnitude. The Secretariat's budget (including the Appellate Body) in 2010 was 194 million Swiss francs (WTO 2010a).

personnel, informatics, languages, documentation and information management, and information and external relations)—are largely self-explanatory.

The third group—*staff dealing with specific subject areas*—provides support to member country representatives in the councils, committees and working parties/groups involved in:

(a) administering the agreements (agriculture, intellectual property, traded services, and so forth) and standing committees (development, trade and environment, accessions, and so forth)
(b) dispute settlement cases, and
(c) the negotiating rounds.

In addition to scheduling meetings, being sure the necessary documents are available and taking minutes, there can be more substantive assignments from committee chairmen—especially those involved in the negotiating rounds—such as preparing 'non-papers' and other material summarizing areas of agreement/disagreement, and making contributions on selected topics. For example, in the Uruguay Round, early work by the Secretariat on policy surveillance was a key input into the development of the Trade Policy Review Mechanism. Apparently, such substantive assignments have become less common in recent years (more on this below).

Two other areas of responsibility for staff members in the third group came out of the Uruguay Round—the Trade Policy Review Mechanism (TPRM) and the Appellate Body. Although they are completely separate and very different activities, they share one important trait, and that is that the member countries have formally delegated to the staff members involved in each activity—and especially to the Appellate Body jurists—much more autonomy, authority, and scope for initiative than has traditionally been the case for staff working in 'policy sensitive' areas.

It is true, in the case of the TPRM, that the member countries control outcomes via the Trade Policy Review Body, where a detailed report prepared by the Secretariat and a more general policy-oriented report prepared by the government under review are discussed. But the staff working on the Secretariat's report, whose responsibilities include a team visit to the country, have considerable independence.

In other words, they don't have the national delegates 'sitting on them' or 'keeping them under the thumb', as happens in many other areas of the Secretariat's work.

The seven jurists on the Appellate Body, which hears appeals of rulings by dispute settlement panels, are—effectively—totally independent of the member countries. Decisions by the Appellate Body can be rejected by the Dispute Settlement Body, but only if there is a consensus to do so, which means it is *very* unlikely to ever happen. That governments have granted this degree of independence to international civil servants in an area so politically sensitive is unprecedented, not only for the GATT/WTO system but for all international economic organizations. It is unique.

Although it might be expected that the member countries would ensure that the number of current staff in the third group provides an adequate level of essential support to the member countries, that is not necessarily the case. Not once during a 19-year period, for example, has the Trade Policies Review Division had the staff needed to produce the mandated number of annual reviews.[14]

Secretariat staff in the fourth group—*specialized support*—have a variety of responsibilities. The Economic Research and Statistics Division prepares two annual reports—*World Trade Report*, reviewing trends in world trade and in trade policies, and *International Trade Statistics*, the WTO's primary outlet for international trade statistics. Cooperation with other international economic organizations and the academic community is also an important part of the staff's activities, as are the special studies, discussion papers and staff working papers. Responsibility for maintaining both the Integrated Data Base and the Consolidated Tariff Schedules are examples of the Division's direct input into the WTO's operational activities. Relative to the rest of the Secretariat, the Division has been subject to very little overt 'oversight' by the member countries (a certain amount of 'self-policing' presumably goes on when selecting research topics).

Low income countries—especially the small and medium-sized ones—are often at a substantial disadvantage when it comes both to understanding their WTO rights and obligations and participating effectively in WTO activities, including trade negotiations. Designing, coordinating and implementing trade-related technical assistance to these countries is the responsibility of the Institute for Training and Technical Cooperation. Its activities, a majority of which are organized in cooperation with other international organizations, take place both in the member countries, as is the case with the three-month regional trade policy courses, and in Geneva—for example, the twice-yearly 'Geneva Weeks', when officials from WTO members and observers without permanent missions in Geneva are briefed on the Doha Round and other WTO activities.[15]

This is a convenient place to comment briefly on the kinds of training and prior experience to be found among the WTO's professional staff members. University degrees in either economics or international law are typical, while prior work experience centres heavily on national civil services, especially economic, trade and foreign ministries, plus (less often) university teaching. New staff members are rarely less than 30 years old and staff turnover is very low.

Anticipating the discussion later in the chapter of the extent of the Secretariat's responsibility to defend and promote the WTO system, it should be noted that it's very difficult to generalize about the views of individual staff members regarding proposals for a more independent and activist Secretariat. Many appear to be comfortable with a career limited to servicing the needs of the member countries. Others see their proper role as being more proactive, and want the Secretariat to show more initiative and independence on promoting freer trade and pursuing a higher profile role for the WTO in cutting-edge trade issues.

---

[14] Ghosh 2010, 447. His data cover 1989–2007. It should also be noted that most of the money for technical assistance activities comes not from the WTO budget but rather from voluntary contributions by a limited number of countries.

[15] The number of staff in the Institute (33) seriously understates the commitment of WTO resources to technical assistance, since the operating divisions—the ones in the third group (*staff dealing with specific subject areas*)—spend a considerable amount of time on technical assistance.

Up to this point, the focus has been on a moderately detailed description of the respective roles of the DG and the Secretariat, as they evolved in the latter part of the GATT years and in the first 15 years of the WTO. In the remainder of this chapter we step back to consider their roles from a broader, more general perspective. This offers a chance, first of all, to examine the extent to which those roles have contributed to the organization's success, and second to explore proposals for improving their respective contributions.

7.3 SECRETS OF SUCCESS

The GATT is widely considered to have been one of the most successful—if not the most successful—of the post-war international economic organizations. At the same time, the member governments not only kept the size of the Secretariat much smaller than that of most other international economic organizations, but also granted less authority and scope for initiative to the DG and the Secretariat than to virtually any other international organization.

On the issue of the authority and scope for initiative, consider the following:

- The DG cannot initiate a dispute settlement case, nor are the DG or the Secretariat permitted to interpret definitively (or publicly) WTO rules, or to pass judgement on the conformity of a country's behaviour with those rules (for example, in the Committee on Balance-of-Payments Restrictions, only the committee members can pass judgement).[16] With very rare exceptions, Secretariat staff are not allowed to chair committees, working parties and so forth.
- Despite its role in servicing a rules-based agreement involving *contractual* obligations, the Secretariat had to wait until 1983—35 years—to have a formal legal adviser and an Office of Legal Affairs. This contrasts with, for example, the IMF, which had a General Counsel and a Legal Division from day one. There is a mind-set behind this—a view of the Secretariat's appropriate role—that has by no means disappeared.
- A quote from the WTO website sums up the situation: 'Since decisions are taken by Members only, the Secretariat has no decision-making powers.'

As the earlier discussion of the roles of the DG and the Secretariat made clear, they played an active role in the run-up to the Uruguay Round, in the negotiations once the round was launched, and in the period since the WTO came into being—although apparently less so in recent years. Obviously, they are by no means powerless to influence member countries' decisions and, more generally, the course of the WTO's work.

---

[16] Secretariat staff from the Legal Division, as well as other divisions, do play a significant role in interpreting WTO rules when they advise dispute settlement panels, often drafting the panel reports. But the final decisions on interpretation are made by the panel members, not by Secretariat staff.

But on a broader level, there is also no doubt that the member countries consciously keep the DG and the Secretariat on a leash that is, if not always very short, never very long. They want the DG and the Secretariat to be helpful—and in past years they have offered a number of opportunities for them to be so—but they insist on maintaining full discretion over when, where and how. The scope for any kind of independent initiative that runs counter to the wishes of the member countries at a particular point in time—especially those of the major players—is extremely limited.[17]

This raises intriguing questions. Did limiting the roles of the DG and the Secretariat contribute to GATT's success? And is it helping or hurting the WTO at a time when a prolonged lack of progress in the Doha Round is giving rise to concerns about the effectiveness and future of the WTO?

Certainly there have been times, for example in the late 1970s and early 1980s, as the trade policy behaviour of the major countries increasingly threatened GATT's survival, when the inability of the DG and the Secretariat to more forcefully protect the integrity of the GATT system could be seen as a serious shortcoming. But this begs the question of exactly what they could have done—beyond what the DG did in the years leading up to the launch of the Uruguay Round—had they had more independent authority? It seems highly unlikely, for example, that a series of dispute settlement cases filed by the DG would have put an end to voluntary export restraint agreements. On the contrary, it's very likely they would have seriously worsened an already stressful situation.

A more compelling view is that the success of the GATT was due in very large part to, first of all, the active leadership and support of the major countries, especially that of the United States in the early years, and second to the decisions to (a) construct the post-war trading system on a foundation of *contractual rules*,[18] and (b) give very little authority and right of initiative to a group of independent international civil servants.

As the Canadian political scientist, Gilbert Winham, has noted:[19]

> In the relatively brief history of international organization, states have made greater efforts to establish strong organizations than to establish strong rules. The success of the GATT/WTO 'contract' regime is a reminder that in an international system with sovereign actors, rules rather than formal organization may be a better basis on which to promote international cooperation.

As for the second decision, in a rules-based organization there is much less need for the DG and the Secretariat to play 'activist' roles such as those played by the heads of the World Bank and the IMF and their respective secretariats (the 'strong organization' model). They exist to help the member countries run a rules-based system, and that obviously requires not only many fewer people than the major international economic organizations with 'activist agendas', but also less authority and scope for independent

---

[17] See Elsig 2010a, 7, for further evidence of this short leash.

[18] GATT's initial rules and disciplines drew heavily on the draft charter of the stillborn International Trade Organization (ITO).

[19] Winham 1998, 366. Elsewhere in the article, he contrasts a 'rules-first' approach with an 'organization-first' approach.

action. Moreover, in policy-sensitive areas a 'member-driven' organization is likely to be more viable precisely because it ensures that the organization is fully—indeed exclusively—responsive to the members' perceived needs. Knowledge that there was no risk of anonymous international officials dictating policy in such a politically sensitive area of the economy was crucial to maintaining political support for the organization in the member countries.

In short, there are good reasons for believing that the limited roles of the DG and the Secretariat—being a member-driven organization, in other words—along with contractual rules, were central to GATT's success.[20]

7.4 IS THE GATT MODEL WORKING FOR THE WTO?

A first step in answering this question is to note five important differences between the GATT years and the WTO period:

- *First*, there are many more members. At the end of 2011, the WTO had 153 members, with another 29 in the accession process, up from the GATT's 91 members at the beginning of the Uruguay Round in 1987. Moreover, the increase of 62 understates the increase in 'actively participating members' because of the big increase in technical assistance to developing countries under the WTO.[21]
- *Second*, trade in services and the protection of intellectual property rights have been added to GATT's traditional focus on trade in goods.
- *Third*, while under the GATT countries could block 'inconvenient' dispute settlement cases, in the WTO the process is automatic and there is no way a country can block an unfavourable decision. This makes countries want to be more involved in what's going on—making less room for the DG and the Secretariat—and more cautious about accepting new obligations.[22]
- *Fourth*, with the dramatic reduction in border restrictions, the search for ways to further liberalize world trade in goods and services has led countries further 'inside the border'—to health and safety regulations, legal systems and other 'values-based' dimensions of modern economies.[23]

---

[20] As is evident at the GATT/WTO, in a member-driven organization the counterpart to a much smaller Secretariat staff is a much larger number of resident national delegates devoted to the organization's work.

[21] Here it is important to note that the WTO does not have an 'executive board' as do, for example, the World Bank and the IMF. All WTO councils, committees and working parties/groups are open to all 153 WTO members.

[22] See, for example, Pauwelyn 2005b.

[23] WTO 2010b.

- *Fifth*, the emergence of rapidly growing, major developing countries—such as China, Brazil, and India—has greatly increased the role of developing countries in the organization's work.[24]

How have these changed circumstances affected the role of the DG and Secretariat under the WTO? Consider a spectrum at the left-hand end of which the roles of the DG and the Secretariat are limited to sharpening pencils, scheduling meeting rooms and translating/reproducing documents, and at the right-hand end of which the member countries have delegated considerable autonomy and authority to the DG and the Secretariat. During the GATT years the situation was between these two extremes—obviously it always will be, the question is where?—with some gradual movement in the direction of the right-hand end over time.

As for the WTO, recent research points convincingly to a leftward shift along the spectrum. Between the autumn of 2006 and spring of 2009, Elsig interviewed a former DG, 20 current and former, mostly senior, members of the Secretariat, and 12 current and former ambassadors to the WTO. Defining the Secretariat to include the DG, he concludes that 'the influence of the WTO Secretariat in international trade negotiations has been declining'.[25] Later he observes, 'The DG, his cabinet and in particular the Secretariat officials in the various divisions, seem to have lost standing during the negotiations as the chairing has been exclusively taken over by [local ambassadors] and in a number of areas their expertise is not adequately "used" by the chair and other [ambassadors]'.[26] Earlier, in 2004, the Consultative Board chaired by former DG Sutherland had already called attention to this trend.[27]

Elsig's interviews suggest that part of the explanation for this trend is 'an inherent rational interest of [WTO ambassadors] to stick to the model of a member-driven organization'.[28] He notes:

> in negotiations the [ambassadors] can actively engage, shape and influence processes...[they] can report to the capital (and domestic stakeholders) on their personal contributions in the form of negotiation proposals, important statements and coalition endeavors...[this] contributes to legitimizing [their] stay in Geneva and helps strengthen their positions within their own organizations...One way for

---

[24] Another change worth noting is the appointment of senior politicians, rather than senior civil servants, as DG. This has coincided with a dramatic shortening of the DG's term in office, from an average of 15+ years under the GATT (excluding Sutherland's brief tenure as GATT DG) to 3+ years under the WTO (the Deputy Director-Generals (DDGs) have suffered a similar dramatic shortening of tenure relative to the GATT years). It's true that under the new rules, the DG has a four-year contract which is renewable for another four years, and that given the typically very contentious selection process for the heads of the international organizations, it's likely the norm will turn out to be eight years—as is the case with the current DG (the first to be selected under the new rules). However, this will only partly redress the WTO's serious loss of 'institutional memory' at the senior management level.

[25] Elsig 2010a, 2; see also 3, 9–10.
[26] Elsig 2010a, 10.
[27] WTO 2004, 73.
[28] Elsig 2010a, 13.

ambassadors to increase influence and enhance reputation is through chairing one of the many Committees…Thus, delegating to the Secretariat means losing influence and deprives the ambassadors and their staff of opportunities to participate in activities within the WTO.[29]

The rational interest explanation gains strength when we factor in the combined impact of the big increase in the membership, the increase in the number of members capable of participating actively, and the emergence of China, India, and Brazil as major players in the global economy—changes that have significantly reduced the scope for the kind of informal politics and deal-making, aided by the DG and the Secretariat, that characterized the GATT era.[30] If so, a diminished role for the DG and the Secretariat may be inevitable.

7.5 A STRENGTHENED DG AND SECRETARIAT?

There is no shortage of proposals to reverse this trend by enhancing the authority and strengthening the roles of the DG and the Secretariat. From the Consultative Board report:

> A helpful starting point may be to see the Secretariat as the guardian of the treaties that comprise WTO law…the Secretariat and Director-General should get back to basics in the manner in which the WTO is presented and defended. On such a basis, the Secretariat could rightly lay claim to more independence of action and enhanced authority.[31]

And:

> It is vitally important to strengthen the role and authority of the Director-General and the Secretariat in the WTO.[32]

> There are various ways to empower the Secretariat. One option would be to formally increase the role of the Director-General and the Secretariat in managing negotiations[33]

> this chapter [identifies] the type of decision-making processes in which the Secretariat should be given a more active role:[34]

> Most participants to the discussion did not question the potential and/or the need for an enhanced role of the Secretariat, although they were critical with respect to the suggestion of the Sutherland Report that the Secretariat should become a 'guardian of the treaties'.[35]

---

[29] Elsig 2010a, 13. See 14–15 for additional supporting anecdotal evidence.
[30] I'm grateful to Manfred Elsig for this point.
[31] WTO 2004, 77.
[32] Steger and Shpilkovskaya 2010, 145.
[33] Elsig 2010b, 72.
[34] Alvarez-Jiménez 2010, 114.
[35] Van den Bossche and Alexoviovà 2005, 689.

However, support for strengthening the roles of the DG and the Secretariat is far from universal. Consider, for example, the following remarks by two GATT/WTO experts:

> The efforts of the Consultative Board to relegate NGO relations to the Secretariat is part and parcel of the general thrust in the CB Report to expand the Secretariat's resources and give it new duties in interface with the public...In my view, this recommendation is not well considered. Selling the benefits of the WTO should be the role of elected officials, cabinet ministers, advocacy organizations, journalists, educators, etc., not the role of international civil servants...The Director-General of the WTO is an exception to some extent and I would give her or him greater latitude to act as a human voice for the WTO. [four footnotes omitted][36]

Or:

> Although the [Sutherland] report is correct that the WTO Secretariat needs to take a more proactive stance in explaining the benefits of liberalized trade and connecting with civil society, it is too early...to confer 'a parallel responsibility' on the WTO Secretariat 'as guardian of the system' or 'Guardian of the Treaties...to act in the common interests of the Members'. Put differently...it would be premature to convert the intergovernmental WTO Secretariat into a supranational EU-Commission type construct with independent powers and heavy handed steering by a Jacques Delors type WTO Director-General. [two footnotes omitted][37]

Two additional issues raised by proposals to increase the authority and independence of the DG and Secretariat concern, first, what new activities might be pursued, and second, whether those new activities would be compatible with current responsibilities.

7.5.1 More authority and independence to do what?

When considering proposals to 'revitalize' the roles of the DG and the Secretariat, it's helpful to keep in mind the distinction between (a) their activities connected to helping the delegations to administer the rules, settle trade disputes, and negotiate reductions in trade barriers, and (b) their activities connected to being 'guardians of the system'.

With respect to both types of activities, there are few, if any, formal constraints on what the DG can do (the flip side of not having a written job description). Presumably more authority and independence would mean that he could engage in more activities— take more initiatives—without risking his relations with the local ambassadors and ministers in capitals.[38] But what new activities and initiatives?

---

[36] Charnovitz 2005, 318–19.

[37] Pauwelyn 2005a, 342. For a more purely political critique of proposals to strengthen the roles of the DG and Secretariat, based on a perceived lack of direct democratic legitimacy, see Petersmann 2005. Shaffer 2005, 435, also touches briefly on legitimacy concerns, linking them to the risk of a political backlash against any attempt to create a stronger and more independent DG and Secretariat.

[38] Elsig 2010a, 14–15, is particularly good on this point.

The Consultative Board report posits a choice between a DG who travels widely and often, developing contacts with ministers and acting as the international advocate for free trade, and a DG who focuses primarily on leading/managing the Secretariat and working with heads of delegations in Geneva. As a practical matter, an effective DG may well have to do both, the challenge being to find the correct balance between the two. As examples of Geneva-based activities, the report mentions giving the DG more of a chairmanship role in various committees and councils (the General Council is specifically mentioned), and, to quote from the report's list of principal conclusions and recommendations, 'The Director-General and Secretariat should have the capacity and the standing to be at the centre of negotiations during Ministerial meetings.'[39]

On a broader level, there is the suggestion that the DG and the Secretariat have a responsibility as 'guardian[s] of the system ... to act in the common interests of Members'.[40] At least three categories of 'guardians of the system' activities can be envisioned. The first involves regularly praising multilateralism, freer trade, and the WTO system in speeches and publications. No problem here—it's already done all the time. In a similar vein, at the request of the member countries the Secretariat has taken the lead on a programme of outreach to journalists and non-governmental organizations.

A second 'guardian' category involves monitoring trade policy developments, alerting members to protectionist trends and other threats to the WTO system, and warning against protectionist reactions to economic disturbances. Again, there are many examples from past speeches and GATT/WTO publications of this kind of activity—from early warnings on voluntary export restraints (VERs) and the spread of preferential trade agreements, to Dunkel's initiative in creating the Leutwiler Group and Supachai's in appointing the Sutherland Group.

The latest example of this kind of activity is especially noteworthy. As the recent financial and economic crises unfolded, and concerns about the risk of protectionist reactions were on the rise, the DG had the Secretariat begin informally monitoring and reporting on trade policy actions more frequently than the annual review mandated under the Trade Policy Review Mechanism—a more frequent monitoring that has become even more important as the debate over possible currency manipulations intensifies. When they became aware of these reports, the member countries liked them and asked the DG to continue the effort, as did the G20, which gave the Secretariat a formal mandate. The Secretariat has considerable independence and discretion over what to publish—for example, it was decided that the reports should cover all trade measures, not just 'illegal' ones. The report appeared four times in 2009, then moved to twice a year beginning in 2010. All this suggests that the member countries are prepared to accept a

---

[39] WTO 2004, 82. After endorsing this recommendation, Elsig continues: 'A more radical approach to strengthening the Secretariat within decision-making would consist of transferring agenda-setting prerogatives to the Director-General.' Elsig 2010b, 72.

[40] WTO 2004, 73.

fair amount of independence and initiative on the part of the DG and the Secretariat for such activities.[41]

From this brief look at the first two categories of guardian activities it is obvious that for at least the past three decades the DG and the Secretariat have been actively engaged as 'guardians of the system'. It's not a new assignment—they've been doing it all along.

A third category of possible 'guardian' activities involves taking positions on important issues on which the member countries are divided. Few, if any, delegations seem to have a problem with this, *provided* the DG and the Secretariat limit themselves to lobbying the delegations privately in their day-to-day dealings with them. Many of Dunkel's and Sutherland's activities during the Uruguay Round, brokering compromises on issues threatening the negotiations, can be put in this category.

Going public with positions on such issues is an entirely different matter. Mention has already been made of the strong reaction of developing countries in 1985 when Dunkel publicly supported the need for a new round of negotiations, and again in 1986 when he openly supported a particular draft of the ministerial declaration to be issued at the end of the ministerial meeting that would launch the new round.

Even more problematic was a GATT Secretariat study on bringing rules and disciplines on foreign direct investment into the GATT, published just before the 1996 Singapore ministerial meeting. Given the reactions this generated among the delegations, it seems very unlikely that they will ever again let the Secretariat publicly 'get out ahead of them' on a major issue (see below for details).

There is a hypothetical fourth category of possible 'guardian of the system' actions—hypothetical in the sense that there have been no past activities that fall in this category, nor are there ever likely to be any—but which nevertheless is worth mentioning to illustrate a point. It's not difficult to find trade policy people, especially in developed countries, who lament the fact that the GATT/WTO system is no longer focused exclusively on reducing barriers to trade on a non-discriminatory basis and resolving trade disputes. For them, being guardians of the system would have involved the DG and the Secretariat in actively and publicly resisting such 'innovations' as:

(a) introducing special and differential treatment for developing countries
(b) providing large-scale technical assistance to developing countries (together with (a), critics say this has turned the GATT/WTO into a development agency, of which there were already several in existence, beginning with the World Bank; note that the WTO negotiating round launched in 2001 bears the overall title of the 'Doha Development Agenda'), and

---

[41] For additional details see Pauwelyn and Berman 2009. Other examples of DG and Secretariat initiative include: (a) in 2001 the WTO, in cooperation with Cambridge University Press, launched a new professional journal entitled *World Trade Review*, the editor of which, and all but one of the editorial board members, are independent academics; (b) the publication of a joint study with the International Labour Organization on trade and employment (see Charnovitz 2008); and (c) the publication of a joint study with the United Nations Environment Programme on trade and climate change (see Charnovitz 2010).

(c) bringing intellectual property into the WTO, making the WTO the enforcement arm of the World Intellectual Property Organization.

Of course, not only did this opposition not happen, it could not have happened. At the first sign of active and public opposition by the DG and Secretariat to any of these new activities, powerful coalitions of member countries would have simply put a stop to it— they would not have tolerated it.

To be 'guardians of the system' implies there is an accepted definition of exactly what the 'system' is that is being guarded. And the answer is clear—it's whatever system the member countries want it to be. If they want to expand the WTO's mandate to include things other than reducing trade barriers and resolving disputes, they will. The DG's and the Secretariat's views are irrelevant.

7.5.2 Can 'honest brokers' also be 'guardians of the system'?

It depends. Guardian activities in the first two of the three categories just described do not interfere with the honest broker role. Those in the third category can interfere, especially when they involve taking a public position on a contentious issue which has direct or indirect implications for members' legal rights and obligations. Dunkel's decision to publicly support the launching of a new round, and his subsequent decision to support a particular draft of the declaration that launched it, simultaneously defended the GATT system and undermined his credibility as an impartial, honest broker at a time when there were high-stakes differences between the member countries.

Another example of an inherent conflict between the two roles, this time involving the Secretariat, draws on a personal experience.[42] Early in 1996 the Economic Research Division proposed, and senior management agreed, that 'trade and investment' would be the special topic for that year's annual report. In anticipation of the Singapore ministerial meeting, scheduled for the end of the year, the question of whether the WTO should write rules governing trade-related investment was being intensely debated, making this (apparently) an excellent choice—one where the Secretariat could contribute to the member countries' decision-making by careful economic analysis of the various aspects of the issue.

Although we began the research with an open mind on the issue, the final report, distributed to the member countries and the press just before the Singapore meeting, ended up providing very strong support for adding rules governing trade-related investment to the WTO—a conclusion which, after some discussion, the senior management agreed to make explicit in the concluding section (a decision with which I very much agreed). A number of important WTO members reacted angrily to what they saw—understandably, in my view—as a serious breach of the Secretariat's

---

[42] The following three paragraphs draw on Blackhurst 2005, 385–6.

obligation to remain impartial.[43] Even the countries whose position on the issue was supported by the report were upset because they worried that next time they could be on the losing side.

Suggestions, such as the one in the Consultative Board report, that the WTO should be making 'a pre-eminent input into public and political debate' on trade-related issues and that 'It can do so without compromising the negotiating positions or policies of Members—nor, indeed, of its own advice' are a bit facile.[44] There will always be important instances in which the gap between the member countries' different aspirations for the WTO is too great for this to be workable.

7.6 CONCLUSIONS

Reviewing the GATT years, it was argued that the success of the GATT was due not only to the active leadership and support of the major countries in the early years, but very importantly to the decisions to base the post-war trading system on a foundation of *contractual rules* and to give very little independence and authority to the DG and the Secretariat—in short, that being a member-driven organization, along with contractual rules, was central to GATT's success.

The chapter then turned to the question of whether the GATT model is working for the WTO. Despite some evidence that the DG and Secretariat officials in the various divisions seem to be playing reduced roles, and that a diminished role may be inevitable, it is evident that for at least the past three decades the DG and the Secretariat have been actively engaged as 'guardians of the system'. As long as they avoid taking public positions on contentious issues on which the member countries are divided, there seems to be sufficient scope for initiative and independent action. The GATT model's approach to the roles of the DG and the Secretariat is working for the WTO.

It's hard not to conclude that calls for further enhancing the authority of the DG and the Secretariat risk being a modern equivalent of tilting at windmills. Meaningful change in this area is unlikely to happen, and it's by no means clear that the WTO would benefit significantly if it did. Put a bit differently, the WTO is confronting a number of serious problems but there are good reasons for believing that the solutions lie elsewhere. Those other areas are where we should be asking whether the GATT model is working for the WTO, and where—if not—we should focus our reform efforts.[45]

[43] Here I would add that I'm convinced that it would have been impossible to produce an economically rigorous analysis that opponents of WTO rules on trade-related investment would have considered even remotely balanced or relevant.

[44] This view receives support from Shaffer 2005, 438.

[45] Discussions of possible reforms include, among other topics, the future of the 'single undertaking' approach to negotiations (where nothing is agreed until everything is agreed), possible exceptions to the consensus approach to decision-making, possible future roles for plurilateral agreements, and enhanced participation of ministers and other senior officials from capitals in WTO activities. See, for example, WTO 2004 and Warwick Commission 2007.

REFERENCES

Alvarez-Jiménez, Alberto. 2010. Improvements to the WTO Decision-Making Process: Lesson from the International Monetary Fund and the World Bank. In *Redesigning the World Trade Organization for the Twenty-First Century*, edited by Debra P. Steger, 91–126. Ottawa: Wilfrid Laurier University Press.

Blackhurst, Richard. 2005. The Future of the WTO: Some Comments on the Sutherland Report. *World Trade Review* 4 (3):379–89.

Charnovitz, Steve. 2005. A Close Look at a Few Points. *Journal of International Economic Law* 8 (2):311–19.

Charnovitz, Steve. 2008. Book Review of: Trade and Employment: Challenges for Policy Research. A Joint Study of the International Labour Organization and the Secretariat of the World Trade Organization. *Journal of International Economic Law* 11 (1):167–76.

Charnovitz, Steve. 2010. Book Review of: Trade and Climate Change: A Report by the United Nations Environment Programme and the World Trade Organization. *World Trade Review* 9 (1):273–88.

Croome, John. 1995. *Reshaping the World Trading System: A History of the Uruguay Round.* Geneva: WTO Secretariat.

Elsig, Manfred. 2010a. Principal–Agent Theory and the World Trade Organization: Complex Agency and 'Missing Delegation'. *European Journal of International Relations* 1–23.

Elsig, Manfred. 2010b. WTO Decision-Making: Can We Get a Little Help from the Secretariat and the Critical Mass? In *Redesigning the World Trade Organization for the Twenty-First Century*, edited by Debra P. Steger, 67–90. Ottawa: Wilfrid Laurier University Press.

GATT. 1985. *Trade Policies for a Better Future: Proposals for Action.* Geneva: GATT Secretariat.

Ghosh, Arunabha. 2010. Developing Countries in the WTO Trade Policy Review Mechanism. *World Trade Review* 9 (3):419–55.

Pauwelyn, Joost. 2005a. The Sutherland Report: A Missed Opportunity for Genuine Debate on Trade, Globalization and Reforming the WTO. *Journal of International Economic Law* 8 (2):329–46.

Pauwelyn, Joost. 2005b. The Transformation of World Trade. *Michigan Law Review* 104 (1):1–65.

Pauwelyn, Joost, and Ayelet Berman. 2009. Emergency Action by the WTO Director-General: Global Administrative Law and the WTO's Initial Response to the 2008–09 Financial Crisis. *International Organization Law Review* 6: 499–512.

Petersmann, Ernst-Ulrich. 2005. Addressing Institutional Challenges to the WTO in the New Millennium: A Longer-Term Perspective, *Journal of International Economic Law* 8 (3):647–65.

Shaffer, Gregory. 2005. The Role of the Director-General and Secretariat: Chapter IX of the Sutherland Report. *World Trade Review* 4 (3):429–38.

Steger, Debra, and Natalia Shpilkovskaya. 2010. Internal Management of the WTO: Room for Improvement. In *Redesigning the World Trade Organization for the Twenty-First Century*, edited by Debra P. Steger, 129–61. Ottawa: Wilfrid Laurier University Press.

Van den Bossche, Peter, and Iveta Alexovioà. 2005. Effective Economic Governance by the World Trade Organization (section summarizing a conference panel session on an 'Expanded Role for the WTO Secretariat in Decision-making'). *Journal of International Economic Law* 8 (3):667–90.

Warwick Commission. 2007. *The Multilateral Trade Regime: Which Way Forward?* Report of the First Warwick Commission. Coventry, UK: University of Warwick.

Winham, Gilbert. 1998. The World Trade Organisation: Institution Building in the Multilateral Trading System. *The World Economy* 21 (3):349–68.

WTO. 1995. *The Results of the Uruguay Round of Multilateral Trade Negotiations.* Geneva: WTO Secretariat. Available on <http://www.wto.org>.

WTO. 2003. Procedures for the Appointment of Directors-General. WT/L/509. Geneva: WTO. Available on <http://www.wto.org>.

WTO. 2004. *The Future of the WTO: Addressing Institutional Challenges in the New Millennium.* Geneva: WTO Secretariat. Available on <http://www.wto.org>.

WTO. 2010a. *Annual Report 2010.* Geneva: WTO Secretariat. Available on <http://www.wto.org>.

WTO. 2010b. The Doha Round Marks a Transition from the Old Governance of the Old Trade Order to the New Governance of a New Trade Order. Speech by DG Lamy at the 10th anniversary of the World Trade Institute, Bern, 1 October. Available at <http://www.wto.org/english/news_e/sppl_e/sppl173_e.htm>. Accessed 6 November 2011.

CHAPTER 8

....

DEFINING THE BORDERS OF THE WTO AGENDA

....

MARION JANSEN[*]

8.1 Introduction

....

DEFINING the borders of the World Trade Organization's (WTO) agenda has been an intensely debated issue for several decades. Although the original General Agreement on Tariffs and Trade (GATT) already reached 'behind the border', early multilateral trade negotiation rounds had the distinctive characteristic of dealing mainly with border measures, in particular tariffs. This has changed over time, and very much so during the Uruguay Round that was concluded in 1995 and led to the creation of the WTO. Since that time a range of multilateral agreements, including the Agreement on Trade-Related Aspects of Intellectual Property Rights (TRIPS) and the Agreement on Sanitary and Phytosanitary Measures, deal explicitly with internal measures—that is, measures mainly intervening in the internal market. For some, the Uruguay Round decisions have gone too far. For many others they are not far-reaching enough. Indeed, the fact that numerous regional trade agreements concluded after 1995 go significantly further 'behind the border' than multilateral agreements signals that at least part of the WTO membership is willing to include themes into their trade agenda that have not reached support at the multilateral level.

In this chapter, the linkages between trade liberalization and internal or 'behind the border' measures are analysed from the point of view of the WTO. The focus is on regulatory measures, although other types of internal measures, like subsidies or public procurement, are touched upon. The term 'domestic regulation' is used to refer to regulatory policies that act behind the border. The terms 'international regulation' or 'international

* The views expressed in this chapter are those of the author and should not be attributed to the International Labour Office. The author thanks Rolf Adlung, Patrick Low, and Gabrielle Marceau for insightful discussions on the topic discussed in this chapter. All errors in the published text are the author's.

standards' will be used to refer to domestic regulatory measures that have been harmonized across countries.

Finding adequate answers to making the links between liberalization and regulation is crucial for the multilateral trading system. It will not only determine whether future negotiations are successful, but may affect the chances of the multilateral trading system surviving. The 2008–9 global financial and economic crisis has illustrated that strong liberalization in a weak global regulatory environment can lead to significant global instability, and can trigger important economic losses. The role of regulation in financial markets is, admittedly, rather special because of its importance for macroeconomic stability. But the interface between regulation and liberalization has also put the multilateral trading system under tension in other areas, notably food safety.

Liberalizing trade in markets where regulation matters can be complex and is often considered sensitive. Designing appropriate regulation for markets that are open is equally complex and sensitive. Trade reform is often perceived as triggering pressure for domestic regulation to change. This pressure is not always well received because approaches to domestic regulation are deeply embedded in cultural heritage and strongly linked to levels of development. Sensitivities also arise because changes to the regulatory status quo can have significant economic effects on individual private sector players. Affected players are thus likely to try and influence policy decisions on these matters. In other words, the risk of government capture is real.

Relevant policy design is complex because the relationship between trade liberalization and domestic regulation is placed at the interface of different academic and technical disciplines. Addressing it adequately requires collaboration between individuals or bodies in charge of trade liberalization and those in charge of domestic regulation. As such, it requires collaboration between different groups of national or international experts, and between different national or international institutions. These types of collaborations are challenging by nature. At the institutional level, they also lead to questions of how the mandates of different institutions relate to each other.

This chapter takes as a starting point the WTO's mandate to provide a forum for the negotiation of agreements aimed at reducing obstacles to international trade and ensuring a level playing field for all.[1] From there, the first question that arises is *why* trade negotiators felt compelled to deal with domestic regulation since the very inception of the multilateral trade system. This question is analysed in the second section of the chapter. The third section then provides an overview of how the relationship between the multilateral trade system and domestic regulation has evolved in subsequent rounds of trade negotiations, and the role that GATT and WTO decision-making processes have played in this evolution. Section 8.4 looks at *how* trade negotiators have chosen to define this relationship in the different trade agreements. In addition to the GATT and the General Agreement on Trade in Services (GATS), the Technical Barriers to Trade (TBT), Sanitary and Phytosanitary Measures (SPS), and TRIPS Agreements will be discussed prominently.

---

[1] See mission statement as available on the WTO website in December 2010.

The discussion in section 8.4 will reveal that WTO legal texts tend to encourage the use of international standards and the recognition of partner countries' regulatory policies. With this approach, the texts automatically enter into the type of work that typically falls under the auspices of regulatory agencies. Not surprisingly, therefore, WTO legal texts have, over the years, contributed to defining a relationship between trade authorities and regulatory authorities. A separate, albeit short, section of this chapter is therefore dedicated to the relationship that arises from those legal texts. As the role of experts or bodies dealing with regulation is also an issue for WTO disputes, the discussion in that section will touch upon the second mandate of the WTO, about providing a legal and institutional framework for the implementation and monitoring of these agreements, and for settling disputes arising from their interpretation.

The challenges the WTO faces in dealing with domestic regulation are multiple. The last section of this chapter focuses on four of them: (a) the challenge to respond to a demand for expansion of the WTO mandate put forward by subsets of the WTO membership; (b) the need to constantly critically assess whether it is appropriate to encourage international harmonization; (c) the challenge to find ways to connect the WTO's mandate with the mandate of regulatory agencies in such a way that the relationship between those institutions works effectively and leads to coherent global policy outcomes; and (d) the challenge to ensure that all WTO members can actively contribute to defining the liberalization–regulation relationship, notwithstanding their different levels of development and technical capacity.

8.2 REASONS FOR LINKING DOMESTIC REGULATION TO TRADE NEGOTIATIONS

From its origins, the multilateral trade system has had implications for national decisions on domestic regulation or internal measures more generally. Indeed, Article III of the GATT concluded in 1947 explicitly deals with internal regulations and national treatment.[2] A variety of justifications for including such references to domestic regulation in trade agreements have been discussed in the academic literature. Most of those arguments are 'trade related', i.e. they are based on the logic that internal measures can affect trade flows, and thus the essence of what trade agreements are about.

Much of the debate around the trade-relatedness of internal measures takes as a starting point the observation that internal measures have the potential to affect trade flows through their effect on relative prices or trade-related fixed costs. This can have three types of policy consequences:

(1) governments have the incentive to circumvent tariff concessions through the use of internal measures in order to protect domestic producers against imports

---

[2] Jackson 2001.

(2) governments have the incentive to use internal measures with a view to engendering new export opportunities for their domestic producers

(3) trade liberalization triggers a 'race to the bottom' in domestic regulation or 'regulatory chilling' through one of the two above-mentioned channels.[3]

The first and third consequences have received quite some attention in the theoretical economic literature. It has been shown (a) that governments will be tempted to use internal measures to substitute for tariffs, if trade agreements contain loopholes that allow them to do so, and (b) that, as a result of (a), the original policy objective will be pursued in a suboptimal manner in order to provide some support for domestic producers with the internal measure,[4] and that those mechanisms can trigger races to the bottom, i.e. a vicious circle where governments iteratively lower regulation in order to control import levels.[5] In other words, by helping to avoid 'prisoner's dilemma'-type situations with respect to trade policy-setting, trade agreements (with loopholes) may end up triggering prisoner's dilemma situations in other policy areas.[6]

Governments may not only face incentives to protect domestic producers against imports, but also incentives to support domestic exporters in their attempt to conquer markets abroad. The argument that subsidies can be used for strategic export considerations, and in support of domestic champions, is quite familiar to trade economists.[7] Albeit less familiar, the same argument can be made for regulatory measures. Sturm, for instance, has shown that governments may opt for domestic product safety standards that are too low if this gives domestic exporters a competitive advantage.[8] Again, this may lead to prisoner's dilemma situations.

The argument that internal measures may affect competitiveness, and thus trade flows, is well known from the political debate and finds support in the above-mentioned theoretical trade models. Empirical work on the effects of internal measures on trade flows has mainly focused on environmental and labour regulations, and the evidence provided so far is mixed.[9] Concern about the possible use of internal measures to circumvent tariff concessions or to distort trade flows in favour of national exporters has, nevertheless, continuously played a role in regional and multilateral trade negotiations.

Negotiations on government procurement, competition policy, and intellectual property rights have often been justified on the grounds that they affect trade flows through a different mechanism, i.e. through their effect on the functioning of national markets.[10] If national markets are not competitive, tariff reductions are unlikely to have a significant impact on trade. If, for instance, a market is dominated by a public or private monopoly, it may prove

---

[3] Jansen 2011.   [4] Copeland 1990.   [5] Bagwell and Staiger 2002.
[6] Maskus 2002.   [7] Brander and Spencer 1985.   [8] Sturm 2006.
[9] Empirical studies on the trade effects of environmental regulations include Jaffe et al. 1995, and Copeland and Taylor 2003. Studies on trade and labour regulation include Kucera and Sarna 2006 and Van Beers 1998.
[10] Maskus and Penubarti 1995, 1997, evaluate the validity of this argument in an empirical exercise, and find significant positive effects of stronger patent rights on trade flows for a number of developing countries, in particular those with strong imitation capacities.

virtually impossible for exporters to enter that market, even if tariffs are low. This explains why the structure of national markets may be of interest to trade negotiators and play a role in trade negotiations.

Not all arguments used in the debate on the borders of the WTO agenda are, strictly speaking, trade-related. Negotiators may simply want to link different types of issues in one single negotiation, because they expect that this increases the scope for finding mutually acceptable agreements.[11] Another argument often put forward in favour of including domestic regulation on the multilateral trade agenda is the strength of the WTO's enforcement mechanism. Indeed, members have equipped the organization with a rather solid dispute settlement mechanism that has proven its effectiveness over the years. Some observers have therefore argued that the enforcement of regulatory measures could be facilitated by including the relevant themes on the multilateral trade agenda.[12]

Last, but not least, it has been argued that regulatory policies need to be linked to trade negotiations because trade reduces the effectiveness of national policymaking. In particular, it has been argued that standard domestic enforcement mechanisms that function in an autarkic setting lose their effectiveness if relevant private sector players can act internationally. Arguments of policy effectiveness have been prominent in the debate on the need for multilateral collaboration on competition policy (possibly but not necessarily within the WTO framework). It has, for instance, been argued that liberalization has led to the creation of international monopolies or cartels.[13] Given that such cartels operate in multiple markets, it would be difficult, if not impossible, for national authorities to discipline possible anti-competitive abuse. To sum up, there is a whole range of economic and political arguments *why* the WTO does not only deal with pure border measures. The rest of this chapter focuses on *how* the WTO agenda has expanded behind the border.

8.3 DEFINING THE BORDERS OF THE MULTILATERAL TRADING SYSTEM: THE PROCESS

Trade negotiators have been searching for ways to discipline the use of domestic regulatory measures since the very inception of the GATT. Article III contains an explicit reference to domestic regulation stipulating that domestic regulation should not treat imported goods less favourably than domestically produced goods. The exact meaning and interpretation

[11] Cross-issue linkages in the context of trade negotiations have been analysed by economists in theoretical frameworks. The relevant literature is rather thin, and focuses on evaluating the benefits of linking negotiations on environmental policy with negotiations on trade policy (e.g. Conconi and Perroni 2002; Abrego et al. 2001).

[12] This argument, though popular in the public debate, has received little attention in the economic literature. An exception to this rule is the paper by Hoekman and Saggi that investigates the feasibility of a deal involving a linkage between specific antitrust disciplines and market access commitments (Hoekman and Saggi 2003).

[13] For example Evenett, Levenstein, and Suslow 2001.

of that Article has been the subject of many disputes and academic debates, the details of which fall outside the scope of this chapter. Suffice to say here that the drafters appear to have wanted to signal that domestic regulation should not be applied in a discriminatory way and with the objective to provide protection. While this principle is perfectly in line with the multilateral trade system's objective to facilitate trade, its application has turned out to be challenging. The rather general language in GATT Article III does not give much concrete guidance as to when domestic regulation is considered to be in conflict with WTO agreements and when it is not.[14] In subsequent rounds of negotiations, lawmakers have gone further and further in providing such guidance.

Since the inception of the GATT, multilateral trade negotiations have taken place within the context of eight negotiation rounds. The ninth round, the Doha Round, was launched in 2001 and is ongoing. The first five rounds—the Geneva (1947), Annecy (1949), Torquay (1950–1), Geneva (1956–6) and Dillon (1960–1) Rounds—dealt exclusively with tariff reductions. Starting with the Kennedy Round, attention began to shift towards non-tariff trade restrictions, though the Kennedy Round dealt only with non-tariff measures that were already covered by the GATT.[15] The Tokyo Round addressed policies that were not subject to GATT disciplines, and resulted in the conclusion of a number of codes, including: (a) subsidies and countervailing measures; (b) technical barriers to trade (only product standards); (c) government procurement; (d) customs valuation; (e) import licensing procedures; and (f) a revision of the Kennedy Round anti-dumping code.[16]

The term 'codes' was used to refer to plurilateral agreements, i.e. legal texts that were not signed by all GATT members. At the time, the use of codes was partly driven by the fact that developing countries objected to the expansion of GATT disciplines. Subsets of members therefore opted for negotiating in smaller groups in order to reach some level of collaboration at the international level.

The trend of expanding the WTO mandate was continued during the Uruguay Round. Some themes, dealt with in plurilateral agreements after the Tokyo Round, resulted in fully fledged multilateral agreements after the Uruguay Round, albeit in revised form. Negotiations on the Tokyo Round code on technical barriers to trade, for instance, resulted in the conclusions of the TBT and the related SPS Agreement. The Subsidies Code became the Agreement on Subsidies and Countervailing Measures.[17] Other agreements dealt with entirely new areas, like the TRIPS Agreement. Negotiations on trade in services also came to a conclusion and resulted in the General Agreement on Trade in

---

[14] It has been argued that GATT Article XX has been introduced in recognition of the fact that the rather general non-discrimination norm in Article III may not in all cases be an adequate dividing line between 'legitimate' public policies and 'cheating' on trade liberalization commitments (see Howse 2002). Article XX provides explicit exceptions for policies that may even entail elements of discrimination, provided that they are justified in terms of certain, explicitly listed, non-protectionist goals and that their application does not entail *unjustified* or *arbitrary* discrimination.

[15] Hoekman and Kostecki 2009.

[16] Ibid.

[17] The Agreement in Public Procurement, instead, remained a plurilateral agreement.

Services (GATS). Other themes that had been under negotiation did not make it into the legal texts concluded as a result of the Uruguay Round. This is notably the case for the theme of labour standards. The fact that regulatory measures related to labour would not fall under the auspices of the WTO was explicitly reconfirmed at the Singapore ministerial meeting in 1996.

In order to understand how different themes make it onto the negotiation agenda and possibly end up being dealt with in legal texts, it is useful to understand the WTO's decision-making process. The topmost decision-making body of the WTO is the Ministerial Conference, which usually meets every two years. It brings together all members of the WTO, all of which are countries or customs unions. The Ministerial Conference can take decisions on all matters under any of the multilateral trade agreements. The WTO's highest-level decision-making body in Geneva is the General Council. The Council is explicitly mandated to carry out the functions of the ministers in the intervals between the meeting of the Conference. The General Council meets at ambassador level about six to eight times a year.[18]

The General Council is assisted by three other councils—for goods, for services, and for trade-related intellectual property rights. Reporting to these three councils are a number of committees, whose primary function is to oversee the functioning of each WTO Agreement and to carry out the work programme. These bodies therefore reflect the main policy areas that were subject to negotiation in the Uruguay Round.

In addition to the committees that report to the three main councils, there are other committees and working parties that report to the General Council and that have functions reflecting the mandates that members have given to the Secretariat to monitor basic obligations and examine other policy issues of interest to them. At the time of writing, those included a Committee on Trade and Environment, a Committee on Trade and Development, and Working Groups on Trade, Debt and Finance, and on Trade and Technology Transfer. Some of the committees mentioned so far meet in so-called 'special sessions' when negotiating issues that are part of an ongoing round of negotiations.

Committees and working groups are created as a result of ministerial declarations following a ministerial conference, or upon decision of the General Council. It can also be decided to stop activities of existing bodies. In the so-called 'July decision' of 2004, for instance, the General Council decided that certain areas of work referred to in the Doha Ministerial Declaration of 2001 would no longer form part of further Doha Round negotiations. This decision concerned the areas of trade and investment, the interactions between trade and competition policy, and transparency in government procurement. The working groups that had been established to deal with those themes are since considered inactive.

Although the existence and level of activity of working groups and committees depends on Ministerial or General Council decisions, the background work for ministerial decisions and WTO legal texts is, to a large extent, conducted within the working

---

[18] Abbott 2007.

groups and committees, in particular in those meeting in 'special session' and thus directly mandated to negotiate specific issues. Indeed, the legal texts of multilateral trade agreements are largely prepared by those bodies, in repeated sessions of meetings that take place in the course of a negotiation round. Depending on their resources, WTO members send representatives with expert knowledge on the relevant topics to meetings of those committees, and—as discussed later on in this chapter—committees and working groups can request advice or information from external experts, for instance from experts of other international institutions that often have observer status in the relevant bodies.

It has been indicated above that the 'upgrading' of a subject area within the multilateral trading system can take the form of a plurilateral agreement becoming multilateral. A theme's prominence is arguably also reflected in the nature of the body that deals with it and the level of activity of that body. An example of a theme that has gained in prominence over time in multilateral negotiations is the relationship between trade and the environment.[19] In 1971, a so-called 'Group on Environmental Measures and International Trade' was established as a standby machinery, which would be ready to act at the request of a GATT contracting party for clarification on the relationship between environmental measures in trade. The first request for the body to meet was, however, only made around 20 years later, by the European Free Trade Association in 1990.[20] The debate on trade and the environment was further institutionalized within the GATT through the Marrakesh Decision on Trade and Environment in 1994, which resulted in the establishment of the Committee on Trade and Environment (CTE) in 1995. The tasks allocated to this committee were to 'identify the relationship between trade measures and environmental measures, in order to promote sustainable development', and 'to make appropriate recommendations on whether any modifications of the provisions in the multilateral trade system are required, compatible with the open, equitable and non-discriminatory nature of the system.'[21] In 2001, a further step was made as the Doha Declaration foresaw the initiation of negotiations—as opposed to mere discussions—on the theme, with a view to 'enhancing the mutual supportiveness of trade and environment.'[22] As a result, the CTE started to meet in 'special session'.

8.4 DIFFERENT APPROACHES TO LINKING WTO LAW TO DOMESTIC REGULATION

Once a theme is on the negotiation agenda, negotiators start to look into the possible design of a legal text dealing with the theme. With respect to regulatory measures, three types of provisions are repeatedly present in the legal texts drafted after GATT 1947. The

---

[19] Jansen and Keck 2011.
[20] See Annex I of Nordström and Vaughan 1999.
[21] Nordström and Vaughan 1999, 72.
[22] WTO 2001.

first type of provisions is meant to enhance the transparency of domestic regulation. The second type sets a benchmark for the regulations themselves, often by specifying specific types of regulation that are unlikely to be in breach of WTO law. The third type of provisions encourages the practice of recognizing the regulation of trading partners, for instance through the use of mutual recognition agreements.

8.4.1 Transparency

Compliance costs can represent an important element of the costs induced by trading partners' regulation. Exporters need to obtain information on the requirements of relevant regulations, which is costly.[23] In addition, the procedures that need to be followed to prove compliance with foreign regulation can represent significant cost factors. WTO legal texts reflect a desire to reduce those costs as far as possible, by encouraging members to provide timely information on new regulations and to be transparent about compliance procedures.[24] Relevant provisions can be found throughout the WTO legal texts. GATT Article X is arguably the most general relevant provision. It requires that 'laws, regulations, judicial decisions and administrative rulings of general application...shall be published promptly' and that they should be administered 'in a uniform, impartial and reasonable manner'. The TBT and the SPS Agreement also contain language requesting members to publish, at an early stage, information on new regulations, and to notify those regulations through the WTO Secretariat. TRIPS Article 63 contains similar provisions. The SPS Agreement also requests members to be transparent on their control, inspection, and approval procedures. Both the TBT and the SPS Agreement request members to establish enquiry points for trading partners, and TRIPS asks for the establishment of 'contact points' for a similar purpose.

With regard to trade in services, GATS Article III is titled 'transparency', and contains provisions similar to the ones in GATT Article X regarding the publication of laws and regulations.[25] Interestingly, that Article also requests members to publish international agreements pertaining to or affecting trade in services to which the member is a signatory. It is worth mentioning that in three sectors—financial services, basic telecommunications and accountancy—WTO members have gone further in elaborating common disciplines with respect to regulatory measures. The Telecommunication Reference Paper, for instance, requests governments who committed to it to make public the procedures for interconnection negotiations, and to ensure that major suppliers will be transparent about the applied interconnection arrangement. Where relevant, licensing criteria and procedures related to obtaining a licence should be made publicly available. In addition, suppliers must have recourse to an independent domestic body to resolve

---

[23] See WTO 2005 for an exhaustive discussion on compliance costs.
[24] See Wolfe 2003 for a more detailed discussion of WTO provisions related to transparency.
[25] GATS Article VI:1 informs members that relevant regulation should be administered 'in a reasonable, objective and impartial manner'.

disputes regarding interconnection. Members adhering to the Reference Paper must, therefore, ensure that such a body exists.

8.4.2 References to international standards or regulations

The second type of references to domestic regulation typically takes the form of references to standards and norms set by recognized regulatory bodies, mostly international ones. There are, however, significant differences across agreements in how those references are made and in how explicit the agreements are about the identity of the relevant bodies. The Agreement on Technical Barriers to Trade (the TBT Agreement), for instance, merely 'encourages' WTO members to apply international standards. No relevant standard-setting body is explicitly mentioned in this context. As a consequence, TBT disputes sometimes had to deal with the question of whether relevant international standards or standard-setting bodies exist. The SPS Agreement is arguably more explicit. It encourages members to use the international standards set by three relevant bodies: the Codex Alimentarius Commission (Codex) for food safety issues, the International Office of Epizootics—now called the World Organization for Animal Health (OIE)—for animal health and zoonoses, and the Secretariat of the International Plant Protection Convention (IPPC) for issues concerning plant health. The SPS Agreement also specifies that members are requested to provide scientific justification if they want to deviate from these international standards.

Yet another approach has been chosen in the case of the Agreement on Trade-Related Aspects of Intellectual Property Rights (TRIPS). In that Agreement, a number of rules on relevant domestic policy are directly defined by the WTO legal texts, and the enforcement of these rules rests with the WTO disputes settlement system. The TRIPS Agreement, for instance, stipulates that patents should be protected for a period of 20 years. In the TRIPS Agreement the WTO thus takes, itself, the role of a regulator, and by doing this brings under the mandate of the WTO an activity that originally fell within the mandate of another international organization: the World Intellectual Property Organization (WIPO). The preamble to the TRIPS Agreement, however, calls for a mutually supportive relationship between the WTO and WIPO. In addition, the Agreement explicitly specifies, in a number of articles, the Agreement's relationship with relevant agreements administered by WIPO. TRIPS Article 9 is, for instance, titled 'Relation to the Berne Convention' and TRIPS Article 35 is titled 'Relation to the IPIC Treaty'.

In much of the public debate, the approach taken in the TRIPS Agreement has been considered as too far-reaching. On the other hand, the text of the TBT Agreement has often been considered too vague, which makes dispute settlement challenging. Both concerns may explain why the approach taken in the SPS Agreement seems to enjoy a certain level of popularity in ongoing negotiations on other areas. In the negotiations on fishing subsidies, for instance, it has been proposed to make reference to the management and conservation practices of the Fish Stocks Agreement in a potential future WTO legal text regarding fishing subsidies.[26]

Like GATT, GATS contains a national treatment provision (GATS Article XVII). But the GATS text already appears to acknowledge that more than a national treatment provision is necessary to discipline the use of internal measures in the domain of trade in services. Indeed, paragraph 4 of GATS Article VI invites the Council for Trade in Services to develop (through appropriate bodies it may establish) any disciplines relating to qualification requirements and procedures, technical standards, and licensing requirements that may be necessary to ensure that such measures do not constitute unnecessary barriers to trade in services. Subsequently, the Council for Trade in Services established two bodies for this purpose: the Working Party on Professional Services and its successor, the Working Party on Domestic Regulation.[27] As mentioned above, in three sectors—financial services, basic telecommunications and accountancy—WTO members have gone further in elaborating common disciplines with respect to regulatory measures. The elaborated provisions appear to mainly pursue the objective of enhancing transparency of domestic regulations, and relevant provisions in the Telecommunication Reference Paper have been mentioned above. In addition, the Annex on Telecommunication to the GATS encourages WTO members to promote the work of standard-setting organizations like the International Telecommunication Union (ITU) and the International Organization for Standardization (ISO).

The legal texts relevant to telecommunication, financial services and accountancy neither refer to international regulations or standards as benchmarks (as in the case of SPS), nor do they set standards (as in the case of TRIPS). But for both financial services and telecommunication they appear to provide some kind of carve-out for domestic regulatory measures addressing specific market failures. The Telecommunication Reference Paper stipulates that any member has the right to 'define the kind of universal service obligation it wishes to maintain', as long as such obligations are administered in an appropriate way (e.g. in a transparent and non-discriminatory way). The Annex on Financial Services to GATS states that 'a Member shall not be prevented from taking measures for prudential reasons...or to ensure the integrity and stability of the financial system'.

8.4.3 Recognition

The third type of provisions referring to domestic regulations are provisions that encourage members to recognize policies used by other members. If applied, regulation would be less prone to distorting trade, even if it differs across countries. The TBT Agreement contains two relevant provisions, one that encourages members to mutually recognize each other's compliance procedures, and one that encourages members to consider accepting as equivalent technical regulations of other members. It has been

---

[26] WTO 2010, paragraph IV.2.
[27] Delimatsis 2008.

argued, though, that the latter approach may lead to adverse selection processes, by which national producers in the country with stronger regulation are driven out of the market if stricter regulation leads to higher production costs.[28] This leads Baldwin to conjecture that mutual recognition agreements (MRAs) are likely to be observed only among similar countries, and in particular among countries with a similar income level, because those countries are more likely to have relatively similar domestic policies in place, which reduces the risk of adverse selection.[29] Indeed, even the European Union, which embraces a group of countries of arguably similar income levels and cultural backgrounds, only applies an approach of mutual recognition that is combined with elements of 'harmonization of essential requirements'.

GATS also contains references to mutual recognition. In GATS Article VII, members are encouraged to recognize the education or experience obtained, requirements met, or licences or certifications granted in other countries. The Article is explicit about the fact that such recognition can be obtained either through harmonization or through mutual recognition agreements. In the accountancy sector, members decided to go a step further and to actively facilitate the use of MRAs, by adopting guidelines for mutual recognition agreements in the accountancy sector. One drawback of MRAs is that they introduce an element of discrimination themselves, as they provide advantages to the members of MRAs vis-à-vis non-members. GATS Article VII therefore asks members to provide adequate opportunity for the extension of MRAs. It has been argued that the trade-distortiveness of MRAs could be further reduced by actively encouraging the use of templates, as has been done in the accountancy sector.[30]

Last, but not least, GATS has a specific characteristic that is highly relevant for regulatory issues. GATS is a rather flexible agreement that allows each member to adjust the conditions of market entry and participation to sector-specific concerns. This is done by following a so-called 'positive list approach', that implies that individual members only liberalize those services sectors that they explicitly list in their commitment. They can also choose different degrees of liberalization for different modes of trade in the listed sectors.[31] Finally, they can make market access conditional on compliance with domestic regulation by explicitly mentioning the relevant regulations in their commitments. Indeed, commitment schedules of individual countries are full of references to domestic laws. They can even contain references to state laws, like in the schedule of the United States. This makes services commitments schedules a rather complex read, at least in the case of industrialized countries. Developing country schedules tend to be much simpler. In particular, when it comes to least-developed countries (LDCs), references to relevant domestic laws are rare. There are two possible explanations for this. One is that regulatory systems are less sophisticated in developing countries, which would allow for fewer references to domestic regulation in commitment schedules. Another possible reason is that developing country trade negotiators found it hard to handle the linkages between

---

[28] Jansen 2010.   [29] Baldwin 2000.   [30] Fink and Jansen 2009.
[31] The GATS distinguishes four modes of services supply: cross-border trade (mode 1), consumption abroad (mode 2), commercial presence (mode 3) and presence of natural persons (mode 4).

liberalization and regulation, and failed to refer to domestic regulation in their schedule. The latter would be a strong argument in favour of strengthening developing country capacity on the linkages between regulatory and trade policies.[32]

8.5 THE WTO AND OTHER INTERNATIONAL (REGULATORY) BODIES

The discussion so far has shown that the expansion of the WTO agenda in previous rounds has had as a consequence that WTO legal texts contain frequent references to domestic and international regulation. As a result, the WTO has also repeatedly needed to define its relationship with regulators or those providing input into regulatory processes. In previous sections, examples have been mentioned of explicit references in WTO legal texts to international regulatory bodies. The WTO has also developed two other avenues for formal relationships with regulators: observer status and the involvement of experts on regulatory issues in WTO disputes.

8.5.1 Observer status and references to regulatory bodies in WTO legal texts

International organizations explicitly mentioned in WTO agreements typically have observer status in the council or committee dealing with the relevant agreement. Codex, OIE and IPPC are, for instance, observers in the Committee on Sanitary and Phytosanitary Measures. WIPO is an observer in the Council for Trade-Related Aspects of Intellectual Property Rights. Observer status enables the organizations to follow discussions of matters of direct interest to them. They are also regularly invited to provide information to the relevant bodies, for instance in the form of presentations to the council or committee.

Also, organizations not explicitly mentioned in the relevant agreement can receive observer status.[33] The International Organization for Standardization (ISO), for instance, has observer status in the Committee on Technical Barriers to Trade, even though the TBT Agreement does not contain any reference to ISO. International organizations can also have observer status in committees that are not linked to any specific WTO agreement. A series of relevant international bodies have, for instance, obtained observer status in the Committee on Trade and Environment, including: the Convention

---

[32] This argument is also made in Jansen 2007.
[33] See WT/L/161, Annex 3 for guidelines on observer status for international organizations. The full list of international organizations with observer status can be found under <http://www.wto.org/english/thewto_e/igo_obs_e.htm>

on Biological Diversity (CBD), the Convention on International Trade in Endangered Species of Wild Fauna and Flora (CITES), the United Nations Environment Program (UNEP) and the United Nations Framework Convention on Climate Change (UNFCCC). In this context, it is interesting to point out that no specific working group or committee has ever been established to analyse the relationship between trade measures and labour measures, which may explain why the International Labour Office does not have observer status at the WTO.[34]

8.5.2 The role of regulatory bodies in WTO dispute settlement

With WTO legal texts making reference to international standards, the latter will inevitably be an issue that comes up in disputes around the relevant agreements. In particular, questions are likely to arise as to the relationship between domestic regulations under dispute and relevant international standards. WTO dispute panels are typically composed of experts in trade law, trade policy or international economy. Such panels, thus, do not necessarily have strong expertise on specific regulatory matters. The Understanding on Rules and Procedures Governing the Settlement of Disputes, therefore, foresees that panels can consult individuals or bodies with the relevant expertise (Article 13). The SPS and the TBT Agreement also contain specific provisions in this respect. Article 11.2 of the SPS Agreement notes that:

> In a dispute under this Agreement involving scientific or technical issues, a Panel should seek advice from experts chosen by the Panel in consultation with the parties to the dispute. To this end, the Panel may, when it deems it appropriate, establish an advisory technical experts group, or consult the relevant international organizations, at the request of either party to the dispute or on its own initiative.

TBT Article 14 contains similar provisions but without the reference to 'relevant international organizations'. The Annex on Financial Services to the GATS Agreement contains a rather different reference to relevant expertise. Paragraph 4 of that annex foresees that 'panels for disputes on prudential issues and other financial matters shall have the necessary expertise relevant to the specific financial service under dispute'. In other words, the panel itself needs to have expertise on financial regulation, whereas references in TBT and SPS only ensure that panels can get access to the relevant expertise through the consultation of external experts.

Seeking expert advice in the context of a dispute is not without challenges.[35] Expert selection and treatment of inputs from experts has, for instance, been a component of all SPS disputes. Typically, panels start their selection process by soliciting suggestions of scientists from relevant international standard-setting bodies. The list of proposed experts is then circulated to the parties for comment and the parties can state any compelling objections to a candidate. The latter has, for instance, occurred in the context of

---

[34] The WTO does have observer status at the ILO.   [35] Jackson and Jansen 2010.

the disputes related to hormone-treated beef, where scientists who had participated in Codex risk assessment processes were apparently perceived to be biased.[36] As a consequence, those scientists could not be consulted by the relevant panel. Allowing, or even requiring, the exclusion of particular experts with links to the regulatory process at stake may, indeed, be one way to guarantee the independence of the WTO dispute settlement system. But the population of experts for specific regulatory matters may be quite limited, and excluding experts who have contributed to designing the relevant international regulation bears the risk of reducing the options of experts to consult to zero.[37]

8.6 CHALLENGES IN HANDLING THE INTERFACE BETWEEN LIBERALIZATION AND REGULATION

It has been mentioned before that there has been a trend of expanding the mandate of the multilateral trade system in the course of subsequent negotiation rounds. The start of negotiations on the linkages between trade and environment in the context of the Doha Round indicates that this trend may continue. Also, the increasingly frequent inclusion of themes like environment, labour and social policies, investment, and competition policy in regional trade agreements (RTAs) indicates that at least part of the WTO membership considers that those areas form part of their trade agenda. Indeed, it has been argued that members use RTAs to handle those themes as they are unable to do so at the multilateral level. Also, the public debate on the need for increased 'coherence' in global policymaking goes in the direction of requesting the multilateral trade system to define its relationship with other multilateral bodies and the policies they promote. In this context, some observers have concluded that 'all aspects of economic regulation' would have to come within the mandate of the WTO.[38]

If it is accepted that there is a strong demand for further expansions of the WTO mandate 'behind the border' among a significant subset of WTO members, a first challenge the WTO faces is how to effectively respond to this demand. Another challenge is the question of how the relationship should be defined between the WTO and other international (regulatory) bodies that deal with the issues that the WTO draws under its mandate. Two other relevant challenges are to define the role of international harmonization of regulatory measures, and to find ways to guarantee that the interests of different countries can be taken into account in the setting and implementation of global standards. The latter question is, above all, relevant when taking into account relevant capacity constraints in developing countries.

---

[36] The EC also raised these types of concerns in the context of expert inputs in *Canada–US–Continued Suspension* from particular Joint FAO/WHO Expert Committee on Food Additives (JECFA) experts.

[37] Jackson and Jansen 2010.

[38] Steger 2007.

8.6.1 Expanding the mandate (in the absence of consensus)

Whether countries do or do not favour the explicit inclusion of a theme on the negotiation agenda has tended to depend, to a large extent, on how countries expect negotiation outcomes to affect their exports. Countries have repeatedly opposed negotiations on certain topics when they expected resulting agreements to reduce their exports. This reasoning is quite strikingly reflected in the 1996 Singapore Declaration that contains the following sentence concerning labour standards: 'We reject the use of labour standards for protectionist purposes, and agree that the comparative advantage of countries, particularly low-wage developing countries, must in no way be put into question.' On the other hand, countries tend to favour the conclusion of agreements if they believe that this will stimulate their exports. Well-organized export interests appear to have supported the conclusion of TRIPS[39] and strongly influenced the design of the SPS Agreement.[40] Export interests also initially provided support for including competition policy on the WTO agenda,[41] but then arguably withdrew that support.[42] In other words, if a certain agenda item does not clearly enough lead to export advantages for some players, it is less likely to end up on the negotiation agenda or ultimately in a legal text.

If a certain policy area has a number of proponents but is opposed by others, negotiations on the theme will not be successful in a system that relies on consensus for decision-making. Consensus decision making became the common practice in the multilateral trade system during the 1960s and was enshrined as a rule in the legal texts at the conclusion of the Uruguay Round.[43] The legal texts allow for voting if consensus cannot be reached within a specified time frame, but that option has very rarely been used.[44] The slow pace of progress in the Doha negotiations—that stands in stark contrast with the continuous increase in regional trade agreements—has led to an increased interest in the public and academic debate on the role that deviations from the consensus rule could play in facilitating progress in negotiations. Different approaches have been suggested, including the use of a 'variable geometry' approach,[45] plurilateral agreements,[46] critical mass decision-making,[47] or revival of the possibility of voting as a potential solution of last resort.[48] Compared to the currently used

[39] Ryan 1998; Maskus 2002.
[40] Croome 1995.
[41] Hoekman and Kostecki 2009.
[42] Bode and Budzinski 2005. In 2004, the area of competition policy had been explicitly excluded from the Doha negotiation agenda in the so-called 'July decision'. Note that the cost of the lack of multilateral competition policy enforcement has been estimated to reach billions of dollars annually. For details and relevant discussion, see Evenett, Levenstein, and Suslow 2001 and Bhattacharjea 2006.
[43] Steger 2007.
[44] Steger 2007; Low 2009.
[45] WTO 2004; Eizenstat and Aldonas 2007.
[46] For example, Hufbauer and Kim 2008.
[47] Low 2009.
[48] Ehlermann and Ehring 2005.

consensus rule, any of those options carries the potential to facilitate the expansion of the multilateral trade agenda.

8.6.2 Forum selection and policy coherence

If the trade agenda goes increasingly 'behind the border', it automatically enters the policy domain of other international bodies that will often have the nature of regulatory agencies. If policy setting was coherent at the global level, there would be a consistency between references in trade agreements to regulations and references made by the relevant regulatory bodies to trade. How to reach such consistency remains an unanswered question.

The discussion above has revealed that the multilateral trading system has defined its relationship with international regulatory bodies differently across subject areas. In TRIPS, the WTO sets international standards and has, to a certain extent, taken a role of standard setter in this domain—a role originally attributed to WIPO. With respect to sanitary and phytosanitary standards, the SPS Agreement encourages the use of international standards set by three standard-setting bodies explicitly mentioned in the Agreement. Although the WTO and the international standard-setting bodies remain separate institutions, the reference to standard-setting bodies in WTO legal texts appears to have affected their way of working. In particular, it has been pointed out that the international trade community has taken an increasing interest in standard-setting bodies like Codex, reflected, for instance, by the participation of trade negotiators in Codex meetings.[49] In the cases of intellectual property rights and sanitary measures, the most important step towards defining the relationship between the WTO and the relevant regulatory agencies has arguably been taken upon initiative of the WTO.

In the case of negotiations on trade and environment, the dynamics appear to have been different. The first step, of creating a link between trade and environment at the level of international law, was made in environmental agreements. Indeed, a number of multilateral environmental agreements (MEAs) contain explicit trade provisions allowing for the use of trade restrictions if terms of the relevant MEA have not been met. Those references to trade restrictions triggered renewed interest by trade negotiators in the theme of environmental regulation, and, in particular, in the legal relationship between the WTO legal texts and MEAs. This issue has been repeatedly on the agenda of the WTO Committee on Trade and Environment. It is also reflected in the 2001 Doha Declaration, where WTO members are called upon 'to negotiate on the relationship between existing WTO rules and specific trade obligations set out in multilateral environmental agreements (MEAs) with a view to enhancing the mutual supportiveness of trade and environment'.[50]

---

[49] Stewart and Johanson 1998; Abdel Motaal 2004.

[50] Doha Ministerial Declaration, paragraph 31. See also the discussion in Jansen and Keck 2011 and UNEP and WTO 2009.

Given that the initiative to make cross-references may come from either side of the institutional spectrum, the question arises as to whether it can be envisaged that different institutions work in parallel on relevant provisions. Taking into account the difficulties individual institutions have to take decisions on their own, making two institutions work in tandem may seem impossible. Yet it may be possible to make some progress if the relevant discussions take place in expert groups like the WTO committees or working groups, and if expert groups in the two institutions regularly exchange information on progress made.[51] Indeed, such an approach could even lead to a substantial amount of cross-fertilization, and progress in one institution could encourage negotiators in the other to further progress too.

Whatever approach is chosen for relating the WTO to standard-setting bodies or vice versa, policymakers need to be wary of the fact that any cross-reference is likely to affect the landscape of international institutions, and to affect their way of functioning. A thorough understanding of the legal and institutional consequences of cross-references could contribute to the construction of a more coherent and effective set of international institutions and legal frameworks.

8.6.3 How much harmonization to encourage?

Optimal domestic regulation is likely to depend not only on countries' level of development, but also on other country-specific factors, like cultural heritage, climate, and ideology.[52] If regulation is harmonized at the international level, this may reduce international transaction costs and facilitate trade, leading to increased gains from trade. But international harmonization may also create a wedge between applied international and optimal domestic regulation, thus leading to welfare losses in some countries,[53] possibly even to welfare loss at the global level. Even when global welfare gains are positive, they are likely to be divided unequally across countries. Here, the rule of thumb is that an individual country is more likely to lose the further away the international standard is from the one that is domestically optimal.

The non-inclusion of environment and labour on the WTO agenda has sometimes been justified by the potential distributional implications of such an inclusion if it involves a commitment to harmonized international environmental or labour policies. In particular, it has been argued that such standards can be harmful for developing countries if international norms are set too high, i.e. too close to the regulatory levels optimal in industrialized countries.

Yet, WTO legal texts make numerous references to international standards in other domains, like the domains of food safety regulation (SPS) and intellectual property rights (TRIPS). The stance WTO agreements take towards the international

[51] See Schemiel 2004 for a discussion of the role of experts in decision-making processes.
[52] See, for example, Howse 2002.
[53] Jansen 2010.

harmonization of regulatory measures is thus ambiguous, with the agreements favouring harmonization in some policy areas and avoiding references to harmonization in others.

Some have argued that the current approach taken in the WTO legal texts has the potential to lead to situations that are perceived as a 'war between public orders',[54] because WTO panels take decisions on whether specific domestic measures are in conflict with the multilateral trading system, or because domestic measures are replaced by international standards. Some have, therefore, argued in favour of a more extensive use of GATT Article XXIII.[55] Article XXIII foresees that a country can ask for compensation if market access obtained from trade negotiations is offset by changes in trading partners' domestic policies.[56] Article XXIII thus offers a way to deal with domestic regulation without reference to international benchmarks. Instead, domestic regulation in force at the time of concluding a trade agreement is taken as the benchmark, and subsequent changes in the relevant domestic legislation could, in theory, trigger a dispute with reference to Article XXIII. WTO case law has, however, advised to refer to this Article only in exceptional circumstances.[57]

8.6.4 Taking into account capacity in developing countries

International standards play an important role in international trade and are likely to do so increasingly if the multilateral trade negotiations follow the trend established in recent rounds.

In order for international regulation to play a positive role in international trade, it is crucial for all relevant trading partners to be actively involved in standard setting and to represent their national interests in the relevant bodies. This is particularly challenging for developing countries, which often lack resources and technical capacity to effectively intervene in standard-setting activities. There is, for instance, evidence of under-representation of developing countries in Codex bodies,[58] and in ISO bodies.[59] International initiatives, like the Standard and Trade Development Facility, try to address this issue, and in recent years important financial means have been devoted by donor countries to strengthening technical assistance on standard-setting matters. These initiatives should be continued, if not scaled up. In the context of continuing

---

[54] Bagwell, Mavroidis, and Staiger 2002.   [55] Bagwell, Mavroidis, and Staiger 2002.

[56] It has been argued in the literature that this Article was originally meant to deal with the trade effects of domestic policies, like labour market policies—see Hudec 1990.

[57] See the discussion of the Fuji-Kodak panel decision in WTO 2007. In this context, it is interesting to note that recent regional trade agreements offer yet another approach to dealing with regulation, by referring only to domestic policies. Numerous RTAs concluded by Asian countries or involving the EU contain explicit commitments not to lower the level of protection of their national labour law below that in force upon conclusion of the agreement, in order to encourage trade or investment. IILS 2009.

[58] Jansen 2010.

[59] WTO 2005.

regional economic integration, developing countries may also want to consider focusing on building and strengthening regional regulatory institutions rather than domestic institutions, as this could be cost-saving, and could allow countries to build a critical mass of regulatory expertise by avoiding that expertise being dispersed over different places.[60]

8.7 Conclusions

In this chapter the evolution of the GATT/WTO agenda has been described and processes that have driven this evolution have been discussed. The focus has been on the way the agenda deals with internal measures, in particular those of regulatory nature. A range of different policy areas have been covered, including food safety, environmental policies, intellectual property rights, financial, and other services sectors. The discussion therefore touched upon different WTO agreements and even drifted into the issue of dispute settlement. Given the broad coverage, the discussion probably does not give full justice to any of the policy areas or agreements. But this broad approach made it possible to identify a number of 'trends'.

Over time, the agreements appear to have become more specific in the way they define what determines whether or not domestic regulations are in conflict with the multilateral trading system. This evolution is best visible when looking at the way the legal texts have dealt with technical barriers to goods trade. The original GATT provisions (Articles III and XX) provided rather general guidelines, the Tokyo Round TBT code was more explicit but not signed by all members, and the TBT Agreement concluded in the Uruguay Round is a fully fledged separate agreement of multilateral nature.

The Uruguay Round agreements also represented a clear shift towards the encouragement of using international standards. This trend is likely to continue, albeit it is more likely to take the form chosen for the SPS Agreement than the one chosen in the TRIPS Agreement. Instead of setting international standards themselves, future trade agreements are likely to refer to the international standards or rules set by other international bodies or agreements, in particular to those having an explicit mandate to set international rules in the respective policy domain. The system that is likely to arise from this is one where the mandates of different national or international agencies are explicitly connected, rather than one where the mandate of one agency is shifted to the other.

Defining these connections in an effective way will be a challenge. But policymakers and lawmakers do not have to start from scratch to meet this challenge. They can build on the experience the multilateral trading system has built up in over 60 years of law-making and dispute settlement related to the interactions between domestic regulation and trade, and on a significant period of collaboration and active information exchange

---

[60] Jansen 2007.

with regulatory bodies. They will also work in an environment that is increasingly conducive to interagency collaboration. In the area of trade-related technical assistance, for instance, international agencies and national donors from different countries increasingly coordinate their efforts. The preparation of G20 summits has implied collaborative work among different international agencies. Last, but not least, the WTO Secretariat has in recent years increased its technical collaboration with other international agencies, leading, for instance, to a range of joint studies.

For a multilateral trading system to deal effectively with internal regulatory measures, though, it will be important that international regulatory counterparts have the capacity to actively play their role. In particular, they need to have the resources and technical expertise to deal with the complex task of making domestic regulation—harmonized or not at the international level—work in economies that are increasingly integrated at the global level. It is in the interest of trade policymakers to provide relevant regulatory bodies with the necessary support. In a world where markets are interconnected, failure in one market will inevitably affect other markets.

REFERENCES

Abbott, Roderick. 2007. The World Trade Organization. In *The New Economic Diplomacy*, edited by Nicholas Bayne and Stephen Woolcock, 315–32. 2nd edition. Aldershot, UK: Ashgate Publishing Company.

Abdel Motaal, Doaa. 2004. The Multilateral Consensus and the World Trade Organization. *Journal of World Trade* 38 (5):855–76.

Abrego, Lisandro, Carlo Perroni, John Whalley, and Randy M. Wigle. 2001. Trade and Environment: Bargaining Outcomes from Linked Negotiations. *Review of International Economics* 9 (3):414–28.

Bagwell, K., P. C. Mavroidis, and R. W. Staiger. 2002. It's a Question of Market Access. *The American Journal of International Law* 96 (1): 56–76.

Bagwell, Kyle, and Robert W. Staiger. 2002. *The Economics of the World Trading System*. Cambridge, MA: MIT Press.

Baldwin, Richard. 2000. Regulatory Protectionism, Developing Nations and a Two-Tier World Trade System. CEPR Discussion Paper 2574. London: CEPR.

Bhattacharjea, Arnab. 2006. The Case for a Multilateral Agreement on Competition Policy: A Developing Country Perspective. *Journal of International Economic Law* 9 (2):293–323.

Bode, Mariana, and Oliver Budzinski. 2005. Competing Ways Towards International Antitrust: The WTO Versus the ICN. Marburg Papers on Economics 3.

Brander, James A., and Barbara J. Spencer. 1985. Export Subsidies and International Market Share Rivalry. *Journal of International Economics* 18 (1/2):83–100.

Conconi, Paola, and Carlo Perroni. 2002. Issue Linkage and Issue Tie-In in Multilateral Negotiations. *Journal of International Economics* 57 (2):423–47.

Copeland, Brian R. 1990. Strategic Interaction Among Nations: Negotiable and Non-Negotiable Trade Barriers. *Canadian Journal of Economics* 23 (1):84–108.

Copeland, Brian R., and M. Scott Taylor. 2003. *Trade and the Environment: Theory and Evidence*. Princeton and Oxford: Princeton University Press.

Croome, John. 1995. *Reshaping the World Trading System*. Geneva: WTO.

Delimatsis, Panagiotis. 2008. Towards a Horizontal Necessity Test for Services: Completing the GATS Article VI:4 Mandate. In *GATS and the Regulation of International Trade in Services*, edited by Marion Panizzon, Nicole Pohl, and Pierre Sauvé, 370–96. Cambridge: Cambridge University Press.

Ehlermann, Claus-Dieter and Lothar Ehring. 2005. Decision-Making in the World Trade Organization: Is the Consensus Practice of the World Trade Organization Adequate for Making, Revising and Implementing Rules on International Trade? *Journal of International Economic Law* 8 (1):51–75.

Eizenstat, Stuart E., and Grant D. Aldonas. 2007. Transatlantic Leadership for a New Global Economy. Policy Paper, April 2007. Washington DC: The Atlantic Council of the United States.

Evenett, Simon J., Margaret Levenstein, and Valerie Suslow. 2001. International Cartel Enforcement: Lessons from the 1990s. *The World Economy* 24 (9):1221–45.

Fink, Carsten, and Marion Jansen. 2009. Services Provisions in Regional Trade Agreements: Stumbling Blocks or Building Blocks for Multilateral Liberalization? In *Multilateralizing Regionalism*, edited by Richard Baldwin and Patrick Low, 221–61. Cambridge: Cambridge University Press.

Hoekman, Bernard, and Michel Kostecki. 2009. *The Political Economy of the World Trading System*. 3rd edition. Oxford: Oxford University Press.

Hoekman, Bernard, and Kamal Saggi. 2003. Trading Market Access for Competition Policy Enforcement. CEPR Discussion Paper 4110. London: CEPR.

Howse, Robert. 2002. From Politics to Technocracy—and Back Again: The Fate of the Multilateral Trading Regime. *The American Journal of International Law* 96 (1):94–117.

Hudec, R. E. 1990. *The GATT Legal System and World Trade Diplomacy*. Salem, NH: Butterworth Legal Publishers.

Hufbauer, Gary Clyde, and Jisun Kim. 2008. International Competition Policy and the WTO. Paper presented at a conference entitled 'One Year Later: The Antitrust Modernization Commission's Report and the Challenges that Await Antitrust', April, New York University.

IILS. 2009. *World of Work Report 2009*. Geneva: International Labour Organization and International Institute for Labour Studies (IILS).

Jackson, John H. 2001. The WTO 'Constitution' and Promised Reforms: Seven 'Mantras' Revisited. *Journal of International Economic Law* 4 (1):67–78.

Jackson, Lee Ann, and Marion Jansen. 2010. Risk Assessment in the International Food Policy Arena: Can the International Institutions Encourage Unbiased Outcomes? *Food Policy* 35 (6):538–47.

Jaffe, Adam B., Steven R. Peterson, Paul R. Portney, and Robert N. Stavins. 1995. Environmental Regulation and the Competitiveness of U.S. Manufacturing: What does the Evidence Tell Us? *Journal of Economic Literature* 33 (1):132–63.

Jansen, Marion. 2007. Services Liberalization at the Regional Level: Does Southern and Eastern Africa Stand to Gain from Economic Partnership Agreements? *Journal of World Trade* 41 (2):411–50.

Jansen, Marion. 2010. Developing Countries, Standards and the WTO. *The Journal of International Trade and Economic Development* 19 (1):163–85.

Jansen, Marion. 2011. Internal Measures in the Multilateral Trading System: Where are the Borders of the WTO Agenda? In *Governing the World Trade Organization*, edited by Thomas Cottier and Manfred Elsig, 49–81. Cambridge: Cambridge University Press.

Jansen, Marion, and Alexander Keck. 2011. National Environmental Policy and Multilateral Trade Law. In *A Handbook of Globalisation and Environmental Policy: National Government Interventions in a Global Arena*, edited by Frank Wijen, Kees Zoeteman, and Jan Pieters, 107–54. 2nd edition. Cheltenham UK: Edward Elgar.

Kucera, David, and Ritash Sarna. 2006. Trade Union Rights, Democracy, and Exports: A Gravity Model Approach. *Review of International Economics* 14 (5):859–82.

Low, Patrick. 2009. WTO Decision-Making for the Future. Draft for Conference: 'Thinking Ahead on International Trade: Challenges for the World Trade System', September, WTO, Geneva.

Maskus, Keith. 2002. Regulatory Standards in the WTO. *World Trade Review* 1 (2):135–53.

Maskus, Keith, and Mohan Penubarti. 1995. How Trade-Related are Intellectual Property Rights? *Journal of International Economics* 39 (3–4):227–48.

Maskus, Keith and Mohan Penubarti. 1997. Patents and International Trade: An Empirical Study. In *Quiet Pioneering: The International Economic Legacy of Robert M. Stern*, edited by Keith E. Maskus, Peter M. Hooper, Edward E. Leamer, and J. David Richardson. Ann Arbor: University of Michigan Press.

Nordström, H., and S. Vaughan. 1999. *Trade and Environment*. Special Studies 4. Geneva: WTO.

Ryan, Michael P. 1998. *Knowledge Diplomacy: Global Competition and The Politics of Intellectual Property*. Washington, DC: Brookings Institution Press.

Schemiel, Yves. 2004. Expertise and Political Competence: Consensus Making within the World Trade Organization and the World Meteorological Organization. In *Decision Making Within International Organizations*, edited by Bob Reinalda and Bertjan Verbeek, 77–89. London: Routledge and ECPR Studies in European Political Science.

Steger, Debra P. 2007. The Culture of the WTO: Why it Needs to Change. *Journal of Economic Law* 10 (5):483–95.

Stewart, Terence, and David Johanson. 1998. The SPS Agreement of the World Trade Organization and International Organizations: The Roles of the Codex Alimentarius Commission, the International Plant Convention, and the International Office for Epizootics. *Syracuse Journal of International Law and Commerce* 26 (29):27–54.

Sturm, Daniel. 2006. Product Standards, Trade Disputes and Protectionism. *Canadian Journal of Economics* 39 (2):564–81.

UNEP and WTO. 2009. *Trade and Climate Change: A WTO-UNEP Report*. Geneva: WTO.

Van Beers, Cees. 1998. Labour Standards and Trade Flows of OECD Countries. *World Economy* 21 (1):57–73.

Wolfe, Robert. 2003. Regulatory Transparency, Developing Countries and the WTO. *World Trade Review* 2 (2):157–82.

WTO. 2001. Ministerial Declaration. WT/MIN(01)/DEC/1. Ministerial Conference, Fourth Session, 9-14 November 2001, Doha.

WTO. 2004. *The Future of the WTO: Addressing Institutional Challenges in the New Millennium*. Report of the Consultative Board to the Director-General Supachai Panitchpakdi. Geneva: WTO.

WTO. 2005. *World Trade Report 2005: Trade, Standards and the WTO*. Geneva: WTO.

WTO. 2007. *World Trade Report 2007: Six Decades of Multilateral Trade Cooperation: What Have We Learnt?* Geneva: WTO Publications.

WTO. 2010. Fisheries Subsidies: Special and Differential Treatment. TN/RL/GEN/163. Communication from Brazil, China, India and Mexico. Negotiation Group on Rules. Geneva: WTO.

CHAPTER 9

COLLECTIVE AGENCY, SYSTEMIC CONSEQUENCES: BARGAINING COALITIONS IN THE WTO

AMRITA NARLIKAR*

9.1 INTRODUCTION

THE phenomenon of collective bargaining in the multilateral trade regime is not new; coalitions of developing countries go back to the days of the General Agreement on Tariffs and Trade (GATT). But coalitions formed by developing countries to negotiate the Doha Development Agenda (DDA) do display two new features, which distinguish them markedly from their predecessors. First, the coalitions themselves have emerged as much 'stronger' actors: not only do they exercise greater external weight (embedded partly in the economic clout of the emerging economies that are active in such coalitions), but they have also developed mechanisms to maintain internal cohesion and thereby present a united front in some difficult bargaining games. Second, the strong coalitions of the DDA have had an institutional impact, demonstrated not only in the recognition that they have received within the World Trade Organization (WTO), but also in their contribution to the proclivity of the system to deadlock.

* Thanks are due to the Université Libre de Bruxelles (ULB), where the author held a Visiting International Chair and parts of this chapter were written. Early versions of the chapter were presented in seminars at ULB and Ghent University, and the author is grateful to the faculty and students in both departments for valuable feedback. She also thanks Steven Woolcock, Martin Daunton, and Robert Stern for detailed comments and suggestions that helped improve the paper.

While coalitions can have several important institutional consequences, they are, first and foremost, agents of the power that stems from collective action. This is especially important from the perspective of developing countries, where coalitions can serve as a vital mechanism for giving voice to the marginalized many. The first two sections of this chapter, Sections 9.2 and 9.3, focus on coalitions as evolving actors in the WTO, while Sections 9.4 and 9.5 examine their institutional consequences. In Section 9.2, I start off by mapping out the evolving rationale and structure of coalitions involving developing countries, comparing and contrasting coalitions of the Uruguay Round against those of the Doha Development Agenda. In Section 9.3, I analyse the strategies that the Doha coalitions have used, both to preserve their own unity and also as they bargain with outside parties. In Section 9.4, I examine the institutional effects of coalitions. I focus particularly on the recognition that they have received from the WTO and how they have been incorporated into the organization's everyday functioning, but also how these strong coalitions have contributed to the recurrence of deadlock in the Doha negotiations. Section 9.5 takes stock of the opportunities and challenges that coalitions generate for WTO negotiations, and explores directions for institutional reform. Section 9.6 concludes the chapters.

9.2 Overview of coalitions from Uruguay to Doha: rationale and features

While there are different kinds of groupings in the WTO, a bargaining coalition is a group of decision makers participating in a negotiation, who agree to act in concert to achieve a common end. The collective defence of a common position by a coalition is the product of conscious coordination, rather than a coincidental alignment of interests.[1] Coalitions are to be distinguished from consensus-building groupings—such as the G4, the Five Interested Parties, the G6, or the G7 in the Doha negotiations[2]—in which key players, representing diverse and often opposing positions, come together to try and find a middle ground.[3] They are also different from groupings of countries that are bound together by regional trade agreements (RTAs); some RTAs may translate into shared bargaining positions for their members, but very few RTAs (with the EU providing the powerful exception to this) have actually served as a springboard for collective bargaining in either the GATT or the WTO.[4]

Even though bargaining coalitions were not new to the GATT—the Uruguay Round was, in fact, a particularly fertile period for experiments with coalition formation—they

---

[1] Narlikar 2003; Odell 2006.
[2] These have usually included the EU, the US, Brazil and India, plus Australia, and often Japan. Additionally, in its G7 form in July 2008, the group also included China.
[3] Narlikar 2009.
[4] Jones 2009; Narlikar 2003.

were an elusive subject for research. Difficulties involved in studying coalitions continued into the early years of the WTO. This author, for instance, recalls being told, in an interview with a WTO official in 1997, that group and coalition diplomacy was a characteristic of the United Nations Conference on Trade and Development (UNCTAD), and the GATT and the WTO were happily free from such forces, where no coalitions were necessary to articulate members' interests or assist in bargaining thereafter. This denial of the very existence of coalitions in the WTO, then, is a far cry from the visibility and recognition that they receive now. The WTO website lists 26 coalitions as active in the negotiations today (see Annex 1). One indication of just how fundamental coalitions have become to the workings of the WTO is found in the references to them in some of its most basic and popular publications.[5] In this section, we explore the changes that coalitions of developing countries have undergone from the Uruguay Round to the Doha Development Agenda, both in terms of their rationale and structure.

9.2.1 Coalitions of the Uruguay Round

While the Informal Group of Developing Countries in the GATT predated the Uruguay Round, the developing world had, until the 1980s, concentrated its trade activism in the UNCTAD. Recognized and formalized coalitions in the organization—for instance through the G77—made collective action easier to organize, while its commitment to heterodox models of economics made it a more sympathetic milieu for developing countries to operate in. Additionally, though, the relatively cautious approach of developing countries to coalitions in the GATT also made strategic sense. The combination of the most-favoured nation (MFN) rule and the principal supplier principle, which underpinned GATT negotiation processes, meant that developing countries could free-ride on the tariff reductions that were exchanged amongst the major players.

The attempt by the US to include the new issues of services, agreements on Trade-Related Aspects of Intellectual Property Rights (TRIPS), and agreements on Trade-Related Investment Measures (TRIMs) into the GATT at the 1982 ministerial catalysed developing countries into more active coalition formation. These issues had greater potential to encroach upon domestic jurisdictions. It is true that the GATT was already dealing with behind-the-border measures, but it had previously done so through plurilateral agreements that countries could join on a voluntary basis; the new issues, however, were likely to enter into the GATT under its multilateral umbrella. Equally,

---

[5] The WTO's publication, *Understanding the WTO*, for instance, has the following to say about coalitions: 'In order to increase their bargaining power, countries have formed coalitions. In some subjects such as agriculture virtually all countries are members of at least one coalition—and in many cases, several coalitions. This means that all countries can be represented in the process if the coordinators and other key players are present. The coordinators also take responsibility for both "transparency" and "inclusiveness" by keeping their coalitions informed and by taking the positions negotiated within their alliances.' Accessed at <http://www.wto.org/english/thewto_e/whatis_e/tif_e/org1_e.htm> on 7 November 2011.

there was a possibility that developing countries might be able to bring certain issues, in which they had an advantage as exporters—such as agriculture and textiles—which had long been governed by exceptions in the GATT, more into the mainstream rules. All this amounted to high stakes in the Uruguay Round, and developing countries realized that they could not afford to sit on the margins.

In principle, in the GATT (and indeed its successor), developing countries enjoyed power that equalled that of their developed counterparts due to the consensus norm of decision-making: even the smallest and weakest contracting party to the GATT could have theoretically blocked consensus. In practice, however, most of the decisions were actually made under 'the shadow of power', where large economic size was used effectively as an 'invisible weighting' of votes.[6] In the face of this invisible weighted voting, pooling their economic power—through coalitions—offered developing countries greater collective voice. Both strategically and normatively, the larger developed economies would find it difficult to ignore the power deriving from large numbers. Coalitions effectively offered two important advantages to developing countries. First, small countries feared reprisals if they attempted to block a proposal on their own; through collective action, they increased the costs of reprisals for developed countries and also enhanced the legitimacy of their claims. Second, coalitions could facilitate a division of labour and information exchange among members. Such an information exchange is important at most times for countries facing problems of small numbers of staff in their Geneva missions and limited resources. It was especially important when dealing with the new issues of services, TRIPS, and TRIMs, which came ridden with many uncertainties and complexities. Coalitions emerged as a natural course of action for dealing with the challenges of the Uruguay Round.

While the rationale for coalition formation was clear, exactly how one's allies should be chosen was not. Coalitions involving developing countries in the Uruguay Round came to span a range of issues, and came to produce a complicated spaghetti bowl of cross-cutting membership loyalties, agendas, and structures.[7] But, broadly, they could be divided for analytic purposes into two types: bloc-type and issue-based. The cement binding the bloc-type coalitions was a set of ideas and identity that went beyond immediate instrumentality; issue-based coalitions were bound together by a more focused and instrumental aim.

The classic example of a bloc-type coalition that emerged in the pre-negotiation phase of the Uruguay Round was the G10.[8] This coalition resembled some of the older blocs that developing countries had formed, such as the Informal Group of Developing Countries in the GATT and the G77 in the UNCTAD. Led by Brazil and India, the group was staunchly opposed to the inclusion of any of the new issues into the GATT, and

[6] Steinberg 2003.

[7] For a detailed history of the coalitions of the Uruguay Round and the early years of the WTO, see Narlikar 2003.

[8] In its hardline version, the G10 came to comprise Argentina, Brazil, Cuba, Egypt, India, Nicaragua, Nigeria, Tanzania, Peru, and the former Yugoslavia.

firmly resisted the launch of the new round until the concerns of the Third World were addressed. Amidst this grandstanding, the coalition also refused to engage with any other coalitions, and turned down overtures from other developing countries to engage in shared research initiatives or draft joint proposals. The successes of the group were limited. Not only was a new round launched, but services were included within the negotiating mandate (initially placed on a dual track, but subsequently included as part of the 'single undertaking'). Other coalitions of developing countries formed along the lines of blocs generated largely similar and poor success rates.[9]

In contrast to the G10, and almost its contemporary, was the more successful informal grouping of the Café au Lait. This began as a modest research initiative amongst 20 mainly developing countries, led by Ambassador Felipe Jaramillo of Colombia.[10] These countries were joined by another nine developed countries.[11] The process that had begun as a research and consultation exercise came to combine developed and developing countries, and became known as the Café au Lait group (so called because of the leading role played in it by Colombia and Switzerland). Its focus was explicitly on services. After some initial meetings between the G10 and the Café au Lait, the two groupings parted ways. Eventually the Café au Lait came to include over 48 countries, and the draft proposal by this group provided the basis for the Punta del Este declaration that launched the Uruguay Round with services within it.

The successes of this issue-based diplomacy were further replicated in the Cairns Group of agriculture-exporting nations,[12] prompting a flurry of many issue-specific coalitions that consciously brought together a mix of developed and developing countries. Not all of these produced comparable successes, however, and the aura of optimism that had come to surround such coalitions proved to be short-lived, as did the coalitions themselves.[13]

The reason for the limited successes of the bloc-type coalition lay in their heterogeneity. Bloc-type coalitions normally bring together countries with some very different underlying interests; the coalition thereby manages to acquire considerable collective market power, but also risks being bought off through side deals.[14] In other words, such coalitions enjoy external weight, but they run the risk of fragmentation due to their limited internal coherence. Issue-based coalitions suffer from the opposite problem. Such

---

[9] Kumar 1993; Narlikar 2003.

[10] This old G20, focusing on services in the Uruguay Round (not to be confused with the G20 of the DDA on agriculture), included Bangladesh, Chile, Colombia, Hong Kong, Indonesia, Ivory Coast, Jamaica, Malaysia, Mexico, Pakistan, Philippines, Romania, Singapore, Sri Lanka, South Korea, Thailand, Turkey, Uruguay, Zambia, and Zaire.

[11] The G9 included Australia, Austria, Canada, Finland, Iceland, New Zealand, Norway, Sweden, and Switzerland.

[12] At the time of its formation in 1986, the Cairns Group brought together 14 developed and developing countries: Australia, New Zealand, Canada, and also Argentina, Brazil, Chile, Colombia, Hungary, Indonesia, Malaysia, Philippines, Thailand, and Uruguay (plus Fiji, which was not a contracting party to the GATT at the time). Higgott and Cooper 1990; Tussie 1993.

[13] Narlikar 2003.

[14] Narlikar and Odell 2006; Narlikar 2003.

coalitions enjoy internal coherence, but are difficult to sustain when large and diversified economies (with multiple and competing issue-specific interests) are involved. If loyalties are shared across multiple coalitions in competing issue areas, they become difficult to sustain.[15] This problem can be overcome by creating very narrow and focused coalitions involving smaller economies, but then such coalitions lack external weight. The Uruguay Round demonstrated the dangers of forming bloc-type coalitions on the one hand, but also issue-specific ones on the other.

9.2.2 Coalitions of the Doha Development Agenda

The mixed record of the coalitions of the Uruguay Round led developing countries to adapt the structures of their coalitions. In good measure, though, the imperatives that had led trade negotiators to turn to coalitions in the Uruguay Round are perhaps even more important in the DDA negotiations.

First, if the stakes of the Uruguay Round were high, those of the DDA—especially in the prelaunch period and the early negotiations—were higher still. Developing countries now had to ensure that any new round in the WTO met the problems of implementation that the Uruguay Round had generated,[16] and also guard against the inclusion of issues such as environment and labour into the WTO (as well as other contested issues). Once the new round was launched, they had to exercise constant vigilance to ensure that the negotiations did not stray from their professed commitment to development. Second, the Seattle Ministerial Conference in 1999 raised some interesting issues of the external legitimacy of the WTO (as reflected in the public riots and demonstrations outside the deliberations), but also highlighted some serious concerns about the internal legitimacy of the organization. In groups and individually, representatives from the developing world complained of marginalization from key decision-making processes. Coalitions formed one strategy that developing countries could adopt to improve their influence, and it was, moreover, a strategy that developing countries could implement themselves without having to depend on any changes in the institution. Driven by a similar rationale to that which had guided negotiators in the Uruguay Round, developing countries recognized that they could achieve more by joining economic forces. Third, particularly at a time when most international organizations were enduring violent criticism of their democratic deficits, the power of large numbers offered greater mileage on the legitimacy front than ever before. And fourth, even though their efforts over the past three decades have contributed to their ability to participate with greater voice and influence in the organization, many developing countries continue to face the problems of

---

[15] This point was first made in Hamilton and Whalley 1989.

[16] A coalition led by India, the Like Minded Group, was at the forefront in highlighting the implementation issues: Narlikar and Odell 2006. The group included Cuba, Dominican Republic, Egypt, Honduras, India, Indonesia, Kenya, Malaysia, Pakistan, Sri Lanka, Tanzania, Uganda, and Zimbabwe, with Jamaica and Mauritius as observers.

small delegations (and, in some instances, no delegations in Geneva), limited technical expertise, and thinly spread out resources. Add to this the originally expansive ambitions of the Doha negotiations, and it is hardly surprising that the importance of coalitions in the WTO persists.

As in the Uruguay Round, coalitions of the DDA continue to be seen as agents of empowerment for developing countries. Only two coalitions in the 26 listed by the WTO (see Annex 1) comprise exclusively developed countries: the EU and non-agricultural market access (NAMA) Friends of Ambition. The fact that 16 of the 26 are constituted entirely by developing countries (defined broadly to include the least-developed countries (LDCs), middle income countries, and economies in transition) offers us at least one interesting observation: contrary to the fashion of the Uruguay Round issue-based coalitions that sought to transcend the developed–developing/North–South divide, the 'stickiness' of Southern activism persists (driven by a mix of ideas, identity, and interests, which varies between coalitions).

Importantly, if the majority of coalitions of the DDA are not the expected pragmatic, issue-specific coalitions that transcended North–South lines, they are not the obsolete bloc-type coalitions committed to Third Worldist ideas either. Dubbed elsewhere as 'smart coalitions', many of the DDA coalitions have managed to combine the strengths of both the issue-based and bloc-type coalitions of the past.[17] Those that restrict themselves to Southern allies benefit from the cement of ideational unity that had united some of the old blocs, and also enjoy external weight. But, unlike the old blocs, several of these also have an issue-specific focus (such as the G20 and G33 on agriculture, or the NAMA-11 on non-agricultural market access).[18] This helps them address some of the problems of internal coherence that had affected former bloc-type coalitions. Other Southern coalitions—such as the LDC group or the African Group—transcend issue areas but consciously emphasize the specificity and distinctiveness of problems that affect their members. Very importantly, having learned from the experiences of the Uruguay Round, when bloc-type coalitions had shown minimal engagement with—and sometimes even hostility to—other coalitions of developing countries, there is considerable pragmatic information exchange and cooperation across diverse coalitions today.[19] And in sharp contrast to the famous defensiveness of the Third World in the past (the G10 providing the classic example of this), the new coalitions of the DDA have emerged as aggressive demanders and agenda setters. Note that the strengths of these 'smart coalitions' are a product of bargaining strategy—particularly internal bargaining among members of a coalition—as discussed in the next section.

Besides the combination of issue-based and bloc-type diplomacy that the DDA coalitions have used, the 'alliances of sympathy' that they form with other coalitions of developing countries, and their successful attempts to move beyond blocking to agenda-setting, the new coalitions of developing countries in the DDA are backed by

---

[17] Narlikar and Tussie 2004, 959.
[18] For the membership composition of these coalitions, see Annex 1.
[19] Ismail 2009; Narlikar and Tussie 2004.

raw economic power. In this context, the rise of the BICs (Brazil, India, and China) is particularly important: coalitions led by the world's fastest growing economies naturally exercise greater external weight. The comparison is striking, especially for Brazil and India, which have clearly come to exercise greater clout, single-handedly and in coalitions, than they did in the Uruguay Round. The clearest evidence for this is the replacement of the old Quad—comprising the US, EU, Canada, and Japan—with new permutations, in which the constants are the US, EU, Brazil, and India. As the next section illustrates, the leadership of large developing countries also has a positive effect on internal coalition dynamics.

It is worth mentioning that not all the coalitions of developing countries in the WTO comprise the large middle-income economies. Some are made up of distinctly weaker players, such as groups comprising the Small, Vulnerable Economies, the LDCs, the Cotton-4, and others (see Annex 1). The strengths of these coalition types are twofold. First, in the era that has seen the launch of the Millennium Development Goals and the Doha Development Agenda, arguments of fairness, distributive justice, and legitimacy have acquired unprecedented mileage in international negotiation. In other words, the external context has changed, and this can be, and has been, used by coalitions to their advantage through effective framing (discussed further in the next section on strategies). Second, to some extent, coalitions with which the BICs profess sympathy and cooperation derive at least some indirect benefits from the changing balance of power.

Perhaps the most striking feature of the coalitions of the DDA is that they are 'strong' coalitions. The problem with coalitions in the GATT and even in the early years of the WTO—irrespective of whether they were bloc-type or issue-based—was that they would often collapse in the endgame. Some of their members would succumb to the temptations of side deals, while others would concede under threats of bilateral retaliation (such as the withdrawal of aid packages). A small minority that continued to adhere to the original demands would find themselves isolated, and would walk away with nothing.[20] Interestingly, many of the coalitions of the Doha negotiations have shown themselves to be resilient against these pressures. This ability to stand united is partly a direct function of greater economic prowess: that Brazil, India, and China are better able to stand up to their opponents today is unsurprising.[21] But so have their smaller allies, and indeed coalitions which do not include the BICs at their helm. Further, several of these coalitions are the same coalitions that had been susceptible to external pressures in the Uruguay Round and in the lead-up to the launch of the DDA (such as the LDC and African groups). The new found strength of the Doha coalitions can be best explained by examining their bargaining strategies.

---

[20] Narlikar and Odell 2006.

[21] The details of the relationship between coalitions and their leaders lies beyond the scope of this study. Suffice it to note, however, that just as developing country coalitions have benefited from the rise of Brazil and India, and more recently China, the new powers too have been better able to back their claims to bigger roles in international negotiations because of the backing that they enjoy from their coalition allies.

9.3 Strategies of bargaining

The negotiation strategies of coalitions of developing countries have evolved in two important ways. First, in negotiations internal to a coalition, we see conscious attempts to preserve internal cohesion. Second, in negotiations with the outside party, we see an effective use of aggressive framing tactics in terms of ideas of fairness, development, and justice. Both strategies help in the creation of strong and united coalitions. But they also incline coalitions towards the use of distributive rather than integrative strategies. The result is the creation of strong coalitions of developing countries that find it difficult to make compromises, and thereby also the creation of a multilateral trading system that is more deadlock-prone.

9.3.1 Bargaining within a coalition

The Doha Round has seen a burgeoning of coalitions of developing countries that are able to pursue the collective agenda through a united front. Prominent examples include the G20 on agriculture, the G33 on Special Products and Special Safeguard Mechanism, the Cotton-4, NAMA-11, the Small, Vulnerable Economies group, and the LDC group (see Annex 1). The first three were formed at the Cancún Ministerial in 2003, NAMA-11 arose at the Hong Kong Ministerial in 2005, while the latter two pre-date the Doha Ministerial. The reason why these coalitions have managed to resist the risk of fragmentation is that members have been persuaded that the gains of the collective agenda represented by the coalition outweigh the potential gains of defection for an individual member. This recognition is not an automatic function of coalition formation. Rather, it has to be cultivated through careful strategy internal to the coalition.[22]

First, the coalition needs to be so constituted that all its members commit to the collective agenda. The case of the G20 is a good example. Based on defections by developing countries from their coalitions in the past, many outsiders predicted that the G20 would collapse at the Cancún Ministerial. They correctly pointed to the rifts in the G20, particularly the great diversity of interests even between its leaders (with Brazil's 'offensive' interests in agriculture as a leading exporter versus India's 'defensive' interests). But they were wrong in predicting the outcome of collapse. The G20 maintained a unified position at Cancún, and is still going strong. The fact that its two leaders—Brazil and India—have become a part of the 'New Quad' (and other key decision-building groups such as the G4, the Five Interested Parties, the G6, and the G7) bears testimony to the influence that the group has achieved. The reason why the G20 was able to stand firm, both at Cancún and beyond, was because of how its collective agenda was formulated. Specifically, this agenda logrolls two sets of demands: an aggressive set of demands on

---

[22] The detailed, theoretical argument for this is made in Narlikar 2009.

greater market access in the North, and also a reduction in their exports subsidies and domestic support mechanisms; plus a defensive set of demands that seeks to protect the agricultural markets of developing countries. The recognition of the G20 members that potential collective gains will outweigh individual gains acquired through defection is explicit. For example, on being asked about the temptation to defect, a negotiator from a small G20 country responded that the collective gains that would accrue, if the G20 were successful, significantly outweighed any gains that the US or EU could offer him through preferential market access.[23]

Second, smaller members from the developing world naturally tend to be more risk-averse, and a preponderance of small allies in a coalition may increase the legitimacy of the group but may also heighten the risk of fragmentation if these smaller members defect. The likelihood of this happening is higher if there is a low level of trust among allies.[24] This risk, however, can be reduced if larger members are able to offer side-payments to smaller allies. The G20 was able to do this effectively. Its leaders offered concessions in the form of preferential market access for LDCs, and also regional trade arrangements (economic and political) with various members, such as the IBSA (India, Brazil, and South Africa) initiative and India's Africa Forum.

9.3.2 Bargaining with the outside party

Besides the two types of bargaining strategies that are internal to the coalition, collective influence in dealing with the outside party can be further enhanced if the coalition comprises a large number of countries, and also includes some large economies. The coalition that enjoys greater external weight is more likely to produce concessions from the outside party. The refusal of a large and diverse group of countries to sign an agreement has a bigger negative impact on the outside party than a similar smaller coalition. Unsurprisingly, the coalitions that have displayed the greatest staying power in the Doha negotiations—such as the G20 and the G33—are those that bring together a diversity of members that include both the small economies (to enhance the legitimacy of the grouping) and the large emerging economies (to increase the external weight of the coalition).

Coalitions of the DDA thus have both internal coherence and external weight, thanks to the way that they have constituted their membership structures and sustained those bargains. Importantly, they have also successfully captured the normative climate to their advantage. The fact that the new round acquired a development

---

[23] Interview, Cancún, 2003.

[24] Jervis 1978, 172, identifies these risks in his discussion of the game of the Stag Hunt in his conceptualization of the Security Dilemma: 'If the failure to eat that day—be it venison or rabbit— means that he will starve, a person is likely to defect in the Stag Hunt even if he really likes venison and has a high level of trust in his colleagues. (Defection is especially likely if the others are also starving or if they know that he is.) By contrast, if the costs of CD are lower, if people are well-fed or states are resilient, they can afford a more relaxed view of threats.'

focus is attributable at least as much to a conducive external environment (in contrast, for example, to the Washington Consensus-dominated discourse in the 1980s) as it is to the bargaining efficacy of developing countries. An example of a particularly successful framing campaign was by the TRIPS and Public Health Coalition. In the run-up to the Doha Ministerial Conference, a large and diverse group of countries, working in cooperation with Northern non-governmental organizations (NGOs), was able to reframe the debate on TRIPS, from one where protection of intellectual property rights (IPR) was seen as an essential safeguard against theft, to one where protection of IPR came to be seen as a killer because it denied the access of essential medicines to poor and sick people. Through this effective reframing, the coalition was able to secure explicit assurances that they would be allowed to use compulsory licensing and other relevant measures to ensure access to medicines in a public health emergency.[25]

9.3.3 Implications for multilateral negotiations

By successfully managing their internal bargains to promote cohesion, and further strengthening the legitimacy of their demands through appealing to appropriate normative frames, developing countries have managed to produce strong coalitions. But both sets of bargaining strategies—internal and external—also make it difficult for these strong coalitions to make the compromises necessary to reach agreement with the outside party.

The first reason why it is difficult for strong coalitions to make concessions, especially when they comprise developing countries, is that the collective agenda of such coalitions is inevitably arrived at through considerable logrolling. Were the collective agenda not ambitious and far-reaching, the benefits of defection would outweigh those of cooperation, leading to a fragmentation of the coalition. But an ambitious agenda also makes it difficult for the coalition to negotiate with flexibility. A concession made in any one issue area, or a sub-issue, risks antagonizing at least some members of the coalition, and thereby triggering defection. Bernard Hoekman has noted this problem: 'The move towards the creation of negotiating coalitions of groups of countries may reduce the number of 'principals' but possibly at the cost of greater inflexibility and a higher risk of breakdown, especially in a setting where there is little time to consult.'[26]

The G20 gives us a classic example of the risks that making concessions can entail for coalition unity and credibility. In the Geneva talks of July 2008, Brazil (the coordinator of the G20), driven by its powerful lobby of agricultural exporters, urged its allies to accept the proposed 'July Package'. China and India, with their defensive inter-

---

[25] Odell and Sell 2006.   [26] Hoekman 2003.

ests in agriculture, along with other allies within both the G20 and the G33, refused to accept the deal until the North improved its offer. At issue were the deep differences within the G20 over the proposed trigger for the Special Safeguard Mechanism, and also over the adequacy/inadequacy of the US offer to cap its overall trade-distorting support to $14.5 billion.[27] China and India took a firm stance against compromise. Brazil was brought round quickly to resume a negotiating position that was sensitive to the concerns of its more defensive allies. The G20 did not collapse in the July 2008 talks, but it certainly came close to it. And by managing to avoid fragmentation, it also lost out on a fairly good deal. Effectively, the G20 faced the problem that afflicts most strong coalitions: a willingness to compromise by some players over particular issues may be seen as a sign of impending defection by allies and as a sign of the coalition's potential weakness by the outside party. The alternative, of standing firm, heightens the systemic problem of deadlock.

The second reason why it is difficult for coalitions to make concessions has to do with framing. Normative framing of demands may help coalitions persuade the other party of the legitimacy of their claims, but it can also lead coalitions to dig their heels in and refuse agreement until all their demands are met. This may be because principles are often regarded as rights not subject to compromise.[28] Max Bazerman and Margaret Neale have argued that 'fairness considerations can lead negotiators to opt for joint outcomes that leave both parties worse off than they would have been had fairness considerations been ignored.'[29] A recent study confirms that ideational considerations tend to exacerbate conflict among parties.[30] Further research needs to be conducted on this in the context of coalition politics. But it seems plausible to argue, for instance, that were coalitions fighting for 'interests' rather than 'causes' (such as development), they would find it easier to make compromises.

9.4 INSTITUTIONAL IMPACT

The last two sections examined coalitions as actors, but it is also important to take into account the effects that these new clusters of power have on the workings of the WTO. Just how deeply embedded coalitions have become in the everyday workings of the organization is evident in the explicit references that one now finds to them. For example, Director General Lamy's model of consensus-seeking in the DDA negotiations is based on 'concentric circles' (see Annex 2). The inclusiveness of this model is justified through the consultation that it requires with all coalitions, while its transparency is

---

[27] Ismail 2009; Narlikar 2009.   [28] Gamble 2010.   [29] Bazerman and Neale 1995.
[30] Narlikar 2010.

rooted in the process whereby coalition representatives present at the consultations report back to the members. Decision-making that involves coalitions allows the WTO to claim that, as the process is driven by the members themselves, it is truly 'bottom-up'. Coalitions have moved from the periphery of the organization into its core.

Mateo Diego-Fernandez identifies three important effects of coalitions on the organization:

> the existence of coalitions makes it easier to determine whether an emerging consensus exists…it reduces the number of interlocutors, since group leaders often speak on behalf of their constituents in smaller sessions, thus facilitating the task of Chairs and of counterparts…as a result of their decision-making processes, positions presented by coalitions will normally already have the more cumbersome components of their proposals resolved, such as steering a Member's radical position towards a more centred approach.[31]

Effectively, coalitions serve as vital mechanisms of rationalization of the complex processes of multilateral negotiation. In other words, they have considerable potential to improve the efficiency of the negotiation process.

The second set of contributions that coalitions make to institutional development is in representation. Coalitions allow greater voice to countries that would otherwise have no say at all in the small group meetings that underpin WTO negotiations. Coordinators of coalitions are expected to work in close cooperation with their members, and inform them of developments in the Green Room and other small group consultations. Coalitions allow members not only greater possibilities of representation but also a more informed participation in the negotiation process. This is especially important for the smaller countries that lack the necessary resources to deal with negotiating technicalities on their own. All this facilitates empowerment of smaller and weaker members, but also improves the legitimacy of an organization that had previously (particularly at the Seattle Ministerial and its aftermath) faced a barrage of criticism for its democratic deficit.

Not all the effects of coalition diplomacy on the workings of the WTO are positive, however. Small group meetings of the WTO are certainly more representative than ever before, directly through the inclusion of the BICs but also indirectly through the coalitions that these new powers represent and report back to. But this diversity generates a cost. Decisions by consensus were much easier to arrive at when the more homogeneous Quad was in charge. Just the BICs bring great variation in patterns of economic development, and also very different ideas of fairness and justice to the negotiating table, in contrast to the old Quad. Plus they represent the development patterns and competing visions of their coalition allies, which include not just middle-income countries but the

---

[31] Diego-Fernandez 2008, 427.

LDCs. To the variable of diversity we must add the variable of multipolarity. Power in the WTO today is more evenly distributed among the leading players, in contrast to the monopoly of power that the US enjoyed when the GATT was created, or the duopoly that emerged with Europe's post-war recovery. And the more equal the power distribution, the harder it is to reach agreement.[32] Of course, having the old norm of consensus as the basis for decision-making in an altered reality does not help. But the limitations of institutional design arise from the new balance of power, which is at least partly a product of effective coalition formation.

Second, as discussed in Section 9.3, strong coalitions are a source of empowerment for developing countries (they have contributed to the entry of the BICs into key decision-making meetings, and have also given voice to the smaller developing countries and LDCs), but they find it difficult to make concessions. Any conciliatory moves may be interpreted by coalition members as a sign of potential defection, and by the outside party as a sign of weakness. As a result, multilateral negotiations based on coalition diplomacy are prone to deadlock. This is certainly an effect that is patently visible in the Doha negotiations.

While the above two costs undermine some of the efficiency gains that coalition diplomacy should generate for the institution, the third cost comes on the legitimacy front. It is true that engaging with its membership via coalitions in small group meetings is a big improvement on the old Green Room meetings, which were largely restricted to the principal suppliers. But having coalition representatives in small group consultations is not always a happy substitute for having a place for one's own country in the consultative exercise. The July 2008 consultations between the so-called G7 (which included Brazil, China, and India as both the rising economies and coalition leaders) brought discontent with this process to the fore. Rather than see the inclusion of the BICs as a positive development, several developing countries complained of marginalization. The African ministers issued a press statement highlighting that they were 'deeply concerned that in the Group of Seven (G7) not one African country was represented in a round that purports to be about development'.[33]

Coalitions have successfully solved several of the old problems that affected developing country participation in the GATT and in the early years of the WTO. But they have also created some new and unanticipated problems for the organization. A WTO in perpetual deadlock creates opportunity costs for all its members, but its costs are highest for the newly empowered developing world. Developing countries have only recently learned to use the multilateral trading system to their advantage; the drift to regionalism

---

[32] In one recent study, the hypothesis that deadlocks are a function of the balance of power was the most popular hypothesis of the six that were analysed, and was confirmed by all the case studies. Narlikar 2010.

[33] Cited in Ismail 2009; also see same chapter for further details on the reasons and forms of protest that the G7 process generated.

and bilateralism will reverse these gains. Insofar as the genie of coalitions will not go back into the bottle, what can be done about it?

9.5 Directions for reform

Coalitions offer research and representation to their members, and thereby contribute to improving their participation in the WTO; by furthering access, they also improve the legitimacy of the organization; at least theoretically, they should also improve the efficiency of the organization by reducing the number of principals and facilitating the process of compromise.[34] The strong coalitions of the South largely fulfil the promise of empowerment, produce somewhat mixed results on the legitimacy front, but seriously fall short as far as improving the functioning of the WTO goes. Could the power of coalitions be harnessed to deliver the goals of legitimacy and efficiency of the organization, and preserve and further enhance the empowerment that they bring to their members? I offer two sets of solutions below. The first solution set operates at the level of the member countries, while the second requires institutional reform of the WTO.

9.5.1 Reforming coalition structures and strategies

As has been argued earlier in this chapter, developing countries have learned to constitute strong coalitions that stand firm in the endgame. But these coalitions find it difficult to make concessions and heighten the proclivity of the WTO to deadlock due to the risk of misinterpretation by both coalition allies and outside parties. If developing countries were to transform their coalitions from veto-wielding blocking coalitions to negotiating ones, both their members and the system would be better off.

The easiest way in which coalitions could overcome the risk of having concessions interpreted as a sign of weakness would be to restructure their coalitions with a narrow issue-specific focus. Such a coalition would automatically be seen as cohesive, and would not involve the complex logrolling associated with the strong coalitions that we see today. However, this would not only deprive the coalitions of the external weight that underpins their bargaining power, but also the legitimacy that they derive from diversity of membership. But structural reform of the coalition is not the only option available to developing countries.

Insofar as coalitions of developing countries find it difficult to make concessions because conciliatory moves might trigger defection, credible signalling mechanisms

---

[34] This section draws on arguments proposed in Narlikar 2009.

offer the simplest solution.[35] One of the central ideas behind credible signalling is to demonstrate a willingness to incur costs to achieve a prized goal.[36] Prioritization of demands can have a similar effect. A visible and public refusal to accept a bilateral deal and to instead adhere to the coalition's position can also serve as a useful signalling device for reassuring allies and demonstrating the strength of the coalition to the outside party. Having taken on the costs of such signalling, the coalition can then engage in actual negotiation (and the compromise and concession that this requires) without leading the outside party or allies to cast doubt on its commitment to a hierarchy of issues in the collective agenda.

In actual practice, an example of such signalling behaviour in the case of the G20 could have involved concessions on special and differential treatment (SDT), accompanied by an even firmer assertion of the coalition's position on agriculture. As concessions on SDT would have jeopardized the coalition's relations with some other coalitions (particularly the LDC group), the signal would have enjoyed credibility. But the costs would not have been high enough to threaten the unity of the coalition itself, and would have thereby allowed the coalition to negotiate from a position of strength.

9.5.2 Formal institutional recognition for coalitions

While signalling mechanisms could improve the ability of coalitions to make concessions, and thereby address the problem of deadlock, formal institutional recognition of coalitions could potentially help address the problems of efficiency and legitimacy of the organization, and also help transform the veto power of strong coalitions into agenda-setting and negotiating power. A two-step process towards this is proposed.

As a first step, countries would build coalitions, which would then receive formal recognition in the second step.[37] Recognizing that in international politics there are no permanent allies, coalitions would be constituted for the duration of a round, and subsequently reconstituted, so that countries do not get locked into outmoded loyalties.

---

[35] One of the reasons why Cancún failed was that developed countries were simply not aware of the strength of the G20 or other coalitions. Similarly, there were several grounds for the North to assume that in later iterations the G20 would be willing to make concessions (given that most coalitions in the North do make such concessions in the endgame). Were coalitions to improve signalling mechanisms, particularly using costly signals to credibly indicate their intentions, the probability of deadlock would be reduced. This would be true even if coalitions had no intentions of making concessions. As long as they credibly communicate their aims and strategies to the North, the likelihood of reaching agreement would improve. This idea is developed more formally in Narlikar and van Houten 2010.

[36] On signalling mechanisms, see Fearon 1994 and Banks 1991.

[37] Jones 2009. Note that Jones provides a related proposal, where issue-based 'platforms' are used as a mechanism for reaching consensus. A key difference, however, is that formalizing coalitions (as per this chapter) rather than issue-specific platforms would allow countries the option to operate in cross-issue blocs, and thereby form coalitions with greater collective market power in some instances, while retaining the possibility to form issue-specific coalitions if they so preferred. See also Vickers 2010 for a comparative analysis of the two sets of proposals.

But for the purposes of the particular round, a coalition, once constituted, would effectively serve as the principal actor for negotiation. Formalization would entail a moratorium on bilateral/regional side-payments, or other institutional guarantees against attempts to buy members off. Alternatively, if such a moratorium could not be placed against attempts to divide and conquer rival coalitions, an MFN rule could be instituted so that side-payments offered to any one member of the coalition would have to be extended to all members. The purpose of having such guarantees in place would help coalitions overcome the risk that any concessions may be interpreted as a sign of weakness, and make it easier for parties to use integrative strategies and seek mutually beneficial solutions. The direct beneficiaries of this formal recognition would be the member countries themselves, who would be able to translate their veto power into effective influence.

Such a process of according formal recognition to coalitions with each new round would facilitate the negotiation process by narrowing the number of principals, and all other associated efficiencies, without translating into the increasing inflexibility that has come to characterize many coalitions today. If developing countries were allowed to formally aggregate their market power, they would come to enjoy a prize place at the negotiating table, even with the principal supplier principle in operation.[38] Once in the formal domain, it would also be easier to establish certain minimal rules on consultation between the coalition coordinator/representative and their members, thereby addressing some of the legitimacy concerns that smaller members of coalitions have brought up recently. The utility of these coalitions could even potentially be extended to the dispute settlement mechanism to improve its accessibility for developing countries as well as their retaliatory capacities.

9.6 Conclusion

In this chapter, I have traced the evolution of coalitions from the Uruguay Round to the DDA. The new found strength of coalitions today, I argue, lies in their structures and bargaining strategies. While coalitions of developing countries have achieved unprecedented importance in the central negotiation processes of the WTO, and brought unprecedented diversity at the High Table of its decision-making, they have also generated some unanticipated costs. The most serious of these is that, while empowering large parts of the developing world, they have contributed to the making of an organization that is much more deadlock-prone and crisis-ridden. I then suggested two sets of solutions. Neither of these solution sets provides a panacea for all the problems that plague the WTO. But they do offer one way of preserving and furthering the strengths of coalitions of developing countries, while simultaneously removing at least one cause of the stasis that afflicts the system today.

---

[38] See Rolland 2007 for an original proposal on the role of coalitions from a legal perspective.

Annex 1 Coalitions Listed on the WTO Website[1]

Groups	Description/issues	Countries
ACP	African, Caribbean, and Pacific countries with preferences in the EU **Issues**: Agricultural preferences **Nature**: Geographical **Website**: http://www.acpsec.org	**WTO members (58)**: Angola, Antigua and Barbuda, Barbados, Belize, Benin, Botswana, Burkina Faso, Burundi, Côte d'Ivoire, Cameroon, Cape Verde, Central African Republic, Chad, Congo, Cuba, Democratic Republic of the Congo, Djibouti, Dominica, Dominican Republic, Fiji, Gabon, Gambia, Ghana, Grenada, Guinea, Guinea Bissau, Guyana, Haiti, Jamaica, Kenya, Lesotho, Madagascar, Malawi, Mali, Mauritania, Mauritius, Mozambique, Namibia, Niger, Nigeria, Papua New Guinea, Rwanda, Saint Kitts and Nevis, Saint Lucia, Saint Vincent and the Grenadines, Senegal, Sierra Leone, Solomon Islands, South Africa, Suriname, Swaziland, Tanzania, Togo, Tonga, Trinidad and Tobago, Uganda, Zambia, Zimbabwe **WTO observers (10)**: Bahamas, Comoros, Equatorial Guinea, Ethiopia, Liberia, Samoa, São Tomé and Principe, Seychelles, Sudan, Vanuatu **Not WTO members or observers (11)**: Cook Islands, Eritrea, Kiribati, Marshall Islands, Micronesia (Federated States of), Nauru, Niue, Palau, Somalia, Timor-Leste, Tuvalu
African Group	African members of the WTO **Issues**: General **Nature**: Regional	**WTO members (41)**: Angola, Benin, Botswana, Burkina Faso, Burundi, Côte d'Ivoire, Cameroon, Cape Verde, Central African Republic, Chad, Congo, Djibouti, Egypt, Gabon, Gambia, Ghana, Guinea, Guinea Bissau, Kenya, Lesotho, Madagascar, Malawi, Mali, Mauritania, Mauritius, Morocco, Mozambique, Namibia, Niger, Nigeria, Rwanda, Senegal, Sierra Leone, South Africa, Swaziland, Tanzania, Togo, Tunisia, Uganda, Zambia, Zimbabwe
APEC	Asia-Pacific Economic Cooperation forum **Issues**: General **Nature**: Regional **Website**: http://www.apec.org	**WTO members (20)**: Australia, Brunei Darussalam, Canada, Chile, China, Chinese Taipei, Hong Kong, China, Indonesia, Japan, Korea (Republic of), Malaysia, Mexico, New Zealand, Papua New Guinea, Peru, Philippines, Singapore, Thailand, United States of America, Vietnam **WTO observers (1)**: Russian Federation

Groups	Description/issues	Countries
EU	European Union **Issues:** General **Nature:** Customs union Website: http://ec.europa.eu	**WTO members (28):** Austria, Belgium, Bulgaria, Cyprus, Czech Republic, Denmark, Estonia, European Union (formerly EC), Finland, France, Germany, Greece, Hungary, Ireland, Italy, Latvia, Lithuania, Luxembourg, Malta, Netherlands, Poland, Portugal, Romania, Slovak Republic, Slovenia, Spain, Sweden, United Kingdom
Mercosur	Common Market of the Southern Cone (Mercosul in Portuguese) **Issues:** General **Nature:** Customs union **Website:** http://www.mercosur.int	**WTO members (4):** Argentina, Brazil, Paraguay, Uruguay
G90	African Group + ACP + least-developed countries **Issues:** General	**WTO members (65):** Angola, Antigua and Barbuda, Bangladesh, Barbados, Belize, Benin, Botswana, Burkina Faso, Burundi, Côte d'Ivoire, Cambodia, Cameroon, Cape Verde, Central African Republic, Chad, Congo, Cuba, Democratic Republic of the Congo, Djibouti, Dominica, Dominican Republic, Egypt, Fiji, Gabon, Gambia, Ghana, Grenada, Guinea, Guinea Bissau, Guyana, Haiti, Jamaica, Kenya, Lesotho, Madagascar, Malawi, Maldives, Mali, Mauritania, Mauritius, Morocco, Mozambique, Myanmar, Namibia, Nepal, Niger, Nigeria, Papua New Guinea, Rwanda, Saint Kitts and Nevis, Saint Lucia, Saint Vincent and the Grenadines, Senegal, Sierra Leone, Solomon Islands, South Africa, Suriname, Swaziland, Tanzania, Togo, Trinidad and Tobago, Tunisia, Uganda, Zambia, Zimbabwe **WTO observers (14):** Afghanistan, Bahamas, Bhutan, Comoros, Equatorial Guinea, Ethiopia, Lao People's Democratic Republic, Liberia, Samoa, São Tomé and Principe, Seychelles, Sudan, Vanuatu, Yemen **Not WTO members or observers (11):** Cook Islands, Eritrea, Kiribati, Marshall Islands, Micronesia (Federated States of), Nauru, Niue, Palau, Somalia, Timor-Leste, Tuvalu

Term	Description	Members
Least-developed countries (LDCs)	Least-developed countries: the world's poorest countries. The WTO uses the UN list. **Issues:** General **Website:** http://www.ldcgroups.org	**WTO members (32):** Angola, Bangladesh, Benin, Burkina Faso, Burundi, Cambodia, Central African Republic, Chad, Democratic Republic of the Congo, Djibouti, Gambia, Guinea, Guinea Bissau, Haiti, Lesotho, Madagascar, Malawi, Maldives, Mali, Mauritania, Mozambique, Myanmar, Nepal, Niger, Rwanda, Senegal, Sierra Leone, Solomon Islands, Tanzania, Togo, Uganda, Zambia **WTO observers (12):** Afghanistan, Bhutan, Comoros, Equatorial Guinea, Ethiopia, Lao People's Democratic Republic, Liberia, Samoa, São Tomé and Principe, Sudan, Vanuatu, Yemen **Not WTO members or observers (5):** Eritrea, Kiribati, Somalia, Timor-Leste, Tuvalu
Small, vulnerable economies (SVEs)—agriculture	This list is based on sponsors of proposals. See also: list in Annex I of the 10 July 2008 revised draft agriculture modalities, and footnote 9 (paragraph 65) and paragraph 151. **Issues:** Agriculture	**WTO members (14):** Barbados, Bolivia, Cuba, Dominican Republic, El Salvador, Fiji, Guatemala, Honduras, Mauritius, Mongolia, Nicaragua, Papua New Guinea, Paraguay, Trinidad and Tobago
Small, vulnerable economies (SVEs)—NAMA	This list is based on sponsors of proposals. See also: definition in paragraph 13 of the 10 July 2008 revised draft NAMA modalities. **Issues:** NAMA	**WTO members (19):** Antigua and Barbuda, Barbados, Bolivia, Dominica, Dominican Republic, El Salvador, Fiji, Grenada, Guatemala, Honduras, Jamaica, Mongolia, Nicaragua, Papua New Guinea, Paraguay, Saint Kitts and Nevis, Saint Lucia, Saint Vincent and the Grenadines, Trinidad and Tobago
Small, vulnerable economies (SVEs)—rules	Sponsors of TN/RL/W/226/Rev.5 **Issues:** Rules (fisheries subsidies) **Documents:** TN/RL/W/226/Rev.5	**WTO members (14):** Barbados, Cuba, Dominica, Dominican Republic, El Salvador, Fiji, Honduras, Jamaica, Mauritius, Nicaragua, Papua New Guinea, Saint Lucia, Saint Vincent and the Grenadines, Tonga
Recently acceded members (RAMs)	Recently acceded members (RAMs), i.e. countries that negotiated and joined the WTO after 1995, seeking lesser commitments in the negotiations because of the liberalization they have undertaken as part of their membership agreements. Excludes least-developed countries because they will make no new commitments, and EU members. **Issues:** General	**WTO members (19):** Albania, Armenia, Cape Verde, China, Chinese Taipei, Croatia, Ecuador, Former Yugoslav Republic of Macedonia, Georgia, Jordan, Kyrgyz Republic, Moldova, Mongolia, Oman, Panama, Saudi Arabia (Kingdom of), Tonga, Ukraine, Vietnam

Groups	Description/issues	Countries
Low income transition	Seeking to secure the same treatment as least-developed countries. (Georgia formally withdrew, but in the agriculture draft the full list is: Albania, Armenia, Georgia, Kyrgyz Republic, Moldova) **Issues**: Agriculture/NAMA	**WTO members (3)**: Armenia, Kyrgyz Republic, Moldova
Cairns Group	Coalition of agricultural exporting nations lobbying for agricultural trade liberalization. **Issues**: Agriculture **Website**: http://www.cairnsgroup.org	**WTO members (19)**: Argentina, Australia, Bolivia, Brazil, Canada, Chile, Colombia, Costa Rica, Guatemala, Indonesia, Malaysia, New Zealand, Pakistan, Paraguay, Peru, Philippines, South Africa, Thailand, Uruguay
Tropical products	Coalition of developing countries seeking greater market access for tropical products. **Issues**: Agriculture	**WTO members (8)**: Bolivia, Colombia, Costa Rica, Ecuador, Guatemala, Nicaragua, Panama, Peru
G10	Coalition of countries lobbying for agriculture to be treated as diverse and special because of non-trade concerns (not to be confused with the Group of Ten Central Bankers). **Issues**: Agriculture	**WTO members (9)**: Chinese Taipei, Iceland, Israel, Japan, Korea (Republic of), Liechtenstein, Mauritius, Norway, Switzerland
G20	Coalition of developing countries pressing for ambitious reforms of agriculture in developed countries with some flexibility for developing countries (not to be confused with the G20 group of finance ministers and central bank governors, and its recent summit meetings). **Issues**: Agriculture **Website**: http://www.g-20.mre.gov.br	**WTO members (23)**: Argentina, Bolivia, Brazil, Chile, China, Cuba, Ecuador, Egypt, Guatemala, India, Indonesia, Mexico, Nigeria, Pakistan, Paraguay, Peru, Philippines, South Africa, Tanzania, Thailand, Uruguay, Venezuela (Bolivarian Republic of), Zimbabwe

Group	Description	WTO members
G33	Also called 'Friends of Special Products' in agriculture. Coalition of developing countries pressing for flexibility for developing countries to undertake limited market opening in agriculture. **Issues:** Agriculture	**WTO members (46):** Antigua and Barbuda, Barbados, Belize, Benin, Bolivia, Botswana, Côte d'Ivoire, China, Congo, Cuba, Dominica, Dominican Republic, El Salvador, Grenada, Guatemala, Guyana, Haiti, Honduras, India, Indonesia, Jamaica, Kenya, Korea (Republic of), Madagascar, Mauritius, Mongolia, Mozambique, Nicaragua, Nigeria, Pakistan, Panama, Peru, Philippines, Saint Kitts and Nevis, Saint Lucia, Saint Vincent and the Grenadines, Senegal, Sri Lanka, Suriname, Tanzania, Trinidad and Tobago, Turkey, Uganda, Venezuela (Bolivarian Republic of), Zambia, Zimbabwe
Cotton-4	West African coalition seeking cuts in cotton subsidies and tariffs. **Issues:** Agriculture (Cotton)	**WTO members (4):** Benin, Burkina Faso, Chad, Mali
NAMA-11	Coalition of developing countries seeking flexibilities to limit market opening in industrial goods trade. **Issues:** NAMA	**WTO members (10):** Argentina, Brazil, Egypt, India, Indonesia, Namibia, Philippines, South Africa, Tunisia, Venezuela (Bolivarian Republic of)
Paragraph 6 (NAMA)	In NAMA (refers to paragraph 6 of the first version of the NAMA text), for reducing the number of new bindings they would have to contribute and to increase the average target from 27.5 per cent. (Except Macao, China). **Issues:** NAMA	**WTO members (12):** Côte d'Ivoire, Cameroon, Congo, Cuba, Ghana, Kenya, Macao, China, Mauritius, Nigeria, Sri Lanka, Suriname, Zimbabwe
Friends of Ambition (NAMA)	Seeking to maximize tariff reductions and achieve real market access in NAMA. (Some nuanced differences in positions.) **Issues:** NAMA	**WTO members (36):** Australia, Austria, Belgium, Bulgaria, Canada, Cyprus, Czech Republic, Denmark, Estonia, European Union (formerly EC), Finland, France, Germany, Greece, Hungary, Ireland, Italy, Japan, Korea (Republic of), Latvia, Lithuania, Luxembourg, Malta, Netherlands, New Zealand, Norway, Poland, Portugal, Romania, Slovak Republic, Slovenia, Spain, Sweden, Switzerland, United Kingdom, United States of America
Middle Ground Group (NAMA)	Moderate ambition, seeking to improve market access into both developed and developing countries. **Issues:** NAMA	**WTO members (12):** Chile, Colombia, Costa Rica, Hong Kong, China, Israel, Malaysia, Mexico, Morocco, Pakistan, Peru, Singapore, Thailand
Friends of A–D Negotiations (FANs)	Coalition seeking more disciplines on the use of anti-dumping measures. **Issues:** Rules (anti-dumping)	**WTO members (15):** Brazil, Chile, Chinese Taipei, Colombia, Costa Rica, Hong Kong, China, Israel, Japan, Korea (Republic of), Mexico, Norway, Singapore, Switzerland, Thailand, Turkey

Groups	Description/issues	Countries
Friends of Fish (FoFs)	Coalition seeking to significantly reduce fisheries subsidies. Previously included Ecuador, Philippines. **Issues:** Rules (fisheries subsidies)	**WTO members (10):** Argentina, Australia, Chile, Colombia, Iceland, New Zealand, Norway, Pakistan, Peru, United States of America
'W52' sponsors	Sponsors of TN/C/W/52, a proposal for 'modalities' in negotiations on geographical indications (the multilateral register for wines and spirits, and extending the higher level of protection beyond wines and spirits) and 'disclosure' (patent applicants to disclose the origin of genetic resources and traditional knowledge used in the inventions). The list includes as groups: the EU, ACP, and African Group. Dominican Republic is in the ACP and South Africa is in the African Group, but they are sponsors of TN/IP/W/10/Rev.2 on geographical indications. **Issues:** Intellectual property (TRIPS) **Documents:** TN/C/W/52	**WTO members (109):** Albania, Angola, Antigua and Barbuda, Austria, Barbados, Belgium, Belize, Benin, Botswana, Brazil, Bulgaria, Burkina Faso, Burundi, Cote d'Ivoire, Cameroon, Cape Verde, Central African Republic, Chad, China, Colombia, Congo, Croatia, Cuba, Cyprus, Czech Republic, Democratic Republic of the Congo, Denmark, Djibouti, Dominica, Dominican Republic, Ecuador, Egypt, Estonia, European Union (formerly EC), Fiji, Finland, Former Yugoslav Republic of Macedonia, France, Gabon, Gambia, Georgia, Germany, Ghana, Greece, Grenada, Guinea, Guinea Bissau, Guyana, Haiti, Hungary, Iceland, India, Indonesia, Ireland, Italy, Jamaica, Kenya, Kyrgyz Republic, Latvia, Lesotho, Liechtenstein, Lithuania, Luxembourg, Madagascar, Malawi, Mali, Malta, Mauritania, Mauritius, Moldova, Morocco, Mozambique, Namibia, Netherlands, Niger, Nigeria, Pakistan, Papua New Guinea, Peru, Poland, Portugal, Romania, Rwanda, Saint Kitts and Nevis, Saint Lucia, Saint Vincent and the Grenadines, Senegal, Sierra Leone, Slovak Republic, Slovenia, Solomon Islands, South Africa, Spain, Sri Lanka, Suriname, Swaziland, Sweden, Switzerland, Tanzania, Thailand, Togo, Tonga, Trinidad and Tobago, Tunisia, Turkey, Uganda, United Kingdom, Zambia, Zimbabwe
Joint proposal	Sponsors of TN/IP/W/10/Rev.2 proposing a database that is entirely voluntary. **Issues:** TRIPS GI register **Website:** http://www.wto.org/english/tratop_e/trips_e/gi_background_e.htm **Documents:** TN/IP/W/10/Rev.2	**WTO members (19):** Argentina, Australia, Canada, Chile, Chinese Taipei, Costa Rica, Dominican Republic, Ecuador, El Salvador, Guatemala, Honduras, Japan, Korea (Republic of), Mexico, New Zealand, Nicaragua, Paraguay, South Africa, United States of America

1 The WTO website not only lists some of the coalitions involved in the current negotiations, but also has the following to say about them: 'A number of countries have formed coalitions in the WTO. These groups often speak with one voice using a single coordinator or negotiating team. These are some of the most active groups in the WTO.' Accessed at <http://www.wto.org/english/tratop_e/dda_e/negotiating_groups_e.htm> on 8 November 2011

Source: <http://www.wto.org>

Annex 2 Coalitions in the Consensus-Building Process

BIG meetings, small meetings, concentric circles:

- *'Inclusive'*: all coalitions represented in consultations
- *'Transparent'*: representatives report back to coalitions
- *'Bottom-up'*: convergence built by members themselves.

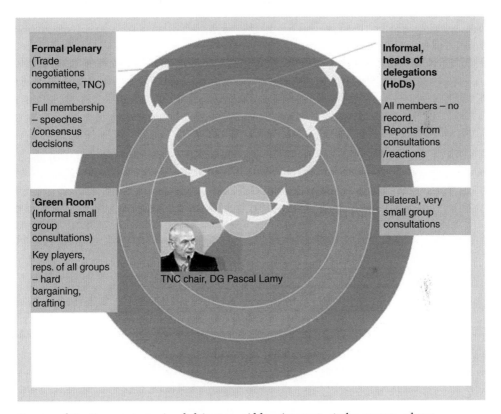

Source: <http://www.wto.org/english/tratop_e/dda_e/meeto8_circles_popup_e.htm>

REFERENCES

Banks, Jeffrey. 1991. *Signaling Games in Political Science*. Chur, Switzerland and New York: Harwood Academic Publishers.

Bazerman, Max, and Margaret Neale. 1995. The Role of Fairness Considerations and Relationships in a Judgemental Perspective of Negotiations. In *Barriers to Conflict Resolution*, edited by Kenneth Arrow, Robert Mnookin, and Amos Tversky, 86–107. New York: W.W. Norton.

Diego-Fernandez, Mateo. 2008. Trade Negotiations Make Strange Bedfellows. *World Trade Review* 7 (2):23–53.

Fearon, James. 1994. Signaling versus the Balance of Power and Interests: An Empirical Test of a Crisis Bargaining Model. *Journal of Conflict Resolution* 38 (2):236–69.

Gamble, Andrew. 2010. The Politics of Deadlocks. In *Deadlocks in Multilateral Negotiations: Causes and Solutions*, edited by Amrita Narlikar, 25–46. Cambridge: Cambridge University Press.

Hamilton, Colleen, and John Whalley. 1989. Coalitions in the Uruguay Round. *Weltwirtschaftliches Archiv* 125 (3):547–56.

Higgott, Richard, and Andrew Cooper. 1990. Middle Power Leadership and Coalition Building: Australia, the Cairns Group, and the Uruguay Round of Trade Negotiations. *International Organization* 44 (4):589–632.

Hoekman, Bernard. 2003. Cancún: Crisis or Catharsis? September 20. Available from <http://siteresources.worldbank.org/.../Hoekman-CancunCatharsis-092003.pdf>. Accessed on 11 November 2010.

Ismail, Faizel. 2009. Reflections on the July 2008 Collapse. In *Leadership and Change in the Multilateral Trading System*, edited by Amrita Narlikar and Brendan Vickers. Leiden: Martinus Nijhoff, and Dordrecht: Republic of Letters Publishing.

Jervis, Robert. 1978. Cooperation Under the Security Dilemma. *World Politics* 30 (2):167–214.

Jones, Kent. 2009. *The Doha Blues: Institutional Crisis and Reform in the WTO*. Oxford: Oxford University Press.

Kumar, Rajiv. 1993. Developing Country Coalitions in International Trade Negotiations. In *Developing Countries in World Trade: Policies and Bargaining Strategies*, edited by Diana Tussie and David Glover. Boulder: Lynne Rienner.

Narlikar, Amrita. 2003. *International Trade and Developing Countries: Bargaining Coalitions in the GATT and WTO*. London: Routledge.

Narlikar, Amrita. 2009. A Theory of Bargaining Coalitions in the WTO. In *Leadership and Change in the Multilateral Trading System*, edited by Amrita Narlikar and Brendan Vickers. Leiden: Martinus Nijhoff, and Dordrecht: Republic of Letters Publishing.

Narlikar, Amrita, ed. 2010. *Deadlocks in Multilateral Negotiations: Causes and Solutions*. Cambridge: Cambridge University Press.

Narlikar, Amrita, and John Odell. 2006. The Strict Distributive Strategy for a Developing Country Coalition: The Like Minded Group in the World Trade Organization. In *Negotiating Trade: Developing Countries in the WTO and NAFTA*, edited by John Odell, 115–44. Cambridge: Cambridge University Press.

Narlikar, Amrita, and Diana Tussie. 2004. The G20 at the Cancún Ministerial: Developing Countries and their Evolving Coalitions in the WTO. *The World Economy* 27 (7):947–66.

Narlikar, Amrita, and Pieter van Houten. 2010. Know the Enemy: Uncertainty and Deadlock in the WTO. In *Deadlocks in Multilateral Negotiations: Causes and Solutions*, edited by Amrita Narlikar, 142–63. Cambridge: Cambridge University Press.

Odell, John, ed. 2006. *Negotiating Trade: Developing Countries in the WTO and NAFTA*. Cambridge: Cambridge University Press.

Odell, John, and Susan Sell. 2006. Reframing the Issue: The WTO Coalition on Intellectual Property and Public Health, 2001. In *Negotiating Trade: Developing Countries in the WTO and NAFTA*, edited by John Odell, 85–114. Cambridge: Cambridge University Press.

Rolland, Sonia. 2007. Developing Country Coalitions at the WTO: In Search of Legal Support. *Harvard International Law Journal* 48 (2):483–551.

Steinberg, Richard. 2003. In the Shadow of Law or Power? Consensus-based Bargaining and Outcomes in the WTO. *International Organization* 56 (2):339–74.

Tussie, Diana. 1993. Holding the Balance: The Cairns Group in the Uruguay Round. In *Developing Countries in World Trade: Policies and Bargaining Strategies*, edited by Diana Tussie and David Glover. Boulder: Lynne Rienner.

Vickers, Brendan. 2010. Decision-Making and Representation through Coalitions in the WTO. Available from <http://www.gtdforum.org/download/Governance%20Brendan%20Vickers.pdf>. Accessed on 14 November 2010.

PART IV

··

AGENCY IN THE WTO

··

CHAPTER 10

....

THE INFLUENCE OF THE EU IN THE WORLD TRADE SYSTEM

....

PATRICK A. MESSERLIN

10.1 INTRODUCTION

....

THIS chapter argues that the EU[1] has had, and may still have, an important influence in the world trade system—a term covering both the preferential trade agreements (PTAs) and the multilateral trade regime based on the General Agreement on Tariffs and Trade (GATT) and its successor, the World Trade Organization (WTO).

But the influence of the EU is markedly different from the role of the United States—and this is why this chapter uses the term of 'influence' for the EU. The EU has never been a leader in the way the US has been: it has never tested grounds for launching new rounds of negotiations in the GATT or in the WTO (with the exception in the late 1990s, largely due to the Trade Commissioner of this time, Lord Brittan) or shaped new agendas. In this respect, the EU has often rather been a somewhat reluctant, or even negative, player at the beginning of every GATT round. And it has turned to be a positive force only late in the rounds, when it finally realized that it could greatly benefit from additional market access. The EU has used its strong attraction to discrimination, with its many PTAs with developing countries, as a way to get allies, reinforcing its weight as a reluctant or negative trading partner at the beginning of the rounds. And when it was ready to shift to more positive attitudes at the end of the rounds, it has generally let down

---

[1] Since the implementation of the Treaty on the Functioning of the European Union (hereafter TFEU, often called the Lisbon Treaty) in 2010, the official name of what used to be the European Community in the GATT/WTO context is now the European Union (EU). For the sake of simplicity, this chapter uses the EU acronym for the whole period.

unceremoniously its many small allies—at a high price for them since they were not induced to grasp the opportunities offered by the final stages of the negotiations.

As a result, the chapter mentions only briefly the influence that the EU may have had on the detailed pace of the negotiations.[2] Rather, it focuses on the influence that the EU may have had on the design of the world trade system. This influence has been both pragmatic and indirect.

First, pragmatic. Contrary to what most European observers have argued,[3] the EU could not develop a 'vision' of the world trade system simply because its political structure has been—and still is—too volatile and fragile. The EU influence has mostly consisted in providing pragmatic tools of negotiations such as 'mutual recognition' in technical barriers to trade or services, 'mutual evaluation' in services, anti-dumping and anti-subsidy rules in goods, and rules on export barriers in goods, to quote the most important ones. In other words, the EU influence has been through the improvement of the technology of negotiations. The EU has had to forge such a technology when coping with the problems that it was facing in its own internal liberalization, often decades earlier than the world trade system. For instance, the EU started to deal with technical barriers to trade and services liberalization in the very early or mid-1970s, and to wrestle with competition policy in a plurilateral environment in the 1980s.

The second feature of the EU influence has been to be largely indirect. Paradoxically, the best advocate of the EU tools of negotiations has not been the EU itself, but other GATT/WTO members, such as Australia, New Zealand, or Georgia. Because these countries have been much bolder in trade policy matters, they have been able to inject the EU tools much more convincingly in the world trade system. If the EU has not been the best advocate—nor indeed the best enforcer—of its own technology, it is largely due again to its fragile political structure and to its increasing heterogeneity since the 1990s.

The chapter is organized as follows. Section 10.2 focuses on the most important issue of modern commercial policy—the balance between regulatory competition and regulatory harmonization. If one excepts agriculture and a very few industrial sectors, negotiations on tariff cuts would be largely over after a successful Doha Round (except for the small developing countries) and the technology of tariff negotiations was very well known—from formula cuts to the design of the exception formulas.[4] As a result, almost all the problems discussed today are of a regulatory nature—technical norms in goods and services liberalization being the two major topics. Section 10.3 describes the sources of the EU improvement of the technology of negotiations: the creativity of the Treaty of Rome, which established the European Community in 1957, and of the first rulings of the European Court of Justice. Section 10.4 examines how the tools created by the EU are slowly percolating through the world trade system (mutual recognition) while others have still not made any progress (anti-dumping and competition, export restrictions), despite a few attempts. Sections 10.5 and 10.6 do the same task for services.

---

[2] For detail on these matters, see Messerlin 2011a.
[3] For a good presentation of this point of view, see Pelkmans 2001.
[4] For more details see Messerlin 2011b.

10.2 MODERN TRADE POLICY: REGULATORY COMPETITION VERSUS REGULATORY HARMONIZATION

From the 1960s to the 1980s, GATT was very successful at cutting tariffs and eliminating quantitative restrictions on imports among developed countries. Here, the US has had clearly the dominant role, with the support of a few small economies (some of them becoming later EU member states before their accession). Two decades ago, this success had induced the major developing countries to undertake unilateral tariff cuts (although without binding their applied tariffs) and to eliminate quantitative restrictions on imports. Here, the dominant role has been clearly played by China—by her decisive and resolute choice of market opening, and by her phenomenal success in terms of growth. A successful Doha Round would basically close this chapter of trade liberalization by binding these unilateral liberalizations for the most important emerging economies. In a post-successful Doha world, only small developing countries will need a traditional GATT/WTO type of tariff negotiations.

All the current hot issues in the world trade system deal with a totally different problem—liberalizing when countries have different regulations—technical regulations in goods, market-related regulations in services. In short, they raise the problem of the balance between regulatory harmonization and regulatory competition. In this chapter, regulatory competition is defined by the use of the mutual recognition principle—according to which, goods lawfully produced in one country cannot be banned from sale on the territory of another country, even if they are produced with different technical or quality specifications.

10.2.1 Two perspectives

When addressing the question of the respective pros and cons of regulatory harmonization and regulatory competition (the latter being defined by the use of the mutual recognition principle), most analysts adopt a 'negative' angle. They focus on what should be done to minimize the consequences of a domestic regulation affecting firms outside of the regulating jurisdiction—that is, on predominantly legal concerns.[5]

What follows argues that an approach at least as interesting raises the question of the pros and cons of competition and harmonization in a 'positive' way. The basic question is then: what would—or should—be the preferred choice of regulators who choose the

---

[5] Sykes 2000.

increase of the welfare of their fellow citizens as the key criterion of their decisions concerning regulations?[6]

When studying the mutual recognition principle, Pincus raises a fascinating paradox:[7]

> through mutual recognition, the States are simultaneously certifying that there are no essential differences in their regulations, while acting as though there are sufficient differences to justify maintaining their own, different regulations.

This section explains Pincus' paradox by providing three arguments which are based on imperfect competition between the many varieties of heterogeneous goods—the type of competition which is dominant in our modern economies—while Pincus' paradox was developed in the context of pure competition among homogeneous products.[8] What follows suggests that an approach based on many differentiated products reinforces considerably the value of regulatory competition.

10.2.2 A Darwinian process of interacting development of markets and regulations

The first argument focuses on the past. In every country, regulations are developed in a broad legal environment built by decades of the country's history. As a result, this environment has shaped the varieties of goods available in a country, with laws making it easy or not to produce some varieties, hence determining the range of varieties. In turn, the existing varieties of goods in the country have generated the varieties of regulations that are needed to support their development. In short, there is a two-way interaction between the varieties of goods and the varieties of regulations, a kind of 'Darwinian' process of development of markets and regulations.

In such a context, the range of varieties of goods available in the world is so wide that a country relying only on its own domestic regulations unduly narrows the range of goods available to its consumers. Regulatory competition aims to keep this range as large as possible, while regulatory harmonization narrows the number of available varieties. The fact that a regulator accepts regulatory competition reflects, thus, the desire to enlarge the range of goods available to the domestic consumers, making it possible for these consumers to fully grab the gains from trade flows, based on differentiated goods, which

---

[6] The difference between the negative and positive approaches is very similar to the one between the way trade negotiators and economists perceive trade liberalization. Trade negotiators see liberalization as requiring concessions to be extracted from negotiating partners, while trade economists perceive it as a source of welfare gains from importing foreign goods.

[7] Pincus 2009.

[8] The discussion thus leaves aside 'political' arguments for harmonization related to 'nation building' captured by Pincus' quote of Alexis de Tocqueville: 'In great centralized nations, the legislator is obliged to give a character of uniformity to the laws'. Pincus 2009, 16.

have been highlighted by the trade theory since the 1980s.[9] But ensuring that domestic consumers fully benefit from 'foreign' goods requires recognition of the 'foreign' varieties of regulations that have shaped these goods, because the regulatory structure 'behind' a product is part and parcel of the characteristics defining the product in question.

This first argument suggests several conclusions.

- It sees mutual recognition primarily as a way to increase domestic consumers' welfare ('positive' approach), not as a way to solve cross-borders spillovers ('negative' approach) of national regulations. Regulatory differences between two countries do not need to be large, but simply large enough to counterbalance the transaction costs generated by the coexistence of different technical norms.
- Second, mutual recognition is likely to have a greater value in larger and/or more heterogeneous entities (like the EU) than in smaller, more homogeneous ones (like Australia). The more heterogeneous the EU becomes, the wider the range of the varieties of products and regulations may be, and the more attractive mutual recognition between EU member states becomes. By contrast, the more homogeneous Australia becomes, the smaller the range of the varieties of products and regulations is likely to be, and the more attractive harmonization of Australian states' norms becomes. In short, the borders between regulatory competition and regulatory harmonization are fluid over time and distance.
- Lastly, economic analysis shows that there are economic forces pushing for an excessive (hence suboptimal) production of varieties. Regulatory competition should also be expected to be excessive in such cases.

10.2.3 Regulatory behaviour and the future

The second argument focuses on the future and on the need to take into account future-related risk assessment. Two countries may recognize that their current regulations could (or should) be easily harmonized today. But one of them could still prefer to keep the mutual recognition option, for the following reason: this country perceives (wrongly or rightly) that the other country is changing its regulations too slowly (or too quickly) because it is more (or less) risk-averse with respect to new goods. In such a context, the value of mutual recognition is related to the possible differences in future regulations. If these differences are expected to be frequent and/or substantial, it makes sense that one country (possibly both, for opposite reasons) keeps alive the mutual recognition option, even if, in the long run, harmonization would effectively prevail. Mutual recognition appears, then, as an instrument which mirrors some kind of 'precautionary principle' with respect to regulations among countries that have different regulatory behaviour.

---

[9] Krugman 1979.

This argument, based on the future, may explain the reluctance of some EU member states (the United Kingdom, for instance) to harmonize. This reluctance may be caused less by the EU member states' regulations existing at a precise moment of time, than by the possible future developments of EU member states' regulations. The reluctance seems also greater when the various EU member states have different ways to cope with risk assessment. For instance, independent 'bodies' for assessing the risks caused by a product or a technology are much more developed and trusted in some EU member states than in the others. The countries asking for harmonization are often those with weak bodies, hence with less capacity to deal with problems requiring the mix of trust and flexibility that an independent body can provide, as best illustrated by many sanitary and phytosanitary crises (mad cow disease, swine flu, etc.). In short, there is some balance between rule-making (imposing norms) and institution-building (the existence of trusted risk-assessing agencies).

10.2.4 Harmonizing regulations and harmonizing their implementation

The third argument focuses on the fact that managing harmonization raises a two-step challenge: first to adopt harmonized regulations, and second to enforce these new regulations in a harmonized way. Any cost-benefit balance of regulatory harmonization should take into account these two steps.

First, harmonizing regulations requires negotiations. The higher the number of countries, the more costly such negotiations are, and the more unlikely that they will lead to better regulations. Though rarely evoked, this point is crucial. It is almost always assumed that harmonized regulations are better than the pre-existing non-harmonized ones. This is due to the assumption that the process of producing new regulations is an ideal one—dominated by technical experts independent from political pressures as well as from vested economic and scientific interests. This is a strong assumption, which ignores the politically-loaded process of producing harmonized regulations.

Second, once adopted, harmonized regulations need to be enforced in a harmonized way. This condition is much more constraining than generally anticipated, because the inertia associated with the pre-harmonization regulations is often ignored. In the EU, this problem is made worse by the fact that failed implementation often induces the European Commission (hereafter, the Commission) to solve such problems by adopting new regulations—generally stricter than the initial ones. Almost all the regulatory impact assessments done by the Commission since 2003 have ended up in new and stricter regulations, while the initial problem was said to be related to a poor enforcement of previous regulations by all or some EU member states. Of course, such a reaction magnifies the implementation problems rather than solves them, to the extent that it generates a spiral of increasingly intrusive regulations.

In short, mutual recognition emerges as the best solution if the benefits of harmonized norms (assuming that they are better than the pre-existing competing norms) are smaller than the costs of enforcing these norms.

This last argument deserves a final—very important, from a policy perspective—remark. It suggests that the best timing for harmonization is when there are significant changes in production technologies, that is, when investments in new infrastructures are necessary. This lesson is often underlined by the participants to the regulatory forum held under the TransAtlantic Business Dialogue and its successors.

10.2.5 The border between harmonization and competition: in constant flux over time and place

The above three arguments make a strong case for the benefits that consumers could get from regulatory competition—i.e. mutual recognition, either unconditional, or conditional to a set of requirements as limited as possible (see Section 10.3). But they also strongly suggest that the optimal balance between regulatory competition and harmonization is not necessarily a stable state over time. Regulatory competition may end up in convergence in some cases (with harmonization being the ultimate state of convergence), while it may prosper in other cases for long periods.

As already said, mutual recognition is not a stable state over geography either—an important point in the WTO context. This fluidity opens, in the case of very large economic entities such as the EU, the US, China, etc., the interesting possibility of harmonization at the level of sub-groups (more homogeneous) of such entities (for instance, groups of EU member states, of US states, of Chinese provinces, etc.) rather than at the level of the whole entity. The larger an entity is, the more likely harmonization within the entity is 'plurilateral'.

10.3 Goods: the creation of the mutual recognition tool

The EU was initially gifted in two essential ways. It benefited from a treaty much in advance of its time—it took almost 40 years for the GATT to become the WTO and to partly 'catch up' with the EU Treaty of Rome in terms of coverage of commercial policy.[10] And, as importantly, the EU benefited from a series of very innovative rulings of the European Court of Justice from the mid-1970s to the mid-1980s.

---

[10] The Treaty of Rome was the first of a long series of evolving versions (no less than 16) as and when the EU was developing. However, the basic structure of the Treaty of Rome is unchanged from an economic perspective.

10.3.1 A treaty much in advance of its time

Signed in March 1957, the Treaty of Rome was much in advance of its time. Figure 2 allows us to compare its main provisions with those of the 1947 General Agreement on Tariffs and Trade (GATT), extended by those of the 1995 World Trade Organization (WTO). The Treaty defines four 'freedoms', that is, four areas of liberalization (goods, services, persons, and capital) which gives the treaty a much more complete coverage than the GATT/WTO regime.

The Treaty provisions have a very special and crucial feature: they are expressed in general terms, giving them a huge capacity to adjust to new circumstances. For instance, the Treaty bans 'quantitative restrictions on imports and all measures having equivalent effects'.[11] If the first term was well defined and already used by the GATT, the second one opened a box of questions, hence the key role of the court of Justice.

10.3.2 A creative Court of Justice

Confirming and clarifying these questions has been the crucial task of the European Court of Justice (hereafter, the 'Court'). For instance, the Court has made a very innovative use of the above-mentioned notion of 'measures having

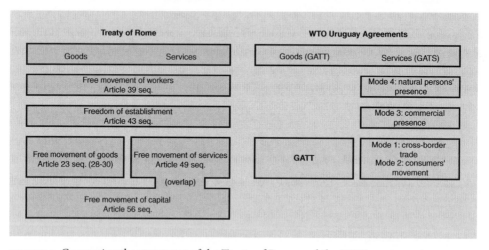

FIGURE 2 Comparing the structures of the Treaty of Rome and the WTO agreements

Sources: Treaty of Rome, WTO Uruguay agreements

[11] The Treaty of Rome had one provision for imports and one for exports, but with exactly the same terms. These two provisions are merged in one provision (Article 28) in the last version of the treaty (the Treaty on the Functioning of the European Union, hereafter TFEU).

equivalent effects' in its 1979 Cassis de Dijon case—probably its most famous ruling. This ruling established the notion of 'mutual recognition' in the EU legal framework.

The Cassis de Dijon ruling is an example of the importance of differentiated products in a modern economy. Cassis de Dijon is a potable spirit which could be freely imported into Germany in the 1970s, but could not be sold there because a German regulation provided that only potable spirits having a wine-spirit content of at least 32 per cent could be marketed in Germany, whereas the wine-spirit content of Cassis de Dijon ranges from 15 to 20 per cent. The Cassis de Dijon ruling posed the legal principle of mutual recognition, according to which goods lawfully produced in one EU member state cannot be banned from sale on the territory of another EU member state, even if they are produced with different technical or quality specifications. By making a wider range of varieties (here potable spirits) sellable in the EU, the Cassis de Dijon ruling has unleashed the intra-EU trade in differentiated products. It should be underscored that this ruling occurred in a broad context where Europeans ranked the increased range of varieties of goods as the number one benefit from the 'Common Market', higher than price competition.

The Cassis de Dijon ruling opened the possibility for the EU to change dramatically its approach to technical norms. It was the legal basis for the so-called 'New Approach' directives. Until the early 1980s, the EU tried to fully harmonize the EU member states' technical norms by adopting the so-called 'Old Approach' directives. These efforts have quickly shown the limits and costs of the Old Approach. For instance, there have been no less than three EU directives and five Commission directives for car rear-view mirrors since the early 1970s.

That said, it is essential to realize that the mutual recognition approach in technical norms still has a harmonization component because it consists of two elements. First, there is a core set of provisions to be fully harmonized, because the Cassis de Dijon ruling recognizes the need to take into account the existence of 'overriding requirements of public interest'. Second, all the other provisions are under the mutual recognition by the EU member states. In such a structure, the norms per se are no more harmonized; it is only the 'essential requirements' which have to be harmonized. This approach was opening a potentially vast degree of freedom for the firms, which could then choose the norms they wanted to use as long as they met the essential requirements.

The innovative impact of the mutual recognition tool depends largely on the scope of the core provisions to be harmonized, compared to the non-core provisions. The larger the scope of the core harmonized provisions is, the closest from harmonization mutual recognition de facto is, and the less successful it can be (for exactly the same reasons as for harmonization). This conclusion explains the increasing frustrations, when mutual recognition goes with a large core of harmonized provisions, which have emerged within the EU and in the world trade system during the last decade.

10.4 GOODS: THE EU INFLUENCE IN THE WORLD TRADE SYSTEM

As said in the introduction to this chapter, the EU influence in the detailed pace of nego-tiations on market access in industrial goods has been relatively secondary, in the sense that the EU has not been a driving force, nor a blocking force in the long run. Much more decisive were the US role or the role of some medium-sized GATT/WTO members (such as the Colombia–Switzerland 'Café au Lait' coalition, which was key to shaping the com-promise allowing to reintroduce agriculture in the GATT negotiations).[12] By contrast, the EU influence in agricultural goods has systematically been very negative. The EU:

- resisted the reintroduction of this sector until the Montreal (1988) and Brussels (1990) Ministerial Conferences
- made every effort to jeopardize the 'tariffication' of the non-tariff barriers (mostly variable levies in the EU case) required by the Uruguay Agreement (1995), by cre-ating a host of specific and seasonal tariffs
- has supported, in the Doha negotiations (up to now), (i) formulas for tariff cuts that have strong perverse impacts, (ii) all kinds of complicated exception formu-las, including tariff-rate quotas which also have strong negative effects
- might still hope to disconnect in some way the so-called 'agricultural' negotiations from the rest of the Doha package.

By contrast, the EU influence has been substantial in technical barriers to trade, where the EU technology is percolating through the world trade system via the influence of other countries. It could have been influential in rules (anti-dumping and anti-subsidy) if the circumstances had been more favourable, and it could become influential in export restrictions in the not so distant future.

10.4.1 Technical barriers to trade

The problem of technical norms as potential barriers to trade is one of the most intracta-ble problems of modern commercial policy.[13] The WTO has put it firmly on its agenda only in the most recent years. Meanwhile, countries have tried to solve this problem, or at least to soften it, through the PTA and their provisions on the mutual recognition of the technical norms of the signatories. That said, there are three ways—very different in their consequences—to tackle the problem: the first way has been opened by the EU, the second way by the Australia–New Zealand Closer Economic Relations agreement (ANZCER), and the third way is illustrated by Georgia.

---

[12] In the GATT/WTO framework, agriculture is a misnomer since it covers both the farm sector (farmers) and the food sector (agribusiness).

[13] Wilson 2002.

10.4.1.1 *The EU incapacity to be the best advocate of its mutual recognition concept in the world trade system*

The EU problem is that its decision-making process has made continuous pressures to expand the core set of provisions to be harmonized, to the detriment of those left under mutual recognition. This is because the core set of mandatory common provisions is subject to intense negotiations between the EU member states when the Council examines the Commission's proposals. During such negotiations, the EU member states (the Council) try to enlarge the core set because they feel that it is the best way to protect their vested economic interests. And the Commission does the same thing because it enlarges the scope of its power. Moreover, these incentives have increased over time: the more numerous the EU member states are, the more the EU member states have vested interests to protect, and the more the Commission may use this situation to strengthen its power.

The arrows labelled 'EU' in Figure 3 summarize what could be called the 'positive' list approach adopted over the years by the EU when dealing with the technical barriers to trade. In the 1970s and early 1980s, the EU defined a few industrial sectors, the norms of which should be fully harmonized (agro-food, cars, chemicals, pharmaceuticals). Since the late 1980s, the EU has subjected new sectors (for instance toys or pressure vessels) to the mix of harmonization and mutual recognition. There is a 'residual' of products that is not subjected to any kind of harmonization. However, the logic of the system suggests inbuilt incentives to reduce this residual.[14]

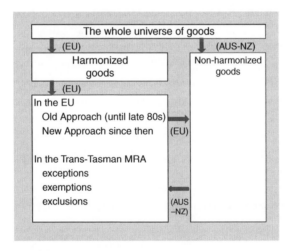

FIGURE 3 The EU and TTMRA approach to the TBT issue

Note: The arrows give a sense of what is done first, and what remains a residual.

---

[14] In 2010, a new step increasing the level of conditionality has been reached with the New Legislative Framework which rules all the activities (certification, laboratory, accreditation) which guarantee that a product put on the market meets the core harmonized requirements. This Framework has created such a web of rules and institutions that it seems that the EU has lost its last chance to influence the thinking of the WTO negotiators in charge of this issue (for detail, see Messerlin 2011b).

Clearly, the positive list approach is hard to sell in the WTO because it imposes strong constraints (a large set of core provisions to be harmonized) on the signatories, that few WTO members would easily accept. By contrast, it is more compatible with PTAs, particularly those where the EU is a signatory. Indeed, it generated a craze for 'mutual recognition agreements' (MRAs) during the 1990s and 2000s. But this craze was followed by a marked sense of disillusion, for the same reason that has happened within the EU: the core set of provisions in these MRAs is often large, meaning that these agreements are, de facto, not so far away from pure harmonization agreements.

10.4.1.2 *The emergence of better advocates of the mutual recognition principle*

Fortunately, a few countries have fully grasped the value of the mutual recognition principle. First is Australia, which in the mid-1990s faced the same problem as the EU, that is, an internal market with many technical barriers to trade between the Australian states and territories. The same problem was faced by ANZCER. In 1998, as illustrated by the arrows labelled 'AUS-NZ' in Figure 3, the Trans-Tasman Mutual Recognition Arrangement (TTMRA) adopted a 'negative' list approach, which defines exceptions, exemptions, and exclusions to the basic rule of unconditional mutual recognition, hence reducing considerably the scope of the core set of provisions to be harmonized. Such a negative list may be easier to sell in the WTO forum (and in PTAs) because it requires far fewer constraints from the signatories although it requires more trust in the regulatory quality of the partner(s).

Very recently, a third way has emerged which could fit the needs of the small economies very well. There are WTO members that apply an unconditional principle of mutual recognition—that is, that recognize unilaterally the norms of other countries. To our knowledge, no WTO member does that on a worldwide scale. But, for instance, Georgia recognizes the norms of all the Organization for Economic Cooperation and Development (OECD) (hence EU) and NIS (newly independent states) countries—a very large chunk of her trade. Such countries maximize the welfare of their consumers in the sense that they put very limited restraints on the varieties of products available to their consumers.

10.4.2 Rules (anti-dumping/anti-subsidy) and competition nexus

The Uruguay negotiations on rules on conditional protection (anti-dumping and anti-subsidy) were held under the influence of increasing pressures to bring them under the broader heading of competition rules.[15] This idea was sound from an economic point of

---

[15] Rules on safeguards are not connectable with competition issues to the extent that they recognize the political constraint and the fact that the importing country has the main responsibility for what is happening. Australian Productivity Commission 2009.

view. There is a large body of economic literature analysing dumping as a largely accept-able pricing strategy, and subsidy as an acceptable or non-acceptable form of public intervention, depending on the circumstances (or objectives). In both cases, competi-tion policy seems to provide the best answer to a complex problem which often needs to be assessed on a case-by-case basis ('rule of reason'), as do competition cases.

Once again, the Treaty of Rome was much in advance of its time, for two reasons. The rules on anti-dumping in the Treaty of Rome had a very simple provision (which has disappeared in the latest versions of the treaty). It consisted in requiring the EU member states to check whether alleged dumped goods face no barriers to going back to their original markets. Such a check would ensure the existence of arbitrage among the markets, and hence eliminate most risks of potentially successful anti-competi-tive behaviour. The remaining risks could then be handled by the competition authorities. The Treaty of Rome rules on subsidies ('state aid' in EU parlance) are much better than the countervailing actions recognized by the GATT/WTO. They consist in imposing the subsidizing EU member states to stop subsidizing—hence taking action at the source of the problem. By contrast, the GATT/WTO counter-vailing measures leave the subsidizing country free to continue to subsidize (by sell-ing goods elsewhere), while hurting the consumers of the importing country (because of the countervailing duties).

During the last year of the Uruguay negotiations, the momentum to tighten the links between anti-dumping/anti-subsidy and competition policy became stronger. The main proponents of such a momentum was not the EU (still one of the two major users of anti-dumping at that time) but the Asian main exporters (Japan, Korea, Hong Kong), which were the main targets of the EU and US anti-dumping and anti-subsidy actions. The result of this momentum was the establishment of a Competition Working Group on competition at the WTO.

Unfortunately, as soon as it was established, this working group rapidly neglected the anti-dumping/anti-subsidy issue, focusing on the other, less trade-related, competition issues. Of course, the US, which was (and still is) adamantly opposed to any deep reform of the anti-dumping and anti-subsidy agreements, was instrumental in this change. But the EU was not opposed to it. As a result, the only EU lasting influence in these areas has been minor, mainly in the way subsidies are defined in the WTO Subsidy Agreement.

10.4.3 Export restrictions

Export restrictions are another illustration of the quality of the Treaty of Rome and of the role of the Court of Justice. Article TFEU 28 defines export restrictions with exactly the same words as the provision on import restrictions, since it bans 'all quantitative restrictions on exports and all measures having equivalent effects'. By contrast, the GATT text bans export quantitative restrictions, but not export taxes or similar meas-ures. This symmetry in the Treaty may be a source of inspiration for the coming discus-sions on disciplines on export restrictions, which are starting in the WTO.

10.5 Services: the EU shift from mutual recognition to mutual evaluation

When the EU started to deal with services in the early 1970s, it first tried, as in goods, to harmonize national regulations—to substitute new EU-wide regulations for the EU member states' regulations—for various services. This approach failed almost totally: after more than a decade of negotiations (from the early 1970s to early 1980s) very few EU-wide regulations were adopted (mostly in insurance and transportation), and their scope and impact were minimal.

10.5.1 The disappointing extension of the mutual recognition principle to services

In the early 1980s, two initiatives—neither of them being from the Commission—unlocked the situation and succeeded in putting services at the core of the Internal Market. First and foremost, a few EU member states (the United Kingdom, Netherlands, Ireland) and future EU member states (Sweden) decided to embark unilaterally on the 'regulatory reforms in services' agenda initiated in the US by President Carter. Second, the same European Round Table of Industrialists (ERT) which was pushing for the elimination of the technical barriers in goods on a mutual recognition basis (see Section 10.3) was advocating a similar approach for dealing with the regulatory obstacles in infrastructure services (telecommunications, transport), which were of prime interest to the ERT members.

As a result, the 'internal market' directives in services have the same structure as the New Approach directives in technical norms in goods: the EU member states mutually recognize their regulations in services, conditionally in respect of a core set of mandatory common rules, to be laid down in directives.

In the late 1990s, it became clear that the Internal Market was far below expectations,[16] although it still took more than half a decade for the Commission to begin to recognize this undesirable evolution. Within 15 years, the initial 50 or so directives—which were supposed to be sufficient to set up the core of the harmonized provisions for all the services targeted—became more than 600 directives. The reasons for such a disappointing evolution are the same as those in technical norms. The intense negotiations between the EU member states for adopting the core set of mandatory common rules enlarged the core provisions, to the detriment of the mutual recognition components.

A recent study captures the limited impact of the Internal Market in services.[17] This study deserves two preliminary remarks. First, it estimates the trade costs in services,

---

[16] Messerlin 2001.
[17] Miroudot, Sauvage, and Shepherd 2010.

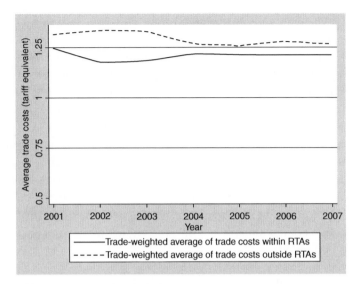

FIGURE 4 Trade costs within and outside PTAs

Source: Miroudot, Sauvage, and Shepherd 2010.

the trade costs being defined as the full range of costs a firm confronts when it decides to sell its services on foreign markets. Second, it does not take into account the flows of foreign direct investments because of lack of data. Figure 4 shows that the trade costs within preferential trade agreements (PTAs) having a service agenda are not substantially different from the trade costs outside these PTAs. As the EU Internal Market is by far the most important PTA in services, Figure 4 shows, de facto, that the trade costs in services within the EU have not evolved differently from those outside the EU. The study also shows that trade costs in the EU services have increased during the 2000s, in contrast with the trade costs in goods.

10.5.2 Shifting to the mutual evaluation principle with the 2006 Services Directive

This very unsatisfactory situation has led to the adoption of a totally new brand of directive—the Services Directive. This adoption (in 2006) was politically very difficult, but the most innovative tool of the Directive (its Article 15) survived the political turmoil.[18]

---

[18] The Services Directive became the symbol of 'ultra-free market' policies and fell hostage to the political turmoil of the referendum on the European Constitution. A softer version of the Directive finally passed. For a detailed legal analysis, see Breuss, Fink, and Griller 2008.

Article 15 lays down the concept of 'mutual evaluation', which requires each EU member state to make a systematic evaluation of its regulations before the entry into force of the directive for the services it covers. These evaluations aim to ensure that the EU member states' laws, regulations, and administrative provisions are compatible with a series of conditions such as non-discrimination according to nationality or to the location of the registered office, necessity requirements which need to be justified by an overriding reason relating to the public interest, and proportionality between the objective pursued and the ways used. These evaluations are then submitted to the other EU member states for evaluation—hence the term of mutual evaluation. If these evaluations do not reveal a problem for the other EU member states, then the member states mutually recognize their regulations with no conditionality. In other words, mutual evaluation is a first step to the adoption of unconditional mutual recognition—hence it is very close to the notion of regulatory competition (indeed, this was one of the main reasons for the strong opposition to its adoption).[19]

It is important to underscore that, by providing a new tool, Article 15 also changes dramatically the perspectives on liberalization in services, and its dynamics. Article 15 shifts the focus from liberalization negotiations with other countries to an internal exercise on the quality of the domestic regulations enforced. The economic literature insists on the fact that most of the benefits from services liberalization are not so much due to the opening of the domestic markets to foreign competitors, as to the opening of these domestic markets to the domestic competitors which have been kept at bay by the existing regulations.[20]

Unfortunately, it is too early to have a sense of how mutual evaluation has really worked in the case of the Services Directive, since the mutual evaluation initial phase was only concluded by the end of the last year.

10.6 Services: the EU influence in the World Trade System

The EU influence is more difficult to assess in services than in goods, because services liberalization in the world trade system is still at an early stage. That said, there is a major difference between what has happened in the WTO and in the PTA context.

---

[19] In addition to Article 15, Article 14 provides a list of 'prohibited requirements', such as those on nationality, on having an establishment in more than one member state, on the freedom to choose between a principal and secondary establishment, on the existence of reciprocity, on economic tests, etc. The value of this Article is that it systematizes—consolidates—the previous Courts' rulings.

[20] Dee 2008.

10.6.1 The EU influence in the WTO

At the beginning of the Uruguay Round (in the mid-1980s) the EU was not a strong supporter of introducing services in the world trade system, because most EU member states believed that they have no comparative advantages in services. This role was played by the US until the late 1980s. But the 'Savings and Loans' financial crisis in the US reached its peak in the late 1980s, leaving the US government with much weaker business support in services. Fortunately, almost concomitantly, the EU attitude changed dramatically. The EU became a supporter of the introduction of services in the multilateral trade regime, largely under the (unrealized) conviction that the Single Market in services was close to being finalized, and would make the EU services more competitive. This influence is reflected by the parallel structures of the GATS and of the Treaty of Rome in services (see Figure 2).

That said, services liberalization per se in the Uruguay Round was very modest: the Uruguay Agreement in services consists mostly in the consolidation of the unilateral liberalizations that a dozen WTO members (this figure includes the major individual EU member states) have undertaken in the 1980s and early 1990s.[21] However, the EU has had a significant influence on two points: first and foremost, the issue of the state-owned enterprises in services liberalization, and second, the tool of the 'reference paper' in the services negotiations.

10.6.1.1 *State-owned enterprises and services liberalization*

At the turn of the 1990s, services were almost exclusively provided by state-owned monopolies in the developing countries. As a result, the US insistence on privatization as a necessary component of services liberalization during the Uruguay negotiations was adamantly opposed by most developing countries, fuelling a deep and long-lasting confusion between competition issues (market structure) and ownership issues (privatization).

In this debate, the EU was an attractive go-between, because many EU member states had just finished going through the same debate as the one experienced by the developing countries. In the late 1980s, most services in Europe were still delivered by state-owned monopolies, and this feature constituted a critical challenge to the creation of an 'Internal Market' in services. Fortunately, the Treaty of Rome has two sets of rules which, combined, provided an economically sound solution.

First, the very few cast-iron competition rules of the Treaty of Rome and its successors (Articles 81 and 82 in the services context) are expressed in a separate chapter and in the typical general wording of the Treaty.[22] As a result, they unambiguously cover serv-

---

[21] Gamberale and Mattoo 2002.

[22] These two Articles also have the very special feature that they are part of the only ten of the Treaty's provisions having 'direct' effect. The Treaty makes a distinction between the few provisions having 'direct effect' (that confer rights on individuals that they can invoke before the national and EU courts) and the other provisions which require additional legislation to be enforced by the EU courts. In other words, the Articles on the competition policy do not need decisions by the Council and the Parliament to be enforced.

ices. This feature was important all the more because the treaty gives a very original definition of services (particularly remarkable for the late 1950s, still enamoured with goods such as cars, concrete, steel or coal, and treating services activities with disdain). Article TFEU 57 states that services are economic activities 'provided for remuneration, in so far as they are *not* governed by the provisions relating to freedom of movement of goods, capital and persons'[author's emphasis].[23]

This definition is quite special: it defines services by what they are not. As a result, the Treaty covers the whole possible universe of goods and services and maximizes the realm of services. This universal coverage leaves open the question of the precise boundaries between goods and services. For instance, is a movie a service (when downloadable) or a product (when available in a DVD format) or both? Such a question has a crucial importance in the WTO negotiations because trade barriers on goods and those on services can differ greatly in nature and intensity, as best illustrated by audio-visuals, where broadcasting movies is highly regulated, but downloading movies enjoys the almost barrier-free Internet environment.

Second, the Treaty of Rome makes a key distinction between state-owned enterprises (ownership) and state-owned monopolies (ownership combined with a monopoly power that the economic analysis considers as costly in the vast majority of cases). In particular, Article TFEU 37 reads as follows:

> Member States shall adjust any State monopolies of a *commercial* character so as to ensure that *no discrimination* regarding the conditions under which goods are procured and marketed exists between nationals of Member States.
>
> The provisions of this Article shall apply to any body through which a Member State, in law or in fact, either directly or indirectly supervises, determines or appreciably influences imports or exports between Member States. These provisions shall likewise apply to monopolies delegated by the State to others [author's emphasis].

The principle of non-discrimination is easy to interpret as requiring competition in the markets in question. However, it was difficult for this interpretation to prevail in the political environment of the early 1980s. It thus required confirmation by the Court of Justice. The Court's British Telecom ruling in 1982 was the landmark case establishing this interpretation and breaching the systemic link between public ownership and monopoly, by stating that, in commercial activities, state-owned enterprises should

---

[23] The four freedoms (free movement of goods, services, people, and capital) are the building blocks of the Treaty. However, the Treaty recognizes some overlap between free movements of services and capital (a feature known as 'parallel applicability'), particularly for financial services. Article 51, on the liberalization in banking and insurance services, stresses that it should be 'effected in step' with the liberalization of movement of capital. The Treaty of Rome has specific provisions on transport (Articles 70 to 80) which balance liberalization with other objectives (a common transport policy and a regional policy), which have, de facto, excluded land transport from the general right of establishment under Article 43, and from competition rules by permitting a long survival of a complex web of price controls, quota licences, public monopolies, state aids, etc.

behave as firms in a competitive market. As one could expect, this case generated a lot of challenges. The main message of the British Telecom ruling was thus confirmed by a series of Court of Justice rulings, while the fuzzy notion of the 'services of general interest' was restated for dealing with cases where it was felt necessary to combine state ownership and monopoly.

The EU approach making the difference between state-owned enterprises and state-owned monopolies was robust enough in the mid/late 1980s to percolate through the Uruguay discussions on these matters, and for incorporating it in the GATS text, as best illustrated by GATS Article VIII paragraph 2:

> Where a Member's monopoly supplier competes, either directly or through an affiliated company, in the supply of a service outside the scope of its monopoly rights and which is subject to that Member's specific commitments, the Member shall ensure that such a supplier does not abuse its monopoly position to act in its territory in a manner inconsistent with such commitments.

10.6.1.2 *The tool of the 'reference paper'*

The EU extension of the mutual recognition approach to services is mirrored, to some extent, by the notion of a 'reference paper' in the GATS context. A reference paper spells out, for the service in question, the regulatory principles and best practices that all the WTO members are invited to follow. In other words, its aim is to define the core principles that every WTO member should follow when regulating the service at stake.

Until now, the tool of the reference paper has been used only once, reflecting the limited role of the WTO in services. In addition, the importance of this reference paper is limited because it deals with fixed telecommunications, a technology that was at the heart of the discussions in the early 1990s Uruguay negotiations, but which since then has become outmoded due to the rise of mobile telecommunications.

10.6.2 The EU influence in the PTA

The EU has pushed for the mutual recognition approach in many PTAs it negotiated and signed. It is difficult to assess the true value of these repeated references without a detailed examination of these bilateral agreements. However, two observations can be made—both suggesting that, as in the technical barriers to trade, the EU is not the best advocate (or enforcer) of the tools it has created.

First, when the EU negotiates bilateral agreements with well-developed economies (e.g. Chile, Korea or Mexico), provisions on services are written in a traditional mould: either they consist of commitments to open some services markets to the firms of the partner, with some mutual recognition provisions; or they are mere expressions of good intent (transparency, etc.), which in fact add very little to the current WTO language.

Second, when the EU negotiates bilateral agreements with its Eastern and Southern neighbours, the EU simply tries to extend the EU regulations to the other negotiating side, leaving little choice to its partners, as best illustrated by the Air Agreement between the EU and Morocco.[24]

10.6.3 Mutual evaluation: a future source of influence for the EU?

To our knowledge, there is no EU-related agreement with a third party which is based on the mutual evaluation approach. Indeed, one may wonder whether such a tool has any chance to be used in the WTO forum, for two reasons. First, the sheer number of WTO members would make such an approach very cumbersome. Second, and more decisively, the huge heterogeneity among the WTO members in terms of size, income level, views on the way to regulate services, and political flexibility suggests that mutual evaluation has little chance to be introduced in the WTO framework.

That said, the Doha Round negotiations have made clear that the WTO should change in order to be able to address the complex issues of services liberalization. More precisely, a two-track approach should be envisaged:

- There is no better place to bind liberalizations undertaken some years before than the whole WTO forum.
- Negotiations on services liberalization (market access) should occur in plurilateral forums, among 'groups of the willing' who would like to open some of their services markets more rapidly than the rest of the WTO members.

The tool of mutual evaluation could be manageable in the context of these plurilaterals. To be compatible with the WTO, it is often suggested that a plurilateral should involve countries representing, altogether, a minimum coverage in terms of world production or trade. However, such a requirement (even if fixed at a level of 80 per cent of the world production) is likely to be easily met by fewer than two dozen WTO members—a number of countries that does not exceed the number of EU member states—which has been already shown compatible with a mutual evaluation exercise.

10.7 CONCLUSION

The EU has exerted a substantial influence in the world trade system, by providing appropriate tools of negotiation that it has had to conceive when it had to address its own processes of internal liberalization. This influence has been particularly noticeable in the old areas that are difficult to crack (technical barriers to trade) or in new areas that the world trade system has just started to tackle (services).

[24] Bertho and Messerlin 2010.

An interesting question is whether this influence will last in the future, or whether it will fade (a question similar to the one on the role of the US). The answer to this question depends on such a wide series of forces that it is beyond the scope of this chapter to look at it in an exhaustive manner. What follows mentions a couple of forces which act in opposite directions—meaning that the future influence of the EU will depend on the respective weights of these conflicting forces. On the one hand, the fact that the EU is much more heterogeneous than it used to be should argue in favour of a permanent influence: the EU economy is becoming more similar to the world economy, hence it should continue to create new tools for the problems that the EU may face more rapidly than the world trade system because it is more advanced in terms of internal liberalization. On the other hand, European policymakers of the twenty-first century seem to be still dominated by the nineteenth-century model of a relatively centralized state (by far the most prevalent model in the EU). This state of mind convinces them that the many setbacks the EU is currently facing are due to too little harmonization, not too much. If this conviction persists, the EU may cease to be a source of innovative tools to deal with the problems faced by the world trade system. This conviction is consistent with the reluctance to recognize the fact that governments could be seen as competing to provide the best regulations, and with the fear that 'competing' governments are doomed to a 'race to the bottom'—a perspective that does not seem realistic, at least for democratic governments.

REFERENCES

Australian Productivity Commission. 2009. *Review of Mutual Recognition Schemes*. Australian Productivity Commission Report. Melbourne, Australia: Productivity Commission.

Bertho, F., and P. Messerlin. 2010. Convergence with the Acquis Communautaire? The Case of Air and Maritime Transport for Egypt. Working paper. Paris: Groupe d'Économie Mondiale at SciencesPo.

Breuss, F., G. Fink, and S. Griller, eds. 2008. Services Liberalisation in the Internal Market. Wien and NewYork: Springer.

Dee, P. 2008. Alternative Growth Strategies in Asia: Liberalization, Deregulation, Structural Reforms. Unpublished mimeo, Crawford School of Economics and Government, Australian National University.

Gamberale, C., and A. Mattoo. 2002. Domestic Regulations and Liberalization of Trade in Services. In *Development, Trade, and the WTO: A Handbook*, edited by B. Hoekman, A. Mattoo, and P. English, 290–303. Washington DC: World Bank.

Krugman, P. 1979. Increasing Returns, Monopolistic Competition, and International Trade. *Journal of International Economics* 9 (4):469–79.

Messerlin, P. 2001. *Measuring the Costs of Protection in Europe: European Commercial Policy in the 2000s*. Washington DC: Peterson Institute for International Economics.

Messerlin, P. 2011a. The European Community Commercial Policy. In *Handbook of International Commercial Policy*, edited by M. Kreinin and M. Plummer. Oxford: Oxford University Press. Forthcoming

Messerlin, P. 2011b. The Doha Round. In *Handbook of Trade Policy for Development*, edited by A. Lukauskas, R. M. Stern, and G. Zanini. Oxford: Oxford University Press. Forthcoming

Miroudot, S., J. Sauvage, and B. Shepherd. 2010. Measuring the Cost of International Trade in Services. Working Paper. Paris: Groupe d'Économie Mondiale at SciencesPo.

Pelkmans, J. 2001. *European Integration*. Harlow, Essex: Financial Times/Prentice Hall.

Pincus, J. 2009. Mutual Recognition and Regulatory Competition. Paper presented at the Samuel Griffith Society 21st Conference, August, Adelaide, Australia.

Sykes, A. O. 2000. Regulatory Competition or Regulatory Harmonization? A Silly Question? *Journal of International Economic Law* 3 (2):257–64.

Wilson, J. S. 2002. Standards, Regulation, and Trade: WTO Rules and Developing Country Concerns. In *Development, Trade and the WTO: A Handbook*, edited by B. Hoekman, A. Mattoo, and P. English, 428–38. Washington DC: World Bank.

CHAPTER 11

....

THE ROLE OF THE UNITED STATES: A MULTILEVEL EXPLANATION FOR DECREASED SUPPORT OVER TIME

....

TODD ALLEE

11.1 INTRODUCTION

....

IT is difficult to summarize the history of the United States' relationship with the World Trade Organization (WTO). John Jackson once referred to the US attitude towards the global trade regime as 'ambivalent', which is perhaps the best one-word description.[1] That the US role within the WTO escapes easy categorization is not surprising. Trade politics is complex, particularly within a country like the US that has a decentralized political system and a diverse economic landscape. Furthermore, the WTO is an evolving entity with more than 60 years of history behind it. Indeed, the many chapters in this volume attest to the range of issues relevant to the organization. Across nearly all of these issues, the United States figures as a prominent player.

One consistent trend is the decreasing US support for the multilateral trade regime over time. The US played an integral role in the development of the General Agreement on Tariffs and Trade (GATT), but, by the time the Tokyo Round was concluded, multiple tensions had surfaced between US priorities and those of a multilateral trading system. US unilateralism, support for trade remedies, and maintenance of agricultural subsidies strained this relationship, and US stances early on at Doha and its policy of 'competitive liberalization' have

[1] Jackson 1987, 379.

added further strain. The US relationship with the WTO is thus a tale of two halves. It played a strong leadership role during the first 30 years of the GATT, but during the past 30 years its role has become more complicated, and at times more contentious.

This chapter employs a multilevel, multi-causal framework to understand the US role in the multilateral trade regime. Systemic factors, namely US hegemony, help to explain initial US leadership as well as the recent decline in US support. The shift from a free trade mentality to one that emphasizes others' unfair policies provides another explanation, as does the increasing political effectiveness of import-competing US interests over time. Perhaps the greatest explanation comes from disaggregating the state into various domestic trade policy institutions, which once served multilateral trade goals but now have shifted to reflect protectionist US ideas and interests.

11.2 EARLY US SUPPORT FOR THE GATT

Amid the mosaic of efforts at international economic cooperation in the late 1940s, it is easy to overlook the United States' leadership role in jump-starting the unprecedented tariff-cutting that resulted from negotiations beginning with the 1947 General Agreement on Tariff and Trade.[2] It made sizeable, and at times asymmetrical, tariff concessions in GATT negotiations during the initial decades, and propelled the launch of several negotiating rounds. It not only pushed for a deepening of the GATT, but also for a widening of the membership and adherence to a multilateral ideal. In short, the United States deserves a significant amount of credit for the successful development of the modern trade regime, particularly in the period from 1947 until the late 1970s. The US was ready to lead multilateral trade liberalization efforts after the Second World War, and as Rhodes notes, 'the international setting was ripe for the success of US leadership', and American trade partners 'were also highly amenable to a cooperative stance towards US ideas.'[3] Several outward and inward forces, including its position as leader of the Western world, the negative experiences of the early 1930s, and widespread domestic support for trade liberalization, are evident in early US efforts within the GATT.

The United States exhibited crucial leadership in support of early multilateral liberalization efforts by making sizeable tariff commitments at Geneva in 1947 and then in subsequent rounds, thus maintaining the GATT's forward momentum even after broader efforts to establish the International Trade Organization (ITO) had failed. Precise data on all countries' tariff commitments during early GATT rounds are elusive, but much is known about US commitments, which are widely viewed as the most substantial among the early members.[4] In the original 1947 Agreement, the US granted tariff concessions on more than half of dutiable import lines, and made average reductions

---

[2] For accounts of the US role in the early GATT years, see Curzon 1965, Evans 1971, Kock 1969, and Low 1993.

[3] Rhodes 1993, 77–8.   [4] For example Curzon 1965; Evans 1971; Kock 1969; WTO 2007.

of 35 per cent.[5] It offered reductions of 15–35 per cent on additional lines during the next four rounds. By 1953, the United States had agreed to bind 80 per cent of its tariff lines through the GATT framework and had reduced tariff levels on 95 per cent of those bound lines.[6]

These initial steps towards multilateral tariff commitments culminated in the more visible success of the Kennedy Round. Curzon claims that although US tariff reductions during the interim 1950s rounds were modest, they nevertheless were 'effective' because they repeatedly brought an expanding number of GATT signatories back to the table, and ultimately prompted them to reciprocate US concessions.[7] Thus, the US deserves credit not only for taking steps to bind and lower its own tariffs, but also for its procedural efforts to keep the GATT moving forward. It pushed strongly for the launch of the aptly-named Kennedy Round, despite a less than favourable global environment.[8] This ongoing leadership paid multilateral dividends, as the US and other leading states reduced tariffs on industrial goods by an additional 35–40 per cent, dropping them to average levels of below 6 per cent.[9] This led US President Lyndon Johnson to proclaim the Kennedy Round the 'most successful multilateral agreement on tariff reduction ever negotiated'.[10]

In addition to being an engine of this early deepening of the GATT, the US also advocated widening the regime to bring in important new members and advanced core principles such as non-discrimination. In the 1950s it provided much needed support for Japanese membership in the face of considerable opposition from other members, 14 of which would continue to discriminate against Japan by invoking Article XXXV.[11] The US also took stances within the institution against other types of discrimination and in support of a more multilateral ideal. For instance, it clashed with the United Kingdom at the regime's outset over the UK's insistence that it be able to maintain colonial preferences. It worked hard to engage the European bloc within the confines of GATT, despite its ambivalence towards early European economic integration. It also was the last major GATT member to extend the potentially discriminatory Generalized System of Preferences (GSP) to developing countries. These behaviours led John Jackson to comment in 1987 that 'in general the United States has been a strong supporter of the principles of multilateralism and non-discrimination as embodied in the unconditional MFN [most-favoured nation] clause of GATT'.[12]

11.3 A MULTILEVEL EXPLANATION FOR EARLY US SUPPORT FOR THE GATT

The explanatory framework in this chapter is inspired by the long-standing idea of levels of analysis in international relations. A loose version of this concept is employed, first to understand initial US support for GATT-based multilateralism and then to explain

---

[5] Evans 1971, 11–12.   [6] WTO 2007, 204.   [7] Curzon 1965, 81.
[8] Eckes 2000, chapter 3.   [9] Preeg 1970; WTO 2007.   [10] Eckes 2004, 66.
[11] Dam 1970, 347–50.   [12] Jackson 1987, 381.

waning US support for the trade regime over time. Ikenberry, Lake, and Mastanduno's application of levels of analysis to US foreign economic policy provides a useful starting point.[13] They distinguish between system-level, state-level, and societal-level explanations for US foreign policy. The approach employed here makes a few modifications to this more conventional organization. First, the argument advanced here is decidedly multi-causal. Various factors at each level help to understand the US relationship with the WTO. Second, the idea of a 'state' level is unpacked and replaced with an emphasis on various state-level *institutions* that make, or affect, US trade policymaking. Third, the societal level is expanded to include the ideas, actors, and interests that shape US interactions with the GATT/WTO regime. The resulting conclusion is that the positive US role during the first decades of the GATT is best understood as resulting from the United States' hegemonic position after the Second World War, a widespread belief among political and business elites in favour of trade liberalization, and, most importantly, a unique set of American policymaking institutions that encouraged a positive role for the US in the GATT.

Characteristics of the early post-Second World War international system, namely the dominant position of the United States as leader of the Western bloc, help to explain the initial positive relationship between the US and the GATT. Hegemonic stability theory provides a useful point of departure.[14] It holds that dominant states in the international system, such as Great Britain in the nineteenth century and the United States for much of the twentieth century, are able and willing to provide public goods such as an open trading system to the international community. As applied to the US and the GATT, it meant that the US had the economic capability, because of its dominant position, to create a multilateral trading system by initiating and supporting the early GATT negotiating rounds and opening its markets to others, by making the aforementioned tariff commitments. As a hegemon, it also was able to sustain this emerging trading system, or in Yarbrough and Yarbrough's terms, it was able to 'enforce' trade multilateralism.[15] Indeed, the early tariff concessions made by the US were asymmetrical, since they were larger than those made by others. Furthermore, many countries were able to 'free ride' by reaping the most-favoured nation (MFN) benefits of others' concessions while making few, if any, of their own.[16] As discussed later, by the 1970s the United States' power had decreased and it was less able, and certainly less willing, to tolerate such differences in commitment-making.

Initial cooperative efforts through the GATT also transpired within a bipolar systemic structure, in which the US was a leader of a market-oriented bloc of countries against a Soviet-led communist bloc. This Cold War bipolarity influenced US support for Japan's early GATT membership, and was a common lens through which trade policy towards

---

[13] Ikenberry, Lake, and Mastanduno 1988.   [14] For example Gilpin 1987; Lake 1988.
[15] Yarbrough and Yarbrough 1992.
[16] Dozens of post-colonial states joined the GATT under Article XXVI:5(c), without completing thorough accession procedures or being asked to make new commitments. Most joined in this way in the 1960s, but a few joined under this provision as early as the 1950s.

the GATT was viewed. As Goldstein notes, the Truman administration frequently claimed that opposition to trade liberalization was a vote against the 'free world'.[17]

In fact, ideas such as the notion of open markets and trade cooperation as a bulwark against communism also drove US support for the GATT. After the tragedy of the Great Depression and the lessons learned from Smoot-Hawley, the idea of open markets gained widespread traction throughout US policymaking circles in the late 1930s and 1940s. Long-standing ideological battles over the desirability of free trade also began to decline. Goldstein claims that by 1948, 'the critics of legislation expanding trade were branded as isolationists—a universally criticized foreign policy stance'.[18] The real-world manifestation of these increasingly dominant free trade beliefs began to evolve, too. Bilateralism in trade cooperation, as illustrated by the 27 agreements the US signed between 1934 and 1945, was replaced by a more multilateral approach as the GATT evolved and the systemic influences above took hold after the war. In sum, from the 1930s into the 1970s, belief in the benefits of free trade was pervasive among major players in the United States. This ideal was advanced by numerous individuals and interests, and was reflected in subsequent trade policy institutions.[19]

Several important individuals at high levels of American politics were strongly committed to the idea of multilateral tariff liberalization in the early post-Second World War era. Secretary of State Cordell Hull served in this post from 1933–44 and was a uniquely strong advocate for free trade, who had long espoused the idea of a multilateral trade organization. His boss, President Franklin D. Roosevelt, condemned the Smoot-Hawley tariff during the 1932 election and gradually developed into a strong proponent of free trade. Subsequent Democratic presidents Truman and Kennedy were similarly supportive, and became closely linked to US tariff reductions in the early GATT negotiating rounds. Equally important is the fact that the first post-war Republican President, Dwight D. Eisenhower, also strongly supported the idea of tariff reduction and US leadership in the GATT. Such support went beyond the Executive branch. Congressman Wilbur Mills, the long-time Democratic chairman of the powerful House Ways and Means Committee, was a staunch supporter of free trade in all forms, including creating the office of the Special Trade Representative, delegation of trade promotion authority to the President, and support for the GATT liberalization agenda more generally.[20]

Moreover, a broad collection of powerful US interests strongly supported the GATT at its outset and beyond. According to Susan Aaronson: 'By the mid-1950s, the GATT developed a special interest constituency consisting of exporters, some labor groups, internationalists, policymakers, journalists, and economists...support of freer trade became a dogma among elites for the next three decades.'[21] Within this coalition, export-oriented firms constituted an important group that has been singled out by political

[17] Goldstein 1993, 164.   [18] Ibid.   [19] Goldstein 1993.
[20] See Eckes 2000, chapter 3, for a retrospective on the Kennedy Round, including numerous statements from former US trade officials and negotiators, who give Mills tremendous credit for supporting their efforts.
[21] Aaronson 1996, 133.

economy scholars.[22] Many multinational firms supported early US efforts through the GATT in the hope of having access to vast new markets, and several later worked in the 1970s and 1980s to limit rising protectionist efforts that might damage the multilateral regime. Although protectionist interests certainly were present during the GATT's first few decades, the number of pro-protection interest groups began to decline and those that remained rebranded themselves and abandoned traditional arguments for protectionism.[23]

Among the many factors that pushed the US towards strong support for the GATT, the role of several domestic trade-promoting institutions was especially important. The most central of these arrangements was the consistent trade negotiating authority delegated to the Executive by the Congress. This authority was included in the 1934 Reciprocal Trade Agreements Act (RTAA), which was extended in 1937, 1940, 1943, 1948, 1949, 1951, 1954, 1955, and 1958. Future extensions in 1962 and 1974 entailed new legislative acts to extend such authority. For all of the post-war era extensions, the granting of such authority was timed to coincide with the various GATT negotiating rounds. In all cases, the President was given pre-authorization to negotiate tariff reductions up to certain amounts, and, most importantly, he was allowed to reach agreements without the onerous requirement of *ex post* legislative approval. This authority greatly facilitated US concession-making in the GATT. In fact, one of the US negotiators who took part in the Kennedy Round claimed that the Europeans were 'stunned' by how much negotiating authority the US negotiating team possessed.[24] This institutional arrangement allowed the US to offer sizeable concessions during many early negotiating rounds, which could then be reciprocated by other major GATT members—all of which was good for the development of the regime. As is discussed later, the lack of such authority in recent years has hampered the Americans' ability to make major concessions thus far during the Doha Round, to the detriment of the broader WTO membership.

Another institutional development was the creation of the special representative for trade negotiations, commonly referred to as the STR.[25] It was established by the 1962 Trade Expansion Act, at the outset of the Kennedy Round, and in 1974 it was renamed the Office of the United States Trade Representative, or USTR. During its first two decades, the STR was an effective extension of US foreign economic policy. It was staffed and headed by some of the most important individuals from the business and political world, who carefully navigated the demands of foreign trade negotiators as well as important interests at home. Most importantly, it played a vital role in driving successful US-led agreements during the Kennedy and, to a lesser extent, Tokyo Rounds. Steve Dryden's illustrative account of these negotiations, appropriately subtitled 'USTR and the American Crusade for Free Trade', illustrates just how skilful those in this office were and how vital this institution was to the GATT.[26]

---

[22] For example Gilligan 1997; Milner 1988.   [23] Goldstein 1993, 164.   [24] Eckes 2000, 61.
[25] Destler 2005; Dryden 1995.   [26] Dryden 1995.

Other US domestic institutions also served the GATT well. The US insisted early on that various trade remedies be allowed in the GATT, which raised fears that such opt-outs might undermine the budding regime.[27] Indeed, contemporary trade remedy procedures in the US, namely those for anti-dumping (AD) and countervailing duties (CVD), have received considerable criticism for the alleged ease with which import-competing industries can receive protection. Often overlooked, however, is how difficult it was to obtain remedies from the 1940s up through the 1970s. Actors who sought protection through anti-dumping, countervailing duties, and escape clause (Article XIX) channels rarely obtained it: success rates for various remedies during this period typically ranged between 10 and 20 per cent.[28] These low rates—which most certainly pleased those in foreign capitals and in the GATT Secretariat—can be attributed to the two primary institutions that rigorously enforced US requirements for using remedies during the majority of the GATT era: the Tariff Commission and the Treasury Department. Both carefully scrutinized petitions for remedies according to the laws on the books at that time. Legislated changes in the US in 1974 and 1979, however, relaxed these laws and removed authority from these institutions in a manner which had deleterious effects on the GATT.

11.4 Changing conditions and a less supportive US role

Much was accomplished under the GATT, and the United States helped to lay the groundwork for the GATT to develop into the modern-day WTO. But at the time of this writing the WTO now faces a number of major challenges, namely the stalemate of the Doha Round and the trend towards bilateral and regional forms of trade cooperation. The United States contributed to these problems, and has done relatively little to help solve them. In the past decade, it has stepped out of the multilateral process and negotiated more than a dozen bilateral agreements. Going back a bit further, other issues have arisen on which US actions and policies have challenged core WTO principles and strained US relations with others within the institution. Most notable are its use of anti-dumping and countervailing duties, efforts at 'aggressive unilateralism', and selective attitude towards non-tariff barriers. In sum, the US role in the multilateral trade regime, which once was instrumental and productive, has become more complicated and less beneficial. There is no precise date or event that marks the shift, but most accounts would suggest that US attitudes and behaviours had changed by the late 1970s or early 1980s. Regardless of the timing, the US role in multilateral trade cooperation is clearly a tale of two halves.

So what drove this deterioration in the US relationship with the global trade regime? Put simply, the same forces that worked towards American leadership in the early

---

[27] On the political benefits of opt-outs in trade agreements, see Rosendorff and Milner 2001.
[28] Destler 2005, 141–2.

decades of the GATT since then have worked in the opposite direction. The prevailing ideational, societal, institutional, and systemic factors that initially brought US trade policy in line with the GATT began to transform by the 1970s and 1980s. The idea of free trade gave way to the idea of policing 'unfair' trade, and protectionist interests became emboldened. These forces were aided by changes in domestic institutions that ran counter to goals of trade cooperation through the GATT/WTO. Finally, slipping US hegemony within the international system also spilled over into the WTO.

11.4.1 Changes in US ideas

A striking ideational change began somewhere in the mid to late 1970s: the shift from a belief in free trade to an espousal of 'fair' trade. Whereas free trade is a simple, universal concept, the notion of fair trade entails selectively confronting others' trade policies that either increase their exports to you or limit your exports to them. This change in the American trade world-view had a major negative effect on US behaviour towards the GATT during its final two decades in existence. It marked a striking reversal of attitudes towards the ideals of non-discrimination and multilateralism, which the US previously had championed, and instead led to discretionary, unilateral policing of others' behaviour. This lengthy episode of what Bhagwati labels 'aggressive unilateralism'[29] ultimately had a positive ending from the point of view of the trade regime, since it was subsumed by the establishment of a strengthened dispute settlement mechanism (DSM) in the WTO. Yet it generated considerable tension for 20 years.

Although the concept of 'fair' trade is nebulous and malleable, the most striking element of this idea is its illiberal tone. It gave the US justification to use retaliatory protectionism against allegedly 'unfair' foreign trade practices, regardless of whether those practices boosted trade or led to enhanced welfare. Bhagwati equates the idea of 'fair' trade to that of 'managed' trade, which in the US meant that the government should play an active role in shaping trade policy. Thus one consequence of this shift in ideas was to provide a post hoc rationale for the trade remedies (AD and CVD) and government support programmes (agricultural subsidies) that would plague US relationships with its trading partners into the next millennium. Most importantly, the idea of fair trade gave the US government the self-endowed right to engage the economic politics of other states outside of multilateral settings. It meant that the US alone would determine, through its own devices, whether a foreign government's policy was legitimate and what unilateral response was appropriate.

Aggressive unilateralism presented a major challenge to the GATT regime. In effect, the fair trade idea shifted the focus from Geneva to Washington, where the US would be judge and jury and would take actions to advance narrow US objectives. The concept of fair trade, as articulated and put into practice by the United States, was strikingly outward-looking. It evoked what Destler calls 'export politics'—the calling out of others'

---

[29] Bhagwati 1990.

barriers—instead of continuing the past practice of working with trading partners to negotiate reciprocal reductions in one's own tariffs.[30] Various 'altruistic' rationales were put forward for why such unilateral measures were needed, either to constrain US protectionism or to advance the Uruguay Round, but these were widely dismissed.[31]

The primary tool of aggressive unilateralism was section 301 of the Trade Act of 1974, as well as the 'super' variant that was authorized more than a decade later.[32] This instrument gave the Executive the authority to take various retaliatory actions against any foreign trade barriers that were 'unjustifiable' and 'unreasonable'. The deliberate vagueness of these ideas, and the way the US determined and pursued them, elevated tensions between the US and its GATT trading partners in the 1980s and early 1990s, as detailed in several scholarly efforts during that time.[33] Although Japan was the primary target of US fair trade rhetoric, from 1975–94 the US pursued nearly twice as many section 301 investigations against the European Community as it did against Japan, along with multiple cases against Korea, Taiwan, Brazil, and even Canada.[34] From the US point of view, the results of the 91 section 301 cases investigated during those two decades are clearly mixed in terms of successful market-opening,[35] but it was the means by which judgement was rendered and punishment was attempted that had the greatest impact.

The establishment of the DSM in 1995 effectively ended the era of fair trade-driven aggressive unilateralism. It became subsumed by 'aggressive multilateralism', as Bayard and Elliott have called it, with the US pledging to use the stronger dispute settlement procedure of the new organization. But the process of taking trade law into its own hands for two decades alienated nearly all major GATT trading partners, and for a time cast doubt on the GATT's effectiveness in dealing with complex non-tariff barriers. It also demonstrated to powerful US interests that working through domestic trade-remedy channels might be preferable to waiting for results from slow, cumbersome GATT negotiating rounds. Furthermore, the fair trade logic that galvanized this process is still evident today in US pronouncements towards current WTO members such as China, and its full implications remain to be seen.

11.4.2 Changes in US trade policy institutions

Major changes within US domestic trade institutions also have had a tremendous impact on the lessened US role within the later GATT and WTO. Within the executive branch, the role of USTR shifted in the 1970s in ways undesirable to the multilateral trade regime.

---

[30] See Destler 2005.   [31] Bhagwati 1991, 30–3.

[32] In the 1988 omnibus trade bill, Congress added a 'super' 301 provision, which required the Executive to single out particular countries for the 'number and pervasiveness' of their 'unfair' trade practices. On the whole, super 301 was more of a continuation of past section 301 practices, and is perhaps most notable for pre-emptive attempts by Taiwan and South Korea not to be pursued under super 301. See Bayard and Elliott 1994, chapters 5–8.

[33] For example Bayard and Elliott 1994; Bhagwati and Patrick 1990.

[34] Bayard and Elliott 1994, 58.   [35] Bayard and Elliott 1994, chapter 3.

On the home front, it became more concerned with trade restriction instead of trade liberalization. According to Dryden, the 'transformed' Office of the US Trade Representative 'by the mid-1970s had become an advocate for ailing US industries and began presiding over a series of deals moderating the flow of imports into the United States'.[36] Furthermore, on the foreign front, USTR also shifted from its original focus on negotiating tariff reductions during GATT negotiating rounds to aggressive export promotion. This is where ideas and institutions came together, since the USTR was charged with enforcing 'fair trade' through section 301. During the last two decades of the GATT, the USTR spent most of its time advancing the strategy of aggressive unilateralism through its pursuit of section 301 petitions. This put the USTR in direct conflict with the multilateral trade regime, and represented a sharp contrast from the role the USTR had played in the GATT previously.

Changes emanating from Congress also counteracted the more free trade inclinations of the Executive branch, which had been a strong force for multilateralism through the GATT.[37] The most notable change was the periodic withholding of fast-track negotiating authority. From the 1930s until the 1970s such authority had been granted frequently and relatively easily, yet in the 1974 Trade Act Congress began to place restrictions on the use of fast-track authority. Debate over renewal of this authority intensified in 1991, in the midst of negotiations over NAFTA and the Uruguay Round. Although granted, the issue became increasingly salient and led to the lapsing of such authority from 1995–2001. Renewal by a razor-thin margin in a December 2001 vote was a pyrrhic victory, since it cast doubt on US commitment to the Doha Round and its ability to follow through on any agreement reached.

Fast-track authority was withdrawn again in 2007, and in the following few years this dealt a near-fatal blow to the Doha Round. The fact that any new multilateral agreement would be scrutinized and amended by the US Congress is a stifling prospect, since individual members would seek exceptions and changes on behalf of numerous protectionist constituents. Implementation of the Uruguay Round was complicated enough, and it occurred under the cover of fast-track authority.[38] The literature on two-level games provides a useful analytic framework.[39] The lack of fast-track authority might increase US bargaining leverage in international negotiations at 'Level 1', but the daunting prospect of ratification at 'Level 2' dramatically shrinks or perhaps eliminates the 'win-set' for any future multilateral agreement. This has led to what Schott calls the 'chicken and egg' problem that has characterized the Doha Round to date. The round needs new concessions by the Americans, but the US cannot obtain trade-promotion authority to make new concessions until other countries make concessions of their own.[40]

[36] Dryden 1995, 7.

[37] The president typically is seen as less protectionist than the Congress, because he represents a national constituency and is responsible for the overall health of the economy as well as relations with other countries. See Baldwin 1988 and O'Halloran 1994, among others.

[38] Croome 1999; Schott 1994.   [39] Evans, Jacobson, and Putnam 1993.   [40] Schott 2006, 4.

Another Congress-driven foray into executive administration of US trade policy, the 1979 Trade Agreement Act, facilitated the use of AD and CVD in ways that have challenged multilateral trade principles. The Act produced several institutional changes in the administration of US AD and CVD, including the relaxation of the injury requirement, faster imposition of preliminary duties and fines, and an overall tightening of the investigation timeline, to the detriment of foreign respondents. The biggest change, however, was the shift in administrative authority for these trade remedies from the seemingly more market-oriented Treasury Department to the more industry-friendly Commerce Department.[41] Consequently, it has become much easier to obtain AD and CVD protection, as the drafters of the 1979 act intended. The large number of AD and CVD impositions since 1979, somewhere in the neighbourhood of 800 unique orders, is widely acknowledged. However, acceptance rates also increased dramatically. Destler reports a greater than 50 per cent acceptance rate of petitions from 1979 to 1994, a number that is three times greater than rates reported for the period before 1979.[42] During the WTO period (1995–2009), between 60 and 65 per cent of US AD and CVD investigations have ended with affirmative decisions.[43] Politics also appears to rear its protectionist head during this quasi-legal process. Hansen and Prusa, for instance, report that affirmative decisions are more likely when petitions involve firms located in districts of important Members of Congress.[44]

US use of AD and CVD measures also has had a negative effect within the WTO. The more lax or pernicious methods of determining AD have been challenged before the WTO dispute settlement mechanism. Disputes over 'zeroing' and the Byrd Amendment have been among the more contentious WTO disputes of the past decade, and, despite panel rulings against US methodologies, both disputes remain largely unresolved. In both cases US intransigence has prompted the suspension of concessions by major US trading partners and put the WTO under added strain. Yet perhaps the biggest negative legacy of changes to US AD/CVD procedures is the spillover effect they have had. Because of their success in producing justifiable protection, dozens of countries have developed new AD procedures, and nearly 40 countries have used AD measures under the WTO.[45]

Single-member districts in the US House of Representatives are another institutional mechanism that protects narrow constituent interests in ways that have fuelled recent US tensions with the global trade regime. Cross-national research shows that countries with single-member constituencies encourage greater protectionism, often in violation

---

[41] See Destler 2005, chapter 6.   [42] Destler 2005, 135.

[43] Data for these calculations are taken from the WTO Anti-dumping gateway (http://www.wto.org/english/tratop_e/adp_e/adp_e.htm) and WTO Subsidies and countervailing measures gateway (http://www.wto.org/english/tratop_e/scm_e/scm_e.htm).

[44] Hansen 1990; Hansen and Prusa 1997.

[45] See data on AD measures from the WTO Anti-dumping gateway, as well as Bown 2010 and Miranda, Torres, and Ruiz 1998.

of their WTO commitments.[46] Moreover, research on American trade politics shows that Members who represent constituents harmed by free trade tend to vote against trade legislation such as implementation of the Uruguay Round agreements.[47] The collection of domestic subsidy programmes for US agriculture is a good illustration of how constituency representation in the US works against cooperation in the WTO. US agricultural interests are incredibly heterogeneous; some are export-competing, while many are import-competing and receive some form of government subsidy. They are also dispersed, which can work in their favour according to Caves's adding machine logic.[48] Most members of both the House and Senate represent one or more subsidy-receiving agricultural interests. Even if a Member does not necessarily support assistance to groups outside his or her district, he or she will support any effort that preserves protection for those he represents. Thus the annual US farm bills are laden with widespread supports to build large political coalitions. As a result, dismantling this extensive support system—a major demand of US trading partners at Doha—is extremely difficult, since most legislators have a stake in maintaining the status quo.

These dynamics are exacerbated by the uncertainty generated by two-year election cycles in the US, which recently have hampered advances in trade negotiations. A common refrain from WTO officials is that concessions from major players are unlikely until after American elections, which seemingly are always on the horizon. US elections caused at least one delay in the Uruguay Round, and the deadline for the conclusion of the Doha Round was originally set for 2007, in part because of the expectation that little could be done in the final year of George W. Bush's presidency. But even after the definitive 2008 US election, actors on all sides were hesitant to fully engage the thorniest negotiating issues as they looked ahead to changing political winds in the 2010 US Congressional elections.

Elements within the US Congress also have become more directly hostile to the WTO. Legislation introduced in the House of Representatives in 2000 and 2005 proposed US withdrawal from the WTO. Although it failed both times, the number of supportive votes increased from 56 to 86 votes over that five-year period, and both times support came almost evenly from Democrats and Republicans. For the first 14 months of the Obama administration, the US had no trade representative to the WTO and no chief agricultural negotiator, which stifled any immediate progress in the Doha Round after the 2008 election, and cast further doubt upon US commitments to the organization. Kentucky senator Jim Bunning blocked the nominees, despite their unanimous support in the Senate Finance Committee, in protest of a Canadian anti-smoking law that could harm tobacco farmers in his state. This example illustrates what a single senator, acting on behalf of narrow interests and using obscure institutional procedures, can do to damage the WTO.

---

[46] For example Magee, Brock, and Young 1989; McGillivray 2004; Rogowski 1987. Rickard 2010 finds that countries with single-member districts, such as the US, are more likely to violate GATT/WTO agreements than countries with other systems of representation.

[47] Baldwin and Magee 2000; Beaulieu and Magee 2004.   [48] Caves 1976.

Such behaviour also reflects the increasing fragmentation of the US Congress, which on balance has lent a more protectionist flavour to US behaviour towards the WTO.[49] In the early years of the GATT, a handful of pro-free trade power brokers in Congress, such as Wilbur Mills, had tremendous institutional influence and could advance the multilateral free trade agenda. But the greater decentralization of US trade policymaking has taken power away from committee chairs and given entrepreneurial Members the ability to advance the narrow interests of their constituents. Moreover, prominent Congressional leaders on trade, who once were staunchly supportive of free trade and the WTO, now include many sceptics. In fact, the legislative figure most closely associated with trade during the 1990s and 2000s is former Democratic House leader Richard Gephardt, who for years pursued a fair trade agenda, introduced trade-restricting legislation, and opposed further US cooperation through the GATT and WTO.

11.4.3 Changes in US domestic interests

Another change evident during the past few decades is the relative effectiveness of narrow, protection-seeking interests within the United States. During the early GATT, when free trade ideas were strong and institutions were favourable, a broad collection of free trade interests pushed forward within the GATT on the relatively straightforward issue of tariff reduction. As discussed earlier, broad protectionist organizations, on the other hand, were marginalized or largely faded from the political scene. Yet by the 1980s an increasing number of narrow, often industry-specific, groups seeking protection had emerged as skilful players.

There are several aspects to this rise of domestic groups whose goals have clashed with the multilateral trade endeavour. The first is what former deputy STR, Alan William Wolff, calls the 'privatization of trade policy formulation in the United States', which means that much of trade policy is demand-driven.[50] This has allowed organized societal actors, who often are protection-seeking, to have a disproportionate say in contemporary US trade policy due to their intense interest in the issue. Groups seeking protection also have become better organized, since peak associations increasingly coordinate the trade policy activities of like-minded individuals and smaller groups.[51] These associations possess the knowledge and resources required to obtain protection within the rules laid down by the WTO. Well-organized groups seeking protection also have become effective in co-opting or neutralizing free trade interests, with Destler providing the example of free-trade Democrats, who are hesitant to take stances against the United Auto Workers (UAW).[52]

---

[49] On fragmentation as it relates to US trade policymaking, see Destler 2005 and Evenett and Meier 2008.

[50] Wolff 1992, 488.

[51] See Shaffer 2003, 32, who notes the increase in the number of national trade associations, from 5,000 in 1955 to 23,000 by the mid 1990s.

[52] Destler 2005, 185.

The use of several types of trade remedies, discussed earlier, is the best example of this shift to demand-driven policymaking that benefits protectionist interests. The major remedies employed by the US since 1975, including 301, AD, and CVD, are primarily driven by requests from narrow, protection-seeking groups. These processes are triggered by formal petitions filed by organized industries seeking protection, based on alleged misdoing by US trade partners. The US has formal requirements that a majority of actors in an industry must participate in AD and CVD actions, which has led to greater coordination and organization among formerly disconnected protectionist interests.[53] Industry associations play a vital role in coordinating behaviour, providing information, and helping to meet the financial demands required to successfully navigate AD and CVD process, which can cost more than $1 million in legal fees alone.[54] Domestic free trade interests, who typically are less organized and more diffuse, participate far less frequently in these narrowly targeted, but increasingly important, AD and CVD processes. Moreover, Allee and Miler also show that Members of Congress of both parties are far more likely to testify before the International Trade Commission in support of AD/CVD protection as opposed to against it.[55] Not surprisingly, AD and CVD are exactly the measures that have drawn the ire of others, and been the source of multiple dispute actions against the US under both the GATT and WTO.

Free trade interests also have become more complacent, narrowly focused, or concerned with issues outside of the WTO. In many ways, the GATT is a victim of its own success in this regard. The major GATT-sponsored tariff reductions from the late 1940s into the 1980s satisfied many free trade interests, who now see little need to push further for broad, multilateral liberalization. Instead, export-oriented firms have begun to direct their attention more narrowly, towards specific elements within WTO negotiations or towards support for selected bilateral and regional agreements. For instance, Destler claims that pro-trade business interests did relatively little to help secure Congressional pass of the Uruguay Round bill as compared to their efforts to gain passage of the contemporaneous North American Free Trade Agreement.[56] Even when pro-free trade interests have been active recently, they have pursued narrow goals as opposed to advancing broader efforts at liberalization. For example, during the Uruguay Round a group called the Intellectual Property Committee pushed hard on the single issue of intellectual property protection, ultimately leading to the Agreement on Trade-Related Aspects of Intellectual Property Rights (TRIPS).[57] But these interests did not necessarily advance the case for broader liberalization, and, if anything, aggressive expansion of the trade regime into this new area has provoked a backlash from important countries like Brazil. Now these types of interests are largely absent from the multilateral process.

[53] Petitions are often filed under unified labels such as the 'Coalition for Fair Lumber Imports' or the 'Blue Crab Coalition'.

[54] Irwin 2009, 149–50.

[55] Allee and Miler 2010.

[56] Destler 2005, 226.

[57] This group included CEOs from 13 globally focused multinationals, such as IBM, Merck, and Monsanto.

Mattoo and Subramanian, in a 2009 piece in *Foreign Affairs*, highlight the lack of participation from pro-liberalization firms from the intellectual property, manufacturing, and service sectors as a telltale sign of how irrelevant the current multilateral trade talks had become.[58]

11.4.4 Changes in US relative power

The most consequential systemic change has been the decrease in US power over time, which has reduced its relative bargaining power and decreased its propensity to bear a high burden for advancing the multilateral trading system. The US has continued to be the world's biggest economic player, but the gap between it and other major players consistently has narrowed, due initially to European integration and Japanese ascendancy, and now to the emergence of the BRIC nations (Brazil, Russia, India, and China). By the time recessions hit in the mid-1970s and early 1980s, many in the US felt it already had gone too far in making disproportionately large concessions during previous GATT rounds. At the Tokyo Round, for instance, there was little American willingness—or capacity—to make sizeable concessions on non-tariff instruments, which were being addressed seriously for the first time. During the Uruguay Round, the US pushed states that had made only modest concessions previously for greater market opening and tariff reduction. Jagdish Bhagwati therefore characterizes US behaviour in the 1980s as being part of 'diminished giant syndrome', noting that Britain also began to make sizeable demands of others as its power waned decades earlier.[59]

Other system-wide dynamics that originated in the later GATT years also contributed to a reduced US role within the global trade regime. A confluence of events pushed many developing countries towards a more active stance in the WTO, thus challenging US superiority. The wave of European decolonization produced a number of newly independent states—from different parts of the world and with very different economies and world-views—who would join the organization in the following years. Many emerging countries that once pursued state-centred economic approaches later moved towards market-oriented models, which pushed them towards greater engagement within the WTO. Alternate multilateral venues, such as the United Nations Conference on Trade and Development (UNCTAD), either became less relevant or changed their role, thus making the WTO the pre-eminent forum for engaging trade issues of widespread importance. Additionally, détente and then the end of the Cold War reduced global security threats and allowed many governments to be less beholden to US influence. All of these factors, then, pushed developing countries to pursue issues of individual and collective interest more actively within the WTO, in ways that inevitably would challenge US interests.

One area in which these power shifts are most evident is in the early negotiations during the Doha Development Round. The various sides involved in the round became entrenched—itself a sign of decreased hegemony—and at the time of writing there is little reason to think the US will achieve a future deal skewed towards its interests. For one, it has relatively less global influence than during previous rounds, as discussed above. Second, its less hegemonic

---

[58] Mattoo and Subramanian 2009.   [59] Bhagwati 1991, 16.

position means it is less able and less willing to make disproportionately large concessions—and domestic interests and unfavourable domestic institutions only reinforce this dynamic. Third, other rising and regional powers have been emboldened by their heightened position and have taken unusually strong bargaining positions. The particularly bold tactics by the G21 in walking away from the table at Cancún are a poignant illustration.

Evidence suggests that these power shifts are impacting outcomes within the WTO. Developing countries achieved a sizeable victory by effectively removing the 'Singapore issues' from the Doha bargaining table. The 2003 patent medicine waiver under the TRIPS Agreement represents another area in which geopolitics shifted against the US position. New, powerful players such as Brazil, India, and perhaps China, have used the DSM to successfully challenge policies by traditional powers such as the United States, thereby changing the negotiating dynamics at Doha and giving them increased bargaining leverage in future negotiations.

US movement towards preferential trade agreements (PTAs) represents a second major area in which power-based considerations have put the US and multilateralism at odds. The failure to make major progress during the first years of Doha, itself a reflection of power dynamics, was a major factor in pushing the US to pursue bilateral agreements with amenable partners. Although US experience with such agreements dates back further, it pursued most of its PTAs simultaneous to the Doha process, successfully negotiating 11 such agreements since 2001, with several others in progress. At least six agreements were launched in 2004, right after former USTR, Robert Zoellick, made his infamous comments about moving away from multilateralism and the 'can't do' countries, and instead seeking agreements with more willing partners.

US pursuit of these PTAs is part of a strategy of 'competitive liberalization', which, at least outwardly, is intended to be mutually reinforcing with multilateral trade liberalization.[60] Ongoing debates exist as to whether these agreements are trade-creating or trade-diverting—and thus helpful or harmful to the WTO.[61] Yet at least one prominent empirical assessment concludes that these PTAs are 'stumbling blocks' for multilateral liberalization.[62] It is increasingly clear that, regardless of their economic impact, US pursuit of these agreements may have negative political implications for the global trade regime by diverting resources away from multilateral negotiations. Evidence also suggests that PTA partners are chosen more selectively for political or foreign policy reasons.[63] Declining US power globally has less of an impact on these narrow trade agreements, many of which are reached with strategic allies, such as Korea, Colombia, and Australia, for whom geopolitical security considerations are still relevant. In fact, the US has been able to obtain more favourable terms in these agreements, including numerous exceptions, opt-outs, and protections for US interests. Regardless of how power politics ultimately plays out in these bilateral and multilateral venues, it is clear that the waning of US hegemonic power has, on balance, had a largely negative effect on the multilateral trading system.

---

[60] See Evenett and Meier 2008 for an overview of this strategy.   [61] Baldwin 2006; WTO 2007.
[62] Limão 2006.   [63] Evenett and Meier 2008.

11.5 Conclusion

The WTO is viewed by many as the most successful post-war international organization, and the United States was a big part of its development and accomplishments. The pathway of multilateral trade liberalization has had several ups and downs in recent decades, and the road is particularly bumpy at present, due in part to US behaviour during recent negotiating rounds and its courtship of bilateral agreement partners.

This chapter has argued that the shifting US role within the WTO can be traced to factors at the system level, as well as to multiple ideational, institutional, and interest-based factors at the domestic level. US hegemony in the international system allowed it to take a leadership role within the GATT, but declining American power has resulted in less trade leadership and a more contentious relationship for the US within the WTO. A US belief in free trade aided the GATT in its early years, but the subsequent pursuit of 'fair' trade challenged the tenets of multilateralism. Certain US institutions, such as fast-track negotiating authority and executive agencies concerned solely with trade policy, once aided in moving the multilateral trade regime forward, but more recently have led to US pursuit of more narrow, and often protectionist, aims.

All of the above factors have shaped the evolving US role within the WTO. Here they have been treated largely as independent forces, yet they certainly interact in unique ways that also affect the course of international trade cooperation. How these external and internal factors within US trade politics will evolve is unknown. The US may lose further economic influence to the European Union or China, or it may maintain its perch atop the global economic order. Congress may provide trade promotion authority to future administrations, or it may work as a protectionist brake on future efforts. However these developments play out, they undoubtedly will affect global trade relations within the WTO. They could rejuvenate the Doha negotiations, or they could put a final nail in the Doha coffin and push WTO members towards even more bilateral trade deals. Regardless, the lessons of the past 60 years suggest that the United States will play a major role in the WTO's future.

References

Aaronson, Susan Ariel. 1996. *Trade and the American Dream: A Social History of Postwar Trade Policy*. Lexington: University of Kentucky Press.

Allee, Todd, and Kristina Miler. 2010. Protecting Your Constituents: Congressional Participation at the International Trade Commission. Paper presented at the 106th Annual Meeting of the American Political Science Association, Washington, DC.

Baldwin, Robert E. 1998. US Trade Politics: The Role of the Executive Branch. In *Constituent Interests and US Trade Policies*, edited by Alan V. Deardorff and Robert M. Stern, 65–87. Ann Arbor: University of Michigan Press.

Baldwin, Robert E. 2006. Multilateralising Regionalism: Spaghetti Bowls as Building Blocs on the Path to Global Free Trade. *The World Economy* 29 (11):1451–518.

Baldwin, Robert E., and Christopher S. Magee. 2000. Is Trade Policy for Sale? Congressional Voting on Recent Trade Bills. *Public Choice* 105 (1/2):79–101.

Bayard, Thomas O., and Kimberley Ann Elliott. 1994. *Reciprocity and Retaliation in US Trade Policy*. Washington, DC: Institute for International Economics.

Beaulieu, Eugene, and Christopher Magee. 2004. Four Simple Tests of Campaign Contributions and Trade Policy Preferences. *Economics and Politics* 16 (2):163–87.

Bhagwati, Jagdish. 1990. Aggressive Unilateralism: An Overview. In *Aggressive Unilateralism: America's 301 Trading Policy and the World Trading System*, edited by Jagdish Bhagwati and Hugh T. Patrick, 1–45. Ann Arbor: University of Michigan Press.

Bhagwati, Jagdish. 1991. *The World Trading System at Risk*. New York: Harvester Wheatsheaf.

Bhagwati, Jagdish, and Hugh T. Patrick, eds. 1990. *Aggressive Unilateralism: America's 301 Trading Policy and the World Trading System*. Ann Arbor: University of Michigan Press.

Bown, Chad. 2010. Global Antidumping Database. *World Bank Policy Research Paper* 3737. Washington DC: World Bank.

Caves, Richard E. 1976. Economic Models of Political Choice: Canada's Tariff Structure. *The Canadian Journal of Economics* 9 (2):278–300.

Croome, John. 1999. *Reshaping the World Trading System*. The Hague: Kluwer.

Curzon, Gerard. 1965. *Multilateral Commercial Diplomacy*. New York: Praeger.

Dam, Kenneth W. 1970. *The GATT: Law and International Economic Organization*. Chicago: University of Chicago Press.

Destler, I. M. 2005. *American Trade Politics*. 4th edition. Washington, DC: Institute for International Economics.

Dryden, Steve. 1995. *Trade Warriors: USTR and the American Crusade for Free Trade*. New York: Oxford University Press.

Eckes, Alfred E. Jr. 2000. *Revisiting US Trade Policy*. Athens, Ohio: Ohio University Press.

Eckes, Alfred E. Jr. 2004. US Trade History. In *US Trade Policy*, edited by William A. Lovett, Alfred E. Eckes, Jr., and Richard L. Brinkman, 36–92. Armonk, NY: M. E. Sharpe.

Evans, John W. 1971. *The Kennedy Round in American Trade Policy*. Cambridge, MA: Harvard University Press.

Evans, Peter B., Harold K. Jacobson, and Robert D. Putnam. 1993. *Double-Edged Diplomacy: International Bargaining and Domestic Politics*. Berkeley: University of California Press.

Evenett, Simon J., and Michael Meier. 2008. An Interim Assessment of the US Trade Policy of 'Competitive Liberalization'. *The World Economy* 31 (1):31–66.

Gilligan, Michael. 1997. *Empowering Exporters: Reciprocity, Delegation, and Collective Action in American Trade Policy*. Ann Arbor: University of Michigan Press.

Gilpin, Robert. 1987. *The Political Economy of International Relations*. Princeton: Princeton University Press.

Goldstein, Judith. 1993. *Ideas, Institutions, and Trade Policy*. Ithaca, NY: Cornell University Press.

Hansen, Wendy L. 1990. The International Trade Commission and the Politics of Protectionism. *American Political Science Review* 84: 22–46.

Hansen, Wendy L., and Thomas J. Prusa. 1997. The Economics and Politics of Trade Policy: An Empirical Analysis of ITC Decision Making. *Review of International Economics* 5 (2):230–45.

Ikenberry, G. John, David A. Lake, and Michael Mastanduno. 1988. *The State and American Foreign Economic Policy*. Ithaca, NY: Cornell University Press.

Irwin, Douglas A. 2009. *Free Trade Under Fire*. 3rd edition. Princeton: Princeton University Press.

Jackson, John H. 1987. Multilateral and Bilateral Negotiating Approaches for the Conduct of US Trade Policies. In *US Trade Policies in a Changing World Economy*, edited by Robert M. Stern, 377–401. Ann Arbor: University of Michigan Press.

Kock, Karin. 1969. *International Trade Policy and the GATT, 1947–1967*. Stockholm: Almqvist & Wiksell.

Lake, David A. 1988. *Power, Protection, and Free Trade: International Sources of US Commercial Strategy, 1887–1939*. Ithaca, NY: Cornell University Press.

Limão, Nuno. 2006. Preferential Trade Agreements as Stumbling Blocks for Multilateral Trade Liberalization: Evidence for the United States. *American Economic Review* 96 (3):896–914.

Low, Patrick. 1993. *Trading Free: The GATT and US Trade Policy*. New York: Twentieth Century Fund Press.

McGillivray, Fiona. 2004. *Privileging Industry: The Comparative Politics of Trade and Industrial Policy*. Princeton: Princeton University Press.

Magee, Stephen, William Brock, and Leslie Young. 1989. *Black Hole Tariffs and Endogenous Policy Theory*. New York: Cambridge University Press.

Mattoo, Aaditya, and Arvind Subramanian. 2009. From Doha to the Next Bretton Woods. *Foreign Affairs* 88 (1):15–26.

Milner, Helen. 1988. *Resisting Protectionism*. Princeton: Princeton University Press.

Miranda, Jorge, Raul A. Torres, and Mario Ruiz. 1998. The International Use of Antidumping, 1987–1997. *Journal of World Trade* 32 (5):5–71.

O'Halloran, Sharyn. 1994. *Politics, Process and American Trade Policy*. Ann Arbor: University of Michigan Press.

Preeg, Ernest H. 1970. *Traders and Diplomats*. Washington, DC: The Brookings Institution.

Rhodes, Carolyn. 1993. *Reciprocity, US Trade Policy, and the GATT Regime*. Ithaca, NY: Cornell University Press.

Rickard, Stephanie J. 2010. Democratic Differences: Electoral Institutions and Compliance with GATT/WTO Agreements. *European Journal of International Relations* 16 (4):711–29.

Rogowski, Ronald. 1987. Trade and the Variety of Democratic Institutions. *International Organization* 41 (2):203–23.

Rosendorff, B. Peter, and Helen V. Milner. 2001. The Optimal Design of International Trade Institutions: Uncertainty and Escape. *International Organization* 55 (4):829–57.

Schott, Jeffrey J., ed. 1994. *The Uruguay Round: An Assessment*. Washington, DC: Institute for International Economics.

Schott, Jeffrey J. 2006. Completing the Doha Round. Policy Briefs in International Economics. Washington, DC: Institute for International Economics.

Shaffer, Gregory C. 2003. *Defending Interests: Public–Private Partnerships in WTO Litigation*. Washington, DC: Brookings Institution Press.

Wolff, Alan W. 1992. The Failure of American Trade Policy. In *Conflict Among Nations: Trade Policies in the 1990s*, edited by Thomas R. Howell, Alan W. Wolff, Brent L. Bartlett, and R. Michael Gadbaw. Boulder: Westview Press.

WTO. 2007. *World Trade Report 2007: Six Decades of Multilateral Trade Cooperation: What Have We Learnt?* Geneva: WTO Publications.

Yarbrough, Beth V., and Robert M. Yarbrough. 1992. *Cooperation and Governance in International Trade*. Princeton: Princeton University Press.

CHAPTER 12

....

THE ROLE OF THE BRICS IN THE WTO: SYSTEM-SUPPORTERS OR CHANGE AGENTS IN MULTILATERAL TRADE?

....

BRENDAN VICKERS

12.1 INTRODUCTION

....

AT the dawn of the twenty-first century, a profound shift of economic and political power from West to East is reshaping international relations. Goldman Sachs's 'BRIC' quartet—Brazil, Russia, India, and China—has become shorthand for the relative rise of the emerging economies as the 'new titans' of the global economy (compared to the economic downturn and slower growth prospects of the high-income economies).[1] With impressive growth rates, expanding consumer middle classes and rapid wealth accumulation, China is projected to become the world's largest economy before 2030, while India could surpass the US by 2050. Collectively, by 2032 the BRIC economies could exceed output in the Group of 7 (G7) industrialized nations.[2] The renewed dominance by 2050 of China and India reflects the rebalancing of the world economy to where it was in earlier centuries, before the Industrial Revolution.

Of all the BRICs, the pace of China's expansion has been the most spectacular. China's accession to the World Trade Organization (WTO) in 2001, preceded by enormous unilateral liberalization in the 1990s, has been the biggest opening of an economy

---

[1] *The Economist*, The New Titans, 16–22 September 2006; see Goldman Sachs 2003.
[2] Goldman Sachs 2007.

the world has ever seen. China has rapidly become the 'workshop of the world': a high-growth economy and investment behemoth, with a globally competitive position in manufacturing, especially processing trade. In 2009, China's total exports were more than $1.2 trillion, overtaking Germany as the world's largest exporter of goods. By 2010, China surpassed Japan to become the world's second largest economy. Given the size of its trade, coupled with concerns over the value of currency and large trade surplus with many countries especially the US since 2004. China has become an increasing target of WTO complaints .

The remaining BRICs have also experienced exponential growth in their output and trade, which has ranked well above the world average. This includes India's exports of software and business services, Russia's sale of oil and natural gas, and Brazil's pre-eminent position in global agricultural and agro-industrial markets. By value, world exports and imports each grew an average 12 per cent per annum from 2000 to 2008 (when the financial crisis struck), but within that Brazil's exports grew 17 per cent and imports 15 per cent, and India's exports 20 per cent and imports 24 per cent in the same period.[3] That said, Brazil and India still account for only 1 per cent and 1.5 per cent of world trade, while Russia's share of world trade is closer to 2 per cent.[4]

This chapter explores the evolving role of Brazil, India, and China—the BICs—in the WTO system, both as leaders of developing country coalitions and individually in their own right. Russia, formally joined the WTO in December 2011 after an eighteen year accession journey. There are two compelling reasons for this enquiry into the BICs' WTO diplomacy. From an economic perspective, the BICs have captured a large and growing share of world trade, which extends from merchandise trade to exports of commercial services. This is reflected in their increasingly favourable balance of trade and payments (mirrored by a deterioration of the US trade balance), coupled with vast foreign currency reserves. The scale of these surpluses—over $3 trillion for China, while Brazil and India hold hundreds of billions of dollars—has caused concerns about global economic imbalances and calls by the G20 Leaders' Forum (distinguished from the trade coalition of the G20 within the WTO) for more balanced global growth. The recent proliferation of regional trading agreements involving the BICs as key players, particularly East Asia's growing number of China-centric free trade agreements (FTAs),[5] have also raised concerns as to whether these new regional initiatives will undermine the established WTO system.

From a political perspective, the rise of these economies from the margins of the world economy has radically reshaped the rules of the game in global trade. There has been a shift of systemic influence from the traditional 'Quad' powers in the previous

---

[3] WTO 2009.   [4] International Trade Statistics, from <http://www.wto.org>.
[5] Eichengreen et al. 2008; Sally 2008. There is no mistaking Asia's new China-centric character. China has signed FTAs with ASEAN, Pakistan, and Singapore in Asia and has promoted closer economic cooperation through ASEAN13 (China, Japan, and Korea).

Uruguay Round (i.e. the US, EU, Canada, and Japan) to an emerging bloc of powers in the Doha Round that includes the US, the EU, and the BICs in various permutations. Compared to its predecessor, the General Agreement on Tariffs and Trade (GATT), the balance of power in the WTO is more multipolar, even multicultural. While it is a credit to the WTO that it has been able to facilitate and accommodate the rise of new powers, this gravitational shift in the governance and management of the world trading system has serious repercussions for the efficient functioning, inclusiveness and future relevance of the organization. As Narlikar cautions:

> No good deed goes unpunished: the WTO's timely responsiveness in accommodating the new powers at the heart of its decision-making has produced new inefficiencies, has heightened its proclivity to deadlock, and has exacerbated disengagement and disillusionment among all its stakeholders.[6]

This chapter therefore explores the evolving role of the BICs in their twin roles as system-supporters and change agents in multilateral trade. The chapter proceeds in three steps. The first section describes the trade policy evolution of the BICs as 'recent globalizers'. Understanding their domestic situations and political economies provides greater insights into their role and behaviour in the WTO, particularly China, as a relative newcomer to the trading system. The second section analyses the impact of the BICs on global trade governance, by focusing on three key areas of the WTO system: rule-making, rule-enforcement and coalition-formation. The chapter concludes by calling for a stronger leadership role from the BICs in multilateral trade, while respecting their vast development challenges.

12.2 THE TRADE POLICIES OF THE BICs

Substantial trade and investment liberalization by the BICs since the 1980s, have been the hallmarks of the second wave of economic globalization. Yet the BICs have pursued different pathways to prosperity. In the case of Brazil and India, domestic reform was crisis-induced, whereas China has gradually and autonomously integrated into the world economy. That reform dynamic appears to have stalled, as BIC governments adopt various stimulus packages and industrial policy measures to address their development challanges following the 2008 financial crisis.

12.2.1 Brazil and India's crisis reforms

Like most developing countries (and strongly informed by dependency theorizing that originated in Latin America), Brazil pursued heavy industrial policies of import-substitution and protectionism from 1930 until the end of the 1980s. This strategy

---

[6] Narlikar 2010b, 724–5.

initially led to rapid industrial development, especially during the two decades of military rule, but at the cost of soaring external debt and hyperinflation. The debt crisis and stagnation of the 1980s, coupled with the transition from authoritarianism to democracy and the emergence of new political elites, provided the catalysts for pro-market reforms in Brazil. Significant unilateral liberalization during the Collor presidency, particularly from 1991–3, was later complemented by President Cardoso's 'Plano Real' macroeconomic stabilization plan.[7] Although the political left won the 2000 and 2006 elections, the Lula government maintained economic policies of greater fiscal discipline and relatively liberalized trade whilst also prioritizing South trade and investment cooperation.

External liberalization and relative openness to foreign direct investment (FDI) and services (more so than China and India) have vastly improved the efficiency of the Brazilian economy and allowed it to profit from favourable global economic conditions, particularly high international commodity prices. The country has emerged as an agricultural powerhouse, with almost unlimited arable land and water, a highly productive agricultural sector, and competitive capacity in transport, storage, distribution, and logistics for farming exports. This explains Brazil's active participation in the Cairns Group of agricultural exporters and its vociferous leadership of the G20 in the WTO.

India shared Brazil's inward-looking trajectory, although Brazil was far more accommodating of foreign investment to develop local industries. For nearly four decades after its independence in 1947, India remained virtually a closed economy. India's post-colonial development strategy was strongly informed by the notion of self-reliance, with little attention to external trade. Notwithstanding piecemeal reforms during the late 1980s, India's marginal growth of around 3 to 5 per cent—the so-called 'Hindu rate of growth'— was insufficient to support a rapidly expanding population. Confronting an extreme balance of payments crisis, in 1991 India launched an ambitious reform programme consisting of short-term stabilization measures alongside longer-term structural reforms.[8]

In a complete paradigmatic shift to policy-making under the 'permit Raj', India reduced tariffs and other trade barriers, scrapped industrial licensing, reduced taxes, devalued the rupee, rolled back currency controls and opened the Indian market to foreign investment. These reforms have been credited with boosting India's economic performance over the past two decades.[9] Indeed, as an emerging global power in IT and business services, India has strongly supported services trade liberalization in the WTO, specifically mode four of the General Agreement on Trade in Services (GATS) regarding better access for the temporary movement of workers and in various areas, including health, education, and call-centres.

In the case of Brazil and India, market-oriented trade reforms were clearly induced by severe macroeconomic crises. Significant autonomous liberalization at home also coincided with the latter years of the GATT's Uruguay Round (1986–94). However, these shifting domestic political economy realities were somewhat removed from Geneva's

---

[7] Marconini 2009.   [8] Ray and Saha 2009.   [9] Panagariya 2008.

multilateral process, where Brazil and India remained cautious participants and reluctant supporters of the round's ambitious agenda. Indeed, both were leaders of intransigent 'Third Worldist' coalitions, such as the Group of 10 (G10) that resisted an inclusion of trade in services within the GATT.[10]

India's positions shifted over time, reflecting changing economic structures (such as the services sector boom, which has driven India's emergence in the world economy) which completely altered its domestic imperatives.[11] From being a vehement opponent of intellectual property rights and services during the Uruguay Round, India later softened its stance on Trade-Related Aspects of Intellectual Property Rights (TRIPS)—largely under duress from the US (Super 301), but also for extracting reciprocal concessions[12]— and is today one of the leading proponents for liberalizing trade in services in the Doha Round. A newly democratized Brazil also adopted a more pragmatic approach to reciprocal bargaining, given the country's competitiveness in agricultural exports.

12.2.2 China's strategic integration

In contrast to Brazil and India's crisis reforms, China has reformed gradually and autonomously since Deng Xiaoping articulated Beijing's 'open door' policy in 1978. During the 1980s and 1990s, China progressively liberalized its trade and FDI regimes, gradually reforming its closed, centrally planned and non-market economy. China's economic boom is historically based on the production and export of manufactured products, with significant investments made by technologically advanced transnational corporations from the developed world and neighbouring Asian countries.[13] This resulted in significant output expansion, particularly 'processing trade': components produced among several East Asian countries, but assembled in and exported from China to the West. Today, expert account for 40 per cent of China's GDP. Ahead of joining the WTO, Beijing accelerated the reform process—including further unilateral liberalization, restructuring of state-owned manufacturing industries, and greater recognition of private enterprise and trading rights—in order to instil confidence about its reformist intentions among its WTO interlocutors.[14] An enlightened cadre of leaders clearly used China's WTO accession in 2001 to accelerate, consolidate and lock in domestic reforms.

China's accession to the WTO, negotiated over 15 years on strictly commercial terms, was unprecedented. It also coincided with the launch of the WTO's maiden trade round, the Doha Development Agenda (DDA) in 2001, with calls on China to exercise greater systemic leadership by offering additional concessions, above and beyond its WTO

---

[10] Narlikar 2003.

[11] During the 1980s, the contribution of services to India's GDP remained quite modest, at 35–40 per cent. Clearly, it was difficult for Indian policymakers to foresee the service-led growth that the country is experiencing currently (Ray and Saha 2009, 107).

[12] Ray and Saha 2009.

[13] It is estimated that foreign-invested enterprises account for more than 50 per cent of China's foreign trade and around 80 per cent of its processing trade.

[14] Lardy 2002; Branstetter and Lardy 2006.

ticket. This coincidence of pressures partly explains China's defensive posturing and largely bystander role during much of the Doha Round.

China's commitments in the WTO are on a par with most developed countries. In many cases, they even exceed the commitments expected of existing members at its stage of economic development.[15] Formal entry came at a very heavy price for China, reflected in the range of 'WTO-plus' and 'WTO-minus' obligations contained in its Accession Protocol.[16] Notwithstanding its tremendous and socio-economic challenges as a developing country, China was, right from the outset, treated differently from its peers. The WTO Agreement places no limits on the terms of accession that the WTO can offer to applicant countries, which must be negotiated bilaterally. China reluctantly agreed, under international pressure, to be treated as a 'non-market economy' in anti-dumping cases against its exports until the end of 2015. Under this arrangement, Chinese exports may be subject to safeguards with a lower trade impact threshold ('market disruption') than normal safeguards applied to other WTO members ('serious injury'). China also agreed to unique product-specific safeguards that could be used against its exports for 12 years (curtailing its right to retaliate),[17] and to submit to annual compliance reviews over the first ten years. These transitional mechanisms are set to lapse soon.

Given these onerous conditions, which in the view of some analysts 'violate fundamental WTO principles',[18] China has demonstrated a remarkable willingness to play by the rules of the game, including dispute settlement. China has bound all its tariffs (compared to India's two-thirds) and significantly reduced the incidence of tariff protection. As a result, China's average tariff level for industrial products has dropped to 9.6 per cent from the pre-accession level of 42.9 per cent, whereas the country's average tariff level for agricultural products now stands at only 15.6 per cent as compared to the pre-accession level of 54 per cent (see Table 4). China, furthermore, agreed to fully enforce the provisions of the Agreement on Trade-Related Investment Measures (TRIMs) and TRIPS upon accession, and is prohibited from imposing any export duties except for those items listed in the Protocol's Index. Although China has implemented the bulk of its accession commitments in timely fashion, some WTO members complain that Beijing is lagging behind in key areas, including intellectual property rights, services, and subsidies or has violated its obligations by restricting exports of rare minerals.[19] When comparing the BICs' tariff profiles and obligations, it becomes evident that China's 'WTO-plus' commitments have considerably constrained Beijing's negotiating space and bargaining chips in the Doha Round. Nonetheless, China's decision to join the world's most important rules-based economic organization, even on onerous terms, is widely regarded as critical for China's 'peaceful development'.[20]

[15] Lardy 2002.
[16] WTO-plus provisions are additional obligations above those in the WTO; WTO-minus provisions are reductions in the normal WTO obligations, specifically with respect to China.
[17] This included an additional safeguard provision for textiles and apparel.   [18] Lardy 2002.
[19] The US maintains a restriction on hi-tech exports to China because of the latter's lack of respect for intellectual property rights.
[20] Sheng 2010.

Table 4 Bound and applied MFN tariffs for the BICs

Country	Year	Tariff binding coverage in % (all goods)	Simple average final bound (all goods)[a]	Simple average applied tariff (manufactures)	Simple average applied tariff (agriculture)	Simple average applied tariff (all goods)	Trade weighted average (all goods)[b]	Maximum MFN applied duties
Brazil	2010	100	31.4	14.2	10.3	13.7	10	35
India	2010	73.8	48.7	10.1	31.8	13	6.9	289
China	2010	100	10.0	8.7	15.6	9.6	4.1	65

Source: International Trade Statistics <http://www.wto.org>
a Simple average of *ad valorem* duties
b 2009

12.3 The role of the BICs in the WTO

The global ascendancy of the BICs in the WTO has been most pronounced on three fronts: rule-making, rule-enforcement and coalition-building. The following section explores their growing voice, agency, and influence in these three critical areas of the WTO system.

12.3.1 Rule-making

Historically, rule-making in multilateral trade was an exclusive and opaque enterprise, initially conducted only among the principal suppliers of products and largely centred on the traditional Quad: the US, EU, Canada, and Japan.[21] Under this 'club model' of diplomacy, many developing countries were excluded from the inner locus of bargaining, presenting the GATT—and later the WTO—with serious participatory and legitimacy deficits. Brazil and India however, have a long history of active participation in multilateral trade, reflecting their recognized status as leaders of the developing world. Their participation dates back to 1947, when both were original contracting parties to the GATT. Even with historically small shares of world trade, Brazil and India were vociferous participants in the GATT's 'Green Room' gatherings and corridor diplomacy, which continued into the WTO. They played a leading role in calling for greater fairness of process and outcomes in the trading system, particularly special and differential treatment (SDT) for developing countries.[22]

---

[21] Wilkinson 2006.

[22] Narlikar 2007. Narlikar argues that in the GATT, developing countries started out by demanding fairness of outcomes and moved on in the Uruguay Round to emphasize fairness of process. Adapting to the lessons from both these campaigns, they have in more recent times demanded fairness of both process and outcomes.

Compared to the 'rich man's club' of the GATT, the BICs have today moved to the front line of rule-making in the WTO, particularly during the Doha Round. A combination of growing confidence as a result of strong economic growth and trade performance, along with institutional adaptation and learning in the WTO (specifically by Brazil and India, and more recently China),[23] has contributed to their greater voice and agency in the organization. Their rising activism is often framed in terms of developmental concerns, specifically rebalancing the trading system's 'asymmetry of economic opportunity'[24] more in favour of developing countries. There have been two major repercussions for rule-making in the WTO, namely agenda-setting and efficiency.

12.3.1.1 *Agenda-setting in the WTO*

Agenda-setting in multilateral trade is no longer the sole preserve of the developed country majors in the WTO. Since the Seattle Ministerial Conference in 1999, which failed to launch the 'Millennium Round', developing countries have shown themselves able and willing to block negotiations under the WTO's consensus rules. In other words, the rise of the BICs is moderating the 'structural power' of the developed countries over the trade regime, namely to set the agenda.[25] Led by the BICs, the formation of the G20 at Cancún in September 2003 formally signalled a 'new politics of confrontation' between the North and the South.[26] Although Brazil and India invited opprobrium from the US by being categorized into the 'won't do' countries,[27] the emergence of the G20 was an important moral and political victory for developing countries. It significantly strengthened their bargaining power vis-à-vis the North, while shifting the terms of the agriculture negotiations towards the G20's well-researched 'middle ground' position on market access, domestic support, and export subsidies. 'As such', conclude Narlikar and Tussie, 'it was not simply a blocking coalition (despite the use of a strict distributive strategy), but in fact a proactive agenda-moving one'.[28]

Whereas Brazil and India have consistently been vociferous champions of developing country interests since the heyday of the GATT, China has only recently shifted from being a low-key actor in the Doha Round negotiations to taking a firmer stand on the side of developing countries.[29] At the July 2008 talks in Geneva, China chose to exercise its influence visibly when it joined India in blocking the consensus that was being negotiated, by refusing to concede on the 'Lamy Package', which proposed a compromise on numbers for agriculture and non-agricultural market access (NAMA). Following the collapse of that meeting, the Brazilian and Indian Foreign and Trade Ministers proclaimed: 'One thing we can celebrate is that rules here are no longer made by the rich countries. They have to take us into account, and that will continue to be so.'[30] Admittedly, this countervailing agency is still largely 'negative' (i.e. the ability and willingness to block an agreement). The BICs still have a long way to go in transforming their veto-

---

[23] Hurrell and Narlikar 2006.   [24] Wilkinson 2006.   [25] Strange 1988.
[26] Hurrell and Narlikar 2006.   [27] Zoellick 2003.   [28] Narlikar and Tussie 2004, 962.
[29] Chin 2009.   [30] Bridges Weekly Trade News Digest 2008.

player status into that of agenda-setters, so as to 'positively' (re)shape global trade governance to support their development. The role of the BICs in facilitating greater flexibility for developing countries in the TRIPS and Public Health negotiations is widely touted as an outstanding example of this positive agency

This changing configuration of bargaining power is reflected in the shift of systemic influence from the established 'Quad' powers in the Uruguay Round (i.e. the US, EU, Japan, and Canada) to an emerging bloc of powers around the US, EU, Brazil and India, and now China. The old Quad has been replaced by new core groups that take the shape of the Group of 4 (G4),[31] the Five Interested Parties (FIPS),[32] the Group of 6 (G6),[33] the Group of 7 (G7) and most recently the Group 11 (G11).[34, 35] Brazil and India, along with the US and the EU, have consistently constituted all permutations of these key consensus-building groups.[36] It is worth noting that these changes are fairly recent, having occurred in tandem with the Doha Round negotiations: until as late as 2001, India had led the Like-Minded Group, a coalition whose agenda included improving the transparency and inclusiveness of the WTO for developing countries.

However, informal small group bargaining has not settled developing countries' demands for an inclusive process and legitimate outcomes, even with the BICs as their interlocutors. Efficiency still remains troubling too, since almost all past 'G-efforts' have resulted in collapse or failure. Substituting the old Quad with a new G7 to reflect the WTO's ground-level multipolarity—as was done in the July 2008 talks—was effectively a return to the de facto 'principal supplier principle'. This led to considerable dissatisfaction on the part of many small developing countries, and threw the legitimacy of any proposed solution via this mechanism into doubt.[37] Others are more perturbed by the apparent 'cooptation' of Brazil and India into the steering club that governs the WTO, and are sceptical that this will presage a more development-friendly trading architecture. Indeed, writes one critic: 'It is paradoxical that the G20, whose formation captured the imagination of the developing world during the Cancún Ministerial, has ended up being the launching pad for India and Brazil's integration into the WTO power structure.'[38] Brazil's initial decision to accept the Lamy Package's proposed agriculture and NAMA compromises in July 2008, which threw the unity of the G20 into question, was seen as vindicating these fears.

[31] The G4 consists of the EU, US, Brazil, and India.
[32] The FIPS consists of the EU, US, Brazil, India, and Australia.
[33] The G6 comprises the EU, US, Japan, Australia (representing the Cairns Group), Brazil, and India.
[34] The G7 consists of the EU, US, Australia, Japan, Brazil, China, and India.
[35] The G11 consists of the EU, US, Canada, Japan, Australia, China, India, Brazil, Argentina, South Africa and Madritius.
[36] To ensure greater transparency and inclusiveness, WTO negotiations are conducted through a concentric circles approach: the first circle involves the WTO majors in various configurations (e.g. G4, G5, G6, and recently G7); the second circle is constituted as a 'Green Room', which accommodates about 30–45 trade ministers; and the third circle encompasses bodies that are open to all participants (e.g. the Trade Negotiation Committee, Heads of Delegation meetings, etc.) Elsig 2006.
[37] Ismail 2009.16.3   [38] Bello 2005.

12.3.1.2 *Efficiency in rule-making*

The second major impact of the BICs' global ascendancy in the WTO relates to the efficiency of rule-making. Greater multipolarity through an altered balance of power has complicated collective action at the global level and made the system prone to deadlock.[39] Though the WTO has demonstrated its institutional maturity by incorporating the BICs at the core of its decision-making, these changes have not improved the efficiency of new rule-making. If anything, more diversity in the Green Room has increased the difficulty of reaching consensus, and has improved the legitimacy of the WTO only marginally at best.

The BICs have not shied away from using their new seats at the 'high table' to vociferously champion the WTO's trade and development objectives, acting as credible veto-players under the organization's consensus rules. This has largely taken the form of distributive, rather than integrative, diplomacy.[40] From the BICs' perspective, developed contries continue to make demands for further market opening in the areas of industrial tariffs and services, while refusing to make reciprocal concessions in agriculture. The BICs have raised their objection to the steady erosion of the DDA's development mandate and hence refused to join what they regard as the 'skewed' consensus of the traditional rule-makers. In doing so, The BICs are unfairly credited for the continuous deadlock in the negotiations and the failure to conclude the Doha Round. While the established powers in the WTO continue to call upon the new powers, particularly China, to exert their growing influence over developing countries, specifically Brazil and India, to conclude the DDA, they too have abdicated their responsibilities to provide systemic leadership.

The BICs have all placed heavy emphasis on agriculture as the centrepiece of a developmental deal in the WTO's DDA. For exporters like Brazil, this means reducing—and ultimately eliminating—the raft of domestic policies and support structures that grossly distort international trade. For countries with large rural subsistence communities, including China and India, rural development, food security, and people's livelihoods are the overriding concerns. Both are very legitimate objectives. As part of the Group of 33 (G33), India—together with China—has backed exempting 'special products' in agriculture from commitments, and the creation of a Special Safeguard Mechanism (SSM), which would temporarily allow developing countries to raise their tariffs in terms of a price fall or import surge. Indeed, it was a trenchant stand-off between the US and India (supported by China) over the trigger for this remedy that provided the proximate cause for the collapse of the July 2008 negotiations in Geneva.[41] Developed countries, which

[39] Narlikar and Vickers 2009.

[40] Negotiation strategies vary across a spectrum, ranging from distributive (i.e. value-claiming) to integrative (i.e. value-creating). Distributive strategies include tactics such as refusing to make any concessions, threatening to hold others' issues hostage, issuing threats and penalties or worsening the other party's best alternative to negotiated agreement (BATNA). Integrative strategies comprise attempts to widen the issue space and explore common solutions, i.e. strategies designed to expand rather than split the pie (Odell 2000).

[41] The US insisted that SSM remedies should be triggered when imports surged by an average of 40 per cent over a three-year period, while India advocated a 15 per cent threshold. China eventually indicated that it could accept something between 20 and 35 per cent, but was not able to persuade the US and India.

had previously called for Chinese leadership as a counterweight to Brazil and India, now blamed China for the collapse of the negotiations. During the Geneva negotiating end-game, the social stability of China's 740 million farming population weighed more heavily on Beijing than actual agricultural trade. China's support for the SSM, as part of the G33, was therefore intended to send a strong signal to Chinese farmers that Beijing had not left them behind in the WTO.

India's behaviour in the Doha Round, particularly in agriculture, thus reflects continuity with its long history of naysaying in the GATT/WTO.[42] This is hardly surprising, since India's farming sector supports the livelihoods of 65–70 per cent of the country's population.[43] Brazil's trajectory in the WTO system, while, overall, similar to the Indian one during the early part of the DDA, showed signs of developing a more conciliatory dynamic in the July 2008 talks. Brazil is reported to have (unsuccessfully) urged its allies within the G20—especially China and India—to compromise on the issue of the SSM and accept the deal that was on offer, which included a cap on US domestic subsidies at $14.5 billion.[44] Brazil's behaviour in the WTO reflects the country's long-standing diplomatic tradition, typical of middle powers, to engage in mediation and bridge-building.[45] This is underpinned by a clear desire to strengthen multilateralism, in which Brazil's own development interests are embedded. In this respect, Brazil's negotiating behaviour in the WTO has been the most integrative of all the BICs.

Still reeling from its 'WTO-plus' accession commitments, this notion of bridge-building initially appealed to China too. As a newcomer to the WTO, Beijing suggested that it would be more appropriate for China to serve as an intermediary between developed and developing countries, while reserving further liberalization. On the one hand, this positioning gave China some temporary respite to implement its accession obligations, while also preoccupying itself mainly with 'learning' the norms and rules of the game.[46] On the other hand, China's reticence in the DDA created an image problem for Beijing as a somewhat detached, if not disinterested, actor, whose reluctance to exercise influence over the developing world was contributing to the parlous state of play in the Doha Round.

However, as Chin observes: 'While China has not tried to take a strong leadership role inside the Doha Round, it would also be inaccurate to call it a passive actor.'[47] Since acceding to the WTO, Beijing has been quite active in advancing a series of proposals for reforming the rules, operational norms and rule-making bodies of the WTO, often speaking on behalf of developing country interests. China has made more than 100

---

[42] Narlikar 2003.   [43] Ray and Saha 2009.

[44] See Washington Trade Daily, 28 July 2008. It was reported that Brazil was canvassing support for the Lamy Package, although this was opposed by India, South Africa, and Argentina. Brazilian Foreign Minister, Celso Amorim, was reported to have stated that Brazil was willing to press ahead, notwithstanding the differences within the G20 and Mercusor on the Lamy Package.

[45] Cooper 1997.   [46] Pearson 2006.   [47] Chin 2009, 136.

proposals altogether in the Doha Round, either alone or through cooperation with other developing countries.[48] In 2003, just two years after acceding to the WTO, China had become the most active developing country (followed by India) and the third most active WTO member, after the EU and the US, in its submissions to the WTO.[49]

12.3.2 Rule-enforcement

The second major area where the impact of the BICs is pronounced is rule-enforcement through the WTO's dispute settlement mechanism (DSM). The BICs have not shied away from enforcing their rights through this system. Brazil and India, followed by Mexico, have historically been the most active developing country litigants in the DSM. After initial years of restraint and substantial investment in developing WTO-related legal capacity, China's recent confidence with trade litigation—increasingly acting as a sole plaintiff—suggests that Beijing is steadily learning to play the dispute settlement game.

Although many developing countries still consider the DSM to be an onerous and costly exercise to settle trade disputes, the security and predictability of the system has worked to the advantage of both big and small members. Notwithstanding the recent upsurge in developing country cases filed at the WTO, the established powers—especially the US, EU, and Canada[50]—are by far the most frequent users of the DSM. While *developed* versus *developed* country cases have been declining, the opposite is evident for *developing* versus *developing* country cases. South–South litigation has grown from 11 per cent (1995–9) to 26 per cent of the total cases (2000–8).[51] Although China has only lodged disputes against the US and the EU, Chinese manufacturers have in recent years been the target of a spate of trade disputes, trade remedies and safeguard actions by developing countries. This partly reflects domestic adjustment pressures in the wake of the BICs' global ascendancy.

While the number of cases filed by *developed countries* against *developing countries* has also been on the decline, there are emerging signs of future contestation. Trade and climate change are an area where the rules are still unclear. Recent industry policy measures by the BICs to stimulate green technology industries, especially wind and solar power, has raised the ire of some developed countries.[52] Conflicts over currencies and current account imbalances are another source of tension. In recent years, China's exchange rate policy has become a major decision in several developed countries, most notably the US. Beijing's intervention in the currency

[48] See 'Official: China has always played active role in WTO talks', Xinhua News Agency, 28 July 2008.

[49] Cited in Chin 2009, 136–7.

[50] The US leads the pack in the DSM, acting as the complainant in 96 cases, the respondent in 110 cases, and a third party in 80 cases. The EU is hard on its heels, with 82, 70, and 98 cases respectively.

[51] Jones 2010, 126. Over the same time period, *developing* versus *developed* country cases rose from 14 per cent to 30 per cent of the total.

[52] The US government has recently complained to the WTO about the Chinese government's subsidies to its export-oriented clean energy manufacturers (mainly solar and wind industries), which Washington claims violate WTO rules banning subsidies to exporters.

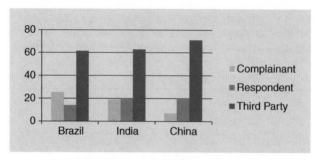

FIGURE 5 The BIC's involvement in the WTO's DSM (as of January 2012)

markets to boost Chinese exports is regarded by the US as a major contributor to the US–China trade imbalance, which reached $252 billion in November 2010. Both the US House of Representatives and the US Senate have passed similar bills that would treat an undervalued currency as an unlawful subsidy. That would open the passage for trade remedies, including tariffs on Chinese goods. But there are broader protectionist concerns too. During 2011, Brazil's Finance Minister warned that the world economy was in the midst of a 'currency war' as countries (particularly the US and China) manipulated their exchange rates to boost exports and recovery from the global recession, which Brazilian authorities claimed could ultimately spark a trade war.[53]

Within the actual DSM, Brazil is the most accomplished developing country player, in terms of being the quantity of cases brought and the cases systemic implications. Brazil has participated in 25 cases as complainant, 14 cases as respondent, and 65 cases as a third party (see Figure 5).[54] Brazil has won landmark cases against the US on cotton, and the EU on sugar. Brazil's case against US upland cotton subsidies is one of the best examples of how developing countries have used the WTO's judicial function to level the playing field, at least to some extent. Brazil's succesful engagement with the WTO's legal order is largely due to the rise of pluralist cooperation between the private sector, civil society, and the government on trade matters.

Brazil's judicial activism is followed by India's—India has participated in 19 cases as complainant, 20 cases as respondent, and 73 cases as a third party. Having only joined the WTO in 2001, China's regular appearances in the DSM are noteworthy. China has participated in the DSM eight times as complainant, 20 times as respondent, and an unprecedented 88 times as a third party. Unlike its defensive negotiating position in the Doha Round, the cases that Beijing has brought against the EU and US allow China to occupy a more offensive role in the WTO system.[55]

---

[53] 'Brazil warns of looming "trade war"', *Financial Times*, 19 January 2011.
[54] The DSM figures for Brazil, India, and China are drawn from the WTO: <http://www.wto.org>.
[55] Chin and Jiang 2009.

China's traditional preference is to settle trader disputes through bilateral consultations without litigation (such as the circuit case). But Beijing is now more prepared to defend its interests using WTO litigation.[56] Some of these disputes, such as China's export restrictions of raw materials (under appeal) are landmark case in WTO jurisprudence. For Chinese officials, third party participation has also offered a valuable opportunity, with little or no risk, to learn the norms and rules of the dispute settlement game, and to draw important tactical and strategic lessons, with an eye to future disputes.[57]

Given the growing prominence of developing countries as plaintiffs against developed countries, the BICs share an interest in a well-functioning DSM to safeguard their interests. The Doha Ministerial Declaration of 2001 mandated negotiations to improve and clarify the dispute mechanism. China and India have been quite active in this review, with proposals that aim at restraining Northern countries from using the DSM to 'harass' Southern members that lack human and financial resources for lengthy litigation. Consistent with its normative framings in multilateral trade, the Indian proposals have largely pertained to special and differential treatment for developing countries in the DSM. China has proposed limiting the number of cases against developing countries to no more than two per year, and the defrayal of costs where a developed country has lost a case. These DSM reform proposals position China as an active and constructive new member, working inside the new institution.[58]

12.3.3 Coalition-formation

The third area of pronounced BIC activity in the WTO is coalition-formation. Developing countries have long used coalition strategies to strengthen their bargaining power through joint positions and collective representation in the GATT and later the WTO.[59] During the Uruguay Round, Brazil and India led the G10, which resisted the inclusion of trade in services within the GATT. India later led the Like-Minded Group, supported by Brazil, which opposed launching a new trade round until the implementation difficulties of developing countries were adequately addressed.

The Doha Round has seen the proliferation of a range of new issue-based alliances, led by the BICs and other large developing countries. These include Indonesia's leadership of the G33, with China and India in tow, and South Africa's role in coordinating the NAMA-11, which counts Brazil and India as members, while China has endorsed many of the group's positions. Reflecting their industrialization ambitions, the BICs have used the

---

[56] Zheng and Kong 2009; Chin and Jiang 2009.
[57] Chin 2009.   [58] Chin 2009.   [59] Narlikar 2003.

NAMA-11 to call for greater 'policy space' in the formula for industrial tariff liberalization; but this has also had the effect of reducing multilateral pressures to open up their industrial goods markets vis-à-vis each other, where some of the highest barriers to South–South trade remain. Of all these coalitions, old and new, the G20 has been the most iconic.

Since its establishment at the time of Cancún in 2003, the G20 has aimed to achieve a more ambitious outcome in the agriculture negotiations, by reducing farm subsidies and trade restrictions in the US and the EU. The G20 has been a formidable alliance, unifying agricultural exporters with liberalizing interests (e.g. Brazil and South Africa) and food importers with sections of their populations dependent on subsistence farming (e.g. China and India). Compared to the more ideological and rigid bloc-type coalitions of the GATT years, which usually splintered during the negotiating endgame,[60] the G20 has broadly survived the politics of the Doha Round, notwithstanding some defections prompted by bilateral pressures from the established powers. This is not to deny the existence of intra-coalitional tensions. Indeed, India's preoccupation with developmental concerns perhaps indicates its greater alignment with the G33, rather than with the G20. This divergence of interests between the coalition members was apparent during the July 2008 talks in Geneva, when Brazil was prepared to accept the terms of the Lamy Package. Brazil attracted considerable flak from many developing countries for taking this position and breaking ranks from the rest of the G20. Several efforts were subsequently made to cover up the rift in the aftermath of the July talks.

Narlikar draws an important distinction between the coalitional behaviour of Brazil and India, within and beyond the WTO,[61] which partly explains the G20's conundrum. Brazil has used its position of leadership and trust in coalitions to facilitate compromise with the outside party. This reflects the country's conception of its middle power role, as a natural mediator and bridge-builder. So, for example, at important junctures in the Doha Round negotiations, Brazil tried hard to persuade its coalition partners in the G20 to make compromises in favour of a deal, particularly the Lamy Package at Geneva in July 2008. In contrast to Brazil's more integrative proclivities, India's distributive 'Just Say No' diplomacy and leadership of the same coalitions has led it to commit to Third Worldist positions and makes it harder for it to make concessions with the outside party. Successful coalition leadership has contributed greatly to India's newfound veto power, but the particular form that this coalition leadership takes has, paradoxically, also undermined its agenda-setting power in the system.

Compared to Brazil and India, China has not actively sought leadership of developing country coalitions, even if it was a founding member of the G20. Despite all the high expectations of it from developing countries in the WTO immediately after its accession, Beijing maintained a low profile in Third Worldist coalitions until July 2008, when it sided with India against the US. China's supportive, yet backseat, role in Southern

---

[60] Narlikar 2003.   [61] Narlikar 2010a.

coalitions partly reflects the fact that Beijing actually shares an interest with the US and the EU in seeking greater access to large developing country markets—including Brazil and India—for its manufactured exports, rather than delaying full external economic liberalization. China has thus adopted a 'two-hand policy',[62] balancing its own interests as a leading importer and exporter with the enduring ideological legacies of the Maoist period, namely Third Worldist foreign policy self-identification.[63]

While lending broad declaratory support to developing country partners, Beijing has carefully picked its own WTO battles. China has been fairly vociferous on one matter, namely special treatment for the group of recently-acceded members (RAMs). As previously noted, China's accession commitments were very demanding. Compared to Brazil and India, China's bound rates are very close to applied rates, leaving little room—or 'water' in 'WTO-speak'—to undertake further reforms so soon after acceding to the system. China has therefore been reserved about additional trade liberalization under the DDA, explaining that it is a developing country that can hardly meet its own people's needs, risking internal peace and stability. Instead, Beijing's mandarins have requested that China be treated as a new member on the basis of the 'four L's'—namely 'less' requests, 'lower' obligations, 'longer' transition periods, and 'later' liberalization.[64] By insisting on no further concessions, China approximates somewhat India's distributive negotiating behaviour in the WTO.

China has been fairly active in another area, namely the Friends of Anti-Dumping Negotiations (FANs) (which also counts Brazil as a member). As the world's most popular anti-dumping target, facing hundreds of such cases, China has lived to regret the 'non-market economy' arrangement of its WTO Accession Protocol. The FANs group thus seeks to strengthen anti-dumping rules to limit arbitrary practices on the part of investigating authorities. Meanwhile, Beijing has also used its 'non-market economy' status as a bargaining chip with other governments, insisting they recognize China as a market economy in return for development aid and the preferential trade deals its Asian neighbours are eager to establish.

12.4 CONCLUSION

Acting alone or in concert, the BICs have clearly emerged as major players in the WTO system. Their growing voice, agency, and influence have been most pronounced in three key areas of global trade governance, namely rule-making, rule-enforcement and coalition-formation. Paradoxically, however, this shift towards greater multipolarity in the WTO, and the inclusion of the BICs at the high table of the Doha negotiations, have not resulted in greater buy-in from the members of the organization—developed or developing. Among the multiple causes for the stasis in the WTO's Doha negotiations is an evident leadership vacuum: neither the established leaders nor the emerging ones,

[62] Huang 2008.   [63] Chin 2009.   [64] Chin and Jiang 2009, 8.

represented by the BICs, are willing to take on the responsibilities of leadership and contribute to the provision of the public good of free multilateral trade.

As Brazil, China, and India, as well as other large developing countries, steadily grow their shares of world trade in goods and services, and hence their interests in an open and stable world economy, these rising powers must assume greater leadership responsibilities in the WTO. This leads to the normative and policy questions of whether these countries, led by the BICs, are able and willing to provide leadership and share the task of exercising a global geopolitical role—or whether their own domestic issues and challenges will take priority.

With regard to the latter, the BICs are still poor and their development challenges large. About 150 million Chinese still live under US$1 per day. Moreover, the gains of global trade growth–measured by trade in sophisticated high-value and high technology content–still accrues largely to the North. The overriding priority for the Chinese authorities is sustaining economic growth and preserving the social and political order. Part of the challenge is to rebalance the country's growth, namely making the Chinese growth path more consumption-led and less export- and investment-driven, which exacerbates overcapacity and risks overheating.[65] China's 1.3 billion consumers potentially provide the country with a major source of internal growth. Stimulating greater domestic demand could also transform China into one of the world's largest importing countries, with important ramifications for the country's bargaining power internationally. Importing countries, as opposed to exporters, generally hold the balance of advantage in international economic relations.[66] Moreover, for the BICs to strengthen their growth prospects and competitiveness, 'second-generation' trade policy reforms may also loom large on the horizon. These are often more difficult to implement than 'first-generation' reforms, since they intrude deeply into domestic trade-related regulations and institutions.[67] How to address these second-generation reforms—unilaterally, regionally, or multilaterally—is likely to determine the BICs' future approach to a post-Doha agenda.

Looking ahead, the ascendancy of these new powers, particularly China, has generated some anxieties for the multilateral trading system. Rising powers are historically revisionist, some even revolutionary, given their subordinate status as rule-recipients of the status quo.[68] After years of obeying Deng Xiaoping's dictum of restrained foreign policy as the best means of advancing its peaceful rise, an emboldened Beijing now appears more comfortable about brandishing its strengths and achievements. Without a

---

[65] A reliance on exports and investments has caused China's domestic consumption to fall to 35 per cent of GDP, the lowest of any major economy, down from 45 per cent a decade ago.

[66] Chin and Jiang 2009.

[67] Sally 2009. Second-generation reforms include services regulation, regulation of food safety and technical standards, intellectual property protection, public procurement, customs administration, and competition rules.

[68] Kennedy 1987.

clear understanding of China's long-term strategic intentions in the WTO, and compounded by its largely passive role in the DDA negotiations, China's rapid rise and weight as an economic powerhouse has stirred uncertainty as to whether Beijing will behave as a responsible WTO citizen, or disrupt and threaten the system.[69] China's support for India at the July 2008 talks was thus interpreted by some commentators as an 'aggressive challenge', intended to impair the functioning of the multilateral trading system.[70] Within that context, 'non-cooperation' with the established powers—or the refusal to join the consensus of the traditional rule-makers—was regarded as troublesome. Others point out that Beijing's willingness to negotiate and promote reform from within the established institutional order should be appreciated as an affirmation of the international trading regime and China's commitment to 'peaceful development', rather than China behaving as an active disabler of multilateralism.[71]

Thus far, Brazil, China, and India have all revealed themselves to be 'system-supporters' to varying degrees, with Brazil being the most regime-confirming.[72] China's position is more nuanced, reflecting its newfound assertiveness in international relations. On the one hand, Beijing has broadly played by the rules of the game, even hosting the 2005 Hong Kong Ministerial Conference, where improved progress was made compared to Cancún. More recently, China and the US have agreed to pursue China's inclusion in the plurilateral Government Procurement Agreement (GPA), bringing China further into the fold. Beijing is presently revising its offer to include all levels of public procurement, namely central, provincial, and local government. On the other hand, China poses key challenges to the world trading regime, ranging from its distributive strategies in the later stages of the DDA negotiations and consistent refusal to make concessions on grounds of having surrendered much in the accession process, and leadership of the RAMs coalition, to its manipulation of its exchange rates to boost exports.

Importantly, however, none of the BICs have behaved as radically revisionist powers. They are certainly beyond status quo, having sought to advance the WTO's trade and development objectives, while championing moderate reform of the international regime. Reflecting this balance between system-supporters and change agents in multilateral trade, the BICs have articulated alternative visions of 'developmentalism', which go hand in hand with a commitment to the cause of 'Third Worldism' (albeit in quite a different form from that of the 1970s). These ideas do not represent a wholesale, revolutionary challenge to the system so much as advance the cause of international reform.

---

[69] Lawrence 2008.   [70] Bergsten 2008.   [71] Chin 2009; Sheng 2010.
[72] See Narlikar 2010a. The BICs have played by the WTO's dispute settlement rules, subjected their trade policies to peer review, and proposed a series of constructive reform measures to strengthen the system. The latter range from improvements to the functioning of the WTO's rule-making and dispute settlement bodies, to more equitable representation of developing countries in the WTO Secretariat.

REFERENCES

Bello, Walden. 2005. The Real Meaning of Hong Kong: Brazil and India Join Big Boys' Club. *Focus on the Global South.* 22 December.

Bergsten, C. Fred. 2008. China and the Collapse of Doha. *Foreign Affairs*, 27 August. Available from <http://www.foreignaffairs.com/articles/64917/c-fred-bergsten/china-and-the-collapse-of-doha>. Accessed on 7 November 2011.

Branstetter, Lee, and Nicolas Lardy. 2006. China's Embrace of Globalization. NBER Working Paper 12373. Cambridge MA: National Bureau of Economic Research.

Bridges Weekly Trade News Digest. 2008. Doha: Close, but Not Enough. 12 (27) 7 August. Available from <http://ictsd.org/i/news/bridgesweekly/18040/>. Accessed on 7 November 2011.

Chin, Gregory. 2009. Reforming the WTO: China, the Doha Round and Beyond. In *Leadership and Change in the Multilateral Trading System*, edited by Amrita Narlikar and Brendan Vickers. Leiden: Martinus Nijhoff, and Dordrecht: Republic of Letters Publishing.

Chin, Leng Lim and Jiang Yu Wang. 2009. China and the Doha Development Agenda. Working paper prepared for the BRICS and the Doha Development Round project of the North–South Institute. Available from <http://www.nsi-ins.ca/english/pdf/China%20at%20Doha.pdf>. Accessed on 7 November 2011.

Cooper, Andrew F. 1997. *Niche Diplomacy: Middle Powers after the Cold War.* Houndmills: Macmillan.

Draper, Peter, Philip Alves, and Razeen Sally, eds. 2009. *The Political Economy of Trade Reform in Emerging Markets: Crisis or Opportunity?* Cheltenham: Edward Elgar.

Eichengreen, Barry et al., eds. 2008. *China, Asia, and the New World Economy.* Cambridge: Cambridge University Press.

Elsig, Manfred. 2006. Different Facets of Power in Decision-Making in the WTO. NCCR Working Paper 23, September.

Goldman Sachs. 2003. Dreaming with the BRICs: The Path to 2050. Global Economics Paper 99, October.

Goldman Sachs. 2007. *BRICs and Beyond.* Goldman Sachs Global Economics Group.

Huang, Zhixiong. 2008. Doha Round and China's Multilateral Diplomacy. Available from <http://www.siis.org.cn/Sh_Yj_Cms/Mgz/200802/2008928112847LJML.pdf>. Accessed on 7 November 2011.

Hurrell, Andrew, and Amrita Narlikar. 2006. The New Politics of Confrontation: Developing Countries at Cancún and Beyond. *Global Society* 20 (4):415–33.

Ismail, F. 2009. Reflections on the WTO July 2008 Collapse: Lessons for Developing Country Coalitions. In *Leadership and Change in the Multilateral Trading System*, edited by Amrita Narlikar and Brendan Vickers. Leiden: Martinus Nijhoff, and Dordrecht: Republic of Letters Publishing.

Jones, Kent. 2010. *The Doha Blues. Institutional Crisis and Reform in the WTO.* Oxford: Oxford University Press.

Kennedy, Paul. 1987. *The Rise and Fall of the Great Powers: Economic Change and Military Confrontation from 1500 to 2000.* New York: Random House.

Lardy, Nicholas. 2002. *Integrating China into the Global Economy.* Washington, DC: Brookings Institution Press.

Lawrence, Robert Z. 2008. China and the Multilateral Trading System. In *China, Asia, and the New World Economy*, edited by Barry Eichengreen et al. Cambridge: Cambridge University Press.

Marconini, Mario. 2009. Brazil. In *The Political Economy of Trade Reform in Emerging Markets: Crisis or Opportunity?*, edited by Peter Draper, Philip Alves, and Razeen Sally, 146–69. 2009. Cheltenham: Edward Elgar.

Narlikar, Amrita. 2003. *International Trade and Developing Countries: Bargaining Coalitions in the GATT and WTO*. London: Routledge.

Narlikar, Amrita. 2007. All's Fair in Love and Trade? Emerging Powers in the Doha Development Agenda Negotiations. In *The WTO after Hong Kong. Progress in, and Prospects For, the Doha Development Agenda*, edited by Donna Lee and Rorden Wilkinson. London: Routledge.

Narlikar, Amrita. 2010a. *New Powers: How to Become One and How to Manage Them*. New York: Columbia University Press, and London: Hurst.

Narlikar, Amrita. 2010b. New Powers in the Club: The Challenges of Global Trade Governance. *International Affairs* 86 (3):717–28.

Narlikar, Amrita, and Diana Tussie. 2004. The G20 at the Cancún Ministerial: Developing Countries and their Evolving Coalitions. *The World Economy* 27 (7):947–66.

Narlikar, Amrita, and Brendan Vickers, eds. 2009. *Leadership and Change in the Multilateral Trading System*. Leiden: Martinus Nijhoff, and Dordrecht: Republic of Letters Publishing.

Odell, John. 2000. *Negotiating the World Economy*. Ithaca, NY: Cornell University Press.

Panagariya, Arvind. 2008. *India: Emerging Giant*. Oxford: Oxford University Press.

Pearson, Margaret M. 2006. China in Geneva: Lessons from China's Early Years in the World Trade Organization. In *New Directions in the Study of China's Foreign Policy*, edited by Alastair Iain Johnston and Robert S. Ross. Stanford: Stanford University Press.

Ray, Amit Shovon, and Sabyasachi Saha. 2009. Shifting Coordinates of India's Stance at the WTO. In *Leadership and Change in the Multilateral Trading System*, edited by Amrita Narlikar and Brendan Vickers. Leiden: Martinus Nijhoff, and Dordrecht: Republic of Letters Publishing.

Sally, Razeen. 2008. *Trade Policy, New Century: the WTO, FTAs and Asia Rising*. London: Institute of Economic Affairs.

Sally, Razeen. 2009. Trade Policy in the BRIICS: A Crisis Stocktake and Looking Ahead. ECIPE Policy Brief 3. Brussels: European Centre for International Political Economy (ECIPE).

Sheng, Ding. 2010. Analyzing Rising Power from the Perspective of Soft Power: A New Look at China's Rise to the Status Quo Power. *Journal of Contemporary China* 19 (64):255–72.

Strange, Susan. 1988. *States and Markets*. New York: Basil Blackwell.

Wilkinson, Rorden. 2006. *The WTO: Crisis and the Governance of Global Trade*. London: Routledge.

WTO. 2009. World Trade 2008, Prospects for 2009; WTO Sees 9% Global Trade Decline in 2009 as Recession Strikes. Press release, Press/554, 23 March. Available from <http://www.wto.org> Accessed 16 June 2010.

Zheng, Yongnian, and Qingjiang Kong. 2009. China in the WTO: From Accession to the Doha Failure. EAI Working Paper 147, 27 March. Singapore: East Asian Institute (EAI).

Zoellick, Robert B. 2003. America Will Not Wait for the Won't-Do Countries. *Financial Times*. 22 September.

CHAPTER 13

....

LEAST-DEVELOPED COUNTRIES IN THE WTO: GROWING VOICE

....

SHISHIR PRIYADARSHI AND TAUFIQUR RAHMAN

13.1 INTRODUCTION

....

THIS chapter examines the issue of least-developed country (LDC) participation in the multilateral trading system (MTS) under three broad sections. The first section looks at the trade profile of the LDCs, not only to see how their share of global trade has evolved, but also to trace their strengths and weaknesses in this sphere; in particular, we detail their reliance on a few products, on a few markets, and often on primary products and commodities. In the second section, we examine their participation in the World Trade Organization (WTO): how the WTO rules, especially those negotiated during the Uruguay Round, have taken into account LDCs' capacity constraints and vulnerabilities, and how members have endeavoured to address their concerns. In the next part of this section, the evolution of LDC issues during the Doha Round have been traced, including the critical issue of providing duty-free and quota-free (DFQF) market access to all products from all LDCs. A brief mention is also made in this section of the complementary and supportive role played by the Enhanced Integrated Framework (EIF), in the broader context of Aid for Trade, in converting these market access opportunities into actual gains for the LDCs. In the third section, the functioning of the LDC Group within the WTO is examined, including the way in which the group dynamics and their collective bargaining power has evolved, and also how the WTO supports the LDC Group institutionally. In addition, we outline some of the key issues in the context of the Istanbul Programme of Action (IPoA) adopted at the Fourth UN Conference on LDCs (LDC-IV) held in May 2011. Finally, the chapter makes some concluding remarks.

13.2 TRADE PROFILE AND KEY CONSTRAINTS FACED BY THE LDCs

There are presently 48 LDCs in the UN list, out of which 31 are WTO members—accounting for one-fifth of the total WTO membership (see Table 5).[1] Ten LDCs are negotiating their accession into the organization, representing more than one-third of all acceding governments. The participation of LDCs in the WTO has increased over the years, reflecting their growing stake and interest in the MTS.

Since the establishment of the WTO in 1995, the trade performance of LDCs as a group has seen a gradual improvement. The share of LDC merchandise exports in world trade stagnated at around half of one per cent throughout the 1990s; it touched one per cent in 2008 but dropped slightly below to 0.97 per cent in 2009—owing to the global economic

Table 5 WTO LDC members and observers

LDCs	WTO members/observers
Angola	M
Afghanistan	O
Bangladesh	M
Benin	M
Bhutan	O
Burkina Faso	M
Burundi	M
Cambodia	M
Central African Republic	M
Chad	M
Comoros	O
Democratic Republic of Congo	M
Djibouti	M
Equatorial Guinea	O
Eritrea	No status
Ethiopia	O
Gambia	M
Guinea	M

[1] The identification of LDCs is based on three criteria, involving income level, stock of human assets, and economic vulnerability, which need to be satisfied at given threshold values. The current threshold levels are: (i) per capita Gross National Income (GNI) of less than $900; (ii) a human asset index (HAI) of less than 58; and (iii) an economic vulnerability index (EVI) of greater than 42. These criteria are reviewed triennially by the Committee for Development Policy (CDP)—a subsidiary body of the UN Economic and Social Council (ECOSOC).

LDCs	WTO members/observers
Guinea-Bissau	M
Haiti	M
Kiribati	No status
Lao People's Democratic Republic	O
Lesotho	M
Liberia	O
Madagascar	M
Malawi	M
Mali	M
Mauritania	M
Mozambique	M
Myanmar	M
Nepal	M
Niger	M
Rwanda	M
Samoa	O
São Tomé and Principe	O
Senegal	M
Sierra Leone	M
Solomon Islands	M
Somalia	No status
Sudan	O
Tanzania	M
Timor-Leste	No status
Togo	M
Tuvalu	No status
Uganda	M
Vanuatu	O
Yemen	O
Zambia	M
Africa=33, Asia=9, Pacific=5, Caribbean=1	
Total = 48	WTO members = 31
	WTO observers = 12

Samoa and Vanuatu have completed their accession process and will become members of the WTO following domestic ratification of their accession protocols.

downturn. However, overall, the LDC economies have exhibited positive trends in the last decade. The share of LDCs in world GDP, as well as in world trade, has been increasing (see Figure 6). The trade–GDP ratio of these countries has also improved, with all categories of LDC exporters experiencing double-digit growth rates during 2000–8. Trade is not only a source of growth, but also a major sector for generating revenues, for many of the

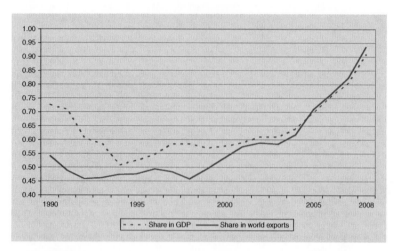

FIGURE 6 LDCs' share in world GDP and exports of goods and commercial services, 1990–2008 (percentage)

Source: WTO Secretariat

governments. Most of the LDCs have embraced trade openness, although positive externalities from such policies are perhaps not accruing to them at the desired level.

LDCs represent the most vulnerable segment of the international community, sharing some common structural handicaps. With a narrow range of export products, coupled with a heavy reliance on limited markets, LDCs remain susceptible to exogenous shocks. Despite a favourable trading environment created by the MTS (see Section 13.3), the production and export structure in the LDCs has not undergone any significant transformation. Export response from non-traditional sectors has been particularly weak. With the exception of a handful of oil-rich countries, most of the LDCs are dependent on a few non-fuel commodity exports, while for some the bulk of their export earnings come from exports of manufactures, particularly textile and clothing products. Structural constraints and inadequate trade-related infrastructure have continued to pose a challenge for LDCs' beneficial integration into the global economy.

13.2.1 LDC participation in world trade

The growth of merchandise exports from LDCs outpaced the world average during 1995–2008 (15 per cent as against the world average of 8 per cent—see Table 6). Despite a drop of 27 per cent in 2009, LDC merchandise exports registered an average annual growth rate of 14 per cent over the period 2000–9, as against a world average of 8 per cent. The exports of goods have increased dramatically since 2003, largely due to the rapid rise of international prices of oil and mineral products. Due to substantial trade surpluses generated by the oil exporters, the LDCs, as a group, registered a positive trade

Table 6 LDC merchandise exports and imports, 1995–2009 (million dollars and percentage)

	Exports				annual % change			Imports				annual % change		
	1995	2000	2008	2009	1995–2000	2000–2008	2008–2009	1995	2000	2008	2009	1995–2000	2000–2008	2008–2009
World	5,164,000	6,456,000	16,097,000	12,461,000	5	12	–23	5,283,000	6,724,000	16,493,000	12,647,000	5	12	–23
LDCs	23,972	36,301	170,501	125,051	9	21	–27	34,267	43,935	161,306	144,252	5	18	–11
Oil exporters	6512	15,087	104,761	63,650	18	27	–39	4754	7685	46,735	40,100	10	25	–14
Angola	3642	7921	63,914	39,000	17	30	–39	1468	3040	20,982	17,000	16	27	–19
Equatorial Guinea	127	1097	15,900	9200	54	40	–42	121	451	3950	4300	30	31	9
Sudan	555	1807	11,671	7800	27	26	–33	1218	1553	9352	8200	5	25	–12
Yemen	1945	4079	8977	4950	16	10	–45	1582	2324	10,452	8500	8	21	–19
Chad	243	183	4300	2700	–6	48	–37	365	317	2000	2100	–3	26	5
Manufacture exporters	6649	11,920	31,707	30,350	12	13	–4	13,539	18,273	47,967	43,743	6	13	–9
Bangladesh	3501	6389	15,370	15,081	13	12	–2	6694	8883	23,860	21,833	6	13	–8
Myanmar	860	1646	6937	6620	14	20	–5	1348	2401	4288	4600	12	8	7
Cambodia	855	1389	4708	4550	10	16	–3	1187	1939	6534	5390	10	16	–18
Madagascar	507	824	1302	1150	10	6	–12	628	1097	3980	2900	12	17	–27
Lao People's Dem. Rep.	311	330	1085	1070	1	16	–1	589	535	1405	1430	–2	13	2
Nepal	345	804	944	680	18	2	–28	1333	1573	3581	3550	3	11	–1
Lesotho	160	220	882	650	7	19	–26	1107	809	2005	1900	–6	12	–5
Haiti	110	318	480	549	24	5	14	653	1036	2315	2140	10	11	–8

	Exports				annual % change			Imports				annual % change		
	1995	2000	2008	2009	1995–2000	2000–2008	2008–2009	1995	2000	2008	2009	1995–2000	2000–2008	2008–2009
Commodities	10,641	9101	33,612	30,651	–3	18	–9	15,706	17,634	65,723	59,669	2	18	–9
Zambia	1040	892	5099	4238	–3	24	–17	700	993	5060	3791	7	23	–25
Uganda	460	460	2703	3560	0	25	32	1056	1536	4526	4410	8	14	–3
Congo, Dem. Rep. of	1563	824	3700	3200	–12	21	–14	871	697	4400	3300	–4	26	–25
Tanzania	682	734	3037	2970	1	19	–2	1675	1524	7125	6347	–2	21	–11
Senegal	993	920	2290	2180	–2	12	–5	1412	1519	6528	5210	1	20	–20
Mali	441	545	1980	2100	4	17	6	772	806	2920	2600	1	17	–11
Mozambique	168	364	2653	1950	17	28	–27	704	1158	3804	3750	10	16	–1
Ethiopia	422	486	1602	1490	3	16	–7	1145	1262	8036	7310	2	26	–9
Mauritania	488	355	1752	1360	–6	22	–22	431	454	1731	1410	1	18	–19
Benin	420	392	1160	1000	–1	15	–14	746	613	2150	1800	–4	17	–16
Guinea	702	666	1430	980	–1	10	–31	819	612	1600	1400	–6	13	–13
Malawi	405	379	860	960	–1	11	12	475	532	1650	1600	2	15	–3
Niger	288	283	880	900	0	15	2	374	395	1500	1550	1	18	3
Burkina Faso	276	209	690	800	–5	16	16	455	611	1950	1900	6	16	–3
Togo	378	363	900	780	–1	12	–13	594	562	1570	1400	–1	14	–11
Afghanistan	166	137	580	530	–4	20	–9	387	1176	3170	4200	25	13	32
Bhutan	103	103	519	280	0	22	–46	112	175	540	550	9	15	2
Rwanda	54	52	262	205	–1	22	–22	236	211	1146	1750	–2	24	53
Sierra Leone	42	13	216	205	–21	42	–5	133	149	534	505	2	17	–5

Liberia	820	329	242	165	−17	−4	−32	510	668	813	640	6	2	−21
Maldives	85	109	331	155	5	15	−53	268	389	1388	967	8	17	−30
Solomon Islands	168	69	203	139	−16	14	−32	154	92	329	276	−10	17	−16
Guinea-Bissau	24	62	125	120	21	9	−4	133	59	195	230	−15	16	18
Central African Republic	171	161	150	110	−1	−1	−27	175	117	300	300	−8	12	0
Djibouti	14	32	69	75	18	10	9	177	207	574	410	3	14	−29
Burundi	105	50	57	65	−14	2	13	234	148	403	410	−9	13	2
Vanuatu	28	26	43	50	−1	7	16	95	87	299	280	−2	17	−6
Eritrea	86	37	15	15	−16	−11	0	454	471	530	515	1	1	−3
Gambia	16	15	14	15	−1	−1	8	182	187	329	310	1	7	−6
Kiribati	7	4	15	15	−14	20	0	35	40	55	54	3	4	−2
São Tomé and Principe	5	3	11	15	−10	17	41	29	30	114	115	1	18	1
Comoros	11	14	13	13	5	−1	2	63	43	180	150	−7	20	−17
Samoa	9	14	11	11	9	−3	−2	95	106	249	195	2	11	−22
Tuvalu	0	0	0	0	−43	40	100	6	5	26	34	−3	23	29

Source: WTO Secretariat

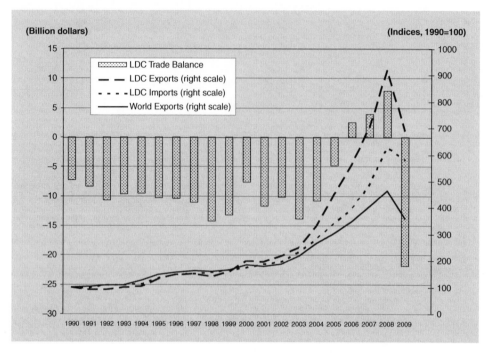

FIGURE 7 LDC merchandise trade, 1990–2009 (value indices and trade balance)

Source: WTO Secretariat

balance for three consecutive years—2006, 2007, and 2008 (see Figure 7). The overall LDC trade balance became negative again in 2009, largely owing to the fall in the value of oil and mineral exports, and because of lower demand from developed countries during the global economic crisis.

However, this rather robust aggregate growth performance hides substantial variations in the export performance of individual LDCs, as oil and mineral exporters weigh heavily in the group's aggregate statistics, masking the weak performance of other LDC exporters. The five oil-producing LDCs (Angola, Chad, Equatorial Guinea, Sudan, and Yemen) recorded an annual increase of 27 per cent in the value of their exports during the period 2000–8 (see Table 6). This is twice the growth rate registered by the manufacture-exporting LDCs (13 per cent). The commodity-exporting LDCs also experienced a more heterogeneous growth pattern, due to sharp fluctuations in international prices of commodities; nevertheless, this group of LDC exporters registered an annual average growth rate of 18 per cent. However, the rate of growth of imports of commodities- and manufacture-exporting LDCs could not cushion the rate of growth of their exports: their coverage ratio of imports to exports remained low, leading to a deterioration of trade balance.

While the LDCs as a group have witnessed an increase in their share of world merchandise trade, the LDCs' share of world trade in commercial services has remained largely static during 2000–9, hovering around the 0.4 to 0.5 per cent mark (see Tables 7a

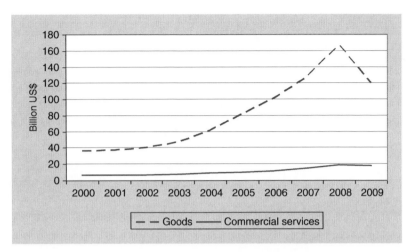

FIGURE 8 Evolution of LDC exports of goods and commercial services, 2000–9 (billion dollars)

and 7b). The structure of LDCs' services exports also remained static, with travel services accounting for about half of LDCs' services trade during this period. Nevertheless, the LDC exports of commercial services grew faster (12 per cent) than the world average of 9 per cent, and accounted for 13 per cent of total LDC exports in 2009 (see Figure 8).

13.2.2 Major products

LDC exports are characterized by a highly concentrated export profile. This concentration is manifested in the composition of their exports as well as in their export destinations. If one constructs a concentration index at HS six-digit level (i.e. share of the top three exports in terms of value in total exports, based on the Harmonized system of six-digit classification), it gives a very illustrative landscape of the narrow export base. On average, the top three export products account for over 70 per cent of each LDC's total merchandise exports.

While concentration levels of exports are high, the leading export product differs across LDCs. Some LDCs have a very high share of agricultural products in their total exports (Burundi, Malawi). At the opposite end, the share of agriculture in total exports is less than one per cent for LDCs like Angola and Bangladesh—the top two LDC exporters in value terms. This implies that despite commonalities, market access interests of the LDCs are quite different.

Since the establishment of the WTO, a distinct shift has taken place in the relative importance of different product groups in the total exports of LDCs. In 1995, food (including fish and fish products) was the principal export, representing more than 20 per cent of all LDC exports. Today, oil is the single most important product in LDC merchandise exports, followed by apparel. The oil exports account for 60 per cent of the

Table 7a Commercial services exports of the LDCs by category, 2000–9 (million dollars and percentage)

	Commercial services	Transportation services		Travel		Other commercial services	
	2009	2000	2009	2000	2009	2000	2009
Least developed countries	17,400	20	18	47	56	33	26
Afghanistan	...	...	...	...	...	...	...
Angola	302	6	...	...	...	94	...
Bangladesh	935	32	15	18	7	50	77
Benin*	328	14	4	61	72	25	24
Bhutan	58	...	...	...	...	...	...
Burkina Faso	114	13	...	67	...	20	...
Burundi*	3	43	27	37	41	20	32
Cambodia*	1613	17	15	72	76	11	10
Central African Republic	28	4	...	51	...	45	...
Chad	87	2	...	65	...	33	...
Comoros*	59	13	10	81	65	6	25
Congo, Dem. Rep. of*	522	...	...	...	...	...	...
Djibouti*	129	76	83	12	6	12	11
Equatorial Guinea*	33	3	...	50	...	47	...
Eritrea	...	18	...	64	...	18	...
Ethiopia*	1775	56	59	15	21	30	20
Gambia*	123	...	17	76	68	...	16
Guinea	68	58	22	7	...	34	...
Guinea-Bissau	54	12	...	...	...	...	...
Haiti	327	...	...	81	96	...	...
Kiribati*	13	12	...	8	...	81	...
Lao People's Dem. Rep.*	372	13	15	76	74	11	11
Lesotho*	60	2	1	67	56	31	43
Liberia*	182	...	11	...	87	...	3
Madagascar	592	16	...	39	...	45	...
Malawi	...	26	...	74	...	0	...
Maldives	629	6	...	93	93	1	...
Mali*	442	36	7	44	62	20	30
Mauritania	176	1	...	20	...	79	...
Mozambique	544	30	28	23	36	47	36
Myanmar	...	17	...	35	...	48	...
Nepal	548	15	7	38	68	47	25
Niger*	126	24	9	64	62	12	28
Rwanda	249	34	22	57	70	8	8
Samoa	...	...	...	...	...	...	...

	Commercial services	Transportation services		Travel		Other commercial services	
	2009	2000	2009	2000	2009	2000	2009
São Tomé and Principe	11	2	2	76	83	22	16
Senegal*	1470	10	...	44	...	47	...
Sierra Leone	53	46	35	27	48	27	16
Solomon Islands	68	3	22	9	64	89	14
Somalia	...	...	...	...	...	...	...
Sudan	370	63	...	22	81	15	...
Tanzania	2220	10	15	65	60	25	25
Timor-Leste	...	...	...	...	...	...	...
Togo*	253	23	43	18	16	59	41
Tuvalu	...	...	...	...	...	...	...
Uganda	876	15	4	81	76	4	20
Vanuatu	217	24	...	47	...	28	...
Yemen	1077	12	...	42	...	46	...
Zambia	239	37	...	58	...	5	...
Memorandum item:							
World	3,350,200	23	21	32	26	44	53

Source: WTO Secretariat

Table 7b Commercial services exports by LDCs, 1995, 2000, and 2009 (million dollars and percentages)

	Value			Share			Annual growth
	1995	2000	2009	1995	2000	2009	2000–2009
Commercial services	5243	6125	17,165	100.0	100.0	100.0	12
Transport	1082	1222	3199	20.6	20.0	18.6	11
Travel	2171	2874	9593	41.4	46.9	55.9	15
Other commercial services	1990	2029	4327	38.0	33.1	25.5	9
Memorandum item:							
World exports of commercial services	1,172,400	1,483,900	3,860,200	100.0	100.0	100.0	9

Source: WTO Secretariat

value of all LDC exports. In fact, the price of oil has been a key factor in the aggregate performance of LDCs in world exports, and excluding oil the LDC exports, as a percentage of world merchandise trade, have increased only marginally, from 0.37 per cent in 2002 to 0.40 per cent in 2008.

13.2.3 Major markets

Another distinguishing feature of LDC exports is their reliance on a very limited number of markets. The top ten markets account for more than 70 per cent of their total merchandise exports. In fact, as the figure below (Figure 9) shows, exports to China, the EU and the US account for over two-thirds of all LDC exports.

Developed countries have remained the dominant destination for LDC exports for a long time. In 2002, nearly 60 per cent of all LDC exports went to the EU and the US. This 'duopsonistic pattern' has started to decline in the last few years. Since 2007, developing countries have been absorbing nearly 50 per cent of all LDC exports. China became the single largest importer of LDC exports in 2008, overtaking the EU, and maintained that top position in 2009. This consolidation of developing countries as a major market for LDC exports reflects the growing importance and potential of South–South trade for the LDCs.

There is also a marked difference in the importance of markets based on the type of product. Developed economies remain the dominant destination for clothing (North America), fish and crustaceans (Western Europe), and some agricultural items. Developing economies have become a major destination for LDC exports of petroleum and minerals.

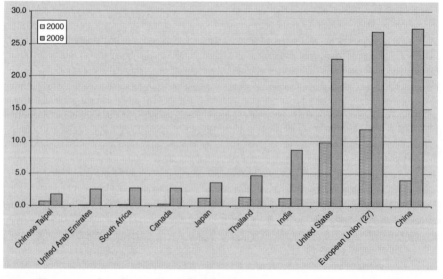

FIGURE 9 Top ten markets for LDC merchandise exports, 2000–9 (billion dollars)

Source: WTO Secretariat

In China, which is an emerging market for the LDCs, the import structure is heavily dominated by fuels. In fact, today the value of LDC fuel exports to developing countries is higher than their fuel exports to developed countries.

13.2.4 Impact of the financial crisis

The sharp contraction in the global economy that began in the second half of 2008 hurt the LDCs during a phase of particularly rapid growth of their exports of goods as well as services. Two factors—price and demand—have been dominant in conditioning the

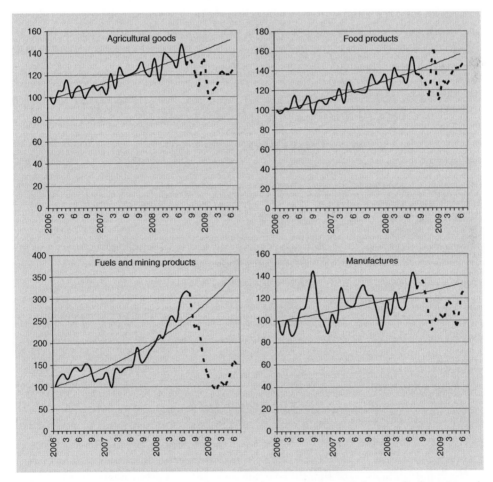

FIGURE 10 LDC exports (by main product groups), January 2006 to July 2009 (Indices, January 2006 = 100)

Note: The dotted line corresponds to the 'crisis period', after September 2008. The trend line shows the extrapolated trend, based on pre-crisis observations. Data are based on statistics obtained from selected developed and developing countries, including the EU.

Source: WTO Secretariat

exports of LDCs, and have led to varying degrees of impact across the different LDCs. For example, the oil and mineral exporters bore the brunt of the crisis due to a salutary price effect. Oil prices dropped by more than 40 per cent during the last quarter of 2008, and remained depressed through the first quarter of 2009, influencing the overall value of LDC exports. The impact on the LDC manufactures exporters came primarily from a fall in global demand, although specialization in the lower range of clothing products helped a few LDCs to weather the storm, as demand for such items remained inelastic. The trade in commercial services, on average, showed some resilience, but some tourism-dependent LDCs experienced a fall in their export earnings as consumers adjusted their consumption patterns in view of falling incomes.

While prices of oil and minerals bounced back in the second quarter of 2009, and the market for primary commodities regained some of the lost ground, the recovery did not match the pre-crisis level of LDC exports. As a consequence, all categories of LDC exporters experienced negative growth rates in 2009 and their exports were below the long-term average registered during 2000–8 (Figure 10).

13.3 LDCs in the multilateral
trading system

13.3.1 WTO provisions giving flexibilities to LDCs

Differential and more favourable treatment for the LDCs are embedded across all WTO agreements and WTO ministerial decisions and declarations, ranging from enhanced market access opportunities to derogations from WTO disciplines. Provisions aimed at increasing trade opportunities for LDCs were contemplated as early as the Tokyo Round, when the then General Agreement on Tariffs and Trade (GATT) contracting parties adopted the Enabling Clause in 1979. This gave developed members a legal cover to provide non-reciprocal preferential market access to the LDCs without requiring them to extend similar treatment on an MFN basis to other members. The legal lacunae in allowing the developing countries to provide similar preferential access to LDCs were also addressed in 1999, with the adoption of a waiver from MFN obligations. Backed by these decisions, there have been significant improvements of preferential schemes in favour of LDCs.

At the same time, there has also been an increasing recognition that lack of market access opportunities was neither the sole cause, nor the only area where action is needed to address the weak performance of LDCs in world trade. The WTO agreements address the special needs of LDCs in a variety of other ways: through exemption from obligations, lower level of commitments than other members, longer transition periods to implement specific agreements, and enhanced technical assistance.

For instance, the Agreement on Agriculture, negotiated during the Uruguay Round, exempted LDCs from undertaking tariff-reduction commitments, even though the average tariff reduction that developing countries were required to make was 24 per cent. The LDCs were therefore able to protect their sensitive products. Also, at that time most of the LDCs took the ceiling binding route to establish their bound rates, with average binding levels being around 78 per cent. In fact, the bound rates of a number of LDCs (the Gambia, Malawi, Myanmar, Zambia) are above 100 per cent.[2] Such flexibilities—which represent an important trade policy instrument—are also proposed to be allowed to the LDCs under the Doha Development Agenda (DDA) negotiations (see Section 13.3.2), demonstrating the accommodative nature of the WTO members towards the LDCs to allow them to integrate into the MTS in a gradual and beneficial manner.[3]

Another example of flexibility from WTO disciplines is the TRIPS Agreement. LDCs had been granted a transition period of ten years to provide protection for trademarks, copyrights and other intellectual property under the TRIPS Agreement, in recognition of the economic, financial, and administrative constraints, as well as the need for a flexibility to create a viable technological base in the LDCs. This transition period, which expired in 2006, has been further extended until 1 July 2013. The LDCs are also not required to provide patents for pharmaceutical products until 2016. In addition to these LDC-specific flexibilities, in 2005 WTO members approved an amendment to the TRIPS Agreement—the first amendment of a multilateral WTO agreement—making it easier for poorer countries, including the LDCs, to obtain cheaper, generic versions of patented medicines.

All these examples show the willingness of WTO members to give policy space to the LDCs to meet their WTO obligations in a way that serves their development needs. It should also be noted that, in addition to global LDC-specific exemptions across the WTO agreements, LDCs can also make use of all the special provisions designed for developing countries.

13.3.2 The Doha Development Agenda and the LDCs

The Doha Development Agenda (DDA) was launched in November 2001, in Doha. As the name suggests, development is at the heart of the DDA. The development focus of the round was a result of the realization by members that better market access and fairer, more transparent rules of trade would be to the benefit of all members, particularly the developing countries and LDCs.

---

[2] Bound tariffs are like a ceiling on the maximum duty that could be applied for any tariff line, thereby providing certainty and market security to exporters and investors alike. Applied tariffs normally cannot exceed these bound rates, which are indicated in every country's schedule to the WTO.

[3] Similarly, more than half of the WTO LDC members have bound less than 35 per cent of their non-agricultural tariff lines.

The conclusion of the Doha Round will result in significant tariff cuts in agriculture, and a substantial reduction in agricultural subsidies, in particular in developed countries. The commitments within the DDA will not only increase market access in developed countries for the LDCs, but will also open up markets in the larger developing countries, thereby facilitating more South–South trade. With the majority membership of the WTO better integrated into the system, strengthened, more transparent regulatory regimes, and the trade facilitation initiatives planned under the DDA, the conclusion of the round is likely to result in smoother and larger trade flows globally, benefiting the global trading system as whole.

A recent study estimates that the boost to global exports from concluding the Doha Round could range between $180 billion and $520 billion annually.[4] LDCs, too, will gain from a successful conclusion of the Doha Round. A number of studies conclude that, on balance, the LDCs stand to gain more from the reforms envisaged in the agricultural sector than in other sectors.[5]

During the course of the negotiations, the LDC Group has made a number of offensive and defensive proposals in different areas of the negotiations, including in the areas of agriculture, non-agricultural market access, services, special and differential (S&D) work programme, dispute settlement, trade facilitation, and in the context of the complementary work programme on Aid for Trade. The LDCs are also seeking an 'early harvest' in some issues, which include the implementation of the decision on DFQF market access for LDC products, adoption of a waiver to receive preferential treatment in services trade, and an ambitious outcome on cotton—all of which they believe are critical for their improved participation in world trade.[6]

Given that the largest gains that the DDA can deliver are in the area of market access, the first and foremost priority identified by the LDCs has been the full implementation of the decision on DFQF market access, which was adopted by WTO members at the Sixth Ministerial Conference in Hong Kong, China, in 2005. In view of the narrow range of products they export, and of the fact that some of their major export items still face higher tariffs, the LDCs have called for the implementation of this decision in a manner that is commercially meaningful to them and which provides long-term security to their exporters. At the same time, they are emphasizing the need to address some of the non-tariff barriers which hinder the full utilization of the preferences granted to them. The call for simplified and transparent rules of origin associated with preference schemes has therefore found a prominent place in all the recent LDC trade ministers' declarations. The LDCs have also submitted specific proposals in the negotiations inviting the

[4] Adler et al. 2009.

[5] Tutwiler and Straub 2008. LDCs are more likely to benefit from subsidy cuts than other developing countries. On average, 18 per cent of their exports are subsidized by at least one OECD member. For example, Benin, Burkina Faso, Chad, Malawi, Mali, Rwanda, Sudan, Tanzania, Uganda, and Zimbabwe have 60 to 80 per cent of their total exports subsidized by one or more WTO members.

[6] A group of four West African cotton-producing countries (Benin, Burkina Faso, Chad, and Mali), commonly known as C-4 or Cotton-4, has been working to put an end to all trade-distorting policies affecting the sector.

preference-granting members to adopt simplified rules of origin criteria, which would facilitate their exports.

Many of the positions taken by the LDCs in the agriculture negotiations are defensive in nature. The LDCs have asked for greater leverage in protecting the agricultural sector, including through the special safeguard mechanism—a tool that would allow countries to increase their tariffs in times of import surges or price declines. The LDCs are seeking flexibility to raise tariffs beyond their bound rates in the WTO without any ceilings being imposed on them. An area where the LDCs are particularly cautious is in the disciplines that are being developed on food aid operations. The LDC Group argue that their governments should retain a key role in the area of food aid, so that the delivery of food aid in emergency situations is unhindered.

One issue that has gained prominence in the course of the negotiations is the likely erosion of preference margins (the difference between the MFN applied duty and the preferential rate of duty) that a majority of LDCs presently enjoy in many of their major markets. Apparel and processed fish, which are two products of particular export interest to LDCs, have some of the highest preference margins—in the range of 20 to 24 per cent in certain markets. The LDCs have identified a number of products where they would like MFN liberalization to take place over a longer time frame, to give them some time to be able to compete on an MFN basis.

The LDCs have also been active participants in the services negotiations. Given their special interest in the movement of natural persons, as defined in mode 4 of the General Agreement on Trade in Services (GATS), LDCs are asking their trading partners to make commitments in those categories of services where they have a comparative advantage.[7] In the course of the DDA negotiations, WTO members have adopted guidelines for LDCs' participation in the negotiations, which give them special treatment in undertaking services commitments and require members to give special priority to facilitate access of LDCs' services and service suppliers to foreign markets. The active persuasion of LDCs for a services waiver culminated into a waiver decision at the Eighth WTO Ministerial Conference held in December 2011, which will allow a WTO member to undertake preferential market access commitments in favour of LDCs.

The trade-facilitation negotiations is another area where LDCs have expressed some offensive interests. LDCs, like other WTO members, are looking at these negotiations as an opportunity to reduce their trade transaction costs. As a result, a number of landlocked LDCs have joined other members to ask for procedural and institutional improvements in cross-border trade, which often delays the movement and clearance of their goods at the border of neighbouring countries.

Another area where the LDCs have shown an interest is the negotiations on the Dispute Settlement Understanding (DSU). Even though, since the establishment of the WTO, very few LDCs have initiated consultations or requested the establishment of a

---

[7] LDCs essentially seek access for natural persons de-linked from commercial presence, such as independent professionals, business visitors and contractual service suppliers.

panel,[8] and also very few complaints have been brought against LDC exports, their interest in this area is increasing. The LDCs have submitted a proposal seeking a number of improvements in the dispute settlement proceedings, including in the terms of reference as well as in the composition of panels. It should be noted that the Advisory Centre on WTO Law (ACWL), which is situated in Geneva, provides free legal advice (on request) and training on legal matters to the LDCs, despite the fact that the LDCs are not members of the ACWL.

While the DDA negotiations are yet to be concluded, the work so far has already provided important pointers that show the round will ensure enhanced market access opportunities as well as adequate flexibilities for LDCs in the MTS. Many of the principal demands of the LDCs made in the Doha Round have been taken on board. The LDCs have been exempted from making any tariff-reduction commitments in the goods negotiations, which gives them the flexibility they desire to pursue some of their development objectives. Both trade and non-trade solutions are being devised to help LDCs address erosion of preferences. Similarly, LDCs are not expected to undertake any new commitments in the services negotiations.[9]

It will be remiss of us if we conclude this section without pointing out the outcome that the LDCs secured in the work programme on S&D. Making the existing S&D provisions more precise, effective and operational is one of the cornerstones of the DDA negotiations. In addition to the decision on DFQF market access for LDC products, a decision was taken at WTO's Hong Kong Ministerial meeting to strengthen a number of S&D provisions contained in WTO legal instruments and agreements, including decisions on improved consideration of LDC waivers and an extended transition period to comply with the Agreement on Trade-Related Investment Measures (TRIMs). While there is further scope for broadening the S&D package in the negotiations, some of the important LDC-specific concerns have now been addressed, providing the LDCs with greater market access opportunities along with the policy space that they have been pressing for.

13.3.3 Market access—the DFQF decision

Securing DFQF market access to both developed and developing country markets has been a prominent issue in the trade agenda of the LDCs for many years. All LDC trade ministers' declarations have put this as a leading priority. The DDA negotiations also embraced this objective, and subsequently, at the WTO Hong Kong Ministerial

---

[8] The first LDC member involved in a dispute as a third party was Bangladesh, which in 2004 requested consultations with India with respect to anti-dumping measures imposed by the latter on imports of lead acid batteries from Bangladesh. In 2006, both parties reached a mutually satisfactory solution to the matter.

[9] LDCs currently have few existing commitments in their GATS schedules, averaging 24 sectors committed out of a possible 155. This compares to an average of 52 sectors for developing countries.

Conference in 2005, a comprehensive decision was adopted to provide DFQF market access to all products from all LDCs. The full implementation of the decision will not only take care of high tariffs that are prevalent on some products of export interest to LDCs (e.g. clothing), but will also address the problems related to tariff escalations, paving the way for export of processed goods from LDCs, thereby also helping them in moving up the value chain. According to the decision, developed countries were required to provide DFQF market access to at least 97 per cent of products originating from LDCs by the end of 2008, or no later than the start of the implementation period of the round. However, in spite of this implementation period not having kicked in, nearly all developed members of the WTO have provided DFQF access to at least this threshold of tariff lines, if not to more. Most LDC exports today enter developed country markets duty-free, with the exception of one market. Developing countries have also been brought into the fold of this decision, although in a flexible manner. A number of LDCs' key developing country trading partners have either adopted or announced schemes which provide a significant degree of DFQF access, through a variety of multilateral, regional and bilateral schemes.

A number of attempts have been made to quantify the gains from the full implementation of the DFQF decision for the LDCs. The discussion on this issue has unfolded a debate on whether the outcome will be a positive sum game for all LDCs, given that LDCs in Africa already enjoy DFQF access in the US market through the African Growth and Opportunity Act (AGOA) scheme, while for instance clothing exports from Asian LDCs enter the market on an MFN tariff, which in certain cases is as high as 15 per cent. Whether the implementation of this decision will cause one group to crowd out another within the LDCs is not yet conclusive, but estimates show that if the US were to grant DFQF to 97 per cent of tariff lines covering export items of interest to LDCs, then their exports to the US are likely to increase by around 10 per cent, or about $1 billion.[10]

13.3.4 Preferential schemes and rules of origin

LDC exports usually enjoy preferential access through unilateral preferential schemes. These preferential schemes have been a salient feature of the international trading regime for a long time. The intent of preferences is to stimulate export diversification, and to convert any comparative advantage that an LDC may have into a competitive advantage. A number of LDC exports have flourished under preferences (e.g. fish, apparel). At the same time, research is replete with examples which show that preferences are not being fully utilized, for a variety of reasons both endogenous and exogenous to the LDCs. Lack of utilization has at times been attributed to the weak productive capacity in the LDCs to produce marketable products, or to lack of institutional infrastructure to comply with international standards. Lack of utilization of preferences has

---

[10] Carrère and De Melo 2009.

also often been attributed to stringent rules of origin associated with some preference schemes, which nullify the intended benefits from the preferences.

Although preferential rules of origin have so far not been subject to WTO rules, the Hong Kong Ministerial Declaration asked members to adopt rules of origin that are simple, transparent and facilitate exports from LDCs. The LDCs, during the course of the negotiations, proposed an across-the-board framework for rules of origin, based on a percentage criterion of the value of local material. Discussions are ongoing in the WTO to suggest a suitable rules of origin framework for LDC exports.

A number of variables—like the threshold for value addition, the rules of cumulation, simple administrative and verification processes—condition the rules of origin. Different schools of thought exist as to the reform of the rules of origin criteria, reflecting the difficulty of having common and universal rules of origin criteria for the LDCs. Some research work suggests a low threshold for value addition,[11] whereas others recommend the 'extended cumulation' route to allow LDCs to source inputs in a cost-efficient manner.[12]

Since the manufacturing capacity varies from LDC to LDC, and especially the way in which the LDCs source the different elements or products that go into the manufacture of the final product to be exported, it has been difficult to conclusively say which rules of origin would be best for LDCs. But what can be conclusively said is that where preferential schemes have been accompanied by flexible rules of origin there has been a definite increase of exports. For instance, with the introduction of the revised Generalized System of Preferences (GSP) scheme for LDCs by Canada in 2003, which came along with product-specific flexible rules of origin criteria for textiles and clothing, imports into Canada from LDCs significantly increased, reaching more than $1 billion in 2009. Similarly, liberal rules of origin under the AGOA scheme (featuring third country fabric provision) also stimulated US imports of clothing from the African LDCs.

13.3.5 Beyond market access—Aid for Trade and the Enhanced Integrated Framework (EIF)

While enhancing market access opportunities is an essential prerequisite it is, by itself, not sufficient to ensure that exports from LDCs will necessarily increase. The ability to produce, as well as adequacy of the trade-related infrastructure, are equally important conditions. This is the reason that the WTO is making a concerted effort to strengthen the productive capacity and trade-related infrastructure in developing countries, including the LDCs. The Aid for Trade initiative, launched in 2005, is intended to assist developing countries and LDCs to build their supply-side capacity to benefit from market access liberalization.

---

[11] Brenton 2006.   [12] Elliott 2010.

Over the past five years, the Aid for Trade initiative has gained momentum. Aid for Trade resources to the LDCs have increased, despite the economic crisis. In 2008, LDCs received $10.5 billion in Aid for Trade, representing a quarter of total Aid for Trade. In fact, three out of the top ten Aid for Trade recipients in 2008 were LDCs (Afghanistan, Bangladesh, and Tanzania). An Aid for Trade Work Programme is currently being implemented by WTO members to maintain the momentum of resource mobilization and to ensure that Aid for Trade makes a visible impact on the ground.

In addition, for LDCs, there exists a unique mechanism through which Aid for Trade resources could be leveraged. The Enhanced Integrated Framework (EIF) is an example where six agencies (IMF, International Trade Centre (ITC), UNCTAD, UN Development Programme (UNDP), the World Bank and the WTO) combine their individual competence to strengthen trade capacity in the LDCs. The programme was launched in 1997 to integrate LDCs into world trade. The achievements in its early years were modest, with only a handful of LDCs receiving support from the initiative. It was revamped in 2001, with the twin objectives of achieving better trade mainstreaming into LDCs' development strategies and ensuring coordinated delivery of Trade-Related Technical Assistance (TRTA). Even the revamped EIF did not go far enough to make the desired impacts on the LDCs, prompting its stakeholders to design the present EIF with improved global governance, strengthened in-country capacity, and, very importantly, the provision of additional resources for the LDCs to implement the recommendations stemming from the EIF process. The EIF is now administered by an Executive Secretariat, and is supported by a multi-donor Trust Fund with the United Nations Office for Project Services (UNOPS) acting as the Trust Fund Manager.

Today, 47 LDCs are at different stages of the EIF process and are benefiting from the different funding tiers available under this initiative. Some LDCs have been able to leverage the EIF process to access broader funding. Other LDCs have been able to establish synergy with other technical assistance programmes, such as the Standards and Trade Development Facility (STDF). Importantly, the EIF process has been accepted as a vehicle to access Aid for Trade resources. Based on a strong analytical foundation, through the Diagnostic Trade Integration Studies (DTISs), the EIF process supports some small-scale projects as identified by the governments while at the same time providing the basis to seek larger-scale funding from traditional channels. While success stories of the EIF are building up, it remains to be seen whether the LDCs and their development partners involved in this process are able to employ the EIF process in triggering the much needed assistance in the area of trade.

13.4 PARTICIPATION OF THE LDCs IN THE WTO

13.4.1 Participation in the WTO

The increased focus on issues of concern to the LDCs, as well as an acknowledgement of their limited institutional and productive capacities—all of which have led to concessions and flexibilities in the rules as well as a drive towards enhanced market access opportunities under the DDA negotiations—can, to a large extent, be attributed to the increasing engagement and participation of the LDCs in the WTO. They are no longer quiet bystanders, dependent on the empathy of their trading partners. They have increasingly sought a voice for themselves, and today command attention and respect from the WTO membership.

The WTO LDC members and observers had set up an LDC Consultative Group in Geneva in 2001. The Geneva-based LDC delegations, often joined by trade officials from their capitals, meet on a regular basis at the WTO. Based on their work in this group, the LDCs articulate and advance their positions in the meetings of various WTO bodies and negotiating groups. As a result, at all formal, informal, and 'Green Room' meetings of the WTO, the Coordinator of the LDC Group speaks on behalf of the LDCs, ensuring that LDC concerns are appropriately focused upon.

The group has pooled resources by creating 'focal points', whereby each such LDC focal point is given a responsibility to follow a specific area and to report periodically to the LDC Coordinator. This is delivering results. Almost all submissions and proposals by the LDCs in the DDA negotiations have been developed at this level. All the more, this group has been playing an instrumental role in organizing and servicing the LDC trade ministers' meetings, which have become a regular feature ever since the formation of the group in 2001. Seven such ministerial meetings have been held so far, and the declarations adopted in these meetings form the basis for the LDC negotiators in Geneva, for their participation in the regular work as well as in the negotiations under the WTO.

Apart from negotiating as a group, members of the LDC Group have also joined different alliances to advance their specific trade interests. The incidence of coalition building has significantly increased with the launch of the Doha negotiations, which has seen developing countries and LDCs assuming considerable bargaining power. For instance, as many as 20 alliances have been formed in the area of agriculture negotiations alone, many of which include the LDCs. One of the most interesting trends of the variable geometry in the post-Doha period has been the formation of issue-based coalitions. The Group of 33 (G33), which includes eight LDCs, advocates securing flexibility to self-designate a number of special products under agriculture negotiations, on which they would not have to make tariff reductions.

The informal group of 'Cotton-4' successfully brought the cotton issue to the forefront of the negotiations during the WTO's Ministerial Conference in Cancún (Mexico) in 2003. A specific mandate on cotton was not part of the Doha mandate in 2001, but today an ambitious result in this area has become vital for the successful conclusion of the round. The LDCs have been actively and effectively coordinating with the African Group and ACP Group—both of which have overlapping memberships with the LDCs. They are also teaming up with a diverse set of countries forming an axis of North–South coalition for strategic purposes. For instance, LDCs have co-sponsored a proposal, initially tabled by an alliance of 11 WTO members in the negotiations on non-agricultural market access (NAMA), where these members seek to have a horizontal mechanism for the facilitation of solutions to non-tariff barriers faced by WTO members.

LDCs have come a long way at the WTO, from being voiceless bystanders at negotiations, to consciously seeking and forging alliances with other members, based on issues of common interest. This, together with the increased participation of LDCs in both the everyday work of the WTO and in trade negotiations, reflects a proactive, as opposed to an erstwhile reactive, approach adopted by the LDCs in the MTS, a development that bodes well for the sustainability of the system.

13.4.2 The WTO's institutional support to the LDCs

The WTO has been helping LDCs to integrate into the rules-based MTS in a concerted manner for a number of years. The Sub-Committee on LDCs, established in 1995, is a dedicated platform in the WTO which has the mandate to address all issues of interest to the LDCs. Soon after the Doha Ministerial Meeting, members in the WTO negotiated a work programme, under which the Sub-Committee is keeping a continuous track on the market access conditions for LDC exports as well as the trade capacity-building efforts undertaken in favour of LDCs. The WTO Secretariat has been preparing annual reports on market access issues covering a wide range of LDC trade data. Over the years, a series of studies of specific interest to the LDCs has also been undertaken by the Secretariat under the aegis of this committee, advancing the interests of the LDCs in the MTS.

Steps have been taken by the WTO Secretariat to help the LDCs participate better in the work of the organization. To service the special needs of the LDCs, an LDC Unit was established in 2003, which serves as the focal point for all LDC issues. Despite being an informal group, the LDC Unit provides day-to-day support to the LDCs' consultative group, which has become an important constituency in the DDA negotiations.

The trade policy reviews (TPRs) are increasingly becoming an important tool, both for understanding LDC concerns and for helping them integrate into the MTS. While the primary objective of the TPR mechanism is to increase the transparency and understanding of WTO members' trade policies and practices, the TPR process in the LDCs also contributes to an assessment and identification of the capacity-building needs, with a view to feeding this into the broader Aid for Trade initiative.

The LDCs have also been a special priority in the delivery of the WTO's training and technical assistance, which continues to be a core function of the WTO. Every year, the LDCs are associated with more than 40 per cent of the technical assistance activities undertaken by the WTO. Specific products have been designed for the LDCs, such as the introductory courses on the WTO. LDCs are entitled to request three national activities per year, while other developing countries can only request two activities per year. In addition, special priority is given to the LDCs in trainee and internship programmes of the WTO as well as in the context of the Reference Centre programmes, which have been designed to disseminate trade-related information to the LDC governments, through technology support and WTO materials, to broaden their understanding of the

WTO. At the same time, the WTO has increased its collaboration with other multilateral institutions equipped with appropriate technical expertise and financial resources to strengthen trade capacity in the LDCs (see Section 13.3.5).

13.4.3 LDC-IV: a time for review and commitment

Contributing to achieving coherent global economic policy making is one of the core functions of the WTO. Under the broad coherence mandate, the WTO works closely with the United Nations to ensure economic growth and development in the LDCs, including through the achievement of the objectives set out in the Istanbul Programme of Action (IPoA) adopted at the LDC-IV Conference in May 2011.

At the LDC-IV Conference is Istanbul, a comprehensive review of the IPoA's predecessor, the Brussels Programme of Action (BPoA), showed that measures taken in the WTO, as well as by LDCs' key trading partners in the last decade, have significantly advanced the trade-related goals for LDCs set by the international community in 2001. In fact, the BPoA's adoption came only months before the launch of the DDA in 2001. As a result, many of the trade-related elements of the BPoA have been embedded in the DDA. For instance, the LDC-III Conference created a momentum for DFQF market access for LDC products, which became an important objective of the DDA and was later concretized in 2005 through a Ministerial Decision (see Section 13.3.3).

While it remains too early to evaluate progress on the IPoA, there has been concrete progress on many fronts in meeting the targets set in the BPoA. For example, the LDCs, as a Group met the threshold of 7 per cent annual GDP growth in 2007 and 2008. While ODA flows to LDCs did not meet the target allocation of 0.15 per cent of GNI of the members of the Development Assistance Committee of the OECD, Aid for Trade of LDCs has seen an increase of more than 50 per cent from US$7 billion in 2005 to US$10.8 billion in 2008.

The IPoA, for its part, builds on the BPoA, setting out measures to accelerate economic development and contribute to poverty alleviation in the LDCs. It aims to halve the number of LDCs by 2020, and puts renewed emphasis on increased ODA, enhanced trade access and improved productive capacity for the LDCs. The hallmark of IPoA is its emphasis on productive capacity, as LDCs need assistance in addressing the multiple dimensions of supply-side contraints they confront-ranging from inadequate physical infrastructure to weak institutional capacity.

The international community also agreed at the LDC-IV Conference to work towards doubling the share of LDC exports in global trade by 2020, including through working for favourable market access conditions for LDC products. To what extent the LDCs could benefit from the IPoA will depend on its effective implementation. The LDCs continue to confront both exogenous and endogenous challenges. There is still scope for further improvement of market access for LDC products. There is a deficit in the capacity of LDCs to meet legitimate standards in their export markets, which stands in the way of commercial exploitation of potential exports. Clearly therefore, trade and economic policies and other support measures need to be crafted in a manner that ensures that international trade plays an increasingly important role in LDCs' development.

13.5 CONCLUSIONS

Since the establishment of the WTO, the MTS has been responsive to the needs and concerns of LDCs. LDCs continue to enjoy a high degree of flexibility in implementing WTO rules and obligations. The special treatment of LDCs in the DDA negotiations, dedicated forum provided by the Sub-Committee on LDCs to address systemic issues, the establishment of the LDC Unit in the Secretariat, day-to-day support to the WTO LDC Consultative Group, and the special priority provided in different components of the WTO's technical assistance programmes are some of the efforts of the WTO to successfully integrate LDCs into the MTS.

During the GATT years, the LDCs were mostly quiet followers of the MTS, perhaps owing to a variety of capacity constraints; even during the initial years of the WTO, the engagement from the LDCs was very limited. The launch of the DDA negotiations in 2001 witnessed the emergence of LDCs on the centre stage of the decision-making process of the WTO. The LDCs have increasingly identified a growing stake in the WTO and have taken a proactive approach, often making alliances with others, to pursue their offensive and defensive trade interests. The greater engagement of LDCs in the DDA negotiations, as well as in the regular work of the WTO, provide ample evidence of their growing human and institutional capacity.

The share of LDC exports in world merchandise trade has seen a gradual improvement over the last decade. This has come along with a significant improvement in market access opportunities for LDC products. Most of the developed countories today grant close to 100 per cent duty-free access to products of LDCs. Developing countries have also become important destinations for LDC exports, and a number of them now grant a significant degree of preferences to the LDCs. The expeditious conclusion of the DDA negotiations could address some of the remaining gaps in achieving greater market access for LDC products, as well as in ensuring the policy instruments that LDCs need to pursue their development objectives.

Notwithstanding some strong economic and trade performance observed in the last decade, the challenges faced by the LDCs are no less formidable. While the trade capacity varies among the LDCs, product and market concentration has been their defining characteristic. In addition, most of the LDCs have not been able to move up the value chain and remained in the low end segment of merchandise exports. These are some of the factors that have prevented them from benefiting from the dynamics of global supply chains. Concerted efforts from the international community are thus essential to help LDCs overcome their production and supply bottlenecks. The Aid for Trade initiative is providing the much needed focus on trade capacity-building to provide developing countries and LDCs with the resources and the platform to build their trade infrastructure to benefit from trade openings.

References

Adler, Matthew, Claire Brunel, Gary Clyde Hufbauer, and Jeffrey J. Schott. 2009. What's on the Table? The Doha Round as of August 2009. Working Paper 09–6. Washington, DC: Peterson Institute for International Economics.

Brenton, Paul. 2006. Enhancing Trade Preferences for LDCs: Reducing the Restrictiveness of Rules of Origin. In *Trade, Doha, and Development: A Window into the Issues*, edited by Richard Newfarmer, 277–84. Washington, DC: World Bank.

Carrère, Céline, and Jaime De Melo. 2009. The Doha Round and Market Access for LDCs: Scenarios for the EU and US Markets. CERDI Publication, E 2009.11. Bangladesh: Central Extension Resource Development Institute (CERDI).

EIF Executive Secretariat. Progress Report for the period 1 November 2009 to 30 April 2010. Available from <http://www.integratedframework.org>. Accessed on 7 November 2011.

Elliott, Kimberly Ann. 2010. *Changing Rules of Origin to Improve Market Access for Least Developed Countries*. CGD Notes, October. Washington, DC: Center for Global Development (CGD).

Tutwiler, M. Ann, and Straub, Matthew. 2008. Making Agricultural Trade Reform Work for the Poor. In *Agricultural Trade Liberalization and the Least Developed Countries*, edited by Niek Koning and Per Pinstrup-Andersen, 25–50. The Netherlands: Springer.

CHAPTER 14

....

AWKWARD PARTNERS: NGOS AND SOCIAL MOVEMENTS AT THE WTO

....

JENS STEFFEK[*]

14.1 INTRODUCTION

....

NON-governmental organizations (NGOs) and social movements have become a third force in international relations, next to states and corporations.[1] By now, at least 25,000 transnationally organized NGOs are active in international politics,[2] plus some more informal social movements that have become vociferous critics of global governance since the 1990s. According to recent surveys, almost all international governmental organizations (IGOs) have institutionalized some form of consultation, cooperation or partnership with NGOs.[3] The density of this interaction and the status and rights accorded to NGOs vary greatly, however. At first glance, the World Trade Organization (WTO) appears to be a relatively hostile environment for NGOs and social movements. The organization continues to define itself as strictly member-driven and, above all, as a venue for confidential negotiation and dispute settlement among states. It is therefore somewhat surprising to see that NGOs have made some inroads into its cloistered bodies in recent years. Step by step, the WTO is opening up at the margins, providing some limited access to its dispute settlement mechanism (DSM), a large number of documents, and some mechanisms of consultation. Many commentators have welcomed this development and called for an increased access for NGOs and other civil society actors to the WTO policy-making process.[4]

[*] The author wishes to thank Usama Ibrahim for valuable research assistance and Jan Beyers for sharing unpublished data on NGO participation in the WTO.
[1] An NGO is defined here as a non-profit organization that is founded and driven by individuals with a common political or social interest that they pursue without resort to violence.
[2] Union of International Associations 2010.   [3] Steffek and Nanz 2008.
[4] See, for example, Charnovitz 2000; Esty 1999, 2002; Shell 1996; Williams 2011.

Their hopes for more NGO access and transparency have been dampened by the resilience of intergovernmentalism in the WTO. The negotiation process proper is still closed, and many negotiators vigorously defend an intergovernmental core of policy-making against too much public scrutiny.[5] Not even the WTO committees, where rather technical debates are taking place, have been opened to civil society actors as observers. In this respect the WTO remains clearly distinct from the United Nations and many of its specialized agencies, which have developed much more transparent and participatory forms of policy-making.[6] Along with the two other global economic multilaterals, the International Monetary Fund (IMF) and the World Bank, the WTO has not fully joined in the turn from intergovernmental bargaining to more participatory modes of governance.

The purpose of this chapter is to analyse the uneasy relationship between the WTO on the one hand, and NGOs and social movements on the other. In the next section, I introduce some theoretical considerations pertaining to the conditions under which intergovernmental organizations, such as the WTO, are likely to interact with NGOs. In Section 14.3, I trace the historical evolution of GATT/WTO relations with NGOs and examine the rules currently governing NGO access to the WTO. Section 14.4 is dedicated to an analysis of the evolution of the NGO population that is active at the WTO, and of its impact on the regulation of global trade. In the concluding section, I summarize the factors that influence the current participatory regime at the WTO, and venture into predictions of likely future developments.

14.2 DETERMINANTS OF INTERACTION BETWEEN WTO AND NON-STATE ACTORS

In historical perspective, the age of the Cold War was the heyday of intergovernmentalism in world politics, as states successfully marginalized non-state actors in policy-making. In the 1940s, the demarcation between the intergovernmental and non-governmental realm solidified, along with the expansion of tasks of international governance and the professionalization of international organizations.[7] The GATT, and more remotely also the WTO, are the offspring of this period in global history, preserving a rigorous spirit of inter-statism. The intergovernmental moment, however, is long over in most issue areas of world politics. Consultation and cooperation arrangements between NGOs and IGOs are mushrooming, and for some policy fields, such as development assistance and environmental protection, students of international organization have found an almost symbiotic relationship between IGOs and NGOs. In other fields progress is noticeable but slower, especially in international security and finance.[8]

---

[5] Loy 2001.   [6] Van den Bossche 2008.   [7] Reinalda 2009.   [8] Steffek 2010.

What determines such variation in interaction between IGOs and non-state actors? I submit that, in an evolutionary perspective, we may usefully distinguish two principally different roads to cooperation. First, there might be pull factors at work, in the sense of an IGO pulling non-state actors in. There are several reasons why this may take place. Many IGOs are miserably funded and understaffed, and hence seek opportunities to prop up their limited in-house capacities.[9] IGOs welcome the technical expertise of non-state actors in research or in drafting their policies. In a similar vein, they rely on NGO capacities for the implementation of projects on the ground. This is evident in the field of development assistance and humanitarian aid. In addition, NGOs may deliver information on local developments, which IGOs are unable to monitor themselves. In the field of human rights protection, NGOs deliver information on violation of international conventions. It hence appears that 'the more an IGO is forced to act in a local context, the more it seeks to influence human behaviour in that context; and the more information it needs about the local context, the more likely it is that it interacts with organized civil society'.[10] The WTO, at first glance, does not seem to need much assistance of this kind.

On the other hand, even in the presence of such pull factors, the willingness to open up to NGOs might be limited due to a perceived need for secrecy. Generally speaking, IGOs and the state actors that populate them have an interest in confidentiality of proceedings.[11] The liberalization of trade is a case in point, as negotiators need to make concessions costly to industries that know how to lobby government and elected representatives. Transparency hence may threaten the viability of international trade negotiations, at least in the phase of quid pro quo bargaining. Not surprisingly, the need for secrecy to secure the success of negotiations is among the most often-cited hindrances to more NGO involvement at the WTO.[12]

The second avenue to participatory governance and inter-organizational cooperation are what one may call 'push dynamics'. NGOs actively seek to perforate the closed settings of international organization to obtain information about their policy-making, and to influence the choices made. Lacking other types of resources, they often rely on attempts at persuasion and, if this fails, public shaming. IGOs, like other collective actors, are susceptible to challenges to their organizational legitimacy. They do not want to be caught violating widely accepted standards of 'good governance', especially if they are propagating such standards themselves.[13] By now, there certainly is a widely accepted norm that policy-making, at whatever level, should be transparent, participatory, and inclusive.[14] The WTO, as I will detail below, experienced such a challenge during the 1990s and responded to it. In summary, in order to explain the evolution of cooperation between the WTO and NGOs, the following factors need to be taken into account:

(1) the demand for information or services that NGOs can deliver
(2) the desire to protect the secrecy of intergovernmental negotiations

---

[9] Raustiala 1997.   [10] Steffek 2010, 82.   [11] Stasavage 2004.   [12] Sutherland et al. 2004.
[13] Woods 2000.   [14] Reimann 2006.

(3)   the push for access by NGOs
(4)   the shifting normative standards of good governance.

However, inter-institutional cooperation is only part of the story about WTO and non-state actors. In international politics in general, and in trade regulation in particular, there is also a group of actors who fundamentally oppose what they consider the neoliberal project of globalization, and that do not want to become involved with IGOs. This is the speciality of more informal social movements[15] that became visible and vociferous during the 1990s. These actors need to be taken into account here, since it was their campaigning and street protest that attracted a lot of media attention and thus helped expose the WTO to critical scrutiny. The movements contributed, even if only indirectly, to institutional change and agenda-setting processes in the WTO.[16] Admittedly, the boundary between NGOs and social movements is an opaque one, and it is shifting over time. Many individual members of social movements also adhere to one or several NGOs, and informal movements tend to breed NGOs as they mature and professionalize. The decisive difference between the two types of actors is that social movements are in fundamental opposition to established authorities and challenge them head on,[17] while many, if not most, NGOs display cooperative attitudes and compromise with power wielders. Unlike the majority of NGOs at the WTO, which approach diplomats and IGO officials directly, the members of social movements critical of liberalization usually prefer to remain outside critics. The logic of involvement sketched above does not apply to them.

14.3 THE RELATIONS BETWEEN GATT/WTO AND NGOS IN HISTORICAL PERSPECTIVE

Some form of participation of non-state actors in the international trading regime was envisaged from the very beginning. When the predecessor of today's WTO, the International Trade Organization (ITO), was negotiated from 1946 to 1948, it was meant to become an encompassing organization in the field of international economic cooperation.[18] During the negotiations, non-state actors were admitted to sit in the meetings of the preparatory committee that was in charge of producing the ITO Charter, and they were allowed to submit documents.[19] The consultation of NGOs by

---

[15] Following Tarrow 1994, I define a social movement as a loosely-knit network of individuals that, based on common purposes and solidarity, sets out to challenge established elites and political authorities.

[16] He and Murphy 2007; Paterson 2011.   [17] Tarrow 1994, 5.   [18] Gardner 1956; Graz 1999.
[19] Charnovitz and Wickham 1995.

the ITO was also considered in the first Charter draft, sponsored by the United States. Article 71, paragraph 3, stipulated that the ITO 'may make suitable arrangements for consultation and cooperation' with NGOs and 'may invite them to undertake specific tasks'.[20] Relating this provision to the determinants affecting participatory arrangements mentioned above, there seems to have been a desire among governments to tap into non-governmental expertise.[21] The reference to 'specific tasks' was dropped later in the negotiation process, but the call for consultation and cooperation remained.[22] As detailed in Chapter 4 of this volume, the ITO project foundered, and the only multilateral framework that remained was the GATT, a side agreement already concluded in 1947. The original GATT was a treaty that dealt almost exclusively with trade in products, and which 'was not intended to be a comprehensive world organization. It was a temporary side affair meant to serve the particular interests of the major commercial powers who wanted a prompt reduction of tariffs among themselves.'[23]

The gestalt shift from ITO to GATT had important consequences for the role and status of non-state actors. The ITO was planned to be an encompassing global organization of the forum type. Such a forum would have been a venue for political debate rather than machinery for the efficient delivery of regulation. A forum organization, by its very nature, is supposed to be open to all interested parties, which today has come to mean also non-state actors. The United Nations is the archetype of such a forum organization and, in fact, through its Economic and Social Council (ECOSOC), provided non-state actors with an access point from the very beginning of its operation.[24] The GATT, by contrast, was built on a 'club model' of international cooperation.[25] Access to a club is limited by definition, and its proceedings are supposed to remain confidential. The mission of the GATT club was to produce agreement among the major Western powers to liberalize commerce, in particular in manufactures, by sidelining protectionist lobbies and minor state parties, such as the newly emerging developing countries.

As a consequence of its limited agenda and its institutional design, the GATT did not develop any formal arrangements for consultation or cooperation with non-state parties. There was little to gain from the presence of NGOs in an organization designed to facilitate tariff bargaining, and greater publicity of proceedings would have hampered the negotiation of compromise deals. It should also be noted that, from the NGO point of view, too, there was little interest in a direct presence at the GATT Secretariat in Geneva. The only non-state actor really seeking participation during these years seems to have been the International Chamber of Commerce.[26] Tariff negotiations were of interest to industry associations that lobbied mainly their national governments. Thus, there was little incentive for member governments to open their club to non-state actors, and, for all we know, there was little demand on the NGO side for such an opening. The GATT thus became a closed shop of national diplomats and experts.[27]

---

[20] United Nations 1946.   [21] Charnovitz and Wickham 1995, 114.
[22] Interim Commission for the International Trade Organization 1948.
[23] Hudec 1990, 57.   [24] Alger 2002.   [25] Keohane and Nye 2001.   [26] Charnovitz 2000.
[27] Weiler 2001.

This situation changed at the beginning of the 1990s, when two crucial developments coincided. First, there was the envisaged expansion of the world trade regime into new issue areas in the Uruguay Round (see Chapter 6). Since the Tokyo Round the GATT had shifted away from pure tariff negotiation into 'behind the border' issues that impacted more heavily on national policies. The massive agenda of the Uruguay Round of negotiations signalled the political will to further extend the competencies of the world trade regime, including also trade in services and questions of intellectual property. This widening of the GATT regime into other issue areas was regarded with suspicion, especially when clashes between trade liberalization and national environmental policies surfaced at the beginning of the 1990s. Environmentalists were infuriated by a recommendation of the GATT dispute settlement panel in the so-called *Tuna–Dolphin* case.[28] Based on the 1972 Marine Mammals Protection Act, the US had banned the import of tuna from the eastern tropical Pacific that was caught without technical devices to save dolphins, which in that region school with tuna. Mexico, a major exporter of canned tuna to the US, brought the case to the GATT, arguing that the prohibition constituted an undue restriction of trade. The panel found that, indeed, the US ban violated the GATT Agreement because it inappropriately discriminated against imported products with reference to the production method.

As Mexico and the US found a negotiated agreement, the panel's recommendation was never formally adopted. Yet it mobilized activists against the GATT. Unlike international commerce, environmental protection was a field in which NGOs had huge interest. Representatives of environmental NGOs as well as academic commentators started to argue that, in tackling disputes such as Tuna-Dolphin, the GATT had gone beyond the scope of its trade facilitation mandate and de facto adjudicated national environmental policies.[29] When in doubt, it seemed, the GATT favoured free trade over ecological concerns. At this point, public attention turned towards the GATT and the regime entered a phase of enhanced (re)politicization.[30]

The expansion of the GATT agenda in the 1980s coincided with a steep increase in numbers and in global political involvement of NGOs. In particular, the global summits of the United Nations had given NGOs new opportunities for transnational operation.[31] Yet there was not only a noticeable increase in numbers, but also the attitude towards international governance changed. In the 1940s, at the time of the San Francisco and Bretton Woods conferences, transnational NGOs were staunch supporters of international organization, constituting part of a multisectoral alliance of progressive internationalists. The early 1990s, by contrast, witnessed the emergence of a transnational social movement that was highly critical of global governance and its institutions. Disillusioned with the failures of development assistance, and alarmed by the ecological consequences of economic growth, these activists were not opposed to the existence of global political organizations as such, but critical of further liberalization. The economic multilaterals,

---

[28] Esty 1994, 29–32.   [29] Esty 1999.   [30] Howse 2002.   [31] Sadoun 2007.

World Bank, IMF, and GATT/WTO, became their prime target. In the words of a prominent critic: 'In the WTO forum, global commerce takes precedence over everything—democracy, public health, equity, access to essential services, the environment, food safety, and more.'[32]

In the early 1990s, transnational social networks started mobilizing against the pitfalls of globalization and the liberal principles that guided the institutions of global governance. A visible output was the campaign '50 Years Is Enough', targeting the 50th anniversary of the foundation of the World Bank and the IMF in 1994.[33] For the first time in their history, IGOs were facing non-governmental opposition on a larger scale. Public protests against GATT/WTO unfolded alongside the campaigns against the other economic multilaterals. In particular, the activities against the Multilateral Agreement on Investment (MAI) served as a catalyst for protests against the WTO.[34] The MAI negotiations were a leftover from the Uruguay Round, in which there had been no consensus on investment issues, notably because of resistance from developing countries. The issue was transferred to the Organization for Economic Cooperation and Development (OECD) where developing countries had no voice. Negotiations had taken place in secret but were exposed to public scrutiny by a coalition of globalization-critical groups, coordinated from Canada. The groups besieged an OECD meeting in Paris, and when MAI was abandoned they claimed victory, although it is plausible that negotiations would have failed in any event.[35]

The loosely connected social movement that had mobilized against MAI turned its attention to the newly founded WTO, facilitated by advances in information technology that allowed for a global coordination of activists via websites and mailing lists.[36] To some extent, the beginning of public protest against the WTO was a spillover effect brought about by a transnational anti-liberalization and anti-privatization movement in search of new targets. In 1998, the first street protests at a WTO Ministerial in Geneva occurred, organized by a short-lived coalition called 'Peoples' Global Action'.[37] The movement gained momentum and mobilized an estimated 40,000 to 60,000 protestors at the next Ministerial in Seattle, in 1999.[38] The organizers were not prepared for such a scenario, and protesters managed to bring the conference proceedings to a halt. Public protests and NGO counter-summits have accompanied WTO ministerials since then, but crowds on the streets never again reached such numbers. The challenge was profound, however, as the WTO felt pressed to publicly justify its mission, its procedures and policies.[39] Not least, activists criticized the WTO for being an opaque organization that violated common standards of transparency and accountability.[40] To summarize, during the 1990s push factors clearly made their mark as external actors pressed the WTO to open its doors and to become accountable to the global public, which implied

[32] Wallach 2004, 13.   [33] Danaher and Yunus 1994.   [34] Mabey 1999.
[35] Trebilcock and Howse 1999, 358.   [36] Barlow and Clark 2001.
[37] Third World Network 1998; Williams and Ford 1999.   [38] Hawken 2000, 14.
[39] Marceau and Pedersen 1999; WTO 2010.   [40] Bonzon 2008, 759; Woods and Narlikar 2001.

giving non-state actors more insight and a voice. In response to the mounting criticism, the WTO launched initiatives to involve the NGO scene in some form of institutionalized dialogue. In the following section, I will scrutinize the terms of engagement.

With heightened levels of public interest and attention, the question of how to deal with the protests carried out by non-state actors became imminent for the WTO.[41] The Marrakesh Agreement included a vague reference to NGOs, stating that 'The General Council may make appropriate arrangements for consultation and cooperation with non-governmental organizations concerned with matters related to those of the WTO.' (Article V, paragraph 2.) This formulation left member governments with ample discretion to determine what these arrangements might be in practice. The General Council in July 1996 adopted some 'Guidelines for arrangements on relations with Non-Governmental Organizations', determining that 'The Secretariat should play a more active role in its direct contacts with NGOs who, as a valuable resource, can contribute to the accuracy and richness of the public debate.'[42] Thus there is something like an 'official' WTO view on the purpose of liaising with NGOs, which is to exploit their capacity to bring trade issues into public debate.[43] The General Council, here at least, implicitly acknowledged a deficit in its relationship with its global constituency. On the other hand, by delegating NGO contacts to the Secretariat, it reaffirmed that there was no place for non-state actors in the inner sanctum of trade policy-making. In fact, the General Council in the document explicitly states that 'there is currently a broadly held view that it would not be possible for NGOs to be directly involved in the work of the WTO or its meetings.'[44]

This attitude is a resilient one among WTO member states and, as a consequence, NGOs are still excluded from almost all meetings of its bodies.[45] This is true even at the level of committees, working parties, and working groups, where technical issues are debated and the need for confidentiality of proceedings is evidently much lower than in actual trade negotiations. There is only one exception to this general no-NGO rule: since 1996, a form of accreditation is possible for NGOs wishing to attend ministerial conferences. It was decided in the preparations for the Singapore Ministerial that NGOs would be allowed to attend the plenary sessions and that the WTO Secretariat would handle applications on the basis of Article V, paragraph 2 of the WTO Agreement. This means that all NGOs that seek accreditation are required to show how they are 'concerned with matters related to those of the WTO'. Since the Singapore meeting, a remarkable number of NGOs have been accredited to ministerial meetings, as detailed in Table 8 below.

In practice, the opportunity to attend plenaries is not the main attraction for NGO representatives travelling to ministerial conferences. A much more important purpose is to meet national delegates, journalists, and other NGO representatives, and to display information material in the designated NGO area that the WTO provides at the conference venue. NGOs also exploit the media attention at these summits to promote their message.[46] In between the ministerial conferences, the WTO Secretariat organizes other

---

[41] Charnovitz 1996.   [42] WTO 1996, paragraph IV.   [43] Ibid., paragraph II.
[44] Ibid., paragraph VI.   [45] Loy 2001; Zutshi 2001.   [46] Steffek and Ehling 2008, 105.

Table 8   Representation of non-state organizations at WTO ministerial conferences, 1996–2009 (figures include NGOs and business groups)

Ministerial	Accredited	Represented	Number of participants
Singapore 1996	159	108	235
Geneva 1998	153	128	362
Seattle 1999	776	686	1500 approx.
Doha 2001	651	370	370
Cancún 2003	961	795	1578
Hong Kong 2005	1065	812	1596
Geneva 2009	435	395	490

Source: Beyers, Hanegraff, and Braun-Poppelaars 2010, based on data furnished by the WTO Secretariat

types of outreach to NGOs. First of all, since 1996, there have been regular public symposia to consult with NGO representatives and other exponents of civil society on topics of concern—in the early years mainly questions of environment and development. The format of these events has changed somewhat over time. In the beginning, all participants were gathered in one conference hall, which limited interaction between them. Now, the symposia have turned into the annual 'WTO Public Forum' and are divided into much smaller panels that take place simultaneously in the meeting rooms of the WTO headquarters. The 2010 symposium stretched over three days and included 40 panel sessions covering a wide range of institutional and political questions. Interestingly, the Secretariat now functions more as a facilitator of these events, with NGOs free to organize and staff panels themselves. The Public Forum is usually attended by a number of government representatives, but by far the most participants come from different branches of civil society, including businesses and law firms.[47] At the Public Forum, the WTO's civil society is hence talking chiefly to other exponents of civil society.

In between these large annual gatherings, there is a certain dialogue with NGOs going on at the WTO Secretariat. NGOs that are conducting research on trade-related issues may be invited for an informal discussion with interested delegations and Secretariat officials. There are also issue-specific discussions and briefings organized by the Secretariat for NGOs, and studies suggest that NGO representatives are quite satisfied with their quality.[48] In 2008, the Secretariat started issuing badges for Geneva-based NGO representatives, which allow them to access the WTO premises on Rue de Lausanne, a measure that had been on the wish list of NGOs for some time.[49] Not all initiatives have proven to be durable, though. The informal NGO Advisory Body that was established by WTO Director-General Supachai Panitchpakdi has not been reconvened

[47] Van den Bossche 2008, 730.   [48] Mason 2003, 15.   [49] Bohne 2010, 183.

since he left the organization.[50] It also needs to be acknowledged that consultative meetings at the Secretariat clearly privilege Geneva-based NGOs over those located abroad, especially those based in developing countries.

Probably the most remarkable progress in terms of external transparency of the WTO was achieved not in terms of participation rights but with regard to public access to documents, where new regulations have supplanted the tight restrictions of the old GATT regime. After years of deliberation, the General Council in May 2002 revised the procedures for the circulation and derestriction of documents.[51] It was agreed that all official WTO documents will be made publicly available via the website in the organization's official languages.[52] Most documents will be published within six to twelve weeks, including the minutes of meetings.[53] An electronic newsletter that anyone can sign up to alerts to events and publication of key documents, especially during negotiation phases. The WTO website is accessible and quite user-friendly, provided that readers master the jargon, and accordingly the WTO has been ranked among the most transparent international organizations.[54]

A development that has thrilled especially international lawyers is that the WTO is also gradually opening its dispute settlement process to public scrutiny. Since 2006 a number of panel meetings and hearings of the Appellate Body have been opened to the public, upon explicit agreement of the parties involved.[55] This opportunity attracted some interest from NGOs, but it wore off considerably when the novelty of the procedure evaporated.[56] Although public hearings render WTO dispute settlement more transparent, they do not allow NGOs to actively intervene. This is possible, at least in theory, by submitting amicus curiae briefs to the Appellate Body. There is no explicit reference to such a practice in the respective agreements, and consequently the issue has spurred a fair amount of controversy among WTO state parties and academic experts.[57] To be precise, at issue are only those NGO briefs that are not attached to the official submissions of the state parties involved in the dispute, which are accepted as a matter of course. In several of its rulings, the WTO Appellate Body affirmed that it has the authority to accept unsolicited statements by NGOs or individuals, even if those do not have a legal right to make such a submission.[58] In one controversial case, the Appellate Body even devised an ad hoc Special Procedure, setting out modalities for the submission of amicus curiae briefs (without considering any of them in the end).[59] Given the ambivalent attitude of an Appellate Body that accepts amicus curiae briefs without considering them, it is difficult to determine if these submissions should be regarded as a valuable tool for non-state actors to make their concerns heard at the WTO, or rather as an exercise in participatory window dressing.

---

[50] Van den Bossche 2008, 735.   [51] WTO 2002.   [52] Ibid., paragraphs 1 and 3.
[53] Ibid., paragraph 2(c).   [54] Kovach, Neligan, and Burall 2003, 15.[55] Ehring 2008.
[56] Van den Bossche 2008, 737.   [57] Appleton 2000; Howse 2003; Mavroidis 2002.
[58] WTO Appellate Body Report 1998, paragraph 104–10; WTO Appellate Body Report 2000, paragraph 42; WTO Appellate Body Report 2002, paragraph 164.
[59] WTO 2000.

To summarize this section, the gradual opening of the WTO towards non-state actors did not take place in revolutionary steps but rather incrementally. The WTO is opening up gradually to NGOs and the public at large, while protecting its intergovernmental core of trade policy-making. NGO participation, it should be stressed, is not equally popular in all quarters. Possible setbacks in terms of effectiveness have already been mentioned. In recent years, misgivings about the alleged lack of accountability and representativeness of NGOs have also been aired.[60] The next section will shed some light on these issues by disaggregating and analysing the group of non-state actors active at the WTO.

14.4 NGOs AT THE WTO: WHO THEY ARE AND WHAT THEY HAVE ACHIEVED

While the formal avenues of NGO participation in the WTO have been studied extensively, there has been much less research on the size and composition of the NGO community active at and around the WTO. The question was addressed only recently by two studies that evaluated the data on NGO participation collected by the WTO Secretariat. Beyers, Hanegraff, and Braun-Poppelaars trace the evolution of the NGO population present at WTO ministerials from Singapore 1996 to Geneva 2009.[61] Piewitt also looks at non-state actors submitting working papers to the WTO Secretariat between 1998 and 2007.[62] The first complication in analysing the data on NGO participation at the WTO is that it can cover only those organizations that seek to engage with the organization and register with the Secretariat. The more radical critics, who prefer to stay at a distance, are not listed there. The second complication is that the Secretariat in its statistics does not distinguish between types of civil society actors. The official register hence is a veritable 'Pandora's Box', with industry associations, think tanks, trade unions, and advocacy NGOs in it. As a consequence, analysts with a specific interest in the NGO community need to disaggregate the data, which is not an easy task as some organizations eschew easy classification. On the other hand, the advantage of having such a comprehensive data set is that it enables researchers to assess the balance between the groups of non-state actors at the WTO.

How many NGOs are directly engaging with the WTO? Table 8 above displayed the evolution of participation figures at ministerial meetings over the years. Beyers et al. identify a total of 1992 non-governmental actors that were eligible to attend at least one of the seven ministerials between 1996 and 2009.[63] The fluctuation over time is relatively high, especially among NGOs. Piewitt reports that only 15 organizations attended all

---

[60] Anderson and Rieff 2004.   [61] Beyers, Hanegraff, and Braun-Poppelaars 2010.
[62] Piewitt 2010.   [63] Beyers, Hanegraff, and Braun-Poppelaars 2010, 5.

WTO ministerials that took place between 1996 and 2005.[64] Both studies find that the venue of ministerial conferences accounts for notable differences in NGO representation. Organizations from the respective region were clearly over-represented at the Ministerial in Seattle, but also at the Cancún and Hong Kong meetings. Another type of venue effect was also visible in Doha 2003, where high prices, limited accommodation capacities, and a restrictive visa policy reduced the number of non-state actors attending the meeting.

With regard to the often-cited dominance of business interests at the WTO, the results are not as unequivocal as one might expect. On the basis of a fourfold typology that divides non-state actors into NGOs, business groups, trade unions, and research institutes, Beyers et al. find that the percentages of business associations and NGOs represented at ministerials is almost equal; for both groups it oscillates between 33 and 44 per cent, with NGOs slightly dominating in numbers at three conferences, and business groups at four.[65] The dominance of business groups at the WTO is hence more felt than measured. What really exists, however, is an enormous North–South gap in non-governmental representation at the WTO. Dividing her data set into OECD and non-OECD countries of origin, Piewitt finds that organizations from the non-OECD world accounted for only 14 to 25 per cent of non-state actors attending ministerial conferences.[66] She also presents interesting figures on the relative strength of business and NGO interests across regions of origin.[67] Only among non-state actors from North America is the business sector constantly better represented than public interests, with agribusiness being particularly active. Among organizations from developing countries, by contrast, the business sector is actually weaker in numbers than NGOs, and the relative dominance of NGOs in the South is increasing over time. The reason for this probably is that Southern NGOs are embedded in, and sponsored by, transnational NGO networks that facilitate their WTO participation.

Since 1998, NGOs and other non-state actors have the possibility to submit working papers on trade-related topics to the WTO Secretariat, which are circulated internally and also posted on the website. Between 1998 and 2007, almost 200 of these papers were filed, in particular during periods of intense intergovernmental negotiation. Piewitt also scrutinized the origins of these written statements and found that sectoral and geographic patterns by and large match the findings about participation in ministerial conferences, with comparable shares of business contributions (48 per cent) and NGO contributions (40 per cent), and a clear dominance of North America and Europe as regions of origin.[68] While there is a persistent North–South imbalance in the representation of non-state actors at the WTO, business associations are not as dominant, at least in numbers, as is sometimes claimed.

Numbers alone are, of course, only a rough first indicator of influence. Who is dominating the NGO scene at the WTO in practice? Arguably, the most influential NGO

---

[64] Piewitt 2010, 478.   [65] Beyers, Hanegraff, and Braun-Poppelaars 2010, 10.
[66] Piewitt 2010, 478.   [67] Piewitt 2010, 479–80.   [68] Piewitt 2010, 483.

players in world trade matters are highly specialized organizations that are based in Geneva, or have an office there, such as the International Institute for Sustainable Development (IISD), the Center for International Environmental Law (CIEL), and the International Centre for Trade and Sustainable Development (ICTSD). The ICTSD's flagship publication is the newsletter 'Bridges', which provides news and analyses with a focus on trade and sustainability issues, and due to its wide circulation is among the most powerful NGO voices in the field of world trade. With regard to non-Western players, the Third World Network sticks out, which is a Malaysia-based platform of NGOs and individuals from the global South. These specialized, think tank-like organizations serve as disseminators of information to a large number of activists all over the world. The specific assets of these institutes and networks are the data they collect, the news they spread, and their expertise that is recognized in the field. In addition, a good number of the big transnational NGO players are also active in the field of world trade, such as Oxfam, the World Wide Fund for Nature (WWF), and Friends of the Earth. Their particular strength is in their ability to mobilize members and to effectively stage public campaigns.

What have these NGOs achieved so far at the WTO? Quite clearly, access to meetings and information does not automatically translate into political influence, nor does the dissemination of information and critical voices. One of the undisputable successes of NGOs is that they have managed to create their own access points at the organization. The fact that the WTO did open up to civil society actors at all is mainly due to the pressure exerted by NGOs and social movements that criticized the violation of common standards of 'good governance' by the WTO.[69] However, when it comes to the substance of political decisions, it is not easy to pin down the influence of NGOs on WTO policy-making.[70] For instance, it has been argued that NGOs are influential mainly through the reframing of certain issues and debates.[71] Such influence is not easy to measure, and most accounts of NGO campaigning successes are narrative and descriptive.

An often-cited example of NGO influence is the campaign for access to affordable medicines against infectious diseases such as HIV/AIDS, malaria, and tuberculosis.[72] Many of the most effective pharmaceuticals against these diseases are protected by patents held by multinational companies, and hence subject to the WTO's TRIPS Agreement about trade-related aspects of intellectual property rights. In 1999, a broad alliance of NGOs launched a massive campaign for the production of affordable generics for patients in developing countries. It supported the government of South Africa, who faced a court case initiated by its domestic Pharmaceutical Manufacturers' Association and international producers because of a law that allowed compulsory licensing for the production of generics. According to the plaintiffs, that law violated TRIPS. Their case was initially supported by the EU and the US but they both backed down once the NGO campaign generated bad publicity.[73] By the year 2001, the pharmaceutical companies

---

[69] Williams 2011.   [70] Paterson 2011.   [71] Van Rooy 2004, 22–3.

[72] Ford 2004.   [73] He and Murphy 2007, 719.

also bowed to the pressure and withdrew the case in South Africa. WTO members in the Doha Declaration affirmed that TRIPS should not prevent countries from protecting public health and promoting access to essential medicines. In 2003, they enabled countries that cannot produce such medicines to import pharmaceuticals made under compulsory licence, and in 2005 this decision was turned into a permanent amendment to the TRIPS. Without the massive intervention of NGOs this outcome would have been rather unlikely. Indeed, WTO Director-General, Pascal Lamy, confirmed that, 'thanks in large part to the light which civil society drew to this issue, in August 2003 the WTO reached an agreement on the use of compulsory licences by developing countries without manufacturing capacity'.[74]

This episode shows that NGOs on certain occasions impacted WTO policies. They did so by producing consensus and alliances within the NGO community, by generating and shaping international debates, and lobbying other international organizations.[75] Their prospect of success, however, crucially depends on the suitability of the case at hand for public campaigning and lobbying. Few issues can trigger emotions and give a human face to trade-related problems like the case of essential medicines. Still, there is another, much more hidden, way by which NGO representatives impact WTO policy-making behind the scenes, and this is membership in official delegations. There is no reliable data on the frequency of this phenomenon, but there is evidence that such 'embedded participation' occurs in delegations of both developed and developing countries, and in the EU.[76] Little is known about the effects of such 'embedded participation' at the WTO or the extent to which NGO representatives are able to shape the position of their delegation.

14.5 CONCLUSION

In this chapter I have outlined the history of NGO participation in GATT/WTO, the possibilities for participation that the WTO currently offers, and the composition of the NGO community active at the WTO. The way that the WTO engages with non-state actors was characterized here as a gradual opening at the margins while the intergovernmental core of WTO policy-making remained untouched. Why is it that the WTO has opened up to non-state actors at all? In this chapter I suggested an explanatory framework that views participatory regimes as a result of a constellation of pull factors (the WTO pulling NGOs in) and push factors (NGOs pushing into the WTO). Generally speaking, pull factors seem to be rather weak at the WTO. With regard to technical expertise, the WTO has some in-house capacity and enlists mainly academic specialists to deliver it. There is rather little in terms of factual information and technical

---

[74] Lamy 2007.   [75] Murphy 2007, 16.   [76] CUTS 2009; Sapra 2009, 90–1.

knowledge that NGO activists could contribute. Second, the WTO clearly belongs to the group of rule-making organizations, not to the project-implementing type. It therefore does not need NGO assistance in implementing its policies. Third, with regard to monitoring of compliance with its rules the WTO can rely on its member states to denounce violations of world trade agreements by other parties.

Hence there is little demand for NGO information, for monitoring or project implementation, which used to be a door opener for NGOs in many other intergovernmental organizations. Due to its intergovernmental and rule-making character, the WTO can do quite well without NGOs in its daily operations. What is more, in the WTO case there are not only few incentives to liaise with NGOs but also some good incentives not to. Policymakers and commentators alike perceive a need for secrecy in trade negotiations to successfully strike intergovernmental deals. What accounts for the opening of the WTO therefore are push factors. The quest for participation was filed by NGOs, who were able to exploit the changing normative environment of global governance. Critics were able to target the organizational legitimacy of the WTO by showing that it violated accepted standards of 'good governance', such as transparency, participation and external accountability. The motivation for including NGOs into the structures of the WTO, I argue, is found here. As the so-called Sutherland Report on 'The Future of the WTO' stated in 2004, 'the issue is no longer whether, but how to partner and collaborate effectively'.[77] The pressure on the WTO to be seen in conformity with good governance standards is very visible in the report, which mentions some 'natural duty'[78] of IGOs to be transparent and to liaise with civil society.

However, the story of the WTO and 'global civil society' is not only about NGOs. As I also emphasized in this chapter, a sole focus on NGOs and their more or less institutionalized participation would be a bit misleading. The public challenge to WTO policies, formulated in the 1990s, was presented by a social movement. The colourful crowd that besieged the WTO at its Seattle Ministerial in 1999 lacked organizational discipline and central choreography by any one organization. How influential are these non-state actors in the intergovernmental arena of the WTO? Non-state actors managed to put topics on the agenda and to spark wider public debate about problematic areas of WTO policy-making, such as the access to essential medicines. On the other hand, due to the resilient intergovernmental character of the WTO, NGOs to date have very little direct influence on shaping policy decisions. Therefore, the landmark successes of NGOs and social movements should not lead us to overstate their general political leverage.

What is the likely future of NGO participation in the WTO? The linkages between trade and non-trade issues that made non-state actors interested in the WTO in the first place are unlikely to disappear any time soon. Simmering conflicts between free trade and environment, development, and social regulation remain largely unresolved. On the intergovernmental side, the cumbersome process of the WTO opening to non-state actors is likely to continue at its slow pace. The normative pressure to engage with civil

---

[77] Sutherland et al. 2004, 41.   [78] Ibid., 43. Also see Charnovitz 2006, 368–72.

society is still there, and will increase rather than decrease as other IGOs are creating more and more precedents of public consultation and multi-stakeholder partnerships. On the other hand, an increasing number of NGOs might become frustrated at achieving very little through their participation at the WTO in Geneva and at the ministerial conferences. As discussed in this chapter, the fluctuation among activist NGOs is already high. With little responsiveness at the WTO, NGOs might just shift their activities to building coalitions with like-minded states and lobbying at more accessible and accommodating intergovernmental venues. This, in the end, might well lead to a net loss of NGOs from the WTO community and thus reduce the demand for participation.

References

Alger, Chadwick. 2002. The Emerging Roles of NGOs in the UN System: From Article 71 to a People's Millennium Assembly. *Global Governance* 8 (1):93–117.

Anderson, Kenneth, and David Rieff. 2004. 'Global Civil Society': A Sceptical View. In *Global Civil Society 2004/5*, edited by Helmut Anheier, Marlies Glasius, and Mary Kaldor, 26–39. London: Sage.

Appleton, Arthur E. 2000. Amicus Curiae Submissions in the Carbon Steel Case: Another Rabbit From the Appellate Body's Hat? *Journal of International Economic Law* 3 (4):691–9.

Barlow, Maude, and Tony Clarke. 2001. *Global Showdown: How the New Activists are Fighting Global Corporate Rule*. Toronto: Stoddart.

Beyers, Jan, Marcel Hanegraff, and Caelesta Braun-Poppelaars. 2010. The Development of the WTO Interest Group Population: Exploring Density, Stability and Diversity over Time. Unpublished manuscript, University of Antwerp.

Bohne, Eberhard. 2010. *The World Trade Organization: Institutional Development and Reform*. Basingstoke: Palgrave Macmillan.

Bonzon, Yves. 2008. Institutionalizing Public Participation in WTO Decision Making: Some Conceptual Hurdles and Avenues. *Journal of International Economic Law* 11 (4):751–77.

Charnovitz, Steve. 1996. Participation of Nongovernmental Organizations in the World Trade Organization. *University of Pennsylvania Journal of International Economic Law* 17 (1):331–57.

Charnovitz, Steve. 2000. Opening the WTO to Nongovernmental Interests. *Fordham International Law Journal* 24 (1–2):173–216.

Charnovitz, Steve. 2006. Nongovernmental Organizations in International Law. *American Journal of International Law* 100 (2):348–72.

Charnovitz, Steve, and John Wickham. 1995. Non-Governmantal Organizations and the Original International Trade Regime. *Journal of World Trade* 29 (5):111–22.

Consumer Unity & Trust Society. 2009. *Towards More Inclusive Trade Policy Making: Process and Role of Stakeholders in Select African Countries*. Geneva: CUTS Geneva Resource Centre.

Danaher, Kevin, and Mohammad Yunus, eds. 1994. *50 Years is Enough: The Case Against the World Bank and the International Monetary Fund*. Boston: South End Press.

Ehring, Lothar. 2008. Public Access to Dispute Settlement Hearings in the World Trade Organization. *Journal of International Economic Law* 11 (4):1021–34.

Esty, Daniel C. 1994. *Greening the GATT*. Washington: Institute for International Economics.

Esty, Daniel C. 1999. Environmental Governance at the WTO: Outreach to Civil Society. In *Trade, Environment, and the Millennium*, edited by Gary P. Sampson and W. Bradnee Chambers, 97–117. New York: United Nations University Press.

Esty, Daniel C. 2002. The World Trade Organization's Legitimacy Crisis. *World Trade Review* 1 (1):7–22.

Ford, Nathan. 2004. Patents, Access to Medicines and the Role of Non-Governmental Organisations. *Journal of Generic Medicines* 1 (2):137–45.

Gardner, Richard N. 1956. *Sterling–Dollar Diplomacy: Anglo-American Collaboration in the Reconstruction of Multilateral Trade*. Oxford: Clarendon Press.

Graz, Jean-Christophe. 1999. *Aux Sources de l'OMC: La Charte de la Havane, 1941–1950*. Geneva: Droz.

Hawken, Paul. 2000. Skeleton Woman Visits Seattle. In *Globalize This! The Battle Against the World Trade Organization and Corporate Rule*, edited by Kevin Danaher and Roger Burbach, 14–34. Monroe, ME: Common Courage Press.

He, Baogang, and Hannah Murphy. 2007. Global Social Justice at the WTO? The Role of NGOs in Constructing Global Social Contracts. *International Affairs* 83 (4):707–27.

Howse, Robert. 2002. From Politics to Technocracy—and Back Again: The Fate of the Multilateral Trading Regime. *American Journal of International Law* 96 (1):94–117.

Howse, Robert. 2003. Membership and its Privileges: The WTO, Civil Society, and the *Amicus* Brief Controversy. *European Law Journal* 9 (4):496–510.

Hudec, Robert E. 1990. *The GATT Legal System and World Trade Diplomacy*. Salem: Butterworth.

Interim Commission for the International Trade Organization, ed. 1948. Havana Charter for an International Trade Organization. *United Nations Conference on Trade and Employment Held at Havana, Cuba from 21/11/1947–24/03/1948—Final Act and Related Documents*. New York: United Nations Organization.

Keohane, Robert O., and Joseph S. Nye. 2001. *Transnational Relations and World Politics*. New York: Longman.

Kovach, Hetty, Caroline Neligan, and Simon Burall. 2003. *Power without Accountability? The Global Accountability Report* 1. London: One World Trust.

Lamy, Pascal. 2007. Keynote address to the WTO Public Forum on 4 October. Available from <http://www.wto.org/english/news_e/sppl_e/sppl73_e.htm>. Accessed 23 September 2010.

Loy, Frank. 2001. Public Participation in the World Trade Organization. In *The Role of the WTO in Global Governance*, edited by Gary P. Sampson, 113–35. Tokyo: United Nations University Press.

Mabey, Nick. 1999. Defending the Legacy of Rio: The Civil Society Campaign Against the MAI. In *Regulating International Business: Beyond Liberalization*, edited by Sol Picciotto and Ruth Mayne, 60–81. Basingstoke: Palgrave Macmillan.

Marceau, Gabrielle, and Peter N. Pedersen. 1999. Is the WTO Open and Transparent? A Discussion of the Relationship of the WTO with Non-Governmental Organisations and Civil Society's Claims for more Transparency and Public Participation. *Journal of World Trade* 33 (1):5–49.

Mason, Michael. 2003. *The World Trade Regime and Non-Governmental Organisations: Addressing Transnational Environmental Concerns*. London: Department of Geography and Environment, London School of Economics and Political Science.

Mavroidis, Petros C. 2002. *Amicus Curiae* Briefs before the WTO: Much Ado About Nothing. In *European Integration and International Coordination: Studies in Transnational Economic Law in Honour of Claus-Dieter Ehlermann*, edited by Armin von Bogdandy, Petros C. Mavroidis, and Yves Mény, 317–29. The Hague: Kluwer Law International.

Murphy, Hannah. 2007. NGOs, Agenda-Setting, and the WTO. Paper presented at the Australasian Political Studies Association Conference, September, Monash University.

Paterson, William B. 2011. *The World Trade Organization and Protest Movements: Altering World Order?* London: Routledge.

Piewitt, Martina. 2010. Participatory Governance in the WTO: How Inclusive is Global Civil Society? *Journal of World Trade* 44 (2):467–88.

Raustiala, Kal. 1997. States, NGOs, and International Environmental Institutions. *International Studies Quarterly* 41 (4):719–40.

Reimann, Kim D. 2006. A View from the Top: International Politics, Norms and the World-wide Growth of NGOs. *International Studies Quarterly* 50 (1):45–67.

Reinalda, Bob. 2009. *Routledge History of International Organizations: From 1815 to the Present Day.* London: Routledge.

Sadoun, Britta. 2007. Political Space for Non-Governmental Organizations in United Nations World Summit Processes. Programme Paper 29. Geneva: United Nations Research Institute for Social Development, Civil Society and Social Movements.

Sapra, Seema. 2009. The WTO System of Trade Governance: The Stale NGO Debate and the Appropriate Role for Non-State Actors. *Oregon Review of International Law* 11 (1):71–107.

Scholte, Jan Aart. 2004. Civil Society and Democratically Accountable Global Governance. *Government and Opposition* 39 (2):211–33.

Shell, Richard G. 1996. The Trade Stakeholders Model and Participation by Nonstate Parties in the World Trade Organization. *University of Pennsylvania Journal of International Economic Law* 17 (1):359–81.

Stasavage, David. 2004. Open-Door or Closed-Door? Causes and Consequences of Transparency in Domestic and International Bargaining. *International Organization* 58 (4):667–703.

Steffek, Jens. 2010. Explaining Patterns of Transnational Participation: The Role of Policy Fields. In *Transnational Actors in Global Governance*, edited by Christer Jönsson and Jonas Tallberg, 67–87. Basingstoke: Palgrave Macmillan.

Steffek, Jens, and Ulrike Ehling. 2008. Civil Society Participation at the Margins: The Case of WTO. In *Civil Society Participation in European and Global Governance: A Cure for the Democratic Deficit?*, edited by Jens Steffek, Claudia Kissling, and Patrizia Nanz, 95–115. Basingstoke: Palgrave Macmillan.

Steffek, Jens, and Patrizia Nanz. 2008. Emergent Patterns of Civil Society Participation in Global and European Governance. In *Civil Society Participation in European and Global Governance: A Cure for the Democratic Deficit?*, edited by Jens Steffek, Claudia Kissling, and Patrizia Nanz, 1–29. Basingstoke: Palgrave Macmillan.

Sutherland, Peter et al. 2004. *The Future of the WTO: Addressing Institutional Challenges in the New Millennium.* Geneva: WTO.

Tarrow, Sidney. 1994. *Power in Movement: Social Movements, Collective Action and Politics.* Cambridge: Cambridge University Press.

Third World Network. 1998. Peoples' Global Action Network Protests Against WTO. Available from <http://www.twnside.org.sg/title/peop-cn.htm>. Accessed 24 September 2010.

Trebilcock, Michael J., and Robert Howse. 1999. *The Regulation of International Trade.* London: Routledge.

Union of International Associations, ed. 2010. *Yearbook of International Organizations* Volume 1. 47th edition. Brussels: UIA/de Gruyter Saur.

United Nations. 1946. Report of the 1st Session of the Preparatory Committee of the United Nations Conference on Trade and Employment, London, October. UN Doc. E/PC/T/33, 1946.

Van den Bossche, Peter. 2008. NGO Involvement in the WTO: A Comparative Perspective. *Journal of International Economic Law* 11 (4):717–49.

Van Rooy, Alison. 2004. *The Global Legitimacy Game: Civil Society, Globalization, and Protest.* Basingstoke: Palgrave Macmillan.

Wallach, Lori. 2004. It's Not about Trade. In *Whose Trade Organization? A Comprehensive Guide to the WTO*, edited by Lori Wallach and Patrick Woodall, 1–17. New York: The New Press.

Weiler, Joseph H. H. 2001. The Rule of Lawyers and the Ethos of Diplomats: Reflections on WTO Dispute Settlement. In *Efficiency, Equity, Legitimacy: The Multilateral Trading System at the Millennium*, edited by Roger B. Porter, Pierre Sauvé, Arvind Subramanian, and Americo B. Zampetti, 334–50. Washington, DC: Brookings Institution.

Williams, Marc. 2011. Civil Society and the WTO: Contesting Accountability. In *Building Global Democracy? Civil Society and Accountable Global Governance*, edited by Jan Aart Scholte. Cambridge: Cambridge University Press.

Williams, Marc, and Lucy Ford. 1999. The World Trade Organization, Social Movements and Global Environmental Management. *Environmental Politics* 8 (1):268–89.

Woods, Ngaire. 2000. The Challenge of Good Governance for the IMF and the World Bank Themselves. *World Development* 28 (5):823–41.

Woods, Ngaire, and Amrita Narlikar. 2001. Governance and the Limits of Accountability: The WTO, the IMF and the World Bank. *International Social Science Journal* 53 (4):569–84.

WTO. 1996. *Guidelines for Arrangements on Relations with Non-Governmental Organizations.* WT/L/162, 23 July 1996. Geneva: WTO.

WTO. 2000b. *EC–Measures affecting Asbestos and Asbestos-Containing Products.* Communication from the Appellate Body. WT/DS135/9. Geneva: WTO.

WTO. 2002a. *Procedures for the Circulation and Derestriction of WTO Documents.* WT/L/452. Geneva: WTO.

WTO. 2003. *Working Procedures for Appellate Review.* WT/AB/WP/7. Geneva: WTO.

WTO. 2010. *10 common misunderstandings about the WTO.* Available from <http://www.wto.org/english/thewto_e/whatis_e/10mis_e/10m00_e.htm>. Accessed 7 November 2011.

WTO Appellate Body Report. 1998. *US–Import Prohibition of Certain Shrimp and Shrimp Products.* WT/DS58/AB/R. Geneva: WTO.

WTO Appellate Body Report. 2000a. *US–Imposition of Countervailing Duties on Certain Hot-Rolled Lead and Bismuth Carbon Steel Products Originating in the United Kingdom.* WT/DS138/AB/R. Geneva: WTO.

WTO Appellate Body Report. 2002b. *EC–Trade Description of Sardines.* WT/DS231/AB/R. Geneva: WTO.

Zutshi, B. K. 2001. Comment. In *Efficiency, Equity, Legitimacy: The Multilateral Trading System at the Millennium*, edited by Roger B. Porter, Pierre Sauvé, Arvind Subramanian, and Americo Beviglia Zampetti, 387–91. Washington, DC: Brookings Institution Press.

CHAPTER 15

··

WHAT HAPPENED TO THE INFLUENCE OF BUSINESS? CORPORATIONS AND ORGANIZED LABOUR IN THE WTO

··

STEVE MCGUIRE

15.1 INTRODUCTION

··

SEATTLE 1999 was for many observers a signal event in the history of global economic governance. The World Trade Organization (WTO) ministerial meeting—the major set piece diplomatic event in the organization's constitution—was essentially abandoned, as a range of protesters representing opposition to the liberalization agenda of the WTO disrupted the meeting. The reason for the breakdown of the negotiations was more complex—and indeed it might have happened without the protests—but Seattle ushered in a new era of heightened public visibility for an organization that, in its earlier guise as the General Agreement on Tariffs and Trade (GATT), was noticeable for its lack of public profile. Piewitt called the Seattle Ministerial a 'milestone' in the precedent it set for subsequent public participation.[1] In the decade since Seattle, major WTO meetings have attracted controversy, protests and, occasionally, significant levels of protest and violence. Why has this become the norm?

---

[1] Piewitt 2010.

Though the specific complaints about the WTO are numerous, they all share a firm rooting in the alleged bias of the organization to business interests. For many critics, the WTO is the manifestation of global market fundamentalism, where all other policy issues, such as labour rights, the environment, and development assistance, are seen through a prism of pro-business, anti-intervention preferences. In one sense the critics are correct: the WTO exists to liberalize trade and, as such, it is not an unbiased organization. Like its fellow international economic organizations, the World Bank and the International Monetary Fund (IMF), the WTO manifests a belief that protectionism is both bad economics and bad politics. Arguably, however, the WTO goes much further in both restricting members' protectionist activities and prescribing domestic rules in areas like intellectual property. This shift in emphasis from proscriptive to prescriptive rule-making, which developed in the Uruguay Round negotiations, has for many civil society organizations dramatically changed the nature of the WTO and has raised searching questions about the legitimacy of the organization, both in the way that it conducts its business and the policy outcomes that flow from its operations. The IMF and the World Bank intervene in domestic politics, but their involvement is episodic and in response to specific events. By contrast, the Uruguay Round agreements signal a move towards deep integration of the international economic system through the articulation and enforcement of multilateral rules. Michael Hart argues that with the Uruguay Round the WTO took a decisive step towards what was desired in 1947: 'a uniform code of practice governing [WTO] members' trade practices'.[2] This, in turn, has raised important questions about the legitimacy of the WTO as a political institution, and efforts by the organization to engage in a range of what might be called 'outreach activities' has been notable. These efforts range from the encouragement of individual participation in WTO consultative processes and the greater use of third party experts on technical issues, to formal agreements with other international institutions. Nonetheless, the WTO continues to be mistrusted by many non-governmental organizations.

Though the WTO is grounded in particular beliefs about the primacy of markets, its actual fidelity to these beliefs is much more problematic, and its operation has revealed a much more nuanced appreciation of the 'politics' of liberalized trade than many critics appreciate. In the first place, WTO member states negotiate about liberalizing trade that is anathema to virtually all economists: economies are opened on the basis of reciprocal concessions with trade partners, rather than via a unilateral opening of markets to the most competitive goods and services, irrespective of their origin. As such, the domestic politics of WTO liberalization involve many of the same rent-seeking dynamics associated with earlier eras of international trade, with domestically-oriented and uncompetitive firms seeking to exempt their sector from enhanced international competition. Second, though trade liberalization has been the prime policy underpinning the WTO, development and, more recently, the environment have not been absent. Developing states received special and differential treatment throughout successive GATT rounds, in recognition of the potential conflict between market openness and broader domestic

---

[2] Hart 2002.

economic and social reforms. The fact the GATT/WTO regime reflects a political compromise rather than a dogmatic pursuit of neoclassical economic liberalization gives
firms (and for that matter other groups) their opening to pursue rent-seeking activity.
This paradoxical situation is lost on many of the organization's critics.

If business is not necessarily as powerful as believed, it remains considerably more
influential in debates about economic governance than organized labour. Twenty years
of neo-liberalism in major economies, combined with the success of economic liberalization in emerging markets such as Brazil and China, undermined the argument that
globalized trade liberalization under the WTO would disadvantage the poorest. In both
business and labour spheres, the growth of a multipolar economic system has increased
the heterogeneity of transnational coalitions and made the adoption of agreed positions
far more difficult.

15.2 Perspectives on corporate political activity

That firms would be interested in engaging with a political process that influenced the
competitive environment for international trade is obvious enough. Yet the broad literature relating to the WTO is remarkably free of detailed analyses of corporate political
activity, and instead relies on macro-level perspectives that assume a high degree of
homogeneity in policy preferences. Capling and Low argue that there is a 'particularly
striking gap in our understanding of domestic trade policy-making'.[3] In one sense, this
is understandable: states, not firms, are signatories to the agreements and an understanding of interstate bargaining is central to unpicking the workings of the WTO.
Nonetheless there are drawbacks. This results in a type of aggregation in the analyses
where vast swathes of corporate opinion are rendered with a single view. In some cases,
even that aggregation is missing. In an overview of the evolution of Brazil's negotiating
stance on agriculture in the Uruguay Round, de Souza Farias barely mentions firms: the
Brazilian diplomatic machinery and farmers take pride of place in the analysis.[4] Given
the growth of Brazilian multinational enterprises (MNEs), not least in the agribusiness
sector, their omission from the story seems odd. Farmers, after all, rarely sell into international markets directly, and instead rely on multinationals as key intermediaries.
Ackrill and Kay argue that Brazil's industry was central to the prosecution of the Dispute
Settlement Understanding (DSU) case against the EU sugar regime, providing extensive
financial support to the then cash-poor Brazilian government.[5] According to Woll, this
inattention to the detail of business preferences flows from the dominant, economics-
based theories used by political economists.[6] In this perspective, firms either engage in

---

[3] Capling and Low 2010, 2.   [4] de Souza Farias 2010.
[5] Ackrill and Kay 2009.   [6] Woll 2008.

rent-seeking activity through lobbying against liberalization, or seek to broaden their foreign market penetration through liberalization. This 'either/or' conception of corporate political activity underestimates the range of responses open to firms when considering involvement in the policy process. Table 9 illustrates the distinctive approaches of political science and management studies.

As Coen, Grant, and Wilson note, political science does not have a micro-theory of business–government relations; most of the scholarship concentrates on the macro-orientation of policy-making and the role of firms (or free market ideology) in this process. 'There are, in fact, substantial differences among businesses—large as well as small—in terms of how much political activity they undertake and, if they become involved, what choices they make on how to pursue their objectives.'[7] Political science literature tends to emphasize firms' homogeneity in respect of demands on public policymakers. This is particularly true of studies underpinned by Gramscian or post-modern perspectives on international political economy. Comparatively little research considers situations where firms either do not participate in the political process, or where that participation fails to secure policy preferences. Susan Sell's work on the political economy of intellectual property protection arguably remains the exception that proves the rule in relation to business-level studies of the evolution of international trade.[8] Her work integrated the meso-level analysis of coalition-building by a small set of intellectual property (IP)-rich multinationals and the broader understanding of the interactions of states in the context of the Uruguay Round.

Political science perspectives, however, do have a conception of power—that firms are engaged in a process of 'mobilization of bias'—to borrow Schattschneider's famous phrase—that has not until recently appeared in management studies-based perspectives on corporate political activity.[9] For many management studies scholars, the political realm is analytically indistinct from other factor markets the firm might operate in. Fuchs and Lederer, for example, note that management studies often adopts a functionalist perspective, seeing firms' political involvement as, paradoxically, 'apolitical' and not concerned with influence but rather compliance with rules and regulations.[10] Mantere, Pajunen, and Lamberg likewise note the tendency of management theory to see involvement in the political sphere as a technical exercise, rather like any other

Table 9 Comparing approaches to corporate political activity

Characteristic	Management studies	Political science
Rationale for corporate lobbying	Competitive advantage vis-à-vis other firms	Profit maximization through rent-seeking or deregulation
Nature of collective corporate interests	Heterogeneous	Homogeneous

[7] Coen, Grant, and Wilson 2010, 12.   [8] Sell 2003.
[9] Schattschneider 1960.   [10] Fuchs and Lederer 2007.

firm-level operation.[11] They note that, while firms 'do politics' in management theory, firms are not 'political actors' in the sense that political science scholars would understand. This perspective, common in business school descriptions of firms' political activity, does not conceptualize a firm's political activity as an exercise in power. Most concepts in the area of competitive strategy—a subfield dedicated to the analysis of corporate behaviour in the market—do not speak to political influence as an important element of firms' strategy: a firm's corporate strategy is comprised of that firm's functional capabilities in marketing, production and finance and their competitiveness vis-à-vis other firms. Strategic management lament literature is comparatively ahistorical, only infrequently querying how a firm came to occupy the competitive position it does, but concentrating instead on how it exploits this existing position. Though business historians such as Jones and Chandler enjoy significant reputations, historically-informed analyses of the evolution of firms' structure and competitiveness are surprisingly few.[12] Oded Shenkar argues that 'political variables and qualifiers were not systematically considered in international business and were neglected altogether in strategy research'.[13]

Until recently, the main exception to management studies' inattention to the firm as a political actor came in studies of foreign direct investment (FDI). Here, several studies have sought to understand how firms interested in investing bargain with potential host governments, and how that initial position of strength is gradually eroded in the 'obsolescing bargain'.[14] However, the obsolescing bargain literature remains a relatively impoverished view of firms' political activity, revolving around one policy area—investment—and concerned mainly with developing country policymakers. Moreover, the obsolescing bargain model perspective was unable to explain the neo-liberal turn in economic policy-making, often manifest with developing states engaging in fierce competition to attract—and retain—foreign direct investment. Eden, Lenway, and Schuler developed the 'political bargaining model' (PBM) as the obsolescing framework could not explain the ability of multinationals to retain significant bargaining leverage vis-à-vis national governments.[15] The PBM framework pushed management studies scholarship to see government–firm relationships as an iterated game rather than a singular interaction. Viewed now as a relationship that persists over time, there is considerably greater scope for corporate political activity across time and issue areas. The emphasis has remained, however, on the national level, with the exception of the work of Brewer and Young, who have analysed ways that the nascent multilateral regime for investment needs to be understood through the lens of corporate strategy.[16]

More recent scholarship in management studies is grounded in a conception of the public policy process as a contest among firms for competitive advantage. Firms, of course, can collude, create coalitions, and otherwise engage in collective action to achieve goals, but the overarching premise of management studies work is that the firm is engaged in a contest—and a zero-sum one at that. Firms' survival can depend on their

---

[11] Mantere, Pajunen, and Lamberg 2009.   [12] Mayer and Whittington 2004.
[13] Shenkar 2009, 1.   [14] Rugman and Verbeke 2008.
[15] Eden, Lenway, and Schuler 2005.   [16] Brewer and Young 2010.

performance vis-à-vis others in the political sphere, and they thus have incentives to develop capacity to deal effectively with politicians and bureaucrats. But that does not mean that firms always participate. Drawing on the economic marketplace as a metaphor, Bonardi, Hillman, and Keim developed the concept of a 'political market' to describe the interactions of firms (demanders of policy preferences) and politicians and bureaucrats (suppliers of policy preferences).[17] They argue that, in the same way that an economic market for, say, housing can be buoyant or stagnant, so too can the marketplace for policy preferences. They argue that a range of structural characteristics shape political markets in ways that diminish or increase the desire of firms to participate. Bonardi, Hillman, and Keim's focus on national-level interactions in democracies limits their analysis somewhat, but their central insight—that firms make nuanced decisions about their participation in the political process—has important implications for our understanding of the Doha Round. Broadly, Bonardi, Hillman, and Keim suggest that a political market is attractive to firms: when the issue is not highly politicized; when the benefits to firms are concentrated; and when the policy issue is new, and governments are unfamiliar with the policy area. Of these, the degree of politicization has long featured in explanations of the increasing complexity and difficulty of successive negotiating rounds.[18] Sell and Prakash noted how, in the case of a TRIPS dispute between large pharmaceutical firms and the government of South Africa in relation to intellectual property protection for anti-retroviral drugs, the tenor of the debate changed dramatically once the issue had been moved off the technical interpretation of IP laws and towards the politically charged fate of the millions of people suffering from AIDS.[19]

In a seminal article on the subject of corporate political activity, David Baron introduced the concept of 'non-market strategy' to conceptualize firms' activity in the public policy arena.[20] The notion that firms engage in market strategy is common sense to many people; firms market goods, hire personnel and make divestitures and acquisitions for the express purpose of gaining competitive advantage over rival firms. All these transactions are governed by market relations, where a price can be established for the transaction. In the non-market environment, the price mechanism either does not work, or works imperfectly, but Baron's insight was to see that just as a new product might alter the competitive landscape, so can changes in government regulations, thus altering the resources and capabilities needed by the firm. Significantly, one of Baron's early case studies about the importance of non-market strategy was a trade dispute: Kodak–Fuji. Baron argued that strategists had to understand that Kodak's failure in the marketplace may not have been due to firm-level processes, but rather to a regulatory issue in Japan. Linking Baron's work with the concept of the political market, we can understand how firms make nuanced decisions about political activity. These decisions are governed by an assessment by the firm of the potential gains and the opportunity cost of involvement in the political process.

---

[17] Bonardi, Hillman, and Keim 2005.   [18] See, for example, Woolcock 2010.
[19] Sell and Prakash 2004.   [20] Baron 1995.

The supranational regulatory process is, however, an area where corporate political activity (CPA) studies remain sparse.[21] This is largely because firms do, in the main, concentrate on national policymakers as the locus of most of the regulation that concerns them. Nonetheless, the increasing legalization of the international political economy should increase the opportunities for firms to engage in transnational corporate political activity.[22] The proliferation of international regulatory regimes has begun to shift attention to corporate political activity above the national level. Manger[23] for example, looked at Japanese corporate preferences for preferential trade agreements in the wake of the creation of the North American Free Trade Agreement (NAFTA). Chase has also done interesting work on how firms seek to exploit regional trade agreements such as NAFTA for competitive advantage.[24] Rugman, though not explicitly considering how the political activities of firms catalyse regional trade agreements, nonetheless highlights how regional strategies of firms map well onto the emergent regionalized international political economy.[25] The implication of his work is that region-specific corporate political activity that reflects the legal and political regime of the area is a co-requisite of market success.

A key element of the problem is that the supranational level is the level of 'soft law' par excellence, in contrast to the hard law of national governments. As Mattli and Woods argue, supranational regulation is 'soft' in the sense that it comprises mainly voluntary codes and the diffusion of best practice, in contrast to the rules and regulations of the national level.[26] In addition, whilst sanctions for non-compliance with rules are generally clear and enforceable at the national level, this clarity diminishes at the supranational level. This can pose a problem for studies of CPA as it becomes relatively more difficult to identify the precise 'target' of firms' non-market strategy. Studies that are informed by regime theory and constructivism do, however, shed light on how firms' political activities shape—and are in turn shaped by—the norms and expectations of other stakeholders with an interest in the regime. In a study of the international regime for the trade in diamonds, the Kimberley Process, Kantz shows how firms were influential in providing both resources and technical expertise central to developing the regime. However, this structural power was to some extent offset by the ability of other stakeholders to socialize firms to the broader, societal expectations about how the regime might operate.[27]

15.2.1 Firms get involved in the WTO

Trade liberalization always affects firms, and to that extent firms' preferences may be said to suffuse policymakers' calculations regarding tariffs and other trade barriers. This conception of firms' activity—that policymakers so completely identify with firms' preferences that there is little need for firms to actively involve themselves—echoes the work

---

[21] Brewer and Young 2010; Lawton and McGuire 2005; Lawton, Lindeque, and McGuire 2009.
[22] Abbott and Snidal 2003.   [23] Manger   [24] Chase 2003.
[25] Rugman and Verbeke 2008   [26] Mattli and Woods 2009, 3.   [27] Kantz 2007.

of Bachrach and Baratz as well as the neo-Gramscian school of political economy.[28] In these conceptions of firm–government relations, CPA (here defined as the purposive use of firms' resources in support of change in the policy environment favourable to the firm) need not exist. Policymakers so internalize market preferences that firms, in a sense, always get what they want. The problem with this conception is that, while it explains the macro-orientation of international trade policy since 1945, the abundant evidence of the growth of corporate political activity suggests that firms' and governments' preferences on specific policy measures did diverge. Formal involvement by firms in the politics of trade liberalization really dates from the 1970s, and owes much to the domestic political economy of the United States.

In the 1970s, two developments shaped the firm–government relationship in profound ways. The first was a change in electoral law, which altered incentives for corporate behaviour, whilst the second was the increasing complexity of GATT negotiations themselves. Amendments to campaign finance laws had a profound effect on the incentives for US firms to lobby government officials. American firms were now able to make campaign contributions, and many quickly saw how this opened a new avenue to influencing policymakers. As Vogel notes, across a swathe of US industry, lobbying activity increased after these changes.[29] The second development concerned the trade system itself. From its inception in 1948 until the 1960s, successive GATT negotiations concerned tariffs. Whilst firms were not indifferent to tariff rates, the widespread belief that beggar-thy-neighbour tariff escalation had contributed to the rise of fascist regimes ahead of the Second World War sustained a strong and shared belief in the efficacy of tariff reductions that overrode the objections of many firms. Moreover, after 1945, the US entered a period of unparalleled dominance of the global economy, and strong domestic growth and rapid overseas expansion made domestic tariff reductions palatable. This began to change in the late 1960s, however; as economic recovery took hold, American firms found themselves in tougher competitive struggles with foreign companies, mainly European and Japanese. The US economy, even by the mid 1960s, had a comparatively small internationally traded sector, equivalent to 5 per cent of GDP.[30] However, the figure would rise dramatically in the latter part of that decade and become politically salient. By the 1970s, established US firms in sectors such as televisions and automobiles were seeing their US and foreign market shares eroded. In emergent sectors such as consumer electronics and computers, US firms faced competitors who worked closely with their home governments in a relationship that US firms alleged gave their foreign competitors significant advantages.

US negotiators of the Kennedy Round came in for considerable criticism for not appreciating the changing nature of international business. Critics argued that the negotiators, as career diplomats, paid too much attention to the high politics of the GATT regime and to the comparatively simple to negotiate issue of tariff reductions. American firms argued that the new competitive landscape required that US policymakers understand how firm–government relations in other states could generate firm-level competitive

---

[28] Bachrach and Baratz 1962.   [29] Vogel 1996.   [30] Hart 2002, 276.

advantage. As American firms increasingly looked to domestic institutional arrangements in foreign states, thus American preferences changed in the Tokyo Round. Non-tariff barriers (NTBs) began to assume paramount importance for the United States, whose negotiators pressed for agreements on a range of domestic economic policies and practices, such as government procurement and sanitary and phytosanitary regulations.

An increasing number of states have developed formal business–government consultative processes that owe at least something to the American practice. As the trade agenda expanded, governments required two things from business. The first was technical expertise about the impact of changes to the international trade regime, and the second was process legitimacy for an intergovernmental process that was increasingly eroding the 'embedded liberal' compromise that underpinned earlier conceptions of the GATT's political legitimacy. As the internal economic arrangement of states became—even indirectly—the focus of GATT/WTO discussions, support from the business community became important in selling globalization to the general public. The growth of complex and durable 'public–private' partnerships in international trade negotiations has been well documented.[31]

When most observers comment on corporate involvement—for good or ill—in the WTO process, most have in mind the extensive firm-level lobbying activity associated with the Uruguay Round negotiations from 1986–94. Indeed, much of the civil society opposition to the WTO stems from the perception that this round was far too beholden to corporate interests. But the success of corporate political activity in the Uruguay Round was arguably exceptional, and has not been repeated since. It depended upon a context in the late 1980s that was particularly favourable to corporate involvement. In the United States there was a widespread view that the Tokyo Round agreements did not sufficiently protect US firms against unfair foreign competition. By the time the Uruguay Round was launched in 1986, the US trade deficit was at politically explosive levels, and major industries, ranging from automobiles and steel to emergent sectors such as the telecommunications, electronics, and computer industries, were lobbying for American policymakers to do more to cancel out foreign economic practices that the US deemed unfair. European firms, like their American counterparts, seeing an opportunity to maintain eroding competitiveness through political action, joined in efforts to push through the Uruguay agenda. In retrospect, the EU–US cooperation in the Uruguay Round was the high point of a Euro-American dominance of the international political economy. If the aim was to 'lock in' Euro-American dominance of the global economy, it failed.[32]

15.2.2 Firms, corporate strategy and the WTO

The WTO's impact on the strategies of internationalized firms has been the subject of debate, with most of the management studies scholarly community ignoring its

---

[31] Shaffer, Sanchez, and Rosenberg 2008.   [32] McGuire and Smith 2008.

influence.[33] Yet, evidence that WTO rules influence corporate strategy is abundant; because the WTO's rules (and disputes process) alter state behaviour and policies, they alter the competitive environment for firms. WTO regulations do incentivize firms to undertake new strategies. For example, one of the key elements of the TRIPS 'bargain' in the Uruguay Round was that higher standards of intellectual property protection in developing countries would incentivize multinational firms to locate high-skilled activities, including basic research and development (R&D), in those countries. Trade liberalization has two potential effects on firms' incentives to undertake R&D: first, it can create positive incentives to invest, as liberalization expands the market (scale effect); but second, it can dampen incentives if new competitors are created (competition effect).[34] As with any other subsidy, research and development incentives risk being captured by organized producer interests, but they can also address the market failures associated with risky investments, and so enhance welfare.[35] Thus, multilateral disciplines on subsidies need to accommodate two demands that are in tension with each other. Unsurprisingly, then, the Subsidies and Countervailing Measures (SCM) Agreement in the WTO is comparatively complex and, when first negotiated, sought to accommodate a range of permissible subsidies—as well as prohibiting export subsidy.[36] As both Evenett and Kang note, WTO disciplines on R&D subsidies are comparatively weak, whereas intellectual property provisions under TRIPS are comparatively strong.[37] This is partly explained by the desire of developed world (or OECD) firms pressing their governments to gain multilateral protection for their *existing* stock of intellectual property. TRIPS has been controversial because of the unfairness implicit in the protection of developed world knowledge, thus restricting the ability of developing states to catch up. Recent experience has, however, called this into question, as Asian countries have demonstrated an ability to develop a range of emergent high-technology sectors. Forero-Pineda, for example, argued that TRIPS has increased incentives to pursue niche technology policies in several developing states.[38]

Similarly, Hu and Matthews observe that innovative activity in China soared after that country's accession to the WTO in 2001 (see Figure 11).[39] They argue that foreign firms had, in effect, been waiting until China joined the WTO before investing in higher value-added activities there.

The SCM Code, in contrast to TRIPS, has not proved problematic for emerging economies, aside from a few high-profile cases such as Embraer's subsidization by the Brazilian government.[40] The language of the SCM—what Evenett refers to as its incompleteness— offers considerable scope for states to develop national programmes under the aegis of environmental technologies or regional economic development.[41] During the Uruguay

---

[33] The exceptions: Aggarwal and Evenett 2010; Brewer and Young 2008; Lawton, Lindeque, and McGuire 2009; Lawton and McGuire 2005.
[34] Teteryatnikova 2008.   [35] Brou, Campanella, and Ruta 2009.
[36] McGuire 2002.   [37] Evenett 2009; Kang 2000.
[38] Forero-Pineda 2006.   [39] Hu and Matthews 2008.
[40] Goldstein and McGuire 2004.   [41] Evenett 2009.

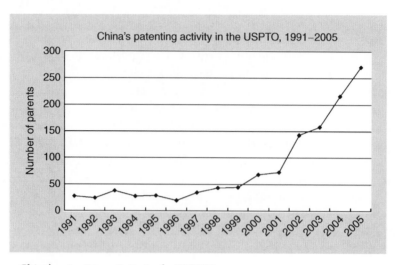

FIGURE 11 China's patenting activity in the USPTO, 1991–2005

Source: Hu and Matthews, 2008

Round negotiations, the United States succeeded in persuading other states of the merits of a specific research and development exemption (i.e. green light) under the SCM Code.[42] The recent economic crisis has merely added to the view that the SCM is not a significant obstacle to governments seeking to promote or protect industries. As Falke notes, the US bailout for the automobile sector was the most costly subsidy in US corporate history.[43] Europe did not retaliate, in large part because several European states went ahead and introduced similar subsidy measures designed to preserve their auto sectors. The European Union essentially suspended its anti-subsidy enforcement activities, fearing a political storm should the Commission be seen as sacrificing member state economies to WTO-inspired regulations.[44] The wide scope of the Subsidies Code has been a boon to nations like India, which have been able to pursue national innovation policies in key areas such as pharmaceuticals and biotechnology.[45] In short, the relatively robust TRIPS Agreement, secured through a highly effective corporate lobbying effort, combined with a relatively loose SCM, has created what Aggarwal and Evenett call 'Murky Protectionism'.[46] A large number of emerging market firms are not remotely interested in a further elaboration of rules that currently give them, and their governments, considerable latitude.

[42] Global Subsidies Initiative (no date).   [43] Falke 2010.   [44] Evenett 2009.
[45] Ramani 2002.   [46] Aggarwal and Evenett 2010.

15.2.3 Explaining the change in business behaviour

The relative absence of corporate political activity in the Doha Round has been noted by many analysts. McGuire and Lindeque observe that corporate support for the EU's activities in the Doha Round has declined as firms have come to the view that the round is, if not doomed, at least unlikely to deliver significant benefits.[47] As Narlikar notes, the corporate sector has chosen 'to invest its energies elsewhere', to the detriment of the round.[48] This seeming disinterest is not easily explained by traditional political economy understandings of corporate behaviour: the WTO seeks to liberalize trade, and firms should wish to pursue the steady deregulation of the international economy. As Bonardi, Hillman, and Keim[49] argue, the political process can be conceptualized as a market, where the number of firms entering the market is a function of the perception of how attractive that market is. Firms do not constantly involve themselves in the political process: their involvement is governed by an understanding of the opportunity cost of devoting resources to political activity that could be deployed elsewhere. Firms are thus keenly interested in political markets for new products and services, where the ability to shape the regulatory terrain does offer the opportunity to erect 'political barriers to entry'.[50] Bonardi notes, too, that firms' non-market strategy is most effective in relatively regulated contexts, where clear bureaucratic barriers to entry exist.[51] Viewed from the perspective of a political market, the declining interest in the WTO is more explicable. Firms have come to view other political marketplaces as more attractive arenas for their activities, and so relegate the multilateral negotiating process to a secondary priority.

The focus on the negotiating rounds of the WTO, and the presumption that these are the main—or even the only—focus for corporate political activity at the international level, has been undermined by recent corporate behaviour. Once we shift the focus from negotiations (what Goldstein and Steinberg call the 'legislative' function of the WTO), it becomes possible to discern new patterns of corporate behaviour, rather than a straightforward absence of interest.[52] It is also useful to draw a distinction between firms from developed economies—particularly the EU and the US—who are typically the firms people have in mind when thinking about CPA, and developing state firms, whose political activity is only now being studied with any seriousness.[53] For many emerging market firms, further elaboration of 'behind the border' issues are, if not unimportant, not nearly as valuable as securing market access to (still, comparatively) affluent Western markets. For many of these firms, their cost advantages vis-à-vis developed country firms are considerable. This, combined with their strong competitive position in fast-growing emerging markets, makes them comparatively uninterested in large elements of the Doha agenda.

---

[47] McGuire and Lindeque 2010.   [48] Narlikar 2010.   [49] Bonardi, Hillman, and Kein 2005.
[50] Mattli and Woods 2009, 14.   [51] Bonardi 2008.
[52] Goldstein and Steinberg 2010, 211–42.   [53] McGuire, Lindeque, and Suder 2010.

One explanation for the relative lack of interest by developed country firms in the new round is the fact that most of what is important to them has already been achieved or is not on the negotiating table. For firms to involve themselves in the Doha process, the potential gains needed to be greater than the firms could have achieved through other, market-based activity. It is not obvious that Doha ever offered this opportunity. Peter Kleen and McGuire and Lindeque both argue that the Doha agenda does not offer the scope for trade-offs among issue areas.[54] In his analysis of a hypothetical Transatlantic Free Trade Agreement (TAFTA), Langhammer notes that business associations on both sides of the Atlantic see the principal obstacles to enhanced European–American trade as largely procedural, best accomplished through greater government to government cooperation. They are not issues of policy that require a bilateral trade pact, let alone integration into the WTO process.[55] At the multilateral level, the removal of the Singapore Issues (trade facilitation, competition policy, procurement, investment) during the early stages of the round made Western MNE support for the round more difficult to sustain. With tariffs increasingly mattering less in swathes of industries, it is precisely the ease of doing business that matters to established multinationals.

The judicialization of the WTO has also had an important effect for firms by making the disputes process a more attractive venue for corporate political activity. Goldstein and Steinberg argue both that the WTO dispute settlement process has engaged in lawmaking to an extent never intended by the national negotiators (most notably the US and the EU), and that litigation through the disputes process has supplanted interstate negotiations as the main driver of evolution in the WTO.[56] 'Forum-shopping' is a widely understood concept in trade policy-making: the desire of an actor to choose a dispute settlement process that most suits them. In trade studies, forum-shopping usually applies to the choice of multilateral or regional trade dispute settlement process. However, it is possible to conceptualize forum-shopping as a process where firms seek to identify the best forum for the execution of their non-market strategy. The WTO offers two main routes for the execution of non-market strategy: the negotiating process, and the disputes process. The WTO disputes process has been one of the Uruguay Round's main success stories, and its ability to generate results—in contrast to the frustratingly slow negotiating process—has not been lost on firms. As Shaffer, Sanchez, and Rosenberg note, 'because of its legalized and judicialized nature, catalysing domestic initiatives to shape international law, the WTO affords significant opportunities to governments and private constituencies, particularly business constituencies'.[57] In a number of countries, firms seem to have concluded that the technical, comparatively less public, disputes process offers better opportunities for their non-market strategy than supporting the negotiating process.

Brazil is a case in point. The country has aggressively used the disputes process as a mechanism to prise open foreign markets. Although much attention is paid to Brazil's highly skilled trade diplomacy, these efforts are, ultimately, undertaken on behalf of firms. As Shaffer, Sanchez, and Rosenberg argue, Brazil has been particularly successful

---

[54] Kleen 2008; McGuire and Lindeque 2010.   [55] Langhammer 2009.
[56] Goldstein and Steinberg   [57] Shaffer, Sanchez, and Rosenberg 2008, 390.

in developing a 'third pillar'—a private sector network of firms, trade associations, civil society and academe—to assist in the prosecution of trade cases and the more general diffusion of knowledge about the international economic systems.[58] Schneider suggests that Brazil has been advantaged in two respects. First, as with other Latin American countries, the development of stable democracy opened up new avenues of corporate political activity for Brazilian business elites. Second, Brazilian business is dominated by diversified business groups with extensive commercial interests across sectors. These two characteristics, when combined with the acceptance of trade liberalization, significantly enhanced the interest of business in foreign economic relations, particularly in areas like agribusiness, where Brazilian companies have dramatically expanded their international presence.[59] Brazil's government invested heavily in a range of research and development programmes for the agribusiness sector during the Cardoso administration. The success of these efforts, combined with the devaluation of the real in 1999, allowed Brazil to emerge as a strong agricultural exporter, not merely of unprocessed commodities, but also processed foods.[60] Indeed, by 2004, processed food exports significantly exceeded raw agricultural produce outputs. BDF, Brazil's largest agribusiness, is among the ten largest agribusiness companies by market capitalization.

The disputes process is in many respects a much more attractive political market than the negotiating rounds. In many ways, the DSU represents a reversion to the less public and more technically orientated negotiating rounds before Uruguay and Doha. Firms have a narrower set of public officials to deal with, and gains can be more easily appropriated by the 'winning' firm. Though Brazilian firms have been particularly prominent, firms from a number of emerging economies have found the WTO disputes process a useful mechanism to press for further market opening and as a means of blunting protectionist measures, such as anti-dumping, by developed states. As many emerging market states have become key suppliers of complex components for established MNEs in Europe and America, concerns about the utility of anti-dumping actions have become more widespread.[61]

Finally, the growth of regional trade agreements has had a significant effect on firms' political activity in the trade realm. As successive WTO negotiations become larger and more unwieldy, the attractions of bilateral or plurilateral approaches increase. In the case of regional agreements, the gains and costs of concluding the pact are more concentrated, providing firms with powerful incentives to participate.[62] Moreover, firms are not nearly as global as is often suggested; most have an identifiable home region, where most of their sales are generated. Ghemawat called regionally based strategies the 'forgotten strategy' for the inattention paid to regional trade agreements (RTAs) by the management studies communities.[63] Firms have never forgotten regional approaches and, as the process in Geneva became more complicated and costly, regional alternatives became more attractive.

---

[58] Shaffer, Sanchez, and Rosenberg 2008, 432.
[59] Schneider 2010.   [60] Pereira, Teixeira, and Raszap-Skorbiansky 2010.
[61] McGuire and Lindeque 2010.   [62] Chase 2003; Manger 2005.   [63] Ghemawat 2003.

15.3 LABOUR GROUPS

In marked contrast to the contentious issue of the WTO's relations with the business community, the organization's relations with the international labour movement have been less controversial—but arguably also far less significant. For much of GATT's existence, labour groups had little reason to engage with the international trade agenda. The early rounds of negotiations focused almost entirely on the reduction of tariffs and, in the post-war economic boom in the United States and, later, other developed economies, relatively strong unions in corporatist political economies meant that the living standards of many workers were well protected. As Perez-Esteve notes, the Tokyo Round of GATT negotiations marked an important break in organized labour's relationship with the trade system.[64] In the United States, just as firms came under increased competitive pressure from the resurgent economies in Europe and Japan, so too did labour. At this juncture, American firms and labour made a common argument, if not common cause: many of the increasing economic pressures faced by the United States had their source in unfair trade, whether cheap labour or foreign government support for their domestic firms. In the years between GATT rounds, the view that some form of core protection for workers ought to be integral to multilateral trade gained a degree of acceptance in the OECD. The OECD's guidelines on member states' foreign investment policies contain commitments to employment standards.[65]

The key development in catalysing labour's interest in the GATT/WTO process was the broadening and deepening of the trade agenda, particularly during the Uruguay Round. By making domestic political economies the subject of international trade negotiations, trade officials invited increased scrutiny of their activities by trade unions and other labour groups. For organized labour in the United States and Europe, the conclusion of the Uruguay Round presented them with an international organization whose disputes process was far more robust than the moral suasion used by the International Labour Organization (ILO). Thus initial response to the creation of the WTO—at least among established unions in the OECD—was broadly positive, as it held out the possibility of gaining international acceptance of the idea of core labour standards.[66]

The linkage between labour standards and international trade is easily made: the price a good commands in a marketplace is a function of the cost of its production, and so cannot be separated from the manner of its production. Moreover, the dominance of neo-liberalism in the international political economy during the 1980s and 1990s allowed many states to erode previous levels of protection in the name of economic competitiveness. Rates of unionization in the United States, for example, went into long-term decline during this period. Spurred on by a concern about races to the bot-

---

[64] Perez-Esteve 2010, 289.   [65] Leary 1997.   [66] Perez-Esteve 2010, 289.

tom in employment standards, organized labour stepped up its lobbying. In the run-up to the first WTO Ministerial, members such as the United States and France, bolstered by political support at home from domestic organized labour, urged the WTO to bring labour standards under the aegis of the WTO. Countries could thus be denied trade concessions by other members for alleged violations of minimum labour standards.[67] The 1996 Singapore Ministerial adopted the first formal language in WTO documents relating to core labour standards, but there is a widespread view that the declaration falls well short of the rigorous commitment sought by organized labour.[68] For many developing states, the articulation and enforcement of core labour standards is simply an unacceptable infringement on national laws and practices, and undermines the comparative advantage these states have in labour-intensive industries. In a clear example of how the accession of large numbers of developing states has tilted the balance of power in the organization, the Singapore Ministerial, whilst acknowledging the importance of labour standards, does little more than provide a facility to keep talking about the issue. Moreover, the apparent success of WTO accession and market opening as a mechanism for alleviating poverty—most notably in China—has undermined the long-held argument that neo-liberalism means impoverishment for the many and enrichment for the few.

In the absence of the full integration of labour standards into its agreements, the WTO has sought to maintain a commitment to the issue through formal associations with the UN. The WTO and the ILO have a formal agreement of cooperation, designed to facilitate information flows and the development of 'soft law' best practice, in the Mattli and Woods sense of the term. Separately, firms have often found it in their interest to engage as social actors, and many actively seek to develop labour standards and employee relations mechanisms that exceed those of the host countries. Many of these efforts, as Brown, Vetterlein, and Roemer-Mahler note, used to hinge on a 'business case': a purely economic consideration that it was more cost-effective—and ultimately more profitable—to treat workers more humanely. This has gradually been complemented (not supplanted) by a broader, socially situated analysis that sees firms in many states, out of necessity, offering services and undertaking activities that used to be the responsibility of the state.[69]

15.4 CONCLUSION

It may be that the business lobbying effort in support of aspects of the Uruguay Round agreements, far from being typical, will come to be regarded as an exceptionally effective instance of corporate political activity. The puzzle for many observers has been to understand how economic agents like MNEs can come to be so disinterested in negotiations about the global economic system. Firms view political activity as a choice, one that

---

[67] Leary 1997, 119.   [68] Baummert et al. 2008.
[69] Brown, Vetterlein, and Roemer-Mahler 2010.

involves trade-offs, costs and risks; as such, the gains from CPA have to outweigh the potential losses. In this sense, the Doha Round has become an unattractive political market. The broad sweep of the negotiations and the numerous participants from civil society make it difficult for firms to keep the focus on relatively defined and technical aspects of business regulation. Similarly, the growth of very strong and confident emerging market firms has made it more difficult for firms to appropriate the gains from CPA. Indeed, the heterogeneity of business interests has been an overlooked feature of the negotiations. Both regional trade agreements and the WTO disputes process have become more attractive markets for firms. It is in these forums that they can narrow the number of participants in the market and more easily appropriate gains.

Organized labour has never had the resources to compete with business interests in the WTO, and the rise of emerging markets has made this competition more difficult. Unions in the developed countries may seek core labour standards out of a profound sense of moral duty, but in emerging economies their advocacy is seen as thinly disguised protectionism. International organizations like the ILO work to keep the issue on the agenda through a range of activities. Finally, the seeming success of trade liberalization in alleviating poverty has blunted labour activists' case in developing states, not least as firms themselves have appropriated the role of government inspector in areas such as working conditions.

References

Abbott, Kenneth, and Duncan Snidal. 2000. Hard and Soft Law in International Governance. *International Organization* 53 (3):421–56.

Ackrill, Roger, and Adrian Kay. 2009. Historical Learning in the Design of WTO Rules: The EC Sugar Case. *World Economy* 32 (5):754–71.

Aggarwal, Vinod, and Simon Evenett. 2010. The Financial Crisis, 'New' Industrial Policy, and the Bite of Multilateral Trade Rules. *Asian Economic Policy Review* 5 (2):221–44.

Bachrach, Peter, and Morton Baratz. 1962. Two Faces of Power. *American Political Science Review* 56 (4):947–52.

Baron, David. 1995. Integrated Strategy: Market and Nonmarket Components. *California Management Review* 37 (2):47–65.

Baummert, Jennifer, Kyle Johnson, Dawn Heushal, and Brendan Lynch. 2008. *International Cooperation on Trade and Labor Issues*. Federal Publications Paper 483. Available from <http://digitalcommons.ilr.cornell.edu/key_workplace/483>. Accessed 10 November 2011.

Bonardi, Jean-Philippe. 2008. The Internal Limits to Firms' Non-Market Activities. *European Management Review* 5 (3):165–74.

Bonardi, Jean-Philippe, Amy Hillman, and Gerald Keim. 2005. The Attractiveness of Political Markets: Implications for Firm Strategy. *Academy of Management Review* 30 (2):397–413.

Brewer, Thomas, and Stephen Young. 2010. Multilateral Institutions and Policies: Implications for Multinational Business Strategies. In *The Oxford Handbook of International Business*, edited by Alan Rugman, 269–306. 2nd edition. Oxford: Oxford University Press.

Brou, Daniel, Eduardo Campanella, and Michele Ruta. 2009. The Value of Domestic Subsidy Rules in Trade Agreements. WTO Staff Working Paper ESRD-2009-12. Geneva: WTO.

Brown, Dana, Antje Vetterlein, and Anne Roemer-Mahler. 2010. Theorizing Transnational Corporations as Social Actors: An Analysis of Corporate Motivations. *Business and Politics* 12 (1):1–39. Available from <http://www.bepress.com/bap/vol12/iss1/art1>. Accessed 10 November 2011.

Capling, Ann, and Patrick Low. 2010. Introduction. In *Governments, Non-State Actors and Trade Policy-Making*, edited by Capling and Low, 2. Cambridge: Cambridge University Press.

Chase, Kerry. 2003. Economic Interests and Regional Trading Arrangements: The Case of NAFTA. *International Organization* 57 (1):137–74.

Coen, David, Wyn Grant, and Graham Wilson. 2010. Political Science: Perspectives on Business and Government. In *The Oxford Handbook of Business and Government*, edited by David Coen, Wyn Grant, and Graham Wilson. Oxford: Oxford University Press.

de Souza Farias, Rogerio. 2010. Sowing the Seeds of Leadership: Brazil and the Agricultural Trade Negotiations of the Uruguay Round. *Journal of World Trade* 44 (3):661–85.

Eden, Lorraine, Stefanie Lenway, and Douglas Schuler. 2005. From the Obsolescing Bargain to the Political Bargaining Model. In *International Business and Government Relations in the 21st Century*, edited by Robert Grosse, 251–72. Cambridge: Cambridge University Press.

Evenett, Simon. 2009. What can be Learned from Crisis-Era Protectionism? An Initial Assessment. *Business and Politics* 11 (3):article 4.

Falke, Andreas. 2010. No Ado About Nothing: Obama's Trade Policies after 1 Year. In *European Yearbook of International Economic Law 2011* edited by Christoph Herrmann and Jörg Philipp Terhechte, 137–50. Berlin: Springer.

Forero-Pineda, Clemente. 2006. The Impact of Stronger Intellectual Property Rights on Science and Technology in Developing Countries. *Research Policy* 35 (6):808–24.

Fuchs, Doris, and Mark Lederer. 2007. The Power of Business. *Business and Politics* 9 (3):article 1.

Ghemawat, Pankaj. 2005. Regional Strategies for Global Leadership. *Harvard Business Review* 83 (12):98–108.

Global Subsidies Initiative. No date. The WTO and Subsidies. International Institute for Sustainable Development. Available from <http://www.globalsubsidies.org/en/media-portal/the-wto-and-subsidies>. Accessed 17 May 2010.

Goldstein, Andrea, and Steven McGuire. 2004. The Political Economy of Strategic Trade Policy and the Brazil–Canada Subsidies Saga. *World Economy* 27 (4):541–66.

Goldstein, Judith, and Ngaire Woods. 2010. Regulatory Shift: The Rise of Judicial Liberalization. In *The Politics of Global Regulation*, edited by Walter Mattli and Ngaire Woods, 211–42. Princeton: Princeton University Press.

Hart, Michael. 2002. *A Trading Nation*. Vancouver: UBC Press.

Hu, Mei-Hsih, and Matthews, J. 2008. China's National Innovative Capacity. *Research Policy* 37 (9): 1465–79.

Kang, M. 2000. Trade Policy Mix under the WTO: Protection of TRIPS and R&D Subsidies. KIEP Working Paper 00-11. Seoul: Korea Institute for International Economic Policy.

Kantz, Carola. 2007. The Power of Socialization: Engaging the Diamond Industry in the Kimberley Process. *Business and Politics* 9 (3):article 2.

Kleen, Peter. 2008. So Alike and Yet So Different: A Comparison of the Uruguay Round and the Doha Round. Jan Tumlir Essay. Brussels: European Centre for International Political Economy.

Langhammer, Rolf. 2009. Why a Marketplace must not Discriminate. *Business and Politics* 11 (3):article 3.

Lawton, Thomas, Johan Lindeque, and Steven McGuire. 2009. Multilateralism and the Multinational Enterprise. *Business and Politics* 11 (3):article 3.

Lawton, Thomas, and Steven McGuire. 2005. Adjusting to Liberalization: Tracing the Impact of the WTO on the European Textiles and Chemicals Industries. *Business and Politics* 7 (3):article 4.

Leary, Virginia. 1997. The WTO and the Social Clause: Post-Singapore. *European Journal of International Law* 8 (1):118–22.

McGuire, Steven. 2002. Between Pragmatism and Principle: Legalization, Political Economy and the WTO's Subsidy Agreement. *International Trade Journal* 16 (3):319–43.

McGuire, Steven, and Johan Lindeque. 2010. Diminishing Returns to Trade Policy in the European Union. *Journal of Common Market Studies* 48 (5):1027–47.

McGuire, Steven, Johan Lindeque, and Gabriele Suder. 2010. Learning and Lobbying: The Acquisition of Corporate Political Capabilities by Emerging Market Firms. Paper presented at the Strategic Management Society Annual Meeting, September, Rome.

McGuire, Steven, and Michael Smith. 2008. *The European Union and the United States: Competition and Convergence in the Global Arena.* Basingstoke: Palgrave Press.

Manger, Mark. 2005. Competition and Bilateralism in Trade Policy: The Case of Japan's Free Trade Agreements. *Review of International Political Economy* 12 (5):804–28.

Mantere, Saku, Kalle Pajunen, and Juha-Antti Lamberg. 2009. Vices and Virtues of Corporate Political Activity. *Business and Society* 48 (1):105–32.

Goldstein, Judith, and Richard Steinberg. 2009. Regulatory Shift: The Rise of Judicial Liberalisation at the WTO. In *The Politics of Global Regulation*, edited by Walter Mattli and Ngaire Woods, 211–241. Princeton: Princeton University Press.

Gomes Pereira, Matheus W., Erly Cardoso Teixeira, and Sharon Raszap-Skorbiansky. 2010. Impacts of the Doha Round on Brazilian, Chinese and Indian Agribusiness. *China Economic Review* 21 (2): 256–71.

Mattli, Walter, and Ngaire Woods. 2009. Introduction. In *The Politics of Global Regulation*, edited by Mattli and Woods, ix. Princeton: Princeton University Press.

Mayer, Michael, and Richard Whittington. 2004. Economics, Politics and Nations: Resistance to the Multidivisional Form in France, Germany, and the United Kingdom 1983–1993. *Journal of Management Studies* 41 (7):1057–82.

Narlikar, Amrita. 2010. New Powers in the Club: The Challenges of Global Trade Governance. *International Affairs* 86 (3):717–28.

Perez-Esteve, Maria. 2010. The Influence of Intergovernmental Non-State Actors in Multilateral and Preferential Trade Agreements: A Question of Forum-Shopping? In *Governments, Non-State Actors and Trade Policy-Making*, edited by Capling and Low, 284–310. Cambridge: Cambridge University Press.

Piewitt, Martina. 2010. Participatory Governance in the WTO: How Inclusive is Global Civil Society? *Journal of World Trade* 44 (2):467–88.

Ramani, S. 2002. Who's Interested in Biotech? R&D Strategies, Knowledge Base and Market Sales of Indian Biotechnology Firms. *Research Policy* 31 (3):381–98.

Rugman, Alan, and Alain Verbeke. 2008. Firms and Public Policy. In *The Oxford Handbook of International Business*, edited by Alan Rugman, 228–56. Oxford: Oxford University Press.

Schattschneider, E. E. 1960. *The Semisovereign People.* New York: Holt, Reinhart and Winston.

Schneider, Ben Ross. 2010. Business Politics in Latin America: Patterns of Fragmentation and Centralization. In *The Oxford Handbook of Business and Government*, edited by David Coen, Wyn Grant, and Graham Wilson, 307–29. Oxford: Oxford University Press.

Sell, Susan. 2003. *Private Power, Public Law: The Globalization of Intellectual Property Rights.* Cambridge: Cambridge University Press.

Sell, Susan, and Aseem Prakash. 2004. Using Ideas Strategically: The Contest Between Business and NGO Networks in Intellectual Property Rights. *International Studies Quarterly* 48 (1):143–75.

Shaffer, Gregory, Michelle Ratton Sanchez, and Barbara Rosenberg. 2008. The Trials of Winning at the WTO: What Lies Behind Brazil's Success. *Cornell International Law Journal* 41 (2):383–501.

Shenkar, Oded. 2009. Business as International Politics. *Business and Politics* 11 (4):article 1.

Teteryatnikova, Mariya. 2008. R&D in the Network of International Trade: Multilateral versus Regional Trade Agreements. WTO Staff Working Paper ESRD-2009-03. Geneva: WTO.

Vogel, David. 1996. The Study of Business and Politics. *California Management Review* 38 (3):146–65.

Woll, Cornelia. 2008. *Firm Interests: How Governments Shape Business Lobbying on Global Trade*. Ithaca: Cornell University Press.

Woolcock, Stephen. 2010. Trade Policy. In *Policy-Making in the European Union*, edited by Helen Wallace, Mark Pollack, and Alasdair Young. Oxford: Oxford University Press.

PART V

SUBSTANCE OF THE AGREEMENTS

CHAPTER 16

....

TRADE IN MANUFACTURES AND AGRICULTURAL PRODUCTS: THE DANGEROUS LINK?

....

HELEN COSKERAN, DAN KIM,
AND AMRITA NARLIKAR

16.1 INTRODUCTION

THE issues of manufactures and agriculture are reassuringly not new to the multilateral trading system. The apparent bane of many trade negotiations is often the newness of issue: recall, for instance, conflicts that arose over the attempts to include services, Trade-Related Aspects of Intellectual Property Rights (TRIPS), and Trade-Related Investment Measures (TRIMs) into the Uruguay Round, or indeed the contestation that engulfed the 'Singapore issues' at the start of the Doha negotiations. The sources of difficulty in negotiating uncharted territory are multiple, and vary with the subject. But there are at least two general concerns that make states wary of exchanging concessions in new areas: the uncertainties that surround the distributive implications of such concessions, and also the fact that regulating these often requires multilateral rules to go behind borders into domestic jurisdictions. Admittedly, trade in manufactures and agriculture is not ridden with these types of controversies. Both areas fit within the General Agreement on Tariffs and Trade's (GATT) conventional domain, i.e. goods; and they are protected, in good part, through border measures (and also subsidies particularly in agriculture). And yet these are the two issues over which the Doha Development Agenda (DDA) negotiations have repeatedly broken down.

In this chapter, we analyse the difficulties that have dogged negotiations over trade in manufactures and agriculture. We examine the successes and failures in these areas historically. The two issues have enjoyed varied levels of success in GATT negotiations, with trade liberalization in manufactures having had more established roots and going further and deeper than agricultural liberalization. Interestingly, however, their different historical tracks notwithstanding, they show some important similarities in the Doha negotiations. While agriculture was always one of the most problematic issue areas in the multilateral trading regime (and remains so in the latest round), even the relatively unproblematic negotiations over manufactures—now known as non-agricultural market access (NAMA)—have begun to encounter unprecedented levels of difficulty. At least some of the testy problems in both areas are a product of the unfinished business of the previous rounds; others are a consequence of the additional expectations created by the DDA's commitment to development concerns. And both streams of liberalization—agriculture and NAMA—have collided in the negotiation process, with one issue area being held hostage to concessions in the other, thereby demonstrating the costs associated with negative issue linkage.

Our analysis divides up into two streams: NAMA and agriculture. Although the two areas involve trade in goods, and have become bound with each other as the Doha negotiations have progressed, via explicit issue linkage, the differing starting points for negotiators lead us to address two different aspects of the puzzle. In Section 16.2, focusing on NAMA, we address the question why, after a history of such success in bringing down trade barriers, have negotiators found themselves in recurrent deadlock? In Section 16.3, focusing on agriculture, we examine the extent to which difficulties today are a continuation of the problems that agricultural trade liberalization has traditionally encountered, and how far they are a product of interests and processes specific to the DDA.

Akin to the negotiation process itself, the discussion of the two issues moves hand in hand. In both the NAMA and agriculture sections, we first identify the importance of the issue and its scope. Our next step is to briefly outline the successes and failures that were achieved in NAMA and agriculture negotiations throughout the history of the GATT, and to also present an account of the interests and processes that contributed to particular outcomes. We then analyse the progress made (or lack thereof) in the Doha negotiations, through an analysis of the key landmark moments in the process so far. As we conduct the analysis for each issue area, we also deal with some cross-cutting issues that include the role of coalitional loyalties and explicit linkage strategies. Section 16.4 concludes.

16.2 NON-AGRICULTURAL MARKET ACCESS (NAMA)

Strictly speaking, non-agricultural market access (NAMA) is a relatively new term; negotiations on industrial and manufactured products prior to Doha functioned under the umbrella of the original GATT mandate, Article 28, entitled 'Tariff

Negotiations'. In rounds prior to the Uruguay Round, products which would now be considered to be covered by NAMA were essentially the only products being negotiated. Only in the Uruguay Round did a distinction of 'industrial tariffs' in contrast to other products (such as agriculture) emerge.[1] The Doha Mandate (paragraph 16) treats 'market access for non-agricultural products' separately from negotiations on agriculture, intellectual property, and investment measures.[2] NAMA negotiations encompass all traded goods not covered by the Agreement on Agriculture.[3] This comprises all industrial or manufactured goods, including chemicals, fuels, mining products, steel, pharmaceuticals, agricultural equipment, fisheries, and forestry products. Despite the increasing attention to issues relating to TRIPS, TRIMs, and agriculture since the Uruguay Round, NAMA covers by far the largest portion of global trade. Products and issues covered in NAMA currently account for approximately 90 per cent of global merchandise exports.[4]

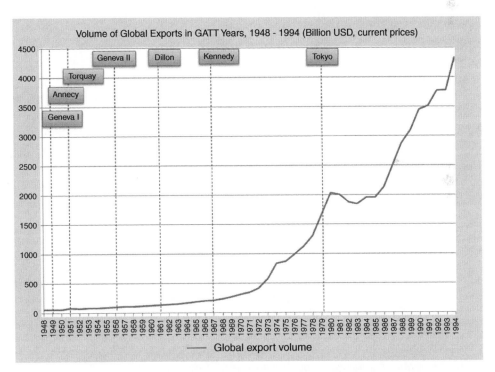

FIGURE 12 Global Exports Volume from 1948–1994 (in billion USD, current prices)

Source: Data from WTO statistics database <http://data.wto.org>

[1] Hoda 2001, 37.
[2] Negotiated in the newly created Negotiating Group on Market Access (WTO 2002a).
[3] Excludes products from chapters 1–24 of the World Customs Organization's Harmonized Commodity Coding and Classification System (HS), but includes fisheries and forestry.
[4] WTO website: <http://www.wto.org/english/tratop_e/markacc_e/nama_negotiations_e.htm>.

Though NAMA has emerged as one of the central causes of the Doha deadlocks (as this chapter illustrates), the roots of issues covered in the NAMA process go back to the GATT's creation in 1947. For decades, industrial goods were the only major issues covered in multilateral trade negotiations. Even after the launch of the Uruguay Round, and despite its focus on new issues, tariff reductions on industrial products formed a large part of the agenda. Figure 12 illustrates the increased global trade due to, at least in part, the significant reductions in tariff barriers that was achieved in previous rounds. Some have argued that because massive tariff cuts have already been achieved in previous GATT rounds and through subsequent unilateral trade liberalization, immediate welfare gains from NAMA might not be as high.[5] This, however, is a dangerous and short-sighted view. While definitively analysing the implications of the NAMA negotiations without a finished deal in place is difficult, several studies point to significant gains from a successful NAMA deal.[6] Patrick Messerlin, for instance, writes, 'one need only look to the real gold mine in the Doha negotiations on industrial products: in the present case, gold means "certainty"... The benefits of binding in the Doha Round stem from the elimination of the possibility that the emerging economies—40 per cent of the GDP of the rich countries—could increase their tariffs on average by 3.5 times (from roughly 8 to 28 per cent for industrial goods, and from roughly 19 to 66 per cent for agricultural products) at any time and without providing compensation to their WTO trading partners.'[7]

The stakes in NAMA negotiations are thus high, and the regime has a successful negotiating history in this area to boot. Why, then, have the current negotiations proven to be so difficult? To answer this, we examine below the factors that contributed to the successes of past negotiations, the limitations of those achievements, and the derivative and new difficulties faced by the Doha negotiators.

16.2.1 Early GATT negotiations: Geneva Round to the Tokyo Round

One of the most compelling warnings regarding the dangers of trade protectionism is captured in the protectionist policies of the interwar period. Following the stock market crash of 1929, the 1930 US Trade Act (the Smoot-Hawley Tariff Act) raised average US tariff rates on imports from 38 to 59 per cent. Trading nations retaliated with restrictions of their own, along with competitive currency devaluation in a spiralling series of 'beggar-thy-neighbour' policies, deepening the Great Depression.[8]

Following the war, the need for international cooperation to avoid such damaging protectionist policies was widely recognized and played a key role in negotiations. The

---

[5] Evenett 2007, for instance, argues that if the Doha gains were foregone, China would lose only three days of economic growth.

[6] Fisher 2006; Legrain 2006.

[7] Messerlin 2008.

[8] Narlikar 2005; Hoekman and Kostecki 2009.

efforts to create the International Trade Organization ran into difficulty, but a less ambitious agreement—the GATT—to negotiate multilateral tariff reductions was established.[9] The Geneva Round (1947), the first negotiating round, involving 23 countries, resulted in 45,000 tariff line concessions in industrial goods. Using an item-by-item negotiations tactic, the original 23 'contracting parties' made significant tariff cuts 'covering about half of world trade', estimated to affect $10 billion worth of global trade.[10] This process helped reduce the significantly inflated tariffs of the Great Depression and the Second World War.

The item-by-item (also known as 'request–offer') approach remained the main negotiation technique for the next four rounds (Annecy, 1949; Torquay, 1950–1; Geneva 1955–6; Dillon 1960–1). Relying on the principal supplier principle, this technique allowed trade negotiators in these early rounds to be precise, because they designated specific domestic products to liberalize. All products not on offer were exempt from liberalization.

The problem with the request–offer technique lay partly in its successes. Countries which already had low tariffs as a result of the first two rounds had little room to manoeuvre with this negotiating method. The Torquay conference generated fewer tariff reductions because of the disparities among tariff levels. Countries with low tariffs, particularly in Europe, had little to offer to 'obtain further concessions from countries with higher level tariffs'.[11] In 1953, France proposed an approach of linear tariff cuts across the board (with exceptions) to replace the 'request and offer' lists. The US negotiators, however, rejected this arguing that they lacked the legal authority from Congress to engage in across-the-board tariff negotiations.[12] In the Dillon Round, the European Economic Community's (EEC) proposal to use a formula-based approach to tariff cuts was again rejected, with negotiators wary of the proposal's ambitious nature.

Due to the 'strong political impetus of the Kennedy Administration and a deteriorating balance of payments', the US adopted the Trade Expansion Act of 1962, which gave the Executive authority to negotiate tariff cuts up to 50 per cent.[13] It is therefore unsurprising that the Kennedy Round (1964–7) introduced the new 'across-the-board formula approach' (linear cuts), where developed countries sought to cut average tariff by 50 per cent. A list of 'sensitive' items was made to allow exceptions to linear cuts, resulting in an overall tariff reduction of 35 per cent. The timing for the change was appropriate: amidst an increased membership of 74 countries, the request–offer method seemed inefficient and impractical.[14]

---

[9] Diebold 1952; Narlikar 2005.
[10] Hoekman and Kostecki 2009, 17.
[11] Hoda 2001, 28.
[12] Jackson 1969.
[13] Ibid, 224.
[14] Canada, Australia, New Zealand, and South Africa were exempt from the linear cuts, at their request, due to their dependence on primary products, but were expected to make equivalent concessions through the request–offer method. Hoda 2001, 36.

The Kennedy Round also saw a significant expansion of membership to include developing countries. They demanded special status within the multilateral trading system (leading to the drafting of Part IV of the GATT) and were allowed relatively high trade barriers and preferential access to export markets. Non-tariff measures were also negotiated, including the codes on anti-dumping and customs valuations.

The Tokyo Round (1973–9) utilized a non-linear 'Swiss formula' by developed countries (albeit with several exceptions). Unlike the linear approach, the non-linear formula essentially created a tariff ceiling at a chosen coefficient. Countries with high tariffs were therefore expected to make sharper tariff cuts in percentage terms. The Round resulted in reductions of about 33,000 bound tariff lines, affecting about $300 billion worth of global trade. Weighted average tariff rates of manufactured products among developed economies were reduced to approximately 6 per cent, representing a 34 per cent reduction in tariff revenues. The Round also introduced 'codes' in which 'like-minded countries were able to cooperate without having all GATT members on board'. This 'GATT à la carte' approach arguably weakened the system by allowing countries to pick and choose the codes which suited their interests.[15]

The formula approach generated large tariff cuts. But not every contracting party was required to participate in the process given the exceptions that were allowed. Of the 76 negotiating parties, only 31 countries and the EEC participated in the Kennedy Round tariff cuts; 36 countries and the EC[16] took on industrial tariff cuts, out of 85 countries in the Tokyo Round.[17]

16.2.2 The Uruguay Round (1986–94)

The Punta del Este Ministerial Declaration, which launched the Uruguay Round in 1986, did not specify a preference for a formula or request–offer approach. Rather, it stated that tariff negotiations 'shall aim, by appropriate methods, to reduce or, as appropriate, eliminate tariffs, including the reduction or elimination of high tariffs and tariff escalation'. It further stated: 'Emphasis shall be given to the expansion of the scope of tariff concessions among all participants.'[18] The main proposals for the industrial tariff negotiations included the traditional request–offer approach to deal with tariff peaks and escalation (US), non-linear formulas (EC, Canada, and Switzerland), and complete elimination of tariffs on all industrial products without exception (Japan). Meanwhile, developing countries demanded 'standstill and rollback': that countries not introduce 'any new restrictive import measures' unless they demonstrated 'strict conformity' with GATT principles, and to 'phase out' trade-distorting practices inconsistent with the GATT, such as non-tariff barriers (NTBs) and voluntary export restraints.[19]

---

[15] Hoekman and Kostecki 2009, 137.
[16] The EEC became the European Commission (EC) on 1 July 1967.
[17] Hoda 2001, 67–8.   [18] GATT 1986b, 9.
[19] GATT 1986a.

Difficulties in reaching a common modality stalled negotiations for years. The Montreal mid-term meeting in 1988 still displayed diverging preferences among developed countries between non-linear formulas (EC) and sectoral approaches (US). The July 1993 Tokyo accord from the Quad (US, Canada, EC, Japan) signalled a major breakthrough.[20] This agreement, at US insistence, included 'zero for zero' proposals to eliminate tariffs in a common list of product sectors. The accord sought to cut tariffs by an average of a third for products outside the listed 'zero for zero' sectors. Only a few developing countries agreed to participate in the sectoral agreements.[21] For most others, concessions involved binding the maximum number of products, usually at a very high rate. In contrast to past negotiations, every country in the Uruguay Round participated in tariff concessions, resulting in significant expansion of product coverage. For developed countries, 99 per cent of tariff lines were bound—up from 78 per cent; meanwhile developing economies bound 73 per cent—up from 21 per cent—as a result of the Round. Tariff averages were decreased overall (from 6.3 per cent to 3.8 per cent for developed countries). But the following trade predictability issues remained:[22]

- The differences between bound and applied tariffs ('water') remained high for both developing and developed economies.
- Tariff peaks (typically +15 per cent) and high tariffs persisted for certain protected products, particularly exports from developing economies. Among developed countries, peaks were particularly problematic for clothing, textiles, and leather goods.[23]
- Tariff escalation (low tariffs for raw materials and higher tariffs for finished products) issues remained.
- Some unbound tariffs remained, especially from developing countries.

Developing countries felt disenfranchised as no credit was given for the unilateral trade liberalization measures that they had already undertaken. Furthermore, the costs of implementing non-tariff measures (such as sanitary and phytosanitary measures (SPS) and technical barriers to trade (TBT)) were much higher than expected. This increased the potential of creating net losers of the multilateral trading system, which contributed to heightened caution among developing countries about furthering market access.[24]

16.2.3 The Doha Development Agenda

In the DDA, NAMA did not start out as a contested issue (compared, for example, to agriculture or the Singapore issues). The unfinished business of the Uruguay Round, along with the implementation costs issue, provided the natural focal points for NAMA negotiations.

[20] GATT 1993. [21] Hoda 2001, 38–9. [22] WTO 2001a.
[23] Hoekman and Kostecki 2009. [24] Finger and Schuler 2000.

The Doha Mandate (2001) assigned the Negotiation Group on Market Access (NGMA) to address NAMA concerns. The Doha Mandate paragraph aimed to not only increase trade liberalization, but also to enhance its predictability and consistency in a comprehensive manner. The 'less than full reciprocity' (LTFR) principle, exempting developing countries from the expectation of providing full reciprocity in trade concessions, would continuously play an important role in the negotiations as well.

North–South and South–South divide—slow decisions on modalities

As the negotiations for the modalities began in 2002, it was clear that no immediate consensus would be found. South Korea and Japan, both export-driven economies with relatively low tariff rates, welcomed a 'formula approach', with limited use of the request–offer approach when necessary.[25] China, India, and Kenya were reluctant to accept a formula approach, and instead preferred the request–offer approach, though they did not necessarily share a common reason for this preference. China argued that its liberalization efforts as part of its accession process were already a heavy burden to bear. India maintained relatively high tariff rates and feared that a formula approach would require serious market openings without much in return; it emphasized the LTFR principle and called for a provision to keep certain domestically sensitive products as unbound.[26] Meanwhile, Kenya (and later Nigeria) shared the fear of many African countries of losing significant tariff revenues upon which their governments relied, and argued that 'tariffs are a tool for developing countries'.[27]

While many developing countries showed reluctance in furthering market access, the US Trade Representative (USTR), in November 2002, proposed eliminating tariffs on almost all consumer and industrial products for all WTO members by 2015.[28] Though Australia and New Zealand, both with low tariffs, approved of this proposal, the European Union (EU)[29] deemed it unrealistic. Japan also supported the idea of a 'zero for zero' tariff approach, submitting a list of products which should bear zero tariffs (but insisted on excluding fisheries and forestry products).[30] The ambition levels among the WTO membership displayed a dominant North–South division, and also latent South–South divisions.

Initial debates revealed the main tensions that would prevail in subsequent negotiations. Four main categories of interests emerged.[31] In the first group were the industrialized countries, which already had low tariffs and aimed for further market access in the developing world (US, Japan, and Australia displaying high ambition, while the EU was more cautious). The second comprised the rising powers (Brazil, India, and South Africa were the most influential), who were reluctant to open their markets without a

---

[25] WTO 2002b; WTO 2002c.   [26] WTO 2002e.   [27] WTO 2003b.
[28] *The Economist*, 30 November 2002: Trading Insults—New Talk of Tariff Cuts.
[29] The EU was established in 1993.   [30] WTO 2003c.
[31] Not to be confused with official negotiating coalitions within NAMA: <http://www.wto.org/english/tratop_e/markacc_e/nama_groups_e.htm>.

balanced outcome between NAMA and agriculture. The third group included developing countries with low tariffs (such as South Korea, Chile, Colombia, Singapore, Thailand, and Mexico), in search of a middle ground. While they did not share the ambition levels of the developed countries, they had some offensive interests in gaining market access as industrial exporters and did not wish to be represented by the rising powers. The fourth group comprised developing countries seeking exemptions. These included least-developed countries (LDCs) and small and vulnerable economies (SVEs) relying on tariff revenues, and recently acceded members (RAMs) who had made significant concessions as part of their WTO accession. The African and African, Caribbean, and Pacific countries (ACP) groups had particularly defensive interests, consistently arguing for special and differential treatment (SDT) to protect their preferential market access.[32]

These four broad divisions, each with markedly varying degrees of ambition, made framing the negotiation itself a difficult issue. The majority of the proposals favoured a formula-based approach, but there was no consensus on this and even less agreement on exceptions allowed.[33] Norway and Chile, for example, favoured the formula approach with a ceiling for all tariffs to prevent tariff peaks.[34] But India and Kenya (among other African countries) opposed a formula-based approach, arguing that it would complicate ensuring LTFR for developing countries.

The sectoral approach, which aimed to significantly reduce or eliminate tariffs on selected production sectors, also proved controversial. For countries which had earlier proposed the elimination of almost all industrial tariffs—primarily the US and Japan—the sectoral approach was a major concession. Developed countries (particularly the US and Canada) demanded mandatory participation in the sectorals, while developing countries maintained that participation should be voluntary. The controversy came in part from the proposal to make no exceptions (not even for LDCs) in the agreed sectors. With such diverging preferences in ambition, a deal looked unlikely.

The Cancún collapse and issue linkage

While the four groupings mentioned above represented broad trade interests, the contestations within the early negotiations mostly displayed a North–South divide. The Singapore issues and agriculture provided the proximate cause of the collapse, but NAMA negotiators fared no better. Disagreements over the use of the formulas and sectorals persisted. Issue linkage between agriculture and NAMA began to emerge as the 'mini G20' expressed reluctance to move on NAMA until 'concrete results' were shown in agriculture.[35]

---

[32] WTO 2005a (African Group); WTO 2005d (ACP Group of States).

[33] WTO 2003d.

[34] WTO 2002d (Norway); WTO 2002f (Chile).

[35] Argentina, Brazil, China, Colombia, India, Indonesia, Malaysia, the Philippines, and Venezuela; *ICTSD Bridges Weekly Trade News Digest*, 21 August 2003: North–South Divide Persists as WTO Market Access Talks Move Towards Cancún.

In June 2004, the US, Canada, and Hong Kong explored a 'critical mass' approach to eliminate tariffs in certain products (such as aluminium), leaving room for some countries to opt out. For them—and in particular the US—the critical mass approach signalled a significant compromise. Brazil countered by stating that any such movement would entirely depend on 'positive outcomes in agriculture' and other NAMA considerations. At the trade negotiations committee, Brazil pledged to 'maintain its position on the principle of total and complete linkage of NAMA to agriculture and on the overall development components of this Round'.[36] Whereas the developed countries preferred the sectoral approach, Brazil stood behind the principle of the 'single undertaking'.[37] Because any significant movement on NAMA was implicitly dependent on the agriculture negotiations, the July 2004 framework on NAMA only offered a vague text.

The July 2004 framework ('Annex B')

'Annex B' of the July 2004 framework identified three negotiation issues: the formula, sectorals, and flexibilities for developing countries. Developing countries refused to negotiate on sectoral aspects of NAMA until the formula was agreed upon. The US and Canada preferred addressing the sectoral approach in parallel with the formula discussions, with the 'critical mass' principle in mind (which allows for exceptions). In March 2005, the US conceded that it would agree to the principle of 'dual coefficients' (where developing countries would make smaller tariff cuts) as long as members accepted the Swiss formula involving the sharper reduction of higher tariffs, and flexibilities would be excluded altogether.[38]

Developing countries, particularly Brazil, China, and India, objected to this proposal on the grounds that it violated the LTFR principle, and remained reluctant to agree to a Swiss formula. In April 2005, Argentina, Brazil, and India submitted a NAMA proposal suggesting a modified version of the Swiss formula, designed to determine the coefficient by reflecting each member's overall (average) tariff level.[39] Such a formula favours countries with existing high tariffs. The proposal also left the door open for exclusion of developing country tariff lines. US negotiators warned that delivery on agriculture would be unlikely without a 'significant commercially meaningful result on NAMA'.[40] Many developing (particularly Latin American) countries were critical of the proposal for inadequately addressing tariff peaks, while the Association of Southeast Asian Nations (ASEAN) countries criticized its treatment of unbound tariffs.[41] These reactions signalled the depth of South–South divisions. While Brazil and India provided the most effective and vocal defensive opposition to the developed countries, the chilly reception to their NAMA proposal showed that they could not take the mantle of leadership of the South for granted.

---

[36] WTO 2004b.   [37] Ibid.   [38] WTO 2005c.   [39] WTO 2005b.
[40] ICTSD *Bridges Weekly Trade News Digest*, 27 April 2005: Members Discuss Argentina–Brazil–India Proposal.
[41] Ibid.

Hong Kong Ministerial (December 2005)

With the Hong Kong Ministerial approaching, there was little convergence on NAMA issues. Many developing countries called for a large gap between the 'dual coefficients' as well as keeping flexibilities to exclude sensitive items from the formula cuts. The US and EU argued that flexibilities should be abolished with lenient formulas if real market access were to be realized.

The Hong Kong Declaration officially adopted the Swiss formula, with coefficients yet to be determined. The US and EU initially called for coefficients of 10 and 15 for developed and developing countries, respectively. The WTO Secretariat had calculated that a coefficient of 15 would require Brazil to cut its average bound tariffs by between 61.7 per cent and 65.2 per cent (depending on product exemptions), while India would be required to make 63.5 per cent to 70.4 per cent cuts. A coefficient of 30 would require both countries to cut tariffs by 45 to 55 per cent.[42] Developed countries argued that such a low coefficient was the only way to ensure enhanced market access, because bound tariff levels were already high and applied tariffs would not be significantly lowered otherwise. Developing countries with high tariffs argued that it was too high a price to pay, especially without a guarantee on agriculture.

The Ministerial also saw the emergence of the NAMA-11 coalition. This coalition pursued issue linkage relentlessly, and was successful insofar as its efforts resulted in the official recognition of a 'comparably high level of ambition in market access for Agriculture and NAMA'.[43] The coalition also argued for 'at least a 25 [Swiss formula] points difference for developed and developing countries'.[44] From this point onwards, the negative issue linkage between agriculture and NAMA was used by both developed and developing countries to dig their heels in.

Developments in 2006 to early 2007

Attempts to negotiate a deal among the G6—the US, EU, Japan, India, Brazil, and Australia—in summer 2006 resulted in further deadlock, with a persistent divergence in the ambitions of the developed and developing countries. Having cut many of their industrial tariffs (weighted average after the Uruguay Round was below 4 per cent), developed countries demanded significant concessions on access to developing country markets. Meanwhile, developing economies had little assurance from developed economies that 'comparable levels of ambition' would be shown in the Lamy 'triangle' of agriculture market access, agriculture domestic support, and NAMA. And the debate on disciplining non-tariff barriers had scarcely begun.

The role of coalitions also provides a key piece of the deadlock puzzle. NAMA-11 was certainly a vocal and cohesive group, but so too were other developing country coali-

---

[42] WTO 2006b.   [43] WTO 2005e.
[44] WTO 2006c; NAMA-11 includes Argentina, Brazil, Egypt, India, Indonesia, Namibia, Philippines, South Africa, Tunisia, and Venezuela.

tions. At least six such groups played a role in the NAMA negotiations: the African group, MERCOSUR, G90,[45] LDC group, SVE-NAMA group, NAMA-11, and Paragraph 6 (NAMA) countries (those with under 35 per cent of NAMA products covered by legally bound tariff ceilings, who wanted more exemptions).

The cohesion between India and Brazil also played an integral part in the negotiations, and the resulting deadlock. These rising powers held their positions well in the G6 negotiations,[46] and continued to do so in the G4 meetings[47] in March 2007. Together (and with the help of NAMA-11), they insisted that the gap between the two coefficients should be at least 25 points to meet the LTFR principle, and resisted pressures from developed countries. Despite the US offering to bind its agricultural domestic support, G4 meetings failed to achieve a consensus. Brazil explained that a Swiss formula coefficient of even 30 would result in a 25 per cent reduction in its tariff lines, whereas the US proposal to cap trade-distorting domestic support (at $17 billion) still allowed room for the US to increase its support from the previous year. In reference to the offers on agriculture and NAMA, the Brazilian Minister, Amorim, declared that 'The exchange rate being asked was too high.'[48]

July 2008 Package

The second half of 2007, and 2008, offered some progress on agriculture negotiations (see below), but the NAMA process became more polarized. MERCOSUR's request in November 2007, led by Brazil and Argentina, to be granted extra flexibilities for developing country customs unions was followed by the threat from China and its allies to block any deal which failed to grant RAMs flexibilities of their own.[49] These requests were met with immediate criticism from developed countries and developing countries alike.[50] The issue of flexibilities for customs unions added further contention to the NAMA debate. In this context, the Chair's text in May 2008 failed to achieve consensus, yet again. The proposal called for a 'sliding scale of coefficients'[51] with the option for further flexibilities. This met with familiar criticism by developed countries, particularly the US, arguing that the sliding scale provided sufficient flexibilities and therefore further flexibilities (that is, ability to exempt products) should not be granted. Meanwhile, the NAMA-11 still believed the burden of tariff cuts was skewed unfavourably towards developing countries.

Deadlock over the Chair's text led to the suspension of talks on 2 June, which did not bode well for the upcoming ministerial in July 2008. While informal NAMA talks in the

---

[45] Including the African Group, the African, Caribbean, and Pacific Group of States (ACP) and least-developed countries (LDCs).

[46] US, EU, Japan, India, Brazil, and Australia.

[47] US, EU, India, and Brazil.

[48] *Bloomberg*, 21 June 2007: WTO Talks Break Down Over Farm Aid.

[49] WTO 2007.

[50] Reuters, 8 November 2007: US, EU Have to Settle for Less in Doha—Mendelson.

[51] Countries would designate product-specific coefficients within a band of coefficients which meets a minimum average tariff reduction; the text proposed coefficients between 8 and 9 for developed countries, and between 19 and 23 for developing countries.

'Green Room' resumed in anticipation of the ministerial, countries were still far apart on the core issues of tariff cuts and flexibilities, with South Africa especially unhappy with the deal at hand.[52]

The July 2008 deadlock centred primarily on agriculture (see next section). But the breakdown in the NAMA process just a month prior to the July talks did not help. The negative linkage between agriculture and NAMA reappeared, with a Chinese official weighing up the concessions proposed by the US on agricultural subsidies against its own NAMA demands: 'Trade-distorting subsidies are illegal while tariffs are legal measures of protection.'[53] Firm opposition to sectoral agreements by China also proved difficult to overcome. Such sudden hardline opposition from China caused a US negotiator to state: 'it was like the man behind the curtain finally came out'.[54] While there would have been significant opposition to any NAMA–agriculture linked deal outside of the 'inner group', even the small inner core failed to reach agreement.[55]

Recent developments

Since the breakdown of talks in July 2008, NAMA negotiators made one more notable text-based attempt to settle the core issues of formula cuts and flexibilities, resulting in the December 2008 text.[56] Developed countries subsequently made renewed efforts to deal with the sectorals issue, attempting to find some product sectors to liberalize with a critical mass. But disagreement persisted on all core issues of tariff formulas, flexibilities, and sectorals. Overall, issue linkage between NAMA and agriculture continued to stall negotiations. A proposal by Mexico in February 2011 to allow negotiators to make trade-offs across agriculture and NAMA was rejected by the US, citing a lack of ambition in market access.[57] Major players in the G11 Ministerial Meeting in late February 2011 struggled to deal with the difficulties of issue linkage between NAMA and agriculture.[58]

16.3 AGRICULTURE

While the previous section analysed the difficulties posed by NAMA, we now examine the politics of agricultural negotiations. Agricultural trade reform is a major priority and source of contention and deadlock in the DDA. And not for the first time. In the following analysis, we focus on attempts in the GATT and WTO to liberalize agricultural trade. In contrast to

---

[52] WTO 2008a; Reuters, 17 July 2008: Industry Talks Edge Forward Before WTO Meeting.

[53] *Wall Street Journal*, 29 July 2008: China Defends its Right on High Tariffs; China joined the US, EU, Australia, Brazil, and India in the 'inner group' of the negotiations.

[54] Ibid.

[55] WTO 2008b.

[56] WTO 2008c.

[57] Reuters, 4 February 2011: US Rejects Mexico Plan for Doha Trade Deal.

[58] Reuters, 22 February 2011: Lamy, WTO Members Say Doha Talks not Fast Enough. G11 consisted of Argentina, Australia, Brazil, Canada, China, EU, India, Mauritius, South Africa, and the US.

NAMA, where we see a record of relative success in the GATT years (versus deadlock in the WTO), agriculture reveals itself to be the bête noire of both the GATT and the WTO.

Annex 1 of the WTO Agreement on Agriculture (AoA) defines 'agriculture' as all products from Chapters 1–24 of the World Customs Organization's Harmonized Commodity Coding and Classification System (HS), excluding fish products and forestry.[59] This covers basic products such as fruit, coffee beans, dairy products, and wheat, but also compound products like chocolate, sausages, wines, spirits, tobacco, fibres, and raw animal skins.[60] The definition of tropical products, of particular interest in developing countries, has been an ongoing point of contention. The less than obvious exclusion and inclusion of certain products in the WTO's definition of agriculture is one indication of its sensitive nature.

As agriculture at the WTO encompasses major agro-food products, its regulation in multilateral trade is seen as vital to governments and their populations. Evidence suggests that overall trade liberalization brought about by concluding the full DDA could result in gains up to $300 billion (63 per cent or $189 billion of which would derive from agriculture liberalization).[61] But, as with any liberalization, some groups face potential losses, including producers which benefit from domestic support and net food-importing countries (NFIC), which could risk a short-term increase in food import prices. Because the global agriculture market has multiple trade distortions (tariffs, subsidies, export restrictions), the outcome of any partial liberalization is difficult to predict. However, these groups could gain through increased export potential for non-agricultural products in which they have a comparative advantage. Further, the long-term benefits of lowered import prices and predictability of trade through increased competition outweigh the potential short-term uncertainties. The conflicting interests of food exporters and importers, developed and developing countries, and large and small states provide a backdrop to understanding the processes and outcomes of agricultural negotiations since 1947.

16.3.1 Early years of the GATT

Trade in agriculture has been governed by exceptions since before the early years of the GATT. Protectionist agriculture policies contributed to the heavy costs of protectionism and beggar-thy-neighbour policies of the interwar years. For example, the US Congress amended its Agricultural Adjustment Act (AAA) as part of the New Deal (in response to the increasingly volatile European export market) in 1935, to give full price support to farmers and provide further protection by permitting import quotas and subsidies for agriculture exports.[62] While many of these measures were repealed after the Second

---

[59] WTO 1995.
[60] Additional products from other chapters included in agriculture are mannitol and sorbitol, certain oils, hides and skin, silk, wool, and cotton. World Customs Organization 2007.
[61] Anderson and Martin 2005.   [62] Porter and Bowers 1989.

World War, such protectionist posturing sent a clear message that governments of major agriculture producers were willing to distort the global market to protect their domestic production. Even the idealistic Havana Charter of 1948 included several notable exceptions to agriculture, including clauses which would allow any protective measures to 'promote the establishment, development or reconstruction' of agriculture production.[63] While the United Kingdom, Canada, India, and Brazil fought to ban export subsidies in the text, the United States ensured exceptions were included on quantitative restrictions and subsidies (Article XX) to protect domestic price support programmes.[64]

The GATT 1947 text further displayed a lack of willingness to tackle agriculture liberalization. Articles 11 and 16 reflect the US demand for, essentially, a comprehensive exemption from regulation for both import restrictions (for 'any agricultural or fisheries product, imported in any form') and subsidies (of 'any primary product').[65] The trade and development principles outlined in Article 36 called for 'more favourable and acceptable conditions' of agriculture markets for developing countries; but the earlier articles allowing for several measures of market distortion would make this particular principle almost meaningless.[66] With these exemptions built in, the GATT was powerless to regulate heavy protectionist measures, such as the US Defense Production Act in the 1950s which allowed protectionist measures in agriculture for national security reasons.[67] A waiver was inserted in the GATT at the request of the US (upon the expiration of the Defense Production Act in 1955) to permit quotas on commodities benefiting from price support programmes. This further weakened the GATT as it gave other contracting parties a precedent to implement similar non-tariff barriers.[68]

Agricultural negotiations became a priority in the Kennedy Round, with the US concern that the EEC's Common Agricultural Policy (CAP) would negatively affect US agricultural exports to Europe.[69] The US and other major grain exporters had four major negotiation objectives for agriculture: increased market access to the EEC, and Japan in particular, by halving agricultural tariffs; increased minimum prices for wheat; better international grain supply; and a multilateral food aid programme.[70] Developing countries wanted more tariff reductions, particularly for tropical products.[71] Though the US recognized that liberalization of its own agricultural trade policy would be necessary to ensure reciprocal concessions from the EEC, the EEC was hesitant about negotiating over agriculture with internal CAP negotiations still at an early stage. The establishment of the CAP further restricted Europe's ability to make concessions.[72] The Round's agricultural negotiations were regarded as a failure by the US due to its dissatisfaction with the International Grain Agreement. And though some progress was made on tropical

---

[63] Havana Charter, Article 14.

[64] United Nations Economic and Social Council 1946a; United Nations Economic and Social Council 1946b.

[65] GATT 1947.   [66] Ibid.   [67] Stiles 1995.   [68] Ibid.

[69] Davis 2004 highlights the irony of this, since the exceptions to agriculture initially encouraged by the US were the very ones now hindering US market access to Europe.

[70] Hedges 1967.   [71] Johnson 1967.   [72] Hedges 1967.

product liberalization, complications due to colonial preferences meant developing countries 'got less than they hoped for'.[73]

The 1972–4 global grain shortage added impetus to the call for multilateral agricultural reform, as did the developing world's call for a New International Economic Order (NIEO) and the negotiation of international commodity agreements.[74] Agriculture was included in the six-point Tokyo Round agenda set in 1973. Here, the US, EC, and Japan were joined by Brazil, Mexico, Australia, and Canada at the inner core of the negotiations.

The six elements of the negotiations were presented as 'one undertaking' in the declaration launching the Round. The EC and Japan supported a separate negotiation strategy for agriculture, however, despite US support for a link between agriculture and manufactures. Ultimately the US conceded, and subgroups on commodities such as dairy, meat, and grains were created. In some cases, agreement was successfully arrived at, such as meat and dairy (though governments could still pick and choose which of these agreements to sign). Other areas proved more complicated: the subgroup on wheat, for example, was made redundant as discussions were conducted in the UNCTAD (not GATT).[75] As a result, the EC and US continued with their wheat support policies, leading to the 1980s 'subsidy wars', during which both increased their domestic support, with significant consequences for their own budgets and with negative implications for agricultural exporters from developing countries.

16.3.2 The Uruguay Round

Against the backdrop of subsidy wars between the US and the EC in the early 1980s, the Uruguay Round was launched. In the early years of the Uruguay Round, the US was adamant that EC export subsidies should be eliminated, with its non-negotiable position on this known as 'zero option'.[76] At the 1988 mid-term review, particularly influenced by domestic dairy and sugar lobbies, the US did not stray from this position. The Cairns Group of agriculture-exporting countries also refused to sign a deal that excluded agriculture. The linkage of agriculture to 14 other working groups caused all talks to break down. The mid-term review established the three separate negotiating pillars of market access, domestic support, and export subsidies.

In an attempt to hammer out differences, Arthur Dunkel (the GATT Director-General) drafted a Chair's text. On agriculture, the draft proposed an export subsidy reduction of 36 per cent, the conversion of non-tariff barriers on agricultural goods to tariffs, and a 20 per cent domestic support reduction.[77] But major and persistent disagreements between the EC and the US rendered agreement elusive. These differences were finally overcome in the November 1992 'Blair House Accord', in which they agreed to the following:

---

[73] Johnson 1967, 330.   [74] Narlikar 2003.   [75] McRae and Thomas 1983.
[76] GATT 1987b; GATT 1987a.   [77] GATT 1991.

- A 21 per cent average export subsidy reduction
- Reduction of subsidy levels would be based on 1991–2, rather than 1986–90, which would initially raise subsidy levels
- An exemption of direct income payments (for example the EC's CAP) from domestic support rules (leading to the creation of the 'blue box')
- An initial agreement to reduce domestic support was replaced with a general commitment to reduce overall support.[78]

These bilateral talks broke the deadlock between the major powers, eventually resulting in the AoA.[79] New export subsidies were forbidden and agricultural tariffs were bound, with the aim of improving market access. Domestic support was tackled in the Aggregate Measure of Support (AMS), which categorized trade-distorting support into three 'boxes' (amber, green, and blue), depending on the degree of trade distortion, support mechanism (such as price supports), and quantitative effect on overall production. The agreement also included provisions on NTBs such as SPS.

These achievements were important, but had many limitations. The EC and US were able to use the domestic support clause to meet overall commitments in products of limited importance while still retaining protectionism on products of interest to developing countries. Developing countries would, moreover, face significant costs of implementing the SPS Agreement.[80] The only evidence of addressing net food importer concerns was the inclusion of Article 16 in the Final Act, requiring a 'Decision on Measures Concerning the Possible Negative Effects of the Reform Programme on Least-Developed and Net Food-Importing Developing Countries'.[81] A North–South divide was evident, with developing countries especially dissatisfied with the overall final outcome.

16.3.3 Doha Development Agenda

Similar to NAMA, much unfinished business remained at the end of the Uruguay Round. Article 20 of the AoA provided for the launch of a new round of agricultural negotiations in 2000. Deep divisions were evident in meetings even before the DDA launch in November 2001, especially on the issue of subsidies. The US argued for a simplification of categories of domestic support into 'exempt support' (minimal trade or production distortion) and 'non-exempt support' (subject to reduction commitment) in order to protect those under its Agricultural Market Transition Payments programme—not substantially different from the AoA's box principles.[82] The EU was willing to negotiate subsidy reductions on the condition that other forms of export competition were included.[83] Japan's reluctance to attempt another major agriculture liberalization while implementing the AoA (especially the box system) was evident in its proposal in

[78] Healy, Pearce, and Stockbridge 1998.   [79] WTO 1995, Annex 1a.
[80] Narlikar 2005.   [81] WTO 1995.   [82] WTO 2000c.   [83] WTO 2000c.

December 2000.[84] The Cairns Group, meanwhile, made it clear that the abolition of subsidies—particularly from the EU—was one of its priorities, and demanded an immediate reduction of 50 per cent.[85] Non-trade concerns were also relevant, with the EU making linkages to animal welfare and food safety[86] (labelled as protectionist by the Cairns Group) and India proposing the inclusion of a 'food security box' for developing countries.[87]

Amidst such disagreement, the Doha Ministerial's proposed commitment to agricultural trade reform was impressive: 'comprehensive negotiations' aimed at the creation of a 'fair and market-oriented trading system through a programme of fundamental reform…in order to correct and prevent restrictions and distortions in world agricultural markets'.[88] With the goal of making substantial progress on all three pillars, plus ensuring LTFR, Doha negotiators had quite a task at hand.

Modalities phase (2002–3)

The modalities debate centred on tariff formulas and a schedule for subsidy reductions. In June 2002, the US proposed elimination of export subsidies within five years,[89] while the Cairns Group argued that this should be done in three years.[90] The EU was opposed, and linked discussion on export subsidies to other forms of export competition such as export credits (which the US used) and state trading enterprises (mainly used in Cairns Group countries).[91] The Cairns Group also demanded phasing out the amber and blue boxes and restricting the green box, whereas the Friends of Multi-functionality[92] were adamant that the blue box be retained.[93]

The Agriculture Chair submitted a draft in February proposing a tariff-cutting formula, abolition of 50 per cent of subsidies in five years and all subsidies in nine years, and maintenance of all boxes, albeit with more disciplines.[94] On all three of these pillars, the LTFR principle was taken into account via SDT. The draft met with disappointment from the EU, who described it as 'unbalanced, spreading the burden very unevenly amongst the developed countries' and showing an 'absence of ambition with respect to tariff- and quota-free access for the least-developed countries'.[95] The US and Cairns Group were similarly disappointed with the text's lack of ambition in domestic support and market access.[96] The 31 March modalities deadline was missed, with continuing discord over the Chair's text.

---

[84] WTO 2000f.   [85] WTO 2000a.   [86] WTO 2000b.
[87] WTO 2001b.
[88] WTO 2001c, Article 13.
[89] Reuters, 4 June 2002: US Urges WTO To Set Farm Export Subsidy Deadline.
[90] Cairns Group 2002.
[91] Reuters, 4 June 2002: US Urges WTO To Set Farm Export Subsidy Deadline.
[92] European Union, Norway, Japan, South Korea, and Switzerland.
[93] *WTO Reporter*, 25 September 2002: Agriculture: Japanese Official sets out Position in Farm Talks, Criticises US, Cairns Group.
[94] WTO 2003a.
[95] European Commission 2003.
[96] United States Trade Representative 2003.

Cancún Ministerial (2003)

Ongoing disagreements on agriculture were primary catalysts for the Cancún Ministerial collapse in September 2003. Leading up to the Ministerial, four LDCs submitted a proposal for a sectoral initiative on cotton.[97] An EU/US joint text on agriculture proposed adjustments to the blue box; a 'blended formula' (a combination of linear and non-linear formulas) with a remaining 'duty-free' category, which would allow countries to decide themselves which products should be subject to which formula; reduction rather than elimination of *de minimis* spending in the amber box;[98] and an extension of the AoA's 'Peace Clause', which would prevent members from bringing disciplinary action on measures legal under the clause but illegal under other WTO agreements.[99]

The text prompted several reactions, including a proposal by the G20 coalition,[100] which advocated more SDT, attention to 'special products', and the inclusion of a special safeguards mechanism (SSM).[101] The G33 coalition emerged at Cancún, with defensive interests (more so than the G20, since the G33 consisted of mainly net importers) supporting special products and SSM proposals. The G90 submitted proposals on behalf of the LDCs, strongly opposing the 'blended formula' and proposing instead an overall target for developed country tariff reductions.[102] The US focused on reducing developing country tariffs in agriculture and lowering EU export subsidies, while the EU wanted to widen the 'export subsidies' pillar to include export competition such as export credits and food aid. The Chair drafted a text on agriculture which attempted a last-ditch compromise, but the talks broke down before this could even be discussed.

July Framework (2004)

Negotiations picked up again in 2004 among a core group of countries known as the Five Interested Parties (FIPs): the EU, US, Brazil, India, and Australia. The process prompted rumblings of discontent by countries not directly involved in these consultations (a pattern that re-emerged in subsequent negotiations). The negotiations resulted in some progress with the creation of the July Package, which laid out the following framework for the negotiations:

- The elimination of export subsidies and disciplines on food aid, while considering the needs of developing NFICs and LDCs.
- Capping blue box spending at 5 per cent of total agricultural production and the reduction of *de minimis* spending (excluding countries supporting subsistence farmers). A review of green box subsidies, with an immediate reduction from major subsidizers.

---

[97] WTO 2003e.

[98] *De minimis* spending refers to the amount allocated to trade-distorting subsidies categorized under the amber box.

[99] WTO 2003.   [100] Narlikar and Tussie 2004.

[101] WTO 2003f.   [102] WTO 2003g.

- The adoption of a tiered approach in tariff-cutting, in which higher tariffs would face deeper cuts, the inclusion of some SDT and LDC exemptions, and an agreement that all countries would be able to choose the products to be treated as 'special'.[103]

While the July Package represented some progress, many serious issues remained. The most contentious details of an agreement on agriculture, including end dates for elimination of subsidies, a formula, SSM, and classification of green box subsidies, were still to be reached.

Hong Kong Ministerial (2005)

The July Framework called for the full modalities to be set at the Hong Kong Ministerial in December 2005, yet little progress was made in the interim. A pre-ministerial EU submission proposed methods and levels for cutting domestic support and tariffs, a request to exempt certain EU products as special products, and a commitment to subsidy elimination.[104] The US proposed the elimination of export subsidies by 2010, while calling for high tariff cuts and substantial reductions in domestic support.[105] The G20 argued that neither proposal went far enough in cutting tariffs.[106] The G33 continued to emphasize the importance of special and differential treatment.[107] The G10 also submitted a paper opposing tariff cuts which would negatively impact their heavily protected agricultural sectors.[108] In an effort to avoid being blamed for the Ministerial's failure, the EU submitted a second paper, which incorporated the proposal made by India and Brazil earlier to link agricultural negotiations to NAMA (as discussed in Section 16.2). However, it also demanded high cuts from the developing world. Unsurprisingly, not much was achieved on agriculture at Hong Kong, except for an agreement on the end date for export subsidy elimination (2013).

Modalities meetings (2006)

Throughout 2006, efforts to resolve the ongoing modalities issues over agriculture continued. In April, the G6 (Australia, Brazil, the EU, India, Japan, and the US) met to discuss the selection of 'special products'. The July Framework stipulated that market access in those products should be improved, based on both tariff cuts and tariff rate quotas (TRQs). Whereas the US and G20 wanted TRQ calculation to be based on domestic consumption, the EU and G10 preferred a 'hybrid' solution based on how much a product was protected. Both the G10 and EU revised this at the April meeting and agreed that domestic consumption would form a part of the calculation. But the link between NAMA and agriculture reappeared; the EU refused to further improve

---

[103] WTO 2004a.   [104] European Commission 2005.
[105] United States Trade Representative 2005.
[106] Hanrahan and Schnepf 2005.   [107] G33 2005.
[108] Hanrahan and Schnepf 2005.

its agriculture offer on the grounds that the developing world was not conceding enough on NAMA. Special products and SSM also continued to play an important role, with the G33 refusing to commit to any modalities which did not include these two subjects.[109]

These issues came together in the July meeting of the Trade Negotiations Committee. Pascal Lamy proposed a '20-20-20 package': a G20 proposal to cut tariffs in agriculture by a 54 per cent average; binding US subsidies at $20 billion; and a Swiss formula with a coefficient of 20 on developing country manufactured products.[110] Once again, the G6 was unable to reach agreement. Lamy blamed this on a 'triangle of issues': EU unwillingness to lower agricultural tariffs, US unwillingness to lower farm subsidies, and India and Brazil's unwillingness to lower industrial tariffs. Much finger-pointing followed.[111] Lamy suspended the Round until February 2007; subsequent talks between the EU, US, Brazil, and India, in Potsdam in June 2007, broke down over the same 'triangle'.[112]

July Package (2008)

Another attempt to agree on modalities was made in July 2008 among the G7 (i.e. the G6 plus China). While NAMA talks had broken down earlier in the summer, a deal on agriculture now looked more promising, with progress on setting specific formulas as well as tariff and subsidy ceilings. However, the talks collapsed again over two issues. First, while Brazil urged its G20 allies to accept the US offer to cap its domestic subsidies at $14.5 billion, China and India firmly refused. The G20 did not collapse, but it came close; its precarious unity at the time was maintained through much negotiation and agreement to follow the Chinese and Indian position (making a deal unlikely). Second, dispute arose over the trigger that would be used for the SSM implementation. China and India demanded lower triggers, whereas the US insisted that the import surge should be considerably higher for countries to utilize the SSM.[113] The negotiations ended in deadlock. And another text by the Chair, circulated in December 2008, was unable to break it.[114]

Recent developments

Since 2008, there has been little significant progress in agricultural negotiations. A larger inner group, the G11, met in February 2011 to bargain over both agriculture and NAMA. But, as mentioned in Section 16.2, disagreement continued on how best to negotiate both issues, with Brazil proposing that linking these would allow reciprocal concessions to be made in each, and the US still favouring separate treatment of the two product categories.[115]

---

[109] *ICTSD Bridges Weekly Trade News Digest.* 12 April 2006: G6 AG Officials Unable to Overcome Divisions on Market Access Flexibilities.

[110] WTO 2006a.

[111] Reuters, 25 July 2006: US, EU Swap Blame for Trade Talks Failure.

[112] Reuters, 21 June 2007: Talks Breakdown Raise Doubts over WTO Pact: EU.

[113] Ismail 2009.   [114] WTO 2008d.

[115] Reuters, 22 February 2011 Lamy, WTO Members Say Doha Talks not Fast Enough.

16.4 CONCLUSION

As discussed in the previous pages, despite the promise of multiple gains from trade liberalization in NAMA and agriculture, neither of these two issues has offered any easy solutions. Agriculture remains unchanged as one of the most difficult areas for multilateral negotiations, while NAMA has thrown up a host of new problems. The strategies that negotiators traditionally use to facilitate agreement—Chair's texts, small-group consultations, variations in formulas that allow a more acceptable distribution of costs, and issue-linkage—have all failed so far. Some strategies, in fact, have unexpectedly heightened the proclivity of the negotiations to deadlock, rather than facilitating the expected solution. Issue linkage, for instance, instead of catalysing a compromise that includes something in it for everyone, has been used by all the major parties to hold up the deal. Why?

First, in good measure, the specific difficulties that NAMA and agriculture have encountered are a reflection of a more general set of problems in the WTO, deriving from the altered balance of power in the organization.[116] Consensus was easy to reach in the 'Rich Man's Club', where major decisions were arrived at amongst the old Quad that comprised a small group of like-minded powers, and developing countries were usually willing to sit on the margins.

Today, the situation looks dramatically different. The old Quad has been replaced by a bigger and diverse group of countries, at very different levels of development. Agreement amidst this diversity and multipolarity is much more difficult to reach. Further, as both the examples of NAMA and agriculture reveal, Brazil, India, and China represent their own interests as well as the interests of their coalition allies. And while these coalitions have proven a source of great empowerment to all their members, they also make it difficult for the rising powers to make concessions.[117] Consensus remains the decision-making rule in the WTO, but is unsurprisingly elusive, even at the core of the organization amidst the New Quad/G7, let alone the rest of the membership (the overwhelming majority of which is now increasingly articulate in its demands, and increasingly sophisticated in its proposals). In other words, the old *process* of negotiation that proved so successful in the days of the GATT is less well suited to the altered balance of power that constitutes the WTO today.

Second, the *substance* of the DDA is controversial, not least because the ambition of the negotiations is deeper than any of the previous rounds (this remains true, even after the narrowing of its agenda in July 2004). The Uruguay Round, even with the single undertaking, had enough loopholes in both agriculture and NAMA for both developed and developing countries to know that many potential costs of commitments could be avoided. That the NAMA and agriculture negotiations today involve addressing the

---

[116] Narlikar 2010.
[117] See Chapter 9 of this volume.

unfinished business of the Uruguay Round automatically takes them into very difficult bargaining terrain. And, as the empirical analysis in this chapter demonstrates, the NAMA–agriculture linkage has repeatedly been used by both sides to hold up the negotiations.[118]

Far too much is at stake in both NAMA and agriculture, and hence the repeated call by the world's leaders to conclude the negotiations. The exact shape that the endgame will take remains unclear. Recurrent deadlocks in these areas, however, do reveal some important issues that go beyond the immediacies of the current round. If the WTO is to reclaim its efficiency and legitimacy, it will have to address the question of institutional reform in response to the changing balance of power. This must involve a careful consideration of the processes that underlie the negotiations, the mandate that guides them, and ways in which issue linkage might be used as a catalyst (rather than a constraint) on agreement.

REFERENCES

Anderson, Kym, and Will Martin. 2005. *Agricultural Trade Reform and the Doha Development Agenda*. London: Palgrave Macmillan.

Cairns Group. 2002. Specific Input: Cairns Group Negotiating Proposal on Export Competition, 20 November. Available at <http://cairnsgroup.org/DocumentLibrary/export_competition_fc.pdf>. Accessed 28 February 2011.

Davis, Christina. 2004. International Institutions and Issue Linkage: Building Support for Agricultural Trade Liberalization. *American Political Science Review* 98 (1):153–69.

Diebold, William. 1952. *The End of the ITO*. Princeton: Princeton University.

European Commission. 2003. First Commission Reaction to Chairman Harbinson's Draft Modalities Paper on Agriculture. EC Press Release IP/03/222. Available at <http://europa.eu/rapid/pressReleasesAction.do?reference=IP/03/222&format=HTML&aged=1&language=EN&guiLanguage=en>. Accessed 14 February 2011.

European Commission. 2005. EU Tables New Offer in Doha World Trade Talks; Calls for Immediate Movement on Services and Industrial Goods. EC Press Release IP/05/1358. Available at <http://europa.eu/rapid/pressReleasesAction.do?reference=IP/05/1358>. Accessed 23 February 2011.

Evenett, Simon. 2007. Doha's Near Death Experience at Potsdam: Why is Reciprocal Tariff Cutting so Hard? Available from <http://www.voxeu.org/index.php?q=node/317>. Accessed on 10 March 2011.

Finger, Michael, and Phillip Schuler. 2000. Implementation of Uruguay Round Commitments: The Development Challenge. *The World Economy* 23 (4):511–25.

Fisher, Bob. 2006. Preference Erosion, Government Revenues and Non-Tariff Trade Barriers. *The World Economy* 29 (10):1377–93.

---

[118] More theoretical analysis is needed on the conditions under which issue-linkage fails to deliver agreement and instead heightens the likelihood of deadlock (and thereby also an analysis of the conditions under which issue-specific critical mass agreements might be more effective).

G33. 2005. G-33 Press Statement Geneva, October 11, 2005. Available from <http://www.
    mission-indonesia.org/modules/article.php?lang=e&articleid=291>. Accessed 20 March
    2011.

GATT. 1947. Available from <http://www.wto.org/english/docs_e/legal_e/gatt47_e.pdf>.
    Accessed 1 December 2010.

GATT 1986a. Standstill, Rollback and Safeguards. PRP.COM(86)W/3/Rev.1. Stanford: GATT
    Stanford Archive.

GATT 1986b. Draft Ministerial Declaration on the Uruguay Round. MIN(86)/W/19. Stanford:
    GATT Stanford Archive.

GATT 1987a. Review of Developments in the Trading System. Minutes of Special Meeting on
    Notification, Consultation, Dispute Settlement and Surveillance, Centre William Rappard.
    C/M/210. Stanford: GATT Stanford Archive.

GATT 1987b. United States Proposal for Negotiations on Agriculture. Multilateral Trade
    Negotiations the Uruguay Round. Group of Negotiations on Goods. Negotiating Group on
    Agriculture. MTN.GNG/NG5/W/14. Stanford: GATT Stanford Archive.

GATT 1991. Draft Final Act Embodying the Results of the Uruguay Round of Multilateral
    Trade Negotiations.

GATT 1993. Trade Negotiations Committee: Report on the Uruguay Round. MTN.TNC/W/113.
    Stanford: GATT Stanford Archive.

Hanrahan, Charles, and Randy Schnepf. 2005. CRS Report for Congress. WTO Doha Round:
    Agricultural Negotiating Proposals. Available from <http://www.policyarchive.org/
    handle/10207/bitstreams/2619.pdf>. Accessed 20 March 2011.

Healy, Stephen, Richard Pearce, and Michael Stockbridge. 1998. *The Implications of the Uruguay
    Round Agreement on Agriculture for Developing Countries: A Training Manual*. Rome: Food
    and Agriculture Organization.

Hedges, Irwin. 1967. Kennedy Round Agricultural Negotiations and the World Grains
    Agreement. *Journal of Farm Economics* 49 (5):1332–41.

Hoda, Anwarhul. 2001. *Tariff Negotiations and Renegotiations under the GATT and the WTO*.
    Cambridge: Cambridge University Press.

Hoekman, Bernard, and Michael Kostecki. 2009. *The Political Economy of the World Trading
    System*. 3rd Edition. Oxford: Oxford University Press.

Ismail, Faizel. 2009. Reflections on the WTO July 2008 Collapse: Lessons for Developing
    Country Coalitions. In Amrita Narlikar and Brendan Vickers eds., *Leadership and Change
    in the Multilateral Trading System*. Leiden: Martinus Nijhoff, and Dordrecht: Republic of
    Letters Publishing.

Jackson, John H. 1969. *World Trade and The Law of GATT: A Legal Analysis of the General
    Agreement of Tariffs and Trade*. Indianapolis: Bobbs-Merrill.

Johnson, Harry G. 1967. The Kennedy Round. *The World Today* 23 (8):326–33.

Legrain, Phillippe. 2006. Why NAMA Liberalisation is Good for Developing Countries. *The
    World Economy* 29 (10):1349–62.

McRae, D. M., and Thomas, J. C. 1983. The GATT and Multilateral Treaty Making: The Tokyo
    Round. *The American Journal of International Law* 77 (1):51–83.

Messerlin, Patrick. 2008. Walking a Tightrope: World Trade in Manufacturing and the Benefits
    of Binding. GMF-GEM Policy Brief. Paris: Groupe d'Économie Mondiale.

Narlikar, Amrita. 2003. *International Trade and Developing Countries: Bargaining Coalitions in
    the GATT and WTO*. London: Routledge.

Narlikar, Amrita. 2005. *The World Trade Organization: A Very Short Introduction*. Oxford: Oxford University Press.

Narlikar, Amrita. 2010. *New Powers: How to Become One and How to Manage Them*. London: Hurst and Company.

Narlikar, Amrita and Diana Tussie. 2004. The G20 at the Cancún Ministerial: Developing Countries and their Evolving Coalitions in the WTO. *The World Economy* 27 (7):947–66.

Porter, Jane M., and Douglas E. Bowers. 1989. A Short History of US Agricultural Trade Negotiations. Staff Report AGES 89–23. Washington DC: Agricultural and Rural Economy Division, Economic Research Service, US Department of Agriculture.

Stiles, Kendall. 1995. The Ambivalent Hegemon: Explaining the 'Lost Decade' in Multilateral Trade Talks, 1948–1958. *Review of International Political Economy* 2 (1):1–26.

United Nations Economic and Social Council. 1946a. Comments on U.S. Proposals for Expansion of World Trade and Employment. E/PC/T/W.14 and E/PC/T/5. Government of India. Stanford: GATT Stanford Archive.

United Nations Economic and Social Council. 1946b. Preparatory Committee of the International Conference on Trade and Employment Memorandum. E/PC/T/C.I/6. GATT Stanford Archive.

United States Trade Representative. 2003. Statement of USTR Spokesman, Richard Mills, regarding WTO Agriculture Report. Available from <http://ustraderep.gov/Document_Library/Spokesperson_Statements/Statement_of_USTR_Spokesman_Richard_Mills_regarding_WTO_Agriculture_Report.html>. Accessed 20 February 2011.

United States Trade Representative. 2005. US Proposal for Bold Reform in Global Agricultural Trade. Available from <http://barbados.usembassy.gov/uploads/images/CqygsLgF8nMR57MUzwpNbA/Doha_fact_sheet4.pdf>. Accessed 20 March 2011.

World Customs Organization. 2007. Harmonized System Nomenclature: General Rules for the Interpretation of the Harmonized System. Available from <http://www.wcoomd.org/home_hsovervi ewboxes_tools_and_instruments_hsnomenclaturetable2007.htm>. Accessed 8 February 2011.

WTO. 1995. Uruguay Round Final Act. Available from <http://www.wto.org/english/docs_e/legal_e/final_e.htm>. Accessed 21 March 2011.

WTO. 2000a. Agreement on Agriculture: Cairns Group Negotiating Proposal, Export Competition. G/AG/NG/W/11. Geneva: WTO Documents.

WTO. 2000b. Agreement on Agriculture: Special and Differential Treatment and a Development Box Proposal to the June Special Session of the Committee on Agriculture by Cuba, Dominican Republic, Honduras, Pakistan, Haiti, Nicaragua, Kenya, Uganda, Zimbabwe, Sri Lanka, and El Salvador. G/AG/NG/W/13. Geneva: WTO Documents.

WTO. 2000c. Proposal for Comprehensive Long-Term Agricultural Trade Reform. Submission from the United States. G/AG/NG/W/15. WTO Documents.

WTO. 2000d. European Communities Proposal: Animal Welfare and Trade in Agriculture. G/AG/NG/W/19. Geneva: WTO Documents.

WTO. 2000e. EC Comprehensive Negotiating Proposal. G/AG/NG/W/90. Geneva: WTO Documents.

WTO. 2000f. Negotiating Proposal by Japan on WTO Agricultural Negotiations. G/AG/NG/W/91. Geneva: WTO Documents.

WTO. 2001a. *Market Access: Unfinished Business—Post-Uruguay Round Inventory*. Special Studies 6. Geneva: WTO.

WTO. 2001b. Negotiations on WTO Agreement on Agriculture: Proposals by India in the Areas of: (i) Food Security, (ii) Market Access, (iii) Domestic Support, and (iv) Export Competition. G/AG/NG/W/102. Geneva: WTO Documents.

WTO. 2001c. Ministerial Declaration. WT/MIN(01)/DEC/1. Adopted 14 November 2001. Geneva: WTO Documents.

WTO. 2002a. Trade Negotiations Committee: Statement by the Chairman of the General Council. TN/C/1. Geneva: WTO Documents.

WTO. 2002b. Negotiating Group on Market Access: Contribution Paper from Japan. TN/MA/W/5. Geneva: WTO Documents.

WTO. 2002c. Negotiating Group on Market Access: Contribution Paper from South Korea. TN/MA/W/6. Geneva: WTO Documents.

WTO. 2002d. Negotiating Group on Market Access: Communication from Norway. TN/MA/W/7. Geneva: WTO Documents.

WTO. 2002e. Market Access for Non-Agriculture Products: Submission by India. TN/MA/W/10. Geneva: WTO Documents.

WTO. 2002f. Negotiating Group on Market Access: The Views of Chile. TN/MA/W/17. Geneva: WTO Documents.

WTO. 2003a. Negotiations on Agriculture. First Draft of Modalities for the Further Commitments. TN/AG/W/1. Geneva: WTO Documents.

WTO. 2003b. Negotiating Group on Market Access: Communication from Egypt, India, Indonesia, Kenya, Malaysia, Mauritius, Nigeria, Tanzania, Uganda, and Zimbabwe. TN/MA/W/31. Geneva: WTO Documents.

WTO. 2003c. Negotiating Group on Market Access: Japan's submission on 'zero-for-zero' and 'harmonization'. TN/MA/W/15/Add.2. Geneva: WTO Documents.

WTO. 2003d. Negotiating Group on Market Access: Overview of Proposals Submitted. TN/MA/6/Rev.1. Geneva: WTO Documents.

WTO. 2003e. WTO Negotiations on Agriculture. Poverty Reduction: Sectoral Initiative in Favour of Cotton. Joint Proposal by Benin, Burkina Faso, Chad, and Mali. Proposal on Implementation Modalities. TN/AG/GEN/6. Geneva: WTO Documents.

WTO. 2003f. Agriculture—Framework Proposal. Joint Proposal by Argentina, Bolivia, Brazil, Chile, China, Colombia, Costa Rica, Cuba, Ecuador, El Salvador, Guatemala, India, Mexico, Pakistan, Paraguay, Peru, Philippines, South Africa, Thailand, and Venezuela. WT/MIN(03)/W/6. Geneva: WTO Documents.

WTO. 2003g. Consolidated African Union/ACP/LDC Position on Agriculture. Communication from Mauritius. WT/MIN(03)/W/17. Geneva: WTO Documents.

WTO. 2004a. Doha Work Programme. Decision Adopted by the General Council. WT/L/579. Geneva: WTO Documents.

WTO. 2004b. Trade Negotiations Committee: Minutes of Meeting. TN/C/M/13. Geneva: WTO Documents.

WTO. 2005a. Negotiating Group on Market Access: Treatment of Non-Reciprocal Preferences for Africa. TN/MA/W/49. Geneva: WTO Documents.

WTO. 2005b. Communication to the Negotiating Group on Non-Agricultural Market Access from Argentina, Brazil, and India. TN/MA/W/54. Geneva: WTO Documents.

WTO. 2005c. Negotiating Group on Market Access: How to Create a Critical Mass Sectoral Initiative. Communication from Canada and the United States. TN/MA/W/55. Geneva: WTO Documents.

WTO. 2005d. Negotiating Group on Market Access: Communication from Benin on Behalf of the ACP Group of States. TN/MA/W/53. Geneva: WTO Documents.

WTO. 2005e. Hong Kong Ministerial Declaration. WT/MIN(05)/DEC. Geneva: WTO Documents.

WTO. 2006a. Lamy Outlines Schedule for 'Moment-of-truth' Meetings. Available from <http://www.wto.org/english/news_e/news06_e/mod06_summary_28june_e.htm>. Accessed 15 February 2011.

WTO. 2006b. Simulation of Tariff Reductions for the Non-Agricultural Products. JOB(06)/210. Geneva: WTO Documents.

WTO. 2006c. NAMA-11 Ministerial Communiqué. TN/MA/W/79. Geneva: WTO Documents.

WTO. 2007. Trade Negotiations Committee: Minutes of Meeting. TN/C/M/27. Geneva: WTO Documents.

WTO. 2008a. Draft Modalities for Non-Agricultural Market Access: Third Revision. TN/MA/W/103/Rev.2. Geneva: WTO Documents.

WTO. 2008b. Declaration of the African Group on the WTO Mini-Ministerial. TN/C/11. Geneva: WTO Documents.

WTO. 2008c. Draft Modalities for Non-Agricultural Market Access: Fourth Revision Negotiating. TN/MA/W/103/Rev.3. Geneva: WTO Documents.

WTO. 2008d. Revised Draft Modalities for Agriculture. TN/AG/W/4/Rev.4. Available from <http://www.wto.org/english/tratop_e/agric_e/agchairtxt_dec08_a_e.pdf>. Accessed 20 March 2011.

CHAPTER 17

TRADE IN SERVICES IN THE WTO: FROM MARRAKESH (1994), TO DOHA (2001), TO . . . (?)

RUDOLF ADLUNG[*]

17.1 INTRODUCTION

17.1.1 Overall scenario

THE General Agreement on Trade in Services (GATS) is a relatively young and, as yet, incomplete agreement. Its main text not only contains four rule-making mandates that are still under negotiation, but also a significant number of new terms and concepts that await clarification. This could be achieved gradually over time via litigation or, to some extent at least, through dedicated conceptual work in relevant committees. The latter option would certainly be preferable. Yet, though the necessary resources would have been available during the Doha Round's repeated stalemates, the political momentum was lacking.

Similarly, the market-access offers submitted in the Doha Round have remained disappointing compared with the liberalization moves undertaken autonomously by WTO members. While the submission of new offers virtually came to a halt in 2005, prior to the Hong Kong Ministerial Conference, many governments continued longer-term reform initiatives in key service sectors. There are thus few countries, apart from recently

[*] The author is grateful for very inspiring comments received from Antonia Carzaniga, Aaditya Mattoo, Peter Morrison, and Elisabeth Türk on an earlier draft. The usual caveats apply.

acceded WTO members, where GATS-committed regimes are close to actual trading conditions. Yet, given the peculiarities of the accession process, it provides little guidance for broad-based trade rounds.

The lack of movement in the WTO stands in stark contrast with zealous negotiating activities in various bilateral and regional settings (investment treaties and preferential trade agreements). There are obvious inconsistencies between the approaches pursued in these settings and WTO negotiating positions. As a common feature, however, definitional and conceptual issues have apparently drawn little attention at regional level either. From a WTO perspective, this must not be cause for concern: decentralized initiatives, within unconnected treaty systems, are more likely to stifle than to promote the search for common solutions. Where could relevant work be conducted, however? Comparable to the early conceptualization stages of the trade-in-services paradigm, there are various conceivable forums; a growing number of governments appear to be ready to explore options.

17.1.2 Looking into the rear-view mirror

The concept of 'trade in services' and the vision of services being covered by an international trade agreement are still relatively new. They were nurtured first by an 'epistemic community' that had emerged in the United States in the course of the 1970s, to culminate two decades later in the creation of the General Agreement on Trade in Services (GATS). From today's perspective, four stages may be distinguished:[1]

(1) Expert discussions since the 1970s, with the Organization for Economic Cooperation and Development (OECD) as an initial catalyst, surrounding the trade-in-services paradigm and the need for multilateral disciplines.

(2) Conceptualization/negotiation of a multilateral agreement since the early 1980s, up to the conclusion of the Uruguay Round in Marrakech in 1994.

(3) Focused negotiations and conceptual refinements during the round's extension in selected service sectors, in particular basic telecommunications and financial services, until the end of 1997.

(4) Intermittent bargaining since the launch of a new round of services negotiations in 2000 and its integration into the Doha Development Agenda (DDA) in late 2001.

---

[1] The following distinction is inspired by Drake and Nicolaïdis' seminal article on this issue. It differentiates between 'issue consolidation', from 1982 to 1986, and the Uruguay Round proper, which, in turn, evolved in three stages: the development of basic principles (until late 1988), their application and testing on a sectoral basis, and the completion of the Agreement and members' schedules of commitments. According to the authors, 'As the negotiations moved from exploring principles to bargaining over concessions, the epistemic community's direct influence on events was increasingly mediated by the mobilization of newly clarified material interests.' (Drake and Nicolaïdis 1992).

There have been no significant achievements since the extended negotiations on basic telecommunications and financial services. The vast majority of current commitments—except those of recently acceded members—reflect the conditions of access, in a limited number of sectors, as they existed in the early 1990s when Uruguay Round participants submitted their schedules. In the same vein, the GATS-mandated negotiations in four rule-making areas (domestic regulation, emergency safeguards, government procurement, and subsidies) have been moving mostly in circles since their start immediately after the round. Apart from a set of competition disciplines in telecommunications, there have been no successful attempts since 1997 to develop common ground on conceptual or interpretational issues surrounding the Agreement.

17.1.3 Current services landscape

Most offers submitted in the DDA negotiations remained significantly below the levels of autonomous liberalization achieved over the years. If the best offers were to be implemented, the outcome would still be significantly more restrictive, by an estimated factor of 1.9, than the applied regimes in key sectors.[2]

The many novel features of the GATS (application of trade rules to non-tradables, distinction between four types of transactions, etc.), combined with the reticence of turf-conscious ministries, may have taken their toll. Given the Agreement's unique ability to accommodate national policy objectives and constraints, governments seem to be lacking direction. There are virtually no measures, whether quantitative restrictions, discriminatory subsidies, or discretionary licensing decisions, that could not be maintained under the GATS. Moreover, from the perspective of current WTO members as distinct from countries in the accession process, there is no particular prize to be gained (i.e. WTO membership) nor threat to be avoided (unilateralism in services trade) any more. Section 17.2 discusses the chilling factors in more detail, while Section 17.3 seeks to explain why, notwithstanding the generally poor substance of GATS offers, a lot has happened in terms of actual liberalization on the ground.

Despite (or because of?) repeated stalemates in the Doha Round, significant strides have been made in other treaty contexts. Since the formal launch of the services negotiations, in 2000, there has been a proliferation of both bilateral investment treaties (BITs) and preferential trade agreements (PTAs) in services.[3] At the same time, the traditional dichotomy in trade policy-making—between agriculture and manufacturing—has gained a new dimension: incoherent positions adopted by the *same actors* on the *same subject matters* in different contexts. For example, although investment-related

---

[2] Gootiiz and Mattoo 2009. Some 70 members tabled initial offers, of which about 30 were improved later (counting the EU as one).

[3] BITs are relevant insofar as their scope overlaps with the GATS' most economically important mode of supply—commercial presence (mode 3)—which is estimated to account for some 55 to 60 per cent of trade under the Agreement (Maurer and Magdeleine 2012).

obligations are covered by the GATS, and more comprehensively by many BITs and recent PTAs, the adoption of a 'trade and investment' agenda was fiercely resisted at WTO ministerial conferences. Another sign of incoherence (or inexperience) is the existence of 'GATS-minus' commitments, i.e. entries that are less stringent than the sig-natories' GATS obligations, in a large number of PTAs (see Sections 17.4 and 17.5). This stands in strange contrast with many members' insistence, in relevant WTO bodies, that the services schedules resulting from the Doha Round must not contain entries that are less favourable than existing commitments—i.e. that there be no 'backtracking'.

Achievements on both fronts—BITs and PTAs—need to be qualified, however. While leading to some additional policy bindings or disciplines, they contributed little, if any-thing, to filling definitional and conceptual gaps still surrounding the trade-in-services paradigm. Neither PTAs nor BITs provide for a forum to advance conceptual clarifica-tion and consensual rule-making. The concluding sections (Sections 17.6 and 17.7) seek to assess the ensuing challenges for the trading system, taking into account initiatives that might play a mitigating role.

17.2 WHY SUCH SCANT PROGRESS IN THE ROUND?

In discussing the results of trade negotiations, it is important to distinguish between lib-eralization moves that go beyond hitherto existing conditions, and bindings that essen-tially confirm and guarantee, in full or in part, current regimes. The focus of the following discussion is on factors that may have prevented governments from negotiating mean-ingful liberalization under the GATS. Yet many of these factors may also work against the binding of—initially autonomous—liberalization moves.

17.2.1 An extremely flexible agreement

The drafters of the GATS were confronted with technical and economic challenges that do not exist in merchandise trade. These included, in particular, the continued need in many service sectors for direct interaction between suppliers and consumers, and thus the limited importance of cross-border trade as well as the absence (or non-applicability) of tariff-type protective instruments. To be economically meaningful, therefore, the GATS had to be broader and deeper in coverage than conventional trade agreements for goods. In turn, this required a particular degree of flexibility to accommodate country-, sector-, and mode-specific policy objectives and constraints. At the same time, it was this 'flexibility factor' that ultimately helped to ensure the Agreement's acceptance by the then 130-odd WTO members. However, if virtually everything is permissible (complete trade bans, all types of quantitative barriers and forms of discrimination, etc.), there is little incentive to overcome domestic political, economic, and institutional rigidities.[4]

Observers have also pointed to a profound change in the structure of international economic relations: the United States' weakening status as a hegemon in the trading system and its growing insistence on negotiating outcomes that were not only balanced overall, but ensured reciprocity in economically important sectors. According to Ahnlid, 'at the creation of the new [GATS] regime, leaders have been more prone to put potential free-riders in straitjackets, than the US was at the establishment of the GATT'.[5] In this context, the author points to the flexibility of the resulting agreement, not least the comparatively weak status of the non-discrimination principle, in terms of both most-favoured nation (MFN) and national treatment.

However, the leverage to exert pressure truly existed only once: prior to the entry into force of the new regimes in high-profile service sectors. It was only at this stage that the acceptance of unfettered MFN treatment could be conditioned on a 'critical mass' of other participants also undertaking commitments deemed appropriate. Similarly, exemptions from MFN treatment, as foreseen in Article II:1 of the GATS, with a view to grandfathering existing discriminations, could be obtained only at the date the Agreement came into force.[6] Once the die had been cast, after the conclusion of the extended negotiations on telecommunications and financial services, in February and December 1997 respectively, MFN treatment was guaranteed across virtually all service sectors.[7] In any future trade rounds, participants may assume policy obligations as they see fit, across sectors, modes of supply, and categories of measures, without being threatened by denials of MFN treatment.

Henceforth, there is thus greater temptation for governments to succumb to vested interests than in merchandise trade under the GATT:

(a) *The sectoral perspective:* Since virtually all members have one or more 'sacred cows'—whether audio-visual services, maritime transport or education—the politically most convenient common denominator is mutual acceptance.[8] And this is particularly tempting in an environment where the coordinating entity has little leverage, in terms of genuine own competencies, resources, etc., to persuade turf-conscious ministries of an outcome that appears to serve the interests of other sectors and/or 'their' departments. In a similar vein, regional governments are naturally averse to the central government encroaching upon their competencies in international trade negotiations.

---

[4] Adlung 2006. For an explanation of the GATS Agreement's four modes of supply—cross-border trade, consumption abroad, commercial presence, and presence of natural persons—see Adlung and Mattoo 2008.

[5] Ahnlid 1996.

[6] For details see Adlung and Carzaniga 2009.

[7] The main exception concerns air transport (measures affecting traffic rights and directly related services). In maritime transport, the MFN obligation remained suspended for those—relatively numerous—members that had not scheduled commitments during extended negotiations in the sector. WTO 2001a.

[8] Jara and Domínguez 2006 refer to an 'exclusions game' with snowball effects.

(b) *The modal perspective*: Deals across different modes of supply may appear tempting in the abstract—e.g. developing countries might concede better conditions for foreign commercial establishment (i.e. direct investment) in return for developed countries compromising on mode 4 (presence of natural persons).[9] Yet this is complicated by the fact that attracting foreign direct investment is a widely shared objective, evidenced by over 2,800 investment treaties across all groups of members,[10] just as the movement of persons is a common sensitivity.

(c) *Absence of a 'negotiating currency'*: Reflecting their highly diverse nature, it is virtually impossible to translate the trade measures that exist in different sectors and modes into one common (tariff-type) indicator.[11] In turn, this rules out the use of horizontal liberalization formulae that, at least in past GATT rounds, have arguably facilitated participants' agreement on what might be considered a balanced or equitable outcome.[12] (Nevertheless, the stalemate in the Doha Round over negotiating modalities for agriculture and NAMA indicates that formulae are no panacea either.)

(d) *The regulators' toolbox*: Even full liberalization, in terms of Articles XVI and XVII of the GATS (market access and national treatment), does not necessarily guarantee effective access. Members remain essentially free to operate 'non-schedulable' regulatory measures, including in the form of licensing or qualification requirements. Their impact may prove particularly stifling in sectors such as professional services, which rely strongly on mode 4 trade, i.e. on the ability of suppliers to move in person into a host market. Hence, why negotiate tough on market access, if essential trade constraints are likely to persist?

Negotiations on (additional) regulatory disciplines, mandated under Article VI:4 of the GATS, are still ongoing.[13] Though there is the possibility that regulatory excesses could be effectively banned, many members seem intent on protecting their current scope for action. Indeed, there is little incentive to change tack, in particular for those participants whose export interests revolve around capital-intensive sectors such as telecommunications or financial services, where regulatory barriers tend to be less pernicious than in labour-intensive segments. Capital is relatively flexible. Large foreign investors may acquire an established company if greenfield investments appear too cumbersome, while service professionals and small firms, which tend to rely on flexible forms of access via modes 1 or 4, have little option but to adjust to whatever regulatory requirements are in force—or stay away.[14]

---

[9] See, for example, Hoekman, Mattoo, and Sapir 2007.

[10] For an overview see UNCTAD 2011.

[11] Nevertheless, for analytical purposes, there have been various attempts in recent years to develop compound indices of market openness in services; see, for example, Francois and Hoekman 2009.

[12] Martin and Messerlin 2007.

[13] Current disciplines and the Article VI:4 mandate are discussed, for example, by Krajewski 2008.

[14] Available evidence suggests that current GATS commitments are also relatively unattractive for enterprises, mostly small and medium-sized companies, that seek to serve foreign markets on a case-by-case basis rather than through establishment under mode 3. Recent preferential trade agreements apparently provide more balanced conditions. Persin 2011.

17.2.2 Competing negotiating interests

In relevant policy declarations, services are not given the same impetus, it appears, as agriculture and Non-Agricultural Market Access (NAMA). Thus, paragraph 24 of the Hong Kong Ministerial Declaration recognizes the importance of advancing the development objectives of the round 'through enhanced market access for developing countries in both Agriculture and NAMA'.[15] To that end, ministers undertook to instruct their negotiators 'to ensure that there is a comparably high level of ambition in market access for Agriculture and NAMA'. Concerning services, the Declaration merely states that the negotiations shall proceed 'with a view to promoting the economic growth of all trading partners and the development of developing and least-developed countries, and with due respect for the right of Members to regulate'.

This discrepancy apparently reflects the political difficulties, in a trade round dedicated to 'development', in treating services in the same way as agriculture and NAMA. As noted by Wolfe, many participants thought 'that the point of a "development round" was unreciprocated concessions by developed countries'.[16] In a similar vein, the Hong Kong Declaration, paragraph 26, completely exempts least-developed countries from the expectation to undertake new commitments, recognizing 'the particular economic situation of these countries, including the difficulties they face'. (On average, the 30 least-developed countries (LDCs) participating in the Uruguay Round scheduled 15 per cent out of some 160 service subsectors, as compared to 25 per cent for developing, and 65 per cent for developed, country members.)[17] Thus, not surprisingly, no LDC has submitted a services offer to date, although some LDCs have concluded rather ambitious investment treaties.[18]

As a possible deterrent from WTO bindings, some observers have also referred to the loss of what might be called 'constructive ambiguity'.[19] In the legally stringent WTO context, governments are hesitant, it is claimed, to assume obligations they might have shouldered in a more flexible environment. Arguably, this is one of the reasons explaining the relative attractiveness of preferential trade agreements, which tend to be less strictly interpreted and enforced. Barring a few exceptions, including in particular the North American Free Trade Agreement (NAFTA), it is difficult indeed to find evidence of disputes adjudicated under PTAs. The parties seem to rely predominantly on the consultation provisions established under the respective agreements.

---

[15] WTO 2005.

[16] Wolfe 2010. See also Deardorff and Stern 2009.

[17] Adlung and Roy 2005. Interestingly, the three LDCs that acceded later to the WTO, Nepal, Cambodia, and Cape Verde, scheduled between 50 and 60 per cent (Cape Verde has since been graduated from LDC status). See also Section 17.3.2 and note 37.

[18] For example, Bangladesh, Democratic Republic of Congo, Rwanda, and Senegal have signed BITs with the United States, under which investors are granted national treatment on a pre- and post-establishment basis across the vast majority of goods and services sectors.

[19] Wolfe 2010.

Nevertheless, other factors must also have been at work. First, available studies suggest that, at least in the case of low-income economies, the risk of trading partners using WTO dispute settlement to enforce compliance is remote as well.[20] Second, if legal stringency was a prevailing concern, why have virtually all governments concluded BITs, which tend to have more bite, in some regards, than WTO obligations (see Section 17.4.1)? Finally, it is surprising to see that members paid relatively little attention to clarifying dubious entries in their Uruguay Round schedules which they might have inscribed out of inexperience at the time.[21] Though background documents explicitly allow for technical clarifications in such cases, and recent dispute rulings, not least in *Mexico–Telecommunications*, point out the risk of ill-specified commitments, many offers still leave significant room for technical refinement.[22]

17.2.3 The devil in the (technical) detail . . .

Significant parts of the classification list (W/120) generally employed for scheduling purposes under the GATS and many preferential agreements are incomplete and outdated.[23] For various reasons, including their intangible nature, services are more difficult to define than goods. Additional problems have resulted from rapid technical and institutional innovation in sectors such as telecommunications, banking, and insurance that are not easily captured by a classification system established almost two decades ago. Though there have been attempts at early stages of the Doha Round to modify the W/120 and incorporate revisions made to the underlying United Nations Central Product Classification, these have led nowhere. Since inconsistencies between the old and the revised classification could not be easily eliminated, for lack of concordance, the whole exercise would have absorbed enormous resources—and required a lot of good faith.

The fact that recent GATS disputes hinged, inter alia, on classification issues—e.g. the United States' failure to clearly circumscribe the sector scope of 'recreational services'[24]—has certainly not encouraged the scheduling of new commitments. Also, there are still uncertainties surrounding key terms and concepts, which may have similar deterrent effects. Cases in point are the scope of 'governmental services', which are excluded per se from the GATS (Article I:3), the coverage of electronic commerce under modes 1 or 2, the definition of subsidies which members frequently exempted from national treatment obligations in their schedules, or the implications of existing subsidy disciplines, and exemptions therefrom, on any safeguards mechanism that might be negotiated under the relevant mandate of Article X of the GATS.[25]

---

[20] Bown and Hoekman 2008.   [21] Adlung and Roy 2005.
[22] Adlung, Morrison, Roy, and Zhang 2012.
[23] Jara and Domínguez 2006; Mattoo and Wunsch-Vincent 2004.
[24] See, for example, Leroux 2007, concerning *US-Gambling*.
[25] These issues are discussed, respectively, by Leroux 2006, Wunsch-Vincent 2005, Poretti 2009, and Adlung 2007b.

While repeated suspensions of the DDA would have provided space for conceptual and definitional clarifications, this has not been used. The absence of relevant initiatives may be attributed, inter alia, to negotiating fatigue, resource problems in missions in Geneva, and/or the lack of institutionally well-established coordinators in capitals.

17.2.4 Domestic policy constraints

Access to many service markets is governed by institutional barriers that are deeply entrenched in domestic legislation; traditional postal or telecom monopolies are cases in point. Yet, while tariff changes may be implemented via government decree, to be issued in a few days, the abolition of public monopolies could require profound legislative changes. Such changes, possibly combined with the creation of new regulatory structures, need to be prepared over years—and may be complicated by further factors. These are, first, the sheer number of ministries with services-related competencies, and, second, the fact that the existence of a particular sector regime may be a ministry's main *raison d'être*. Who would want to contribute to their own demise? Interestingly, concerning the first factor, delegates in Geneva have confirmed the existence of a link between the number of ministries involved and the restrictiveness of their countries' negotiating positions.[26]

For services reforms to succeed, therefore, significant political capital has to be invested over extended periods of time. This might prove more difficult today than one or two decades ago; democratic majorities in many countries have become thinner and more volatile.[27] Yet the position of governments is not as hopeless as it might appear. As noted below, many have been able to advance services reforms in response to user pressure that was fuelled, in turn, by frustration over inefficient domestic services regimes and the lure of successful reforms abroad.

From that perspective, the prime focus of services negotiations could—or should?—be on the binding of policy changes where and when these have been decided for domestic reasons and, possibly, been tested in practice.[28] Available research suggests that, at least in merchandise trade, such bindings can be economically highly effective. For example, the impact of tariff bindings under the GATT or PTAs appears to be comparable to an autonomous cut of the average nominal tariff by 1.5 percentage points.[29] Nevertheless, such an outcome would remain significantly below the GATS' professed

---

[26] Zahrnt 2008.   [27] Messerlin 2008.

[28] Moreover, as indicated before, there is significant scope in a number of schedules for technical amendments that would align existing commitments more closely with relevant provisions of the Agreement and the Scheduling Guidelines (WTO 2001b).

[29] Mansfield and Reinhardt 2008. There are caveats, however. For example, in the absence of effective regulatory disciplines in services trade, it is easier under the GATS to use behind-the-border measures with a view to avoiding access bindings than would be the case under GATT.

aspirations. The negotiating mandate in Article XIX:1 is not about binding existing regimes, but 'achieving a progressively higher level of liberalization'.[30]

17.3 Services liberalization: where the momentum came from

17.3.1 Autonomous policy reforms: 'mainstream' WTO members

Services liberalization is expected to be more economically beneficial than (further) tariff reductions for goods, given high continued barriers in many sectors.[31] Nevertheless, significant strides have already been made over the past two or three decades. Basic infrastructural services, such as telecommunications and possibly banking, insurance, as well as segments of transport, are now widely provided under more open conditions than in the early 1990s.

The driving forces were, first and foremost, new technologies, including the advent of the Internet. It has not only enabled dramatic cost savings across a wide range of user industries—goods and (other) services producers alike—but also increased their geographic mobility, and thus leverage vis-à-vis reform-averse governments. In turn, tariff liberalization exposed a number of manufacturing industries, in high-income countries at least, to stronger competition on their home markets, thus limiting their ability to absorb the cost of overpriced services. This necessarily created a *domestic* constituency for reform. While there are tariff-refund regimes in many countries, which allow exporters to reclaim the duties paid on imported components, it is inconceivable to devise equivalents in the form of compensation regimes for protected, and thus overpriced, telecom or financial services. There is thus little other option for (industrial) users but to push for domestic policy reforms—or to relocate abroad.[32]

In only one decade, during the 1990s, the share of outgoing telecom traffic originating from competitive markets more than doubled to reach some 75 per cent.[33] The extended telecom negotiations, completed in early 1997, thus predominantly reflected the results of ongoing reform efforts, rather than being a causal factor. Nevertheless, as indicated

---

[30] The objective of progressive liberalization, with 'due respect for national policy objectives' and 'appropriate flexibility for individual developing country Members' (Article XIX:2), has been reiterated over time, including in the Hong Kong Ministerial Declaration.

[31] Hoekman 2006; Hoekman 2008; Hoekman, Mattoo, and Sapir 2007.

[32] A broad range of studies deal with the efficiency gains associated with the liberalization of infrastructural (producer-oriented) services. An overview, with a focus on commercial presence, is contained in Council for Trade in Services 2010.

[33] Rossotto et al. 2004.

before, it was also the US insistence on a 'critical mass' of economically meaningful commitments, as a condition for accepting an MFN-based outcome, that contributed to the breadth and depth of the bindings achieved. By the same token, the extended negotiations offered an opportunity to protect from reversals, and thus add credibility to, regime changes that had already been devised for domestic economic reasons.[34]

A high share of phase-in commitments—i.e. of commitments that applied only from specified future dates—testifies to the transitional nature of many telecom regimes in the mid 1990s. Overall, 60 per cent of the 70-odd participants in the extended negotiations scheduled such commitments, with implementation periods of ten years and more. In contrast, the extended negotiations on financial services, concluded in late 1997, resulted predominantly in improved commitments within the spectrum of applied regimes; phase-in commitments were virtually absent. The same is true for the DDA offers submitted to date.[35] However, there has been one more important catalyst for phase-in commitments: WTO accessions (see Section 17.3.2).

Key social services, such as health or education, have been widely ignored in current schedules as well as DDA offers (see Figure 13). One explanatory factor is the absence of vocal consumer groups with a stake in liberal policy bindings. In turn, this may be attributed to an imbalance in the domestic lobbying process, often referred to by political economists, whenever the costs of a particular policy regime are incurred by a large number of individuals who, given their comparatively small shares, have little incentive to form coalitions and confront focused producer interests. The situation in sectors like health or education may be particularly lopsided since, for obvious reasons, these services are typically provided for free or under tightly regulated conditions. Efficiency gains associated with policy reforms might thus not even arrive at the consumer level, but translate into (not widely discernible) fiscal savings. Interestingly, among DDA offers, there are no developed countries, but only a handful of developing economies that envisage new or improved commitments on health and social services.[36]

17.3.2 Negotiated policy reforms: recently acceded members

The members that have joined the WTO after 1995 undertook almost as many sector commitments, about 100 on average, as the most economically advanced countries during the Uruguay Round. Even more significantly, there are also indications that the accession process was combined with liberalization moves in a number of cases.

---

[34] Wolfe 2007. Wolfe opined that 'Services negotiations cannot drive domestic policy change. Rather, in many developing countries, there is an endogenous dynamic for the regulatory reform of telecommunications. It affects a small number of economic actors, requires few trained officials, and has highly visible benefits in increased investment in vital modern infrastructure. Endogenous reform makes it easier for a country to participate in exogenous multilateral negotiations.'

[35] Adlung 2007a.   [36] See also Adlung 2010.

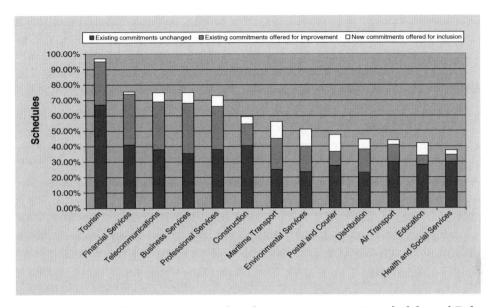

FIGURE 13 Patterns of commitments in selected service sectors: existing schedules and Doha Round offers, September 2005 (per cent)

Note: 'Air Transport' consists of three auxiliary services only (repair and maintenance, selling and marketing, computer reservation systems).

Source: Adlung and Roy 2005.

Virtually all 25 accession schedules submitted between January 1996 (Ecuador) and July 2008 (Cape Verde) contain phase-in commitments.[37] It appears reasonable to assume that significant elements of *negotiated* policy reforms were involved. China, to take an example, might have been reticent to make as many strides on an autonomous basis as are reflected in the form of phase-in commitments in its 2001 schedule;[38] some 60 per cent of all subsectors inscribed, 93 in total, contain such commitments. Across all WTO accession cases since 1995, phase-in provisions appear most frequently in telecommunications, followed by insurance, banking, and distribution services. Interestingly, the implementation periods tend to be far shorter in these cases than those bound in the extended negotiations on basic telecommunications.

Given its particular nature, the accession process affords current members an opportunity to seek commitments in return for a 'concession'—WTO membership, and the related benefits.[39] Accession schedules are thus likely to mirror the incumbents'

---

[37] By end-2011, there had been no further accessions.

[38] According to Mattoo, China's GATS commitments 'represent the most radical services reform program negotiated in the WTO' (Mattoo 2003).

[39] For a broader discussion of the 'costs' and 'benefits' involved, including in the form of WTO-plus commitments in accession protocols, see Cattaneo and Primo Braga 2009.

priorities, or rather those of governments that have the resources to engage actively in the working parties concerned, as much as the priorities of the applicants. Lack of information and expertise arguably played a role as well.[40]

Some additional factors might explain the particularly numerous commitments, on up to 95 per cent of all subsectors (Moldova), undertaken by some Commonwealth of Independent States (CIS) republics, i.e. the successor states of the former Soviet Union. First, the governments concerned might have valued rapid and smooth WTO accession also from a particular political perspective, as additional confirmation of national independence. Second, following the collapse of the old economic regimes, there was certainly less resistance from sector incumbents against new entrants than would otherwise have been the case. And, finally, liberal policy bindings might be expected to promote foreign investment which, in turn, is key to economic transformation. It is thus more than mere coincidence that the schedules of countries like Georgia, the Kyrgyz Republic, or Moldova are even more ambitious, in terms of both sectoral coverage and levels of openness than, for instance, those of OECD countries. As indicated before, the implementation of DDA offers would not fundamentally change the picture.

17.4 DEVELOPMENTS AT BILATERAL/ REGIONAL LEVEL

17.4.1 Bilateral investment treaties

The modal extension of the GATS has blurred the borderline between trade and investment issues. Commercial presence (mode 3) is defined as the supply of a service 'by a service supplier of one Member, through commercial presence in the territory of any other Member' (Article I:2(d)). Such supply is normally based on foreign direct investment, which, in turn, is covered as well by over 2,800 BITs. Almost all WTO members are involved.[41]

Investment treaties have been traditionally promoted by European countries, especially Germany, Switzerland, and the United Kingdom, which each account for over 100 treaties. China has joined this group more recently. The overlap between BITs and the GATS is a potential source of tension. This is particularly evident in the case of the national treatment obligation, post-establishment, which is a key element of most treaties. The obligation is normally without sector- or policy-related exclusions, and thus extends to subsectors not subjected to commitments under mode 3 of the GATS.

---

[40] Kavass 2007.   [41] Adlung and Molinuevo 2008.

The 40-odd treaties concluded by the United States, and, with variations, by a few other members, cover the pre-establishment phase as well. Accordingly, the signatories—including four LDCs and a range of developing and transition economies—are committed to extending any policy reforms immediately to foreign investors. On the US side, the sectoral coverage of such 'liberalization treaties' is subject to certain reservations, concerning mainly the insurance, banking, and certain transport and communication sectors. While many co-signatories inscribed a similar range of reservations, others failed to do so.

A typical example of GATS-plus provisions in virtually all BITs is a compensation requirement for expropriations, which may even extend to intangible assets such as the right to make profits and distribute dividends.[42] Under most BITs, compliance with this and other treaty requirements is not enforceable between states only, but also via investor-to-state arbitration. Further, as distinct from WTO dispute settlement, BITs also provide for the possibility of retroactive monetary compensation for damages suffered. The treaties thus tend to have more bite than the GATS in many situations, with potentially costly consequences for governments launching regulatory reforms for whatever policy reasons.[43] Tellingly, no more than a handful of GATS-related disputes since 1995 compares with an estimated 150 services-related arbitrations under BITs.[44]

Whenever BITs affect trade in services, the MFN obligation under Article II of the GATS applies. Only those treaties that form part of a preferential trade agreement, or those for which a party has listed an MFN exemption under the relevant annex to the GATS, are exempt. The latter possibility existed at the date of the Agreement's entry into force or, in the case of acceding countries, the date of acceptance (see Section 17.2.1). Yet, BIT-related exemptions have been listed only by some 10 per cent of current WTO members. One possible explanation for this relatively low share, apart from inexperience and lack of intragovernmental coordination, is the fact that the majority of BITs (over 1,800 out of a total of over 2,800 treaties) were concluded only after the inception of GATS, and thus might not have been anticipated in the early 1990s.

While the scope of most BITs, and thus their overlap with the GATS, has remained open-ended in terms of sectors, their modal coverage is narrowly confined: commercial presence.[45] It is this absence of a clear sector addressee, combined with a horizontally relevant policy interest (investment promotion), that might have prompted the ministry in charge, typically finance or foreign affairs, to forge ahead without much intragovernmental coordination.

---

[42] Choudhury 2008.   [43] Kulkarni 2009; Adlung 2010.
[44] UNCTAD 2011. By the end of 2010, UNCTAD counted 390 arbitration cases lodged under BITs. Of these, very few dated from before 1995. Using information from preceding UNCTAD studies, it may be assumed that about two-fifths of all claims concern services.
[45] Some BITs also contain limited commitments with regard to mode 4, concerning mostly senior executives.

17.4.2 Preferential trade agreements

The number of PTAs in services has increased rapidly in recent years, for various reasons (lack of multilateral achievements, bandwagon effects, competition for (political/economic/cultural) influence, etc.).[46] Some 90 such agreements had been notified to the WTO by the end of 2011, concluded mostly after the start of the DDA in December 2001. A recent study points out 'vast advances' compared to what has been bound in current schedules and offered in the round.[47] Interestingly, this study also indicates that sectors that proved difficult in the WTO, including postal/courier, audio-visual, health, and transport services, plus mode 4 (presence of natural persons), proved difficult in PTAs as well. The picture for financial services is mixed: fewer gains under mode 1 (cross-border trade), but significantly improved bindings for mode 3 (commercial presence).

The general finding that PTAs replicate familiar patterns of commitments, sometimes at significantly advanced levels, may not come as a surprise. Why should the interplay, across sectors and modes of supply, of commitment-friendly and commitment-adverse forces within the same countries be different? Indeed, the key actors—producer associations, trade unions, parliaments, government agencies, etc.—are the same. If there is one significant difference, it is the higher *political* impetus: negotiators have a stronger tailwind at their disposal. Apparently, it was sufficient in a number of cases to agree on commitments that actually improved on the status quo.[48]

The political attractiveness of PTAs, compared to WTO rounds, may be attributable not least to the short time frame within which they are negotiated. It may not exceed the tenures of the governments concerned. For example, the average negotiating time of the eight PTAs covering goods and services that the United States concluded between January 1995 and November 2005 was 2.2 years, ranging from a mere 0.7 years in the case of Oman to 3.1 years for the agreements with Singapore and Chile.[49] In contrast, the DDA was launched in late 2001...

While the proliferation of PTAs may reflect frustration over (non-)events in the WTO, among other factors, their negotiation further deflects attention and resources from the Geneva-based process, including from rule-making areas in services. Moreover, in order not to increase the appetite of potential PTA partners, governments may hesitate to submit substantive offers as long as the round's conclusion is not within reach—a vicious circle?

It may be argued, in defence of services PTAs, that they are less distortive than their counterparts in merchandise trade. For practical reasons, many concessions will ultimately be extended on an MFN basis. Even if they wanted to do so, governments will hardly be able to enforce various forms of regulatory discrimination, from differences in equity participation to composition requirements for company boards, vis-à-vis investors of different nationality. Also, the origin criterion contained in Article V:6 of the

---

[46] See the discussion in Chauffour and Maur 2010.   [47] Marchetti and Roy 2008.
[48] See, for example, Fink 2008.   [49] Ferrantino 2006.

GATS makes it relatively easy for third-country firms, once established within the PTA area, to share in the benefits agreed between the parties.[50] Doubts have been raised, however, whether this Article is always properly translated into PTA provisions.[51]

Moreover, there are pitfalls that have drawn little attention to date. The advances made in many PTAs, compared to the signatories' GATS schedules, are tempered by 'GATS-minus' commitments. These are entries that are more restrictive, for example because of the inclusion of new limitations or sector definitions, than the same countries had committed to under the GATS.[52] A recent study, examining 56 PTAs, found that some 80 per cent contained such elements on the part of at least one signatory, though they may well coincide with significant improvements in respect of other measures, sectors or modes.[53]

The existence of 'negative preferences' does not easily square with the expectations surrounding regional *liberalization* initiatives. This might explain, in part, why GATS-minus commitments have been widely ignored in the literature. Some may be attributable to lax scheduling practices, possibly reflecting the parties' lack of experience or time constraints during the negotiating process, while others may have been designed deliberately to shield particular policy regimes or sectors. If so, however, the question arises whether the agreements concerned are still compatible with the benchmarks of GATS Article V:1—i.e. whether they provide for 'substantial sectoral coverage' and, in the sectors covered, for 'the absence or elimination of substantially all discrimination in the sense of Article XVII [national treatment]'. If challenged by a frustrated non-participant, how many agreements would be found to be deficient?[54]

The situation would be less problematic, from a WTO perspective, if all PTAs contained comprehensive MFN clauses that extend to the signatories' respective GATS commitments without policy exclusions. However, such clauses exist only in a limited number of agreements.[55] Of course, should GATS-minus commitments be actually enforced under PTAs, the affected party remains free to defend its rights under the GATS, with reasonable chances of success. However, in such a case, would the other party still feel itself bound to extend the GATS-plus elements contained in the PTA, possibly including undertakings for which no WTO equivalents exist (e.g. development funding)?

17.5 POLICY INCOHERENCE AT MULTIPLE LEVELS

The political and institutional divide in many governments between agriculture and industry has multiple equivalents in services. As noted before, there are not only two, but many more ministries (and paradigms) at work: from telecoms, transport, and

---

[50] Fink 2008; Fink and Molinuevo 2008.   [51] Emch 2006.
[52] Adlung and Morrison 2010.   [53] Miroudot, Sauvage, and Sudreau 2010.
[54] Potential complainants are the home country governments of foreign-invested firms within the PTA area if their activities are hampered by GATS-minus commitments.
[55] Adlung and Morrison 2010; Miroudot, Sauvage, and Sudreau 2010.

finance to construction, education, and so forth—and the trenches can be as deep as between agriculture and industry.

Many ministries may be more used to interacting with their counterparts abroad, bilaterally or in international organizations, than with other government entities at home. The question arises whether the positions expressed in the WTO and other forums reflect coordinated government views rather than those of the departments that happen to be in charge. The trade and investment interface is a case in point—with different facets.

First, WTO members agreed in the aftermath of the Cancún Ministerial Meeting, in 2003, not to pursue a trade and investment agenda further in the context of the DDA.[56] Nevertheless, mostly the same governments have since concluded hundreds of new investment treaties that are potentially more ambitious than might have emerged from a WTO project. As indicated before, virtually all developing countries have signed and ratified BITs that guarantee national treatment at least post-establishment, compensation in the case of expropriation, etc. These treaties have proven to be highly effective instruments for aggrieved investors. Some three-quarters of the 390 arbitration cases lodged under BITs by the end of 2010 were targeted against developing and transition economies.[57]

Second, the overlap of BITs with mode 3 of the GATS tends to be widely ignored in trade policy circles. Otherwise, why do some of the same countries that concluded BITs with national treatment guarantees, post-establishment, seek to create a safeguards mechanism under the GATS, under which foreign-invested companies could be prevented from further expansion?[58] Why do BIT-promoting countries modify individual provisions in their treaty templates over time without taking into account that, pursuant to the MFN obligation under the GATS, their most ambitious BIT is due to trump all others as far as services are concerned?[59] And why have several LDCs, normally keen to defend the concept of 'policy space', concluded investment treaties that even provide for national treatment on a pre-establishment basis, thus automatically extending the treatment afforded to domestic companies to potential foreign entrants?[60]

The picture for PTAs is no more encouraging either. As indicated before, a large number of current agreements contain GATS-minus commitments. Such commitments are not only problematic in view of relevant GATS provisions (Article V:1), but might have broader systemic implications. In particular, their existence could prevent members, for example in the context of the DDA, from 'multilateralizing regionalism' by simply incorporating relevant PTAs, which may be more liberal overall, into their GATS schedules. There is a widely shared view that these schedules must not contain any backtracking in the form of new entries that would be less favourable than existing ones.

---

[56] WTO 2004. For a discussion of the underlying reasons, see Evenett 2007.
[57] Calculation based on UNCTAD 2011.
[58] Adlung 2007b.
[59] Note that some two-thirds of world foreign investment stocks are in services (WTO 2010).
[60] See note 18 above.

Thus, without cumbersome renegotiations of current GATS commitments—not realistically conceivable—many PTAs would remain incompatible. They would continue to represent balances of concessions, depending on the respective MFN clauses, that remain disconnected from the WTO/GATS system. Has this ever been discussed within the governments concerned?

Both the existence of scheduling flaws in PTAs and deliberate departures from GATS-committed conditions may have similar causes:

- First and foremost, the absence of a clearly dominant entity—comparable to the status of a department of trade and industry ('DTI') in merchandise trade—that is responsible in a significant number of service sectors for the internal coordination of trade policies, their external representation, and the ensuing implementation and monitoring processes. This certainly complicates efforts to persuade potential contributors to the country's schedule of the need to comply with relevant GATS provisions, and to ensure consistency across the commitments prepared for individual sectors.
- At the same time, it is conceivable that domestic interest groups in services now pursue their views more actively than they used to, for lack of experience and political influence at the time, in the final stages of the Uruguay Round. The services landscape has certainly become larger and more diversified, increasing the temptation for government coordinators to accommodate vested interests at the expense of consistency. At the same time, parliamentary majorities in many countries have become more volatile (see Section 17.2.4).

Nevertheless, in the absence of egregious departures from GATS obligations, the risk of trade disputes appears relatively low. Neither the PTA partners nor third-country governments, many of which are involved in similar initiatives, are likely to take a strong stance. Yet, from a WTO perspective, this is of only limited consolation.

17.6 Consequences for WTO rule-making

Given its broad modal coverage and many related conceptual innovations, the GATS continues to offer far more scope for interpretation than its counterpart in merchandise trade, the GATT. Over time, existing gaps may gradually be filled by dispute rulings. However, this is a highly time- and resource-intensive option. Its main focus would be on issues that are controversial between members with significant economic potential in the sectors and modes concerned. Commitments related to mode 3 might attract more attention than those for mode 4: they are more commercially significant, and interested exporters (i.e. internationally oriented service companies) tend to be better informed and have easier access to 'their' governments than individual professionals who might want to work abroad. Legislation via dispute settlement is thus likely to be selective.

To a certain degree, this is also true for rule-making—or, rather, rule-refining processes in a WTO context. Many members do not have the resource base that would allow them to participate effectively and voice their views in relevant meetings. Nevertheless, WTO-based initiatives offer scope for negotiating economies between like-minded governments that does not exist in other contexts, whether PTAs or BITs.

The last such initiatives took place more than a decade ago, during the extended negotiations on basic telecommunications and financial services, completed in 1997. In both cases, experts from relevant ministries and regulatory agencies were closely involved. It would have been inconceivable in telecommunications, for example, to devise the 'reference paper' with competition disciplines without the sector specialists cooperating in a problem-solving spirit.[61] Their tacit approval to undertaking commitments in relevant sectors would not have sufficed. Regulation- and competition-related trade barriers, not captured by market access and national treatment obligations, might have persisted.

The slack in the market-access segments of the DDA has apparently spilled over. Members seem to have lost sight of a particular function of the multilateral system: fostering dialogue in order to (a) improve the knowledge base for informed decisions; (b) sensitize individual participants to the needs, priorities, and perspectives of others; and (c) engage in a collective search for solutions.[62] As indicated before, given the novelty and complexity of the GATS and its overlap with other sets of treaty obligations, filling this 'missing middle' is a more urgent task in services than in traditional merchandise trade.

On issues where the GATS concedes the existence of (potential) gaps—in the form of rule-making mandates on domestic regulation, emergency safeguards, government procurement, and subsidies—PTAs do not generally provide solutions either. In most cases, they remain silent or cross-refer to outcomes that might be achieved later under the GATS.[63] On the one hand, this may be considered a missed opportunity since PTAs could have been used as a testing ground for regulatory innovation. On the other hand, once such decentralized initiatives are pursued in earnest, they could complicate the search for multilateral solutions. For example, if the United States or the EU started developing subsidy rules and definitions under their respective agreements, this would certainly affect their negotiating flexibility in Geneva. The longer the slack in the WTO continues, the larger the risk that PTAs take over, however.

17.7 IS THERE A SILVER LINING?

17.7.1 Initiatives at the WTO

The preceding discussion suggests that the widening and deepening of the WTO's mandate to services and beyond has not found a domestic equivalent in the form of members reorganizing the allocation of competencies across service sectors/modes and, possibly,

---

[61] For the historical context and main provisions of the reference paper, see Bronckers and Larouche 2008.
[62] Low 2009; Evenett 2009.   [63] Fink and Molinuevo 2008; Mattoo and Sauvé 2008.

federal levels. While the scope for international policy-making has expanded, domestic structures and processes have remained largely unchanged. One conceivable exception, concerning the federal/subfederal allocation of competencies, is the EU internal reforms in the wake of the Lisbon Treaty, which, however, remain to be tested.

From the WTO's perspective, the question arises to what extent it could serve, in current circumstances, as a common platform for trade policy analysis and conceptual clarification. There have been various potentially relevant initiatives in recent years. Cases in point are the creation of the Trade Policy Review Mechanism (TPRM), an early result of the Uruguay Round, and, on a provisional basis, the Transparency Mechanism for Regional Trade Agreements (TRTA) in 2006.

Among other functions, the TPRM is a potentially important analytical instrument, unmatched in terms of country, sector, and policy coverage. As has been noted elsewhere,[64] however, it tends to suffer from resource shortages, the influence of trade diplomacy-related constraints, and possibly the absence of sector experts in review meetings. Moreover, the prime focus is on a member's policy conduct during the reporting period, as distinct from the type of issues raised in Sections 17.4 and 17.5. In turn, as the name implies, the TRTA is intended mainly to enhance transparency, rather than promote discussions on the legal or economic repercussions of particular agreements or policy approaches.[65] Thus, though GATS-minus commitments have been identified in various secretariat presentations, the implications have not been explored in any depth. And BITs have remained virtually absent from the WTO's radar screen.

17.7.2 Other forums

It may be useful in the present context to distinguish between attempts to refine or expand existing policy disciplines and others intended to explore new conceptual ground. The WTO may not be equally well suited for both types of initiative. Typically, early work on the trade-in-services paradigm took place outside the then GATT system before being included, in the mid 1980s, in the Uruguay Round (see Section 17.1.2). By the same token, not all current challenges that may be associated with the WTO and its 'missing middle', i.e. the dearth of exploratory conceptual work, might be best approached within the organization.

Tellingly, a work programme on international investment agreements was recently launched at UNCTAD. It brings together governmental experts, legal practitioners, and academics with a view to promoting an informal exchange in a non-negotiating

---

[64] See Chapter 21 of this volume.

[65] The decision creating the TRTA instructs the Secretariat, 'on its own responsibility and in full consultation with the parties', to prepare a factual presentation of notified PTAs and, in this context, to 'refrain from any value judgement'. The PTAs are then to be 'considered' by members (WTO 2006). As noted by Evenett 2009, had the intention been to equip the TRTA with teeth, the mandate would have called for an 'examination' or 'evaluation' of the agreements.

setting.[66] Though the outcome is open, it would be unrealistic, given failed attempts in the OECD and WTO context, to expect common rules to emerge from this exercise. Nevertheless, from the perspective of 'treaty takers', there is significant potential for improving transparency on BITs, identifying various treaty options, and assessing the economic and legal implications. An increasing number of governments appear to be sufficiently frustrated with non-anticipated arbitration rulings under BITs, the absence of appeals procedures, and other flaws, apparent or real, to be ready to contribute.[67]

With a somewhat different focus, the World Bank has pursued a variety of initiatives in recent years to explore, and assess the consequences of, the services regimes maintained by individual countries and country groups.[68] In turn, this has been a potential source of inspiration for the governments concerned, and set incentives for corrective action. In a similar vein, the OECD Secretariat has been mandated recently with various projects dealing with GATS-related issues which, once delegations are in 'bargaining mode', would prove very difficult to launch in a WTO setting. Under consideration are country- and sector-specific trade restrictiveness indicators for services, allowing for a comparison of individual countries' policy profiles, and comparative studies evaluating the scope and content of PTAs in services. The results are being discussed in the OECD Trade Committee.

WTO Members' focus on the DDA has certainly affected the choice of forums as well. The negotiating process not only absorbed significant resources, which could have been used for exploring definitional and conceptual issues, but also awakened suspicion regarding the proponents' motives. Are such issues brought up simply to blur the offers' (possible) lack of substance or to settle accounts over non-developments in other areas of the DDA? A successful outcome, in the end, depends on a few basic ingredients: mutual trust, political foresight and resolve, and adequate settings for a staged conceptualization/negotiation/bargaining process.

REFERENCES

Adlung, Rudolf. 2006. Services Negotiations in the Doha Round: Lost in Flexibility? *Journal of International Economic Law* 9 (4):865–93.

Adlung, Rudolf. 2007a. The Contribution of Services Liberalization to Poverty Reduction: What Role for the GATS? *Journal of World Investment and Trade* 8 (4):549–71.

Adlung, Rudolf. 2007b. Negotiations on Safeguards and Subsidies in Services: A Never-Ending Story? *Journal of International Economic Law* 10 (2):235–65.

Adlung, Rudolf. 2010. Trade in Healthcare and Health Insurance Services: The GATS as a Supporting Actor? *Intereconomics* 45 (4):227–38.

---

[66] UNCTAD has also organized high-level discussions on international investment policies, for example the Second World Investment Forum (WIF) in Xiamen (China) in September 2010.

[67] *Financial Times*, 12 March 2008: 'Concern grows over global trade regulation'.

[68] The results are reflected in studies such as Mattoo and Patton 2007, and Gootiiz and Mattoo 2009.

Adlung, Rudolf, and Antonia Carzaniga. 2009. MFN Exemptions under the General Agreement on Trade in Services: Grandfathers Striving for Immortality? *Journal of International Economic Law* 12 (2):357–92.

Adlung, Rudolf, and Aaditya Mattoo. 2008. The GATS. In *A Handbook on International Services Trade*, edited by Aaditya Mattoo, Robert M. Stern, and Gianni Zanini, 48–83. Oxford: Oxford University Press.

Adlung, Rudolf, and Martin Molinuevo. 2008. Bilateralism in Services Trade: Is there Fire behind the (BIT-) Smoke? *Journal of International Economic Law* 11 (2):365–409.

Adlung, Rudolf, and Peter Morrison. 2010. Less than the GATS: 'Negative Preferences' in Regional Services Agreements. *Journal of International Economic Law* 13 (4):1103–43.

Adlung, Rudolf, Peter Morrison, Martin Roy, and Weiwei Zhang. 2012. FOG in GATS Commitments—Why WTO Members Should Care. *World Trade Review* (in preparation).

Adlung, Rudolf, and Martin Roy. 2005. Turning Hills into Mountains? Current Commitments under the General Agreement on Trade in Services and Prospects for Change. *Journal of World Trade* 39 (6):1161–94.

Ahnlid, Anders. 1996. Comparing GATT and GATS: Regime Creation Under and After Hegemony. *Review of International Political Economy* 3 (1):65–94.

Bown, Chad P., and Bernard Hoekman. 2008. Developing Countries and Enforcement of Trade Agreements: Why Dispute Settlement is Not Enough. *Journal of World Trade* 41 (1):177–203.

Bronkers, Marco, and Pierre Larouche. 2008. A Review of the WTO Regime for Telecommunications Services. In *The World Trade Organization and Trade in Services*, edited by Kern Alexander and Mads Andenas, 319–79. Leiden and Boston: Martinus Nijhof.

Cattaneo, Olivier, and Carlos A. Primo Braga. 2009. Everything You Always Wanted to Know about WTO Accession (But Were Afraid to Ask). Policy Research Working Paper 5116. Washington, DC: World Bank.

Chauffour, Jean-Pierre, and Jean-Christophe Maur. 2010. Beyond Market Access—The New Normal of Preferential Trade Agreements. Policy Research Working Paper 5454. Washington, DC: World Bank.

Choudhury, Barnali. 2008. Recapturing Public Power: Is Investment Arbitration's Engagement of the Public Interest Contributing to the Democratic Deficit? *Vanderbilt Journal of Transnational Law* 41 (3):775–832.

Deardorff, Alan V., and Robert M. Stern. 2009. Alternatives to the Doha Round. *Journal of Policy Modeling* 31 (4):526–39.

Drake, William J., and Kalypso Nicolaïdis. 1992. Ideas, Interests, and Institutionalization: 'Trade in Services' and the Uruguay Round. *International Organization* 46 (1):37–100.

Emch, Adrian. 2006. Services Regionalism in the WTO: China's Trade Agreements with Hong Kong and Macao in the Light of Article V(6) GATS. *Legal Issues of Economic Integration* 33 (4):351–78.

Evenett, Simon J. 2007. Five Hypotheses Concerning the Fate of the Singapore Issues in the Doha Round. *Oxford Review of Economic Policy* 23 (3):392–414.

Evenett, Simon J. 2009. Aid for Trade and the 'Missing Middle' of the World Trade Organization. *Global Governance* 15 (3):359–74.

Ferrantino, Michael J. 2006. Policy Anchors: Do Free Trade Agreements and WTO Accessions Serve as Vehicles for Developing-Country Policy Reform? Working Paper. Washington, DC: US International Trade Commission.

Fink, Carsten. 2008. Services PTAs: Friends or Foes of Multilateralism? In *Opening Markets for Trade in Services: Countries and Sectors in Bilateral and WTO Negotiations*, edited by Juan A. Marchetti and Martin Roy, 113–48. Cambridge: Cambridge University Press.

Fink, Carsten, and Martin Molinuevo. 2008. East Asian Free Trade Agreements in Services: Key Architectural Elements. *Journal of International Economic Law* 11 (2):263–311.

Francois, Joseph, and Bernard Hoekman. 2009. Services Trade and Policy. Discussion Paper 7616. London: Centre for Economic Policy Research.

Gootiiz, Batshur, and Aaditya Mattoo. 2009. Services in Doha: What's on the Table? *Journal of World Trade* 43 (5):1013–30.

Hoekman, Bernard. 2006. Liberalizing Trade in Services: A Survey. Policy Research Working Paper 4030. Washington, DC: World Bank.

Hoekman, Bernard. 2008. The General Agreement on Trade in Services: Doomed to Fail? Does it Matter? *Journal of Industry, Competition and Trade* 8 (3–4):295–318.

Hoekman, Bernard, Aaditya Mattoo, and André Sapir. 2007. The Political Economy of Services Trade Liberalization: A Case for International Regulatory Cooperation? *Oxford Review of Economic Policy* 23 (3):367–91.

Jara, Alejandro, and M. del Carmen Domínguez. 2006. Liberalization of Trade in Services and Trade Negotiations. *Journal of World Trade* 40 (1):113–27.

Kavass, Igor I. 2007. WTO Accession: Procedures, Requirements and Costs. *Journal of World Trade* 43 (3):453–74.

Krajewski, Markus. 2008. Article VI GATS. In *WTO: Trade in Services*, edited by Rüdiger Wolfrum, Peter-Tobias Stoll, and Clemens Feinäugle, 165–96. Max Planck Commentaries on World Trade Law. Leiden: Koninklijke Brill NV.

Kulkarni, Parashar. 2009. Impact of the GATS on Basic Social Services Redux. *Journal of World Trade* 43 (2):245–83.

Leroux, Eric. 2006. What is a 'Service Supplied in the Exercise of Governmental Authority' under Article I.3(b) and (c) of the General Agreement on Trade in Services? *Journal of World Trade* 40 (3):345–85.

Leroux, Eric. 2007. Eleven Years of GATS Case Law: What Have We Learned? *Journal of International Economic Law* 10 (4):749–93.

Low, Patrick. 2009. Potential Future Functions of the World Trade Organization. *Global Governance* 15 (3):327–34.

Mansfield, Edward D., and Eric Reinhardt. 2008. International Institutions and the Volatility of International Trade. *International Organization* 62 (4):621–52.

Marchetti, Juan A., and Martin Roy. 2008. Services Liberalization in the WTO and in PTAs. In *Opening Markets for Trade in Services: Countries and Sectors in Bilateral and WTO Negotiations*, edited by Juan A. Marchetti and Martin Roy, 61–112. Cambridge: Cambridge University Press.

Martin, Will, and Patrick Messerlin. 2007. Why is it so Difficult? Trade Liberalization under the Doha Agenda. *Oxford Review of Economic Policy* 23 (3):347–66.

Mattoo, Aaditya. 2003. China's Accession to the WTO: The Services Dimension. *Journal of International Economic Law* 6 (2):299–339.

Mattoo, Aaditya, and Lucy Patton, eds. 2007. *Services Trade and Development: The Experience of Zambia*. Washington DC: Palgrave Macmillan and World Bank.

Mattoo, Aaditya, and Pierre Sauvé. 2008. Regionalism in Services Trade. In *A Handbook on International Trade in Services*, edited by Aaditya Mattoo, Robert M. Stern, and Gianni Zanini, 221–86. Oxford: Oxford University Press.

Mattoo, Aaditya, and Sacha Wunsch-Vincent. 2004. Pre-Empting Protectionism in Services: The GATS and Outsourcing. *Journal of International Economic Law* 7 (4):765–800.

Maurer, Andreas, and Joscelyn Magdeleine. 2012. Measuring Trade in Services in Mode 4. In *Reforming Services for Inclusive and Sustainable Development of Asia and the Pacific*, edited by Mia Mikic, Gloria Pasadilla, and Pierre Sauvé. Asian Development Bank Institute and ARTNeT. Bangkok: United Nations (forthcoming).

Messerlin, Patrick. 2008. Reviving the Doha Round: The Agenda for the Developed Countries. In *Monitoring International Trade Policy: A New Agenda for Reviving the Doha Round*, edited by Bruce Blonigen, 1–31. London: Centre for Economic Policy Research, and Kiel: Kiel Institute.

Miroudot, Sébastien, Jehan Sauvage, and Marie Sudreau. 2010. Multilateralising Regionalism: How Preferential are Services Commitments in Regional Trade Agreements? OECD Trade Policy Working Paper 106 (TAD/TC/WP(2010)18/FINAL).

Persin, Daniela. 2011. Market Access for Small versus Large Service Enterprises: The Preferential and Multilateral Trade Liberalization Tracks Compared. *Journal of World Trade* 45 (4):785–819.

Poretti, Pietro. 2009. *The Regulation of Subsidies within the General Agreement on Trade in Services of the WTO*. Alphen aan den Rijn: Kluwer Law International.

Rossotto, Carlo, Björn Wellenius, Anat Lewin, and Carlos R. Gomez. 2004. Competition in International Voice Communications. Working Paper 42. Washington, DC: World Bank.

UNCTAD. 2011. *Latest Developments in Investor–State Dispute Settlement*. IIA Issues Note 1. Geneva, UNCTAD/WEB/DIAE/IA/2011/3. Geneva: UNCTAD.

Wolfe, Robert. 2007. Can the Trading System be Governed? Institutional Implications of the WTO's Suspended Animation. CIGI Working Paper 30. Waterloo, Ontario: Centre for International Governance Innovation.

Wolfe, Robert. 2010. Sprinting During a Marathon: Why the WTO Ministerial Failed in July 2008. *Journal of World Trade* 44 (1):81–126.

WTO. 2001a. *Market Access: Unfinished Business*. Special Studies 6. Geneva: WTO Publications.

WTO. 2001b. Council for Trade in Services. *Guidelines for the Scheduling of Specific Commitments under the General Agreement on Trade in Services*. S/L/92. Geneva: WTO.

WTO. 2004. General Council. *Doha Work Programme*. Decision Adopted on 1 August 2004. WT/L/579. Geneva: WTO.

WTO. 2005. *Doha Work Programme—Ministerial Declaration*. WT/MIN(05)/DEC. Ministerial Conference, 22 December 2005, Doha.

WTO. 2006. General Council. *Transparency Mechanism for Regional Trade Agreements*. Decision of 14 December 2006. WT/L/671. Geneva: WTO.

WTO. 2010. Council for Trade in Services. *Mode 3: Commercial Presence*. Note by the Secretariat. S/C/W/314. Geneva: WTO.

Wunsch-Vincent, Sacha. 2005. *WTO, E-Commerce and Information Technologies*. Edited by Joanna McIntosh. New York: United Nations ICT Task Force.

Zahrnt, Valentin. 2008. Domestic Constituents and the Formulation of WTO Negotiating Positions: What the Delegates Say. *World Trade Review* 7 (2):393–421.

CHAPTER 18

....

TRADE-RELATED INTELLECTUAL PROPERTY RIGHTS

KEITH E. MASKUS

18.1 INTRODUCTION

....

THE Agreement on Trade-Related Aspects of Intellectual Property Rights (TRIPS) was adopted as Annex 1C of the single undertaking establishing the World Trade Organization (WTO) in 1995. TRIPS is the most important international accord on intellectual property rights (IPRs), for three reasons. First, it is easily the most comprehensive agreement ever reached regarding government standards and actions in the realm of intellectual property. Second, because membership of the WTO is virtually universal it extends minimum protection norms to a truly global scale.[1] Third, being subject to the WTO's dispute settlement mechanism it is the only multilateral accord on IPRs that can be enforced through legal action and trade sanctions.[2] As such, TRIPS is the bulwark of the international regime governing IPRs, and the basis on which most national legal systems are now built.

Before turning to specifics, there are some central principles that must be understood about IPRs and TRIPS. First, IPRs are (generally) privately-owned *exclusive* rights. This means that intellectual property (IP) owners may exclude others from activities that would infringe their rights in some way. Thus, a patent is an exclusive grant that permits

---

[1] As noted below, there are many other international treaties covering IPRs, but they generally do not mandate minimum standards and their membership is far from global.

[2] Note, however, that the Agreement includes a moratorium on so-called 'non-violation complaints', by which one country can allege that another government has deprived it of anticipated benefits by virtue of a separate action that does not violate TRIPS. This moratorium originally existed for five years and was extended in 1999; it remains in place.

the owner to decide who may produce, distribute, import, or license a protected good or technological process for a given period of time. A copyright prevents unauthorized copying of a literary or artistic work, whether it is produced in print, digital, or virtual forms, including broadcasts. A trademark allows its owner to exclude others from using the same, or a confusingly similar, mark. There are numerous other forms of IPRs, including, inter alia, design patents, plant variety rights, geographical indications, protected semiconductor topographies, collective marks, and performance rights, all of which are variants on the basic theme of exclusion. The fact that IPRs are exclusive rights means that they are really *negative* rights in the legal parlance, for they permit owners to prevent actions, but do not compel them actually to place their creative goods on the market. Nevertheless, the implicit bargain nations make in providing IPRs is the expectation that owners will divulge the technical information underlying patents, license their technologies, and place goods and services on the market in return for this exclusivity.

Second, IPRs, or rather the standards and policies defining them, are commercial regulations applying to all firms and institutions wishing to utilize them. They are fundamentally different from tariffs, trade subsidies, and other elements of trade regulation that arise at national borders. Trade restrictions are almost uniformly recognized as inefficient and costly, tending to reduce welfare in both the importing and exporting countries. Their mutual reduction or removal can be counted on to raise well-being and efficiency in all trading partners, even if it redistributes income within countries. In contrast, there is no uniform standard of economic optimality in the case of IPRs. When a country expands the scope of patent or copyright protection, it favours current and potential rights-holders, but also reduces the direct access of consumers and makes imitative competition more difficult. These short-run costs may be offset by long-term gains in dynamic competition, though that outcome depends on many circumstances. Even this fundamental trade-off depends on where a country is situated in terms of national income levels, technological development, output mix, social preferences, and even demographic factors. Put simply, countries do not have universal preferences over IPRs, and an agreement to raise standards everywhere may raise or reduce well-being in different trading partners.

Third, although TRIPS is a multilateral agreement, the precise specification for how IPRs are protected remains the province of individual countries. Indeed, a core principle is that WTO members can implement TRIPS according to their own legal systems and practices (Article 1). It has always been the case that patents, copyrights, trademarks and other IPRs exist as *national* rights, not *international* rights. A few examples illustrate the point. A company may register a patent or trademark in the United States but must also register it in all other countries or jurisdictions where it desires protection. Definitions of what is patentable subject matter can vary across countries, as can other limitations and exceptions on patent scope. Copyrights generally do not require registration formalities, but there are different national limitations on the scope and duration of protection. Some countries permit rights-holders to exclude unauthorized re-importation of their goods, while others do not.

The fact that rights are national, rather than international, has been true throughout the history of IPR regulation and cross-border agreements. Indeed, the modern global system is based on two fundamental international conventions established in the nineteenth century. These are the Paris Convention for the Protection of Industrial Property (1883) and the Berne Convention for the Protection of Literary and Artistic Works (1886), both of which are maintained by the World Intellectual Property Organization (WIPO).[3] Both affirm that any rights granted are national in scope.

The TRIPS Agreement does not change that situation, and, in fact, incorporates both conventions by reference. Where TRIPS goes beyond them is in mandating that WTO member nations establish and enforce a set of minimum legal standards in their IPRs systems. In several cases, TRIPS also establishes basic protection norms in new areas of intellectual property, such as computer software. These minimum requirements have frequently prompted significant legislative and administrative changes in particular members, especially the developing and least-developed countries. However, they leave considerable room for variations in precise standards, limitations, and exceptions. Thus, there are numerous so-called 'TRIPS flexibilities' that remain widely discussed in public debates. For example, WTO parties have the right to employ measures needed to protect public health and nutrition, and to pursue the public interest in sectors that are deemed critical to social and technological development (Article 8.1). TRIPS, therefore, hardly settles the issue of how strongly rights-holders should be protected. Indeed, in some cases it focuses attention on how to use its proffered flexibilities for social development or industrial policy purposes.

While this fact is crucial, it should not be overemphasized. Thus, the fourth point to keep in mind is that, flexibilities aside, TRIPS both markedly raises the average level of IPRs protection in the world and holds countries more accountable for their laws and enforcement regimes. In that regard, it is unlikely that the minimum standards required in the Agreement would have been voluntarily adopted in the bulk of developing countries, had they been left to their own devices. While quantitative assessments of the net impacts of TRIPS are extremely difficult to make, on qualitative grounds it seems evident that the primary medium-term beneficiaries are major intellectual property developers, which reside overwhelmingly in the wealthy post-industrial economies and, to a lesser extent, the emerging industrialized countries.

It is often claimed that developing economies were willing to accept this arrangement in return for improved market access in rich countries in agricultural and primary commodities, and textiles and apparel.[4] Another motivation was the expectation that

---

[3] WIPO is a specialized UN organization that performs a variety of tasks associated with the international system of IPRs. In addition to these two basic conventions, WIPO manages another 21 treaties regarding protection norms, registration protocols, and classification systems. Among the most important are the Patent Cooperation Treaty, which permits inventors to file patent applications in numerous countries with a single instrument, and the WIPO Copyright Treaty and WIPO Performance and Phonograms Treaty, both of which set out basic norms of copyright protection in digital goods and electronic transmissions.

[4] Maskus 2000a; Sell 2003; Stiglitz and Charlton 2005.

implementing TRIPS standards would encourage expanded flows of international investment and technology.[5] To date, neither of these anticipated gains appears to have been realized significantly, at least in the poorest nations, although there has been liberalization of textiles and apparel trade. At the same time, authorities in countries adopting stronger IPRs laws recognize the potential restrictions those laws impose on public health systems, agricultural supports, and other areas of social concern. It is little wonder that TRIPS remains considerably controversial.

18.2 MAJOR REQUIREMENTS IN TRIPS

There are numerous published treatments that extensively describe the details of TRIPS, which would take too many pages to replicate here.[6] However, it is worth noting the primary standards it sets out for WTO members.

A primary foundation is that WTO members must have IPRs laws and procedures that are non-discriminatory. Both national treatment and most-favoured nation (MFN) are basic principles of TRIPS, subject to minor exceptions based on provisions in prior international intellectual property conventions (Articles 3 and 4). The MFN plank requires that any country adopting more extensive protection for intellectual property than is set out in TRIPS, which they are free to do, must immediately and unconditionally apply the stronger rules to entities of any WTO partner. The idea is to avoid discriminatory IPRs application becoming a barrier to trade and investment. Note that this principle means, in particular, that developing countries adopting so-called 'TRIPS-plus' standards in the context of a bilateral trade agreement do not do so on a preferential basis.[7] Rather, the intellectual property provisions of bilateral agreements necessarily ratchet up protection for all comers. This feature establishes a bias over time towards more rigorous IPRs in a broader set of countries, moving the baseline up from TRIPS.

18.2.1 Patents

With respect to patents, several notable minimum standards exist in TRIPS. First, patent protection must endure for at least 20 years from the application date, making TRIPS the first international agreement with a minimum duration. Second, patents must be

---

[5] Maskus 2004.

[6] The WTO itself offers a good overview at <http://www.wto.org/english/tratop_e/trips_e/trips_
e. htm>, where readers can find the full text, while UNCTAD-ICTSD 2005 offers an extensive discussion. See also Maskus 2000a, World Bank 2001, Watal 2001, Deere 2009, and several chapters in both Cottier and Mavroidis 2003 and Maskus and Reichman 2005.

[7] For descriptions of the TRIPS-plus process and its impacts on IPRs within free trade agreements, see Fink and Reichenmiller 2005, Maskus 2006, and Roffe and Spennemann 2006.

made available for both products and processes. The relevance is that many countries, prior to the Agreement, had offered protection only to processes for making pharmaceuticals and chemicals, which are far easier to invent around than the compositions of the products themselves. Third, all fields of technology must be eligible for patents, without discrimination in duration or scope. Significant exceptions exist here: countries can exclude from patentability inventions that, if used domestically, might damage public order or morality, pose a threat to human, animal, or plant health, or seriously harm the environment.[8] They also can exclude diagnostic, therapeutic, and surgical methods for treatment of humans and animals. Further, countries may refuse patents for animals and plants other than microorganisms and for methods of biological reproduction, except for microbiological processes.[9]

18.2.2 Plant variety rights

This form of intellectual property provides exclusive rights to developers of new plant varieties to control use of their propagating material (primarily seeds) and harvested products. To garner protection, the variety must be new, distinct, uniform across plantings, and stable over time. Such rights are important for seed companies and increasingly for developers of agrobiotechnological inventions. Relatively few developing countries had a legal system for defining and protecting plant variety rights prior to TRIPS, which requires some means of registration and protection, an entirely new obligation in international commercial regulation. Countries were obliged to implement either a *sui generis* system of protection, patents for new plant varieties, or both. In adopting the former, nations had available as models the provisions of the UPOV Treaty. UPOV stands for the French acronym of the International Union for the Protection of New Varieties of Plants.

There are two relevant versions of UPOV. Under UPOV 1978, countries could enact the so-called farmers' privilege, which permits farmers to retain seeds for their own use and to exchange them under non-commercial circumstances, and the breeders' exemption, which allows rival plant breeders to use existing varieties in their experimentation without licence or compensation. The provisions in UPOV 1991 disallowed the exchange of seeds (and made it optional for countries to permit farmers to replant seeds harvested on their own land) and required that breeders gain authorization from rights-holders for use of their varieties. The majority of developing countries have implemented legal systems based on the earlier version, even though UPOV 1978 is no

---

[8] The authority to limit protection in order to sustain public health and nutrition, and to pursue policies promoting socio-economic and technological development, actually applies to all forms of IPRs (Article 8).

[9] The language on patenting of life is in Article 27.3(b), which has proved both confusing and controversial.

longer open for accession. Others have acceded to UPOV 1991, with its more rigorous provisions, sometimes in the context of negotiating a free trade agreement with the United States or the EU.

18.2.3 Copyrights

Put simply, a copyright is the legal ability of an author or composer, or the entity to which she assigns the right, such as a publishing company, to prevent others from making or distributing copies of their original works. The TRIPS Agreement incorporates the substantive obligations of the Berne Convention, thereby extending its rules to all WTO members. That Convention essentially defines copyrightable subject matter, describes the exclusive rights inherent in copyright, and indicates minimum time periods of protection. Thus, for example, TRIPS now obliges nations to respect copyrights for a period covering the life of an author plus 50 years, or, where no author is identified (as in the case of many corporate creations), for 50 years. Member states are free to adopt longer periods, as many have done.

Moving beyond the Berne Convention, TRIPS introduces significant new obligations. For example, it requires that computer programs be copyrighted as literary expressions. It also extends copyrights to compilations of data where their accumulation and arrangement can be considered intellectual creations. While these are important new rights, note that the Agreement does not require patent protection for software, as in the United States, nor does it obligate governments to erect patent-like, *sui generis* protection for databases, as in the European Union. It also requires that rights-holders be permitted to exclude copyrighted movies and computer programs from rental markets. Finally, TRIPS defines rights of artists to prevent recording and broadcasting of their performances, of music producers to prevent direct or indirect reproduction of phonograms, and of broadcasters to prevent recording or rebroadcasts of their products, such as television programmes.

Despite these additional rights, TRIPS falls short of dealing effectively with issues of copyright protection in the digital age, especially as regards unauthorized downloading and file-sharing. Thus, the music, film, and proprietary software industries have worked tirelessly in the intervening period to expand and sharpen such rights, while opposition has been raised by certain non-governmental organizations (NGOs) and university and public libraries.

18.2.4 Trademarks and geographical indications

The trademark provisions in TRIPS are largely uncontroversial, and essentially incorporate basic practices in major developed economies that combat misleading or fraudulent use of registered marks, logos, symbols, and the like. One difficult element in some developing nations has been the implementation of laws protecting well-known trademarks, such as 'Intel Inside' and 'Chanel No. 5', which are often copied by local imitators but are familiar to firms in relevant sectors. The definition of what is well known is not entirely clear, leading to some variability in legal standards and enforcement.

More controversial was the introduction into TRIPS of protection for geographical indications (GIs), which identify a product as being produced (at least partially) in a particular region, and where some quality attribute of the product is associated with that location. Obvious examples are Burgundy wines, Scotch whisky, and Parma ham. WTO members are required by TRIPS to establish procedures permitting owners of GIs to prevent misleading or unfair use of their place names, and to preclude registration of GIs that attach to products that do not originate in the territory indicated. At the insistence of the EU, a stronger set of requirements was put into place to protect GIs for wines and spirits, though prior use in good faith remains permissible under some circumstances. Notably, TRIPS calls for additional negotiations to establish an international registry and notification system of wines and spirits. Such registration among members that adopt it would amount to a list of GIs that must be protected.[10] These negotiations are now underway as a component of the Doha Round. They form a key component of the IPRs deliberations, as discussed below.

18.2.5 Trade secrets and confidential test data

Although there are no precise substantive obligations with respect to trade secrets or confidential business information, TRIPS does require members to permit firms to take legal measures to prevent their disclosure through means that are contrary to honest practices. In practice, this means implementing laws that define such unfair practices and establish judicial procedures for adjudicating disputes about whether means of unauthorized disclosure were within the law. TRIPS is otherwise silent on the extent of this obligation.

A more precise, and decidedly more controversial, obligation (Article 39.3) was to state that member governments had to protect confidential data submitted in the process of gaining marketing approval for pharmaceuticals and agricultural chemicals against unfair disclosure, or at least to ensure that the data could not be used unfairly for commercial purposes. This provision refers largely to test data from expensive clinical trials, which many governments require to be submitted for marketing approval. The notion is that such data should be protected for some period of time in order to give the originator firms a lead time advantage over generic firms, which could otherwise use the data to demonstrate quickly and cheaply that their drug versions are therapeutically equivalent. However, the agreement does not mention a minimum period of protection,

---

[10] Fink and Maskus 2006.

leaving governments free to decide what it should be in their own legislation. This issue has been at the centre of debates over TRIPS-plus provisions in free trade areas.

18.2.6 Enforcement obligations

One of the unique features of TRIPS, in comparison with other components of the WTO agreements, is that it clarifies that rights-holders, which are primarily private concerns, must have access to a legal system for enforcing their rights. Thus, TRIPS states that there must be an administrative and judicial system within which owners may sue suspected infringers and take other deterrent actions. Indeed, public enforcement authorities such as customs agents and police are often involved in raids against counterfeit and pirate operations. The legal enforcement procedures must permit effective action against infringement and include remedies to prevent and deter infringing activity, including criminal sanctions in the case of wilful counterfeiting and piracy on a commercial scale. However, TRIPS does not define the meaning of 'effective' in this context, nor does it require countries to erect procedures that go beyond their general framework for law enforcement. This latter issue was central in the US–China dispute over copyrights, discussed later in this chapter.

   Among its enforcement provisions, TRIPS calls for government agencies to have the authority to issue injunctions, order fines and monetary damages, dispose of infringing commodities and production equipment, and employ provisional measures to address infringement in a timely manner. There also need to be border measures—the first time such a requirement has appeared in a multilateral agreement—that permit customs authorities, upon request by rights-holders who present sufficient evidence of infringement, to prevent exports of suspected goods and ensure that imported counterfeit products are not released into general circulation. Some safeguards exist to discourage rights-holders from engaging in abuses of these enforcement measures so that they do not become illegitimate barriers to trade.

18.3 Limitations to IPRs: the 'TRIPS flexibilities'

While setting out these general standards and expectations in support of IPRs, the TRIPS Agreement also recognized the importance of striking a balance between the scope of private rights and the need for user access. This discussion offers a brief overview of the general limitations and exceptions described in the Agreement.[11]

---

[11] Interested readers may consult Deere 2009 and UNCTAD-ICTSD 2005 for detailed information.

18.3.1 Exhaustion and parallel imports

The exhaustion doctrine is a legal principle setting out the circumstances under which the rights of an IPRs owner to prevent further distribution of a good are exhausted.[12] For the vast majority of goods, these rights are exhausted upon first sale within a country. If a consumer purchases a car or a book it is his to sell to others. The exception arises with respect to digital products: when someone legally downloads a movie or computer program, the transaction is generally a licensing agreement that prevents resale or other distribution by the consumer.

Exhaustion becomes an international trade issue because IPRs are nationally defined, and a country may choose to prevent re-importation of goods that were legitimately placed on the market in another country by the rights-holder or her licensees. Such re-imported goods are referred to in the economics literature as parallel imports (PI) because they are transacted in a parallel distribution channel, without the authorization of the rights owner. In the United States, for example, it is illegal to import, beyond certain *de minimus* exceptions for personal use, products that are protected by US patents, designs, and copyrights, though goods protected solely by trademarks are generally open to parallel trade. Thus, the US policy is to ensure free circulation of protected goods within its territory by virtue of the first-sale doctrine, but to prevent competition from PIs. This is an example of national exhaustion. The EU pursues a policy of regional exhaustion, permitting free parallel importation among its members but preventing it from outside the region. Still other countries follow international exhaustion, where distribution rights are eliminated on first sale anywhere in the world, and PI are legal. There is considerable variation across countries and forms of intellectual property in this regard.

The TRIPS Agreement essentially states, in Article 6, that determination of the exhaustion regime is up to individual governments and there is no obligation to permit or prevent PI, so long as the system meets the non-discrimination principles of national treatment and MFN. In the early years after TRIPS was introduced, there was considerable discussion about the legal meaning of Article 6, but the consensus now is that it permits national choice in this matter. Thus, WTO members are free to pursue their own laws governing parallel trade. Again, this has been a key issue with respect to TRIPS-plus provisions in US free trade agreements, for the American position in recent accords has been to ask its partners to ban PI in patented and copyrighted goods.

18.3.2 Compulsory licences and unauthorized use

Developed countries have for a long time featured in their law provisions for permitting unauthorized uses of patented technologies. In one form, such uses are permitted as

---

[12] Maskus 2000b; Ganslandt and Maskus 2008.

limitations on patent rights to encourage competition. A prominent example is the so-called Bolar exception (or early working exception), under which generic drug companies can use protected formulations during the patent term in order to achieve rapid marketing approval when the patent expires.[13] Another is the research exception, which permits others to experiment on a patented product or process in order to invent around protected inventions and bring new innovations to the marketplace faster.

In a second form, firms may be subject to compulsory licences, or non-voluntary licences. Non-voluntary licences may be issued for a variety of reasons.[14] Governments can claim the need to use patented information for public and non-commercial purposes, including ensuring national security, dealing with a public health emergency, building infrastructure, or even developing a vital economic sector. Thus, the government may wish to have multiple producers of a key medicine during a public health emergency. A prominent example happened in 2001 when, in the wake of the 9/11 scare, the United States ordered the Bayer Company to reduce its price and expand supply of Ciprofloxacin, a treatment for the symptoms of anthrax poisoning, or else share its production rights with designated producers. Governments may issue a public use licence for critical technologies that offer national security benefits or address other public goods.

Governments may also compel the owners of patents or copyrights to share some or all of their rights with third parties, generally in return for compensatory royalties. Most commonly, antitrust authorities may compel a firm with a dominant technology to license its use to other firms as part of a competition order. For example, in 1998 the US Department of Justice, concerned about the potential anti-competitive effects of a merger between Monsanto and DeKalb Genetics, ordered the former to license its patented corn germplasm to over 150 seed companies to encourage development of transgenically improved hybrid varieties.[15]

The TRIPS Agreement has a general exceptions clause (Article 30), permitting governments to recognize limited exceptions to exclusive rights so long as they do not unreasonably conflict with the legitimate interests of the patent owner, or unreasonably interfere with the ability to exploit a patent. In practice, many developing countries have interpreted Article 30 as a broad authorization to extend legal limitations on patent rights.

TRIPS also has extensive language (Article 31) setting out conditions under which compulsory licences to third parties may be issued. Among other elements, these conditions require that reasonable efforts have been made to license the technology, but without success, that the use will be temporary and cease when the conditions supporting it

---

[13] This provision was first introduced by the United States in the US Drug Price Competition and Patent Term Restoration Act of 1984.

[14] Reichman and Hazensahl 2003.

[15] See 'Justice Department Approves Monsanto's Acquisition of DeKalb Genetics Corporation: Divestiture of Transformation Technology Rights and Licensing of Corn Germplasm Implemented', 30 November 1998, at <http://www.usdoj.gov/atr/public/press_releases/1998/2103.htm>.

no longer exist, that the licence is non-exclusive (and, in particular, remains available for use by the patent owner), and that adequate remuneration be paid based on the economic value of the compulsory licence. Article 31 also provides scope for compulsory licences so that a dependent patent (one on a new good or technology that requires access to the initial patented technology to work effectively) may be exploited, and also to remedy anti-competitive licensing practices by rights-holders. The most controversial TRIPS provision is Article 31.f, which states that a compulsory licence can only be authorized for production and sale aimed predominantly at the domestic market. This provision made it impossible for small countries with little production capacity to issue a compulsory import licence in medicines—a problem discussed later.

A survey of implementation laws in 49 developing countries found that virtually all had adopted provisions for issuing compulsory licences.[16] However, the reasons for their use varied considerably. Most established that the failure of a rights owner to work the patent by providing adequate domestic supply within three or four years was sufficient grounds, as was the need to invigorate a dependent patent. Somewhat fewer explicitly recognized public interest, national security, and public health grounds. Fewer than half listed the need to remedy anti-competitive practices or the failure of domestic firms to obtain licences under reasonable terms.

18.3.3 Anti-competitive practices

A third general area limiting the scope of actions that rights-holders may take is the ability of governments to employ competition actions to discipline abusive practices in licensing intellectual property (Article 40). The logic is that anti-competitive actions can restrict trade or diminish prospects for technology transfer. While three potentially abusive practices were listed in the provision, the list is not exhaustive and countries are free to deploy their own competition rules within their legal systems. To date, however, relatively few developing countries have adopted extensive anti-monopoly laws with provisions aimed at licensing abuses.

18.3.4 Fair use of copyrighted material

Over time copyrights have been extended beyond the creative outputs of authors and composers to recorded performances, broadcasts, satellite transmissions, software, and digital products and databases. However, the scope of copyrights was limited by permitting nations to enact limitations and exceptions (L&Es), subject to principles listed in the Berne Convention. In essence, this doctrine permits countries to adopt L&Es to exclusive copyrights so long as they do not interfere with the normal commercial exploitation of the rights and do not unreasonably prejudice the rights owners' legitimate interests. Copyrights are

---

[16] Musungu and Oh 2006.

further narrowed by the doctrine of fair use, which permits certain unauthorized uses lying outside legislated L&Es. Prominent examples include making limited copies for personal use, using short quotations for criticism and reviews, permitting teachers to use extracts of copyrighted works for educational purposes, allowing libraries to reproduce works for preservation purposes, letting the press make copies necessary for the reporting of events, and supporting free access by persons with disabilities, such as the visually impaired.[17] This list is not exhaustive, and provisions vary widely across nations.

The TRIPS Agreement, by incorporating these broad exceptions, permits considerable latitude to countries in setting their limitations on copyrights. For example, while TRIPS requires that computer programs be protected by copyrights at a minimum, it is silent on the issue of whether program code may be copied and decompiled for purposes of reverse engineering and promoting interoperability. It also permits governments, under certain circumstances, to issue compulsory licences for copying imported products to promote access to works published abroad.

Perhaps most significantly, TRIPS does not address limitations on copyright protection for digital products, such as recorded music, movies, and e-books, presumably because it was negotiated before the Internet made such goods easily downloadable and available on file-sharing services. This thorny issue was addressed in two further treaties negotiated at the World Intellectual Property Organization, but remains highly controversial. Many developing countries have yet to define their available limitations and exceptions in this regard.

18.3.5 The Doha Declaration and the TRIPS waiver for public health

It did not take long after TRIPS was adopted for observers to note that its provisions may have raised roadblocks against the ability of developing countries to promote widespread and inexpensive access to patented medicines, some of which could prove essential in dealing with endemic diseases. Specifically, the obligation to provide patents for new drugs and biotechnological treatments expanded the exclusive rights available in many developing countries. In itself, this raised the prospect of higher drug prices, as pharmaceutical companies would enjoy longer periods of exclusive production and distribution rights free from generic competition. This prospect was compounded by the limits placed on the ability of countries to promote early generic competition through compulsory licensing or other means. Government-use licences are not of much help if the authorities are unwilling to invoke an emergency, and if no domestic entity is capable of producing the drugs. Most starkly, TRIPS Article 31(f) ruled that a compulsory licence could be ordered only for products that would be made substantially for the domestic market. This provision effectively eliminated the possibility of issuing such a licence to import production from generic firms abroad. In combination with an

---

[17] Okediji 2006; Deere 2009.

obligation to protect confidential test data and the ambiguity surrounding the scope for parallel importation, it seemed that governments would find it difficult to gain low-cost access to new medicines.

The essential question posed by this dilemma was whether commercial WTO rules would trump the perceived needs of individual countries to pursue public health goals. This conflict was brought into early sharp relief by the dispute between South African representatives of global pharmaceutical companies and the South African government, which passed legislation in 1997 to deal with the burgeoning population of HIV-AIDS patients. Under the 'Medicines Act', the government adopted measures to reduce drug prices through compulsory licensing, generic substitution, and parallel importing. The US government pressured the South African authorities to withdraw the legislation. The government refused, despite threats of trade sanctions and a listing on the Special 301 Watch List, and ultimately the United States backed down, recognizing that these legal provisions were in compliance with TRIPS.

In the wake of such concerns, WTO members met in November 2001 to launch the Doha Development Round of trade negotiations. A component of that agreement was the Doha Declaration on the TRIPS Agreement and Public Health, which affirms that, 'the TRIPS Agreement does not and should not prevent Members from taking measures to protect public health'. It therefore confirmed that countries could take advantage of TRIPS safeguards and provisions to attain health goals, including enhanced access to medicines in poor countries.[18] In particular, it referenced the ability of countries to grant compulsory licences, the right to determine what constitutes a national health emergency, and to establish a regime of exhaustion of IPRs. The Declaration also extended the TRIPS implementation period for the least-developed countries from 2006 to 2016, though only as regards drug patents and marketing rights and protection of test data in medicines. Thus, the Doha Declaration clarified that poor countries were permitted to find ways to ensure access to patented drugs, even as TRIPS attempts to preserve the role of patents in incentivizing R&D in the industry.

Despite these modifications, the problem with Article 31(f) remained: poor countries with limited or no production capacity could not benefit from granting a compulsory licence on a patented drug. In paragraph 6 of the Doha Declaration, the TRIPS Council was instructed to find a solution to this problem. On 30 August 2003 a General Council decision was announced to waive Article 31(f) under certain circumstances and thereby permit countries with production capacity to export drugs made under compulsory licence to those without manufacturing capability. This waiver was converted into a formal amendment to the TRIPS Agreement in December 2005.

To implement the waiver, the developed countries agreed not to take advantage of its importation provision, while it is understood that developing countries with sufficient production capacity remain bound by Article 31(f). Thus, it applies only to small and poor nations with limited manufacturing potential. Several countries, including Canada

---

[18] See World Health Organization, 'The Doha Declaration on the TRIPS Agreement and Public Health', at <http://www.who.int/medicines/areas/policy/doha_declaration/en/index.html>.

and India, have passed legislation permitting their generic drug companies to export under the provision. It should be noted that the circumstances under which the waiver may be invoked are complex, and some observers consider them to constitute a remaining barrier to access. To date, just one country has availed itself of the procedure. In July 2007 Rwanda announced it would import 260,000 packs of Apo-Triavir, a generic version of a patented AIDS drug, produced in Canada by the generic firm Apotex. The licence was issued for two years, exclusively for use in the Rwandan market.[19] It was not extended beyond this initial period.

18.4 DISPUTE SETTLEMENT UNDER TRIPS

As a fundamental component of the WTO agreements, TRIPS is fully subject to the dispute settlement procedures of the WTO. By the end of 2010, 29 disputes involving TRIPS rules or TRIPS enforcement had been notified to the Dispute Settlement Body, though panels were formed in just a subset of those cases.[20] It is interesting to note that the United States appeared as complainant in 17 of these suits, seven of which were levied against developing countries. The United States was the respondent in four cases, one of which was brought by a developing country. The European Communities (EC) was the complainant in seven cases, of which two were filed against developing nations. The EC or one of its member nations was respondent in 12 cases, just two brought by developing countries. Among other respondents, Canada appeared twice, Japan twice, and developing countries nine times. Among the latter were Argentina, Brazil, China, India, Indonesia, and Pakistan. Brazil filed one case against the United States, while Brazil and India each complained once about the EC. So far, at least, TRIPS-based litigation has taken place largely among major developed economies.

While each of these cases is interesting, only six are summarized here in order to conserve space. These instances are described because they establish or illuminate important points with respect to TRIPS obligations.

18.4.1 US–Brazil: patent working requirements

In 2000, the United States requested consultations with Brazil regarding Article 68 of Brazil's industrial property law, adopted in 1997. Under that provision, Brazil established a local 'working requirement' that firms needed to satisfy in order to enjoy exclusive patent rights. Brazil defined a failure to work as either not manufacturing the patented product or not making full use of the patented process in that country within a certain

---

[19] International Centre for Trade and Sustainable Development 2007.
[20] See 'Disputes by Agreement' at <http://www.wto.org/english/tratop_e/dispu_e/dispu_agreements_index_e.htm?id=A26#selected_agreement>.

time period. Not meeting this requirement would subject the patent to a possible compulsory licence. The United States argued that this provision required local production, rather than importation, to satisfy legal working needs, and that this was inconsistent with Articles 27 and 28 of TRIPS. Indeed, Article 27 states that patent rights shall be 'enjoyable without discrimination as to the place of invention, the field of technology, and whether products are imported or locally produced'. Brazil countered that its law complies with TRIPS, while NGOs painted the dispute as another instance of US trade authorities attempting to limit the scope of compulsory licensing in medicines.

A dispute panel was set up in early 2001, but in July of that year the two parties reached a settlement and the United States withdrew the complaint. In particular, Brazil promised not to grant a compulsory licence against an American-held patent, based on inadequate domestic production, without engaging in prior consultations with the US government. The US recognized that Brazil had never invoked its industrial property law to issue such a licence, and therefore saw little risk of future use. Furthermore, Brazil agreed to suspend its counter-dispute against the United States regarding sections of the US patent law that, in essence, require that if a small firm or non-profit organization licenses its patented technology it must be to an entity that will manufacture the associated products 'substantially in the United States'.[21]

This case demonstrated that many countries have explicit or implicit production-based working requirements and also discriminate between domestic and international interests, despite the language in TRIPS Article 27. As a result, this US–Brazilian resolution in effect permits developing countries to define working requirements as they wish.

18.4.2 EC–Canada: regulatory review exception

In 1997, the EC requested consultations with Canada over terms of its Patent Act as they applied to pharmaceuticals. In particular, the EC challenged two provisions that it alleged were inconsistent with the exclusive rights of patent owners during the full term of protection. First, under the regulatory review exception, the Canadian law permitted potential generic competitors to use the drug, without authorization of the patent owner, in order to demonstrate that their versions were effective and safe and thereby gain official marketing rights approval upon expiry of the patent term. Second, it allowed generic firms to produce and stockpile quantities of patented drugs so that they could be sold immediately when the patent expired. A dispute panel was formed in 1999 and it reported its findings a year later. In brief, it found that the regulatory review exception is acceptable under TRIPS as a general exemption meeting the terms of Article 30. However, it also ruled that the stockpiling exception was an inappropriate use of the product during the patent term, and ordered its dissolution. Canada implemented this ruling in 2000.

---

[21] Provisions of this kind apply, for example, to university-owned patents on technologies developed using federal grants as set out in the Bayh-Dole Act.

This case is noteworthy for its clarification that experimental use by rival firms during the patent term for purposes of marketing approval was not inconsistent with TRIPS, so long as it did not support production or stockpiling in marketable quantities. The regulatory review exception is an important means by which generic firms can achieve rapid approval, and is widely in place in developing nations.

18.4.3   EC–US: copyrights

In 1999, the EC challenged Section 110(5) of the US Copyright Act. That provision contains two exceptions to the law requiring that bars, restaurants, and retail establishments procure authorized licences to play music and display copyrighted material for the benefit of their patrons. The so-called 'business exemption' permitted small establishments (those under a certain square footage) to play radio and television broadcasts without authorization and without paying a fee. The accompanying 'homestyle exemption' allowed small restaurants and retailers the same exception if they used equipment like that found in private homes, rather than commercial equipment. The EC took exception to these limitations, noting in particular that the business exemption applied to the majority of US restaurants and bars, and to nearly half the retail stores in the country. The dispute settlement panel found, in 2000, that the business exemption was inconsistent with TRIPS Article 13 and constituted a practice that interfered with normal exploitation of copyrighted works and unreasonably prejudiced the owners' interests. In effect, the exception applied to too large a swathe of US businesses, and could not be construed to be a minor limitation on the economic value of copyrights. However, the homestyle exemption was found to be acceptable because it is a significantly limited provision.

There followed a series of meetings in which the United States claimed to be working with Congress towards a legislative implementation of the panel recommendations, and the EC (and Australia, as an interested party) expressed frustration with the slow progress of that process. In 2003, the main parties reached a temporary resolution of the dispute, in which the United States agreed to pay the EC $3.3 million as compensation for lost royalties of European music and television rights-holders over the period 1996–8. In fact, this was the first instance of monetary compensation being paid as a resolution of a WTO dispute. However, as of mid 2009, the United States still had not adopted new legislation to change its copyright act in compliance with the dispute settlement ruling.

18.4.4   US and Australia–European Communities: registration of geographical indications

In 1999, the United States requested consultations with the EC over its legal registration procedures as regards geographical indications. This request was followed in 2003 by a similar inquiry from Australia. These countries complained that EC Regulation 2081/92, as amended, and its administrative and enforcement procedures, discriminated against non-EU nationals, and therefore violated the national treatment and MFN requirements of both GATT 1994 and TRIPS. A WTO panel was established in early 2004, with several countries reserving third party rights in the case.

The panel ruled in favour of the basic claims made by the complainants. Specifically, the EC rule was found not to provide national treatment to other WTO member rights-holders. First, the regulation made GI registration in the EU contingent on the home government of the applicant adopting a protection system identical to that in the EU and providing reciprocal protection to GI holders from the EC. Second, it mandated that firms from outside the EU apply for GI protection through their own governments, and that the authorities in those home countries have inspection systems like those in EU members. This provision thereby denied identical access procedures to non-nationals compared to those that existed for EU firms, and raised an additional hurdle to protection. The panel otherwise sided with the EC, specifically in finding that its practice of registering GIs, even where they may conflict with prior trademarks or cause confusion for consumers, was an acceptable limitation on trademark rights. The panel report was adopted in 2005. In response, the EU implemented a new regulation in March 2006 that it claimed complied with the Dispute Settlement Body's recommendations. However, the United States and Australia argued that the new rule is not in full compliance, and continue to press the case.

18.4.5 US–China: protection and enforcement of intellectual property rights

In 2007, the United States lodged a dispute with China regarding aspects of its IPRs protection and enforcement. Specifically, the United States alleged first that China's thresholds for criminal penalties against trademark counterfeiting and copyright piracy were too low to be an effective deterrent, while the scope of activities subject to criminal enforcement was too narrow. A second complaint was that the practice of customs authorities to auction seized infringing goods after removing the offending labels was inconsistent with TRIPS language on disposal outside commercial channels. Finally, the denial of copyrights and related rights to creative works, such as sound recordings, movies, and books, that were not approved for distribution within China was inconsistent with TRIPS rules regarding an absence of copyright formalities. Moreover, Chinese works were subject to less rigorous procedures on censorship and other predistribution reviews, violating the national treatment obligation.

A WTO panel was formed, and issued its report in early 2009. In brief, the decision could be read as a victory by either side. The criminal penalty thresholds were found not to be a TRIPS violation, nor was the scope of the law found to be overly restrictive. However, the public auctioning of seized goods was inconsistent with the need to dispose of items outside normal market channels. As for the copyright regulations, China's denial of protection to goods not authorized for distribution was found to be inconsistent with

TRIPS obligations. In March 2010, China implemented revisions of its copyright law and customs regulations to come into compliance with these rulings.

These findings essentially affirm that countries retain essential sovereignty over the scope of penalties associated with enforcing IPRs, so long as they remain consistent with the overall legal framework. However, authorities cannot establish procedures that interfere with the market opportunities of IPRs owners, nor can they use other forms of regulation, such as censorship, to deny copyright protection. This case constitutes an important interpretation of the TRIPS enforcement provisions.

18.4.6 Ecuador–European Communities: bananas

Before completing this review of particular dispute resolution cases, it is important to note the unique situation raised within a dispute over a non-TRIPS issue, the EC banana import regime. Specifically, in 1999 a WTO panel found that the import regime favoured producers in the African, Caribbean, and Pacific (ACP) nations in ways that violated several GATT rules. The EC made only token attempts to reform the system. Ecuador requested that a panel be established in 2007 to assess the compliance with prior recommendations of the Dispute Settlement Body regarding changes in the EC's banana import regime. The new panel found again that the system was in violation of several GATT rules.

Less well known is that in May 2000 Ecuador, one of the complainants, requested and was granted the authority to suspend trade obligations to the EU in the amount of $202 million. Among the particulars of this suspension were certain copyrights for EU performers and producers of recorded music and broadcasts, geographical indications, and industrial designs. To date, Ecuador has not implemented this retaliation but the authorization remains in place. The possibility is significant in economic terms, for it addresses a particular imbalance facing smaller countries proposing to retaliate against illegal trade restrictions in larger nations. Ecuador's market is probably too small for the country to damage the EU's interests by simply raising tariffs. In contrast, the discriminatory suspension of copyrights and GIs could permit significant copying of EU-owned IPRs, and perhaps a considerable expansion of regional trade in these legal copies, which would present a greater market-access problem for the affected EC firms.

18.5 Continuing TRIPS issues and IPRs in the Doha Round

Although TRIPS has been in place for 15 years, it remains subject to potential revisions. The Agreement itself left some issues open for subsequent analysis by the TRIPS Council at the WTO and ultimate renegotiation by member states. Other elements have emerged that are the subject of intense debate regarding their inclusion in the Doha Round.

18.5.1 Technology transfer mandate

One of the selling points that prompted adherence of developing countries to TRIPS during its negotiation was the promise of greater technology transfer, which is seen by many as central to achieving gains from IPRs reforms. This notion was in part an implicit bargain, with many policy authorities in developed nations and independent observers noting the enhanced prospects for technology flows to reforming countries.[22] It was also explicit, with a number of TRIPS provisions mentioning technology transfer. Article 7, for example, lists as a basic objective of TRIPS, 'the promotion of technological innovation and…the transfer and dissemination of technology'. Most directly, Article 66.2 requires that developed members provide incentives to their enterprises and institutions to encourage and promote technology transfer to the least-developed countries (LDCs).

The TRIPS Council monitors the implementation of this mandate through inspection of periodic reports about such incentives submitted by authorities in developed nations. Several analysts have read some of these reports and commented on the nature and effectiveness of the policies.[23] They find little evidence that new incentives have been put in place or that procedures are effective at encouraging technology transfer to the LDCs. Indeed, representatives of LDCs are frustrated at the lack of progress in achieving inward technology transfer in the period since TRIPS was agreed.[24] This ineffectiveness is unsurprising because the economic characteristics of LDC markets generally do not attract private technology flows. Nonetheless, figuring out how to make Article 66.2 more effective, via enhanced actions by developed members, remains a priority item for the LDCs.

18.5.2 Geographical indications

As noted earlier, TRIPS recognizes GIs as globally protectable subject matter. In principle, GIs could apply to wines, spirits, beverages and food products, textiles and clothing with artisanal designs or weaving characteristics, and other goods where regional characteristics matter. WTO members must provide means for GI owners to prevent others from making false or misleading claims about the origin of their goods. However, the particular means by which this protection is offered is at each country's discretion. Thus, for example, GIs are protected in the United States largely as trademarks, collective marks, and certification marks (such as 'California Almonds), rather than through a special regime. Also used in various countries are elements of consumer protection law and common law.

---

[22] Maskus 2000a.   [23] Maskus 2004; Moon 2008.
[24] Statements by delegations to WIPO High-Level Forum on Intellectual Property for the Least Developed Countries, Geneva July 2009.

In negotiating TRIPS, the European Union succeeded in achieving stronger protection for wines and spirits. In essence, where firms have not already been using names such as 'Champagne' or 'Scotch Whisky' in good faith for an extended period prior to TRIPS, countries must prevent such use, even if accompanied by qualifiers such as 'kind' or 'imitation'. However, the EU saw this solution as insufficient protection. Therefore, inserted in Article 23.4 is a mandate for additional negotiations within the TRIPS Council over the establishment of a multilateral system of registration and notification of GIs in this industry.

This requirement now forms one element of ongoing negotiations within the Doha Round over GIs. The EU's position is that TRIPS should be amended to say that a product entered into the multilateral register would enjoy a legal presumption that the name must be protected in all members unless it is a generic term or does not fit the definition of a GI. Specifically, registration with the WTO Secretariat would constitute prima facie evidence that the name fits the TRIPS definition of a geographical indication, and this fact must be taken into account when the reviewing country decides whether to accept the application and how to protect it. Opponents, led by the United States, Australia, Argentina, Chile, Canada, and other 'new world' wine-producing nations, argue that there is no need to amend TRIPS. Rather, the TRIPS Council could establish a voluntary registry and only those countries that join the system would be obliged to consult the database when considering a GI registration.

The second element relates to proposals to extend the higher level of protection beyond wines and spirits to other products. Numerous developing countries, led by India, Indonesia, Brazil, China, Thailand, Turkey, and the African Group, believe that their producers of location-based food products and designs can gain greater global marketing reach, and earn additional economic value, through registration and protection of GIs. They are joined by the EU and Switzerland in supporting this extension, which gives them greater leverage in pushing for the registry on wines and spirits.

18.5.3 Disclosure of origin of genetic resources in patent applications

One of the most perplexing components of TRIPS is Article 27.3(b), relating to intellectual property protection for plants and animals. This provision permits countries to exclude from patentability plants and animals and 'essentially' biological processes for producing them (i.e. biological reproduction techniques). However, this exclusion does not apply to microorganisms or microbiological processes, or non-biological processes of production. The intent was to make biotechnological inventions widely available for patenting. Article 27.3(b) reflected an awkward compromise between the needs of biotechnology producers and those who are uncomfortable with the idea of firms owning private rights to life forms and processes. However, the language on life patents is so vague that there has been considerable confusion in interpreting its meaning as countries implement new patent regimes.[25] Moreover, commercial interests found it unsatisfying. Accordingly, negotiators included a provision for review of this Article within four years of TRIPS being passed.

In that review it quickly became evident that 27.3(b) raises difficult issues regarding its consistency with the United Nations Convention on Biological Diversity (CBD). In particular, the CBD states that countries have sovereign rights over the genetic resources, including plants and animals, found in their jurisdictions. States can, therefore, regulate the extraction of such resources for use in any capacity, including scientific and industrial activities that may generate patentable inventions. Further, the CBD posits that extracting firms and institutions should achieve prior informed consent with the owners of such resources (typically national governments) and ensure that benefits from their use are shared with those owners or citizens.

TRIPS is silent on all these issues, requiring only that microbiological inventions be patented and plant varieties be protected, with no requirements for consent or benefit sharing. In principle, then, a foreign firm or university could take plant material from a developing country, use it to develop new biogenetic processes and medicinal products, and patent these inventions wherever it wants, without benefit sharing. That would block inventors in the originator nation from developing competing products based on their own formulations and exporting to those markets. It could even be possible for that firm or university to patent them in the country where the resources originate, if permitted by the patent law, and enforce those patents against similar medicinal uses that may have existed in a village's traditional practices for a long time. This possibility motivated some developing countries to adopt laws governing the use of genetic resources and traditional knowledge, with provisions for prior consent and benefit sharing. Among others, Peru and India have implemented extensive legislation in this regard.

Facing such concerns, WTO members in the Doha Declaration called for the TRIPS Council to consider the relationship between TRIPS and the CBD, along with means of protecting traditional knowledge and folklore.[26] Over time, this consideration evolved into proposals by some countries to negotiate a change in TRIPS that would mandate a particularly contentious rule: that patent applications must include statements identifying the sources of genetic materials on which the inventions are based. Positions taken to date are widely separated, reflecting the controversial aspects of this issue. At one extreme are a group of countries, including the United States, Australia, Japan, Canada, and Korea, that argue there is no inconsistency between TRIPS and the CBD and that both agreements can be implemented at the national level without conflict. In particular, they claim that proper recourse to existing patent application protocols will ensure that invalid patents are not issued, thereby safeguarding the prior knowledge of others. Further, these patent rules do not prevent applicants from engaging in prior informed consent and benefit sharing.

---

[25] Deere 2009.   [26] See WTO 2006.

At the other extreme are countries that see inherent conflicts between TRIPS and the CBD on two grounds. The first is that TRIPS offers scope for appropriation and ownership of genetic materials without recognizing the sovereignty of countries over their use. The second is that TRIPS does not require prior informed consent or benefit sharing. Countries in this camp, including the African Group, Bangladesh, and Zambia, argue that Article 27.3(b) should be amended to state that life forms and inventions from genetic materials cannot be patented.

Other countries are arrayed between these poles, with most developing countries taking the view that, while there may be no inherent inconsistency between TRIPS and the CBD, the global patent system needs to be reformulated to make sure that both Agreements may be respected in practice. From this logic flows the proposal for disclosure in patent applications of the source and country of origin of any biological resources or traditional knowledge involved, as advocated by the Andean Community, Brazil, China, India, the Philippines, and many other developing countries, along with Switzerland and Norway among rich nations. These proposals would also require patent applicants to demonstrate that they had achieved prior informed consent from appropriate authorities and entered into fair and equitable benefit-sharing arrangements.

These are complex negotiating issues, on which little progress has been made. The United States and Japan, for example, seem unyielding in their opposition to a disclosure requirement, arguing that this would become an additional condition of patentability and overturn centuries of legal tradition. Their commercial and innovative interests are concerned that such a requirement would destroy a valuable trade secret, which is confidential information about material's location.

The EC and Switzerland have joined forces with many developing countries to push for incorporating both of the GI provisions and the disclosure requirement into formal revisions of TRIPS at the Doha Round.[27] This reflects an alliance of cross-issue interests that may be sufficiently broad and powerful to overcome the opposition of other major countries.

18.6 CONCLUDING REMARKS

The TRIPS Agreement at the WTO is the most comprehensive global agreement covering protection and enforcement norms in IPRs. To comply with its provisions, numerous developing and emerging nations have implemented legal reforms, with the effect of strongly expanding the scope of protection for patents, copyrights, and related rights.[28] However, the language of TRIPS is sufficiently flexible that countries may sustain significant exceptions and limitations to the exercise of exclusive rights. The Agreement also failed to address a number of complex questions, such as copyrights in digital goods and

[27] WTO 2008.   [28] Park 2008.

internet transmissions, the relationship of patents to national sovereignty over genetic resources, and the full scope of GIs protection. The Doha Round of negotiations is supposed to resolve these issues, though without success to date.

Whether the TRIPS Agreement has achieved an appropriate balance between incentives for innovation and licensing on the one hand, and the needs for access to new goods and information on the other, remains an open question. There are reasons to be optimistic about the medium-term impacts on international technology diffusion.[29] However, stronger IPRs raise fundamental concerns about the ability of governments and international organizations to procure needed public goods at reasonable cost.[30] In this sense, the international system remains controversial and subject to further revisions.

REFERENCES

Cottier, Thomas, and Petris C. Mavroidis. 2003. *Intellectual Property: Trade, Competition and Sustainable Development*. Studies in International Economics. The World Trade Forum Volume 3. Ann Arbor: University of Michigan Press.

Deere, Carolyn. 2009. *The Implementation Game: The TRIPS Agreement and the Global Politics of Intellectual Property Reform in Developing Countries*. Oxford: Oxford University Press.

Fink, Carsten, and Keith E. Maskus. 2006. The Debate on Geographical Indications at the WTO. In *Trade, Doha and Development: A Window into the Issues*, edited by Richard Newfarmer, 197–207. Washington, DC: World Bank.

Fink, Carsten, and Patrick Reichenmiller. 2005. *Tightening TRIPS: The Intellectual Property Provisions of Recent US Free Trade Agreements*. Trade Note 20. Washington, DC: World Bank. Available from <http://www.worldbank.org/trade>. Accessed on 7 November 2011.

Ganslandt, Mattias, and Keith E. Maskus. 2008. Intellectual Property Rights, Parallel Imports and Strategic Behavior. In *Intellectual Property, Growth and Trade, ii: Frontiers of Economics and Globalization*, edited by Keith E. Maskus, 263–88. Amsterdam: Elsevier-North Holland.

International Centre for Trade and Sustainable Development. 2007. Rwanda Tests Public Health Waiver. *News and Analysis* 11 (6). Available from <http://ictsd.org/i/news/bridges/4095>. Accessed on 7 November 2011.

Maskus, Keith E. 2000a. *Intellectual Property Rights in the Global Economy*. Washington, DC: Institute for International Economics.

Maskus, Keith E. 2000b. Parallel Imports. *The World Economy: Global Trade Policy 2000* 23 (9): 1263–84.

Maskus, Keith E. 2004. Encouraging International Technology Transfer. Project on IPRs and Sustainable Development. Issue Paper 7. Geneva: International Centre for Trade and Sustainable Development.

Maskus, Keith E. 2006. Intellectual Property Rights in the U.S.–Colombia Free Trade Agreement. In *The Free Trade Agreement between Colombia and the United States*, edited by Jeffrey G. Schott. Washington, DC: Peterson Institute for International Economics.

[29] Ibid.   [30] Maskus and Reichman 2005.

Maskus, Keith E., and Jerome H. Reichman, eds. 2005. *International Public Goods and Transfer of Technology under a Globalized Intellectual Property Regime*. Cambridge: Cambridge University Press.

Moon, Suerie. 2008. Does TRIPS Art. 66.2 Encourage Technology Transfer to LDCs? Project on IPRs and Sustainable Development. Policy Brief 2. Geneva: International Centre for Trade and Sustainable Development.

Musungu, Sisule, and Cecilia Oh. 2006. The Use of Flexibilities in TRIPS by Developing Countries: Can They Promote Access to Medicines? WHO Study on Intellectual Property Rights, Innovation and Public Health. Geneva: World Health Organization.

Okediji, Ruth L. 2006. The International Copyright System: Limitations, Exceptions and Public Interest Considerations for Developing Countries. Project on IPRs and Sustainable Development. Issue Paper 15. Geneva: International Centre for Trade and Sustainable Development.

Park, Walter G. 2008. Intellectual Property Rights and International Innovation. In *Intellectual Property, Growth and Trade, ii: Frontiers of Economics and Globalization*, edited by Keith E. Maskus, 289–328. Amsterdam: Elsevier.

Reichman, Jerome H., and Catherine Hazensahl. 2003. *Non-Voluntary Licensing of Patented Inventions: Historical Perspective, Legal Framework under TRIPS, and an Overview of Practice in Canada and the United States*. Project on IPRs and Sustainable Development. Geneva: International Centre for Trade and Sustainable Development.

Roffe, Pedro, and Christoph Spennemann. 2006. The Impact of FTAs on Public Health Policies and TRIPS Flexibilities. *International Journal of Intellectual Property Management* 1 (1–2):75–93.

Sell, Susan K. 2003. *Private Power, Public Law: The Globalization of Intellectual Property Rights*. Cambridge: Cambridge University Press.

Stiglitz, Joseph E., and Andrew Charlton. 2005. *Fair Trade for All: How Trade Can Promote Development*. Oxford: Oxford University Press.

United Nations Conference on Trade and Development and International Centre for Trade and Sustainable Development. 2005. *Resource Book on TRIPS and Development*. Cambridge: Cambridge University Press.

Watal, Jayashree. 2001. *Intellectual Property Rights in the WTO and Developing Countries*. The Hague: Kluwer Law International.

World Bank. 2001. *Global Economic Prospects and the Developing Countries 2002: Making Trade Work for the World's Poor*. Washington, DC: World Bank.

WTO. 2006. Council for Trade-Related Aspects of Intellectual Property Rights. *The Relationship Between the TRIPS Agreement and the Convention on Biodiversity*. IP/C/W/368/Rev.1. Geneva: WTO.

WTO. 2008. Trade Negotiations Committee. *Draft Modalities for TRIPS-Related Issues*. TN/C/W/52. Geneva: WTO.

CHAPTER 19

··

FLEXIBILITIES, RULES, AND TRADE REMEDIES IN THE GATT/WTO SYSTEM

··

J. MICHAEL FINGER

An institution is an imperfect agent of order and of purpose... Intent and chance alike share in its creation.

Walton H. Hamilton[1]

19.1 INTRODUCTION

··

GENERAL Agreement on Tariffs and Trade (GATT)/World Trade Organization (WTO) provisions such as safeguards and anti-dumping provide procedures through which a member government can apply a new trade restriction. Within a system intended to promote and to defend an open international trading system, the logic of such provisions is that a controlled step back may sometimes be necessary to preserve two steps forward.

In practice, these provisions have served the system well. They have provided process and flexibility for WTO member governments to manage internal pressures for protection within a generally liberal trade policy. They have helped to keep the application of new restrictions under sufficient discipline that their use has minimally compromised the momentum of liberalization the reciprocal negotiations have created, and they have managed the application of new restrictions in such a way that unsuccessful protection-seekers have not organized to overturn the system—they have brought protection-seekers to accept 'No' for an answer.

---

[1] Hamilton 1963, 89.

The form of these provisions (e.g. a restriction may be imposed when dumped imports injure a domestic industry) suggests that they limit members to applying restrictions only in the circumstances, or in a form, that 'makes sense' in relation to some standard of social or economic welfare—this appearance is intensified by the rhetoric of policing against 'unfair' trade. In practice, however, they do not do this. The discipline the system applies is about fewer restrictions versus more, not about 'good' restrictions versus 'bad'. Anti-dumping is perhaps the classic example of a pragmatically successful flexibility instrument with pretensions—but no more than pretensions—to a real economic rationale.

What is this chapter about? As an essay, it advances the position on trade remedy usage that is stated in the two paragraphs above. The chapter is not a survey of the literature on trade remedies—several recent and comprehensive ones are already available.[2] But these are, in large part, surveys of trade remedy *analysis*, and thus are only tertiary sources of information on trade remedy *use*. I hope in this chapter to shift attention more directly to trade remedy usage, and particularly to national practice. National practice, I posit, applies discipline, while WTO rules are only one of the forces that shape national practice. To think simply of WTO rules as specifying what a member can and cannot do overlooks a good deal of what makes the WTO system work.

As to how the chapter's argument is laid out, Section 19.2 reviews how trade remedy use has shifted from GATT's early decades—when renegotiation dominated—to the post-Uruguay Round era, in which anti-dumping has become by far the most popular instrument. Section 19.3 documents that the application of new restrictions in the WTO era has been small relative to the extent of trade remedy usage in the 1980s, when negotiated export restraints were the most popular flexibility. Section 19.4 points out that the discipline the system imposes is different from that it appears to impose. A wealth of research supports the conclusion that trade remedy protection is not limited to the circumstances specified in the agreements—and draws from this the incorrect conclusion that it is not limited, that trade remedies constitute a leading obstacle to free and fair trade.[3]

Section 19.5 illustrates that WTO rules are only one of the influences that have guided the evolution of national trade remedy practice. It does so by reviewing the safeguard restrictions imposed by the United States in 2002–3 on imports of steel. It outlines the interaction of national management of protectionist pressures with the WTO agreements; it also shows that, as trade remedies continue to evolve, import users are creating for themselves an increasing role in the management of pressures for protection.

Section 19.6 presents my conclusions and my speculations about questions on which further research might prove interesting.

---

[2] WTO 2009—this recent WTO Secretariat survey lists over 350 references. Other notable surveys are Blonigen and Prusa 2003 and Nelson 2006 on anti-dumping, and Sykes 2007 on trade remedy law.

[3] Kucik and Reinhardt 2008, 478, review such interpretations.

19.2 THE EVOLUTION OF TRADE REMEDY USE

Historically speaking, trade remedy instruments such as the escape clause, anti-dumping, and countervailing duties existed in national legislation before there was a GATT or WTO. The initial GATT Agreement of 1948 did little more than to reserve the right of countries to impose such restrictions. These provisions were simply compromises—different in legal form and in political rhetoric from not reducing tariffs in some sectors, e.g. textiles—but compromises none the less. Without their inclusion, the domestic politics of trade would not have accepted the liberalization that was achieved.

In form, these provisions are regulations or rules. They allow restrictions, but limit them to particular conditions or response to particular problems, e.g. anti-dumping measures, or measures in response to balance of payments problems. In the WTO Secretariat, anti-dumping, safeguards, and countervailing duties are within the ambit of the 'Rules Division'.

From a more functional perspective, such provisions provide flexibility for governments to respond to pressures for protection that, if not accommodated, might undo a generally liberal trade policy framework. The cliché 'one step backward to preserve two steps forward' describes this linkage. The foreword by Pascal Lamy in the WTO Secretariat review of contingency measures provides a useful exposition of this perspective.[4]

Generally speaking, the provisions the GATT provides for imposing import restrictions include:

- provisions for renegotiating previous tariff concessions and commitments
- restrictions that can be imposed unilaterally, but only in particular circumstances, i.e. contingent or administered protection
- measures that may have trade effects but are imposed for different reasons, e.g. to protect human, animal, or plant life and health[5]
- provisions for specific, one-off approval such as a waiver.

The changes of usage, from reliance in GATT's early decades on tariff renegotiations to the modern era in which anti-dumping is the predominant vehicle, were part of the evolution of the GATT/WTO system from a diplomatic process towards a more judicial one.

---

[4] WTO 2009.

[5] The Uruguay Round agreements on technical barriers and on sanitary and phytosanitary barriers stem from concern that standards were being used to provide protection not justified by the principal purposes a standard serves. This chapter will not, however, take up use of these agreements.

19.2.1 A diplomat's jurisprudence

GATT's early decades were characterized by what Robert Hudec described as a 'diplomat's jurisprudence'.[6] This diplomat's jurisprudence was a compromise between jurisprudence as understood by lawyers and the reality of the limited influence trade negotiators had over national trade policy decisions. In an era in which there was sometimes a greater sense of shared objective among trade negotiators than between these negotiators and government officials at home, not pinning down trade differences with legal precision could allow the working out of a mutually acceptable solution before the matter reached domestic politics.

As to dealing with domestic parties who pressed for protection, trade policy officials tried to keep decisions out of the give and take of domestic politics, and exploited the discretion the trade remedies mechanisms allowed to avoid applying them. Irwin's study, for example, documents[7] that the US Treasury Department did not find less-than-fair-value pricing in a large share of anti-dumping cases.[8]

I have documented elsewhere that renegotiations under GATT Article XXVIII were, in the GATT's early decades, the most used means for obtaining GATT clearance for new restrictions.[9] We know little about the domestic processes through which officials

---

[6] Particularly in Hudec 1970, generally in Hudec 1975 and Hudec 1978.

[7] Irwin 2005.

[8] Blonigen and Prusa 2003, 254, after noting the relatively few anti-dumping actions before 1980, attribute this to (or conclude from this that) 'the GATT rules for imposing anti-dumping duties were difficult to satisfy'.

This, however, cannot be the explanation. First, in an era in which positive consensus was required to adopt a panel report, it was difficult to establish through the dispute settlement procedure that a national practice was in violation of a country's Article VI obligations. The respondent could simply block adoption of the panel report. In the absence of such adoption, the consequent steps, possibly authorized retaliation, would never come into play.

Second, there is little 'GATT jurisprudence' that demonstrates active enforcement of 'GATT rules' on anti-dumping. GATT 1994, which covers the entire history of the GATT from 1948 to 1994, lists only five panel reports in which Article VI anti-dumping obligations were referenced.

In three of the five, reference to Article VI by the respondent had about it the air of a last gasp attempt to find legal cover for something that was quite different from what we think of today as anti-dumping. 'Swedish anti-dumping actions' and 'US exports of potatoes to Canada' were about reference price tariff systems, in which a tariff surcharge was added if the price of an import shipment was below the reference price. A third case, 'Japan trade in semiconductors', was about Japanese government export restraints on semiconductors. In its defence (in a case that was basically about Article XI obligations to avoid quantitative restrictions), Japan argued that its export restraints were to prevent dumping by Japanese enterprises, referring to Article VI's hortatory condemnation of dumping.

The other two cases, 'New Zealand anti-dumping duties on imports of electrical transformers from Finland' and 'US anti-dumping duties on imports of cement from Mexico', did involve issues central to anti-dumping enforcement. In the New Zealand case, the panel took up the way in which the New Zealand government had determined injury and a causal link. In the US cement case, the panel found that the US government had not adequately 'satisfied itself' that the request for the anti-dumping investigation was on behalf of all or most of the producers in the relevant regional market. The US cement panel report was not adopted.

[9] Finger 2002.

managed protectionist pressures, or decided in which instances a tariff rate would be renegotiated.

The thrust of Hudec's analysis is that in this era the contribution trade remedies made to the development of an open international trading system was more a matter of how trade policy officials used them to manage the domestic politics of trade than of the legal limits the relevant GATT Articles imposed. Julio Nogués and I, in our study of Latin American liberalization, found a similar role for the acceptance of GATT/WTO commitments. For Latin American reformers, a significant attraction of full entry into GATT/WTO system was that such entry supported the domestic politics of removing administration mechanisms that they had been unable to control. Almost the entirety of the protection that was removed had been 'administered protection', applied through such mechanisms. (There would thus be some naivety in treating trade remedy notifications by developing countries since the Uruguay Round as an increase of protection.) The GATT/WTO system of bindings and trade remedy rules was critical to the success of these liberalization programmes; but equally critical was the skill and the courage of reformers in Latin America to use these rules in support of liberalization.[10]

19.2.2 Negotiated export restraints

In the mid 1970s, the negotiation of 'voluntary' export restraint (VER) agreements became the favoured instrument for handling trade problems. A GATT Secretariat tabulation identified 249 such arrangements in place in 1989—these in addition to restraints sanctioned by the Multi-Fiber Arrangement (MFA).[11] Laird estimated that in 1988 about 15 per cent of US and EC imports were under VERs or orderly marketing arrangements.[12] (Laird's figure includes MFA sanction restrictions.)

Except for those sanctioned by the textile arrangements, VERs were GATT-illegal.[13] Nevertheless, they accorded well with its ethic of reciprocity, and their negotiation controlled for the possibility of chain reaction of import restrictions from one country to another, as had been disastrous in the 1930s. The reality of power politics was at play, but compensation was involved. Reduced export volumes were compensated by higher prices, the result often being a net gain for exporters. Sometimes the quid pro quo was foreign aid or some other non-trade consideration.

The Uruguay Round Agreements on Safeguards and on Textiles and Clothing required existing VERs to be phased out, and banned further use of such restrictions. One might speculate that the reasons behind this elimination of VERs included the shift

---

[10] Finger and Nogués 2006.

[11] GATT 1991, Appendix Table 2.

[12] Laird 1992: Laird reports that it was difficult to identify restraints applied by EC member states. Some such restraints, he reports, were negotiated between EC member state governments and foreign enterprises rather than foreign governments. These had limited degrees of transparency and differing degrees of official sanction.

[13] GATT 1994, 494.

of Congressional power in the United States away from the Southern delegations who represented textile manufacturing states, the increasing weight of developing countries in world trade, and their increasingly active role in the GATT system. They also included the growing realization in developed economies that a VER was a costly form of protection; the long-term legal pressure of the GATT rules; and—not to be underestimated—the availability of an attractive, GATT-legal alternative, anti-dumping.

19.2.3 Anti-dumping ascends

Anti-dumping measures and VERS proved to be effective complements; the threat of formal action under the anti-dumping law provided leverage to force an exporter to accept a VER. Nearly half of the anti-dumping investigations opened in the United States in the 1980s were superseded by VERs; agreed price undertakings were the end result of EC cases more often than were anti-dumping duties.[14]

Once anti-dumping action proved itself to be applicable to any case of troublesome imports, its other attractions for protection-seeking industries became apparent. The rhetoric of foreign unfairness provides a vehicle for building a political case for protection. Additionally, GATT/WTO rules allow specific exporters to be targeted by anti-dumping measures and the usual practice has been to target the newer, more dynamic ones. Traditional exporters—who often were being displaced by them—would often serve as passive, if not active, allies of such restrictions.

Before the Uruguay Round agreements came into effect in 1995, application of anti-dumping was almost exclusively by the major industrialized countries. Since, anti-dumping use has become widespread among developing members as well as developed (see Table 10), and anti-dumping has dominated use of other provisions that sanction import restrictions: 2,374 anti-dumping measures as compared with 99 safeguard measures, 139 countervailing duty measures and 32 renegotiations (see Table 11). WTO Balance of Payments Committee reports (WT/BOP/R/10 and WT/BOP/R/19) for 1995 and 1996 reported balance of payments measures in place in 18 members; subsequent reports (through 2008) indicate that all such measures have been removed.

Countervailing measures have remained an instrument primarily of industrialized countries. Over the period 1995–2009, three-quarters of countervailing duty investigations notified to the WTO have been by three members: Canada, the United States, and the European Union. Countervailing duty investigations have often been the complement of disputes in which the complainant has likewise taken up the allegedly illegal subsidy under WTO subsidy rules.

Again, the minimal use of countervailing duties can be explained by the administrative convenience of anti-dumping. Strictly as a matter of providing import relief, anti-dumping can cover the same problems. In addition, the standards for demonstrating that the exporter receives a subsidy are more difficult to meet than the standards for demonstrating dumping.

[14] Finger 2002; Stegemann 1991.

Table 10 Numbers of WTO members who have notified trade remedy measures, 1995–2009

Trade remedy		Developing members	Developed members	All members
Anti-dumping	Investigations initiated	30	13	43
	Measures applied	26	13	39
Safeguards	Investigations initiated	26	19	45
	Measures applied	14	14	28
Countervailing measures	Investigations initiated	12	8	20
	Measures applied	9	6	15

Source: Tabulated from data in the WTO website database.

Table 11 Numbers of anti–dumping, safeguard, and countervailing investigations undertaken and measures applied by developed and developing WTO members, 1995–2009

	Investigations			Measures		
	Developed	Developing	All	Developed	Developing	All
Anti-dumping	1325	2350	3675	815	1559	2374
Safeguards	62	136	198	39	60	99
Countervailing measures	200	45	245	107	32	139
Totals	1587	2531	4118	961	1651	2612

Source: Tabulated from data in the WTO website database.

19.3 THE MAGNITUDE OF TRADE REMEDY USAGE

Though the numbers of countries who have applied trade remedy measures and the number of measures applied have increased notably, such measures, in fact, have been applied to a limited amount of trade. Chad Bown,[15] building from a World Bank database,[16] has put together a careful year-by-year tabulation of the number of products and the value of imports on which 'temporary trade barriers' were in place. The tabulation includes safeguards, anti-dumping, countervailing duties, and special safeguards against China (as allowed in China's protocol of accession to the WTO). For a representative sample of countries (that account for 86 per cent of anti-dumping measures applied in 2007–9), he found that the share of imports subject to such measures has remained flat

---

[15] Bown 2010.
[16] World Bank 2010. Bown was one of the principal constructors of the database.

or even declined since the 1990s, minimally affected by the Asian crisis of 1997 or the global downturn that began in 2007.[17]

Tables 12 and 13 are constructed from Bown's findings and provide a profile of restrictions as of 2009. They show that across the countries in his sample well below 2 per cent of import value was subject to trade remedy measures; for only four of the 14 countries in the sample were there trade remedy measures on as much as 2 per cent of import value.

This coverage is well below the 15 per cent of imports Laird found to be subject to VERs by major trading countries before the Uruguay Round agreements eliminated VERs.[18]

Table 12 Imports of selected economies subject to temporary trade barriers in 2009

Economy applying measure	Percentage of product lines*	Percentage of import value**
Developing economies		
Turkey	5.3	3.1
India	6.1	2.9
Argentina	2.8	2.0
Brazil	1.5	1.7
China	0.9	1.7
Mexico	1.1	0.7
Indonesia	0.5	0.7
South Africa	0.8	0.3
Simple average of above developing economies	2.4	1.6
High-income economies		
United States	4.7	2.3
European Union	2.5	1.6
Japan	0.1	1.1
Canada	1.3	0.6
Australia	0.6	0.4
South Korea	0.9	0.4
Simple average of above high-income economies	1.7	1.1

* Percentage of six-digit (HS-06) lines with at least one measure in place.
** In the HS-06 lines where measures have been applied.
Source: Bown 2010, Table 1.

[17] Bown 2010, Figure 1.
[18] Laird 1992.

Table 13 Percentages of exporters' products* subject to the anti-dumping measures of selected importers,** 2009

Exporting economy	Products exported to developing economies	Products exported to developed economies
Developing economy exporters		
China	2.6	1.6
India	0.5	0.6
Thailand	0.8	0.4
Indonesia	1.0	0.6
Ukraine	1.3	1.7
Brazil	0.5	0.7
Russia	1.1	0.9
South Africa	1.2	0.5
Malaysia	0.6	0.1
Vietnam	0.3	0.3
Kazakhstan	7.9	0.7
Mexico	0.1	0.2
Turkey	0.2	0.1
Argentina	0.0	0.1
Pakistan	0.0	0.1
Other developing economies	0.1	0.0
Simple average of above developing economies	1.1	0.5
High-income economy exporters		
South Korea	1.1	0.6
European Union	0.4	0.6
Taiwan, China	0.7	0.5
Japan	0.3	0.5
United States	0.3	0.1
Other high-income economies	0.1	0.0
Simple average of above high-income economies	0.5	0.4

*Note that these are percentages of product lines (HS-06) on which anti-dumping measures are imposed, not of import values.
**These data cover anti-dumping measures imposed by the following: developing economies: Argentina, Brazil, China, India, Indonesia, South Africa, Turkey; high-income economies: Australia, European Union, Japan, South Korea, United States. These economies account for 86 per cent of anti-dumping measures in place 2007–9.
Source: Bown 2010, Table 5.

These restrictions, by the way, display a pattern that has been noted before: developing country restrictions have the same bias (against developing countries) as do developed country restrictions, and they are more severe. Another familiar result is that restrictions are relatively high against the more dynamic exporters, e.g. China and South Korea.

19.4 THE LIMITS ON TRADE REMEDY APPLICATION ARE NOT WHAT THEY APPEAR TO BE

As noted in the introduction, a considerable amount of research has been done on the application of trade remedies. A major conclusion that has emerged from this work is that trade remedy application is not limited to sets of circumstances defined by WTO agreements.

Anti-dumping—by far the most frequently used trade remedy—is not about 'dumping' in any specialized economic sense. Operationally speaking, the law specifies the conditions under which an industry is eligible for *anti-dumping* protection, and 'dumping' is—implicitly—whatever you can get the government to act against under the anti-dumping law. Similarly, safeguard action, in practice, is not limited to those instances in which it has been demonstrated in an econometrically meaningful way that 'injury' has resulted from imports that themselves result from 'unforeseen developments'—as GATT Article XIX demands.

Different people have stated this conclusion in different ways. Finger concluded[19] that 'Anti-dumping is ordinary protection with a grand public relations programme';[20]

---

[19] Finger 1993, 34.

[20] Nelson severely castigated this statement. He described it as 'hysterical rhetoric', as being 'wrong in virtually every essential way', and concluded, 'It does not help' (Nelson 2006, 582, footnote 68).

On the contrary, it helped tremendously. In the late 1970s when I first began to think about anti-dumping, it had about it an aura of righteousness. An objective that soon emerged for me was to 'desanctify' it. When I first presented at the World Bank a tabulation of protection against developing country exports, a prominent economist objected to my including anti-dumping measures. In his words, 'anti-dumping is GATT-legal'. When I replied, 'so are tariffs', he saw my point immediately. It took longer in political circles.

The statement, 'anti-dumping is ordinary protection with a grand public relations programme', first came to mind in 1991 as I drove into the parking lot of a Canberra radio station. The talk show moderator looked at me as if she expected another technocrat she would have to carry through the session. She opened by asking 'What's anti-dumping?' My response set the tone for the discussion, and put the industry people on the panel on the defensive. The programme provided a few licks in support of the ongoing attempt by the Hawke government to rein in Australia's then copious application of anti-dumping measures.

By the early 1990s, several studies had pointed out technical biases in trade remedy procedures and professionally the proposition was being accepted that anti-dumping, as economics, was little different from ordinary protection. Boltuck and Litan 1991 is an example. My phrase helped to elevate such studies from technicalities to a political force—turned the tide so that anti-dumping's supporters, rather than its opponents, were on the defensive. In support of this point, I draw on two examples from my own experience. First, Greg Mastel's book (Mastel 1998) in defence of anti-dumping begins by arguing that, contrary to what Michael Finger has asserted, anti-dumping does not have a favourable public image. The second concerns an appearance I made at a US Congressional subcommittee hearing. In response to the 'public relations' point (and others), one of the big-time trade lawyers with a long list of anti-dumping-protected clients circulated a few days later a 30-page rejoinder to my eight-page testimony. (My second reaction to the rejoinder was pique. The lawyer probably billed his clients a handsome fee for preparing it. My appearance at the hearings had cost me—a day of unpaid leave from the World Bank to prepare the statement, and a second to appear at the hearings.)

I had begun in 1982 (Finger 1982) my effort to shift the rhetoric, from protection's advocates sounding like people and its opponents like college professors, to the other way around.

Hoekman and Kostecki that 'Anti-dumping constitutes straightforward protectionism that is packaged to make it look like something different.'[21] Blonigen and Prusa, in the opening paragraph of their survey of research on anti-dumping, specify that their work 'is about anti-dumping, not dumping... anti-dumping has nothing to do with keeping trade "fair"'.[22]

Horlick and Shea present the same conclusion from the perspective of motive rather than effect: 'From the perspective of a US industry seeking protection, those laws [the various trade remedies] simply represent different ways of reaching the same goal—improvement of the competitive position of the complainant against other companies.'[23] Similarly, Sykes concludes that 'the political constituency for anti-dumping policy is not (and never has been) an anti-monopoly constituency, but is instead much the same as the political constituency for safeguard measures—declining industries.'[24]

A related conclusion to which I want to call attention is that, in practice, the 'causal link' between the injury that an import restriction relieves and the imports which are its ostensible cause is (at best) inexact. A number of studies have investigated whether affirmative results in trade remedy investigations are explained strictly by 'injury from imports' rather than by 'bad times—whatever the cause'. They found that 'bad times'—as proxied by general macroeconomic conditions such as movements of GDP, employment, and capacity utilization—is the dominant explanation.[25]

Other studies have looked into the 'econometrics' applied in trade remedy investigations. They examine how these investigations actually attempt to determine if the injury in evidence is the result of increased imports and to ensure that injury resulting from other causes is not attributed to imports. In the language of the investigations, the first of these is to demonstrate a 'causal link', the second is to demonstrate 'non-attribution'.

Sykes provides a detailed and perceptive analysis of these matters.[26] He begins by questioning the economic logic of treating imports as a causal or exogenous factor. In

---

[21] Hoekman and Kostecki 2001, 322.

[22] Blonigen and Prusa 2003, 253.

[23] Horlick and Shea 2002, 202. As the number of trade agreements and arrangements has increased, the number of administrative procedures available to solicit changes in the terms of importation have likewise increased. For example, there are administrative procedures in the United States by which an industry can petition for removal of a product from the list eligible for tariff preferences. The mechanisms taken up in this chapter are only a few from the long menu of alternatives a trade attorney can offer an industry seeking protection.

[24] Sykes 2007, 101. Sykes, in his analyses of safeguards, does not acknowledge their fungibility with anti-dumping. In the two papers on safeguards (Sykes 2003 and Sykes 2004), he refers 21 times to voluntary export restraints as where governments will turn if safeguards requirements continue to be impossible to meet—only once, and that parenthetically, to anti-dumping: 'WTO members may return to extra-legal alternatives such as voluntary restraint agreements (or to the excessive use of other protectionist devices such as anti-dumping measures)' (Sykes 2003, 262).

If safeguards are considered the better instrument for managing import problems that do not involve predation, then nearly every one of the 3,752 anti-dumping investigations WTO members have notified is an 'excessive use' of anti-dumping.

[25] Nelson 2006, 561–3 and WTO 2009, 147–8 summarize these findings.

[26] Sykes 2003, 2004.

economic logic, imports are an endogenous variable, simultaneously determined with domestic output, domestic production, and imports. In raising this point, Sykes questions whether it is even possible to frame the conditions imposed by the WTO Safeguards Agreement and GATT Article XIX as workable econometrics. Going further, his evaluation of the guidance provided by the WTO panel and WTO Appellate Body as to how such analysis should be done leads to his scepticism on the workability of the safeguard mechanism. He concludes that 'WTO rules, as interpreted by recent Appellate Body decisions and applied by the dispute panel in the steel case, pose nearly insurmountable hurdles to the legal use of safeguard measures by WTO members.'

Durling returns a generally positive evaluation of the quality of the WTO Appellate Body and panel evaluations of the pricing parts of anti-dumping investigations, but he raises questions similar to those raised by Sykes about Appellate Body and panel treatment of the causal link and of non-attribution.[27]

Sykes also has presented serious criticism of the way in which causal link and non-attribution are treated in anti-dumping cases;[28] Hindley, and also Vermulst, Pernaute, and Lucenti, point out a number of problems with European Commission analysis of these matters.[29]

Trade remedy application, these studies show, is not limited to the specific economic circumstances specified in the GATT/WTO texts.

Finding, however, that the system does not impose the discipline its legal structure appears to impose does not demonstrate that there is no discipline. (Not finding the lost keys in the most obvious place does not establish that there are no keys.) The following section looks into the application and subsequent lifting of US safeguard measures on imports of steel in 2002–3 for insights as to the disciplines that keep trade remedy application in check.

19.5 US SAFEGUARD MEASURES AGAINST IMPORTS OF STEEL, 2002–3

The ascent of anti-dumping took place at the same time as the rules for applying trade remedies were being both extensively and intensively elaborated. In the United States, the Congress saw the Executive as exploiting the discretion in trade remedy laws to administer them in a manner that was increasingly neglectful of their intent. The basic economics of the trade remedies, to neutralize 'injury', is, at its core, the premise that imports may be restricted when they displace domestic production. As trade remedy use became important, analysts complained that it was biased, e.g. 'tilted systematically against importers, [t]he results...difficult to square with economic theory or with the interests of American consumers.'[30]

---

[27] Durling 2003.   [28] Sykes 2007, 92–4.
[29] Hindley 2009; Vermulst, Pernaute, and Lucenti 2004.   [30] Boltuck and Litan 1991, 7.

While the bias that irritated analysts was that the law overdid what economic theory intended, in my days at the US Treasury Department the bias that irritated Congress was that we did not do what the law intended. Over time, Congress imposed a series of amendments that: (a) eliminated obvious loopholes such as the lack of time limits on investigations; (b) expanded the scope for affirmative determinations; (c) subjected administration to judicial appeal; (d) shifted administration of anti-dumping and countervailing duties from the US Treasury Department to the US Commerce Department, which was expected to offer a more sympathetic ear to US industry.

Contrary to what such changes, viewed in isolation, might suggest, the data cited above indicate that administered protection has not become more readily available.

The imposition of US safeguard restrictions on imports of steel, and their subsequent lifting, illustrate well how trade policy institutions in the United States have evolved. In 1962, US President John Kennedy, to win negotiating authority for what became the Kennedy Round, had to accept protection for the US textile industry that lasted 40 years. To obtain negotiating authority for the Doha Round, President George Bush in 2001 accepted import restrictions on steel products that lasted 13 months.

19.5.1 Background to the case

The US steel industry has been one of the more frequent appellants for import restrictions, always alert for an opportunity. President George W. Bush's seeking 'trade promotion authority' in 2001 provided such an opportunity. The Doha negotiations were under way, and scheduled to end by 1 January 2005. Trade negotiations are a prestigious platform for a US president—those in a position to give this authority to the President will bargain for something in return.

The steel-producing states of Pennsylvania, Ohio, and West Virginia had been hotly contested in the presidential election of 2000, and were shaping up as battleground states for the Congressional elections of 2002. Richard Cheney, the Republican vice-presidential candidate, had emphasized in campaigning in these states the willingness of a Bush–Cheney administration to vigorously enforce US anti-dumping laws on behalf of steel producers. In spring 2001, the United Steelworkers of America and the Congressional delegations from these states issued statements that any support for legislation to grant negotiating authority to the President would be directly related to action on steel imports.

19.5.2 Pre-empting anti-dumping

The steel industry had traditionally petitioned for and received protection through the unfair trade laws, anti-dumping and countervailing duties. Bown reports over 200 anti-dumping or countervailing duty investigations between 1989 and 2003 that led to restrictions on steel imports.[31] US unfair trade laws, however, allow the President no discretion. If the dumping and injury determinations are affirmative, the restriction is automatic.

To pre-empt anti-dumping or countervailing duty petitions from the industry, the United States Trade Representative (USTR) in June 2001 petitioned the US International Trade Commission (USITC) to undertake a safeguards investigation. (The political/managerial skill, of course, included selling this option to the industry and its supporters.) An affirmative USITC determination would leave to the President the final decision; perhaps more important, it would provide for several 'events' that would (1) allow resistance to import restrictions to come forward, and (2) provide the President the legal authority to modify the restrictions. These events are taken up below.

19.5.3 Affirmative determination from the USITC

General conditions indicated that the industry had a good case. Employment at furnaces, mills, and foundries dropped from almost 470,000 in 1995 to less than 400,000 in 1999, and more than 30 steel companies had gone bankrupt between 1997 and 2001. No one was surprised when the Commission in December 2001 submitted to the President affirmative determinations on 16 different categories of steel products.

An affirmative determination by the USITC in a safeguard case gives the President the legal authority to restrict imports. It does not, however, mandate such action. The President could impose or not impose restrictions—of whatever form he chose, on whatever of the covered products he chose.

After the Commission returns an injury determination it then turns to deliberations and recommendations over remedy. The President is not required by law to follow the Commission's recommendations, but the deliberations over remedy do serve a useful function. They provide a venue for interested parties to enter into the debate over what the President's action will be.

19.5.4 Managing the application of safeguard restrictions

Another element of judicious management was that the period for which the President imposed restrictions (a combination of tariff rates and quantitative restrictions) was three years *and one day*. Why the extra day? Because, as mandated by the WTO Safeguards Agreement, US safeguard law specifies that when restrictions of more than three years' duration are imposed, there must be a mid-term review. The review provides another focal point, along with the opportunity to ease or withdraw the restrictions.

---

[31] Bown 2004, 28.

Exporters affected by the restrictions claimed immediately that unless satisfactory compensation was provided, they would retaliate.[32] The WTO Safeguards Agreement suspends the right of compensation/retaliation only if the safeguard measures are taken in response to an absolute increase of imports, and the USITC report itself provided a basis to argue that there had not been an absolute increase of imports.[33] Over the period the USITC used for its investigation, 1996–2000, imports tended to peak in the middle, then decline sharply in 1999 and 2000.

To deal with such threats, the President's March 2002 order instructed the USTR to consider exemption requests from other countries. The initial order had already exempted free trade agreement partners Canada, Mexico, Israel, and Jordan, along with a number of smaller developing countries.

Steel-using companies had been an organized political element throughout; the resulting consultations were driven by partnerships of steel-using US companies combined with their foreign sources. CITAC, the Consuming Industries Trade Action Coalition, was perhaps the most active organization of steel users. They claim on their website to 'employ more workers and have a greater positive impact on the US economy than the industries that advocate frequent use of trade restrictions'.[34]

Casual information suggests that more than 60 Washington law firms were involved in the resulting bargaining. Politically speaking, the outcome of these consultations represented a balancing of the three interests at play: US producers who had petitioned for protection, US steel users, and foreign exporters. As a result of these negotiations, some 37 per cent of US steel imports subject to the March 2002 order were exempted.[35]

Taking user interests into account did not begin with the steel case. US administrative practice has for more than a decade incorporated the concept of 'short supply'. Even an anti-dumping restriction could be suspended if the administering agency determined that the product subject to restriction was important to a US buyer and that domestically produced substitutes were unavailable or 'in short supply'. Bown points out that in the steel case the basis for many of the requests for exemption was that the product was trademarked or patented—this to demonstrate that a domestically made substitute was not available.[36]

19.5.5 WTO case

In May 2002, a number of exporting countries (Brazil, China, the European Communities, Japan, Korea, New Zealand, Norway, and Switzerland) requested consultations with the US concerning the WTO-legality of the measures. When these

---

[32] Under the Safeguards Agreement (Article 8.2), exporters can retaliate 120 days after the date of imposition of the restrictions.

[33] United States International Trade Commission 2001.

[34] 3 February 2011 at <http://www.citac.info/about/whoweare.php>.

[35] Hufbauer and Goodrich 2003, 4.

[36] Bown 2004, 7.

consultations and the exemptions negotiated with USTR (re the previous paragraph) did not resolve the issue, the exporters requested that a panel be established. The panel found against the United States, the US appealed, and the Appellate Body upheld the panel on every major point. The Appellate Body's report was adopted by the WTO Dispute Settlement Body on 10 December 2003.

Though some had questioned the earlier claim of exporters to a right to retaliate— and no country had retaliated—it was clear that exporters now held a right to do so. Exporting countries began soon to publicly identify US exports on which they might retaliate, focusing on US producers/exporters in sensitive states and Congressional districts. In short, they followed the same politics as the steel industry had used to put pressure on the President to restrict imports.

19.5.6 USITC mid-term review

In March 2003, the USITC announced the opening of its mid-term review.[37] Shortly after announcing this investigation, the Commission received a request from the US House of Representatives Committee on Ways and Means to investigate also the impact of the import restrictions on US steel-consuming industries.

The Commission's conclusions on the impact on US steel producers were even-handed. The President could draw on it to support either a decision to continue the restrictions or to terminate them. As to the need for continuing protection, the report pointed out continuing weaknesses in demand for vehicle parts, appliances, and construction. While profitability had improved, it was not up to the level in the base period chosen for comparison. Selling prices were well short of their 2000 and 2001 levels. On the other hand, imports had fallen in many categories not covered by the restrictions, and there was an indication that world demand was picking up. Moreover, the restructuring of the industry was continuing. Several more of the less efficient factories had been closed, four of the largest steel producers had merged into two, and these had announced significant investments to increase productivity.

The companion report on the effects on steel-consuming industries was in structure the mirror image of an injury investigation: it measured how the restrictions had affected employment, wages, prices, profitability, sales, productivity, and capital investment in steel-using industries and in port facilities. (Facilities relevant to internal distribution—of imported or domestically produced products—were not included.) A survey of steel-using companies (in parallel with a survey of US producers) added information on such factors as abrogation of contracts by export suppliers when the restrictions were applied, and the continued availability of inputs needed to produce their outputs.

---

[37] US law requires that the mid-term review be completed by the midpoint of the restrictions in place. That would have been July 2003.

The report also provided the results of a modelling exercise that estimated economy-wide returns to capital to go down by $294.3 million, and returns to labour to go down by $386.0 million as a result of the restrictions. Tariff revenues increase by $649.9 million, the net impact on annual GDP being then a loss of $30.4 million. (US gross domestic product (GDP) in 2003 was over $11 trillion.)

19.5.7 Decision to terminate the restrictions

The study sparked a surge of articles and press statements that provided the political base for a presidential decision to terminate the restrictions. Perhaps the threat of retaliation from foreign exporters did influence the decision, but the announcement that the restrictions would be terminated did not mention that factor.

The announcement[38] began with a review of the circumstances that warranted safeguards: thousands of jobs were at stake, many steel firms were in or facing bankruptcy—this caused by a surge in imports due, in part, to global overproduction. In response, the President decided that the US steel industry needed breathing space—the chance to adapt.

Turning to the present, the announcement reported that 'as the ITC's analysis clearly demonstrated, the safeguard worked'. The lines that followed (a third of the announcement) reported the mid-term review's findings on restructuring, higher productivity, profitability, US exports at a historically high level, etc.

The announcement then explained that the risk of a foreign surge of exports had abated; demand was up in China, Russia, and other parts of the world.

The announcement then turned to user costs:

> In the first 21 months of the safeguard, the benefits to the industry outweighed the marginal costs to consumers. Going forward, however, this is not the case. For these reasons, the President has concluded that the safeguard has done its job and can now be lifted.[39]

As to lessons one might draw from steel imports' experience, the first is that an institutionalized role for user costs is emerging in US administrative procedures, though this role is not mandated by WTO rules or even by US law. Given the role that import users forged for themselves in this case, it is not likely that their interests could be passed over in the next safeguard case taken up in the US. Institutionally speaking, their success in the steel case is more appropriately interpreted as building political capital than as using it.

Foreign exporters' interests also have a role. In practice, the influence of foreign exporters on the US decision depended on the partnerships (foreign exporters and US users) that US process allows. In appearance, removing the restrictions was a concession

---

[38] United States International Trade Commission 2003.
[39] USTR 2003, 3.

to the interests of US users, not to foreign exporters. USTR Zoellick's announcement of the termination of the steel safeguards mentioned twice the costs to users. Though the WTO decision and the USITC mid-term review created a synergetic relationship between domestic users and foreign exporters, the final announcement did not mention the cost to US exporters of potential retaliation.

Not to be overlooked, the managerial skill of the US administration, to take up this issue as a safeguard case rather than an anti-dumping case and to use the various events the process allowed to end the restriction at a minimal loss of domestic political capital, was critical.

19.6 CONCLUSIONS, CLOSING COMMENTS, AND THOUGHTS ABOUT FURTHER RESEARCH

Economic analysis, by instinct, tends to ask if a policy decision system isolates interventions that make economic sense—e.g. that produce a net increase in 'economic welfare' or 'the national economic interest'. Legal analysis starts with such a standard, but is willing to step back to a lesser one: does the regulatory system at least tell the regulated what is and is not allowed, so they can get on with their business?

I conclude from my looks at their use and at their analytical literature that trade remedies serve the WTO system well, but are an embarrassment to both legal and economic theory.

What follows from this conclusion are not suggestions for policy reform, but suggestions for analytical reform. One suggestion is for more attention to be paid to national institutions for managing trade remedies. The discipline in the system is less a matter of how the WTO regulates, more a matter of how the WTO has helped to shape the domestic institutions that regulate. A second suggestion is that getting protection-seekers to accept 'No' for an answer is principally about their sharing the procedural values of the system. (This point is taken up again below.)

A related point: the subject is how institutions *evolve*. I am increasingly uncomfortable with interpretations of the WTO system that amount to creationist models of intelligent design.[40] Bauer, Pool, and Dexter, in the prologue to their classic study, remind us that 'individual and group interests get grossly redefined by the operation of the social institutions through which they must work'.[41]

Recalling the quote from Walton Hamilton at the beginning of this chapter, I would add, 'and so do the social institutions through which they work'.

I have focused here on US institutions, and I apologize for doing so. (My excuse is that I have stayed with what I know best.) I do not want to suggest that other countries'

---

[40] My views on the usefulness of seeking the intrinsic rationale of things in the GATT/WTO system are expressed in Finger 2009.

[41] Bauer, Pool, and Dexter 1972, ix.

experiences are similar. Though national experiences are all linked with the GATT/WTO system, from what I know they are quite different one from other. Each member's experience merits study.

Another lesson I draw is that, at least in US experience, unintended consequences have been a significant part of the evolution of trade remedies—and this is why I began with the statement from Walton Hamilton. Three I will list are:

(1) After the first Reciprocal Trade Agreements Act (RTAA) of 1934, the Congress never went back to direct tariff writing. It is hard to imagine that the RTAA would have been passed had it been presented as abandonment of the old system, but trade remedies became, by default, the only outlet for protection-seekers.

(2) Congressional reforms of trade remedies failed to increase the amount of protection granted—even though the reforms were explicitly about expanding the scope for protection and for management of the instruments in a manner that paid closer attention to industries asking for relief.

(3) The interests of import users are increasingly influential in processes that formally give expression only to the interests of protection-seekers.

As to explaining the first of these, there is an extensive literature that explains how the trade negotiations process built momentum. A major element in the United States was that foreign policy and export interests dominated. This analysis, however, leaves unexplained why the Congress did not go back to direct tariff writing. Were there ever serious proposals to go back to direct tariff writing, and if so, how were they managed?

A related question, in GATT's early decades, when renegotiation was a frequently used flexibility instrument, was how did the US government manage pressures for protection, and channel them eventually to renegotiations? Generally, how were pressures for protection managed domestically in the era in which the international system was the diplomat's jurisprudence, that Hudec has explored?

Congressionally mandated reforms of trade remedies brought with them considerable technical complexity. Establishing that the injury from which the importer asked relief was really 'caused' by imports may involve bad economic theory and bad econometrics, but that does not mean that it is easy, nor that the discretion that remains in the system can be exploited without a high level of technical expertise. There is a tendency, however, in the analytical literature to view anything inconsistent with the professional standards of the analysts as 'political', and anything 'political' as standard-less or even capricious.

Analysis, up to now, has paid more attention to the looseness in the administrative process than to the tightness. Seth Kaplan provided an excellent analysis of the ways in which different members of the USITC have structured their analysis of the link between imports and injury.[42] The paper is often cited as evidence of the primitive econometrics that goes into such determinations. The next step might be for someone with such

---

[42] Kaplan 1991.

intimate knowledge of how things are done (perhaps Kaplan) to write a 'yes, but' paper, documenting (a) the things that one must nonetheless show and the steps one must go through to win an affirmative determination, and (b) examples of shortcuts such as casualness in data management that would render information valueless as trade remedy evidence. Members of the trade bar know that it is not easy to win an affirmative determination. The literature is, perhaps, biased towards examples from respondents of their losing for reasons that economic theory or econometrics might find wanting. The reasons for petitioners losing would round out the story.

Nelson suggested that a sense of fairness is another part of the explanation;[43] I would add that the sense of fairness keeping unsuccessful protection-seekers from kicking over the table and saying 'We will not play this game any more' is probably a procedural one. The trade remedies follow standards of administration generally considered to be appropriate. The result is accepted because the process is accepted, not because it satisfies an intrinsic sense of what the result should be.

Moreover, having to go through a mandarin class (the trade bar) in order even to identify alternative courses of action helps to promote acceptance of negative outcomes. The trade bar evolving symbiotically with the trade remedies is another part of the story.

To some degree, Congress' intended shift towards protection-seekers might have been overcome by the more general changes of governance standards that took place over the same period as the trade remedies were being restructured.

The third unintended consequence is that import users have pushed their interests into the determination of trade remedy outcomes. The steel case of 2001 illustrates this well.

The United States, however, has not undertaken a safeguard investigation since the steel case. A relevant question, then, is if the steel case has influenced whether or how import user interests are taken into account in anti-dumping cases.

Import user interests are not formally recognized in anti-dumping cases, but they are not formally recognized in safeguard cases either. On the positive side here, the role of import users in the steel case reflects the growing prosperity of import users in the US economy—and with it the money they have for political contributions. It also documents the entrepreneurial skill of members of the trade bar who saw them as potentially profitable clients.[44] Mechanisms through which user interests influence anti-dumping

---

[43] Nelson 2006.

[44] This recalls another of my attempts to change the rhetoric of trade policy politics. Andrei Zlate and I explained in a paper several years ago (Finger and Zlate 2005) that the 'lesser duty rule' treated import users as bastard children. After the legitimate children got what they wanted—sufficient protection to remove injury—the illegitimate ones could have what was left. Accepting that we had no power to make things better, we closed by telling import users, 'You bastards will have to look out for yourselves.' It seems they did.

Some years before, I had pointed out to a group of users of imported steel that pornography is protected under the law so long as it has redeeming social value. I advised them to paint dirty pictures on what they imported, then present it as pornography—pornography receiving better treatment under the law than imports.

administration are evolving. For example, the 'short supply rule' explained in Section 19.5.4 has been around for more than a decade. Another is that the US Congress, by direct vote on 2 August 2010, suspended tariff rates on more than 600 products, mostly imported manufacturing inputs. President Obama signed the action into law on 11 August.[45]

In conclusion, the trade remedy system works. The discipline the WTO system imposes on new import restrictions is about less versus more import restrictions, not about import restrictions in this circumstance but not in that. Economic theory suggests that, in a universe of all possible import restrictions, there are probably more bad ones than good ones, and in that universe a mechanism that reduces the number is, by economic theory, a useful thing.

References

Bauer, Raymond, Ithiel de Sola Pool, and Lewis Dexter. 1972. *American Business and Public Policy: The Politics of Foreign Trade*. Chicago: Aldine Atherton.

Blonigen, Bruce A., and Thomas J. Prusa. 2003. Antidumping. In *Handbook of International Trade*, edited by E. Kwan Choi and James C. Hartigan, 252–84. Oxford: Blackwell.

Boltuck, Richard D., and Robert E. Litan. 1991. *Down in the Dumps: Administration of the Unfair Trade Laws*. Washington, DC: Brookings Institution Press.

Bown, Chad P. 2004. How Different are Safeguards from Antidumping? Evidence from US Trade Policies Toward Steel. Brandeis University Working Paper. Available from <http://people.brandeis.edu/~cbown/papers/steel_mfn.pdf>. Accessed on 12 May 2009.

Bown, Chad P. 2010. Taking Stock of Antidumping, Safeguards and Countervailing Duties, 1990–2009. Photocopied manuscript dated July 2010.

Durling, James P. 2003. Deference, But Only When Due: WTO Reviews of Anti-Dumping Measures. *Journal of International Economic Law* 6 (1):125–53.

Finger, J. Michael. 1982. Incorporating the Gains from Trade into Policy. *The World Economy*. 5 (4):367–77.

Finger, J. Michael. 1993. *Antidumping: How it Works and Who Gets Hurt*. Ann Arbor: University of Michigan Press.

Finger, J. Michael. 2002. Safeguards: Making Sense of GATT/WTO Provisions Allowing for Import Restrictions. In *Trade Negotiations and the Developing Countries: A Handbook*, edited by Bernard Hoekman, Aaditya Mattoo, and Philip English, 195–205. Washington, DC: World Bank.

Finger, J. Michael. 2009. Review of Douglas A. Irwin, Petros C. Mavroidis and Alan O. Sykes, *The Genesis of the GATT*, (Cambridge University Press for The American Law Institute, 2008, pp. xiv, 314). *Journal of World Trade* 43(4):893–5.

Finger, J. Michael, and Julio J. Nogués. 2006. *Safeguards and Antidumping in Latin American Liberalization: Fighting Fire with Fire*. Basingstoke: Palgrave Macmillan, and Washington DC: World Bank.

Finger, J. Michael, and Andrei Zlate. 2005. Antidumping: Prospects for Discipline from the Doha Negotiations. *Journal of World Investment and Trade* 6 (4):531–52.

---

[45] World Trade Interactive 2010.

GATT. 1991. *The International Trade Environment: Report By the Secretary General, 1989–90*. Geneva: GATT.

GATT. 1994. *Analytical Index: Guide to GATT Law and Practice*. 6th Edition. Geneva: GATT.

Hamilton, Walton H. 1963. Institution. In *Encyclopaedia of the Social Sciences*, volume 8, edited by Edwin R. A. Seligman and Alvin Johnson, 84–9. New York: Macmillan.

Hindley, Brian. 2009. Cause-of-injury Analysis in European Anti-Dumping Investigations. ECIPE Working Paper 05/2009. Brussels: European Centre for International Political Economy (ECIPE).

Hoekman, Bernard M., and Michel M. Kostecki. 2001. *The Political Economy of the World Trading System*. 2nd edition. Oxford: Oxford University Press.

Horlick, Gary N., and Eleanor Shea. 2002. Dealing with US Trade Law. In *Development, Trade and the WTO: A Handbook*, edited by Bernard Hoekman, Aaditya Mattoo, and Philip English, 206–12. Washington, DC: World Bank.

Hudec, Robert E. 1970. The GATT Legal System, A Diplomat's Jurisprudence. *Journal of World Trade Law* 4: 615–65.

Hudec, Robert E. 1975. *The GATT Legal System and World Trade Diplomacy*. New York: Praeger. Second edition, 1990. Salem, NH: Butterworth.

Hudec, Robert E. 1978. *Adjudication of International Trade Disputes*. Thames Essay 16. London: Trade Policy Research Centre.

Hufbauer, Gary Clyde, and Ben Goodrich. 2003. *Steel Policy: The Good, the Bad, and the Ugly*. Policy Brief PB03–1. Washington, DC: Institute for International Economics.

Irwin, Douglas. 2005. The Rise of US Anti-Dumping Activity in Historical Perspective. *The World Economy* 28 (5):651–68.

Kaplan, Seth. 1991. Injury and Causation in USITC Antidumping Determinations: Five Recent Approaches. In *Policy Implications of Antidumping Measures*, edited by P. K. M. Tharakan, 143–73. Amsterdam: North Holland.

Kucik, Jeffrey, and Eric Reinhardt. 2008. Does Flexibility Promote Cooperation? An Application to the Global Trade Regime. *International Organization* 62 (3):477–505.

Laird, Sam. 1992. Recent Trends in the Use of Export Restraint Arrangements. Paper prepared for the Trade Policy Research Center Conference on the Political Economy of Export Restraint Arrangements, September 1988, Washington, DC. Updated December 1992.

Mastel, Greg. 1998. *Antidumping Laws and the U.S. Economy*. Armonk, NY: M. E. Sharpe.

Nelson, Douglas. 2006. The Political Economy of Antidumping: A Survey. *European Journal of Political Economy* 22 (3):554–90.

Stegemann, Klaus. 1991. Settlement of Antidumping Cases by Price Undertakings: Is the EC More Liberal than Canada? In *Policy Implications of Antidumping Measures*, edited by P. K. M. Tharakan. Amsterdam: North Holland, and New York: Elsevier Science Publishers.

Sykes, Alan O. 2003. The Safeguards Mess, a Critique of WTO Jurisprudence. *World Trade Review* 2 (3):261–95.

Sykes, Alan O. 2004. The Persistent Puzzle of Safeguards: Lessons from the Steel Dispute. *Journal of International Economic Law* 7 (3):523–64.

Sykes, Alan O. 2007. Trade Remedy Laws. In *Research Handbook in International Economic Law*, edited by Alan O. Sykes and Andrew T. Guzman, 62–102. Northampton, MA: Edward Elgar.

United States International Trade Commission. 2001. *Steel*, volumes I, II, III. Investigation TA 201–73, Publication 3479.

United States International Trade Commission. 2003. *Steel: Monitoring Developments in the Domestic Industry* (Investigation TA-204-) and *Steel-Consuming Industries: Competitive*

Conditions with Respect to Steel Safeguard Measures (Investigation 332-452), Publication 3632.

Vermulst, Edwin, Marta Pernaute, and Krista Lucenti. 2004. Recent European Community Safeguards Policy: Kill Them and Let God Sort Them Out? *Journal of World Trade* 38 (6):955–84.

World Bank. 2010. *Temporary Trade Barriers Data Base.* Available from <http://econ.world-bank.org/ttbd>. Accessed 23 August 2010.

World Trade Interactive. 2010. President Signs MTB, Touts Duty Breaks as Part of Effort to Increase Exports. *World Trade Interactive* 17 (161). Available from <http://www.strtrade.com/wti/wti.asp?pub=0&story=35245&date=8%2F13%2F2010&company=>. Accessed 7 November 2011.

WTO. 2009. *World Trade Report 2009: Trade Policy Commitments and Contingency Measures.* Geneva: WTO.

CHAPTER 20

....

REGULATORY MEASURES

....

ROBERT HOWSE[*]

20.1 INTRODUCTION

....

FROM the beginning of the post-war multilateral trading system, it was recognized that negotiated tariff reductions and disciplines on other 'border' measures (such as quotas or bans on the import and export of particular products: General Agreement on Tariffs and Trade (GATT) Article XI) could be undermined by internal regulations of governments.[1] As tariffs were progressively reduced over rounds of negotiations, increasingly trade disputes became focused on internal policies (regulations on matters such as health and safety, subsidies, government procurement practices, etc.) that restricted market access or altered the competitive relationship between domestic and imported products in favour of the former. Many new legal disciplines were introduced to address these policies where they had trade effects.

But disciplining internal regulations in a multilateral system to which states with many different political and social systems adhere is a complex and sensitive matter. While usually advancing legitimate, non-protectionist governmental objectives, such policies may be more trade-restrictive than necessary to achieve those objectives; and there are cases where they are intentionally designed to advantage domestic interests. In legislating and regulating, governments, particularly in pluralist liberal democracies, attempt to balance the interests of diverse constituencies. Regulations serve diverse objectives and reflect compromises between different groups. In such circumstances, it is not simple to draw a line between internal policies that are legitimate exercises of domestic regulatory autonomy (even if they have some trade-restrictive effects) and

---

[*] In this chapter, I have freely drawn on more than a decade of diverse scholarly writing on these issues, including co-authored work with, among others, Henrik Horn, Lisi Tuerk, Jane Earley and Steve Charnovitz.

[1] For a lucid economic analysis of the general problem of regulatory protectionism, see Sykes 1999.

those that can be considered a form of protectionism or 'cheating' on the WTO bargain, in that they undermine the market access reasonably expected from commitments on liberalization of border measures in the multilateral trading system.

The challenge of such line drawing is left, in significant measure, to the WTO's judges, the Appellate Body, and the panels of first instance below them. This chapter considers how the WTO judiciary has met this challenge so far, examining the techniques of legal interpretation and approach to review of domestic regulation that they have used, and whether and to what extent the result has been one of adequate sensitivity to domestic regulatory autonomy, focusing primarily on WTO rules with respect to trade in goods. In light of this analysis, the conclusion examines whether there nevertheless remains a 'democratic deficit' in the WTO, to the extent that judicial review against the norms in the WTO treaties remains overly or inappropriately intrusive in or constraining of domestic democratic outcomes in the regulatory process.

During the earlier era of the multilateral trading system, based on the General Agreement on Tariffs and Trade (GATT) 1947, the concern with domestic regulation was largely focused on problems of discrimination: against imports in favour of domestic products (national treatment), and between imports from different member states (most-favoured nation (MFN)). The multilateral trading system was viewed as, mostly, a framework for negotiated bindings on the reduction or elimination of discriminatory border measures restricting trade, such as tariffs or quotas. In order to sustain such a bargain, it was necessary to ensure that member states did not 'cheat' on, or circumvent, these commitments through reintroducing measures amounting to import discrimination in their domestic policies. The official theology of the trading system sanctioned complete regulatory autonomy and wide regulatory diversity: as long as they did not discriminate, member states were free to adopt whatever approach to domestic regulation they saw as appropriate. This outlook was well suited to an international regime like the GATT, which lacked the institutions, expertise, or explicit mandate to engage in 'positive integration' through regulatory rapprochement or harmonization.[2]

It is notable, however, that not even the non-discrimination norm is an absolute constraint on regulatory autonomy in the GATT regime. In practice, it is largely impossible to determine, in a given case, which regulatory distinctions amount to impermissible 'discrimination', and which do not, without reference to *some* benchmarks or standards for, crudely speaking, 'legitimate' regulation. Consider debates about the meaning of like products in the National Treatment obligation, such as whether social, environmental, ethical, and health considerations may be taken into account in determining whether products are like for purposes of domestic regulatory treatment. Moreover, policies that violate National Treatment or Most-Favoured Nation might be justified under certain conditions, where necessary or rationally related to particular policy objectives such as public morals, health, or the conservation of exhaustible natural resources. Judging the necessity or rationality of a particular regulatory device necessarily

[2] For an economic perspective on the non-discrimination norm as a basis for addressing regulatory trade 'barriers', see Horn 2006.

entails reviewing and appraising a set of domestic regulatory choices informed by diverse concerns (culture, social and community structures, administrability, the constitutional system, etc.).

In part due to recognition of this difficulty, as well as the related instability of the non-discrimination norm as a means of disciplining domestic policy, two of the specialized agreements that emerged out of the Uruguay Round[3] gave a significant role to international standards as a means of managing the interface between domestic regulation and trade liberalization in the case of trade in goods. These were the Agreement on Technical Barriers to Trade (TBT) and the Agreement on Sanitary and Phytosanitary Measures (SPS). The international standards were imported in various ways from non-WTO standardization regimes, such as the International Organization for Standardization (ISO) or the Codex Alimentarius Commission, as normative benchmarks for judging the acceptability of WTO members' domestic regulations from the viewpoint of trade liberalization.

The Uruguay Round negotiations coincided with an era of regulatory reform and privatization, where many traditional approaches to regulation and the public sector (such as public monopolies in services like telecommunications) were put in question, and changed or dismantled in a number of important jurisdictions within the multilateral trading system. Particularly with respect to service industries, the traditional approaches were viewed as too restrictive of market forces; legitimate public policy goals, it was thought, could be attainable through more market-friendly regulatory instruments. The durability of the older approaches was often attributed to vested interests in the status quo. This mindset migrated to the multilateral trading system, where non-discriminatory domestic regulatory policies began to be questioned as 'barriers' to market access. It was thought that shifting to less restrictive regulatory instruments could, at the same time, make domestic markets more efficient and open up the possibility of international trade.

Thus, the interests of those most intent on pushing for liberalization of trade in services (such as the United States) lay with inducing trade partners to lock in, as binding concessions, pro-competitive or pro-market regulatory changes. Many countries, especially developing countries, tried to resist the insertion of the 'deregulation' agenda into the multilateral trading system. The resulting set of legal instruments, the General Agreement on Trade in Services (GATS) and related agreements, reflects a messy compromise between these points of view.

20.2 National Treatment in the GATT

Article III:4 of the GATT sets out the National Treatment obligation with respect to non-fiscal laws, regulations, and requirements that affect imported products. Such non-fiscal measures must accord no less favourable treatment to imports than to like domestic

---

[3] The Uruguay Round negotiations ran from 1986–94, culminating in the Marrakesh Declaration and Final Act of 15 April 1995, announcing the creation of the WTO.

products. The determination of whether a measure is in violation of Article III:4 entails two distinct steps. The first is to ascertain whether the imported product and the domestic product are 'like'. The analysis of likeness under Article III:4 entails a weighing and evaluation of the same kinds of factors as for fiscal measures—including physical characteristics, end uses, and consumer habits—with the possibility that other factors may, in certain cases, also be probative of likeness (*EC–Asbestos*[4]). In *EC–Asbestos*, the Appellate Body took into account health impacts that can influence consumer behaviour, finding that asbestos, which France had banned, was not like permitted substitute products that were non-carcinogenic. If the domestic and the imported product are determined to be like, the adjudicator will normally then determine whether the regulatory distinction between the two products results in less favourable treatment of imports (*EC–Asbestos*; *Dominican Republic–Cigarettes*[5]); however, if there is no prima facie evidence of discrimination on the basis of the foreign origin of the products, the adjudicator may dismiss the claim without proceeding to the determination of likeness in the first place (*EC–Biotech*). As the Appellate Body has emphasized in *EC–Asbestos*, not all regulatory distinctions between like products are impermissible under Article III:4, only those which result in less favourable treatment for the *group* of imported products in comparison to the *group* of like domestic products. In other words, like products can be treated differently, if there is no systematic discrimination based on national origin.

20.3 PRODUCT–PROCESS

Of historical importance in debates over the meaning of the National Treatment obligation (and also the MFN obligation) in the GATT has been the so-called product–process distinction—the notion, reflected in the infamous unadopted *Tuna–Dolphin* GATT panel rulings,[6] that the GATT does not permit differential treatment of products based on their method of *production* as opposed to their properties as products for *consumption*. Without rehashing this controversy here,[7] we note to begin with that the approach to 'likeness' and 'directly competitive and substitutable' articulated by the Appellate Body does not predetermine a conclusion one way or another concerning methods of production.

There is no textual provision of the GATT prohibiting states from regulating imported products based on the impacts of their process and production methods (PPMs). But, nevertheless, this assumption has had a profound influence on the debate on trade and environment.

The only textual reference to the PPMs concept in the WTO treaties is in the Agreement on Technical Barriers to Trade (TBT), establishing that technical regulations

---

[4] WTO Appellate Body Report 2001a.
[5] WTO Appellate Body Report 2005a.
[6] GATT Panel Report 1991, 1994.
[7] For a full discussion, see Howse and Regan 2000; see also Bronckers and McNelis 2000.

for purposes of the Agreement *include* regulations that address not only the characteristics of products but their 'related' process and production methods. The word 'related' here indicates that, since the TBT Agreement deals with trade in goods, regulation of process and production methods apart from the goods that are there as a result is not a TBT issue. Such regulation may well be a services or intellectual property matter, and thus fall under some WTO agreement not concerned with trade in goods as such.

As noted, the PPMs notion was brought into being in the context of the GATT era *Tuna–Dolphin* dispute. The United States had imposed a ban on sale in the US of both domestic and imported tuna that was fished in a manner that led to excessive incidental killing of dolphins. In theory, assuming that the ban were imposed *even-handedly* on both domestic and imported tuna, under the law of the GATT it would be viewed as an 'internal law, regulation or requirement' that met the national treatment obligation in Article III:4 of the GATT that such measures provide 'no less favourable' treatment to imports than to like domestic products. The GATT dispute panel found such a consequence unacceptable. The underlying thinking was apparently that such a measure, even if even-handed, unilaterally imposed American environmental standards on the country of export, which would be an illegitimate exercise of extraterritoriality. The panel considered it intuitively obvious that such measures could not be consistent with the GATT regime. In order to create a legal foundation for this intuition, the panel suggested that the National Treatment obligation in Article III:4 of the GATT pertained only to measures that directly regulated the imported 'product' as a physical commodity, in this case tuna; measures that purported to regulate how a 'product' was produced would need to be assessed, not as 'internal laws, regulations or requirements' under Article III:4, but rather as quantitative restrictions under Article XI. While Article III:4 allows even-handed measures that fall within its ambit, Article XI operates differently; once a measure is determined to fall within Article XI, then it is per se illegal under GATT, subject only to certain exceptions. In this regard, the panel also found that the ban could not be justified under either the animal health and life (Article XX(b)) or conservation (Article XX(g)) exceptions in the GATT. Here, the panel was more direct in its reasoning, asserting the view that measures that are somehow 'extraterritorial' cannot be justified under GATT Article XX exceptions.

Moreover, in the second *Tuna–Dolphin* ruling the panel held that, even if Article III:4 were applicable, domestic and imported products are like, even if they have different PPMs. Only different physical characteristics can distinguish products as not 'like'. Thus, dolphin-unfriendly imported tuna is like dolphin-friendly domestic tuna and must be treated the same. The *Tuna–Dolphin* rulings were controversial and never adopted, but the idea of PPMs as illegal in the GATT stuck and became conventional wisdom. In the WTO era, a case came before the dispute settlement system not dissimilar to *Tuna–Dolphin*. The *Shrimp–Turtle* dispute concerned a US ban on shrimp fished without technologies that prevented killing of endangered species of sea turtles. In that case, the US did not challenge the PPM construction as such, but instead invited the WTO Appellate Body to overrule the aspect of *Tuna–Dolphin* that suggested PPM-related measures could not be justified under Article XX exceptions. In broad measure, the Appellate Body agreed with the United States, as discussed in the next section.

The impact of the *Shrimp–Turtle* case is to blunt the importance of the PPM assumption, since the very kinds of measures supposedly prohibited through that assumption may well be justifiable under the conservation or life and health exceptions in Article XX. If one considers carefully our discussion above of the recent jurisprudence of the WTO Appellate Body on like products in Article III:4 (the *Asbestos* case), consumer habits and tastes may be of decisive importance in determining whether products are 'like', belying the notion that only physical differences in themselves count in the analysis. In addition, the recent jurisprudence on 'treatment no less favourable' indicates that, even if products were considered like, regulatory distinctions between them would not violate Article III:4, provided they are even-handed with respect to the group of domestic and imported like products.

20.4 ARTICLE XX EXCEPTIONS

Contrary to some broad constitutionalist understandings of the WTO system, it does not represent a delegation or allocation of regulatory authority from sovereign states to the WTO institutions. As the Appellate Body held in the recent *China–Audio-visual* case: 'we see the "right to regulate"…as an inherent power enjoyed by a Member's government…With respect to trade, the *WTO Agreement* and its Annexes…operate to, among other things, discipline the exercise of each Member's inherent power to regulate by requiring WTO Members to comply with the obligations that they have assumed thereunder …We observe, in this regard, that WTO Members' regulatory requirements may be WTO consistent in one of two ways. First, they may simply not contravene any WTO obligation. Secondly, even if they contravene a WTO obligation, they may be justified under an applicable exception.'(Paragraphs 222–3)[8]

The Article XX exceptions provide that a member may impose otherwise GATT-illegal measures under two distinct conditions. First, the measure must fall into one of ten categories, including:

(a) necessary to protect public morals;
(b) necessary to protect human, animal or plant life or health; …
(d) necessary to secure compliance with laws or regulations which are not inconsistent with the provisions of this Agreement, including those relating to customs enforcement, the enforcement of monopolies operated under paragraph 4 of Article II and Article XVII, the protection of patents, trade marks and copyrights, and the prevention of deceptive practices.

---

[8] WTO Appellate Body Report 2009.

Second, a trade-restrictive measure must comply with Article XX's *chapeau*: it cannot be 'applied in a manner which would constitute a means of arbitrary or unjustifiable discrimination between countries where the same conditions prevail', and it cannot be 'a disguised restriction on international trade'. As just noted, during the GATT era, the *Tuna–Dolphin* rulings, never adopted by the GATT membership as binding on the parties to the dispute, established the notion that Article XX of the GATT could not be used to justify trade measures that conditioned imports on the adoption by the exporting country of particular kinds of public policies; later, in the *Shrimp–Turtle* case,[9] however, the Appellate Body of the WTO held exactly the reverse, stating:

> It appears to us, however, that conditioning access to a Member's domestic market on whether exporting Members comply with, or adopt, a policy or policies unilaterally prescribed by the importing Member may, to some degree, be a common aspect of measures falling within the scope of one or another of the exceptions (a) to (j) of Article XX. Paragraphs (a) to (j) comprise measures that are recognized as **exceptions to substantive obligations** established in the GATT 1994, because the domestic policies embodied in such measures have been recognized as important and legitimate in character. *It is not necessary to assume that requiring from* **exporting countries** *compliance with, or adoption of, certain policies (although covered in principle by one or another of the exceptions) prescribed by the importing country, renders a measure a priori incapable of justification under Article XX. Such an interpretation renders most, if not all, of the specific exceptions of Article XX inutile, a result abhorrent to the principles of interpretation we are bound to apply.* (Paragraph 121)

The Appellate Body makes clear that, in principle, a measure may be covered by Article XX, not only if the measure is to facilitate a *domestic* policy in the *importing* country, but also if the measure conditions imports on the existence of certain policies maintained by the *exporting* country. Here, notably, the Appellate Body refers to all of paragraphs (a) to (j) of Article XX.

20.5 ARTICLE XX(A) PUBLIC MORALS

In *US–Gambling*, the WTO Dispute Settlement Body addressed the concept of public morals for the first time,[10] in the course of interpreting an exception in the General Agreement on Trade in Services (GATS) that has broadly similar, though not identical, wording to that in GATT XX(a). In *US–Gambling*, the dispute settlement organs had to decide whether the US prohibition on Internet gambling was a measure 'necessary to protect public morals'. In its approach to the interpretation of this language, the WTO panel displayed considerable deference to the value choices of the WTO member defending its

[9] WTO Appellate Body Report 1998b.
[10] WTO Appellate Body Report 2005b.

measures, in this case the United States.[11] 'The content of these concepts for Members can vary in time and space, depending upon a range of factors, including prevailing social, cultural, ethical and religious values.' Analogizing to past Appellate Body decisions concerning similar provisions, the panel concluded that 'Members should be given some scope to define and apply for themselves the concepts of 'public morals'...in their respective territories, according to their own systems and scales of values.'

This flexibility notwithstanding, the panel determined that 'we must nonetheless give meaning to these terms in order to apply them to the facts of in [sic] this case.' Considering the definitions of 'public' and 'morals' from the *Shorter Oxford English Dictionary*, the panel at length concluded that '"public morals" denotes standards of right and wrong conduct maintained by or on behalf of a community or nation.' Although this portion of the panel's decision was not appealed, the Appellate Body quoted this definition in its final decision, indicating some support for this reasoning. Finally, to add context to the definition, the panel looked at past precedent by other WTO members, as well as similar language in other international agreements. The panel first noted that several other WTO members had used the public morals exception to justify gambling-related restrictions. Next, it examined the use of 'moral' in a League of Nations draft convention, noting that this exception was thought to include lottery tickets. The panel also discussed past decisions of the European Court of Justice, which had allowed EU member states to restrict gambling-related activities, despite EU free trade rules. The panel held that gambling-related restrictions fell under the 'moral' exception as long as they were enforced 'in pursuance of policies, the object and purpose of which is to "protect public morals"'.

Applying the *US–Gambling* panel's reasoning, social or labour rights criteria that relate to human rights clearly fall within the concept of 'public morals'. As the panel indicated, public morals will 'vary in time and space', and 'Members should be given some scope to define and apply [them] for themselves.' When based on fundamental human rights, social criteria are clearly 'standards of right and wrong conduct maintained by or on behalf of' the member that is imposing the measure.[12]

20.6 THE 'NECESSITY' TEST

In *US–Gambling*, the Appellate Body held that whether a measure is 'necessary' is to be assessed by a three-pronged test. First, a panel must assess the 'relative importance of the interests or values furthered by the challenged measure'. Next, it must 'weigh and

[11] WTO Panel Report 2004b.

[12] Prior to the *US–Gambling* decision, some scholars (for example, Francioni 2001) had rather confusingly argued that the public morals exception would only apply with respect to human rights where the human rights in question were a matter of international morality. This may have been based on a misinterpretation of some of my own earlier scholarship, where I suggested that international legal instruments such as human rights or labour rights treaties could be used to interpret the general scope of the concept of public morals.

balance' other factors, particularly the 'contribution of the measure to the realization of the ends pursued by it' and 'the restrictive impact of the measure on international commerce'.[13] Finally, a panel must compare the measure with possible alternatives, 'and the results of such comparison should be considered in the light of the importance of the interests at issue'. The Appellate Body is clearly sensitive to the legitimacy and competence issues involved in a specialized international trade tribunal assessing complex domestic regulatory choices. Consider the text of paragraph 151 in *Brazil–Tyres*:

> We recognize that certain complex public health or environmental problems may be tackled only with a comprehensive policy comprising a multiplicity of interacting measures. In the short term, it may prove difficult to isolate the contribution to public health or environmental objectives of one specific measure from those attributable to the other measures that are part of the same comprehensive policy. Moreover, the results obtained from certain actions—for instance, measures adopted in order to attenuate global warming and climate change, or certain preventive actions to reduce the incidence of diseases that may manifest themselves only after a certain period of time—can only be evaluated with the benefit of time.[14]

A measure need not be 'indispensable' to be justified as 'necessary' (*Korea–Beef*),[15] and a member can choose among various possible measures with different levels of cost, feasibility and predicted effectiveness, as long as its choice is reasonable, taking into account not only the achievement of its objective but the need to minimize trade restrictiveness (*Brazil–Tyres*).

20.7 THE REQUIREMENTS OF THE *CHAPEAU*

A condition of maintaining measures based on an Article XX justification is that they may not be applied so as to constitute unjustifiable or arbitrary discrimination between countries where the same conditions prevail, or a disguised restriction on international trade (this is based on the 'chapeau' or preambular paragraph of Article XX). This condition, it must be emphasized, deals only with *application* through administrative or judicial action, not the scheme as such (*US–Shrimp, US–Shrimp 21.5*).[16] In its initial ruling in the *Shrimp–Turtle* case, the Appellate Body found, under the chapeau, several shortcomings in respect of the application of the environmental conditionalities at issue in that case. The United States had pursued a negotiated agreement with some countries in the Western Hemisphere whose practices raised the environmental concerns in question, but had not done so with

---

[13] Some careless readings of the case law (for example, Cremona 2001) present this as a matter of balancing the actual interests of different WTO members, rather than considering the contribution of the measure to the interests or values protected by Article XX itself.

[14] WTO Appellate Body Report 2007.

[15] WTO Appellate Body Report 2000.

[16] WTO Appellate Body Report 1998b, 2001b.

the Asian countries, who were the complainants in the case. This finding led to a conclusion that the United States had engaged in 'unjustifiable discrimination'. While the Appellate Body was very clear that the problem here was treating different groups of countries differently, some scholars, who did not read the decision carefully, jumped to the conclusion that negotiation was being imposed as a *general precondition* for exercising rights under Article XX.[17] However, in the *US–Gambling* case, the Appellate Body made it clear that attempting negotiations is not a precondition to the justification of measures under Article XX: 'Engaging in consultations with Antigua, with a view to arriving at a negotiated settlement that achieves the same objectives as the challenged United States' measures, was not an appropriate alternative for the Panel to consider because consultations are by definition a process, the results of which are uncertain and therefore not capable of comparison with the measures at issue in this case.' (Paragraph 317)

20.8 THE AGREEMENT ON TECHNICAL BARRIERS TO TRADE AND THE ROLE OF INTERNATIONAL STANDARDS

The Agreement on Technical Barriers to Trade (TBT) covers technical regulations and standards, and imposes obligations additional to those in the GATT. It is possible that the obligations of the TBT could apply simultaneously to those of GATT, provided the measure in question falls under the definitions in both agreements. The TBT Agreement's provisions are aimed at government regulations, and they also include a Code of Conduct for non-governmental standardizing bodies. As interpreted by the Appellate Body, the TBT Agreement applies to a very wide range of domestic regulations,[18] arguably only excluding those measures that deal with certain aspects of food and agricultural health and safety regulation which are defined as falling within the exclusive province of the WTO Agreement on Sanitary and Phytosanitary Measures (SPS). One of the key disciplines of the TBT Agreement is the obligation for WTO members to use 'international standards' as a 'basis' for their technical regulations, unless the international standards are ineffective or inappropriate (Article 2.4). Yet international standards themselves are mostly of a voluntary nature and do not result, in most cases, in binding treaty commitments; quite a few of these standards are the creation of non-governmental bodies, or private–public partnerships where industry is the driving force. By virtue of Article 2.4 of the TBT Agreement, a very broad range of normative material, including privately generated norms in some cases, is converted or transformed into international legal obligation.

---

[17] A particularly egregious example of such a misreading is Cremona 2001.
[18] WTO Appellate Body Report 2002.

In dicta in the *EC–Sardines* ruling, the Appellate Body has suggested that a 'very strong and substantial' relationship may be required between domestic regulations and international standards to satisfy the obligation under TBT Article 2.4 to use international standards as a basis. The Appellate Body has clearly implied that international standards have considerable, automatic legal force in the WTO. However, the TBT Agreement nowhere defines international standards, nor does it attempt to list the international regimes that qualify to promulgate international standards within the meaning of TBT Article 2.4.[19]

The question of importing normative material from other international legal and policy sources into WTO adjudication related to internal regulations is broader than the TBT Agreement itself, although raised most pointedly by TBT given the open-ended notion of 'international standards' combined with the strong 'importation' effect that the Appellate Body has conferred on TBT 2.4.

Even where not specified in the WTO agreements themselves, the use of certain kinds of normative material external to the treaty text is mandated by Article 31 of the Vienna Convention on the Law of Treaties (VCLT). Thus, this Article provides that the treaty interpreter shall take into account, as context, 'any agreement relating to the treaty which was made between all the parties in connection with the conclusion of the treaty' and 'any instrument which was made by one or more of the parties in connection with the conclusion of the treaty and accepted by the other parties as an instrument related to the treaty'. In addition, the treaty interpreter is to take into account '(a) any subsequent agreement between the parties regarding the interpretation of the treaty or the application of its provisions; (b) any subsequent practice in the application of the treaty which establishes the agreement of the parties regarding its interpretation; (c) any relevant rules of international law applicable in the relations between the parties'. In a recent decision, *EC–Aircraft*, the Appellate Body has held that, under Vienna Convention 31(3)(c), it is possible to take into account non-WTO treaties, even if not all WTO Members are parties to those treaties; however, caution should be exercised where doing so.

A range of issues needs to be addressed in order to develop an adequate conceptual framework for a broader use of non-WTO legal norms.

A first perspective, common in the WTO epistemic community, is that the 'telos' of the WTO is *full international competition*, facilitated by progressively deeper or more complete deregulation[20] and/or privatization. From this perspective, the accommodations in these agreements to more traditional regulatory approaches represent concessions to political reality, which is likely to change as the trend for deregulation and free markets continues to spread globally.

---

[19] This and many other questions of interpretation may well be clarified by rulings of the Appellate Body that are expected spring 2012 in three separate appeals, all concerning the main provisions of the TBT Agreement. The cases are: *US–Clove Cigarettes, US–Tuna, and US–COOL*.

[20] The concept of deregulation here in fact denotes the reform of regulation in the direction of 'lighter', more market-friendly or incentive-oriented regulatory instruments. In some instances, the market access approach to the WTO implies more or higher regulatory standards, for instance intellectual property and competition-related regulatory standards. Thus, the turn to 'deregulation' really means a tendency to minimize regulation that limits competition or market access and to maximize regulation that enhances or guarantees competition and market access.

A second perspective, the one generally speaking underlying the analysis in this chapter as a whole, is that the WTO treaties represent a careful *balance of values*, with those public policy values that may be in tension with full liberalization given significant play, and with considerable policy space guaranteed for a diversity of regulatory approaches at the domestic level.

A third perspective, broadly speaking consistent with the second, is that liberalization of global markets may lead to increased spillovers, or negative effects of regulatory failure in one jurisdiction on the interests of other jurisdiction; from this point of view, liberalization of trade may well imply or require *upward harmonization of regulation*.

Depending upon which of the three perspectives, or combination thereof, the WTO adjudicator adopts, the function that she sees the importation of standards as achieving will differ.

Standards can have a wide range of intended normative effects within regulatory regimes. First of all, standards may be viewed as *minimum requirements*, prescribing a threshold level of regulation that parties to the regime undertake not to go below, though upward regulatory diversity—in regulating more strictly or extensively—may be encouraged. A different normative function of standards could be described as *aspirational*—that is, intended to demarcate the level or kind of regulation that parties are encouraged eventually to attain, with regulatory diversity being tolerated or encouraged to the extent that it refers to the speed and/or the means by which the regulatory objective is attained. Third, standards may be *facilitative*, but not directive, of a particular regulatory approach. This role of standards is, in principle, quite consistent with deep regulatory diversity.

Fourth, some standards may serve the function of 'boilerplate' or *default rules*. These standards do not express a normative preference for harmonization, even in principle. They may serve to reduce the costs of regulation, and facilitate regulatory cooperation, where particular states desire it, but entail no negative judgement upon states that formulate domestic regulations without regard to the default rules.

Finally standards may be expressed as *guidelines* or other material that is intentionally under-determined in its normative effect. The expectation is that the standards will provide some shaping guidance for domestic regulation, but the substantive regulatory outcome will be the product of the domestic political and/or administrative process. This is the case, frequently, with standards that are procedural in nature—suggesting certain inputs in the regulatory process or evoking certain best practices. In such instances, it is arguably the case that accountability for the substantive balance of values and interests reflecting in regulatory outcomes is expected to remain at the domestic level.

Unlike domestic regulations, international standards are often the product of informal, non-transparent, expert elite-driven processes that are not subject to direct or effective democratic control. A much debated question is whether in fact this matters, given that in most cases the standards only acquire a determinative, binding, coercive effect through being translated into regulations. There is an increasing appreciation that standard-setting at the international level may nevertheless shape the behaviour and opportunities of various agents, as well as increasing awareness of the difficulty of *ex post* democratic control through the regulatory process, given the agency costs and information asymmetries entailed in relying on expert elites to shape the standards in the first place.

20.9 Unnecessary obstacle to trade

The TBT Agreement also requires that technical regulations do not constitute an unnecessary obstacle to trade. While this test is not couched in exactly the same language as the necessity test that pertains to Article XX exceptions in the GATT, it is unlikely that a measure found to meet the necessity test in GATT would fail this requirement in TBT. One feature of this TBT provision is that it is couched in language that relates the necessity of trade restrictiveness to the attainment of a (non-exhaustive) list of 'legitimate objectives'. This list partly, but not entirely, overlaps with Article XX of the GATT. The list is as follows: 'national security requirements; the prevention of deceptive practices; protection of human health or safety, animal or plant life or health, or the environment'. One possible interpretation of the absence of public morals from this list is that moral regulations that relate to imported products, such as human rights or labour rights conditionalities, are not 'technical regulations' within the meaning of the TBT Agreement, and are to be assessed only under the GATT. However, the meaning of 'technical regulation' under TBT explicitly includes regulations concerning production processes in as much as they relate to traded products (as opposed, for example, to regulations on production processes that concern intellectual property or services, for example consulting engineering). Various provisions of TBT appear to assume that 'technical regulations' are in the nature of risk regulation, which is not how human rights or ethical standards are typically understood. Nevertheless, in the *EC–Gambling* case, the public morals exception in the GATT was held to apply to a ban on Internet gambling that was explicitly argued by the US to address some of the social risks or harms from gambling, especially to young people. This suggests that there may be overlap between risk regulation as a concept and the regulation of public morality. And, of course, as already noted, the list of 'legitimate objectives' in the TBT Agreement is not exhaustive.

20.10 SPS: food and agriculture regulation

One of the most visible and controversial areas where trade rules constrain regulatory diversity is that of food safety. The World Trade Organization (WTO) Agreement on Sanitary and Phytosanitary Measures (SPS Agreement), negotiated in the Uruguay Round and enacted in 1994, requires that countries either adopt harmonized international standards or, if they choose to maintain stricter regulations, base these on risk assessment, scientific principles, and scientific evidence. The SPS Agreement also requires that the regulations adopted be the least trade-restrictive available to achieve the desired level of protection. The above provisions apply even to non-discriminatory regulations that would not fall foul of the most-favoured nation and national treatment provisions of the GATT itself. The SPS Agreement also prohibits 'arbitrary' and 'unjusti-fied' distinctions in levels of protection in situations that are comparable, where these distinctions lead to 'discrimination' or 'disguised restriction on trade'.

More specifically, Article 2.2 of the SPS Agreement requires that members ensure, inter alia, that each SPS measure is 'based on scientific principles and is not maintained without sufficient scientific evidence'. Measures that 'conform to' international standards, however, are deemed to conform to this, as well as the other provisions of the SPS Agreement. Article 3.3 of the SPS Agreement allows members to maintain a higher level of protection than would be achieved by international standards if there is a 'scientific justification'.

In the original *Hormones* case,[21] the Appellate Body viewed the language 'based on' in Article 5.1 as implying the existence of a justified, rational basis for a measure in assessed risks; a measure could still be based on a risk assessment, even if scientific opinion were divided or uncertain. All that was required in the evidence represented by a risk assess-ment was evidentiary support for the connection being drawn by the government between the measure in question and the reduction or elimination of the identified risks. It is worth citing the Appellate Body's analysis at length:

> We do not believe that a risk assessment has to come to a monolithic conclusion that coincides with the scientific conclusion or view implicit in the SPS measure. Article 5.1 does not require that the risk assessment must necessarily embody only the view of a majority of the scientific community

Further, again being sensitive to democratic perspectives on risk regulation and reject-ing a narrow technocratic view, the Appellate Body eschewed a strict separation between risk assessment and risk management—the former based on quantitative analysis of risks themselves, and the latter involving judgements of value as well as fact in the deter-mination of the best strategy to manage risk. As the Appellate Body observed, 'It is essential to bear in mind that the risk that is to be evaluated in a risk assessment...is not only risk ascertainable in a science laboratory operating under strictly controlled condi-tions, but also risk in human societies as they actually exist, in other words, the actual potential for adverse effects on human health in the real world where people live and work and die.' Here, the issue was whether a risk assessment could take into account risks that might arise from the use of the hormones in question in an abusive fashion, contrary to sound veterinary practice. It was, in fact, this kind of risk that played an important role in the public outcry that had led to the EC ban in the first place. The Appellate Body nevertheless held that the ban on hormone-injected beef violated the SPS Agreement because the European Community had not offered a risk assessment that dealt specifically enough with the risks posed by the use of hormones in a manner inconsistent with sound veterinary practice.

Revisiting the *Hormones* dispute recently,[22] in light of claims by the EC that it had now had actual evidence of the risks of abusive use of hormones, the Appellate Body, in

---

[21] WTO Appellate Body Report 1998a.
[22] WTO Appellate Body Report 2008.

reversing the panel decision, emphasized that there is an important element of deference to the bona fide judgements of national regulators entailed in the application of
Article 5:[23]

> 590. Where a panel goes beyond this limited mandate and acts as a risk assessor, it
> would be substituting its own scientific judgement for that of the risk assessor and
> making a *de novo* review and, consequently, would exceed its functions under
> Article 11 of the DSU. Therefore, the review power of a panel is not to determine
> whether the risk assessment undertaken by a WTO Member is correct, but rather to
> determine whether that risk assessment is supported by coherent reasoning and
> respectable scientific evidence and is, in this sense, objectively justifiable.
>
> 591. This scientific basis need not reflect the majority view within the scientific
> community but may reflect divergent or minority views.

The Appellate Body further noted:

> 592. The purpose of a panel consulting with experts is not to perform its own risk
> assessment. The role of the experts must reflect the limited task of a panel.

Article 5.6 requires that 'Members shall ensure that…measures are not more trade-
restrictive than required to achieve their appropriate level of sanitary or phytosanitary
protection, taking into account technical and economic feasibility.' A footnote to this
provision indicates that, for a measure not to be the least trade-restrictive, another measure must be 'reasonably available, taking into account technical and economic feasibility, that achieves the appropriate level of sanitary or phytosanitary protection and is
significantly less restrictive to trade'. In the recent *Australia–New Zealand Apples* dispute,[24] the Appellate Body clarified the meaning of this provision, making it very clear
that the *complainant* must do much more than merely asserting that, hypothetically, an
alternative measure is reasonably available; they must show, on the basis of scientific
evidence, that the alternative would achieve the defending member's chosen level of
protection.

Article 5.7 of SPS allows a member to take provisional measures to address a risk
where there is insufficient scientific evidence to regulate based on a full scientific assessment of risk. In the recent *Hormones–Suspension* case, the Appellate Body explained
that judgements about the insufficiency of scientific evidence may change over time, as
the nature of the risk is better understood and the limits of existing scientific risk assessment become evident. The Appellate Body also suggests that it is prepared to afford a
certain deference in the application of the criteria for provisional measures where there
is an emergency situation, and/or where the risk is potentially life-threatening, based on
the precautionary principle.

---

[23] Having found that the panel erred in inter alia not being sufficiently deferential to the EC, the
Appellate Body also held that, given the complexity of the factual record, it was unable to complete the
analysis by applying the correctly deferential standard to the EC's measures. The dispute was later
settled by an agreement between the EC and the US that allowed the EC to maintain its measures.

[24] WTO Appellate Body Report 2010.

20.11 THE GATS

As already noted, domestic regulatory activities are crucial to attaining legitimate policy goals intertwined with the provision of services. There are important public good aspects to many service sectors, such as telecommunications, education, health, or the provision of water, with a corresponding need for extensive regulation.[25] Even where there are justifications for de-monopolization and regulatory reform, new regulations are needed to address access to 'networks', consumer protection, and equitable access to basic services. So far, the case law concerning such 'network' regulatory issues has been sparse; the *Telmex* ruling, concerning Mexico's pricing of interconnection for purposes of incoming long distance calls from the United States, showed little sensitivity to or understanding of public interest regulation in this area.[26] GATS Article I:3(b) excludes 'services supplied in the exercise of governmental authority'. However, a closer look reveals that the exact scope of this governmental/public services exception is far from clear. In order to be exempt from the GATS, a service has to be provided neither 'on a commercial basis' nor 'in competition with one or more services suppliers'. To date, the precise meaning of these provisions remains unclear. In the case of basic health services, for example, it remains unclear whether user fees or even insurance premiums charged for public health care would result in these services being found to be provided on a 'commercial basis', and thereby subject to general GATS disciplines.[27]

Similar lack of clarity surrounds some of the rules based on which members enter into specific commitments for individual services subsectors and modes of supply. For example, the GATS national treatment obligation (Article XVII) establishes that a member, once it has accepted that one of its subsectors and modes of supply is bound by this provision, may not discriminate between domestic and foreign like services and service suppliers. In that case, the scope of permissible regulatory action depends upon whether two services or service suppliers are 'like'. Although feasible in theory, it is virtually impossible for a WTO member to reverse specific commitments: the 'modification of schedule' process may start only three years after a commitment has been taken, and it entails lengthy and difficult negotiations about the level of compensation for affected trading partners. Again, this bargaining process promises to be particularly difficult for developing country members, which, because of their lack of negotiating expertise and their difficult economic situations, might be those countries most in need of quick and easy modification processes. In addition, the GATS 'lock in' effect may also bring about ramifications for citizens' democratic right to decide how services are regulated in the future. Citizens who have elected a government upon its promise to reverse or adapt certain steps towards economic liberalization in the services sector will realize that the

---

[25] See the magisterial study by Krajewski 2003a.
[26] WTO Panel Report 2004a. For a compelling critique, see Mavroidis and Neven 2006.
[27] The authoritative study on public services and the GATS is Krajewski 2003b.

latter may have virtually no means of taking back measures if preceding governments had enshrined them as binding GATS commitments.

20.12 Conclusion: is there a democratic deficit in the WTO approach to internal regulations?

This last observation brings us back to the fundamental question of the relationship between WTO trade liberalization disciplines and democratic control of the regulatory state. GATT/WTO law is also an area where information asymmetries have traditionally been very severe—there is very little understanding about trade rules and how they function, even among other agents of the people, such as legislators and senior bureaucrats concerned with domestic matters directly affected by trade rules. Negotiations have taken place in secret, making the account by negotiating agents of what went on in the room very difficult to verify independently. Further, governments (and ultimately citizens) have been highly dependent, in most cases, on the expert community to which the negotiating agents belong in making judgements about what the rules being negotiated 'mean', or, more precisely, the future consequences of those rules for various relevant interests.

Those who believe that the WTO is adequately 'democratic' usually point to the process of *ex post* legislative approval of negotiated WTO rules as an appropriate and effective democratic safeguard. However, those who have examined the role of *ex post* legislative control in the case of the Uruguay Round agreements tend to the conclusion that in all jurisdictions apart from the United States, *ex post* legislative scrutiny of negotiated rules was largely perfunctory.

The mere fact, however, that such scrutiny was perfunctory in this case does not itself show that it was not optimized in the Uruguay Round, nor that it is *in principle* ineffective in controlling agency costs.[28] For instance, one reason why such scrutiny might have been perfunctory and yet optimal is that legislators might have perceived agency costs to be small—that is to say, they might have trusted negotiators to have closely reflected the interests of citizens in bargaining to an agreement. Legislators have scarce resources—it could well be that the opportunity cost of using legislative time and money to closely scrutinize the Uruguay Round bargain was simply too high. There are *many* international negotiations where legislative oversight is minimal, just as legislative oversight of domestic agency rule-making varies greatly from agency to agency and regulatory context to regulatory context.

Here, it makes a great deal of difference how one perceives the choices of trade negotiators as they make WTO rules. Is this largely a matter of applying some kind of

---

[28] On agency costs in representative government, see Coglianese and Nicolaïdis 2001.

expertise—technical economics, for instance—to further a relatively uncontested conception of the public interest? Or do the rules in question, or the choices about the content of the rules, engage directly competing public values and constituencies? Especially after the Uruguay Round, WTO rules have been increasingly perceived, and rightly so, as conforming more to the latter description.

On the other hand, if we look at the problem from the point of view of the effects of WTO rules on regulatory democracy, the picture may be somewhat different. In the case of the WTO, the kind of rules characteristic of the GATT could plausibly be presented as largely democracy-enhancing, on the theory that these rules largely constrain trade protectionism. Since protectionism is often considered by trade economists and policy analysts to be almost always an inefficient instrument for achieving legitimate public aims, it is often assumed that it is a result of distortions or imperfections in the democratic process that allow concentrated interest groups to capture government policy-making and win rents. To the extent that GATT-type rules either constrain protectionism, or require a justification of trade protection as a necessary or legitimate public policy in the circumstances, they could be argued to prevent the corruption of the democratic process of special interests. As discussed above, at least in recent years, the interpretation of the rules such as National Treatment by the WTO adjudicator has been reasonably deferential or sensitive to the need to preserve policy space for legitimate, non-protectionist regulations (the *Asbestos* ruling for example).[29] However, it is clear that many of the newer WTO rules pose particular challenges in this regard, such as those in SPS that appear to place science over democracy as the ultimate test of legitimate food safety policies. Here the Appellate Body appears to be aware of the difficulty, as we have seen. In the application of these rules it has emphasized the precautionary principle, the importance of giving democratic regulators the ability to choose between divergent scientific opinions, and, most recently, the importance of an appropriately deferential standard of review—which considers the reasonableness and objectivity of the reasons for a member's regulators, rather than engaging in a *de novo* review of the correctness of the scientific basis for its policies.

In the case of TBT, as we have seen, the Appellate Body has not so far been so sensitive to regulatory democracy, interpreting the rules to give considerable normative force to standards created in bodies (some of them entirely private) that are not subject to normal democratic processes and oversight. Despite various attempts at cooperation and exchange of information between the Secretariats of the WTO and specialized regulatory regimes, what one might call a regulatory culture has not yet emerged within the administrative and diplomatic/political organs of the WTO. The committees within the WTO charged with implementing WTO agreements that concern specialized regulatory fields have generally avoided profound or sustained dialogue with either domestic or international regulatory agencies. There is no effective administrative or regulatory process in the WTO for

---

[29] In a recent book, Dani Rodrik has, along these lines, argued that review of domestic regulations by WTO adjudicators should be limited to scrutiny of the democratic process that produced the measures. See Rodrik 2011, 254–5.

adaptation of normative material from other regulatory regimes to the purposes of the WTO. Under these circumstances, the burden is likely to fall largely on the WTO adjudicator to define the appropriate relationship between those regimes and the WTO.

It is worth considering some of the practices and procedures that can facilitate the adjudicator playing this role. Participation of officials or experts from specialized regulatory regimes on WTO panels, solicitation of interpretations or opinions from the secretariats of such regimes, the use of international or domestic regulators as experts in WTO panel proceedings, and amicus curiae briefs from domestic and international regulatory agencies to both the panel and the Appellate Body (as well as stakeholders) are all possibilities, consistent with the existing Dispute Settlement Understanding as interpreted in the Appellate Body jurisprudence.

REFERENCES

Bronckers, Marco and Nathalie McNelis. 2000. Rethinking the 'Like Product' Definition in WTO Law: Anti-dumping and Environmental Protection. In *Regulatory Barriers and the Principle of Non-Discrimination in World Trade Law*, edited by Thomas Cottier and Petros C. Mavroidis, 345–85. Ann Arbor: University of Michigan Press.

Coglianese, Cary, and Kalypso Nicolaïdis. 2001. Securing Subsidiarity: The Institutional Design of Federalism in the United States and Europe. In *The Federal Vision: Legitimacy and Levels of Governance in the United States and the European Union*, edited by Kalypso Nicolaïdis and Robert Howse, 277–99. Oxford: Oxford University Press.

Cremona, Marise. 2001. Neutrality or Discrimination? The WTO, the EU and External Trade. In *The EU and the WTO: Legal and Constitutional Issues*, edited by Grainne de Burca and Joanne Scott, 151–84. Oxford: Hart Publishing.

Francioni, Francesco. 2001. Environment, Human Rights and the Limits of Free Trade. In *Environment, Human Rights and International Trade*, edited by Francesco Francioni, 1–26. Oxford: Hart Publishing.

GATT Panel Report. 1991. *US–Restrictions on Imports of Tuna*. DS21/R, DS21/R. Unadopted, BISD 39S/155. Geneva: GATT.

GATT Panel Report. 1994. *US–Restrictions on Imports of Tuna*. DS29/R. Unadopted. Geneva: GATT.

Horn, Henrik. 2006. National Treatment in the GATT. *American Economic Review* 96 (1): 394–404.

Howse, Robert, and Donald Regan. 2000. The Product/Process Distinction—An Illusory Basis for Disciplining 'Unilateralism' in Trade Policy. *European Journal of International Law*. 11:2. pp. 249–89.

Krajewski, Markus. 2003a. *National Regulation and Trade Liberalization in Services: The Legal Impact of the General Agreement on Trade in Services (GATS) on National Regulatory Autonomy*. The Hague: Kluwer.

Krajewski, Markus. 2003b. Public Services and Trade Liberalization: Mapping the Legal Framework. *Journal of International Economic Law* 6 (2):341–67.

Mavroidis, Petros, and Damien Neven. 2006. El Mess in TELMEX: A Comment on Mexico–Measures Affecting Telecommunications Services. *World Trade Review* 5 (2):271–96.

Rodrik, Dani. 2011. *The Globalization Paradox: Democracy and the Future of the World Economy*. Norton: New York.

Sykes, Alan. 1999. Regulatory Protectionism and the Law of International Trade. *University of Chicago Law Review* 66 (1):1–46.

WTO Appellate Body Report. 1998a. *EC–Measures Concerning Meat and Meat Products (Hormones)*. WT/DS26/AB/R, WT/DS48/AB/R. Adopted 13 February 1998. DSR 1998:I, 135. Geneva: WTO.

WTO Appellate Body Report. 1998b. *US–Import Prohibition of Certain Shrimp and Shrimp Products*. WT/DS58/AB/R. Adopted 6 November 1998. DSR 1998:VII, 2755. Geneva: WTO.

WTO Appellate Body Report. 2000. *Korea–Measures Affecting Imports of Fresh, Chilled and Frozen Beef*. WT/DS161/AB/R, WT/DS169/AB/R. Adopted 10 January 2001. DSR 2001:I, 5. Geneva: WTO.

WTO Appellate Body Report. 2001a. *EC–Measures Affecting Asbestos and Asbestos-Containing Products*. WT/DS135/AB/R. Adopted 5 April 2001. DSR 2001:VII, 3243. Geneva: WTO.

WTO Appellate Body Report. 2001b. *US–Import Prohibition of Certain Shrimp and Shrimp Products—Recourse to Article 21.5 of the DSU by Malaysia*. WT/DS58/AB/RW. Adopted 21 November 2001. DSR 2001:XIII, 6481. Geneva: WTO.

WTO Appellate Body Report. 2002. *EC–Trade Description of Sardines*. WT/DS231/AB/R. Adopted 23 October 2002. DSR 2002:VIII, 3359. Geneva: WTO.

WTO Appellate Body Report. 2005a. *Dominican Republic–Measures Affecting the Importation and Internal Sale of Cigarettes*. WT/DS302/AB/R. Adopted 19 May 2005. DSR 2005:XV, 7367. Geneva: WTO.

WTO Appellate Body Report. 2005b. *US–Measures Affecting the Cross-Border Supply of Gambling and Betting Services*. WT/DS285/AB/R. Adopted 20 April 2005. DSR 2005:XII, 5663 (Corr.1, DSR 2006:XII, 5475). Geneva: WTO.

WTO Appellate Body Report. 2007. *Brazil–Measures Affecting Imports of Retreaded Tyres*. WT/DS332/AB/R. Adopted 17 December 2007. DSR 2007:IV, 1527. Geneva: WTO.

WTO Appellate Body Report. 2008. *US–Continued Suspension of Obligations in the EC–Hormones Dispute*. WT/DS320/AB/R. Adopted 14 November 2008. DSR 2008:X, 3507. Geneva: WTO.

WTO Appellate Body Report. 2009. *China–Measures Affecting Trading Rights and Distribution Services for Certain Publications and Audiovisual Entertainment Products*. WT/DS363/AB/R. Adopted 19 January 2010. Geneva: WTO.

WTO Appellate Body Report. 2010. *Australia–Measures Affecting the Importation of Apples from New Zealand*. WT/DS367/AB/R. Adopted 17 December 2010. Geneva: WTO.

WTO Panel Report. 2004a. *Mexico–Measures Affecting Telecommunications Services*. WT/DS204/R. Adopted 1 June 2004. DSR 2004:IV, 1537. Geneva: WTO.

WTO Panel Report. 2004b. *US–Measures Affecting the Cross-Border Supply of Gambling and Betting Services*. WT/DS285/R. Adopted 20 April 2005, as modified by Appellate Body Report WT/DS285/AB/R. DSR 2005:XII, 5797. Geneva: WTO.

PART VI

IMPLEMENTATION AND ENFORCEMENT

CHAPTER 21

....

THE TRADE POLICY
REVIEW MECHANISM

....

SAM LAIRD AND RAYMUNDO VALDÉS[*]

21.1 INTRODUCTION

....

THE Trade Policy Review Mechanism (TPRM) is the main transparency instrument of
the World Trade Organization (WTO), affording as it does opportunities for a process
of collective evaluation of the trade policies and practices of individual members.[1]
Transparency has historically been one of the main pillars of the multilateral trading
system because of its power to provide crucial information to market participants about
the conditions under which commercial transactions take place, thus allowing markets
to function more efficiently.[2] Transparency has also been critical to the effective functioning of the multilateral system by allowing participants to monitor the adherence to,
and the impact of, its provisions. The TPRM is not part of the enforcement processes of
the WTO in the way that is served by the dispute settlement mechanism, although it
provides information that may be used to assess compliance, as discussed further below.

Efforts to enhance transparency have thus been a feature of the multilateral trading
system since its creation in 1947, as denoted by the various requirements concerning notification and publication of information contained in the original General Agreement on
Tariffs and Trade (GATT).[3] The broader concept of transparency underpinning the

* The views expressed are those of the authors and do not necessarily represent the views of any
organization to which they are affiliated.

[1] The WTO uses the term 'members' rather than countries, since there are a number of members
that are customs territories rather than states. However, in this paper we occasionally use the word
'countries' where constant use of 'members' seems excessively legalistic.

[2] WTO 2002.

[3] The basic provision on transparency was contained in Article X of the GATT 1947, which called for
members to publish promptly any laws and regulations relating to trade matters in order to allow
traders to become familiar with them. Under present multilateral rules, in addition to Annex 3 of the
Marrakesh Agreement, the main transparency provisions are contained in Article X of the GATT 1994,

present TPRM can be traced back to the ad hoc surveillance schemes established under the GATT, and the discussions to establish a wider ranging multilateral surveillance mechanism during the Uruguay Round negotiations. These led to the establishment of the TPRM, on a provisional basis, within the GATT in 1989, and its placement on a permanent footing as one of WTO's basic functions when the Round was concluded in 1994.

Since its creation in 1989, the TPRM has become a major source of information on the trade policies of individual members as well as global trade developments. The information and analysis provided by the TPRM may be seen as a public good, contributing to a more secure trading environment that fosters investment and trade. In addition, the idea of using transparency to assist good policy-making is founded in the public choice literature, so that, for individual countries, the mechanism helps to foster an atmosphere in which rent-seekers find it more difficult to operate.[4]

While the mechanism is generally perceived as having worked satisfactorily, it has been criticized for not being tough enough or analytical enough. However, this goes somewhat against the culture of the GATT/WTO, which has discouraged the Secretariat from taking a hard line against its own members in anything other than the most diplomatic language. The trade policy review (TPR) process also faces a number of other practical challenges in carrying out its mandate, mostly linked to resource constraints. In particular, it is not clear how best to carry out the full programme of reviews, especially in the light of the WTO's increasing membership and number of meetings.

The organization of the chapter is as follows: Sections 21.2 and 21.3 cover the origins and objectives of the TPRM, Section 21.4 discusses the TPR process (the cycle of reviews, the stages of a review, the review meetings, the Secretariat and government reports, and other review documents and dissemination), Section 21.5 describes the overview and monitoring functions of the TPRM, Section 21.6 covers domestic transparency, Section 21.7 provides an evaluation of the mechanism, and Section 21.8 discusses some of the challenges facing the mechanism.

21.2 ORIGINS OF THE MECHANISM

Several ad hoc surveillance schemes existed under the GATT, most of whose bodies can be said to have played a surveillance role if this function is interpreted in a broad sense. More specific forerunners of the TPRM were the biannual special meetings of the GATT Council, which were introduced in 1980 to carry out reviews of developments in the trading system. From 1983 onwards, the scope of these Council meetings was broadened to include monitoring of paragraph 7(i) of the 1982 Ministerial Declaration, in which

Article III of the General Agreement on Trade in Services (GATS), and Article 63 of the Agreement on Trade-Related Aspects of Intellectual Property Rights (TRIPS). More detailed provisions spelling out procedural rules can be found in many other WTO agreements.

[4] An analogy sometimes used by some trade policy review (TPR) staff is that rent-seekers are like vampires that cannot flourish in the light of day—or so it is said!

contracting parties (GATT members) agreed 'to make determined efforts to ensure that trade policies and measures are consistent with GATT principles and rules and... to make determined efforts to avoid measures which would limit or distort international trade'.[5] The main documentation for the special Council meetings consisted of a Secretariat note which surveyed developments in trade policies and related matters over the last semester. The Secretariat note was comprehensive in its coverage, drew both on notified and non-notified material, and included an introductory 'overview' and other analysis. GATT 1987 points out, however, that the note deliberately refrained from suggesting that particular actions conformed or failed to conform with GATT obligations, on the ground that such judgements were reserved to the contracting parties.[6]

In 1983, in the context of supporting the recovery of the global economy from the then ongoing debt crisis and identifying options for strengthening the multilateral trading system, an Eminent Persons Group was set up, chaired by Fritz Leutwiler. In 1985, this group recommended, among other things, that 'countries should be subject to regular oversight or surveillance of their policies and actions, about which the GATT Secretariat should collect and publish information'.[7] The transparency element of the Leutwiler report filtered into the Punta del Este Declaration of 1986, which committed to 'enhance the surveillance in the GATT to enable regular monitoring of trade policies and practice... and their impact on the functioning of the multilateral trading system'. To fulfil this mandate, the negotiating group on the Functioning of the GATT System (FOGS) engaged in a series of discussions concerning surveillance during 1987 and 1988.

Compared with other areas negotiated during the Uruguay Round, the FOGS discussions proceeded speedily. As part of those discussions, developed countries submitted proposals for improving the notes prepared by the Secretariat for the biannual special Council meetings by placing greater emphasis on economic analysis and the verification of compliance with contractual obligations. Although developing countries did not want to create new obligations, Ghosh notes that they agreed to the early establishment of the TPRM seeking to close the gap between their surveillance capacity and that of developed countries, improve their trade and investment policies and obtain international recognition for these improvements, and ensure that the trade measures applied by major trading countries would be regularly monitored.[8]

At the Montreal Mid-Term Review of the Uruguay Round, ministers recommended the creation of the TPRM, which was established on a provisional basis within the GATT in 1989. The TPRM was placed on a permanent footing by Annex 3 of the agreement establishing the WTO. Reflecting the broadening of the multilateral trading system itself, Annex 3 also expanded the scope of the TPRM to include, not only policies and measures related to trade in goods, but also those linked to trade in services and trade-related aspects of intellectual property rights.

---

[5] GATT 1982.   [6] GATT 1987.
[7] Leutwiler et al. 1985.   [8] Ghosh 2008.

21.3 OBJECTIVES OF THE MECHANISM

Annex 3 of the Marrakesh Agreement set up the purpose of the TPRM as to 'contribute to improved adherence by all Members to rules, disciplines and commitments made under the Multilateral Trade Agreements and, where applicable, the Plurilateral Trade Agreements, and hence to the smoother functioning of the multilateral trading system, by achieving greater transparency in, and understanding of, the trade policies and practices of Members'. Annex 3 goes on to note that 'the function of the review mechanism is to examine the impact of a Member's trade policies and practices on the multilateral trading system'. Hence, the mechanism's stated purpose is to shed light on the systemic effects of the trade policies and practices of individual WTO members.

There has been some debate in the literature concerning the practical interpretation of the TPRM objectives, with some highlighting the transparency and other non-legal objectives of the mechanism, while others emphasize the importance of the mechanism as part of the enforcement of GATT/WTO legal obligations.

According to Annex 3, 'the assessment carried out under the review mechanism takes place, to the extent relevant, against the background of the wider economic and developmental needs, policies and objectives of the Member concerned, as well as of its external environment'. The non-legal objectives of the mechanism are also noted by Blackhurst.[9] Richard Blackhurst, Director of the GATT's Economic Research and Analysis Unit at the time the TPRM was established, traces the concept of a transparency mechanism at the national and international levels to the economic literature on public choice.[10] The basic line of argument in this literature is that elected officials and civil servants may become influenced by vested interests ('rent-seekers') to make decisions which help such groups and run counter to the promotion of general public welfare. Transparency is said to lead to better decision-making by alerting the public at home to the potential costs and benefits of policies, as well as signalling potentially harmful changes to trading partners. For these reasons, there is 'a very strong case for surrounding all facets of economic policy-making with a high degree of transparency and surveillance'.[11]

In the same vein, Curzon Price argues that TPRM surveillance will apply peer group pressure to help overcome the natural tendency of countries to want to be free-riders, encouraging them to cooperate for enhanced international welfare.[12] In this same respect, the second appraisal of the operation of the TPRM (see below) concluded that 'The Mechanism had demonstrated that it had a valuable public-good aspect, and had been a vehicle for Members to reflect on their policies, served as an input into policy formulation, and highlighted general technical assistance needs.'[13]

---

[9] Blackhurst 1988.   [10] See, for instance, Olson 1965 and Tullock 1987.
[11] Ibid.   [12] Curzon Price 1991.   [13] WTO 2005.

The views of some delegations in the FOGS echo the economic interpretation. Thus, the United States noted that the TPR process is broader than a limited review of GATT obligations: 'its aim is to improve understanding of the total context of trade policies and make contracting parties reflect on their economic policies'.[14] A number of developing countries, including China (which was party to the negotiations although not a GATT contracting party), emphasized the importance of looking at policies in a development context. However, there were also differences about the extent to which the wider context of policies should be taken into account.

In relation to the legal objectives of the mechanism, the text of the Marrakesh Agreement is quite explicit that the mechanism 'is not intended to serve as a basis for the enforcement of specific obligations under the [WTO] agreements or for dispute settlement purposes or to impose new policy commitments on Members'. However, certain aspects of the legal texts, in particular the phrase 'improved adherence...to rules, disciplines and commitments', have led to a legal interpretation of those objectives. Thus, Qureshi essentially argues that the mechanism is intended to ensure compliance with GATT obligations.[15] It may be noted that, in a later article, Qureshi places greater emphasis on the transparency aspect, while arguing that reviews should take fuller account of GATT/WTO provisions for developing countries in reviews of those countries.[16] Mavroidis, also a jurist, recognizes the importance of the transparency element, but is disappointed by the reluctance of the Secretariat to express more forceful views on the GATT-consistency of measures.[17]

There is also some support for the legal interpretation among statements made by some GATT contracting parties in the FOGS group.[18] Thus, India, in particular, suggested that the surveillance should contribute to improved adherence to GATT disciplines and obligations. In this respect, it is useful to recall that the widespread use of 'grey areas measures', such as voluntary export restraints, and subsidy wars in the area of agriculture had been seen as undermining the GATT system, to the point that Lester Thurow was to declare 'GATT is dead'.

In practice, the WTO Secretariat reports, while generally focusing on economic issues, also look at the consistency of certain trade measures with multilateral principles. Thus, for example, the Secretariat reports normally identify instances of applied tariffs exceeding bound rates, or of when the domestic legislation falls short of the minimum protection laid down in the Agreement on Trade-Related Aspects of Intellectual Property Rights (TRIPS), albeit without making an explicit assessment of the degree of consistency with WTO rules. Members themselves pay attention to legal issues during the review meetings, routinely questioning the member under review on its compliance with WTO agreements. However, rather than clarifying the objectives set up in Annex 3 and their revealed interest on compliance issues, members have preferred to simply reaffirm 'the relevance of TPRM's mission as defined in Annex 3 of the Marrakesh Agreement'.[19]

---

[14] GATT 1988.   [15] Qureshi 1990, 1992.   [16] Qureshi 1995.
[17] Mavroidis 1992.   [18] GATT 1988.   [19] WTO 2008a.

On the other hand, it is clear from the earlier discussions, as well as repeated statements by a wide range of members, that at no time was there any view held that the mechanism would be part of the formal dispute settlement system. Indeed, one of the strengths of the TPRM is its role as a forum where policies can be explained and discussed, where information can be sought, and concerns can be expressed on a largely non-legalistic (and non-confrontational) basis. This was confirmed by the panel established in relation to the dispute brought by Brazil against Canada concerning measures affecting the export of civilian aircraft. Noting that Annex 3 provides that the mechanism 'is not, however, intended to serve as a basis for the enforcement of specific obligations under the Agreements or for dispute settlement procedures', the panel decided to 'attach no importance to the Trade Policy Review of Canada in considering Brazil's arguments concerning IQ [Investissement-Québec] assistance to the regional aircraft industry'.[20]

Several authors have focused on the benefits of the TPRM for improved domestic policies—emphasizing the public choice aspect.[21] They see the TPRM as the multilateral complement to national transparency mechanisms, which they maintain can help improve domestic policy-making and the allocation of resources in the domestic economy. Recognizing this complementarity, Annex 3 calls for members 'to encourage and promote greater transparency within their own systems', while at the same time underscoring that 'the implementation of domestic transparency must be on a voluntary basis and take account of each Member's legal and political systems' (see below).

21.4 THE TPR PROCESS

21.4.1 Cycle of reviews

Trade policy reviews are conducted by the Trade Policy Review Body (TPRB), which is in fact the General Council under another name and meeting under different terms of reference. This means that reviews are conducted by WTO's highest-level body responsible for day-to-day decision-making. At its first meeting of the year, the TPRB elects its own chair from among the representatives of members; the chair holds office for one year.

The TPRB undertakes the regular collective 2011 appreciation of the trade policies and practices of all WTO members. By the end of 2011, the TPRB had conducted 338 trade policy reviews since its formation (counting the European Union as one), at 254 review meetings (see Table 14). The reviews have covered 141 of the 153 WTO members, representing some 89 per cent of the share of world trade.[22] Overall, there has now been extensive coverage of all regions and members at different levels of development.

---

[20] WTO Panel Report 1999.
[21] Spriggs 1991; Laird and Messerlin 1990; Banks 1992.
[22] Excluding significant double counting and intra-EU trade.

Table 14 Trade policy reviews: WTO members reviewed under GATT 1947 and WTO provisions, 1989–2011

Europe/Middle East	Asia/Pacific	Africa	America
Albania	Australia (6)	Angola*	Argentina (3)
Armenia	Bangladesh* (3)	Benin*[2] (3)	Antigua and Barbuda[2] (2)
Austria[1]	Brunei Darussalam (2)	Botswana[2] (3)	Barbados (2)
	Cambodia*		
Bahrain (2)	China (3)	Burkina Faso*[2] (3)	Belize (2)
Bulgaria[1]	Fiji (2)	Burundi*	Bolivia (3)
Croatia	Georgia	Cameroon[2] (3)	Brazil (5)
Cyprus[1]	Hong Kong, China (6)	Chad*	Canada (9)
Czech Republic[1] (2)	India (5)	Central African Republic*	Chile (4)
European Union (10)	Indonesia (5)	Congo, Dem. Rep.	Colombia (3)
Finland[1]	Japan (10)	Congo, Rep. of	Costa Rica (3)
Hungary[1] (2)	Korea, Rep. of (5)	Côte d'Ivoire	Dominica[2] (2)
Iceland (3)	Kyrgyz Republic	Djibouti*	Dominican Republic (3)
Israel (3)	Macao, China (3)	Egypt (3)	Ecuador (2)
Liechtenstein[2] (3)	Malaysia (5)	Gabon[2] (2)	El Salvador (3)
Norway (5)	Maldives* (2)	Gambia* (2)	Guatemala (2)
Poland[1] (2)	Mongolia	Ghana (3)	Grenada[2] (2)
Qatar	New Zealand (4)	Guinea* (3)	Guyana (2)
Romania[1] (3)	Pakistan (3)	Kenya[2] (3)	Haiti*
Slovak Republic[1] (2)	Papua New Guinea (2)	Lesotho*[2] (3)	Honduras (2)
Slovenia[1]	Philippines (3)	Madagascar* (2)	Jamaica (3)
Sweden[1] (2)	Singapore (5)	Malawi* (2)	Mexico (4)
Switzerland[2] (5)	Solomon Islands* (2)	Mali[2] (3)	Nicaragua (2)
Turkey (4)	Sri Lanka (3)	Mauritania* (2)	Panama
United Arab Emirates	Chinese Taipei (2)	Mauritius (3)	Paraguay (3)
Jordan	Thailand (6)	Morocco (4)	Peru (3)
Oman		Mozambique* (2)	St Kitts and Nevis[2] (2)
		Namibia[2] (3)	St Lucia[2] (2)
		Niger*[2] (2)	St Vincent & Grenadines[2] (2)
		Nigeria (4)	Suriname
		Rwanda*	Trinidad and Tobago (2)
		Senegal*[2] (3)	United States (10)
		Sierra Leone*	Uruguay (3)
		South Africa[2] (4)	Venezuela (2)
		Swaziland[2] (3)	
		Tanzania*[2] (2)	
		Togo* (2)	
		Tunisia (2)	

		Uganda*[2] (3)	
		Zambia* (3)	
		Zimbabwe (2)	
42 members	26 members	40 members	33 members (95 reviews)
(60 reviews)	(91 reviews)	(92 reviews)	

( ) Number of reviews completed where this is greater than one.
*Least-developed member.
[1]Now included in European Union (EU).
[2]Joint review but counted as individual members for statistical purposes from 2009.
Source: WTO 2011a.

There is a predetermined rhythm of reviews under which all WTO members must be reviewed. The four largest trading entities (counting the European Union as one) are reviewed every two years, the next 16 trading entities (in terms of their share of world trade in goods and services) are reviewed every four years, and the remainder of the membership is reviewed every six years. Once a member is included in the process, its next review should take place according to this cycle, except that a leeway of six months may be allowed. The essential idea behind the differential cycles is that traders with the greatest impact on world trade and the multilateral system should be reviewed more frequently; acceptance of this principle by the larger traders was also seen as important in drawing developing members into the review process.

The ranking of members is based on the average value of their trade in goods and services over a period of three years. Hence, their review cycles can change in several ways. For example, until 2003 the members on the two-year cycle included Canada, the European Union, Japan, and the United States; thereafter, the rapid expansion of China's trade led to Canada being replaced by China in the group of the four largest trading entities. The repeated enlargement of the European Union has also caused several changes, with various countries dropping out of the group of 16 members on the four-year cycle, thus making space for others to move into the group. In addition, variations in trade in goods and services flows may affect the rankings—for example, as a result of changes in commodity prices. This can affect, in particular, the ranking of large petroleum-exporting countries, and the composition of the four- and six-year cycle groups.

There has been some sporadic discussion in the TPRB on possible changes to the cycle of reviews. Proposals include a modification to provide for a three-year cycle for members currently on a two-year review pattern, but there was no support from other members for such a change. However, it was agreed that, in the case of two-year reviews, every second review might have an 'interim' character, although this was not to detract from the comprehensive nature of reviews of such members. The allowance of six months of leeway for all members may be seen as a compromise on the proposal for changes in the cycle.

There was a progressive build-up of the review programme from 1990, when only six reviews were held, to 1999, when 12 reviews were conducted. During 2000–11, the number of reviews ranged between 16 and 21 (2009) each year. Despite this increase, the number of reviews still falls short of the total required annually to meet the mandate in Annex 3. Thus, two members in the two-year cycle must be reviewed each year, plus four members in the four-year cycle. In addition to the 20 members that fall within the two-and four-year cycles, there are 133 WTO members (January 2011), of whom 27 are members of the European Union and are not reviewed separately. Thus, 106 members need to be covered on the six-year cycle. This gives a total of some 24 reviews per year. In addition, with 30 countries in the process of acceding to the WTO (January 2011), the annual number of reviews should eventually expand to about 30 a year.

In fact, there is some latitude for reviewing least-developed members on a longer cycle,[23] but the number of reviews must continue to increase if the current cycles are to be met. In the meantime, members have decided that 'all Members, including LDCs [least-developed countries], should be reviewed at least once as soon as possible'.[24] Accordingly, priority is given in the TPRB calendar to including members that have not been previously reviewed. Efforts to expand the coverage of least-developed countries stems from a perception that the reviews can be of benefit to the members under review in taking stock of and planning their trade policies, as discussed later. As at early 2011, 12 WTO members had never been reviewed, although four of these were being proposed for review in 2011.[25] Most of the other members yet to be reviewed were relatively recent accessions.[26]

21.4.2 Stages of a review

The reviews by the TPRB are conducted on the basis of a report prepared by the WTO Secretariat and a 'policy statement' by the member under review. An overview of the process is given in Table 15. The scheduling is agreed between the Secretariat and the member under review, with the date of the review meeting determining the timing of other steps, including translation into WTO's official languages.

Today, the WTO Secretariat reports are largely based on published sources, including WTO notifications and official reports from the member, with increasing reliance on the Internet to obtain the information. The Secretariat has acknowledged that its task is made easier by availability of reports from organizations such as the International Monetary Fund (IMF), the World Bank, the Organization for Economic Cooperation and Development (OECD), UN regional commission, and so on. During a visit or

---

[23] Annex 3 of the Marrakesh Agreement, paragraph C (ii) provides that a 'longer period' (than six years between reviews) may be fixed for least-developed country members. In addition, paragraph D contains provision for 'particular account [to] be taken of difficulties presented to least-developed country members in compiling their reports'.

[24] WTO 1999.

[25] WTO 2011a.

[26] There is an informal understanding that the period between an accession and a first review corresponds to the review cycle in which a member falls.

Table 15 Stages in preparing a trade policy review

Time before/after the review meeting	Stage
12 months before	Secretariat and the authorities of the member under review agree on the work programme for the preparation of the review.
11 months before	Authorities nominate contact points in Geneva and the capital.
11 months before	Secretariat submits its initial request for information to the authorities.
8 months before	First technical assistance visit to member under review, if any.
7–4 months before	Secretariat progressively sends sections of its report for comment by the authorities, with observations requested within two to four weeks later, depending on the section.
14 weeks before	Main visit to member under review (five working days) to hold high-level and detailed technical discussions aimed to complement and clarify the authorities' written comments.
11 weeks before	Secretariat report sent to the editor, following the incorporation of comments and additional information provided by the authorities, as appropriate.
10 weeks before	Deadline to receive the government report.
9 weeks before	Secretariat and government reports are sent for translation so they may be distributed in the three official WTO languages.
5 weeks before	Secretariat and government reports must be distributed to members.
4 weeks before	Selection of the discussant for the review meeting.
2 weeks before	Deadline to receive advance written questions for which answers should be provided at the start of the review meeting.
Review meeting	Chair opens the meeting, followed by the initial statement by the member under review, then the discussant and delegates. The formal review process ends with the chair's concluding remarks.
2 weeks after	Secretariat prepares and distributes in draft form the record of the meeting.
4 weeks after	Deadline for the member under review to submit in writing any answers not provided during the meeting.
6 weeks after	Secretariat issues a revised version of the reports.

mission to the capital, the Secretariat team sometimes collects information and gets a take from the private sector (e.g. Chambers of Manufacturers or Commerce) and research institutes on policies and developments in the economy. Academic economists have often made studies of aspects of the trade regimes in their home countries, and these can provide useful background, but contact with the academic community on visits to the capital is today rather limited.

The Secretariat prepares a draft, which is submitted progressively to the authorities of the member being reviewed; this text typically includes extensive questions on policy and details on how policy measures are applied in practice. The authorities' comments on the Secretariat draft are then the subject of the discussions with the authorities during the Secretariat's main (policy) visit to the capital. This approach represents a considerable shift from earlier practice, which involved the Secretariat preparing a detailed questionnaire and conducting an early fact-finding visit to the member under review. Comments are taken into account by the Secretariat in the preparation of the final report, which remains fully under the responsibility of the Secretariat and is not a negotiated text. In general, despite the fact that it has no powers to subpoena information, the Secretariat receives good cooperation from members. Occasionally, information is not forthcoming, and the Secretariat sometimes notes this in its reports.

Secretariat reports adopt a more or less standard chapter structure and use standardized tables. This promotes full coverage, while also making it easier for users to find information. It also facilitates the collation of information for the periodic overviews of the world economy. There have been some criticisms about the inclusion of detailed macroeconomic data, and thus this information has been condensed. However, the Secretariat has continued to include other detailed information on trade measures and economic sectors, which provides valuable background to policy developments. This has been important most recently, for example, in identifying and understanding new protectionist measures taken during the financial crises, e.g. the increase in anti-dumping actions to reduce pressures on domestic firms. It is important to note that the preparation of the Secretariat report requires more detailed documentation of the legal basis of policies and practices than is evident in the reports of other organizations, reflecting the different character of the WTO as an organization based on a core of legal texts governing almost all aspects of international economic relations.

On the whole, Secretariat reports have been welcomed by WTO members as well as academia. For example, periodic special issues of *The World Economy* are based on these reports. However, as might be expected, members under review occasionally indicate their disagreement with the more critical aspects of the Secretariat's assessment, sometimes maintaining that the Secretariat should limit itself to a mere factual reporting of the existence of measures rather than the evaluation of policies and their implementations. By contrast, the academic community has expressed concern that the reports are not sufficiently analytical or critical. However, Keesing notes that the reports have evolved from 'largely descriptive catalogues of countries' protectionist measures into more thorough, incisive and analytical surveys of trade policies and practices'.[27] Nevertheless, he argues that the reports have sometimes been over-optimistic, and should comment more forthrightly on the credibility and sustainability of policy reforms, while acknowledging that the cautious tone relates to the diplomatic environment of the WTO.

Keesing argues that reports need to pay more attention to the 'bottom line', attempting to calculate the total costs of protection. It is hard to argue with this, but such computations are complex and resource-intensive, and would require a quite different level of resource input from that which is available to the Trade Policies Review Division (TPRD) (the WTO division with responsibility for the TPR process). Keesing also

---

[27] Keesing 1998.

identifies a number of areas which he believes need more comprehensive and critical treatment in Secretariat reports. In this regard, he singles out anti-dumping, regional trade agreements (RTAs), and export promotion schemes, as well as bribery and corruption, as obstacles to trade, investment, and government procurement. Some of these issues have indeed been expanded in subsequent reports, for example in relation to RTAs, investment, procurement, and so on—as well as the major expansion in the area of services since the establishment of the WTO.

The Reports by the member under review have evolved over time and now usually take the form of policy statements, outlining the objectives and direction of trade policies. They often contain a short presentation of recent trends and problems, including those encountered in foreign markets, e.g. concerns about protectionist measures taken by others. Preparation for and participation in a trade policy review can be onerous for small developing members, and the WTO Secretariat has, on request, assisted such members at different stages of the process.

The reports by the Secretariat and by the country under review are provided to all WTO members at least five weeks before the review meeting, giving other members the time to submit questions in writing before the start of the TPRB meeting. Questions submitted at least two weeks before the meeting are to be answered in writing by the member under review by the start of the meeting, while questions posed subsequently are to be answered to the extent possible during the meeting itself. The Secretariat identifies the main points contained in the questions submitted in advance and posts them on the non-public members' website one week before the meeting.

21.4.3 TPRB review meeting

In a TPRB review meeting, the member whose policies are being examined is not in the dock, although it may sometimes feel like it. Rather, the process is an opportunity for the member to provide information on the evolution of their trade policies and explain what is driving the process at home. It also provides the opportunity for other members to inquire about such policies—a learning process—and to express concern about issues that affect their trading interests. In this process, other members learn what works and what does not work. But they also have the occasion to offer advice on what works for them, and indeed comments—however diplomatically expressed—may be a plea for the member under review to put its house in order.

Review meetings normally take place in two sessions (each typically half a day), with a day in between to give the delegates from the member under review the chance to get more information from home and prepare responses to questions posed during the first day of the meeting.

TPRB meetings are open to all WTO members and to accredited observers including other intergovernmental organizations, such as the IMF, World Bank, OECD, and United Nations Conference on Trade and Development (UNCTAD). However, like most other WTO meetings, TPRB meetings are not open to the public. This arrangement is curious for a transparency mechanism. A case can be made that the member under review may be more forthcoming in a private dialogue with other WTO members. However, this argument is undermined by the fact that there is a detailed public reporting of the meetings—even with copies of statements—posted on the Internet. Indeed, members have discussed the webcasting of TPRB meetings but have reached no agreement to do so, apparently because of the precedent that this would establish for the conduct of other WTO meetings.

The meeting process is designed to be as fair as possible, giving the member under review and other members the chance to provide/elicit information and express their views. After a brief introduction by the chair, there is a statement by the representative of the member under review—often at the ministerial or deputy ministerial level—followed by comments and questions from a discussant chosen from among Geneva-based delegates, acting in his/her personal capacity. Other members then make statements and raise questions, with priority being given to members that submit advance questions. This process has acquired something of a ritualistic quality, playing out set roles.

The second session starts with the replies by the member under review, followed by further requests for clarification and comments by the discussant and other TPRB members. At the end of the meeting, the chair presents his or her concluding remarks, which are meant to represent his or her assessment of the collective views of the meeting. This is not a negotiated text, but is delivered on the chair's own authority, drafted with the assistance of the Secretariat. There are no formal recommendations on actions to be taken by the member under review. As is sometimes noted, unlike in other international organizations, there are no recommendations and no loans!

Over recent years, it has been observed that there is a trend towards increasing participation by members in the first session, which in a few cases requires extending it to a whole day. In contrast, second sessions have tended to become shorter, seldom lasting more than one and a half hours. This reflects, mostly, the fact that attendance has been falling at second sessions, and is now generally poor, in part due to other meetings taking place at the same time. Moreover, except during the reviews of the largest members, a real interactive exchange of views is seldom in evidence during the second session. To some degree, this reflects a feeling that the documentation is very comprehensive, and observers of the process sometimes have the impression that delegates see the point of the meeting as the opportunity to make known their views in a semi-public way, perhaps to increase pressure to resolve issues that are also being pursued through direct diplomatic representation.

Once the review meeting is over, the member has up to one month to respond in writing to questions left unanswered at the end of the second session, with some latitude for members reviewing a very large number of questions. Staff in member administrations admit that, while they have learned a great deal about their own countries in the process, the preparation involved and participation in a TPR impose a considerable burden on them.

The reports by the Secretariat and the member under review are made public through the Internet at the end of the first session of the review meeting (the two reports are made available to the press beforehand, subject to embargo).

Sometimes the review meeting is followed up with a seminar in the country that has just been reviewed to disseminate the results, adding to the transparency process at home and furthering a policy debate, but this has not been the general practice. See further below.

21.5 Overview and monitoring of trade developments

Apart from the reviews of individual WTO members, the TPRB is also required to conduct an annual overview of developments in the international trading environment which are having an impact on the multilateral trading system (WTO Agreement, paragraph G of Annex 3). These overviews were suspended after 2005 because of duplication with other WTO publications, such as the World Trade Report and the Annual Activities Report. However, as the global financial crisis deepened in 2009, the WTO Secretariat decided to start monitoring on a regular basis the trade and trade-related developments of members and observer governments, and issued a series of reports as a preparatory contribution to the annual overview called for in paragraph G of Annex 3. Members welcomed this exercise, finding that it added transparency to trade policy developments around the world, and was a useful instrument to highlight the need to resist protectionism, particularly during the crisis.[28]

The overview reports usually receive a flurry of comments in the press. These reports also serve a useful purpose internally, in that they may be used to develop a more structured approach by looking at the composite picture emerging from individual reviews and identifying wider themes for consideration by members and committees.[29] In fact, synergies can probably be generated in both directions: individual reviews can contribute to piecing together the global picture of trade-related developments, while the annual overview can help put in context and interpret developments in individual members.

Complementing both the annual overviews and individual trade policy reviews is the reporting provision contained in paragraph D of Annex 3, which requires members to provide regularly information to the TPRB in order to achieve the fullest possible degree of transparency. This provides a potential tool to follow up developments after individual reviews are completed, including any domestic actions undertaken by a member as a result of a trade policy review. However, exploiting the full potential of the three different facets of the TPRM would require a closer integration of the processes involved in carrying out individual trade policy reviews, monitoring policy changes, and preparing the annual overview.

[28] WTO 2009.   [29] WTO 1996.

21.6 DOMESTIC TRANSPARENCY

As noted at the outset, the TPRM was founded to some degree in public choice theory, and Annex 3 of the Marrakesh Agreement recognizes the inherent value of domestic transparency of government decision-making, stating that this is important for both members' economies and the multilateral trading system. Annex 3 thus encourages greater transparency within members' own systems, while acknowledging that this must be on a voluntary basis. Consistent with this, members have supported paying greater attention to transparency in government decision-making on trade policy matters.[30] Accordingly, the Secretariat reports have regularly touched on issues of due process and public governance in domestic administrations as part of their coverage of the institutional framework governing trade policy in members under review.

Domestic transparency also relates to the need to enhance awareness, among governments and other domestic stakeholders, of the costs of protection and the benefits of reducing trade barriers. This is of immediate relevance to meeting the objective in Annex 3 of smoothing the functioning of the multilateral trading system. After all, persuading domestic groups that liberalization is in the national interest is, as a general rule, a prerequisite for liberalization at the multilateral level.

Members have acknowledged that the TPRM has served as an input into policy formulation.[31] However, the capacity of the TPRM to feed into domestic change has enjoyed little visibility, and strengthening this function would smooth the functioning of the multilateral trading system. The seminars that are occasionally organized in capitals to present the results of a review and generate domestic debate can be seen as a concrete step towards achieving this. For example, in 2009, such seminars took place as a follow-up to the trade policy reviews of Dominican Republic and Guyana; no such seminars took place in 2010 or 2011.

Overall, the impact of the TPRM on trade policies of WTO members is not clear and not easily quantified. Officials in some countries have expressed appreciation for the TPR process as helping to boost their arguments within government for more rational policies. But the main idea behind public choice theory is that it is harder for rent-seekers to operate in a more public environment, where their self-seeking actions are more obvious. The same applies to politicians and officials, who may benefit from the favours they are in a position to grant to the private sector.

To some degree, then, the TPRM is preventative medicine with longer-term benefits. But if the process can identify those who benefit from protection and measure the costs to the nation, then it can also help roll back protection and other more discreet forms of assistance to the private sector, including by marshalling those negatively affected to start lobbying for change. Regrettably, many countries, especially in the developing

---

[30] WTO 1999.   [31] WTO 1996, 2005.

world, do not have effective lobbies to promote consumer interests. It is, of course, possible that the TPRM is too far divorced from what happens in individual members, or simply that the reviews often examine a policy regime 'as is', without winners and losers from distortion in the use of scarce resources. Again, the reviews may not go far enough in identifying explicitly the changes that have taken place over time, nor those resulting from an earlier review. To address this point, members have called for the Secretariat reports to highlight policy modifications relative to the previous review.[32] This has been done with some success, but to spot policy modifications in a systematic manner requires familiarity with a trade policy regime at two different periods or constant tracking, for either of which the Secretariat has limited resources.

21.7 EVALUATION OF THE TPRM

Annex 3 required the TPRB to undertake an initial appraisal of the operation of the TPRM not more than five years after the establishment of the WTO, and subsequent appraisals at intervals to be determined by the TPRB or a ministerial conference. Accordingly, the TPRB appraised the operation of the TPRM in 1999, 2005, and 2008.[33] These appraisals have found that the TPRM was operating effectively, noting in 2008 that 'the TPRM had functioned effectively and was achieving satisfactorily its mission'.[34] At this last appraisal, the TPRB resolved that the next one should take place within three years, i.e. in 2011.

The first appraisal of the operation of the TPRM noted that 'There is a clear value for WTO Members in having a forum where they can openly discuss each other's trade and trade-related policies, elicit information, and register concerns. The benefits for the Member under review are also significant: the TPRM can provide a valuable input into national policy-making, serving as an independent, objective assessment of trade and economic policies. Members have also commented on the extent to which the experience of review has helped to strengthen interagency discussion and cooperation in their own countries. The trading system as a whole benefits in that the process can sometimes assist governments in pursuing desirable trade policy reforms; it also frequently illuminates areas of WTO obligations which may have received insufficient attention to date and thus helps to ensure that these are addressed.'[35]

The three appraisals have resulted in a number of procedural changes, subsequently incorporated in revised Rules of Procedure for Meetings of the TPRB.[36] They called for,

---

[32] WTO 1999, 2008a.

[33] The text of the adopted reports may be found in WTO 1999, 2005, and 2008a. After the completion of this chapter, the TPRB finalized the Fourth Appraisal of the TPRM. The respective report may be found in WTO 2011b

[34] WTO 2008a.   [35] WTO 1996.

[36] The current Rules of Procedure are contained in WTO 2008b. Following the adoption of the Fourth Appraisal of the TPRM, the TPRB was revising its Rules of Procedure.

among other things: priority to be given to reviewing all members at least once as soon as possible; improvements in the focus and readability of reports; greater use of grouped reviews; the reports by the Secretariat and the member under review to be distributed, and advance questions to be sent to the member under review, five and two weeks, respectively, before a review meeting; the member under review to provide written answers at the start of the first session; and the Secretariat reports to highlight the changes to policies and measures during the period under review. The appraisals also concluded that steps should be taken to make the review meetings more interactive.

Members have also discussed a number of operational changes that have not been adopted, but remain of interest to several of them. Reflecting this, members have set shorter periods between appraisals to offer new opportunities to discuss further improvements to the TPRM. Among areas for improvement considered at the latest appraisal were: the coverage and critical level of Secretariat reports, the possible opening to the public of review meetings, participation in press conferences, and the number of sessions for a meeting and the time between them.[37]

The presentation of the trade policies of the larger members provides ample opportunity for the examination of their effects on trading partners and the system as a whole. Much of that information is already in the public domain, but the TPR process brings together the information in a systematic manner and the review meeting gives the authorities an opportunity to explain the evolution of, and rationale for, their trade policies. Indications from the authorities in a number of members suggest that the process has also helped them take stock of their policies on the basis of an independent analysis, contributing to the internal debate on policy development. The review process has strengthened the hands of domestic agencies promoting liberalization, supporting trade reforms, and thus helping individual members become better integrated into the multilateral trading system and the global economy. Members engaged in an active process of trade policy reform have also used the opportunity of the review to present their achievements to a world audience. The dual aspects of self-analysis and external audit underpin the effectiveness of the TPRM exercise for all members.[38]

The benefits to developing members from their involvement in the TPRM were examined in some detail in a Note of 12 July 1996, circulated to all WTO members, from the chair of the TPRB to the Chair of the Committee on Trade and Development. The summary conclusion in that Note was: 'Involvement in the TPRM is an important way for developing countries, particularly least-developed countries, to develop confidence and experience with the WTO. This needs to be borne in mind in (a) planning the TPRM timetable and (b) ensuring that technical assistance is available to those LDCs who would otherwise have difficulty in preparing for and undergoing review. With increased participation of developing countries in the TPRM, it will be particularly important to ensure that lessons learned from these reviews are channelled into the WTO machinery.'

---

[37] WTO 2008a.
[38] WTO 1996.

The report to the Singapore Ministerial Meeting also noted that the TPRM occupied a unique place within the WTO in promoting non-confrontational discussion of key trade policy issues. 'Its specific de-linkage from dispute settlement procedures is an essential feature which must be safeguarded.'[39] However, it also noted that further opportunities might be sought for encouraging greater cross-fertilization between TPRB discussions and those undertaken in other WTO bodies.

Another benefit of the TPRM is that it has led the way in increasing the transparency in the trade policies and practices of WTO members, and in some degree paved the way for much greater transparency in the WTO as a whole. In doing so, albeit outside the framework of specific legal commitments, the process has often highlighted weaknesses in the fulfilment of WTO obligations, including notifications, and thus helped to ensure that these are addressed. The mechanism's spotlight has effectively focused on all the main players in the WTO trading system, and has illuminated the most significant trends in trade policy.

One aspect of the reviews has been a learning process about trade reforms and the linkages between trade and other policies. Thus, the lessons of trade reforms are being passed on to other members within the WTO system. Dealing with lessons from the TPRM, one particularly important feature has been the linkage between macroeconomic policies and performance and trade policies and performance. Largely under IMF or World Bank programmes, many developing country members have started to put the emphasis on macroeconomic policy to redress savings–investment imbalances as the source of current account deficits; as a result, there is much less frequent use of import restrictions to attempt to resolve balance of payments difficulties.

In an echo of one of the criticisms by Keesing,[40] noted above, a related comment has been that the process can focus too much on detail, at the cost of giving insufficient attention to policy direction. However, the TPRM is not just intended to give an idea of the broad sweep of policies but also to cover the practices of members—that is, the implementation of policy. Often, the broad policy thrust is unexceptionable, but this can be undermined at the level of implementation by lower-level officials. This is why shortening reports would not necessarily save time or resources: it is still necessary to explore the detailed implementation of policy to allow an assessment to be phrased accurately, albeit in fewer words—as George Bernard Shaw famously apologized for a lengthy letter to a friend, he did not have time to be shorter!

One benefit from the TPR process has been the development of an extensive source of material on trade policies and a source of learning experiences with trade policy at all levels of development. The TPRB has not made systematic use of this material in recent years to draw lessons, although Valdés used the Secretariat reports prepared for the TPRs conducted in the Western Hemisphere during 1989–2009 to analyse the evolution of trade policies in the Americas over the first two decades of operation of the TPRM.[41]

---

[39] Ibid.   [40] Keesing 1998.   [41] Valdés 2010.

A broader overview of the lessons from the first eight years of operation of the TPRM, provided in Chapter III of the WTO *Annual Report 1997*, highlights the importance of outward orientation for growth and for overcoming the anti-export bias of protectionist policies, including industrial targeting.[42] The report also stressed the importance for durable trade reforms of a transparent and stable long-term policy framework, avoiding slippages through exemptions for particular sectors of the economy with political leverage or through the abuse of contingency measures such as anti-dumping.

Individual TPRs also highlighted problems facing the private sector, such as cumbersome bureaucracy and paperwork, high taxes, and high rates of interest because of dysfunctional capital markets. Some of these issues have been the reason for the emphasis now being given to issues of governance in some national programmes. The TPRs also drew attention to large-scale privatizations—sometimes under financial pressures, but also to improve competitiveness—as well as poor frameworks for domestic competition, which is also needed to build international competitiveness. And the TPRs were quick to identify the growing trend towards regionalism that saw the quadrupling of growth in the number of regional trade agreements in the period since the TPRM was instituted.

However, there have been no such overarching comments on the linkage between trade policy and development in recent years. It can certainly be argued that there is not much left to say now that major trade reforms have largely completed globally, whether under World Bank/IMF lending programmes or as a result of unilateral reforms under a different model in China and India. It is also the case that the implementation of the results of the Uruguay Round saw the progressive elimination of major trade distortions, such as the textile and clothing restraints, Trade-Related Investment Measures (TRIMs), variable levies, voluntary export restraints, and so on, while paving the way for further liberalization in agriculture and services, and stricter protection of intellectual property. There is a case that today the main issues, at least in trade in goods, are potentially WTO-consistent measures such as anti-dumping and sanitary/phytosanitary measures.

On the other hand, in other international institutions today there is now much greater caution about trade reforms after some negative experiences, especially in Africa. The World Bank, in a major review of 20 years of trade policy lending, admits to a number of mistakes,[43] and the Commission on Growth, urging the need for caution on reforms, cites Deng Xiaoping's oft-quoted dictum to 'cross the river by feeling for the stones'.[44] However, there is little in the TPRs or elsewhere in the WTO that highlights these policy failures. The major work in the WTO that recognizes the problem of structural adjustment and problems of implementation of the WTO agreements is in its efforts for Aid for Trade—hence the more detailed coverage of this theme in recent TPRs.

---

[42] WTO 1997.   [43] World Bank 2006.
[44] Commission on Growth and Development 2008.

21.8 Challenges for the TPRM

On the whole, WTO members and the Secretariat can take a good deal of satisfaction from the operation of the TPRM since its establishment just over two decades ago. The operation of this looking glass on trade policies has been very effective and useful for the trading community, generally drawing favourable comments from within the academic community and from other organizations. Its value as a public good and in fostering good practices is not easy to estimate, but should not be underestimated.

The WTO has also made serious efforts over the years to improve the functioning of the processes, as documented in this chapter, but the lack of interaction in review meetings of members other than the major players has arguably become the least satisfactory aspect of the TPRM operation.

The Secretariat reports are, of course, also central to the quality of the debates in the TPRB. As noted, the most frequent criticisms of the reports have been that they are insufficiently analytical, that they need to sharpen their focus, and that they should be tougher in identifying the cost of protection, who pays and who gains, if they are to meet their public choice objectives. Efforts have been made to address these criticisms throughout the years; however, conducting extensive background and econometric studies such as those sometimes done at the World Bank would require a major increase in resources. Moreover, it is far from certain that this would be appreciated by the large majority of WTO members, who may well see this as requiring a reinterpretation or revision of the purpose of the TPRM as stipulated in Annex 3 of the Marrakesh Agreement. Also, given the juridical and negotiating environment of the WTO, it is to be expected that the language of Secretariat reports will continue to reflect a degree of caution that will not satisfy academic and business readers.

In addition, if the TPRM is to use the public choice concept to foster the adoption of good policy practices and root out the rent-seekers, this needs to be nurtured through a greater effort at dissemination and dialogue in the members that have been reviewed. At the very least, this requires as much effort on communication as other well-publicized activities of the WTO. Seminars and workshops in the members' capitals are one way to do this, but a greater effort is needed.

Another concern is whether the WTO Secretariat has enough resources to meet existing programme requirements for an expansion of the number of reviews so that all members are covered as scheduled in the agreed cycle of reviews. This preoccupation has intensified with the increased need for resources to review complex trade-related regulations in services as well as new wave non-tariff measures, not to mention the growing number of WTO members. A partial solution has been the occasional use of consultants to help in the preparation of the reports by the Secretariat, but this shifts the nature of the resources rather than changing the requirement. Recent efforts to try to increase the number of regular staff involved in the TPR process are thus steps in the right direction.

Another challenge arises from the need to reduce the burden on delegations imposed by the increased number of meetings (not only in the TPRB but also other WTO bodies). An option for this might be to have fewer review meetings, covering a number of members in each session, similar to board meetings of the IMF and the World Bank. With this aim, the TPRB introduced the concept of group reviews, i.e. reviews covering more than one member during a single meeting.[45] Experience shows that, provided the focus remains firmly on national trade policies, group reviews can help achieve a more efficient use of resources, and enhance the visibility of the reviews of smaller members. It would thus appear that a much greater use of group reviews should be made to avoid the proliferation of review meetings observed in recent years.

Finally, there is a challenge for the TPRM to fulfil a technical assistance role, particularly for smaller, developing members. With this in mind, the Secretariat reports for LDC reviews have typically included a section on technical assistance needs and priorities, as identified in cooperation with the member concerned, with a view to feeding this into the Enhanced Integrated Framework process. More recently, changes are being introduced to the Secretariat reports in order to place Aid for Trade needs within the context of a country's trade policy framework.

References

Banks, G. 1992. The Industry Commission: Australia's Domestic Transparency Institution. Introductory Remarks to a special session of the UNCTAD Trade and Development Board on Domestic transparency procedures, October, Geneva.

Blackhurst, R. 1988. Strengthening GATT Surveillance of Trade-Related Policies. In *The New GATT Round of Multilateral Trade Negotiations: Legal and Economic Aspects*, edited by Meinharf Hilf and Ernst-Ulrich Petersman. Deventer, The Netherlands: Kluwer Law and Taxation Publishers.

Commission on Growth and Development. 2008. *The Growth Report: Strategies for Sustained Growth and Inclusive Development*. Washington, DC: World Bank.

Curzon Price, V. 1991. GATT's New Trade Policy Review Mechanism. *The World Economy* 14 (2):227–38.

GATT. 1982. Ministerial Declaration of 29 November 1982. BISD 29S/11. Geneva: GATT.

GATT. 1987. *Existing Surveillance Functions in the GATT*. Note by the Secretariat. MTN.GNG/ NG14/W/3. Geneva: GATT.

GATT. 1988. Trade Policy Review Mechanism. Compendium of comments made in discussion of Chair's discussion paper (second revision) in formal and informal discussions in March 1988 (27 April).

Gosh, Arunabha. 2008. Information Gaps, Information Systems, and the WTO's Trade Policy Review Mechanism. GEG Working Paper 2008/40. Oxford: Global Economic Governance Programme.

[45] WTO 1995, 1999.

Keesing, D. B. 1998. Improving Trade Policy Reviews in the World Trade Organization. Policy Analyses in International Economics 52. Washington DC: Institute for International Economics.

Laird, S., and P. Messerlin. 1990. Institutional Reform for Trade Liberalization. *The World Economy* 13 (2):230–49.

Leutwiler, F., B. Bradley, P. G. Gyllenhammar, G. Ladreit de Lacharrière, I. G. Patel, M. H. Simonsen, and S. Djojohadikusumo. 1985. *Trade Policies for a Better Future: Proposals for Action*. Geneva: GATT.

Mavroidis, P. 1992. Surveillance Schemes: The GATT's New Trade Policy Review Mechanism. *Michigan Journal of International Law* 13 (2):374–414.

Olson, M. Jr. 1965. *The Logic of Collective Action*. Cambridge, MA: Harvard University Press.

Qureshi, A. H. 1990. The New GATT Trade Policy Review Mechanism: An Exercise in Transparency or 'Enforcement'? *Journal of World Trade* 24 (3):142–60.

Qureshi, A. H. 1992. Some Reflections on the GATT TPRM, in the Light of the Trade Policy Review of the European Communities—A Legal Perspective. *Journal of World Trade* 26 (6):103–20.

Qureshi, A. H. 1995. Some Lessons from Developing Countries' Trade Policy Reviews in the GATT Framework: An Enforcement Perspective. *The World Economy* 18 (3):489–503.

Spriggs, J. 1991. Towards an International Transparency Institution: Australian Style. *The World Economy* 14 (2):165–80.

Tullock, G. 1987. Public Choice. *The New Palgrave: A Dictionary of Economics*, volume 3: 1040–4. Palgrave Macmillan.

Valdés, Raymundo. 2010. Lessons from the First Two Decades of Trade Policy Reviews in the Americas. WTO Staff Working Paper ERSD-2010–15. Geneva: WTO.

World Bank. 2006. *Assessing World Bank Support for Trade 1987–2004—An IEG Evaluation*. Washington, DC: World Bank.

WTO. 1995. *Procedural Improvement to the Trade Policy Review Mechanism*. Note by the Chair. WT/TPR/13. Geneva: WTO.

WTO. 1996. *Trade Policy Review Mechanism—Report to the Singapore Ministerial Conference*. WT/TPR/27. Geneva: WTO.

WTO. 1997. *Annual Report 1997*. Geneva: WTO.

WTO. 1999. *Appraisal of the Operation of the Trade Policy Review Mechanism*. Report to Ministers. WT/MIN(99)/2. Geneva: WTO.

WTO. 2002. *Transparency*. Note by the Secretariat. WT/WGTI/W/109. Geneva: WTO.

WTO. 2005. *Second Appraisal of the Operation of the Trade Policy Review Mechanism*. Report to Ministers. WT/MIN(05)/1. Geneva: WTO.

WTO. 2008a. *Third Appraisal of the Operation of the Trade Policy Review Mechanism*. WT/TPR/229. Geneva: WTO.

WTO. 2008b. *Rules of Procedure for Meeting of the Trade Policy Review Body*. WT/TPR/6/Rev.2. Geneva: WTO.

WTO. 2009. *Report of the Trade Policy Review Body for 2009*. WT/TPR/249. Geneva: WTO.

WTO. 2011a. *Report of the Trade Policy Review Body for 2011*. WT/TPR/284. Geneva: WTO.

WTO. 2011b. Fourth Appraisal of the Trade Policy Review Mechanism. WT/MIN(11)/6.

WTO Panel Report. 1999. *Canada—Measures Affecting the Export of Civilian Aircraft*. WT/DS70/R. Geneva: WTO.

CHAPTER 22

....

DISPUTE SETTLEMENT MECHANISM—ANALYSIS AND PROBLEMS

....

THOMAS BERNAUER, MANFRED ELSIG, AND
JOOST PAUWELYN[*]

22.1 INTRODUCTION

....

WHEN the WTO came into being in 1995, its dispute settlement mechanism (DSM) was widely heralded as the 'jewel in the crown'. Sixteen years later, the DSM has moved further towards centre stage. Public attention has increasingly turned to the ways in which the WTO has dealt with trade disputes. Similarly, the academic study of the litigation mechanisms of the WTO has grown substantially.

Three main factors have contributed to the prominence of the DSM. First, the designers of the WTO have created one of the most legalized interstate dispute settlement systems worldwide, thus changing incentives structures of governments and increasing the number of cases being brought before the DSM.[1] The prospect of winning cases where the losing party cannot block the process and prevent a formal verdict (as was the case under the General Agreement on Tariffs and Trade (GATT)) has appealed to many WTO members. Second, since progress in the Doha Round has been very slow, some WTO members have tried to affect these negotiations by resorting to litigation. Third, the potential increase in judicial law-making and the difficulties of overturning DSM rulings through formal WTO treaty amendments or interpretations have given rise to perceptions of imbalance

    [*] We wish to thank Todd Allee, Chad Bown, Susan Kaplan, Gregory Shaffer, and the editors for their valuable comments. We acknowledge support from the NCCR Trade Regulation of the Swiss National Science Foundation.
    [1] Weiler 2001.

between litigation and negotiation. Critics claim that the 'Geneva judges' tend to overstep their mandates by engaging in law-making through the back door, providing faulty interpretations of WTO commitments, and embarking on 'gap filling'.

While the Uruguay Round negotiations sought to solve some of the problems with dispute resolution in the GATT system, there was continued emphasis on non-judicial mechanisms for avoiding trade conflicts. The WTO Dispute Settlement Understanding (DSU) stipulates that 'recommendations and rulings...shall be aimed at achieving a satisfactory settlement' (Article 3.4 DSU), and that 'the aim of the dispute settlement mechanism is to secure a positive solution to the dispute' (Article 3.7 DSU). Special emphasis was put on the desirability of trying to settle the issue bilaterally before using the litigation machinery.[2] Consequently, consultations remain the cornerstone of dispute settlement. The designers of the DSU also provided multiple tools, ranging from consultation procedures and mediation to arbitration and third party adjudication. The various options described in the DSU can be regarded as separate venues or mechanisms, but may also be seen as sequential steps. The empirical record shows that some dispute settlement tools have rarely been used (e.g. good offices, conciliation, mediation (Article 5), special procedures for least-developed countries (Article 24), or arbitration as defined in Article 25), whereas other dispute settlement tools dominate within the DSM (consultation at one end and third party adjudication at the other). Given the lack of data on consultations prior to the launching of a case, research has focused predominantly on the cases that have been brought, and has analysed the evolving case law.

This chapter provides an overview of issues and progress in research on WTO dispute settlement. For reasons of space, the focus is primarily on research by political scientists and legal scholars. We pay only passing attention to the burgeoning normative literature on the legal accuracy of WTO rulings and the legitimacy and accountability of WTO dispute settlement. The following section (Section 22.2) describes how the DSM works, notes the key differences from the older GATT dispute mechanism, and discusses some trends in WTO dispute settlement. Section 22.3 offers various conceptualizations as to the functioning of the DSM. In Section 22.4 we look at some key findings from recent research, and in Section 22.5 we identify some remaining research gaps. The final section links research on the DSM with ongoing debates on reforming WTO dispute settlement.

22.2 THE WTO'S DISPUTE SETTLEMENT SYSTEM

22.2.1 How it works and how it differs from the GATT system

Notwithstanding its rudimentary legal basis (two Articles in the GATT) and the right of defendants to block the process, GATT dispute settlement (1948–95) has been described

---

[2] Article 3.7 DSU stipulates: 'Before bringing a case, a Member shall exercise its judgment as to whether action under these procedures would be fruitful', and 'A solution mutually acceptable to the parties...is clearly to be preferred.'

as surprisingly successful.[3] Two key problems were, however, recurrent. First, recalcitrant defendants (especially the European Community and Japan) would block the establishment or adoption of panels. Second, determined complainants (especially the United States), frustrated with lack of progress in obtaining desired outcomes through the GATT, would unilaterally decide that another party had breached its obligations and impose trade sanctions without the GATT's approval. It was this dual problem that gave rise to the DSU revolution:[4] in exchange for dropping the veto (a US request), WTO members committed to stopping unilateral enforcement and to bringing all WTO claims exclusively to the WTO DSM (a demand by the EC and developing countries). As an insurance policy against 'runaway panels' within such a veto-free system, panel reports could now also be appealed. In addition, to limit the consequences of a more legalized DSM and further rein in unilateral retaliation, the remedy for WTO violation was restricted to prospective, state-to-state retaliation, capped and multilaterally controlled through arbitration.[5] Hence the three key novelties of the new system: the right to a panel (no more vetoes), strengthened multilateralism (no more unilateral sanctions), and the establishment of an Appellate Body (to soften the blow of automatic panel adoption).

The WTO DSM foresees up to four steps. First, consultations to attempt to settle the dispute amicably. Second, third-party adjudication by a three-member, ad hoc appointed panel, that decides whether a WTO member's conduct violates the WTO treaty. For each case, the WTO Secretariat proposes possible panellists who the disputing parties may reject. If there is no agreement on the composition of the panel after 20 days, however, either party may request that the Director-General of the WTO appoints the panellists (which, so far, has occurred in 60 per cent of cases). Third, the possibility of an appeal (at the request of either party) to be submitted to a newly established Appellate Body. The Appellate Body is composed of seven members, each of whom is appointed for a term of four years (renewable once) but whose examination is limited to legal questions. Fourth, implementation of adverse rulings, monitored by the Dispute Settlement Body (on which all WTO members have a seat), with the possibility of reverting to a compliance panel and, as a last resort, bilateral retaliation by the winning party against the member delaying implementation. A separate arbitration process ensures that this retaliation is equivalent or proportional to the original violation (no punitive sanctions). Crucially, moving from one step to the next in this new system requires a decision by the DSB (except for appeals), but such a decision is taken by reverse consensus: only if all WTO members vote against moving forward can the process be blocked. In other words, the new system is automatic as soon as one party wants to move forward.

[3] Hudec 1990.   [4] Pauwelyn 2005.
[5] See also Van den Bossche 2005.

22.2.2 Some trends

Between 1995 and 22 September 2010 (i.e. within 15 years), 414 requests for consultations were filed.[6] After ten years of operation, more requests had already been filed with the WTO than with the GATT (around 300). Of these 414 requests for consultations filed with the WTO, (so far) only 125 led to a panel examination and adopted panel reports. Of these 125 panel reports, 78 have been appealed, and in 85 per cent of appeals, panel reports were reversed or modified. This, in turn, demonstrates a high level of appeals and a high success rate of appeals. Finally, only 19 arbitrations on retaliation have been entered into (and 17 retaliations have actually been authorized). Most recently, Brazil was authorized to restrict US imports and protection of US intellectual property rights following non-compliance by the US in the US–Cotton dispute. This means that retaliation is a formal tool for enforcing DSM rulings that WTO members rarely resort to. The overwhelming majority of dispute rulings have been implemented without resorting to retaliation.[7]

Although, on average, 28 requests for consultations have been filed per year, the overall trend in the number of cases per year has been downward (with a peak of 50 requests in 1997 and a low of 11 requests in 2005). There are some indications that, with the end of the financial crisis and the renewed pressure for protectionism brought on by the crisis, the number of requests may be rising (14 in 2009; 12 in the first nine months of 2010 alone). Panel proceedings take on average 12 months. The Appellate Body must conclude its proceedings in 90 days (although on occasion it has taken longer).

Most requests continue to raise claims of violation of the original GATT (316) or focus on anti-dumping (85) or subsidy (80) matters. Only 29 requests have been filed under the new Agreement on Trade-Related Aspects of Intellectual Property Rights (TRIPS), and 20 requests under the equally new General Agreement on Trade in Services (GATS). Although most complaints have been filed by developed countries, participation by developing countries is important and increasing. Between 1995 and 2009, developing countries were complainants in more than 45 per cent of cases and defendants in more than 43 per cent. That said, few cases have been filed by or against low-income countries (respectively, 27 and 24 of the 414). The most active participants have been the US (22 per cent of requests filed; 27 per cent of requests filed against) and the EU (19 per cent of requests filed; 21 per cent of requests filed against). Although China joined the WTO only in 2001, it already ranks fourth in numbers of cases defended (20; the same amount has been filed against India, a WTO member since 1995).

When it comes to who was selected to serve on WTO panels, of the 459 panel positions only 66 were held by women. Given the rule that nationals of either parties or third parties cannot serve on a panel (unless the parties so agree), only 12 panel positions have

---

[6] Data obtained from the WTO website and <http://www.worldtradelaw.net>. Accessed on 30 September 2010.

[7] Bown and Pauwelyn 2010.

been taken by US nationals, but 41 by New Zealand nationals, 38 by Swiss nationals, and another 38 by Australian nationals. In almost 90 per cent of adopted dispute reports, at least one violation of legal obligations under the WTO was found.

22.3 CONCEPTUAL AND THEORETICAL ISSUES

22.3.1 Why dispute settlement?

Why are dispute settlement provisions in international trade agreements needed? International relations (IR) scholars started to look at this question in the 1980s. Keohane, for example, suggested that mistrust and lack of transparency are major obstacles to international cooperation.[8] At the heart of the analysis in liberal institutional IR theory has been the game-theoretic model of the prisoner's dilemma, which serves as a starting point for illustrating the difficulties of cooperation. An important way to address incentives for free-riding or reneging on commitments, then, is to provide states with a functioning system of settling disputes that enhances trust and information (e.g. an enforcement mechanism).[9] Even if, as in the WTO case, dispute settlement is not associated with centralized enforcement, it establishes a system of reciprocity and creates a normative reference system that imposes significant constraints on the unilateral exercise of power ('right over might'). From a liberal institutionalist viewpoint, the WTO thus facilitates global trade liberalization by deterring non-compliance with WTO rules, imposing multilateral legal pressure on states reneging on their commitments, and by disciplining enforcement if non-compliance is established through the multilateral judicial process (e.g. by limiting retaliation to a level proportional to a formally established violation of legal rules).

Realist theories of IR, for their part, tend to downplay the importance of dispute settlement in multilateral treaties as long as obligations for states remain weak.[10] Within the realist tradition, there is also a widely held view that only hegemonic power politics can impose some discipline on the international community. By implication, realists assume that compliance with international commitments is strong only when such commitments are weak and basically reflect what states would do anyway, or when a hegemonic power acts as an enforcer (e.g. as the US presumably did in the GATT system). From this perspective, key features of international institutions, such as dispute settlement, are simply

---

[8] Keohane 1984.

[9] The economic trade theory literature focuses largely on decentralized sanctioning to overcome the problem of the prisoner's dilemma. Institutions in economic models are usually agreements. Different strands of economic theories (e.g. the terms-of-trade school or the political externalities school) have so far not addressed variation in forms of dispute settlement and in particular the existence of strong third party delegation for enforcement (Keck and Schropp 2007).

[10] Downs, Rocke, and Barsoom 1996.

part of the general international landscape in which power politics plays out, but do not have important effects of their own. Hence they are considered epiphenomenal.

The WTO dispute settlement system creates a challenge for both realists and liberal institutionalists. From a realist perspective, the move towards a highly legalized system (e.g. automatic adoption, the creation of an appeal institution) and substantial concessions accepted by powerful nations calls for an explanation. From a liberal institutionalist perspective, the creation of a strong DSM remains a puzzle given the positions of GATT contracting parties at the onset of the Uruguay Round.[11]

22.3.2 Conceptualizing the DSU

Beyond general debates in IR research, many approaches embedded in the broader literature on law and economics, as well as on delegation, have inspired and advanced the study of WTO dispute settlement.

The law and economics view of dispute settlement adds several new elements to the liberal institutionalist perspective in IR theory, the most important being the notion of incomplete contracts.[12] When comparing WTO agreements, however, there are important differences in terms of their 'incompleteness'. In some issue areas, negotiators have clearly defined what contractors are allowed to do (in particular when expected or unexpected 'events' occur). In other areas, obvious gaps in the original contracts exist. Recourse to dispute settlement instruments is likely when one contracting party questions the fulfilment of contractual obligations by another (breach of contract). This leads to a delegation of interpretative power to adjudicating bodies to assess whether an alleged *ex post* non-performance (e.g. a national policy measure) is a legal breach or violation of the contract.[13] What drives overall demand for dispute settlement is not so much the need to enforce unambiguous obligations under a certain WTO agreement (sanctioning of known defectors), but the existence of contractual silence on issues (clear gaps) or ambiguous wording that creates different expectations as to the interpretation of the contract (strategic ambiguity).[14] Seen in this light, the dispute settlement system addresses the conflict and might (depending on the standpoint) fill contractual gaps. From the perspective of the adjudicator, the

---

[11] The main arguments put forward to explain the overall deal are US-centric: first, a transatlantic plot inducing others to follow (Steinberg 2002), second, a successful lock-in strategy applied by the US Trade Representative (USTR) in order to bind the hands of US Congress (Brewster 2006; Thompson 2007). Yet, negotiation dynamics over time involving a number of actors with salient positions on dispute settlement (e.g. India, Japan, and Canada) have been largely overlooked so far.

[12] See Horn, Maggi, and Staiger 2006; the IR literature has focused more on how to explain opt-outs and assumes that incomplete contracts are endogenous decisions in the first place (Rosendorff and Milner 2001).

[13] Schropp 2010.

[14] Maggi and Staiger 2008.

question arises as to what type of interpretation should assist in addressing incomplete contracts.[15]

In IR research, a fruitful debate among scholars relying on delegation theories has emerged. These types of middle range theories (e.g. principal–agent theory) assist in conceptualizing the functions and the politics of dispute settlement. Within delegation theories, views differ as to the most accurate conceptualization of the two main bodies of WTO dispute settlement (panels and the Appellate Body). It is largely undisputed from a functional perspective, following liberal institutionalism, that the main function of the DSM is to make commitments more credible. Yet, alleged variation in delegation (e.g. mandate, discretion) from WTO members (principals) to panels and the Appellate Body (agents) leads to different expectations as to the functioning of the DSM. While there is general agreement that panel members are less autonomous and work as arbitration agents, the members of the Appellate Body have more discretion, individually and as a group. How much autonomy the Appellate Body possesses and how it reads principals' signals, however, is the subject of continued debate among scholars, and calls for further empirical analysis. For some scholars, the Appellate Body is a trustee beyond the control of WTO members.[16] This view is based on the argument that recontracting or sanctioning is not possible given high thresholds.[17] For other scholars, the Appellate Body is a group of agents with substantial autonomy, whereas principals influence agents through *ex ante* control tools, such as nomination and selection.[18] In sum, delegation theories assist in better grasping the conditions under which principals successfully use control tools to affect the behaviour of those mandated to adjudicate disputes.

Finally, legal scholars have analysed the DSM not only as a commitment and enforcement device that makes defection more costly, but also as a stabilizing factor that promotes peaceful relations between countries by identifying breaches in an impartial manner and putting a cap on retaliation,[19] by offering legal clarification and predictability to private traders,[20] and by fulfilling a domestic constitutional function of protection against government abuse.[21] Legal scholars have generally applauded the move from a power-based or diplomatic approach to a rules-based judicial approach. However, some of them have highlighted that legalization is not a unidirectional process away from politics, but rather requires a careful balance between more law (reduced exit options) and more politics (increased voice).[22]

---

[15] See also Chapter 24 of this volume.

[16] Alter 2008; Grant and Keohane 2005.

[17] In order not to accept a panel or Appellate Body ruling, WTO members would have to reject it by consensus, or indirectly they could attempt to engage in an 'authoritative interpretation', for which a three-quarters majority is necessary.

[18] Elsig and Pollack 2010.

[19] Schwartz and Sykes 2002.

[20] Jackson 1997.

[21] Petersmann 1986.

[22] Pauwelyn 2005.

22.4 PROGRESS IN RESEARCH

Beyond broader conceptual issues that have guided studies on the DSU, a number of specific research activities have emerged over time. In this section we discuss what we regard as the most important areas of research on WTO dispute settlement from a political science and international law perspective.

22.4.1 Does increased legalization matter?

An important question in research on WTO dispute settlement has been whether legalization or judicialization matters.[23] Research on this issue has been embedded in a wider quest for an understanding of how international law works. To the extent that legalization can be regarded as an independent factor, research has focused on various effects thereof, and has illuminated several causal mechanisms. Goldstein and Martin have theorized about the effect of increased legalization on the incentives of domestic groups to mobilize.[24] In their view, greater legalization goes along with more transparency, which changes the balance of the domestic political economy in favour of import-competing groups. This change leads to less willingness to liberalize further.[25] Along similar lines, Pauwelyn has argued that a stronger DSM (reduced options to exit from treaty commitments) requires a corresponding need for more political participation and contestation (more voice and insistence on consensus in overall WTO affairs), making further trade liberalization more difficult (e.g. because of the consensus requirement) and increased transparency and input into the DSM inevitable (to allow for this increased demand in participation and contestation).[26] While often referred to as an argument as to why the Doha Round is deadlocked,[27] the evidence that 'legalization has gone too far' is still limited.[28] Instead, a number of scholars have conjectured about indirect causal effects of existing rules enforced through a strong dispute settlement system. For instance, Allee argues that the existing DSM (the shadow of harder law) can serve as a buffer against protectionist policies.[29] Focusing on US trade remedy measures demanded by import-competing industries, he finds that the existence of the WTO DSM deters US authorities from accepting demands for protectionist measures where the merits of a legal case under the WTO are weak. Zangl focuses on implementation of actual rulings.[30] He provides evidence, relying on pairwise GATT and WTO cases across time, that while it is still far from being a system of rule of law, legalization has contributed to a better implementation record.[31]

---

[23] Stone Sweet 1999; Goldstein and Martin 2000; Zangl 2008.   [24] Goldstein and Martin 2000.
[25] For a similar argument, see Stasavage 2004.   [26] Pauwelyn 2005.
[27] See Chapter 26 of this volume.   [28] Rosendorff 2005; Poletti 2011.
[29] Allee 2005.   [30] Zangl 2008.
[31] Zangl relies on a least-likely case design. He focuses on the US (and EU). Put differently, if judicialization matters in these cases, it is assumed to affect outcomes for less powerful states.

22.4.2 Dispute initiation

Most quantitative (i.e. large-N statistical) research has focused on explaining the initiation of dispute proceedings.[32] Three types of determinants of dispute initiation have received particular attention: economic factors, legal capacity, and power.[33] Several studies have found substantial evidence that countries of greater economic size, with significant trade flows, are more likely to become involved in trade disputes, both as complainants and defendants.[34] In addition, for smaller states, the removal of trade barriers via WTO adjudication needs to lead to sufficient economic benefits; otherwise launching a case is too costly.[35] This pre-litigation assessment hinges on an estimation of the chances of winning the case and the likelihood of concessions by the defendant.[36]

Other research has emphasized the role of legal capacity in the decision to launch a case. The underlying argument assumes an entry barrier due to high litigation costs as disputing countries need to rely on specialized law firms (assisting litigants throughout the entire process). However, legal capacity is also required before and after litigation.[37] Kim, for example, argues that legal capacity is likely to play an even bigger role in the WTO DSM than in the corresponding GATT system.[38] The more legalized WTO DSM, he argues, has created the unanticipated effect that litigation costs are a substantial barrier, privileging developed countries over others. Studies examining the implications of variation in legal capacity have worked with a variety of proxies for this concept. Most researchers have used indirect measures, such as income (gross domestic product (GDP) per capita) or domestic bureaucratic quality.[39] As a reaction to criticism about the validity of these proxies, a number of contributions have relied on more direct measures, such as the size of countries' WTO delegations in Geneva or actual resources of national missions to the WTO.[40] The results of this research, thus far, do not offer any robust evidence for a legal capacity bias in WTO dispute initiation.[41]

---

[32] The large-N literature has struggled for some time with the 'iceberg' issue. The difficulties in clearly defining the potential universe of cases (as actual cases are only the visible tip of the iceberg) has led to concerns of selection bias. More recent studies have attempted to remedy this by focusing on pre-litigation conflict data (Young 2005 on sanitary and phytosanitary measures; Allee 2008 on trade remedies), or estimating the likelihood of cases that potentially qualify for litigation (Horn, Mavroidis, and Nordström 1999; Sattler and Bernauer 2011).

[33] Other arguments exist in the literature, e.g. that cases are launched in reaction to cases suffered, or that parties learn from experience and therefore the likelihood of launching a case is affected by past involvement (Davis and Blodgett Bermeo 2009). There has so far been less evidence to support these claims.

[34] Horn, Mavroidis, and Nordström 1999; Sattler and Bernauer 2011.

[35] Guzman and Simmons 2005.

[36] The second point is linked to the possibility of using retaliatory measures in cases of non-compliance (Bown 2004a; Bown and Pauwelyn 2010).

[37] Bown 2009.

[38] Kim 2008.

[39] Guzman and Simmons 2005.

[40] Horn, Mavroidis, and Nordström 1999; Busch, Reinhardt, and Shaffer 2009; Sattler and Bernauer 2011.

[41] Sattler and Bernauer 2011.

Yet other research has investigated the effects of power and power differentials. In these contributions, the underlying argument for non-entry into litigation has been that small states 'abstain from launching disputes due to fear that they either will not be able to enforce rulings in their favor, or will be subjected to some form of revenge from more powerful states'.[42] Most studies find that power, measured in terms of economic size of countries, existing trade relations, or dependence on bilateral aid flows, significantly impacts on the decision to initiate a WTO dispute.[43] Sattler and Bernauer, for instance, show that there is a substantial power preponderance effect: pairs of countries that differ more in terms of power are less likely to litigate in the WTO.[44] Whether this means that the big powers are able to coerce smaller powers into concessions outside the WTO and small powers do not dare to formally challenge the big powers in the WTO remains to be examined more systematically. Elsig and Stucki use a qualitative case study approach to illuminate how power works in highly asymmetrical cases.[45] Their contribution calls for the development of a typological theory, as the nature of obstacles to litigation entry vary widely across types of countries (e.g. least-developed countries, emerging economies, small industrialized countries, and countries that offer substantial market access).

22.4.3 Dispute escalation

Most quantitative work on WTO dispute settlement conceptualizes the dependent variable in binary terms, measuring whether a pair of countries (dyad) experiences a WTO trade dispute in a given year, or in terms of how many such disputes are observed in a given year or since the WTO DSM was set up. Similarly, research on dispute escalation has also defined the phenomenon to be examined in binary terms (whether a dispute is settled at the consultation stage or escalates to the panel stage), or in terms of three stages (consultation, panel/Appellate Body, compliance dispute).

On the explanatory side, existing studies have focused primarily on the implications of the characteristics of trade issues. Guzman and Simmons code whether the nature of the dispute is 'continuous' or 'lumpy' (their coding of dispute escalation is also binary).[46] They argue that disputes of the second, all-or-nothing type are more likely to escalate to the panel stage (escalation is coded as a two-step process) because it is more difficult to arrange gradual concessions and side-payments in such cases. This argument implies that, for example, disputes about tariff levels are easier to settle than disputes about health and safety regulations. The authors find some empirical support for this argument among democratic countries.

[42] Francois, Horn, and Kaunitz 2008, 4.
[43] Bown 2005a; Zejan and Bartels 2006.
[44] Sattler and Bernauer 2011.
[45] Elsig and Stucki 2012.
[46] Guzman and Simmons 2002.

Bernauer and Sattler, defining WTO disputes as a three-step process, examine whether WTO trade disputes over environment, health and safety (EHS) issues are more likely to escalate than other types of disputes.[47] They argue that such disputes should be more likely to escalate because gradual concessions by the defendant to the complainant are more difficult in such cases, and because side-payments to domestic interest groups in the defendant country, which are often used by defendant countries to buy political support for concessions, are more difficult to arrange. They test this argument on 506 WTO conflict dyads in 1995–2003. In contrast to conventional wisdom, they find that EHS disputes are not more likely to escalate from the consultation to the panel stage. However, once they have escalated to that stage, they are more likely than other types of disputes to escalate into compliance disputes.

In a recent paper, Sattler, Spilker, and Bernauer develop a more generic typology of dispute types and derive the implications of dispute types for dispute escalation.[48] This typology connects to the general perspectives on WTO dispute settlement discussed above. One perspective views the WTO's DSM as an enforcement device (see realist and liberal institutionalist perspectives above), the other argues that the DSM is primarily a complexity-reducing and rule-clarification device (see law and economics perspective above). They set up a strategic model that reflects the essential steps in WTO dispute settlement and then estimate the empirical model using statistical backward induction. The results offer more support for the enforcement than the rule-clarification argument. More politicized disputes are more prone to escalation throughout the first two stages of dispute settlement (up to the panel or Appellate Body). The same, however, applies to more complex disputes, for which one could have expected escalation primarily up to the panel ruling stage, but not beyond. The main implication of these results is that the second perspective, which views dispute settlement primarily as a rule-clarification and compliance-management device, is probably too optimistic, and that the WTO's ability to settle disputes is significantly circumscribed both by domestic economic interests and by the types of countries involved in these disputes.

22.4.4 Third parties in litigation

Some research has also looked at the conditions under which other WTO members influence dispute settlement. In terms of participation in DSM proceedings, the WTO creates the possibility for interested members to invoke their right as a third party. Third parties receive other parties' first written submissions and are invited to express their views during panel or Appellate Body hearings. Third parties have, however, no right to appeal a panel ruling, nor can they retaliate against a defendant who was found guilty (only the complainant(s) can suspend trade concessions).

---

[47] Bernauer and Sattler 2006.
[48] Sattler, Spilker, and Bernauer 2010.

WTO members use their third party rights for different reasons (e.g. signalling interests, supporting the complainant or the defendant). Some large economies have become third parties in almost every case (e.g. China, the US, and the EU). Others have selectively chosen this status. Third party rights can easily be invoked, and offer WTO members partial participation during the litigation process. Bown argues that, in statistical terms, there is no significant evidence that the decision to participate as third party differs from complainant status.[49] Elsig and Stucki find, however, that the weakest countries in the system are more likely to become third parties than complainants.[50] Third party status allows for a form of strategic signalling of some legitimate interests to the involved parties, and amounts to partial free-riding. Busch and Reinhardt find evidence that more participation of third parties is associated with a lower probability of early settlement.[51] They argue that audience costs lower the prospects for success in pre-trial negotiations. By extension, they argue that the higher the number of third parties the greater the likelihood that the dispute will end in a ruling.

22.4.5 Implementation

Research on the implementation of WTO dispute verdicts is, arguably, least advanced. This is not surprising, however, because measuring implementation of WTO rulings is far from easy. Data coding of dispute initiation and escalation is able to follow the procedural steps of the WTO DSM, from requests for consultations up to the level of disputes over compliance with WTO verdicts. Using such data to measure implementation (or compliance with) WTO DSM verdicts is useful as a rough approximation. With this approach, the empirical findings in the existing literature are equivalent to what is observed in studies that conceptualize trade dispute escalation in terms of three stages. As noted above, for instance, Bernauer and Sattler find that EHS disputes are particularly likely to run into implementation problems after they have made it through the consultation and panel/Appellate Body stages.[52] Sattler, Spilker, and Bernauer also find that disputes over complex trade issues and disputes over issues involving politically important domestic sectors are more likely to run into implementation problems.[53]

Based on data for 181 disputes between 1995 and July 2002, and using a more direct coding of implementation, Davey observes a successful implementation rate of adopted panel and Appellate Body reports of 83 per cent.[54] He finds prompt implementation, especially in safeguards and TRIPS cases, but more problems in disputes over trade remedies, sanitary and phytosanitary (SPS) measures, agriculture, and subsidies. Implementation that requires a legislative act also appears to be more difficult than implementation in cases where compliance can be achieved by executive decree.

---

[49] Bown 2005a.   [50] Elsig and Stucki 2012.
[51] Busch and Reinhardt 2006.   [52] Bernauer and Sattler 2006.
[53] Sattler, Spilker, and Bernauer 2010.   [54] Davey 2007.

22.4.6 Outside-in and inside-out effects

A new literature on overlapping jurisdictions has emerged in recent years.[55] In the WTO context, such research has focused on the interaction between the multilateral trading regime and preferential trade agreements (PTAs) as well as the interplay between trade law and public international law. One key question has been how the relationship between GATT/WTO law and public international law has transformed the formerly self-contained GATT regime into a WTO system that is more firmly embedded in the broader landscape of international law. More so than the GATT, the WTO DSM is placed within the context of public international law (Article 3.2 DSU). Whereas GATT dispute settlement panels limited themselves to the four corners of the GATT Agreement, WTO panels and the Appellate Body increasingly refer to other rules of international law. These other rules can be of a procedural nature (burden of proof, due process, good faith) or substantive content (rules set out in environmental treaties, bilateral agreements, customary international law and other non-WTO documents). Normative debates have focused on how far such references to 'outside' international law should go. Some stakeholders in this debate have taken the position that outside rules can only be referred to in the interpretation of ambiguous WTO provisions, and, in the end, unambiguous WTO rules always prevail.[56] Others have expressed the view that panels and the Appellate Body can apply outside norms more broadly and that, on occasion, WTO rules must give way to provisions in other treaties.[57]

22.4.7 Forum-shopping

In view of the increased number of PTAs in recent years and the existence of multiple forums for dispute settlement, research has also focused on the interaction between courts and on the strategic choice of forums. Busch looks at forum-shopping and argues that this practice concerns not only the likelihood of success of the complainant, but also where to set a precedent that is useful for case law development.[58] Drezner argues that more powerful states are better able to cope with overlapping jurisdictions, and that increased legalization empowers stronger states that were meant to be controlled by legalization in the first place.[59] Pauwelyn describes how the WTO and regional dispute settlement mechanisms increasingly overlap, and offers rules on how to address sequencing and conflict, arguing that the WTO cannot remain indifferent to forum exclusion clauses in PTAs.[60]

---

[55] Pauwelyn 2003; Raustiala and Victor 2004; Alter and Meunier 2007; Shaffer and Pollack 2010.
[56] Trachtman 1999.   [57] Pauwelyn 2001.   [58] Busch 2007.
[59] Drezner 2006.   [60] Pauwelyn 2009.

22.5 WHAT REMAINS?

The preceding sections show that existing research offers a wealth of insights into the causes and implications of a wide range of phenomena within the realm of WTO dispute settlement. In this penultimate section we touch upon some of the research gaps that remain—some refer to specific measurement issues, others are more conceptual in nature.

The 'non-cases'. When studying the disputes that have been filed at the WTO, it remains difficult to set the benchmark in terms of how many cases should have been filed. Why does a country violate WTO law? What makes other countries file a case or not file a case? Specifically, of all WTO cases filed, why do only 3 per cent concern the TRIPS Agreement and 2 per cent GATS, even though both agreements (and in particular TRIPS) cover a broad range of regulatory policies?[61] Similarly, in view of the hundreds of bilateral or regional PTAs involving (in varying compositions) almost every one of the 153 WTO members, why, after 16 years, has there been only one single Appellate Body ruling that focuses on whether a PTA meets the requirements outlined in GATT Article XXIV?[62]

Who won the case? While some important advances in research have been made by counting (and defining outcomes of) all individual claims,[63] we lack a convincing set of measures that define overall 'success' in the WTO litigation process. In particular, the increasing tendency by disputing parties to provide panels with a 'shopping list' of claims, in the hope that some of these claims (and the corresponding Articles) will be interpreted in their favour, creates difficulties in analysing the success of disputing parties.

Interaction between panels and the Appellate Body. In the context of the WTO, the two litigation stages display some clear differences. While panels address issues of facts, the review by the Appellate Body is (meant to be) restricted to legal questions applied to those facts. The way panels deal with cases therefore creates certain path-dependent effects as to the development of Appellate Body case law. Put differently, this sequential game (without the possibility for the Appellate Body to remand the case, that is, to send the dispute back to the panel), impacts on the direction of legal interpretation. In addition, panellists are cognizant that their rulings can be overturned and Appellate Body members presume they are not selected simply to rubber-stamp panel decisions. Anecdotal evidence suggests that this creates strategic interaction between the judicial bodies that has not been studied systematically.

How to measure implementation? Another measurement problem concerns implementation. As noted above, the existing literature views escalation into compliance

---

[61] See Pauwelyn 2010; on trade remedies, see Bown 2005b.

[62] Article XXIV states the conditions under which PTAs are allowed as an exception to the MFN rule—see Mavroidis 2006.

[63] Hoekman, Horn, and Mavroidis 2008; they do not weigh claims, but treat them all equally notwithstanding whether it is a procedural or substantial matter (there is no hierarchy); see also Horn, Johannesson, and Mavroidis 2011.

disputes as a sign of implementation problems. However, this approach creates the potential for false positives or false negatives. In a number of disputes the parties notify the WTO that the dispute has been resolved. It is possible, however, that there has been some 'horse-trading' outside the WTO process; if so, this could imply a false negative, in the sense that we do not record an implementation problem when there is in fact such a problem. False positives (where disputing countries formally escalate the dispute further, even though the defendant has made the requested trade concessions) are also possible, though arguably less likely. In any event, reliable measurement of implementation, and thus of successful dispute resolution, will ultimately require an assessment of whether the defendant has implemented what the applicable DSM ruling has asked for.

Do WTO dispute rulings foster trade? One of the criteria for determining how well the DSM works could, arguably, be whether dispute rulings have a trade-increasing effect. Assuming that the DSM helps in removing trade restrictions, we should assume that judicial verdicts by the WTO increase trade flows, particularly between those countries involved in a dispute. There has been very little research on this issue.[64] In a recent paper, Bechtel and Sattler examine the effect of WTO rulings on sectoral trade flows. They find that WTO verdicts have a delayed positive effect on sectoral exports of the countries that initiated a dispute. Third parties tend to benefit as well.[65]

The role of panellists/the role of the judge. How are panellists or members of the Appellate Body selected and how do they behave? What does this tell us about how the court system addresses incomplete contracts? There has been very little research on internal decision-making in the various WTO judicial bodies,[66] notably on whether the type of deliberation, discourse, and the preferences of judicial appointees matter. The main obstacle is lack of data. From the insights of past Appellate Body members, we know that the first seven people appointed to the Appellate Body built some buffers against member governments' attempts to influence their work (e.g. working towards collegiality in decision-making to pre-empt division).[67] But, generally, scholars have to second-guess causal processes based on observable outcomes. For example, for the heated amicus curiae debate, we can observe over time how the Appellate Body steered a course between maintaining its original position and allowing for some flexibility.[68] Some research on these issues is beginning to emerge. Busch and Pelc, for example, show that the experience of the chair of the panel has a significant effect on whether panel decisions are appealed.[69] They also investigate the conditions under which the Appellate Body uses specific legal tools to abstain from ruling (e.g. relying on judicial economy).[70]

---

[64] Bown 2004a, 2004b.   [65] Bechtel and Sattler 2011.

[66] Alvarez-Jimenez 2009.   [67] Ehlermann 2002, 2003; Bacchus 2004.

[68] Mavroidis 2001. 'Amicus curiae briefs' are submissions by actors that are not a party to the case. There was a debate in the WTO on whether panels or the Appellate Body can or should accept such briefs.

[69] Busch and Pelc 2009.

[70] Busch and Pelc 2010. 'Judicial economy' refers to a court's refusal to decide on specific claims raised by any of the parties. This is mostly done on the grounds that deciding on a particular claim is not necessary to rule on a case.

Other work attempts to trace the ways in which appointment procedures in the WTO potentially affect the preferences of court members, and subsequently the rulings.[71] Again, the major challenge pertains to missing data on the behaviour of individual panellists or Appellate Body members; only dissenting views offer partial indications as to important disagreements amongst adjudicators, blocking ways to reach a compromise and affecting outcomes.[72]

What is the influence of private actors? The dispute settlement system is intergovernmental, and private actors have no standing before the 'court'. However, there is plenty of anecdotal evidence that the influence and participation of interest groups is important. The lack of more systematic empirical work on the role of private actors, in particular firms, and their participation throughout the process of settling disputes in the WTO, is puzzling.[73] There is very little research beyond a small number of case studies that look at the firm level and study how companies and associations lobby and gain access to decision makers. Few contributions stand out. For instance, Shaffer focuses on the ways firms and state authorities work in a type of public–private partnership approach in WTO litigation, studying the US, the EU, and Brazil.[74] In addition, we know little about the way firms affect implementation. In sum, more research is needed on the conditions under which firms participate: how the institutional set-up affects interest aggregation (through access points for business groups to governments), what determines firms' relative influence on decisions to file, and how firms react to demands by the WTO system (and through domestic public authorities) to change established practice.

The role of information. We lack theoretical and empirical work on how information affects dispute settlement. This debate is only in its initial stages.[75] Information has different facets, such as how courts deal with submissions by interest groups (amicus curiae briefs), how transparent litigation procedures are and to what degree information provided by the parties is shared, or under what conditions dissenting views are articulated in panel or Appellate Body reports.[76] In relation to the Appellate Body, Steinberg conjectures that the Appellate Body pushed to open up the proceedings to other players and to improve their access (in particular to provide easier access for developing countries, invite expert testimony, and allow private lawyers to represent the litigating party), also as a potential way to gather more information.[77] Yet the proper role of information poses some normative questions, such as protecting courts from too much public scrutiny and politicization, and addressing a potential trade-off between transparency and performance.[78]

---

[71] Elsig and Pollack 2010.   [72] Flett 2010.   [73] Bown 2009.

[74] Shaffer 2003; Shaffer, Sanchez, and Rosenberg 2008.

[75] Elsig 2010.

[76] In a move towards more transparency, some hearings have been public. However, this only occurs when both the complainant and the defendant in a dispute agree on such a step (Ehring 2008).

[77] Steinberg 2004. The decision to allow private lawyers to represent governments, while changing established GATT practice, also helped to empower developing countries (Goldstein and Steinberg 2008, 268–9).

[78] Stasavage 2004.

The negotiation–litigation nexus. Our understanding is also wanting as to the dynamic interaction between negotiations and dispute settlement. Most research overlooks subtle spillover effects between these functions of the WTO. Dispute settlement not only takes into account a growing body of existing case law,[79] it also strategically interacts with current or future negotiations. Some limited judicial law-making may well impact on the scope and direction of negotiations, allowing for particular focal points to emerge. Yet the causal story is still not adequately theorized, and we have not yet seen much empirical work. Some clues have been offered by Fearon about how the strength of the dispute settlement system (the existence of binding laws with long-term distributional effects) may impact negatively on the search for common zones of agreement.[80]

Cultural or regional aspects? A brief look at the empirical evidence on who launches cases also suggests important variance across regions. This could be explained by differing attitudes as to 'how to settle disputes', rooted in domestic traditions of resolving disputes or variance in foreign policy traditions. Some states are more inclined to use legal means of dispute settlement, while others prefer conciliatory approaches.[81] Insight from anthropology, psychology, or foreign policy analysis might inspire new research on the cultural barriers to litigation. In addition, we might ask whether we will observe more convergence over time (also linked to outside-in effects through participation in international organizations, allowing for certain types of diffusion processes to occur).

22.6 Conclusions

This chapter has addressed past and present scholarly work on the WTO DSM, including a mapping of gaps that might be of interest for future research in this area. The literature is already quite developed and research is venturing into areas that are empirically and conceptually more challenging. Yet much of the research also has important stories to tell in terms of policy implications, and research into the politics and law of WTO dispute settlement will also be beneficial for current reform debates. Research on least-developed countries shows that the legal and financial constraints are not pivotal in explaining the reluctance to launch disputes; therefore a fund for the poorest countries is likely to have little effect on actual usage of the system.[82] Busch and Pelc address the proposal by the European Union to create a permanent body of panellists and discuss the implications of such a change.[83] Another example is a proposal by Mexico for an auctioning system for allocating the right to sanction. This idea was largely inspired by research on tradable remedies.[84]

---

[79] On the role of precedence, see for example Bhala 2001.
[80] Fearon 1998.
[81] Porges 2003.
[82] Elsig and Stucki 2012.
[83] Busch and Pelc 2009.
[84] Bagwell, Mavroidis, and Staiger 2006.

And the question of reform will not go away. Members of the WTO are constantly discussing and negotiating potential changes to the existing dispute settlement mechanism. A review of the functioning of the DSU was part of the final deal during the Uruguay Round negotiations, and started in 1998 (but continues to this day without any amendment of the DSU). The most recent attempt was launched with—but separate from—the Doha Round negotiations. Very active in this debate has been the US, which advocated reform in the direction of constraining the overall legal nature (e.g. limiting gap-filling, defining how panels and the Appellate Body should use interpretative methods, and partial acceptance of recommendations), and giving more support to Appellate Body members (as a reaction to criticism of too much influence by the Appellate Body Secretariat) by allowing for individual legal assistance (e.g. clerks). In recent years, we have witnessed some potential agreement on procedural issues (e.g. sequencing, remand option), and on strengthening third party rights and developing countries' participation. Yet, other issues remain stalled (e.g. increased control by members over the process, monetary or collective retaliation, list of permanent panellists).[85] A particularly thorny issue is how to deal with 'hit and run' practices, where a member enacts an inconsistent measure, goes through the entire DSU proceeding and then removes the measure, without having to pay any compensation or suffer any retaliation given that the WTO remedy of last resort is prospective retaliation only. In this respect, a balance needs to be found between increasing the cost of violation and leaving the DSU enough flexibility to allow it to continue to muster high levels of support and implementation. However, given the consensus rule and substantial support for the current system, it is unlikely that WTO members will agree on any grand reform.

References

Allee, Todd. 2005. The 'Hidden' Impact of the World Trade Organization on the Reduction of Trade Conflict. Paper presented at the 2005 Midwest Political Science Association Conference, Chicago, Illinois.

Allee, Todd. 2008. Developing Countries and the Initiation of GATT/WTO Disputes. Paper prepared for delivery at the 1st Conference on the Political Economy of International Organizations, February, Monte Verità, Switzerland.

Alter, Karen. 2008. Agents or Trustees? International Courts in their Political Context. *European Journal of International Relations* 14 (1):33–63.

Alter, Karen, and Sophie Meunier. 2007. The Politics of International Regime Complexity. Working Paper 3. Illinois: Roberta Buffett Center for International and Comparative Studies, Northwestern University.

Alvarez-Jimenez, Alberto. 2009. The WTO Appellate Body's Decision-Making Process: A Perfect Model for International Adjudication. *Journal of International Economic Law* 12 (2):289–331.

Bacchus, James. 2004. *Trade and Freedom*. London: Cameron May.

---

[85] See for instance Zimmermann 2006.

Bagwell, Kyle, Petros Mavroidis, and Robert Staiger. 2006. The Case for Tradable Remedies in WTO Dispute Settlement. In *Economic Development and Multilateral Trade Cooperation*, edited by Simon Evenett and Bernard Hoekman, 395–413. Washington, DC: Palgrave Macmillan and World Bank.

Bechtel, Michael, and Thomas Sattler. 2011. The Effect of the WTO Dispute Settlement Body on Bilateral Trade Relations. Unpublished manuscript, ETH Zurich, Center for Comparative and International Studies (CIS).

Bernauer, Thomas, and Thomas Sattler. 2006. Sind WTO-Konflikte im Bereich des Umwelt- und Verbraucherschutzes Eskalationsträchtiger als Andere WTO-Konflikte. *Zeitschrift für Internationale Beziehungen* 13 (1):5–37.

Bhala, Raj. 2001. The Power of the Past: Towards De Jure Stare Decisis in WTO Adjudication. *George Washington International Law Review* 33:873–978.

Bown, Chad. 2004a. On the Economic Success of GATT/WTO Dispute Settlement. *Review of Economics and Statistics* 86 (3):811–23.

Bown, Chad. 2004b. Trade Policy under the GATT/WTO: Empirical Evidence of the Equal Treatment Rule. *Canadian Journal of Economics* 37 (3):678–720.

Bown, Chad. 2005a. Participation in WTO Dispute Settlement: Complainants, Interested Parties, and Free Riders. *The World Bank Economic Review* 19 (2):287–311.

Bown, Chad. 2005b. Trade Remedies and World Trade Organization Dispute Settlement: Why are so Few Challenged? *Journal of Legal Studies* 34 (2):515–55.

Bown, Chad. 2009. *Self-Enforcing Trade: Developing Countries and WTO Dispute Settlement*. Washington, DC: Brookings Institution Press.

Bown, Chad, and Joost Pauwelyn, eds. 2010. *The Law, Economics and Politics of Retaliation in WTO Dispute Settlement*. Cambridge: Cambridge University Press.

Brewster, Rachel. 2006. Rule-Based Dispute Resolution in International Trade Law. *Virginia Law Review* 92 (2):251–88.

Busch, Marc. 2007. Overlapping Institutions, Forum Shopping, and Dispute Settlement in International Trade. *International Organization* 61 (4):735–61.

Busch, Marc, and Krzysztof Pelc. 2009. Does the WTO Need a Permanent Body of Panelists? *Journal of International Economic Law* 12 (3):579–94.

Busch, Marc, and Krzysztof Pelc. 2010. The Politics of Judicial Economy at the World Trade Organization. *International Organization* 64 (2):257–79.

Busch, Marc, and Eric Reinhardt. 2006. Three's a Crowd: Third Parties and WTO Dispute Settlement. *World Politics* 58 (3):446–77.

Busch, Marc, Eric Reinhardt, and Gregory Shaffer. 2009. Does Legal Capacity Matter? A Survey of WTO Members. *World Trade Review* 8 (4):559–77.

Davey, William. 2007. Evaluating WTO Dispute Settlement: What Results Have Been Achieved through Consultations and Implementation of Panel Reports? In *The WTO in the Twenty-First Century*, edited by Yasuhei Taniguchi, Alan Yanovich, and Jan Bohanes, 98–140. Cambridge: Cambridge University Press.

Davis, Christina, and Sarah Blodgett Bermeo. 2009. Who Files? Developing Country Participation in GATT/WTO Adjudication. *The Journal of Politics* 71 (3):1033–49.

Downs, George, David Rocke, and Peter Barsoom. 1996. Is the Good News about Compliance Good News about Cooperation? *International Organization* 50 (3):379–406.

Drezner, Daniel. 2006. The Viscosity of Global Governance: When is Forum-Shopping Expensive? Paper presented at 102nd Annual Meeting of the American Political Science Association, Philadelphia, PA.

Ehlermann, Claus-Dieter. 2002. Six Years on the Bench of the 'World Trade Court'. *Journal of World Trade* 36 (4):605–39.

Ehlermann, Claus-Dieter. 2003. Experiences from the WTO Appellate Body. *Texas International Law Journal* 38 (3):469–88.

Ehring, Lothar. 2008. Public Access to Dispute Settlement Hearings in the World Trade Organization. *Journal of International Economic Law* 11 (4):1021–34.

Elsig, Manfred. 2010. The World Trade Organization at Work: Performance in a Member-Driven Milieu. *Review of International Organizations* 5 (3):345–63.

Elsig, Manfred, and Mark Pollack. 2010. Agents, Trustees, and International Courts: Nomination and Appointment of Judicial Candidates in the WTO Appellate Body. Paper presented at the SGIR Pan-European International Relations Conference, Stockholm.

Elsig, Manfred, and Philipp Stucki. 2012. Low-Income Developing Countries and WTO Litigation: Why Wake Up the Sleeping Dog? *Review of International Political Economy* forthcoming.

Fearon, James. 1998. Bargaining, Enforcement, and International Cooperation. *International Organization* 52 (2):269–306.

Flett, James. 2010. Collective Intelligence and the Possibility of Dissent: Anonymous Individual Opinions in WTO Jurisprudence. *Journal of International Economic Law* 13 (2):287–320.

Francois, Joseph, Henrik Horn, and Niklas Kaunitz. 2008. Trading Profiles and Developing Country Participation in the WTO Dispute Settlement System. Issue Paper 6. Geneva: ICTSD.

Goldstein, Judith, and Lisa Martin. 2000. Legalization, Trade Liberalization, and Domestic Politics: A Cautionary Note. *International Organization* 54 (3):603–32.

Goldstein, Judith, and Richard Steinberg. 2008. Negotiate or Litigate? Effects of WTO Judicial Delegation on U.S. Trade Politics. *Law and Contemporary Problems* 71:256–82.

Grant, Ruth, and Robert Keohane. 2005. Accountability and Abuses of Power in World Politics. *American Political Science Review* 99 (1):29–43.

Guzman, Andrew, and Beth Simmons. 2002. To Settle or Empanel? An Empirical Analysis of Litigation and Settlement at the WTO. *Journal of Legal Studies* 31 (1):205–35.

Guzman, Andrew, and Beth Simmons. 2005. Power Plays and Capacity Constraints: The Selection of Defendants in WTO Disputes. *Journal of Legal Studies* 34 (2):557–98.

Hoekman, Bernard, Henrik Horn, and Petros Mavroidis. 2008. Winners and Losers in the Panel Stage of the WTO Dispute Settlement System. Working Paper Series 769. Stockholm: Research Institute of Industrial Economics.

Horn, Henrik, Lowise Johannesson, and Petros Mavroidis, 2011. The WTO Dispute Settlement System 1995–2010; Some Descriptive Statistics. *Journal of World Trade* 45(6): 1107–38.

Horn, Henrik, Giovanni Maggi, and Robert Staiger. 2006. Trade Agreements as Endogenously Incomplete Contracts. Working Paper 12745. Cambridge, MA: National Bureau of Economic Research.

Horn, Henrik, Petros Mavroidis, and Hakan Nordström. 1999. Is the Use of the WTO Dispute Settlement System Biased? Discussion Paper 2340. London: CEPR.

Hudec, Robert. 1990. *The GATT Legal System and World Trade Diplomacy*. Salem, NH: Butterworth Legal Publishers.

Jackson, John. 1997. *The World Trading System: Law and Policy of International Economic Relations*. Cambridge, MA: MIT Press.

Keck, Alexander, and Simon Schropp. 2007. Indisputably Essential: The Economics of Dispute Settlement Institutions in Trade Agreements. *Journal of World Trade* 41 (2):411–50.

Keohane, Robert. 1984. *After Hegemony*. Princeton: Princeton University Press.

Kim, Moonhawk. 2008. Costly Procedures: Divergent Effects of Legalization in the GATT/WTO Dispute Settlement Procedures. *International Studies Quarterly* 52 (3):657–86.

Maggi, Giovanni, and Robert Staiger. 2008. On the Role and Design of Dispute Settlement Procedures in International Trade Agreements. Working Paper 14067. Cambridge, MA: National Bureau of Economic Research.

Mavroidis, Petros. 2001. *Amicus Curiae* Briefs Before the WTO: Much Ado About Nothing. Jean Monnet Working Paper 2. New York: School of Law, NYU.

Mavroidis, Petros. 2006. If I Don't Do It, Somebody Else Will (or Won't). *Journal of World Trade* 40 (1):187–214.

Pauwelyn, Joost. 2001. The Role of Public International Law in the WTO: How Far Can We Go? *American Journal of International Law* 95 (3):535–78.

Pauwelyn, Joost. 2003. *Conflict of Norms in Public International Law: How WTO Law Relates to Other Rules of International Law*. Cambridge: Cambridge University Press.

Pauwelyn, Joost. 2005. The Transformation of World Trade. *Michigan Law Review* 104:1–70.

Pauwelyn, Joost. 2009. Legal Avenues to 'Multilateralizing Regionalism': Beyond Article XXIV. In *Multilateralizing Regionalism: Challenges for the Global Trading System*, edited by Richard Baldwin and Patrick Low, 368–400. Cambridge: Cambridge University Press.

Pauwelyn, Joost. 2010. The Dog that Barked but Didn't Bite: Fifteen Years of Intellectual Property Disputes at the WTO. *Journal of International Dispute Resolution* 1 (2):389–429.

Petersmann, Ernst-Ulrich. 1986. Trade Policy as a Constitutional Problem. On the 'Domestic Policy Functions' of International Trade Rules. *Aussenwirtschaft* 41:405–39.

Poletti, Arlo. 2011. WTO Judicialization and Preference Convergence in EU Trade Policy: Making the Agent's Life Easier. *Journal of European Public Policy* 18 (3):361–82.

Porges, Amelia. 2003. Settling WTO Disputes: What do Litigation Models Tell Us? *Ohio State Journal on Dispute Resolution* 19 (1):141–84.

Raustiala, Kal, and David Victor. 2004. The Regime Complex for Plant Genetic Resources. *International Organization* 58 (2):277–309.

Rosendorff, Peter. 2005. Stability and Rigidity: Politics and Design of the WTO's Dispute Settlement Procedure. *American Political Science Review* 99 (3):389–400.

Rosendorff, B. Peter, and Helen V. Milner. 2001. The Optimal Design of International Trade Institutions: Uncertainty and Escape. *International Organization* 55 (4):829–57.

Sattler, Thomas, and Thomas Bernauer. 2011. Gravitation or Discrimination? Determinants of Litigation in the World Trade Organization. *European Journal of Political Research* 50 (2):143–67.

Sattler, Thomas, Gabriele Spilker, and Thomas Bernauer. 2010. Dispute Settlement as Rule Clarification or Enforcement? Evidence from the World Trade Organization. Unpublished manuscript, ETH Zurich, Center for Comparative and International Studies (CIS).

Schropp, Simon. 2010. *Trade Policy Flexibility and Enforcement in the World Trade Organization: A Law and Economics Analysis*. Cambridge: Cambridge University Press.

Schwartz, Warren, and Alan Sykes. 2002. The Economic Structure of Renegotiation and Dispute Resolution in the WTO. *Journal of Legal Studies* 31 (1):179–204.

Shaffer, Gregory. 2003. *Defending Interests: Public–Private Partnerships in W.T.O. Litigation*. Washington, DC: Brookings Institution Press.

Shaffer, Gregory, and Mark Pollack. 2010. Hard vs Soft Law: Alternatives, Complements and Antagonists in International Governance. *Minnesota Law Review* 94 (3):706–99.

Shaffer, Gregory, Michelle Ratton Sanchez, and Barbara Rosenberg. 2008. The Trials of Winning at the WTO: What Lies Behind Brazil's Success. *Cornell International Law Journal* 41 (2):383–501.

Stasavage, David. 2004. Open-Door or Closed-Door? Transparency in Domestic and International Bargaining. *International Organization* 58 (4):667–703.

Steinberg, Richard. 2002. In the Shadow of Law or Power? Consensus-Based Bargaining and Outcomes in the GATT/WTO. *International Organization* 56 (2):339–74.

Steinberg, Richard. 2004. Judicial Lawmaking at the WTO: Discursive, Constitutional, and Political Constraints. *American Journal of International Law* 98 (2):247–75.

Stone Sweet, Alec. 1999. Judicialization and the Construction of Governance. *Comparative Political Studies* 32 (2):147–84.

Thompson, Alexander. 2007. The Power of Legalization: A Two-Level Explanation for US Support of WTO Dispute Settlement. Paper presented at the Annual Convention of the International Studies Association, Chicago, Illinois.

Trachtman, Joel. 1999. The Domain of WTO Dispute Resolution. *Harvard International Law Journal* 40 (2):333–77.

Van den Bossche, Peter. 2005. From Afterthought to Centerpiece: The WTO Appellate Body and its Rise to Prominence in the World Trading System. Working Paper 1. Maastricht: Faculty of Law, Maastricht University.

Weiler, Joseph. 2001. The Rule of Lawyers and the Ethos of Diplomacy. *Journal of World Trade* 35 (2):191–207.

Young, Alasdair. 2005. Picking the Wrong Fight: Why Attacks on the World Trade Organization Pose the Real Threat to National Environmental and Public Health. *Global Environmental Politics* 5 (4):47–72.

Zangl, Bernhard. 2008. Judicialization Matters! A Comparison of Dispute Settlement under GATT and the WTO. *International Studies Quarterly* 52 (4):825–54.

Zejan, Pilar, and Frank Bartels. 2006. Be Nice and Get Your Money—An Empirical Analysis of World Trade Organization Trade Disputes and Aid. *Journal of World Trade* 40 (6):1021–47.

Zimmermann, Thomas. 2006. The DSU Review (1998–2004): Negotiations, Problems and Perspectives. In *Reform and Development of the WTO Dispute Settlement System*, edited by Dencho Georgiev, and Kim van der Borght, 443–72. London: Cameron May.

CHAPTER 23

THE DISPUTE SETTLEMENT MECHANISM AT THE WTO: THE APPELLATE BODY—ASSESSMENT AND PROBLEMS

MITSUO MATSUSHITA

23.1 A BRIEF HISTORICAL BACKGROUND OF THE DISPUTE SETTLEMENT SYSTEM IN THE WTO

23.1.1 The dispute settlement system under the GATT 1947

THE World Trade Organization (WTO) dispute settlement mechanism has taken great strides towards establishing the rule of law in international trade, i.e. a rule-oriented international trading system.[1] In the old dispute settlement system under the General Agreement on Tariffs and Trade (GATT) 1947, which preceded the present dispute settlement system, the contracting parties established panels to resolve disputes when they arose among Contracting Parties regarding the interpretation and application of rules of the GATT 1947. Panels, which consisted of three to five individuals appointed by the Contracting Parties, examined issues in dispute and submitted reports in which solutions were suggested. However, the adoption of panel reports was made by consensus and the parties in dispute could also vote. As long as one of the Contracting Parties

---

[1] Industrial Structure Council 2008, 3–7.

objected to adopting the report, there was no adoption. This meant that the losing party in a dispute had a de facto veto power in the adoption process. This was a fatal defect in the dispute settlement system under the old GATT, and the framers of the WTO dispute settlement system wanted to remedy this defect and establish a more stable procedure for settling disputes.

23.1.2 An increase of trade disputes in the 1970s and 1980s

The need for a stable dispute settlement system in international trade was felt to be more and more necessary as trade relationships among nations came to be closely knit together and more disputes among trading nations arose. In the late 1970s, 1980s, and 1990s, products exported from newly industrialized countries such as Japan, Korea, China, Taiwan, and Brazil began to pour into the markets of developed countries such as the United States and the European Communities. Threatened by competition on these products, domestic industries in those countries initiated trade remedy actions to prevent and slow down the inflow of products—those actions included, inter alia, anti-dumping and countervailing duty actions, requests to invoke safeguard measures, and claims based on intellectual property rights against such imports. Indeed the period from 1970 to the establishment of the WTO in 1995 could be characterized as that of trade disputes.

Just to give a few examples, the United States requested Japan and other exporting nations to limit exports to the United States through 'voluntary export restraint' (VER) with the threat that protectionist measures might be taken if exports were not restrained. Examples are the Steel VER, the Textile VER and the Auto VER.[2] Also, in the 1980s, the United States often applied Section 301 of the Trade Act and imposed sanctions against trading partners whose trade policies the United States regarded as 'unfair'.[3] Whether a trade policy of a trading partner was unfair or not was judged by the United States and, when so judged, a penalty was imposed by the United States. In this system, prosecutor and judge became one entity, the US Government, and this could be characterized as 'unilateralism'.[4]

With large domestic markets, big countries such as the United States and the European Communities had strong bargaining powers vis-à-vis smaller trade partners such as Korea, Taiwan, and other developing countries, and imposed terms disadvantageous to them. Smaller countries had no choice but to succumb to the

[2] On issues of voluntary export restraint, see Matsushita 1987, 29–58; Matsushita 1999, 131–54.

[3] On Section 301 of the Trade Act, see US Congress 2008.

[4] The European Communities brought a case against the United States with the WTO on the grounds that the existence of Section 301 of the Trade Act in the United States was per se contrary to the Dispute Settlement Understanding (DSU). The panel held that Section 301 was not a violation of the DSU in itself but, depending on the way it is put into effect, it can be held to be inconsistent with provisions of the DSU. See WTO Panel Report 1999d.

pressure of such big trade partners. This was a power-oriented international trade system. In a power-oriented international trading system, it is a nation's power, whether political or economic, that counts. In this system, trading partners with less power had to suffer disadvantages due to their lack of power in relation to more powerful trade partners. In this system, fairness, objectivity, and predictability were somewhat lacking.

23.1.3 The move towards a rule-oriented international trading system

The establishment of the Bretton Woods System in the late 1940s signalled the advent of the time when international economies would be disciplined through an international framework such as the IMF and the World Bank. The GATT was signed in 1947 and this signified that international trade rules rather than powers should govern the trade relationships among nations.[5] Although, as discussed earlier and as stated by John Jackson, the GATT 1947 started with 'flawed constitutional beginnings',[6] nevertheless the GATT was successful to a degree in establishing a set of rules in the international trading system. In fact, the GATT was a great success compared with the international trade system before the Second World War, in which bloc economies separated trading nations and protectionism prevailed. This eventually led to the Second World War.

Since its establishment in 1947, the GATT initiated international trade negotiations (known as 'rounds'), and the eighth round was the Uruguay Round. In the Uruguay Round, the negotiating parties decided to create the WTO—this was indeed an epoch-making event in the history of the international trading system. As discussed in other chapters of this book, the WTO widened the coverage of disciplines to not only trade in goods but also to trade in services and trade-related aspects of intellectual property rights. As touched upon above, the WTO created a more powerful dispute settlement mechanism which would act as an 'international trade court'. With the establishment of the WTO, trading nations saw the advent of a rule-oriented international trading system.

One advantage of a rule-oriented international trading system is that the rule of law prevails over the powers of nations, and fairness and predictability in international trade are maintained. This provides security and advantage to developing country members, which lack bargaining powers compared to developed countries. This system also provides advantage to developed country members because it has more predictability and stability.

---

[5] For a general account of the Bretton Woods System and early days of the GATT 1947, see Wilcox 1949; Wilson 1947.
[6] Jackson 1997, 35.

23.2 THE WTO DISPUTE SETTLEMENT SYSTEM

23.2.1 An overview of the WTO dispute settlement system

The WTO has achieved remarkable success in settling trade disputes through its dispute settlement mechanism. Since its establishment, about 450 cases have been filed with this procedure and WTO panels and the Appellate Body have handed down decisions in more than 80 cases. Principles of interpretation of WTO agreements, as established by the Appellate Body, have become the cornerstones of the stability and predictability of the international trading system. Indeed, the WTO dispute settlement mechanism is the most effective international tribunal for settling disputes among international tribunals such as the International Court of Justice (ICJ).

The WTO dispute settlement mechanism is composed of the Dispute Settlement Body (DSB), panels, and the Appellate Body.[7] The DSB (which is the General Council of the WTO acting as a dispute settlement body) is the decision-making body which resolves disputes. Article 23 of the Dispute Settlement Understanding (DSU) requires that every dispute that arises under WTO agreements has to be brought to the dispute settlement mechanism and settled through the WTO dispute settlement procedures. Members of the WTO are prohibited from resorting to unilateral retaliations without going through this mechanism against other members which they deem to be violating WTO agreements.

When a dispute arises among members of the WTO, the parties must engage in consultation (for 60 days), and if the dispute is not resolved through consultation one of the parties (or both) can request the DSB to establish a panel to settle it. Three panellists are appointed to resolve a dispute. No particular qualifications are required as a panellist, but they should be individuals who have knowledge on international trade and law. Members of the WTO have submitted indicative lists of panellists to the WTO. The WTO can select panellists from among those in the indicative lists but does not necessarily have to choose from these lists. Often diplomats stationed in Geneva are appointed to act as panellists.

The DSB must establish a panel at the second request by a party. The panel conducts an investigation and hearing regarding the dispute in question, and prepares a report in which it applies the relevant WTO agreement and decides whether the measure complained about is a violation or not. The DSB adopts the report by a negative consensus.[8] Once adopted by the DSB, panel reports become decisions of the WTO and the parties in dispute are obliged to comply with the terms of the report.

---

[7] For a summary of the WTO dispute settlement mechanism, see WTO 2009.

[8] This means that the panel report is adopted by the DSB unless the adoption is unanimously opposed. Consensus is seldom established because the winning party generally favours its adoption. Therefore, deciding the case by negative consensus is called 'automaticity'.

If a party is not satisfied with the panel report, it can appeal to the Appellate Body. If an appeal is made, a panel report is not adopted until the appellate process is finished. The Appellate Body is a standing body composed of seven members, which reviews panel reports and can uphold, modify, or reverse them. The Appellate Body is authorized to review legal questions, i.e. to interpret WTO agreements but not to deal with factual questions. An Appellate Body report is submitted to the DSB and the DSB adopts it by negative consensus together with the panel report as upheld or modified by the Appellate Body report. The DSB issues a recommendation to the losing party and requests that it puts in place the trade measures and policies in question to conform to the WTO rules.

How are members of the Appellate Body selected? A selecting committee established by the DSB selects candidates for the Appellate Body members and the DSB appoints Appellate Body members as recommended by the selecting committee. In fact, WTO members recommend certain individuals to the DSB as candidates for the Appellate Body. Appellate Body members are appointed for the term of four years which is renewable only once. They must be individuals of recognized authority in international law and trade. Former judges, lawyers, diplomats, and academic scholars have been appointed to act as members of the Appellate Body.

Formally, panels and the Appellate Body are not decision-making bodies. Their functions are to prepare reports for the resolution of a dispute to be submitted to the DSB, and it is the DSB which adopts the reports and resolves the disputes. Therefore, formally, panels and the Appellate Body are auxiliaries attached to the DSB whose function is to recommend resolution of disputes. However, as stated earlier, reports of the Appellate Body are adopted by negative consensus and, therefore, adopted automatically (or almost automatically). Therefore, reports of the Appellate Body are effectively the final resolution of disputes. If a losing party does not implement the DSB's recommendations, the prevailing party can request authorization from the DSB for suspension of concessions (retaliation). Suspension of concessions is a measure taken by the prevailing party against the losing party in which the prevailing party imposes trade restrictions (such as increase of tariffs, imposition of quantitative restrictions on imports or exports) on the losing party. The amount and extent of suspension of concessions should be roughly equivalent to the amount and extent of damage that the prevailing party has suffered due to the infringement in question.

Article IX: 2 of the WTO Agreement states that ministerial conferences shall have the exclusive authority to adopt interpretations of WTO agreements by a decision of a three-fourths majority of the members. Therefore, a ministerial conference could overrule reports of the Appellate Body through this procedure. However, no ministerial conference has ever exercised this power.

The above system is somewhat akin to a judicial system in that disputes are settled through application of relevant provisions of international agreements by judgment of neutral arbiters, and there is an enforcement mechanism although this is not as sophisticated as that in domestic courts. Indeed, the establishment of this dispute settlement mechanism was intended to bring 'the rule of law' into the international trading system and to create stability, predictability, and fairness in international trade.

23.2.2 The WTO dispute settlement system and developing countries

There are some examples in which developing country members successfully challenged trade measures of developed country members that violated WTO agreements by using the WTO dispute settlement mechanism. Such examples include the *US–Underwear* case,[9] the *US–Shrimp–Turtle* case,[10] the *US–Shirts and Blouses* case,[11] the *US–Gambling* case,[12] and the *EC–Sardines* case.[13] Most of those cases are discussed later, but three of these cases are discussed briefly here.

In the *US–Underwear* case, the United States invoked a safeguard measure under the Agreement on Textiles and Clothing (the ATC Agreement, which is now defunct) and restricted imports of underwear from Costa Rica. Costa Rica brought a claim against the United States and argued that this was contrary to the safeguard provision of the ATC Agreement. The Appellate Body accepted Costa Rica's claim and ruled that the US measure was a violation of the ATC Agreement, and the United States revoked the measure.

In the *US–Gambling* case, the United States prohibited internet gambling services provided by operators in Antigua-Burbuda to US customers. Antigua-Burbuda claimed that this prohibition was contrary to the principle of national treatment because the United States prohibited international transfer of gambling services while permitting interstate transfer of gambling services within the United States. The Appellate Body held that the United States had violated the provisions of the General Agreement on Trade in Services (GATS) by discriminating against international gambling services in favour of domestic services. The Appellate Body permitted Antigua-Burbuda to retaliate against the United States by suspending intellectual property rights of US citizens in Antigua-Burbuda. This is an example of cross-retaliation.

In the *EC–Sardines* case, the EC prohibited the use of the label 'sardines' on canned foods made of fish caught in any area other than the North Sea, the Mediterranean Sea, and the Black Sea. Peru argued that this was a violation of Article 2.4 of the Agreement on Technical Barriers of Trade (TBT) because this provision mandates WTO members to base their compulsory standards on international standards, and the relevant international standard permitted the use of this expression with some conditions. Here, again, the Appellate Body agreed with Peru and held that the EC was in violation of the TBT Agreement.

---

[9] WTO Panel Report 1997c; WTO Appellate Body Report 1997b.
[10] WTO Panel Report 1998b; WTO Appellate Body Report 1998c.
[11] WTO Panel Report 1997b; WTO Appellate Body Report 1997a.
[12] WTO Panel Report 2004; WTO Appellate Body Report 2005.
[13] WTO Panel Report 2002; WTO Appellate Body Report 2002.

The above three examples show that smaller and less powerful states can prevail over more powerful trade partners as long as their legal claims are correct and persuasive. If, in the above cases, the petitioners (developing countries) had had to settle the dispute by bilateral negotiations, the outcome would have been less advantageous to them than a total withdrawal of the measures in question. Antigua-Burbuda is a country with a population of only about 70,000, but it still could win the case by presenting valid legal arguments.

23.3 MAJOR JURISPRUDENTIAL PRINCIPLES ESTABLISHED BY THE APPELLATE BODY

23.3.1 WTO jurisprudence established by the Appellate Body

Principles of WTO jurisprudence established by the Appellate Body are many, and it is hard to present them all in this chapter. Instead of making a comprehensive study of the subject matter, a review of some principles as set out by the Appellate Body will be made in the following sections. It should be noted, however, that this is not a comprehensive survey of the Appellate Body jurisprudence but an illustrative review.

23.3.2 Like products and directly competitive products

'Like products' is one of the most essential concepts in WTO law.[14] One of the most fundamental principles of the WTO regime is non-discrimination, i.e. the principles of most-favoured nation treatment and of national treatment. The former requires a WTO member to accord a product of one member treatment no less favourable than it accords to a like product imported from another member. The latter requires a member to accord treatment to a product imported from another member no less favourably than it accords to a like domestic product. The term 'like products' appears in many other provisions of WTO agreements, such as the Anti-dumping Agreement and the Safeguards Agreement.

The *Japan–Alcohol* case[15] is a landmark decision of the Appellate Body on this issue. Japan imposed a high liquor tax on vodka, gin, rum, whisky, and wine and imposed a low liquor tax on 'shochu', a Japanese traditional liquor—a distilled liquor of about 25 per cent alcoholic content. The United States, European Communities, and Canada brought claims against Japan at the DSB and argued that the liquor tax system in Japan was contrary to the national treatment principle in Article II of the GATT.

---

[14] A detailed and comprehensive study of like products is Choi 2003.
[15] WTO Panel Report 1996a; WTO Appellate Body Report 1996a.

The panel and the Appellate Body held that a question of whether or not an imported product is discriminated against in relation to a domestic product should be determined by a two-stage analysis—i.e. (a) that there should be a determination that an imported product is a like product or directly competitive product of a domestic product, and (b) that, if so, there should be a determination of whether there is less favourable treatment of the imported product than the domestic product. Also, the panel held that whether a product is like another product is decided by reference to (a) physical characteristics, (b) end use, (c) perception of users or consumers, and (d) tariff classification.

The panel and the Appellate Body made a distinction between Article III, paragraph 2, sentence 1, on the one hand, and sentence 2 on the other. They stated that while sentence 1 refers to a situation where the issue is whether two products are like products, sentence 2 refers to a situation where the issue is whether two products are directly competitive products. Whether two products are directly competitive or not should be determined by using 'cross-elasticity of demands'—the test that demand for one product declines as its price goes up, demand for the other product goes up in response to this, and a mutual responsiveness of increase or decline of prices and demands exists between the two products. Using this test, the Appellate Body decided that shochu and vodka were like products, and shochu and whisky, wine and other alcoholic beverages were directly competitive products.

If two products (one a domestic product and the other imported) are like products, any difference in domestic liquor taxation is inconsistent with Article III, paragraph 2, sentence 1, and if two products are directly competitive products, a difference in taxation is unlawful if this difference is made so as to afford protection to a domestic industry. In the latter situation, whether or not differential taxation is unlawful depends on how much difference there is, i.e. a difference is not unlawful per se.

The decision of the Appellate Body in this case denied 'the aims and effects test', which had been set out in a panel ruling under the old GATT (1947),[16] according to which the question of whether one product is like other should be determined in reference to the aims and effects of the laws and policies involved in a particular dispute.

Another important decision with respect to like product issues is the *EC–Asbestos* case,[17] in which the French Government prohibited use and imports of asbestos because of its danger to health. Canada challenged the EC at the WTO on the grounds that asbestos could be used without much danger in its 'controlled use' form and, while several products whose physical characteristics were similar to those of asbestos were permitted for sale, asbestos was prohibited and this amounted to a violation of Article III, paragraph 2, sentence 1.

In resolving this issue, the Appellate Body emphasized that the danger of asbestos had been recognized by international organizations such as the World Health Organization (WHO) and the International Labour Organization (ILO), by national governments and in professional circles, and that the perception of the public and among users of the

---

[16] GATT Panel Report 1992.
[17] WTO Appellate Body Report 2001b.

risk of asbestos was determinative of the question of whether asbestos and other similar products were like products or not.

This decision is important in that it established the principle that the perception of users was one of the determinative considerations in deciding whether a product was like others. This ruling will have far-reaching implications in resolving some environmental cases and food safety cases. There will be questions in future as to whether biofuel is a like product of petroleum fuel, or whether genetically modified (GMO) foods are like products of non-GMO foods. If these are not like products, there will be no problem of violating Article III, paragraph 2, sentence 1 of the GATT even if a WTO member treats biofuel more favourably in terms of taxation than petroleum fuel for environmental purposes.

23.3.3 Procedural issues

The Appellate Body has established a number of important procedural principles to be applied when engaging in dispute settlement. Some of them will be touched upon below.

23.3.3.1 *Burden of proof*

Burden of proof is a rule of procedure to decide who is responsible for proving what in litigation processes. Often it has a decisive effect on the outcome of litigation. The *US–Shirts and Blouses* case[18] is the landmark decision rendered by the Appellate Body on this issue. In this case, India brought a complaint against the United States because it imposed quantitative restrictions on imports of shirts and blouses coming from India. While the panel decided that the US imposition of these quantitative restrictions violated the safeguards provision contained in the ATC Agreement, it held that India had a burden of proving that the United States had violated this provision. India appealed and argued that, since the safeguards were an exception to the general rule of free trade, it should be the responsibility of the party invoking the exception to prove that it was necessary.

The Appellate Body held that whoever asserts the positive of a claim (i.e. the existence of the legal requirement in question) has the burden of proof on this matter. Once this burden is accepted, a prima facie case is established with regard to the existence of this legal requirement. Then the burden of rebuttal is shifted to the other party to disprove the existence of the requirement.[19]

23.3.3.2 *Standard of review*

In disputes under the WTO dispute settlement procedures, it is a governmental measure of a WTO member which is the subject of dispute. The facts have been found and

---

[18] WTO Panel Report 1997b; WTO Appellate Body Report 1997a.
[19] For details of the burden of proof issues, see Grando 2006.

determined by the national authority of that member in charge of enforcement of this measure and the authority has made a judgment based on those facts. When this measure is the subject of the WTO dispute settlement procedure, a question arises as to how much deference a panel dealing with the case should give to the fact-findings of the national authority.[20]

There are two principles to regulate the standard of review of facts found by a national authority. One is the *de novo* principle—the principle that a panel can make its own fact-findings with regard to the matter before it, independently of the fact-finding made by the national authority. The other is the deference principle—according to which a panel respects the fact-finding of the national authority and defers to it.

In the *EC–Hormones* case,[21] the Appellate Body dealt with this issue. The Appellate Body stated that it was neither the *de novo* principle nor the deference principle that should be applied, and that it should be Article 11 of the DSU which should apply. Article 11 of the DSU states: 'a panel should make an objective assessment of the matter before it, including an objective assessment of the facts of the case and the applicability of and conformity with the relevant covered agreements'. It seems that the principle enunciated in the above provision contains both the *de novo* principle and the deference principle. The Appellate Body's decision implies that both of these principles should be applied on a case-by-case basis, depending on the situation involved in the case before a panel.

23.3.3.3 *Quantitative/qualitative test*

Article XX (b) of the GATT states that a measure necessary to protect human, animal, or plant life and health is exempted from the prohibitions of the GATT. The issue here is how to prove whether a measure is necessary or not, e.g. the question of whether such a test is a quantitative or qualitative test. In the *Brazil–Tyres* case,[22] the issue was whether Brazil would be justified when it prohibited imports of retreaded tyres and used tyres in order to slow down the accumulation of waste tyres. The accumulated discarded waste tyres catch water and this is a breeding place of mosquitoes, causing a spread of dengue, yellow fever, and malaria. The precise legal question was whether Brazil needed to establish a quantitative linkage between the prohibition of imports of retreaded tyres and a decline in the disease (a quantitative test), or if it was sufficient for Brazil to establish that the prohibition had a likelihood or quality to reduce disease (a qualitative test).

The Appellate Body held that a qualitative test should be sufficient to prove that a measure was necessary to protect human, animal, and plant life. Therefore, it was sufficient for Brazil to establish that the import prohibition on retreaded tyres had features, or a likelihood, of reducing disease, even without the evidence that a quantitative relationship was established between the prohibition of imports of retreaded tyres and a decline of disease.

---

[20] On issues of the standard of review, see Bohanes and Lockhart 2009, 344 *et seq.*
[21] WTO Panel Report 1997a; WTO Appellate Body Report 1998a.
[22] WTO Panel Report 2007; WTO Appellate Body Report. 2007.

This decision made it much easier for a member to invoke Article XX (b) of the GATT 1995, because for a member to establish a quantitative link between a measure and the consequence was often difficult. A measure may have been initiated recently and it would take time before the consequence became clear.

23.3.3.4 *Adverse inferences*

Article 15 of the DSU requires that disputing parties cooperate with panels with respect to production of documents and other necessary information. Parties to a dispute are required to cooperate fully with a panel dealing with the case, and produce documents and other pieces of information if requested by the panel. What happens if a party refuses to cooperate, and withholds documents that are essential for addressing the dispute? This is what happened in the *Canada–Aircraft* case,[23] in which Brazil challenged Canada on the grounds that Canada had granted a subsidy to a Canadian aircraft company. The panel asked Canada to produce certain documents on the subsidy that Canada might have given to the company, but Canada refused to supply them for the reason that the documents contained confidential and proprietary business information of the company. The panel drafted a special procedure for the production of documents, to be applied to this case. In order to protect confidential information from being disclosed to outside parties, the panel provided detailed restrictions regarding the treatment of the documents.

However, Canada still refused to supply them. Brazil alleged that this refusal amounted to a violation of Article 15 of the DSU and the panel should draw a negative inference for the refusal, i.e. that the panel should assume that the information withheld from production was adverse to the interests of Canada. The panel refused to accept this claim and held that it would draw no negative inference from this refusal because, in the view of the panel, there was sufficient information to hold that Canada had violated the Agreement on Subsidies and Countervailing Measures (SCM).

Brazil appealed this decision and argued that the panel had erred by not drawing a negative inference from Canada's refusal to supply this information. The Appellate Body stated that the panel did not make a legal error in this, but that the panel could have drawn a negative inference and also that Brazil could have brought another complaint on the basis of Article 15 of the DSU.

Availability of pieces of evidence in litigation is essential for dispute settlement at any tribunal, and this applies to the WTO dispute settlement mechanism as well. Therefore, it is significant that the Appellate Body clarified that the principle of negative inference applied to the dispute settlement process at the WTO.

23.3.4 Anti-dumping—zeroing

Anti-dumping is one of the areas where many disputes occur with regard to interpretation of the Anti-Dumping Agreement (the Agreement on Implementation of Article VI

---

[23] WTO Panel Report 1999b; WTO Appellate Body Report 1999b.

of the GATT), and many rules have been formulated by the Appellate Body. One of these rules—zeroing—is discussed below.

Dumping in WTO law is a practice in which an exporter sets the price of a product in the domestic market at a high level, sets a lower price of a like product for an export and, by exporting the product with this price differential, causes a material injury to a domestic industry in the market of the importing country. Article VI of the GATT states that such dumping 'should be condemned', i.e. it is an unfair practice. In order to offset the advantage of an exporter engaged in dumping, the government of the importing country is authorized to impose an anti-dumping duty, where the maximum is the differential between the domestic price and the export price (dumping margin).

'Zeroing' is a practice in which an anti-dumping authority of an importing country calculates minus dumping margins as zero, and thereby artificially inflates the dumping margin. A hypothetical example is given below.

Exporter A exports product B (linen) to the importing country C. A sells in the domestic market three types of product B, that is, product b(1), b(2), and b(3) (for example, large, medium, and small size linen). The three types of product B are imported into the market of the importing country C. In the domestic market, b(1) is priced $100, b(2) $120, and b(3) $100 per unit. In exporting to country C, b(1) is priced $80, b(2) $120, and b(3) $120. The dumping margin for b(1) is plus $20, for b(2) 0, and for b(3) minus $20. When domestic prices and export prices are averaged and compared, the domestic price is $106 and the export price is $106, and there is therefore no dumping margin. However, the anti-dumping authority disregards the minus dumping margin of $20 with respect to b(3) and calculates this margin as zero. This is zeroing and, as the result, the dumping margin of $20 is artificially created. This is indeed a way to create or inflate dumping margin artificially by disregarding margins of export prices that are higher than the corresponding domestic prices.

This practice was widely used in the European Communities and the United States. The *EC–Bed Linen* case decided by the Appellate Body is, among appellate cases which dealt with this issue, the first and landmark case to outlaw this practice.[24]

The EC was challenged by India for the reason that the EC imposed anti-dumping duties on imports of bed linen coming from India and, in doing so, disregarded minus dumping margin with respect to bed linen products. The panel held in favour of India and the EC appealed. The Appellate Body held that the EC's zeroing practice was unlawful under the Anti-Dumping Agreement because it requires that an investigating authority is required to establish whether there is dumping with regard to 'a product' and calculate the dumping margin in the sale and export of this product as a whole. In this case, the product in question is bed linen but the EC disregarded part of the dumping margins with respect to the product, and imposed anti-dumping duties. This is contrary to the requirement of the Anti-Dumping Agreement.

This decision is important in that it made clear that evasive conduct such as zeroing would be held as a violation of the Anti-Dumping Agreement.

[24] WTO Panel Report 2000; WTO Appellate Body Report 2001a.

23.3.5 Subsidies

In the SCM Agreement, subsidies given by governments are classified into three categories: *export subsidy*, which is prohibited per se, *actionable subsidy*, whose amenability under the SCM Agreement depends on whether it produces a material injury to a domestic industry of an importing country or otherwise seriously prejudices its interest, and *non-actionable subsidy*, which cannot be countervailed. The last category lapsed five years after the establishment of the WTO. Like the anti-dumping area, many disputes have arisen under the SCM Agreement and many important principles of interpretation have been formulated. Space permits only a limited examination of the totality of such cases and so the *US–Steel Bar* case[25] will be touched upon.

In this case, the British Government conferred a subsidy to the British Steel company and the company built a production facility using the subsidy. Later, British Steel was privatized and the facility was sold to a third party at market price. The United States imposed countervailing duties on steel products coming from the United Kingdom on the grounds that the subsidy given to British Steel had caused injury to a US industry and the effect of this subsidy still existed after the privatization.

An important question in this case was when the subsidy which had been given ceased to exist. The EC argued that the subsidy ceased to exist when the facility was sold, because the purchaser paid the market price to procure the facility, and therefore whatever special benefit had been bestowed to build this facility did not pass on to the purchaser. The Appellate Body decided that the subsidy did cease to exist when the subsidized facility was sold to a purchaser at market value.

This decision raises an interesting question of whether a subsidy ceases to exist when the purchaser of a facility, which had been built by the subsidy, paid the market price to procure it. One might raise the argument that the facility in question could only come into being because of the subsidy, and it would not have been built but for the subsidy and, for this reason, the facility is in excess of what the market could have permitted. When the facility was purchased at the market price, that market price had already been depressed by the existence of the subsidized facility. Therefore, the purchaser paid less than it would have had to pay if there had not been the subsidy and, in this sense, the purchaser also benefited from the subsidy. It is not suggested here that the Appellate Body is mistaken in this decision, but the decision raises interesting issues regarding the concept of subsidy.

23.3.6 Safeguards

Safeguards are temporary measures to impose tariffs or quantitative restrictions on imports in order to give a domestic industry breathing space when it is seriously injured due to the pressure of imports. Although the GATT is designed to promote and maintain

---

[25] WTO Panel Report 1999c; WTO Appellate Body Report 2000b.

free trade, it is necessary to provide safety nets so that domestic industries which are being seriously damaged due to imports can get temporary relief, in the form of safeguards. There are a number of important decisions rendered by the Appellate Body with regard to conditions under which WTO members can invoke safeguards. Here, again, space permits an examination of only one issue.

In WTO law, safeguards are provided for in Article XIX of the GATT 1994 and in the Safeguards Agreement. Article XIX states that safeguards can be applied if (a) there is an increase in imports because of unforeseen developments and as the result of concessions (reduction of tariffs) made in accordance with negotiations at the GATT, and (b) a serious injury has been caused to a domestic industry or there is threat of this due to the import. Therefore, according to Article XIX of the GATT 1994, a safeguard measure can be applied only when there are 'unforeseen developments' together with other requirements. However, in the Safeguards Agreement, which is regarded as implementing Article XIX of the GATT, there is no requirement that the administering authority of safeguards presents evidence of unforeseen developments.

In the *Argentina–Footwear* case,[26] Argentina imposed safeguards by way of tariffs on imports of footwear coming from abroad, including the EC. The EC brought a complaint against Argentina to the WTO on the grounds that the administering authority of safeguards in Argentina did not present evidence that the domestic industry was seriously injured by an increase of imports of footwear caused by unforeseen developments. Argentina responded by arguing that the Safeguards Agreement contained no requirement that the increase of imports must be because of unforeseen developments. The panel held that the Safeguards Agreement was a subsequent agreement in relation to Article XIX of the GATT and, therefore, if there was a difference between the two, the Safeguards Agreement would prevail.[27]

The Appellate Body reversed this finding of the panel, and held that 'safeguards' was used in the Safeguards Agreement in the sense of Article XIX of the GATT, and concluded that the Safeguards Agreement and Article XIX of the GATT should be read together. In this interpretation, administering authorities invoking safeguards must prove that an increase in imports has been caused by unforeseen developments.

When this decision was made, in both the United States and the EC, two major jurisdictions in international trade, unforeseen developments were not required for safeguards. Therefore, this decision had a big impact on the practices of administering authorities of safeguards in these countries.[28]

This decision raises an interesting question of what is a conflict of provisions in WTO agreements. As stated above, Article XIX requires that a member invoking safeguards

---

[26] WTO Panel Report 1999a; WTO Appellate Body Report 1999a.

[27] Annex 1A, 'Multilateral Agreements on Trade in Goods', in the Agreement Establishing the World Trade Organization, contains a conflict rule, which states: 'In the event of conflict between a provision of the General Agreement on Tariffs and Trade 1994 and a provision of another agreement in Annex 1A to the Agreement Establishing the World Trade Organization . . . the provision of the other agreement shall prevail to the extent of the conflict.'

[28] WTO Appellate Body Report 2003.

must prove that an increase in imports has been caused by unforeseen developments and the Safeguards Agreement does not require it. In a sense, it might be argued that while a WTO member is permitted to invoke safeguards without the requirement of unforeseen developments under the Safeguards Agreement, this right is restricted by Article XIX of the GATT. Looked at in this way, there might be a conflict between these two provisions. If there is a conflict between the two, the Safeguards Agreement prevails over Article XIX of the GATT.

In WTO law, a typical conflict of laws is a situation where one violates one provision of law by following the other provision—i.e. this is a 'damned if you do and damned if you don't' situation.[29] The situation surrounding the relationship between Article XIX of the GATT and the Safeguards Agreement is not quite this situation because, by following Article XIX of the GATT, a member does not violate any provision in the Safeguards Agreement, although that member is deprived of the right to enjoy the benefit conferred by the Safeguards Agreement that it can invoke safeguards without proving the existence of unforeseen developments. This might be called an imperfect conflict or disharmony between the two provisions. Whether this situation may be elevated to the level of conflict in the sense of the Conflict Rule is a question that future appellate decisions might have to tackle.

23.3.7 Environment

Environment and trade is becoming more and more an important issue, both for the WTO and the world at large.[30] There are several landmark decisions by the Appellate Body on trade and environment. Major decisions are the *US–Reformulated Gasoline* case,[31] *US–Shrimp-Turtle* case,[32] and the *Brazil–Tyres* case.[33] Among those decisions, *US–Shrimp-Turtle* is probably the most well known, and a brief discussion of this case follows.

In this case, the United States imposed a ban on import of shrimps from India, Pakistan, Thailand, and Malaysia for the reason that those countries did not require their fishing vessels to install TED (turtle exclusion devices)—a device to exclude sea turtles from being caught accidentally when harvesting shrimps. Those countries brought claims to the WTO on the grounds that such measures amounted to a violation of Article XI of the GATT, which prohibited an imposition of quantitative restriction of imports. The United States argued that, even if it fell under Article XI of the GATT, it would still be justified by Article XX (g) of the GATT, which states that a measure relating to the conservation of exhaustible natural resources was exempted from prohibitions of the GATT.

---

[29] WTO Panel Report. 1998a; WTO Appellate Body Report. 1998b.
[30] On trade and environment, see Hufbauer, Charnovitz, and Kim 2009; Tamiotti et al. 2009.
[31] WTO Panel Report. 1996b; WTO Appellate Body Report. 1996b.
[32] WTO Panel Report 1998c; WTO Appellate Body Report 1998c.
[33] WTO Panel Report 2007; WTO Appellate Body Report 2007.

The panel did not examine whether the US measure would be justified by Article XX (g) for the reason that the US measure amounted to a violation of the *chapeau* of Article XX of the GATT (which requires that a measure should not be an arbitrary or unjustifiable discrimination between countries where the same conditions prevail, nor a disguised restriction of international trade) because the United States invoked the ban without consulting with those four countries. The United States appealed, and the Appellate Body reversed this holding of the panel and stated that the first stage of examination should be whether the US measure fell under Article XX (g) and, after this had been established, there should be an examination of the compatibility of the US measure with the chapeau. The Appellate Body stated that the US measure fell under Article XX (g) and could have been justified, but held that it was a violation of the chapeau because the US measure was invoked unilaterally and without any consultation with the countries that would be affected by the measure.

This holding is important in that it recognized that environmental measures are covered by Article XX (g) and, therefore, environmental policies and their implementing measures can be justified under the WTO regime. This holding accords with the preamble to the Marrakesh Agreement, which declares the importance of sustainable development and the protection and preservation of the environment.[34]

Another important ruling of this decision is that it recognized the production and process method (PPM), i.e. that a WTO member can apply a measure to control imports of a product for the reason that the product was manufactured in a way that would adversely affect the environment. Also, this decision recognized that a WTO member can apply a measure to control situations that occur outside its territory (extraterritorial application) as long as these have some consequences within their territory.

23.3.8 Technical barriers to trade

Technical barriers to trade refer to trade issues arising from differences in national standards relating to product safety, product testing, product representation, and related matters. Differences among trading nations in technical standards (especially mandatory standards) may adversely affect the smooth flow of international trade by erecting artificial barriers. At the same time, it is an important duty and right of trading nations to establish technical standards and ensure that the safety of citizens in regard to various products be maintained. The Agreement on Technical Barriers to Trade (TBT) aims harmonize national standards by requiring, in Article 2.4, that national mandatory standards be based on international standards if there are any. There is a dearth of dispute

---

[34] The preamble of the Marrakesh Agreement, which established the WTO, emphasizes the importance of economic developments while 'seeking both to protect and preserve the environment and to enhance the means for doing so in a manner consistent with their respective needs and concerns at different levels of economic development'.

cases in this area. In fact, the only full-scale TBT case is the *EC–Sardines* case and this will be briefly touched upon.

In the *EC–Sardines* Case,[35] the EC required by regulation that the label 'sardines' could be used only on canned foods made of fish caught in the North Sea, the Mediterranean, and the Black Sea. Therefore, Peru was prevented from using the label 'sardines' on canned seafoods made of fish caught in its neighbouring sea areas when exporting them to the EC. The international standard on seafood representation, the Codex Alimentarius, permits that, although the mark 'sardines' should be used on seafoods produced from fish caught in the North Sea, the Mediterranean Sea, and the Black Sea, canned foods made of similar fish caught in other areas can be labelled with the mark 'sardines' if an appropriate prefix is attached such as 'Pacific sardines' or 'Peruvian sardines'. Therefore, there was a difference between the EC standard and the international standard.

Peru brought a claim against the EC and argued that, whereas Article 2.4 of the TBT Agreement requires that a mandatory national standard should be based on international standards, the EC standard in question prohibited a use of the label 'sardines' which was permitted by the international standard, the Codex Alimentarius, and was therefore inconsistent with it.

The EC standard came into being in 1989 and Article 2.4 of the TBT Agreement took effect on 1 January 1995 and, therefore, the EC standard preceded Article 2.4 of the TBT Agreement in time. The question in this case is whether a provision in the TBT Agreement can prevail and nullify a national regulation which already existed at the time when that provision came into being. The Appellate Body stated that, regardless of whether or not a provision in the TBT Agreement came into being before a national regulation, the TBT provision overruled the national regulation.

Article 2.4 states that national standards should be based on international standards 'when such standards exist or their completion is imminent'. The words 'exist' and 'completion is imminent' seem to suggest that Article 2.4 applies only to national standards that come into being after Article 2.4 took effect, or at best on national standards when applicable international standards are close to completion. This interpretation may be contrary to the wording of Article 2.4 and also the literal interpretation adopted by the Appellate Body.[36]

Article 2.4 of the TBT Agreement cuts deeply into the realm of national jurisdiction of trading nations to regulate domestic matters, and a determination of how much Article 2.4 can intervene is a delicate matter. The framers of the Article may have found a balance between the Article and the power of domestic authorities by limiting the scope of application of Article 2.4 to situations in which national standards come later in time, or at best when an applicable international standard is about to be completed. The intention of the framers may have been that the rest is reserved to the realm of national authorities.

---

[35] WTO Panel Report 2002; WTO Appellate Body Report 2002.
[36] Matsushita 2006.

23.3.9 Food safety

Trade issues relating to national regulations on food safety are akin to those of product safety as discussed in connection with the TBT Agreement. However, the Agreement on Sanitary and Phytosanitary Measures (SPS) provides specifics of food safety regulation, and when the SPS Agreement applies, the application of the TBT Agreement is excluded. Article 5.1 of the SPS Agreement requires that a WTO member should operate a risk assessment when it takes an SPS measure (a measure to protect human, animal, and plant life and ban or regulate production and sale of a product).

Among several cases dealing with SPS issues, the *EC–Hormones* case is by far the most famous and important. In this case, the EC banned sale and import of meat taken from animals treated with hormones for their growth. Since about 70 per cent of beef produced in the United States and Canada was taken from animals treated with hormones, exports from the United States and Canada to the EC were seriously damaged. The United States and Canada brought claims against the EC to the WTO.

These claims were raised by the United States and Canada in 1997 and the Appellate Body rendered the first judgment in 1998, in which the decision went against the EC and the WTO recommended that the EC make its measure conform to the recommendation.[37] However, the United States alleged that the EC did not implement the recommendation and requested a retaliation, and this was granted by the WTO. In 2003, the EC enacted a new Council regulation and claimed that the WTO requirements were fulfilled. However, the United States did not cease to apply the retaliation and the EC brought a claim that the United States was violating provisions of the DSU by continuing the retaliation even though the EC had complied with WTO requirements.[38] In 2009, a compromise was reached between the United States and Canada on the one hand and the EC on the other, and the dispute was resolved.

This dispute lasted for about ten years and several panel and Appellate Body reports were issued to resolve it. Many detailed rules were enunciated during the process of resolving this dispute. Some highlights are discussed below.

In the original case, the panel commissioned several scientists to provide opinions as to the risk that hormones would cause to human health, and the majority of the scientists stated that, as long as the residue of hormones in meat remained within the range permitted by the international standard, the Codex Alimentarius, there was no recognizable sign of risk. However, one of the scientists expressed the opinion that, even if the residue of hormones in meat remained within the range stipulated by the Codex Alimentarius, there is still a risk of humans getting cancer in one out of one million people. The panel went along with the majority opinion and held that there would be no risk as long as hormones contained in meat stayed within the range stipulated by the international standard. Since the EC did not prove by scientific evidence that there would be

---

[37] WTO Panel Report 1997a; WTO Appellate Body Report 1998a.
[38] WTO Panel Report 2008; WTO Appellate Body Report 2008.

a risk even in situations in which the content of hormones remained within this range, the EC measure was contrary to Article 5.1 of the SPS Agreement.

The EC appealed and argued that the panel ignored the view of the scientist who expressed the opinion that, even in the above situation, there would be a risk to human life and health. It argued that this amounted to an unreasonable distortion of evidence in violation of Article 11 of the DSU. The Appellate Body decided that it was a power of the panel to adopt a certain scientific opinion out of differing opinions and decide the case on the basis of this, and therefore the panel did not err in this respect. However, the Appellate Body stated that even a minority opinion deserved to be respected under some circumstances. When a dispute arose again in 2003 in connection with the implementation of the 1989 appellate decision, the Appellate Body declared this point more clearly by stating that a minority opinion can be respected and relied upon if it comes from respectable sources.

In the compliance panel, the panel commissioned scientists and made its own risk assessment as regards the question of whether the 2003 EC regulation was based on proper risk assessment. The Appellate Body reversed this ruling and held that it was beyond the power of the panel to make its own judgment as to whether there was still a risk involved in hormone-treated beef under the new EC regulation. The Appellate Body held that the power of the panel was limited to examining whether there was a reasonable linkage between scientific evidence produced by the EC and this new regulation and, as long as this relationship was established, the EC measure would be justified.

The Appellate Body limited the power of panels in dealing with SPS measures, and prohibited panels from substituting judgments of SPS authorities of trading nations with its own judgment based on opinions of the scientists it commissioned. In this way, the Appellate Body recognized the sovereign power of trading nations in dealing with SPS matters.

23.3.10 Developing countries

The majority of WTO members are developing countries. Developing countries claim that their economic and political conditions are relatively weaker than those of developed countries, more vulnerable to crisis and depressions, and they deserve special treatment in the WTO regime compared with developed country members. Reflecting this situation, the Enabling Clause was agreed upon in 1979. This decision was adopted by the GATT in 1979 and formally titled 'GATT Contracting Parties, Decision of 28 November 1979 on Differential and More Favourable Treatment'. It permits developed country members to provide preferential and more favourable treatment in tariffs and other trade terms to developing country members by granting GSP (Generalized System of Preferences)—i.e. reduced tariffs and eased other trade restrictions applied to imports from developing countries which are more favourable than those that are applied generally to non-developing countries. The *EC–Tariff Preferences* case[39] raises one issue regarding preferential treatment in connection with the Enabling Clause.

[39] WTO Panel Report 2003; WTO Appellate Body Report 2004.

In the *EC–Tariffs Preferences* case, the EC provided special preference tariffs to developing countries that were struggling with drug problems. India was not given this treatment, petitioned to the WTO and alleged that this would be a violation of Article I of the GATT (the most-favoured nation (MFN) principle). Footnote 3 to paragraph 2 (a) of the Enabling Clause requires that preferential treatment should be given on a non-discriminatory basis. The panel interpreted this provision to mean that there should be an identical treatment among developing countries, and held the EC measure to be contrary to Article I of the GATT.

The Appellate Body reversed this panel ruling on the grounds that interests of developing countries could be promoted by giving preferential treatment to a certain category of developing countries, based on their specific needs, and that the identical preferential treatment need not be given to all developing countries.

It can be observed that, in this decision, the Appellate Body adopted a teleological interpretation of WTO agreements. This interpretation may have a far-reaching consequence in other areas, such as trade and environment, which has been briefly discussed above. A developed country member might give special and preferential treatment in tariffs and other terms of trade to those developing country members striving to accomplish certain environmental objectives, such as producing biofuel instead of coal fuel or taking measures to reduce greenhouse gases for the purpose of improving the environment.

23.4 CRITICISMS OF THE APPELLATE BODY

As discussed above, the Appellate Body has accomplished much in establishing jurisprudential rules, on the basis of which disputes regarding WTO agreements are regulated. This has contributed much towards maintaining stability and predictability in international trade. However, like any human institution, the Appellate Body is not immune to infirmities and criticisms. In fact, there are many such criticisms. Some critics say that interpretations adopted by the Appellate Body are too literal and stick too much to grammatical meanings of words in the texts of WTO agreements. Some others say that the Appellate Body has overstepped the boundary of what has been assigned to it by 'making law' rather than interpreting law. On the surface, these two criticisms seem to be contradictory to each other.[40] However, those criticisms address different aspects of activities of the Appellate Body. In the following paragraphs, a review of such criticisms will be made, to see how much they are justified.

23.4.1 Literal interpretation

Some critics argue that the Appellate Body has interpreted provisions of WTO agreements too literally and this literal interpretation has deprived the Appellate Body of

---

[40] For criticisms and assessment of the activities of the Appellate Body, see Mavroidis 2008.

necessary flexibility and adaptability to interpret and apply provisions of agreements in such a way that current and newly arising issues are properly addressed. It is true that the Appellate Body has taken a literal or textual approach in interpreting provisions of agreements. In the *Japan–Alcohol* case,[41] which has been discussed already, the Appellate Body analysed the grammatical structure of Article II, paragraph 2, sentence 1 and sentence 2, and arrived at the conclusion that there should be a distinction between like products and directly competitive products, and with respect to the former any difference of treatment is per se unlawful, whereas with respect to the latter differential treatment is unlawful only when the differential treatment has been made so as to afford protection to domestic industry and there is more room to allow differential treatment. There may be a question as to whether or not this interpretation makes sense economically. However, this interpretation is faithful to the grammatical structure of the provisions in question.

It should be noted, however, that the DSU requires that panels and the Appellate Body interpret provisions of WTO agreements in accordance with the rules of customary international law on treaty interpretation, and such customary rules are reflected in the Vienna Convention on the Law of Treaties (VCLT). Article 31 of the VCLT requires treaty interpreters to abide by the words of a treaty in their ordinary meanings, their context, and purposes and objectives. It is, therefore, a mandate given to interpreters of WTO agreements to observe faithfully the dictionary meanings of words in a treaty and, in this sense, a certain degree of literalism is inevitable in WTO law.

This attitude of the Appellate Body towards literal interpretation probably originated from the position of the Appellate Body in the WTO structure. As stated earlier, although the Appellate Body has de facto the power to decide cases, formally it is an auxiliary body in relation to the DSB. Panels and the Appellate Body assist the DSB by providing reports on disputes, and it is the DSB which has the power to decide.

There is a delicate balance between this formality and the substance. The negotiators who established the WTO dispute settlement mechanism were well aware that there should be 'something like' a judiciary with a strong enforcement mechanism. On the other hand, members of the WTO have had a strong sense that the WTO is a member-run organization and it should be the members who made important decisions, including determinations in dispute settlement. WTO members would jealously defend their sovereign rights to decide matters bearing on their interests and would reject an establishment of omnipotent judiciary which hands down decisions on matters which vitally affect their domestic interests.[42]

Therefore, the establishment of the Appellate Body is a compromise between the two requirements—that there should be a strong dispute settlement body with the

---

[41] WTO Panel Report 1996a; WTO Appellate Body Report 1996a.
[42] On the delicate position of the Appellate Body in early days of the WTO, see Matsushita 2005.

power to decide cases on the one hand, and that WTO members control the process of dispute settlement mechanism on the other. Article 3:2 of the DSU, which states 'Recommendations and rulings of the DSB cannot add to or diminish the rights and obligations provided in the covered agreements', is meant to ensure that the WTO dispute settlement mechanism would not unduly interfere in the realm of domestic jurisdictions of WTO members. Again, Article 3:9 states 'The provisions of this Understanding are without prejudice to the rights of Members to seek authoritative interpretation of provisions of a covered agreement through decision-making under the WTO Agreement.' From the above, one can see that, at least in the early days of the Appellate Body, its position within the WTO organization was rather delicate.

When the Appellate Body was established, it was well aware of this potential tension between the membership and the dispute settlement mechanism, and this is probably one of the reasons that the Appellate Body took a literal approach to interpretation of WTO agreements. To be on the safe side, the Appellate Body interpreted provisions of WTO agreements literally and tried to be faithful to the intention of the membership because the intention of members is best expressed in the words of agreements and, by interpreting them literally and not deviating from the textual meaning of words in agreements, the Appellate Body could show its faithfulness to the membership. It could be said that the Appellate Body has adhered to strict literalism due to the reality that the only common ground for the members with diverse sense, social norms, culture, etc., is the agreed texts of the agreements.

It has been about 15 years since the WTO was established and the reputation of the Appellate Body is now more firmly established than it was in 1995. It is probably time for the Appellate Body to be free from this preoccupation and engage in flexible interpretation.

23.4.2 Making law rather than interpreting law

Another criticism of the Appellate Body is that it has 'made law' rather than interpreted law. Of course, any interpretation of law cannot be just a mechanical process. Interpretation necessarily involves some value judgement, whether it is a value in economic policy, or for other reasons. So the distinction between interpreting law and making law is often subtle indeed. The Appellate Body has had to interpret provisions of WTO agreements where the meaning is unclear due to the fact that a provision in an agreement that is the subject of interpretation is a political compromise and thus unclear. Therefore, some elements of making law inevitably come in when interpreting provisions of law unless the provision in question is absolutely crystal clear and just a mechanical interpretation suffices.

Heated debates were made in the DSB when the Appellate Body made a ruling on the issue of whether an amicus curiae brief submitted by a person other than the disputing parties and third parties to a dispute could be accepted and considered.[43] The Appellate Body decided affirmatively on this issue and many WTO members strongly criticized the Appellate Body as having overstepped the jurisdictional boundary assigned to it.

There is no provision in the DSU on whether panels and the Appellate Body can accept and consider an amicus brief from persons other than disputing parties and third parties. This issue was raised first in connection with panels. In the *US–Shrimp-Turtle* case,[44] amicus briefs were submitted to the panel by NGOs. With respect to the question of whether the panel can accept amicus briefs from persons other than parties to the dispute, the Appellate Body ruled that Article 13 of the DSU empowered panels to 'seek' information from any sources, and the power to seek necessarily includes the power to receive any information, including amicus briefs. The question of whether or not the Appellate Body was empowered to accept and consider amicus briefs came up in the *US–Steel Bar* case.[45] The Appellate Body decided that the DSU gave more power to the Appellate Body than it did to panels and, since panels were empowered to accept and consider amicus briefs, it followed by logical necessity that the Appellate Body was empowered to accept and consider such briefs.

It should be noted that the Appellate Body is cautious about not making law, especially when the issue is under negotiation. In a dispute between the United States and the EU which involved the interpretation of DSU Articles 21 and 22, known as the 'sequence issue', the Appellate Body, after noting that there had been a proposal to the General Council to amend both Articles, clearly stated that 'Only WTO Members have the authority to amend the DSU or to adopt such interpretations... Determining what the rules and procedures of the DSU ought to be is not our responsibility.'[46]

Provisions of the DSU are rather scanty and they do not provide sufficient guidance to panels and the Appellate Body when they deal with disputes. In resolving disputes, procedural principles such as burden of proof, standard of review, and evidence that they could consider (including amicus briefs) are essential. Such basic principles of litigation were largely formulated by the Appellate Body through its rulings. It is fair to say that, given the fact that there was little provision in the DSU, the Appellate Body has had to 'create' procedural principles by relying on scanty language in the DSU. It is, therefore, lacunas in the DSU which promote the Appellate Body to 'make law' in the enforcement of WTO agreements. It should be the responsibility of the WTO membership to provide sufficient rules and provisions so that arbiters in WTO disputes would not have to overexpand the powers given to them.

[43] For details, see Donaldson 2005, especially 1332–5.
[44] WTO Panel Report 1998b; WTO Appellate Body Report 1998c.
[45] WTO Panel Report 1999c; WTO Appellate Body Report 2000b.
[46] WTO Appellate Body Report 2000a, paragraphs 91–2.

23.5 Conclusion—some suggestions for the future

In spite of the criticisms of the Appellate Body as touched upon above, it is fair to say that it has made a tremendous accomplishment in building the WTO jurisprudence and this has provided stability and predictability in the international trading system. As stated earlier, the Appellate Body contributed much towards establishing a rule-oriented international trading system. It tends to provide fairness in resolving disputes among WTO members.

However, like any human institution, the Appellate Body is not without problems and some suggestions are worth thinking about with regard to possibilities for improving this institution. In view of the good performance of the Appellate Body and the WTO dispute settlement mechanism, the best policy towards this system is, as the Sutherland Report suggests, 'to do no harm' to it.[47] However, the writer would suggest some possibilities for improvement.

One criticism raised against the Appellate Body is that it is engaged in 'making law' rather than interpreting law. There are sentiments behind this criticism that the Appellate Body's power is in fact unlimited and there may be aggrandizement of power on the part of the Appellate Body, and this may in turn lead to usurpation of powers reserved to the WTO membership. Therefore, this criticism is a cry for a constitutional check mechanism which would moderate exercises of power by the Appellate Body.

There are some critics who argue that the WTO dispute resolution system has been too much judicialized and the international trade communities are not mature enough to adopt it. This view argues that the WTO dispute settlement system should adopt 'political resolution', i.e. resolution of disputes through negotiation.[48] In fact, the dispute settlement system under the GATT 1947 was characterized by a less judicialized and more politically oriented format for the resolution of disputes. However, experience shows that dispute settlement through political negotiations tends to be a power-oriented negotiation and to create instability and injustice. Therefore, this should be regarded as a regress rather than a progress.

It is unfortunate for the WTO dispute settlement mechanism and for the Appellate Body that there is no effective system of 'checks and balances' in the WTO system. In domestic jurisdictions, if the Supreme Court makes a mistake, the legislature can correct it by legislation. In the WTO, the role of legislature should be played by the ministerial conference. However, unfortunately, the political situations surrounding the ministerial conference do not allow it to play such a role. In this respect, there are no effective checks and balances of power with regard to dispute settlement and legislation in the WTO.

---

[47] World Trade Organization 2004, 49.
[48] One of the most prominent among such critics is Barfield 2001.

One suggestion may be to create a group of experts within the WTO, a peer group which would periodically review decisions rendered by the Appellate Body. This group may applaud or criticize decisions of the Appellate Body, but it would have no power to overrule decisions of the Appellate Body. However, the Appellate Body would be expected to take into account the views expressed in reports of this group. The group would be established within the WTO, and would be more informal than formal. The members of this group should be appointed from among respected professional persons such as lawyers, judges, academics, and others. This is not meant to create a formal checks and balances system within the dispute settlement mechanism but just to give the Appellate Body chances of reflecting on its own decisions.

Another idea is to promote the use of Article XI: 2 of the Marrakesh Agreement, which states: 'The Ministerial Conference and the General Council shall have the exclusive authority to adopt interpretations of the Agreement and the Multilateral Trade Agreements ... The decision to adopt an interpretation shall be taken by a three-fourths majority of the Members.' Under this Article, the WTO membership is given the power to overrule decisions of the Appellate Body. A question is whether or not the requirement of a three-fourths majority is too strict to meet. Should this be a simple majority or two-thirds majority rule? The ministerial conference and the General Council are political bodies and, for the sake of maintaining stability, predictability, and fairness, it is probably not desirable to make this process too easy, because then judicial or quasi-judicial decisions are easily overturned by political decisions. Therefore, a simple majority rule may be too prone to political abuses. The idea of introducing a two-thirds majority rule may be worth thinking about.

REFERENCES

Barfield, Claude. 2001. *Free Trade, Sovereignty, Democracy: The Future of the World Trade Organization.* Washington, DC: American Enterprise Institute Press.

Bohanes, Jan, and Nicholas Lockhart. 2009. Standard of Review in WTO Law. In *The Oxford Handbook of International Trade Law*, edited by Daniel Bethlehem, Donald McRae, Rodney Neufeld, and Isabelle Van Damme, 378–436. Oxford: Oxford University Press.

Choi, Won-Mog. 2003. *'Like Products' in International Trade Law: Towards a Consistent GATT/ WTO Jurisprudence.* Oxford: Oxford University Press.

Donaldson, Victoria. 2005. The Appellate Body: Institutional and Procedural Aspects. In *The World Trade Organization: Legal, Economic and Political Analysis*, volume I, edited by Patrick F. J. Macrory, Arthur E. Appleton, and Michael G. Plummer, 1279–339. New York: Springer.

GATT Panel Report. 1992. *US–Measures Affecting Alcoholic and Malt Beverages.* Adopted on 19 June 1992. DS23/R, BISD 39S/206. Geneva: GATT.

Grando, Michelle T. 2006. Allocating the Burden of Proof in WTO Disputes: A Critical Analysis. *Journal of International Economic Law* 9 (3):615–56.

Hufbauer, Gary, Steve Charnovitz, and Jisun Kim. 2009. *Global Warming and the World Trading System.* Washington, DC: Peterson Institute for International Economics.

Industrial Structure Council. 2008. *2008 Report on Compliance by Major Trading Partners with Trade Agreements—WTO, FTA/EPA, BIT.* Japan: Ministry of Economy, Trade and Industry. Available from <http://www.meti.go.jp/english/report/data/gCT08_1coe.html>. Accessed 11 November 2011

Jackson, John H. 1997. *The World Trading System: Law and Policy of International Economic Relations.* 2nd edition. Cambridge, MA: MIT Press.

Matsushita, Mitsuo. 1987. A Japanese View of United States Trade Laws. *Northwestern Journal of International Law and Business* 8 (1):29–58.

Matsushita, Mitsuo. 1999. Section 301 of the Trade Act of 1974: The Impact of US Unilateral Measures on Japan and Asian Countries. In *North America & the Asia-Pacific in the 21st Century,* edited by K. S. Nathan, 131–54. London: ASEAN Academic Press.

Matsushita, Mitsuo. 2005. Some Thoughts on the Appellate Body. In *The World Trade Organization: Legal, Economic and Political Analysis,* volume I, edited by Patrick F. J. Macrory, Arthur E. Appleton, and Michael G. Plummer, 1390–403. New York: Springer.

Matsushita, Mitsuo. 2006. Sovereignty Issues in Interpreting WTO Agreements: The Sardines Case and Article 2.4 of the TBT Agreement. In *Reform and Development of the WTO Dispute Settlement System,* edited by Dencho Gorgiev and Kim van der Borght, 191–9. London: Cameron May.

Mavroidis, Petros C. 2008. Legal Eagles? The WTO Appellate Body's First Ten Years. In *The WTO: Governance, Dispute Settlement & Developing Countries,* edited by Merit E. Janow, Victoria Donaldson, and Alan Yanovich, 345–67. New York: Juris Publishing Company.

Tamiotti, Ludivine, Robert Teh, Vesile Kulaçoğlu, Anne Olhoff, Benjamin Simmons, and Hussein Abaza. 2009. *Trade and Climate Change: A Report by the United Nations Environment Programme and the World Trade Organization.* WTO/UNEP, Geneva.

US Congress. 2008. Omnibus Trade and Competitiveness Act of 1988. Conference Report: Report 100–576. 100th Congress, 2nd Session, April.

Wilcox, Clair. 1949. *A Charter for World Trade.* New York: Macmillan.

Wilson, R.R. 1947. Proposed ITO Charter 1947. *American Journal of International Law* 41(4):879–85.

WTO. 2004. *The Future of the WTO: Addressing Institutional Challenges in the New Millenium.* Report of the Consultative Board to the Director-General Supachai Panitchpakdi. Geneva: WTO.

WTO. 2009. *A Handbook on the WTO Dispute Settlement System.* WTO Secretariat Publication prepared for publication by the Legal Affairs Division and the Appellate Body. Cambridge: Cambridge University Press.

WTO Appellate Body Report. 1996a. *Japan–Taxes on Alcoholic Beverages.* WT/DS8/AB/R, WT/DS10/AB/R, WT/DS11/AB/R. Geneva: WTO.

WTO Appellate Body Report. 1996b. *US–Standards for Reformulated and Conventional Gasoline.* WT/DS2/AB/R. Adopted 29 April 1996. Geneva: WTO.

WTO Appellate Body Report. 1997a. *US–Measures Affecting Imports of Wool Shirts and Blouses from India.* WT/DS33/AB/R, 97-1973. Geneva: WTO.

WTO Appellate Body Report. 1997b. *US–Restrictions on Imports of Cotton and Man-Made Fibre Underwear.* WT/DS24/AB/R. Adopted 25 February 1997. DSR 1997. Geneva: WTO.

WTO Appellate Body Report. 1998a. *EC–Measures Concerning Meat and Meat Products (Hormones).* WT/DS26/AB/R, WT/DS48/AB/R. Adopted 13 February 1998. Geneva: WTO.

WTO Appellate Body Report. 1998b. *Guatemala–Anti-Dumping Investigation Regarding Portland Cement from Mexico*. WT/DS60/AB/R. Geneva: WTO.

WTO Appellate Body Report. 1998c. *US–Import Prohibition of Certain Shrimp and Shrimp Products*. WT/DS58/AB/R. Geneva: WTO.

WTO Appellate Body Report. 1999a. *Argentina–Safeguard Measures on Imports of Footwear*. WT/DS121/AB/R. Geneva: WTO.

WTO Appellate Body Report. 1999b. *Canada–Measures Affecting the Export of Civilian Aircraft*. WT/DS70/AB/R. Geneva: WTO.

WTO Appellate Body Report. 2000a. *US–Import Measures on Certain Products from the European Communities*. WT/DS165/AB/R. Geneva: WTO.

WTO Appellate Body Report. 2000b. *US–Imposition of Countervailing Duties on Certain Hot-Rolled Lead and Bismuth Carbon Steel Products Originating in the United Kingdom*. WT/DS138/AB/R. Geneva: WTO.

WTO Appellate Body Report. 2001a. *EC–Anti-Dumping Duties on Imports of Cotton-Type Bed Linen from India*. WT/DS141/AB/R. Adopted 12 March 2001. DSR 2001: V, 2049. Geneva: WTO.

WTO Appellate Body Report. 2001b. *EC–Measures Affecting Asbestos and Asbestos-Containing Products*. WT/DS135/AB/R, 01-1157. Geneva: WTO.

WTO Appellate Body Report. 2002. *EC–Trade Description of Sardines*. WT/DS231/AB/R. Adopted 23 October 2002. Geneva: WTO.

WTO Appellate Body Report. 2003. *US–Definitive Safeguard Measures on Imports of Certain Steel Products*. WT/DS248/AB/R, WT/DS249/AB/R, WT/DS253/AB/R, WT/DS254/AB/R, WT/DS259/AB/R. Adopted 10 December 2003. Geneva: WTO.

WTO Appellate Body Report. 2004. *EC–Conditions for the Granting of Tariff Preferences to Developing Countries*. WT/DS246/AB/R. Geneva: WTO.

WTO Appellate Body Report. 2005. *US–Measures Affecting the Cross-Border Supply of Gambling and Betting Services*. WT/DS285/AB/R. Adopted 20 April 2005. Geneva: WTO.

WTO Appellate Body Report. 2007. *Brazil–Measures Affecting Imports of Retreaded Tyres*. WT/DS332/AB/R. Geneva: WTO.

WTO Appellate Body Report. 2008. *Canada/US–Continued Suspension of Obligations in the EC–Hormones Dispute*. WT/DS320/AB/R, WT/DS321/AB/R. Adopted 14 November 2008. Geneva: WTO.

WTO Panel Report. 1996a. *Japan–Taxes on Alcoholic Beverages*. WT/DS8/R, 96-2651. Geneva: WTO.

WTO Panel Report. 1996b. *US–Standards for Reformulated and Conventional Gasoline*. WT/DS2/R. Adopted 29 April 1996. Geneva: WTO.

WTO Panel Report. 1997a. *EC–Measures Concerning Meat and Meat Products (Hormones)*. WT/DS26/R/USA, WT/DS48/R/CAN. Adopted 13 February 1998. Geneva: WTO.

WTO Panel Report. 1997b. *US–Measures Affecting Imports of Wool Shirts and Blouses from India*. WT/DS33/R, 97-0001. Geneva: WTO.

WTO Panel Report. 1997c. *US–Restrictions on Imports of Cotton and Man-Made Fibre Underwear*. WT/DS24/R. Adopted on 25 February 1997. DSR. Geneva: WTO.

WTO Panel Report. 1998a. *Guatemala–Anti-Dumping Investigation Regarding Portland Cement from Mexico*. WT/DS60/R, WT/DS156/R. 19 June 1998. Geneva: WTO.

WTO Panel Report. 1998b. *US–Import Prohibition of Certain Shrimp and Shrimp Products*. WT/DS58/R, 98-1710. Geneva: WTO.

WTO Panel Report. 1999a. *Argentina–Safeguard Measures on Imports of Footwear*. WT/DS121/R. Geneva: WTO.

WTO Panel Report. 1999b. *Canada–Measures Affecting the Export of Civilian Aircraft*. WT/DS70/R. Geneva: WTO.

WTO Panel Report. 1999c. *US–Imposition of Countervailing Duties on Certain Hot-Rolled Lead and Bismuth Carbon Steel Products Originating in the United Kingdom*. WT/DS138/R. Geneva: WTO.

WTO Panel Report. 1999d. *US–Sections 301–310 of the Trade Act of 1974*. WT/DS152/R. Adopted on 27 January 2000. Geneva: WTO.

WTO Panel Report. 2000. *EC–Anti-Dumping Duties on Imports of Cotton-Type Bed Linen from India*. WT/DS141/R. Adopted on 12 March 2001. DSR 2001: VI, 2077. Geneva: WTO.

WTO Panel Report. 2002. *EC–Trade Description of Sardines*. WT/DS231/R. Adopted 23 October 2002. DSR 2002: VIII, 3451. Geneva: WTO.

WTO Panel Report. 2003. *EC–Conditions for the Granting of Tariff Preferences to Developing Countries*. WT/DS246/R. Geneva: WTO.

WTO Panel Report. 2004. *US–Measures Affecting the Cross-Border Supply of Gambling and Betting Services*. WT/DS285/R. Adopted on 20 April 2005. Geneva: WTO.

WTO Panel Report. 2007. *Brazil–Measures Affecting Imports of Retreaded Tyres*. WT/DS332/R. Geneva: WTO.

WTO Panel Report. 2008. *Canada/US–Continued Suspension of Obligations in the EC–Hormones Dispute*. WT/DS320/R, WT/DS321/R. Adopted 14 November 2008. Geneva: WTO.

CHAPTER 24

WTO JUDICIAL INTERPRETATION

GREGORY SHAFFER AND JOEL TRACHTMAN[*]

24.1 INTRODUCTION

THIS chapter develops a comparative institutional analytic framework for studying approaches to interpretation of the agreements of the World Trade Organization (WTO). The aim is to provide an analytic framework for describing and assessing the consequences of choices in treaty interpretation, referring to examples from WTO case law. Judicial interpretation implicates a range of interacting social decision-making processes, including domestic, regional, and international political, administrative, judicial, and market processes—which we refer to collectively as *institutions*. Our definition of institutions expands on those used in institutional economics, in order to focus attention not just on institutions as constraints on future decision-making established to increase welfare, but also on the way that institutions determine *social decision-making processes*.

Alternative interpretive choices regarding the meaning of texts can be viewed in terms of institutional choices—that is, in terms of their implications for different social decision-making processes, affecting the articulation and mediation of individual preferences, and, ultimately, social welfare. These interpretive choices can be viewed through a comparative institutional lens—that is, in comparison to the implications of the alternative drafting and interpretive choices for different institutions. By comparatively analysing the institutional dynamics associated with different interpretive choices, in which individuals participate or are otherwise represented to varying extents, we can begin to understand how choices in treaty drafting and interpretation affect the articulation and

* The authors are grateful to Gabrielle Marceau, Petros Mavroidis, and Joost Pauwelyn for their comments. Errors are ours.

institutional mediation of individual preferences, and (in this way) domestic and global economic welfare. In the case of the WTO, interpretive choices implicate the interaction of institutions for domestic, regional, and global governance.

Like any dispute settlement body confronting a legal text, WTO panels and the Appellate Body have choices in applying the text to particular factual scenarios that are not specifically addressed by the text. More than one WTO provision or WTO agreement may apply to the factual situation, whether the provisions are drafted as fairly precise rules, more open-ended standards, or exceptions. Interpretive claims are made before panels, and the resolution of these interpretive arguments has important consequences, not only regarding who wins or loses a particular case, but also regarding broader systemic issues of domestic and international policy.

These consequences of treaty interpretation can be viewed in *welfare terms* (regarding the efficiency and distributive consequences of a particular interpretation) and in *participatory terms* (regarding the quality and extent of participation in the decision-making processes at issue). In terms of participation, we refer to the effect of a WTO interpretive choice on the allocation of authority over a particular issue to different social decision-making processes, such as domestic political and administrative processes, international political and administrative processes, markets, and judicial bodies. In each of these social decision-making processes, individuals' perspectives are directly or indirectly represented and mediated in different ways. The institutional effects of interpretive choices can thus be viewed in comparative participatory terms. Regardless of how imperfect participation may be in each alternative social decision-making process implicated by WTO texts and their interpretation, the imperfections will not be the same.

These two approaches to analysis (welfare-based and participation-based) are related, and not opposed. In fact, they have significant overlaps, and the addition of the participation-based criteria may be understood in welfarist terms.[1] In a system where welfare consequences are difficult to calculate, the quality and extent of participation can serve as a proxy for both efficiency and distributive consequences. The different dynamics of participation characterizing different institutional forums will determine the pursuit of a particular social goal, whether it be resource allocation efficiency, justice as fairness, human rights, sustainable development, or whatever other goal might be sought. All of these goals are susceptible to inclusion in a welfarist analysis.

The remainder of this chapter is divided into three sections. Section 24.2 presents an analytical template for comparative institutional analysis of treaty design and interpretive choice regarding dispute settlement. Section 24.3 assesses the implications for social decision-making processes of the interpretive choices made within WTO dispute settlement. It assesses each of these choices in comparative welfare and participatory terms, and provides examples from WTO case law. Section 24.4 concludes.

---

[1] Komesar 1996, 2008.

24.2 The parameters of institutional choice in dispute settlement and interpretation

New institutional economics proposes that individuals, firms, and states select institutional devices in order to maximize welfare benefits, net of transaction costs and strategic costs.[2] We may understand not only private ordering decisions, but also mechanisms for majority voting, administrative delegation, and dispute settlement, in these terms. We may also understand and compare different interpretive approaches in these terms, although there has been much less work in this area. The designers of international dispute settlement do not exercise extensive control over the second order decision-making of judicial bodies, which is probably why new institutional economics has attended less to this phenomenon. Yet general interpretive approaches and particular interpretive choices can be examined in terms of their costs and benefits in social welfare terms. In a related way, they can be understood in terms of their effect on the form and level of participation in decision-making, which can serve as a proxy for assessing social welfare.

Our discussion of welfare effects will be relatively straightforward. While we are normatively interested in public interest-type economic welfare, we also recognize, descriptively, that in the international relations context, institutions may be chosen to promote public choice-type welfare: the welfare of government officials. To the extent that the domestic political system successfully aligns public choice-type welfare with public interest-type welfare—that is, to the extent that the domestic political system is responsive—these measures of welfare are congruent. We also recognize that, in the trade context, the fundamental theorem of welfare economics will often (but not always) align national and global public interest welfare with free trade. A particular challenge arises when trade liberalization goals interact with other social policy preferences. In addition to considering the welfare and public choice efficiency of interpretive choices, we must also consider their distributive effects.

While we examine welfare and public choice efficiency separately from participation, we believe that participation can be understood in welfarist terms, and so this separation is in important respects artificial. Welfare analysis is based on methodological and normative individualism: welfare only exists in terms of the preferences of individuals. If we are to analyse welfare from outside the mind of an individual, we must refer to revealed preferences. In the economics of market behaviour, these revealed preferences are analysed through purchases and sales, and equilibrium pricing. But preferences can be inferred from other behaviours as well. One such behaviour, which affects and interacts with market activity, is political participation, which involves both individuals and interest groups. In this sense, participation is not an alternative to welfare, but a method of gauging welfare through revealed preferences.

---

[2] North 1990; Williamson 1985.

Turning to judicial interpretation, different interpretive choices with respect to a legal text can be viewed as affecting participation by allocating authority over an issue to different social decision-making processes. Individuals are able to participate to different degrees in these social decision-making processes, affecting the articulation, mediation, and attainment of their preferences, and thus of social welfare.

In addition, participation may be understood intrinsically as a preference: individuals may value the possibility for participation, separately from the ability that participation gives them to affect decisions. We do not have an empirical method by which to separate this second welfare role for participation, but we recognize that it may be significant in many contexts. Our discussion of participation generally recognizes that greater accountability, transparency, and opportunities for input in different social decision-making processes will often be valued in themselves, as well as for the articulation and furtherance of individual preferences.

Within the overall category of participation, we examine the relative degree of transparency, accountability, and legitimacy that a particular interpretive choice entails. By 'transparency', we mean the extent to which the decision-making is observable by citizens. By 'accountability', we mean the extent to which decision-making can be influenced by citizens. By 'legitimacy', we mean the overall extent to which citizens believe that the interpretive choice has been structured so as to provide a fair and accurate method by which to reflect citizens' preferences.

Finally, we stress that institutions interact. Judicial interpretation is part of this dynamic process of institutional interaction, horizontally and vertically, across different levels of social organization. In this chapter, we set forth an institutional understanding of certain choices made in connection with WTO judicial interpretation. Our focus is on alternative social decision-making processes, ultimately affecting *who decides* a policy issue, and thereby affecting social welfare.

24.3 JUDICIAL INTERPRETIVE CHOICE WITHIN WTO DISPUTE SETTLEMENT AS INSTITUTIONAL CHOICE

Legal texts are always indeterminate at some level, which is why their meaning is intensely debated and reasonable interpreters often disagree. Under all interpretive theories and methodologies, there are inevitably disagreements regarding a WTO text's meaning. What, for example, is the meaning of 'like product' in the various agreements? The Appellate Body has found that it varies depending on the context, writing in the *Japan–Alcoholic Beverages* case that, 'The concept of "likeness" is a relative one that evokes the image of an accordion. The accordion of "likeness" stretches and squeezes in different places as different provisions of the WTO Agreement are applied . . . [in relation to] the context and the circumstances that prevail in any given case.'[3] Similarly, what is the meaning of 'exhaustible natural resources' in Article XX of the GATT? The Appellate Body said that the meaning of the term 'natural resources' is 'not "static" but is rather *"by definition, evolutionary"*'.[4] What if two provisions potentially apply, potentially leading to different results, with one setting forth a more general standard and the other a more specific rule?

In short, the analysis of a text's 'ordinary meaning' can only get an interpreter so far. In some cases, that meaning is generally settled among all affected parties, which makes that case 'easy'. In many cases, however, the meaning of a particular provision, including in the light of other provisions in the WTO texts and other international law, may be highly contested as applied to different factual contexts. What does a panel do in such cases? Although constrained in the interpretation of WTO texts, the WTO Appellate Body and panels retain important interpretive choices, and these choices implicate the operation of other social decision-making processes, and ultimately affect social welfare.

This section takes the subsequent analytical step: to examine the implications for other social decision-making processes of different interpretive choices made by the WTO Appellate Body and panels. The section examines how panels and the Appellate Body make interpretive decisions that can effectively delegate responsibility to different social decision-making processes, including to national political and administrative processes, WTO political bodies, other international organizations with specific functional mandates (such as standard-setting organizations), international market processes (by stringently reviewing and ruling against national decisions that adversely affect imports), and the dispute settlement panels themselves (by engaging in judicial balancing and process-based review). In making these institutional choices, the Appellate Body and panels can reallocate decision-making authority over the issues at stake, including by delegating the determination of some underlying factual issues in disputes to experts with technical expertise, such as scientists and economists.

Each of these interpretive choices, with its institutional implications, has different effects on welfare and participation. We look at each of these choices individually and comparatively in terms of their welfare, distributive, and participation implications, giving examples in each case from WTO case law. None of these institutional choices is perfect from the perspectives of social welfare maximization, distributive fairness, or the direct or indirect participation in decision-making of affected stakeholders. Under each alternative, stakeholder positions will be heard and affected in different and imperfect ways. Different interpretive choices can thus be analysed using a comparative institutional analytic method that focuses on the relative implications of interpretive choices for welfare and participation.

---

[3] WTO Appellate Body Report 1996.

[4] WTO Appellate Body Report 1998b, paragraph 130 (emphasis added). It also held that the words 'must be read ... in the light of contemporary concerns of the community of nations about the protection and conservation of the environment'. Id., paragraph 129.

We leave for another work discussion of the institutional choices made by treaty-writers in connection with interpretation of texts in dispute settlement. These choices include reference to the rules of interpretation of customary international law, including a focus on text as opposed to *travaux préparatoires*, the selection of specific rules as opposed to broader standards, specific reference to non-WTO sources of rules, retention of capacity for 'legislative veto', and member state defiance or civil disobedience.

24.3.1 Allocation of decision-making to WTO political processes, or to subsets of WTO members

It is possible to evaluate the allocation of authority within the WTO using a structural model of horizontal and vertical allocation of powers: examining the relationship and checks and balances between legislative, executive, and adjudicative components. While the WTO's executive function is handled largely by the WTO Secretariat and is relatively limited, the relationship between adjudication and legislation—between the judicial branch and the legislative branch—is of particular interest. The legislative branch, understood here as the members in their treaty-making and treaty-oversight capacity, is presumably omnipotent, but it only exercises its power after long rounds of negotiations, or in very limited and infrequent amendments and interpretive understandings. The interpretive choices of the Appellate Body and panels in a dispute settlement system which is automatic and binding can thus easily affect this allocation of powers.

The practice of voting by consensus makes it practically impossible for WTO members to override an Appellate Body or panel decision. This difficulty affects the horizontal allocation of powers provided in the WTO agreements. The WTO agreements provide for specific types of decision-making by the parties, and delegate this decision-making authority to certain committees within the WTO, such as the Committee on Balance of Payments and the Committee on Regional Trade Agreements. Although still subject to the constraint of voting by consensus, the extensive WTO committee system represents a form of political decision-making that can be used to elaborate and guide the meaning of texts and help mediate disputes before they result in full litigation. In one anti-dumping case, for example, a dispute settlement panel referenced a recommendation of the Committee on Anti-Dumping Practices in 2000 as providing the applicable norm to guide interpretation.[5] Moreover, approximately 75 international organizations hold observer status within the WTO, and WTO Secretariat members reciprocally attend the meetings of many of these international organizations. These arrangements permit the WTO Secretariat and the trade representatives of the WTO members to be aware of developments in other areas of international law, and permit the secretariats and state representatives of other international organizations to be aware of the implications of WTO law for their areas.

---

[5] WTO Panel Report 2003, paragraph 7.321 and n.272.

These political processes within WTO committees, however, have yet to exclude the dispute settlement system from exercising jurisdiction in matters falling within their areas of concern. For example, the Appellate Body has found that specific WTO treaty provisions confirm the availability of dispute settlement regarding the issues of whether a balance of payments exception or customs union exists, and it has thus interpreted and enforced these provisions.[6] The specific assignment of decision-making authority to these political bodies has thus not stopped the Appellate Body from issuing rulings over a claim in these areas. The WTO Appellate Body has generally so far declined to recognize a form of 'political question' doctrine, pursuant to which it will defer questions to the WTO's political branches and thus refrain from ruling on particular WTO claims, at least in cases where it finds that the agreement at issue specifically confirms the availability of dispute settlement. Nor has it recognized a concept of *non liquet*, pursuant to which it will refuse to issue a ruling where it finds that existing WTO law does not cover an issue.[7] As a result, WTO dispute settlement is available to interpret and enforce WTO provisions even where the application of these provisions is also expressly assigned to political decision-making or there is an alleged 'gap' in the law. Importantly, the practice of voting by consensus has prevented political decision-making in these cases, so that the judicial process can be viewed as deciding them by default.

Through interpretation, the WTO Appellate Body and panels can allocate decision-making implicitly to other political processes by signalling that they will take into account other agreements between the parties to a dispute. This issue arose, for example, in the *US–Shrimp–Turtle* case. There, the Appellate Body's report noted that the United States had successfully negotiated the signature of an Inter-American Convention for the Protection and Conservation of Sea Turtles, which demonstrates that 'multilateral procedures are available and feasible'.[8] The Appellate Body found that the United States never seriously attempted to negotiate a similar agreement with the four Asian complainants. In this way, in the particular context of the *chapeau* of Article XX of the GATT, the Appellate Body tried to foster an ad hoc political approach by requiring the United States to attempt to negotiate harmonized substantive rules before implementing a ban that could trigger a dispute before the WTO judicial process. When Malaysia subsequently challenged the United States for failing to reach a negotiated settlement through such a multilateral process, the Appellate Body held that the United States only needed to engage in good faith negotiations, but was not required to conclude an agreement.[9]

In other words, in the *US–Shrimp–Turtle* case, the Appellate Body implicitly accepted the possibility that a subset of WTO members themselves might define, in its words, the 'line of equilibrium' between regulatory restrictions and liberalized trade under the

  [6] WTO Appellate Body Report 1999a, paragraph 87; WTO Appellate Body Report 1999b, paragraph 9.50–9.51.
  [7] Steinberg 2004.
  [8] WTO Appellate Body Report 1998b, paragraphs 166–70.
  [9] WTO Appellate Body Report 2001c, paragraphs 122–3.

chapeau of Article XX.[10] This decision can be viewed as setting a factual standard as to what types of national efforts will satisfy the requirements of the *chapeau*, while also re-delegating to subsets of members implicated in a dispute the authority to decide on an arrangement, pursuant to which the national trade-restrictive measure would be able to meet Article XX requirements. This allocation of authority is, nonetheless, significantly more circumscribed, and more provision-specific, than allowing subsets of members to vary their obligations *inter se*, which does not appear to be formally permissible under the WTO charter.

It is impossible to evaluate this institutional choice of allocating authority to a subset of WTO members from the standpoint of economic welfare without addressing the competing priorities held by the affected parties, because this type of decision involves commensuration between diverse values. From the standpoint of political efficiency, in a public choice sense, such sub-multilateral arrangements are likely to be efficient, so long as they do not confer negative externalities on the governments of other states. Similarly, if the arrangements do not result in negative externalities to other constituencies, then they can be viewed as more appropriate from a participatory perspective, again depending on the domestic politics of the subset of WTO members for their transparency, accountability, and legitimacy. By virtue of the political consensus among the contending states, concerns regarding both efficiency and participation are to some extent addressed. A number of commentators have thus contended that such international political processes should become institutionalized within the WTO,[11] or outside of it and in collaboration with it.[12] It should be mentioned, however, that it is likely that a rule of consensus or unanimity could frequently result in a minority blocking what might otherwise be an efficient outcome, or an outcome that would enhance stakeholder participation.

Overall, delegation of decision-making authority to an international political process is, like other institutional alternatives, subject to trade-offs from the standpoints of welfare and participation. Even if international political processes were made more robust, they are subject to biases on account of resource and power imbalances, collective action problems, and general citizen apathy towards a distant forum. The bureaucracies of large, wealthy countries have greater resources, and larger, more experienced staffs. Interest groups from these countries are more likely to have greater funds to represent their views at the international level than do developing country interest groups. The development of international political governance mechanisms can nonetheless provide a focal point for political negotiations that can make the conflicting norms, priorities, and interests at stake in trade social policy conflicts more transparent, potentially

---

[10] WTO Appellate Body Report 1998b, paragraph 170 ('the parties to the Inter-American Convention marked out the equilibrium line'). The obligation to negotiate was rejected by the Appellate Body in the *Gambling* case, in the context of the subheadings of Article XIV of GATS—in a provision equivalent to the necessity requirement of Article XX(b) of GATT. WTO Appellate Body Report 2005.

[11] Guzman 2004.

[12] Esty 1994; Shaffer 2001.

enhancing global welfare. By bringing developing country perspectives, that might otherwise be suppressed in a litigation context, to the fore, political bargaining might facilitate targeted financial transfers that would be more equitable and efficient in addressing environmental and development goals. Yet political bargaining also brings to the fore the role of power as compared to legal right, and may provide better opportunities for strong states to prevail over the interests of weaker ones in the resolution of disputes.

24.3.2 Recognition of other international political processes through taking account of other international law

One way for the judicial process to allocate authority to other political processes is through its treatment of other (non-WTO) international law. The question of what law is to be applied and interpreted in WTO dispute settlement raises both treaty design and interpretive questions which have significant institutional implications. Application of, or reference to, non-WTO international law can be viewed as a way of effectively delegating decision-making authority to the non-WTO source of other international law. The drafters of the WTO agreements made certain choices clear, but left others open. Some of these have been raised in WTO disputes and have also been the subject of considerable academic commentary.

It is clear, and undisputed, that when states agreed, in the Uruguay Round, to the Dispute Settlement Understanding (DSU), they did not create a court of general jurisdiction. As a result, only claims based on WTO law may be adjudicated under the DSU. This choice of international treaty design is certainly an important institutional one: the creation of a court capable of interpreting and applying claims under WTO law, but not authorized to entertain claims under other international law, empowers certain institutions, laws, and values in relation to others.

Yet there may be circumstances in which non-WTO law is relevant to a claim based on WTO law, raising questions of interpretive choice having institutional implications. For example, it may be that a multilateral environmental treaty or a customary rule of human rights law could apply as a defence to a WTO obligation. That is, under certain circumstances, a norm of customary international law (including but not limited to *jus cogens*) or another international treaty provision could trump a claim under WTO law, should the two conflict. There is no question that these non-WTO rules of international law may apply to state conduct. The more difficult question is whether, when states agreed to the DSU, they meant panels and the Appellate Body to apply non-WTO international law. Panels and the Appellate Body are not courts of general jurisdiction, but what is the law that they are assigned to interpret and apply?

The DSU does not explicitly specify the body of applicable law that WTO adjudicators are assigned to interpret and apply, although it does provide that the mandate to panels and the Appellate Body is 'to clarify the existing provisions of the [WTO-covered agreements]', which are listed in Appendix 1 to the DSU.[13] The Appellate Body has said clearly that WTO adjudicators are not empowered to interpret non-WTO international law for purposes of applying non-WTO international law. In the *Mexico–Soft Drinks* case, the Appellate Body stated that it would be inappropriate for a panel to make a determination on whether the United States had acted inconsistently with its North American Free Trade Agreement (NAFTA) obligations.[14] It declined to accept 'Mexico's interpretation [which] would imply that the WTO dispute settlement system could be used to determine rights and obligations outside the covered agreements.'[15] While the Appellate Body determined that it could not 'determine rights and duties outside the covered agreements', it did not explicitly state that it could not give effect to rights and duties outside the covered agreements in assessing claims based on WTO law.

Article 31(3)(c) of the Vienna Convention on the Law of Treaties (VCLT) specifically instructs that interpreters shall 'take into account...any relevant rules of international law applicable in the relations between the parties'. In the *EC–Biotech* case, the panel determined that 'Article 31(3)(c) should be interpreted to mandate consideration of rules of international law which are applicable in the relations between all parties to the treaty which is being interpreted.'[16] Therefore, only those international legal rules to which all WTO members are party, such as general, customary international law or treaties that include all WTO members, would be *required* to be taken into account. The panel observed that 'Requiring that a treaty be interpreted in the light of other rules of international law which bind the States parties to the treaty ensures or enhances the consistency of the rules of international law applicable to these States and thus contributes to avoiding conflicts between the relevant rules.'[17] The panel thus limited the authority of other international political processes, constituting an institutional choice. In the *EC–Biotech* case, since the complainants (as well as many other WTO members) had not ratified the Biosafety Protocol, the panel found that the language of Article 31(3)(c) did not require it to take the Biosafety Protocol into account in the interpretation of the WTO treaty.

The Panel in the *EC–Biotech* case nonetheless left open the possibility that a panel would have *discretion* to take into account another international treaty where the parties to the dispute had each ratified that other treaty.[18] In addition, it recognized that other rules of international law might inform the interpretation of WTO law as applied to a particular factual context, rather than as rules of law.[19] This limited use of other international law in interpretation constitutes (once more) an implicit institutional choice: a decision to focus WTO dispute settlement, at least formally, on interpretation of the

---

[13] Understanding on Rules and Procedures Governing the Settlement of Disputes, Article 2.2, 15 April 1994; Marrakesh Agreement Establishing the World Trade Organization, Annex 2, 1869 U.N.T.S. 401.

[14] WTO Appellate Body Report 2006, paragraph 56.

[15] Id.

[16] WTO Panel Report 2006, paragraph 7.70.

[17] Id., paragraph 7.70.

[18] Id., paragraph 7.72.

[19] WTO Panel Report 2006, paragraph 7.91.

covered agreements in the light of their context, object, and purpose, while limiting the scope for taking into account other international law. This decision not to take other international law generally into account in judicial interpretation constitutes an institutional choice to assign to the political processes the job of reconciliation of diverse rules of international law.

From a welfare perspective, is this current arrangement for dispute settlement of WTO and other international law efficient? Its efficiency depends in part on the relative efficiency of the substance of WTO law compared to other international law. In economics, trade liberalization is viewed as economically efficient for all states, enhancing both national and global welfare, subject to the caveat that some powerful states can, in some circumstances, enhance their economic welfare through trade restrictions at other states' expense.

Furthermore, from a welfare perspective, if we assume states are acting rationally in their welfare-based self-interest, and if we assume that international law is not biased due to the exercise of asymmetric power or subject to other strategic problems (two large assumptions), then we can infer that states have determined that it would increase efficiency to provide for stronger enforcement of WTO law, while implicitly determining that it would not be as valuable to provide for equally strong enforcement of other international law. Given the need to make strong assumptions here, such an inference of efficiency in a welfare sense rests on shaky ground. There are stronger reasons to infer efficiency from the standpoint of maximizing the political welfare of government officials, in a public choice sense.[20] From the perspective of political welfare, those constituencies interested in WTO rules have been able to elevate the importance of WTO rules among government priorities.

While it is clear that a limited mandate for the Appellate Body's and panels' jurisdiction accentuates the phenomenon of 'fragmentation' of international law, pursuant to which different types of international law are separated, both at the negotiation and at the implementation stages, it is also possible that states would prefer different types of dispute settlement mechanisms for different types of international law. Thus, the acceptance of this type of fragmentation could be viewed as an acceptance of an institutional choice made by states: a choice to differentiate among different types of international law in terms of the available institutional infrastructure.

There are, nonetheless, welfare-oriented arguments for recognizing other international law in WTO dispute settlement in order to constrain trade liberalization. This choice can be understood from an 'embedded liberalism' perspective that recognizes that, in order to establish the political conditions for liberalism, it is necessary to engage in some measure of redistributive and other social regulation. The embedded liberalism concept links considerations of welfare economics with other political considerations. Redistributive regulation is viewed as necessary to induce those who would otherwise be hurt by liberalization to accept liberalization that will increase aggregate social welfare, and thus legitimize the regime.

---

[20] Schwartz and Sykes 1996; Sykes 1991.

Finally, if WTO law always trumps other international law in WTO dispute settlement, it raises issues of institutional choice from the perspective of participation. Those participating in other international law regimes that do not benefit from automatic and binding dispute settlement are disfavoured. This move, therefore, again raises questions of the legitimacy of establishing a de facto structural hierarchy through negotiations among trade officials, without extensive participation of officials responsible for other substantive areas.

In sum, the exclusion of the determination of rights and duties under other international law from the mandate of WTO dispute settlement can be understood as an implicit institutional decision, whether made by treaty design or through interpretive choice: a decision to leave other international law to the general institutional mechanism for application and enforcement of international law (or to other discrete mechanisms), while providing a special mechanism for application and enforcement of WTO law. This move may be viewed as an implicit elevation of WTO law above other international law, as a type of 'structural supremacy', and it therefore raises questions regarding the legitimacy of establishing a de facto structural hierarchy of international law through negotiations among trade officials, without extensive participation of officials responsible for other functional subjects. It can thus be argued that if the WTO dispute settlement process declines to give effect to broadly accepted values embodied in other international law, the WTO itself will lose legitimacy.[21]

24.3.3 Textual incorporation of other international law; delegation to international standard-setting bodies

The authors of the WTO treaties decided to delegate certain decision-making to external standard-setting bodies under the Agreement on Sanitary and Phytosanitary Measures (SPS) and the Agreement on Technical Barriers to Trade (TBT). However, the terms of this delegation left important room for interpretation by panels and the Appellate Body. In the *EC–Sardines* case,[22] the Appellate Body examined the effect within the WTO legal system of an international standard for labelling in connection with sardines. The EC argued that the EC regulation was 'based on' Codex Stan 94, as required by Article 2.4 of the TBT Agreement, because it adopted the portion of Codex Stan 94 that reserves the term 'sardines' exclusively for *sardina pilchardus*.[23] It argued that this relationship satisfies the requirement for a 'rational relationship' between the international standard and the technical regulation, as required by Article 2.4 of the TBT Agreement. The Appellate Body ruled against the EC, finding that the Codex standard could not be the 'basis' for the EC regulation since the EC regulation and the Codex

---

[21] Howse 2001.

[22] WTO Appellate Body Report 2002.

[23] European Communities Appellant's Submission, paragraph 150, quoted by WTO Appellate Body Report 2002, paragraph 241.

standard were contradictory.[24] This interpretation of the meaning of 'basis' delineates the institutional relationship between the WTO and Codex Alimentarius. The Appellate Body agreed with the panel's use of the earlier *EC–Hormones* decision, which had applied an analogous provision under the SPS Agreement. In the *EC–Hormones* case, the Appellate Body found that, in order for an international standard to be used 'as a basis for' a technical regulation under Article 3.1 of the SPS Agreement, that standard must be 'used as the principal constituent or fundamental principle for the purpose of enacting the technical regulation.'[25]

The authors of the WTO agreements also incorporated other international treaties by reference in the Agreement on Trade-Related Aspects of Intellectual Property Rights (TRIPS). Incorporation by reference to other international treaties generally entails interesting interpretive problems regarding the meaning of these treaty provisions. Appellate Body interpretations of the Paris Convention and the Berne Convention have been subject to academic scrutiny and critique.[26]

These interpretive choices can be assessed as to whether they have been faithful to the intent of the drafters of these provisions as to the requirements to utilize rules produced outside the WTO. The use of these rules may be understood as adding to the welfare efficiency of these provisions, to the extent that these other organizations appropriately bring expertise to bear in the formulation of the rules. We discuss the role of expertise in more detail in Section 24.3.4 below. The Appellate Body also seems to have been careful to ensure that members are not able to depart from these rules too widely, in keeping with the goal of minimizing protectionist use of technical standards. This seems to promote both welfare efficiency and political efficiency. To the extent that these rules are produced under circumstances of limited transparency, accountability, and legitimacy, however, the Appellate Body's applications of these provisions may raise issues of participation. Indeed, in the *EC–Sardines* case, the Appellate Body accepted that international product standards may include not only those adopted by consensus, but also those that are adopted based on majority voting.[27]

24.3.4 Delegation to experts on factual issues

In determining how to interpret textual language as applied to a specific factual setting, judicial bodies often seek to hear expert advice. They do so, in the WTO context, when deciding whether to defer to national regulatory decisions or subject them to stricter scrutiny, whether in terms of the substance of the claims or the domestic procedures used.

This form of delegation of institutional authority can be viewed as technocratic, or expert-based. In requesting experts' views and taking them into account, panels can be

---

[24] Id., paragraph 248.
[25] WTO Appellate Body Report 1998a; WTO Appellate Body Report 2002, paragraph 243.
[26] Dinwoodie and Dreyfuss 2009; Evans 2007; Gervais 2009.
[27] WTO Appellate Body Report 2002.

viewed as engaging in a form of delegation, although this delegation is only a partial one, as the panels retain authority to determine how to make use of the experts' views. Nonetheless, to the extent that the experts shape the perspectives of the panels on the factual contexts, they may wield considerable authority.[28]

In cases that raise environmental and health-related issues, WTO panels have typically called on experts to testify about these issues in order for the panels to weigh the factual evidence. Under Article 13.2 of the DSU, panels are permitted to establish 'expert review groups'. This facility has not yet been used to create 'expert review groups' per se, but it has been used by panels to receive testimony from experts on an individual basis regarding complex scientific and other determinations.[29] Panels have done so in eight cases involving environmental, food safety, and phytosanitary questions: *Japan–Apples*, *Australia–Salmon*, *EC–Asbestos* (initial panel and Article 21.5 panel), *Japan–Agricultural Products*, *US–Shrimp*, *EC–Hormones*, *EC–Biotech*, and *US–Continued Suspension* (a follow-up to the *EC–Hormones* case). For example, in the *EC–Biotech* case, the panel called on six scientific experts to testify, asking them detailed questions regarding the risks posed by individual genetically modified varieties, and whether the EU member state bans were supported by risk assessments.

The use of such expertise in decision-making can be controversial. On the one hand, WTO panels can better check the reasoning of the regulating member against expert opinion to address whether the regulatory rationales pass muster. Yet, as shown in debates over risk regulation between rationalists[30] and culturalists,[31] expertise-based accountability mechanisms (focused on effectiveness) are in tension with those of democratic politics (focused on responsiveness). In the context of multilevel governance, internal accountability mechanisms within national democracies are in tension with the external accountability mechanisms of WTO technocratic review through partial delegation of fact-finding to experts.[32]

Panels, however, have not consulted individual experts on economic issues, in contrast to their consultation of scientific experts on environmental and food safety issues. The determination of evidence invoking economic concepts, such as the causation of significant price suppression by competitive products, would seem amenable to a report from an expert review group comprised of economists with expertise in trade economics and econometrics.

Of course, expertise is no guarantee against bias or ideology, and affected stakeholders will be concerned, in particular, if questions raising value judgements, such as economic development policy, are being delegated to unaccountable economic experts, who help to justify in technocratic terms judicial decisions with political implications. There are, in short, important limits to the usefulness of expert methods. In particular, when diverse values are required to be balanced, economics cannot assist in commensuration among them. Panels may use experts to justify their decisions from a technical

---

[28] Chalmers 2003.   [29] Pauwelyn 2002.   [30] For example Sunstein 2005.
[31] For example Kahan et al. 2006.   [32] Keohane 2003.

perspective, but such deference to technical judgement will not necessarily avoid legitimacy challenges where particular social priorities are at stake. Stakeholders will inevitably raise questions about the participation characteristics or legitimacy of assigning even partial decision-making to expert groups of economists and scientists. Experts' assessments of the underlying facts, nonetheless, can assist panels in making the ultimate institutional choices at stake, such as whether to defer to a national measure, to engage in judicial balancing, to turn to process-based review, or to issue a clear bright-line rule against categories of measures, thus leaving ultimate outcomes to market processes.

We now look at cases of judicial interpretation delegating authority to each of the alternative institutional processes.

24.3.5 The institutional choice of judicial balancing

WTO panels and the Appellate Body face particularly difficult institutional choices where WTO disputes raise conflicts between diverse values and social priorities. This situation is evident in cases involving Article XX of the GATT and its analogue for trade in services, Article XIV of the General Agreement on Trade and Services (GATS). In some cases, the Appellate Body has explicitly interpreted certain of these provisions as requiring a balancing approach. In others, it has appeared to back off from a full balancing approach by permitting the member to choose its 'level of protection' (such as a zero tolerance) and then asking if this level can be reached through a less trade-restrictive means of regulation (finding that nothing is as effective as an import ban to achieve it).

The Appellate Body most notably formulated and applied a judicial balancing approach in a case involving a requirement of the Republic of Korea that retailers make a choice of selling only Korean or foreign beef.[33] Korea's alleged regulatory rationale was to ease monitoring of the labelling of the origin of beef sold in Korea to ensure compliance with regulations against deceptive marketing practices, as there was evidence that Korean retailers were selling lower-priced US beef as Korean beef. The Appellate Body responded by applying a judicial balancing test involving (at least) three variables in determining whether the Korean measure was 'necessary' to secure compliance with Korea's anti-fraud regulations under its Unfair Competition Act for the purposes of Article XX(d) of the GATT. The Appellate Body concluded:

> In sum, determination of whether a measure, which is not 'indispensable', may nevertheless be 'necessary' within the contemplation of Article XX(d), involves in every case a process of *weighing and balancing* a series of factors which prominently include the contribution made by the compliance measure to the enforcement of the law or regulation at issue, the importance of the common interests or values protected by that law or regulation, and the accompanying impact of the law or regulation on imports or exports.[34]

---

[33] See WTO Appellate Body Report 2000.
[34] See id., paragraph 164 (emphasis added).

It explicated each of these three listed variables individually in relation to the question of whether a member's regulatory measure is 'necessary' for purposes of GATT Article XX, maintaining:

- 'The more vital or important those common interests or values are, the easier it would be to accept as "necessary" a measure designed as an enforcement instrument.'[35]
- 'The greater the contribution [to the realization of the end pursued], the more easily a measure might be considered to be "necessary".'[36]
- 'A measure with a relatively slight impact upon imported products might more easily be considered as "necessary" than a measure with intense or broader restrictive effects.'[37]

After reiterating that WTO members have the right to determine for themselves the level of enforcement of their domestic laws, the Appellate Body 'assume[d] that in effect Korea intended to *reduce considerably* the number of cases of fraud', and not '*totally eliminate* ... fraud with respect to the origin of beef', as Korea had contended.[38] It then found that Korea's measure was not 'necessary', since a less trade-restrictive alternative was reasonably available to achieve this aim, such as 'devot[ing] more resources to enforcement'.[39]

Yet the Appellate Body did not fully articulate how to conduct the balancing test, and, in particular, did not prescribe explicit cost–benefit analysis from a law and economics perspective. It appears that the balancing test prescribed is to proceed by a kind of gestalt, rather than by aggregating the value of costs and benefits in quasi-mathematical form. It was, moreover, not clear in *Korea–Beef* how this balancing test relates to the traditional test which asks whether an alternative measure which is less restrictive of trade is reasonably available to meet the member's policy goal.

In other cases, the Appellate Body, while consistently referring to the *Korea–Beef* balancing test, has avoided engaging in explicit judicial balancing by applying the least trade-restrictive alternative test after finding that the purpose of the regulatory measure was to reduce a given risk as much as possible. It is not clear how the Appellate Body will reconcile the right of a WTO member to determine its chosen level of protection with the criterion in a balancing test of evaluating the importance of the value protected.[40] The Appellate Body attempted to do so partially in the *EC–Asbestos* case, where it referred to its decision in *Korea–Beef*. There, the Appellate Body pointed out that the protection of human life from the risk of asbestos 'is both vital and important in the highest degree', suggesting that, as for the *Korea–Beef* balancing criteria, the more important the common interests or values pursued, the easier it would be to accept the national measure as necessary.[41]

---

[35] Id., paragraph 162.   [36] Id., paragraph 163.   [37] Id., paragraph 176.
[38] Id., paragraph 178.   [39] Id., paragraph 180.
[40] Cf. Marceau and Trachtman 2002; Regan 2007.
[41] WTO Appellate Body Report 2000, paragraph 172.

In this line of cases, the Appellate Body can be viewed as arrogating to itself a great deal of authority to balance substantive concerns implicated by a trade restriction. In the cases that hold a member's policy goals inviolate, in contrast, it can be viewed as deferring to a greater extent to the importing member's policy goals and measures to achieve them. From an economic welfare perspective, insights from a full cost–benefit analysis may improve economic efficiency, leading to increased economic welfare. However, there are important arguments for a retreat from cost–benefit analysis, and even from an imprecise balancing test, based on the difficulty of commensuration between diverse values and concerns, as well as on the expertise of WTO tribunals for such a task.[42] To the extent that the WTO Appellate Body's legitimacy would be challenged if it were to engage in explicit balancing in such cases, then such an approach is probably not desirable from the perspective of the political welfare of the overall system, and thus of the political welfare of the officials of individual members.

From the perspective of participation, open-ended judicial balancing tests privilege the judicial process compared to determinations by a political process. In contrast to either deference to national decision-making or to a bright-line rule as applied in the GATT *U–Tuna–Dolphin* case discussed next, judicial balancing creates greater uncertainty. This approach can thus be viewed as favouring those best able to engage in full-scale litigation on a case-by-case basis. Large and wealthy states who are repeat players in WTO litigation are able to mobilize legal resources more cost-effectively than smaller and poorer ones. The dynamics of full-scale litigation can thus favour them, and, indirectly, the constituents that they represent in these disputes.

Yet, in creating uncertainty, the Appellate Body can also potentially open space for multilateral political negotiations in other forums, fostering the political institutional alternative discussed above. Through an in-depth examination of rival policy claims and their impacts, the Appellate Body and panel can help frame subsequent bilateral and multilateral negotiations between disputing parties. In other words, institutional choices should not be viewed as static, since institutional processes can dynamically interact.

24.3.6 Delegation to markets

In a number of contexts, the meaning of critical WTO legal terms can be found in the light of market practice. In other cases, judicial interpreters can apply interpretive choices that directly allocate decisions to market processes. For example, in evaluating national measures under GATT Articles I, III, and XI, together with the exceptions of Article XX, we have seen how panels and the Appellate Body often review them in relation to alternative measures that are less restrictive of trade. Import bans can be particularly scrutinized because of the frequent availability of more market-friendly means to inform consumers of foreign environmental and other social impacts, such as product labelling. Product labelling, in particular, can inform consumption decisions (and,

---

[42] Trachtman 1998.

indirectly, foreign production decisions) in a less draconian manner. Taking such a labelling approach effectively shifts decision-making over the appropriate balance between trade, environmental, development, and other social goals from a national political process to the market. The GATT *US–Tuna* case took this route, accepting environmental labelling regimes as not in violation of the Article I MFN obligation of GATT.[43]

WTO judicial decision makers can apply interpretive choices that delegate decision-making away from national political processes to markets. Arguably, the most famous example of this situation is WTO panels' handling of domestic regulatory measures based on production and process methods (PPMs) in the absence of multilaterally agreed rules. The (in)famous *US–Tuna* case and the initial WTO panel in the *US–Shrimp–Turtle* case took this route—both involved US regulatory restrictions based on fishing methods, a type of PPM. Both cases addressed US regulatory bans on the import of products from countries that did not have a marine species conservation programme comparable in effectiveness to the relevant US regulatory programme. Neither panel showed deference to the US national regulation which restricted the marketing of foreign products in the US on account of the alleged lack of adequate regulation of the PPMs abroad.[44]

Similarly, the initial WTO panel in the *US–Shrimp–Turtle* case found that, although the US regulation was not discriminatory on the face of it, by 'conditioning access to the US market' on a change in a foreign government's environmental regulatory policy, the US measure 'threatens the multilateral trading system'.[45] The panel's broad ruling was based on the type of measure affecting trade, a PPM, and not on the measure's social purpose or the details of its implementation. The two panel decisions effectively maintained that PPM-based measures that did not affect products (as such) were in violation of GATT rules, so that foreign products using different PPMs could not be restricted. As a result, these products would effectively be in competition with each other, and consumers would decide between them based on advertising and (potentially) labelling regimes regarding the PPM.

This type of market-based model has many benefits from the perspective of participation in the decision-making process. A market-based decision-making mechanism can permit more individualized participation in determining the proper balance between trade, environmental, and other social goals. In this manner, markets can enhance democratic voice. Marketers can label their products in terms of social preferences. Consumers, informed through advertising campaigns, can choose which products to buy on the basis of how they are produced, such as 'dolphin-safe' tuna, or 'GMO-free' foods. In choosing between products, consumers implicitly choose among alternative regulatory regimes for the production of particular products. Such a WTO approach

---

[43] GATT Panel Report 1991.

[44] See GATT Panel Report 1991, 35–6, paragraphs 5.27–5.28.

[45] It repeated this assertion of a threat to the system nine times. See paragraphs 7.44, 7.45, 7.51, 7.55, 7.60, 7.61. See Shaffer 2005.

could stimulate not only product competition, but also regulatory competition.[46] Different regulatory approaches would be in competition when consumers select which product to buy. In purchasing a product, one would effectively be voting for one regulatory system over another.

From a welfare perspective, this interpretive approach to the handling of regulatory measures based on PPMs in the absence of multilateral agreements can foster greater commercial certainty, thereby facilitating cross-border trade, promoting development, and protecting a liberal international trading system. The market decision-making mechanism, however, is also subject to bias, resulting in skewed participation in the determination of the appropriate balance of the policy concerns. Markets are subject to information asymmetries, externalities, and collective action problems. Information costs would be high. The labels could be misleading. Even if the labels were accurate, many consumers would not take the time to review them. Some consumers, even if informed, might decide to buy the cheaper product and 'free-ride' on more socially concerned purchasers. Other purchasers might refrain from buying a product which is produced in a particular way because they doubt that their purchasing decisions would be effective in the light of other consumers' actions. The views of consumers who do not plan on consuming a particular product (however it is produced) would not be represented in the market process. Social activists thus fear that competition between socially protective regulations and non-socially protective regulations would result in a 'race to the bottom' towards less protective regulations.

Other types of cases in which market or consumer preferences are critical are those that refer to market competition for a determination of the 'likeness' of products.[47] The reference to competition as the determinant of 'likeness' leaves little room for considering the types of regulatory distinctions that might not be made by the market. Indeed, the economic theory of regulation suggests that regulation would often be necessary precisely where the market fails to make important distinctions. In these cases, reference to markets might suffer from deficiencies in welfare and political efficiency. While consumer preferences are incorporated in market decision-making, regulatory preferences might be seriously underweighted, diminishing political participation as well.

24.3.7 Vertical (re)allocation: deference to states

One interpretive choice that some commentators favour is for the WTO judicial body to show deference to a country implementing a trade restriction on social policy grounds in reflection of local values, thereby effectively allocating decision-making authority to a national political process. Some scholars contend that WTO rules should be interpreted in deference to the 'local values' of the country imposing the trade restriction.[48]

---

[46] Bratton et al. 1996.
[47] See WTO Appellate Body Report 2001a; WTO Appellate Body Report 1996.
[48] Nichols 1996.

Environmental activists and many legal scholars further maintain that WTO rules (and, in particular, GATT Articles III.4 and XX) should be interpreted to permit trade restrictions imposed on account of foreign production processes that are environmentally harmful, as long as the same ban is applied domestically.[49] For example, a WTO panel could hold that as long as a national regulatory purpose is facially valid, then the panel will look no further at the regulatory measure chosen, in terms of its impact on trade, its effectiveness, its proportionality, or otherwise. This choice was implicitly made by the Appellate Body in *Brazil–Tyres*.

However, in general, the Appellate Body's approach to standards of review has eschewed special deference to states. Rather, in the *EC–Hormones* decision, the Appellate Body explained that the appropriate standard of review is that expressed in Article 11 of the DSU: an objective assessment of the facts.[50] Even where the drafters of the WTO treaty seem to have intended an especially deferential standard of review, under Article 17.6(ii) of the Anti-Dumping Agreement, the Appellate Body has not so far accorded extensive deference.

The institutional choice of deference would entail particular institutional consequences in terms of social and political welfare, and the participation of affected stakeholders. There are sometimes strong policy grounds for deferring to domestic regulatory choices, given the remoteness of international institutional processes. Participation in democratic decision-making at the national level is of a higher quality than at the international level because of the closer relationship between the citizen and the state, the consequent reduced costs of organization and participation, and the existence of a sense of common identity and communal cohesiveness—that is, of a demos. National and subnational processes are better able to tailor regulatory measures to the demands and needs of local social and environmental contexts. They are more likely to respond rapidly and flexibly to new developments. This approach applies a principle espoused in a variety of scholarly disciplines, from law, to political science, to institutional economics.[51]

Yet national and subnational political decision-making processes can be highly problematic from the perspectives of participation, accountability, and global social and political welfare. First, producer interests may be better represented than consumer interests on account of their higher per capita stakes in regulatory outcomes, which can give rise to economic protectionist legislation, reducing national as well as global social welfare. Second, even where national and local procedures are relatively pluralistic—involving broad participation before administrative and political processes that are subjected to judicial review—they generally do not take account of adverse impacts on unrepresented foreigners. International law comes into play precisely where other states have concerns about how these domestic political choices affect them. If the WTO judicial process showed complete deference to national political processes, permitting them

---

[49] Howse and Regan 2000.
[50] WTO Appellate Body Report 1998a, paragraphs 115–7.
[51] Tullock 1969; Williamson 1967.

to ignore significant effects on foreign interests in a manner contrary to the obligations set forth in the WTO Treaty, then accountability would suffer in a reciprocal sense: the affected foreign states' political processes, and the political process of international law, would be prevented from inducing states to take account of the foreign effects of their actions.

WTO members with large markets, such as the United States and European Union, are often favoured by such a deferential approach, which is why developing countries tend to be wary of such deference on social policy grounds. This institutional choice can permit countries with large markets to use their market leverage to compel foreign regulatory change in the light of the large country's particular preferences. If the WTO Appellate Body deferred to national legislation and its administrative application, then it would effectively allocate decision-making over the appropriate balance of the trade and other regulatory concerns at stake to national political and administrative processes.

24.3.8 Process-based review

As a result, instead of simply deferring to a member's policy goals or engaging in judicial balancing of substantive concerns, the WTO Appellate Body has sometimes reviewed national decision-making processes to attempt to ensure that they take into account the views of affected foreign parties. Since the WTO's creation, Article X of the GATT, which provides for transparency of regulatory measures, has been increasingly applied by panels. While it was considered to be 'subsidiary' to the substantive provisions of the GATT prior to the WTO, it has now been regularly enforced by WTO panels and the Appellate Body, as have its more detailed analogues in the GATS, TRIPS, SPS and TBT Agreements.[52]

The WTO Appellate Body has applied this process-based approach in a number of cases involving defences based on social concerns. For example, in the *US–Shrimp–Turtle* case, the Appellate Body returned the substantive issue to a lower vertical level of decision-making—that is, back to the US Department of State which was responsible for implementing the US legislation—subject to certain procedural conditions. By reviewing the due process and transparency of the State Department's implementing procedures, the Appellate Body attempted to enhance the representation of affected foreign parties and thereby counter the national biases of domestic legislative and administrative bodies.

In this case, the Appellate Body faulted the United States for the national biases in its procedures, and can be viewed as effectively requiring the United States to create an administrative procedure pursuant to which foreign governments or traders have an opportunity to comment on US regulatory decisions that affect them. The Appellate Body held that the application of the US measure was 'arbitrary' in that the certification process was not 'transparent' or 'predictable', and did not provide any 'formal opportunity for an

---

[52] Stewart and Badin 2009.

applicant country to be heard or to respond to any arguments that may be made against it.[53] The Appellate Body admonished the United States for failing to take 'into consideration the different conditions which may occur in the territories of…other Members', and required the United States to assure that its policies were appropriate for the local 'conditions prevailing' within the complainant developing countries.[54] Similarly, in the *EC–Preferences* case, the EC's lack of procedural transparency was the primary ground for the Appellate Body's finding against the EC's scheme.[55]

In cases involving members' use of trade remedies against dumping and subsidies, panels and the Appellate Body likewise have sought refuge in procedural criticisms of national economic analyses, rather than engaging with the substantive determinations.[56] Panels, for example, have examined whether national authorities have created a record evidencing that they considered the required factors.[57] Were panels to use the institutional alternative of expert review groups, as discussed above, they might feel more comfortable engaging in a full substantive review, but instead they have often turned to this process-based form of review.

Process-based review may seem desirable, since it is relatively less intrusive than substantive review and it directly focuses on the issue of participation of domestic and foreign parties. However, process-based review also raises serious concerns, in particular because processes can be manipulated to give the appearance of consideration of affected foreigners without in any way modifying a predetermined outcome. Even if international case-by-case review were possible (which it is not), it will be difficult, if not impossible, for an international body to determine the extent to which a national agency actually takes account of foreign interests. The challenge remains that WTO members, and in particular powerful ones, can thus go through the formal steps of due process without meaningfully considering the views of other affected parties. As a result, WTO panels and the Appellate Body may retain the interpretive alternatives of judicial balancing and the application of bright-line rules.

24.4 CONCLUSION: THE CENTRALITY OF INSTITUTIONAL CHOICE

This chapter has assessed the institutional implications of the interpretive choices confronting the WTO judicial bodies. These choices may be evaluated in terms of which social decision-making process decides a policy issue, affecting the participation of stakeholders. This form of institutional analysis helps us to evaluate the comparative

---

[53] WTO Appellate Body Report 1998b, paragraph 180.   [54] Id., paragraph 164.
[55] WTO Appellate Body Report 2004, paragraph 182–9.
[56] See, e.g. WTO Appellate Body Report 2003.
[57] See, e.g. WTO Panel Report 2002; WTO Appellate Body Report 2001b; WTO Panel Report 2001; WTO Panel Report 2000.

distributive and efficiency consequences of treaty interpretive choices, both in social welfare and public choice terms.

In this chapter, we have provided an analytical framework for assessing the consequences of alternative interpretative choices in comparative institutional choice terms. We have evaluated interpretive decisions by examining how they allocate authority between different social decision-making processes. We have suggested the consequences of these allocations for efficiency and distribution of economic and political welfare, as well as in participatory terms. First, these choices affect the degree of transparency, accountability, and legitimacy of social decision-making. Second, by deciding among such institutional alternatives as incorporation of international standards, judicial balancing, delegation to markets, national deference, and process-based review, they can determine which social decision-making process decides a particular policy issue, thereby affecting the institutional mediation of individual preferences. We have shown how each of these alternative institutional choices has been applied by WTO panels and the Appellate Body in case law, explaining the comparative welfare and participatory implications at stake.

REFERENCES

Bratton, William, Joseph McCahery, Sol Picciotto, and Colin Scott, eds. 1996. *International Regulatory Competition and Coordination: Perspectives on Economic Regulation in Europe and the United States*. Oxford: Clarendon Press.

Chalmers, Damian. 2003. Food for Thought: Reconciling European Risks and Traditional Ways of Life. *Modern Law Review* 66 (4):532–62.

Dinwoodie, Graeme B., and Rochelle C. Dreyfuss. 2009. Designing a Global Intellectual Property System Responsive to Change: The WTO, WIPO, and Beyond. *Houston Law Review* 46 (4):1187–234.

Esty, Daniel C. 1994. *Greening the GATT: Trade, Environment, and the Future*. Washington, DC: Peterson Institute for International Economics.

Evans, Gail E. 2007. Recent Developments in the Protection of Trademarks and Trade Names in the European Union: From Conflict to Coexistence? *Trademark Reporter* 97 (4):1008–48.

GATT Panel Report. 1991. *US–Restrictions on Imports of Tuna*. DS21/R, DS21/R. Unadopted, BISD 39S/155. Geneva: GATT.

Gervais, Daniel. 2009. International Decision, China–Measures Affecting the Protection and Enforcement of Intellectual Property Rights. *American Journal of International Law* 103 (3):549–55.

Guzman, Andrew T. 2004. Global Governance and the WTO. *Harvard International Law Journal* 45 (2):303–52.

Howse, Robert. 2001. The Legitimacy of the World Trade Organization. In *The Legitimacy of International Organizations*, edited by Jean-Marc Coicaud and Veijo Heiskanen, 355–407. Tokyo: United Nations University Press.

Howse, Robert, and Donald Regan. 2000. The Product/Process Distinction—An Illusory Basis for Disciplining 'Unilateralism' in Trade Policy. *European Journal of International Law* 11 (2):249–89.

Kahan, Dan, Paul Slovic, Donald Braman, and John Gastil. 2006. Review of *Fear of Democracy: A Cultural Evaluation of Sunstein on Risk*, by Cass R. Sunstein. *Harvard Law Review* 119 (4):1071–109.

Keohane, Robert. 2003. Global Governance and Democratic Accountability. In *Taming Globalization: Frontiers of Governance*, edited by David Held and Mathias Koenig-Archibuigi, 130–59. Cambridge: Polity Press.

Komesar, Neil K. 1996. *Imperfect Alternatives: Choosing Institutions in Law, Economics, and Public Policy*. Chicago: University of Chicago Press.

Komesar, Neil K. 2008. The Essence of Economics: Law, Participation and Institutional Choice (Two Ways). In *Alternative Institutional Structures: Evolution and Impact*, edited by Sandra S. Batie and Nicholas Mercuro, 165–86. London: Routledge.

Marceau, Gabrielle, and Joel P. Trachtman. 2002. The Technical Barriers to Trade Agreement, the Sanitary and Phytosanitary Measures Agreement, and the General Agreement on Tariffs and Trade—A Map of the World Trade Organization Law of Domestic Regulation of Goods. *Journal of World Trade* 36 (5):811–81.

Nichols, Philip M. 1996. Trade Without Values. *Northwestern University Law Review* 90 (2):658–719.

North, Douglass C. 1990. *Institutions, Institutional Change and Economic Performance*. Cambridge: Cambridge University Press.

Pauwelyn, Joost. 2002. The Use of Experts in WTO Dispute Settlement. *International and Comparative Law Quarterly* 51 (2):325–64.

Regan, Donald H. 2007. The Meaning of 'Necessary' in GATT Article XX and GATS Article XIV: The Myth of Cost–Benefit Balancing. *World Trade Review* 6 (3):347–69.

Schwartz, Warren F., and Alan O. Sykes. 1996. Toward a Positive Theory of the Most Favored Nation Obligation and its Exceptions in the WTO/GATT System. *International Review of Law and Economics* 16 (1):27–51.

Shaffer, Gregory C. 2001. The World Trade Organization under Challenge: Democracy and the Law and Politics of the WTO's Treatment of Trade and Environment Matters. *Harvard Environmental Law Review* 25 (1):1–94.

Shaffer, Gregory C. 2005. Power, Governance and the WTO: A Comparative Institutional Approach. In *Power in Global Governance*, edited by Michael Barnett and Bud Duvall, 130–60. Cambridge: Cambridge University Press.

Steinberg, Richard H. 2004. Judicial Lawmaking at the WTO: Discursive, Constitutional, and Political Constraints. *American Journal of International Law* 98 (2):247–75.

Stewart, Richard B., and Michelle Ratton Sanchez Badin. 2009. The World Trade Organization and Global Administrative Law. In *Constitutionalism, Multilevel Trade Governance, and Social Regulation*, edited by Christian Joerges and Ernst-Ulrich Petersmann. 2nd edition, 2011. Oxford: Hart Publishing.

Sunstein, Cass R. 2005. *The Laws of Fear: Beyond the Precautionary Principle*. Cambridge: Cambridge University Press.

Sykes, Alan O. 1991. Protectionism as a 'Safeguard': A Positive Analysis of the GATT 'Escape Clause' with Normative Speculations. *University of Chicago Law Review* 58 (1):255–306.

Trachtman, Joel P. 1998. Trade and…Problems, Cost–Benefit Analysis and Subsidiarity. *European Journal of International Law* 9 (1):32–85.

Tullock, Gordon. 1969. Federalism: Problems of Scale. *Public Choice* 6 (Spring):19–29.

Williamson, Oliver E. 1967. Hierarchical Control and Optimum Firm Size. *Journal of Political Economy* 75 (2):123–38.

Williamson, Oliver E. 1985. *The Economic Institutions of Capitalism*. New York: Free Press.

WTO Appellate Body Report. 1996. *Japan–Taxes on Alcoholic Beverages*. WT/DS8/AB/R, WT/DS10/AB/R. Adopted 1 November 1996. Geneva: WTO.

WTO Appellate Body Report. 1998a. *EC–Measures Concerning Meat and Meat Products (Hormones)*. WT/DS26/AB/R, WT/DS48/AB/R. Adopted 13 February 1998. Geneva: WTO.

WTO Appellate Body Report. 1998b. *US–Import Prohibition of Certain Shrimp and Shrimp Products*. WT/DS58/AB/R. Geneva: WTO.

WTO Appellate Body Report. 1999a. *India–Quantitative Restrictions on Imports of Agricultural, Textile and Industrial Products*. WT/DS90/AB/R. Adopted 22 September 1999. Geneva: WTO.

WTO Appellate Body Report. 1999b. *Turkey–Restrictions on Imports of Textile and Clothing Products*. WT/DS34/AB/R. Adopted 19 November 1999. Geneva: WTO.

WTO Appellate Body Report. 2000. *Korea–Measures Affecting Imports of Fresh, Chilled and Frozen Beef*. WT/DS161/AB/R, WT/DS169/AB/R. Geneva: WTO.

WTO Appellate Body Report. 2001a. *EC–Measures Affecting Asbestos and Asbestos-Containing Products*. WT/DS135/AB/R. Adopted 5 April 2001. Geneva: WTO.

WTO Appellate Body Report. 2001b. *Thailand–Anti-Dumping Duties on Angles, Shapes and Sections of Iron or Non-Alloy Steel and H-Beams from Poland*. WT/DS122/AB/R. Adopted 5 April 2001. Geneva: WTO.

WTO Appellate Body Report. 2001c. *US–Import Prohibition of Certain Shrimp and Shrimp Products—Recourse to Article 21.5 of the DSU by Malaysia*. WT/DS58/AB/RW. Geneva: WTO.

WTO Appellate Body Report. 2002. *EC–Trade Description of Sardines*. WT/DS231/AB/R. Adopted 23 October 2002. Geneva: WTO.

WTO Appellate Body Report. 2003. *US–Definitive Safeguard Measures on Imports of Certain Steel Products*. WT/DS248/AB/R, WT/DS249/AB/R, WT/DS251/AB/R, WT/DS252/AB/R, WT/DS253/AB/R, WT/DS254/AB/R, WT/DS258/AB/R, WT/DS259/AB/R. Adopted 10 December 2003. Geneva: WTO.

WTO Appellate Body Report. 2004. *EC–Conditions for the Granting of Tariff Preferences to Developing Countries*. WT/DS246/AB/R. Adopted 20 April 2004. Geneva: WTO.

WTO Appellate Body Report. 2005. *US–Measures Affecting the Cross-Border Supply of Gambling and Betting Services*. WT/DS285/AB/R. Adopted 20 April 2005. Geneva: WTO.

WTO Appellate Body Report. 2006. *Mexico–Tax Measures on Soft Drinks and Other Beverages*. WT/DS308/AB/R. Adopted 24 March 2006. Geneva: WTO.

WTO Panel Report. 2000. *Mexico–Anti-Dumping Investigation of High-Fructose Corn Syrup (HFCS) from the United States*. WT/DS132/R. Adopted 24 February 2000. Geneva: WTO.

WTO Panel Report. 2001. *EC–Anti-Dumping Duties on Imports of Cotton-Type Bed Linen from India*. WT/DS141/R. Adopted 12 March 2001, as modified by Appellate Body Report WT/DS141/AB/R). Geneva: WTO.

WTO Panel Report. 2002. *Egypt–Definitive Anti-Dumping Measures on Steel Rebar from Turkey*. WT/DS211/R. Adopted 1 October 2002. Geneva: WTO.

WTO Panel Report. 2003. *EC–Anti-Dumping Duties on Malleable Cast Iron Tube or Pipe Fittings from Brazil*. WT/DS219/R. Adopted 7 March 2003. Geneva: WTO.

WTO Panel Report. 2006. *EC–Measures Affecting the Approval and Marketing of Biotech Products*. WT/DS291/R, WT/DS292/R, WT/DS293/R, Add.1 to Add.9, and Corr.1. Adopted 21 November 2006. Geneva: WTO.

CHAPTER 25

THE DISPUTE SETTLEMENT MECHANISM: ENSURING COMPLIANCE?

ALAN O. SYKES

25.1 INTRODUCTION

WHAT is the purpose of the World Trade Organization (WTO) dispute settlement mechanism (DSM)? This seemingly simple question has become a source of considerable academic debate. All commentators agree that one purpose of the system is to encourage compliance with WTO obligations, at least some of the time. Beyond this point of partial agreement, however, lie a variety of additional perspectives.[1] Some commentators argue that the limits on retaliation under the rules of the DSM are intended to facilitate 'efficient breach' of WTO obligations. Another theme is that the DSM serves to 'rebalance' concessions following breach of obligations, or to 'compensate' aggrieved members for the harm done to them by breach. The proposition that the DSM affords a 'safety valve' for protectionist pressures, akin to arrangements such as the General Agreement on Tariffs and Trade (GATT) 'escape clause', is a further hypothesis.[2]

---

[1] Surveys of the various perspectives may be found in Pauwelyn 2010; Charnovitz 2001; Lawrence 2003; and Schropp 2009.

[2] This list is not exhaustive. Some commentators also view the system as a potential 'gap-filling' mechanism for an inevitably incomplete bargain. See Horn, Maggi, and Staiger 2010; Maggi and Staiger 2011. Others see the system as, in large part, an information revelation mechanism, publicizing deviant behaviour so that various informal sanctions may work more effectively. See Schwartz and Sykes 2002. Each of these perspectives has merit, but my emphasis here is on the debate among proponents of the various perspectives noted in the text about the function of the 'equivalence' standard for countermeasures.

Much of the commentary on the subject proceeds as though these various hypotheses are mutually exclusive, when in fact they are to a great extent complementary—the DSM can in fact be understood to promote all of these objectives in varying degrees. A forti-ori, the question posed in the title to this chapter—is the goal one of *ensuring compliance?*—must be answered in the negative. The discussion to follow elaborates this claim, clarifies the relationship among the various competing hypotheses, and addresses many of the arguments advanced for and against various notions of what the system seeks to accomplish.

Section 25.2 provides a quick sketch of the DSM, including its pre-WTO history dur-ing the GATT era. Section 25.3 then reviews the legal debate over the 'purpose' of the DSM and authorized countermeasures, and shows how the treaty text, as interpreted by WTO arbitrators, affords WTO members the option to violate WTO obligations for a measured 'price' tied to the harm done by the violation to complaining members. Section 25.4 then argues that the essential logic of the system can be understood primarily as a way to facilitate efficient adjustment of the bargain over time, and thereby suggests why 'ensuring compliance' is not the goal of the DSM.

25.2 THE HISTORY AND STRUCTURE OF THE DSM

The now 15-year-old DSM was preceded by 47 years of dispute resolution under GATT. The GATT Treaty text on dispute resolution was sparse to say the least. It introduced the concept of 'nullification or impairment' of GATT benefits in GATT Article XXIII, which provided that any party suffering nullification or impairment could raise the matter with other interested parties. In the event that the concerned parties failed to reach a 'satisfac-tory adjustment' on their own, the GATT membership as a whole (the contracting par-ties) could investigate the matter and 'make recommendations'. Thereafter, if the circumstances were 'serious enough', the Contracting Parties could authorize an aggrieved party or parties to 'suspend…concessions or other obligations' determined to be 'appropriate under the circumstances'.

Despite its sketchy quality, therefore, the text of GATT did authorize collective sanc-tions for breach of obligations in 'appropriate' cases. What the text did not anticipate, however, was the evolution of the 'consensus rule' in GATT, under which decisions taken by the membership on these matters had to be unanimous (and thus had to have the support of any member that had violated GATT). Unsurprisingly, the result was that centrally authorized sanctions played no material role in the system (they were author-ized only once, in 1952).[3] Indeed, the consensus rule even allowed an accused violator to 'block' an investigation of alleged violations for much of the history of GATT. Only in

---

[3] See Hudec 1975.

1989 did the GATT membership agree to eliminate the power of members to block the formation of an investigative panel. And for the entire duration of GATT, any member (including a violator) could block the 'adoption' of dispute panel findings by the membership—adoption is a legal step that is necessary under GATT for decisions to become binding and gain the force of law.

Given the frailty of its formal enforcement mechanism, one might have expected GATT to collapse due to rampant cheating. But it did not, and indeed GATT was extraordinarily successful in reducing average tariff rates in the developed world. Plainly, the incentive for compliance lay not with a formal dispute mechanism and attendant collective sanctions, but with other incentives for compliance. Such incentives had two dimensions—a breach of obligations might result in a direct unilateral retaliatory response in the form of trade or other sanctions, or it might result in diminished opportunities for the violator to secure desired cooperation in the future.[4]

Dissatisfaction with the system nevertheless arose in the later years of GATT, for two reasons. First, 'blocking' under the consensus rule allowed some prominent disputes to drag on for years with no resolution from the complaining party's perspective. Second, frustration with the dispute process led some members (most notably the United States) to engage in unilateral retaliation outside the formal GATT system to a degree that became objectionable to many other members.[5]

Accordingly, the Uruguay Round negotiations that created the WTO ushered in a dramatically new DSM, governed by an extensive text known as the Dispute Settlement Understanding (DSU). As in the days of GATT, dispute resolution under the DSM begins with consultations among the concerned members. Failing a resolution of the dispute during consultations, a complaining member has a right to the establishment of an arbitral panel. The panel is obliged to decide the case within a given time frame (often extended), and a party losing on any issue of law has a right of appeal to the Appellate Body. Panel decisions, as modified in any appeal, and decisions of the Appellate Body, are automatically 'adopted' and gain the force of law unless the WTO membership unanimously rejects them (which never happens).

A member found to be in violation of WTO rules has a 'reasonable period of time' to bring its policies into conformity with its obligations. The duration of this period is subject to arbitration if the parties do not agree on it.[6] Disputes over whether compliance has occurred are also subject to arbitration and appeal through a 'compliance panel' process.[7] In the absence of compliance within the reasonable period, complaining nations have a right to negotiated compensation or to a retaliatory suspension of concessions. If compensation negotiations do not succeed, an aggrieved party can propose a suspension of concessions, which must be 'substantially equivalent' to the harm caused

---

[4] See Schwartz and Sykes 2002; Bown 2004.
[5] See, generally, Bhagwati and Patrick 1990.
[6] See DSU Article 21:3 ('If it is impractical to comply immediately with the recommendations and rulings, the Member concerned shall have a reasonable period of time in which to do so.')
[7] See DSU Article 21:5.

by the violation.[8] An arbitration procedure exists to examine the 'substantial equivalence' question if the member faced with such a suspension of concessions objects that the suspension is excessive.[9]

25.3 THE OPTION TO VIOLATE WTO OBLIGATIONS, IN LAW AND IN PRACTICE

WTO members can and do choose to violate their obligations for extended periods of time; prompt compliance with adverse rulings in the dispute process is frequent, but by no means universal. This section discusses the uncertain legality of such behaviour, and explains in detail how the DSM permits it as a practical matter, regardless of its legality.

25.3.1 The legality of breach

The genesis of the debate over the legality of breach, coupled with compensation or retaliation, can be traced to an exchange in the *American Journal of International Law* between Judith Hippler Bello and John Jackson. In response to arguments made during the US ratification debate that the WTO might intrude unduly on US sovereignty, Bello argued that the WTO did not compel the United States to act contrary to its interests. Rather, the United States would always have the option, she contended, to deviate from its WTO commitments and to compensate other members or suffer retaliation: 'the only truly binding WTO obligation is to maintain the balance of concessions'.[10]

Jackson disagreed with Bello's notion that WTO rules are 'not binding in the traditional sense'.[11] He pointed to 11 separate passages in the WTO Dispute Settlement Understanding that, in his view, support the existence of an obligation to comply with dispute settlement rulings. Central among them were the following:

> The first objective of the dispute settlement mechanism is usually to secure the withdrawal of the measures concerned (Article 3:7)
>
> Where a panel or the Appellate Body concludes that a measure is inconsistent with a covered agreement, it shall recommend that the Member concerned bring the measure into conformity (Article 19:1)

---

[8] See DSU Article 22:4 ('The level of the suspension of concessions or other obligations authorized by the DSB shall be equivalent to the level of nullification or impairment.') The Agreement on Subsidies and Countervailing Measures contains somewhat different language, however, and the standards for retaliation there have been held by various dispute panels to be somewhat looser. See Grossman and Sykes 2011.

[9] See DSU Article 22:6–7.

[10] Bello 1996, 418.

[11] Jackson 1997. See also Jackson 2004.

> Prompt compliance with recommendations or rulings of the DSB [Dispute Settlement Body] is essential in order to secure effective resolution of disputes. (Article 21:1)
>
> Compensation and the suspension of concessions are temporary measures available in the event that the recommendations and rulings are not implemented within a reasonable period of time. However, neither compensation nor the suspension of concessions or other obligations is preferred to full implementation of a recommendation. (Article 22:1)
>
> The DSB shall continue to keep under surveillance the implementation of adopted recommendations...[while] the recommendations to bring a measure into conformity...have not been implemented. (Article 22:8)
>
> Where a measure is found to 'nullify or impair' benefits under the agreement without violating its letter, 'there is no obligation to withdraw the measure'. (Article 26:1(b))

From these passages, Professor Jackson finds that the DSU 'clearly establishes a preference for an obligation to perform'.[12]

But there is another side to the argument, as argued by Sykes.[13] It is possible to interpret each of these passages as consistent with Bello's suggestion that WTO members have a legal (as well as a practical) option to choose between compliance, compensation, and retaliation.

If the objective of the system is 'usually' to secure the withdrawal of the offending measure (Article 3:7), this implies that it is not always the objective. This passage seemingly opens the door to other options. The fact that panels and the Appellate Body must recommend withdrawal of the offending measure says nothing about the existence of an obligation to follow the recommendation, in preference to paying compensation or suffering retaliation as an alternative. The importance of 'prompt compliance' with recommendations can be read as an admonition against dilatory tactics, and not a statement that by itself forecloses the compensation/retaliation option. The fact that compensation and retaliatory measures are 'temporary' might simply underscore the fact that they will end when the breach of obligation has been cured, *if* cure is the option chosen by the member who has been found in violation. And if compensation and retaliatory measures are not 'preferred', neither does the text say that they are unacceptable, or that a member who elects for compensation or retaliation is in violation of the rules.

The last two snippets of treaty text perhaps offer the strongest support for Professor Jackson's position. Regarding the first, the ongoing surveillance of cases where a violation persists indeed suggests that a decision to compensate or accept retaliation does not 'end' the dispute, and that members will thereafter be badgered until they are in compliance. Yet, another interpretation is possible. The alternative to compliance under the WTO involves ongoing compensation or trade retaliation, the latter calibrated to be roughly

---

[12] Jackson 1997, 63.   [13] Sykes 2000.

'equivalent' to the harm done by the violation in question.[14] Because circumstances change and the proper calibration of the 'damages' measure may change as well, it is perhaps not surprising that the Dispute Settlement Body (DSB) should exercise some continuing oversight in these cases, much as a conventional court might retain jurisdiction over a case where damages are payable over time (such as child support payments under family law or medical monitoring costs in tort). Likewise, ongoing violations may have an impact on parties other than the original disputants. Continued publicity and oversight may thus serve to alert other members who might suffer redressable harm. Finally, ongoing oversight serves to check periodically on whether the impasse that led to compensation or retaliation may have lifted. But its existence by no means excludes the possibility that members have the legal right to opt for compensation or retaliation.

Regarding the last passage emphasized by Professor Jackson, the absence of an obligation to change behaviour in so-called 'non-violation' cases (in which certain behaviours upset market access expectations but do not violate the letter of GATT) might indeed be read as supporting the existence of an obligation to comply in the much more common cases involving violations. But here, again, another interpretation can be offered. The 'non-violation' cases involve actions that do not offend the letter of any WTO agreement, but that frustrate market access expectations associated with tariff concessions. It could prove quite awkward for the WTO to recommend that otherwise permissible measures be discontinued simply because a member establishes that their effects were unexpected and upset the anticipated balance of concessions—such recommendations might well tend to offend the proponents of legitimate and valuable domestic regulation, and heighten domestic opposition to WTO liberalization. This possibility may explain why the WTO simply provides that in these cases the parties to the dispute should undertake to restore the balance of concessions through a mutually satisfactory settlement. The absence of an 'obligation to withdraw the measure' can simply be read as a provision that prevents dispute panels from making politically undesirable recommendations in non-violation cases. And, as noted, the fact that panels routinely recommend withdrawal of measures in *violation* cases does not by itself establish a legal obligation to obey the recommendation in preference to compensation or retaliation.

In short, as Jackson ultimately concedes,[15] the treaty text is not entirely conclusive regarding the 'legality' of the choice by a violator to maintain a violation over time and then to compensate or suffer countermeasures. A number of passages offer support for the existence of such an obligation, but the support is not unequivocal, and other passages suggest a looser standard.[16]

More importantly, even if Professor Jackson is right as a formal, 'legal' matter, so what? Nothing in Jackson's argument negates the fact that violators can simply choose

---

[14] Article 22:4 provides that 'The level of the suspension of concessions or other obligations authorized by the DSB shall be equivalent to the level of nullification or impairment.'

[15] Jackson 1997.

[16] Howse and Staiger 2006 concur on the issue of textual ambiguity, but argue that an obligation of compliance can nevertheless be inferred by reading WTO law in the 'context' of customary international law.

not to comply with rulings as a practical matter. The reason is quite simple—as the next section elaborates, the DSM considerably circumscribes the magnitude of countermeasures, and thereby allows violations to continue for a limited 'price' that violators may well be willing to pay.

25.3.2 The option to breach in practice

DSU Article 22 provides, as noted, that violations which continue beyond the 'reasonable period of time' for compliance can be addressed through negotiated compensation, and that in lieu of compensation an aggrieved member is entitled to impose countermeasures 'equivalent to the level of nullification or impairment'. Article 22 then proceeds to establish an elaborate arbitration system to review proposed countermeasures to ensure their 'equivalence'.

What is meant by the phrase 'equivalent to the level of nullification or impairment'? As noted earlier, GATT Article XXIII contemplates situations in which a 'benefit accruing to [a GATT member] . . . is being nullified or impaired', triggering certain rights of redress. 'Nullification or impairment' is thus a detriment to one member resulting (typically) from the violation of some WTO obligation by another member. Thus, the natural interpretation of the equivalence requirement is that countermeasures should be comparable in their effects to the harm done by the violation. In calibrating them, the focus is then on the damage done by the violation to aggrieved members, rather than on the gains to the violator from the violation. Concomitantly, the harm done to aggrieved members affords a rough cap on their countermeasures, regardless of the gains to the violator—and, thus, regardless of whether such countermeasures will suffice to induce the violator to cease.

This interpretation of the text has generally been confirmed in practice. During the course of various arbitrations over countermeasures, complaining nations have urged that violators should be subjected to stiff measures that will induce their compliance with a ruling against them—in effect, complaining nations have suggested that sanctions be set at a sufficiently high level to coerce compliance. But, with the exception of some 'prohibited subsidies' cases that are arguably subject to a different standard for countermeasures, the arbitrators have insisted on close calibration of countermeasures to the harm caused by the violation.

For example, in the *EC–Bananas* dispute, the EC had declined to comply with a panel ruling finding that its tariff preferences for bananas from certain nations violated WTO law. The United States then invoked its retaliation rights, and proposed substantial sanctions, which the EU challenged before an arbitration panel as excessive. In defending its proposed sanctions, the United States argued that its 'suspension (of trade concessions) is an incentive for prompt compliance . . . precision in measuring trade damage is not required'. The arbitrator rejected this position: 'We agree with the United States . . . that it is the purpose of countermeasures to *induce compliance*. But, this purpose does not mean that the DSB should grant authorization to suspend concessions beyond what is equivalent to the level of nullification or impairment. In our view there is nothing in [the relevant provisions of the DSU] that could be read as a justification for countermeasures of a punitive nature.'

More recently, the arbitrators in *US–Byrd Amendment* remarked that 'the DSU does not expressly explain the purpose behind the suspension . . . On the one hand, the general obligation to comply with DSB recommendations and rulings seems to imply that suspension of concessions or other obligations is intended to induce compliance . . . On the other hand, the requirement that the level of such suspensions be equivalent to the level of nullification or impairment suffered by the complaining party seems to imply that suspension . . . is only a means of obtaining some form of temporary compensation.'[17]

This perspective has held fast throughout the history of WTO countermeasures arbitration, save for a few cases involving prohibited subsidies. The Agreement on Subsidies and Countervailing Measures (SCM) contains its own language about the remedies for breach, which various complaining nations have urged should be read to authorize a higher level of countermeasures. Arbitrators in some subsidies cases have thus allowed retaliation based not on the harm to the complaining member, but on the value of the illegal subsidy, in part based on the logic that such retaliation might be more effective at inducing compliance. In the most dramatic case, *US–Foreign Sales Corporations*, the arbitrator allowed Europe to retaliate against the United States in an amount based on the worldwide value of the US subsidy at issue, even though other nations could have filed cases and sought retaliation rights as well. In the most recently completed arbitration over sanctions, however, *US–Upland Cotton*, the arbitrator rejected this more 'punitive' approach to retaliation. With reference to the principle in the SCM Agreement that countermeasures against prohibited subsidies should be 'appropriate', the arbitrator concluded:

> countermeasures, in order to be 'appropriate', should bear some relationship to the extent to which the complaining Member has suffered from the trade-distorting impact of the illegal subsidy. Countermeasures are in essence trade-restrictive measures to be taken in response to a Member's application of a trade-distorting measure that has been determined to nullify or impair the benefits accruing to another Member. Countermeasures that would ensure a relationship of proportionality between the extent to which the trade opportunities of the Member applying the countermeasures has been affected and the extent to which the trade opportunities of the violating Member will in turn be adversely affected would notionally restore the balance of rights and obligations arising from the covered agreements that has been upset between the parties. This would ensure a proper relationship between the level of the countermeasures and the circumstances out of which the dispute arises.[18]

Thus, at the time of writing, even the subsidies area has for the moment been brought into line with the general principle that retaliation should be broadly commensurate

---

[17] 6.2–6.4.
[18] *United States—Subsidies on Upland Cotton, Recourse to Arbitration Under Article 22.6 of the DSU and Article 4.11 of the SCM Agreement by Brazil* WT/DS267/ARB/1, 31 August 2009, 4.190.

with the harm to the complaining nation, and should not go beyond that level to 'punish' the violator, even if the allowed countermeasures are insufficient to ensure compliance.

In short, the treaty text on countermeasures in the DSU, and now in the SCM Agreement as well, as interpreted by the arbitrators, links the magnitude of counter-measures to the harm done by violations. The arbitrators are well aware that counter-measures at this level may not suffice to induce compliance, but see themselves as lacking the authority to authorize stiffer measures. The practical result is that WTO members have an option to breach their obligations on an ongoing basis as long as they are willing to pay the attendant 'price' grounded in some estimate of harm to others. Some com-mentators, such as Professor Jackson, may regard such behaviour as 'illegal' as a matter of international law, but the system plainly permits it to happen nonetheless.

It is important to note that this feature of the DSM is not unavoidable. The drafters could easily have designed a system to coerce compliance more effectively. As past arbi-trations indicate, complaining members can, and apparently would, impose stiffer sanc-tions than those 'equivalent to the level of nullification or impairment' if they were permitted to do so by the arbitrators, who routinely cut back on the sanctions proposed by complaining members. The limitation on countermeasures in the treaty text has thus proven a binding constraint on a regular basis.

Likewise, it is often noted that smaller nations may lack retaliatory capacity and have a difficult time devising meaningful countermeasures (although the potential availabil-ity of cross-retaliation under the Agreement on Trade-Related Aspects of Intellectual Property Rights (TRIPS) may empower small nations quite significantly, as discussed below). If the goal of the DSM were to 'ensure compliance', its drafters might have devised a solution to this problem by authorizing collective retaliation against violations rather than limiting retaliation rights to members who bring a successful complaint.[19] It simply does not do so.

Thus, the limits on countermeasures in the DSM are a matter of choice by the drafters and are by no means inevitable. Why should the drafters of the DSU have designed such a system? The most plausible answer, in my view, is that countermeasures at a level suffi-cient to ensure compliance are at times undesirable. The next section considers why.

25.4 THE ECONOMIC RATIONALE FOR THE OPTION TO BREACH

A trade agreement is a treaty, and a treaty is in many ways analogous to a contract. To assess the objective of the DSM, it is thus useful to begin with the economic logic of dis-pute settlement in contract law.

---

[19] See Maggi 1999 for a formal model in which collective retaliation plays a useful role. See also Pauwelyn 2000.

25.4.1 The contract analogy: property rules and liability rules

The remedial system for breach of contract in the private sector begins with a basic choice of remedy. One option is for the court to order the breaching party to perform its contractual obligations, backed by the threat of severe punishment should the party in breach refuse to comply (hefty fines, seizure of assets, time in jail). This option is broadly known as the remedy of 'specific performance', whereby the breaching party must either cure the breach or suffer the full force of the legal system. It is a member of the general class of remedies known as 'property rules', pursuant to which the law effectively forces parties who seek to impair legal rights of others to secure permission.

The alternative remedial option is to provide the breaching party with the option to pay damages in lieu of performing the contract. Several different measures of damages may be observed. Damages can restore the other party to its original position before the contract was made (rescission), compensate the other party for the costs of changing its position in reliance on the contract (reliance damages), or place the party in the position it would have enjoyed had the contract been performed (expectation damages). It is impossible to say in general which damages remedy is best, although the reliance option is generally known to be inferior.[20] A well-known advantage of the expectation measure, however, is that it tends to result in breach of contract only when breach is 'efficient'—if the breaching party can compensate the other party for the lost value of contractual performance and still remain better off, the result is a Pareto improvement. Contract damages remedies belong to the broader class of remedies known as 'liability rules'. Such rules allow parties to act in a manner that diminishes the legal rights of others without securing permission, allowing them instead to pay a 'price' *ex post*.

The choice between the property rule and liability approaches in contract law is not an easy one, as each has its disadvantages. The property rule approach trusts renegotiation to adjust the bargain when aspects of it become inefficient. Renegotiation, in turn, may be costly, lengthy, and subject to strategic behaviour. The liability rule approach avoids the difficulties that may arise with renegotiation but requires a mechanism to value damages, a mechanism that is itself costly and potentially error prone, even if the appropriate damages rule is in place.

These observations suggest some basic considerations that may favour one approach over the other. When damages are extremely difficult to calculate, for example, the property rule approach may be more appealing. By contrast, if renegotiation is problematic due to a prospect of holdouts or other likely sources of bargaining failure, the liability rule approach may be superior.

---

[20] The classic paper on contract damages remedies is Shavell 1980.

25.4.2 The 'equivalence' standard and efficient breach

As Schwartz and Sykes argue, the DSM functions in practice as a 'liability rule' rather than a 'property rule'.[21] At no point does the DSM compel a violator to seek permission to initiate or continue a violation, nor does it confront a violator with stiff 'punitive' sanctions.[22] Rather, a party found to be in violation of particular obligations may, if it so chooses, continue to violate them, even in perpetuity, and the price to be paid is the withdrawal of substantially equivalent concessions (failing negotiated compensation). Such a system does not 'ensure compliance', nor does it appear to be designed for that purpose. If compliance were the only objective, the remedial system would impose a penalty for breach high enough to discourage it altogether.

Further, the calibration of countermeasures is based on the harm done by the violation to complaining members—the level of 'nullification or impairment'. This fact suggests an immediate analogy to a particular damages remedy in contract law—expectation damages—pursuant to which a party in breach must compensate the other party for the harm suffered due to the breach (even though the penalty for violation here is plainly not monetary).[23] Schwartz and Sykes proceed from this observation to argue that the DSM utilizes 'equivalent' countermeasures in order to secure a well-known benefit of the expectation damages remedy—if a party that breaches its obligations must pay a 'price' equal to the value of the harm suffered by others, breach will occur if and only if the benefits to the breaching party exceed the harm done to others, i.e. if and only if breach is efficient.[24]

The use of the term 'efficiency' here requires some clarification. The efficient breach hypothesis is not a normative claim about the DSM. It is instead a *positive* claim about the retaliation mechanism chosen by the drafters of the DSU. The claim is that the 'substantial equivalence' standard was chosen because it tends to encourage breach when breach is efficient *from the perspective of the WTO negotiators*, and to discourage breach otherwise. The normative appeal of such a system depends in substantial part on whether the negotiators' maximand is normatively justifiable, an issue that the efficient breach hypothesis does not address.

25.4.2.1 *Ex ante and ex post efficiency*

The efficiency gains from a mechanism that optimizes the breach decision arise both *ex post* and *ex ante*. From the *ex post* perspective, efficient breach confers an aggregate gain on the parties to the bargain (Kaldor-Hicks efficiency), which can be converted into a gain for all affected parties (Pareto efficiency) if the parties injured by breach receive

[21] Schwartz and Sykes 2002.

[22] Similarly, members may revoke tariff concessions without permission under Article XXVIII, and may employ safeguard measures without permission under Article XIX.

[23] The monetary option is always possible as an element of negotiated compensation, to be sure, and has now been used in connection with settlements in both *US–Section 110 of the Copyright Act* and *US–Subsidies on Upland Cotton*.

[24] Schwartz and Sykes 2002.

compensation. And because efficient breach confers gains *ex post*, the parties to the bar-gain enjoy greater expected welfare *ex ante*. Indeed, a mechanism that ensures efficient breach *ex post* will maximize joint welfare *ex ante*, other things being equal.

The immediate implication of this proposition is that the possibility of efficient breach makes bargains more attractive. In the context of a trade agreement, it will produce a greater number of reciprocal trade concessions. A mechanism to facilitate efficient breach of trade agreements thus serves as a useful 'safety valve' in the terminology of Lawrence.[25] Parties to the WTO bargain know that they can respond to strong political pressures to deviate *ex post* as long as they pay the agreed price, which reduces the riski-ness of concessions and leads to an increased willingness to make them. An efficient breach mechanism thus resembles an efficient 'escape clause' mechanism, the difference being that an escape clause undertakes to specify *ex ante* the conditions under which deviation from the bargain is efficient, while the efficient breach mechanism recognizes that the ideal *ex ante* contingent contract is infeasible, so that occasional deviation from the agreement *ex post* may be desirable.[26]

25.4.2.2 *Formal analysis of the efficient breach hypothesis*

In the past few years, various economic commentators have begun to analyse formally the capacity of trade sanctions to facilitate efficient breach when shocks may render the original bargain inefficient.[27] Howse and Staiger consider the possibility of a shock that causes a government to seek to raise its tariff above the level of its current tariff commit-ment. In their 2-country, 2-good model, a retaliation rule somewhat akin to the rule WTO arbitrators employ, which allows a complaining nation to reduce its imports from the violator in an amount equal to its lost volume of exports due to the violation, evalu-ated at pre-violation prices, approximates the level of retaliation that will yield efficient breaches *if* the original tariffs were 'politically efficient' and the contemplated breach is 'small'. This level of retaliation also has the property that it preserves the original terms of trade between the violator and the complaining nation. Bown and Ruta extend this approach to consider violations other than illegal tariff increases.[28] Grossman and Sykes show that the equal track volume rule does not restore the terms of track in a more gen-eral setting (say, more than 2 trade of goods).[29]

These models raise the broader question of whether retaliation rules that allow WTO members to reverse the damage done by a violation to their terms of trade may be use-ful in providing proper incentives for breach. The answer is not fully developed,[30] but it is clear that such a retaliation rule is not in general 'first best'. Lawrence anticipates the

---

[25] Lawrence 2003.

[26] See Sykes 1991.

[27] See Howse and Staiger 2006; Bagwell and Staiger 2002; Limão and Saggi 2008; Bown and Ruta 2010; Beshkar 2010; Grossman and Sykes 2011.

[28] Bown and Ruta 2010.

[29] Grossman and Sykes 2011.

[30] Indeed, the notion that deterioration in the terms of trade is always a key issue in disputes is clearly wrong—consider a nation that complains about an illegal subsidy that damages its import-competing industry yet improves its terms of trade!

problem by noting that if retaliation simply restores the terms of trade, it nevertheless introduces the inefficiency of the higher (retaliatory) tariff.[31] Lawrence thus likens this rule for retaliation (or 'rebalancing', another term often used to describe the role of trade sanctions in the WTO) as akin to rescission of a contract rather than to a system of expectation damages. When the breaching party withdraws a concession, the other party responds by withdrawing a reciprocal concession, thus undoing the bargain and leaving each party at its pre-agreement welfare level. The party aggrieved by breach thus loses the benefits of the agreement and is not fully compensated.

Bagwell, and Grossman and Sykes put the point slightly differently.[32] Retaliation to restore the terms of trade eliminates the welfare loss associated with the deteriorated terms of trade, but the gains from a trade agreement also, in general, include benefits from an expanded volume of trade. In particular, if tariffs are initially politically efficient, and if the breach is 'small' (in a calculus sense), retaliation to restore the terms of trade will restore the welfare of the non-breaching party. But if the breach is 'large', such retaliation will still leave the aggrieved party worse off due to a decline in the volume of trade. Likewise, if the initial tariffs are not politically efficient and the aggrieved nation strictly prefers a larger volume of trade than is generated by the original bargain, retaliation to restore the terms of trade will also be insufficient to restore the welfare of the aggrieved party.

Beshkar makes the further argument that optimal retaliation is actually somewhat smaller than the level that fully restores the terms of trade because sanctions are costly.[33] Intuitively, the fact that trade sanctions are a source of dead weight loss implies that they should be used more sparingly.[34] Grossman and Sykes offer the related observation that if the sanctions mechanism requires the breaching party to restore fully the lost welfare of the party harmed by breach, while at the same time introducing a dead weight cost, then the penalty for breach is too high in relation to a Kaldor-Hicks efficiency standard.[35]

These observations clearly point to the difficulty of implementing an ideal rule to facilitate efficient breach. The approach to retaliation in the DSM will never be more than a crude mechanism towards this end, although further attention to the economics of retaliatory measures may enable it to attain greater precision. But the initial formal work on the subject does show how trade sanctions may, in principle, create useful incentives regarding the decision to comply or breach.

25.4.2.3 *Objections to the efficient breach hypothesis*

The hypothesis that the DSM is designed to calibrate the price for breach efficiently has nevertheless met with a considerable amount of criticism. This section considers the various objections to it, and offers some observations about their strengths and weaknesses.

---

[31] Lawrence 2003.
[32] Bagwell 2008; Grossman and Sykes 2011.
[33] Beshkar 2010.
[34] See also Limão and Saggi 2008.
[35] Grossman and Sykes 2011.

Breach is never efficient because other mechanisms for adjusting the bargain are adequate   As Schwartz and Sykes acknowledge, a mechanism to facilitate efficient breach has no utility if breach is never efficient.[36] In this respect, one must consider the possibility that other mechanisms for adjusting the WTO bargain over time are adequate to allow WTO members to avoid commitments that become inefficient.

Indeed, many mechanisms for adjusting the bargain are built into WTO law. Article XXVIII permits members to withdraw tariff concessions. If negotiations over concession withdrawal reach impasse, members may nevertheless proceed to withdraw them, subject to the ability of other members with a 'principal supplying interest' or 'substantial interest' to withdraw 'substantially equivalent concessions' in response.[37]

Similarly, GATT Article XIX (the 'escape clause'), as elaborated by the WTO Agreement on Safeguards, permits members to suspend concessions temporarily under circumstances where, as a result of 'unforeseen developments', 'increased quantities' of imports have caused or threaten to cause 'serious injury' to an import-competing industry. The Agreement on Safeguards allows such measures to be taken, without any obligation to compensate adversely affected trading partners, for a period of three years if certain conditions are met.[38] Thereafter, for a limited period, safeguard measures can be continued, but a member using them must negotiate compensation or again suffer the withdrawal of 'substantially equivalent concessions'.

Thus, tariff concessions may be revoked subject to a liability rule mechanism that in many ways resembles the DSM. Temporary suspension of concessions is also possible, also subject to a modified liability rule mechanism. GATT Article XX adds some exceptions to commitments for measures to protect public morals, public health, and so on.

Further, renegotiation is possible with respect to any WTO obligation. Rounds of negotiations have been undertaken throughout the history of the GATT/WTO system, and at the time of writing the latest (Doha) Round is ongoing. Negotiating rounds frequently revisit and modify or elaborate prior treaty commitments.

Are these options for modification of the WTO bargain collectively sufficient to address any obligations that may become inefficient? The answer is subject to some uncertainty, but there are good reasons to suspect that it may be 'no'. Perhaps the best way to make the point is by example.

One of the longest running disputes in the WTO system involves the importation of hormone-treated beef into Europe. The European Communities have prohibited domestic production and imports of such products, insisting that the prohibition is a legitimate health measure. Beef exporters, including the United States and Canada, argue that the policy is protectionist and not justified by any legitimate scientific evidence of health issues. In past proceedings, the WTO dispute process has sided with the United States and Canada, but Europe has declined to remove the prohibition and has instead been

---

[36] Schwartz and Sykes 2002.
[37] GATT Article XXVIII(3).
[38] Agreement on Safeguards, Article 8(3).

subject to ongoing retaliation. The dispute seems to have been settled for the moments, but only after decades of wrangling.

Suppose, *arguendo*, that Europe is indeed in violation of its WTO obligations, but that domestic political pressures to continue its policy are so great that breach is efficient (the benefits to Europe exceed the costs to other nations). Can Europe employ the above-mentioned devices to avoid its commitments on hormone-treated beef without the need for formal breach?

An increase in the most-favoured nation tariff on beef imports under GATT Article XXVIII cannot do the job of screening out hormone-treated beef. Europe might attempt to create a new tariff classification for hormone-treated beef and then impose a prohibi-tive tariff, but this action would trigger retaliation rights under GATT Article XXVIII much like those involved in the ongoing dispute, and would not materially alter things. Indeed, from Europe's perspective, that option would be worse because it would forfeit the opportunity to continue arguing that its current policies are legal under the WTO Agreement on Sanitary and Phytosanitary Measures (SPS). Likewise, Europe cannot address its desire for a permanent ban on hormone-treated beef through an Article XIX action—among other things, because the prerequisites for such action are not present, and such actions are temporary.

Does renegotiation offer a solution? The answer is likely to be no against the backdrop of the existing DSM. The United States and Canada hint at no willingness to revise the SPS Agreement in Europe's favour, and indeed the hormone-treated beef dispute pro-vided much of the impetus for the negotiation of that Agreement. It is possible that Europe might offer some side-payment to buy its way out of obligations under the SPS Agreement during the course of a negotiating round, but of course it has had that option under the DSM since the beginning of the dispute. The fact that the dispute has been around for many years, pre-dating the formation of the WTO, casts considerable doubt on the likelihood of a change in WTO rules to resolve the dispute. Instead, Europe must realistically choose between three options: compliance, retaliation, or negotiated com-pensation (the present solution).

To be sure, if the DSM were designed differently—perhaps with stiff punitive sanc-tions for violations instead of sanctions based on 'equivalence' (the property rule approach)—Europe might have beeen pressed sooner into making an offer that mem-bers such as the United States and Canada might accept. But would such a system be superior? The obvious difficulty is that the United States, Canada, and other interested members might well hold out for a large share of the surplus from Europe's action. The possibility of bargaining breakdown is obvious, doubly so with multiple members (and thus multiple potential holdouts) involved as complainants. Because of these problems, efficient breaches might not occur.

In short, the built-in mechanisms for adjusting the WTO bargain appear inadequate to address all of the scenarios in which breach may be efficient. Renegotiation is always a fallback option, but a highly imperfect one, especially given the potentially large number of players who may need to agree on any changes in obligations. If this analysis is right, then something is to be said for a mechanism that permits breach to occur subject to an appropriate liability rule mechanism.[39]

Trade sanctions do not compensate *firms and workers* **harmed by violations**   Various commentators make the point that neither trade sanctions nor trade compensation afford any relief to the firms and workers injured by the breach of WTO obligations (unless, of course, such measures eventually lead to compliance).[40] Rather, the beneficiaries of trade sanctions will be firms and workers in import-competing industries that receive retaliatory protection, while the beneficiaries of trade compensation will be the purchasers of goods on which compensatory tariff concessions are made. Thus, Pauwelyn states: 'a violation in, for example, the beef sector is not in any way compensated by a tariff concession or reciprocal suspension in, for example, the textile sector. As a result, it is difficult to speak of breach with the victims of breach being fully compensated, a true *conditio sine qua non* for there to be "efficient breach".'[41]

Although it is certainly correct that firms and workers injured by a violation are not made whole by trade sanctions or compensation in other industries, the conclusion drawn by Pauwelyn and others from this observation does not follow. 'Efficient breach' implies that the benefits of breach to the breaching party exceed the costs to the non-breaching party (or parties). This condition can hold irrespective of whether the non-breaching party is in fact compensated for breach.

Perhaps the implicit premise of this criticism is that the term 'efficient breach' refers exclusively to cases in which breach yields an *ex post* Pareto improvement for all affected individuals. If that is the claim, it simply misunderstands the argument put forward by the proponents of the efficient breach hypothesis.

As noted, the efficient breach hypothesis uses the term 'efficiency' from the perspective of the political officials who negotiate trade agreements—the claim is that trade agreements will maximize the joint welfare of those officials (or of their governments, as in the modern literature on the political economy of trade policy). An 'efficient breach' is one that benefits the government that commits the breach more than it harms the governments of adversely affected trading partners. This condition can hold even if the firms and workers harmed by the breach receive no compensation.

Indeed, it is not even necessary for the *governments* adversely affected by a breach to receive compensation *ex post*—compensation can occur *ex ante*, as noted earlier. If all governments have the opportunity to engage in efficient breaches, it is possible that the *ex ante* gains for every nation are positive, even with zero compensation *ex post*. Of course, it is important that breaches not become opportunistic, and some mechanism is needed to ensure that they tend to be efficient. But it can suffice for such a mechanism

---

[39] See also chapter 6 of Schropp 2009 for a concurring view on the superiority of a liability rule approach.

[40] For example Anderson 2002.

[41] Pauwelyn 2010.

simply to *penalize* the party in breach by an appropriate amount, even if it does not *compensate* the party harmed by breach.[42] The opportunity for political officials to use trade sanctions in response to a breach by another WTO member, however, indeed affords them a form of compensation, as argued below.

Trade sanctions harm the *nations* that employ them and cannot compensate them for breach   A related objection to the efficient breach hypothesis stems from the claim that trade sanctions injure the nations that employ them.[43] Pauwelyn argues that 'non-compliance in combination with reciprocal suspensions is *not* a situation of 'efficient breach' in any economic sense of the word: by their very nature WTO suspensions do not compensate the victim (like other sanctions, they are costly to the victim and intended rather to punish the wrongdoer)'.[44]

As Mercurio notes, the foundation of such objections to trade sanctions lies in the belief that tariff increases are economically inefficient.[45] To be sure, positive tariffs indeed reduce national income for a 'small' country that lacks any ability to influence its terms of trade. But the proposition that trade sanctions are 'inefficient' in general, that they cannot provide 'compensation', or that they cannot be part of a mechanism that facilitates efficient breach 'in any economic sense of the word', hardly follows.

First, to reiterate the points above, it is a fallacy to assume that retaliatory measures must benefit or 'compensate' the nations that employ them in order for a retaliatory mechanism to play a role in facilitating efficient breach (and discouraging inefficient breach). All that is necessary is that the retaliatory mechanism causes potential violators to bear a cost that approximates to the injury that a violation will cause to others (thereby inducing potential violators to 'internalize the externality').

To be sure, when the retaliatory mechanism entails measures that create dead weight losses, these costs must be taken into account in designing a retaliation mechanism, and some subtle issues may arise.[46] The notion of 'efficient breach' itself may require adjustment when breach necessarily triggers a costly enforcement mechanism in addition to the harms that arise directly from the breach. One can even imagine scenarios where the available enforcement mechanism is so costly that it is better not to use it at all. But the mere fact that sanctions entail some dead weight losses does not establish that they cannot be used to confront potential violators with an appropriate price for breach.

---

[42] Pelc makes the same conceptual error when, for example, he argues that the WTO system has moved away from trying to facilitate efficient deviations from the bargain by reducing the compensation requirement under the WTO Agreement on Safeguards (Pelc 2010). The safeguards mechanism may afford *ex ante* gains to WTO members and therefore be efficient, regardless of the degree to which compensation occurs *ex post*.

[43] For example Charnovitz 2001; Anderson 2002.

[44] Pauwelyn 2010.

[45] Mercurio 2009.

[46] See Beshkar 2010; Grossman and Sykes 2010.

Second, a nation that employs conventional trade sanctions is (for reasons discussed below) likely to be 'large' (able to influence its terms of trade), and such a nation may well have bound its tariffs under GATT below their 'optimal' level. Such a nation can increase its national income by increasing tariffs, and thereby receive compensation from retaliatory tariff increases. A reduction in global income ensues from such measures, of course, but the net loss may be borne entirely by the violator that is the target of sanctions, which, of course, makes the sanction more useful.

Third, sanctions *may* take the form of measures that have little effect on global efficiency, or even enhance it. Cross-retaliation under the TRIPS Agreement, for example, may primarily transfer rents from intellectual property interest groups in a violator country to interest groups in a complaining nation, with little welfare impact (if it is not large enough to materially affect innovation incentives) or even positive welfare impact (if it draws down excessively monopoly rents to intellectual property). Likewise, in the cases where a violator offers trade compensation to avert retaliation, the resulting trade liberalization can be efficiency-enhancing from a global perspective.

Finally, and most importantly, national (or global) income is not the relevant welfare metric, as has been noted at length above—even when trade sanctions are 'inefficient' from the standpoint of traditional welfare economics, they are nevertheless valuable to political officials who are empowered to use them. The modern trade literature typically postulates that governments maximize a welfare function that incorporates political economy weights.[47] A common presumption is that producer welfare receives more weight than consumer welfare. If so, protection that benefits import-competing producers can increase national 'welfare' even if it reduces national income.

The same point may be put slightly differently: what do the parties to trade agreements maximize? As suggested above, it is plausible to assume that the objective of trade negotiators is to maximize the political welfare of officials in power. The victims of 'breach' are not the firms and workers who lose rents, but the political officials who suffer a loss of political support. The question of whether trade sanctions can 'compensate' for breach is not a question of whether sanctions can raise national income or restore the welfare of firms and workers, but a question of whether they can be used to restore lost political support. In that regard, political officials who receive the authority to use sanctions can restore their support by using them to coerce a violator towards compliance, or by using them to afford protection to producer interest groups who will reward them for it. Indeed, a political official with the power to use trade sanctions is, by definition, less constrained than a political official without such power, and can use this power in a way that enhances political support. In this sense, trade sanctions are almost certainly (at least partially) compensatory.

---

[47] For example Grossman and Helpman 1994; Bagwell and Staiger 2002.

WTO retaliation in practice is poorly calibrated in relation to the efficient breach objective   Another objection to the efficient breach hypothesis is the suggestion that, in practice, WTO arbitrators follow arbitrary, incoherent, or inconsistent approaches to setting the level of retaliation. They do not agree on the objectives of retaliation or how to calculate it, and their calculations are full of dubious assumptions and crude guesswork.[48]

Indeed, it is often unclear what 'compliance' means, and it is thus unclear what counterfactual to use in deciding what amount of harm has been caused by the violation. *US–Gambling* is illustrative of this, in which the United States was found to have violated its commitments to afford market access to offshore service providers, including providers of Internet gambling services. The United States sought to justify its policies under GATS Article XIV (which provides exceptions to GATS obligations), a defence that was accepted in principle but that could not save the ban on offshore betting on horse races given that the United States permitted remote gambling on horse racing domestically. The United States nevertheless refused to repeal the ban. In the arbitration over sanctions, the arbitrator was faced with the problem of deciding what compliance counterfactual to use. The complainant (Antigua) argued that compliance required the United States to open all forms of gambling to offshore providers (as it had ostensibly promised under GATS), while the United States ultimately urged that it could comply merely by removing the ban with respect to horse racing (invoking its Article XIV rights with respect to other forms of gambling). The arbitrator ultimately sided with the United States with a dissenting vote, more or less on the grounds that the US proposal reflected the most plausible way that the United States might comply.

These concerns about the arbitration process in practice have considerable force. The WTO legal system is in its infancy, and the number of arbitrations to date is small. Given the lack of tight textual guidance and the confusion engendered by the different language on retaliation in the SCM Agreement, it is hardly surprising that arbitrators have struggled with issues concerning the proper counterfactual and the challenges of quantifying 'nullification or impairment'. Neither is it a surprise that the arbitral decisions are not always consistent with each other. In time, one can reasonably expect the jurisprudence to improve as thoughtful legal and economic commentators offer critique and suggestions for improvement, so that eventually arbitrations can more reliably set a proper price for breach. But the fact that arbitrations to date include findings that may rest on dubious assumptions does not seriously undercut the hypothesis that the *objective* of the equivalence standard is to create appropriate incentives for breach, or that a proper approach to calibrating retaliation can achieve that objective reasonably well.

Prospective trade sanctions are undercompensatory   Numerous commentators have noted that sanctions under the WTO are not available until a violation has been formally

---

[48] See Spamann 2006 and various essays in Bown and Pauwelyn 2010.

adjudicated and the 'reasonable period of time' for the violator to comply has elapsed.[49] Indeed, even that time frame is subject to slippage, as violators may insincerely claim that they have complied with a ruling, and force the complaining nation to obtain a favourable ruling from a 'compliance panel' before sanctions can be imposed.[50] As a result, violators can avoid any sanctions for a few years after the violation is first detected, a situation colloquially known in WTO parlance as the 'three-year free pass'. Likewise, the current understanding in WTO jurisprudence is that sanctions, once authorized, should be equivalent to the *prospective* nullification or impairment of the ongoing violation, and are not intended to compensate for harm suffered up to that point. Plainly, this system appears undercompensatory in relation to the total harm suffered from a violation. Indeed, if a violator cures the violation after the reasonable period for compliance, there is no sanction at all, and no requirement to provide any compensation.

This feature of the DSM is indeed puzzling, although commentators have offered some conjectures about its rationale. Schwartz and Sykes argue that many disputes in the WTO (although by no means all) appear to involve good faith disagreements about the content of obligations.[51] Because sanctions in the system are costly, and because litigation can provide useful clarification of the bargain for all members (a positive externality), it may make sense to encourage parties to litigate these good faith disputes to conclusion. The DSM plainly does so by insulating parties from sanctions until litigation concludes. In a related way, some nations may have limited compliance capacity due to a lack of technical expertise, especially developing countries, and it may not make sense to impose costly sanctions on them for their 'accidental' violations, as long as they cure them once they are clearly identified.

These thoughts are speculative at best, however, and may paint an excessively rosy picture. It is not difficult to think of actual disputes involving fairly flagrant violations of WTO law, for example, which are quite difficult to characterize as 'good faith disputes'. Thus, as many commentators have argued, it is entirely possible that the existing dispute resolution system may unduly encourage temporary cheating.

Even if the system is unduly lenient on violations, however, it does not follow that the efficient breach hypothesis should be rejected. Indeed, if the competing hypothesis is that the system is designed to 'ensure compliance', then undue leniency is even more puzzling.

Trade sanctions are of no use to small countries   Numerous commentators make the point that economically 'small' nations cannot use conventional trade sanctions effectively.[52] Such countries lack the market power to move world prices and thus to affect the returns to exporters in a violator nation. Accordingly, the argument runs, the

---

[49] See, e.g. Schwartz and Sykes 2002; Pauwelyn 2010; Schropp 2009.
[50] Brewster 2010.
[51] Schwartz and Sykes 2002.
[52] See, e.g. Mercurio 2009; Mavroidis 2000; Bagwell 2008.

DSM does not protect small countries and they may become the victims of inefficient breach. Various reform proposals follow from this observation, such as shifting to monetary compensation in lieu of trade sanctions or allowing retaliation rights to be auctioned.[53]

This concern about the strategic position of small countries is certainly justified to some extent, but it is important not to overstate it. The DSU provides for cross-retaliation when retaliation in the same sector or under the same agreement as that involving the violation is not 'practicable or effective'. Small countries such as Ecuador (in *EC–Bananas)* and Antigua (*US–Gambling*), and not so small countries such as Brazil (*US–Upland Cotton*), have thus received authorization to retaliate against violations involving trade in goods with sanctions pertaining to intellectual property rights. Although such measures have not to date been implemented, and it is unclear precisely how they would work, it does seem that even a small country can in principle be quite an effective and profitable pirate of intellectual property. Thus, it is perhaps a mistake to imagine that small countries are entirely helpless.

To the degree that small countries are at a strategic disadvantage under the DSM, however, it is only because the concessions they make under a trade agreement lack value to others—if small countries cannot affect world prices through trade sanctions, they are also unable to affect them through tariff concessions. The fact that the DSM is not designed well to protect the interests of countries whose concessions are of little importance to others is a natural outcome of the bargaining process, and does not pose a serious challenge to the hypothesis that the DSM seeks to create efficient incentives for breach among the more important players.

Likewise, one must again ask: what is the competing hypothesis? If the system were designed to 'ensure compliance', the lack of protection for smaller nations seems even more problematic.

The efficient breach hypothesis fails to take account of informal sanctions   Pauwelyn criticizes the efficient breach hypothesis on the grounds that the incentives for compliance in the system do not depend entirely on a prospect of 'equivalent' sanctions following a breach.[54] He argues that breach results in other, informal sanctions, some of which he terms 'community costs', and further observes that when these informal sanctions are combined with formal retaliation, the penalty for breach may exceed the level that would produce efficient breach, and push the system closer to 'ensuring compliance'.

Pauwelyn is surely right that informal sanctions for breach have played a role in the trading system. Indeed, in the days of GATT, formal retaliation was non-existent, and the bargain held together nonetheless because of some combination of actual or threatened unilateral retaliation, coupled perhaps with a concern on the part of GATT members for avoiding damage to their reputations as reliable trading partners.

---

[53] See Bronckers and van den Broek 2005; Davey 2005; Bagwell, Mavroidis, and Staiger 2007.
[54] Pauwelyn 2010.

With the advent of the WTO, however, unilateral retaliation has been supplanted, under the DSU, with collectively authorized retaliation. Indeed, an end to unilateralism was a key objective of the DSU.[55] To date, WTO members have respected, at least formally, their commitment under the DSU not to 'take the law into their own hands', and have avoided retaliatory measures outside the purview of the DSM. To be sure, the suspicion arises that WTO members may at times employ less transparent forms of unilateral retaliation, such as the initiation of WTO-legal proceedings under the anti-dumping laws. But, at a minimum, it appears that unilateral retaliation has been greatly circumscribed.

The other informal sanction relates to a trading nation's 'reputation', and corresponds to Pauwelyn's notion of community costs. The importance of reputational considerations in the WTO system has always been questionable, however, and is even more questionable after the advent of the DSU.

In economics, reputation games involve conditions of asymmetric information. Actors wish to deal with 'reliable' types and to avoid dealing with 'unreliable' types, but cannot identify an actor's type directly and must draw an inference based on each actor's history of reliable or unreliable behaviour. Thus, when an actor behaves 'reliably', it gains a reputation for such behaviour and is able to engage in a greater degree of useful cooperation with others. The notion that trading nations must rely on reputation to decide which nations are worthy of cooperation on trade matters, however, is dubious. Particularly with the transparent democracies such as the United States, Canada, Australia, Japan, the members of the European Union, and so on, the propensity of a nation to keep to its commitments on particular trade issues can be gleaned more reliably from the newspapers, from political speeches, from legislative hearings, and the like than from past behaviour. It is questionable whether the occasional violation of treaty commitments adds much additional information. Likewise, the fact that a nation has violated one commitment because of domestic political pressures says little about its propensity to violate others. And, as Brewster argues, it seems implausible that 'reputation' crosses issue areas or survives changes in political administrations.[56]

Furthermore, a violation of WTO law need not beget any loss of reputation at all after the enactment of the DSU. The DSU provides that a violation shall be followed by certain consequences, including, eventually, compensation or measured retaliation. As argued above, the retaliation mechanism can be understood to allow for efficient breach. If that claim is right, why should a nation that breaches and pays the requisite price suffer any loss of reputation? It is simply behaving in a fashion that the DSM was designed to permit.

Accordingly, it is questionable whether any substantial informal sanctions for breach survive the enactment of the DSM. It is even less clear that any remaining informal sanctions, when added to the prospect of 'equivalent' countermeasures, are enough to 'ensure

---

[55] Schwartz and Sykes 2002.
[56] Brewster 2009.

compliance'. The fact that some members elect not to comply with their obligations despite ongoing countermeasures indeed suggests otherwise.

25.5 CONCLUSION

A remarkable amount of academic attention has been devoted to analysing the objectives of the DSM and to its practical consequences. The most controversial suggestion, both from a legal and an economic standpoint, is the hypothesis that the 'equivalence' standard for retaliation under DSU Article 22 serves to (crudely) optimize the incentives for WTO members to breach their obligations, thus serving (in part) as a mechanism for adjusting the bargain to changing circumstances. A corollary of this hypothesis is that the goal of the DSM is not to 'ensure compliance', but only to ensure 'efficient' compliance. This chapter has addressed both the legal and economic objections to this line of thinking, arguing that many of the objections result from error or misunderstanding, while others have greater merit. The debate will no doubt continue, and I hope only to have made some further contribution to its precision and clarity.

REFERENCES

Anderson, Kym. 2002. Peculiarities of Retaliation in WTO Dispute Settlement. *World Trade Review* 1 (2): 123–34.

Bagwell, Kyle. 2008. Remedies in the WTO: An Economic Perspective. In *The WTO: Governance, Dispute Settlement and Developing Countries*, edited by Merit E. Janow, Victoria J. Donaldson, and Alan Yanovich, 733–70. Huntington, NY: Juris Publishing.

Bagwell, Kyle, Petros C. Mavroidis, and Robert W. Staiger. 2007. Auctioning Countermeasures in the WTO. *Journal of International Economics* 73 (2):309–32.

Bagwell, Kyle, and Robert W. Staiger. 2002. *The Economics of the World Trading System.* Cambridge, MA: MIT Press.

Bello, Judith H. 1996. The WTO Dispute Settlement Understanding: Less is More. *American Journal of International Law* 90 (3):416–18.

Beshkar, Mostafa. 2010. Optimal Remedies in International Trade Agreements. *European Economic Review* 54 (3):455–66.

Bhagwati, Jagdish, and Hugh T. Patrick. 1990. *Aggressive Unilateralism: America's 301 Trade Policy and the World Trading System.* Ann Arbor: University of Michigan Press.

Bown, Chad P. 2004. On the Economic Success of GATT/WTO Dispute Settlement. *Review of Economics and Statistics* 86 (3):811–23.

Bown, Chad P., and Joost Pauwelyn, eds. 2010. *The Law, Economics and Politics of Retaliation in WYO Dispute Settlement.* Cambridge: Cambridge University Press.

Bown, Chad P., and Michele Ruta. 2010. The Economics of Permissible WTO Retaliation. In *The Law, Economics and Politics of Retaliation in WTO Dispute Settlement*, edited by Chad P. Bown and Joost Pauwelyn, 149–93. Cambridge: Cambridge University Press.

Brewster, Rachel. 2009. The Limits of Reputation on Compliance. *International Theory* 1 (2):323–33.

Brewster, Rachel. 2010. The Remedy Gap: Institutional Design, Retaliation, and Trade Law Enforcement. Unpublished mimeo.

Bronckers, Marco, and Naboth van den Broek. 2005. Financial Compensation in the WTO: Improving the Remedies of WTO Dispute Settlement. *Journal of International Economic Law* 8 (1): 101–26.

Charnovitz, Steve. 2001. Rethinking WTO Trade Sanctions. *American Journal of International Law* 95 (4):792–832.

Davey, William J. 2005. The Sutherland Report on Dispute Settlement: A Comment. *Journal of International Economic Law* 8 (2):321–8.

Grossman, Gene M., and Elhanan Helpman. 1994. Protection for Sale. *American Economic Review* 84 (4):833–50.

Grossman, Gene M., and Alan O. Sykes. 2011. Optimal Retaliation in the WTO-A commentory on the Upland Cotton Arbitration, *Word Trade Review* 10: 133–64.

Horn, Henrik, Giovanni Maggi, and Robert W. Staiger. 2010. Trade Agreements as Endogenously Incomplete Contracts. *American Economic Review* 100 (1):394–419.

Howse, Robert, and Robert W. Staiger. 2006. United States—Anti-Dumping Act of 1916 (Original Complaint by the European Communities)—Recourse to Arbitration by the United States under 22.6 of the DSU, WT/DS136/ARB, 24 February 2004: A Legal and Economic Analysis. In *The WTO Case Law of 2003: The American Law Institute Reporters' Studies*, edited by Henrik Horn and Petros C. Mavroidis, 254–79. Cambridge: Cambridge University Press.

Hudec, Robert E. 1975. *The GATT Legal System and World Trade Diplomacy*. New York: Praeger Publishers.

Jackson, John H. 1997. The WTO Dispute Settlement Understanding—Misunderstandings on the Nature of Legal Obligation. *American Journal of International Law* 91 (1):60–4.

Jackson, John H. 2004. Editorial Comment: International Law Status of WTO DS Reports: Obligation to Comply or Option to 'Buy-Out'? *American Journal of International Law* 98: 109–25.

Lawrence, Robert Z. 2003. *Crimes and Punishments? Retaliation Under the WTO*. Washington, DC: Peterson Institute for International Economics.

Limão, Nuno, and Kamal Saggi. 2008. Tariff Retaliation Versus Financial Compensation in the Enforcement of International Trade Agreements. *Journal of International Economics* 76 (1):48–60.

Maggi, Giovanni. 1999. The Role of Multilateral Institutions in International Trade Cooperation. *American Economic Review* 89 (1):190–214.

Maggi, Giovanni, and Robert W. Staiger. 2011. The Role of Dispute Settlement Procedures in International Agreements. *Quarterly Journal of Economics* 126: 475–515.

Mavroidis, Petros C. 2000. Remedies in the WTO Legal System: Between a Rock and a Hard Place. *European Journal of International Law* 11 (4):763–813.

Mercurio, Bryan. 2009. Why Compensation Cannot Replace Trade Retaliation in the WTO Dispute Settlement Understanding. *World Trade Review* 8 (2):315–38.

Pauwelyn, Joost. 2000. Enforcement and Countermeasures in the WTO: Rules are Rules—Toward a More Collective Approach. *American Journal of International Law* 94 (2):335–47.

Pauwelyn, Joost. 2010. The Calculation and Design of Trade Retaliation in Context: What is the Goal of Suspending WTO Obligations? In *The Law, Economics and Politics of Retaliation in WTO Dispute Settlement*, edited by Chad P. Bown and Joost Pauwelyn, 34–65. Cambridge: Cambridge University Press.

Pelc, Krzysztof J. 2010. Eluding Efficiency: Why do we Not See More Efficient Breach at the WTO? *World Trade Review* 9 (4):629–42.

Schropp, Simon A. B. 2009. *Trade Policy Flexibility and Enforcement in the WTO: A Law and Economics Analysis*. Cambridge: Cambridge University Press.

Schwartz, Warren F., and Alan O. Sykes. 2002. The Economic Structure of Renegotiation and Dispute Resolution in the WTO. *Journal of Legal Studies* 31 (1):179–204.

Shavell, Steven. 1980. Damage Measures for Breach of Contract. *Bell Journal of Economics* 11 (2):466–90.

Spamann, Holger. 2006. The Myth of 'Rebalancing' Retaliation in WTO Dispute Settlement Practice. *Journal of International Economic Law* 9 (1):31–79.

Sykes, Alan O. 1991. Protectionism as a 'Safeguard': A Positive Analysis of the GATT 'Escape Clause' with Normative Speculations. *University of Chicago Law Review* 58 (1):255–306.

Sykes, Alan O. 2000. The Remedy for Breach of Obligations Under the WTO Dispute Settlement Understanding: Damages or Specific Performance? In *New Directions in International Economic Law: Essays in Honour of John H. Jackson*, edited by Marco Bronckers and Reinhard Quick, 347–57. The Hague: Kluwer.

PART VII

CHALLENGES TO THE SYSTEM

CHAPTER 26

PERSISTENT DEADLOCK IN MULTILATERAL TRADE NEGOTIATIONS: THE CASE OF DOHA

MANFRED ELSIG AND CÉDRIC DUPONT[*]

26.1 INTRODUCTION

NEGOTIATIONS over distributive issues are naturally characterized by periods of progress and of stagnation. Therefore, it is not unusual that, from time to time, negotiations over the way countries open their economies to trade appear deadlocked. The history of GATT (General Agreement on Tariffs and Trade) negotiations is full of anecdotes on missed deadlines, failed ministerial conferences, and brinkmanship situations. Tactics such as walking away from the table or sleep-depriving night sessions are legendary in the context of attempting to overcome impasse in negotiations. The last hurdles for concluding the Uruguay Round were addressed by contracting parties' highest office-holders far from Geneva. The final sticking point cleared in the last night of negotiations was the European (French) reluctance to further liberalize audio-visual services. Before US President Bill Clinton accepted the deal on the table, he called 'Hollywood' to make sure they would not later torpedo the agreement.[1] Yet, while this issue was the last to be resolved between the transatlantic partners to conclude the Round, the more important deadlock was overcome earlier. The G2 (the US and the European Union) announced that the old rules of the GATT would no longer apply, and therefore states had to join the

[*] We wish to thank Susan Kaplan and Amrita Narlikar for their valuable comments. We acknowledge support from the NCCR Trade Regulation of the Swiss National Science Foundation.
[1] Interview with Leon Brittan, November 2000.

World Trade Organization (WTO) (and the agreements it covered).[2] This drastically changed the status quo options for many contracting parties to the GATT.

This chapter takes issue with the current deadlock (at the time of writing) of the Doha Round negotiations. After the Round started in 2001 and deliberations picked up in the various negotiation committees, the Ministerial Conference in Cancún culminated in a first major failure to agree how to move forward.[3] Momentum was restored in summer 2004 as negotiators agreed, in Geneva, on a framework to tackle a number of thorny issues, including agriculture. And in autumn 2004 and spring 2005 a number of small group meetings, building upon the framework agreement, searched for common ground in three main areas—agriculture, services, and industrial goods (in WTO language: non-agricultural market access (NAMA). These attempts, however, failed to move the complex Geneva negotiation machinery forward, and since the Ministerial Conference in Hong Kong in late 2005 progress has been hardly visible. In summer 2008, an informal ministerial meeting with selected members attempted to address some of the obstacles. But in the end, ministers failed to reach an agreement once more. At the most recent Ministerials in Geneva in 2009 and 2011, members abstained from engaging in any meaningful type of negotiations.[4]

Members' deliberations have over time oscillated across the different concentric negotiation circles, including various sizes of WTO membership. However, in recent years the Geneva process has been stalled and dependent on the momentum to be achieved in small group negotiations, in particular among four countries (which are those called upon to offer concessions and which also make substantial demands): the US, the European Union, Brazil, and India.[5] Strong divisions within this small group have hindered progress and contributed to the lowering of overall ambitions as to the market-liberalizing outcome. And, at the time of writing, there is still no outcome in sight, despite the efforts of the WTO Director-General (DG), Pascal Lamy, to push negotiations forward. The DG has on various occasions told the members: 'we have talked the talk, now we should walk the walk'.

Different expressions have been used along the way to give meaning to the difficulties in progressing in the negotiations. With the passage of time, the notions have moved from a failed opportunity, delay or postponement, taking time out for reflection, to stronger wording such as stalling of the round, or (persistent) deadlock, to the writing of post-mortems. The aim of this chapter is to go beyond an exercise in creating additional labels, and to examine the structural dynamics of deadlock throughout the Round. To do so, we approach the negotiation dilemmas faced by WTO members through game-theoretic lenses. From this perspective, we view deadlock in the Doha Round as the result of a series of overlapping and chronologically sequential games, rather than as a

---

[2] Steinberg 2002.

[3] Narlikar and Tussie 2004.

[4] The WTO treaties stipulate that members meet every two years at the level of the ministers. There was no ministerial meeting in 2007.

[5] China is a special case. While there are expectations by other members that China should more actively engage in concessions-trading, China has remained critical about additional leadership.

single overall stalemate game. Game theory, in this light, might assist in disentangling complex situations of cooperation, and in conceptualizing deadlock as a process of ongoing negotiations over issues that are hard to settle within the context of a decision-making machinery characterized by consensus. The chapter is structured as follows: first, we offer our definition of deadlock and discuss a set of factors highlighted in the international relations literature that explain the existence and persistence of deadlock. Second, with the help of game theory, we attempt to illustrate the challenges actors face in negotiations. Finally, we sketch two general scenarios for the future of the Doha Round.

26.2 THE CONCEPT OF DEADLOCK AND ITS DETERMINANTS

One important lesson learned from the study of trade negotiations in the context of a multilateral trade round is that this type of business takes time. The Dillon Round lasted from 1960–2, the Kennedy Round was concluded in just over three years (1964–7), the Tokyo Round stretched over a six-year period, and the Uruguay Round was not concluded until eight years of intensive bargaining had taken place. The Doha Round is currently in its eleventh year. Given the increase in the number of actors and topics, while there has been no change in the consensual decision-making processes, the length of negotiations is, in itself, not surprising.[6] In addition, it usually takes a long time before negotiators get nervous and see absence of progress as a malign development. Negotiators usually do not act under immense pressure—the exception being when the negotiations pick up speed and the final showdown approaches. Thus, trade negotiators do not perceive deadlock as threatening, which stands in sharp contrast to bargaining situations that decide on war and peace (e.g. if negotiations on a ceasefire break down, this could trigger more conflict, creating huge social and human costs).

Conceptually, we use Odell's definition of deadlock as 'a period during a negotiation when parties stand firm on inconsistent positions'.[7] Actors wait for each other to move and make little effort to revive negotiations, while expectations grow that actors should move towards producing a tangible outcome.[8]

What are the factors that explain the existence and persistence of deadlock? Based on the vast array of work on international negotiations and on international cooperation

---

[6] Elsig 2011.

[7] Odell 2009, 274–5.

[8] In order to differentiate deadlock from other pauses in negotiations, Narlikar suggests this situation to be one in which an internal or an external event exists that puts pressure on parties. Such an event can be described as 'a landmark moment...which may be an "action-forcing event" in the shape of a chair's text or a deadline imposed by a mediator, or may be a natural landmark endogenous to the negotiation and recognized as such by the parties involved' (Narlikar 2010, 2–3).

more generally, we identify four sets of 'structural/contextual' factors that cut across research paradigms in international relations: interests, institutions, ideas, and information. Understanding the impact of these sets of factors helps to anticipate potential deadlocks, but a finer analysis needs to take into account the mitigating/intervening impact of actors' behavioural choices (tactics, strategies).[9] We delay such a discussion to the next section, which is devoted to games played by actors.

26.2.1 On interests

An interest-based reading can either draw from a realist or a liberal paradigm. While for the liberal school, states' positions are shaped by domestic interest groups (the pluralist story), for the realist camp, power considerations largely determine the interest calculation of political elites and therefore foreign policy (the national interest story). What is important is that the interests of states will guide the negotiators, as these interests define what is acceptable at home. Moving to international bargaining, in the realist version, states' behaviour is driven by a quest to increase, or preserve, relative power.[10] But following a kind of circular reasoning, states' ability to achieve such an objective depends on existing power resources, mostly material ones. These resources are translated to the negotiations in indirect forms. In the trade policy area, power is often equated with how much parties can affect trade relations (in the absence of international rules) by resorting to unilateral trade policy instruments to limit market access, bluntly privileging some trading partners over others (through preferential trade agreements), or using alternative means of influence through other foreign policy tools (e.g. foreign aid or investment). If the most important actors wish for a particular outcome, they will find ways to push their preferences through.[11] Put into the negotiation analytic jargon, powerful actors impact on the bargaining dynamics through their ability to create best alternatives to a negotiated agreement (BATNAs).[12] Yet, as power becomes more equally distributed in the area of trade, single actors are less successful at dominating outcomes, and deadlock becomes a frequent outcome.[13]

The liberal version also takes as a starting position that interests (defined as a result of domestic competition among interest groups) predetermine the possible outcomes in international negotiations. Demands from specific interest groups delimit what is acceptable at home, which in turn affects what is agreeable at the international level (a 'landing zone' in the words of the current DG of the WTO), as argued by Putnam in his seminal piece on 'two-level games'.[14] From this perspective, governments remain

---

[9] Odell 2000.   [10] Krasner 1976, 1978.   [11] Gruber 2000.
[12] Raiffa 1982; Lax and Sebenius 1991.   [13] Dupont 1994; Drezner 2007.
[14] Putnam 1988. For an application of the two-level game metaphor to a range of international economic negotiations, see Evans, Jacobson, and Putnam 1993. For a discussion of the complexity of the interplay between domestic and international constraints under various contextual dimensions, see Iida 1993; Dupont 1994; Mo 1995.

very attentive to BATNAs. Such options may become the solution to the absence of a 'win-set' of agreements agreeable at the international level and feasible at the domestic level. BATNAs also serve as benchmarks to help design a cooperative solution to the bargaining problem.[15] Crucial in this process of choosing among various solutions is the saliency of domestic economic interests.[16] Those who rely on a deal and are not well positioned as to BATNA will be less influential at the international bargaining table as they will have to make more concessions. From a liberal viewpoint, variation in the number of international and domestic actors thus has a potentially large impact. In particular, an increase in membership and new economic powers has led to additional constraints to finding a common zone of agreement. The way the conventional liberal argument usually runs is that there is no overlap of interests among the key trading nations, which leads to deadlock. By extension, this argument implicitly assumes that overcoming deadlock will be difficult as long as domestic veto players do not 'move'.[17]

26.2.2 On institutions

International institutions can be thought of in a variety of ways; most importantly, institutions aggregate the interests of the multiple actors involved in negotiations. Since Keohane's contribution to the liberal school, institutions are conceptualized as platforms that allow cooperation to occur.[18] Institutions make deals possible and credible. As states face incentives to free-ride or to renege on past agreements, the exact design (and level of legalization) is important for understanding *ex ante* and *ex post* willingness to commit. International institutions can also be approached within a realist perspective. In particular, analysts following the tradition of neorealist institutionalism focus on how international regimes affect the distribution of costs and benefits of state interaction. Institutions have distributional consequences, and can be used as devices to seek and maintain asymmetric gains.[19] They can more broadly help control other actors' behaviour, both at home and abroad.[20]

We can differentiate a number of explanations as to how various types of 'institutions' affect outcomes. First, we find explanations that focus on the way negotiation procedures are defined. These include institutions that determine who has a seat at the table in the most important subject-related discussions and how the dominating modes of decision-making procedures (voting or consensus) are to be applied. A constituent

---

[15] BATNAs impact on the status quo point, and hence potentially affect the determination of the Nash bargaining solution (Nash 1950) that underlies the so-called negotiation analytic approach to bargaining (Raiffa 1982; Lax and Sebenius 1991).

[16] Lax and Sebenius 1991; Moravcsik 1997; Landau 2000; Schneider 2005.

[17] Yet, see Davis 2003 for a liberal argument, where the international level and linkages assist in overcoming domestic dominance of some interest groups.

[18] Keohane 1984.

[19] Aggarwal 1985; Krasner 1991; Knight 1992.

[20] Aggarwal 1985.

feature in the WTO context—in addition to consensus-seeking—is the single under-taking, where all issues are linked and 'nothing is agreed until everything is agreed'.[21] The choice of such 'micro-institutions' has important implications for the conditions under which coalitions are built, and affects overall negotiations.[22] Furthermore, the role assigned to the chairs of the respective negotiation groups, or to the DG and the Secretariat staff, may also matter.[23] Second, international institutions may reverberate at the domestic level. Recent work has focused on how legalization in the WTO context has affected the balance of interest group powers at home.[24] Moreover, given that increasing legalization affects enforcement, parties are becoming more reluctant to commit to new obligations.[25]

The literature shows that some institutions are more likely to lead to deadlock (e.g. consensus decision-making vs majority voting), while institutional changes (e.g. through coalition-building and procedural inventions) might act as a necessary condition for advancing negotiations. Whereas one could consider these changes to be part of actors' strategies and tactics rather than structural or contextual factors, we discuss them under this section given that the types of micro-institutions mentioned above are sticky and do not change overnight.

26.2.3 On ideas

A third determinant of deadlock can be found in the realm of ideas. As Keynes famously wrote: 'The ideas of economists and political philosophers both when they are right and when they are wrong, are more powerful than is commonly understood. Indeed the world is ruled by little else.'[26] Ideas come in many different forms.[27] More recent research in international relations has focused on the conditions that lead to change of dominating ideas (norm change).[28] There is some disagreement between different theoretical orientations as to how ideas causally affect outcomes. A number of scholars have used the concept of the 'focal point' to illustrate ideational power.[29] Two different views stand out. In the liberal tradition, focal points are perceived as a 'road map' that influences outcomes in cases where no clear-cut preferences or multiple equilibriums exist.[30] In a constructivist reading, by contrast, focal points are conceptualized as a 'mental map', which can help actors incorporate confirmatory information, while simultaneously filtering out non-confirmatory information. From this perspective, one would see the negotiation

---

[21] Elsig and Cottier 2011.   [22] Narlikar 2003.   [23] Elsig 2011.
[24] Goldstein and Martin 2000.   [25] Fearon 1998.   [26] Keynes 1936, 383.
[27] For a general overview, see Goldstein and Keohane 1993; Wendt 1999.
[28] Keck and Sikkink 1998; Checkel 2007.
[29] Schelling 1960, 70. According to Schelling, a focal point can be defined as any outcome that enjoys 'prominence, uniqueness, simplicity, precedent, or some rationale that makes it qualitatively differentiable from the continuum of possible alternatives'.
[30] Goldstein and Keohane 1993.

process as a 'contest of partisans trying to establish the dominant frame of reference'.[31] Parties try to get their preferred frame adopted through tactics of persuasion and argumentation.

In relation to the Doha Round, there are various driving ideas that affect negotiations (so it is difficult to disentangle the liberal from the social-constructivist argument). There exists a dominating idea among negotiators that has been coined, 'Smith abroad and Keynes at home'. Put differently, liberalization is advocated in areas where states judge their industries to be competitive, at the same time keeping all options open for sectors that are facing difficult competition due to increased imports.

There are other ideas that impact on the daily business in the WTO. Let us mention two: first, informal decision-making modes have become entrenched in the organization. For example, members share the normative view that 'we don't vote in this organization', while it would be formally possible. So strongly held beliefs (and the fear that the US could walk away) prevent engagement in the exploration of voting options. Second, the success of launching the Round in Doha has come at a price. As the Round was rebranded from a Millennium to a Development Round, legitimate expectations arose, on the part of the developing countries, that Doha will have to deliver on development. The tricky issue related to the concept of development is that, while all agree on the principle, wide disagreement exists on how to design trade rules to assist development.

26.2.4 On information

Information is a critical and challenging factor in international negotiations. A fundamental dilemma for negotiators stems from the incentive to reveal as much information as possible to allow for an 'objective' joint assessment of the zone of mutual agreements, coupled with the fear of being exploited by the others who may use biased information to push the agreement closer to their ideal stance. In particular, common wisdom considers that allowing the other parties to figure out the 'reservation point' turns out to be a disadvantage in most cases, unless the party is very strong and can credibly signal to other parties that, due to the domestic circumstances, the reservation point is fixed.[32] Another problem with wide dissemination of information was raised by the collective work on two-level games.[33] Information may not be easily available. Negotiators not only face the problem of understanding the other parties' reservation points (and conditions for shifting them), but most often they are not able to grasp their own reservation point (what will be acceptable at home to get a treaty

---

[31] Odell and Sell 2006, 88. In a social-constructivist reading, frames can be defined as 'specific metaphors, symbolic representations and cognitive clues used to render or cast behaviour and events in an evaluative mode and to suggest alternative modes of actions' (Zald 1996, 262).
[32] Putnam 1988. The reservation point is the outmost limit for a negotiator.
[33] Evans, Jacobson, and Putnam 1993.

ratified). In the context of GATT/WTO negotiations, one would assume that over time information increases and the likelihood of information asymmetry impacting on negotiations decreases; yet, novel challenges posed by the nature of the negotiation topics have come up. During the high days of the GATT negotiations, which predominantly focused on tariff concessions, it was more straightforward for negotiators to understand the impact of their decisions, given the potential losses for some parts of the industries and the benefits for export industries that a lowering of tariffs would bring about.[34] Yet, in the Doha Round, tariff negotiations are increasingly relegated to the back burner (so-called negative integration through lowering of tariffs), while cooperation on new rules to regulate market integration moves to the forefront (positive integration). The challenges of positive integration reveal at least three new obstacles negotiators face: first, given general provisions on rules (e.g. on competition, trade facilitation, subsidies, intellectual property rights), it becomes tricky for negotiators (and their industries at home) to assess the likelihood of gaining market shares through new rules. This depends on many intermediate steps and on the ways parties interpret and implement their obligations. Second, many of these rules have important (but not clear) distributional effects on societies in the long run. Third, WTO members already have certain rules in place and would face significant adjustment costs if they changed the existing rules (e.g. more stringent sanitary and phytosanitary measures, flexibility of labour markets, or competition policy). These considerations lead to cautious approaches by negotiators knowing of potential distributive consequences but lacking a better proxy.

Drawing upon the assumption that information is limited, information exchange becomes crucial on the way towards a negotiated agreement. But as recent studies based on experimental work have shown, information exchange can quickly become a bumpy ride and can be derailed by a host of factors and tactics. In addition to facing the temptation to bluff, actors may fall into an overconfidence trap, into self-serving biases and other forms of cognitive closure.[35] The more players fall into such decision-making traps, the more likely deadlocks become, and the more difficult it will be to get out of them. We now turn to strategic choices that actors make in the multidimensional context outlined in this section.

26.3 Games that are Played

As our discussion above suggests, a major difficulty in getting out of a deadlock consists in identifying the key blocking factor(s). In complex negotiations with a large number of actors, this is easier said than done, even when there is plenty of information available to

---

[34] Firms usually consider losses as more important than benefits. This, in turn, affects the intensity of lobbying. On exporter discrimination, see Dür 2010, 30–4.

[35] For a specific application to trade negotiations, see Dupont, Beverelli, and Pézard 2006.

Table 16 Prisoner's dilemma game (ordinal form)

		Player Beta	
		Cooperation	No cooperation
Player Alpha	Cooperation	3, 3	1, 4
	No cooperation	4, 1	**2, 2**

Note: Nash equilibrium in bold; the numbers in the various cells indicate the preferences of players on an ordinal ranking scale, with four being the most preferred situation and one the least preferred. In this and the following tables, the first number in each box refers to Player Alpha's preference, while the second number refers to Player Beta's preference (thus '4, 1' is Alpha's most preferred outcome and Beta's least preferred outcome).

negotiators. Rather than hide behind the complexity of reality, we propose here to think about the essence of the negotiation interaction using simple game-theoretical tools. To keep this section's discussion as parsimonious as possible, we focus on simple games with two actors and two strategies per actor. We further restrict our analysis of these games to a mostly static perspective, without delving deeply into problems of limited information. Our modelling choices may appear to oversimplify real-life examples but, as several authors have already shown, simple models can clearly reveal the essence of strategic dilemmas that governments face in attempting to deal with fundamental aspects of interdependence.[36]

Difficulties associated with trade liberalization processes have often been analysed through the prism of the famous game of the prisoner's dilemma.[37] In the prisoner's dilemma game (see Table 16), each actor has a dominant strategy not to cooperate (right column for player Beta and lower row for player Alpha in Table 16), leading to an outcome—no cooperation—that is socially suboptimal. In the context of trade liberalization, each country prefers, for political reasons, to gain greater market access in foreign markets while keeping more control over access to its own market, hence pleasing both export-oriented groups and import-competing ones. As a consequence, a cooperative solution (upper left cell in Table 16) is both unlikely and unstable. To overcome this unfortunate situation, parties could either rely on a third party to induce and enforce an agreement or be lured by the long-term prospect of an interaction. The design of the WTO aims at addressing these issues; notably the dispute settlement system, the Trade Policy Review Mechanism (TPRM), and the work of various committees facilitating

---

[36] For a broader discussion of the use of simple game-theoretic models to enhance our understanding of cooperation and collaboration in international economic relations, see Aggarwal and Dupont 1999, 2011.

[37] Grossman and Helpman 1995; Maggi 1999.

implementation. These mechanisms aim to foster cooperation over a long, and unde-fined, period of membership.

The prisoner's dilemma game is, however, of limited use for the analysis of deadlocks in bargaining situations.[38] Indeed, rather than considering players' willingness to engage or not to engage in trade liberalization, deadlocks may result from differences in negoti-ators' individual ranking of multiple outcomes that the parties would prefer to no agree-ment.[39] At best, we could conjecture—based on the well-established result that mutual concessions may come out of a long repetition of the game—that a deadlock corre-sponds to a situation of scattered unreciprocated attempts by actors to offer some concessions.

To understand persistent deadlock in the ongoing Doha Round of talks, one thus needs to go beyond the simple overarching view of the prisoner's dilemma and think of the deadlock as the result of several other games played between actors. The resort to a multiplicity of game structures comes from the decentralized process of discussions in the GATT/WTO, with sub-groups of members engaging in a series of sequential or par-allel talks on issues that have varying sensitivity to the whole membership. Different game structures may reflect these various sub-processes, and deadlock in any of them may explain deadlock at the overall level of the Round, given the choice of a single undertaking—that is, 'nothing is agreed until everything is agreed'. From this perspec-tive, we identify six specific interactions, past, current, or potential (at the time of writ-ing), that have impacted, or may impact, on deadlock episodes in the Doha Round. We first identify them empirically and then highlight strategic issues within a game-theo-retic setting.[40]

We begin with two games that have already been played. The first relates to the diver-gence between the EU and the US over the agenda-setting of the Round. Even though both pushed for the beginning of a new round, the Europeans wanted a Millennium round, including deep trade issues beyond the classical border regulation—the so-called Singapore issues—whereas the US was particularly eager to discuss market access issues.[41] This interaction had the features of a coordination game, as illustrated in Table 17.

---

[38] We do not consider either the game of 'deadlock', in which actors' dominant choice of no concessions leads to a stable and collectively optimal outcome of no agreement. This corresponds better to a situation of negotiation breakdown, with both actors finding better alternatives to any negotiated agreement.

[39] Schelling 1960; Fearon 1998.

[40] In the various games, we focus on the essence of the interactions, which explains our choice to use complete information models. From this perspective, we do not engage with issues such as information updating and learning. From an empirical viewpoint, given the issues at stake, actors have tended to go from one problem to the next (and at the same time to switch interlocutor), and thus learning is anything but a key feature of bargaining in the Doha Round.

[41] The EU proposed already at the first WTO Ministerial Conference, in Singapore in 1996, to start negotiations on competition, investment, public procurement, and trade facilitation.

Table 17 US–EU on general orientation of the Round (ordinal form)

		US	
		Millennium issues	Market access
EU	Market access	1, 1	**3, 4**
	Millennium issues	**4, 3**	2, 2

Note: Nash equilibrium in bold

Unlike the situation of the prisoner's dilemma, none of the players has a dominant strategy. Given the need to converge on one solution or another, the EU prefers to support a market access round when it is clear that the US will choose this option and, symmetrically, the US prefers to opt for a Millennium round when the EU sticks to that choice. The interaction has two possible outcomes—the upper right and lower left cells in Table 17—corresponding to a mutually agreed choice of a Millennium or a market access round. These two outcomes were clearly better than the absence of an agreement, and thus the failure to launch a new round.[42] But, given the difference in ranking between the two outcomes, both players engaged in some tough discussions, explaining the slow start of the round, including the fiasco in Seattle in 1999.[43] The EU and the US eventually settled their differences with one side largely converging on the other's position—in this case, this meant the EU dropping the Singapore issues and largely siding with the choice of a market access round. The need to agree on one solution (e.g. to send a strong message to the international community that multilateralism was still important for the big powers) and the firmness of the US attitude drove the process out of its initial deadlock.[44] The US position was further supported by the considerable scepticism of many developing countries vis-à-vis the Singapore issues. This led the EU to engage in a gradual withdrawal of its demands (with the notable exception of trade facilitation) with a view to saving face.[45]

The second (but rather less visible) episode of deadlock came from the confrontation between the US and the EU—the so-called G2—on one side, and China on the other. As China had just entered the WTO in 2001, the G2 tried to engage it in the liberalization dynamics and invited it to join the small group negotiations to induce a concessionary attitude. But China resisted this push by the G2 and quickly signalled its resolve not to commit to an additional liberalization position. It helped create and organize a new group called RAMs (recently acceded members), united by the willingness not to engage in new concessions over the ones already associated with accession.[46] The group was

---

[42] On attempts between the US and EU to agree prior to going to Doha, see Blustein 2009.

[43] Elsig 2002.   [44] Blustein 2009.   [45] Elsig 2009.

[46] See on the membership of the RAMs group <http://www.wto.org/english/tratop_e/dda_e/negotiating_groups_e.pdf> accessed on 27 October 2010.

Table 18 China–G2 (ordinal form)

		China	
		Concessions	No concessions
G2	Concessions	3, 3	**2, 4**
	No concessions	**4, 2**	1, 1

Note: Nash equilibrium in bold

able to get its concerns reflected in the July framework agreement of 2004, and later in the Declaration of the Ministerial Conference in Hong Kong in 2005.[47] Furthermore, China teamed up with Brazil and India, prior to the Cancún Ministerial Meeting in 2003, to push the agenda of the G20, challenging the G2 view of the Round.[48] In game-theoretic terms, the G2–China interaction had features of a chicken game, as illustrated in Table 18.

In this game, each side tries to pull the discussion towards its preferred outcome, similarly to the coordination game described earlier, but with an added possibility of settling on a compromise solution—the upper left cell. Indeed this outcome is socially interesting, but it is an unstable outcome, sensitive to the desire of each actor to win it all, which tends to create deadlocks. To escape the situation, both players need to clearly signal their willingness to resist the other's attempts to impose its preferred solution. The one most able to do so, or alternatively the one that is least sensitive to the absence of agreement, is likely to obtain its prize. In the case of the G2–China interaction, China made credible signals (through coalition-building), pushing the G2 to give in for the sake of keeping the Round alive.

But if the G2–China interaction has come to an end (for now), the tensions between the G2 and the South, organized around the G20, have remained very much alive, severely impacting upon the negotiation dynamics since the July 2004 framework agreement. After that agreement, the EU was able to convince the other main parties to widen the discussions and link the debates on agriculture with market access for industrial goods (NAMA) and services liberalization.[49] Yet there was disagreement about the relative importance of those three sets of issues. The G20 position was to give priority to agriculture and seek a differentiated engagement for liberalization in industrial products and services. They were guided by the notion that they would have to offer 'less than

---

[47] Paragraph 58 of the Hong Kong Ministerial Declaration states that: 'We recognize the special situation of recently-acceded members who have undertaken extensive market access commitments at the time of accession. This situation will be taken into account in the negotiations.'

[48] The G20 emerged as a new developing country coalition in the WTO Ministerial Conference in Cancún, led by the key emerging economies Brazil, India, China, and South Africa. The coalition's objective was to counter the dominance of the G2 in relation to the agricultural negotiations.

[49] Elsig 2009.

Table 19 North–South divide after Cancún (ordinal form)

		G20	
		Flexible	Agriculture
G2	Flexible	3, 3	**2, 4**
	Services, NAMA	**4, 2**	1, 1

Note: Nash equilibrium in bold

full reciprocity'. The G2, for their part, pushed for substantial liberalization in services and NAMA. In order to sell the Round at home, the G2 needed tangible concessions in these areas. This cooperation situation also resembled a game of chicken as illustrated in Table 19.[50]

The natural result of the distributive tension in this setting was a deadlock, with both sides trying to flex their muscles. The South did so with the help of coalitional dynamics[51] and the North by negotiating new preferential trade agreements. The deadlock proved rigid, which led DG Lamy to officially 'suspend' the Round between July 2006 and February 2007.[52] In spring 2007, talks resumed and small group meetings tried to push issues forward again. However, a mini-ministerial meeting comprising the G4 (US, EU, Brazil, and India) at Potsdam in July 2007 was still characterized by little movement. Yet, with time, some key players on each side have demonstrated some willingness to end the stalemate. In particular, Brazil and the EU signalled some flexibility. Given the prospects of additional market access in the agricultural sector, Brazil started to drive a more proactive negotiation strategy.[53] The EU addressed some of the existing criticism on its agricultural policy by sending signals that it may be prepared to accept further cuts in farm subsidies.[54] This clearly helped to diffuse the general disagreement on the 'negotiation triangle' consisting of NAMA, services, and agriculture.

The next important negotiation event was another mini-ministerial meeting, this time comprising an enlarged group. The negotiations took place in Geneva in July 2008. After days of negotiating within a small group setting and making progress on a number

---

[50] There are alternative ways to address the credibility issue in North–South bargaining. For instance, Narlikar and van Houten use an asymmetric incomplete information game, where the North is unsure about the resolve of the South (Narlikar and van Houten 2010). In such a game, deadlock is the result of the game as long as the South has no ability to credibly signal its commitment not to make concessions. This is essentially the same strategic dilemma as the one captured by our more parsimonious modelling choice.

[51] Narlikar 2009.

[52] At about the same time, the EU abandoned its moratorium on launching negotiations for concluding new trade agreements and embraced a new market access-driven approach through bilateral agreements (Elsig 2007).

[53] Padua Lima 2009.

[54] Elsig 2009.

Table 20 India–US on agricultural safeguards (ordinal form)

		India	
		Limited	Special safeguard
US	Limited	3, 3	**2, 4**
	Special safeguard	**4, 2**	1, 1

Note: Nash equilibrium in bold

of open questions, a specific issue proved divisive between India and the US. The more bloc-type deadlock between the G2 and the G20 was replaced by a two-country deadlock on the issue of special safeguard mechanisms for agriculture, and in particular under what conditions these mechanisms would apply. Given the strong distributive tensions and the room for potential joint concessions, we also consider this game to preserve the characteristics of a chicken game (see Table 20).

How could the deadlock—which is prolonged by the fact that each member is resolved to push for its own preferred outcome—be overcome? One possibility, the most likely, is that the US will become convinced that India will not give in, unlike in previous negotiations, and therefore will accept a relatively large application range for specific safeguard mechanisms on farm trade. Pressure exerted by export-oriented groups in the US in favour of the conclusion of the Round would surely be a facilitating factor. Another possibility is that India could give in on this issue in order to get some concessions in another issue area, for example fewer commitments on NAMA or more on the liberalization in specific service sectors (potentially including movement of natural persons). As a third possibility, both actors may lose any interest in a general agreement, either for domestic political reasons (India) or because better alternatives are obtainable via preferential trade agreements (US). The last scenario seems most likely at this stage and contributes to prolonged deadlock (close to breakdown).

Now what if the India–US deadlock is resolved? The road towards a general agreement would not be guaranteed. The next delicate interaction could most likely take place among developing countries. Even though all developing countries would prefer a multilateral extension of the rule of law, there is disagreement about how to achieve this. Big emerging countries are willing to pay the price of some tariff liberalizations (in exchange for improved market access), whereas poorer developing countries are adamant in their wish to avoid any liberalization commitments. The desire for a multilateral solution is further hampered by the fear of many developing countries which are currently benefiting from preferential market access for some of their strategic products exported to the North. This fear is related to the potential effects of a type of preference erosion as a result of general tariff liberalization across the board.[55] In particular, the African,

---

[55] Rahman and Shadat 2006.

Table 21 South–South divisions (ordinal form)

		ACP and others	
		Multilateral agreement	Alternatives
G20	Multilateral agreement	**4, 4**	1, 3
	Alternatives	3, 1	**2, 2**

Note: Nash equilibrium in bold

Caribbean, and Pacific countries (ACP) and a number of low-income Asian states have on various occasions voiced concerns that when tariffs go down they will lose market share to other emerging economies (e.g. G20) which are more competitive. So far, the strong preference for a multilateral option has united developing countries; this may not be sufficient in the future, especially if each side starts to doubt the commitment of the other to stick to this position. Such a dynamic can be illustrated within the setting of an assurance game as presented in Table 21.

In the game of assurance, players share a single most preferred outcome, represented in the upper left cell in Table 21, but they do not have dominant strategies. As a result, there is a second, socially suboptimal, equilibrium outcome: deadlock. In such a game, reaching an agreement on the single most preferred outcome, the upper left cell in Table 21, is not a foregone conclusion. Doubts about the willingness of one's counterpart to stick to the common position might prevent one from adopting a positive attitude. Such doubts are ubiquitous in this game, because every player always has a strong interest in pushing the other one to act cooperatively. Previous disappointment in each other's attitude (ACPs not reassured by deals between emerging countries and developed economies; emerging countries doubting willingness of least-developed countries (LDCs) to reach a multilateral agreement) may push individual, defective, action. Big emerging countries may give in and go for preferential trading arrangements, leaving the LDCs out in the cold. In anticipation, LDCs may seek to renew or prolong special treatment from developed countries through preferential schemes outside the WTO.[56]

Finally, assuming that the game between India and the US is resolved and all parties wait for the South–South issue to be 'untied', what could we expect from those powerful trading nations that have compromised and are now ready to conclude the deal? One scenario could be inspired by the developments that occurred at the end of the Uruguay Round. When the US and the EU were converging on their positions towards the end of the Round (e.g. the Blair House Agreement over agriculture) and felt comfortable about having a package deal that reflected their overall interests, they worked towards

---

[56] See Narlikar 2009 for using a game-theoretical approach to address the stability of South–South coalitions, in particular the G20.

Table 22 'Go it alone' end game (ordinal form)

| | | Small developing countries | |
		Cooperate	Resist
G6	Cooperate multilateral	3, 2	1, 4
	Plurilaterals	**4, 3**	2, 1

Note: Nash equilibrium in bold

concluding the Round quickly. In that situation, the G2 agreed to 'go it alone'.[57] They put other parties to the test by changing developing countries' BATNAs dramatically. They argued that countries better join the newly created organization and accept all negotiated agreements, because old GATT agreements would no longer be applicable in the foreseeable future.[58] This created uncertainty and many recalcitrant developing countries saw no other choice than to embrace the G2 compromise and join the consensus.

Now, while in this Round the power of the G2 will not be sufficient to overcome potential deadlock caused by some developing countries' threat of using their veto power, one can imagine that a group of like-minded established and emerging states could become interested in achieving a final result and decide to go it alone. They could explore new ways of decision-making, including negotiating plurilateral agreements within the WTO, de facto sidelining a number of laggards by excluding them from benefits as a result of liberalizing further. A critical mass-type approach was used during the Tokyo Round negotiations. For some of the Codes negotiated, the industrialized countries did not fully multilateralize benefits (they restricted the application of the most-favoured nation (MFN) clause).[59] If played, this game would look like the one depicted in Table 22. One side, the new G6 (US, EU, Brazil, India, China, and Japan), has a clearly dominant choice to go ahead no matter what, and thus the other side can either choose to stay out, with a very poor payoff, or to give in and follow suit. It would no longer have the option of prolonging the current Round and waiting for additional concessions to be tailored to its needs (upper right cell in Table 22). This, of course, would substantively change the way decisions are made in the multilateral forum.

26.4 CONCLUSION: DEADLOCK, AND NOW?

Whereas deadlock has been a recurring phenomenon in multilateral trade negotiations, the literature has so far attempted to capture it either in very general terms (prisoner's dilemma-type approach) or in very specific ones (linked to specific issues or

[57] Gruber 2000.   [58] Steinberg 2002.

[59] For a discussion on the subtle differences between plurilaterals and critical mass, see Elsig 2010.

specific countries). In this chapter, we have tried to combine both extremes by tracing the dynamics of deadlock through a set of overlapping and sequential games. Persistent deadlock is made up of a series of different episodes with different logics and impacts.

Where is the Doha Round going to end up? Beyond the hypothetical game-theoretical situations presented above, we suggest two general scenarios. In scenario 1, overcoming deadlock is a question of time (and *ex post* deadlocks are seen as benign). The G6 will not have to take recourse to 'go it alone' strategies. However, a necessary condition for this scenario to materialize is, as mentioned above, that parties are willing to settle on a multilateral agreement and have not already taken the exit option spurred by loss of belief in the legitimate role of the WTO.[60] A key factor that might bring movement to negotiations (slowly tipping them towards the point of final negotiations) is the growing consensus that the WTO's agenda of negotiations dates back to the 1990s, yet new additional challenges abound, ranging from climate change and export taxes to natural resources. Therefore there is a need to conclude the Doha Round with the elements that seem to have a large backing ('Doha lite'). This could lead to the situation where the leftovers are directly transferred to the next round (a new in-built agenda). Whether this additional difficult 'heritage' would be good news for a next round to have to start with is another question.

Scenario 2 sees extended deadlocks leading to complete breakdown (e.g. ending the Round without results). In this scenario, short-term gains for some may be largely outweighed by long-term losses for a substantial number of WTO members.[61] In particular, the institution itself (the WTO) would be called into question and other forums (probably less legitimate ones) would be increasingly used by powerful actors to impose their philosophies as to how to regulate global trade. In addition, existing incentives to apply unilateral trade measures (to please domestic constituencies) would be less controlled for by the existing multilateral toolkits backed up by a strong dispute settlement system. What has been overlooked in the study of the WTO litigation arm is that the buffering effect of WTO dispute settlement is dependent on WTO members' perceptions of the reputation and role of the institution. If the institution does not produce any outcomes, or worse, fails in concluding a Round, its overall legitimacy is at stake.

References

Aggarwal, Vinod. 1985. *Liberal Protectionism*. Berkeley: University of California Press.

Aggarwal, Vinod, and Cédric Dupont. 1999. Goods, Games and Institutions. *International Political Science Review* 20 (4):393–409.

Aggarwal, Vinod, and Cédric Dupont. 2011. Collaboration and Coordination in the Global Political Economy. In *Global Political Economy*, edited by John Ravenhill, 67–95. Oxford: Oxford University Press.

---

[60] Hirschman 1970.   [61] Narlikar 2010.

Blustein, Paul. 2009. *Misadventures of the Most Favored Nations: Clashing Egos, Inflated Ambitions, and the Great Shambles of the World Trade System*. Cambridge, MA: Public Affairs.

Checkel, Jeffrey. 2007. *International Institutions and Socialization in Europe*. Cambridge: Cambridge University Press.

Davis, Christina. 2003. *Food Fights over Free Trade: How International Institutions Promote Agricultural Trade Liberalization*. Princeton: Princeton University Press.

Drezner, Daniel. 2007. *All Politics is Global: Explaining International Regulatory Regimes*. Princeton: Princeton University Press.

Dupont, Cédric. 1994. Domestic Politics and International Negotiations: A Sequential Bargaining Model. In *Game Theory and International Relations*, edited by Pierre Allan and Christian Schmidt, 156–90. Cheltenham: Edward Elgar.

Dupont, Cédric, Cosimo Beverelli, and Stéphanie Pézard. 2006. Learning in Multilateral Trade Negotiations: Some Results from Simulation for Developing Countries. In *Developing Countries and the Trade Negotiation Process*, edited by John Odell, 145–74. Cambridge: Cambridge University Press.

Dür, Andreas. 2010. *Protection for Exporters: Power and Discrimination in Transatlantic Trade Relations, 1930–2010*. Ithaca: Cornell University Press.

Elsig, Manfred. 2002. *The EU's Common Commercial Policy: Institutions, Interests and Ideas*. Aldershot: Ashgate.

Elsig, Manfred. 2007. The EU's Choice of Regulatory Venues for Trade Negotiations: A Tale of Agency Power? *Journal of Common Market Studies* 45 (4):927–48.

Elsig, Manfred. 2009. The EU in the Doha Negotiations: A Conflicted Sponsor? In *Leadership and Change in the Doha Negotiations*, edited by Amrita Narlikar and Brendan Vickers, 23–43. Dordrecht: Martinus Nijhoff Publishers.

Elsig, Manfred. 2010. WTO Decision-Making: Can We Get a Little Help from the Secretariat and the Critical Mass? In *Redesigning the World Trade Organization for the Twenty-first Century*, edited by Debra Steger, 67–90, Ottawa: Wilfrid Laurier University Press, CIGI and IDRC.

Elsig, Manfred. 2011. Principal–Agent Theory and the World Trade Organization: Complex Agency and 'Missing Delegation'. *European Journal of International Relations* 17(3): 495–517.

Elsig, Manfred, and Thomas Cottier. 2011. Reforming the WTO: The Decision-Making Triangle Revisited. In *Governing the World Trade Organization: Past, Present and Beyond Doha*, edited by Thomas Cottier and Manfred Elsig. Cambridge: Cambridge University Press.

Evans, Peter B., Harold K. Jacobson, and Robert D. Putnam, eds. 1993. *Double-Edged Diplomacy: International Bargaining and Domestic Politics*. Berkeley: University of California Press.

Fearon, James. 1998. Bargaining, Enforcement, and International Cooperation. *International Organization* 52 (2):269–306.

Goldstein, Judith, and Robert Keohane, eds. 1993. *Ideas and Foreign Policy*. Ithaca: Cornell University Press.

Goldstein, Judith, and Lisa Martin. 2000. Legalization, Trade Liberalization, and Domestic Politics: A Cautionary Note. *International Organization* 54 (3):603–32.

Grossman, Gene, and Elhanan Helpman. 1995. The Politics of Free-Trade Agreements. *American Economic Review* 85 (4):667–90.

Gruber, Lloyd. 2000. *Ruling the World*. Princeton: Princeton University Press.

Hirschman, Albert. 1970. *Exit, Voice and Loyalty: Responses to Decline in Firms, Organizations and States*. Cambridge, MA: Harvard University Press.

Iida, Keisuke. 1993. When and How Do Domestic Constraints Matter? *Journal of Conflict Resolution* 37 (3):403–26.

Keck, Margaret, and Kathryn Sikkink. 1998. *Activist Beyond Borders: Advocacy Networks in International Politics*. Ithaca: Cornell University Press.

Keohane, Robert. 1984. *After Hegemony*. Princeton: Princeton University Press.

Keynes, John Maynard. 1936. *The General Theory of Employment, Interest and Money*. London: Macmillan.

Knight, Jack. 1992. *Institutions and Social Conflict*. Cambridge: Cambridge University Press.

Krasner, Stephen. 1976. *Structural Conflict: The Third World Against Global Liberalism*. Berkeley: University of California Press.

Krasner, Stephen. 1978. *Defending the National Interest*. Princeton: Princeton University Press.

Krasner, Stephen. 1991. Global Communications and National Power: Life on the Pareto Frontier. *World Politics* 43 (3):336–66.

Landau, Alice. 2000. Analyzing International Economic Negotiations: Towards a Synthesis of Approaches. *International Negotiation* 5 (1):1–19.

Lax, David, and James Sebenius. 1991. The Power of Alternatives or the Limits of Negotiations. In *Negotiation Theory and Practice*, edited by William Breslin and Jeffery Rubin, 97–114. Cambridge, MA: The Program on Negotiation at Harvard Law School.

Maggi, Giovanni. 1999. The Role of Multilateral Institutions in International Trade Cooperation. *American Economic Review* 89 (1):190–214.

Mo, Jongryn. 1995. Domestic Institutions and International Bargaining: The Role of Agent Veto in Two-Level Games. *American Political Science Review* 89 (4):914–24.

Moravcsik, Andrew. 1997. Taking Preferences Seriously: A Liberal Theory of International Politics. *International Organization* 51 (4):513–54.

Narlikar, Amrita. 2003. *International Trade and Developing Countries: Bargaining Coalitions in the GATT and WTO*. London: Routledge.

Narlikar, Amrita. 2009. A Theory of Bargaining Coalitions in the WTO. In *Leadership and Change in the Multilateral Trading System*, edited by Amrita Narlikar and Brendan Vickers, 183–201. Leiden: Martinus Nijhoff, and Dordrecht: Republic of Letters Publishing.

Narlikar, Amrita, ed. 2010. *Deadlocks in Multilateral Negotiations: Causes and Solutions*. Cambridge: Cambridge University Press.

Narlikar, Amrita, and Diana Tussie. 2004. The G20 at the Cancún Ministerial: Developing Countries and their Evolving Coalitions in the WTO. *World Economy* 27 (7):947–66.

Narlikar, Amrita, and Pieter van Houten. 2010. Know the Enemy: Uncertainty and Deadlock in the WTO. In *Deadlocks in Multilateral Negotiations: Causes and Solutions*, edited by Amrita Narlikar, 142–63. Cambridge: Cambridge University Press.

Nash, John. 1950. The Bargaining Problem. *Econometrica* 18 (2):155–62.

Odell, John. 2000. *Negotiating the World Economy*. Ithaca: Cornell University Press.

Odell, John. 2009. Breaking Deadlocks in International Institutional Negotiations: The WTO, Seattle, and Doha. *International Studies Quarterly* 53 (2):273–99.

Odell, John, and Susan Sell. 2006. Reframing the Issue: The WTO Coalition on Intellectual Property and Public Health, 2001. In *Negotiating Trade: Developing Countries in the WTO and NAFTA*, edited by John Odell, 85–114. Cambridge: Cambridge University Press.

Padua Lima, Maria L. 2009. Brazil's Multilateral Trade Policy in the WTO. In *Leadership and Change in the Doha Negotiations*, edited by Amrita Narlikar and Brendan Vickers, 75–95. Dordrecht: Martinus Nijhoff Publishers.

Putnam, Robert. 1988. Diplomacy and Domestic Politics: the Logic of Two-Level Games. *International Organization* 42 (3):427–60.

Rahman, Mustafizur, and Wasel Bin Shadat. 2006. NAMA Negotiations in the WTO and Preference Erosion: Concerns of Bangladesh and other Asia-Pacific LDCs. *South Asia Economic Journal* 7 (2):179–203.

Raiffa, Howard. 1982. *The Art and Science of Negotiation*. Cambridge, MA: Harvard University Press.

Schelling, Thomas. 1960. *The Strategy of Conflict*. Cambridge, MA: Harvard University Press.

Schneider, Gerald. 2005. Capacity and Concessions: Bargaining Power in Multilateral Negotiations. *Millennium* 33 (3):665–89.

Steinberg, Richard. 2002. In the Shadow of Law or Power? Consensus-Based Bargaining in the GATT/WTO. *International Organization* 56 (2):339–74.

Wendt, Alexander. 1999. *Social Theory of International Politics*. Cambridge: Cambridge University Press.

Zald, Mayer. 1996. Culture, Ideology, and Strategic Framing. In *Comparative Perspectives on Social Movements: Political Opportunities, Mobilizing Structures, and Cultural Framings*, edited by Doug McAdam, John McCarthy, and Mayer Zald, 261–74. Cambridge: Cambridge University Press.

CHAPTER 27

....

THE ROLE OF DOMESTIC COURTS IN THE IMPLEMENTATION OF WTO LAW: THE POLITICAL ECONOMY OF SEPARATION OF POWERS AND CHECKS AND BALANCES IN INTERNATIONAL TRADE REGULATION

....

THOMAS COTTIER[*]

27.1 INTRODUCTION

....

DISPUTE settlement in the context of the World Trade Organization (WTO) was greatly enhanced with the advent of the Dispute Settlement Understanding (DSU) in 1995. Mandatory participation in proceedings, a two-tier system allowing for legal appeals to the Appellate Body and relatively effective enforcement of adopted decisions, profoundly altered the role of law and legal dispute settlement within the WTO. It funda-

[*] This chapter partly draws upon Cottier 2007. The author is most grateful and indebted to Rachel Liechti-McKee (lic. iur.), Research Fellow, Department of Economic Law, University of Bern, and to Susan Kaplan, Scientific Editor at the World Trade Institute for their most valuable support in preparing this chapter.

mentally altered the relationship of negotiations and judicial dispute resolution in the WTO. While the former continues to operate on the basis of consensus and faces increasing difficulties in a multipolar world, judicial dispute resolution operates on reverse consensus or consensus-minus-one, and emerged as a key factor in international relations. It has increasingly attracted attention in international relations theory.[1]

At the same time, the role of domestic courts in assessing claims brought before them on the basis of WTO law has attracted less attention beyond discussions among trade lawyers. However, it raises equally profound questions about the function of courts in international affairs and the role of power in international relations. It raises profound questions of separation of powers and checks and balances, both horizontally and vertically. It entails questions relating to the interaction between different branches of government. It raises questions as to what extent independent courts may enforce international law and, in doing so, oblige the executive branch and legislator to comply with international law. It raises questions as to what extent individuals and corporations are and should be entitled to invoke WTO disciplines and be in a position to challenge domestic laws and regulations before domestic courts. Finally, it raises comparative questions as to the effectiveness of WTO law in different jurisdictions and the implications of diverging roles of the judiciary and judicial review in terms of international competitiveness of economies. This issue raises the problem of reciprocity and the international balance of powers.[2]

All these questions arise independently of WTO dispute settlement. Cases before domestic courts rarely relate directly to WTO dispute settlement, except when claims are based upon decisions of the Dispute Settlement Body (DSB). The ways and means of treating WTO law before, and by, domestic courts are thus a self-standing and important issue in the process of reinforcing and implementing the rule of law in international economic relations. It is at the heart of defining power and the role of law in foreign affairs. In doing so, it is important to recall the history of a limited, but growing, role of courts in international affairs, before turning to assess their role in the context of international law and WTO law. This chapter seeks to analyse the role of courts—*the least dangerous branch of government*[3]—in international trade regulation. It focuses on the relationship of law and power, but does not seek to offer a detailed legal account and discussion of the relevant case law.

27.2 DOMESTIC COURTS AND FOREIGN AFFAIRS

The judicial branch of government has traditionally been concerned with domestic affairs. Courts dealt with disputes between private parties, and with disputes between state and individuals in penal and administrative law. They fine-tuned and shaped the relationship of public and private spheres, between state, society, and individuals in

---

[1] See Chapter 22 of this volume.   [2] Cottier 2009a.   [3] Bickel 1986.

constitutional law. Foreign affairs, on the other hand, belonged to the realm of the sovereign kings or the executive branch. International relations were perceived in terms of realism and power politics, subject to weak and hardly enforceable rules and emerging principles of public international law. Foreign policy was essentially considered unsuitable for the judicial branch in the nation state.[4] It was perceived as, and dominated by, power politics, including warfare, under a loose framework of international law, mainly shaped by broad—and often vague—principles of customary law, devoid of enforcement mechanisms. Treaty law, while gradually increasing, essentially used to deal with relations among states. These issues were considered political questions, on which the powers of government should not be restricted in their pursuit of national interests. Domestic courts, therefore, had little business in international affairs. People generally had no standing to challenge governmental acts relating to foreign affairs. And where such matters arose, courts adopted policies of judicial restraint, deferring the business to the executive branch.[5] Most of the case law in the field relates to the allocation of powers under the constitution, and not to the policies and course of action and decisions taken.[6] The doctrine of sovereignty and the prerogative of the executive branch has remained a powerful ingredient of the debate, limiting the role of courts despite the process of regionalization and globalization. It has not changed much under national constitutions since they were shaped in the nineteenth and twentieth centuries, except for the increasing influence of international law in defining the roles of courts and judges in foreign affairs.

The established patterns and roles of the contemporary judiciary were essentially shaped by eighteenth, nineteenth and twentieth century constitutionalism. While based upon a long tradition of adjudication, the judicial function was separated from the political branches of government, in particular from the executive and legislative functions, and was given an independent status within the overall constitutional framework. Rulers would no longer be responsible for passing judgement on individuals. In this process, courts were no longer limited to the traditional functions of settling disputes between private parties. They were increasingly given the job, and assumed the task, of controlling the government and administration. In some countries, such powers extended to the control of legislative powers under constitutional review. Constitutional law, and fundamental rights guaranteed in, and by, constitutional law, evolved as the major benchmark of justice in the delineation of public and private spheres.[7] Additional dimensions were added in federalist structures, delineating powers of different layers of governance, in particular between federal and subfederal entities.[8] A substantial body of law emerged and profoundly established the courts as a branch of government. Whether developed under doctrines of the separation of powers, or of institutional checks and

---

[4] Cottier and Oesch 2003, 289–90.
[5] For example *United States v. Curtiss-Wright Export Corp.*, 299 US 304, 1936.
[6] Henkin 1996, 141–8; Yoo 2005; Trone 2001, 16; Eeckhout 2004, 281–314.
[7] Johnson 1995, 46; Oakeshott 1983.   [8] Aubert 1991, 60–72, 424–30.

balances, courts assumed essential functions in the process of law-making. Case law today is an indispensable source of law in all Western countries, whether they emerged from the tradition of common law or continental law. Led by US law, constitutional law witnessed a profound revival and evolution after the Second World War.

The rise of constitutional law, however, did not extend to foreign and international relations to the same extent, for the reasons stated above. Constitutions were framed and shaped on introverted patterns, all essentially deriving from the principles of no taxation without representation, and the protection of liberty and property rights. Constitutional law was preoccupied with defining the legal status of private persons and subfederal entities in a purely domestic context of the nation state.[9]

The exclusion of foreign policy from legal protection also largely extended to international economic relations, even though private operators were apparently often affected—courts were barred from developing, or failed to develop, a body of law comparable to domestic constitutional law. Fundamental rights stopped at national borders, and the impact of policies on human rights abroad was not a proper concern.[10] At the time, treaties on trade, investment, and navigation did not manage to provide for the effective settlement of disputes between states, let alone to make such mechanisms available to private operators. Constitutionalism per se has remained an essentially introverted concept when it comes to international economic relations. Even today, the external reach of fundamental rights remains unclear, and the domestic legal remedies against economic sanctions imposed by the international community and states remain weak, if not nonexistent. Judicial review of administrative law affecting foreign relations often remains excluded, or is subject only to limited judicial review.[11] This said, domestic courts today increasingly encounter foreign policy in several ways. The application of domestic law may affect international relations. Courts may deal with the allocation of powers between different branches of government relevant to foreign affairs. First and foremost, they are confronted with an ever-increasing body of international law, including general principles, customary law, and treaty law.

The evolution of European Union (EU) law, as well as the law of the WTO, in the past few decades has profoundly changed the relationship of constitutional and international relations.[12] The process of regionalization and globalization no longer allows clear distinctions to be drawn between domestic and international law. Issues formally pertaining to domestic law affect foreign relations as much as external relations affect domestic law. And constitutional law and domestic law increasingly overlap with instruments pertaining to European or international economic law. Private operators derive rights from these instruments, in law and in fact.

The pace of development and integration in trade regulation, both regional and global, derives from enhancing market access through law. Trade regulation is part of the

---

[9] Cottier 1993, 409, 413–16; Petersmann 1993, 6–7.   [10] Franck 1992; Kälin 1986, 252.
[11] Oesch 2004a, 285.   [12] Jackson 2006, 57–8. Cf. also Peters 1997.

law of transactions of goods and services which are suitable to be traded and exchanged regionally and worldwide. Unlike the law relating to resources, it cannot be successfully dealt with within the confines of state territories alone. The penetration of markets by economic operators and investors is bound to touch domestic law at some stage. And the obstacles encountered will be addressed by means of international negotiations, resulting in new disciplines which, in return, affect domestic regulation. The interaction of international law with domestic law is inevitable.[13] It eventually extends to other fields of law as they cannot be separated from transactions and trade regulation. At the same time, most treaties and constitutions alike still fail to address this interaction in a comprehensive manner. Diplomats and legislators refrain from addressing it, due to its complexity and political sensitivity. Its definition is mainly left to the judicial branch of governments. Judges are called upon to fine-tune the relationships of rights and obligations, of rules and exceptions, of economic and non-economic concerns, to watch over checks and balances between different branches of government, both horizontally and vertically, and to define, in doing so, the relationship of international and domestic law within an emerging system of global governance and its various layers. With this assignment, the traditional role of judges inevitably expands in the pursuit of justice, fairness, and legal security. While politics change day by day, judges play a key role in building long-term structures, and stabilizing the overall legal order.

27.3 THE ADVENT OF WTO LAW

The advent of WTO law has had a strong influence on the legal nature of external economic relations. The basic principles of progressive liberalization—non-discrimination and transparency—are at the heart of it. While the General Agreement on Tariffs and Trade (GATT) 1947 laid down the foundations of a rule-based system, the voluntary nature of GATT dispute settlement, which allowed the establishment of panels and of panel reports to be vetoed, left international relations mainly to the realm of diplomacy and political relations.[14]

The new Dispute Settlement Understanding, negotiated during the Uruguay Round and adopted in 1995, brought about fundamental changes. Building upon the customary procedures developed under GATT, the power to veto the establishment of panels and the adoption of panel reports was removed. Instead, a right to a panel and the obligation to accept the findings of the Appellate Body—a standing body of seven jurists—was introduced. The failure to implement adopted decisions ultimately results in the suspension of market access rights. It leads to painful retaliatory measures against members

---

[13] Cottier and Hertig 2003, 267–71.   [14] Van den Bossche 2005, 176–80.

found to be violating legal commitments, and thus also against operators within the countries concerned. The WTO dispute settlement system achieved a remarkable record during its first decade.[15] By 2005, more than 310 disputes had been dealt with, of which approximately 92 were adjudicated by panels and approximately 56 by the Appellate Body.[16] In only a few cases (albeit of major political importance) did members fail to bring about implementation and compliance with international law.

The advent of the WTO dispute settlement system, in combination with a greatly expanded scope of WTO law encompassing not only goods, but also services and intellectual property protection, has been a major force in reassessing the role of law in international economic relations. As seen some years earlier in European law, a new legal culture is gradually emerging. WTO law is enriched by case law, and a lawyer dealing with it can no longer afford to ignore the fine-tuning brought about by the reports of the panels and the Appellate Body. Overall, it is fair to say that WTO law and its precedents have emerged as a rule-oriented system, pushing back power politics and the perception that international trade relations ultimately rely upon the barrel of a gun. Of course, it would be wrong and naïve to exclude the impact of power based upon the market size of a country. Effective retaliation continues to rely upon it. Yet, these power relations today are tempered by law. Sovereignty is being redefined into what John Jackson has termed 'sovereignty modern'.[17] Undoubtedly, international law defining the exercise of sovereign rights has been reinforced. For some, in particular from a European angle, a process of constitutionalization of WTO law and of integration can be observed, while others—mainly from a US viewpoint—prefer a more modest perception of embedded liberalism. In terms of practical results, however, the two schools both defend the rule of law and the importance of creating a balance between market access and non-economic concerns in international trade regulation.[18]

27.4 THE STATUS OF WTO LAW IN DOMESTIC LAW AND COURTS

27.4.1 Pacta sunt servanda

WTO law is part of international law. Members of the WTO are therefore obliged to comply with rights and obligations in international relations vis-à-vis other members of the organization. Nullification and impairment of benefits, which today mainly entail the breach of particular obligations but may also be rooted in so-called non-violation

---

[15] Wolfrum, Stoll, Kaiser 2006; Ortino and Petersmann 2004.
[16] Leitner and Lester 2005; Davey 2005, 17; Jackson 2005, 5.
[17] Jackson 2006, 57–78.   [18] Cottier and Oesch 2003, 289–90.

complaints, trigger international responsibility and obligations to comply with the decisions of the Dispute Settlement Body, based upon recommendations and findings of panels and the Appellate Body. These are obligations under international law and rooted in the fundamental principle of *pacta sunt servanda* enshrined in Article 26 of the Vienna Convention on the Law of Treaties. Members of the WTO are obliged to honour their commitments; they cannot escape them by taking recourse to domestic law inconsistent with international obligations.[19] While the relationship between members is thus defined by international law, it is altogether a different matter when it comes to defining the position of international law in domestic law. The boundaries for international law remain set by domestic law.[20]

The two levels need to be clearly distinguished. Unless international law specifically prescribes the relationship of international and domestic law in a particular context, mainly in treaty law, the relationship is defined by the constitutional law of the member concerned. At its present stage of development—and unlike EU law—WTO law does not define that relationship. In *US—Sec 301–310 Trade Act*, the panel held in 1999 that 'neither the GATT nor the WTO has so far been interpreted by GATT/WTO institutions as a legal order producing direct effect' (paragraph 7.72). This finding has remained unquestioned as of today; albeit, it can be argued that specific provisions may produce direct effect. Article XX of the Government Procurement Agreement (GPA) thus requires domestic judicial review as to whether a determination is in accordance with the Agreement. It is difficult to see how this obligation can be respected without giving domestic effect to the provisions of the GPA. In the absence of a general doctrine, members define the relationship of WTO law and domestic law on their own terms. In doing so, they also define the role of domestic courts. Members essentially follow one of the two doctrines of dualism or monism, or a combination of both. Overall, they have shown considerable reluctance in giving domestic effect to WTO law, and limit its effect to the doctrine of consistent interpretation.

27.4.2 The status in constitutional law

27.4.2.1 *The doctrine of consistent interpretation*

In line with the general obligations of *pacta sunt servanda*, it is generally accepted that courts should apply and read domestic law consistently with obligations incurred under WTO law. The doctrine of consistent interpretation obliges courts to adopt an interpretation of domestic law consistent with international law.[21] Unlike with direct effect, international law does not overrule domestic law. But it informs domestic law within a given framework. Often, WTO law is more detailed than generally framed provisions in

[19] Bhuiyan 2007, 33–41.   [20] Cottier and Nadakavukaren 1998, 83, 91–119.
[21] Eeckhout 2004, 314–16.

domestic law. It is therefore of considerable importance in the process of interpretation, and must be taken into account in litigation before domestic courts. The so called 'Charming Betsy' doctrine was established in the US.[22] Today, it is, in general, widely accepted around the world, including in the EU and in Swiss law.[23]

In the trade remedy area in the US there seems to be a contest between the Charming Betsy doctrine and the canon of interpretation deriving from the *Chevron* case,[24] which divides the process of review into two stages: if the intention of Congress is clearly reflected in the statute, there is no room for interpretation. If a statute is ambiguous or incomplete, the court will defer to any agency interpretation that is reasonable.[25] In the *Corus* case,[26] the court found that US legislation neither requires nor prohibits the practice of zeroing, and therefore the Charming Betsy doctrine was of no use. In the examination of *Chevron* stage two, the court came to the conclusion that the practice of zeroing was 'technically compatible' with the Anti-Dumping Agreement and therefore it should defer to Commerce's interpretation. This was in spite of the fact that the Appellate Body had, in *Bed Linen* 2001 and *Softwood Lumber* 2004, found the zeroing methodology to have violated the Anti-Dumping Agreement.[27]

The crucial question remains whether WTO law may overrule domestic law in cases of inconsistencies. What needs to be done in cases where convergences of domestic and international law cannot be found, or where domestic rules are simply missing? Are domestic courts allowed to apply WTO law in such constellations? The issue raises fundamental questions of separation and balance of powers, and is generally discussed in terms of dualist and monist traditions of international law.

27.4.2.2 *The dualist tradition*

The dualist tradition conceptually separates the spheres of international law and domestic law. It reflects the classical divide of domestic and foreign affairs. Domestic courts are not entitled to apply international law short of transformation into domestic law by Parliament.[28] It is therefore not possible to assess in court whether domestic law is consistent with international law unless this is particularly provided for, as is the case in bilateral investment agreements. Under WTO law, importers and investors are not able to challenge domestic law by referring to international law obligations of the country.[29]

---

[22] *Murray* v. *The Schooner Charming Betsy*, 6 US (2 Cranch) 64 (1804).

[23] See Case C-70/94, *Fritz Werner Industrie—Ausrüstungen GmbH* v. *Germany* (1995), ECR I-3189; Case C-83/94, *Peter Leifer and others* (1995), ECR I-3231; Case C-61/94, *Commission* v. *Germany* (1996), ECR I-3989; Case C-14/83, *Von Colson* (1984), ECR 1891; Case C-106/89, *Marleasing/La Comercial International de Alimentación* (1990), ECR I-4135; see also *Frigerio* v. *Eidg. Verkehrs- und Energiewirtschaftsdepartement*, BGE (Swiss Federal Court Reporter) 94 I 669, at 678.

[24] *Chevron USA, Inc.,* v. *Natural Res. Def. Council, Inc.,* 467 US 837, 104 S.Ct. 2778.

[25] Davies 2007; Barceló 2006.

[26] *Corus Staal BV and Corus Steel USA Inc.* v *United States Department of Commerce*, 259 F.Supp.2d 1253 CIT, 2003.

[27] Davies 2007.

[28] Bhuiyan 2007, 29–33.

[29] Cottier 2001, 2009b.

Accordingly, courts are not empowered to review domestic law. Dualism has its roots in the Westminster system, securing the prerogatives and powers of Parliament vis-à-vis the Crown. While the latter was empowered to conduct foreign affairs and to conclude treaties, no such treaty should deploy any effect without the consent of Parliament. Dualism thus emerged as a doctrine of separation of powers, safeguarding the rights of the electorate and Parliament in nineteenth century constitutional monarchies. It is interesting to note that dualism today is still strongly rooted in monarchies and applied in the United Kingdom and members sharing the tradition of the Commonwealth and common law, in particular India. Many developing countries sharing this tradition follow the dualist approach. In Europe, it is applied in particular by the Nordic countries. It is important to emphasize the rooting of dualism in monarchy and the struggle for domestic constitutionalism. These roots no longer offer a convincing rationale for dualism. Modern monarchies are limited to representation, and foreign policy powers are all shared between the executive branch and Parliament. The divide of domestic and foreign affairs no longer exists in terms of law-making and treaty-making powers.[30] Except for countries where foreign policy remains detached from control and influence of Parliament, it would seem that the dualist conception is outdated and no longer responds to principles of democratic accountability of foreign policy.

27.4.2.3 *The monist tradition*

The monist tradition does not separate international and domestic law. Both are inherent parts of the law of the land. It stresses the unity of law, whatever its sources and modes of generation. Courts of law are thus allowed to apply international law as much as they apply domestic law.[31] It is a matter of defining the relationship of international law and domestic law, and of terms and criteria under which this application may take place. It is also a matter of properly defining the relationship between international law and domestic law. Different constitutional systems have adopted diverging principles and rules. Some accept the primacy of international law in general. Others accept international law as being equal to statutory law. It is subject to constitutional law and responds to a 'later in time' rule. Again, it is a matter of constitutional law to define the relationship between different instruments, both in terms of hierarchy and temporal scope. Whatever the differences, countries operating under the monist system allow courts to review domestic law under international law, unless this is specifically excluded. Monism reflects a doctrine of checks and balances rather than the separation of powers. Courts are empowered to watch and ensure that other branches of government stay within the bounds of international commitments made. Even here, however, domestic law has often barred courts from adjudicating matters relating to foreign affairs.[32]

Monist doctrines and the unity of law emerged in the United States of America after the Revolution. Since treaties were concluded by an elected president and subject to

---

[30] Gaja 2007.   [31] Bhuiyan 2007, 30.

[32] Jacot-Guillarmod 1993, 47; Morrison and Hudec 1993, 91.

approval by a two-thirds majority of the Senate, the risk of jeopardizing the rights of Parliament did not exist at the outset. It is interesting to observe that countries operating under democratic and liberal constitutions formed after the Revolution—such as France, the Netherlands, or Switzerland—tend to operate under monist doctrines. These traditions, equally, shaped the doctrine developed by the European Court of Justice (ECJ). In the EU, international law is part of domestic law and no fundamental divide exists.

27.4.2.4 *The predominance of de facto dualism in WTO law*

The fundamental differences between the dualist and monist traditions suggest that the role of domestic courts and legal protection relating to international trade before domestic courts must be fundamentally different. While importers enjoy no protection in international law under dualism as a matter of principle, they are able to call upon WTO law in monist countries. But, for a number of reasons, such differences have not developed in the real world. Monist countries have been reluctant to give full effect to monism in the field of international economic law. Partly, this is the doing of Parliament. And partly, it is due to self-restraint of the courts. In the US, the doctrine of monism was applied to GATT 1947 in the early days of the Agreement by domestic courts.[33] Self-execution of the Agreement was later challenged on the grounds that the GATT merely amounts to an executive agreement. The Supreme Court never ruled on the matter. Instead, Congress barred direct effect in the implementing legislation of the results of the Uruguay Round. WTO agreements are defined to be non-self-executing. Despite the underlying monist doctrine, no court in the US is entitled to review US legislation under WTO law. Importers are therefore barred from invoking WTO law in defence of their interests, and are limited to legal remedies offered by domestic legislation.[34] The same doctrine also applies to free trade agreements concluded by the US. The US policy strongly influenced attitudes in Europe and in other parts of the world. The denial of direct effect does not create incentives for others to fully comply with WTO law, and foreign policy goals to seek compliance abroad are impaired.[35]

While the European Council merely advised that WTO law would not be suitable for direct effect, it was the Court of Justice which, in a series of cases following precedents under GATT,[36] excluding direct effect except when the EU directly referred to GATT law[37] and in cases under the trade barrier regulation,[38] denied direct effect of WTO law

---

[33] *Territory of Hawaii* v. *Harry M. Y. Ho*, Supreme Court of Hawaii, No. 3078, 31 January 1957.

[34] Leebron 1997; Barceló 2006, 154, 167–8.

[35] Henkin 1979.

[36] ECJ 12 December 1972, Cases 21–24/72, *International Fruit Company NV and others* v. *Produktschap voor Groenten en Fruit*.

[37] ECJ 7 May 1991, Case C-69/89, *Nakajima All Precision Co. Ltd* v. *Council of the European Communities*.

[38] ECJ 22 June 1989, Case 70/87, *Fédération de l'industrie de l'huilerie de la CEE (Fédiol)* v. *Commission of the European Communities*.

in relation to EU legislation across the board, irrespective of the particular context. The Court also denied direct effect not only of WTO law, but also of rulings under the WTO dispute settlement system.[39] In particular, it denied any responsibility of the EU incurred for the lack of implementation of WTO rulings.[40] Private actors are not entitled to compensation, albeit they suffer losses from continued inconsistencies of EU law with WTO obligations assessed in WTO dispute settlement.[41] The Court essentially built its rationale on two grounds: firstly, it affirmed its views, developed under GATT 1947, that the WTO is primarily an instrument of negotiations with rights and obligations not sufficiently defined. Secondly, the Court stressed the importance of reciprocity in granting direct effect—an element lacking in the light of existing US legislation and practice.[42] The Court, however, limited its findings to EU law. Member states remain free to give direct effect to WTO agreements with respect to their own jurisdictions.

The finding and open door is of particular importance in the field of standards and enforcement of intellectual property rights.[43] Eventually, domestic courts gave direct effect to the Agreement on Trade-Related Aspects of Intellectual Property Rights (TRIPS). The Barcelona Commercial Court Number 4 applied the TRIPS Agreement in assessing the problem of retroactive application of the Agreement.[44] The ECJ confirmed *Dior* and allowed for direct effect of the TRIPS Agreement in areas not yet harmonized by EU law, such as patent duration.[45]

The evolution of WTO-related case law in the fields of EU competence contrasts with a strong tradition of direct effect granted to preferential trade agreements.[46] This striking difference can be explained in terms of political economy. Firstly, regional agreements reflect the predominance of EU law and do not run the risk of producing results contrary to internal EU legislation, unlike under WTO law. Secondly, the Court maximized the effect of international agreements in relationship to member states, and minimized the impact when it was called upon to review EU legislation: 'When invoked in challenges to Member State action the ECJ has all too often adopted the boldest of stances, often in the face of powerful Member State submissions, in a manner which shares a marked parallel with the maximalist treaty enforcement logic that characterizes the treatment accorded to "Community law proper". Challenges to Community action, although uncommon, have in contrast led to a judicial willingness to acquiesce in the submissions advanced by the Community's political institutions in order to shield Community action from review'.[47]

---

[39] ECJ 23 November 1999, Case C-149/96, *Portuguese Republic* v. *Council of the European Union*.

[40] Case C-93/02, *Biret International* v. *Council* (2003), ECR I-10497; Case T-19/01, *Chiquita Brands and others* v. *Commission* (2005), ECR II-315.

[41] Cottier 2009b; Bronkers 2005; Holdgaard 2008; Trachtman 1999.

[42] Van den Broek 2001; Zonnekeyn 2008; Griller 2000; Hilpold 2009; Brand 1997.

[43] ECJ 14 December 2000, Case C-300/98 and C-392/98, *Dior and others*.

[44] *Alfa Wassermann* v. *Valeant Pharmaceuticals*, 29 January 2007. Documents on file with author.

[45] ECJ 11 September 2007, Case C-431/05, *Merck Genéricos–Produtos Farmacêuticos Lda* v. *Merck & Co. Inc. And Merck Sharp & Dohme Lda*.

[46] ECJ 26 October 1982, Case 104/81, *Hauptzollamt Mainz* v. *C.A. Kupferberg & Cie KG a.A.*

[47] Mendez 2010, 104.

Legislation and judicial policy in the US and the EU largely result in de facto dualism. In the field of multilateral trade, both jurisdictions exclude direct effect categorically; in the US, this also applies to preferential trade agreements, which enjoy a long tradition of direct effect in the EU.[48] Recent developments in EU law see a further expansion of excluding direct effect from other areas of international law, further aligning it to the practices of the US.[49] At the same time, there is evidence that courts actually and informally take WTO decisions and precedents into account, yet without citing them, in what was called a 'muted dialogue'.[50] This trend, while beneficial to achieving greater coherence, poses problems of transparency and legal security. Courts are obliged to faithfully and transparently reason their decisions without hidden agendas and considerations. It remains to be seen whether this will also reverse direct effect granted to regional and preferential trade agreements, which so far has been a mainstay of EU external economic relations. The possibility cannot be excluded that the trend towards power politics will increase in the light of a new generation of bilateral agreements containing dispute settlement mechanisms built after the model of the WTO.

In China, the issue of granting direct effect to WTO law before domestic courts is controversial and still unresolved. According to a statement made by the Vice President of the Supreme Court, China rules out direct effect of WTO law.[51] As a practical result, this amounts to an effect equivalent to dualism, which also excludes direct effect in India. The High Court of Judicature of Madras distinguished the case from the application of the UK European Community Act, and held that the existence of international dispute settlement under the WTO agreements barred the Court from reviewing the contractual arrangements under the TRIPS Agreement entered into by the Union of India.[52] This, as a result, amounts to the de facto application of a dualist doctrine.

While the field and discussions so far are dominated by US and EU judicial policy, it is important to note that other monist countries avoid strict exclusion of direct effect and operate on a more flexible mode of trial and error. Switzerland—a middle-sized trading country, much less powerful but highly dependent on open markets in goods and services—may show the way,[53] although the Swiss Federal Court has so far, in some cases, held the line with the ECJ that the GATT and GATS were not available to an individual in Swiss courts of law.[54] Courts and appeal boards also regularly apply WTO law,

---

[48] Dražen 2000.

[49] Mendez 2010, 97.

[50] Bronckers 2008.

[51] Jianming 2002.

[52] *Novartis AG v. Union of India*, WP No. 24759 and 24760, 6 August 2007.

[53] Engelberger 2004; Cottier and Oesch 2004b, 121ff.

[54] *Maison G. Sprl. c. Direction general des douanes*, BGE (Federal Court Reporter) 112 Ib 183, 189–90; *Commcare AG Communications & Networks c. Swisscom AG*, BGE 2A 503/2000, BGE (Swiss Federal Reporter) 125 II 613 effectively applied the Agreement on Import Licensing Procedures in agriculture (*ASA c. Bundesamt für Landwirtschaft*, judgment of 14 July 1997, BGE 2A 496/1996, not reported, reprinted in Cottier and Oesch 2005, 225–6, 677).

in particular the Government Procurement Agreement. The Swiss government affirmed direct effect of some provisions of the WTO law, emphasizing that this cannot be decided on in general, but only on a case-by-case basis.[55] The government also stated that several provisions of the TRIPS Agreement have a direct effect.[56] The view was similarly stated before the WTO.[57] Overall, jurisprudence and judicial policy shows a more nuanced, and less categorical, attitude than within the EU. It has the potential to lead to the development of a more sophisticated jurisprudence in the coming years.

27.4.3 The debate on direct effect

The denial of direct effect in EU case law triggered a lively debate at the outset of the new century, which coincided with the emerging debate on constitutionalization of international economic law. Pros and cons of direct effect of WTO were widely discussed in the legal literature.[58] Many of the arguments, however, relate to issues of substantive law and are not truly to the point.

Arguments against direct effect of WTO law, other than those relating to power politics, often point to the need for domestic policy space. Members should not be unduly restrained in the pursuit of their own democratically defined policies.[59] Yet, these are issues of substance and need to be addressed in shaping appropriate rules. The Appellate Body has repeatedly demonstrated that these rules can be construed and applied in a balanced manner and that these concerns are largely unfounded.

The argument is made that WTO law is not sufficiently precise, and domestic courts will adopt diverging interpretations. Yet, autonomous interpretation is inherent to all international agreements and if taken seriously would bar the doctrine of direct effect in general terms. Moreover, the increasing body of WTO precedents offers guidance and reduces the risk of conflicting interpretation. Another reason given relies upon an alleged lack of democratic legitimacy. But it should be stressed that negotiators act upon the instructions of their governments and no rules are adopted without consent. Moreover, the legitimacy of WTO law relies upon a number of additional factors which are critical in preserving peace and stability and long-term growth, in particular of developing countries.[60]

In procedural terms, it is argued that direct effect is barred due to the right and possibility to offer compensation and to take retaliation into account. This argument ignores

---

[55] Message relatif à l'approbation des accords du GATT/OMC du 19 septembre 1994, BBl. 1994 IV 1, 418.

[56] Ibid., 282(3).

[57] WTO 2001, chapter III.2.v, with regard to the Anti-dumping Agreement and the Subsidies and Countervailing Measures Agreement; WTO 1998, paragraph 44, concerning Article 53 (2) of TRIPS.

[58] Cottier and Nadakavukaren 1998.

[59] Howse 2008; Eeckhout 2002; Kuijper and Bronckers 2005; Van den Broek 2001; Cass 2005.

[60] Cottier 2009b; Cottier 2009c.

the fact that genuine cases of direct effect are unrelated to WTO dispute settlement and the special case of implementing a particular decision. We return to this point below.

Another argument relates to the protection of human rights: direct effect granted to trade rules may impair them. Yet, this is a matter of primacy and not of direct effect. It is conceivable to operate a doctrine of direct effect which takes into account the relative value of fundamental rights and principles at stake. Nothing impairs a doctrine of direct effect to preserve the protection of fundamental rights in constitutional law. As in EU law, this may lead to the inclusion of such rights within the WTO body, or the possibility of operating on the basis of primacy of constitutional law and limiting the implications of direct effect to the level of legislation, even subject to a later in time rule. There are ample options to fine-tune the balance of domestic and international law in combating economic protectionism and state failures while preserving the fundamental rights of individuals. The example of the Kadi case[61] has shown the way in defining the relationship between EU and UN law.[62] The policy could equally apply to WTO law, comparable also to the *Solange* doctrine of the German Constitutional Court.[63] The German Constitutional Court ruled that it would protect fundamental rights as long as this was not sufficiently done within European law—a judicial policy which eventually encouraged the European Court of Justice to implicitly protect fundamental rights long before they were included in the EU treaties or the Charter of Human Rights.[64]

While most of the arguments against direct effect are therefore not compelling and need to be addressed in substantive law, the implications for the horizontal and vertical allocations of powers within a constitutional framework amount to the true reasons for denying direct effect in the real world.

27.4.4 The underlying political economy

The exclusion of judicial review of domestic legislation, both in the US and the EU as well as in many other countries, is essentially rooted in the allocation of powers and a perceived balance of power between different branches of governments. Direct effect of WTO law implies powers of the courts to review acts of domestic legislation and to bar their application in case of conflict with WTO obligations of that member. It equally and indirectly reinforces powers of the executive branch, as it negotiates international agreements which the courts eventually apply. In the US, concerns that judicial review would undermine the constitutional foreign policy powers of Congress in trade loom large and explain the mercantilist and categorical exception of direct effect in trade regulation.

---

[61] ECJ 3 September 2008, Cases C-402/05 P and C-415/05 P, *Yassin Abdullah Kadi and Al Barakaat International Foundation v. Council of the European Union.*

[62] Besson 2009.

[63] BVerfGE 29 May 1974, BVerfGE 37, 271, *Solange I* and BVerfGE 22 October 1986, BVerfGE 73, 339, *Solange II.*

[64] Slaughter, Stone Sweet, and Weiler 1998.

In the EU, judicial restraint imposed by the European Court of Justice can be explained by the trauma caused in both the *Bananas* and *Hormones* disputes. At the heart of agricultural policy, the Court was keen to avoid a major conflict with the Commission, the Council and Parliament. We should not forget that major transatlantic tensions in GATT and the WTO traditionally concerned agriculture and the Common Agricultural Policy, and were therefore politically sensitive. The Court's judicial policy reflects a strategy to avoid both internal conflict and the limelight, leaving the matter to the political branches of government.

It is interesting to observe that the doctrine of direct effect and reliance upon international agreements in domestic law emerged at a time when the US was an emerging power in the nineteenth century, before the status as a superpower allowed the country to impose its rules on others while shielding off their influence at home. It would seem that the prevailing doctrine in the EU follows the same pattern. Denial of direct effect is considered beneficial by Kuijper to an emerging global power.[65] This doctrine is therefore clearly related to power politics and realism, reinforcing traditional perceptions of foreign policy and a division of domestic and international law. It will be seen whether the judicial policy today applied by the European Court of Justice, including the denial of compensation to those affected by adjudicated violations of EU law,[66] runs the risk of undermining the impressive doctrine of direct effect and primacy in domestic EU law. It should be recalled that the tensions caused by the protracted implementation of the *Bananas* rulings equally triggered challenges to EU law in domestic courts.[67] There is a lack of coherence of judicial policy on different layers of governance, which undermines the legitimacy of EU law.[68] Domestic courts, in particular constitutional courts, may be tempted to play the cards of power politics and of judicial protectionism again.

27.5 TOWARDS A COMMON THEORY OF JUDICIAL REVIEW

The current status of WTO law in domestic law in most countries, including the US and the EU, thus either reflects an outdated conception of dualism or a monism categorically excluding the application of WTO law beyond the doctrine of consistent interpretation. Overall, the judicial system still suffers from the legacy and tradition of power politics and the absence of coherent judicial policies linking domestic and foreign affairs.

---

[65] Kuijper and Bronckers 2005, 1,317.
[66] ECJ 9 September 2008, Case C-120/06 P and C-121/06 P, *FIAMM and FIAMM Technologies* v. *Council and Commission*.
[67] Griller 2000.
[68] Cottier 2009b.

As a result, the current state of play in major trading nations grossly undermines the authority and effectiveness not only of WTO law, but of international law and the concept of law in general. It ignores the fact that international trade and global governance depend upon a stable legal framework on the international and domestic level, and that coherence cannot be achieved by denying legal effect. It ignores the fact that WTO law is a crucial ingredient in bringing about equal conditions of competition, combating economic protectionism at home. It ignores the fact that lawyers will only take WTO law seriously if it is of relevance in domestic relations as well as in interstate disputes. Students and corporate lawyers will only turn to study the matter in greater depth if the body of law is of as much critical use in domestic litigation as it is before panels and the Appellate Body.

At the same time, it is evident that progress on the status of WTO law in domestic law has to take into account the underlying problem of separation and balance of powers within a given constitutional setting. Also, it needs to take into account the overall requirement of political reciprocity in terms of offering legal protection at home.[69] As long as the majority of countries exclude direct effect as a matter of principle or as a matter of judicial expediency, progress is very difficult to achieve. The matter therefore should not be entirely left to constitutional law, but also be addressed in WTO law itself. Legal protection before domestic courts is an important ingredient of the rule of law and of transparency. The past dichotomy of dualism and monism, and the categorical restraints imposed on monism in trade regulation, do not offer an appropriate foundation for defining the proper role of domestic courts in coming years.

The European Court of Justice of the EU, in an impressive and consistent jurisprudence, developed the doctrine of primacy and direct effect of EU law, both in relation to freedoms and secondary law.[70] Such jurisprudence is the essence of constitutionalization of EU law, from a trade agreement establishing a customs union to an instrument granting rights to individuals. It is not suggested simply to follow this route, as realities and conditions on the global level are fundamentally different and do not allow for simple analogies. Yet, lessons may be partly learned from drawing on the concept of justiciability of norms, which has a long tradition both in EU law and in domestic constitutional law. It is not a matter of defining entire agreements as to having or not having direct effect. It is not a matter of defining such effects even for single provisions in general terms. It is a matter of assessing the context and constellations of a particular case in order to decide whether the application of a particular rule may properly fall within the province of the court. This is not a technical operation of assessing the structure or clarity of the rule concerned. Much more, it is a matter of assessing the implications of a decision on the overall constitutional framework—on the allocation of powers between the political and the judicial branches of government. In doing so, the courts

---

[69] Ibid.   [70] Cottier 2009b.

will find that some WTO rules are suitable for direct effect in particular constellations, while not in others. While it is reasonable to exclude direct effect in the context of major international disputes, the same rule may apply in a different and more limited context. It is necessary to develop a doctrine of judicial review which allows different interests to be balanced more carefully.

27.5.1 Justiciability, political questions and judicial restraint

In the age of globalization and regionalization, the fundamental divide between international law and domestic law no longer permits a response to the complex regulatory needs of interlinked economies depending on legal security and mutual market access.[71]

The notion of law cannot be divided. It is conceptually outdated to question the legal nature of international law, and in particular of WTO law in the light of existing mechanisms of international dispute settlement and enforcement of WTO law. No longer are Austinian and positivist doubts appropriate. Instead, the body of law needs to be considered as a whole, and it is a matter of defining the mutual relationship between different sources and layers of regulation in defining primacy and the effect of norms. This is the essence of an emerging doctrine of multilayered governance, seeking to establish a proper balance between international and domestic law.[72] Within this concept, norms—whatever the layer of governance—may be of a programmatic nature, calling upon the legislator for implementation and barring direct effect. Such norms may be found in international law and in constitutional law alike. They may also be found in legislation. At the same time, other norms are suitable for direct effect, again independently of whether they belong to the realm of international or domestic law.[73] Whether or not a norm is of such a quality depends upon what we call the doctrine of justiciability.[74]

Courts need to ask whether the norm is justiciable—whether, in other words, it is suitable for judicial decision-making. Courts can refer to criteria in assessing whether the matter pertains to their province or not. These criteria not only include the textual precision and clarity of a rule, whether it allocates rights and obligations, but mainly whether it is suitable for judicial application, concretization, and refinement in case law. The matter before the court must be apt to be assessed by the court, and a decision taken suitable to be implemented without further legislation. Clearly, there are areas of WTO law, such as intellectual property enforcement procedures, which are readily suitable for application by courts. Equally clearly, there are areas which are more suitably dealt with by the legislative process as they entail large and complex programmes and need to engage the political process.[75] The issues in *EC–Bananas* are a case in point. They entail

---

[71] Cottier 2009a.   [72] Johnston 2005.   [73] Cottier 2009c.
[74] Cottier 2009b; Wüger 2005.   [75] Cottier 2009c.

basic problems of development policies, and cannot be solved by simply removing preferential tariffs without engaging, at the same time, in substantial programmes of structural reform in support of the communities affected.[76] Lifting import restrictions is legally less of a problem for traditional importers, but may affect other treaty obligations and, foremost, seriously affect the livelihood of millions. It would imply substantial foreign policy interference, which the courts cannot contain. Courts should thus leave the matter to the political process and WTO adjudication by declining direct effect or deploying a political question doctrine, both on the basis of lack of suitability. In *EC–Hormones, US–Continued Suspension of Obligations in the EC Hormones Dispute,* and *EC–Biotech Products* on the other hand, domestic courts would be able, in applying the Agreement on the Application of Sanitary and Phytosanitary Measures (SPS), to assess what essentially amounts to procedural obligations in setting domestic food standards which deviate from agreed international standards. Relying upon a test of suitability of courts to deal with the issue in light of their constitutional relations to the Council, Parliament, and Commission, the Court of First Instance and the European Court of Justice are in a position to define their province in WTO matters.

In assessing justiciability, the implications of a ruling on the allocation and balance of powers within a constitutional framework thus play an important role. These considerations are today often taken into account silently and implied in reasons given to deny direct effect. They need, however, to be discussed in explicit terms. Separations of powers and checks and balances form an important ingredient of judicial reasoning in assessing justiciability.[77] A political question doctrine and a doctrine of judicial restraint offer appropriate rationales.

It is submitted that the exclusion of judicial review, and thus of direct effect, should be framed and placed within a future *political question doctrine*. Such a doctrine would be based upon criteria defining the lack of suitability of judicial review. It would not be limited to the exclusion of programmatic norms, which necessarily require action in legislation, but also entail constellations where a ruling on the basis of specific rules such as national treatment or Most-Favoured Nation (MFN) would incur substantial foreign policy ramifications. The theory could build upon the doctrine of direct effect, but eventually would no longer depend on it. In the long run, WTO rules and principles would simply be applicable (as much as primary law applies within the internal market). It would, however, remain subject to exclusions on the basis of the criteria of the political question doctrine. It would be far more convincing to decline justiciability on the basis of thorough arguments relating to the proper role of courts and their limitation under the facts of a particular case, than seeking to explain denial to rule by recourse to alleged (and in fact often nonexistent) general vagueness of rules.[78] Within an overall constitutional framework of multilayered governance, these steps would allow the achievement

---

[76] Breuss, Griller, and Vranes 2003. See also Trachtman 1999.

[77] Cottier 2009b.

[78] Cottier 2009c.

of greater coherence and consistency. They would overcome the basic divide which currently reigns within the law.

Within norms found suitable for judicial review, and thus not subject to the political question doctrine, the legal process may now take recourse to additional components of the doctrines of judicial review. In assessing the legality of domestic law in the light of WTO rules, courts are in a position to exercise *judicial restraint*, much as such restraint is exercised in examining the legality of legislative and administrative decisions in EC law. In complex cases of international economic law, courts equally and inherently depend upon expertise found within the Commission and domestic administrations.[79] They may limit full review to procedural issues while applying the standards on manifest error, misuse of powers, or excessive exercise of discretion. At the same time, courts will need to bear in mind that judicial review in WTO panels and the Appellate Body is full review, and extensive limitation of domestic review creates the paradox that standards of review are more intrusive on the global than the domestic level.[80] EC and domestic courts therefore need to develop standards of review which are more elaborate than the current limitations to abuses of power and capricious decisions. Proper standards remain to be developed.

27.5.1.1 *Implementation of DSB decision*

In the field of WTO law, it is important to clearly distinguish disputes which have been the subject of WTO dispute settlement from constellations of genuine and independent application of WTO law before domestic or EC courts. Both constellations pose different legal issues and should not be intermingled. The existence of international dispute settlement under the DSU does not exclude genuine examination. Nonetheless, the European Court of Justice recognized that the two constellations are separate and need distinction.[81] The general denial of direct effect was essentially developed without making that fundamental distinction. The same is true for the High Court of Judicature of Madras,[82] which stated that it did not have jurisdiction to rule on the TRIPS issue because of the mere existence of dispute settlement under the WTO agreements. In the case of implementing DSB decisions, WTO law is authoritatively defined in a precise manner in case law and the decision. It cannot be a matter of denying legal effects due to imprecise rules. In the Corus case, the US Court of Appeals actually cited earlier reports of the Appellate Body before coming to the conclusion that it was sufficient to clearly deny any binding effect to WTO reports, noting that 'Congress has enacted legislation to deal with the conflict presented here'.[83]

---

[79] Cottier 2009b.
[80] Oesch 2004b.
[81] Case C-93/02, *Biret International v. Council* (2003), ECR I-10497; Case T-19/01, *Chiquita Brands and others v. Commission* (2005), ECR II-315.
[82] *Novartis AG v. Union of India*, WP N 24759 and 24760, 6 August 2007.
[83] *Corus Staal*, 1,349; Davies 2007.

The problem lies with the mechanism of implementation under the DSB, which limits direct effect prior to the exhaustion of all the avenues provided: compensation, retaliation, or implementation. In such constellations, it is evidently a matter for the political bodies to define the agenda, and direct effect of WTO law may only take place upon failure to act in accordance with the procedures of the DSB as a matter of denial of justice or abuse of law. If Commission, Council, and Parliament persistently fail to act and refuse to adjust the WTO inconsistency, and thus to support the removal of retaliatory surcharge tariffs, courts should eventually lift import restrictions in accordance with the DSB report or grant financial compensation to importers affected.[84] Evidently, these conditions will be met only in very exceptional cases. They primarily have a preventive effect and serve as an incentive to engage in legislative change without delay.

27.5.1.2 *Genuine cases before domestic courts*

Matters are completely different when WTO provisions are before domestic or EC courts outside, and without ongoing WTO dispute settlement in the specific matter. A court of law may be called upon by a private party with an issue to which WTO rights and obligations are relevant and in which they need to be taken into account. It is here that a court is bound to ask to what extent it is genuinely required to assess domestic law on the basis of WTO law. The relationship to the political branches of government is different from the constellation discussed above. In applying standard doctrine of justiciability, political question and judicial restraint as discussed above, courts are able to assess the issue on a case-by-case basis, examining in detail the scope and content of the norms invoked and taking into account the WTO case law. They will be able to take into account existing WTO jurisprudence and case law, as well as doctrinal writings on the subject. They are able to discuss and reason why a norm is given effect or not, in light of the balance of powers and checks and balances, in a transparent manner.

27.5.2 Towards common rules on judicial review in WTO law

In the pursuit of rendering WTO law more effective around the world, the issue of judicial review should no longer be entirely left to domestic law. Common rules should be developed in future negotiations, relating both to the implementation of DSB reports and to the role of WTO law in disputes before domestic courts, following the example of Article XX of the WTO Government Procurement Agreement. The basic problem of reciprocity can be tackled by suggesting domestic recourse by individuals to WTO law as a market access concession in WTO terms. Members willing to claim such rights before their courts, where suitable, would in return obtain additional commitments in fields of their interest, since direct effect as a principle amounts to enhanced market

---

[84] Cottier 1988.

access rights for importers of foreign products by reinforcing the rule of law and of legal security.

27.6 CONCLUSIONS

Courts continue to have difficulties in defining an appropriate role in combining traditional constitutional layers and emerging layers of international economic law in the process of shaping rights and obligations in a comprehensive and coherent manner. The role of courts in WTO law has been shaped by a long tradition of the judicial branch abstaining in foreign affairs. Traditional doctrines of judicial review in foreign relations continue to prevail, and courts still need to find their proper and future role in international economic relations.[85] Current trends incline even more towards less protection at home, and a renaissance of dualism. This may well be explained in terms of power politics, and the difficulties in shaping appropriate relations among different branches of government in foreign affairs. It is hardly to the benefit of international law and the role of law to contain power and economic protectionism at home.

Traditional doctrines of dualism and monism in international law no longer provide an adequate framework in dealing with WTO law and a complex relationship among different branches of government and, horizontally, between the WTO and members.[86] In the process of constitutionalization, courts play the leading role. To the extent that they deal with international affairs, they affect traditional patterns of separation of powers, checks and balances, and thus traditional patterns of constitutionalism. As much as being a matter of protecting rights and interests, the task entails a constant and delicate balancing of the prerogatives of different branches of government. Adjudication in international law cannot be separated from the constitutional allocation of powers. Doctrines of judicial review which are explicitly based upon, and take into account, separations of powers and checks and balances therefore need to be developed.

Based upon the premise of unity of all law, whether international or domestic, a doctrine of justiciability takes into account the nature of particular norms and the implication its application has for the allocation of powers among the different branches of government and among different layers of governance.[87] Criteria of justiciability, a political question doctrine, and the doctrine of judicial restraint allow an appropriate balance to be achieved without excluding the effectiveness of WTO rules before domestic courts *ex ante* and as a matter of principle. In doing so, it is important to clearly distinguish constellations of implementing DSB decisions from cases where WTO law is being

---

[85] Slaughter 2003.
[86] von Bogdandy 2008.
[87] Cottier 2009b.

invoked before a domestic court independently of the existence of an international dispute. A common doctrine should be developed in the process of dialogue and interaction of courts, which may eventually also find its way into explicit principles and rules within the WTO.

REFERENCES

Aubert, Jean-François. 1991. *Bundesstaatsrecht der Schweiz*, volume 1. Basel: Helbing & Lichtenhahn.

Barceló III, John J. 2006. The Paradox of Excluding WTO Direct and Indirect Effect in U.S. Law. *Tulane European & Civil Law Forum* 21: 147–72.

Besson, Samantha. 2009. European Legal Pluralism after Kadi. *European Constitutional Law Review* 5 (2):237–64.

Bhuiyan, Sharif. 2007. *National Law in WTO Law: Effectiveness and Good Governance in the World Trading System*. Cambridge: Cambridge University Press.

Bickel, Alexander M. 1986. *The Least Dangerous Branch: The Supreme Court at the Bar of Politics*. New Haven: Yale University Press.

Brand, Ronald A. 1997. Direct Effect of International Economic Law in the United States and the European Union. *Northwestern Journal of International Law and Business* 17 (2–3):556–608.

Breuss, Fritz, Stephan Griller, and Erich Vranes. 2003. *The Bananas Dispute: An Economic and Legal Analysis*. Vienna, NY: Springer.

Bronckers, Marco. 2005. The Effect of the WTO in European Court Litigation. *Texas International Law Journal* 40 (3):443–8.

Bronckers, Marco. 2008. From 'Direct Effect' to 'Muted Dialogue'. Recent Developments in the European Courts' Case Law on the WTO and Beyond. *Journal of International Economic Law* 11 (4):885–98.

Cass, Deborah Z. 2005. *The Constitutionalization of the World Trade Organization*. Oxford: Oxford University Press.

Cottier, Thomas. 1988. Dispute Settlement in the World Trade Organization: Characteristics and Structural Implications for the European Union. *Common Market Law Review*. 35 (2):325–78.

Cottier, Thomas. 1993. Constitutional Trade Regulation in National and International Law: Structure–Substance Pairings in the EFTA Experience. In *National Constitutions and International Economic Law*, edited by Meinhard Hilf and Ernst-Ulrich Petersmann, 409–42. The Hague: Kluwer Law International.

Cottier, Thomas. 2001. A Theory of Direct Effect in Global Law. In *European Integration and International Co-ordination: Studies in Transnational Economic Law in Honour of Claus-Dieter Ehlermann*, edited by Armin von Bogdandy, Petros C. Mavroidis, and Yves Mény, 99–123. The Hague: Kluwer Law International.

Cottier, Thomas. 2007. The Judge in International Economic Relations. In *Economic Law and Justice in Times of Globalization, Festschrift für Carl Baudenbacher*, edited by Mario Monti et al., 99–122. Nomos: Baden-Baden.

Cottier, Thomas. 2009a. The Constitutionalization of International Economic Law. In *Economic Law as an Economic Good*, edited by Carl M. Meessen, 317–36. Munich: Sellier: European Law Publishers.

Cottier, Thomas. 2009b. International Trade Law: The Impact of Justiciability and Separations of Powers in EC Law. *European Constitutional Law Review* 5 (2):307–26.

Cottier, Thomas. 2009c. The Legitimacy of WTO Law. In *The Law and Economics of Globalization: New Challenges for a World in Flux*, edited by Linda Yueh, 11–48. Cheltenham: Edward Elgar.

Cottier, Thomas, and Maya Hertig. 2003. The Prospects of 21st Century Constitutionalism. *Max Planck Yearbook of United Nations Law* 7 (1):261–328.

Cottier, Thomas, and Krista Nadakavukaren. 1998. The Relationship between World Trade Organization Law, National and Regional Law. *Journal of International Economic Law* 1 (1):83–122.

Cottier, Thomas, and Matthias Oesch. 2003. The Paradox of Judicial Review in International Trade Regulation. In *The Role of the Judge in International Trade Regulation*, edited by Thomas Cottier and Petros C. Mavroidis, 287–306. Ann Arbor: University of Michigan Press.

Cottier, Thomas, and Matthias Oesch. 2004. Die Unmittelbare Anwendbarkeit von GATT/WTO Recht in der Schweiz. *Szier* 14 (2): 121–54.

Cottier, Thomas, and Matthias Oesch. 2005. *International Trade Regulation: Law and Policy in the WTO, the European Union and Switzerland*. Bern: Cameron May and Stämpfli.

Davey, William J. 2005. The WTO Dispute Settlement System: The First Ten Years. *Journal of International Economic Law* 8 (1):17–50.

Davies, Arwel. 2007. Connecting or Compartmentalizing the WTO and United States Legal Systems? The Role of the Charming Betsy Canon. *Journal of International Economic Law* 10 (1):117–49.

Dražen, Petrović. 2000. *L'effet Direct des Accords Internationaux de la Communauté Européenne: à la Recherche d'un Concept*. Geneva: Presses Universitaires de France.

Eeckhout, Piet. 2002. Judicial Enforcement of WTO Law in the European Union—Some Further Reflections. *Journal of International Economic Law* 5 (1):91–110.

Eeckhout, Piet. 2004. *External Relations of the European Union: Legal and Constitutional Foundations*. Oxford: Oxford University Press.

Engelberger, Lukas. 2004. *Die Unmittelbare Anwendbarkeit des WTO-Rechts in der Schweiz. Grundlagen und Perspektiven im Kontext Internationaler Rechtsentwicklungen*. Studies in Global Economic Law, 7. Bern: Peter Lang.

Franck, Thomas M. 1992. *Political Questions Judicial Answers: Does the Rule of Law Apply to Foreign Affairs?* Princeton: Princeton University Press.

Gaja, Giorgio. 2007. Dualism—a Review. In *New Perspectives on the Divide Between National and International Law*, edited by J. Nijman and A. Nollkaemper, 52–62. Oxford: Oxford University Press.

Griller, Stefan. 2000. Judicial enforceability of WTO law in the European Union: Annotation to Case C-149/96, Portugal v. Council. *Journal of International Economic Law* 3 (3): 441–72.

Henkin, Louis. 1979. *How Nations Behave: Law and Foreign Policy*. 2nd edition. New York: Columbia University Press.

Henkin, Louis. 1996. *Foreign Affairs and the US Constitution*. 2nd edition. Oxford: Oxford University Press.

Hilpold, Peter. 2009. *Die EU im GATT/WTO System*. 3rd edition. Innsbruck: Innsbruck University Press, Schuthess, Nomos.

Holdgaard, Rass. 2008. *External Relations Law of the European Community: Legal Reasoning and Legal Discourse*. Alphen aan den Rijn: Kluwer Law International.

Howse, Robert. 2008. Human Rights, International Economic Law and Constitutional Justice: A Reply. *European Journal of International Law* 19 (5):945–53.

Jackson, John H. 2005. The Changing Fundamentals of International Law and Ten Years of the WTO. *Journal of International Economic Law* 8 (1):3–15.

Jackson, John H. 2006. *Sovereignty, the WTO, and Changing Fundamentals of International Law*. Cambridge: Cambridge University Press.

Jacot-Guillarmod, Olivier. 1993. *Le Juge National Face au Droit Européen*. Basel: Helbing & Lichtenhahn.

Jianming, Cao. 2002. WTO and the Rule of Law in China. *Temp In't L & Cop. J.* 16: 379.

Johnson, Nevil. 1995. Constitutionalism: Procedural Limits and Political Ends. In *Constitutional Policy and Change in Europe*, edited by Joachim Jens Hesse and Nevil Johnson. Oxford: Oxford University Press.

Johnston, Douglas M. 2005. World Constitutionalism in the Theory of International Law. In *Towards World Constitutionalism: Issues in the Legal Ordering of the World Community*, edited by Roland St John Macdonald and Douglas M. Johnston, 3–30. Leiden: Martinus Nijhoff Publishers.

Kälin, Walter. 1986. Verfassungsgrundsätze der Schweizerischen Aussenpolitik. *Referate und Mitteilungen des Schweizerischen Juristenvereins*.

Kuijper, Peter Jan, and Marco Bronckers. 2005. WTO Law in the European Court of Justice. *Common Market Law Review* 42: 1313–355.

Leebron, David W. 1997. Implementation of the Uruguay Round Results in the United States. In *Implementing the Uruguay Round*, edited by John H. Jackson and Alan Sykes, 175–242. Oxford: Clarendon Press.

Leitner, Kara, and Simon Lester. 2005. WTO Dispute Settlement 1995–2004: A Statistical Analysis. *Journal of International Economic Law* 8 (1):231–52.

Mendez, Mario. 2010. The Legal Effect of Community Agreements: Maximalist Treaty Enforcement and Judicial Avoidance Techniques. *European Journal of International Law* 21 (1):83–104.

Morrison, Fred L., and Robert E. Hudec. 1993. Judicial Protection of Individual Rights under the Foreign Trade Laws of the United States. In *National Constitutions and International Economic Law*, edited by Meinhard Hilf and Ernst-Ulrich Petersmann. The Hague: Kluwer Law International.

Oakeshott, Michael Joseph. 1983. The Rule of Law. In *On History and Other Essays*, edited by Michael Joseph Oakeshott. Oxford: Basil Blackwell, and New York: Barnes and Noble.

Oesch, Matthias. 2004a. Gewaltenteilung und Rechtsschutz im Schweizerischen Aussenwirtschaftsrecht. *Schweizerisches Zentralblatt für Staats- und Verwaltungsrecht* 105: 285–321.

Oesch, Matthias. 2004b. *Standards of Review in WTO Law*. Oxford: Oxford University Press.

Ortino, Federico, and Ernst-Ulrich Petersmann. 2004. *The WTO Dispute Settlement System 1995–2003*. The Hague: Kluwer Law International.

Peters, Anne. 1997. The Position of International Law within the European Community Legal Order. *German Yearbook of International Law* 40: 9–77.

Petersmann, Ernst-Ulrich. 1993. National Constitutions and International Economic Law. In *National Constitutions and International Economic Law*, edited by Meinhard Hilf and Ernst-Ulrich Petersmann. The Hague: Kluwer Law International.

Slaughter, Anne-Marie. 2003. A Global Community of Courts. *Harvard International Law Journal* 44 (1):191–219.

Slaughter, Anne-Marie, Alec Stone Sweet, and Joseph Weiler, eds. 1998. *The European Courts and National Courts: Doctrine and Jurisprudence*. Oxford: Hart Publishing.

Trachtman, Joel P. 1999. Bananas, Direct Effect and Compliance. *European Journal of International Law* 10 (4):655–78.

Trone, John. 2001. *Federal Constitutions and International Relations*. St Lucia: University of Queensland Press.

Wolfrum, Rüdiger, Peter-Tobias Stoll, and Karen Kaiser, eds. 2006. *WTO: Institutions and Dispute Settlement*. Max Planck Commentaries on World Trade Law. Leiden: Martinus Nijhoff Publishers.

Wüger, Daniel. 2005. Anwendbarkeit und Justiziabilität Völkerrechtlicher Normen im Schweizerischen Recht: Grundlagen, Methoden und Kriterien. In *Abhandlungen zum Schweizerischen Recht*, edited by Heinz Hausheer. Bern: Stämpfli Verlag.

von Bogdandy, Armin. 2008. Pluralism, Direct Effect, and the Ultimate Say: On the Relationship between International and Domestic Constitutional Law. *International Journal of Constitutional Law* 6 (3–4):397–413.

Van den Bossche, Peter. 2005. *The Law and Policy of the World Trade Organization*. Cambridge: Cambridge University Press.

van den Broek, Naboth. 2001. Legal Persuasion, Political Realism, and Legitimacy: The European Court's Recent Treatment of the Effect of WTO Agreements in the EC Legal Order. *Journal of International Economic Law* 4 (2):411–40.

WTO. 1998. Council for Trade-Related Aspects of Intellectual Property Rights. *Review of Legislation on Enforcement*. Switzerland. IP/Q4/CHE/1. Geneva: WTO.

WTO. 2001. Trade Policy Review Body. *Joint Trade Policy Review*. Switzerland and Liechtenstein. Minutes of Meeting—Addendum. WT/TPR/M/77/Add.1. Geneva: WTO.

Yoo, John. 2005. *The Powers of War and Peace: The Constitution and Foreign Affairs after 9/11*. Chicago: Chicago University Press.

Zonnekeyn, Geert A. 2008. *Direct Effect of WTO Law*. London: Cameron May.

CHAPTER 28

··

PREFERENTIAL
TRADING
ARRANGEMENTS

··

RICHARD BALDWIN

28.1 INTRODUCTION

PREFERENTIAL trade agreements have been important features of the world trade system since the General Agreement on Tariffs and Trade's (GATT) inception in 1947. The challenges and contributions to this system, however, have evolved over the decades. For the GATT/World Trade Organization (WTO)'s first 50 years, regional trade agreements (RTAs) were mainly, or exclusively, about preferential tariff reduction. The traditional, preference-centric perspective, however, is no longer sufficient. This traditional view, however, forms the core of received wisdom on RTAs and their relationship with the WTO, so the bulk of this chapter is devoted to it. Issues raised by the so-called twenty-first century regionalism are addressed in the last sections.

The key issues surrounding RTAs and the WTO turn on political issues, not economic ones, but the politics is driven by economic effects, so the next section, Section 28.2, briefly covers the quintessential economics of preferential tariffs. Section 28.3 uses the economics to inform a discussion of the relevant political economy theory. Section 28.4 looks at the systemic implications of RTAs for the WTO. To transit from the traditional view to the twenty-first century regionalism view, Section 28.5 presents the basic facts that show that tariff preferences are now a marginal feature of global trade. Section 28.6 presents the main lines of the twenty-first century regionalism analysis. The final section presents the concluding remarks.

28.2 BASIC ECONOMICS

The key feature of regionalism in the traditional view is tariff preferences. While the traditional view occasionally acknowledged non-tariff measures, such barriers were generally thought of as affecting outcomes in a tariff-like manner. This strategic simplification led scholars to rely almost exclusively on the Vinerian framework when studying the economics and political economics of regional trade agreements. This section reviews that framework and related extensions.

28.2.1 Vinerian framework

There are only three elemental effects in the Vinerian framework—all well known since 1950.[1] The first general point, namely 'Smith's certitude', was made by Adam Smith.[2] When a nation 'exempt[s] the good of one country from duties to which it subjects those of all other...the merchants and manufacturers of the country whose commerce is so favoured must necessarily derive great advantage'.[3]

The economic logic behind Smith's certitude is straightforward and easily illustrated with an example of a world where firms from two nations—call them Partner and Rest-of-World (RoW)—are competing in a third nation—call it Home. Without preferences, Home charges the same tariff on imports from Partner and RoW. After Home and Partner sign a free trade agreement, Partner firms pay no tariff on their sales to Home but RoW firms do. The incidence of the removed tax is shared, as usual, between consumers and producers. Home consumers see lower prices and Partner exporters see higher prices. As RoW firms must match the consumer price of their competitors, they lower their border prices and some import shifts from RoW to Partner. In short, Smith's certitude stems from the fact that Partner firms enjoy a rise in both prices and sales to Home.

The second elemental effect was identified when Gottfried Haberler asserted that third nations — those excluded from the preferences—must lose.[4] This is 'Haberler's spillover', and it can be illustrated with the same simple case. To remain competitive in the Home market while still paying the tariff, RoW firms must accept a lower producer price for their exports. This pushes them down their export supply curve so RoW exports fall. Thus the spillover is that third nation exports suffer a drop in both prices and sales to Home; what is preference to one nation is discrimination to another.

As we shall see in the next sections, Smith's certitude—and especially Haberler's spillover—are the linchpins of the political economy of the traditional view of regionalism.

---

[1] For a more formal treatment, see Baldwin and Venables 1995.   [2] Smith 1776.
[3] Smith 1776, as quoted in Pomfret 1997.   [4] Haberler 1937.

After the war, Jacob Viner demonstrated that preferential liberalization might harm the preference-giving nation; this is 'Viner's ambiguity'.[5] Viner, who was blissfully ignorant of post-war mathematical economics, couched his argument in the enduring but imprecise concepts of 'trade diversion' and 'trade creation'.[6] The basic economics, nevertheless, is clear. Discriminatory liberalization is both 'liberalization'—which removes some price wedges and thus tends to improve economic efficiency and Home welfare—and 'discrimination'—which introduces new price wedges and thus tends to harm efficiency and welfare. Specifically, the ambiguity turns on three effects: substitution of lower-cost Partner goods for Home goods, improved terms of trade vis-à-vis RoW, and worsened terms of trade vis-à-vis Partner.

A fourth effect is not elemental but is critical in thinking about regionalism–multilateralism interactions, namely the Kemp–Wan–Meade theorem.[7] The theorem states that when formation of an RTA is teamed with the right amount of multilateral tariff-cutting, all nations may gain from the combination of regionalism and multilateralism—i.e. Haberler's spillover can be neutralized by partial multilateral tariff-cutting. Of course, real world RTAs do not adjust external tariffs in a Kemp–Wan–Meade manner, but the theorem is an important intellectual lighthouse for policymakers. It also helps us understand why the duo of multilateral and preferential tariff-cutting—in operation since the 1950s—has had relatively benign effects on the world trade system.

28.2.2 Scale and growth effects

Real world discussions of the merits of RTAs almost always mention scale, pro-competitive, and growth effects. This section introduces the relevant economics.[8]

A frequent justification of RTAs turns on the belief that market size matters; access to a large market helps a nation's industrial competitiveness. The logic is simple. National barriers mean national firms are more successful in their home market—a situation known as market fragmentation. This reduces competition, raises prices and keeps too many small, inefficient firms in business. Tearing down trade barriers defragments the markets, producing a 'pro-competitive effect'. This then puts pressure on profits, the result of which is industrial restructuring. The least efficient firms are driven out; the most efficient flourish. In the end, the integrated region has a more competitive industrial structure with fewer, bigger, more efficient firms.

A second effect that is frequently observed is investment-led growth following the formation of an RTA. Again the economics is straightforward. The RTA-linked efficiency enhancements also improve the investment climate and thus attract more investment. While this is typically a one-off effect—the one-off improvement in static

---

[5] Viner 1950.

[6] The problem is that the terms suggest that trade volumes are the key, while Viner's words clearly indicate that price changes are what matter.

[7] Meade 1955; Kemp and Wan 1976.   [8] See Baldwin and Wyplosz 2009 for details.

efficiency induces a medium-run investment boom—the effect can be to raise aggregate growth rates for many years.

28.3 Political economy of RTAs

Starting from the premise that tariffs are the endogenous outcome of an interaction between a nation's economy and its political system, trade liberalization is a puzzle.[9] Why would nations find it politically optimal to reduce tariffs that they had previously found it optimal to impose? As a first step towards answering this, it is useful to set out the determinants of the politically optimal tariff.[10]

28.3.1 Political economy of tariff choices

The tariff choice question can be framed as an equilibrium interaction between the supply and demand for protection.[11] Walrasian supply curves are marginal cost curves, so the supply of protection is the marginal cost to the government of imposing a tariff (i.e. damage to the economy is a marginal political cost). Walrasian demand is the marginal utility curve, so the demand for protection is the marginal lobbying expenditures by import-competing firms brought forth by a small tariff hike (i.e. such expenditures are a political benefit).

The supply of protection curve thus traces out the marginal damage done by raising tariffs. Higher tariffs lower consumer surplus, raise producer surplus, and change tariff revenues; the net cost always rises with the tariff level, but it is negative for very low tariffs (optimal tariff argument). This is why the supply curve (see Figure 14) intersects the horizontal axis at a positive number and is upwards sloping.

The demand for the tariff is linked to lobbying, which itself is linked to profitability of import-competitors (their producer surplus). The tariff raises domestic production, and the more domestic production there is to protect, the higher is the marginal gain of a tariff hike. This means the demand curve is also upwards sloping, but it starts at a positive intersection with the vertical axis.

The politically optimal tariff is the intersection of the supply and demand curves.[12]

---

[9] See Baldwin and Baldwin 1996 on political economy of endogenous trade liberalization.

[10] For a more formal treatment of this, see the original treatments by Findlay and Wellisz 1982, Grossman and Helpman 1994, articles or reviews in Hillman 1989; see Baldwin and Robert-Nicoud 2006 for a simplified presentation of Grossman and Helpman 1994.

[11] See Hillman 1989 for a review of the main approaches, and Grossman and Helpman 2002 for mathematical refinements of several of the basic approaches.

[12] See Grossman and Helpman 1994, or Baldwin and Robert-Nicoud 2007 for details.

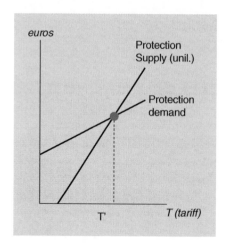

FIGURE 14 Supply and demand for protection

28.3.2 Liberalization: juggernaut effects and MTNs

Starting from an initial situation where tariffs are chosen unilaterally as in Figure 14, announcement of multilateral trade negotiations (MTN) changes the political calculation facing all participating nations in such a way that they find it politically optimal to reduce tariffs that they had previously found it optimal to impose. The reason is that reciprocity confronts old-fashioned protectionism with old-fashioned mercantilism. In this context, the old-fashioned protectionists are import-competing firms who want a tax placed on the products of their foreign rivals; old-fashioned mercantilists are exporting firms who would like a reduction in the taxes they pay in foreign markets. The key point is that under a reciprocal trade agreement, mercantilists win lower foreign tariffs only if domestic tariffs also fall. This enables governments to counterbalance protectionist lobbies (who opposed domestic tariff-cutting) with exporter lobbies (who don't care directly about domestic tariffs, but who know they have to fight protectionists in their own nation to win better foreign market access).[13]

But this is not the end. The agreed tariff reductions slice into political support for protection in a scissor-like fashion. Domestic liberalization downsizes import-competing industries as firms shed workers, lose sales, or go broke. Foreign tariff cuts boost output, employment, and profits in export sectors. As political influence follows economic clout to some extent, the upsizing of export interests and the downsizing of import-competing interests tilts future political calculations towards more liberalization. The shift may take years, however, since the induced entry and exit can take years.

---

[13] An early reference is Cooper 1971, 410, but also see Roesseler 1978, Blackhurst 1979, Baldwin 1980, Moser 1990, or Hillman and Moser 1996. The best known reference is the parameterization by Grossman and Helpman 1995.

The ineluctable outcome is that reciprocal tariff cuts agreed at one GATT round alter national political-economy landscapes in a way that fosters continued liberalization at the next GATT round. Trade-induced economic growth also eases economic adjustment, thus rendering liberalization easier politically.

This mechanism is called the juggernaut effect; once the tariff-cutting ball starts rolling, political economy momentum keeps it rolling until all tariffs in its path are crushed. At that point it runs out of 'fuel' and stops.[14] Plainly, the logic only applies to tariffs that are subject to reciprocal negotiations. Sufficiently strong special interest groups in key nations, e.g. agriculture, managed to keep their protection off the negotiating table until 1986, so the juggernaut had little effect on them.

28.3.3 Dominos and RTAs

The juggernaut effect concerns all tariff-cutting; Haberler's spillover means that an additional effect operates when it comes to preferential liberalization.

The logic starts with the immediate impact of an idiosyncratic deepening of integration among two or more nations. Once the deal is done, third nations face a new situation—one in which pro-RTAs are strengthened. The point is that now joining the newly created RTA would give third nations two political economy pluses—they would enjoy Smith's certitude and redress the loss from Haberler's spillover. Previously, they would have enjoyed only Smith's certitude, so it is entirely possible that membership becomes politically optimal even though it was not before the idiosyncratic deepening among the initial members.

Returning to our three-nation example (Section 28.2)—where the initial political equilibrium has no preferences, an RTA between Home and Partner (assume it is forged for reasons outside the model) creates *de novo* political economy forces in RoW. If RoW exporters are politically strong enough, the pro- and anti-RTA forces can shift so that the RoW government finds the RTA politically optimal even though the RTA was suboptimal previously. As with the juggernaut, there is a second round of effects (but for this we need more than three nations).

If one non-member actually does join the preference area, discrimination facing other non-members expands in a way that shifts their pro- and anti-RTA forces towards membership. The cycle repeats itself until a new political equilibrium is reached—in the meantime, tariff walls fall in what looks like a domino-like fashion. This is what Baldwin called the domino theory of regionalism.[15]

---

[14] 'Juggernaut' is a mispronunciation of the Hindu deity of the Puri shrine, Jagannath, whose chariot—an enormous and unwieldy construction—requires thousands to get rolling; once in motion, it is hard to stop. See Baldwin 1994, 73, for the first presentation of the idea, Baldwin and Robert-Nicoud 2007 for formal modelling, and Fugazza and Robert-Nicoud 2010 for empirical evidence.

[15] See Baldwin 1993 for the original formulation of the domino theory, Baldwin 2006 for an early application, and Baldwin and Jaimovich 2009 for a formal model; empirical support is provided by Egger and Larch 2008. Also see Bond and Syropoulos 1996; Freund 2000; Yi 1996; McLaren 2002; Levy 1997; Krishna 1998.

So far there has been no mention of the 'supply side' membership—i.e. thinking about whether the incumbents would allow the applicants to join. Considering the supply side is rather a difficult matter. The best effort to date is by Aghion, Antràs, and Helpman.[16] To make progress, however, they must assume a highly structured model in which only one nation is allowed to make offers of FTAs while all other nations simply accept or reject. In order to employ the tools of cooperative game theory directly, they assume that lump-sum transfers among nations are costless. In this setting they find that critical issues are the extent of what game theorists call 'coalition externalities' (i.e. Harberler's spillover) and 'grand coalition superadditivity' (i.e. global free trade maximizes global welfare). In this setting, they find that regionalism can lead to global free trade under certain circumstances, and not in others. Given the highly stylized game they use to study the problem, the results are difficult to apply to the real world, but in any case one possibility they highlight as possible is the domino effect outcome.

28.3.4 Dominos and juggernauts

In the post-war period, dominos have helped push the juggernaut and vice versa. Indeed, the major RTA- and MTN- pushes line up remarkably well. The 1940s and 1950s saw a sequence of MTNs and important steps towards European preferential trade. Formation of the European Economic Community (EEC) customs union (1958–68) occurred in tandem with the Dillon and Kennedy Rounds, as well as the US–Canada preferential deal, the 1965 Auto Pact. Preferential and multilateral tariff-cutting went hand in hand again in 1973—the year of the first EEC enlargement and launching of the Tokyo Round. The last successful MTN was launched in 1986, the same year that the US–Canada FTA and EU's Single Market Programme began.

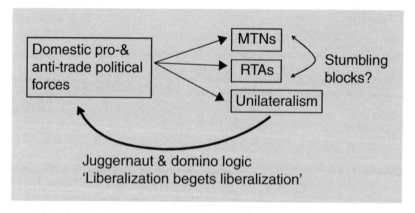

FIGURE 15 Political economy feedback: Regionalism and multilateralism

[16] Aghion, Antràs, and Helpman 2007.

This synchronicity is quite in line with the juggernaut model. Periodic tariff-cutting induces industrial restructuring that makes further liberalization politically optimal a few years down the road—both multilateral and preferential liberalization. This feedback and the interactions are illustrated in Figure 15. The basic point is that a nation's stances on RTAs and MTNs are jointly endogenous variables, and both are affected by the balance of pro- and anti-liberalization forces.

28.4 REGIONALISM AND MULTILATERALISM

Until the late 1980s, regionalism comprised highly effective European arrangements (which encompassed a third of world trade but were driven by strategic motives), and a bouquet of developing nations RTAs that covered little trade and affected even less. A volte-face by Canada (1986) and Mexico (1990) changed this; Canada proposed an FTA with the US in 1985 that entered into force in 1989. Mexico proposed an FTA with the US in 1990 that evolved into NAFTA at Canada's insistence (the first domino effect in the Western Hemisphere). The US, which had long been interested in expanding preferential North American trade beyond its 1965 US–Canada Auto Pact, readily agreed. The US–Mexico initiative triggered a wave of Latin American requests for bilateral FTAs, and gave greater urgency to arrangements among Latin Americans, most notably Mercosur.[17]

This Western Hemisphere domino effect, combined with one in Europe triggered by the collapse of the Soviet Union, contrasted sharply with the acrimonious collapse of the Uruguay Round's 'final' summit in December 1990. Many scholars looked at this correlation and saw causality with regionalism viewed as a threat to the world trading system. Up to then, thinking about regionalism was largely confined to the 'small think' question: 'Should a nation join?'; afterwards, 'big think' questions arose such as: 'Is regionalism bad for the multilateral system?', or 'Are trade blocs building blocks or stumbling blocks on the road to global free trade?'

Krugman introduced the new approach by asking whether an exogenous increase in RTAs raises world welfare—the 'Is bilateralism bad?' literature.[18] Bhagwati, alluding to political economy factors, asked whether trading blocs were stumbling blocks or building blocks on the road to global free trade.[19] This literature looks distinctly odd today as it uses simple theory to address an empirical question. The theory, however, is deeply embedded in the current debate, so it needs to be reviewed.

28.4.1 Building or stumbling blocks?

In its clearest form the question is: would forbidding RTAs hasten multilateral tariff-cutting (stumbling blocks) or slow it (building blocks)? There are three main examples

[17] See Baldwin 1997 or Serra et al. 1997 for an account of this domino effect.
[18] Krugman 1991a.   [19] Bhagwati 1991.

of the former: the preference-erosion logic, the goodies-bag logic and the cherry-picking logic.

The preference-erosion logic is a simple application of Smith's certitude.[20] A preferential tariff helps Partner exporters in two ways: directly, as they no longer pay the tax, and indirectly, as their competitors continue to pay it. If third nations are also granted the preference, part of Smith's certitude is lost to Partner exporters. As the same is true for Home exporters in the Partner market, it is easy to see that there might be a coalition of Home and Partner exporters that would oppose extension of the preferences to RoW (i.e. the move to global free trade).

The goodies-bag logic is related,[21] but more relevant to a situation where Home is the dominant partner, say the US in North America, or the EU in Europe, where Partner values the preferential market access more than Home. As Partner firms (and, by political economy reasoning, the Partner government) value the preference, the Home government can extract a political price for the special market access. This could involve, for example, cooperation with Home's anti-drugs or anti-terror policies. Multilateral tariff-cutting in this situation reduces Home's leverage.

The cherry-picking logic turns on an entirely distinct mechanism. Moving to global free trade will typically involve some pluses and some minuses from the national political economy perspective. The logic suggests that there can be groups of nations whose trading pattern means that an RTA among them would have many of the pluses and few minuses. If these groups form trade blocs, then the move from RTAs to global free trade is likely to involve more minuses and fewer pluses than if the move was from non-cooperative tariffs everywhere to global free trade. In particular, Levy suggests that the trade blocs formed in North America and Europe took much of the steam out of the drive for global free trade, as exporters in these nations won lower foreign tariffs via the RTAs rather than via multilateral trade talks.[22]

The building blocks side of the debate highlights situations where RTAs make MFN tariff-cutting easier. The first is an extension of the juggernaut effect described above. RTAs involve reciprocal liberalization that typically makes export sectors larger and import-competing sectors smaller in the member nations. Thus the RTA can alter the member governments' stance in MFNs, making it politically optimal to cut MFN tariffs to levels that would not have been politically optimal without the RTA. Of course, if an RTA results in higher external tariffs (as in the case of the EU's agriculture tariffs), then an RTA can start the juggernaut rolling backward.

A second building block logic is the obverse of the preference-erosion stumbling block logic. Consider a situation of so-called hub-and-spoke bilateralism, where the large nation has bilateral RTAs with several small nations that depend upon it heavily for trade. Returning to our example, suppose Home has bilaterals with Partner and RoW. This situation provides Home firms with preference rents in both Partner and RoW markets, but Partner and RoW firms have access to the Home market identical to that of

---

[20] The idea can be found in Riezman 1985; Kennan and Riezman 1990; Krishna 1998; Freund 2000.
[21] Limão 2006.   [22] Levy 1997.

global free trade. Clearly, moving to global free trade would harm Home and help Partner and RoW, so Home might veto global free trade. Observe, however, that if the two 'spoke' economies sign a bilateral, the matrix of bilaterals achieves the same effect, namely zero tariffs globally. See Lloyd for a clear development of this so-called veto-avoidance building-block logic,[23] and note that it is one strand in the widely discussed 'competitive liberalization' logic of Bergsten.[24]

A third line of thinking considers the impact of an RTA on the MFN tariff a nation would find unilaterally optimal to impose. This is called the 'complements or substitutes' approach. If preferential tariff-cutting makes MFN tariff-cutting more attractive, they are complements, otherwise substitutes. For example, an RTA makes a nation's import taxes more distortionary, so cutting MFN tariffs may become politically optimal after a preferential cut. Countering this is the possibility that the RTA members—especially if it is a customs union—may seek to exploit their joint market power. That is, the 'optimal tariff' of the enlarged bloc may be larger than it was for the individual members. Of course, this would violate GATT/WTO rules and has not been observed on a large scale in the last 60 years, but it is a theoretical possibility.[25]

A closely related line of reasoning considers the impact of a non-customs union RTA on the external protection of RTA members, when members impose different tariffs on third nations. Under some circumstances, the FTA effectively lowers the higher MFN tariff (imported MFN liberalization); in other circumstances, the FTA effectively raises the lower MFN tariff (imported MFN protection). A good example is the US–Mexico FTA. The FTA equalized prices in the two nations. As the US's low MFN tariffs on most goods had brought US prices close to the world level, the FTA meant Mexico's internal prices were as if they had the US's external tariff schedule (which is far more open than Mexico's). Combining this observation with the second part of the juggernaut effect suggests that the US–Mexico FTA made the Mexican government less resistant to MFN free trade than it was previously. Shibata, Vousden, Krueger, Richardson, and Grossman and Helpman are all important contributors to or users of this line of analysis.[26]

The final line of argumentation worth mentioning is the so-called 'terms of trade' approach by Bagwell and Staiger,[27] which follows up on the insight by Krugman.[28] This assumes that nations act like firms in a game theory model of collusion. Collusion (i.e. high prices) is sustained by the threat of retaliation against cheating (price undercutting by one firm). Here, the collusion is on keeping MFN tariffs low and the threat is retaliation if one nation raises its tariffs unilaterally. A long series of papers study whether the presence of an RTA makes it harder or easier to sustain low MFN tariffs in this sort of set-up. The logic, however, is fatally flawed as it requires that tariffs go unobservable for

---

[23] Lloyd 2002.   [24] Bergsten 1996.

[25] Notable contributions include Riezman 1985; Kennan and Riezman 1990; Richardson 1993; Krugman 1991a, 1993; Bond and Syropolous 1996; Freund 2000a; Ornelas 2005, 2008.

[26] Shibata 1967; Vousden 1990; Krueger 1993; Richardson 1993, 1994, 1995; Grossman and Helpman 1995.

[27] Bagwell and Staiger 1993.

[28] Krugman 1991b, 1993.

a significant period of time. As tariffs are instantaneously observed the first time they are paid, the approach's logic collapses in the case of real world tariff agreements.

There are other contributions exploring the RTA–MTN linkages. Lawrence and Sapir argue that the threat of regionalism was a critical element in inducing GATT members to initiate the Uruguay Round and to accept the final Uruguay Round Agreement.[29] Winham makes the same argument for the Tokyo Round.[30] Bergsten dubs this 'competitive liberalization'.[31] A somewhat related idea, which has not been formalized, is that RTAs are testing grounds for the GATT/WTO.[32] The prime example here is the EU, which dealt with deeper than tariff-cutting liberalization for decades before the issues arrived on the GATT agenda in the Tokyo and Uruguay Rounds. See Ludema for a partial formalization of the idea.[33] Finally, Ethier and Freund view regional initiatives as a consequence of the success of multilateralism.[34] Ethier asserts that this is a benign consequence, since RTAs intensify world investment and create incentives for economic reforms in less developed countries. Freund studies the incentives for and the sustainability of preferential liberalization when multilateral tariffs are lower. She finds that deeper multilateralism provides greater incentives to form RTAs due to forces akin to the complementarity discussed above.

28.4.2 Exogenous RTAs and world welfare

The other major strand in the big-think regionalism is the 'is bilateralism bad?' literature started by Krugman.[35] These studies take RTAs as exogenous (i.e. not the outcome of a political economy choice), and consider the world welfare effects of raising the number. A large number of studies arrived at different findings depending upon the underlying economic structure assumed. The basic economics is almost identical to that of the complements-versus-substitutes literature. As RTAs are plainly not exogenous, this literature died out after a burst of enthusiasm generated by the initially seductive logical framework.[36]

28.4.3 Empirical evidence

To date there is no evidence that regionalism has been a major stumbling block to free trade, and some evidence that it has promoted broad liberalization. Irwin shows that bilateral agreements during the nineteenth century induced broader liberalization.[37]

---

[29] Lawrence 1991; Sapir 1993.   [30] Winham 1986.   [31] Bergsten 1996.
[32] Lawrence 1996; Bergsten 1996.   [33] Ludema 1996.   [34] Ethier 1998; Freund 2000.
[35] Krugman 1991a.
[36] Krugman 1991a. For example, see Frankel, Stein, and Wei 1995, 1996; Frankel 1996; Nitsch 1996; Schiff 2000; Spilimbergo and Stein 1996; Bond and Syropoulos 1996; Sinclair and Vines 1995.
[37] Irwin 1993.

Using data on trade and trade policy in 50 countries from 1965–95, Foroutan studies how RTA members adjusted their external tariffs, finding that both integrating and non-integrating countries reduced trade barriers. Foroutan does not control for other factors.[38] Baldwin and Seghezza show that nations with high MFN tariffs also have high preferential tariffs, suggesting that nations either find liberalization politically optimal— and do it regionally and multilaterally—or they find liberalization politically suboptimal and so do neither.[39]

Using a detailed cross-industry dataset on Argentina for 1992, 1993, and 1996, Bohara, Gawande and Sanguinetti examine the influence of imports from Mercosur's partner, Brazil, on Argentina's external tariffs. They find that increased preferential imports vis-à-vis the value added of the domestic industry led to lower external tariffs in Argentina, especially in industries that experienced trade diversion.[40] This is consistent with the complementarity of tariffs identified in the theoretical literature.

Estevadeordal, Freund, and Ornelas investigate the impact of preferential tariffs on developing nations' MFN tariffs. They find that preferences lead to lower external tariffs, implying that regionalism is a building block to free trade. Like Bohara and Gawande, they find that the complementarity effect is stronger in sectors where trade bloc partners are more important suppliers, precisely where trade discrimination would be more disrupting.[41] Using a similar methodology for ASEAN, Calvo-Pardo, Freund and Ornelas also find evidence that regionalism is associated with unilateral tariff reduction.[42]

Limão and Karacaovali and Limão find a stumbling block effect at the tariff-line level. Specifically, they show that the US and EU were less likely to lower tariff lines where they had previously granted preferences, although the overall tariff cuts were about 30 per cent on average, as agreed at the launch of the Uruguay Round. The suggestion is that goodies-bag logic was in effect for a small number of tariff lines. For example, the data shows US tariffs decreasing for all but 12 of the thousands of tariff lines (defined at the HS-8 products level in the WTO's database).[43]

28.5 Stylized facts

This section presents a snapshot of regionalism in 2009. The presentation is structured around three reasons for which RTAs are a concern: economic inefficiency stemming from discrimination, injustice and power asymmetries, and threats to support for multilateral liberalization.

Looking at RTAs from the perspective of economic inefficiency suggests a focus on the degree of discrimination involved. Figure 16 shows the evolution of the number of RTAs and the amount of trade covered. The number rose steadily, with an acceleration

---

[38] Foroutan 1998.   [39] Baldwin and Seghezza 2007.
[40] Bohara, Gawande, and Sanguinetti 2004.   [41] Estevadeordal, Freund, and Ornelas 2008.
[42] Freund and Ornelas 2009.   [43] Limão 2006; Karacaovali and Limão 2007.

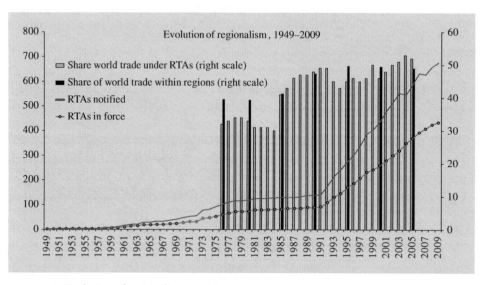

FIGURE 16 Evolution of regionalism, 1949–2009

Source: WTO database for RTA count, Baldwin and Carpenter 2010 for trade shares

in 1992 (due to a domino effect of the announcement of the US–Mexico FTA, and the unrelated velvet revolutions in Central and Eastern Europe).

The figure shows the share of world trade covered by RTAs on a yearly basis and the share of world trade taking place within WTO-defined regions for five-year intervals (only for 1976 to 2005 due to computational constraints). The first salient point is that the regionalization of world trade has tracked the rise in the share of regional trade under RTAs rather well. This suggests that it might be the regionalization of trade driving the RTAs rather than, or in addition to, the usual direction of causality (i.e. RTAs lead to trade regionalization). The second point is that the share of world trade under RTAs is rising much more slowly than the number of RTAs. This is due to the fact that many recent RTAs cover very little trade (Table 23).

The table shows that the two big RTAs—the EU and NAFTA—are very large, but other arrangements are modest or tiny. Over 200 RTAs cover less than one-tenth of one per cent of world trade (not shown in table). These are typically bilaterals between economically small nations. While each is minuscule, taken together they add up to about 8 per cent of world trade. See Box 1 for RTA abbreviations.

In gauging the degree of discrimination, the second thing to look at is the size of the margins of preference. Two types of measures are available: crude indicators of the margins for a wide range of nations, and a precise calculation for the largest traders.

The crude measures look first at the share of imports allowed in duty-free regardless of origin (preferences are not possible on this trade) and the average MFN applied tariff rate (a rough indicator of the upper bound of average preference margins). Figure 17 shows the facts for 2009.

Table 23 The size of selected RTAs, share of world trade, 2009

Largest bilateral RTAs		Selected plurilaterals		Largest plurilateral–nation	
China–Hong Kong China	1.5%	EU27	21.9%	ASEAN–Japan	1.4%
US–Singapore	0.4%	NAFTA	6.4%	EC–Turkey	0.9%
China–Singapore	0.4%	ASEAN	1.4%	ASEAN–Korea	0.6%
Japan–Thailand	0.4%	MERCOSUR	0.3%	ASEAN–Australia– New Zealand	0.6%
Japan–Malaysia	0.3%	GCC	0.1%	EC–South Africa	0.4%
Japan–Indonesia	0.3%	SADC	0.1%	EC–Algeria	0.4%
US–Australia	0.2%	ANZCER	0.1%	EC–Mexico	0.4%
Japan–Singapore	0.2%	SAPTA	0.05%	ASEAN–India	0.3%
US–Israel	0.2%	CACM	0.05%	EC–Israel	0.3%
Russia–Belarus	0.2%	COMESA	0.02%	EC–Morocco	0.2%
Brazil–Argentina	0.2%	ECOWAS	0.02%	EC–Egypt	0.2%
Russia–Ukraine	0.2%	EFTA	0.02%	EC–Tunisia	0.2%
Korea–Singapore	0.2%	CARICOM	0.01%	EC–Croatia	0.2%
China–Chile	0.2%	WAEMU	0.002%	EC–Chile	0.1%
Japan–Mexico	0.1%				
US–Chile	0.1%				

Source: Baldwin and Carpenter 2010

Note: The numbers are a crude measure in that they reflect all the trade among the nations that share the RTA mentioned, even if not all trade (e.g. agriculture) is covered by the agreement; there is no adjustment for preference margins, or MFN zero tariff rates.

As the left panel shows, about half of all imports face no tariffs regardless of origin for the three largest RTAs (EU, NAFTA, and ASEAN). The average MFN tariff rates (right panel) show that the upper bounds on preferences are low or modest for most of the plurilateral RTAs and all of the large ones. Of course, there are plenty of high MFN tariffs applied by these nations (especially on agriculture and light manufactures) but these products are often excluded from the RTA's coverage.

Using tariff line data and matching import flows, it is possible to display preference margins exactly for large trading nations (Figure 18). This shows that large preference margins—defined as those over 10 per cent—are quite rare. Indeed, even in the moderate or low categories of margins (5–10 per cent, and 0–5 per cent), the extent of preferences is modest for all the nations except Switzerland, Mexico, and Canada. Apart from Mexico, these exceptions have margins for the most part below 10 per cent and thus are not very distortionary.

Overall, the evidence is that tariff preferences are no longer very important. This observation flies in the face of the widespread concern about RTAs. This paradox—the manifest importance of RTAs despite the lack of preference margins—is what leads to the new view of RTAs—the subject of the next section.

Box 1 RTA abbreviations

ANZCER, Australia-New Zealand Closer Economic Relations Agreement
ASEAN, Association of Southeast Asian Nations
CACM, Central American Common Market
CARICOM, Caribbean Community and Common Market
CEFTA, Central European Free Trade Agreement
CEMAC, Communauté Économique et Monétaire de l'Afrique Centrale
COMESA, Common Market for Eastern and Southern Africa
EAC, East African Community
ECOWAS, Economic Community of West African States
EFTA, European Free Trade Association
EU15, European Union (15 members)
EU27, European Union
GCC, Gulf Cooperation Council
MERCOSUR, Southern Common Market
NAFTA, North American Free Trade Agreement
SACU, Southern African Customs Union
SADC, Southern African Development Community
SAPTA/SAFTA, South Asian Preferential (Free) Trade Arrangement (Bangladesh,
    Bhutan, India, Maldives, Nepal, Pakistan, Sri Lanka)
UEMOA, Union Économique et Monétaire Ouest Africaine
WAEMU (UEMOA), West African Economic and Monetary Union (Benin, Burkina
    Faso, Côte d'Ivoire, Guinea Bissau, Mali, Niger, Senegal, Togo).

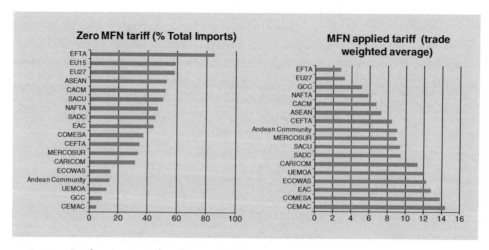

FIGURE 17 Crude measures of preference margins, 2009

Source: Baldwin and Carpenter 2010

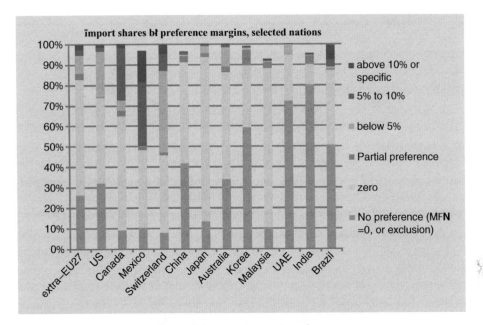

FIGURE 18 Preference margins and import coverage, selected nations, 2009

Source: Carpenter and Lendle 2011

28.6 TWENTY-FIRST CENTURY REGIONALISM

A good deal of the world's trade is a much more complex phenomenon than trade was in the 1980s and earlier. This 'twenty-first century trade' arose from 'production unbundling', also known as production sharing, internationalization of the supply chain, or fragmentation. In essence, production bays that used to be grouped in a single factory within a single jurisdiction now are dispersed across multiple nations. The resulting flows of things, people, information, and investment require deeper international disciplines than the WTO provides. Twenty-first century regionalism is the name for the policies that arose to fill this governance gap—mainly deep RTAs, a matrix of bilateral investment treaties, and massive unilateral tariff-cutting by developing nations.[44]

To better understand twenty-first century regionalism, and its implications for world trade governance, consider how the changed nature of trade that drove it fits into the broad landscape of economic history. The cost of moving goods, people, and ideas has always forced the geographical bundling of production and consumption. Before the industrial revolution, each village made most of what it consumed. The radical reduction in transportation cost due to steam power meant goods could be produced far away

---

[44] Baldwin 2010.

from consumers. Once this possibility arose, scale economies and comparative advantage made it inevitable, and production shifted towards the most efficient locations. This created what might be called twentieth century trade. The GATT was set up to provide international discipline for this simple form of international commerce—basically, goods crossing borders.

The post-steam power dispersion of production globally was, however, accompanied by a local clustering—the emergence of large-scale factories and industrial districts within nations. The reason is simple. Think of a stylized production line with a sequence of production bays. Coordinating the manufacturing process involves a continuous two-way flow of things, people, and information among the bays. These two-way flows are cheaper, faster, and more reliable when the bays are in close proximity.

In the 1980s and 1990s, the radical reduction in information management and communication costs that came with the Information and Communication Technology (ICT) revolution partly melted the 'coordination glue' holding the bays in close proximity. Cheaper communication triggered a suite of information-management innovations that made it easier, cheaper, faster, and safer to coordinate complex activities at distance. This triggered what could be called the 'second unbundling', i.e. the spatial unbundling of factories' production bays. Once this became feasible, scale economies and comparative advantage made it inevitable; manufacturing stages were moved offshore. ICT was to the second unbundling what steam power was to the first.

Internationalization of the supply chain did not end the two-way flows; it just meant that they occurred across jurisdictions, thus giving rise to a very much more complex form of international commerce—twenty-first century commerce (sharing tacit and explicit technology and intellectual property, training workers and managers, physical investment, the development of long-term business relationships, time-sensitive shipping, world-class telecoms, and short-term movement of managers and technicians). Trade in goods and foreign direct investment are the most easily measured aspect of this multifaceted, multidirectional commerce.

This more complex international commerce required deeper governance, especially as it grew between developed and developing nations. Three sets of bilateral disciplines arose to underpin the new international commerce: those signed by the US (NAFTA-type agreements), those signed by Japan (EPA-like agreements), and those signed by the EU (Association Agreements). Some emerging economies have also sought to fill the gap with unilateral 'pro-market' reforms; unilateral tariff-cutting[45] and WTO membership are key parts of this.

Table 24 shows some of the deeper disciplines that are features of this twenty-first century regionalism.

---

[45] Vézina 2010.

Table 24 Deeper disciplines in Japanese EPAs

	Mex	Mala	Phil	Thai
Liberalization & promotion of investment	X	X	X	X
Harmonization of custom procedures		X	X	X
Protection of intellectual property rights		X	X	X
Mutual recognition and testing		X	X	X
Movement of natural persons	X		X	X
Government procurement	X			X
Competition	X	X	X	X
Enhancement of business environment	X	X	X	X
Environment				
Labour				
Exchange of information, intellectual property rights	X			
Financial services	X	X	X	
Information technology		X	X	X
Science and technology	X	X	X	X
Education and human resource development	X	X	X	X
Trade and investment promotion	X		X	X
Small and medium enterprises	X	X	X	X
Transportation			X	
Energy			X	X
Agriculture, forestry and fishery	X	X		X
Road development	X		X	

Notes: Columns show the topics addressed in Japan's EPAs with Mexico (Mex), Malaysia (Mala), the Philippines (Phil) and Thailand (Thai).

Source: Balboa 2008.

28.7 CONCLUDING REMARKS

For most of the GATT/WTO's history, regionalism was all about tariff preferences. At first, the key concern was whether an individual nation would gain from joining an RTA. From the 1990s, concern shifted to the more systemic question of whether regionalism was good or bad for the multilateral trading system. More recently, fundamental changes in international commerce has led to a dramatic reduction in tariff preferences, but no reduction in worries that RTAs are undermining the WTO. The new perspective, the so-called twenty-first century regionalism, is really about defining new international disciplines necessary to underpin twenty-first century international commerce, i.e. international production networks and flows of people, things, and information that they generate.

This is the challenge to the WTO — twenty-first century regionalism is creating new rules governing international commerce, including international trade. These are being decided outside of the WTO, in a setting of massive power asymmetries and without basic principles of non-discrimination and reciprocity in concessions. The challenge facing the WTO today is whether it can respond by multilateralizing some of the deeper disciplines, or alternatively, remaining vibrant even as its disciplines remain limited to those laid out in the 1994 Marrakesh Agreement that established the WTO.

References

Aghion, P., P. Antràs, and E. Helpman. 2007. Negotiating Free Trade. *Journal of International Economics* 73 (1):1–30.

Bagwell, K., and R. W. Staiger. 1993. Multilateral Tariff Cooperation during the Formation of Regional Free Trade Areas. NBER Working Paper 4364. Cambridge MA: National Bureau of Economic Research.

Balboa. 2008. Negotiated Trade Liberalization in East Asia: Examining Japan's Economic Partnership Agreement (EPA): Focusing on the Japan–Philippines Economic Partnership Agreement (JPEPA). Unpublished manuscript.

Baldwin, Richard. 1993. A Domino Theory of Regionalism. CEPR Discussion Paper 857; NBER Working Paper 4465. Published in *Expanding Membership in the European Union*, edited by Baldwin, Haaparanta, and Kiander, 25–48, Cambridge: Cambridge University Press, 1995.

Baldwin, Richard. 1994. *Towards an Integrated Europe*. London: CEPR.

Baldwin, Richard. 1997. The Causes of Regionalism. *The World Economy* 20 (7):865–88.

Baldwin, Richard. 2006. Managing the Noodle Bowl: The Fragility of East Asian Regionalism. CEPR Discussion Paper 5561. London: CEPR.

Baldwin, Richard. 2010. 21st Century Regionalism: Filling the Gap Between 21st Century Trade and 20th Century Trade Governance. HEID working paper. Geneva.

Baldwin, Richard, and Theresa Carpenter. 2010. The Evolution of Regionalism. Unpublished manuscript, Graduate Institute.

Baldwin, Richard, and Dany Jaimovich. 2009. Are Free Trade Agreements Contagious? Global COE Hi-Stat Discussion Paper gd09-057. Tokyo: Institute of Economic Research, Hitotsubashi University.

Baldwin, Richard, and Frédéric Robert-Nicoud. 2006. Protection for Sale Made Easy. CEPR Discussion Paper 5452. London: CEPR.

Baldwin, Richard, and Frédéric Robert-Nicoud. 2007. A Simple Model of The Juggernaut Effect of Trade Liberalisation. CEPR Discussion Papers 6607. London: CEPR.

Baldwin, Richard, and Elena Seghezza. 2007. Are Trade Blocs Building or Stumbling Blocks? New Evidence. CEPR Discussion Paper 6599. Published in *Journal of Economic Integration* 2–25.

Baldwin, Richard E., and Anthony J. Venables. 1995. Regional Economic Integration. In *Handbook of International Economics*, volume 3, edited by G. M. Grossman and K. Rogoff, 1597–644. Amsterdam: Elsevier.

Baldwin, Richard, and Charles Wyplosz. 2009. *The Economics of European Integration*. 3rd edition. New York: McGraw-Hill.

Baldwin, Robert. 1980. The Economics of the GATT. In *Issues in International Economics*, edited by Peter Oppenheimer. Stocksfield, England and Boston: Oriel.

Baldwin, Robert Edward, and Richard Edward Baldwin. 1996. Alternate Approaches to the Political Economy of Endogenous Trade Liberalization. European Economic Review 40 (3–5):775–82.

Bergsten, Fred. 1996. Globalizing Free Trade: The Ascent of Regionalism. *Foreign Affairs* 75 (3):105–20.

Bhagwati, Jagdish. 1991. *The World Trading System at Risk*. Hemel Hempstead: Harvester Wheatsheaf.

Blackhurst, Richard. 1979. Reciprocity in Trade Negotiations under Flexible Exchange Rates. In *Trade and Payments Adjustment under Flexible Exchange Rates*, edited by John Martin and Alasdair Smith, 212–44. London: Macmillan.

Bohara, Alok, Kishore Gawande, and Pablo Sanguinetti. 2004. Trade Diversion and Declining Tariffs: Evidence from Mercosur. *Journal of International Economics* 64 (1):65–88.

Bond, Eric, and Constantine Syropoulos. 1996. The Size of Trading Blocs: Market Power and World Welfare Effects. *Journal of International Economics* 40 (1):411–37.

Carpenter, T., and A. Lendle. 2011. How Preferential is World Trade? CTEI Working Paper. Geneva: Centre for Trade and Economic Integration. Available from <http://graduateinstitute.ch/webdav/site/ctei/shared/CTEI/working_papers/CTEI-2010-32.pdf>. Accessed on 10 November 2011.

Cooper, Richard. 1971. Tariff issues and the Third World. *The World Today* 27 (9):401–10. London: Chatham House publication.

Egger, Peter, and Mario Larch. 2008. Interdependent Preferential Trade Agreement Memberships: An Empirical Analysis. *Journal of International Economics* 76 (2):384–99.

Estevadeordal, Antoni, Caroline Freund, and Emanuel Ornelas. 2008. Does Regionalism Affect Trade Liberalization toward Non-Members? *The Quarterly Journal of Economics* 123 (4):1531–75.

Ethier, William. 1998. Regionalism in a Multilateral World. *Journal of Political Economy* 109 (6):1214–45.

Findlay, Ronald, and Stan Wellisz. 1982. Endogenous Tariffs, the Political Economy of Trade Restrictions, and Welfare. In *Import Competition and Response*, edited by J. Bhagwati, 223–44. Chicago and London: University of Chicago Press.

Foroutan, Faezeh. 1998. Does Membership in a Regional Preferential Trade Arrangement Make a Country More or Less Protectionist? World Bank Policy Research Working Paper 1898. Washington DC: World Bank.

Frankel, Jeffery. 1996. *Regional Trading Blocs*. Washington, DC: Institute for International Economics.

Frankel, Jeffery, Ernesto Stein, and Shang-Jin Wei. 1995. Trading Blocs and the Americas: The Natural, the Unnatural, and the Super-Natural. *Journal of Development Economics* 47 (1):61–95.

Frankel, Jeffery, Ernesto Stein, and Shang-Jin Wei. 1996. Continental Trade Blocs: Are They Natural and Super-Natural? In *The Regionalism of the World Economy*, edited by Frankel, Chapter 4. Chicago: Chicago University Press.

Freund, Caroline. 2000. Different Paths to Free Trade: The Gains from Regionalism. *Quarterly Journal of Economics* 115 (4):1317–41.

Freund, Caroline, and Emanuel Ornelas. 2009. Regional Trade Agreements. CEP Discussion Paper 0961. London: Centre for Economic Performance, LSE.

Fugazza, Marco, and Frédéric Robert-Nicoud. 2010. The Emulator Effect of the Uruguay Round on US Regionalism. CEP Discussion Paper 0973. London: London School of Economics.

Grossman, Gene, and Helpman, Elhanan. 1994. Protection for Sale. *American Economic Review* 84 (4):833–50.

Grossman, Gene, and Elhanan Helpman. 1995. The Politics of Free Trade Agreements. *American Economic Review* 85 (4):667–90.

Grossman, Gene M., and Elhanan Helpman. 2002. *Interest Groups and Trade Policy*. Princeton: Princeton University Press.

Haberler, Gottfried. 1937. *The Theory of International Trade with its Applications to Commercial Policy*. New York: Macmillan.

Helpman, Elhanan. 1995. Politics and Trade Policy. CEPR Discussion Paper 1269. London: CEPR.

Hillman, Arye. 1989. *The Political Economy of Protection*. Chur, Zurich: Harwood Academic Publishers.

Hillman, Arye, and Peter Moser. 1996. Trade Liberalization as Politically Optimal Exchange of Market Access. In *The New Transatlantic Economy*, edited by M. Canzoneri, W. J. Ethier, and V. Grilli, 295–312. Cambridge: Cambridge University Press.

Irwin, Douglas. 1993. Multilateral and Bilateral Trade Policies in the World Trading System: A Historical Perspective. In *New Dimensions in Regional Integration*, edited by Jaime de Melo and Arvind Panagariya, 22-51. New York: Cambridge University Press.

Karacaovali, Baybars, and Nuno Limão. 2007. The Clash of Liberalizations: Preferential vs Multilateral Trade Liberalization in the European Union. CEPR Discussion Paper 4973. London: CEPR.

Kemp, Murry, and Henry Wan. 1976. An Elementary Proposition Concerning the Formation of Customs Unions. *Journal of International Economics* 6 (1):95–7.

Kennan, James, and Raymond Riezman. 1990. Optimal Tariff Equilibria with Customs Unions. *Canadian Journal of Economics* 23 (1):70–83.

Krishna, Pravind. 1998. Regionalism and Multilateralism: A Political Economy Approach. *Quarterly Journal of Economics* 113 (1):227–50.

Krueger, Anne. 1993. Free Trade Agreements as Protectionist Devices: Rules of Origin. NBER Working Paper 4352. Cambridge MA: National Bureau of Economic Research.

Krugman, Paul. 1991a. Is Bilateralism Bad? In *International Trade and Trade Policy*, edited by Elhanan Helpman and Assaf Razin, 9–23. Cambridge MA: MIT Press.

Krugman, Paul. 1991b. The Move Toward Free Trade Zones. *Economic Review*, Federal Reserve Bank of Kansas City, November:5–25.

Krugman, Paul. 1993. Regionalism versus Multilateralism: Analytic Notes. In *New Dimensions in Regional Integration*, edited by J. De Melo and A. Panagariya. Cambridge: Cambridge University Press for CEPR.

Lawrence, Robert. 1991. Emerging Regional Arrangements: Building Blocs or Stumbling Blocks? In *Finance and the International Economy, 5: The AMEX Bank Review Prize Essays 1991*, edited by O'Brien, 23–35. New York: Oxford University Press.

Lawrence, Robert. 1996. *Regionalism, Multilateralism and Deeper Integration*. Washington: Brookings Institute.

Levy, Philip. 1997. A Political–Economic Analysis of Free-Trade Agreements. *American Economic Review* 87 (4):506–19.

Limão, Nuno. 2006. Preferential Trade Agreements as Stumbling Blocks for Multilateral Trade Liberalization: Evidence for the United States. *American Economic Review* 96 (3):896–914.

Lloyd, Peter John. 2002. New Bilateralism in the Asia-Pacific. *The World Economy* 25 (9):1279–96.

Ludema, Rodney. 1996. On the Value of Preferential Trade Agreements in Multilateral Negotiations. *Journal of International Economics*.

McLaren, John. 2002. A Theory of Insidious Regionalism. *The Quarterly Journal of Economics* 117 (2):571–608.

Meade, James. 1955. *The Theory of Customs Unions*. Amsterdam: North Holland.

Moser, Peter. 1990. The Political Economy of the GATT. PhD thesis, University of St Gallen, St Gallen.

Nitsch, Volker. 1996. Do Three Trade Blocs Minimize World Welfare? *Review of International Economics* 4 (3):355–63.

Ornelas, Emanuel. 2005. Endogenous Free Trade Agreements and the Multilateral Trading System. *Journal of International Economics* 67 (2):471–97.

Ornelas, Emanuel. 2008. Feasible Multilateralism and the Effects of Regionalism. *Journal of International Economics* 74 (1):202–24.

Pomfret, R. W. T. 1997. *The Economics of Regional Trading Arrangements*. Oxford: Clarendon Press.

Richardson, Martin. 1993. Endogenous Protection and Trade Diversion. *Journal of International Economics* 34 (3–4):309–24.

Richardson, Martin. 1994. Why a Free Trade Area? The Tariff Also Rises. *Economics and Politics* 6 (1):79–96.

Richardson, Martin. 1995. Tariff Revenue Competition in a Free Trade Area. *European Economic Review* 39 (7):1429–37.

Riezman, Raymond. 1985. Customs Unions and the Core. *Journal of International Economics* 19 (3–4):355–65.

Roesseler, Freider. 1978. The Rationale for Reciprocity in Trade Agreements under Floating Currencies. *Kyklos* 31 (2):258–74.

Sapir, André. 1993. Discussion of Chapter 7. In *Schattschneider, E.E. 1935. Politics, Pressures and the Tariff*, edited by De Melo and Panagariya, 1491–506. New York: Prentice-Hall.

Schiff, Maurice. 2000. Multilateral Trade Liberalization and Political Disintegration— Implications for the Evolution of Free Trade Areas and Customs Unions. Policy Research Working Paper 2350. Washington DC: World Bank.

Serra, Jaime, Guillermo Aguilar, Jose Cordoba, Gene Grossman, Carla Hills, John Jackson, Julius Katz, Pedro Noyola, and Michael Wilson. 1997. Reflections on Regionalism: Report of the Study Group on International Trade. New York: Carnegie Endowment for International Peace.

Shibata, Howard. 1967. The theory of economic unions: A Comparative Analysis of Customs Unions, Free Trade Areas and Tax Unions. In *Fiscal Harmonization in Common Markets*, volume I, edited by C. S. Shoup, 145–264. New York: Columbia University Press.

Sinclair, Paul, and David Vines. 1995. Bigger Trade Blocs need not Entail more Protection. Unpublished mimeo, University of Birmingham.

Smith, Adam. 1776. *The Wealth of Nations*. MetaLibri edition, 2007.

Spilimbergo, Antonio, and Ernesto Stein. 1996. The Welfare Implications of Trading Blocs among Countries with Different Endowments. NBER Working Paper 5472. Cambridge MA: National Bureau of Economic Research.

Vézina, Pierre-Louis. 2010. Race-To-The-Bottom Tariff Cutting. IHEID Working Paper 12-2010. Geneva: Economics Section, The Graduate Institute of International Studies.

Viner, Jacob. 1950. The Customs Union Issue. New York: Carnegie Endowment for International Peace.

Vousden, Neil. 1990. *The Economics of Trade Protection*. Cambridge: Cambridge University Press.

Winham, Gilbert. 1986. *International Trade and the Tokyo Round Negotiation*. Princeton: Princeton University Press.

Yi, Sang-Seung. 1996. Endogenous Formation of Customs Unions under Imperfect Competition: Open Regionalism is Good. *Journal of International Economics* 41:151–75.

CHAPTER 29

....

NEW TRADE ISSUES IN FOOD, AGRICULTURE, AND NATURAL RESOURCES

....

TIM JOSLING[*]

29.1 INTRODUCTION

....

INTERNATIONAL trade in foodstuffs, agricultural products and natural resources is at the heart of several emerging challenges to the multilateral trade system and the parallel systems being developed at a regional level.[1] In these sectors issues of economic development, equity and national sovereignty become entangled with safety and security concerns. Property rights and access to raw materials mix with price stability and terms of trade trends as drivers of policy. This chapter touches on some of the most significant of these challenges and explores some questions that will be high on the agenda in this broad area of international commerce.

Trade rules need to be revised and reinforced periodically to keep up with emerging market developments and policy responses. The chapter starts with the food trade issues that have been elevated in public awareness in the past three years as a result of concerns about the significant rise in commodity prices. Issues of food safety and food security have pushed their way to the front of the agenda. Many of these issues stem from the transition from the time when national food markets were more self-contained than the present global food system. The growth of sophisticated supply chains built around product differentiation and private labelling has left the World Trade Organization's

* The author would like to thank the participants in the TAIT Inaugural Workshop held at the Graduate Institute of International and Development Studies, Geneva (September 2009) for helpful comments on an early draft of this chapter.

[1] The term 'primary products', as used in the GATT Articles, covers most of this group of traded goods, but would not include those foods that are highly processed.

(WTO) framework for constraining government policies to avoid the protectionist use of regulations looking less relevant to current issues. In the area of agriculture the current rules reflect heavily the time when agricultural problems revolved around surpluses and declining prices. In agriculture the focus on reigning in the domestic farm policies of industrial countries needs to meld into a broader approach that includes the policies that will be needed in developing countries to increase their production and productivity. Climate change and the legislation that is being introduced create some challenges as well as opportunities for agriculture. There is a strong link between food trade and agricultural trade, though the issues in the latter case are somewhat different. Agricultural trade issues have focused on the disciplines applied to industrial country farm policies and the associated market access for products considered 'sensitive'. The Doha Round addresses in a significant way the further reform of agricultural trade rules, though it is not certain whether the Round will eventually reach a conclusion.

Natural resource issues are much more diverse, ranging from fisheries access and forest management, to the extraction of minerals, and to oil and natural gas trade. Each of these questions is tied up with environmental objectives, including pollution, environmental degradation, and greenhouse gas emissions. They raise fundamental issues as to when a domestic product becomes subject to trade rules and how to handle common access resources. Trade issues in this area often have to do with subsidies granted to domestic firms, either directly, or through the restraints on the export of raw materials. Other issues include property rights to indigenous resources, trade rules governing biofuels, and the investment in and ownership of land and mineral rights in resource-rich countries. Rapid growth in emerging countries has revived concerns about the reliability and stability of markets for raw materials. More assurance of such supplies without the threat of export embargoes and taxes would help to lubricate the trade system in times of high commodity prices. Many of these natural resource issues have been traditionally absent from the WTO agenda, though this appears to be in the process of change.

29.2 FOOD TRADE ISSUES

The global food system has seen dramatic changes over the past 20 years, and the trade rules are in the process of catching up with these developments. The main manifestation of globalization of the food sector has been the establishment of global supply chains, with the driving force behind such chains being supermarkets and food processors.[2] The increasingly aware consumer has played a willing role in this development. In developed countries the successful attempt by retailers to package attributes of health and

---

[2] For a fuller discussion of the process of globalization of the agricultural and food sector, see Coleman, Grant, and Josling 2004.

environmental responsibility with foodstuffs—along with animal welfare, and in some cases labour conditions—has transformed the economics of food trade. This has been supported by radical changes in the management of information as reflected in the development of private standards and the certification schemes necessary to make such standards credible. The spread of supermarkets in developing countries has been particularly striking: consumers in those countries have increasingly embraced the availability of non-local foods and the better reliability and quality control that can come with firm size and management expertise.[3]

Another, somewhat contradictory, trend is noticeable in developed country markets, as consumers seek to express social choices through food purchases. Many search out local foods and embrace more diverse distribution systems—such as farmers' markets. Others buy 'fair trade' products certified to be free of economic exploitation of farmers in developing countries. Organic food production, sustainable farming methods, and animal-friendly livestock systems have their adherents, and suppliers are ready to respond to such demands. Though still accounting for a small part of total food consumption, this trend poses some interesting questions for international food trade. They all emphasize the method of production, rather than the characteristics of the product itself—a problem that has bedevilled trade rules based on product standards for years.

The balance between increased globalization of the food system and the differentiation of affluent consumer tastes has further implications for developing country food suppliers. Longer food chains have integrated many developing countries into the global marketplace, though this has also led to a bifurcation of suppliers into those that have the capacity to meet strict standards, and those that don't. But the push for specific food attributes in developed countries has made it somewhat harder for overseas suppliers to compete. The organic foods movement has exacerbated this problem by a series of private standards that are both market specific and costly to adopt. Governments have added their own standards and certification schemes. Once again, foreign suppliers often struggle to meet the conditions for entry into lucrative markets.

The challenge to the WTO is not in the spread of supermarkets in developing countries or farmers markets in rich countries, but in the adoption of private standards in both these areas that appear to overlap with government regulations. Governments negotiated at length to establish the rules for national health and safety regulations contained in the Sanitary and Phytosanitary (SPS) Agreement. This circumscribed the ability of governments to set import standards that were not justified by risk assessment and based on scientific evidence. But in many cases consumers decided that governments and their scientific advisers were underplaying certain subjective risks to health and to the environment. Headline issues—such as the possible dangers of biotech crops—became grist for the mill in the competition for market shares among retailers. But this was merely the tip of the iceberg, as private standards tied to particular marketable attributes

---

[3] The striking growth of supermarkets in developing countries is discussed in Traill 2006; Reardon et al. 2003; Swinnen 2007.

began to proliferate. Most of these attributes relate to 'production and processing methods' as opposed to more easily verifiable 'product standards'. The once-bright line between safety and quality standards is increasingly blurred. And the fact that private standards are unconstrained by the need to exhibit scientific justification further complicates an already difficult corner of the trade system.[4]

The SPS Agreement has been very successful in increasing transparency, particularly in the area of animal and plant diseases, and curbing the egregious use of SPS barriers for the protection of domestic producers, but has not been so effective in cases where public sentiment has dominated scientific consensus.[5] The question that countries will have to face in the next few years is whether to try to amend the SPS Agreement to allow government regulations to respond to consumer concerns that have not been found to have scientific merit. Exporting countries clearly see this as a possible end to the SPS Agreement as an effective constraint on governments: who is going to arbitrate on whether subjective fears pass some test of credibility and legitimacy? But in the absence of some sort of solution to this problem the SPS Agreement might increasingly become irrelevant for global food (as opposed to agricultural commodity) trade. This could be compounded by the adoption of standards related to such longer-term health topics such as obesity. The SPS Agreement relates to regulations governing the safety of foods, but eating too much of a 'safe' food can cause health problems. So it is not inconceivable that agencies such as the World Health Organization could find itself advocating policies that are in contradiction to the SPS Agreement.[6]

The other food issue that has become more visible in recent years is that of food security. Part of this concern is a reflection of the high prices for basic food commodities on world markets in 2007–8 and again in 2010. Certainly the price spikes overwhelmed the ability of governments in developing countries to cushion low-income groups, and poverty and malnutrition jumped. Food riots in several countries gave a reminder of the sensitivity of food price developments. But one question that was suggested by the experience of the price spikes was the extent to which the current WTO rules are adequate to deal with trade-distorting policies of governments in times of high prices. From an institutional viewpoint the question of food security has fallen within the realm of the Committee on World Food Security (CFS), a product of the 1974 World Food Conference and administered by the Food and Agriculture Organization of the United Nations (FAO). The CFS has recently been reformulated with a wider range of stakeholders and a renewed mandate to coordinate national-level plans for improving food security. So the role for the WTO in specific food security actions, if any, is likely to be to monitor and assist this institution, rather than add new programmes. This does not of course preclude measures that improve the workings of international markets and make it easier for countries to provide for a more stable and affordable food supply for their citizens.

[4] The characteristics of private food standards are discussed in Henson and Humphrey 2009.
[5] Josling, Roberts, and Orden 2004.   [6] Josling, Orden, and Roberts 2009.

The WTO has taken a more active role in the link between food aid and commercial trade. Food aid, an important aspect of food security, has been the province of the Food Aid Convention (FAC), originally negotiated in 1967 as a part of the outcome of the General Agreement on Tariffs and Trade (GATT) Kennedy Round, and renegotiated in 1986. This body acquired some additional responsibility as a result of the 1994 WTO Ministerial Decision on the possible negative effects of the Uruguay Round on least-developed and net food-importing developing countries.[7] It was renegotiated in 1999 and subsequently renewed pending the outcome of the Doha Round. However, the FAC has lacked monitoring capacity and enforcement authority. There have therefore been calls for more active involvement by the WTO in the institutional supervision of food aid. Indeed, it has been identified as a trade issue of concern to several food-exporting countries. As a result, the WTO rules regarding the elimination of the subsidy element of food aid would be tightened up if the Doha Round is concluded. This is at least one area where the WTO has found a role in the management of the global food trade in conjunction with other multilateral agencies.

29.3 AGRICULTURAL TRADE ISSUES

The questions raised above about the trends in the food sector have implications for agricultural trade. But in addition there are a number of underlying agricultural issues that are only indirectly tied to food trade. These issues include the future of developed country farm policies and the path that emerging and developing countries will follow in this area. Together these two issues will continue to provide the political tensions that will keep agriculture in the trade headlines for decades to come—regardless of the outcome of Doha.

The period since 1985 has seen some major changes in the domestic agricultural policies of the developed countries. Reform started in countries such as New Zealand and Chile with the notion that the government could not artificially provide the demand for farm products in small exporting countries in the face of macroeconomic distortions and locational disadvantages. It spread to those countries that were stifling their farm sectors with marketing arrangements that provided little incentive for quality and led to unwanted surpluses of basic products. Together with the paradigm shift in the management of the economy towards deregulation and the provision of more appropriate incentives, the change in agricultural policies away from market intervention towards direct payments has now transformed those policies and provided a new environment for agricultural trade.

---

[7] Ministerial Decision on Measures Concerning the Possible Negative Effects of the Reform Programme on Least-Developed and Net Food-Importing Developing Countries, WTO, LT/UR/D-1/2, 15 April 1994.

In the EU this process accelerated over the 1990s as farm policy shifted to include environmental and quality aspects of food production, culminating in the reforms of 2003 that virtually eliminated for arable agriculture any link between farmer support payments and commodity market conditions.[8] Progress in the US has been less linear, with a move in 1996 to delink payments and production, but some recidivism in 2002 and 2008 as commodity-based price support programmes proved to have strong support in the farm lobby and in Congress.[9]

So a key issue for the next decade or so is whether the reform process will continue, so that all developed countries will in essence have rural policies that emphasize land stewardship and rural development, nutrition policies that focus on quality and food safety, and agricultural policies that are aimed specifically at issues of productivity enhancement and risk management. Such a world would be consistent with a more open trade system and the removal of the many impediments that developing countries face in supplying food to the industrial country markets.

But reform could become unhinged if attitudes changed, perhaps as a result of widespread food shortages or a collapse of world trade. It would not be difficult for those who would prefer the old policies of protection of producers by governmental management of markets to make the case that the 'free market' had not worked. And the benefit of keeping the major developed countries moving along the same path, albeit at different speeds, is clear. It would be difficult to imagine the EU following a reform agenda that removed government from involvement in commodity markets if the US were moving in the other direction by increasing that involvement. So this is one area where the back-stopping of the multilateral trade system is particularly useful.

The Doha Round will play a major role in ensuring that the market-oriented reforms of the past 20 years in developed country farm policies are not reversed. The Round, if successful, will have eliminated export subsidies and other export-stimulating policies such as export credit guarantees, aid to parastatal exporters, and export enhancement through food aid.

Domestic support will have been reduced to a fraction of existing limits, and no longer allow countries to maintain expensive trade-distorting price support systems. Tariffs will have been sharply cut, and will be weakened even further by the multiple concessions granted through regional and bilateral trade agreements. What will remain is relatively high protection for a small group of products, including rice, cotton, dairy and sugar (sometimes called the white goods). The reduction of these tariffs will presumably have to wait until the next set of trade negotiations.

What will be left of the domestic support programmes is direct payments (not linked to output or to price) and infrastructure support for the sector. It is likely that some clarification of the way in which domestic support is notified may be needed within a year or two.

---

[8] A full discussion of the significance of the remarkable 2003 Common Agricultural Policy reforms are found in Swinnen 2008.

[9] More analysis on the recent changes in US farm policy in relation to the WTO can be found in Blandford and Orden 2011.

Market price support (in the Aggregate Measurement of Support) is now virtually without meaning for most developed countries: the administered prices, the eligible quantities, and the reference prices are increasingly irrelevant to the question of policy reform. And the green box, that was intended to capture trade-neutral subsidies, now includes a raft of payments tied to environmental aims with little regard to their actual output effect.[10]

The more fundamental question is whether developing countries will follow the same pattern with respect to the protection of domestic markets and producers.[11] Much of the impetus for public intervention in developed country markets came as a reaction to different rates of growth in the agricultural and the non-agricultural sectors. Strong growth in manufactures and services in developing countries can put pressure on the government to intervene to help agriculture. But how that assistance is given, and under what conditions, is important. The WTO Agreement on Agriculture will be significant in its constraints on this choice.

There are two 'models' of agricultural trade strategy that seem to be embraced by developing countries. The first is that typical of Latin America, which entered the 1980s with considerable protection for its agriculture and highly regulated domestic markets. These countries, often with the support of the World Bank, the Inter-American Development Bank and the International Monetary Fund began a process of 'structural adjustment' that emphasized opening up the agricultural sector along with other parts of the economy. As a result, applied tariffs even on agricultural products are now relatively low, though the bound rates are often higher. This type of agricultural policy has been conducive to growth of trade and to stronger regional markets. However, the process could always go in reverse: serious income problems in rural areas of Latin America could spur a resurgence of protectionism. A serious disruption of exports to the US and Europe may be enough to bring two decades of relatively open trade policies to a close.

The second model that may be followed is more typical of Asia, where agricultural trade policy owes more to debates about the livelihood of the rural population, the degree of self-sufficiency, and the need for poverty alleviation than about access into the lucrative US market. This has led to an increase in agricultural protection as countries experience rapid economic growth. The pattern has been repeated in several countries since the 1960s, first in Japan, then in Korea, and now in China and India. How the emerging countries manage the stresses of relative agricultural decline will determine the extent to which they will agree to further liberalization in agricultural trade. The hold-up in the Doha Round in July 2008 illustrated the problem posed by the Asian model. Negotiators failed to agree on modalities that included a special safeguard mechanism for developing countries that would have allowed them to raise tariffs to protect their agriculture when world prices fell. The main proponents for such a safeguard were Indonesia, the Philippines, India, and other Asian countries. The resolution to this issue is still a key to the completion of the current set of trade negotiations in agriculture.

---

[10] For an extensive review of the experience with the Green Box, see Melendez-Ortiz, Bellman, and Hepburn 2009.

[11] This question is addressed in detail in Anderson 2009.

Preoccupation with the task of constraining developed country farm policies, the key agricultural trade issue over the past 40 years, has led governments to neglect some more fundamental long-run agricultural trade issues. The recent period of high food prices has refocused the attention of countries on the extent to which investments are needed to maintain and increase the capacity of the agricultural sector to meet the demands of a growing population.[12] Expenditure on agricultural research has been lagging in recent years as a result of shifting priorities for public investment and lack of financial incentives for private investment.

One might expect there to be a resurgence of public investment in the production of basic foodstuffs if price levels were to stay reasonably high, but this may not be enough. To complement the investment in production there needs to be an increased focus on infrastructural improvements that are often the main constraint on the marketing of local foods in developing countries. Such infrastructure includes quality schemes and biosafety systems. The ability for small and medium-sized farms to be incorporated into the supply chains of modern food retailing will be dependent on such investments. If this is forthcoming, the demand-driven growth in agricultural output and productivity will have a beneficial impact on trade and be consistent with a continued opening up of markets, particularly in the developing world. South-south trade will grow under such conditions to the advantage of the balance in the global economy.

Whether or not public investment in agriculture is increased, private investment will also be needed to fully develop the capacity of global agriculture. This will undoubtedly include the use of advanced technology to optimize crop yields and adapt varieties to different climate conditions. The experience of investment in biotechnology, where consumer acceptance has been slow in many parts of the world, has undoubtedly had a salutary effect on the attitude of private companies. The public authorities may have to become more engaged as a partner in private sector investment in new technologies that are based on genetic advances. The ability to steer the genetic make-up of plants and animals to improve their productivity will certainly increase, but the extent to which this ability is translated into products acceptable to consumers is still uncertain. The role that trade rules play in such matters is crucial. Investment is unlikely to be forthcoming if global markets are fragmented by regulations on biotech and on other scientific approaches to increasing food supplies.

29.4 AGRICULTURE, ENERGY, AND ENVIRONMENTAL ISSUES

The most significant development in agricultural trade in the past decade has undoubtedly been the emergence of a new market for agricultural products as biomass for ethanol and biodiesel. This has transformed the markets for corn, sugar cane, rapeseed, and

---

[12] See, for instance, United Nations Food and Agriculture Organization 2008.

palm oil in developed and some developing countries. The rapid growth in production of biofuels was mainly as a result of the adoption of biofuel mandates by major countries, though stimulated in part by a spike in oil prices in 2007–8. If oil prices were to remain high there would be many more opportunities open up for the use of agricultural crops in energy production. But again there is the potential for a backlash from civil society: already the uncertain contribution of biofuels to environmental goals, and the undoubted exacerbation by ethanol production of the recent spike in food prices, has taken some of the bloom off the biofuels expansion.[13] In this respect, private investment will follow directly from changes in government policy. If the various subsidies and tax breaks for ethanol and biodiesel were to be reduced, along with the mandates for the incorporation of biofuels in transportation requirements, the private sector would find many of its investments unrewarding.

This is rapidly becoming a trade issue: domestic production of biofuels is often protected from competition from abroad. So the development of the market is distorted by domestic energy policy. A strong case can be made for trade liberalization in biofuel products. If these products were more freely traded (and produced in ways that minimized environmental impacts) the investment in renewable fuels from agricultural biomass could be considerable. For this to occur a significant reduction in biofuel subsidies would be helpful: when subsidies are paid there will always be a tendency to restrict imports to control the domestic price. In this regard it is unfortunate that the Doha Round is not likely to provide much in the way of market opening for ethanol and biodiesel, even though the negotiations were charged with stimulating trade in environmental goods and services.

The need for greater transparency in biofuel fuel subsidies is becoming more evident. The transparency could start with the WTO notifications. Until now this has not been forthcoming from the system of notification to the WTO Subsidies and Countervailing Measures (SCM) or the Agriculture Committees. In both cases the information needed to estimate the trade impact of the subsidies has been lacking. The SCM Committee has not been able to persuade WTO members to report all subsidies in enough detail to allow analysis. The Agriculture Committee seems to have been content to ignore subsidies to ethanol through biofuel mandates, even though a case can be made that these should have been reported.[14]

Behind many of these issues is the question of the response of the trade system to the challenges related to global warming. This is the link that has emerged between

---

[13] The impact of the use of corn for ethanol on agricultural markets and world food prices became a matter of concern in 2007–8, when commodity process surged. The Organization for Economic Cooperation and Development (OECD) estimated the effect at an increase in prices of 10–17 per cent; other estimates show somewhat higher impacts in the tight market situation of that period. This confirms the finding of several studies that price instability may have increased as a result of the ethanol boom, and the price of gasoline is seen as an additional source of variation in demand for corn that may exacerbate price swings from income-related demand (Josling, Blandford, and Earley 2010).

[14] Josling, Blandford, and Earley 2010.

agricultural trade policy, energy policy, and the environment.[15] Many governments have already enacted legislation in response to the need to contain the emission of greenhouse gases. The promotion of ethanol as an alternative energy source that would reduce greenhouse gas emissions has been set back by the realization that secondary impacts of shifting corn to energy production could in part offset the benefits of substituting for fossil fuels. But the indirect land use changes themselves pose a challenge for trade rules. Once the concept of life cycle analysis of products takes hold in national legislation the differentiation of goods at the border by their method of production becomes inevitable. The trade system is set up to recognize goods by their product attributes, not by the process attributes that one needs to evaluate a carbon footprint. So until this disconnect can be resolved, one would expect increasing conflicts over the issue of the environmental impact of the production and processing methods of traded goods.

At the global level the debate has centred on whether to work purely through environmental institutions, or to build environmental considerations into trade rules. The negotiations on the trade in 'environmental goods and services' in the current Doha Round suggests that the WTO may become more involved. On the other hand, the talks have for now floundered on the definition of environmental goods.

29.5 NATURAL RESOURCES

Issues related to trade in natural resources have their own set of conceptual and analytical challenges. Anticipating trade problems that might emerge in the future is made more difficult by the lack of engagement in the GATT, and subsequently in the WTO, on the pressing trade issues.[16] At a fundamental level, natural resources are as much a part of the reason for trade than a tradable item as such. Many natural resources form the economic basis for other sectors of the domestic economy and so are involved in trade only in an indirect way. Trade models commonly define countries by their resource endowment. But mineral resources and oil can of course be extracted and enter directly into trade. Climate and scenery can be exported through tourism or exploited through inward investment. Traditionally, this sector has not been blessed by an abundance of rules related to trade. But this could change. This section will highlight a few such areas of natural resource production and distribution where trade issues are likely to arise in the near future.

One natural resource tied intimately to the agricultural potential of a country is its farmland, packaged with climate and soil attributes and subject to land tenure and property rights laws. As an archetype 'fixed' resource, it is hardly ever considered in the

---

[15] For more detail on the links between agricultural trade and global warming see Blandford and Josling 2009.

[16] The unratified Havana Charter contained rules specifically related to natural resource trade, but these were primarily concerned with the establishment of international commodity agreements.

context of international trade. Agricultural labour and entrepreneurs have, of course, often moved to farm better or more abundant land in other countries. One tends to think of these migrations as being in the past, with only limited and controlled movements of farm labour still tolerated. But investment in overseas farmland is by no means an historical relic. Many countries have benefited from allowing foreign nationals to hold land and operate farms, and this trend could well intensify. Indeed, one would expect that foreign investment in farming activities, as opposed to the processing or marketing of food, could be a growth area in the international economy in the next decades to come. One would not expect such a trend to pose many problems for the WTO.

However, one aspect of this renewed interest in farmland investment has commanded some attention. In recent years, governments and parastatal bodies have begun to explore such investments (labelled somewhat pejoratively as 'land grabs') as an aspect of food security policy. Under certain conditions, one would expect this model to work well to the advantage of both investor and host country.[17] This purchase of farmland by other governments or private corporations reached a peak in 2008 when commodity prices were high, and several governments feared being caught in a situation where supplies of basic foodstuffs were not available. The trade implications are yet to be seen. Private firms can of course sell products to whoever they wish. But what privilege would a firm owned by a foreign government have when supplies were tight and that government wished to import at less than the going price? Would this constitute state-trading? Or would it be a case of discrimination and hence a potential violation of Article I? This would certainly pose problems for the WTO.

Another natural resource closely aligned to food and agriculture is that of the world's fisheries. The sector has a vital and increasing role in world trade in foodstuffs. Several features make this a rich if understudied aspect of international trade. The harvesting of fish is conveniently (if not precisely) divided between 'capture fisheries' and 'fish farming'. The first, more traditional, method has been growing slowly since the 1970s: the production from aquaculture has increased rapidly over the past 40 years until it is now almost equal to that of wild fisheries. The policy environment differs greatly between these two types of fish production. The main problem with respect to the capture fisheries is that of open access to a common resource, leading to overfishing.[18] For years the issue of fishing rights was contentious, but the implementation of 200-mile exclusive economic zones since 1977 has changed the nature of coastal fisheries, stimulating the development of many local fish exporting industries at the expense of the 'deep sea' fleets of a handful of countries. But management of stocks is by no means uniform or effective: most fisheries are better classified as 'regulated open access' and still subject to problems of stock management.[19]

[17] This point is made coherently in World Bank 2010.
[18] Alternatively one can define this as a case of insecure property rights. With such property rights the incentives to manage the stocks should lead to a more sustainable outcome.
[19] For a concise account of the international aspects of the fisheries management problem, see Asche and Smith 2010.

Added to the common pool problem for capture fisheries is that of the conservation of marine diversity. This is often where trade issues arise. The method of fishing has become the focus for regulations, with particular attention to the impact on other species. Governments have used trade policy to protect the marine environment. Two landmark cases have hinged on such policies and have set the background for subsequent policies. The first case concerned the US attempt to impose trade restrictions on countries that did not follow the US regulations (mandated by the Marine Mammals Protection Act) aimed at the prevention of dolphin capture by tuna fishing boats. The case was brought by Mexico in 1991, under the GATT. The panel did not find fault with the objective of saving dolphin, but considered the methods used by the US to be in violation of GATT Article III, as it imposed restraints based on production methods on Mexican tuna that violated national treatment.[20] A second complaint was brought by the EU in 1994, charging that the US has imposed a secondary embargo on fisheries products coming from countries that traded with Mexico. This too was found to contravene the GATT. The second case was about the inconsistent application of US policy to require turtle excluder devices on shrimp boats in certain fisheries. The WTO panel found no problem with the aim, but ruled that the US had treated different shrimp exporters in different ways. These two cases have, in essence, determined the interface between environmental and trade laws. In both instances the panel showed a preference for multilateral environmental agreements, and in both cases the ability to take into account the method of capture was upheld.

The growth of aquaculture in the past three decades has been remarkable for its ability to turn relative luxury foods, such as shrimp and salmon, into commodities. Transport and packaging improvements have also contributed to the global expansion of the market for quality seafood at a low price. Trade problems stem largely from the integration of this sector into the global food economy described above. Fish from Africa has found markets in Europe, and fish from Asia is now widely available in the US. For aquaculture the problem is not so much management as the potential environmental damage—from run-off, to the escape of genetically-modified salmon.[21] And the stricter regulations related to human health have provided another hurdle for trade in farmed fish.

Historically, the links between fisheries policy and the trade rules in the WTO have been tentative: however, a more direct approach has been tried in the Doha Round. The discussion in the Doha Round has been about restricting fisheries subsidies on environmental grounds. This reflects the view that the many subsidies that are given to the fisheries industry are a contributory cause of overfishing. Such an approach may be

---

[20] The report of the panel was not adopted, but Mexico introduced regulations similar to those of the US, and the industry began certifying tuna as dolphin-safe.

[21] The introduction of fast-growing genetically modified (GM) salmon onto the market in the US has been delayed by an involved regulatory process, but also by the fear of consumer resistance. The environmental issue is whether an escaped GM salmon would outcompete the local salmon population into which it introduced itself.

insufficient to resolve the broader problem, but it represents a degree of engagement in this sector of trade that has been lacking to date. One would expect this area of natural resource trade to be more prominent in future, with additional institutional innovation needed.

Trade in forestry products has a long history and generally gives rise to few problems. Import tariffs are generally not high. As a renewable resource it does not suffer from problems of over-production.[22] But environmental issues focusing on the destruction of tropical forests have come to the fore in the past two decades. Governments have sometimes given support to private non-governmental organization (NGO) initiatives to label timber on the basis of whether it was sustainably harvested, or whether it represented the destruction of habitats deemed worthy of preservation. Some of these issues hinge on process characteristics that may pose problems of discrimination. But enshrining such actions in a multilateral environmental agreement could make the apparent conflict with trade rules of less consequence.

Different ownership patterns of forestry assets can also cause international problems. A long-standing trade complaint in the area of forest products has surrounded the question of access by domestic firms to state-owned timber at concessional rates. These low 'stumpage' charges were at the heart of the series of US–Canada softwood lumber disputes, which were (temporarily) resolved in 2006. The US maintained that Canadian softwood lumber producers were being subsidized by having favourable access to publicly owned forests.[23] Litigation under the North American Free Trade Agreement and the WTO on the possible Canadian subsidy, and the US countervailing charges on imports from Canada, dominated bilateral trade relations for nearly a decade.

Facing somewhat different challenges is trade in non-renewable resources, such as minerals and oil.[24] Compared to the renewable resources discussed above, the distribution of non-renewables is set by geology. Some 20 countries earn over three-quarters of their export earnings from the sale of oil, gas, or minerals.[25] Many of these countries are poor despite the rents from commodity exports, and the internal distribution of these rents is often somewhat uneven. Extractive industries pose their own set of problems with respect to trade rules. First, there is the basic problem of ownership of the land and the allocation of extraction rights. Countries often have rules on the purchase of land for mineral and oil extraction, and almost universally control the allocation of licences for exploitation. The distribution of the economic rents is the principal focus of market participants, and is fixed by (usually) long-term contracts.

---

[22] Some types of exploitable forests take so long to grow back that these are subject to the economics and biology of population dynamics.

[23] A balanced account of the softwood lumber disputes is given in Zhang 2007.

[24] The WTO considered this area of trade significant enough to justify extensive consideration in the 2010 edition of the World Trade Report (WTO 2010). Non-renewables account for about 15 per cent of world trade.

[25] Collier and Venables 2010.

This gives rise to a number of issues for trade. First is the question of transparency.[26] If such contracts are the result of confidential bilateral relations it may be difficult to demonstrate non-discrimination.[27] The second question relates to the point at which a natural resource becomes a tradable good. Are standing trees and lakes to be counted as lumber and water waiting to be exported, and is oil in the ground a tradable good waiting to be pumped? On the surface one would say that natural resources are purely domestic concerns until harvested or extracted. But the WTO panel in *US–Software Lumber IV* argued that trees are indeed goods and have a trade classification. A third issue is whether taxes on the export of natural resources are covered by Article XI (that allows such restraints on exports in order to relieve critical shortages)? Export taxes are common on natural resources, as mentioned above, often to keep down prices to domestic users. And which other provisions of the WTO cover such products? The definition of 'primary products' in GATT Article XVI (which includes any product of farm, forestry, or fisheries, or any mineral, in its natural form or transformed for international trade) would appear to apply? But in the case of agricultural products, that definition may have been in effect replaced by that in the Agreement on Agriculture.

The distribution of non-renewable natural resources around the world is particularly uneven. This increases the value of trade, but leads to tension—ranging from disputes over ownership (for instance of offshore oil reserves), to the use of revenue for illicit activities (such as conflict diamonds). Many developing countries, as mentioned before, have a compelling interest in exports of these products. So, to the extent to which trade rules appear to help these countries to develop their extractive industries, they will be more satisfied with the multilateral trade system.

A further issue emerging with regard to trade in natural resources such as timber, as well as minerals and ores, has to do with the question of security of supply. Governments of exporting countries have increasingly used export taxes, quantitative restrictions, and embargoes to restrict trade, often when prices are high and supplies scarce. The motives for such restrictions vary from the desire to keep raw material costs down for local processors (often through differential export taxes), to the need for revenue sources for other programmes. But firms dependent on secure supplies of minerals and rare earths have become increasingly worried about the spread of what has been called 'resource nationalism'. Markets are distorted, and developed and developing countries alike can suffer. Importing regions, including the EU, have begun to formulate strategies that would reduce the likelihood of shortages in raw materials as a result of intense competition from faster growing economies. China is often cited as a country that has been assiduous in lining up long-term supply relations with other countries, through investment

---

[26] An important development that addresses the transparency issue is the creation of the Extractive Industries Transparency Initiative in 2002. This international coalition of countries, companies, and NGOs emphasizes full disclosure of gas, oil, and mining company payments to host governments.

[27] WTO 2010.

and ownership. The US, Mexico, and the EU have challenged the policy of China with regards to export restrictions on several key raw materials.

The WTO will obviously tread cautiously in this high-stakes debate. It has so far avoided delving into issues of trade in oil, in part because many of the largest oil producers have not until recently felt it necessary to become WTO members. But the climate change dimension of fossil fuels use may be the trigger for a more active role of the WTO in energy policy. In particular, the issue of subsidies for the production and use of fossil fuels is rising fast on international agendas. The International Energy Agency (IEA) recently estimated the amount of such subsidies in 37 developed and emerging countries at about $557 billion.[28] The Organization for Economic Cooperation and Development (OECD) estimates that eliminating such subsidies would reduce greenhouse gas emissions by 10 per cent. The G20 has gone on record as encouraging governments to curb such subsidies, and the US administration has lent its support to such an initiative.[29] But any move that would increase the price of energy is likely to face domestic opposition, particularly in the current economic climate.

29.6 PRICE VOLATILITY

Trade policy in agriculture may be as much a reaction to price variability as it is to price levels, though the two reinforce each other. Price volatility is a function in the main of production fluctuations, and is particularly acute in periods when the level of stocks is low. Production fluctuations in agricultural markets may well increase in the future, as global warming changes weather patterns and makes agriculture more marginal in certain regions. More extreme weather events are also expected to be a product of global warming. Price variability in other commodities, such as minerals and oil, is less due to production fluctuations than it is to shifts in demand. Such demand-induced price fluctuations in natural resource markets have implications for producers, governments, and firms that use the products. So one has to ask the question whether the WTO has any role to play in avoiding or ameliorating such instability problems?

Adequate stocks would act to smooth out these fluctuations, but the levels of carryover stocks tend to have been lower in recent years. During a period of low prices the cost of holding stocks increases, and the benefit of having those stocks decreases. Neither the

---

[28] 'Energy Subsidies: Getting the Prices Right', accessed at the IEA website, 7 June 2010. This amount is over twice the OECD estimates of support for agriculture ($252.5 billion, for 2009) as reported in 'Agricultural Policies in the OECD Countries: At a Glance 2010' accessed on the OECD website, 8 July 2010.

[29] WTO Deputy Director-General Harsha V. Singh recently stated that: 'Fossil fuel subsidy reform is undoubtedly one of the important tools in the hands of the international community in the fight against climate change' (Singh 2010).

private nor the public sector has the incentive to hold stocks through these low-price periods. However, as prices rise, the lack of stocks leads to panic buying. The political reaction in exporting countries can also exacerbate price spikes, as export controls and taxes operate to keep supplies at home. Past international actions to deal with price instability in commodity markets have included buffer stocks and funds, usually incorporated in international commodity agreements. Such policies have not been noticeably successful, as they tend to break down at the very time they are most needed. Selection of stock trigger prices is difficult and often reflects political considerations: allocation of the costs of holding stocks is also problematic.

Commodity market conditions are themselves a reflection of the underlying performance of the global economy. Such growth also increases the price of oil and other energy sources as well as primary commodities in general. Oil importers may suffer even as the global economy prospers. Volatility of prices also has political and economic implications in the area of trade in raw materials and commodities: in foodstuffs the impact may be devastating on vulnerable populations. So the question of the response to price variations, and the responsibility for ameliorating them, is once again (as in the 1970s) on the table. Secular price trends of primary products relative to manufactured goods has also become a topic for speculation and concern in the recent past, linked to growth in emerging economies and to underlying productivity growth.

Price instability can undermine the legitimacy of the global market as a place in which countries can buy food supplies on a regular basis and make use of trade to supplement domestic production. Even exporters benefit little from price fluctuations, and will drive prices down when surpluses begin to appear. The WTO rules are currently unbalanced: they spring into action when prices are low, but do little to constrain government action when prices rise.[30] So export subsidies are constrained and tariffs are bound, but export taxes are not limited and export embargoes barely mentioned. The ability of the world trade system to respond in times of price volatility is likely to be tested severely in the future, and some creative institutional arrangements may be needed.

Whether these problems of price instability persist, and international action is needed, may depend in part on the longer-term price trends. Are the terms of trade for primary products likely to resume their downward trend? In 2008 it was becoming plausible to argue that food and agricultural prices were on a secular upward trend as a result of strong demand from emerging markets and slower growth in productive capacity. Similarly, the prospects for metals and minerals looked as if strong demand would be the dominant force in the market. Even though many commodity prices have fallen back, they are still high by historical standards. Whether these prices (including that of oil) rise again as the global economy resumes vigorous growth is likely to have a fundamental impact on the demands put on the trade system.

---

[30] For a discussion of the WTO rules on export restraints and taxes, see Mitra and Josling 2009.

29.7 CONCLUSION

One theme links the areas of food, agriculture, and natural resources: they are all strongly linked to the health of the global economy. Continued strong growth in the emerging countries would seem to be a prerequisite for further liberalization of trade, though it could also generate price spikes. Economic growth facilitates the shift of labour from agriculture and reduces adjustment costs. When off-farm jobs are available the improvement in market access for farm products is politically more acceptable and economically more advantageous. Consequently, it might be reasonable to assume that steady growth in the world economy, particularly in the developing world, would be a fertile environment for the further liberalization of trade in agricultural products, and an eventual convergence between the treatment of agricultural and of non-agricultural goods in multilateral trade rules.

However, such growth can bring with it pressures that constrain the opening up of markets. A frequent by-product of growth is its uneven impact on rural–urban income distribution. If the growth is concentrated in urban-based export industries then the political demands for assistance for rural areas will tend to increase. As exchange rates will tend to appreciate in rapid-growth countries, farmers will face growing competition from imported products. So growth brings further pressures on domestic producers to become more efficient or move to non-farm jobs. And the reaction of the government may well be to try to protect rural industries to alleviate the pressure for migration. Rising demand for raw materials could lead to shortages that again could lead to interruption of trade through export restrictions. The present period of more modest growth would seem to be appropriate to design rules that could protect trade against the tensions of rapid growth.

WTO trade rules in food, agriculture, and natural resources have a double task: to keep up with developments in the markets themselves, and to prevent government actions that damage the careful construct of the multilateral trade system. The developments that have been mentioned above include the increased global scope of the food industry, the widespread reform of developed country farm policies, and the challenges posed by the public reaction to biotechnology applied to foodstuffs, and each of these developments will require changes in trade rules. But, in addition, the reaction of governments to the possibility of raw material shortages, such as the purchase of land by foreign entities, and the use of export taxes to keep food prices low in times of shortage, suggests that the present imbalance between importer and exporter obligations in WTO rules may need to be addressed.

The links between these issues of food, agriculture, and natural resources, and broader development questions, has always added to their significance. Many of the tensions surrounding trade in primary products and commodities arise because of their implications for development. Indeed, the developing countries as a whole appear to have the most interest in maintaining an open trade system in these areas.

But the interests of developed countries have generally driven the trade agenda in food, agriculture, minerals, fisheries, and timber in the past. So the rebalancing of the multilateral agenda, as developing countries increasingly press for their own priorities to be included, could lead to new demands for rule-making activity in some of these areas of trade.

REFERENCES

Anderson, Kym, ed. 2009. *Distortions to Agricultural Incentives: A Global Perspective 1955–2007*. London: Palgrave Macmillan, and Washington, DC: World Bank.

Asche, Frank, and Martin D. Smith. 2010. Trade and Fisheries: Key Issues for the World Trade Organization. Staff Working Paper ERSD-2010-03. Geneva: World Trade Organization.

Blandford, David, and Tim Josling. 2009. Greenhouse Gas Reduction Policies and Agriculture: Implications for Production Incentives and International Trade Disciplines. ICTSD/IPC Policy Issues No. 1. Geneva: ICTSD.

Blandford, David, and David Orden. 2011. United States. In *WTO Disciplines on Agricultural Support: Seeking a Fair Basis for Trade*, edited by David Orden, David Blandford, and Tim Josling, 97–152. Cambridge UK: Cambridge University Press.

Coleman, William, Wyn Grant, and Tim Josling. 2004. *Agriculture in the New Global Economy*. Cheltenham: Edward Elgar.

Collier, Paul, and Anthony J. Venables. 2010. International Rules for Trade in Natural Resources. *Journal of Globalization and Development* 1 (1): Article 8.

Henson, Spencer, and John Humphrey. 2009. Understanding the Complexities of Private Standards in Global Agri-Food Chains. Unpublished manuscript.

Josling, Tim, David Blandford, and Jane Earley. 2010. Biofuel and Biomass Subsidies in the US, EU and Brazil: Towards a Transparent System of Notification. IPC Discussion Paper. Washington, DC: International Food & Agricultural Trade Policy Council.

Josling, Tim, David Orden, and Donna Roberts. 2009. National Food Regulations and the WTO Agreement on Sanitary and Phytosanitary Measures: Implications for Trade-Related Measures to Promote Healthy Diets. In *Trade, Food Diet and Health: Perspectives and Policy Options*, edited by Corinna Hawkes et al, 219–37. Oxford: Wiley-Blackwell.

Josling, Timothy E., Donna Roberts, and David Orden. 2004. *Food Regulation and Trade: Toward a Safe and Global System*. Washington, DC: Institute for International Economics.

Melendez-Ortiz, Ricardo, Christophe Bellman, and Jonathan Hepburn, eds. 2009. *Agricultural Subsidies in the WTO Green Box: Ensuring Coherence with Sustainable Development Goals*. Cambridge: Cambridge University Press.

Mitra, S., and T. Josling. 2009. Agricultural Export Restrictions: Welfare Implications and Trade Disciplines. IPC Position Paper, Agricultural and Rural Development Policy Series. Washington, DC: International Food & Agricultural Trade Policy Council.

Reardon, T., C. Peter Timmer, C. B. Barrett, and J. A. Berdegué. 2003. The Rise of Supermarkets in Africa, Asia, and Latin America. *American Journal of Agricultural Economics* 85 (5):1140–6.

Singh, Harsha V. 2010. Opening address by the Deputy Director-General at a conference held at the WTO, 14 October, Geneva. Available from <http://www.wto.org/english/news_e/news10_e/ddg_14oct10_e.htm>. Accessed 3 November 2010.

Swinnen, J., ed. 2007. *Global Supply Chains, Standards and the Poor*. Wallingford: CABI Publishing.

Swinnen, J. F. M., ed. 2008. *The Perfect Storm: The Political Economy of the Fischler Reforms of the Common Agricultural Policy*. Brussels: Centre for European Policy Studies Publications.

Traill, B. 2006. The Rapid Rise of Supermarkets? *Development Policy Review* 24 (2):163–74.

United Nations Food and Agriculture Organization. 2008. *The State of Food Insecurity in the World 2008 (SOFI)*. Rome: UNFAO.

World Bank. 2010. *Rising Global Interest in Farmland: Can it Yield Sustainable and Equitable Benefits?* Washington, DC: The World Bank.

WTO. 2010. *World Trade Report*. Geneva: WTO.

Zhang, Daowei. 2007. *The Softwood Lumber War: Politics, Economics and the Long U.S.- Canadian Trade Dispute*. Washington, DC: Resources for the Future.

PART VIII

NORMATIVE ISSUES

CHAPTER 30

··

FAIRNESS IN THE WTO TRADING SYSTEM

··

ANDREW G. BROWN AND
ROBERT M. STERN

30.1 INTRODUCTION

··

IN this chapter, we first comment on the fairness of the multilateral trading system as conducted under the rules and procedures of the World Trade Organization (WTO).[1] Having been dominated until quite recently by a small number of developed countries, the system has focused heavily on managing the conduct of trade relations among these countries. Ideas of fairness, like non-discrimination and national treatment, have played a part in these relations and are woven into the system. However, with the great expansion in membership to include most developing countries, the distinctly different economic conditions of these countries have put the rules and procedures of the system under fresh scrutiny. There is more emphasis on the relevance of fairness in trade relations, but these relations also have to be understood in a broader, more global setting. However, discussion of the issue so far is lacking in coherence. What we attempt in this chapter is to offer a framework within which the fairness of the current system can be assessed.

As a first step, we should state what we understand by fairness. We do so in full recognition that there is no objective, universal definition to which all reasonable persons are likely to agree. We begin from a view of fairness espoused by philosophers

---

[1] The WTO came officially into existence on 1 January 1995, following the conclusion of the Uruguay Round (1986–94) of multilateral trade negotiations. It subsumed the General Agreement on Tariffs and Trade (GATT), which was created after the Second World War, and which provided the framework for seven rounds of multilateral trade negotiations from 1947 to the beginning of the Uruguay Round.

since Kant, and most recently by Sen,[2] that finds its roots in the impartiality with which we make judgements about the distribution of rights and obligations, income and wealth, or other valued attributes. Impartiality demands that we put aside our own preferences or prejudices, and that we take account of the interests and concerns of others.[3] Arriving at an impartial judgement calls for a reasoned scrutiny of the evidence and arguments. However, as Sen has observed, the reasoning need not result in only one judgement.[4] There is 'a plurality of unbiased principles' that may inform the judgements of reasoning persons. Thus, in the present context of the multilateral trading system, there are two widely known underlying principles that vie with each other for primacy—the utilitarian principle, and the principle of economic equity. The former is explicitly or implicitly favoured by most mainstream economists, but we consider the latter the more persuasive and relevant. As discussed more fully later, we see economic equity as composed of two subsidiary principles: equality of opportunity and distributive justice.

Were the rules and procedures of the multilateral trading system the outcome of an impartial process, they could be declared to be fair (by some impartial standard). As we know, however, they have emerged from numerous rounds of negotiations among countries that not only have diverse interests, but also differ greatly in bargaining power. However, because the system is based on voluntary cooperation, considerations of fairness have never been entirely absent from these negotiations (though neither have they been dominant).

It is through the successive rounds of negotiations that a fairer system can gradually be realized. If the initial position was unfair, then the rounds of negotiations, if fair in themselves, should lessen the distortions and move the system towards greater fairness.[5] But what constitutes fair negotiations? Trade agreements reached through multilateral negotiations amount to binding contracts that confer certain rights and obligations on all the participating countries. The process of negotiation is critical for the fairness of the outcome. In principle, the extent to which participants respect each other's autonomy and engage willingly in the reciprocal exchange of benefits goes far towards defining the fairness of the process. As we know, however, and explore later, respect for autonomy and reciprocity is by no means always present.

We begin our discussion with a brief critique of the utilitarian principle as a guide to fairness in the world trading system. We then turn to the alternative of economic equity, exploring the meaning of its two components: equality of opportunity and distributive

---

[2] Sen 2009.

[3] Rawls realizes impartiality in his theory of justice as fairness by postulating an 'original position' in which participants decide on a system of justice before they know what their position in society will be (Rawls 1971).

[4] Sen 2009.

[5] It may, however, leave some initial biases untouched because they are not part of the negotiating agenda. This, for instance, is what happened to agricultural tariffs and subsidies from the 1950s until the Uruguay Round in the 1990s.

justice. We thereafter proceed to discuss the conditions of autonomy and reciprocity that have to be met in order to realize greater fairness in multilateral trade negotiations. Next, we comment briefly on aspects of procedural justice that are necessary for the functioning of a fair trading system. Finally, we conclude with a brief assessment of considerations of the fairness achieved in the Uruguay Round of multilateral trade negotiations and discuss implications for the conclusion of the Doha negotiations.

30.2 THE UTILITARIAN PRINCIPLE AS A GUIDE TO FAIRNESS

The mainstream utilitarian principle applied to the trading system derives from the view of rational behaviour as the maximization of utility. There is a tacit acceptance that the realization of a more efficient global economy can be a practically acceptable criterion of fairness. Greater efficiency is defined as a movement towards Pareto optimality and, in the context of international trade, that state is reached if no country can be made better off without some other country being made worse off. Even in that circumstance, if the losing country can be compensated by the gaining country while still leaving the latter better off, that qualifies as a gain in efficiency. This utilitarian view of fairness posits that, so long as no country suffers a net loss, there are no rational grounds for resisting measures to liberalize trade that benefits the global economy.

But in our view, this criterion has serious limitations as a basis for assessing fairness in the multilateral trading system. That is, the multilateral trading system consists of a set of agreements among trading partners that has evolved over the decades, and these agreements define how the governments of these countries will conduct themselves in their trade relations. It is thus a form of cooperation entered into by independent countries for their mutual advantage and is not necessarily compatible with the utilitarian principle, since all the participants in the system expect some benefit from their participation, and none seek per se to maximize global welfare.

But even if we chose to disregard that independent countries cooperate to obtain mutual advantage, the utilitarian principle would be a poor guide to fairness. In practical application, the analysis is based on welfare maximization; it compares the initial situation with the final situation after the policy change has been put into effect and equilibrium has been restored. The difficulty here is that the initial situation is taken as given with respect to the existing distribution of income and wealth and the structure of institutions and policies that will reflect the inequities built into the system. Thus, for many emerging developing countries, a system of trade rules and procedures based on allocative efficiency may well seem unfair to them without consideration of the initial conditions. Strongly held differences of opinion on this issue may therefore limit the possibilities of agreement about the fairness of rules and procedures based on the efficiency criterion.

The mainstream efficiency criterion has dominated much of the commentary on the multilateral trading system. Unfortunately, this viewpoint abstracts from the world of nation states that constitute the key actors in the WTO system. It does not conceive of the trading system as an evolving body of rules and procedures that nations have entered into to manage their relations in expectation of mutual advantage.

30.3 ECONOMIC EQUITY AS A GUIDE

We favour economic equity as the relevant guiding principle in assessing the fairness of the trading system. It focuses on the distribution among nations of the rights and obligations that constitute the WTO trading system. As already stated, economic equity breaks down into two subsidiary, and related, principles—equality of opportunity and distributive justice. We first explore the meaning of equality of opportunity and thereafter consider how it needs to be qualified to take account of distributive justice.

30.3.1 Equality of opportunity

In some of its specific manifestations, such as non-discrimination, national treatment, and fair competition, the principle of equality of opportunity has a long history in trade relations. These norms or rules have evolved over time, being adapted to changing circumstances and being extended to cover a widening range of inter-governmental conduct. Their practical application has undoubtedly enhanced the fairness of the trading system.

By ensuring that countries extend the same treatment to all their most favoured trading partners, non-discrimination has been of great importance in the evolution of the multilateral trading system. From the mid-nineteenth century onward, adherence to non-discrimination did much to lessen trade rivalries and to provide a foundation for multilateral trade cooperation. However, while still an important principle of the General Agreement on Tariffs and Trade (GATT)/WTO agreements, it has lost some of its practical significance in recent years as regional and bilateral free trade agreements (FTAs) have multiplied. Taken at face value, these agreements run counter to the whole idea of non-discrimination and so detract from equality of opportunity. Through the trade diversion that they cause, these regional or bilateral agreements may penalize third countries in ways that, for them, are quite arbitrary. However, in recognition that political and trade relations among countries are not set in stone, the formation of customs unions (CUs) and free trade areas has long been accepted under the GATT/WTO agreements. Member countries are free to enter into these preferential arrangements without legally breaching the principle of non-discrimination. An intellectual defence of this formal inconsistency would be that this is a situation in which the principle of the greater good should override that of equality of opportunity. So long as the trade created by the

CU or FTA is greater than the trade that is diverted, the world is better off.[6] Still, harm is nonetheless done to individual third countries.[7] Worse, being negotiated outside the framework of the WTO disciplines and procedures, some FTAs reveal a deliberate disregard for the idea of fairness as understood in multilateral trading relations. When drawn up between a powerful country and a small and weak country (or countries), the former has not always resisted the temptation to impose conditions on the latter that would not be acceptable in less asymmetric multilateral negotiations.[8] The larger political reality, however, is that, since virtually every nation state has entered into at least one FTA, very few voices have been raised denouncing such agreements as breaches of non-discrimination.

National treatment, which is also embedded in the GATT/WTO rules, is another limited expression of the principle of equality of opportunity. National treatment has been closely associated with the negotiation of reductions in border barriers since countries have wanted assurances that concessions won in reducing these barriers would not be defeated by the use of discriminatory domestic measures. In recent decades, as border barriers have diminished and increasing attention given to the role of domestic regulations in impeding trade, scrutiny of national practices that might be deemed to be discriminatory has intensified. Indeed, a substantial number of the complaints brought to the WTO Dispute Settlement Body (since its establishment in 1995) have turned around the question of national treatment.

Fair competition, though lacking the formal standing of non-discrimination or national treatment, is another norm that has further extended the idea of equality of opportunity. Countries have wanted to be assured that their firms would be able to compete fairly with foreign enterprises, whether in foreign or domestic markets, and rules have been introduced to discipline the use by governments of particular measures that distort competition. A long-standing complaint, for instance, had been the use of subsidies that give foreign firms a competitive edge, and subsidy agreements now limit or prohibit the use of specific forms of subsidies.

At least since the initiation of the Uruguay Round in 1986, a decidedly more expansive view of equality of opportunity has come to permeate the discussion of multilateral trade relations. Equality of opportunity, at its extreme limit, would imply that the firms of different countries are able to have access to, and to do business in, each other's markets under the same regulatory conditions as they have in their own domestic market.

---

[6] While raising few objections to such regional agreements as the European Common Market or the North American Free Trade Agreement (NAFTA), most trade economists emphasize that the proliferation of FTAs is likely to have adverse effects because the tangle of differential tariffs and rules of origin would distort trade flows and diminish global efficiency.

[7] It is a fact, however, that affected third countries have quite often been able to take countermeasures—notably, negotiating their own FTAs—to lessen the damage.

[8] For example, the conditions that the United States included in its FTAs with Chile and Singapore were intended to prevent these countries from resorting to controls over capital outflows even in the event of a financial crisis. In other bilateral agreements, the United States has also insisted on the enforcement of stricter intellectual property rights than prevail under the WTO agreement.

There would, in effect, be a single, integrated market. Such a 'level playing field' virtually exists for some products in the markets of some participants in the trading system, but it is very far from being the rule. To insist on such an extreme interpretation of the principle of equality of opportunity would be to make a wholly integrated world market the ultimate standard of fairness in multilateral trade. In a world of nation states which differ vastly in power, in levels of development, in institutions, and in their histories of trade relations, that seems too great an abstraction to be useful. Although the trend has been both towards the reduction of barriers at the border and towards some limited convergence in domestic regulations, wide differences in the content of countries' border and domestic regulations remain.

These differences sometimes have origins of an administrative or technical nature, such as in customs procedures or technical standards. In these cases, there can be sizable practical difficulties in formulating common rules, not least in overcoming entrenched interests in long-established practices. Arriving at a solution is, for the most part, a matter of finding an equitable sharing of the burden of adjustment that countries have to make in order to introduce more comparable practices.

Differences in national regulations or practices, however, may also arise from strongly held social preferences that reflect countries' social mores, their institutions, or particular level of economic development. These national preferences place valid limits on the scope of the multilateral rules that can be negotiated to realize greater equality of opportunity. For instance, in the name of fairness, many in the United States and European Union have advocated the inclusion of labour standards in the WTO agreements as a way of countering competition from 'sweatshop labour'. Others, especially from emerging countries, have argued strongly against such an action. One fear is that such standards would be abused for protectionist purposes. A more intrinsic objection is that it is very difficult to arrive at definitions of labour standards that are both sufficiently specific for dispute settlement purposes and would be widely acceptable. The particular labour standards acceptable in individual countries are shaped uniquely by their own social and political histories. As the experience of including labour standards in FTAs has demonstrated, the accommodation of distinctively different social norms and practice in common rules has defeated negotiators, and at best, they have agreed that each trading partner will actively undertake to enforce its own labour standards.[9] Again, there are numerous complaints directed against the trading system about unfair pricing, and many of these instances imply some form of restrictive business practice.[10] However, because of national differences in views about acceptable forms of business organization, a consensus on competition policy has so far been beyond the reach of WTO members, and there is no corresponding set of rules that can be applied.

---

[9] For a fuller discussion, see Brown and Stern 2008.

[10] Anti-globalization critics find some business practices unfair—for example, the displacement of smallholders by agro-businesses—that are nonetheless accepted or condoned by governments of the trading countries. These are more in the nature of criticisms of the social system and lie outside our discussion.

Clearly, there are many national regulations and procedures that presently lie outside the scope of WTO disciplines. The firms and individuals of each country may sometimes choose to regard the different regulations and procedures of the other countries as unfair but, from the viewpoint of the impartial spectator, they can only be described as different. It has to be accepted that when the differences reflect strongly held national preferences, these limit the scope for multilateral rules that would enhance equality of opportunity (at least so long as the autonomy of the individual countries participating in rules formation is respected).

30.3.2 Distributive justice

In the view that we espouse, the principle of equality of opportunity has to be qualified to take account of distributive justice. For most of us, the great disparity in levels of living among countries imposes a moral obligation on the richer countries to assist the poorer countries in the alleviation of dire poverty. While the provision of financial aid is the most obvious expression of this obligation, foreign trade is also widely accepted as a major means of economic betterment; there are therefore grounds for extending favourable trading conditions to these countries.

But what do favourable conditions mean in the context of the multilateral trading system? Distributive justice patently does not mean the utilization of the system to transfer resources from rich to poor nations. The trading system is not a vehicle for the transfer of resources but an arrangement for promoting commercial relations among firms and individuals in different countries to their mutual benefit. What it can only mean in this context is that the system should specially favour the economic growth of the poorer countries, and this can only happen in two ways. First, it can improve the access of these countries to foreign markets. This potentially contributes to their economic growth by enlarging the market for domestic producers and enhancing specialization, and it can have such beneficial longer-term consequences as the promotion of learning, the realization of economies of scale, and the introduction of technological improvements. Second—and, for some, more controversially—the system can allow the poorer countries to practice greater protection of their domestic markets. This, especially in the earlier stages of development, potentially encourages new domestic firms (whether nationally or foreign owned) to establish themselves, to expand production, and to make innovations, so that they can form the core of an expanding modern sector. How far the GATT/WTO system, which has historically focused primarily on the reciprocal improvement of market access among trading partners, should be adapted to accommodate these two developmental objectives, has been, and remains, a matter of controversy—it has been a theme running through the faltering Doha Development Round, and the positions taken on this issue deeply affect views about the fairness of the system.

Preferred access for developing countries to the markets of the richer countries has long been a formal feature of the trading system. Several non-reciprocal preferential programmes are features of the system. The richer countries launched the Generalized

System of Preferences (GSP) in the 1970s. In addition, the United States, the European Union, and other developed countries operate other, still more favourable schemes for particular groups of countries, such as the countries of sub-Saharan Africa under the US African Growth and Opportunity Act (AGOA), or the EU Cotonou Agreement that favours the African, Caribbean, and Pacific former colonies. Further, the developed countries generally provide still more extensive preferences to the least developed countries.

There are grounds for scepticism about the practical value of these preferential arrangements for developing countries as a whole. The evidence is that the possibilities of preferential access are far from having been fully utilized, probably because exporters have had difficulty in complying with rules of origin, or because the transactions cost of the certification process have outweighed the saved preferential margin. More fundamentally, a number of emerging countries—China being the outstanding instance in recent years—have achieved a remarkable export performance without the benefit of any preferential treatment. This only emphasizes that, in the relatively open trading system that now prevails, the dominant determinants of export performance lie in the internal economic growth, structural change, and export-oriented policies of the exporting countries themselves. Such doubts about the practical value of broad-based preferences[11] may even apply, in some degree, to the more generous preferential arrangements for the least developed countries at their earlier stage of development.[12]

In aiming to ease market access on grounds of distributive justice, the rich countries are open to the major criticism that they have confined their efforts to preferential arrangements for tariffs on a range of industrial products (with these countries excluding some of the more 'sensitive'—and usually labour-intensive—products.) This has entirely failed to address some of the more deeply embedded discriminatory trade barriers that developing countries face in exporting to the rich countries. The most stubborn is the tariffs and subsidies with which the rich countries protect their agricultural markets. The Agriculture Agreement of the Uruguay Round, and the uncompleted negotiations of the Doha Development Round, have left this bias against developing country agricultural exports largely unchanged. Other embedded features of rich countries' trade barriers are relatively high tariffs on labour-intensive products and the escalation of tariffs by degree of processing on primary products.[13]

---

[11] For a review of the literature on the benefits of preferences for developing countries, see Hoekman and Ozden 2006. For a more detailed discussion of these doubts, see Brown and Stern 2007.

[12] At a forum marking the 10th anniversary of the passage of the African Growth and Opportunity Act, the US Secretary of State, Hilary Clinton, told delegates: 'We all know, despite the best of intentions, AGOA has achieved only modest results and has not lived up to the highest hopes of a decade ago.' *Financial Times*, 8 September 2010.

[13] Removal of these biases would, it might be noted, be better described as steps towards greater equality of opportunity, rather than as measures taken in the name of distributive justice to provide particularly favourable market access.

On the other side of the coin—the protection of their own markets—developing countries have sought in multilateral trade negotiations to preserve their margin of protection by insisting that they grant less-than-full reciprocity to the rest of the world. In addition, they have sought to retain flexibility by binding their tariffs at relatively high levels, even though many have made substantial cuts in their applied tariffs. Developing countries, however, face a quandary, since bargaining to gain improved access to the markets of rich countries means offering concessions in their own tariffs.

It is, however, not only more favourable tariff regimes that concern developing countries. Equally important—or perhaps more so—is that these countries should enjoy greater flexibility in the use of domestic measures that may promote their development, but that are subject to WTO disciplines. This is discussed more fully in the next section.

30.4 FAIRNESS IN THE NEGOTIATION OF TRADE AGREEMENTS

In the real world, what matters is how far the principle of economic equity is translated into practice through multilateral negotiations, and that depends on the fairness of the negotiating process. The participating countries have to enjoy both autonomy in their decision making and reciprocity in the negotiation of benefits.

30.4.1 Autonomy

Multilateral negotiations are conducted on the premise that all member countries will concur in the final package of negotiated agreements as a 'single undertaking'. The agreements are thus based on the consent of the participants, so that the obligations which they accept are self-imposed. The voluntary nature of the agreements, however, is by no means sufficient to ensure that they are fair. Participants differ greatly in their bargaining power as well as in their bargaining skills. The weaker participants may consent to a negotiated agreement simply because of their lack of acceptable alternatives. It is quite possible, for example, for a weaker participant to accept the outcome of a round of negotiations that leaves it worse off than before. A government could therefore consider, in such a circumstance, the alternative of withdrawing from membership of the WTO. But this would mean the loss of more fundamental rights like most-favoured nation and national treatment, which would be difficult to give up.

While there has been a significant shift since the Uruguay Round in the negotiating power of participating countries, the balance of advantage still lies markedly with the most developed countries of North America, Europe, and Japan. Supported by their technological leadership and political power, they have hoped that the regime of open-market access which—leaving aside agriculture—they have developed among themselves, could be enlarged to embrace the developing countries as well. The developing countries, however, have the more complex aim of wanting to improve their market access to other countries while defending the firms in their emerging modern sectors from being eclipsed by highly competitive, and more experienced, foreign enterprises.

Many suggestions have been made for improvements in the negotiating process so that the smaller and weaker countries have a larger voice in the deliberations. Some of the larger emerging countries—Brazil, China, India, and South Africa—acquired a new eminence in the suspended Doha Development Round. However, 'mini-ministerial' meetings deciding common positions have still excluded the smaller and weaker countries from participation. Even relatively large countries have complained strongly about some negotiating procedures. For example, in the Uruguay Round, the major content of the Agreement on Agriculture was drafted by the United States and the European Communities—known as the Blair House Agreement—and presented to the other participants, some of whom were major traders in agricultural products, as a *sine qua non* of the final agreement.[14] A more open and inclusive process would undoubtedly contribute towards improving the perception that the negotiating process was not unduly weighted in favour of the most powerful countries; it should be noted that the Director-General of the WTO has made efforts in the course of the Doha Development Round to effect some improvements—such as inviting more countries to participate in the formerly exclusionary 'Green Room' negotiations.

The real test, however, of the fairness of the negotiating process lies in whether the outcome is seen to be mutually beneficial for all participants. In other words, if the agreements arising out of a round of negotiations are to approach our idea of fairness, it is not enough that the member countries should participate in the negotiations and willingly consent to the decisions; it is also necessary that the agreements should yield benefit to all. How far such reciprocity is met is by no means always easy to determine in actual practice. We explore what reciprocity has practically meant in the following section.

30.5 WHAT RECIPROCITY MEANS PRACTICALLY

30.5.1 Regarding market access

In the context of international trade relations, reciprocity has usually been taken to mean that the participants in any negotiations enjoy roughly equivalent benefits or bear roughly equivalent costs. These benefits and costs, it should be remembered, do not correspond to the economist's concept of economic welfare. Mainstream economists are

---

[14] Cedro and Vieira 2010.

interested in the consequences of trade liberalization—both the gain in access to foreign markets, and the reduction in trade barriers on imports—in enhancing the efficient use of productive resources in the economy. But trade negotiators tend to take a more limited view of benefits and costs; these refer primarily to the prospective increases in trade flows that follow from the greater market access granted by other trading partners, or conceded to other partners.

In the early post-Second World War days of multilateral trade negotiations, it was relatively clear what the realization of equivalence in market access meant. Countries, which were almost all developed countries, negotiated reductions of industrial tariffs or quantitative restrictions on a product-by-product basis that involved comparable amounts of trade. Introduction of across-the-board cuts of tariffs did not seriously impair this perception of equivalence. An equal percentage cut in tariffs across the board was taken to imply equivalent gains in market access, an assumption made more plausible by the fact that trade among the developed countries was largely intra-industry trade. The effects of the tariff-cutting formulae, however, became more complicated as they endeavoured to take account of differences among countries in tariff peaks, and to differentiate among developed and developing countries and as countries sought to exempt lists of specific products from the cuts. It can very reasonably be maintained that the greater complexity in the formulae evolved as a consequence of efforts to improve the fairness of trade-liberalization agreements. However, the effect of the adopted methodology combined with the increasing number of countries participating in the negotiations has, for many individual countries, been that any close correspondence between the gains in market access granted and received has ceased to be apparent. Finger, Reincke, and Castro demonstrated this clearly for the Uruguay Round.[15] They found that the tariff cuts and affected trade flows that were granted and received by many individual countries failed to balance out.

There is a further complication in the assessment of reciprocity. It is quite often an oversimplification to say that the benefits and costs of gains in market access can be equated with the expected changes in trade volumes. Trade negotiators often have also to take into account the political costs of the domestic adjustments that are generated by the lowering of import barriers. The question then becomes whether the proposed gains in market access more than balance the political and social costs of the adjustments that have to be made. For instance, in the negotiations conducted on agricultural market access during the suspended Doha Development Round, the United States negotiators were concerned that US farmers would not accept the proposed reductions in agricultural subsidies unless they were compensated by sufficiently large gains in access to foreign markets. Again, the EU was reluctant to reduce its agricultural tariffs significantly if its firms in the manufacturing and service industries failed to enjoy sufficient gains in market access and act as a counterweight to the agricultural interests. For their part, India and China (as well as more developed countries like Japan and South Korea) were

---

[15] Finger, Reincke, and Castro 2002.

concerned with the social and political effects of lowering their agricultural tariff barriers on their huge peasant populations. The question for negotiators from each country was whether the balance of conflicting domestic interests was acceptable.

Still, despite these complications, it does appear that in the bargaining to improve market access through tariff reductions, inter-country reciprocity is not entirely forgotten. Though equivalence may not be a primary concern in the final stages of negotiations, countries nonetheless want to be assured that all participants have made 'an appropriate contribution' to the enhancement of market access.[16]

When it comes to the service industries, equivalent gains in market access have again been a relevant concern in negotiations among the rich countries. Having highly developed service industries, most of these countries have been able to see opportunities for expansion in each other's markets if market access is improved. Between developed and developing countries, however, the possibilities for negotiating equivalent gains in market access are much more limited, since the latter's service industries are generally less developed (though there are some notable exceptions such as some IT services or construction services). As a consequence, the market opening of service industries in developing countries has tended to be a more one-sided gain for the rich countries.

The conclusion we can draw is that, when trade negotiations to improve market access were very largely among the developed countries, the idea of reciprocity—understood to imply equivalence—may have worked well enough. But when the participating countries are as numerous and varied as they are today, it becomes a much less transparent and effective guide to fairness. The dissimilarities among countries in productive structures are too great to allow for intra-sectoral reciprocity. There is further the fact that, as discussed in the next section, the supporting rules of the WTO system also have both effects on market access, and create costs for countries. Thus, the assessment of reciprocity has to be made not only on the basis of border barriers, but also in regard to changes in the system as a whole. We will return to this point after commenting on the process of rule formation.

30.5.2 Regarding rule formation

Besides drawing up agreements on reductions in tariffs and other principal barriers to market access, the rounds of GATT/WTO negotiations have produced a growing number of other rules that improve equality of opportunity. These rules may seek to remove impediments to trade that arise from complex or opaque domestic regulations; or they try to prevent the discriminatory use of these regulations; or they prohibit or limit the use of measures by governments that are considered to constitute unfair interventions in freely competitive private-enterprise markets. Some major examples are customs procedures and valuation methods, health and safety standards, and subsidies.

---

[16] Finger, Reincke, and Castro 2002.

While governments have collectively consented to these rules, the adoption of specific rules has not necessarily been to the benefit of all. Since it is the agendas of the most powerful countries that primarily drive rule formation, there is evidently no assurance of reciprocity in the negotiation of particular rules. This said, we should nonetheless first note that some rules do give rise to net benefits that are generally shared. This is most probably the case where the impediments to trade have arisen largely from technical differences among countries. Customs procedures and standards are instances. The agreements reached during the Tokyo Round on standards, for example, brought greater uniformity into the technical regulations that were applied nationally to individual products. While recognizing the right of countries to devise their own regulations in matters like health, the environment, and consumer safety, the agreements encouraged countries to move towards internationally agreed standards that would facilitate the flow of trade. Greater transparency in national inspection and certification procedures has also been required, lessening the fear that technical standards might be used in a discriminatory way. Countries have recognized a common benefit in conforming their regulations.

A significant qualification, however, to the fairness of introducing such new rules arises from the fact that numerous developing countries face considerable practical problems in implementing them. It has, for instance, often proved burdensome for countries to have to comply with technical standards set by developed countries that require complex certification and testing procedures. Moreover, there are numerous countries that do not have long histories as independent states and are without well-established central administrations, or whose small size gives rise to administrative diseconomies; they also have difficulty meeting their formal obligations without undue strain on their resources. It is true that some leeway has generally been granted the poorest countries under clauses according 'special and differential treatment', but these have often been unrealistically time limited.

The fairness of rules is less clear cut when these attempt to reconcile different national practices that are rooted in strongly held national preferences. It has long been recognized, for instance, that subsidies could nullify or impair market-access commitments made by countries in trade negotiations, and that some multilateral discipline was accordingly needed. But, while virtually all countries make use of subsidies for diverse economic or social purposes, their practices vary widely. The differences in the economic use of subsidies turn essentially on the perceived role of the state in the economy. The United States has emphasized reliance on market-based decisions (at least in buoyant times) and, in the Uruguay Round, it sought a broad definition of what constitutes a subsidy, and a narrow definition of subsidies that were not 'actionable' under GATT/WTO rules. Most other countries, both developed and emerging, sought a more restricted definition of a subsidy and a more inclusive definition of non-actionable subsidies. Compromises were made for the sake of reaching some agreement, but that clearly left room for a range of views—based on different economic beliefs—about the fairness of the adopted rule.

Some new rules introduced by developed countries, however, have patently not been based on any recognition of mutual advantage. They have been advanced on the basis of superior bargaining power and are particularly hard to defend as fair. A major criticism voiced by the emerging countries of the rules formed during the Uruguay Round is that some placed undue constraints on their development-policy options. The new subsidy rule just mentioned was one source of concern. So too was the Agreement on Trade-Related Investment Measures (TRIMs) that place restrictions on national development policies, most especially in prohibiting the use of restrictions on import content of foreign direct investment in order to promote backward linkages. In this context, acknowledgment by the developed countries of the principle of distributive justice has largely been confined to the 'special and differential treatment' accorded to the least developed countries.

The Agreement on Trade-Related Aspects of Intellectual Property Rights (TRIPS) stands on its own as a particularly egregious instance of a new condition being introduced into the WTO system of rules and procedures without an adequate basis of common consent. For a number of countries, the TRIPS Agreement lacked any evidence of net benefit and, indeed, was clearly negative for some. Moreover, until later modified, it rode roughshod over the public-goods preferences of many countries for the health of their populations.

30.6 A MORE INCLUSIVE ASSESSMENT

Given the comprehensive nature of trade negotiations covering both market access agreements and rules agreements, we need to ask whether fairness is respected when we take all the agreements together as a single package. Do the negotiations promote greater equality of opportunity and do they enhance distributive justice? There is unfortunately no common measure of the gains in opportunity to trade of individual countries or groups of countries, and only subjective, qualitative assessments can be made. Moreover, a comprehensive assessment has to allow for the possibility of large differences in adjustment costs and for possible restrictions in the freedom to pursue developmental measures that restrict market access.

Take the Uruguay Round as an example. If we look at its outcome, it would be reasonable to conclude that at least the rich countries moved towards greater equality of opportunity through the roughly comparable reciprocal measures that they adopted in each of the major areas of negotiation. In industrial tariffs, for example, though the average reduction was not identical, the differences were small and tariff levels were, in any case, low. In a number of service industries, negotiators gained comparable treatment in each other's markets, an improvement that their comparably developed service industries were able to take advantage of. In agricultural trade, both the US and the European Communities very largely succeeded in preserving most of the measures that protected their own industries. In the formation of new rules, it is true that they did not always share the same views—as, for example, on subsidies—but they mostly had similar concerns, and neither side dominated the final agreements.

In assessing the outcome of the negotiations between the rich countries and the emerging or developing countries, the question is more complicated. We have to ask not simply whether the negotiations brought reciprocal gains for both groups of countries (in terms of improved market access), but also whether the gains favoured the emerging or developing countries; we have further to ask whether there were large adjustment costs or loss of freedom to utilize developmental measures. The task is made yet more difficult by the fact that there is not the same intra-sectoral comparability in the concessions given and received as there is among developed countries alone.

In the trade of manufactures, the most dramatic gain for the developing countries was purportedly the gradual dismantling of the Multifibre Arrangement (MFA). They also benefited from the general tariff reduction of the rich countries. In return, many developing countries bound their tariffs and removed quotas, or made limited reductions in their bound tariffs. (However, the wide gap between bound and applied tariffs robbed some tariff concessions of much practical significance. On the other hand, numerous countries were unilaterally reducing their tariffs.) In agriculture, the developed countries made little in the way of concessions, thus failing to improve market access for the appreciable number of developing countries with a strong comparative advantage in agricultural products. While developed countries appreciably liberalized access to some service sectors—notably, the financial and telecommunications industries—there were substantially fewer concessions made by developing countries since their service sectors were less developed. Still, the concessions made on both sides very largely benefited the service industries of the developed countries.

Among the new rules adopted in the Uruguay Round, some had market-opening effects in developing countries. But there were also other, and probably more important, consequences of the new rules that were introduced. First, some deprived developing countries of flexibility in the measures they could use to promote their development. Second, the introduction into the system of trade rules of a new regime on intellectual property rights placed new restrictions and costs on the developing countries in the use of new technologies. Third, for many smaller countries, the new rules added to the administrative costs of participating in the system.

What can we conclude then about the fairness of the Round? In terms of the other principle of equality of opportunity, when considered alone, both developed and developing countries won some improvements in access to each other's markets, and the gains may possibly not have been too dissimilar. The difficulty comes when we introduce the principle of distributive justice. The improvements in market access made by developed countries did little to remove major trade barriers like agricultural protection, or other biases like tariff peaks on labour-intensive products. In supporting rules, while the developmental status of the poorer countries was formally recognized through such measures as special and differential treatment, the broad thrust of the agreements adopted in the Round was to restrict the space that developing countries had to use developmental measures.

30.6.1 Procedural justice

We have already commented on procedural justice in the negotiation of trade agreements. But if fairness is to be respected, it is not less important in the implementation of these agreements. A fair dispute settlement procedure is necessary to resolve the differences in interpretation of rules that inevitably arise.

Most commentators would agree that the dispute settlement procedure established in the WTO has worked well. No one has seriously questioned the impartiality of the Dispute Settlement Body. Moreover, it has been careful in its judgments not to venture beyond the limits set by the rules that were established consensually by the member countries. Of course, trade lawyers and diplomats have often disagreed with the particular judgments made in specific cases. Each adjudicator brings his or her own normative or causal beliefs to the interpretation of the rules and the review of the evidence, but—as we observed in the introduction—so long as the process is conducted impartially, its fairness is not in question.

One major complaint that can be made against the dispute settlement procedure is that it demands specialized legal and informational expertise to present and argue a case. Many smaller and poorer countries are thus put at a serious disadvantage since they have numerous other competing claims on their limited resources.[17] It has also sometimes been argued that smaller countries are at another disadvantage in disputes with large countries because their power to enforce any ruling by the Dispute Settlement Body is slight. If a small country is authorized to raise its import duties against a large country because the latter fails to conform to a ruling, the effect of its action will be much less than if the positions are reversed. However, the experience so far has been that—for reputational reasons—the powerful have been willing to respect the rulings of the Dispute Settlement Body.[18]

30.7 CONSIDERATIONS OF FAIRNESS IN THE URUGUAY ROUND

The completion of the Uruguay Round and the founding of the WTO were a milestone in the long struggle to establish a rules-based system governing multilateral trade relations. The evolution of this system has made possible, though it has not assured, the advancement towards greater economic equity in trade relations.

Ideas of fairness have been translated into practice through successive rounds of negotiations. For the large developed countries—primarily the United States and the

---

[17] For a discussion of this point, see Hoekman and Mavroidis 2000.
[18] For a more detailed discussion of fairness in the dispute settlement process, see Brown and Stern 2009.

European Union—a key issue in the negotiation of greater market access and improved rules has been whether benefits have been perceived to be reciprocal. Through these negotiations, they have moved gradually towards the realization of greater equality of opportunity in their trade relations. However, for the growing membership of emerging or developing countries—many of whom were non-members or only passive members until the Uruguay Round—we have argued that, in the name of fairness, equality of opportunity should also be qualified by the principle of distributive justice.

Taking greater equality of opportunity on its own, its realization in negotiations between developed and developing countries has been difficult to assess. The differences between these countries, and among the developing countries themselves, in levels of living and economic structures, have not allowed any close matching of reciprocal benefits. Still, though there have not necessarily been reciprocal gains in market access or in the improvement of rules, the imbalances may not have been too great for most countries. The rounds of negotiations conducted so far, however, have left some long embedded impediments to trade on both sides largely untouched.

In qualifying the principle of equality of opportunity to meet the demands of distributive justice, the weight given by an impartial spectator to distributive justice depends on his or her causal, as well as normative, beliefs. There are valid differences of view about the place of protectionist trade measures in national economic development. The same spectator may, moreover, very reasonably modify his or her causal beliefs in the light of the size and resource endowment of the specific country or countries being considered. In other words, if fairness is defined by equality of opportunity qualified by a sense of distributive justice, we have to accept that there is always scope for differences in impartial judgements about the fairness of any trading system. The best we can do is to ensure that the system accommodates these differences of view by not allowing one viewpoint to dominate the rules and procedures.

30.8 ACHIEVING EQUALITY OF OPPORTUNITY AND DISTRIBUTIVE EQUITY IN THE DOHA ROUND

We have presented our interpretation of fairness under the heading of two criteria: equality of opportunity and distributive equity. At the present time, it cannot be said that the global trading system corresponds closely to these two criteria, and there is ample scope for improvement if and when the Doha Round negotiations are activated and concluded. Some of the rules supporting market access, as we have indicated earlier, do not sufficiently accommodate different national conditions, institutions, or policy preferences to be generally accepted as fair, even when taken as a package. Procedural justice is also far from having been reached. However, we will confine our remaining comments to the primary issue of fairness in the market-access arrangements prevailing between developed and developing countries.[19]

Equality of opportunity in the negotiation of gains in market access is a definition of reciprocity. We have noted earlier that reciprocity has served well enough in past negotiations among developed countries but that, when applied to negotiations between developed and developing countries in the Uruguay Round, it appeared to be a very vague and uncertain criterion. The reason was that, whereas for the developed countries, the criterion could be applied within each of the sectors or issues on which mutual concessions were negotiated, between developed and developing countries there was much less symmetry in the sectors and issues being negotiated, and large trade-offs were made across them. This is unfortunate since fairness can be more readily assessed when negotiations relate to like sectors or issues. However, so far as market-access negotiations are concerned, some bargaining across sectors is inescapable—though there could possibly be merit in striving for reciprocity within sectors.[20] Still, there would be some gain in clarity if the fairness of market-access negotiations were assessed separately from those relating to rule-making and procedural justice. As we have already argued, other standards of fairness apply to the latter.

A move to adhere more closely to market-access gains, of course, does not address the biases inherent in pre-existing trade barriers, or the great disparity in national economic conditions that give rise to the call for distributive equity. There is, as we have noted, a recognized bias in the trade barriers of developed countries against many of the products in which the developing countries have a comparative advantage. Developed countries can claim that the bias is offset by their non-reciprocal preferential programmes and by the less-than-full reciprocity that they concede to developing countries in tariff negotiations. We suggest, however, that both fairness and efficiency would be better served if, over time, the bias in trade barriers were progressively removed, while developing countries—apart from the low-income and least developed countries—moved closer towards full reciprocity.

An alternative to removal of the bias in developed countries' trade barriers is to make their non-reciprocal preferential programmes larger and more effective. But it is highly improbable that these programmes are ever likely to be made a more extensive instrument of promoting development in most developing countries. The successful export performance of a number of these countries alone militates against their more extensive use. Moreover, if the rationale of these programmes is to encourage the formation and

---

[19] It is an anomaly of the present arrangements that removal of some of the existing distortions could seriously penalize some small countries. The reduction of subsidies and trade barriers to agricultural products is likely to have adverse effects on a number of countries that now enjoy preferred access to developed country markets or benefit from subsidized food imports. For some small countries, heavily dependent on a single export crop, the consequences may be particularly severe. The most elementary notion of fairness dictates some form of compensation.

[20] An obvious example in services is the right to make temporary transfers of low cost labour in order to fulfill construction contracts.

expansion of export-oriented firms, and not to transfer income to developing countries, then the programmes seem largely relevant for low-income and least-developed countries in the early stages of diversifying their production and exports. These programmes have, in addition, undesirable characteristics when measured by the efficiency criteria. They generate inefficiencies in diverting trade from the lowest cost producers, and they create overlapping rules of origin. Further, they are not necessarily stable, since they are extended unilaterally and can be arbitrarily withdrawn. In comparison with multilateralism, weaker countries are less protected from the use (or abuse) of trade measures by the powerful for non-trade aims.

We can also ask whether less-than-full reciprocity in tariff negotiations best serves the criterion of distributive equity if that is taken to mean favourable treatment of developing countries in order to promote their development. Developing countries appear to have been deterred from full reciprocity in part because of their belief that they should be able to protect their domestic production more than developed countries, both for infant-industry reasons, and because of the limitations on their capacity to adjust. There are good arguments, however, in moving towards full reciprocity, not least of which is that larger tariff cuts would encourage trade with other developing countries. But concerns about infant industries and sensitive lines of production also need to be taken into account if some weight is to be given to distributive equity. This might be accomplished by more specific measures than less-than-full reciprocity in across-the-board tariff cuts. For example, exclusion of a proportion of tariff lines from the tariff-cutting formula, as proposed by India at one stage, makes more specific provision for branches of production that countries may continue to want to protect. On agriculture, a similar proposal has been made that certain 'special products', mostly crops of subsistence of semi-subsistence smallholders, should be excluded from liberalization measures.[21]

Another still more specific measure would be revision of the rules governing the ability of countries to alter their tariff commitments on infant-industry grounds. GATT/WTO rules have long allowed countries to break their bound tariff commitments on these grounds, but the relevant part of Article (XVIII A) has been largely unused. This was mostly because, when the need arose, it was possible to invoke balance-of-payments reasons for breaching commitments, though the obligation to compensate affected trading partners for the losses sustained from raising tariffs has surely been an added deterrent. With conditions for use on balance-of-payments grounds made more rigorous, the issue of compensation comes to the fore. It is a highly restrictive condition, and it is accordingly difficult to say that the rule provides significant freedom to developing countries in the use of tariffs as a development measure. One possible solution would be waiver of the commitment under specified circumstances, possibly providing for a

---

[21] The protection of agriculture is, as we have suggested, something of a special case. The costs of adjustment to agricultural liberalization can be heavy in many developing countries, even threatening social cohesion. Particularly when staple crops are affected, there may be grounds for protection that are not developmental in the familiarly understood sense.

permissible number of waivers over a ten-year period. This is not far removed from the provisions in the present Agreement on Safeguards in which the protection of injured industries may be instituted in developing countries for a period of up to ten years.

The rules on subsidies and countervailing measures would similarly require revision. The present Agreement recognizes, in general terms, that domestic subsidies may play an important role in the economic development programmes of developing countries. This, however, is not explicitly allowed for in the operational provisions of the Agreement. Domestic subsidies that may be challenged by trading partners include any that nullify or impair the benefits they are accorded through the binding of tariffs; this again gives developing countries an incentive not to bind their tariffs or not to lower them. A provisional clause in the Agreement defined 'actionable subsidies' to include subsidies such as those for regional development within countries, or to support the implementation of environmental regulations, but it contained no reference to developmental subsidies. The clause was allowed to lapse in 2000, and its replacement would be the opportunity for a more development-oriented definition.

References

Brown, Andrew, and Robert M. Stern. 2007. Concepts of Fairness in the Global Trading System. *Pacific Economic Review* 12 (3):293–318.

Brown, Andrew, and Robert M. Stern. 2008. What are the Issues in Using Trade Agreements to Improve International Labor Standards? *World Trade Review* 7 (2):331–57.

Brown, Andrew G., and Robert M. Stern. 2009. Issues of Fairness in Dispute Settlement. In *Trade Disputes and the Dispute Settlement Understanding of the WTO: An Interdisciplinary Assessment*, edited by James C. Hartigan, 33–72. Frontiers of Economics and Globalization, Volume 6. Bingley, UK: Emerald Publishing Ltd.

Cedro, Rafael Rosa, and Bruno Furtado Vieira. 2010. John Rawls' Justice as Fairness and the WTO: A Critical Analysis on the Initial Position of the Multilateral Agricultural Negotiation. *The Law and Development Review* 3 (2): Article 5.

Finger, Michael J., Ulrich Reincke, and Adriana Castro. 2002. Market Access Bargaining in the Uruguay Round: Rigid or Relaxed Reciprocity. In *Going Alone: The Case for Relaxed Reciprocity in Freeing Trade*, edited by Jagdish Bhagwati, 111–36. Cambridge MA: MIT Press.

Hoekman, Bernard, and Petros Mavroidis. 2000. WTO Dispute Settlement, Transparency and Surveillance. *The World Economy*. 23 (4):527–42.

Hoekman, Bernard, and Çaglar Özden, eds. 2006. *Trade Preferences and Differential Treatment of Developing Countries*. Cheltenham: Edward Elgar Publishing.

Rawls, John. 1971. *The Theory of Justice*. Cambridge MA: Harvard University Press.

Sen, Amartya. 2009. *The Idea of Justice*. Cambridge MA: Harvard University Press.

CHAPTER 31

··

LABOUR STANDARDS
AND HUMAN RIGHTS

··

DRUSILLA K. BROWN

31.1 INTRODUCTION

The integration of global goods and services markets facilitated first by the General Agreement on Tariffs and Trade (GATT), and subsequently by the World Trade Organization (WTO), is correlated with economic prosperity and a fall in poverty.[1] Women and children, particularly adversely affected by extreme poverty, have enjoyed considerable improvement in economic status and human capital formation following integration into global supply chains. For women earning $2 or less per day, the global apparel industry provides employment opportunities that pay a higher wage under more humane conditions of work than the next best alternative.[2] For children, globalization is correlated with a decline in child labour and increased schooling.[3]

Nevertheless, news of human rights violations in global supply chains abound. Violations of the most egregious sort such as human trafficking, child enslavement, mortally hazardous conditions of work, verbal and physical abuse, exhausting hours of work, non-payment of wages, etc. are common occurrences.[4]

The establishment of international labour standards linked to market access within the WTO is among the proposals intended to remedy the gross violations of human rights that accompany international trade. Yet the WTO Charter and, previously, the GATT, are virtually silent on the potential inhumanity of globally integrated goods and services markets. The only labour standard currently in the WTO Charter is embedded in Article XX, permitting member nations to prohibit imports of goods produced by prison labour.

---

[1] Harrison 2007.   [2] Robertson et al. 2009.
[3] Edmonds and Pavcink 2006.   [4] National Labor Committee 2006.

Cross-country harmonization of labour market regulations was first advanced by Switzerland in 1881.[5] Following a series of international conferences, several west European countries agreed to ban international trade in white phosphorous matches and place limits on night work for women. Article 7 of the 1948 Havana Charter established a 'fair labour standards' clause and was to be included in the charter of the moribund International Trade Organization (ITO). However, only the general exceptions provisions limiting trade in goods produced by prison labour (Article XX(e)) survived into the GATT.

Following the failure of the ITO, international harmonization of labour standards was removed to the United Nations. The Universal Declaration of Human Rights of 1948 was adopted by the UN General Assembly without dissent. The Declaration provides for 'civil and political rights (the right to life, liberty, freedom from torture, freedom of opinion and expression, freedom from slavery and servitude, right to peaceful assembly and association) and economic, social and cultural rights (right to join and form trade unions, right to work, right to equal pay for equal work, right to education)'.[6]

Further coordination of labour laws within the multilateral system was proposed by the European Parliament in 1983 and 1994, by the US Government in 1986, and at every WTO Ministerial between 1996 and 2001. Despite intense pressure from the United States and the European Union, the Singapore Ministerial Declaration (December 1996), while acknowledging the importance of international labour standards, identified the International Labour Organization (ILO) as the competent body to establish and monitor labour standards.[7] On balance, the WTO Ministerial is implicitly reflecting a view that the agitation in favour of labour standards is motivated principally by a desire to protect domestic labour interests, rather than a humanitarian concern for workers in global supply chains. Following the Singapore Ministerial, the effort to link the establishment of labour standards in the ILO to enforcement within the WTO *multilateral* framework was not pursued further.

The only exception is the Waiver Concerning Kimberly Process Certification Scheme for Rough Diamonds[8] issued by the WTO General Council in 2003. The Kimberly Process certifies diamonds not originating from countries in which illegal trade in diamonds is funding gross human rights violations. The waiver allows WTO members participating in the Kimberly Process to prohibit imports of uncertified diamonds, normally a violation of the *non-discrimination* provisions of the WTO Charter.[9] However, while some of the human rights violations targeted by the Kimberly Process concern the treatment of labourers in diamond mines, the role that diamond profits play in human rights violations that arise during armed conflict is the principle focus of the Waiver.

Advocates for international labour standards ultimately gained access to the process of rule-setting in the WTO indirectly through Article XXIV governing the creation of customs unions and free trade agreements and, more importantly, the 1971 Generalized

---

[5] Engerman 2003.   [6] OECD 1996.   [7] Stern 2003.
[8] Decision of 15 May 2003, WT/L/518 (27 May 2003).   [9] Schefer 2005.

System of Preferences (GSP) Decision[10] permitting *special and differential treatment* of developing country exports. The GSP waiver permits all WTO members to extend preferential tariff treatment to the exports of developing countries. The principle of special and differential treatment for developing countries was made a permanent feature of GATT 1994 by the adoption of the Enabling Clause of 1979.[11, 12] While the WTO charter establishes some of the terms limiting the use of preferential trade agreements, there are no restrictions on conditionality relating to labour standards and enforcement for countries invoking Article XXIV or the Enabling Clause.

The determined practice of imposing minimum conditions of work in trade agreements emerged in legislation establishing the 1983 Caribbean Basin Economic Recovery Act (USA), the 1984 renewal of the US GSP, and the 1988 Community Charter of the Fundamental Social Rights for Workers, ultimately adopted by all European Union (EU) members. The US GSP Renewal Act of 1984 specifically sought to protect:

(1) the right to freedom of association
(2) the right to organize and bargain collectively
(3) a prohibition on the use of any form of forced or compulsory labour
(4) a minimum age for the employment of children, and
(5) acceptable conditions of work with respect to minimum wages, hours of work, and occupational safety and health.[13]

The Act also provided for enforcement. The established mechanism identified a threshold for petition review by the Office of the United States Trade Representative (USTR). Domestic workers, trade unions, and religious and human rights activists could file a complaint, present evidence, and argue for removal or suspension of benefits based on labour rights violations.[14] Between 1984 and 2001, 13 countries were suspended from US GSP status, and 17 were placed on temporary extension with continuing review.[15]

Labour standards in the Chile–US (2003) and Singapore–US (2003) free trade agreements (FTAs) are limited to requiring governments to enforce their own domestic labour law, and a fine may be imposed for non-compliance.[16] The text of the agreements also includes respect for the ILO's Declaration on Fundamental Principles and Rights at Work, but failure to comply is excluded from dispute resolution.[17] Somewhat more expansive terms have been included in the North American Free Trade Agreement

---

[10] GATT document, *Generalized System of Preferences* ('GSP Decision') (25 June 1971) BSD 18S/24 (reproduced in Annexe).

[11] GATT document, *Differential and More Favourable Treatment, Reciprocity and Fuller Participation of Developing Countries* ('Enabling Clause') (28 November 1979) L/4903 (reproduced in Annexe) paragraph 2(a).

[12] Hoekman and Özden 2005.

[13] GSP Renewal Act of 1984, Pub. L. No. 98–573, 98 Stat. 3019 (1984).

[14] Compa and Vogt 2001.

[15] Suspensions: Romania (1987), Nicaragua (1987), Paraguay (1987), Chile (1987), Burma (1989), Central African Republic (1989), Liberia (1990), Sudan (1991), Syria (1992), Mauritania (1993), Mauritania (1993), Maldives (1995), Pakistan (1996), and Belarus (2000).

[16] Stern 2003; Polaski 2004.   [17] Elliott 2004.

(NAFTA) and the US Trade Agreement with Jordan (2001). Under the terms of the Jordan–US FTA, each country has the right to challenge the partner's protection of labour rights. Adjudication is undertaken by a neutral international dispute resolution panel. Penalties for an adverse finding include imposition of tariffs.[18]

More expansive terms have been imposed through conditions in the European Union (EU) GSP. The EU GSP requires the ratification and implementation of the ILO's Fundamental Rights at Work: (a) freedom of association and collective bargaining; (b) elimination of forced labour; (c) eradication of child labour; and (d) abolition of discrimination. GSP beneficiaries are subject to supervision through the standard enforcement mechanisms of the ILO—member state reports, and tripartite reports of non-compliance.[19]

A mechanism for linking ILO-established labour standards, monitoring by the ILO, and enforcement through the threat of lost trade concessions emerged fully operational in the 1999 US–Cambodia Bilateral Textile Trade Agreement. The ILO Better Factories Cambodia[20] (BFC) programme engages in monitoring and reporting on working conditions in Cambodian garment factories according to ILO core labour standards and Cambodian labour law. Under this trade agreement, the United States provided Cambodia access to US markets by giving expanded apparel and textile quotas conditional on improved working conditions in the garment sector.[21]

The ILO and the International Finance Corporation (IFC) jointly agreed to extend Better Factories Cambodia into a global programme in 2006. The ILO/IFC Better Work Programme, inaugurated in 2008, establishes labour standards in eight areas: child labour, forced labour, freedom of association and collective bargaining, discrimination, contracts, compensation, occupational safety, and health and work hours.

Better Work country programmes are currently operational in Cambodia, Vietnam, Jordan, Lesotho, Haiti, Nicaragua, and Indonesia, though each country programme varies with national labour law and applicable trade agreements. For Vietnamese factories, participation in Better Work is entirely voluntary unless required by a principal buyer. For Jordan, participation by apparel factories was initially voluntary. However, as in Cambodia, the Jordanian government is promulgating rules requiring apparel factories producing for export to the United States to enrol in Better Work Jordan. The Haitian Hemispheric Opportunity through Partnership Encouragement (HOPE II) legislation requires Haitian factories to enrol in Better Work Haiti. In addition, each factory in Haiti must reach a minimum level of compliance in order to receive preferential access to the US apparel market.

Thus, Article XXIV and the Enabling Clause have allowed for the establishment of labour standards within the WTO. As anticipated by the 1996 Singapore Ministerial Declaration, the ILO has been tasked with promulgating and monitoring compliance with international labour standards. However, contrary to Ministerial dictates, labour

---

[18] Polaski 2004.   [19] Cavaglia 2010.
[20] For more information, see <http://www.betterfactories.org>.   [21] Polaski 2009.

standards are now routinely enforced by the prospective loss of preferential tariff concessions and market access.

Critics of labour standards provisions in trade agreements typically argue that domestic protectionism is masquerading as humanitarian concern for workers in developing countries. While it is likely true that domestic labour interests are one of the driving forces behind international labour standards, it remains the case that there are market failures that are aggravated by integration of global markets, may have severe adverse consequences for workers in developing countries, and can be remedied through the imposition of labour standards. I begin in Section 31.2 with a survey of the human rights issues that emerge in a globalizing world economy, the market failures that produce human rights violations, and the role of labour standards in mitigating the most grievous of consequences. Section 31.3 is devoted to a presentation of the evidence on the impact labour standards in international trade agreements have on trade, firms, and workers. Conclusions follow.

31.2 HUMAN DIGNITY IN AN INTEGRATED GLOBAL ECONOMY

The case for or against including labour standards in trade agreements depends, in part, on the market process each standard is intended to constrain. The theoretical case in favour of linking labour protections and international trade is advanced by Bagwell and Staiger. They note that tariffs and labour protections are policy substitutes. A government that commits to tariff reductions during a round of international trade negotiations can *ex post* achieve its protectionist objectives by reducing costly protections for workers in the import-competing sector. As a consequence, negotiating over tariffs alone will give rise to inefficiently weak domestic protection of labour and inefficiently low openness to international trade.[22]

However, despite the strategic link between domestic labour protections and trade policy, Bagwell and Staiger's analysis does not suggest coordination of trade and labour protections should take the form of labour standards in the WTO. Rather, WTO members who do not realize the expected market access from a round of trade negotiations as a consequence of *ex post* changes in the labour law of its trade partner can lodge a *non-violation* complaint under Article XXVIII. Article XXVIII allows the plaintiff to retract tariff concessions made in a previous round if promised market access is not realized due to subsequent actions by the partner's government. A complaint can be lodged even if the action of the protecting government is legal within the rules of the WTO. The threat of retaliation, then, for changes in labour protections that limit market access, will eliminate the strategic benefit of the domestic policy change. Thus, the efficient configuration of

---

[22] Bagwell and Staiger 2001.

labour protections and tariffs can be achieved without incorporating labour standards directly into trade negotiations.

The analysis of Bagwell and Staiger focuses on the *strategic* link between labour standards and trade. Srinivasan considers *humanitarian* motivations for international labour standards. He first argues that cross-country standards heterogeneity is reasonably the consequence of variations in tastes and income. Free trade is the optimal policy in the face of such working conditions heterogeneity-driven trade. To the extent that standards heterogeneity gives rise to human rights violations, Srinivasan, citing Rawls, argues that the most efficient mechanism for addressing human rights concerns in trade partners is simply to allow for free international migration of labour. A second mechanism for internalizing the external effect of poor conditions of work on those with a concern for human rights is to provide for income transfers reflecting the willingness to pay for humanitarian conditions of work.[23] [24]

Despite the theoretical elegance of the Bagwell–Staiger and Srinivasan analyses, little of their proposed mechanisms have been adopted to address concerns with working conditions in global supply chains. The only exception concerns the use of transfers to compensate developing countries for the adoption of labour protections.

The first and most direct transfer emerges as a consequence of the adoption of labour standards in preferential trade arrangements. To the extent that the developing countries in preferential trade arrangements are small relative to their preferential trading partners, the agreements generate a transfer from the developed to the developing country. Small developing countries are able to sell to their larger partners at the world price plus the tariff applying to exports of non-members. The transfer of tariff revenue to the developing country trade partner can be thought of as compensation for their agreement to adopt certain labour standards.

Though, it should be noted that transfers generated through preferential trading arrangements are not first best. Preferential trading arrangements introduce distortions between member and non-member trade partners, giving rise to a loss of efficiency relative to a multilateral agreement.

A second strategy has been to employ market-based mechanisms to improve conditions of work in developing countries.[25] Consumer product labels detailing conditions of work can, in principle, allow consumers with a disutility for consuming goods produced under inhumane conditions to increase utility by choosing goods produced under humane conditions. However, if the consumer demand for humane conditions of work is small relative to the overall market, it is possible for the market to direct goods already produced under humane conditions of work to those consumers concerned with working conditions. While consumers may be better off, there is no consequence for workers either in terms of wages or conditions of work.[26]

Furthermore, market-based mechanisms cannot remedy the more likely case in which the humanitarian concern for the well-being of workers is a public good. A consumer

---

[23] Srinivasan 1998.   [24] Rawls 1993.
[25] Elliott and Freeman 2003; O'Rourke 2003.   [26] Brown 2006.

product label potentially allows a human rights-sensitive consumer to choose goods produced under humane conditions of work. However, the external effect generated from the consumption by others onto the human rights-sensitive consumer is not internalized by a product label.

Given the political and practical challenges of a right to international migration, tariff retaliation, and a system of income transfers for addressing human rights violations, labour standards have emerged as the preferred option in this constrained policy environment. Linking market access and labour standards has at least two theoretical justifications. Spagnolo argues that linkage should occur when trade and labour standards are viewed as policy *substitutes*. Policy objectives are substitutes when failure to achieve an agreement on one issue increases the value of achieving agreement on the other. In this setting, linking negotiations increases the cost of a negotiating failure, providing greater incentive for negotiating parties to reach agreement.[27]

Linkage may also be desirable if negotiating parties are having more difficulty establishing an enforcement mechanism for labour standards than for trade standards. Using trade punishments to enforce trade and labour agreements transfers some enforcement power from trade to labour. The consequence, of course, is that a linked agreement will have stricter labour standards, but less trade liberalization than two unlinked agreements.[28]

Below I detail seven labour standards categories, the link between globalization and human rights violations, and the market inefficiency or inequity that a standard would remedy.

Forced labour and human trafficking. Human trafficking typically involves kidnapping, inducing workers to migrate based on false pretences, or physically preventing workers from abrogating a labour contract. The most egregious cases concern trafficking of women or children into sex slavery. Less horrific, but still a violation of human rights, are the cases of migrant workers who do not control their travel documents, working papers, or residency permit. Such restrictions on the freedom of movement is a violation of the core labour standard prohibiting forced labour.

Clearly human rights violations related to forced labour arise due to a governmental failure to protect each individual's property rights claim to her or his own body. Domestic legal structures that permit forced labour generate a transfer from the individual to the trafficker and incidentally exert downward pressure on wages and employment opportunities for workers with fully protected *auto* property rights.[29] Following Srinivasan, human rights activists may attempt to transfer wealth to a government which is failing to protect *auto* property rights or buy the right to the worker from the trafficker. However, in both cases, the use of a positive transfer provides a perverse incentive to increase trafficking in order to elicit a larger payment from the human rights activist. A negative penalty attached to the failure to prohibit forced labour, such as a refusal to

[27] Spagnolo 2001.   [28] Limão 2005.
[29] 'Auto property rights' are property rights to one's own body and labour.

trade in goods produced with trafficked labour, provides a well-targeted tax on the human rights violation.[30]

Child labour. In contrast, a standard prohibiting the employment of children, while profoundly morally compelling, is challenging to establish from an efficiency or equity perspective. Theory and evidence on the causes, consequences, and effective policies targeting child labour have been exhaustively studied and surveyed.[31]

The level of child labour may be inefficiently high as a consequence as several market failures. From an efficiency perspective, the decision between work and school depends on the wage the child could earn in current employment relative to the present discounted value of the future earnings as an educated adult. Binding credit constraints, however, limit the ability of a family to make efficient education investments.[32] Multiple remedies exist, including providing credit, replacing earnings for children attending school, improving school quality and availability, and relieving poverty. In fact, cross-country empirical evidence finds strong support for the hypothesis that poverty is the decisive determinant of the work–school choice.[33] Income growth associated with trade liberalization is correlated with a decline in child labour and increased schooling.[34]

Labour standards that prohibit the employment of children without addressing the root causes of poverty and credit constraints pose a risk of unintended consequences. Empirical inquiry on the impact of prohibitions against child labour and mandatory education provide little evidence that a regulatory approach is likely to have a significant positive effect on working children. Lleras-Muney finds evidence that US laws regulating the minimum age for obtaining a work permit during the early part of the twentieth century increased the school completion rate for white males.[35] However, Goldin and Katz argue that mandatory education and minimum age of work laws accounted for no more than 5 per cent of the increase in school enrolment during the first four decades of the twentieth century.[36]

The lone exception to the above analysis concerns the case in which a child is sold into bonded servitude and compensated only with subsistence housing, food, and water. In this case, the guardian selling the bond has extracted all of the value of the child's labour for his own purposes. Such contracts violate prohibitions against forced labour and exploitative child labour.

Discrimination and sexual harassment. Similarly, an efficiency-based justification for linking market access and non-discrimination is difficult to establish. No demographic group has been more positively affected by globalized markets than women. The pro-competitive effect of international trade has been one factor in narrowing the gender gap in industrialized countries. Globalizing firms are highly motivated to minimize the cost of production, an objective incompatible with a taste for discrimination on the part of managers and supervisors.[37] Further, Busse and Spielmann find that gender

---

[30] Srinivasan 1998.   [31] Basu 1999; Brown, Deardorff, and Stern 2003; Edmonds 2008.
[32] Baland and Robinson 2000.   [33] Edmonds and Pavcnik 2005a.
[34] Edmonds and Pavcnik 2005b; 2006.   [35] Lleras-Muney 2002.
[36] Goldin and Katz 2003.   [37] Black and Brainard 2004.

wage inequality is a significant factor in explaining the comparative advantage of developing countries.[38] Global supply chains appear to seek out markets in which the alternative employment opportunities for women are limited. To the extent that discrimination is observed in sectors such as the apparel industry, it is against men and pregnant women.[39]

The poorest women in the world have discovered new employment opportunities in apparel, footwear, jewellery, electronics, and call centres, etc.[40] For example, in Bangladesh, two-thirds of the two million newly created jobs in the apparel industry are held by women.[41] For many of these women, employment opportunities created in global supply chains are the first formal work experience other than prostitution. For example, 85 per cent of women newly employed in the Madagascar apparel industry had never previously received compensation in the form of cash. The comparable figure for men was 15 per cent.[42] Earning wages raises the status of women, which has long-run consequences, particularly for the educational attainment of girls.

Yet the impact of globalization is not monotonically positive. As women make the transition from traditional non-market work to market work, there is evidence that men in traditional societies continue to process the market activity of women through a traditional lens. Prior to the arrival of a garment factory in a traditional society, prostitution is often the only paid occupation in which women have previously participated. As a consequence, women employed in a newly opened apparel factory are seen as equivalent to prostitutes, and thus are often subjected to sexual harassment.[43] Women are also disproportionately negatively affected when globalized industries shift to a lower-wage market.[44]

Labour standards prohibiting sexual harassment could potentially speed the transition to a modern perception of paid female employment. In the interim, monitoring sexual harassment in a factory setting will increase the willingness of community elders to permit the market employment of women.

Freedom of association and collective bargaining. The right to join a union is the standard that evokes the most intensely negative response among labour standards critics. Unions can be anti-competitive and corrupt and limit the flexibility of a firm to adapt to a changing market environment. The empirical evidence, though, paints a less toxic picture of the effect of unions on economic performance. Aidt and Tzannatos survey research on the impact of the rights to freedom of association and collective bargaining on economic growth and find no systemic relationship. The only significant effect appears to be that high union density reduces wage inequality.[45]

It has been argued that integrated labour markets improve the cost-benefit ratio of union activity.[46] First, unions subject to the competitive pressure of international trade enhance the *voice* face while constraining the *monopoly* face of unions.[47] Unions provide a voice to workers in developing countries for several reasons:

---

[38] Busse and Spielmann 2006.   [39] Warren and Roberts 2010.
[40] World Bank 2004.   [41] Paul-Muzumdar and Begum 2000.
[42] Nicita and Razzaz 2003.   [43] Khosla 2009.   [44] Levinsohn 1999.
[45] Aidt and Tzannatos 2002.   [46] Elliott 2004.   [47] Freeman and Medoff 1984.

(1) Migrant labour with restricted movement lacks a meaningful market mechanism for disciplining employers. As will be discussed below, migrant workers are typically tied to a single employer, limiting their ability to move to an employer that pays a higher wage and/or offers better conditions of work.

(2) Conflict over reasonable hours of work, and the trade-off between wages and working conditions, can only be resolved through negotiation between workers and firms.

(3) Low literacy workers with limited market experience may lack the communication and bargaining skills necessary to guarantee that they are paid as promised, are not subject to excessive hours of work, nor exposed to extremely hazardous working conditions.

Compensation, contracts and hours. Critics of international labour standards harmonization commonly focus intense attention on 'cash' or 'outcome' standards. Such standards involve the terms of employment particularly related to hours and wages. The outcome of bargaining between workers and firms must, by necessity, reflect underlying technology and constraints imposed by goods and factors markets. Heterogeneity in wages and working conditions across industries and countries is an inevitable reflection of cross-country variations in productivity and income.

However, labour standards, as implemented by the ILO in connection with trade agreements, do not impose uniform wages or hours on all markets or industries. Rather, firms in each country are required only to adhere to national law. Nevertheless, the question still remains: what market failure are 'outcomes' standards designed to address?

Labour management practices in developing countries often follow the *traditional* human resource (HR) model, including extremely fine division of labour, piece-rate pay, close monitoring of work effort, one-directional communication, etc.[48] Arguably, technology is determining the HR choice since work effort in simple production processes is easily observable and, therefore, perfectly contractible.[49] However, the empirical evidence on the use of high-powered incentives such as piece-rate pay is mixed. Bandiera et al. find that piece-rate pay increases productivity in traditional industries relative to hourly pay.[50] However, Hamilton et al. find that HR innovations, including production teams, increase productivity and workplace satisfaction relative to use of alienating, high-powered individual piece-rate pay.[51]

More seriously, labour management practices in developing countries commonly fall below even the traditional system. Workplaces employing a *sweatshop* HR system characterized by non-payment of wages, extreme hours of work, and physical and sexual abuse, etc., are common.[52] Such factory managers pay workers the reservation wage, and then employ non-pecuniary motivational techniques such as verbal and physical abuse to elicit work effort. These sweatshop labour management practices are unrelated to the

---

[48] Ichniowski, Shaw, and Prennushi 1997.   [49] Lazear and Oyer 2007.
[50] Bandiera, Barankay, and Rasul 2007.   [51] Hamilton, Nickerson, and Owan 2003.
[52] National Labor Committee 2006.

nature of technology, stemming rather from an ability to exploit low-literacy docile female workers with limited market experience.

HR innovations that improve efficiency may also enhance a sense of worker agency and perceptions of fairness, increasing labour's relative bargaining power and reducing capital's share of any economic rents earned by the firm.[53] The tension between economic efficiency and firm profits is highlighted by Freeman and Kleiner.[54] In one factory-based intervention, Nike worked with a Chinese footwear factory to experiment with the use of pay incentives for line workers. Despite the fact that pay incentives were found to increase productivity, the factory reverted to pre-experiment pay practices at the end of the study.

Labour standards designed to require employers to pay workers as promised, and prohibit verbal and physical abuse, impose a binding constraint on the range of HR systems available to a factory. *Efficiency-enhancing* HR innovations in the presence of labour market imperfections characteristic of developing countries may be *profit-maximizing* only within the confines of a set of clearly articulated and enforced binding constraints, such as laws, corporate codes, or international labour standards.[55] Employers no longer able to employ an exploitative sweatshop model will be required to adopt innovations that include the use of pay incentives to elicit work effort, and respectful communication and problem-solving. Such labour standards will not constrain the management options of firms employing a traditional (or more complex) HR system.[56]

Occupational safety and health. Hazardous conditions of work range from the exposure to lint dust in an apparel factory, to exposure to toxic chemicals in the recycling of electronic waste. Workplace hazards can be efficiently managed through the provision of protective equipment and/or the payment of a compensating differential for employment involving health risks. A market failure may arise in the presence of an information asymmetry between the worker and the employer. The cost of acquiring information and monitoring employer compliance with agreements to manage workplace hazards may be prohibitively high for a low-literacy worker lacking employment experience.

At a minimum, efficiency would require the employer to disclose known health risks associated with a particular task. However, a worker's *ex ante* evaluation of the trade-off between monetary compensation and occupational health may differ from the *ex post* evaluation once the worker has had an opportunity to realize the negative health consequences associated with a particular task. In such a case, a labour standard prohibiting certain types of work contracts may produce an efficiency gain.

Poverty. The textbook Heckscher–Ohlin model of international trade leads us to expect that international trade will increase economic welfare and narrow the distribution of income in unskilled, labour-abundant countries. Trade creates the opportunity to specialize in the production of goods in which a country has a comparative advantage, thereby increasing equilibrium income. To the extent that relative factor abundance determines comparative advantage, international trade should raise demand for

[53] Falk, Fehr, and Zehnder 2006; Lazear and Oyer 2007.   [54] Freeman and Kleiner 2005.
[55] Weil 2005.   [56] Brown, Dehejia, and Robertson 2010.

the abundant factor and increase its return. For low income countries, the abundant factor (unskilled labour) is also the poor factor. Thus, international trade should raise the income of the poorest workers in the world both absolutely and relative to other factors of production.[57] Indeed, Warcziarg and Welch find compelling cross-country evidence that trade liberalization increases economic growth.[58]

Evidence of the positive impact of globalization on poverty alleviation is nowhere more evident than in the apparel industry. The positive impact emerges in the form of a wage premium in apparel employment, expanded formal employment opportunities for women, better conditions of work, less hazardous employment, job security, and higher educational attainment, particularly for girls. Robertson et al., analyzing household survey data in Cambodia, El Salvador, Honduras, and Indonesia, find that the apparel industry pays a wage premium even after controlling for worker characteristics. For example, workers in the Cambodian apparel industry earn 80 per cent more than the average worker with similar skills, experience, and gender. The wage premiums in other developing countries are smaller, but still quite significant—such as El Salvador (18.8% in 2000), Honduras (21.5% in 2004), and Indonesia (7.4% in 2004). Robertson et al. also find that the apparel industry is characterized by lower accident rates and better employment and social security. Work hours are longer than in other occupations, though it is unclear whether this is a worker or employer choice.[59]

The end of the Multifibre Arrangement (MFA) provides additional evidence of the positive and negative consequences of globalization. Nicita and Razzaz simulate a five-year expansion of the textile industry in Madagascar and find that purchasing power for a household with a member employed in the textile industry could potentially rise by 24 per cent.[60] Yet, following the end of the MFA, workers in the Zone Franche in Madagascar suffered a 20 per cent decline in pay relative to workers outside the zone.[61]

Higher wages and expanded employment opportunity for women in the apparel industry has had deep consequences for the social outcomes for women and girls. Khosla, surveying the literature on the impact of the ready-made garment industry in Bangladesh, find evidence of greater economic independence, respect, social standing, and *voice* for women.[62] More strikingly, Bajaj[63] reports on research by Mobarak[64] which finds that the school enrolment rate of Bangladeshi girls aged 5 to 18 is approximately seven percentage points higher in villages with a garment factory, as compared to other villages. Similarly, Oster and Millett find that the introduction of a call centre in India raises the number of children in school in the local community by 5.7 per cent.[65]

Yet, rightly or wrongly, the WTO has acquired a *corporatist* reputation in which the rules appear to greatly favour the interests of producers. The 'social clause' advocated

---

[57] Krueger 1983; Bhagwati and Srinivasan 2002.   [58] Warcziarg and Welch 2008.
[59] Robertson et al. 2009.   [60] Nicita and Razzaz 2003.
[61] Cling, Razafindrakoto, and Roubaud 2009.   [62] Khosla 2009.
[63] <http://economix.blogs.nytimes.com/2010/07/21/garment-factories-changing-womens-roles-in-poor-countries/>
[64] <http://www.som.yale.edu/faculty/am833/>   [65] Oster and Millett 2010.

during the Uruguay Round was intended to provide the same type of protection for labour that the Agreement on Trade-Related Aspects of Intellectual Property Rights (TRIPS) provides to the owners of intellectual property.[66] Under the prevailing set of rules in the WTO, globalization alters the power relationship between capital and labour by protecting (a) market access for exports; (b) physical and intellectual property rights; and (c) the international mobility of capital. Labour, by contrast, is not guaranteed any protections within the WTO and is subject to considerable restrictions on international migration. Economic integration under the terms in the WTO charter could, in principle, lower labour's cost share as capital moves or threatens to move to markets with the lowest labour costs and weakest restrictions on the employment of labour. Labour standards are proposed, first and foremost, to lower the probability that labour loses absolutely as the consequence of globalization, and secondarily to preserve labour's current share of income.

Indeed, despite the overall positive picture in evidence at the macro-level, there remains considerable evidence that trade lowers the *relative* wages of unskilled workers, particularly in developing countries, and there are notable episodes in which liberalization has increased poverty. Though there are many potential explanations, unskilled labour in developing countries is less mobile than other factors, and is therefore unable to take advantage of new employment opportunities created by international trade.[67]

More importantly, the poorest workers in the world with limited literacy, savings, and market experience are vulnerable to exploitation. Harrison and Scorse, notably, find that prior to the anti-sweatshop campaign that struck Indonesia during the mid-1990s, foreign-owned and export-oriented firms had poorer compliance with minimum wage laws than comparable domestic firms supplying the domestic market. Pressure by international buyers to raise wages in the textile, footwear, and apparel industries improved minimum wage compliance and lowered profits *without* lowering employment. These findings are consistent with the hypothesis that successful exporters are more effective in monopsonistic wage-setting behaviour than other firms.[68]

Jordan provides a second example in which firms producing for export are seeking regulatory settings in which monopsonistic employment practices are feasible. The Qualified Industrial Zone (QIZ) Agreement, signed by the United States and Jordan in 1999, was developed as part of the US-facilitated Palestinian–Israeli peace process. Tariff concessions were provided to Jordanian exports provided they had 11.7 per cent value-added in Jordan and 8 per cent from Israel.[69] The expectation was that the QIZ Agreement would provide economic incentives for Israeli capital to work with Palestinian labour, thereby creating economic interdependence between these two factions.

The weakness in the QIZ Agreement, however, is that there was no requirement that eligible factories hire Palestinian workers to obtain preferential treatment. Nor was there any requirement that the capital be Israeli owned. While the Agreement had some initial

---

[66] Maskus 1997.   [67] Harrison 2007.   [68] Harrison and Scorse 2009.

[69] In addition, the collective value-added by the United States, Jordan, Israel, and the West Bank and Gaza must be 35 per cent.

success, creating 17,654 jobs for Jordanians by 2004, since that time the Jordanian share of apparel employment has steadily declined. This is the case, even though the unemployment rate for Jordanian women is over 25 per cent.

Factory owners prefer to import migrants from Bangladesh, India, Sri Lanka, and China. The preference for migrant labour stems in part to an asymmetry between the legal treatment of Jordanians and migrants in laws regulating work, residency permits, and rights to freedom of association and collective bargaining. Jordanian workers are permitted to join a union and are free to move from one employer to another. However, a migrant receives a work permit for employment only at a sponsoring firm. A migrant worker can change jobs, though only with the permission of the sponsoring employer. As a consequence, migrant labour is not free to move to a factory with higher pay and/or more desirable working conditions. Thus, the competitive mechanism that normally protects workers from monopsonistic exploitation is disabled.

More generally, ILO monitoring in Cambodia, Vietnam, Jordan, and Haiti have found frequent compensation-related violations including (a) failure to comply with minimum wage law; (b) failure to provide information about the wage calculation; (c) excess deductions; (d) excessive payment *in-kind*; (e) failure to pay wages as promised; (f) failure to pay on time; and (g) improper calculation of overtime compensation. Violations related to hours of work are also common, including forced overtime, excess overtime, and failure to provide weekly rest.[70]

A set of labour standards that requires employers to clarify payment calculations, and monitors compliance with basic pay requirements—such as paying wages as promised, and setting wages consistent with the statutory minimum wage—could inhibit the ability of employers to engage in monopsonistic wage setting behaviour and improve the overall competitiveness of the labour market. Such standards allow the market to set the wage level consistent with labour productivity, while providing workers the information required to choose the employer with the constrained utility-maximizing pay and benefits package.

31.3 EMPIRICAL EVIDENCE OF THE IMPACT OF LABOUR STANDARDS IN THE INTERNATIONAL TRADING SYSTEM

The implications of labour standards can be most readily seen from their implementation in practice. Below, I provide detailed experience from the Generalized System of Preferences (GSP) and Better Factories Cambodia.

The early use of the violations petitioning process provided for by the US GSP highlight the connection between labour rights generally, and freedom of association

---

[70] Warren and Robertson 2010.

specifically, with emergent democracy. The first two successful petitions were brought against Chile (1986) and Guatemala (1988). Both cases involve the downfall of violently repressive military regimes targeting labour organizers.

The petition filed in 1986 by the American Federation of Labor and Congress of Industrial Organizations (AFL–CIO) against Chile followed more than a decade of violent repression of union rights, the murder in 1982 of Tucapel Jimenez (a public employee workers union member), and the 1985 murder of three teachers' union leaders. The Chilean government argued against suspension of GSP status, claiming that they were taking 'positive steps', halting the killing, jailing, and harassment of union leaders. However, violations continued, leading to Chile's suspension from the US GSP in February 1988.[71] Compa and Vogt argue that loss of preferential treatment of Chile's exports to the US market undermined business support of the government and was a factor in the transition to democracy.[72]

The petition against Guatemala was filed with the Office of the United States Trade Representative (USTR) in 1988. The petition provided evidence of assassination, arrests, and torture of trade union activists and repressive provisions of the Guatemalan Labor Code. Yet despite the compelling evidence of labour rights violations, USTR rejected all petitions. USTR staff argued that the human rights violations were not a direct reprisal for their trade union work.[73] Yet, faced with mounting evidence and repeated petitions, the US Trade Policy Staff Committee (TPSC) accepted a petition for review in 1992.

Shortly thereafter, Guatemala's GSP status became a factor in restoring democratic rule. In mid-May 1993, Guatemala's president Jorge Sarrano dissolved the Parliament and the Supreme Court. By mid-June 1993, under threatened loss of GSP status, human rights advocate Ramiro Deleon Carpio was installed as the President, and Serrano was exiled. The loss of support from the business community linked to Guatemala's GSP status was a critical factor.

By contrast, petitions involving Malaysia, Indonesia, and Pakistan were less successful. Compa and Vogt argue that business opposition marshalled by the US–Asean Council for Business and Technology successfully blocked review of Indonesia by the USTR.[74][75] The Clinton administration did suspend GSP treatment of Pakistani exports of sporting goods, surgical instruments, and hand-woven rugs in 1996 over the concern with child labour. However, Pakistan's pivotal role in the war in Afghanistan became an overriding concern, and GSP treatment was reinstated by the Bush administration.

Despite the failure of the Clinton administration to deploy the loss of GSP preferences against Indonesia, Harrison and Scorse document a significant impact of the attendant anti-sweatshop campaign on minimum wage law compliance, as discussed above. By

---

[71] Amending the Generalized System of Preferences, 52 FED. REG. 49, 129 (30 December 1987).
[72] Compa and Vogt 2001.
[73] USTR, GSP Subcommittee of the Trade Policy Staff Committee, *Workers Rights Review Summary: Petitions Not Accepted for Review* (Guatemala 1988, 1989, 1990 and 1991).
[74] Compa and Vogt 2001.
[75] The US–Asean Council includes Mobil, Texaco, Chevron, American Express, General Electric, General Motors, Nynex, Caterpillar, etc.

1997, exports from factories in districts from which Nike sourced were more compliant than domestic firms.[76]

One of the most significant weaknesses of the US GSP stems directly from the binary link between working conditions and preferential treatment. A finding of non-compliance and a loss of GSP status had a dramatic impact on government stability, local businesses, American business interests, and the implementation of US foreign policy during the 1980s and 1990s.

Intentionally or not, evolution of the labour standards in the international trading system addressed the consequences of such high stakes implementation. A revised labour standards framework employed in agreements between the United States and Mexico, Chile, and Jordan dramatically lowered the level of tension over working conditions in developing country trade partners. These agreements typically require each government to enforce their own labour law, and failure to do so is not the subject of dispute resolution.

Perhaps more importantly, removal of monitoring to the ILO ratcheted down the power of the incentives embedded in the US GSP scheme. The ILO employs a consultative tripartite approach rather than confrontation. Factories are inspected against the set of core standards and national labour law. Factories are offered an opportunity to respond, and non-compliance is publicly disclosed. The ILO then engages factories in consultation and training aimed at remedying non-compliance. However, for most factories (excluding those in Haiti) the main consequence of non-compliance is the impact that reports have on current and prospective business relationships and the public embarrassment of disclosure of non-compliance.

Furthermore, beyond the core labour standards, the ILO relies on national labour law to establish the baseline against which factories are monitored. The ILO issues a report determining whether a factory is in compliance with the local minimum wage law and whether workers are paid as promised, thus removing the common criticism of *cash* standards which reflect industrialized country expectations of pecuniary and non-pecuniary compensation.

The ILO monitors are also less vulnerable than the USTR to the pressures that emanate from geopolitical concerns and business interests. Regulatory independence is obviously a consequence of the fact that ILO monitors are not employees of any government.

Finally, considerable attention has also been paid to establishing and demonstrating a business case for workplace organization that are also compliant. Monitoring imposes a binding constraint on the human resource management system selected by a factory manager. Evidence discussed above supports the case that the exploitative model, an initial labour management strategy typically chosen by factory managers, is not the most efficient, and may not be the most profitable.

Evidence from the experience of Better Factories Cambodia (BFC) illustrates the impact of the *softer* enforcement approach employed by the ILO. The US Cambodia

---

[76] Harrison and Scorse 2009.

Textile Agreement provided for unequivocal linkage between labour rights enforcement and market access. Following steady improvement in labour law compliance, Cambodia's apparel and textile quota allocation was increased by 12 per cent in each of 2002 and 2003, and by 14 per cent in 2004.[77]

Empirical analysis of BFC is supportive of the positive impact on Cambodia. First, BFC monitoring and reporting appears to have given Cambodia a reputation for acceptable conditions of work among large reputation-sensitive international buyers. Polaski reports that Cambodian exports of quota constrained apparel expanded by 44.8 per cent between 1999 and 2002. By comparison, non-quota constrained apparel exports expanded by 302 per cent. While not definitive, this evidence is consistent with the hypothesis that international buyers were attracted by Cambodia's demonstrated reputation for protecting workers rights. The expansion in exports is mirrored in new job opportunities for Cambodian workers. Apparel employment in Cambodia expanded from 80,000 in 1998 to 350,000 in 2008. The overwhelming majority of these workers are young women aged 18 to 25 who have migrated from impoverished rural households. These workers received $50 per month, which is 25 per cent higher than the average *household* income in rural Cambodia.[78]

The most common compliance violations uncovered by the ILO concerned (a) incorrect payment of wages; (b) excess hours of work and forced overtime; (c) occupational safety and health; and (d) the right to form a union.[79] Warren and Robertson, analyzing compliance data between 2001 and 2008, find improved average compliance rates across all compliance dimensions.[80]

Further analysis of the BFC compliance data is indicative of either an efficiency wage, monopsonistic exploitation, and/or a business case for improved conditions of work. Similar to findings by Harrison and Scorse, Warren and Robertson find no evidence of a trade-off between pecuniary and non-pecuniary forms of compensation. That is, compliance improves across all dimensions even as employment expanded and the unit value of apparel fell after the end of the MFA. These two findings are consistent with a business case for compliance.

Brown, Dehejia, and Robertson employ two natural experiments to identify the impact of compliance on factory performance. First, prior to November 2006, points of non-compliance were publicly disclosed. From November 2006 forward, BFC reported summary compliance statistics only. Subsequently, the financial crisis of 2008 provided an exogenous shock. Prior compliance behaviour was used to predict the probability of survival.[81]

Several findings are consistent with a business case for compliance.

(1) The threat of factory-level public disclosure of non-compliance deterred retrogression in compliance. This effect was stronger for factories supplying a reputation-sensitive buyer than for other factories. However, all factories were deterred

---

[77] Polaski 2004.   [78] Polaski 2009.   [79] Polaski 2009.
[80] Warren and Robertson 2010.   [81] Brown, Dehejia, and Robertson 2010.

from retrogression by public disclosure. These findings are consistent with the hypothesis that public disclosure helped Cambodian apparel factories coordinate away from a prisoner's dilemma in non-compliance. Following the end of the public disclosure period, the rate of improved compliance slowed, and retrogression occurred in factories lacking a reputation-sensitive buyer. However, compliance did not return to the baseline, even for factories lacking any incentive to remain compliant.

(2) Factories which were more likely to comply than a statistical model predicted were also more likely to survive the financial crisis of 2008 than other firms. That is, idiosyncratic compliers are more resilient than other factories.

(3) Further evidence of the inefficiency of sweatshop conditions was found by analyzing the correlation between compliance on wages and the probability of closure during the financial crisis. Factories that pay wages as promised, control sexual harassment, and find peaceful mechanisms for management disagreement were more likely to survive the financial crisis. By comparison, factories engaged in more sophisticated human resource management practices were not more likely to survive.

31.4 CONCLUSIONS

Over the last three decades, the international trade community has undertaken an exhaustive and exhausting discussion as to whether access to global markets should be conditioned on an acceptable record of labour protections and human rights. As of the Singapore Ministerial (1996), weak labour protections and their accompanying human rights violations are formally excluded as a basis for restricting imports within the WTO *multilateral* system. The sole exception applies to goods produced by prison labour. However, trade-linked labour standards are not prohibited in preferential trading agreements as provided for in WTO Article XXIV governing the creation of customs unions and free trade agreements and the Enabling Clause of 1979[82] governing special and differential treatment for developing country exports. While the WTO charter establishes some terms limiting the use of preferential trade agreements, there are no restrictions on conditionality relating to labour standards and enforcement. As a consequence, most current preferential trade agreements involving developed and developing countries contain labour standards provisions.

The pure theory of labour standards setting establishes cross-country heterogeneity of labour law, free trade, and humanitarian transfers as the first best policy configuration. The pure theory, however, does not address optimal international standards setting

---

[82] GATT document, *Differential and More Favourable Treatment, Reciprocity and Fuller Participation of Developing Countries* ('Enabling Clause') (28 November 1979) L/4903 (reproduced in Annexe) paragraph 2(a).

in the presence of certain market and government failures. The most egregious government failure involves the inability to enforce the property claim that each individual has over his or her own body, giving rise to forced labour and human trafficking. Less severe human rights violations involve the exercise of monopsony power that occurs with government failure to enforce labour agreements. Firms employing low education docile female workers with limited market experience may find that the profit-maximizing human resource management system consists of payment of a reservation wage, failure to pay wages as promised, excess hours of work, and verbally and physically abusive motivational techniques. Additional human rights violations as they pertain to extremely hazardous conditions of work may arise as a consequence of information asymmetries between workers and managers. Workers may only appreciate the dangers of locked exit doors and toxic materials after the dangers have been realized. As a consequence, an employer will not have a pecuniary incentive to adopt the *ex post* efficient configuration of workplace hazard mitigation and compensating pay differentials.

International labour standards that prohibit forced labour, require the enforcement of agreed upon terms of employment, and require employers to provide a safe workplace, or disclose and compensate for occupational dangers, can improve market efficiency and equity in a global trading context. Basic labour protections also increase the probability that the gains from trade are not procured exclusively by employers.

The first cases of strict enforcement of trade-linked labour standards involved high stakes confrontations with non-democratic regimes violently repressing union rights. However, standards of enforcement were inconsistently applied as developed country government objectives concerning security, business interests, and human rights came into conflict.

Since 1999, labour standards setting and monitoring has fallen largely under the purview of the ILO, with preferential access to developed country markets the enforcement mechanism. Several aspects of ILO standards conform with the pure theory of international labour standards setting. Core standards which penalize firms engaging in forced labour address the government failures involving the protection of each individual's property right to their own body. Labour standards that focus on workplace practices and terms of employment address government failure to enforce labour contracts and informational asymmetries that produce inefficient work contracts.

However, beyond core labour protections, the ILO adopts local labour law as the reference standard. Standards pertaining to regular work hours, overtime, and compensation are determined by national labour law, thus providing the cross-country heterogeneity of standards required for economic efficiency.

References

Aidt, Toke, and Zafiris Tzannatos. 2002. *Unions and Collective Bargaining: Economic Effects in a Global Environment*. Washington, DC: World Bank.

Bagwell, Kyle, and Robert W. Staiger. 2001. Domestic Policies, National Sovereignty, and International Economic Institutions. *Quarterly Journal of Economics* 116 (2):519–62.

Baland, Jean-Marie, and James A. Robinson. 2000. Is Child Labor Inefficient? *Journal of Political Economy* 108 (4): 663–79.

Bandiera, O., I. Barankay, and I. Rasul. 2007. Incentives for Managers and Inequality Among Workers: Evidence from a Firm-Level Experiment. *Quarterly Journal of Economics* 122 (2):729–73.

Basu, Kaushik. 1999. Child Labor: Cause, Consequence, and Cure, with Remarks on International Labor Standards. *Journal of Economic Literature* 37 (3):1083–119.

Bhagwati, Jagdish, and T. N. Srinivasan. 2002. Trade and Poverty in the Poor Countries. *American Economic Review Papers and Proceedings* 92 (2): 180–3.

Black, Sandra, and Elizabeth Brainerd. 2004. Importing Equality? The Impact of Globalization on Gender Discrimination. *Industrial and Labor Relations Review* 57 (4):540–59.

Brown, Drusilla K. 2006. Consumer Product Labels, Child Labor and Educational Attainment. *The B. E. Journal of Economic Analysis & Policy* 5 (1): Article 23.

Brown, Drusilla K., Alan V. Deardorff, and Robert M. Stern. 2003. Child Labor: Theory, Evidence, and Policy. In *International Labor Standards: History, Theory, and Policy Options*, edited by Kaushik Basu, Henrik Horn, Lisa Román, and Judith Shapiro, 195–247. Oxford: Basil Blackwell.

Brown, Drusilla K., Rajiv Dehejia, and Raymond Robertson. 2010. *Better Factories Cambodia, Summary of Findings, 13 September 2010.*

Busse, Matthias, and Christian Spielmann. 2006. Gender Inequality and Trade. *Review of International Economics* 14 (3):362–79.

Cavaglia, Chiara. 2010. *Trading with the European Union: The Impact of Decent Work in Developing Countries.* Manchester: University of Manchester.

Cling, Jean-Pierre, Mireille Razafindrakoto, and François Roubaud. 2009. Export Processing Zones in Madagascar: The Impact of the Dismantling of Clothing Quotas on Employment and Labor Standards. In *Globalization, Wages, and the Quality of Jobs*, edited by R. Robertson, D. Brown, G. Pierre, and M. Sanchez-Puerta. Washington, DC: World Bank.

Compa, Lance A., and Jeffrey S. Vogt. 2001. Labor Rights in the Generalized System of Preferences: A 20-Year Review. *Comparative Labor Law & Policy Journal* 22 (2/3):199–238.

Edmonds, Eric. 2008. Child Labor. In *Handbook of Development Economics*, Volume 4, edited by T. P. Schultz and J. Strauss, 3607–710. Amsterdam: North Holland.

Edmonds, Eric, and Nina Pavcnik. 2005a. Child Labor in the Global Economy. *Journal of Economic Perspectives* 19 (1):199–220.

Edmonds, Eric, and Nina Pavcnik. 2005b. The Effect of Trade Liberalization on Child Labor. *Journal of International Economics* 65 (2):401–19.

Edmonds, Eric, and Nina Pavcnik. 2006. International Trade and Child Labor: Cross-Country Evidence. *Journal of International Economics* 68 (1): 115–40.

Elliott, Kimberly Ann. 2004. Labor Standards, Development and CAFTA. International Economics Policy Briefs, Number PB04-2. Washington, DC: Institute for International Economics, Center for Global Development.

Elliott, Kimberly Ann, and Richard B. Freeman. 2003. Vigilantes and Verifiers. In *Can Labor Standards Improve Under Globalization?*, edited by Kimberly Ann Elliott and Richard B. Freeman. Washington, DC: Institute for International Economics.

Engerman, Stanley. 2003. 'The History and Political Economy of International Labor Standards,' in Kaushik Basu, Henrik Horn, Lisa Roman and Judith Shapiro (eds.), *International Labor Standards*, Malden, MA: Blackwell Publishing Ltd., 9–83.

Falk, A., E. Fehr, and C. Zehnder. 2006. Fairness Perceptions and Reservation Wages—The Behavioral Effects of Minimum Wage Laws. *Quarterly Journal of Economics* 121 (4):1347–80.

Freeman, R., and M. Kleiner. 2005. The Last American Shoe Manufacturers: Changing the Method of Pay to Survive Foreign Competition. *Industrial Relations* 44 (2):307–30.

Freeman, Richard, and James L. Medoff. 1984. *What Do Unions Do?* New York: Basic Books.

Goldin, Claudia, and Lawrence Katz. 2003. Mass Secondary Schooling and the State: The Role of State Compulsion in the High School Movement. Working Paper 10075. Cambridge MA: National Bureau of Economic Research.

Hamilton, B., J. Nickerson, and H. Owan. 2003. Team Incentives and Worker Heterogeneity: An Empirical Analysis of the Impact of Teams on Productivity and Participation. *Journal of Political Economy* 11 (3):465–97.

Harrison, A. 2007. *Globalization and Poverty*. Chicago: University of Chicago Press.

Harrison, Ann, and Jason Scorse. 2009. Multinationals and Anti-Sweatshop Activism. *American Economic Review* 100 (1):247–73.

Hoekman, Bernard, and Çaglar Özden. 2005. Trade Preferences and Differential Treatment of Developing Countries. World Bank Policy Working Paper 3466. Washington, DC: World Bank.

Ichniowski, C., K. Shaw, and G. Prennushi. 1997. The Effects of Human Resource Management Practices on Productivity: A Study of Steel Finishing Lines. *American Economic Review* 87 (3):291–313.

Khosla, Nidhi. 2009. The Ready-Made Garments Industry in Bangladesh: A Means to Reducing Gender-Based Social Exclusion of Women. *Journal of International Women's Studies* 11 (1):289–304.

Krueger, Ann. 1983. *Trade and Employment in Developing Countries*, iii: *Synthesis and Conclusions*. Chicago: University of Chicago Press.

Lazear, E. P., and P. Oyer. 2007. Personnel Economics. Working Paper 13480. Cambridge MA: National Bureau of Economic Research.

Levinsohn, James. 1999. Employment Responses to International Liberalization in Chile. *Journal of International Economics* 47 (2):321–44.

Limão, Nuno. 2005. Trade Policy, Cross-Border Externalities and Lobbies: Do Linked Agreements Enforce More Cooperative Outcomes? *Journal of International Economics* 67 (1):175–99.

Lleras-Muney, A. 2002. Were Compulsory Attendance and Child Labor Laws Effective? An Analysis from 1915 to 1939. *Journal of Law and Economics* 45 (2):401–35.

Maskus, Keith E. 1997. *Should Core Labor Standards Be Imposed Through International Trade Policy?* Washington, DC: World Bank, Development Research Group.

National Labor Committee. 2006. *U.S.–Jordan Free Trade Agreement Descends into Human Trafficking and Involuntary Servitude*. Pittsburgh, PA: National Labor Committee.

Nicita, Alessandro, and Susan Razzaz. 2003. Who Benefits and How Much? How Gender Affects Welfare Impacts of a Booming Textile Industry. World Bank Policy Research Working Paper 3029. Washington, DC: World Bank.

OECD. 1996. Trade, Employment and Labor Standards: A study of Core Workers' Rights and International Trade, COM/DEELSA/TD(96)8/FINAL. Paris: Organization of Economic Cooperation and Development.

O'Rourke, Dara. 2003. Outsourcing Regulations: Analyzing Nongovernmental Systems of Labor Standards and Monitoring. *Policy Studies Journal* 31 (1):1–29.

Oster, Emily, and M. Bryce Millett. 2010. Do Call Centers Promote School Enrollment? Evidence from India. NBER Working Paper 15922. Cambridge MA: National Bureau of Economic Research.

Paul-Muzumdar, Pratima, and Anwara Begum. 2000. The Gender Imbalances in the Export Oriented Garment Industry in Bangladesh: Policy Research Report on Gender and Development. Working Paper 12. Washington, DC: World Bank.

Polaski, Sandra. 2004. Protecting Labor Rights Through Trade Agreements: An Analytical Guide. *Journal of International Law and Policy* 10 (13).

Polaski, Sandra. 2009. *Harnessing Global Forces to Create Decent Work in Cambodia*. Geneva: International Institute for Labor Studies, Better Work, International Labour Office.

Rawls, John. 1993. *Political Liberalism*. New York: Columbia University Press.

Robertson, Raymond, Drusilla Brown, Gaëlle Pierre, and María Laura Sanchez-Puerta. 2009. *Globalization, Wages, and the Quality of Jobs*. Washington, DC: World Bank.

Schefer, Krista Nadhakavukaren. 2005. Stopping Trade in Conflict Diamonds: Exploring the Trade and Human Rights Interface with the WTO Waiver for the Kimberley Process. In *Human Rights and International Trade*, edited by T. Cottier, J. Pauwelyn, and E. Bürgi, Oxford: Oxford University Press.

Spagnolo, Giancarlo. 2001. Issue Linkage, Credible Delegation, and Policy Cooperation. CEPR Discussion Paper No. 2778. London: CEPR.

Srinivasan, T. N. 1998. Trade and Human Rights. In *Constituent Interests and U.S. Trade Policy*, edited by A.V. Deardorff and R. M. Stern. Ann Arbor: University of Michigan Press.

Stern, Robert M. 2003. Labor Standards and Trade Agreements. *Revue d'Economie du Developpement* 17: 125–50.

Warcziarg, Romain, and Karen Horn Welch. 2008. Trade Liberalization and Growth: New Evidence. *World Bank Economic Review* 22 (2):187–231.

Warren, Cael, and Raymond Robertson. 2010. Do Wages Serve as a Compensating Differential for Adverse Non-wage Working Conditions in Cambodia's Garment Sector? Working Paper. Macalester College.

Weil, David. 2005. Public Enforcement/Private Monitoring: Evaluating a New Approach to Regulating the Minimum Wage. *Industrial and Labor Relations Review* 58 (2):238–57.

World Bank. 2004. The Impact of International Trade on Gender Equality. PremNotes, Number 86. Washington, DC: World Bank.

CHAPTER 32

TRADE AND THE ENVIRONMENT

GARY HUFBAUER AND MEERA FICKLING[*]

32.1 INTRODUCTION

THE relation between international trade and environmental protection has engaged policymakers for decades. Claims that open international trade would worsen environmental conditions erupted in the 1990s over the North American Free Trade Agreement (NAFTA) and the World Trade Organization (WTO). The debate over trade and the environment continues to this day. A substantial theoretical and empirical literature has sprung up to analyse both the impact of freer trade on the environment, and the relationships between institutions that foster global economic integration and those that advocate global environmental protection.

New challenges loom on the horizon. In particular, the prospect of climate change raises the stakes—the potential costs of inaction could be devastating, yet the costs of mitigation will be considerable.[1] The appearance of trade-related climate change measures on the international agenda transforms the debate from a discussion over policy to an existential battle. Each country has an enormous incentive to shift the cost burden of mitigation from itself to other nations. Accordingly, climate change has the potential to sharpen existing frictions over trade and the environment, and this at a time when public support for the international trading system is already at a low ebb.[2]

We begin this chapter with an overview of empirical evidence regarding the relationship between trade and the environment. We then move to an overview of the relations

[*] The authors are associated with the Peterson Institute for International Economics; however, the views expressed are their own and not necessarily the views of the Institute.

[1] See Stern 2006; Weitzman 2007; Cline 1992.
[2] See 'Americans Sour on Trade', *Wall Street Journal*, 4 October 2010.

between the pre-eminent global trade institution, the WTO, and the existing array of international environmental institutions. Our third section focuses on the challenges posed by climate change. We lay out our recommendations for reconciling greenhouse gas controls with the international trading regime, and our thinking about the global governance of geoengineering. A fourth section concludes.

32.2 EMPIRICAL EVIDENCE

A predominant theme in public discourse is that business firms are likely to move production from countries of high environmental regulation to countries of low environmental regulation when low tariff barriers permit the back flow of exports to high regulation countries. Indeed some studies conclude that firms in an open economy are more likely to locate in poorly regulated jurisdictions, after controlling for other variables.[3] Nevertheless, the relevant question is whether the effect of environmental regulation on trade patterns, and the corresponding effect of open trade on the environment, are significant enough to justify serious concern. Most of the literature concludes that other factors substantially outweigh environmental regulation in determining the location of business firms.[4] Environmental regulation might be a significant factor in instances where production conditions in two countries are very similar, but this appears to be the exception rather than the rule.[5] A wealth of empirical evidence argues against the 'race to the bottom' hypothesis—namely the argument that open trading systems will prompt well-regulated countries to lower their standards in an effort to remain competitive, triggering a vicious cycle of deregulation.[6]

In fact, some studies suggest that open trade can improve the environment in certain cases.[7] An open economy can stiffen the competition that domestic industries face, encouraging innovation and more efficient use of resources. Liberalization leads to production at scale, which tends to decrease the amount of pollution per unit of output.[8] In general, greater efficiency means less polluting and less resource-intensive production methods.[9] Moreover, Dasgupta et al. point out that pollution data signals to investors whether a firm is efficient, thereby increasing the incentive for firms based in an open economy to abate pollution.[10]

---

[3] Cole and Elliott 2005; Levinson and Taylor 2004.

[4] Copeland and Taylor 2004; Ederington, Levinson, and Minier 2004; Cole and Elliott 2005.

[5] Cole and Elliott 2005 find that capital and labour endowments largely determine the location of production and foreign direct investment (FDI). However, US pollution abatement costs for a given industry are a positive and statistically significant predictor of FDI from the United States to Brazil and Mexico, which have weaker pollution regulations.

[6] For starters, see Copeland 2008, Copeland and Taylor 2004, Cole and Elliott 2005, Frankel and Rose 2003, Wheeler 2001, Mani and Wheeler 1998, and Jaffe et al. 1995.

[7] Frankel and Rose 2003 find that, for a given level of income, trade openness significantly reduces ambient SO_2 concentrations and moderately reduces ambient NO_2 concentrations. However, there is a significant positive effect on CO_2 emissions.

[8] Dasgupta, et al. 2002.   [9] Frankel 2009.   [10] Dasgupta et al. 2002.

In short, international trade can spark a 'race to the top', or 'California effect'. Often, the engineering costs of adapting products and production methods to local conditions will outweigh the savings from using less environmentally friendly methods that might be permitted in less regulated jurisdictions. As a result, increased foreign direct investment from developed to developing countries can lead multinational companies to transfer cleaner production approaches from their home countries to developing countries. The same principle applies to firms selling products to multiple jurisdictions with a diversity of environmental regulations. Just as US automakers often adopt California emissions standards for entire lines of cars, an integrated international economy can cause a multinational firm to conform its products to the strictest environmental standards.[11]

Likewise, Porter and Van der Linde suggest that environmental regulations could actually benefit firms exposed to a global market, if they are designed to spur innovation.[12] Some recent studies corroborate this hypothesis. McAusland finds that regulation of domestic consumption can give domestic industries a boost.[13] Antweiler et al. find, all else equal, that trade increases the concentration of SO2-intensive industries in high-income countries.[14]

32.2.1 Environmental Kuznets Curve

Trade can also affect the environment by increasing income.[15] Several studies have found an 'Environmental Kuznets Curve',[16] or inverse-U relationship between pollution and income.[17] There are a number of reasons for this relationship. As a country industrializes, it is likely to shift from capital-driven growth to total factor productivity-driven growth. As a result, the economy might shift from resource-intensive manufacturing to less resource-intensive and more skill-intensive goods, lowering pollution per unit of output.[18] Higher income also increases resources available for environmental protection.[19] Another possible explanation could be that countries become more efficient at controlling pollution over time, so that they are able to achieve more 'bang for every buck' of pollution control as they develop.[20]

Copeland and Taylor find that economic growth of one per cent raises pollution concentrations on average by 0.25 to 0.50 per cent due to increased production, but lowers pollution concentrations by 1.25 to 1.50 per cent due to cleaner production methods.[21]

---

[11] Frankel 2009.   [12] Porter and van der Linde 1995.

[13] McAusland 2007.   [14] Antweiler, Copeland, and Taylor 2001.

[15] A number of studies have shown the positive relationship between free trade and economic growth, including Bradford, Grieco, and Hufbauer 2005, Balassa 1978, and Dollar and Kraay 2002.

[16] Kuznets 1955. The name derives from Simon Kuznets's conjecture that income inequality follows an inverse U-shaped curve when graphed against income per person.

[17] See Grossman and Kruger 1995, Shafik and Bandhyopadhay 1992, Selden and Song 1995, Copeland and Taylor 2004, and Dean 2002.

[18] Grossman and Kruger 1995; Copeland and Taylor 2004.   [19] Esty 1994.

[20] Andreoni and Levinson 2000.   [21] Copeland and Taylor 2004.

Taken together, these coefficients suggest that economic growth reduces pollution. However, sources of growth are important: a country whose growth is fuelled by technological progress can improve environmental quality by better techniques, whereas a country whose growth is fuelled by capital accumulation will often be saddled with greater production through capital-intensive and dirty processes.

Several studies suggest that decreased pollution at higher levels of income is largely a function of the political process, rather than an automatic effect of income growth.[22] These studies caution that higher income alone does not magically abate pollution, but rather spurs the enactment of appropriate policies. Copeland and Taylor also find that the effects of trade liberalization on the environment depend on whether environmental policy is set in stone, or adjusts to trade influences.[23]

Damania, Fredriksson, and List report that the effects of trade liberalization on the environment depend heavily on a third factor—corruption.[24] In their study, open trade policies and low corruption are both associated with strong environmental policy. If corruption is particularly rife, then an open trade policy has an even greater positive effect on the environment. However, if corruption is very low to begin with, trade openness is associated with less stringent environmental regulations.

Taken as a whole, recent research calls into question the robustness of the Environmental Kuznets Curve. Many water pollutants do not seem to share the Kuznets relationship, and greenhouse gas emissions appear to increase monotonically with income.[25] Even for air pollutants, the results do not seem robust. Pollutant data is scarce, so most Environmental Kuznets Curve studies only examine select pollutants, notably SO_2, while other pollutants such as toxics cannot be analysed.[26] The selection of sample countries, the methodology used, and the dataset at hand seem to significantly impact the results.[27] For example, Stern and Common expand their sample and find a positive, monotonic relationship between income and sulphur emissions, in sharp contrast to earlier Environmental Kuznets Curve findings.[28]

We conclude that the Environmental Kuznets Curve is not a deterministic relationship between growth and environment, but simply a statistical assertion about the strength of political and economic forces for and against certain pollutants at different

---

[22] Panayotou 1997; Mani, Hettige, and Wheeler 2000.   [23] Copeland and Taylor 2004.

[24] Damania, Fredriksson, and List 2003. See also Torras and Boyce 1998.

[25] Both Shafik and Banyopadhay 1992 and Grossman and Krueger 1995 find a positive and statistically significant relationship between income and total coliform concentrations for incomes above $11,000. Shafik and Bandhyopadhay 1992 find that carbon dioxide pollution and municipal solid waste rise with income across the sample, and dissolved oxygen in waterways—an indicator of ecosystem health—declines monotonically. Holtz-Eakin and Selden 1995 obtain the same findings for CO_2, though they also find that marginal propensity to emit diminishes with income. Mani, Hettige, and Wheeler 2000 find an asymptotic relationship between income and water pollution: pollution increases, but levels out with higher income.

[26] See Dasgupta et al. 2002. The authors also point out that the curve is sensitive to the inclusion of higher order polynomials.

[27] See Harbaugh, Levinson, and Wilson 2002 and Stern and Common 2001.

[28] Stern and Common 2001.

levels of income. Environmental regulation is necessary to reinforce whatever market forces might exist to curtail pollution. We now turn to the interaction between environmental regulatory institutions and the General Agreement on Tariffs and Trade (GATT), and its successor, the World Trade Organization (WTO).

32.3 INSTITUTIONAL FRAMEWORK

A number of multilateral environmental agreements (MEAs) use trade restrictions as tools of enforcement, or have other implications for trade (Table 25). None of these MEAs have yet been directly challenged in the World Trade Organization (WTO) dispute settlement mechanism, but frictions have emerged as a result of trade-related environmental measures adopted by individual countries.

Concerns about WTO–environment linkages have been present for some time. Trade and environmental issues arose frequently during GATT negotiating rounds. In the Marrakesh Agreement that established the WTO, the Ministerial Declaration on Trade

Table 25 A guide to trade-restrictive multilateral agreements

Agreement	Trade restrictions included in agreement
Convention on International Trade in Endangered Species	Imposes trade restrictions on endangered species. Restrictions range from a general prohibition on commercial trade, to a licensing system.
Montreal Protocol	Controls production and trade in ozone-depleting substances and trade in products containing controlled substances. Bans trade in products containing ozone-depleting substances both between parties and non-parties.
Basel Convention	Countries must explicitly consent to imports of hazardous wastes. Parties may not trade hazardous waste with non-parties.
	Parties may not trade hazardous wastes unless they believe that the hazardous wastes will be treated in an environmentally sound manner at their destination.
Cartegena Protocol on Biosafety (2000)	Establishes a procedure for restriction of imports of live genetically modified organisms.
Rotterdam Convention on the Prior Informed Consent Procedure for Certain Hazardous Chemicals and Pesticides in International Trade (1998)	Exporters must provide importers with information about hazardous chemicals and allow countries the option of restricting imports. This agreement is the subject of discussion in a GATT working group, so far without resolution.
Stockholm Convention on Persistent Organic Pollutants	Restricts trade in certain chemicals.

and the Environment emphasized the importance of sustainable development and created the Committee on Trade and Environment (CTE) as a forum for dialogue.

In 2001, WTO members agreed to launch negotiations that would address the nexus between trade and environment. Negotiations were mandated to focus on three issues: (a) the relationship between WTO rules and specific trade obligations set out in MEAs; (b) procedures for regular information exchange between MEA secretariats and the relevant WTO committees; and (c) the reduction or elimination of tariff and non-tariff barriers to environmental goods and services. Cooperation between the WTO and MEAs to fulfil the first two negotiating goals is underway, although there is still substantial disagreement over the relationship between MEAs and the WTO. In addition, the CTE was instructed to focus on (a) the effect of environmental measures on market access, especially in relation to developing countries; (b) the relevant provisions of the Agreement on Trade-Related Aspects of Intellectual Property Rights (TRIPS); and (c) labelling requirements for environmental purposes. Here, much work remains to be done.

Though environmental issues have been discussed frequently in the WTO context, the politics remain difficult. North–South frictions over the correct balance between the environment and economic growth continue to plague negotiations. Developed countries have long feared that free trade without environmental conditions would lead firms to relocate in areas with weaker environmental regulation, as discussed in the first section of this paper. Developing countries, meanwhile, tend to view inclusion of environmental provisions in trade agreements as a front for protectionism.

The WTO contains a number of provisions that have implications for the environment. GATT Article I requires countries to extend the same treatment to like products from all countries, known as most-favoured nation (MFN) treatment. Article III, the principle of national treatment, requires countries to treat imported products no less favourably than like domestic products. Particularly in the environmental context, there is much debate over what constitutes a 'like' product. The Appellate Body, deciding *EC–Asbestos*, required the text of WTO rules to consider a broad range of characteristics in determining 'likeness', including effects on human health.[29] However, it remains unsettled whether production processes and methods (PPMs) can or should be taken into account in determining 'likeness'. The answer to this question has significant implications for environmental legislation, since a product's life cycle environmental impact is often determined by its PPM characteristics.

The Agreement on Technical Barriers to Trade (TBT) prohibits countries from maintaining technical regulations that restrict trade, if their concerns can be addressed in a less trade-restrictive manner. However, Article 2.5 of the TBT permits the application of technical regulations if they are applied for environmental reasons in accordance with international standards. It remains unclear whether energy regulations are covered by the TBT Agreement.[30]

---

[29] WTO Appellate Body Report 2001, paragraphs 98–100, 103.   [30] Hufbauer, et al. 2009.

GATT Article XX, the General Exceptions clause, allows for certain measures even when they violate other GATT rules. Among the measures excepted are those 'necessary to protect human, animal, or plant life or health' or 'relating to the conservation of exhaustible natural resources if such measures are made effective in conjunction with restrictions on domestic production or consumption'. Such measures may include import bans related to another country's environmental regulation.[31] In *US–Shrimp*, the Appellate Body ruled that 'conditioning access to a Member's domestic market on whether exporting Members comply with, or adopt, a policy or policies unilaterally prescribed by the importing Member may, to some degree, be a common aspect of measures falling within the scope of one or another of the exceptions (a) to (j) of Article XX'.[32]

However, Article XX measures are subject to the *chapeau*, which prohibits them from being 'applied in a manner which would constitute a means of arbitrary or unjustifiable discrimination between countries where the same conditions prevail, or a disguised restriction on international trade'. The test of whether a measure complies with the *chapeau* is based largely on the way the measure is applied.[33] Measures should allow foreign governments to contest their application, and international negotiations should be pursued before trade restrictions are imposed on other countries.[34]

There has been much debate over the appropriate roles of MEAs and the WTO in international politics. Hudec notes that the ultimate power to interpret GATT rules rests in the WTO, not in MEAs.[35] However, the WTO often takes notice of other international agreements when making its own interpretations. In an early case, *US–Gasoline*, the Appellate Body stated that WTO rules may 'not ... be read in clinical isolation from public international law'.[36] Moreover, Hudec argues that, following the rules of *lex posterior*[37] and *lex specialis*,[38] signatories of MEAs with trade restrictions are assumed to waive their right to free trade that conflicts with those MEAs. To date, as we have said, no MEA has been challenged in a WTO dispute settlement proceeding; the closest the Appellate Body ever came, in *Brazil–Tyres*, was to rule that the provisions of the Mercosur Agreement did not excuse Brazil from its WTO obligations.

In fact, few legal challenges to environmental regulations have actually been brought in the history of the WTO. As to those that were brought, the Appellate Body has made narrow rulings, generally preserving the ability of countries to regulate their own environments, provided that trade discrimination was incidental. Frankel[39] points out that most cases, including those regarding Canadian asbestos, Venezuelan reformulated gasoline, and Malaysian shrimp, were decided in ways that allowed countries to pursue

---

[31] Esty 1994, cited in Hufbauer, et al. 2009.
[32] WTO Appellate Body Report 1998, paragraph 121.
[33] WTO Appellate Body Report 1996, 22; WTO Appellate Body Report 1998, paragraph 160.
[34] Hufbauer, Charnovitz, and Kim 2009.
[35] Hudec 1996.
[36] WTO Appellate Body Report 1996, 17, as cited in Steger.
[37] The latter agreement carries more weight.
[38] The more specific agreement carries more weight.
[39] Frankel 2009.

their environmental interests.[40] Countries have responded to negative rulings, not by abandoning their environmental regulations, but rather by tweaking them into compliance with the WTO.[41]

Nevertheless, several commentators have suggested ways to lessen friction between the WTO and environmental protection. Weinstein and Charnovitz[42] and Esty[43] suggest that the WTO should show greater deference to trade MEA restrictions on trade, and Esty[44] further suggests that trade measures taken pursuant to MEAs should not be limited to WTO members that are parties to the MEAs.[45] Weinstein and Charnovitz suggest that the WTO should explicitly authorize eco-labelling, and should create a commission of experts to report on potential environmental impacts of trade agreements.

A number of experts have exhorted the WTO to improve the transparency of its proceedings. Esty, Weinstein and Charnovitz, and Barfield argue for the written evidence and arguments submitted to dispute settlement panels to be made public,[46] and Esty, Weinstein, and Charnovitz argue for amicus curiae briefs filed by NGOs to be read by the panels and Appellate Body.[47] Environmental experts argue that current procedures contribute to the WTO's reputation—deserved or otherwise—of catering to a closed trade community.

Finally, WTO members could adopt a more active role in environmental protection by pushing liberalization in areas that could be environmentally beneficial. A sectoral agreement eliminating tariffs on environmental goods could boost world exports by $6 billion, while reducing the cost of environmentally friendly technologies.[48] A renewed focus on environmentally harmful subsidies—for example, agriculture, fish, and fossil fuels—could carry even greater environmental and economic benefits. The International Monetary Fund (IMF) estimates that halving global petroleum product subsidies could not only reduce fiscal deficits by a large sum, but also cut greenhouse gas emissions by 15 per cent over the long run.[49]

32.4 NEW CHALLENGES: CLIMATE CHANGE

Most studies of the relationship between trade and the environment and most of the WTO case law has dealt with localized environmental problems. Even when global action has been required—as with species loss and ozone depletion—the scope of action

---

[40] However, in *US–Standards for Reformulated and Conventional Gasoline*, the United States was asked not to discriminate unnecessarily against Venezuela.

[41] Young 2005.

[42] Weinstein and Charnovitz 2001.

[43] Esty 1994.

[44] Esty 1994.

[45] Elliott 2001 also suggests that the WTO clarify its relationship with MEAs.

[46] Esty 1994; Weinstein and Charnovitz 2001; Barfield 2001.

[47] Esty 1994; Weinstein and Charnovitz 2001.

[48] Hufbauer, Schott, and Wong 2010.

[49] See Coady 2010. G20 countries have already committed to phase out fossil fuel subsidies over the medium term, without a specific timetable. See the G20 Pittsburgh Declaration.

has been relatively narrow. The trade implications of these measures are real, but they are limited to a small, well-defined subset of goods.

By contrast, climate change is a global problem requiring large-scale changes in the production and consumption of energy and goods. The warming effects of greenhouse gases (GHGs) are not confined to the locality in which they are emitted. While pockets of dissent remain, most countries agree on the need for action, but specific obligations are hotly debated. Almost every country has multiple economic interests that would be harmed, at least in the short term, by curbing fossil fuels.

Responsibility for climate change abatement is difficult to assign in an objective and broadly agreed fashion. Should developed countries be held accountable for greenhouse gases emitted *before* scientists knew global warming was a threat? Should developing countries be held accountable for their emissions, even if the use of fossil fuels will assist their escape from poverty? Should a single per capita limit on carbon emissions be imposed on all countries, or should countries instead adopt an *equal carbon price*? These alternatives have given rise to sharp international debate.

In part because there is little agreement on who should do what to reduce GHG emissions, and in part because the economic stakes are so high, the potential trade problems associated with climate change mitigation are unprecedented. At the core of trade issues is the concept of 'carbon leakage'. Because GHG emissions come from all parts of the globe, it is aggregate global emissions that matter to a country's welfare, not a country's own emissions. Consequently, each country's emissions reductions have at best a modest impact on its own felt damage from climate change, and will have no impact if they are offset by emissions increases elsewhere.

A key fear of countries which adopt climate legislation is that carbon-intensive production will not desist, but simply shift to countries without comparable regulation. In that scenario, the country adopting GHG limits will incur economic cost without any corresponding environmental gain. Politically, this concern has hampered efforts to reduce GHG emissions.

The United States has been the main driver behind the movement to allow countries to include border measures in climate legislation to 'level the playing field'.[50] For economic reasons, the United States has long been reluctant to take action on climate change. The US view on reducing GHG emissions was clearly articulated by the 1997 Byrd–Hagel Resolution (Senate Resolution 98), which stated that the Senate would ratify the Kyoto Protocol only if developing countries took on GHG limits and the Protocol proved benign for the US economy.

The authors of recent US climate change bills have been faced with the task of conforming their proposals to these expectations, without the benefit of an international agreement in place. Most legislators have addressed the problem by introducing methods of pricing the carbon content of imports from countries that do not adopt comparable GHG targets. This approach accomplishes two objectives. First, it gives foreign

---

[50] Some European Union members have also proposed border adjustment measures to level the playing field, but their suggestions have not made it past the discussion stage.

countries an incentive to take comparable action. Second, it levels the playing field between domestic and foreign producers—at least when they compete for domestic consumers—mitigating the potential economic impact of a climate change bill.

Developing countries have reacted sharply to this move for a number of reasons. First, they argue that historical responsibility for climate change lies with developed countries, not with developing countries. Thus, they argue, it is unfair to expect developing countries to take on emissions commitments like those of developed countries. Second, per capita emissions are far lower in developing countries than in developed countries, particularly the United States. The average Chinese emits only one-fifth of the GHGs emitted by the average American, and the average Indian emits less than one-tenth. Third, they argue that border provisions violate the principle of 'common but differentiated responsibilities' enshrined in the United Nations Framework Convention on Climate Change (UNFCCC), which stipulates that the more financially able countries should be the first to take on stringent climate change commitments.

Even though no border measure has yet passed the US Congress, developing countries are already seeking ways to prevent developed countries from using trade measures against them. At an informal group meeting under the Ad Hoc Working Group on Long-Term Cooperative Action (AWG–LCA) held in August 2009 in Bonn, India proposed the inclusion of a draft paragraph in the negotiating text, which reads as follows:

> Developed country Parties shall not resort to any form of unilateral measures including countervailing border measures, against goods and services imported from developing countries on grounds of protection and stabilization of climate. Such unilateral measures would violate the principles and provisions of the Convention, including, in particular, those related to the principle of common but differentiated responsibilities (Article 3, paragraph 1); trade and climate change (Article 3 paragraph 5); and the relationship between mitigation actions of developing countries and provision of financial resources and technology by developed country Parties (Article 4, paragraphs 3 and 7).

Based on this reaction, it is likely that China and India would litigate border measures under the WTO. Below, we describe the proposals included in recently proposed US legislation, illustrate potential frictions with WTO law, and propose a compromise solution that could forestall costly litigation in WTO dispute settlement.

32.4.1 Competitiveness proposals in US legislation

Legislative proposals for carbon pricing in the United States and elsewhere fall into two broad categories: carbon taxes and cap-and-trade programmes. Carbon taxes levy charges in proportion to the carbon content of fuels and products. The price imposed on carbon (technically, the carbon dioxide equivalent, or CO_2e) is uniform (although the resulting price increase for goods would vary considerably depending on their carbon content), and it rises over time according to a set schedule. In other words, a carbon tax offers price certainty.

A cap-and-trade programme, by contrast, offers quantity certainty. It sets annual limits, or caps, on the overall number of tons of GHGs (measured in CO2e) that regulated entities can emit. These caps are ratcheted downward according to a set schedule. The government then issues permits to emit GHGs; one permit generally corresponds to one ton of CO2e, and the number of permits printed in a given year is equal to the overall annual cap. These permits can be either allocated for free or auctioned to regulated emitters, who may then use them or buy and sell the permits between themselves. The market price of the permits, once issued, is determined by their overall supply (set by the cap) and the demand of the regulated entities. At the end of the year, each regulated entity must retire enough permits to cover its own emissions.

Most legislation proposed after 2007 contains provisions that attempt to equalize costs between entities that are regulated under these measures and companies exporting to the United States from unregulated jurisdictions. Carbon taxes proposed by Representatives Fortney Pete Stark (Democrat, California) and John Larson (Democrat, Connecticut) would both rebate taxes to exporters and impose taxes on imports.[51] Almost every cap-and-trade programme introduced after 2007 includes an 'international reserve allowance programme'. Such a programme would require importers to purchase enough allowances at the border to cover the emissions involved in manufacturing the product.

The two most prominent cap-and-trade proposals to date, the American Clean Energy and Security Act introduced by Representatives Henry Waxman (Democrat, California) and Ed Markey (Democrat, Massachusetts) (the Waxman–Markey bill), and the American Power Act introduced by Senators John Kerry (Democrat, Massachusetts) and Joe Lieberman (Independent, Connecticut) (the Kerry–Lieberman bill), both adopt a two-pronged approach. For the first decade or so of implementation, both bills would rebate to vulnerable firms the full cost of their compliance—both the cost of buying allowances for direct emissions, and the increased cost of energy inputs. To qualify for rebates, industries must be both energy-intensive and trade-exposed; that is, energy costs must comprise at least 5 per cent of the total value of shipments, and imports and exports must comprise at least 15 per cent of the products consumed in the sector.

The second prong is the international reserve allowance programme described above, which is scheduled to begin in 2020 in the Waxman–Markey bill, and after 2025 in the Kerry-Lieberman bill. Starting in 2018 in the Waxman-Markey bill and 2023 in the Kerry-Lieberman bill, the president must make a determination as to whether a sufficient number of imports in a given sector come from countries that have made international commitments to reduce emissions. A certain percentage of imports must come from countries that:

(1) are a party to an international agreement to which the United States is a party, and have made commitments as strong as those of the United States; or

---

[51] See H.R. 594, the 'Save Our Climate Act of 2009' introduced by Representative Stark, and H.R. 1337, 'America's Energy Security Trust Fund Act of 2009' introduced by Representative Larson.

(2) have entered a sectoral emissions reduction agreement with the United States; or

(3) have a sectoral energy or greenhouse gas intensity less than or equal to that of the United States.

When the proposed rebate programme begins to fade, starting in 2025, imports from countries that do not meet the stated conditions must buy allowances at the border to compensate for the cost differential between producing in the United States and producing abroad, factoring the rebates into the calculation.[52] Neither bill gives a specific formula for calculating the allowance purchase requirement. The Environmental Protection Agency is given wide discretion to determine how many allowances must be submitted for imports, and this might have become a significant source of contention if the bills had passed Congress.

As Hufbauer, Charnovitz, and Kim point out, there are a number of flaws in this strategy.[53] First, any comparability tests imposed on foreign countries can be turned around and imposed on the United States. Countries most incensed by the threat of border measures—India and China, for example—have far lower per capita emissions than the United States, and could easily fashion a retaliatory tariff based on per capita emissions rather than the price of carbon.

Second, Hufbauer et al. show that the largest foreign suppliers of carbon-intensive goods to the United States are such jurisdictions as Canada and the European Union, whose manufacturing firms emit fewer GHGs per unit of output than their US competitors.[54] If the United States adopts a border adjustment scheme in climate legislation, these countries might follow suit, harming some US exporters. Target countries such as China, by contrast, do not export enough to the United States to be seriously threatened by restrictive US trade measures. In 2007, imports from China made up only 11 per cent of total US carbon-intensive imports, and India was even smaller. China and India might ignore the US system, while Canada and the European Union might retaliate.

Finally, the measures could interrupt the broad agenda of trade liberalization that has proven enormously successful in boosting world economic growth since the Second World War. At the Bali Roadmap conference in December 2007, US Trade Representative Susan Schwab correctly warned that efforts to address climate change through trade measures could lead to tit-for-tat restrictions and slow global economic growth.[55]

To make matters worse, the international trade law governing GHG controls is murky. We now turn to the WTO consistency of proposed border adjustment measures.

---

[52] Importers from least developed countries and *de minimis* emitters are exempt from the requirement to purchase allowances.

[53] Hufbauer, Charnovitz, and Kim 2009.

[54] Hufbauer, Charnovitz, and Kim 2009. While Canada emits more GHGs overall per unit of gross domestic product (GDP), its manufacturing sector emits fewer GHGs per unit of output due to the large amount of electricity generated from renewable resources in Canada.

[55] See *Inside US Trade* 25, no. 49, 14 December 2007.

32.5 Border measures and the WTO

32.5.1 Border tax adjustments

WTO rules allow governments to impose product taxes on imports and rebate them on exports, but the adjustability of taxes on production processes or inputs is more doubtful. Hufbauer, et al. note that in *US–Taxes on Petroleum and Certain Imported Substances (Superfund)*, the WTO dispute settlement panel ruled that the United States could legally tax imported substances made from chemicals that were taxed in the United States.[56] Hufbauer et al. also conclude that the annexes to the Agreement on Subsidies and Countervailing Measures (SCM) allow taxes on energy inputs to be rebated upon export.[57] However, the authors warn that the application of a border tax adjustment to exports could contradict the environmental justification for applying an adjustment to imports, if the government tries to justify the adjustment under the GATT Article XX exemption (see below).

The exact taxes and rebates for the greenhouse gases emitted during production would be tricky to calculate, as greenhouse gas emissions can differ among firms and even between units of firms producing like products. The United States could require a certificate of carbon content to be attached; however, the administrative difficulty of verifying the certificates would be formidable.[58]

32.5.2 International reserve allowance provisions

Unlike the border tax adjustment, the international reserve allowance programme clearly violates GATT Article I:1, as it discriminates against products based on country of origin when assigning reserve allowance purchase requirements to imports. As a result, the reserve allowance programme would need to be justified under GATT Article XX. The international reserve allowance programme would probably qualify as 'relating to the conservation of exhaustible natural resources', and would probably qualify as a measure 'necessary to protect human, animal, or plant life or health'. However, the legislation must be for the purpose of environmental protection, and not for the purpose of industrial competitiveness or fairness. Although the latest climate change legislation has made this clear in the text, public statements made by legislators endorsing the legislation—which understandably tend to emphasize support for manufacturers—could prove problematic if the provision is brought before a WTO panel.[59]

In addition, measures must not condone 'arbitrary and unjustifiable discrimination', and the case law suggests that a dispute settlement panel might look askance at border

---

[56] Hufbauer, Charnovitz, and Kim 2009.   [57] Ibid.   [58] Ibid.   [59] Maruyama 2010.

allowance purchase requirements. The Appellate Body, in the *Shrimp–Turtle* case, suggested that in order to comply with Article XX, measures must provide administrative flexibility to take into account different conditions in different WTO members, and must provide due process protections so that foreign firms are given an opportunity to appeal decisions limiting their exports to the United States. Though small emitters and least developed countries are automatically exempted from the contemplated US border allowance purchase requirements, the bills provide minimal administrative flexibility to respond to different conditions and contain no due process provisions.[60] In particular, the bills contain no explicit exception for firms that produce in unregulated jurisdictions but with clean technologies. In other words, recent legislation discriminates against foreign firms that exhibit good behaviour, but have the misfortune of being located in a 'non-compliant' country.

Moreover, the border allowance proposals were crafted unilaterally, with no attempt at collaboration with other WTO members. The Appellate Body, in *US–Shrimp*, strongly commended efforts to gain the concurrence of the international trading community, or to follow internationally agreed-upon rules, when a WTO member creates environmental measures that limit trade. The flaw in proposed US legislation might be corrected by inviting foreign governments to participate in a new commission established to design and administer an international reserve allowance programme.

32.5.3 Allowance rebates

Though the export rebate system has received less attention, it could also fall foul of WTO rules. Article 1 of the SCM Agreement defines a 'subsidy' as a 'financial contribution' with a 'benefit' to the recipient. There is no jurisprudence on whether the free allocation of an emissions allowance constitutes a subsidy.[61] However, a panel might find an emissions allowance to be a subsidy, in part due to the potential for governments to avoid subsidy disciplines in the future by allocating free emissions allowances to favoured producers.

If a free allowance is a subsidy, then it is subject to the provisions of the SCM—which does not contain an Article XX exception.[62] Article 3 prohibits subsidies contingent upon export performance. Although the rebates for vulnerable manufactures are not contingent upon a firm's export performance, one criterion for choosing eligible sectors refers to their export and import volumes. As a consequence, the rebates appear to contravene the SCM on their face.

Even if the rebates do not count as export subsidies, they are subject to the rest of the SCM provisions. The most relevant of these provisions is Article 6.3, which prohibits

---

[60] Ibid.   [61] Hufbauer, Charnovitz, and Kim 2009, 61.
[62] It could be argued that Article XX applies to *all* WTO agreements, protocols of accession, and other legal obligations. This position has not been litigated, and seems a stretch.

subsidies that cause 'serious prejudice', or in other words 'displace or impede the imports of a like product of another Member into the market of the subsidizing Member'.[63] It remains to be seen whether a rebate system would cause serious prejudice; however, the potential clearly exists.

Because they are allocated on a product–output basis, the rebates could create incentives to produce more goods from the carbon-intensive sectors receiving the allowances. In the version of the bill that was enacted by the House, firms with average carbon intensities would have 100 per cent of their costs subsidized by rebates. By implication, firms that were less carbon-intensive than average—roughly half the firms in any given sector—would have over 100 per cent of their costs subsidized. Since these subsidies are given on a product–output basis, they could be trade-distorting.[64]

In fact, Dworsky, Hafstead, and Goulder estimate that trade-vulnerable industries would receive three times as many allowances between 2012 and 2030 as needed to retain the same level of profits.[65] Other analysts arrive at different results. A 2009 US interagency report estimates that the rebates would be just enough to fully offset the effect of the cap-and-trade programme on production costs; net US imports could decrease depending on other countries' actions, but the decline would not exceed one per cent.[66] All such calculations are subject to wide margins of error; if the rebates did turn out to have a measurable impact on imports, they could be successfully challenged in the WTO.

32.5.4 A trade and climate change code

Leaving GHG control disputes up to the WTO Dispute Settlement Body could cause a host of problems. Given the uncertain character of existing rules, and the high stakes involved, any Appellate Body decision is sure to spark discontent from a large number of stakeholders. A strict decision against climate-related trade measures could produce heated criticism of the dispute settlement process, whereas a lenient decision could inspire rent-seeking protectionism. Moreover, the sheer number of cases that trade-related climate change measures might generate could seriously burden the dispute settlement mechanism.

We suggest that major emitting countries agree on a 'code of good practice' to guide their trade-related climate change measures. Two plausible options are a plurilateral agreement under Annex 4 of the WTO, or a code outside the WTO altogether. There are of course drawbacks to either approach; a plurilateral agreement would not bind

---

[63] Agreement on Subsidies and Countervailing Measures Article 6.3(a).

[64] Rebates could be smaller if the 15 per cent maximum allocation of allowances for this purpose were insufficient to compensate firms for 100 per cent of increased costs. However, an interagency report concludes that this is unlikely. See: <http://www.epa.gov/climatechange/economics/pdfs/InteragencyReport_Competitiveness-EmissionLeakage.pdf>.

[65] Dworsky, Hafstead, and Goulder 2009.

[66] Environmental Protection Agency et al. 2009.

non-parties, and a code negotiated outside the WTO would require its own dispute settlement mechanism in order to be enforceable. However, if it attracted a critical mass of signatories, a Code of Good Practice could provide all countries with useful guidance on acceptable means of implementing trade-related GHG control measures and forestall a wave of litigation within the WTO.

Whatever form the Code of Good Practice takes, we suggest that it should contain certain elements, summarized below.

(1) It should encourage, but not require, members to adopt GHG taxes or to auction emissions permits, as the preferred control measures. Market-based mechanisms would greatly simplify the task of comparing costs across countries.

(2) 'Like' domestic products should be defined as all goods belonging to the same four-digit harmonized tariff system (HTS) code, including the ancillary goods used in making the final domestic products.

(3) Countries should make producers responsible for GHG emissions, but allow importing countries to impose border adjustments to offset disparities between home and foreign regimes. Border adjustments should give credit for carbon taxes imposed directly and indirectly on like products by the exporting country.

(4) Members should extend national treatment to imports with respect to their own performance standards. If exporters do not furnish adequate information regarding their PPMs, the importing country may use its best assessment to calculate the exporter's GHG emissions.

(5) Allocations of free allowances should not be treated as subsidies under the SCM, unless they are linked to exportation. No restriction should be placed on the transfer or purchase of emissions allowances by qualifying firms in other member countries.

(6) Comparability between regimes should be assessed by an independent international entity such as the compliance committees of the United Nations Framework Convention on Climate Change (UNFCCC). Comparability should be determined at the most specific level possible—at the firm level, if feasible.

(7) Members may give preferences to least developed countries or *de minimis* exporters. These preferences should not be considered to violate most-favoured nation (MFN) obligations.

Alternative approaches to trade and the environment within the WTO should also be considered. For example, tariff lines in the harmonized tariff system could be labelled to designate products that are climate-friendly, and these could be scheduled for zero duties along the lines of the environmental goods negotiations now underway in the Doha Round.

It might also be possible to initiate sectoral agreements that would restrict international trade in certain commodities produced with excessive GHG emissions. The sectoral agreements could be sanctioned under GATT Article XX, which contains an exception for measures 'undertaken in pursuance of obligations under any intergovernmental commodity agreement that conforms to the criteria submitted to the contracting parties and not disapproved by them'.

32.6 Geoengineering

Many have suggested that a 'plan B' might be required in the case of unsuccessful climate change mitigation efforts. Though unlikely in the near term, 'geoengineering' has been proposed as a means to mitigate the effects of excessive GHG concentrations, once GHGs have been emitted into the environment. There are two major kinds of proposals: carbon dioxide removal (CDR) from the atmosphere, and solar radiation management (SRM) to reflect a portion of sunlight back into space. CDR may include, inter alia, land management techniques and increase of biomass cover, enhancement of oceanic uptake through the addition of scarce nutrients, or direct capture of CO_2 from the air. SRM might include the injection of sulphur aerosols into the atmosphere, the placement of solar reflectors in space, or painting structures with reflective material. Both kinds of proposals have uncertain consequences.

These techniques pose serious global governance problems. One is risk management: when it comes to implementing geoengineering techniques, who should decide the acceptable level of risk or uncertainty regarding the outcome? Another is the distribution of the consequences. Even if a particular geoengineering technique promises a net global benefit, it may have significant costs for some regions. For example, Jones, Haywood, and Boucher find that SRM via cloud brightening over the South Atlantic could produce drought in the Amazon,[67] and Hegerl and Solomon also warn about risks to the water supply.[68] Whereas Lin and Shepherd et al. point out that geoengineering may be folded into existing climate regimes such as the UNFCCC and the Kyoto Protocol,[69] it is difficult to see how international consensus might be reached on geoengineering given these uncertainties and costs. Moreover, SRM techniques, once begun, might need to be continued for several hundred years in order to prevent abrupt warming.[70] Therefore, in order to prevent serious political or climatic instability, global institutions governing SRM must also last for centuries. It is hard to imagine global institutions with this longevity.

The governance difficulties of implementing geoengineering would almost certainly spill over into international economic institutions. Should countries disadvantaged by certain geoengineering techniques be financially compensated, and if so should this be done through cash aid, trade preferences, carbon credits, or other mechanisms? Problems may arise in the WTO regarding whether subsidies and trade restrictions may be used to address the competitive disadvantages (particularly in agriculture) that some countries might face due to geoengineering. There may be substantial debate regarding whether geoengineering techniques fall under GATT Article XX exceptions. If geoengineering

---

[67] Jones, Haywood, and Boucher 2009.   [68] Hegerl and Solomon 2009.
[69] Lin 2009; Shepherd et al. 2009.   [70] Bengtsson 2006.

eventually becomes a widespread response to global climate change, the trade issues arising from climate change could become far more difficult than they are today.

32.7 CONCLUSION

The tension between trade and environment has escalated since the battle over NAFTA two decades ago. Although fears of a 'race to the bottom' proved unfounded, GHG controls, with their potential cost and their dependence on global cooperation, have given legislators pause. Consequently, measures to reduce carbon leakage and protect domestic industries feature prominently in the climate change debate.

It is not clear to what extent carbon leakage poses a threat to the environmental integrity of GHG control regimes. Morgenstern, Pizer, and Shih conservatively estimate that environmental legislation up to the late 1990s had cost 1.5 to 2 per cent of gross domestic product (GDP), yet much of the literature shows that even this cost burden has been outweighed by other factors in determining the location of industry.[71] While it is likely that some carbon-intensive sectors will experience trade dislocation as a result of climate change policies, past experience suggests that this effect might not be as large as feared.[72] In this light, a cautious approach to GHG trade measures seems prudent. On the other hand, every country that takes the initiative in GHG controls has an incentive to encourage other countries to do likewise.

GATT Article XX provides an exception for measures taken to protect the environment and human health, but it is uncertain whether measures under consideration would comply with the Article XX *chapeau*. Further, the SCM could limit the use of free allowances, without an escape hatch through Article XX. Countries should attempt to clarify these issues through international negotiations before conflicting national controls erupt in trade wars.

REFERENCES

Andreoni, James, and Arik Levinson. 2000. The Simple Analytics of the Environmental Kuznets Curve. *Journal of Public Economics* 80 (2):269–86.

Antweiler, Werner, Brian R. Copeland, and M. Scott Taylor. 2001. Is Free Trade Good for the Environment? *American Economic Review* 91 (4):877–908.

Balassa, Bela. 1978. Exports and Economic Growth: Further Evidence. *Journal of Development Economics* 5: 181–9.

Barfield, Claude. 2001. *Free Trade, Sovereignty, Democracy: The Future of the World Trade Organization*. Washington, DC: American Enterprise Institute Press.

---

[71] Morgenstern, Pizer, and Shih 1998.

[72] Some models of carbon taxes also do not show a large 'carbon leakage' effect. See for example Winchester, Paltsev, and Reilly 2010.

Bengtsson, Lennart. 2006. Geo-Engineering to Confine Climate Change: Is it at all Feasible? *Climatic Change* 77 (3/4):229–34. Cited in Lin 2009.

Bradford, Scott, Paul Grieco, and Gary Hufbauer. 2005. The Payoff to America from Global Integration. In *The United States and the World Economy: Foreign Policy for the Next Decade*, edited by C. Fred Bergsten. Washington, DC: Peterson Institute for International Economics.

Cline, William. 1992. *The Economic Effects of Global Warming*. Washington, DC: Institute for International Economics.

Coady, David, et al. 2010. Petroleum Product Subsidies: Costly, Inequitable, and Rising. IMF Staff Position Note, February 25. Washington DC: IMF.

Cole, Matthew, and Robert Elliott. 2005. FDI and the Capital Intensity of 'Dirty' Sectors: A Missing Piece of the Pollution Haven Puzzle. *Review of Development Economics* 9 (4):530–48.

Copeland, Brian. 2008. The Pollution Haven Hypothesis. In *Handbook on Trade and the Environment*, edited by Kevin Gallagher. Cheltenham: Edward Elgar.

Copeland, Brian, and M. Scott Taylor. 2004. *Trade and the Environment: Theory and Evidence*. Princeton: Princeton University Press.

Damania, Richard, Per G. Fredriksson, and John A. List. 2003. Trade Liberalization, Corruption, and Environmental Policy Formation: Theory and Evidence. *Journal of Environmental Economics and Management* 46 (3):490–512.

Dasgupta, Susmita, Benoit Laplante, Hua Wang, and David Wheeler. 2002. Confronting the Environmental Kuznets Curve. *Journal of Economic Perspectives* 16 (1):147–68.

Dean, Judith. 2002. Does Trade Liberalization Harm the Environment? A New Test. *Canadian Journal of Economics* 35 (4):819–42.

Dollar, David, and Aart Kraay. 2002. Spreading the Wealth. *Foreign Affairs* 81 (1):120–33.

Dworsky, Michael, Marc A. C. Hafstead, and Lawrence H. Goulder. 2009. Profit Impacts of Allowance Allocation under the American Clean Energy and Security (ACES) Act. Available from <http://www-siepr.stanford.edu/GoulderSep2009.pdf>. Accessed 7 October 2010.

Ederington, Josh, Arik Levinson, and Jenny Minier. 2004. Trade Liberalization and Pollution Havens. NBER Working Paper 10585. Available from <http://www.nber.org/papers/w10585>. Accessed 7 October 2010.

Elliott, Kimberly Ann. 2001. Dealing with Labor and Environment Issues in Trade. Policy Brief 01-08. Washington, DC: Peterson Institute for International Economics.

Environmental Protection Agency et al. 2009. The Effects of H.R. 2454 on International Competitiveness and Emission Leakage in Energy-Intensive Trade-Exposed Industries: An Interagency Report Responding to a Request from Senators Bayh, Specter, Stabenow, McCaskill, and Brown. Available from <http://www.epa.gov/climatechange/economics/pdfs/InteragencyReport_Competitiveness-EmissionLeakage.pdf>. Accessed 7 October 2010.

Esty, Daniel. 1994. *Greening the GATT: Trade, the Environment, and the Future*. Washington, DC: Peterson Institute for International Economics.

Frankel, Jeffrey. 2009. Environmental Effects of International Trade. Expert Report No. 31 to Sweden's Globalisation Council. Available from <http://www.hks.harvard.edu/fs/jfrankel/Swenvirinlaga31proofs.pdf>. Accessed 7 October 2010.

Frankel, Jeffrey, and Andrew Rose. 2003. Is Trade Good or Bad for the Environment? Sorting out the Causality. *Review of Economics and Statistics* 87 (1):85–91.

G20. 2009. Leaders' Statement, Pittsburgh Summit, September 24–25.

Grossman, Gene, and Alan Kruger. 1995. Economic Growth and the Environment. *Quarterly Journal of Economics* 110 (2):353–77.

Harbaugh, William, Arik Levinson, and David Wilson. 2002. Reexamining the Empirical Evidence for an Environmental Kuznets Curve. *Review of Economics and Statistics* 84 (3):541–51.

Hegerl, Gabriele, and Susan Solomon. 2009. Risks of Climate Engineering. *Science* 325: 955–6.

Holtz-Eakin, Douglas, and Thomas Selden. 1995. Stoking the Fires? CO_2 Emissions and Economic Growth. *Journal of Public Economics* 57 (1):85–101.

Hudec, Robert. 1996. The GATT/WTO Dispute Settlement Process: Can it Reconcile Trade Rules and Environmental Needs? In *Enforcing Environmental Standards: Economic Mechanisms as Viable Means?*, edited by Rudiger Wolfrum. Berlin: Springer-Verlag.

Hufbauer, Gary, Steve Charnovitz, and Jisun Kim. 2009. *Global Warming and the World Trading System*. Washington, DC: Peterson Institute for International Economics.

Hufbauer, Gary, Jeffrey Schott, and Woan Foong Wong. 2010. *Figuring Out the Doha Round*. Washington, DC: Peterson Institute for International Economics.

Jaffe, Adam B., Steven R. Peterson, Paul R. Portney, and Robert N. Stavins. 1995. Environmental Regulation and the Competitiveness of U.S. Manufacturing: What Does the Evidence Tell Us? *Journal of Economic Literature* 33 (1):132–63.

Jones, Andy, Jim Haywood, and Olivier Boucher. 2009. Climate Impacts of Geoengineering Marine Stratocumulus Clouds. *Journal of Geophysical Research* 114 (D10106).

Levinson, Arik, and M. Scott Taylor. 2004. Unmasking the Pollution Haven Effect. NBER Working Paper 10629. Cambridge, MA: NBER. Available from <http://www.nber.org/papers/w10629>. Accessed 7 October 2010.

Lin, Albert. 2009. Geoengineering Governance. *Issues in Legal Scholarship* 8 (3): Article 2.

McAusland, Carol. 2007. Trade, Politics, and the Environment: Tailpipe vs Smokestack. *Journal of Environmental Economics and Management* 55 (1):52–71.

Mani, Muthukumara, Hemamala Hettige, and David Wheeler. 2000. Industrial Pollution in Economic Development: The Environmental Kuznets Curve Revisited. *Journal of Development Economics* 62 (2):445–76.

Mani, Muthukumara, and David Wheeler. 1998. In Search of Pollution Havens? Dirty Industry in the World Economy, 1960–1995. Paper presented to the OECD Conference on FDI and the Environment, 28–29 January 1999, The Hague.

Maruyama, Warren. 2010. Trade and WTO Aspects of U.S. Climate Change Legislation: Cap-and-Trade or Carbon Tax? Hogan and Hartson LLP. Draft paper prepared for the Fair Trade Center.

Morgenstern, Richard D., William A. Pizer, and Jhih-Shyang Shih. 1998. The Cost of Environmental Protection. RFF Discussion Paper 98-36. Available from <http://www.rff.org/documents/RFF-DP-98-36.pdf>. Accessed 7 October 2010.

Panayotou, Theodore. 1997. Demystifying the Environmental Kuznets Curve: Turning a Black Box into a Policy Tool. *Environment and Development Economics* 2: 465–84.

Porter, Michael, and Claas van der Linde. 1995. Toward a New Conception of the Environment–Competitiveness Relationship. *Journal of Economic Perspectives* 9 (4):97–118.

Selden, Thomas M., and Song Daqing. 1995. Neoclassical Growth, the J Curve for Abatement, and the Inverted U Curve for Pollution. *Environmental Economics and Management* 29 (2):162–8.

Shafik, Nemat, and Sushenjit Bandyopadhyay. 1992. Economic Growth and Environmental Quality: Time Series and Cross-Country Evidence. World Bank Policy Research Working Paper 904. Washington DC: World Bank.

Shepherd, John et al. 2009. *Geoengineering the Climate: Science, Governance, and Uncertainty.* Report produced by the Royal Society. Available from <http://royalsociety.org/geoengineering-the-climate/>. Accessed 7 October 2010.

Stern, David, and Michael Common. 2001. Is There an Environmental Kuznets Curve for Sulfur? *Journal of Environmental Economics and Management* 41: 162–78.

Stern, Nicholas. 2006. *The Economics of Climate Change: The Stern Review.* Cambridge: Cambridge University Press.

Torras, Mariano, and James K. Boyce. 1998. Income, Inequality, and Pollution: A Reassessment of the Environmental Kuznets Curve. *Ecological Economics* 25: 147–60.

Weinstein, Michael, and Steve Charnovitz. 2001. The Greening of the WTO. *Foreign Affairs* 80 (6):147–56.

Weitzman, Martin. 2007. A Review of the *Stern Review on the Economics of Climate Change*. *Journal of Economic Literature* 45 (3):703–24.

Wheeler, David. 2001. Racing to the Bottom? Foreign Investment and Air Pollution in Developing Countries. *Journal of Environment & Development* 10 (3):225–45.

Winchester, Niven, Sergey Paltsev, and John Reilly. 2010. Will Border Carbon Adjustments Work? MIT Joint Program on the Science and Policy of Global Change Report No. 184. Cambridge MA: MIT.

WTO Appellate Body Report. 1996. *US—Standards for Reformulated and Conventional Gasoline.* WT/DS2/AB/R. Adopted 20 May 1996. Geneva: WTO.

WTO Appellate Body Report. 1998. *US–Import Prohibition of Certain Shrimp and Shrimp Products.* WT/DS58/AB/R. Geneva: WTO.

WTO Appellate Body Report. 2001. *EC—Measures Affecting Asbestos and Asbestos Containing Products.* WT/DS135/AB/R. Adopted on 5 April 2001. Geneva: WTO.

Young, Alasdair. 2005. Picking the Wrong Fight: Why Attacks on the World Trade Organization Pose the Real Threat to National Environmental and Public Health Protection. *Global Environmental Politics* 5 (4):47–72.

PART IX

REFORM OF
THE WTO

CHAPTER 33

PROPOSALS FOR WTO REFORM: A SYNTHESIS AND ASSESSMENT

BERNARD HOEKMAN[*]

33.1 INTRODUCTION

THE Uruguay Round was a landmark for the trading system. Agriculture and textiles and clothing were reintegrated, voluntary export restraints outlawed, rules on protection of intellectual property rights and trade in services added, and the dispute settlement system was strengthened. Because of the single undertaking rule, all countries desiring to become a member of the new World Trade Organization (WTO) were obliged to accept all of the disciplines embodied in the WTO and its multilateral agreements, ending the General Agreement on Tariffs and Trade (GATT) à la carte practice (under the GATT, countries were free not to sign on to newly negotiated disciplines, and most developing countries exercised this option).

The creation of the WTO can be seen as one dimension of a gradual process of global liberalization of trade. Across all countries, average tariffs in 1950 were in the 20–30 per cent range.[1] A variety of non-tariff barriers, including quantitative restrictions and exchange controls, augmented the effects of tariffs. Starting in the mid 1980s, however, average levels of protection in both industrialized and developing countries were gradually lowered. As of 2010, the average level of import protection was some 10 per cent or less in many developing countries, and the average uniform tariff equivalent of merchandise trade policies in Organization for Economic Cooperation and

* This paper is an output of the UK-supported Global Trade and Financial Architecture project. I am grateful to Petros Mavroidis, Patrick Messerlin, Amrita Narlikar, and Robert Wolfe for helpful comments. The views expressed are personal and should not be attributed to the World Bank.

[1] WTO 2007.

Development (OECD) countries had fallen to less than 4 per cent.[2] Imports of many manufactures are now duty free.

The policy reforms helped generate a boom in world trade. The value of global trade in goods and services passed the $15 trillion mark in 2006, up from around $1 trillion in the late 1970s (measured in current dollars). The global value of the stock of foreign direct investment (FDI) rose more than six-fold between 1990 and 2008, substantially faster than the growth in trade, which increased 'only' three and a half times over the same period.

Domestic policy reform was largely driven by autonomous decisions by governments, not least because many of the key reforms that were implemented in the 1980s and 1990s were not subject to GATT rules (e.g. privatization, exchange rates, fiscal and macroeconomic policy, most areas of domestic economic regulation). But the trade regime played an important role in facilitating an exchange in trade policy commitments between countries and establishing a mechanism through which commitments could be enforced.

The WTO has proved to be quite effective in sustaining cooperation between members. Most of what was agreed in the Uruguay Round was implemented. The dispute settlement mechanism has worked: there have been over 350 disputes that have gone beyond consultations, most of which were concluded with the losing party bringing its measures into compliance. The robustness of the regime was put to the test during the 2008 financial crisis and proved to be resilient—there was only limited recourse to the type of protectionist policies that characterized responses to the last global recession in the late 1970s and early 1980s. Some 25 countries acceded to the WTO between 1995 and 2010, and another 20+ are in the process of negotiating accession.

All this suggests the WTO has been, and is, a resounding success. But the institution has been subject to widespread criticism by governments, civil society, industry, and academics. A cottage industry sprung up in the late 1990s that argued the WTO:

- lacked 'legitimacy' and had a 'democratic deficit'
- is too democratic as a result of the practice of consensus-based decision-making
- is hobbled by 'medieval' procedures
- allows the largest traders to impose their will
- permits even the smallest countries to block the majority from moving forward
- has a dispute settlement system that gives too much discretion to unelected judges to write law
- does not give enough scope to judges to interpret agreements and help complete the WTO contract.

As is obvious from this very incomplete list many of the criticisms are orthogonal to each other, reflecting the very different objectives and perspectives of the heterogeneous set of interest groups and stakeholders in the trade regime.

---

[2] Kee, Nicita, and Olarreaga 2009.

It is useful to classify arguments for institutional reform of the WTO along three dimensions: (a) the rule-making and decision-making process (the 'legislative function'); (b) the management of day-to-day activities (the 'executive function'); and (c) the enforcement of negotiated commitments and rules of the game (the 'judicial function'). Proposals for reform focus on all three functions, but since 2005 increasingly centre on the first. Since its creation in 1995, attempts to expand the coverage of the institution have not been very fruitful. Efforts to negotiate rules on competition, investment, and transparency in government procurement failed. As of the time of writing, the Doha Round has gone on for ten years. Many argue that while this is a serious problem in and of itself, given the opportunity costs of the lack of movement, it also endangers the trade regime.[3] The fear is that without progress on further liberalization there is an increased danger of backsliding: the WTO is often likened to a 'bicycle' that needs to keep moving if it is not to fall over.

This paper reviews proposals for WTO institutional reform as opposed to proposals regarding specific rules for trade policies, criteria for differentiation and special and differential treatment of developing countries, and so forth. Most of the proposals for institutional reform have come from former government and WTO officials, civil society groups, and the academic community.[4] A number of suggestions have been taken up in two expert group reports that considered WTO reform priorities—Sutherland et al. and the Warwick Commission.[5] To date, however, the revealed preference of most WTO members, whether developing or developed, has been to limit reforms to pragmatic, incremental changes in procedures and practices.

The plan of the chapter is as follows. Section 33.2 starts with a summary of some of the key operating principles of the WTO that reform proposals suggest need to be changed. Section 33.3 briefly reviews the economic literature on the rationale for trade agreements, as a benchmark is needed to understand whether proposals for reform will help achieve the underlying objective of WTO members. Many critics impose their own value judgments regarding what they believe the WTO should pursue, or base arguments for reform on the mention of a particular desirable aim listed in the WTO Preamble (e.g. sustainable development, full employment, etc.).[6] An understanding of the preconditions for cooperation in trade is needed to assess whether and how reform proposals will help make cooperation more effective or efficient. Sections 33.4–33.8 then discuss arguments and proposals to reform the WTO. The discussion is organized around the five major functions of the WTO as defined by Article III WTO: (a) to

---

[3] As illustrated in the call by Ernesto Zedillo to 'save the WTO from Doha' (Zedillo 2007).

[4] No attempt is made to be comprehensive in surveying the extensive literature on WTO reform. Reform proposals and analysis of the WTO by the academic community primarily spans scholarship in the fields of international relations, public law and economics. These disciplines utilize distinct frameworks and methods, and often tend to build on (refer to) literature from within their specific discipline, with limited interdisciplinary cross-fertilization.

[5] Sutherland et al. 2004; Warwick Commission 2007.

[6] See, for example, Ismail 2009a, who argues that in his view development must be the objective of the WTO and calls for a discussion in the WTO to reassess what the goals of the institution should be.

facilitate the implementation, administration, and operation of the Agreement; (b) to provide a forum for negotiations; (c) to administer the Dispute Settlement Understanding; (d) to administer the Trade Policy Review Mechanism (TPRM); and (e) to cooperate with the International Monetary Fund (IMF) and World Bank Group to achieve greater coherence in global economic policy-making. Some proposals span more than one of these functions, but this classification is nonetheless a useful organizing device. Section 33.9 concludes.

33.2 CORE ELEMENTS OF THE WTO's MODUS OPERANDI

There are a number of core aspects of the WTO that are the focus of many reform proposals. These include the consensus practice; the 'single undertaking' in multilateral negotiations; the non-discrimination principle; member-driven, 'collective management' through a ministerial conference and various councils comprising the whole membership; a Secretariat without power of initiative; and a 'self-enforcing' dispute settlement system that is limited to maintaining the negotiated balance of concessions, with compliance ultimately a function of (the effectiveness of) the threat of retaliation by the party (parties) winning a case.[7]

Decision-making in the WTO operates by consensus. Voting is technically possible, but in practice does not occur.[8] Consensus implies that any motion or decision can be blocked if any member objects. While in principle this ensures that no country can be steamrollered into accepting decisions or agreements it objects to—giving it leverage to seek either concessions to agree to a matter, or to refuse to consent to a change in the rules of the game—in practice the largest players carry more weight than do small ones.[9] One way small countries seek to increase their weight in decision-making is through coalitions.[10]

In negotiations the analogue to consensus is the single undertaking: 'nothing is agreed until everything is agreed', i.e. the results of a multilateral round are a package deal. Both

---

[7] See Hoekman and Kostecki 2009 for a detailed discussion of the various WTO agreements and disciplines.

[8] See Ehlermann and Ehring 2005 for a discussion of the history of the consensus rule and voting in the GATT/WTO. Article X WTO specifies that if voting occurs—which is on a one member, one vote basis—unanimity is required for amendments relating to general principles such as non-discrimination; a three-quarters majority is needed for interpretations of provisions of the WTO agreements and decisions on waivers; and a two-thirds majority for amendments relating to issues other than general principles. Where not otherwise specified, and consensus cannot be reached, a simple majority vote is sufficient. No member is bound by an amendment that passes a vote if it alters its rights and obligations. In such instances the ministerial conference may decide to request that the member withdraw from the WTO, or to grant it a waiver.

[9] See, e.g. Steinberg 2002.   [10] Narlikar 2003; Grynberg 2006; Odell 2007.

are practices, not formal rules. The consensus practice has a long history in the GATT/WTO, whereas the single undertaking is a practice that was central to the Uruguay Round and the creation of the WTO (i.e. the WTO was a package deal, take it all or leave it). It has been applied in the Doha Round as well.[11]

The non-discrimination principle requires that any concession or commitment be accorded to all members. WTO members may not grant a subset of countries with which they have negotiated concessions better treatment than countries that have not been offered such concessions. The only exception is if members conclude free trade agreements with each other or negotiate a so-called plurilateral agreement. Under such an agreement, a subset of WTO members can agree to specific disciplines that apply only to signatories, and need not apply the associated benefits to non-signatories. However, a plurilateral agreement can only be appended to the WTO on the basis of consensus (and unanimity if there is recourse to voting—Article X:9 WTO). Thus, the plurilateral option offers a mechanism for groups of WTO members to agree to rules in a policy area that is not covered by the WTO, or goes beyond existing disciplines, as long as the membership as a whole perceives this is not detrimental to their interests.

The management of the WTO is collective. The WTO is headed by a ministerial conference of all members that is supposed to meet at least once every two years. Between such meetings the WTO is managed by a general council at the level of officials. This meets about 12 times a year, with WTO members usually represented by delegations based in Geneva. The General Council turns itself, as needed, into a body to adjudicate trade disputes (the Dispute Settlement Body (DSB)) and to review trade policies of the member countries (the Trade Policy Review Body (TPRB)). Three subsidiary councils operate under the general guidance of the General Council: the Council for Trade in Goods, the Council for Trade in Services, and the Council for Trade-Related Aspects of Intellectual Property Rights. Separate committees, working parties, and subcommittees deal with specific subject areas covered by multilateral agreements.

All councils, committees, and so forth, as well as all negotiating groups, are chaired by a WTO member. The only exception is the Trade Negotiations Committee, the body that oversees multilateral trade talks, which is chaired by the Director-General. The Director-General does not have a defined role in the Agreement Establishing the WTO. This is left to the Ministerial Conference to determine, which to date it has not done.

The main actors in day-to-day activities of the WTO are the officials that are affiliated with the delegations of members. Geneva in turn is the hub of a large network of officials, agencies, and ministries in member countries.[12] The member-driven and network nature of the organization puts a considerable strain on the delegations in Geneva and officials in capitals. There are over 5,000 meetings in the WTO every year. This level of activity makes it very difficult, if not impossible, for citizens of members to keep track of what is happening.

---

[11] As already noted, under the GATT contracting parties were free not to sign on to certain parts of what was negotiated in a trade round.

[12] Blackhurst 1998.

At the time of writing there are 157 members. Few, if any, members participate in all meetings and activities. Committees are open to all members, but in practice those that care most about a subject will be most active. WTO practice is for members to organize in informal small groups to develop proposals that may subsequently be put forward to the broader membership, either formally through existing bodies and committees, or informally to other members/groups. In WTO speak this process is described as the 'concentric circles' approach to agenda-setting.

The Secretariat supports the members, providing technical and logistical support when requested by committees or councils. It has very little formal power of initiative. It is prohibited from identifying potential violations of the WTO by members and may not interpret WTO law or pass judgment on the conformity of a member's policy with WTO rules. These are matters that are the sole prerogative of members. Similarly, dispute settlement panels are staffed by members of WTO delegations, or outside experts drawn from a roster that has been pre-approved by the membership. Specific panellists from this roster are generally nominated by the Secretariat.

Dispute settlement in the WTO aims at maintaining the balance of negotiated concessions. If a member is found to have violated a commitment, the remedy is *prospective*: the offending member is simply called upon to bring its measures into compliance. How this should be done is left to the WTO member to determine. There is no requirement to compensate for losses incurred while a violation occurred. In cases where a member does not comply with the DSB, those who won the case may be authorized to retaliate in an amount that is equal in effect to the action that was taken by the country that violated a commitment. This introduces a significant asymmetry in that small countries that cannot affect their terms of trade cannot exercise much pressure on large countries that do not wish to comply with the DSB.

33.3 MATCHING INSTRUMENTS TO OBJECTIVES: WHAT PROBLEMS DO PROPOSED REFORMS FIX?

Economists often stress the importance of the terms of trade in providing a theoretically consistent rationale for the formation of trade agreements. The argument is that countries negotiate away the negative terms-of-trade externalities created by the imposition of trade restrictions in partner countries.[13] A consequence is that agreements will (need to) be among countries that can affect their terms of trade. Small countries will generally have much less power to do so, although if products are differentiated even a small state may be able to affect its terms of trade. As a result of this asymmetry, trade agreements

---

[13] Bagwell and Staiger 2002. As such negative externalities can be created by domestic policies as well, the terms of trade theory also offers guidance regarding what types of policies could be the subject of multilateral negotiations and cooperation.

will tend to reflect the concerns of large countries.[14] An implication of the terms-of-trade theory is that there is no prospect for cooperation on new rules or market access deals if the large countries cannot agree on a mutually beneficial (balanced) exchange of policy commitments. No possible reform of process or the institutional structure of the WTO will make a difference. Calls to put in place mechanisms that will force these countries to 'do the right thing' are irrelevant: the WTO is a self-enforcing agreement; there is no central or supranational enforcement agency. Cooperation must be in the self-interest of all members.[15]

Assume instead that there is a potential agreement that benefits the large players but that a small country opposes this—it wants to get more out of a deal. Given the consensus practice and the single undertaking principle this may block agreement. An obvious solution to this possibility is to shift away from consensus—e.g. shift towards a weighted voting type approach. An empirical question of some importance is how often such 'blocking' in fact occurs given that large countries could either go ahead and accept free riding, or conclude free trade agreements among themselves. We do not observe much of the latter: trade agreements tend to be North–South or South–South; there are no agreements between the major players (EU, US, Japan, China, etc.).

Terms of trade theories cannot explain why small country governments negotiate limits on their own use of trade policies. Another strand of the economic literature provides an alternative rationale: trade agreements may offer a mechanism to governments that want to commit to a set of policies that otherwise may not be (politically) feasible to adopt or maintain.[16] This line of theory has trade agreements serving as a lock-in mechanism or anchor for trade and related policy reforms. By committing to certain rules that bind policies, a government can make its reforms more credible: officials can tell interest groups seeking the (re-)imposition of trade policies that doing so will violate its commitments and generate retaliation by trading partners.

A related strand of theory combines elements of both the terms of trade and commitment theories and stresses domestic political economy dynamics.[17] It builds on a long tradition that starts from the premise that governments seek to maximize political support: they will respond to and seek to satisfy the domestic constituencies that they need to stay in power. Taking as given that governments are conservative in the sense that they put greater weight on prospective losses for groups in society than on the expected

---

[14] Of course, governments of small countries still have an interest in being a member of the WTO because exporters will benefit from the tariffs that larger countries negotiate reciprocally with one another and then extend to all members under the most-favoured nation (MFN) rule. They can also benefit from active participation in the operation of the regime by combining forces and acting as brokers—see e.g. Narlikar 2003, and Odell 2005, 2010.

[15] The economic theories of trade agreements are positive in nature—they seek to understand the preconditions for, and drivers of, cooperation. They are not normative models of how the world should be. Much of the literature suggesting reforms of the WTO is, in contrast, often explicitly normative in nature, frequently disregarding the reality of power relationships and the fact that any trade agreement must be self-enforcing.

[16] For example Tumlir 1985; Maggi and Rodriguez-Clare 1998.   [17] See Ethier 2007.

gains from liberalization, governments have incentives to impose or maintain protection because this raises the incomes of the groups from which they derive political support. If foreign governments could be induced to liberalize, that provides a direct gain for existing exporters. This changes the government's incentives as it affects the balance of political support. A more liberal stance becomes optimal.

Complementary explanations for the formation of trade agreements have been offered in the international relations and political science literature.[18] These place emphasis on the role of power, on domestic political considerations and the structure of institutions, as well as on 'non-economic' objectives such as the avoidance of war. All the more political and political economy driven rationales for trade agreements are conditional on agreements being enforced. This leads back to the central insight of the terms of trade theory of trade agreements, where the incentive to enforce agreements is created by the fact that defection generates an incentive to retaliate. In practice, small countries may not confront a retaliation threat because the incentives for trading partners to invest the required resources are too weak—that is, enforcement costs exceed expected benefits. If this is the case, cooperation is conditional on anchoring reforms in domestic institutions. From a 'WTO reform' perspective this suggests a focus on increasing compliance incentives, be it through external or internal mechanisms. This might revolve around provision of information, enhancing domestic processes to bolster support for ('ownership' of) making trade policy commitments, reducing the costs of—increasing incentives for—enforcement, etc.

A necessary condition for both negotiations and enforcement of agreements is information. Any negotiation requires the parties to understand the others' positions. A process of learning is required to identify what is negotiable and what is not. Negotiations are multilevel games with a complex process of domestic interactions between interest groups (including lobbying, advocacy, etc.) determining what a country can offer/wants. On the enforcement side of the equation information is needed to determine if countries are implementing commitments, or if an action by a partner is a violation. An independent process of monitoring and collective discussion of trade policies can help both identify and diffuse potential disputes. This 'transparency function' can be supplied by an independent secretariat, raising a question of the effectiveness and efficiency of the WTO Secretariat in fulfilling this role.

33.4 OPERATION OF THE WTO

As noted above, the modus operandi of the WTO revolves around regular and numerous meetings of WTO members, generally chaired by a member representative, supported by the Secretariat. Agenda-setting occurs through a decentralized, bottom-up

---

[18] See WTO 2007 for a review.

process ('concentric circles'). Although large players often take the lead, this need not be the case. Small countries often organize themselves into informal groups or more formal coalitions to defend their interests and put forward proposals.

33.4.1 Consensus

Many proposals for reform have focused on the consensus norm. Consensus has been argued to be a major source of inefficiency and deadlock, impeding the ability of the majority to move forward and giving excessive scope for a small minority to block a decision.[19] Conversely, supporters of the consensus norm argue that given 153 members with vast differences in per capita incomes, capacity, and economic interests, consensus is a critical mechanism through which to ensure the legitimacy of the organization and the support that is needed in domestic polities of members.[20] Developing countries in particular are strong supporters of the consensus practice as it provides them with some assurance that they will not be confronted with decisions that may be detrimental to their interests.[21]

A necessary condition for consensus to have the purported benefits is that there is informed participation. In practice, small or poor countries confront serious information and resource constraints that impede effective participation. This can have costs, both in an opportunity forgone sense, and in a direct sense if countries agree (or do not object) to initiatives that have adverse consequences for them. While the value of consensus to smaller and poorer members should not be exaggerated,[22] it does provide a significant element of security.

Three types of proposals have been made. The first is to stick with consensus as a basic practice, but to introduce some procedural changes that would require those countries blocking adoption of a measure in instances where the majority is in favour of proceeding to explain why they are doing so. Specifically, the Sutherland report recommended that a member seeking to block a decision be required to declare in writing that the matter is of vital national interest to it.[23]

---

[19] See, for example, Cottier and Takenoshita 2003, Ehlermann and Ehring 2005, Hufbauer 2005, Lawrence 2006, Steger 2009, Steger and Shpilkovskaya 2010.

[20] See Howse and Nicolaidis 2003, Pauwelyn 2005, Wolfe 2005, 2007, 2009, and Tijmes-Lhl 2009 for analyses and defences of the consensus norm.

[21] For example Ismail 2009a.

[22] Narlikar 2006, for example, argues that the value of the consensus practice to small players is reduced as a result of limited representation, exclusion from the key upstream parts of the concentric circle process (such as Green Room meetings), and intimidation by developed economies (often providers of aid and other forms of assistance). See also Evenett 2005 and Wilkinson 2006. Capacity constraints and the adverse incentive effects of aid dependence are also often mentioned in the literature focusing on the operation of the Dispute Settlement Understanding (DSU) (e.g. Hoekman and Mavroidis 2000; Lawrence 2003; Nordstrom 2005; Nordstrom and Shaffer 2008; Bown and Hoekman 2008).

[23] Sutherland 2004.

A second approach is to shift to a system of weighted voting, or to adopt a 'critical mass' approach. The weighted voting approach is generally linked to the creation of an executive board, but need not be. The critical mass approach has been described as 'a practice where countries refrain from blocking consensus when a critical mass of countries supports a proposed change. This critical mass of countries could be expressed as an overwhelming majority of countries and an overwhelming amount of the trade weight in the world, such as 90 per cent of both of these factors'.[24]

A third set of proposals revolve around the creation of an executive board or committee. There are two flavours to proposals along these lines. One is to emulate the management structure of the IMF or World Bank, in which a board of 20 to 30 representatives is given decision-making powers.[25] The other is to use a board as an instrument through which to identify compromise positions in negotiations, suggest solutions when WTO councils or committees fail to achieve consensus, engage in strategic thinking, and help to set priorities to further the mandate of the organization.[26] In this model the membership would still take decisions on the basis of consensus.[27] Most proposals would make permanent membership of the executive body a function of 'economic weight', with a subset of members serving on a rotating basis to ensure representativeness. Those on the Board would speak on behalf of groups of countries that they were chosen to represent.

Developing countries object strongly to an IMF or World Bank model, as they believe that the consensus principle maximizes their ability to safeguard their interests. There is also little appetite among most developed countries to move in this direction. Thus, if there will be any move towards an executive committee-type structure it is more likely to be on the lines of what has been proposed by Blackhurst and Blackhurst and Hartridge and the 2004 Sutherland report.[28] The latter proposed the establishment of a consultative group of no more than 30 members, in which some members would have permanent membership and others would rotate. The purpose of the group would be to give political guidance to negotiators 'when appropriate' and map out possible areas of agreement/proposals for moving forward on WTO business. Meetings of the group at the senior official level would occur before every ministerial meeting to prepare the ground/agenda, etc. One rationale offered for the creation of such a group was that it would formalize the ad hoc 'mini-Ministerial meetings' that had frequently been called by subsets of WTO members to deal with Doha Round questions. The report argued that

---

[24] Jackson 2001, 74–75.

[25] For example, Matsushita, Schoenbaum, and Mavroidis (2003) call for an executive, decision-making body that reports to the General Council, comprising a mix of permanent and rotating members. Permanent membership would be determined by criteria such as gross domestic product (GDP), population, and share of world trade, with supplementary criteria used to ensure low-income and small countries are represented.

[26] Steger 2009.

[27] Blackhurst (1998) and Schott and Watal (2000) are early proponents of such a mechanism.

[28] Blackhurst 2001; Blackhurst and Hartridge 2004. Blackhurst and Hartridge argued that the WTO needs an 'efficient-size subgroup of members for the purpose of discussing, debating and negotiating draft decisions that can be put to the entire membership for adoption' with criteria to ensure that participation be 'fully transparent, predictable, equitable and legitimate in the eyes of all WTO members'.

formalization of what was in any event emerging on an informal, ad hoc basis would help enhance the effectiveness of a smaller group interaction.[29]

As noted by Pascal Lamy, there is a consensus about consensus among WTO members.[30] The existing provisions for voting are not used, making proposals to shift to different types of voting moot. Wolfe makes a compelling case in favour of consensus, noting that it is difficult to envisage a different decision rule that would do a better job in ensuring the 'ownership' of what is decided or negotiated in national polities.[31] Shifting to a system of weighted voting, or an Executive Board with decision-making powers, would most likely result in a resurgence of the types of critiques that characterized the debates on the WTO in the late 1990s and early 2000s.[32]

33.4.2 Internal transparency and the role of chairs

The 'concentric circles' approach to agenda formation and deliberations in the WTO is cumbersome but has the advantage of allowing those who care most about an issue to launch an initiative. But to be effective and acceptable to members the process requires parties to understand what their interests are, and what the implications of an initiative would be for them, as well as extensive communication and transparency. Once a matter has been put on the agenda of a formal group, the role of the chair becomes particularly significant in ensuring that different views on an issue are reflected and considered.

The critical importance of internal transparency was crystallized by the Seattle Ministerial meeting,[33] and led to many proposals for procedural improvements to ensure that small group meetings (such as the Green Room) are transparent, that consultations be open-ended, and that members are informed about the results of small(er) group meetings on issues that affect the membership as a whole in a timely fashion.[34] Following the Seattle Ministerial meeting the Chairman of the General Council launched a process of consultations on WTO processes. This revealed no strong support for radical reform of the WTO. Members indicated that the system of informal consultations was a fundamental element of the WTO process. A variety of procedural improvements were adopted by the WTO Secretariat in the post-2000 period to enhance internal transparency, many of them along the lines of what had been suggested by observers.[35] Compared to Seattle, subsequent Ministerial meetings were organized in a way that greatly increased transparency, including through briefings of

---

[29] The Sutherland report also proposed increased high-level participation in Geneva talks by capital-based policy-makers, annual meetings of the WTO Ministerial Conference (as opposed to every two years), and a WTO summit of the heads of state of members every five years.

[30] Lamy 2009.

[31] Wolfe 2007, 2009.

[32] Wolfe 2007 concludes a detailed analysis of WTO operating practices with the observation that if the WTO is medieval, it is because the world is as well.

[33] See, e.g. Hoekman and Kostecki 2009 and Wilkinson 2006.

[34] For example Schott and Watal 2000; Luke 2000.   [35] Pedersen 2006.

heads of delegations by Ministers who were appointed to be 'Friends of the Chair' on various negotiating issues.

With very few exceptions, WTO bodies are chaired by a WTO member. Chairs play an important role in the WTO given the limited formal role of the Secretariat.[36] It has been argued that a more empowered Secretariat could help ensure that all views are reflected, that the distributional dimensions of proposals are better understood (made more transparent), and that alternative potential compromises are put on the table. Ismail argues that the WTO should consider the use of 'supranational' chairs drawn from the ranks of the Secretariat where a suitable chair is unavailable from among the members.[37] More generally, Odell notes that there is little in the way of formal terms of reference or a code of conduct for chairs: all that is required in the relevant WTO document addressing this matter is that 'chairpersons should continue the tradition of being impartial and objective, ensuring transparency and inclusiveness in decision-making and consultative processes; and aiming to facilitate consensus'.[38]

33.4.3 The Secretariat

The role of the WTO Secretariat extends beyond merely servicing the membership. As noted by Esty, the Secretariat plays a role in agenda-setting and structuring the interactions that occur in formal meetings.[39] It also acts as the institutional memory for the trading system—an important role given regular turnover of delegations in Geneva and capitals—and provides much of the documentation/drafting for dispute settlement panels.[40]

The Sutherland report called on members to bolster the role of the Secretariat, permitting it to do more in terms of providing intellectual leadership and undertaking policy analysis. Proposals to expand the remit of the Secretariat to strengthen its monitoring role, undertake analysis, and provide better access to data, have been pursued to a greater extent than have suggestions to give the Secretariat greater powers of initiative. As noted by Lamy, echoing the Sutherland report, to be more effective in supporting the trading system the Secretariat needs stronger research, analysis and dissemination capacity, and must do more to compile and publish data on trade and

---

[36] Odell 2005; Tallberg 2008; Ismail 2009b. Chairs also play an important role in dispute settlement panels. Busch and Pelc 2009 find that panels led by experienced chairs are far less likely to have their rulings reversed by the Appellate Body; the experience of the other panellists, by comparison, is inconsequential. The implication they draw is that the WTO would be well served by establishing a pool of permanent chairs.

[37] Ismail 2009a.

[38] Odell 2005.

[39] Esty 2007.

[40] In part, this reflects the fact that panellists fulfil the job on a part-time basis. See Nordstrom 2005 for an analysis of the roles played by the WTO Secretariat.

trade policies.[41] Lamy's vision is one where the WTO becomes more of a source of knowledge and analysis on global trade statistics and policy, thereby becoming more effective in its support for negotiations, monitoring, dispute settlement, technical cooperation, and outreach. The WTO membership has been taking steady steps in this direction, as reflected in the launch of an annual analytical report by the Economic Research and Statistics Division on a trade policy topic; closer collaboration with academic institutions in developing countries, including a programme of WTO 'chairs' (support for academics focusing on training and research in trade); as well as initiatives to expand monitoring (discussed below).

Following the creation of the WTO in 1995, many developing country governments, as well as numerous non-governmental organizations (NGOs) based in both poor and rich countries, suffered from a 'Uruguay Round hangover'—a perception that the results of the Round were unbalanced.[42] Analysis of the outcome of the negotiations suggested that the net benefits for many developing countries in narrow market-access terms were limited, and that the costs of implementation of some WTO disciplines could be significant. The result was a push for more effective and more technical assistance. One response was the creation of a special trust fund in which grants for technical assistance would be placed by donors, with the Secretariat reporting to the WTO Committee on Trade and Development on the use of funds. At the time of writing, the trust fund had an annual budget of some CHF 25 million, equivalent to some 10 per cent of the WTO budget.[43] This has supported an extensive programme of technical assistance seminars in developing countries. While a response to demand, this has imposed a significant burden on WTO staff. Greater reliance on third parties and outsourcing would free up the Secretariat for other tasks.

33.4.4 Access and participation by civil society

An active debate was initiated towards the end of the 1990s on the legitimacy, governance, and coherence of the multilateral trading system. In the first decade of the WTO many NGOs held the view that the WTO did not allow them to express their views and engage with the institution. WTO members countered that the WTO is an intergovernmental organization, and that NGOs should engage on the substance of matters covered by the WTO through the domestic processes that determine national policies and positions. This argument was less than compelling to civil society, given that other organizations such as the OECD, the International Labour Organization (ILO), and the United Nations (UN) had developed mechanisms through which NGOs could be accredited and express their views on substantive issues. NGOs such as Consumers International

---

[41] Lamy 2009.   [42] See, e.g. Finger 2007.
[43] Esty 2007 argues that a more robust structure of administrative law would help improve the institutional effectiveness of the WTO, and overcome perceptions of a 'democratic deficit' and the WTO's reputation for opaque decision-making that is susceptible to special interest manipulation.

proposed that the WTO introduce accreditation of international NGOs to grant them observer status, following the example of other international organizations and release draft agendas of meetings to facilitate national consultation.

Various initiatives were taken by the WTO in response to NGO pressure for greater openness and access. An annual public forum has become one of the platforms for dialogue with NGOs, with participation from around the globe.[44] Decisions by WTO members to derestrict many documents more rapidly, and to make them accessible to the public through the Internet, have done a lot to improve transparency relative to the GATT years. In 2008, a pilot project was implemented granting Geneva-based NGOs permanent access to the WTO premises. Decisions by parties, panels, and the Appellate Body in specific disputes have also increased the scope for NGOs to express views in cases (see below). Overall, the criticism of the WTO by NGOs is today much more muted than ten years ago, reflecting the various steps that have been taken to enhance transparency.

33.4.5 Linkages to national parliaments

A number of commentators and NGOs have argued that the legitimacy of what is negotiated in the WTO would be enhanced if there was more direct and formal involvement of national parliaments in the deliberations of the WTO.[45] Given that legislatures generally must ratify agreements, one rationale for stronger links to parliaments is that it would generate more support for the WTO in national polities. The most far-reaching proposals on this front call for the creation of a 'WTO Parliament' with representatives from all member states.[46] Shaffer addresses the policy arguments for and against the addition of a parliamentary dimension to the WTO.[47] He argues that one criterion to assess the merits of such an initiative is whether it would increase the voice (enhance participation) of developing countries and thus offset some of the asymmetry in power and capacity that prevails in the WTO.

The suggestion for greater engagement by legislators in the WTO has been opposed by many WTO members, including developing countries. Their view is that the WTO is an intergovernmental institution and that negotiating trade policy is a matter that falls in the purview of governments, with the role of national legislatures being to provide the mandate for, and approval of, what is negotiated. Here, as in other areas of proposed reform, the approach that has been taken by WTO members has been pragmatic. Starting in 2001, international parliamentary conferences on the WTO have been organized by the Inter-Parliamentary Union in cooperation with the European Parliament, both in Geneva and at WTO ministerial conferences. A network approach has emerged, with parliamentarians working through bodies such as the Inter-Parliamentary Union to engage on WTO issues.

---

[44] Piewitt 2010.   [45] Mann 2004; Steger 2009.
[46] Bellmann and Gerster 1996.   [47] Shaffer 2004.

33.5 FORUM FOR NEGOTIATIONS

Whereas in the first years of the WTO the focus of institutional reform proposals was mostly on the executive functions of the organization, starting in the mid 2000s concerns were increasingly directed at the efficacy of negotiating procedures and mechanisms.

33.5.1 Agenda-setting and trade negotiating rounds

The trading system historically has developed the rules of the game and defined national commitments through broad 'rounds' of negotiations. The premise of this approach is that by spanning many subjects and products, issue linkages can be made that increase the potential gains from trade. An often remarked upon consequence is that rounds can (and do) take a long time—the more issues, the more complex the negotiation. Many have argued that a smaller negotiation set would reduce the length of negotiations and enhance the interest of the private sector in the WTO.[48] However, the experience to date has been that WTO members have a revealed preference for broader negotiations.

The key issue here is defining an agenda. This generally emerges from informal interactions among WTO members (via the concentric circle/coalition approaches) and/or is determined by prior agreements embedded in the results of past negotiations. Thus, the Uruguay Round agreements called for new negotiations to be launched on agriculture and services in the year 2000. One reason for the launch of the Doha Round was a perception by many WTO members that the prospects of success would be enhanced by expanding the agenda to additional issues.

Getting the agenda 'right' is obviously critical—there must be something for everyone, in the sense that any agenda must include subjects that matter to important constituencies in each WTO member. Establishing the agenda therefore requires extensive consultations within countries and between countries. If the process results in an agenda that does not have broad-based support, or includes issues that are (or are seen to be) zero-sum, the prospect of success will be greatly reduced.

It can be argued that in the case of the Doha Round the agenda was badly crafted, helping to explain why the round has lasted so long. Thus, developing countries and large parts of the global business community were not convinced that extending the WTO to cover competition, investment, and procurement policies would generate meaningful benefits. Having papered over a lack of consensus at the Doha ministerial meeting to include these subjects on the agenda of the new round, Ministers agreed to revisit the question at their next meeting, two years down the road. As a result, the first years of the Doha Round were more about the agenda than substantive negotiations.

---

[48] For example Messerlin 2010.

One lesson from the Doha experience is that the agenda-setting process could benefit from a more formal process of consultation with national stakeholders regarding what matters most to them. At the end of the day trade agreements must be ratified, which implies that they need domestic political support.

33.5.2 Negotiating coin—binding of policies versus liberalization

Policy commitments are the negotiating coin in the WTO—enforceable promises not to use certain policies or not to exceed a certain level of protection for a product or sector. This may not do much to interest the business community if what is being committed to by a government does not imply an actual reduction in barriers to trade. But binding has value: it reduces uncertainty regarding the conditions of competition on a market, which is beneficial to investors. An important source of tension between WTO members concerns what a commitment to bind policy is 'worth'. Many countries may reduce barriers to trade unilaterally in the period between negotiations. How much 'credit' should be given for such autonomous reforms in a subsequent negotiation has been a source of contention. The absence of clarity can have perverse effects in that a government may delay beneficial reforms if it thinks that trading partners will simply 'bank' its reforms and not recognize them as 'concessions' in a future multilateral trade round. Explicit agreement to 'count' unilateral liberalization as much as what a country may agree to liberalize at the end of a round would help remove this distortion.

33.5.3 The single undertaking

One of the premises of the single undertaking rule in multilateral negotiations is that it ensures that all participants will obtain a net benefit from an overall deal. By allowing for issue linkages and requiring a package deal, countries can make trade-offs across issues and increase the overall gains from cooperation. However, the approach also creates potential 'hold-up' problems and can have the effect of inducing negotiators to devote (too) much time to seeking exceptions and exemptions. The failure to conclude the Doha Round has led many to raise questions about the single undertaking approach to negotiations and to propose that WTO members shift towards 'variable geometry'. Proponents argue that a shift back to a club-type approach in considering new disciplines offers the opportunity for a subset of the membership to move forward on an issue, while allowing others to abstain.[49] A difference between proposals to relax the single undertaking constraint is whether this should allow for agreements that apply only to signatories, or whether the most-favoured nation (MFN) principle should continue to apply.

---

[49] For example Lawrence 2006; Levy 2006, 2010; Martin and Messerlin 2007; Jones 2010; Messerlin 2010.

33.5.4 Variable geometry with MFN: critical mass

The notion of critical mass used in the context of negotiations differs from that discussed earlier. It is equivalent to what Schelling called a 'k-group strategy'[50]—seek to identify the minimum number of countries ('K') out of a larger set ('N') that internalize enough of the total potential gains from cooperation for them to permit free riding by the remaining $N–K$ players. The practice has always been a major feature of trade negotiations as a result of the MFN rule: those countries that are asked to make concessions in an area have a clear interest to minimize free riding and will therefore seek to ensure that all the major players are part of a deal. Finger showed that such 'internalization'—defined as the sum of all imports originating in countries with whom a country exchanges concessions as a percentage of total imports of goods on which concessions are made—was some 90 per cent for the US in the Dillon (1960–1) and Kennedy (1964–7) Rounds.[51] A similar ratio was required to conclude the Information Technology Agreement.[52]

As argued by several ex-WTO officials—Gallagher and Stoler and Harbinson, among others—an explicit shift towards 'critical mass' negotiations that aim at agreements that are applied on a MFN basis would move the WTO back towards a negotiating modality that has a proven track record of success.[53] However, the basic question is to what extent this would entail a change in modus operandi.[54] Arguably it would not, as effectively it is how the GATT always operated in the pursuit of market access negotiations. In the case of services, a critical mass approach is de facto the modus operandi.[55] Thus, the approach would only make a difference if applied to the decision-making process at the end of a negotiation, or to approve a rule change—i.e. allowing a majority to move forward without the consent of a (small) minority. This was discussed above.

33.5.5 Variable geometry without MFN: plurilateral agreements

The presumption of the critical mass approach to negotiating agreements is that any agreement must be applied on an MFN basis. An alternative is to relax the non-discrimination constraint and let a subset of countries conclude agreements that they apply only to fellow signatories.[56] Such plurilateral agreements are already allowed for in the WTO, although there is effectively only one such agreement in effect: the Government Procurement Agreement (GPA).[57]

---

[50] Schelling 1978.   [51] Finger 1974, 1979.   [52] Hoekman and Kostecki 2009.
[53] Gallagher and Stoler 2009; Harbinson 2009.   [54] Wolfe 2009.
[55] Hoekman and Mattoo 2010.   [56] Levy 2010.
[57] The only other plurilateral agreement, on civil aircraft, is no longer effective following US objections to what it regarded as excessive launch aid and other support for the development of the Airbus A380 by the EU, and the launch of a formal dispute. See Hoekman and Kostecki 2009.

Plurilateral agreements are a vehicle for like-minded countries to cooperate in areas not (yet) addressed by the WTO. They allow countries not willing to consider new disciplines in a policy area to opt out. Accommodating diversity in interests through greater use of plurilateral agreements was one of the recommendations of the Warwick Commission report. Lawrence discusses what he calls the 'club of clubs' option, and argues that this approach can help the WTO address the diverging interests of its members in an efficient way.[58] He suggests a number of criteria, including that:

- clubs be restricted to subjects that are clearly trade-related
- any new agreement is open to all members in the negotiation stage—i.e. participation in the development of rules should not be limited to likely signatories
- club members be required to use the Dispute Settlement Understanding (DSU) to settle disputes, with eventual retaliation being restricted to the area covered by the agreement (as is the case under the GPA).

While greater use of plurilateral agreements will result in a multi-tier system with differentiated commitments and some erosion of the MFN principle—as club members would have the right to restrict benefits to other members—there is already significant differentiation in the level of obligations across countries. A constraint in pursuing the plurilateral route is that the incorporation of a plurilateral agreement into the WTO requires unanimity. Thus, for this approach to become feasible a necessary condition is likely to be that this rule be relaxed.[59] Others argue that no such change is needed and that non-members should be comfortable with the terms of any plurilateral agreement that is introduced.[60] Wolfe raises a number of objections to the 'club of clubs' idea, noting that clubs would be 'parasitic on limited WTO resources', will invariably include OECD countries that often will already have achieved whatever level of cooperation/discipline is suggested for a new issue, and that many non-OECD countries are not going to have the capacity to participate in negotiations that will set a precedent.[61] Clubs will define the rules of the game in an area that will be difficult to change subsequently if and when initial non-signatories decide to participate.[62]

33.5.6 Accession

Some two dozen countries have joined since the WTO was established, the majority of them developing and transition economies. The process of accession to the WTO is a long, hard road for most countries, often requiring major policy changes, adoption of new legislation, and establishment or strengthening of domestic institutions. This compares to the accession at a stroke of a pen that applied to former colonies when they acceded to GATT upon independence—the result of Article XXVI:5(c) GATT, a provision that expired with the creation of the WTO. A December 2002 decision by the

---

[58] Lawrence 2006.   [59] Tijmes-Lhl 2010.   [60] Lawrence 2006.
[61] Wolfe 2007.   [62] Hoekman 2005.

General Council called for the exercise of restraint by WTO members in seeking concessions and commitments from acceding least-developed countries (LDCs). In practice, this decision has not appeared to have had much impact—the post-2002 accession process for LDCs has remained arduous. Of the 29 countries in the accession queue at the end of 2009, 16 had been engaged in the process for over a decade.

Alternative approaches that have been put forward in the literature would use the WTO accession process more as a vehicle to identify and implement national reforms that reduce trade costs and improve competitiveness. Imposing a one-size-fit-all set of legal obligations through a long and costly accession process entails a potentially serious opportunity cost for governments of small, poor countries (in terms of scarce administrative capacity/personnel) while not necessarily generating much in the way of benefits for traders—thus resulting in less 'ownership' and support of the institution.[63]

33.6 Administering the Dispute Settlement Understanding

The operation of the WTO dispute settlement system is the subject of a huge literature. A review of the DSU launched in 2000 (based on a Uruguay Round Ministerial Decision) became part of the Doha Round agenda, although it is not formally part of the single undertaking. The review generated various proposals to strengthen the DSU through:

- the establishment of a permanent panel body (i.e. a true first instance court)
- explicit multilateral review of bilateral settlements
- additional rights for third parties in disputes
- making the dispute settlement process more transparent—e.g. by making the taking of evidence open to the public.[64]

What follows briefly summarizes some of the proposals for reform. Most members and observers agree that the system—warts and all—is functioning reasonably well.

Professionalization of the panel stage. As mentioned above, panellists are part-timers, nominated by the Secretariat from a roster that has been approved by WTO members. Proposals have been made for a permanent body of panellists, on the basis that this would improve the quality and consistency of reports and reduce the discretion of/reliance on the Secretariat in the selection of panellists and drafting of findings.

Standing. Only governments can bring disputes in the WTO. This implies that those directly affected by a violation of a WTO commitment—exporters—cannot go to the WTO directly. They must convince their government to bring the case, which may decide that it is not in the general interest to do so. This arguably reduces the relevance of the WTO to the trade community. One option to address this potential problem is to give export interests

---

[63] Jones 2010.   [64] Esty 2007.

direct access to the WTO. In an analysis of the likely effects of such a change in modus oper-andi, Levy and Srinivasan argue that in addition to the obvious point that a government may have good reasons not to pursue a trade case from a national welfare perspective, removing a government's discretion to decide whether to prosecute a case can also make it more difficult to make commitments in the first place.[65]

Third parties. WTO members can participate in disputes as third parties. (By partici-pating as a third party a WTO member reserves its rights in a dispute and can make submissions to the panel.) In the DSU review, a number of proposals were made to make it easier for any country to participate in disputes, including in the consultations stage. The DSU limits participation by third parties in consultations to members that have a substantial trade interest (Article 4.11 DSU). Busch and Reinhardt argue that widening access for third parties may make it more difficult to negotiate a settlement.[66] Thus, the apparent advantages on greater inclusion and 'multilateralization' of disputes may come at the cost of fewer early settlements and more disputes. This matters because early set-tlements tend to be 'better', not just in the sense of generating compliance at lower cost, but also because they result in greater concessions than if a case is litigated.[67]

Remedies. A government found to be in violation of the WTO is generally told to bring its measures into compliance with the rules. This may not provide enough incen-tive to the private sector to pursue a dispute given the length of time associated with the process—some three years—and the lack of any prospect for compensation for damages incurred. WTO members have been unwilling to go down the compensation track due to uncertainty regarding the possible repercussions (potential liability). Some countries have also argued that their legal systems prohibit compensation. Historically, develop-ing countries have favoured the introduction of rules that would allow for claims for monetary damages to be paid to them in instances where illegal measures are imposed against them by industrialized nations. Not surprisingly, GATT contracting parties always rejected this. 'Money damages, said the developed countries, were simply outside the realm of the possible. In effect, they were saying, GATT was never meant to be taken seriously.'[68]

---

[65] Levy and Srinivasan 1996. Private parties can participate in dispute settlement to a limited extent through so-called amicus curiae briefs. This was a hotly contested matter in the early WTO years, but is an example where the WTO has been responsive. Multiple decisions by the Appellate Body have ruled that such briefs may be considered by panels as they have the power to seek information and advice, and are free to ignore any brief sent to them. Many WTO members have opposed consideration by panels of such briefs on the basis that the WTO is government to government. Rulings on this matter have been regarded as an example of the adjudicating bodies overstepping their mandate. However, such briefs have proven to be useful. For example, in the *EC–Sardines* dispute the brief submitted by the UK Consumers' Association was an important piece of evidence that showed the EU claim—that the contested measure was justified on the basis of consumer protection—to be spurious (Hoekman and Kostecki, 2009).

[66] Busch and Reinhardt 2006.

[67] Busch and Reinhardt 2001.

[68] Hudec 2002. The DSU review generated a number of proposals by developing countries for retroactive remedies, including payment of legal costs by the losing party. However, such proposals were all limited to situations where a WTO member does not implement a DSB ruling.

Enforcement capacity. There are asymmetric incentives for countries to deviate from the WTO, as the ultimate threat that can be made against a member that does not comply with the DSB is retaliation. Small countries cannot credibly threaten this because raising import barriers will have little impact on the target market, while being costly in welfare terms. A possible way out of this dilemma is for small trading nations affected by a dispute to form alliances and retaliate as a group whenever one of the members is affected. More generally, one can conceive of the rules being enforced through retaliation by all WTO members, not just affected members. However, under WTO rules, only countries with a trade interest may bring a case. Those not affected cannot participate.

Collective retaliation—a standard recommendation by economists for many years—has always been resisted by WTO members on the basis that the objective is not to punish, but to maintain a balance of rights and obligations (the reciprocal bargain). A practical problem with collective retaliation is that it implies a direct intrusion in sovereignty—the WTO would be requiring its members to raise tariffs. This explains why proposals along these lines[69] have not gone anywhere.

A number of suggestions have been made in the DSU review and in the literature to address both the asymmetric retaliation capacity constraint, and the economic inefficiency/costs of raising tariffs. An innovative proposal to address both problems was suggested by Mexico in 2003: permit WTO members to trade their rights for retaliation in instances where a losing party refuses to implement a ruling. Bagwell, Mavroidis, and Staiger argue this makes sense from the perspective of developing countries as long as the non-complying party can also bid for the rights.[70] However, they stress that their analysis does not imply that introducing the possibility of tradable remedies into the WTO system is necessarily a good idea given the likely political ramifications of a government imposing WTO-sanctioned retaliatory tariffs against other governments with whom it has no unresolved WTO dispute.

A basic problem with retaliation is that it involves raising barriers to trade, which is generally detrimental to the interests of the country that does so. Lawrence has suggested a shift to trade compensation and proposed adoption of what he terms contingent liberalization commitments.[71] In a trade round, WTO members would designate sectors or methods for liberalization in the event that they should fail to comply with DSB findings. This would make retaliation redundant, thus improving global welfare, and level the playing field by addressing the problem of asymmetric capacity to retaliate.

An alternative is direct compensation. Bronckers and van den Broek argue in favour of financial payments between governments to address 'contract violations', and note that there are examples of this in the trade area, in particular bilateral trade agreements.[72] Thus, free trade agreements (FTAs) between the US and Australia, Chile, and Singapore, as well as the Dominican Republic–Central America Free Trade Agreement (DR–CAFTA) provide for fines (monetary compensation) when intellectual property rights are violated.

---

[69] For example Pauwelyn 2000.   [70] Bagwell, Mavroidis, and Staiger 2006.
[71] Lawrence 2003.   [72] Bronckers and van den Broek 2005.

A practical advantage of financial transfers is that they do not need to be applied on an MFN basis. However, a number of arguments have been made suggesting that, in practice, compensation may not do much to alleviate the 'retaliation constraint' and could have the perverse effect of increasing non-compliance with the WTO.[73]

Resource constraints and costs of dispute settlement. There are obvious asymmetries in capacity and resources between WTO members that affect their ability to use the DSU. Article 27:2 DSU calls for technical assistance to be provided to developing countries by the WTO Secretariat. The Secretariat's ability to satisfy this mandate is very limited, in part because assistance can only be provided *after* a member has decided to submit a dispute to the WTO. The ability of developing countries to use the DSU was enhanced with the creation of the Advisory Centre on WTO Law (ACWL), one of the few concrete outcomes of the 1999 Seattle ministerial meeting. Many proposals have been made that would complement such efforts to augment access to legal expertise by reducing the need for it. Examples include putting in place a 'fast-track' mechanism for smaller disputes—what Nordstrom and Shaffer call a small claims procedure[74]—under which disputes involving only a small value of trade would be dealt with by a standing body of panellists on an expedited time frame with decisions not subject to appeal and remedies that include payment of damages—i.e. binding arbitration. Other possibilities that have been proposed include an ombudsman or 'special prosecutor'[75] that would have the mandate to identify and contest potential WTO violations on behalf of developing countries. Such outsourcing of enforcement could help address both the resource constraints and the incentive problems (fear of cross-issue linkage) that may impede developing country governments from pursuing cases. Although cases brought by the special prosecutor could not be backed by the threat of retaliation (as they are not brought by or on behalf of a government), findings against a WTO member could generate moral pressure to bring measures into conformity.

Summing up, many proposals have been made to improve the dispute settlement system. A recurring theme in the economic analyses of the relatively weak enforcement mechanisms in the WTO is that this is endogenous—it reflects the incomplete nature of the WTO contract.[76] As a result, governments do not want to subject themselves to a process where they may be subject to penalties that they deem inappropriate given the absence of *ex ante* specificity on the rules that will apply. Given that countries will be both complainants and respondents over time, Ethier argues that this gives governments an incentive to agree to remedies that are limited in scope,[77] i.e. one that does no more than maintain the original negotiated balance of concessions. Stronger enforcement—whether

---

[73] Mercurio, 2008. Limão and Saggi 2008 show that a system of monetary fines that is supported by the threat of tariff retaliation is more efficient than one based on retaliation alone, but note that if the ultimate threat to enforce compensation payments is to raise tariffs, nothing will have been achieved. In order to make a system of monetary compensation 'work' without the threat of retaliation, agreement is needed *ex ante* to contribute to a multilateral 'escrow account' (in effect, each WTO member would post a bond).

[74] Nordstrom and Shaffer 2008.   [75] Hoekman and Mavroidis 2000; Warwick Commission 2007.
[76] Horn, Maggi and Staiger 2010.   [77] Ethier 2009.

it takes the form of more effective remedies, greater collective action, expansion of standing, etc.—can have the perverse effect of inducing countries to make fewer commitments in the first place, resulting in an outcome that is inferior to one where there is weaker enforcement, in the sense that the expected benefits of cooperation are higher.[78] However, taking the set of commitments that governments are willing to make as given, there remains an important asymmetry in the capacity of WTO members to participate in the dispute settlement mechanism. The cotton dispute between Brazil and the United States is illustrative: the US agreed to provide some compensation to Brazil to avoid imposition of retaliatory measures, but did not extend this to the West African cotton producers that were equally affected by the illegal US subsidies. The latter were not formal co-complainants and in any event did not have the capacity to retaliate.[79]

33.7 TRANSPARENCY: THE TRADE POLICY REVIEW MECHANISM, NOTIFICATIONS, AND SURVEILLANCE

Transparency is a critical input into WTO processes as well as an important output of the organization. Many of the WTO processes and requirements aim at the generation of information through notification requirements, formal surveillance, the possibility of cross-notification, review of proposed measures in committees, etc. There are over 200 notification requirements embodied in the various WTO agreements and mandated by Ministerial and General Council decisions.[80] The Secretariat is required to provide a listing of notification requirements and members' compliance on an ongoing basis, and to circulate this semi-annually to all members. It is generally recognized that members are not taking notification requirements seriously enough—in many cases notifications are incomplete, and are often not made on a timely basis when they occur.

The WTO has important surveillance functions. The membership as a whole periodically reviews the trade regimes of members through the Trade Policy Review Mechanism (TPRM). The reviews are supplemented by an annual report by the Director-General that provides an overview of developments in the international trading environment. In recent years, two initiatives have been taken to improve the surveillance function: a December 2006 decision by the General Council to provisionally establish a new transparency mechanism for preferential trade agreements (PTAs), and an initiative under the auspices of the trade policy review (TPR) to monitor trade policy responses to the financial crisis that had erupted in late 2008. The latter followed on the creation of an internal task force by the Director-General to assess the trade implications of the crisis.

---

[78] Lawrence 2003.   [79] The two factors are, of course, interrelated. See Baffes 2010.
[80] Hoekman and Kostecki 2009.

The crisis monitoring initiative revealed that the Secretariat could not rely on notifications to the WTO for up-to-date information, and that publication of the analysis was important to improve quality and coverage.[81]

The TPR process for WTO members has had less impact than originally envisaged when it was put in place. In a recent analysis, Ghosh concludes that reviews do not generate peer pressure and are often silent on important matters—as reflected in a limited correlation between disputes initiated against a country, and whether these were identified in a TPR report. In part, this is explained by Secretariat staffing and resource constraints.[82]

Many economists have long argued that the public good of information is currently underprovided by the WTO, and that this reduces its value as a tool to promote better policies in members.[83] Large lacunae in information exist on a variety of relevant policies affecting international integration. Even in the area where information is the best— barriers to goods trade—the focus of data collection (and thus analysis) is mostly on statutory MFN tariffs. Data on the types of non-tariff policies that are increasingly used by countries—such as subsidies or excessively burdensome product standards—are not collected on a comprehensive and regular basis. Matters are much worse when it comes to information on policies affecting services trade. Steps to remedy these gaps — through strengthening and more effective enforcement of notification requirements, cross-notification, as well as direct collection of data (including from secondary sources)—are a precondition for better policy analysis and monitoring of policies. For the Secretariat to do more to compile data on a comprehensive basis, WTO members must give it the mandate and resources to do so, and permit the results to be made publicly available in a format that lends itself to analysis by third parties.[84]

For greater transparency of policies and outcomes to have an impact on policy in WTO members it is important that it feeds into, and is used in, domestic policy formation and assessment processes, and is relevant for traders and other stakeholders in each country. Greater involvement of think tanks, policy institutes, and private sector associations in both the production and dissemination process of TPRs would increase their impact at the national level. One way of stimulating greater engagement would be for WTO members to commit to establish an entity that would have the mandate to review

---

[81] The first WTO monitoring report was kept restricted. The lack of public provision of information by the WTO in the early stage of the crisis played a role in inducing other entities to step in, most prominently the Global Trade Alert, a joint venture of think tanks around the world.

[82] Ghosh 2010.

[83] See, e.g. Messerlin 2010; Stoeckel and Fisher 2008.

[84] Hoekman and Kostecki 2009. An alternative is to bolster transparency through institutions that extend beyond the WTO membership. Proposals have been made to create an international public interest body that would act as a forum to explore the technical (economic, scientific) and social impacts of WTO rules and national trade policies. Such a body could also analyse aspects of specific contentious issues or proposed areas for action at the WTO (Hoekman and Mavroidis 2000). Cottier 2007 proposes the creation of a consultative committee comprising a mix of officials and outside experts that would act as a think tank and develop conceptual ideas and proposals on systemic questions.

and report on national trade and related regulatory policies. A good example of a model that has proven to be very effective is the Australian Productivity Commission.

33.8 ENHANCING COHERENCE OF GLOBAL ECONOMIC POLICY-MAKING

A precondition for greater coherence in international and national trade-related policy-making is that WTO rules support development, are *seen* to do so by stakeholders, and that WTO rules are complemented by supply-side initiatives to address trade capacity constraints, supported by 'aid for trade'.[85] Clearly the substance of WTO disciplines—which is not the focus of this paper—matters a lot. But the importance of complementary inputs ('flanking measures') illustrates why enhanced coherence of policies is a legitimate concern: the WTO has no financial resources to help poor members improve their trade capacity—this must come from private investment, governments, and development organizations.

Significant achievements during the Doha Round were the launch of a multilateral aid for trade initiative and the establishment of the Enhanced Integrated Framework for trade-related technical assistance. Although not formally tied to the negotiations and not legally enforceable, these initiatives signify recognition on the part of the membership that market access and rules were not enough. What the aid for trade initiative did was to engage development agencies (bilateral and multilateral) more in the trade integration agenda and raise the profile of trade issues in the process of determining priorities for investment and policy reform at the national level—an example of the WTO fulfilling its coherence mandate.[86]

The trade facilitation negotiations in the Doha Round illustrate how the WTO can be used by developing countries to make a difference on the ground for traders and producers. A key innovation that was introduced in the trade facilitation talks by developing countries was to link implementation of any agreement to the provision of financial and technical assistance. Another feature of the negotiations was to engage the specialized agencies with expertise in the area—such as the World Customs Organization, the World Bank, the United Nations Conference on Trade and Development (UNCTAD), and the IMF—in the process. These agencies, together with the WTO, undertook assessments at country level of the trade facilitation situation, gaps, and priorities. The process raised national awareness of the importance of trade facilitation. This awareness raising affected the development (donor) community as well. As a result, the number of projects

---

[85] Hoekman 2002.

[86] Winters 2007 argues that coherence starts (and mostly ends) at home in that national governments must define priorities and engage with the various international organizations extant to pursue their objectives.

and level of resources allocated to this area increased significantly relative to the late 1990s and early 2000s. Independent of what happens with the Doha Round, this is a positive outcome that is due in part to the launch of the negotiations and the focal point they provided.

The focus of the WTO is primarily on discriminatory policies, not on the substance of domestic regulation (the Agreement on Trade-Related Aspects of Intellectual Property Rights (TRIPS) being the major exception). Insofar as the WTO deals with regulatory 'behind the border' policies, the aim is to ensure that these are not impediments to market access (are applied on a non-discriminatory basis, and are not more trade-restrictive than necessary). The specifics of regulation are left to the discretion of governments. In practice, the 'benign neglect' of domestic regulation implies that there are no assurances that liberalization will in fact be beneficial (increase national welfare) as trade negotiations are not concerned with the adequacy of national regulation and enforcement institutions.

Greater effort by WTO members to put in place mechanisms to increase information and dialogue on regulatory impacts and alternative options/good practices is needed to complement the WTO negotiating process. International relations scholars—e.g. Abbott and Snidal, Chayes and Chayes—have argued that 'soft law' mechanisms are needed to sustain cooperation.[87] These can aim at learning about an issue, sharing experiences with regulation and reform, generation of information on what has been done in different countries, what works and why, and what did/does not. An important function of such mechanisms is to bring in sectoral regulators who may not think about trade, but are the 'owners' of the policies that affect trade opportunities. Learning is critical when it comes to the substance of policy rules—officials and stakeholders need to understand what the implications are of a given proposed rule and how it will impact on the economy. Establishment of forums aimed at fostering a substantive, evidence/analysis-based discussion of the impacts of sector-specific regulatory policies could help build a common understanding of where there are large potential gains from opening markets to greater competition, the preconditions for realizing such gains, and options to address possible negative distributional consequences of policy reforms. This need not be done in or by the WTO. Existing institutions that perform such functions include the Asia-Pacific Economic Cooperation (APEC) and the OECD. The challenge is to extend such mechanisms to cover all interested countries, which may be most effectively pursued by building on existing regional instruments.[88]

33.9 CONCLUSION

On the occasion of his reappointment as Director-General of the WTO, Pascal Lamy argued that no major surgery or overhaul was needed in terms of the governance of the institution; instead, there was 'rather a long to-do list to strengthen the global trading

---

[87] Abbott and Snidal 2000; Chayes and Chayes 1995.   [88] Hoekman and Mattoo 2010.

system'.[89] Others disagree. Those calling for more structural reforms span a wide spectrum, including ex-WTO officials, negotiators, and a significant cross section of academics.

The fact that the WTO was seen to be a closed shop in its early days, and did a poor job of organizing Ministerial Conferences, gave rise to numerous proposals to improve external and internal transparency. Many changes on this front were in fact made, and most observers would recognize that the WTO has responded to the criticisms that were generated in the run-up and aftermath of Seattle. Despite a large number of suggestions to bolster the DSU, most members appear to be satisfied with the status quo in this area. Concerns with the WTO more recently have centred more on the apparent inability to get to 'yes' in the Doha Round. Proposals to address what analysts regard as contributing factors to the failure of efforts to conclude a deal have centred on the single undertaking practice and consensus-based decision-making.

It is not at all clear, however, that suggestions to move away from these norms would be effective. There are strong reasons why these practices have become core WTO operating principles. The fact of the matter is that the lack of progress in the Doha Round reflects the assessment of major players that what has emerged on the table is not of sufficient interest to them—it is not that a small group of small countries are holding up a deal. Trade agreements are self-enforcing treaties: if the large players do not see it in their interest to deal, no amount of fiddling with alternative institutional arrangements will make a difference. Any outcome, even if endorsed by a majority, will not be implemented if one or more large countries find it unacceptable.

Some of the proposals for institutional reform of the WTO appear to ignore incentive constraints. The WTO is an incomplete contract. One result is that governments have a revealed preference for maintaining tight control over the functioning of the organization. There are good reasons why there seems to be a 'consensus on consensus', panellists are not full-time professionals, why dispute settlement is strictly an intergovernmental affair and remedies are not retrospective, why chairs of WTO bodies are drawn from the membership, why the Secretariat has limited right of initiative, etc. Proposals to reduce the role and influence of individual members are therefore not likely to have much resonance. Indeed, much of the economic analysis of specific proposals for WTO reform suggests that the effects of moving away from the status quo on the incentives to cooperate may be perverse, reducing the willingness to agree to rules and to make commitments.[90]

Given that there is already significant scope to apply critical mass and analogous approaches that allow differentiation across the membership, these considerations suggest reform efforts could more productively centre on mechanisms to assist in the process of 'getting to yes'. The various proposals to establish a consultative body of some

---

[89] Lamy 2009.

[90] Indeed, some have argued that the increased 'legalization' of the WTO relative to the GATT has already had that effect, in part by putting too much of a burden on the DSU. See, e.g. Barfield 2001, 2010 and Evenett 2010.

type do not touch on the sovereignty of individual WTO members. A consultative entity could play a variety of roles, ranging from helping to define a negotiating agenda, to identifying possible compromises and trade-offs. It could also contribute to the needed process of (re)considering what the role of the WTO should be as the agenda shifts increasingly towards 'behind the border' policies.

Information, knowledge, and understanding of the effects of trade and regulatory policy are critical inputs into international cooperation. This applies to the agenda-setting, the negotiating, and the implementation-cum-monitoring stages of trade agreements. Whereas export interests have an incentive to monitor implementation of agreements by trading partners, a key insight of the economic literature on trade agreements as domestic commitment devices is that there must be domestic enforcement if the country is small.[91] Not enough attention has been devoted to this by the WTO, and the literature on WTO reform.

More and better data on applied policies, on the countries affected/targeted, and the specific products (tariff lines) involved is a public good. This public good is underprovided by the WTO, a gap that is only partly offset by efforts by other organizations (such as UNCTAD, the International Trade Centre (ITC), and the World Bank) and civil society initiatives such as the Global Trade Alert (see http://www.globaltradealert.org/). The 2008–09 financial crisis revealed the importance of timely data on trade policies, trade finance and trade flows—and that there were important lacunae in all three areas. Generation, compilation, and publication of such information arguably should be a core task of the WTO and thus the focus of institutional reform, including clarification/ strengthening of notification requirements and more regular monitoring of—and reporting on—compliance.

The negotiation literature stresses that negotiators need to learn about the preferences and interests of other parties, as well as their own, a process that takes time. Learning is also critical when it comes to the substance of policy rules—it often may not be clear to officials and to stakeholders what the implications are of a given rule and how it will affect their policy options. Analysis of reform should focus more on how to bolster the role of the WTO in promoting this 'learning dimension'. Better understanding and related mobilization of domestic constituencies in favour of specific policies and policy disciplines will also benefit negotiations and enforcement, in part by identifying where the traditional mechanism of negotiating binding, enforceable disciplines is appropriate, and where it is not.[92] This is a non-trivial challenge as it requires institutional mechanisms that encourage dialogue and communication, informed by objective analysis and country experiences.

Whether such mechanisms can be created within the WTO is an open question given the culture of negotiation and the mercantilist spirit that often appears to dominate

---

[91] Bown and Hoekman 2005.
[92] See, e.g. Hoekman and Vines 2007, Wolfe 2007, Feketekuty 2010, and Hoekman and Mattoo 2010 for elaborations on this theme.

interactions between members.[93] But complementary mechanisms are clearly needed to promote regular dialogue and cooperation on regulatory matters as these are increasingly the source of market segmentation and the focus of concern of firms. One explanation for the proliferation of deeper integration (regional) agreements is that the institutions that are associated with such arrangements focus much more explicitly on this agenda than does the WTO. Even if there are no binding (legally enforceable) rules (as is the case in APEC for example, and many of the provisions of association agreements negotiated between the EU and trading partners), the working groups, committees, and councils that operate under the auspices of such initiatives over time help to promote a process of gradual improvement and convergence in regulatory regimes. The challenge looking forward is to determine whether, how, and to what extent the WTO can play a role in 'multilateralizing' what is happening in regional and other forums, and fill the gaps in terms of what is not being (and cannot be) done among subsets of countries.

REFERENCES

Abbott, K., and D. Snidal. 2000. Hard and Soft Law in International Governance. *International Organization* 53 (3):421–56.

Auboin, M. 2009. Restoring Trade Finance During a Period of Financial Crisis: Stock-taking of Recent Initiatives. WTO Working Paper ERSD-16. Geneva: World Trade Organization.

Baffes, J. 2010. Learning from the 'Cotton Problem': Settling Trade Disputes. Carnegie International Economic Bulletin. Available from <(http://www.carnegieendowment.org/publications/index.cfm?fa=view&id=41003)>. Accessed 5 November 2011.

Bagwell, K., P. Mavroidis, and R. Staiger. 2006. The Case for Tradable Remedies in WTO Dispute Settlement. In *Economic Development and Multilateral Trade Cooperation*, edited by S. Evenett and B. Hoekman, 395–414. London: Palgrave-McMillan.

Bagwell, K., and R. Staiger. 2002. *The Economics of the World Trading System*. Cambridge: MIT Press.

Barfield, C. 2001. *Free Trade, Sovereignty and Democracy*. Washington DC: American Enterprise Institute.

Barfield, C. 2010. Overreach at the WTO. VoxEU (30 September). Available from <http://voxeu.org/index.php?q=node/5581>. Accessed 5 November 2011.

Bellmann, C., and R. Gerster. 1996. Accountability in the World Trade Organization. *Journal of World Trade* 30 (6):31–74.

Blackhurst, R. 1998. The Capacity of the WTO to Fulfill Its Mandate. In *The WTO as an International Organization*, edited by A. Krueger, 31–58. Chicago: University of Chicago Press.

---

[93] Recent experience suggests the WTO can play an effective role in facilitating exchanges of information. In the 2009–09 crisis it used a WTO Expert Group on Trade Finance to bring together representatives of the financial sector active in trade finance, multilateral banks, and export credit agencies. This helped lead to a multilateral initiative under G20 auspices to expand support for trade finance during the crisis (Auboin, 2009).

Blackhurst, R. 2001. Reforming WTO Decision Making: Lessons from Singapore and Seattle. In *The World Trade Organization Millennium Round: Freer Trade in the Twenty-First Century*, edited by K. Deutsch and B. Speyer, 295–310. London: Routledge.

Blackhurst, R., and D. Hartridge. 2004. Improving the Capacity of WTO Institutions to Fulfill Their Mandate. *Journal of International Economic Law* 7 (3):705–16.

Bown, C., and B. Hoekman. 2005. WTO Dispute Settlement and the Missing Developing Country Cases: Engaging the Private Sector. *Journal of International Economic Law* 8 (4):861–90.

Bown, C., and B. Hoekman. 2008. Developing Countries and Enforcement of Trade Agreements: Why Dispute Settlement Is Not Enough. *Journal of World Trade* 42 (1):177–203.

Bronckers, M., and N. van den Broek. 2005. Financial Compensation in the WTO. *Journal of International Economic Law* 8 (1):101–26.

Busch, M., and K. Pelc. 2009. Does the WTO Need a Permanent Body of Panelists? *Journal of International Economic Law* 12 (3):579–94.

Busch, M., and E. Reinhardt. 2001. Bargaining in the Shadow of Law: Early Settlements in GATT/WTO Disputes. *Fordham International Law Journal* 24 (1):158–72.

Busch, M., and E. Reinhardt. 2006. Three's a Crowd: Third Parties and WTO Dispute Settlement. *World Politics* 58 (3):446–77.

Chayes, A., and A. H. Chayes. 1995. *The New Sovereignty: Compliance with International Regulatory Agreements*. Boston: Harvard University Press.

Cottier, T. 2007. Preparing for Structural Reform in the WTO. *Journal of International Economic Law* 10 (3):497–508.

Cottier, Thomas, and Satoko Takenoshita. 2003. The Balance of Power in WTO Decision-Making: Towards Weighted Voting in Legislative Response. *Aussenwirtschaft* 58: 171–96.

Ehlermann, C., and L. Ehring. 2005. Decision-Making in the World Trade Organization: Is the Consensus Practice of the World Trade Organization Adequate for Making, Revising and Implementing Rules on International Trade? *Journal of International Economic Law* 8 (1):1–75.

Esty, D. 2007. Good Governance at the World Trade Organization: Building a Foundation of Administrative Law. *Journal of International Economic Law* 10 (3):509–27.

Ethier, W. 2007. The Theory of Trade Policy and Trade Agreements: A Critique. *European Journal of Political Economy* 23: 605–23.

Ethier, W. 2009. Trade Agreements and Dispute Settlement in the WTO System. In *Trade Disputes and the Dispute Settlement Understanding of the WTO: An Interdisciplinary Assessment*, edited by H. Beladi and E. K. Choi, 349–67. Bingley, UK: Emerald Group Publishing.

Evenett, S. 2005. Can the WTO's System of Governance Rise to the Challenge of Sustainable Development? Available from <http://www.ycsg.yale.edu/focus/gta/wto_rise.pdf>. Accessed 5 November 2011.

Evenett, S. 2010. A Future Agenda for EU Trade Policy as if the Real World Really Mattered. VoxEU (25 September). Available from <http://www.voxeu.org/index.php?q=node/5560>. Accessed 5 November 2011.

Feketekuty, G. 2010. Needed: A New Approach to Reduce Regulatory Barriers to Trade. VoxEU (19 June). Available from <http://www.voxeu.org/index.php?q=node/5208>. Accessed 5 November 2011.

Finger, J. M. 1974. GATT Tariff Concessions and the Exports of Developing Countries. *The Economic Journal* 84 (335):566–75.

Finger, J. M. 1979. Trade Liberalization: A Public Choice Perspective. In *Challenges to a Liberal International Economic Order*, edited by R. Amacher, G. Haberler, and T. Willett. Washington DC: American Enterprise Institute.

Finger, J. M. 2007. Implementation and Imbalance: Dealing with the Hangover from the Uruguay Round. *Oxford Review of Economic Policy* 23 (3):440–60.

Gallagher, P., and A. Stoler. 2009. Critical Mass as an Alternative Framework for Multilateral Trade Negotiations. *Global Governance* 15 (3):375–92.

Ghosh, A. 2010. Developing Countries in the WTO Trade Policy Review Mechanism. *World Trade Review* 9 (3):419–55.

Grynberg, R., ed. 2006. *WTO at the Margins: Small States and the Multilateral Trading System*. Cambridge: Cambridge University Press.

Harbinson, S. 2009. The Doha Round: 'Death-Defying Agenda' or 'Don't Do it Again'? ECIPE Working Paper. Brussels: ECIPE.

Hoekman, B. 2002. Strengthening the Global Trade Architecture for Development: The Post-Doha Agenda. *World Trade Review* 1 (1):23–46.

Hoekman, B. 2005. Operationalizing the Concept of Policy Space in the WTO: Beyond Special and Differential Treatment. *Journal of International Economic Law* 8 (2):405–24.

Hoekman, B., and M. Kostecki. 2009. *The Political Economy of the World Trading System*. Third edition. Oxford: Oxford University Press.

Hoekman, B., and A. Mattoo. 2010. Services Trade Liberalization and Regulatory Reform: Re-invigorating International Cooperation. World Bank Policy Research Working Paper 5517. Washington DC: World Bank.

Hoekman, B., and P. Mavroidis, 2000. WTO Dispute Settlement, Transparency and Surveillance. *The World Economy* 23 (4):527–42.

Hoekman, B., and D. Vines. 2007. Multilateral Trade Cooperation: What Next? *Oxford Review of Economic Policy* 23 (3):311–34.

Horn, H., G. Maggi, and R. Staiger. 2010. Trade Agreements as Endogenously Incomplete Contracts. *American Economic Review* 100 (1):394–419.

Howse, R., and K. Nicolaidis. 2003. Enhancing WTO Legitimacy: Constitutionalization or Global Subsidiarity? *Governance* 16 (1):73–94.

Hudec, R. 2002. The Adequacy of WTO Dispute Settlement Remedies for Developing Country Complainants. In *Development, Trade and the WTO: A Handbook*, edited by B. Hoekman, A. Mattoo, and P. English, 81–92. Washington DC: World Bank.

Hufbauer, G. 2005. Inconsistency Between Diagnosis and Treatment. *Journal of International Economic Law* 8 (2):291–7.

Ismail, F. 2009a. Reforming the World Trade Organization. *World Economics* 10 (4):109–46.

Ismail, F. 2009b. The Role of the Chair in the WTO Negotiations from the Potsdam Collapse in June 2007 to July 2008. *Journal of World Trade* 43 (6):1145–71.

Jackson, J. H. 2001. The WTO 'Constitution' and Proposed Reforms: Seven 'Mantras' Revisited. *Journal of International Economic Law* 4 (1):67–78.

Jones, K. 2010. *The Doha Blues: Institutional Crisis and Reform in the WTO*. Oxford: Oxford University Press.

Kee, H. L., A. Nicita, and M. Olarreaga. 2009. Estimating Trade Restrictiveness Indices. *Economic Journal* 119 (534):172–99.

Lamy, P. 2009. Strengthening the WTO as the Global Trade Body. Statement by the Director-General on his reappointment. Available from <http://www.wto.org/english/news_e/news09_e/tnc_chair_report_29apr09_e.htm>. Accessed 5 November 2011.

Lawrence, R. 2003. *Crimes and Punishment: Retaliation under the WTO*. Washington DC: Institute for International Economics.

Lawrence, R. 2006. Rulemaking Amidst Growing Diversity: A 'Club of Clubs' Approach to WTO Reform and New Issue Selection. *Journal of International Economic Law* 9 (4):823–35.

Levy, Philip. 2006. Do We Need an Undertaker for the Single Undertaking? Considering the Angles of Variable Geometry. In *Economic Development and Multilateral Trade Cooperation*, edited by S. Evenett and B. Hoekman, 417–438. London: Palgrave Macmillan.

Levy, Philip. 2010. Alternatives to Consensus at the WTO. VoxEU (19 June). Available from <http://www.voxeu.org/index.php?q=node/5209>. Accessed 5 November 2011.

Levy, P., and T. N. Srinivasan. 1996. Regionalism and the (Dis)advantage of Dispute Settlement Access. *American Economic Review* 86 (2):93–8.

Limão, N., and K. Saggi. 2008. Tariff Retaliation Versus Financial Compensation in the Enforcement of International Trade Agreements. *Journal of International Economics* 76 (1):48–60.

Luke, D. 2000. African Countries and the Seattle Ministerial Meeting: A Personal Reflection. *Journal of World Trade* 34 (3):39–46.

Maggi, G., and A. Rodriguez-Clare. 1998. The Value of Trade Agreements in the Presence of Political Pressures. *Journal of Political Economy* 106 (3):574–601.

Mann, E. 2004. A Parliamentary Dimension to the WTO—More Than Just a Vision? *Journal of International Economic Law* 7 (3):659–65.

Martin, W., and P. Messerlin. 2007. Why is it so Difficult? Trade Liberalization Under the Doha Agenda. *Oxford Review of Economic Policy* 23 (3):347–66.

Matsushita, M., T. Schoenbaum, and P. Mavroidis. 2003. *The World Trade Organization: Law, Practice and Policy*. Oxford: Oxford University Press.

Mercurio, B. 2008. Why Compensation Cannot Replace Trade Retaliation in the WTO Dispute Settlement Understanding. *World Trade Review*. 8 (2):315–38.

Messerlin, P. 2010. The Doha Round. GEM Policy Brief. Paris: SciencesPo. Available from <http://gem.sciences-po.fr/content/publications/pdf/Messerlin_DohaRound102010.pdf>. Accessed 5 November 2011.

Narlikar, A. 2003. *International Trade and Developing Countries: Coalitions in the GATT and WTO*. London: Routledge.

Narlikar, A. 2006. Fairness in International Trade Negotiations: Developing Countries in the GATT and WTO. *The World Economy* 29 (8):1005–29.

Nordstrom, H. 2005. The World Trade Organization Secretariat in a Changing World. *Journal of World Trade* 38 (5):819–53.

Nordstrom, H., and G. Shaffer. 2008. Access to Justice in the WTO: The Case for a Small Claims Procedure. *World Trade Review* 7 (4):587–640.

Odell, J. 2005. Chairing a WTO Negotiation. *Journal of International Economic Law* 8 (2):425–48.

Odell, John. 2007. Growing Power Meets Frustration in the Doha Round's First Four Years. In *Developing Countries and Global Trade Negotiations*, edited by L. Crump and S. J. Maswood, 7–40. London: Routledge.

Odell, J. 2010. Negotiating from Weakness in International Trade Relations. *Journal of World Trade* 44 (3):545–66.

Pauwelyn, J. 2000. Enforcement and Countermeasures in the WTO: Rules are Rules—Toward a More Collective Approach. *American Journal of International Law* 94 (2):335–47.

Pauwelyn, J. 2005. The Transformation of World Trade. *Michigan Law Review* 104 (1):1–70.

Pedersen, P. 2006. The WTO Decision-Making Process and Internal Transparency. *World Trade Review* 5 (1):103–31.

Piewitt, M. 2010. Participatory Governance in the WTO: How Inclusive is Global Civil Society? *Journal of World Trade* 44 (2):467–88.

Schelling, T. 1978. *Micromotives and Macrobehavior*. New York: W.W. Norton.

Schott, J., and J. Watal. 2000. Decision-Making in the WTO. International Economic Policy Brief 00-2. Washington DC: Institute for International Economics.

Shaffer, G. 2004. Parliamentary Oversight of WTO Rule-Making: The Political, Normative, and Practical Contexts. *Journal of International Economic Law* 7 (3):629–54.

Steger, D. 2009. The Future of the WTO: The Case for Institutional Reform. *Journal of International Economic Law* 12 (4):803–33.

Steger, D., and N. Shpilkovskaya. 2010. Internal Management of the WTO: Room for Improvement. In *Redesigning the World Trade Organization for the Twenty-First Century*, edited by D. Steger. Waterloo, Ontario: Wilfred Laurier University Press.

Steinberg, R. 2002. In the Shadow of Law or Power? Consensus-Based Bargaining and Outcomes in the GATT/WTO. *International Organization* 56 (2):339–74.

Stoeckel, A., and H. Fisher. 2008. *Policy Transparency: Why Does it Work? Who Does it Best?* Canberra and Sydney: Center for International Economics.

Sutherland, P. et al. 2004. The Future of the WTO: Addressing Institutional Challenges in the New Millennium. Report by the Consultative Board to the Director-General. Geneva: World Trade Organization.

Tallberg, J. 2008. The Power of the Chair: Formal Leadership in International Cooperation. Unpublished mimeo, Stockholm University.

Tijmes-Lhl, Jaime. 2009. Consensus and Majority Voting in the WTO. *World Trade Review* 8 (3):417–37.

Tumlir, J. 1985. *Protectionism: Trade Policy in Democratic Societies*. Washington, DC: American Enterprise Institute.

Warwick Commission. 2007. *The Multilateral Trade Regime: Which Way Forward?* Coventry: University of Warwick.

Wilkinson, R. 2006. *The WTO: Crisis and the Governance of Global Trade*. London: Routledge.

Winters, L. A. 2007. Coherence and the WTO. *Oxford Review of Economic Policy* 23 (3):461–80.

Wolfe, R. 2005. Decision-Making and Transparency in the 'Medieval' WTO: Does the Sutherland Report have the Right Prescription? *Journal of International Economic Law* 8 (3):631–45.

Wolfe, R. 2007. Can the Trading System Be Governed? Institutional Implications of the WTO's Suspended Animation. CIGI Working Paper 30. Waterloo, Ontario: Centre for International Governance Innovation.

Wolfe, R. 2009. The WTO Single Undertaking as Negotiating Technique and Constitutive Metaphor. *Journal of International Economic Law* 12 (4):835–58.

WTO. 2007. *World Trade Report 2007: Six Decades of Multilateral Trade Cooperation: What Have We Learnt?* Geneva: WTO Publications.

Zedillo, Ernesto. 2007. Surviving the Doha Round. In *Impacts and Implications of Global Trade Reform on Poverty*, edited by B. Hoekman and M. Olarreaga. Washington DC: Brookings Institution.

CHAPTER 34

....

THE WTO AND INSTITUTIONAL (IN)COHERENCE IN GLOBAL ECONOMIC GOVERNANCE

....

STEVEN BERNSTEIN AND ERIN HANNAH*

34.1 INTRODUCTION

....

THE creation of the World Trade Organization (WTO) in 1995 marks one of the most significant advances towards legally rigorous economic integration in the global political economy. The scope of trade rules has expanded well beyond managing barriers to trade at the border to shaping national labour, environmental, human health, food safety, and development policies. The range of actors affected by WTO rules has grown exponentially, and the WTO's focus on national legal and regulatory systems has raised a chorus of legitimacy concerns. These dramatic changes were accompanied by a commitment to achieve greater coherence in global economic governance and to establish mechanisms by which institutions can address each other. Yet, these commitments only singled out the WTO's relationship to the World Bank and the International Monetary Fund (IMF). The exclusive focus on international financial institutions is unfortunate given the dramatic changes in the multilateral trade regime since 1995.

In this chapter, we map institutional cooperation in global economic governance across a range of areas—finance and aid, intellectual property rights, environmental and

* The authors gratefully acknowledge helpful comments and suggestions from Alan Alexandroff, John Hancock, Louis Pauly, and the editors of this volume, and research assistance from Summer Thorp.

social regulations—in order to address two primary questions. First, where do the rules of the WTO overlap or compete with those of other institutions? Second, what explains institutional coherence and incoherence between the WTO and other international and transnational organizations? We recognize that extending the scope of our inquiry beyond macroeconomic coordination moves well beyond the WTO's formal mandate for economic coherence. Such a move is justified, however, because any discussion of economic coherence must acknowledge that the WTO's challenge extends to the relationship among global economic, environmental, and social stability.

We make three interlinked arguments below. First, the WTO is well-equipped to support the coordination of policies aimed specifically to facilitate trade liberalization with institutions of relatively equal size and power. However, states have been unwilling to provide the WTO the capacity or mandate to play a significant role in reconciling broader inconsistencies on macroeconomic policies or mandates across global economic institutions that might indirectly undermine the goals of the trade regime. Second, the complexities of the international trade regime, imbalances in institutional power, a fairly narrow normative underpinning to the trade regime, and persistent, though shifting, structural asymmetries between North and South render the WTO normatively and legally constrained in its attempts to navigate institutional conflicts in non-traditional trade areas. These factors also create tensions in how best to achieve coherence. In areas that parties have directly targeted to facilitate trade liberalization, such as intellectual property rights, aid, and finance, the WTO can and should play the role of regulatory institution in cooperation with other relevant international institutions, and increase the scope of its Coherence Mandate to improve performance and better reconcile tensions or contradictions in global economic governance. Third, as a corollary, in areas such as social and environmental regulation where the goal of regulation is to 'embed' economic governance in broader societal goals,[1] coherence is best achieved if states ensure WTO rules continue to leave space for a global division of labour and allow other institutions to do the regulating. The legitimacy and coherence of global economic governance is increasingly at risk if the WTO's mandate or rules make it unable to manage these tensions.

The chapter proceeds in three parts. First, we provide a brief account of the WTO's Coherence Mandate, which focuses exclusively on its relationship to the Bretton Woods institutions and is aimed at coordinating trade, finance, and aid policies. We examine its limited success at promoting macroeconomic consistency in the global economy, but greater success in two key initiatives focused more narrowly on liberalization: the Enhanced Integrated Framework and Aid for Trade. Second, we look beyond the formal Coherence Mandate to examine regime complexity in the international intellectual property rights (IPR) regime. This serves to illustrate and assess the challenges of coherence in an area of new economic regulation, but one still close to the core economic underpinnings of the global marketplace. Third, moving still further from the traditional

---

[1] Ruggie 2007; Bernstein and Hannah 2008.

trade agenda, we examine the tensions that arise between WTO rules and social and environmental standards and regulations designed to 'embed' economic governance within broader societal values.

34.2 The Coherence Mandate:
COORDINATING TRADE, FINANCE,
AND AID POLICIES

34.2.1 Context

Improving the coherence of global economic policy-making is a core function of the WTO, especially in the area of trade liberalization. The 1994 Ministerial Declaration on Achieving Greater Coherence in Global Economic Policy-Making established the Coherence Mandate of the WTO and emphasized the special relationship between the WTO and the Bretton Woods Institutions.[2] Article III, 5 of the Marrakesh Agreement Establishing the World Trade Organization states that 'the WTO shall cooperate, as appropriate, with the International Monetary Fund and with the International Bank for Reconstruction and Development and its affiliated agencies', and the Doha and Hong Kong Ministerial Declarations reiterate this commitment.[3] Achieving coherence makes sense because all three institutions share a normative commitment to sustainable growth, development, and poverty reduction through the further liberalization of the global economy.[4] Although major work remains to be done, cooperation between the WTO and Bretton Woods institutions has resulted in more coordinated trade, financial, and aid policies directly relevant for trade liberalization. However, that cooperation has not extended significantly into coordination on broader macroeconomic policy.

The origins of the WTO's Coherence Mandate date back to the launch of the Uruguay Round in 1986. The General Agreement on Tariffs and Trade (GATT), its successor, the WTO, and the Bretton Woods institutions were designed to bring stability to the international economy by managing international economic affairs in their respective policy domains—trade, finance, and monetary policy. The architects of the post-Second World War international economic institutions explicitly acknowledged that trade and finance are inextricably linked and viewed them as complementary.[5] Indeed, according to Curtis:

> There was no problem of 'coherence': the basic principles of a gradual reduction of barriers to trade, the freeing up of international payments, and the 'binding' of liberalization gains by commitments not to raise tariffs matched by parallel

---

[2] WTO 1994c.   [3] WTO 2001a, 2005a.   [4] Sampson 1998, 259.
[5] For discussion of linkages between the GATT (1947) and the IMF, see Zapatero 2006, 598–600; Auboin 2007, 5–6; Sampson 1998, 259–61. Notably, no comparable basis for cooperation exists between the GATT (1947) and the World Bank, largely because the latter's core competency at its inception was post-Second World War reconstruction.

disciplines against competitive devaluation of currencies, were designed to be coherent and were seen to be so.[6]

Nonetheless, there have been important inconsistencies and competition between the goals of these institutions in the post-Second World War period.

These inconsistencies stem from shifts over time in how states and international financial institutions have responded to the well-known 'trilemma' identified in the Mundell–Fleming model, which argues that autonomy can only be maintained in two of the three macroeconomic policy areas of exchange rates, capital flows, and domestic monetary policy.[7] Daunton suggests that these choices also have implications for trade policy, which in practice have created an 'inconsistent quartet'.

The architects of the post-war economic order believed that trade liberalization was the key to peace, prosperity, and an end to 'beggar-thy-neighbour' competitive economic nationalism, but liberalization required increased liquidity and relatively stable exchange rates. The challenge was how to achieve these conditions while carving out exceptions that allowed states enough national economic autonomy to respond to payment imbalances and the havoc they could play with important national economic goals such as full employment. John Ruggie famously characterized the resulting compromise as 'embedded liberalism', or the idea that liberal markets must be premised on exceptions and exemptions necessary to maintain domestic stability. The Bretton Woods monetary order aimed to achieve this balance via a fixed exchange rate regime under IMF supervision, but that allowed currency devaluations and the imposition of export capital controls to counter balance-of-payment disequilibria. These trade-offs meant that states could pursue active domestic monetary policy: interest rates rather than capital mobility would be used to achieve stability. The rules of the GATT were constructed on this premise.

This solution began to unravel in the late 1960s under the weight of inflationary pressures associated with full-employment policies and enormous budget deficits, especially in the United States. The story of the subsequent 'collapse' of the Bretton Woods fixed exchange rate regime is well known,[8] but its most significant implication for the discussion here is that it signalled that national capital controls had become increasingly obsolete by the early 1970s owing to the increased costs of such controls to domestic economies and the problem of leakage.[9] As a result, leading states began to actively encourage the liberalization of financial markets and short-term capital mobility. The GATT, IMF, and World Bank had no institutional capacity to interact with one another to adapt to this shift in the trilemma trade-off, which limited states' ability to independently use interest rates to stabilize domestic economies. This problem became acute when massive global imbalances and macroeconomic problems of the early 1980s threatened to undermine the international trade regime.

[6] Curtis 2007, 212.
[7] Discussed in historical context in Chapter 2 of this volume; Pauly 1997.
[8] For example, Ruggie 1982; Bordo and Eichengreen 1993, 3–109.
[9] Goodman and Pauly 1993.

A series of external shocks in the 1970s and early 1980s, including the collapse of the dollar-gold convertibility standard, the oil price shocks of 1973 and 1979, the related debt crisis in developing countries, and massive inflation and fiscal deficits in developed countries, exposed widespread policy incoherence at the national level. In an effort to manage these shocks, central banks tightened monetary policy—a move followed by growing global imbalances, dramatic exchange rate swings, and a period of new protectionism, particularly in developed countries.[10]

From 1974 onward, the favouring of capital mobility in the 'trilemma' established an entirely new context for international trade policy. GATT commitments, reinforced later by the creation of the WTO, largely kept trade barriers in check. However, the IMF adapted to the shift in the trilemma trade-off by allowing backdoor strategies to achieve protection in global markets. For example, through competitive currency devaluations or currency manipulation, various countries increase their exports' competitiveness abroad while decreasing the competitiveness of imports at home. This can erode the achievements of trade liberalization and there is little recourse under the GATT/WTO to do anything about it. This situation persists to the present despite the enormous implications of currency manipulation for trade imbalances. A case in point is the sidelining of the WTO in the dispute over whether China artificially suppressed the value of its currency, the renminbi, against the US dollar after the onset of the 2008–2009 global financial crisis.[11]

With some irony, currency manipulation remained outside the GATT/WTO purview even as the core responsibilities of the IMF, World Bank, and GATT began to blur with the debt crisis of the early 1980s; the IMF waded into the World Bank's traditional domain of microeconomic policy-making with its conditionality loans, the World Bank duplicated the work of the IMF by issuing 'soft loans', and both institutions tied lending to further trade liberalization. The launch of the Uruguay Round created the Negotiating Group on the Functioning of the GATT System (FOGS) to address these challenges.[12]

34.2.2 The FOGS response

Governments mandated FOGS negotiators to examine the linkages between 'trade, money, finance, and development' in the international economy.[13] Specifically, FOGS aimed to determine whether extreme exchange rate fluctuations were responsible for the rise in new protectionism and large current account imbalances.[14] These issues put the predictability of international trade rules at risk.[15] Moreover, market access restrictions made it extremely difficult for developing countries to service their large external

---

[10] Curtis 2007; Sampson 1998.

[11] For a discussion of how the trade regime should address currency manipulation, see Staiger and Sykes 2010.

[12] GATT 1986, A(iii).   [13] GATT 1986, Preamble.

[14] Ostry 1999; Curtis 2007, 213; Sampson 1998, 261–2.   [15] Auboin 2007, 6–7.

debts with export earnings. Negotiators also explicitly recognized the adjustment costs to trade liberalization encountered by developing countries, the need to coordinate short-term support to ease the transition to more open markets, and the need to align GATT requirements and the trade policy recommendations made by the Bretton Woods institutions.[16]

By 1989, the original objectives of the FOGS Negotiating Group were, according to Ostry, 'pretty well dead'.[17] Consultations between the Director General of the GATT and heads of the Bretton Woods institutions found insufficient evidence to link exchange rate misalignments, global imbalances, and protectionism. Even if such links could be made, they deemed these areas 'least amenable to improvement through action by the international agencies themselves'.[18] After seven years, the main outcome of FOGS negotiations was the Ministerial Declaration on Achieving Greater Coherence in Global Economic Policy-Making, or Coherence Mandate. Analyses have described it as 'largely rhetorical' and lacking substantive, binding commitments on issues that require coordination.[19]

In essence, the Coherence Mandate:

(1) re-articulates the importance of 'achieving harmony' between 'structural, macro-economic, trade, financial, and development aspects of trade policy-making' at both the national and international level

(2) highlights the important role to be played by the IMF and World Bank in 'supporting adjustment to trade liberalization, including support for net food-importing developing countries'

(3) emphasizes the need to pursue and develop cooperation between the Bretton Woods institutions and the newly created WTO in order to achieve 'consistent and mutually supportive policies'

(4) 'invite[s] the Director General of the WTO to review, with the Managing Director of the International Monetary Fund and the President of the World Bank, the implications of the WTO's responsibilities for cooperation ... [and] the forms that such cooperation might take'.[20]

Subsequently, the WTO signed cooperation agreements with the IMF and World Bank in 1996.[21] The agreements provide for procedural coordination between the three institutions, including procedures for consultation, staff participation in meetings, information sharing, and the provision of 'soft services' such as research and analysis of trade policy. The Doha Ministerial Declaration reiterates the commitment to fulfil the Coherence Mandate and WTO members agreed to set up a working group to further examine links between trade, debt, and finance.[22] The 2005 Hong Kong Ministerial Declaration advanced the Mandate by making specific recommendations on capacity building in developing countries and, in Annex F, against the practice of

---

[16] Sampson 1998, 262; Auboin 2007, 8.   [17] Ostry 1999.   [18] Sampson 1998, 267.
[19] Ostry quoted in Winters 2007, 465.   [20] WTO 1994c, paragraphs 1–5.
[21] WTO 1996a.   [22] WTO 2001a, paragraphs 5 and 36.

cross-conditionality. Specifically, it asks donors and international economic institutions not to subject least-developed countries to conditions 'inconsistent with their
rights and obligations under WTO agreements'.[23]

Much has been written about efforts to fulfil the Coherence Mandate.[24] Since 1995, the
scope for cooperation has widened as the institutions try to cope with the impact of new
trade rules for national and regulatory systems and cope with financial crises in the global economy. Low-level, ad hoc cooperation has helped the institutions present a coherent public face.[25] However, there is little evidence that these institutional linkages have
resulted in greater consistency between trade liberalization and macroeconomic policies promoted and supported through the IMF, nor is it any clearer how controlling currency manipulation—a difficult enough task on its own—could be realistically joined
institutionally to international trade goals. To paraphrase Daunton (this volume), the
policy 'quartet' remains inconsistent and the levers to produce consistency did not materialize through linkages generated by the Coherence Mandate. Rather, the Coherence
Mandate's most substantive impact has been in the provision of technical assistance for
least-developed countries (LDCs)[26] and in mainstreaming trade into development and
poverty reduction strategies.

34.2.3 Aid for Trade, the Enhanced Integrated Framework, and the Doha Development Round of multilateral trade negotiations

The Enhanced Integrated Framework (EIF) and Aid for Trade (AfT) initiatives grew out
of the Coherence Mandate, and are clear attempts to harmonize policies between institutions of relatively equal size and power by mainstreaming trade into development and
poverty reduction policies. In our view, these initiatives are both consistent with the
scope and legitimate purpose of the WTO and likely to produce more coordinated trade,
financial, and aid policies.

The EIF has its roots in early attempts by the WTO to help LDCs integrate more fully
into the global economy through the provision of coordinated, trade-related technical
assistance. At the Singapore Ministerial Conference in December 1996, WTO members
adopted the Comprehensive and Integrated WTO Plan of Action for the Least-
Developed Countries which 'envisage[d] a closer cooperation between the WTO and
other multilateral agencies assisting least-developed countries'.[27] Subsequently, six

---

[23] WTO 2005b, Annex F, paragraph 38.

[24] See for example Auboin 2007; Zapatero 2006. The WTO Director-General also produces annual
reports on progress made in the Coherence Mandate. See WTO 2008, 2009a.

[25] See for example, WTO 2004. There are some obvious exceptions. Most notable is the very public
dispute between the World Bank and IMF over the management of the Asian financial crisis.

[26] Though the effectiveness and limited scope of such assistance has been subject to criticism,
discussed in part below.

[27] WTO 1997a, Preamble.

organizations—the WTO, IMF, World Bank, UN Conference on Trade and Development (UNCTAD), United Nations Development Programme (UNDP), and International Trade Centre (ITC)—collaborated to establish the Integrated Framework (IF) in 1997.[28] It was designed to offer a broad range of services, including assistance in acceding to the WTO, implementing Uruguay Round commitments, improving the capacity of LDCs to participate in multilateral negotiations, and strengthening export supply capabilities, trade support services, and trade facilitation.[29] This proved a more difficult challenge than anticipated.

A mandated, independent review of the IF in 2000 found it largely ineffectual in its primary mission to provide technical assistance to LDCs.[30] These findings prompted the six agencies to restructure and relaunch the IF in 2001, alongside the Doha Development Round, with a new purpose: to promote LDCs' full integration into the multilateral trading regime by mainstreaming trade into national development plans such as the World Bank's Poverty Reduction Strategy Papers (PRSPs), facilitating the coordinated delivery of trade-related assistance, and linking assistance to conditional debt financing.[31]

The major innovation in 2001 was the Diagnostic Trade Integration Study (DTIS); each LDC would qualify for an initial DTIS that 'evaluates internal and external constraints on a country's integration into the world economy, and recommends areas where technical assistance and policy actions can help the country overcome these barriers'.[32] A new IF Trust Fund would finance the preparation of the DTIS and provide bridge financing to jump-start the policy actions identified in the DTIS.

The reformed IF also added a steering committee to overcome problems associated with inter-institutional coordination. Located at the WTO, it consists of a tripartite group of donors, LDCs, and the six international agencies. An internal working group manages its day-to-day operations and the UNDP manages the IF Trust Fund consisting of donations from both bilateral and multilateral donors.[33] These changes increased the mandate of the IF, targeted a wider range of countries, and aimed to improve LDC ownership over the delivery of trade-related technical assistance.

Despite these changes, independent evaluations of the IF in late 2003 found they did little to correct the problems identified in the first IF evaluation and, in some respects, exacerbated process inefficiencies; the evaluations identified implementation gaps across LDCs and highly variable effectiveness of the IF as a whole.[34] In response, intensive negotiations between the three stakeholders—agencies, donors, and LDCs—in 2004 and

---

[28] WTO 1997b.   [29] WTO 1997b.

[30] WTO 2000c. Winters 2007, 470, provides a thorough discussion of the main issues with the IF during this period.

[31] For more information about the IF, see <http://www.integratedframework.org/about.htm>.

[32] For information on country trade diagnostic studies, see <http://web.worldbank.org/WBSITE/EXTERNAL/TOPICS/TRADE/0,,contentMDK:20615178~menuPK:1574524~pagePK:148956~piPK:2166 18~theSitePK:239071,00.html>.

[33] For information regarding the IF Governance Structure, see <http://www.wto.org/english/tratop_e/devel_e/teccop_e/if_e.htm>.

[34] WTO 2003; OED 2004.

2005, led to the creation of an IF Task Force at the WTO to recommend how to enhance the IF. The 2005 Hong Kong Ministerial Conference endorsed its recommendations and singled out three essential elements for an Enhanced IF (EIF): (a) increased, additional, predictable financial resources to implement Action Matrices; (b) strengthened in-country capacities to manage, implement, and monitor the IF process; and (c) enhanced IF governance.[35] In June 2006, the IF Steering Committee adopted its recommendations on the EIF.[36] Although much work remains to be done to implement the recommendations and to overcome concerns about the IF's scope, effectiveness, and funding deficiencies, the EIF was formally launched in July 2009 and shows better prospects of fulfilling its mandate.[37] This is largely owing to its partnership with the global AfT initiative.

The 2005 Hong Kong Ministerial Declaration endorsed the new AfT programme and a Task Force to operationalize and implement it[38] in response to a growing consensus at the time that developing countries were ill-equipped to participate effectively in international trade, that improvements in market access alone were insufficient to set them on a path towards sustainable economic growth, and that they required Official Development Assistance (ODA) to help correct human, institutional, and infrastructural capacity deficits.[39] The Task Force had a mandate to provide recommendations on 'how Aid for Trade might contribute most effectively to the development dimension of the DDA [Doha Development Agenda]' and to 'consult with Members as well as with the IMF and World Bank, relevant international organizations and the regional development banks with a view to reporting to the General Council on appropriate mechanisms to secure additional financial resources for Aid for Trade'.[40]

AfT is the provision of ODA—concessional loans and grants—for trade-related programmes and projects. The EIF and AfT are meant to be complementary processes to enable developing countries to use trade to achieve economic growth and poverty reduction.[41] The broad scope of AfT reflects the complex challenges developing countries face. It includes technical assistance to improve the negotiating capacity of developing countries, infrastructure such as roads and telecommunications, investment in industries across a broad range of sectors, and financial assistance to compensate for short-term costs of trade liberalization or losses owing to preference erosion.[42]

---

[35] WTO 2005a, paragraph 31.

[36] WTO 2006a. Modalities for achieving these recommendations are discussed in detail in WTO 2006b.

[37] For more information see <http://www.wto.org/english/tratop_e/devel_e/teccop_e/if_e.htm> and http://www.integratedframework.org/>. Current projects and financial pledges are detailed in Integrated Framework 2009.

[38] Notably, Aid for Trade is a complement to the Doha Development Round, but it is not conditional upon its successful conclusion.

[39] MDG Gap Taskforce 2010 recently re-articulated this consensus.

[40] WTO 2005a, paragraph 57.

[41] WTO 2006c, F.1. For further discussion concerning the rationale behind Aid for Trade, see Prowse 2006; Hoekman 2007.

[42] Details of the AfT initiative are available at: <http://www.wto.org/english/tratop_e/devel_e/a4t_e/a4t_factsheet_e.htm>.

For LDCs, AfT is the supply side of the EIF. Through the EIF diagnostic process (the DTIS), LDCs identify and prioritize their trade-related assistance needs. AfT also aims to redress major funding deficiencies that plague the EIF Trust Fund, which only provides bridge financing for projects and priorities identified in DTIS. Through the AfT process, development partners can provide additional, predictable, and sustainable funding. It is the process through which trade-related diagnostics requiring technical assistance are converted into funded and implemented projects. In other words, the EIF leads LDCs to access AfT.[43]

Although the provision of ODA for trade was not new in 2005, the explicit acknowledgment that these issues require the cooperation of both the trade and development communities was. Moreover, the initiative aims to dramatically increase the mobilization of financial resources over time, mainstream trade into national development plans and poverty reduction strategies, and respond to developing countries' priorities. The WTO's role is to work with bilateral donors, multilateral agencies, and international financial institutions, especially the World Bank and IMF, to ensure they understand the trade-related needs of its Members and to improve the effectiveness, coordination, and overall coherence of the disbursement of aid.[44] It is also responsible for monitoring and evaluating AfT in order to 'strengthen mutual accountability between donor and recipient countries through improved transparency'.[45] To this end, it publishes jointly with the Organization for Economic Cooperation and Development (OECD) the biannual Global Review of Aid for Trade, which takes stock and evaluates the impact of existing AfT flows and highlights the needs of particular regions.[46] Improving quantitative and qualitative criteria for AfT evaluation also forms a core element of the WTO's AfT work programme.[47] Overall, according to WTO Director General Pascal Lamy, the WTO serves as both a catalyst and a facilitator of aid flows to developing countries.[48]

The EIF and AfT clearly hold promise as important vehicles for coordinating the priorities and policies of the WTO, donors, multilateral agencies, and Bretton Woods institutions. They also increase awareness of the linkages between trade and development and monitor progress in the delivery of aid. However, there is wide-ranging debate over their effectiveness and efficiency. While the supply of AfT has increased significantly since 2005, concerns persist about its distribution and impact.[49] Winters suggests that

[43] WTO 2007a.

[44] The WTO's partners in the global AfT initiative are: the African Development Bank, Asian Development Bank, European Bank for Reconstruction and Development, IMF, Inter-American Development Bank, Islamic Development Bank, ITC, OECD, UNCTAD, UNDP, United Nations Economic Commission for Africa (UNECA), United Nations Industrial Development Organization (UNIDO), and the World Bank. The key challenges to the coherent provision of AfT are detailed in WTO 2006c, e.

[45] WTO 2007b, 4.

[46] OECD and WTO 2007; 2009. The conference programme and submissions for the second AfT Global Review are available at: <http://www.wto.org/english/tratop_e/devel_e/a4t_e/global_review09_prog_e.htm>.

[47] WTO 2009b.

[48] Lamy 2006.

[49] For comprehensive assessments, see Hoekman and Wilson 2010; Hallaert 2010.

the WTO should abandon its foray into development policy and the provision of aid because the transaction costs far outweigh the tangible returns.[50] Indeed, the precise role of the WTO as a 'development' institution is a growing preoccupation of scholars.[51] Critics contend that conditionality and a market-driven approach to development are inappropriate to reduce poverty in LDCs.[52] Advocacy organizations in the South have also raised concerns that the EIF and AfT initiatives will lead to cross-conditionality, inadequate policy space, and an erosion of special and differential treatment.[53]

Given that the EIF and the AfT initiatives are still in their genesis phases, the jury is still out on their long-term implications for development. However, it is clear that these initiatives will be litmus tests for the WTO's ability to coordinate policies with institutions of relatively equal size and power in the global economy.[54] The World Bank, IMF, and WTO are institutions that align ideologically, their work is mutually supportive, and they have engaged in extensive, formal efforts to enhance the coherence of global economic policy-making, at least with respect to trade and aid. These efforts are consistent with a growing post-Washington consensus that development should be the foremost priority in the global economy. They are also consistent with the scope and legitimate purpose of the WTO. In light of the global economic downturn, the related liquidity crisis, and the lack of progress being made in the DDA, the need for coordination in the areas of trade, finance, and aid is more important than ever.[55]

While EIF and AfT show some promise, broadening the perspective on economic governance even slightly beyond the attempts to build coherence among the core international economic institutions reveals even greater challenges, owing to power imbalances and North–South politics. Take the Financing for Development initiative that emerged out of the 2002 Monterrey Consensus, for example.[56] It operates in parallel to the EIF, although they are meant to be complementary, and the 2008 Doha Declaration on Financing for Development explicitly identifies EIF and AfT as means of fulfilling the Consensus. One important output from the 2002 Monterrey Conference—largely unnoticed at the time—was a commitment to high-level dialogue of the three core international economic institutions with the UN Economic and Social Council (ECOSOC). On one hand, bringing together these institutions reflects an ideological rapprochement on development policy when compared to the 1980s and 1990s.[57] On the other hand, despite the apparent unity of purpose, almost ten years later, calls for greater coherence among international financial, monetary, and trading systems is still a major theme. In the context of the 2008–2009 financial crisis, such meetings have focused especially on a desire for a more coherent approach to addressing global financial and trade imbalances, as well as limiting currency speculation. However, according to a report by the President of ECOSOC on the March 2010 high-level meeting, 'there [remains] no agreed international

[50] Winters 2007.   [51] See, for example, Qureshi 2009.
[52] Saner and Paez 2006; Grabel 2007.   [53] South Centre 2005.
[54] Evenett 2009.   [55] Hoekman and Wilson 2010, 4.
[56] On the history of UN, WTO, and Bretton Woods coordination in the follow-up to the Monterrey Conference on Financing for Development, see Pauly 2007.
[57] Thérien 2007.

regulatory system for enabling trading partners to avoid distortions stemming from financial shocks and exchange rate misalignments'.[58] Nor was there consensus at the meeting that exchange rates are a major component or cause of trade imbalances.

With discussions on coordination and cohesion occurring in multiple institutional settings, the question arises not only of where coherence might ideally be facilitated, but also where it is most likely to be achieved in practice. Arguably, a forum like the G20 would facilitate negotiations toward such a new regulatory framework better than ECOSOC. However, while participants at the ECOSOC meeting recognized the 'importance of having a mechanism for dialogue between the United Nations and the G20', many participants 'stressed the central role of the United Nations in achieving a greater coherence and coordination among different actors and areas of global governance' and suggested that 'ECOSOC should serve as the principal international body for coordinating all economic and social issues'.[59] This preference likely reflects that long-standing ideological and interest divides between North and South have not been entirely washed away, despite significant convergence on development policy. It should not be surprising, then, that developing countries might prefer ECOSOC, where they hold a majority and where their understandings of social justice and equity hold more sway in economic discussions.[60] Such preferences expose the challenge, and perhaps the need to move beyond the formal Coherence Mandate.

34.3 THE WORLD INTELLECTUAL PROPERTY ORGANIZATION (WIPO)–WTO RELATIONSHIP: A REGIME COMPLEX

The extension of WTO rules into services, investment, and intellectual property rights increased the density and complexity of international institutions governing these areas. The concept of 'regime complex', developed by Kal Raustialia and David Victor to describe 'an array of partially overlapping and non-hierarchical institutions governing a particular issue-area', nicely captures the resulting institutional terrain in these areas.[61] Regime complexes are inherently competitive environments because there is no agreed-upon hierarchy for resolving disputes between overlapping legal agreements. They often lack clear mechanisms for coordination, or there are stark inequalities in size and power among the relevant institutions. Actors exploit these features by proposing rules and norms in forums that favour their concerns and strategic interests through forum shopping,[62] and sometimes may even shift rule-making processes or the scope of authority of regimes that favour their interests in what Hefler labels 'regime shifting'.[63]

---

[58] ECOSOC 2010, 10.   [59] ECOSOC 2010, 10.   [60] Thérien 2007.
[61] Raustialia and Victor 2004, 279.   [62] Raustialia 2007, 1021, 1025.
[63] Hefler 2004, 2009 argues that, unlike forum shopping, which is limited to single episodes, regime shifting is a long-term, iterative strategy.

Regime complexity can be found in a range of issue areas. In this section, we focus exclusively on the international IPR regime because it provides one of the clearest illustrations of the challenges complexity poses in global economic governance.[64] The relationship between the WTO and the World Intellectual Property Organization (WIPO), in particular, engenders conflict, forum shopping, regime shifting,[65] and the emergence of counter-regime norms. Power differentials between institutions, and structural asymmetries between developed and developing countries, have thus far prohibited effective coordination in these areas.

Until 1995 and the introduction of the Agreement on Trade-Related Aspects of Intellectual Property Rights (TRIPS), the WIPO had primacy and near exclusive responsibility for rule-making in the international IPR regime.[66] It is a specialized agency of the United Nations established in 1970 to protect IP and promote the development and harmonization of IPR rules among its members.[67] It currently administers 24 international treaties on IP protection and classification.[68]

The WIPO came under fire from IP-based industry in the early 1980s for failing to prescribe minimum substantive IP standards and for lacking the necessary enforcement mechanisms to ensure members' compliance with those treaties. Industry groups also criticized it for identifying too closely with developing countries that, from the perspective of IP-based industry, 'abet the theft of intellectual property'.[69] Prior to the TRIPS Agreement, businesses in a wide range of sectors faced substantial losses due to inadequate IP protection abroad. Indeed, Sell and Prakash estimate that US industry lost between $43 billion and $61 billion in 1986 alone.[70] Consequently, IP-based industry forged a powerful private sector coalition aimed at securing more stringent international IP protection, linking it to the multilateral trade regime, and establishing enforcement and dispute settlement mechanisms.[71] The result was the 1994 TRIPS Agreement.

The TRIPS Agreement incorporates treaties administered by the WIPO, but broadens the scope of IP protection in significant ways.[72] It has commonly been referred to as a Berne–Plus or Paris–Plus agreement because it imposes greater and more stringent

---

[64] Similar challenges can be located in services and investment regime complexes, but space limitations prevent a discussion on those issues here.

[65] Ibid.

[66] For the history and evolution of the WIPO, see May 2009; Okediji 2008; Sell and May 2006.

[67] For an overview of the purpose and key activities of the WIPO, see <http://www.wipo.int/about-wipo/en/core_tasks.html>.

[68] Details of the treaties administered by the WIPO are available at <http://www.wipo.int/treaties/en/>.

[69] Sell and Prakash 2004, 158.

[70] Sell and Prakash 2004, 154.

[71] Controversy over the appropriate scope and forum for IP protection has a long history. However, this was the first time IP was recognized as a 'trade issue'. Yu 2009a; Sell and May 2006.

[72] TRIPS incorporates the Paris Convention for the Protection of Industrial Property and the Berne Convention for the Protection of Literary and Artistic Works, which were the cornerstones of the global IPR regime for over 100 years. It also incorporates the Rome Convention for the Protection of Performers, Producers of Phonograms and Broadcasting Organizations, and the Treaty on Intellectual Property in Respect of Integrated Circuits. WTO 1994b, Article 1(3).

obligations on member states. First, most-favoured nation and national treatment principles now constitute the cornerstones of the global IPR regime. Second, the TRIPS Agreement treats IP as a commodity and is designed to ensure that IP protection works to encourage innovation and the transfer of technology. It provides a universal blueprint that sets minimum standards of protection and enforcement for intellectual property (patents, trademarks, geographic indicators of source, industrial designs) and copyright (literary and artistic works).[73] All WTO signatories are required to provide 20-year minimum patent protection 'for any [new] inventions, whether products or processes, in all fields of technology without discrimination.[74]

Third, while WIPO members grant IP protection at their discretion, TRIPS requires all WTO members to implement minimum levels of IP protection in their national legislation and to bring national patent regimes into line with their TRIPS obligations. It also requires the same levels of IP protection regardless of members' level of development,[75] although it grants gradated grace periods for implementation.[76] Finally, IP rules are virtually unenforceable under the WIPO. By contrast, TRIPS introduced the possibility of inflicting retaliatory commercial measures for non-compliance through the WTO's mandatory dispute settlement system. Since 1995, members can impose punitive trade sanctions in any field of trade (not just IP) on violators of the Agreement. For the first time, stringent intellectual property rules were legalized and married to the international trade regime.

The WIPO remains an important actor in the IP arena. Some even claim that the growing dominance of the WTO rejuvenated the WIPO,[77] which today has three primary tasks in the global IPR regime. First, it processes and registers applications for patents, trademarks, designs, and appellations of origins. Second, it provides technical assistance to help developing countries build sufficient capacity to implement their international obligations. Finally, and most significantly for this chapter, it works to develop new international IP treaties and harmonize existing IP rules. For example, it facilitated new treaties in response to the increasingly global reach of digital communications,[78] and its ongoing work addresses IP issues in areas of particular concern to indigenous communities not covered by the TRIPS Agreement, including traditional knowledge, traditional cultural expressions, and genetic resources.[79]

---

[73] For an extensive discussion of the ways in which the TRIPS Agreement adds to the requirements of the WIPO Agreement, see Dinwoodie and Dreyfuss 2009.

[74] WTO 1994b, Article 27(1).

[75] For a discussion of the implications of a 'one size fits all' approach to intellectual property rules for developing countries, see Fink and Maskus 2005.

[76] Developing countries had until 2005 to bring their national patent legislation into line with TRIPS. LDCs have until 2013, and they do not have to provide protection for pharmaceutical patents until 2016. See <http://www.wto.org/english/tratop_e/trips_e/ldc_e.htm>.

[77] Yu 2009b, 12.

[78] The so-called WIPO 'Internet Treaties', the WIPO Copyright Treaty, and the WIPO Performances and Phonograms Treaty pertain to copyright protection for digital media.

[79] See <http://www.wipo.int/tk/en/>.

The WIPO and the WTO have a joint mandate to set rules in the international IPR regime. However, the relationship—especially the law-making relationship—between the two institutions, is ill-defined. While the TRIPS Agreement incorporates provisions of WIPO treaties, it provides few explicit directives on devising a consultative or cooperative framework. It does mandate the TRIPS Council to build cooperative arrangements,[80] but it leaves details of these arrangements to future negotiations.[81] It may also 'consult with and seek information from any source it deems appropriate', though the WIPO only has observer status in these consultations.[82]

The WTO–WIPO Agreement is the main instrument of coordination, but it focuses exclusively on administrative coordination to exploit the WIPO's administrative competency in the provision of technical and legal assistance.[83] Article 2 provides mechanisms to facilitate transparency of rules and laws in the international IPR regime,[84] and Article 3 formally integrates the WIPO into the TRIPS administrative framework. The Agreement also directs the WIPO and WTO Secretariat to cooperate in the provision of technical and legal assistance to developing countries to help them meet their international obligations.[85] In addition, the WIPO conducts its development agenda, adopted in 2007, through a formal agreement with the WTO that links it to the DDA.[86] These links support its aim to help developing countries implement their TRIPS obligations, increase protection for 'domestic creations, innovations and inventions', and make use of flexibilities contained in the TRIPS Agreement and reaffirmed in the Doha Declaration.[87]

Notably, however, the provision of technical assistance has been a source of controversy. As in the case of the WTO more generally, critical analyses charge that technical assistance is too focused on socializing developing countries rather than enabling them to adapt policies that suit their needs or better formulate their negotiating positions.[88]

---

[80] WTO 1994b, Article 68. The TRIPS Council was also directed to explore the relationship between the TRIPS Agreement and the Convention on Biological Diversity (CBD), but no formal agreement has developed.

[81] WTO 1995.

[82] Dinwoodie and Dreyfuss 2009, 1196.

[83] WTO 1995.

[84] Article 2 (1, 2) requires the WIPO's International Bureau to provide all WTO members, including those who are not members of the WIPO, with copies and translations, and access to electronic databases, of laws and regulations. Okediji 2008, 98.

[85] Article 4(1) specifies that the WIPO 'shall make available to developing country WTO Members which are not Member States of the WIPO the same legal-technical assistance relating to the TRIPS Agreement as it makes available to Member States of the WIPO which are developing countries. The WTO Secretariat shall make available to Member States of the WIPO which are developing countries and are not WTO Members the same technical cooperation relating to the TRIPS Agreement as it makes available to developing country WTO Members.' While Membership in WTO and the WIPO is not coextensive, few countries do not belong to both.

[86] See de Beer 2009; Netanel 2008.

[87] The WIPO's Development Agenda work programme is divided into six clusters and 45 recommendations. Cluster 'A' concerns technical assistance and capacity building. See WIPO 2007.

[88] Grabel 2010; Ostry 2009.

Specifically in the context of IP, Sell argues that, 'not surprisingly, through technical assistance programmes developing countries' patent offices have been set up to resemble those of their OECD counterparts. Emphasizing property protection and enforcement tilts the balance toward foreign rights holders.'[89] Sell suggests there is some irony in technical assistance institutionalizing a form of IP protection in developing countries that is 'under attack' in the North for overly favouring industry interests, while industry associations from the North are controlling the focus of technical assistance to promote administrative convergence.[90]

The introduction of the TRIPS Agreement also increases regime complexity, creates conflict, and raises legitimacy issues in the IP arena. These tensions play out in a variety of ways. First, the cooperation agreement contains no substantive provisions for the lawmaking relationship between the WTO and the WIPO. Conflicts may arise owing to discrepancies between the TRIPS Agreement and incorporated WIPO treaties, or when TRIPS standards differ from WIPO Treaties' provisions.[91] Only the WTO has the capacity to interpret the rules and authorize trade sanctions for non-compliance, and it provides no direction on when and how it ought to seek the WIPO's expertise and opinion; it leaves such decisions entirely to the discretion of each dispute panel or Appellate Body.[92]

Article 31 of the Vienna Convention on the Law of Treaties may provide some guidance, however. It states that a treaty or rule of international law may be used to interpret another agreement provided that 'agreement . . . was made between all parties'[93] or they accept an interpretive relationship between the treaties.[94] Few countries do not belong to both the WTO and the WIPO,[95] and the TRIPS dispute panel ruling in *US–Section 110(5) Copyright Act* reinforced this view when it agreed with the United States that the WIPO Copyright Treaty, adopted in 1996, sheds light on the exceptions test in the TRIPS Agreement.[96] Nonetheless, with very few IP cases adjudicated so far,[97] there remains considerable legal ambiguity about how subsequent TRIPS dispute panels would treat WIPO treaty developments. Notwithstanding vigorous scholarly debate over which institution should have primacy over the future development and interpretation of IP rules, this relationship will likely only be defined through future TRIPS disputes.

Second, IP issues often emerge rapidly, which creates a need to frequently recalibrate the rules in response to new knowledge production and changing realities. Conflict also

---

[89] Sell 2010b, 7.
[90] Ibid.
[91] These potential conflicts are dealt with extensively by Dinwoodie and Dreyfuss 2009, 1201–11.
[92] Okediji 2008, 116–17 discusses the circumstances under which TRIPS dispute panels or appellate bodies have referenced the WIPO.
[93] UN 1969, Article 31(2a).
[94] UN 1969, Article 31(3a).
[95] May 2006, 435.
[96] WTO Panel Report 2000.
[97] 28 cases to date. For details see: <http://www.wto.org/english/tratop_e/dispu_e/dispu_subjects_index_e.htm>.

exists over which is the appropriate negotiation forum for new rules. Incremental, or even experimental, rule changes are difficult to achieve at the WTO because of its consensus decision-making rules. Moreover, according to Dinwoodie and Dreyfuss, the '[Dispute Settlement Body] DSB has interpreted the TRIPS Agreement so narrowly that Member States cannot otherwise adapt their laws to new circumstances'.[98] The slow pace of Doha Round negotiations is also a source of frustration for developed countries at the WTO. Meanwhile, developing countries are generally unwilling to negotiate more stringent commitments at the WTO because they view the TRIPS Agreement rules as 'maximalist'. This impasse encourages regime shifting.[99]

Frustrated by the inertia at the WTO, developed countries—especially the United States and the European Communities (EC)—have shifted their efforts to achieve more stringent IP protection to bilateral and regional trade and investment agreements. In exchange for market access in developed countries, developing countries agree to comply with more stringent IPR commitments than the TRIPS Agreement requires. In many cases, these 'TRIPS-Plus' agreements require developing countries to introduce a range of provisions, including those that extend patent terms beyond 20 years, limit the use of compulsory licences, and lead to the erosion of flexibilities or policy space provided for in the TRIPS Agreements. Unlike the GATT Article XXIV, there is no general exception for free trade agreements or customs unions in the TRIPS Agreement. Developing countries that grant TRIPS-Plus favours to one country must extend those favours to all WTO members.[100] The profusion of TRIPS-Plus agreements, when combined with the most-favoured nation (MFN) principle, has the effect of setting new minimum standards for IP protection.[101]

By contrast, developing countries are shifting to other international institutions, including the Convention on Biological Diversity (CBD), World Health Organization, Food and Agriculture Organization and, most notably, the WIPO. Attention has shifted from the WTO to the WIPO as the forum for ongoing IP rule negotiation, in large part because developing countries view it as the more responsive, inclusive institution; it can expeditiously address new issues,[102] introduce soft law or experimental measures to address new issues,[103] and provide opportunities for a more diverse range of inputs. The WIPO also prioritizes developing country concerns and provides them with a voice in IP rule-making. The WIPO's development agenda (DA) is most significant in this regard.

---

[98] Dinwoodie and Dreyfuss 2009, 1191.

[99] Hefler 2009, 39.

[100] WTO 1994b, Article 4.

[101] Drahos 2007 and Sell 2010a refer to this as the 'global IP ratchet effect'.

[102] The WIPO decision-making process is not bound by a requirement for consensus and the WIPO Secretariat may take a more active role in rule-making. The WIPO Internet Domain Name Process provides an excellent example of these features. See Abbott 2000, 71–4.

[103] See, for example, the Uniform Domain-Name Dispute-Resolution Policy (UDRP) adopted by the Internet Corporation for Assigned Names and Numbers (ICANN) to deal with 'cybersquatting'. This soft-law instrument has gradually hardened as its usefulness is tested. See Dinwoodie 2007, 80–4.

Argentina and Brazil proposed the DA in 2004, with enthusiastic support from 11 other developing countries, to address the shortcomings of the TRIPS Agreement, the costs of increased IP protection for developing countries, and concerns about the harmonization of substantive patent law.[104] The six clusters of 45 recommendations that form the core of the DA were adopted by consensus in 2007. They take into account the special needs and interests of developing countries, explicitly reject a one-size model of international IP rules, and improve the participatory process at the WIPO by introducing mechanisms to widen the involvement of 'all WIPO members and their stakeholders, including accredited intergovernmental organizations (IGOs) and non-governmental organizations (NGOs)'.[105] The DA aligns the WIPO's work with aims of the UN system by mainstreaming development into the international IPR regime. While the WIPO continues to promote the protection and enforcement of IP rules, it explicitly recognizes that IP protection is not an end in itself.[106] The DA is in its early implementation phase, and the precise details of how to operationalize the recommendations are yet to be determined. Thus, it remains unclear whether it will successfully mainstream development, or have any 'teeth' in the international IPR regime. However, there is no doubt that the WIPO's DA marks a paradigm shift in the international IPR regime that conflicts fundamentally with the trend towards bilateralism and TRIPS-Plus agreements.

In short, whereas achieving coherence in new areas of international trade rules, such as intellectual property rights, is important, regime complexity engenders conflict and inhibits coordination. Imbalances in institutional power and legal traction, legitimacy concerns, and persistent structural asymmetries between developed and developing countries have thus far rendered the WTO unable to successfully navigate institutional conflicts in these areas.

34.4 SOCIAL AND ENVIRONMENTAL REGULATION AND STANDARD SETTING: THE CASE FOR REGULATORY SPACE

Whether by design or effect, the expanded scope of WTO rules has created implications for policy areas that, on the surface, appear distant from its core competencies.[107] As in cases of new economic regulation discussed above, these implications stem in part from

---

[104] The Group of Friends of Development was comprised of Argentina, Brazil, Bolivia, Cuba, the Dominican Republic, Ecuador, Egypt, Iran, Kenya, Sierra Leone, South Africa, Tanzania, and Venezuela.

[105] WIPO 2007.

[106] WIPO 2007, Cluster F, 45.

[107] This section draws heavily from Bernstein and Hannah 2008.

the GATT/WTO's evolution from an institution primarily concerned with controlling barriers at borders, to one that, in order to address barriers to access in new areas of competency, may require 'behind-the-border' reforms to domestic legal and regulatory systems. The problem is exacerbated, however, when its rules affect ostensibly non-economic areas where WTO rules do not explicitly dictate policy, but may interact with those policies nonetheless. Such interactions are a major source of the WTO's legitimacy problems.[108] In particular, environmental, food safety, and health issues have been focal points for criticism as governments increasingly ask the WTO to adjudicate in areas where the original architects of the GATT system had purposely carved out space for domestic intervention and policy development.[109] A dilemma is thereby created. At the same time as new agreements—on food safety, intellectual property, services, and technical barriers to trade—open the door to trade challenges that touch on ostensibly non-trade areas with fragmented regulatory structures, governments show increasing reluctance to advance issues related to the environment or social standards on the agenda of WTO negotiations.

There is a dynamic scholarly debate over whether social and environmental standards should be incorporated into the WTO through positive rule-making.[110] For instance, Trachtman argues that the strength of the DSM and the enhanced possibility of issue linkage make the WTO the ideal institutional framework for negotiating and enforcing new rules in these areas.[111] In our view, this approach is wrong-headed. Rather, WTO members should ensure that the trade regime leaves international and transnational 'regulatory space' for social and environmental regulation and standard setting in the global polity and marketplace rather than try to create additional rules on what standards to accept. These issues fall outside the legitimate social purpose of the WTO and developed and developing countries alike lack the political will to bring them under the auspices of the WTO. Therefore, coherence in environmental and social regulation of the global economy is best achieved if the WTO carves out negative policy space and defers authority for positive rule-making to other institutions, whether intergovernmental or non-state.

We favour a non-interventionist approach based on our reading of WTO negotiating history on environmental and social concerns. More overt action, such as amending the exceptions delineated in GATT Article XX, are not only unlikely to succeed, but will unnecessarily politicize the issue or risk causing undesirable spillovers in the eyes of many members. Consistent with the minimalist approach, we found in an earlier study[112] a general consensus among European Commission, WTO, and NGO officials we interviewed, supported by a wide variety of commentators, that the WTO is not the appropriate body to develop social and environmental standards. Environmental and social policies are simply outside its competency.

---

[108] Ostry 2009; Howse 2001.   [109] Ruggie 1982.
[110] For example, Thomas 2004; Shahin 2009.   [111] Trachtman 2005.
[112] Bernstein and Hannah 2008.

Some may suggest that carving out regulatory space—whether intergovernmental or non-governmental—from WTO disciplines will lead to the widespread proliferation of standards with no concrete or effective way of adjudicating between them. Our proposal should not be read as encouraging a thousand flowers to bloom. On the contrary, we suggest that existing rules already offer sufficient leeway and guidance. For example, where standardization bodies meet or exceed commonly accepted norms of democratic procedures and comply with relevant WTO provisions, they should be allowed to operate without the impending risk of Members who adopt or support them being subject to trade disputes. In addition, other, better qualified organizations—both non-governmental and intergovernmental—are filling the regulatory gap, and doing so in ways that are consistent with WTO rules. A norm of 'regulatory space' prevents WTO members from being drawn into collectively having to pick and choose among potential international social and environmental standards. Given the controversies over the WTO's record on environmental and social issues, simple prudence suggests governments and the WTO Secretariat should avoid allowing the institution to be thrust further into the position of having to adjudicate social and environmental regulation.[113]

Environmental and social standard setting highlights the dual tension in the WTO between positive and negative rule-making. In areas that liberalize trade, such as intellectual property rights, aid, and finance, the WTO should play the role of regulatory institution, making positive rules and coordinating its work with other institutions. In other areas, coherence in global economic policy-making is best achieved if the WTO makes space for a global division of labour and allows other institutions to do the regulating. This argument builds on the basic premise of John Ruggie's idea of embedded liberalism that informed the original Bretton Woods negotiations. In that era, the compromise was to allow exceptions and exemptions for national policies to ensure social stability—especially labour and welfare policies—which might be otherwise viewed as protectionist. In a more globalized era, a new locus of attempts to socially regulate or buffer the effects of pure laissez-faire liberalism is international and transnational environmental and social regulation.[114] Thus, while there are other facets to the trade and environment or social regulation debate, we limit our focus to the problem of (in)coherence between the WTO and these international instruments or standards.

---

[113] Aaronson (2007), in contrast, argues that WTO members and staff can actively research and provide clarity on which standards or corporate social responsibility (CSR) initiatives ought to be supported, and which are trade distorting, rationalize the plethora of initiatives, and thereby help promote CSR. We are more sceptical that such efforts would lead to rules or processes to clearly differentiate or choose among mechanisms, with anything but a lowest common denominator outcome. In only one sector—'conflict diamonds'—has anything approaching such a process led to members endorsing a particular initiative. They did so through a waiver allowed under current rules, not through a new norm or rule that could offer future guidance. Moreover, this example is exceptional owing to its high political profile and narrow target, among other factors, which make it unlikely to be replicated in other sectors.

[114] Ruggie 2007; Bernstein and Hannah 2008.

34.4.1 Multilateral environmental agreements (MEAs) and the WTO

Much has been written about the overlap and compatibility between multilateral environmental agreements (MEAs) and international trade rules.[115] Currently there are 250 MEAs in force, 14 of which are considered by the WTO to have implications for international trade.[116] The WTO deals with the potential conflict between MEAs and WTO rules in three ways.

First, WTO members agreed to negotiate the relationship between MEAs containing 'specific trade obligations' (STOs) and WTO rules at the 2001 Doha Ministerial Conference.[117] Despite the convening of a special session of the Committee on Trade and Environment (CTESS) to oversee these negotiations that were supposed to conclude by 2005, WTO members' positions on what constitutes a relevant MEA, measures that constitute STOs, and the appropriate relationship between WTO rules and relevant MEAs, remain intractable. The CTESS has done little more than compile summaries that report the disparate submissions of WTO member states.[118] Negotiations on MEAs have been stalled since 2008,[119] and the likely outcome is a general statement about the mutual supportiveness of MEAs and WTO rules.

Second, WTO members are working to establish procedures for information exchange between the WTO and MEA Secretariats.[120] The WTO Secretariat sponsors information sessions with select MEA Secretariats, it invites the Secretariats of the United Nations Environment Programme (UNEP), UNCTAD, and MEAs to participate in WTO trade and environment seminars, and members of the WTO Secretariat attend and give presentations at side events at MEA negotiations.[121] The WTO Secretariat also grants observer status to several MEAs.[122] While these interactions provide useful opportunities to exchange information, they fall short of coordination. With the exception of vague promises by MEAs to ensure the rules are 'mutually compatible' with WTO rules, no concerted efforts have been made to harmonize rules.

---

[115] Conca 2000; Sampson 2001; Winham 2003; Eckersley 2004; Carlarne 2006.

[116] WTO 2007c.

[117] The mandate is quite narrow as paragraph 31(i) specifies that 'negotiations shall be limited in scope to the applicability of such existing WTO rules as among parties to the MEA in question. The negotiations shall not prejudice the WTO rights of any Member that is not a party to the MEA in question.' Paragraph 32 further qualifies that 'the outcome of this work...shall not add to or diminish the rights and obligations of members under existing WTO agreements...nor alter the balance of these rights and obligations'. WTO 2001a.

[118] One notable exception is the Matrix of Trade Measures Pursuant to MEAs, designed by the CTESS to help WTO members identify STOs. However, there remains considerable disagreement between WTO members over what constitutes an STO or 'relevant' MEA.

[119] Notably, the CTE has not received a WTO member submission on paragraph 31(i) since May 2008. WTO 2010.

[120] WTO 2001a, paragraph 31 (ii).   [121] WTO 2007d.

[122] See Jinnah 2010, 62–9 on the role of the WTO Secretariat in managing trade and environmental interactions within the CTE/CTESS.

Third, the relationship between WTO rules and MEAs could be clarified through the interpretation and enforcement of rules and principles in dispute settlement. To date, no party has brought a formal dispute involving a trade-related measure under an MEA to the DSB, and there is a general lack of political will to do so.[123] However, in the event that WTO–MEA compatibility is raised in a dispute, we suggest the panel is best advised to consider trade-related measures adopted under an MEA to constitute legitimate measures under Article XX exceptions (interpreted broadly). This would ensure that Members can meet their MEA obligations without the threat of being challenged in a WTO dispute.

Whether one agrees with this position, the lack of jurisprudence suggests that the issue is unlikely even to arise unless one of the parties is not a member of the MEA. As in our earlier example of the panel decision in *United States–Section 110(5) of the US Copyright*, existing jurisprudence, consistent with the Vienna Convention, suggests that the MEA would not be invoked in the ruling. This is precisely what occurred in the *EC–Approval and Marketing of Biotech Products* panel report, which used the Vienna Convention to justify not taking into account the Convention on Biological Diversity or Biosafety Protocol in its decision, because the United States was not a party.[124]

However, this position leaves unaddressed the thornier problem of the potential of a future dispute to involve unilateral trade measures—such as a border tax adjustment to combat unregulated carbon emissions in the production, or processing methods, of imports—that might be imposed and justified on the basis of a climate change MEA, even if it contains no specific trade provisions. There also remains much disagreement in the literature over whether such future measures, even if endorsed in a successor agreement to the Kyoto Protocol, could be justified under WTO rules.[125] Such controversies point to potential future tensions if the stalemate on addressing potential conflicts between MEAs and trade rules continues.

34.4.2 Non-state governance systems and the WTO

An added level of complexity for coherence arises in environmental and social regulation owing to the proliferation of transnational non-state mechanisms designed to create authoritative social and environmental standards in the global marketplace. These mechanisms—usually in the form of producer certification and product labelling systems that include third-party auditing—are a subset of the broader 'corporate social responsibility' (CSR) category, but are remarkable for their similarity to state-based regulatory and legal systems.[126] Such mechanisms can now be found in sectors including

---

[123] For a discussion of the three disputes adjudicated at the WTO involving the environment, unilateral trade measures, and the application of GATT Article XX, see Charnovitz 2007, 695–705.

[124] WTO Panel Report 2006, paragraphs 7.70–7.95; Charnovitz 2007, 705 fn. 103.

[125] Eckersley 2009; Werksman and Houser 2009; Hufbauer, Charnovitz, and Kim 2009.

[126] Meidinger 2007.

forestry (e.g. Forest Stewardship Council), apparel (e.g. Fair Labour Association), tourism (e.g. Sustainable Tourism Stewardship Council), agriculture and food (e.g. Fair Trade Labelling Organization), and fisheries (e.g. Marine Stewardship Council). Coined 'non-state market driven' (NSMD) governance systems,[127] they aim not only to create standards for products and services, but also to regulate processes of production, environmental and social impacts, and working conditions. Because they operate largely independently from states, they differ from more traditional standard-setting bodies that derive their authority from governments or intergovernmental organizations, such as Codex Alimentarius (established by the Food and Agricultural Organization and World Health Organization), or from national standard-setting bodies such as the International Organization for Standardization (ISO).

As long as non-state governance systems only affect niche markets for environmentally or socially responsible products and services, and are truly voluntary for firms to join, they are unlikely to conflict with international trade rules and can operate outside the purview of WTO law. However, four issues complicate this relationship. First, NSMD systems are vying for recognition as international standard setting bodies. Normally, recognition of international standards could either occur through explicit references in relevant international trade agreements, such as Technical Barriers to Trade (TBT), or Sanitary and Phytosanitary Measures (SPS), or through WTO dispute settlement rulings. As we have argued elsewhere, WTO law is not definitive on the requirements for recognition of NSMD standards.[128]

Second, NSMD environmental or social standards are likely to fall under the rules of the TBT. The Agreement aims primarily to ensure that (mandatory) technical regulations and (non-mandatory) standards[129] do not 'create unnecessary obstacles to international trade'.[130] The TBT permits national technical regulations, including those for environmental purposes and those based on international standards, as long as they do not discriminate on the basis of national origin, are necessary for the stated objective, and are the least trade restrictive to achieve that objective.[131] Under a strict reading of the TBT, voluntary standards, including NSMD standards, are not actionable under WTO law even if governments promote or endorse them. However, potential conflicts arise when voluntary standards segment the market, deny exporters access, and thereby become de facto mandatory.[132]

Third, there is disagreement over whether non-product-related production and processing methods (npr-PPMs) (e.g. life-cycle analysis that takes into account values or effects not directly related to production) are covered by the TBT Agreement and

---

[127] Cashore 2002. Others' labels include 'transnational regulatory systems' (Meidinger 2007) and 'civil regulation' (Vogel 2008).

[128] Bernstein and Hannah 2008, 586–7.

[129] WTO 1994a, Annex 1

[130] WTO 1994a, Preamble, Article 2.2. Note, Article 2.2 applies only to technical regulations.

[131] WTO 1994a, Article 2.

[132] Voluntary standards determined to be mandatory in practice have been the subject of several trade disputes. See, for example, GATT Panel Report 1984; WTO Appellate Body Report 2000.

therefore subject to dispute under the TBT. This matters for NSMD systems because many include npr-PPMs. And fourth, some governments and commentators see environmental, social, labour, and human rights standards as potentially disguised forms of discrimination, especially against developing country products or services, and therefore this may constitute the basis of a future dispute at the WTO.[133]

In the absence of an official process or body that determines which standards are authoritative, NSMD systems are engaged in a multi-pronged strategy to conform to every possible relevant international rule to increase their legitimacy and uptake, and the chances that their standards would survive a trade challenge. The International Social and Environmental Accreditation and Labelling (ISEAL) Alliance plays a leading role in establishing and monitoring compliance with a Code of Good Practices for Setting Social and Environmental Standards.[134] The Code is designed to help NSMD systems conform with, or surpass, any requirements under WTO rules for recognition as legitimate standardization bodies.[135] Another prong of the strategy of gaining recognition is to register with the World Standards Services Network (WSSN), a publicly accessible network of web servers of standardization bodies administered by the ISO Information Network.[136] NSMD systems hope these efforts, among other advocacy activities to increase their exposure and support, will ensure their standards stand up to the legal scrutiny they may encounter if referenced by a WTO member government.

Meanwhile, WTO members have shown little willingness or ability to address the consistency of environmental and social standards with WTO rules, especially those that include npr-PPMs, in either the Trade and Environment (CTE) or TBT Committees.[137] Indeed, developed and developing countries alike have staunchly opposed any attempt to work through the Committees to consider whether the TBT Agreement permits or legitimizes the use of standards based on npr-PPMs.[138]

One way that WTO members may deal with uncertainties about the compatibility of social and environmental standards with WTO rules is by writing environmental or social standards into regional and bilateral trade agreements. The EU's Forest Law Enforcement, Governance, and Trade (FLEGT) initiative is one such example.[139] In the absence of any international agreement on forestry, the FLEGT initiative aims to combat illegal logging in countries that export to the EU. The EU is currently negotiating bilateral, voluntary partnership agreements (VPAs) with timber exporting countries

---

[133] WTO 1996b; Joshi 2004, 72.   [134] ISEAL 2010.

[135] Discussed at length in Bernstein and Hannah 2008, 595–7.

[136] See World Standards Services Network (WSSN), 'About WSSN', at <http://www.wssn.net/WSSN/aboutwssn.html>.

[137] The negotiating history is covered in detail in Bernstein and Hannah 2008, 601–3.

[138] Joshi 2004, 82–3.

[139] The 'Forest Annex' in the US–Peru FTA is an example of mandatory provisions being written into an FTA to address illegal logging. Notably, it also requires both parties to fulfil their obligations in MEAs to which they are both party. See Del Gatto et al. 2009.

wishing to access the EU market.[140] The VPA will establish a licensing system in each country designed to distinguish between legally and illegally harvested timber; unlicensed timber will be denied entry at the EU border.

Negotiated in this way, it is doubtful that FLEGT standards will be successfully challenged in a WTO dispute. Parties to a VPA that have mutually agreed to the FLEGT licensing measure are unlikely to mount a challenge at the WTO, especially because the EU will provide capacity-building assistance to help implement the licensing system and minimize the cost to the exporter.[141] The EU does not require exporting states to sign a FLEGT agreement to gain market access; thus, the FLEGT is voluntary and non-discriminatory even though, once signed, forestry products will be tracked and certified, and if found to be illegal, banned. However, one could imagine a different interpretation from the perspective of an exporting country government unwilling to sign a FLEGT agreement. It could argue that the policy would act as a de facto barrier to trade because it segments the marketplace and denies its exporters access to the 'non-illegally logged products' segment.[142] Under this interpretation, the standard is de facto mandatory and could possibly be subject to dispute. However, since FLEGT agreements fall within VPAs, it is likely that a general exception for free trade agreements under GATT Article XXIV would be invoked. It appears as though writing environmental or social standards into bilateral or regional trade agreements may be one way of ensuring they are WTO compliant. Of course this is largely speculation, since no such dispute has been brought to the WTO.

Adding to the complexity of the environmental and social standard-setting landscape are increasing linkages between domestic environmental regulations and NSMD systems. For example, the 100-year-old US Lacey Act makes it illegal to 'import, export, transport, sell, receive, acquire, or purchase in interstate or foreign commerce' illegally harvested fish and wildlife.[143] In 2008, Section 8204 of the US Farm Bill broadened the Act's coverage to plants and plant products, including timber.[144] The US is the first country to make it illegal under a domestic criminal code to trade in illegally harvested timber.[145] The act does not aim to apply US law extraterritorially; 'illegally sourced' is defined by the exporting country's laws and the onus is on US importers to vet their imports and 'declare the species, country of harvest, and other information related to timber imports.'[146] Given the looming prospect of criminal and civil prosecution, US importers now have a powerful incentive to eliminate all illegally harvested wood from their supply chains by exercising what the Act refers to as 'due care.'[147] As the Lacey Act is implemented,

---

[140] VPAs have been concluded with the Republic of the Congo, Cameroon, and Ghana. Negotiations are going on with Democratic Republic of Congo, Gabon, Liberia, and the Central African Republic. For updates see <http://www.eu-flegt.org/>.

[141] Brack 2009, 3.

[142] Switzerland expressed precisely this concern to the CTE and TBT committees. See WTO 2001b.

[143] Brack 2009, 10.

[144] United States Department of Agriculture (USDA) 2008.

[145] McClanahan 2010, 11.

[146] USDA 2008; and details and background for the Lacey Act are provided by the US Environmental Investigation Agency: <http://www.eia-global.org/forests_for_the_world/Lacey_Act_Background.html>.

[147] Salzman 2010.

a number of observers note an increased reliance on third party NSMD certification systems such as the Forest Stewardship Council and Smartwood, run by the Rainforest Alliance.[148] Given that the Lacey Act is not a trade measure applied at the border, and it applies equally to imported and domestically harvested fish, wildlife and plant products, it is doubtful a dispute will be raised at the WTO.[149] Measures like the Lacey Act may constitute a backdoor through which WTO members can promote NSMD systems without explicitly referencing their standards in national regulations or procurement policies, and thereby running afoul of WTO rules.

In our view, WTO members should not develop rules that militate against the use or adoption of NSMD standards. Neither should the WTO be pulled into the political game of overtly deciding which standards are authoritative. Instead, the WTO should adopt an approach akin to the notion of 'policy space', but for transnational non-state governance in the environmental and social areas and not simply for national governments and policy development. Essentially, transnational regulatory space should be preserved or carved out from WTO disciplines such that these standards can proliferate—and in effect regulate directly in the marketplace—outside the direct purview of WTO disciplines. An exhortation by WTO members to refrain from making further WTO rules on standard setting, or a simple endorsement of existing rules for environmental and social standards that preserves room for experimentation and promotes good practices, may suffice, since rules found in the TBT and its annexes already set the bar high for recognition of such standards as international standards.[150]

34.5 CONCLUSION

This chapter advanced three main arguments. First, the WTO is well equipped to achieve policy coherence in areas that directly facilitate trade liberalization. Coordination between institutions that share an ideological commitment to market liberalization, pursue mutually supportive policies, and are relatively equal in size and power, show good prospects for success on specific policy initiatives. The AfT and EIF are crucial tests for the formal Coherence Mandate between the WTO and the Bretton Woods institutions and show promise because they focus on areas where specific levers exist to mobilize resources and build on expertise within their existing, overlapping, mandates. Despite debates over the efficiency, effectiveness, and appropriateness of these initiatives, they can go some distance to produce more coordinated trade, financial, and aid policies.

However, the wider challenge of trade and coherence in global economic governance may require an expanded Coherence Mandate beyond those institutions, especially to include the G20 and ECOSOC. So far, little evidence points to support among leading

[148] Brack 2009, 9; McClanahan 2010, 11.
[149] Brack 2009 shares this observation.
[150] Bernstein and Hannah 2008.

states for an expanded WTO mandate to play a more active role in resolving inconsistencies among trade and macroeconomic policies. The recent experience of responses to the 2008–2009 global financial crisis, in which the WTO has been essentially a non-player, is a case in point. While there may be good economic reasons to improve such coordination in principle, ongoing disagreements over the relationship between exchange rates and trade imbalances, among a variety of political reasons, have kept the WTO on the sidelines compared to the G20, IMF, Basel Committee, or the Financial Stability Board in macroeconomic policy coordination.

Second, the extension of WTO rules into new trade areas increased the regime complexity of global economic governance. The international IP regime provides one example of the WTO's inability to successfully mitigate the conflicts caused by the power dynamics in a regime complex. Regime shifting, imbalances in institutional power, and structural asymmetries between developed and developing countries have thus far inhibited effective coordination in the international IP regime. Similar dilemmas are arising in a range of other areas including agriculture, services, and investment. The coherence of global economic governance is at risk if the WTO neglects to renegotiate its relationships with other institutions operating in these domains.

Third, there are dual tensions in the WTO between positive and negative rule-making that have serious implications for the coherence of global economic governance. In areas that facilitate trade liberalization, coherence is best achieved if the WTO acts as a regulatory institution and works to coordinate the rules among the relevant international institutions. However, the development of positive rules on environmental or social regulations falls outside the scope or legitimate social purpose of the WTO. In these domains, coherence is best achieved if the WTO leaves international and transnational 'regulatory space' for other institutions to make positive rules. In other words, coherence is achieved by creating a global division of labour.

References

Aaronson, Susan Ariel. 2007. A Match Made in the Corporate and Public Interest: Marrying Voluntary CSR Initiatives and the WTO. *Journal of World Trade* 41 (3):629–60.

Abbott, Frederick M. 2000. Distributed Governance at the WTO–WIPO: An Evolving Model for Open-Architecture Integrated Governance. *Journal of International Economic Law* 3 (1):63–81.

Auboin, Marc. 2007. Fulfilling the Marrakesh Mandate on Coherence: Ten Years of Cooperation Between the WTO, IMF and World Bank. Discussion Paper no. 13. Geneva: WTO.

Bernstein, Steven, and Erin Hannah. 2008. Non-State Global Standard Setting and the WTO: Legitimacy and the Need for Regulatory Space. *Journal of International Economic Law* 11 (3):575–608.

Bordo, Michael, and Barry Eichengreen, eds. 1993. *A Retrospective on the Bretton Woods System: Lessons for International Monetary Reform*. Chicago: University of Chicago Press.

Brack, Duncan. 2009. Combating Illegal Logging: Interaction with WTO Rules. Chatham House Briefing Paper, June. Available from <http://www.chathamhouse.org.uk/.../papers/.../14185_bp0609illegal_logging.pdf>. Accessed 25 October 2010.

Carlarne, Cinnamon. 2006. The Kyoto Protocol and the WTO: Reconciling Tensions between Free Trade and Environmental Objectives. *Colorado Journal of International Environmental Law and Policy* 17 (1):45–88.

Cashore, Benjamin. 2002. Legitimacy and the Privatization of Environmental Governance: How Non-State Market-Driven (NSMD) Governance Systems Gain Rule-Making Authority. *Governance* 15 (4):502–29.

Charnovitz, Steve. 2007. The WTO's Environmental Progress. *Journal of International Economic Law* 10 (3):685–703.

Conca, Ken. 2000. The WTO and the Undermining of Global Environmental Governance. *Review of International Political Economy* 7 (3):484–94.

Curtis, John M. 2007. The Quest for Coherence: Pessimism of the Intellect, Optimism of the Will. In *Trends in World Trade: Essays in Honor of Sylvia Ostry*, edited by Alan S. Alexandroff, 207–18. Durham: Carolina Academic Press.

de Beer, Jeremy, ed. 2009. *Implementing WIPO's Development Agenda*. Waterloo, Ontario: Wilfrid Laurier University Press.

Del Gatto, Filippo, Bernardo Ortiz-von Halle, Braulio Buendía, and Chen Hin Keong. 2009. Trade Liberalisation and Forest Verification: Learning from the US–Peru Trade Promotion Agreement. Verifor Briefing Paper 9. Available from <http://www.verifor.org/.../briefing.../9-perutradeliberalisation.pdf>. Accessed 25 October 2010.

Dinwoodie, Graeme. 2007. The International Intellectual Property System: Treaties, Norms, National Courts, and Private Ordering. In *Intellectual Property, Trade, and Development*, edited by Daniel J. Gervais, 61–114. Oxford: Oxford University Press.

Dinwoodie, Graeme and Rochelle Dreyfuss. 2009. Designing a Global Intellectual Property System Responsive to Change: The WTO, WIPO, and Beyond. *Houston Law Review* 46 (4):1187–234.

Drahos, Peter. 2007. Four Lessons for Developing Countries from the Trade Negotiations Over Access to Medicines. *Liverpool Law Review* 28 (1):11–39.

ECOSOC. 2010. Summary by the President of the Economic and Social Council of the Special High-Level Meeting of the Council with the Bretton Woods Institutions, the World Trade Organization and the United Nations Conference on Trade and Development (New York, 18–9 March 2010) 20 May 2010. Available from <http://www.un.org/esa/ffd/documents/10-ECOSOC-BWI-Summary-Final_AUV_20.05.10.pdf>. Accessed 20 November 2010.

Eckersley, Robyn. 2004. The Big Chill: The WTO and Multilateral Environmental Agreements. *Global Environmental Politics* 4 (2):24–40.

Eckersley, Robyn. 2009. Understanding the Interplay between the Climate Regime and the Trade Regime. In *Climate and Trade Policies in a Post-2012 World*, 11–18. Geneva: United Nations Environment Programme (UNEP).

Evenett, Simon J. 2009. Aid for Trade and the 'Missing Middle' of the World Trade Organization. *Global Governance* 15 (3):359–74.

Fink, Carsten, and Keith R. Maskus. 2005. *Intellectual Property and Development: Lessons from Recent Economic Research*. Oxford: Oxford University Press.

GATT Panel Report. 1984. *Canada–Administration of the Foreign Investment Review Act (Canada–FIRA)*. BISD 30S/140. Adopted 7 February. Geneva: GATT.

General Agreement on Tariffs and Trade. 1986. *Ministerial Declaration on the Uruguay Round*. Adopted 20 September. MIN.DEC. Geneva: GATT.

Goodman, John B., and Louis W. Pauly. 1993. The Obsolescence of Capital Controls?: Economic Management in an Age of Global Markets. *World Politics* 46 (1):50–82.

Grabel, Irene. 2007. Policy Coherence or Conformance? The New World Bank–International Monetary Fund–World Trade Organization Rhetoric on Trade and Investment in Developing Countries. *Review of Radical Economics* 39 (3):335–41.

Grabel, Irene. 2010. Cementing Neoliberalism in the Developing World: Ideational and Institutional Constraints on Policy Space. In *Towards New Developmentalism: Market as Means Rather than Master*, edited by Shahruku Rafi Khan and Jens Christiansen, 100–18. New York: Routledge.

Hallaert, Jean-Jacques. 2010. Increasing the Impact of Trade Expansion on Growth: Lessons from Trade Reforms for the Design of Aid for Trade. OECD Trade Policy Working Papers 100. OECD Publishing. Available from <http://www.oecd.org/dataoecd/55/55/45620314.pdf>. Accessed 9 October 2010.

Hufbauer, Gary, Steve Charnovitz, and Jisun Kim. 2009. *Global Warming and the World Trading System*. Washington, DC: Peterson Institute for International Economics.

Hefler, Laurence R. 2004. Mediating Interaction in an Expanding International Intellectual Property Regime. *Case Western Reserve Journal of International Law* 36 (1):123–36.

Hefler, Laurence R. 2009. Regime Shifting in the International Intellectual Property System. *Perspectives on Politics* 7 (1):39–44.

Hoekman, Bernard. 2007. Aid for Trade: Helping Developing Countries Benefit from Trade Opportunities. In *Aid for Trade and Development*, edited by Dominique Njinkeu and Hugo Cameron, 27–45. New York: Cambridge University Press.

Hoekman, Bernard, and John S. Wilson. 2010. Aid for Trade: Building on Progress Today for Tomorrow's Future. Policy Research Working Papers 5361. Washington, DC: World Bank. Available from <http://www-wds.worldbank.org/external/default/WDSContentServer/IW3P/IB/2010/07/19/000158349_20100719153619/Rendered/PDF/WPS5361.pdf>. Accessed 9 October 2010.

Howse, Robert. 2001. The Legitimacy of the World Trade Organization. In *The Legitimacy of International Organizations*, edited by Jean-Marc Coicaud and Veijo Heiskanen, 355–407. Tokyo: The United Nations University Press.

Integrated Framework. 2009. The Enhanced Integrated Framework: Supporting LDCs to Develop Trade. Geneva: WTO.

International Social and Environmental Accreditation and Labelling (ISEAL) Alliance. 2010. ISEAL Code of Good Practice for Setting Social and Environmental Standards. P005, Public Version 5. Available from <http://www.isealalliance.org/resources/p005-iseal-code-good-practice-setting-social-and-environmental-standards-v50>. Accessed 25 October 2010.

Jinnah, Sikina. 2010. Overlap Management in the World Trade Organization Secretariat Influence on Trade–Environment Politics. *Global Environmental Politics* 10 (2):54–79.

Joshi, Manoj. 2004. Are Eco-Labels Consistent with World Trade Organization Agreements? *Journal of World Trade* 38 (1):69–92.

Lamy, Pascal. 2006. It's Time for a New 'Geneva Consensus' on Making Trade Work for Development. Emil Noel Lecture at the New York University Law School, 30 October, New York. Available from <http://www.wto.org/english/news_e/sppl_e/sppl45_e.htm>. Accessed 9 October 2010.

McClanahan, Paige. 2010. The Lacey Act: Timber Trade Enforcement Gets Some Teeth. *Bridges Trade BioRes Review* 4 (1):11–13.

May, Christopher. 2006. The World Intellectual Property Organization. *New Political Economy* 11 (3):435–45.

May, Christopher. 2009. The Pre-History and Establishment of the WIPO. *The WIPO Journal* 1 (1):16–27.

MDG Gap Taskforce. 2010. *MDG Gap Taskforce Report 2010: The Global Partnership for Development at a Critical Juncture*. Geneva: United Nations.

Meidinger, Errol. 2007. Beyond Westphalia: Competitive Legalization in Emerging Transnational Regulatory Systems. In *Law and Legalization in Transnational Relations*, edited by Christian Brütsch and Dirk Lehmkuhl, 121–43. Oxford and New York: Routledge.

Netanel, Neil Weinstock, ed. 2008. *The Development Agenda: Global Intellectual Property and Developing Countries*. Oxford: Oxford University Press.

Okediji, Ruth. 2008. WIPO–WTO Relations and the Future of Global Intellectual Property Norms. *Netherlands Yearbook of International Law* 39: 69–125.

OED. 2004. *Integrated Framework for Trade-Related Technical Assistance. Addressing Challenges of Globalization: An Independent Evaluation of the World Bank's Approach to Global Problems*. Washington, DC: World Bank, OED.

OECD and WTO. 2007. Aid for Trade at a Glance 2007: 1st Global Review. Available from <http://www.oecd.org/dataoecd/24/63/39638213.pdf>. Accessed 8 October 2010.

OECD and WTO. 2009. Aid for Trade at a Glance 2009: Maintaining Momentum. Available from <http://www.oecd.org/document/56/0,3343,en_2649_34665_42835064_1_1_1_1,00.htm>. Accessed 8 October 2010.

Ostry, Sylvia. 1999. Coherence in Global Policy-Making: Is This Possible? *Canadian Business Economics* 7 (3):20–5.

Pauly, Louis W. 1997. *Who Elected the Bankers*. Ithaca: Cornell University Press.

Pauly, Louis W. 2007. The United Nations in a Changing Global Economy. In *Global Liberalism and Political Order: Toward a New Grand Compromise?*, edited by Steven Bernstein and Louis W. Pauly, 91–108. Albany: SUNY Press.

Prowse, Susan. 2006. Aid for Trade: A Proposal for Increasing Support for Trade Adjustment and Integration. In *Economic Development and Multilateral Trade Cooperation*, edited by Simon J. Evenett and Bernard M. Hoekman, 229–67. Washington, DC: Palgrave Macmillan and World Bank.

Qureshi, Asif H. 2009. International Trade for Development: The WTO as a Development Institution? *Journal of World Trade* 43 (1):173–88.

Raustialia, Kal. 2007. Density and Conflict in International Intellectual Property Law. *UC Davis Law Review* 40 (3):1021–38.

Raustialia, Kal, and David Victor. 2004. The Regime Complex for Plant Genetic Resources. *International Organization* 58 (2):277–309.

Ruggie, John Gerard. 1982. International Regimes, Transactions, and Change: Embedded Liberalism in the Postwar Economic Order. *International Organization* 36 (2):379–415.

Ruggie, John Gerard. 2007. Global Markets and Global Governance: The Prospects for Convergence. In *Global Liberalism and Political Order: Toward a New Grand Compromise?*, edited by Steven Bernstein and Louis W. Pauly, 23–50. Albany, NY: SUNY Press.

Salzman, Rachel. 2010. Establishing a 'Due Care' Standard Under the Lacey Act Amendments of 2008. *Michigan Law Review First Impressions* 109 (1):1–8.

Sampson, Gary P. 1998. Greater Coherence in Global Economic Policymaking: A WTO Perspective. In *The WTO as an International Organization*, edited by Anne O. Krueger, 257–70. Chicago: University of Chicago Press.

Sampson, Gary P. 2001. Effective Multilateral Environmental Agreements and Why the WTO Needs Them. *The World Economy* 24 (9):1109–34.

Saner, Raymond, and Laura Paez. 2006. Technical Assistance to Least-Developed Countries in the Context of the Doha Development Round: High Risk of Failure. *Journal of World Trade* 40 (3):467–94.

Sell, Susan. 2010a. The Global IP Upward Ratchet, Anti-Counterfeiting and Piracy Enforcement Efforts: The State of Play. PIJIP Research Paper no. 15. Washington, DC: American University Washington College of Law.

Sell, Susan. 2010b. The North–South Politics of Intellectual Property, Technology Transfer, and Climate Change. Paper presented to the workshop on Transnational Governance: Transforming Global Environmental Politics, 27–8 September, Durham University, Durham, UK.

Sell, Susan, and Christopher May. 2006. *Intellectual Property Rights: A Critical History*. Boulder, CO: Lynne Rienner.

Sell, Susan, and Aseem Prakash. 2004. Using Ideas Strategically: The Contest Between Business and NGO Networks in Intellectual Property Rights. *International Studies Quarterly* 48 (1):143–75.

Shahin, Magda. 2009. To What Extent Should Labor and Environmental Standards Be Linked to Trade? *The Law and Development Review* 2 (1):27–52.

South Centre. 2005. *Changing Gears on Global Economic Policymaking Coherence: Policy Choices, Flexibility and Diversity in Development Strategies*. Trade Analysis, October. SC/TADP/TA/GEG/11. Geneva: South Centre.

Staiger, Robert W., and Alan O. Sykes. 2010. Currency Manipulation and World Trade. *World Trade Review* 9 (4):583–627.

Thérien, Jean-Philippe. 2007. The Politics of International Development. In *Global Liberalism and Political Order: Toward a New Grand Compromise?*, edited by Steven Bernstein and Louis W. Pauly, 71–89. Albany, NY: SUNY Press.

Thomas, Chantal. 2004. Should the World Trade Organization Incorporate Labor and Environmental Standards? *Washington & Lee Law Review* 61: 347–404.

Trachtman, Joel P. 2005. The Missing Link: Coherence and Poverty at the WTO. *Journal of International Economic Law* 8 (3): 611–22.

United Nations. 1969. *Vienna Convention on the Law of the Treaties*. Vienna: United Nations.

United States Department of Agriculture. 2008. Food, Conservation, and Energy Act of 2008. H.R. 6124 of the 110th Congress. Available from <http://www.usda.gov/documents/Bill_6124.pdf>. Accessed 23 November 2010.

Vogel, David. 2008. Private Global Business Regulation. *Annual Review of Political Science* 11: 261–82.

Werksman, Jacob, and Houser, Trevor G. 2009. Competitiveness, Leakage and Comparability: Disciplining the Use of Trade Measures under a Post-2012 Climate Agreement. Washington, DC: World Resources Institute. Available from <http://pdf.wri.org/working_papers/competitiveness_leakage_and_comparability.pdf>. Accessed 20 November 2010.

Winham, Gilbert R. 2003. International Regime Conflict in Trade and the Environment: The Biosafety Protocol and the WTO. *World Trade Review* 2 (2):131–55.

Winters, Alan. 2004. Coherence with No 'Here': WTO Cooperation with the World Bank and IMF. In *The Political Economy of Policy Reform: Essays in Honor of J. Michael Finger*, edited by Douglas Nelson, 329–51. Oxford: Elsevier.

Winters, Alan. 2007. Coherence and the WTO. *Oxford Review of Economic Policy* 23 (3):461–80.

WIPO. 2007. The 45 Adopted Recommendations under the WIPO Development Agenda. Available from <http://www.wipo.int/ip-development/en/agenda/recommendations.html>. Accessed 21 November 2010.

WTO. 1994a. *Agreement on Technical Barriers to Trade*. Marrakesh: WTO.

WTO. 1994b. *Agreement on Trade-Related Aspects of Intellectual Property Rights*. Marrakesh: WTO.

WTO. 1994c. *Ministerial Declaration on the Contribution of the World Trade Organization to Achieving Greater Coherence in Global Economic Policymaking*. Geneva: WTO.

WTO. 1995. *Agreement Between the World Intellectual Property Organization and the World Trade Organization*. Geneva: WTO.

WTO. 1996a. *WTO Agreements with the Fund and the Bank, Approved by the General Council at its Meetings on the 7, 8, and 13 November*. WT/L/195. Adopted 18 November. Geneva: WTO.

WTO. 1996b. Committee on Trade and Environment. *Conclusions and Recommendations of the CTE to the 1996 Singapore Ministerial Conference*. WT/CTE/1. Geneva: WTO.

WTO. 1997a. *Comprehensive and Integrated WTO Plan of Action for the Least-Developed Countries*. WT/MIN(96)/14. Adopted 13 December 1996. Singapore: WTO.

WTO. 1997b. *An Integrated Framework for Trade-Related Technical Assistance, including for Human and Institutional Capacity-Building, to Support Least-Developed Countries in their Trade and Trade-Related Activities*. WT/LDC/HL/1/Rev.1. Adopted 23 October. Geneva: WTO.

WTO. 2000. Sub-Committee on Least-Developed Countries. *Report of the Review of the Integrated Framework for Technical Assistance for Trade Development of Least-Developed Countries*. WT/LDC/SWG/IF/1. Adopted 29 June. Geneva: WTO.

WTO. 2001a. *Doha Ministerial Declaration*. WT/MIN(01)/DEC/1. Adopted 14 November. Geneva: WTO.

WTO. 2001b. Technical Barriers to Trade Committee. *Marking and Labelling Requirements*. Submission by Switzerland. G/TBT/W/162. Geneva: WTO.

WTO. 2003. Integrated Framework Steering Committee. *Final Report of the Evaluation of the Integrated Framework*. WT/IFSC/6/Rev.2/Add.1. Adopted 3 December. Geneva: WTO.

WTO. 2004. *Coherence in Global Economic Policymaking and Cooperation Between the WTO, IMF and the World Bank*. Note by the Secretariat. WT/TF/COH/S/9. Adopted 11 October. Geneva: WTO.

WTO. 2005a. *Doha Work Programme. Hong Kong Ministerial Declaration*. WT/MIN(05)/W/3/Rev.2. Adopted 18 December. Geneva: WTO.

WTO. 2005b. *Hong Kong Ministerial Declaration: Annexes*. WT/MIN(05)/DEC. Adopted 18 December. Geneva: WTO.

WTO. 2006a. *An Enhanced Integrated Framework: Report of the Chairman of the Task Force on an Enhanced Integrated Framework, Including Recommendations*. WT/IFSC/W/15. Adopted 29 June. Geneva: WTO.

WTO. 2006b. *An Enhanced Integrated Framework: Report of the Chairman of the Task Force on an Enhanced Integrated Framework, Including Recommendations*, Appendix III. WT/IFSC/W/15(Appendix III). Adopted 29 June. Geneva: WTO.

WTO. 2006c. Aid for Trade Task Force. *Recommendations of the Task Force on Aid for Trade*. WT/AFT/1. Adopted 12 October. Geneva: WTO.

WTO. 2007a. *Aid for Trade Regional Reviews. The Integrated Framework for Least-Developed Countries (LDCs): How Does it Fit Into Aid For Trade*. Note by the WTO Secretariat. Available from <http://www.integratedframework.org/files/non-country/A4T_IF-e.pdf>. Accessed 8 October 2010.

WTO. 2007b. *WTO Work Programme on Aid-For-Trade*. Background Note prepared by the WTO Secretariat. WT/AFT/W/26. Geneva: WTO.

WTO. 2007c. Committee on Trade and Environment, Special Session. *Matrix on Trade Measures Pursuant to Selected Multilateral Environmental Agreements.* Note by the Secretariat—Revision. WT/CTE/W/160/Rev.4, TN/TE/S/5/Rev.2. Geneva: WTO.

WTO. 2007d. *Existing Forms of Cooperation and Information Exchange Between UNEP/MEAs at the WTO.* Note by the Secretariat—Revision. TN/TE/S/2/Rev.2. Geneva: WTO.

WTO. 2008. *Coherence in Global Economic Policymaking.* Report (2007) by the Director-General. WT/TF/COH/S/13. Adopted 18 February. Geneva: WTO.

WTO. 2009a. *Coherence in Global Economic Policymaking.* Report (2008) by the Director-General. WT/TF/COH/S/14. Adopted 7 May. Geneva: WTO.

WTO. 2009b. Committee on Trade and Development, Aid for Trade. *Aid for Trade Work Programme 2010–2011.* WT/COMTD/AFT/W/16. Geneva: WTO.

WTO. 2010. Committee on Trade and Environment in Special Session (CTESS). *List of Documents.* Note by the Secretariat—Revision. TN/TE/INF/4/Rev.14. Geneva: WTO.

WTO Appellate Body Report. 2000. *WTO Canada–Certain Measures Affecting the Automotive Industry (Canada Autos).* WT/DS139/AB/R, WT/DS142/AB/R. DSR 2000:VI, 2995. Adopted 19 June 2000. Geneva: WTO.

WTO Panel Report. 2000. *United States–Section 110(5) of the US Copyright Act.* WT/DS160/R. Geneva: WTO.

WTO Panel Report. 2006. *European Communities–Measures Affecting the Approval and Marketing of Biotech Products.* WT/DS291/R, WT/DS292/R, WT/DS293/R. Adopted 21 November 2006. Geneva: WTO.

Yu, Peter K. 2009a. The Objectives and Principles of the TRIPS Agreement. *Houston Law Review* 46 (4):979–1045.

Yu, Peter K. 2009b. The Global Intellectual Property Order and its Undermined Future. *The WIPO Journal* 1 (1):1–16.

Zapatero, Pablo. 2006. Searching for Coherence in Global Economic Policymaking. *Penn State International Law Review* 24 (3):595–627.

INDEX

Printed and bound by CPI Group (UK) Ltd, Croydon, CR0 4YY